1001

MICROSOFT®
VISUAL C++®
PROGRAMMING TIPS

CHARLES WRIGHT

CONTRIBUTING EDITOR
KRIS JAMSA, PH.D., M.B.A.

A Division of Prima Publishing

Prima Publishing and colophon are registered trademarks of Prima Communications, Inc. PRIMA TECH is a trademark of Prima Communications, Inc., Roseville, California 95661.

Publisher:	Stacy L. Hiquet
Associate Marketing Manager:	Jenni Breece
Managing Editor:	Sandy Doell
Book Production:	Argosy
Technical Reviewer:	Greg Perry
Cover Design:	Prima Design Team

Microsoft and Visual C++ are either registered trademarks or trademarks of Microsoft Corporation in the United States and/or other countries.

Important: Prima Publishing cannot provide software support. Please contact the appropriate software manufacturer's technical support line or Web site for assistance.

Prima Publishing and the author have attempted throughout this book to distinguish proprietary trademarks from descriptive terms by following the capitalization style used by the manufacturer.

Information contained in this book has been obtained by Prima Publishing from sources believed to be reliable. However, because of the possibility of human or mechanical error by our sources, Prima Publishing, or others, the Publisher does not guarantee the accuracy, adequacy, or completeness of any information and is not responsible for any errors or omissions or the results obtained from use of such information. Readers should be particularly aware of the fact that the Internet is an ever-changing entity. Some facts may have changed since this book went to press.

ISBN: 0-7615-2761-3

Library of Congress Catalog Card Number: 0-010540

Printed in the United States of America

01 02 03 04 GG 10 9 8 7 6 5 4 3 2 1

Contents at a Glance

Contents

Exploring the Visual C++ Environment

Getting Started With Programming

C++ Operators

Windows and Visual C++ Fundamentals

The Graphics Device Interface

The Microsoft Foundation Class Library

The Wizards of the Developers Studio: Creating Projects

Debugging Techniques

The Resource Workshop

The Windows Common Dialogs

Windows Common Controls

Basic Common Controls

1. *Understanding the Concept of Software*

A computer is only a machine. It can deal only with numbers. Actually, it can deal only with electric-states that we humans refer to as 0 and 1; we put groups of these electrical states together and call them a number. A computer can do little more than add 1 and 1 and come up with 10 (binary, of course). We group these 0s and 1s into a bundle and call it a byte. One or more bytes make a word, and so forth. The logic circuitry of computer processors determines what will happen when particular numbers are encountered, either from memory or by register operations.

Software is the mechanism by which computers get their instructions. Left to its own devices and randomly initialized memory, a computer would fall into an endless loop (perhaps a large loop, but a loop nonetheless). When you create a program, you specify the instructions you want the computer to execute by using a programming language such as C or C++. Another program, such as a word processor or spreadsheet program, converts those instructions into the numbers a computer can use, and you have software.

In the following tips, you will learn about aspects of the C and C++ languages, explore a program from Microsoft called the Developers Studio, and learn how to use it to program in C and C++. At least some exposure to programming is assumed. I assume you have read, or have for reference, a programming primer on the C or C++ language and that you have turned to this book for practical applications of the standard textbook explanations. I'll show you some unusual aspects of the language and how to apply them in ways the textbook probably doesn't. This book is primarily concerned with the Developers Studio and developing projects with it. For a more detailed Tips list on the C++ language itself, you might explore *Jamsa's C++ Programmer's Bible*.

2. *Understanding How a Computer Runs a Program*

When you load a program into memory on a PC, the operating system sets aside enough memory to hold the program in a code segment and provides space for data the program needs to run in a data segment. Variables and objects declared in the data segment are called *global* and usually are initialized to 0 or whatever value your program assigns to them. Most operating systems also set aside an area of memory called the *heap*. Objects in the heap are almost never initialized, and your program must give them initial values before using them. A stack segment is allocated for the program to save register information when functions and subroutines are executed. In most languages used on personal computers, temporary variables also are stored on the stack. The operating system also adjusts important pointer references in the program to reflect the memory location in which the program was loaded.

The stack and heap are important concepts in programming. You'll find references to them throughout the Visual Studio documentation, and understanding their purpose and use will make your programming and debugging tasks easier.

Putting something onto the stack is called a *push*; removing it from the stack is a *pop*. In C and C++, for example, when your code calls a function *SecondFunction(x,y)* from function *FirstFunction()*, the code generated by the compiler instructs the computer first to push the value of variable y onto the stack, then the value of variable x, and finally the address of the next statement to execute in *FunctionOne()*. The order in which the variables are pushed onto the stack is important because other languages might use a different sequence and C/C++ enable you to call routines written in a different language, for example, in library code. Pascal, for example, would push the variable x first and then the variable y. For this reason, throughout the Visual Studio documentation, you'll see functions declared as "PASCAL" or

"C." These declarations tell the compiler to compensate for the different push methods, and your program keeps track of the variables properly.

3. Understanding Low-Level Languages

The first computers were programmed by entering the 0s and 1s directly into the registers, which is an extremely time-consuming process. Mnemonic codes for the instructions were devised so that the code would be more readable for programmers and *assembly* was born. Still, hand assembly was tedious, and assemblers were written to convert the assembly language into machine code. That made programming a lot easier, but each computer design had its own set of mnemonics, essentially its own programming language. Putting a value into the accumulator might be *LD* on one machine, *MOV* on another, and *MVA* or *LDA* on yet another. If a programmer started working on a different machine, he essentially had to learn a new language. Several languages were invented to isolate the programmer from the assembly code, but they still remained closely tied to the hardware. These languages, including assembly language, today are considered *low-level* languages to reflect those ties to the machinery. For a long time assembly remained the primary language for computers.

4. Understanding High-Level Languages

As computers became more common (well, by no means as common as they are now) it was clear that some easier method had to be devised to instruct the computer. Computers were very expensive (costing well into the millions of dollars), and it took a room full of programmers to produce applications in a reasonable time. Thus, higher-level languages, such as FORTRAN (*FORmula TRANslator*) in the mid 1950s, COBOL (*COmmon Business Oriented Language*) about 1960, and later BASIC (*Beginners All-purpose Symbolic Instruction Code*), were developed to provide a machine-independent method of programming. Each implementation contained some machine-specific symbols for practical reasons, but porting a program from one machine to another meant only translating those specific instructions. These languages were robust enough—and companies invested enough money programming applications with these languages—that they survive today. Object-oriented versions of them have been developed, and many are available for personal computers.

5. Running an Interpreted Language Program

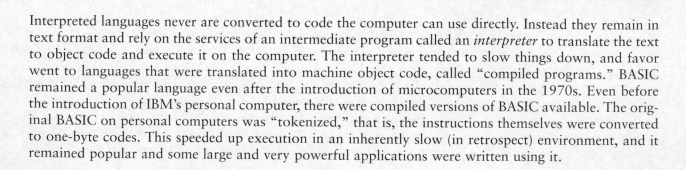

Interpreted languages never are converted to code the computer can use directly. Instead they remain in text format and rely on the services of an intermediate program called an *interpreter* to translate the text to object code and execute it on the computer. The interpreter tended to slow things down, and favor went to languages that were translated into machine object code, called "compiled programs." BASIC remained a popular language even after the introduction of microcomputers in the 1970s. Even before the introduction of IBM's personal computer, there were compiled versions of BASIC available. The original BASIC on personal computers was "tokenized," that is, the instructions themselves were converted to one-byte codes. This speeded up execution in an inherently slow (in retrospect) environment, and it remained popular and some large and very powerful applications were written using it.

6. *Running a Compiled Language Program*

COBOL and FORTRAN are compiled languages. After the programs are written, another program called a "compiler" is run to read the text and translate it into machine object code, which then is stored for later execution. When the compiled program is run, the computer takes its instructions directly from the program code rather than relying on an intermediary program. Compiled programs are inherently fast compared to interpreted code, and compilers for various languages were available for microcomputers. Ellis Computing produced such jewels as Nevada FORTRAN and Nevada COBOL, and Digital Research had CBASIC, a compiled version of BASIC. The machinery might have been slow compared to today's personal computers, but the inherent speed of compiled code and the relative ease of programming in mainframe languages made microcomputers attractive for projects that did not require expensive time on their bigger brothers.

7. *Where Does C++ Fit In?*

C is a compiled language developed in the early 1970s by Dennis Ritchie and Brian Kernighan primarily for the UNIX operating system. Their book, *The C Programming Language*, contains a brief history of the language. C contains a relatively small number of control instructions and is considered by many to be a machine-independent assembly language.

Many of the functions programmers associate with the language are actually contained in a runtime library. There have been interpreted versions of C available, but most have disappeared from the market in favor of compiled code. C was the basis for Bjarne Stroustrup's development of C++.

To say that C++ is a refinement or enhancement of C would not be quite right. Many C++ features such as encapsulation are possible in C, but it was not designed as an object-oriented language, whereas C++ was. Other languages such as FORTRAN and COBOL only recently became object oriented. Kernighan and Ritchie describe C as "not a very high-level language." C++ introduces higher language programming concepts, including object orientation, but still retains the low-level language aspects of C.

8. *Understanding Program Files in Visual C++*

Program files contain the C++ "source code," which is the statements the programmer writes according to the syntax rules of the language. Program files are ordinary text files with an extension of .cpp. C language files have an extension of .c; the compiler handles both types and uses the file extension to determine which rules to apply.

9. *Creating Source Code Files*

The Developers Studio includes a program called Integrated Development Environment (IDE). From within the IDE, you can create and edit source code files by choosing the New item on the Files menu.

Before you can compile and test your program, however, you must first create a project. For small programs, you don't have to use the IDE. The compiler and linker can be run from the command line by using the command *CL* followed by the source code file name. From the command line, create a source code file using the *DOS EDIT.COM* program or the Windows *NotePad.Exe*.

Source code files must be plain-text files. Do not use a word processor such as Microsoft Word or WordPerfect because these programs embed formatting information in the file. Instead, use the basic file editing tools that come with Windows.

10. Understanding and Creating Header Files

Programs generated from C++ source code rarely are contained in a single file. Header files with extensions of .hpp or .h contain declarations and definitions that are common to the files containing the programming code. The header files are made a part of the program by using the *#include* directive in a source code file. The compiler recognizes this statement as a directive to read in the requested file. Even the simplest of C or C++ programs include at least a header file named *stdio.h*, which contains definitions and directives for standard input and output. Although source code files must include the extension, header files can have any extension or no extension at all. Programming practice is to give them the .h or .hpp extension to identify them as header files.

11. Understanding Computer Languages

Computer languages are not unlike languages used by humans. They contain a body of symbols or words known as "keywords" or "reserved" words and their own grammatical rules for putting these symbols together.

In English, for example, the grammar rules put the subject of the sentence first, the verb next, and the object of the verb following it; any other construction tends to confuse the reader. If you want to say "He put the cat in the hat," it wouldn't make much sense to write "Cat he the box put hat in the." Although a human reader might read the line and eventually come up with the correct meaning, compilers are created by humans to expect certain grammatical sequences, and anything out of the ordinary will raise an error flag.

In C and C++, the rules generally require an object (called the lvalue) at the beginning of the statement, an operator, and an expression. As with any language, there are exceptions. In C, for example, the statement x = x + 1 increments the value of x, but you also can write x++ or even ++x to achieve the desired result (as you will learn, there are differences between x++ and ++x, but the effect is to increment the variable x).

12. Understanding Syntax in a Computer Language

Syntax is the set of grammatical, sequence, and punctuation rules that are applied to a language to cause a statement to convey a particular meaning. For C and C++, the syntax is defined by the American National Standards Institute (ANSI), and compilers usually apply the rules strictly.

In English, you use a period to signify the end of a statement; omitting it creates a run-on sentence. In C and C++, you use a semicolon (;) to signal the end of a simple statement; omitting it generates an error (I have seen C compilers that assume the end of a statement at the newline character and simply generate a warning, but the rules for C++ are much more strict). A "compound" statement, one that contains additional statements, should begin and end with curly braces ({}).

As your programming skills develop, the syntax will become more natural to you, so don't be discouraged by occasional syntax errors; even seasoned programmers slip from time to time. The compiler will rap you on the hand with a ruler to remind you to fix the problem.

13. *Understanding Tokens*

"Tokens" are portions of the source code text that the compiler does not break down into smaller component items. These include the language keywords, identifiers, operators, and punctuation, along with constants and string literals defined in the source code. Although the implementation is up to the compiler creator, tokens often are assigned a numeric value to make them easier to arrange and search. Tokenizing is transparent to the programmer, but you need to understand how the word is applied when you encounter it in documentation.

14. *How C and C++ Use White Space*

In any language, there needs to be some method of identifying the end of an element. In spoken language, this is done with a slight pause between words and longer pauses between sentences; in written English, a period and a space character signify the end of an element. In C and C++, you use white space characters (which can be a space, a tab, or a newline) to separate the elements and a semicolon to mark the end of a statement. No separator is needed between operators and other elements, however. Writing *x <space> = <space> 2;* is the same as writing *x=2;*. The compiler ignores multiple white space characters and, except for comments beginning with // in C++, newlines are not required.

Programmers use multiple white space characters to make a program more readable simply for human convenience. The following code is easily readable:

```
for (x = 1; x < 10; ++x)
{
        y = x + 1;
        z = y + 4;
}
```

What the compiler sees is *for(x=1;x<10;++x){y=x+1;x=y+4}*. Obviously, the example above is easier to read.

Tab characters in a C or C++ program generally are four spaces, although some programmers use three or even two spaces for a tab and others use more than four because they are used to it in languages such as FORTRAN or COBOL. Four seems to be a happy medium, producing readable code without introducing too much white space. When indenting, remember to use the tab key rather than multiple spaces, for two reasons:

- **Efficiency of storage.** A tab character requires only one byte in a source code file; four spaces need four bytes. Using tabs results in source files that are 10- to 20-percent smaller than files using spaces. This means the file will be written and read more quickly.

- **Compiler speed.** It makes no difference to the compiler, but it must spend more time detecting and ignoring multiple spaces where it could dispense with a single tab character in one-fourth the time.

If you download source code that contains multiple spaces, the Developers Studio has a menu item to "tabify" a selected block of text. For inclusion in email (Outlook, for example, isn't very friendly toward tabbed source code), there is a menu item to "untabify" the selection.

15. *Understanding Variables*

Variables are identifiers used to store information. In C/C++, variables are cast to a specific data type, such as *int*, *float*, or *long*, and cannot be directly assigned information of a different data type. If variable *x* is cast as an integer, it cannot be used to hold floating values or string types, for example.

A variable is not the same as an object, although programmers generally treat them the same. A variable is of a fundamental data type and contains only value or state information but no information about how the value is assigned. An object as defined in Visual C++ can contain the means for setting or changing the value. For example, *int i;* followed by *i = 2;* declares a variable and sets its value.

An object such as a C++ class or C++ structure can contain the means to set the value before it is used. Objects are almost always user-defined data types. A class might declare an integer variable as a member and then set its initial value in an initialization function called a constructor. Thus, the class object both contains the value and defines the behavior of the variable.

In addition to their data types, variables are classified according to their storage class, which determines the lifetime of the variable and how it is assimilated into the code. Table 15 lists the storage classes in Visual C++.

Name	Creation	Persistence
Automatic	On the stack when declared within a block of code	Until the end of the block in which they are declared
Static	In the data segment when the program is loaded into memory	Lifetime of the program
Register	On the stack when declared within a block of code	Until the end of the block in which they are declared
External	When the code unit or enclosing scope is created	Duration of the program or enclosing scope

Table 15   Storage classes

When you declare a variable or an instance of an object from within a function, space is set aside for it on the stack. Its initial value is whatever happens to be in that memory location when it is allocated, so your program must give it the desired value to start. Declaring a variable this way is called "creating it on the stack," a phrase you'll see often. Your function can use the variable or object, but when the function completes and returns to its calling point, the stack register is adjusted and the variable is destroyed automatically. You'll often see the term "automatic variable" (or object) to describe these variables.

Your program also might create objects on the heap, but it is responsible for destroying the objects when they are no longer needed. Several things happen when your program executes the following line from within a function:

```
CMyClass *MyObject = new CMyClass;
```

First, enough memory for an object of *CMyClass* is set aside in the heap. Then, an automatic variable containing a pointer to the object is created on the stack. A function called a *constructor* (a member of all class definitions in C++) is executed to initialize the storage space. Creating an object this way is called "creating it on the heap." Your program then can use the object by referencing it through the automatic variable containing a pointer to it. It is important to understand that when your function containing the variable declaration returns to a calling function (or your program exits), the pointer variable is lost and the object no longer is available to your program, but the memory allocation in the heap remains. Your program must free the memory space by using the *delete* operator before the variable is lost:

```
delete MyObject;
```

If it does not, the memory area remains allocated and cannot be used until the next time you reboot your computer. This situation is called a "memory leak."

16. *Naming Variables*

As long as they do not conflict with reserved words or keywords, C/C++ allows you to give a variable any name you want as long as it conforms to a few basic rules:

- **A variable name cannot begin with a digit.**

- **A variable name cannot begin with or contain a C/C++ operator.** For example, *int MeAndYou;* or *int Me_And_You;* are valid variable declarations, but *int Me&You;* is an illegal declaration because it contains the *&* operator.

- **A variable name cannot duplicate a C/C++ reserved word or keyword or a user-defined data type.** Names within the language are case sensitive, so *int Int;* would be a legal (although confusing) declaration.

Although the underscore character is a valid character for a variable name, it is best not to begin variable names with it to avoid conflict with runtime and system variables.

By default, variable names are case sensitive, so *int stuff;* and *int Stuff;* declare two different variables. A common error is to declare a variable beginning with an uppercase letter and then later use it as lowercase. If the compiler gives you an error such as "undeclared identifier" and you know it was declared, this is a good point to check.

Generally, use variable names that describe the purpose of the variable. One-letter variables such as *i* or *j* are commonly used for index variables and as loop counters, but if you have a large program, they can get confusing. Programming is hard enough, and debugging sometimes can be downright nasty, so give yourself the edge in making your code understandable.

17. *Understanding Expressions*

In C/C++, an *expression* is any combination of variables, operators, functions, or constants that evaluate to a value.

The statement *var = 12* is a valid expression, as is *var < 12* and *var != 12*. Notice that the terminating semicolon is not part of the expression. The semicolon terminates a statement, but an expression might be only a part of a single statement, as in the conditional operator:

```
int x = var < 12 ? 18 : 6;
```

In this case *var < 12* is a complete expression, but it is only part of the statement, which itself is another expression because it equates to a single value.

An expression might also be a single variable because it evaluates to a distinct value. The following code, although basically useless, is perfectly legal:

```
int Hey = 12;
    // Some lines of code;
    Hey;
```

Using *Hey;* by itself as a valid expression is an important property because a requirement of a loop or conditional is that the controlling element be a valid expression. This makes it possible to use a variable name only as a control element:

```
int Hey = 12;
while (Hey)
    {
    //Some statements that modify Hey
    }
```

As long as the variable is non-zero, the loop will continue executing.

Generally, however, an expression will contain at least one operator with numbers, constants, variables, or functions as operands:

```
int x = 12;
int y = x / 6;
```

Expressions might contain calls to functions, and complex mathematical expressions might contain several operators, parentheses, and functions calls. An expression also might be used as a argument to a function call, in which case the expression is evaluated before the body of the function is called.

You can combine simple statements on a single line by using the comma operator. In English, you often can replace a comma with the word "and." The same is true in C++. The third line in the following code means "Set the value of x to 12 THEN set the value of y to 14."

```
int x;
int y;
x = 12, y = 14;
```

The expression to the left of the comma is evaluated completely before any operations in the expression to the right are performed. If the left expression modifies a variable used in the right expression, the modified value is used when the right expression is evaluated. If the left expression does not store the result with an assignment operator, the result is lost and the value of the result is the value of the right expression. To prove it, try the following code:

```
#include        <stdio.h>
#include        <iostream.h>
void FunctionOne(int z);
void main (void)
{
    int x, y;
    FunctionOne (x = 12, y = 14);
    cout << "\nThe value of x is " << x;
}


void FunctionOne (int z)
{
    cout << "The value passed is " << z;
}
```

When you compile the code, you get an error stating that *FunctionTwo* does not take two parameters. Modify the code to read *FunctionOne ((x = 12, y = 14));*, introducing a second set of parentheses. The compiler is happy because it sees a single parameter, and the value passed to the function is 14—the value of the right expression—yet the left expression was evaluated.

Such tactics are not good programming practice, of course, and I mean only to show you the flexibility of the C++ language. This example should convince you that C++ syntax is robust. "Be careful what you say because someone might take you literally" translates in C++ as "Be careful what you code because the compiler *will* take you literally."

18. *Statements in C/C++*

A statement is any combination of zero or more expressions *and* one or more tokens. The "and" is emphasized here because an expression by itself cannot constitute a complete statement; it must at least include the terminating semicolon, which is a token (remember that the definition of what constitutes a token includes the language punctuation). So *x = 12* is a valid expression but not a valid statement. Adding the semicolon, *x = 12;*, makes it a valid statement. Of course, you could combine it with other tokens like this:

```
if (x == 12)
    y = 13;
```

The preceding examples show simple statements; each of them contains only a single statement. Translated into English, the latter example would read "If the value of x is equal to 12, then set the value of y to 13."

Statements can be compound and contain other statements. A compound statement is enclosed in curly braces ({ and }) and itself can constitute the body of another statement. The braces are optional if only one statement is included in the compound statement.

```
if (x == 12)
    y = 13;
```

The preceding statement is syntactically the same as the following:

```
if (x == 12)
{
    y = 13;
}
```

Overall, this is a single statement, and the compound statement is the body of the first statement.

Compound statements often are referred to as blocks and can include variable declarations. If variables are declared within a compound statement, their lifetimes are limited to the extent of the compound statement. Consider the following:

```
int x = 12;
{
int x;
    x = 13;
}
// Next statement;
```

Notice that *x* is declared twice. This is a legal construction in C++. The second declaration of *x* is said to "mask" or "hide" the earlier declaration and has meaning only between the curly braces. After the compound statement ends, the second declaration has "gone out of scope" and its meaning is lost; any later references to *x* will use the first declaration.

19. *Understanding Program Flow*

A C/C++ program executes statements sequentially in the order they appear in the source file and, within a statement, evaluates expressions before they are used. This might sound self evident, but it isn't always apparent in C++ source code. It's pretty obvious what is happening in the following statement:

```
int x = 12;
```

The expression "12" is evaluated, and then the variable *x* is set to the result. But what happens in the following code?

```
void FunctionOne ()
{
    int x = 12;
    FunctionTwo (x = 14);
}

void FunctionTwo (int x)
{
    if (x)
        // Do something
    else
        // Do something else
}
```

What is the value of *x* when the program enters *FunctionTwo()*? It's 14. Instead of the code executing *x = 12*, calling *FunctionTwo()*, and finally executing *x = 14*, the order has changed to the following:

Evaluate *x = 12*

Evaluate *x = 14*

Call *FunctionTwo()*

I point this out because C++ syntax, although it might seem rigorous and unbending, really is dynamic and allows statements such as this. However, such statements can be the source of insidious and hard-to-find program errors. Suppose you really meant to write *FunctionTwo(x == 14);*, sending the result of the test (a 0 or a 1, in this case a 0 because the expression is false) to the function? The compiler won't warn you because from its point of view there is nothing wrong with the statement. You might scratch your head for a long time trying to figure out why *x* is never false. Program flow is sequential from line to line, but it isn't necessarily sequential within a line.

20. Breaking the Program Flow: Understanding the goto Statement

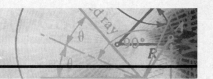

Sequential program flow can be interrupted by a number of C/C++ statements, the most basic of which is the unconditional jump. Virtually every computer language has some form of unconditional jump because it is an indispensable part of any computer's assembly language; it is built into the processor's microcode (the very low-level instructions that reside within the CPU).

In C/C++, the unconditional jump is the *goto* statement. The *goto* is always used with a label, which in C++ is an identifier followed by a colon. The label is a point to which control will be transferred and cannot be used alone; it must be attached to a statement, which can be an empty statement consisting only of a semicolon.

The following code transfers control to the statement labeled *ErrorAbort* if thc function *OpenAFile()* and the *return(false)* statement are executed. Otherwise, execution continues to the *return(true)* statement.

```
        if (!OpenAFile(FileName))
                goto ErrorAbort;
      return (true);
ErrorAbort: return (false);
```

By using an empty statement, the label can be rewritten as the following and accomplish the same result:

```
ErrorAbort:;
      return (true);
```

The *goto* has gotten a lot of bad press and many programmers shun it, claiming it breaks the normal flow of a program. In many cases, it is more of a convenience than a necessity, and you can rewrite your code to avoid it. The example can be rewritten as

```
if (!OpenAFile(FileName))
      return (true);
else
      return (false);
```

This is more obvious and easier to read. Your eyes naturally flow to the *else* statement rather than having to search the code for a label.

21. Breaking the Program Flow: Calling Functions

A function call is an interjection into the program flow; it really doesn't change the sequence of execution, but a single function call can insert a large body of functions into the flow of the program. A function can call other functions, which in turn might call other functions, including library functions of which you might be unaware.

Conceptually, when the program flow comes to a function call, the instruction sequence jumps to the first line in the function and execution continues. At the end of the function, program flow returns to the next instruction in the code that called the function.

If an expression is used as a parameter in the function call, the expression is evaluated before the function call. The expression might contain a call to another function, such as the following *printf* statement:

```
printf ("The length of the string is %d\n", strlen (str));
```

The expression *strlen (str)* is evaluated before the *printf()* function is called.

You should be aware that other code might be executed even before the code in the function. For example, it is common in the Microsoft Foundation Class for function calls to include a copy of a *CString* object. In this case, the function call will invoke the copy constructor of the *CString* class.

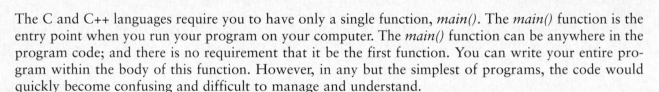

22. *Understanding Program Structure*

The C and C++ languages require you to have only a single function, *main()*. The *main()* function is the entry point when you run your program on your computer. The *main()* function can be anywhere in the program code; and there is no requirement that it be the first function. You can write your entire program within the body of this function. However, in any but the simplest of programs, the code would quickly become confusing and difficult to manage and understand.

The syntax of these languages allows you to break the code down into smaller units, or functions. Solving a big problem, for example, involves breaking code down into smaller, more manageable problems, solving them, and then applying the results of these solutions to the larger problem. Functions allow you to encapsulate the code and data required to solve the smaller problems and then apply their results to the overall objective of the program.

Often in C you use the *main()* function to process information passed to the program from the command line and test that needed resources are available to the program (as you will see later, in Windows programming even these tasks are managed in a separate function). After the program completes the initial setup and testing, it then branches out to other functions.

Many programs can be thought of as an iterative process of collecting data, processing data, and then applying the data to the given task. In a program that looks up client information in a database, for example, you might write a function that waits for the user to enter information, such as the client's name. Then, you branch off to a function that searches the database and retrieves the client information. Next, you display the information for the user and go back to waiting for the user to enter another client's name until the program is told to exit.

Functions themselves can break tasks into even smaller component tasks and call other related functions to solve them. C++ allows you to create and use objects that further encapsulate tasks and data as they are needed and then discard them when they no longer are needed. Just getting a client's name from the user is another iterative task of waiting for a keystroke, applying it to an object that build's the name, and then waiting for another keystroke. After the name is built and the user presses the Enter key, the name is passed on for processing. When it is no longer needed, you discard it and create another name object and wait for the user to enter another name to process.

When you set about writing a program, think of it this way: Break it down, decide what tasks need to be done and in what order, and then start solving the smaller tasks in order. It makes little sense to work on the code to look up client information before you solve the problem of how to get the client's name.

23. *Understanding Functions in C/C++*

Some languages provide a large body of operations called functions to support file manipulation, mathematical calculations, printing, and the like. Program routines are performed in procedures (in COBOL, for example, a routine is called a procedure and is executed with the *PERFORM* statement; in FORTRAN, a program routine is a subroutine and is executed with the *CALL* statement).

C++, on the other hand, has a very small number of built-in operations and does not support formal procedures. All routines are functions, and functions in the runtime library provide many of the operations you connect with a programming language.

Functions are a mechanism for compartmentalizing code and isolating program elements. Conceptually, in C++ they are custom extensions to the programming language. You don't perform or call them explicitly. Instead, you write the function name and include parameters in a statement. A program requires only one function, *main()*, which is the entry point to the program. A program that is anything other than "short and sweet" would be unwieldy without functions.

Before you can use a function in C++, you must declare or define it. Declaring a function is much the same as declaring a variable: You state its return type, the name of the function, and the number and type of its variables enclosed in parentheses. This is also called *prototyping* a function. A declaration is a statement and requires a terminating semicolon. You can include the names of the parameters in a declaration, but they are only for the ease of understanding the code; the parameter names are not binding on the definition or use of the function. You are free to use other names for the parameter when you actually define and call the function, but they must be of the same data type as in the declaration.

C does not require you to list the variables in a function declaration, but C++ treats them as separate functions if the function definition and declaration do not match. If you get an unresolved external error on a function that has been declared and defined, check that the number and data type of the parameters match in the declaration and definition.

```
// Function declaration
   void MyFunction (int Param1, long Param2);
// Function definition
void MyFunction (int Param1, long Param2)
{
    // Some program statements
}
```

In the preceding example, you could write the function prototype, or declaration, without the parameter names, using their data types only:

```
void MyFunction (int, long);
```

Alternatively, you might define the function before you call it and skip the declaration altogether. Defining a function includes writing the body of the code for it within a set of curly braces. You declare the return type, the name of the function, and the parameters and their data types. A function definition is a compound statement, so you do not include a terminating semicolon.

Avoid any problems before you start by getting into the habit of declaring all functions. It might not be required in all cases, but there's no code penalty for making a declaration. When you create your own classes, prototyping is required.

24. *Writing Reusable Code in Functions*

Depending on the occupation or favorite hobby that is the subject of most of your programs, you might find yourself writing the same functions over and again in projects you create, perhaps making only minor changes to them in each project. My programs use a number of file, text, and string manipulation functions that are not included in the standard runtime library because most of my programming is for the newspaper industry.

Reusable code is one of the strengths of C++. It is an important concept in the principle of inheritance in classes. Code in a parent class is available to derived classes without you having to write it again, and even without having the source code.

The idea of reusable code can be carried over to ordinary functions. Rather than doing a lot of cutting and pasting between files to put these functions into your projects, make the code as generic as possible. If there are subtle differences in the various implementations, try building the code so that the adjustments can be made before or after the function calls. Keep the functions together in a single source file and the declarations in a separate header file. When you need the functions in a project, you can add the source and header files to your project, or put the functions in a library file and link it at compile time.

To be reusable, follow a few simple rules when writing your code:

- **Avoid using a lot of global variables.** These might have to be declared as external in your project code, and you want to be able to use these functions with a minimum of coding.

- **Avoid static variables where possible.** Even in functions, only one copy of a static variable is created, and calls to your function might change it unexpectedly.

- **All the data needed by your function should be passed to it through parameters, and all data returned by it should be in the return statement.** If you need more than one return value, use the reference operator for parameters and pass the data back through them.

25. *Using Library Functions*

In C and C++, even such basic functions as screen output and keyboard input or printing are not a part of the language specification. Instead, these are handled by *library* functions that can be linked into your program as needed.

Library functions are reusable functions whose code has been placed in a library file, which has a .lib extension. Rather than rewrite the language specification as technology and usage change, only the library functions need to be updated. Library files are usually accompanied by a header file that declares the functions. To use a library in a command-line program, you must add the header file to your project and then include the library file in the linker commands. Within the Visual Studio IDE, you need only include the header file and links to the proper libraries. Standard input and output functions such as *printf()* and *scanf()* are contained in the standard C++ runtime library and declared in the *stdio.h* header file. Even the most basic program needs to include *stdio.h*; without it, you have to write your own functions to get keyboard output and to write to the screen.

C++ contains no specification for complicated math operations such as finding a hyperbolic tangent. The *math.lib* library file, however, contains a rich set of advanced math functions, including *tanh()* for hyperbolic tangents. To use the function, include the header file by using the *#include* directive in your source file:

```
#include    <math.h>
```

Your program code might override library functions, so you can write a custom *printf()* function and still link the standard runtime library to your program. The linker sees a local function and does not include the library function.

Visual C++ also includes a number of dynamic link libraries, or DLLs. These library files have an extension of .dll, and are not included in your program when it is linked. Instead, the compiler adds code to your program to load the DLL into memory when you run your program. Often, you can choose between LIB and DLL versions of a library. Including the LIB file is called statically linking the library. The Microsoft Foundation Class library, for example, is contained in a DLL, but the Professional and Enterprise editions of Visual C++ also include a static library. Statically linking a library means you don't have to ship the corresponding DLL with your code to run it on another computer.

The Visual Studio package includes a Library Manager, *LIB.EXE*, to create and modify library files.

26. *Understanding the Data Type*

Data types are the fundamental units of storage in a programming language. Data type specifications usually describe the amount of storage that is set aside for a variable, the minimum and maximum values, and the way in which values are stored. The American National Standards Institute established a set of requirements for computer languages that specifies the minimum amount of storage required for basic data types and their basic behavior. In C and C++, the minimum and maximum values that can be contained in a data type are specified in a standard header file, *limits.h*.

27. *Data Types in the C/C++ Language*

Data types in C and C++ fall into two groups: fundamental and derived. The fundamental set includes the basic variable types for characters, integers, and floating-point numbers. The *char* and several *int* types form the *integral* data types and the *float*, *double*, and *long double* form the *floating* data types.

The derived set includes types that can be formed by combining one or more of the fundamental types; these include arrays, structures, classes, functions, and pointers. Conceptually, there is no limit on the number of derived data types in C++.

A programmer can declare new data type names from the fundamental and derived sets by using the *typedef* statement.

The language specifications only give minimum storage requirements for the various data types; the actual sizes might vary from one operating system to another. In DOS and Windows prior to Windows 95, an *int* was contained in only two bytes. In Windows 95 and later and Windows NT, it occupies four bytes. A type *char* as required by the language must be large enough to store any member of the basic character set. In Windows, that is one byte, but on many operating systems, and in Windows NT when using Unicode, it is two bytes.

Data types used in C and C++ and their sizes in Visual C++ are listed in Table 27. Derived types have no size specification.

Data Type	C/C++	Type	Size (bytes)
char	Both	Integral	1
unsigned char	Both	Integral	1
short int	Both	Integral	2
unsigned short int	Both	Integral	2
int	Both	Integral	4
long int	Both	Integral	4
unsigned long int	Both	Integral	4
float	Both	Floating	4
double	Both	Floating	8
long double	Both	Floating	10
enum	Both	Integral	4
void	Both	Empty	0
array	Both	Derived	
array	Both	Derived	
pointer	Both	Derived	
structure	Both	Derived	
union	Both	Derived	
reference	C++	Derived	
class	C++	Derived	
pointer to class member	C++	Derived	

Table 27   C and C++ data types

Notice that there are no corresponding *unsigned* types for floating data types. The minimum and maximum values that can be contained in data types, and hence their sizes, can be found in the standard header file *limits.h*.

28. *Defining Your Own Data Types*

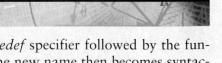

A programmer can declare a user-defined data type by using the *typedef* specifier followed by the fundamental or derived data type and the name of the new data type. The new name then becomes syntactically equivalent to the original data type.

To declare a new data type *ULONG* to represent the unsigned version of the fundamental type *long*, you would write

```
typedef   unsigned long   ULONG;
```

After this statement, you might declare a variable of type *ULONG* and use it in the same manner you would declare and use any other unsigned *long* variable:

```
void MyFunction ()
{
ULONG  ulMyLong;
    ulMyLong = 42;
}
```

The *typedef* mechanism is handy for declaring data types for structures and unions. You can data type a structure at the time it is defined or after the definition:

```
typedef struct tagMYSTRUCT
{
    int    MyInt;
    long   MyLong;
    char   MyString[12];
} MYSTRUCT, *PMYSTRUCT;
```

This definition makes *MYSTRUCT* represent a structure of type *tagMYSTRUCT* and *PMYSTRUCT* represents a pointer to a *tagMYSTRUCT* structure.

In C++, classes, structures, and unions are automatically given a type definition when they are defined. You could have written the definition without a *typedef* for *MYSTRUCT*, as shown in the following example:

```
struct MYSTRUCT
{
    int    MyInt;
    long   MyLong;
    char   MyString[12];
};
typedef   MYSTRUCT   *PMYSTRUCT;
```

Here, you need only *typedef* the pointer type to achieve the same result. The same is not true in C, as discussed in Tip 40, "How C and C++ Handle Structures and Unions."

After you declare a data type, you cannot use other type modifiers on it. If you define a data type *INT* and then try to declare a variable as *unsigned int*, as in the following two lines, the compiler will reject it.

```
typedef     int  INT;
unsigned INT MyUI;
```

Instead, you should declare it of type *unsigned int*, or declare a new data type name *UINT* to represent an unsigned *int*.

29. *Understanding Operators*

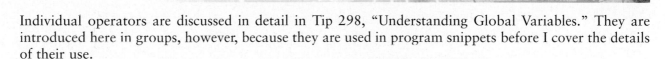

Individual operators are discussed in detail in Tip 298, "Understanding Global Variables." They are introduced here in groups, however, because they are used in program snippets before I cover the details of their use.

An operator is a word borrowed from mathematics that means a symbol that is used to describe an operation on one or more elements. When you write x = 12, the equals sign is the assignment operator and x and 12 are the operands, the elements being used in the operation. The x element is called the *lvalue*, a word derived from the fact it is on the left side of the operator. The language syntax determines the use of an operator; you could not write 12 = x to set the value of x to 12 according to the rules of C++.

Unlike most high- and low-level languages, C and C++ have a rich set of operators. Although they might seem confusing and ambiguous at first, the intent and effect of the multiple operators is to make programming easier.

C and C++ use what is known as *infix* notation, in which the operators appear between their operands. There are other forms of notation, such as Reverse Polish, or outfix, notation, in which the operator appears after the operands. Infix notation, however, is a natural, left-to-right reading notation and most people are familiar with it.

30. *Assignment Operators*

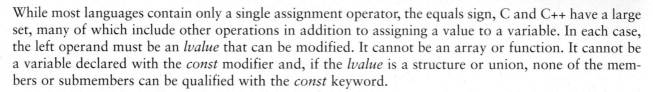

While most languages contain only a single assignment operator, the equals sign, C and C++ have a large set, many of which include other operations in addition to assigning a value to a variable. In each case, the left operand must be an *lvalue* that can be modified. It cannot be an array or function. It cannot be a variable declared with the *const* modifier and, if the *lvalue* is a structure or union, none of the members or submembers can be qualified with the *const* keyword.

Finally, the expression on the right side of the assignment operator must evaluate to the same data type as the *lvalue* unless both operands are integral or floating (arithmetic) types. You cannot set an integral or floating type equal to a pointer, for example. If both operands are arithmetic types, the result of the expression will be cast automatically to the type of the *lvalue* variable. In Visual C++, the compiler will issue a warning if an automatic cast would result in a loss of data.

```
int x;
double pi;
pi = 3.14159;
x = pi / 2;
```

The preceding operation would truncate the fractional portion of the division and result in a conversion warning from the compiler.

```
warning C4244: '=' : conversion from 'double' to 'int', possible loss of data
```

In a valid assignment, the value of the left operand is set to the result of the expression in the right operand.

In addition to the equals sign, C and C++ contain a number of assignment operators that combine arithmetic operations. In this case, the *lvalue* becomes a part of the expression in the right operand. Table 30 lists the assignment operators and their results.

Operator	Result
=	The *lvalue* is set to the result of the expression in the right operand.
*=	The *lvalue* is multiplied by the result of the right operand expression and then set to the result of the multiplication.
/=	The *lvalue* is divided by the result of the right operand expression and then set to the result of the division.
%=	The *lvalue* is divided by the result of the right operand expression and then set to the remainder of the division.
+=	The result of the right operand expression is added to the value of *lvalue*.

Table 30   C and C++ assignment operators (continued on following page)

Operator	Result
-=	The result of the right operand expression is subtracted from the value of *lvalue*.
<<=	The value in *lvalue* is shifted left logically by the number of places specified by the result of the expression in the right operand.
>>=	The value in *lvalue* is shifted right logically by the number of places specified by the result of the expression in the right operand.
&=	The *lvalue* is logically *AND*ed with the result of the right expression and then set to the result of the *AND* operation.
^=	The *lvalue* is logically *XOR*ed with the result of the right expression and then set to the result of the *XOR* operation.
|=	The *lvalue* is logically *OR*ed with the result of the right expression and then set to the result of the *OR* operation.

Table 30   C and C++ assignment operators (continued from previous page)

The various assignment operations provide a convenient shorthand for C/C++ programming. The operations are so common in programming that it only seems natural to combine the operations with the assignment operator. For example, instead of writing x = x + 5, you could simply write x += 5. The result of both is to increase the value of x by 5.

31. *Understanding Unary Operators*

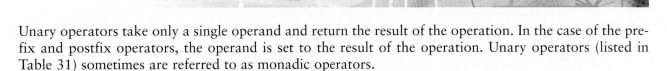

Unary operators take only a single operand and return the result of the operation. In the case of the prefix and postfix operators, the operand is set to the result of the operation. Unary operators (listed in Table 31) sometimes are referred to as monadic operators.

Unary Operator	Meaning	Returns
*	Indirection	The variable, object, or function pointed to by the operand.
&	Address	The address of the operand, which cannot be a bitfield or register class variable.
&	Reference	An address that acts like an alias to another variable.
–	Minus	The negative value of the operand, which must be an arithmetic data type.
()	Cast	The data type of the operand following the operator is temporarily changed to the data type inside the parentheses.
sizeof	Data Type Size	The size in bits required to store a datatype specified in the operand.
~	One's complement	All the data bits in the operand are toggled; 0s are set to 1 and 1s are set to 0. If the operand is signed, it is first cast to an unsigned type, the operation is performed, and the result is cast back to a signed type.

Table 31   The C++ unary operators (continued on following page)

Unary Operator	Meaning	Returns
prefix ++	Increment	The value of the operand is incremented before the expression is evaluated.
postfix ++	Increment	The expression is evaluated before the value of the operand is incremented.
prefix −−	Decrement	The value of the operand is decremented before the expression is evaluated.
postfix −−	Decrement	The expression is evaluated and the value of the operand is decremented.

Table 31   The C++ unary operators (continued from previous page)

The indirection (*) and address (&) operators are the same characters used for the multiplication and logical *AND* operators. In the C syntax, their usage determines their exact meaning.

Used in a statement such as $y = x * 5$, the operator can only mean multiplication. Used in $y = *x$, it can only mean to assign y the value pointed to by the pointer variable x. The effect of the indirection operator is to return the object at the memory address pointed to by the value in the operand.

The address operator returns a pointer to a variable, which is the memory address at which its value is stored. In C++, the & operator also is used as the reference operator, and shares the same position in the table as the address operator.

The casting operator (the open and close parentheses) allows you to temporarily modify the data type of a variable. C and C++ perform automatic casts when operations are done on arithmetic variable types, but not on object types such as arrays, structures, and classes. Often you need to cast one type to another, such as the type of a derived class to that of its parent.

The *sizeof* operator enables you to determine the amount of storage in bytes required to store an object type specified in the operand. The expression *sizeof(int)* returns the value *4*, which means it will take four bytes to store an integer variable. Knowing the size of an operand can be useful in certain cases. The *sizeof* operator is discussed in more detail in Tip 209, "Understanding the *sizeof* Operator."

The increment (++) and decrement (−−) operators have different results depending on whether they are used as prefix (the operator precedes the operand) or postfix (the operator appears after the operand). Used as a prefix (such as $++x$), the variable is incremented or decremented before its value is taken. Used as a postfix (such as $x++$), the value of the variable is taken and used before the variable is incremented or decremented. In the following snippet, the loop will execute four times:

```
int x = 5;
while (--x)
{
    // Some statements
}
```

In the first test, the value is decremented to four before the test is made. The next time around it is decremented to three. On the fifth test, the value is decremented from 1 to 0; the test is false and the loop terminates.

Using a postfix operator ($x--$), the loop will execute five times. On the first test, the value nested is 5 and the variable is decremented to 4. On the fifth test, its value is 1 and the test is true, the variable is decremented to 0, causing the loop to terminate on the sixth iteration.

Incrementing or decrementing a variable is a common statement in programming. As with many common operations in C and C++, incrementing and decrementing variables have their own syntax. You could write $x = x + 1$ instead of $++x$ or $x = x – 1$ for $x--$, but the shorthand is so common that you will encounter it in sample code and in snippets in the Visual C++ documentation.

Understanding how the increment and decrement operators work is important and sometimes will determine where you place the statements in your code. Also notice that their behavior makes them unsuitable for use in many macro definitions.

Together, the unary operators give the language some assembly-like qualities that are not found in most high-level languages.

32. *Understanding Arithmetic Operators*

Arithmetic operators fall into two groups: the multiplicative operators and the additive operators. All arithmetic operators require two operands of an arithmetic type.

The multiplicative group includes the multiply operator (*), the division operator (/), and the modulo division operator (%). The operators are grouped as they are because division is simply the reverse of multiplication.

The division operator returns the quotient of the operation. Both operands should be of the same data type, but you won't receive an error if they are not. If the division is of two integers, the result is an integral value, regardless of whether the expression is cast to a floating type. If you mix data types (such as an *int* and a *double*) the compiler will promote all of the variables or values to the type in the expression with the highest precision. For example, if you write 42. 0/2, the compiler automatically will promote the denominator to a double type.

The modulo operand returns the remainder of a division, and both operands must be integral types. You cannot perform modulo division if either of the operands is of data types *float* or *double*. In mathematics, the result of modulo division normally is not signed, even if one of the operands is negative. C and C++ guarantee the sign of the result will be positive only if both the left and right operands are positive (unless the result is 0). If either or both operands are negative, the sign of the result depends upon the implementation. In Visual C++, if the left operand is negative, the sign of the result will be negative (unless the result is 0). The sign of the right operand (the dividend) has no effect on the operation.

The additive group includes the addition operator (+) and the subtraction operator (−). The value of the operation is the result of the addition or subtraction, and if one of the operands is a pointer variable, the rules for pointer arithmetic apply.

33. *Other Operators*

C++ contains a number of operators for comparing values and manipulating bits in variables. Table 33 summarizes the operators, and a detailed discussion is provided in the section called, "C++ Operators" (Tips 135–160).

Operator	Group	Returns
<	Relational	Boolean value. True if the left operand is less than the right operand.
>	Relational	Boolean value. True if the left operand is greater than the right operand.

Table 33   Other C and C++ operators (continued on following page)

Operator	Group	Returns
<=	Relational	Boolean value. True if the left operand is less than or equal to the right operand.
>=	Relational	Boolean value. True if the left operand is greater than or equal to the right operand.
==	Equality	Boolean value. True if both operands have the same value.
!=	Equality	Boolean value. True if both operands do not have the same value.
<<	Shift	The value in the left operand is shifted to the left the number of bits contained in the right operand.
>>	Shift	The value in the left operand is shifted to the right the number of bits contained in the right operand.
|	Bitwise	The bits in the right operand are logically ORed with the corresponding bits in the left operand.
&	Bitwise	The bits in the right operand are logically ANDed with the corresponding bits in the left operand.
^	Bitwise	The bits in the right operand are logically XORed with the corresponding bits in the left operand.
||	Logical	Boolean value. True (1) if either operand is non-zero.
&&	Logical	Boolean value. True (1) only if both operands are non-zero.
? :	Conditional	The result of an expression to the left or right of the : depending on whether the expression to the left of the ? is true or false. Requires three operands.
,	Comma	The value of the right operand. The left operand is fully evaluated before the right operand.

Table 33   Other C and C++ operators (continued from previous page)

34.   *Understanding How the Compiler Evaluates Expressions*

In any computer language there must be rules that govern how the grammar is applied. Chief among these is the order in which the language's operators are applied. Some of the rules are lifted directly from mathematics; multiplication and division take place before addition or subtraction, for example.

In C and C++, identifiers (for example, variables) are evaluated first. If they weren't, the other operations couldn't be performed. Next on the list are constants, followed by strings and expressions in parentheses. Within a set of parentheses, the precedence of operators is followed.

The unary operators get the next highest priority because they signal operations on single variables that might affect the outcome of the entire expression.

Table 34 lists the operators, their precedence, and their order of evaluation in descending order. For operators that share the same precedence, they are evaluated in the order in which they are encountered.

Group	Operator	Name	Precedence	Direction
Primary		Identifiers	1	
		Constants	1	
		Strings	1	
	()	Parentheses	1	
Unary	++	Postfix Increment	2	Left to right
	−−	Postfix Decrement	2	Left to right
	++	Prefix Increment	2	Right to left
	−−	Prefix Decrement	2	Right to left
	&	Address	2	Right to left
	*	Indirection	2	Right to left
	+	Plus Sign	2	Right to left
	−	Minus Sign	2	Right to left
	~	One's Complement	2	Right to left
	!	Logical Negation	2	Right to left
	sizeof	Size of	2	Right to left
	(*type*)	Cast	2	
Multiplicative	%	Modulo Division	3	Left to right
	*	Multiplication	3	Left to right
	/	Division	3	Left to right
Additive	+	Addition	4	Left to right
	−	Subtraction	4	Left to right
Shift	<<	Bitwise Shift Left	5	Left to right
	>>	Bitwise Shift Right	5	Left to right
Relational	<	Less Than	6	Left to right
	>	Greater Than	6	Left to right
	<=	Less Than or Equals	6	Left to right
	>=	Greater Than or Equals	6	Left to right
	==	Equality	7	Left to right
	!=	Not Equal To	7	Left to right
Bitwise	&	*AND*	8	
	^	*XOR*	9	
	|	*OR*	10	
Logical	&&	*AND*	11	Left to right
	||	*OR*	12	Left to right
Conditional	? :	Conditional	13	

Table 34   C++ operator precedence (continued on following page)

Group	Operator	Name	Precedence	Direction
Assignment	=	Equals	14	Right to left
	*=	Multiply and Assign	14	Right to left
	/=	Divide and Assign	14	Right to left
	%=	Modulo and Assign	14	Right to left
	+=	Add and Assign	14	Right to left
	–=	Subtract and Assign	14	Right to left
	<<=	Left Shift and Assign	14	Right to left
	>>=	Right Shift and Assign	14	Right to left
	&=	Bitwise *AND* and Assign	14	Right to left
	*=	Bitwise *XOR* and Assign	14	Right to left
	|=	Bitwise *OR* and Assign	14	Right to left
	,	Comma	15	Left to right

Table 34   C++ operator precedence (continued from previous page)

35. *Using Parentheses to Group Operators*

Expressions within parentheses are considered *primary* expressions, and are evaluated before any other expression or operator in a statement. Ordinarily, in a statement such as the following, the program evaluates the $b * c$ part of the expression first:

```
int a = 4, b = 6, c = 8;
int d = a + b * c;
```

Then the program adds the variable a to the result of $b * c$, *48*, and the value of d is set to 52.

If you want the variable c to multiply both a and b, however, you would write with two multiply operators:

```
int d = a * c + b * c;
```

This isn't very efficient because it involves two multiplication operations, and multiplication uses a lot of processor time. When you can combine time-consuming operations, you speed up your code. In mathematics, you can factor out the multiplier and declare $d = (c + b) * c$. The same holds true in programming. You write

```
int d = (a + b) * c;
```

to get the desired result, 80. The primary expression inside the parentheses is evaluated and its value, 10, is multiplied by 8 and placed in the d variable.

As in mathematics, parentheses can be nested and the innermost expression evaluated first. If unnested groups of parentheses are found in an expression, they are evaluated in the order in which they are encountered, but before any other operations are performed.

36. *Understanding C/C++ Keywords*

Every computer language has a set of words known as "keywords" that it reserves for its own use. Programmers cannot declare any identifier (variables, functions, and constants, for example) that duplicates a keyword.

C and C++ contain a small set of keywords, all of which are lowercase. Identifiers are case sensitive, so duplicating a keyword with at least one character in uppercase is not considered an error.

The following are keywords in C and cannot be used in any other way:

auto	break	case	char	const
continue	default	do	double	else
enum	extern	float	for	goto
if	int	long	register	return
short	signed	sizeof	static	struct
switch	typedef	union	unsigned	void
volatile	while			

Some implementations of C also can reserve *asm* and *fortran* as keywords. The same keywords are used in C++, which has a number of additional keywords. Many of the additional keywords are not keywords in the sense that they declare basic types or operations, but are created using *typedefs* and other mechanisms.

and	and_eq	asm	bitand	bitor
bool catch	class	compl	const_cast	delete
dynamic_cast	explicit	export	false	friend
inline	mutable	namespace	new	not
not_eq	operator	or	or_eq	private
protected	public	reinterpret_cast		static_cast
template	this	throw	true	try
typeid	typename	using	virtual	wchar_t
xor	xor_eq			

In addition, identifiers that contain a double underscore (__) are reserved for use by the compiler implementation and should be avoided. Identifiers beginning with a single underscore are used by libraries and programmers should avoid them. In either case, no error is generated if they are used unless the names conflict with other identifiers, but it's good programming practice to avoid them.

37. *Compiler Directives*

A C/C++ compiler breaks down the process of converting program code into object code into several steps. The first step is the preprocessor, which can be a separate program file started by the compiler. In the days when memory was at a premium, the compiler often was broken into several executables that would fit into available memory. The first to execute was the preprocessor. Today, machines typically have plenty of memory and the preprocessor is not a separate program. Thus, preprocessor directives often are called simply compiler directives, but preprocessing still takes place.

The preprocessor prepares the source file for compilation by performing macro substitution, reading header files, and evaluating condition compilation statements. Instructions interpreted by the preprocessor are called preprocessor, or compiler, "directives" and begin with the poundal character (#), sometimes called the "pound sign." The poundal must be the first non-white character on the line containing the directive; the line can be indented, but general practice is to place the poundal in the first position on the line. There can be optional white space between the poundal and the directive.

The preprocessor also uses several predefined names that you cannot redefine.

The following list summarizes the use of preprocessor directives. Notice that there is no ending semicolon after a preprocessor directive.

- *#define*. Used as a definition. Causes the preprocessor to replace all unquoted occurrences of an identifier with the specified sequence of tokens. Note that the identifier cannot contain spaces and usually is entered in all uppercase letters to distinguish it from ordinary identifiers declared in the program. The directive is followed by an identifier and an optional expression.

```
#define   identifier   token-sequence
```

- *#define*. Used as a macro definition. If the identifier is followed by an open parenthesis, the identifier is understood to be a macro. There can be no intervening white space between the identifier and the opening parenthesis, but in subsequent use in the program you can use a separating space. Unlike the first form, parameters can be given after the opening parenthesis and the parameter list can contain spaces. The companion closing parenthesis signals the end of the macro identifier. The following line shows the general syntax of a macro:

```
#define   identifier(identifier-list)   token-sequence
```

- *#undef*. Undefines a previous definition or macro declaration and frees it for use by the program. It can be used with only one identifier, as shown in the following line:

```
#undef   identifier
```

- *#if*. Marks the beginning of a conditional compilation block. If the expression following the directive equates to non-zero, the statements following the *#endif* are included in the source compilation until a matching *#endif*, *#else*, or *#elseif* is encountered. If the expression is zero, the block, including any other preprocessor directives within it, is ignored.

- *#ifdef*. Tests whether the identifier has already been defined. If it has been defined, the following block is included in the compilation until a matching *#endif*, *#else*, or *#elseif* is encountered. The *#ifdef* directive can be written as *#if defined*.

- *#else*. Alternate conditional compilation. If the expression of a preceding *#if* equates to 0 or the identifier specified in a preceding *#ifdef* directive has not been defined, the block following the *#else* directive is included in the compilation. Otherwise, it is ignored.

- *#elseif*. Alternate condition. Used for stacking conditional compilation directives. The syntax is the same as the *#if* directive. It can also be written as *#elif*.

- *#endif*. Ends conditional compilation. All *#if* and *#ifdef* statements must be terminated by a matching *#endif* or an error will result.

Note: Conditional compilation directives can be nested. A conditional block can contain another conditional directive or any other compiler directive. If conditions are nested, there must be a matching #endif *for each condition, and they must be written on separate lines.* #endif *directives work outward; the first* #endif *encountered is paired with the last conditional directive encountered.*

- *#line*. Sets the internal number of the line being processed. The preprocessor maintains a line counter and the name of the current file for diagnostic purposes. This directive resets the internal number to the specified constant value. If the directive contains an optional file name, the internal name of the "remembered" file is set to the new file name. The *#line* directive is written in one of two forms:

```
#line      constant
#line      constant    "file-name"
```

- *#error*. The compiler outputs a diagnostic message. In some implementations, including Visual C++, this directive can cause compilation to terminate.

- *#pragm*. Directs the processor to perform an implementation-specific action.

- *# --*. Null directive. Has no effect.

The following identifiers are used by the compiler and cannot be redefined by preprocessor directives:

- *__LINE__*. A decimal constant containing the current source code line number.

- *__FILE__* . A string literal containing the name of the file being compiled.

- *__DATE__*. A string literal containing the date of compilation. The date is in the form "MM DD YYYY."

- *__TIME__*. A string literal containing the time of compilation. The time is in the form "HH:MM:SS."

- *__STDC__*. Set to the constant 1 to indicate Standard C code is being compiled. If this identifier is 1, the implementation must conform to standard C rules.

- *_cplusplus*. Set to the constant 1 to indicate C++ code is being compiled. Both *__STDC__* and *_cplusplus* are never set to 1 at the same time.

The preprocessor uses three specific operators:

- \ – Backslash. Used at the end of a line to notify the preprocessor that the directive continues on the next line. The following newline is ignored and the lines are concatenated as if they were written as a single line. A directive can span several lines if all but the last line ends with the backslash operator.

- # -- Replacement. In a macro definition, if a poundal appears in the replacement expression, string quotes are placed around the parameter *before it is evaluated* and the poundal is removed.

- ## -- Concatenation. In a macro definition, this operator and all leading and trailing white spaces are removed from the directive. This is used to join two identifiers to produce a new identifier.

The replacement and concatenation operators are examined in more detail in Tip 48, "Understanding the *#define* Compiler Directive: Defining Macros," where some examples are presented.

38. *Introduction to Structures and Unions*

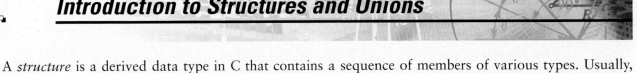

A *structure* is a derived data type in C that contains a sequence of members of various types. Usually, structures are used to encapsulate data elements that are related so that they can be passed in a function call as a single parameter. The members don't *have* to be related, but the structure wouldn't make much sense if they weren't. A structure can contain any number of data types except its own. It can, however, contain a pointer to a data type of itself.

Structures are defined by using the keyword *struct* followed by the name by which the structure will be identified and a block delimited by curly braces. A structure definition is a statement, and when defined alone (say, without a *typedef* instruction), the ending brace must be followed by a semicolon. The *tm* structure in the standard library is a good example. All of its members are integer members that indicate information about a specific time. It is defined in the header file *time.h*.

```
struct tm
{
    int tm_sec;     /* seconds after the minute - [0,59] */
    int tm_min;     /* minutes after the hour - [0,59] */
    int tm_hour;    /* hours since midnight - [0,23] */
    int tm_mday;    /* day of the month - [1,31] */
    int tm_mon;     /* months since January - [0,11] */
    int tm_year;    /* years since 1900 */
    int tm_wday;    /* days since Sunday - [0,6] */
    int tm_yday;    /* days since January 1 - [0,365] */
    int tm_isdst;   /* daylight savings time flag */
};
```

To declare an object of a structure, use the *struct* keyword followed by the name of the structure:

```
struct tm SomeTime;
```

To access a structure member, use the structure member operator, which is represented by a period (.). Write the name of the structure variable, the period, and then the member name:

```
SomeTime.tm_hour = 9;  // Set the hour to 9 o'clock
```

After you initialize the members, you can construct a time string by calling the *asctime()* function using just a pointer to the structure:

```
char *TheTime = asctime (&SomeTime);
cout << TheTime;
```

The previous code produces the following output (assuming you set the member variables to the proper values):

```
Wed Apr 08 09:12:42 2000
```

All the information needed by the call to *asctime()* is contained in the structure members (the returned string pointer is to a static string that is overwritten by each call to *asctime()*).

A *union* is a C object that contains any one of several members of different types. Like a structure, you can define it with several members of various data types. Unlike a structure, an instance union can contain only one of those members at any given time. A union is handy when you have to declare a variable ahead of time, but you don't know what the data type will be.

A union is declared in the same manner as a structure but instead uses the *union* keyword. You access members using the same syntax as a structure. A union can contain more than one member of the same data type, but it doesn't make much sense because only one of them can be used at any given time. Usually, all the members of a union are of different data types.

```
union ThisUnion
{
    int     AnInteger;
    long        ALong;
```

```
      float   Afloat;
      char        Astring[32];
      char    *AstrPointer;
};
```

When you declare a variable of a union, the compiler reserves enough space to contain the largest member, in this case the *Astring* member. It requires 32 bytes, whereas in 32-bit Windows an *integer*, *long*, or string pointer requires only four bytes and a *float* requires eight bytes.

Be careful when using a union. If you store a variable of one type and then access it using another member, no automatic type casing is performed and the results are unpredictable, and the compiler will not generate an error. In the preceding example, if you set the *AnInteger* member to 0 and then try to copy a string to or from the *AstrPointer* member, the code will compile without error, but you'll get an access violation from Windows when you run the program.

A good example of a union in Visual C++ is the *VARIANT* data type used to pass variables to and from Visual BASIC. *VARIANT* is a structure that contains a union member. The definition is long and involved, so I won't list it here, but you can find it in the help file by typing *VARIANT* in the Index tab of MSDN. In BASIC, you declare a variable simply by using it, no type checking is performed. But C++ strictly requires type casting when variables are declared. *VARIANT* helps to resolve this difference when calling a routine in a module written in Visual BASIC. The union member contains members of all possible data types, and the interface between the languages sets the data type and stores the proper data.

Structure and union member identifiers must be unique within the definition itself, but they can be duplicated outside or in other structures and unions.

Unions also can be "anonymous" if they are defined within other unions or structures. When you define another structure or union, you can include a member by using only the keyword *union* followed by the name of the union. The union members become integral parts of the new structure and don't have to be qualified. An example of a non-anonymous union is as follows:

```
union EmployeeID
{
    int     EmployeeID;
    long Department;
};
struct Employee
{
    char    FirstName[24];
    char    LastName[24]
    union EmployeeID  Number;
} Joe;
```

To refer to Joe's *EmployeeID* union member, you have to write *Joe.Number.EmployeeID*. To make the union anonymous in the structure, simply redefine the union members (it doesn't matter if the definition matches an earlier union outside the structure; you aren't giving it an identifier, so no conflict exists):

```
struct Employee
{
    char    FirstName[24];
    char    LastName[24]
    union
    {
        int    EmployeeID;
        long   Department;
    };
} Joe;
```

The union members become an integral part of the structure, and you can now write *Joe.EmployeeID*. Of course, it's still a union, so only *EmployeeID* or *Department* can be used at a given time, but it is a convenient shortcut.

Visual C++ also supports anonymous structures. For portability, I don't recommend you use them because anonymous structures are not a part of the C++ definition (anonymous unions are), but you can look them up in the MSDN help.

39. *Introducing the C++ Class*

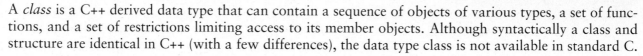

A *class* is a C++ derived data type that can contain a sequence of objects of various types, a set of functions, and a set of restrictions limiting access to its member objects. Although syntactically a class and structure are identical in C++ (with a few differences), the data type class is not available in standard C.

A class is defined in the same manner as a structure but using the *class* keyword:

```
class ThisClass
{
public:
    ThisClass();        // A Constructor
    ~ThisClass();       // The Destructor
    int     m_x;        // an integer member
    char    m_char[42]; // a string member
};
```

Notice that the class definition includes at least two member functions that have the same name as the class. The first is the "constructor," which is called automatically when an object of the class is created. The second, preceded by a tilde, is the "destructor," called automatically when an object of the class is destroyed. The definition also includes a new keyword, *public*, which is not used in standard C. The *public* keyword grants access to the following members to any outside function. Two other C++ keywords, *private* and *protected*, limit access to members.

Notice also that I precede the member variables with *m_*. This is not required, but it is standard practice in programming to designate them as members of a class.

A detailed discussion of the class and its members is in the section, "The C++ Class" (Tips 332–357). The class introduces object-oriented programming constructs to C++. Like the structure, the class is a container that allows you to manage groups of variables and objects and treat them as a single object. A major difference between a class and a structure in C++, however, is that structure members by default are given public access, but class members by default are declared private.

40. *How C and C++ Handle Structures and Unions*

Although they are used the same, there are some major differences between structures and unions in C and C++.

In C++, a structure can contain functions, including constructors and destructors. In C, a structure cannot contain a function, although it can contain a pointer to an external function.

In C++, once you define a structure or union, you can declare variables of it simply by using the name used in the definition. In C, you must use the *struct* or *union* keyword unless you specifically *typedef* an identifier for the structure or union. In C, the compiler uses a different *namespace* to store the names of structure types; in C++, the identifiers are included in the same namespace as the program code.

A "namespace" is a mechanism for grouping identifiers. Identifiers in namespaces do not conflict with one another. You can have an object called Stuff in one namespace, and another by the same name in a different namespace. Using a namespace is as simple as declaring it and using a set of curly braces.

```
namespace blerbi
{
int     Stuff;
}
namespace klaetu
{
    int    Stuff;
}
```

You can then refer to these variables as *blerbi::Stuff* and *klaetu::Stuff*. From within another namespace, you can access and use a member of another namespace with the *using* keyword, as shown in the following example:

```
using blerbi::Stuff;
```

After this statement, all references to the variable *Stuff* are to the variable in the *blerbi* namespace. Namespaces are subject to scope limits, so if you declare a namespace or *using* keyword from within a function, it will revert to the previous namespace when the function exits.

41. *Understanding Naming Conventions*

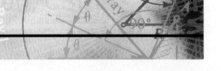

Neither C nor C++ places any restrictions on how you name identifiers except that you cannot duplicate a language keyword. The languages are case sensitive and all keywords are lowercase, so duplicating a keyword in uppercase is not an error. If you are a FORTRANphile and are used to using uppercase for identifiers, you can continue the practice in C and C++.

C comes to us from UNIX, which is a case-sensitive operating system, so more often than not you'll see identifiers in lowercase, which is a general practice in UNIX, or a mixture of upper- and lowercase. Macros and #*define*ed constants are identified in all uppercase.

However you decide to program in C and C++, you should use a standard naming convention or develop one of your own so that you can recognize the type and use of an identifier to make your code more readable. There's a good chance that eventually your code will be read by someone else, so a standard naming convention is recommended. In Windows programming, the Hungarian Notation, discussed in the next tip, is recommended.

42. *The Hungarian Notation System*

Before ANSI set standards for the C language, type checking was not as rigorous, and programmers developed various schemes to identify the type of variable as part of its name. The most common system, and the one used by Microsoft, is called Hungarian notation (so named because the creator was from Hungary). In this system, you add a prefix to the variable name to signify its data type. In addition, this system is almost certain to avoid duplicating the names of keywords or data types.

Today, with the strong type checking of C++, such notations are anachronisms, but they remain useful for keeping track of a large number of variables. It is worth learning and using the notation because it is so prevalent in the Microsoft documentation. Table 42 lists the prefixes and data types used in Hungarian notation and includes data types defined by Microsoft as well as basic C/C++ data types.

Prefix	Data Type
c	*char*
by	*BYTE* (type unsigned *char*)
n	short *int*
i	*int*
x, y	short when used as coordinates
cx, cy	short when used to signify the length (count) of a coordinate
b	*BOOL* (type *int*)
w	unsigned *int* or *WORD* (type unsigned short)
l	*long* or *LONG*
dw	unsigned *long* or *DWORD*
p	Pointer to an object or variable
fn	Pointer to a function
s	Character array (string)
sz	A null-terminated string

Table 42   The Hungarian notation prefixes

You can see these prefixes combined. For example, "psz" to identify a pointer to a null-terminated string. You can also see something like "lpsz" to identify a "long" pointer to a null-terminated string. The latter is a holdover from the 16-bit DOS and Windows operating systems in which pointers were either *NEAR* (pointing to an address in the current memory segment) or *FAR* (pointing to an address in another segment). With modern processor chips and a 32-bit operating system, much more memory can be addressed and the *NEAR* and *FAR* keywords are not necessary. You will, however, see them from time to time in the documentation.

43. Understanding the Difference Between a Declaration and a Definition

It has been mentioned and you have probably read it elsewhere that a variable must be declared before it is used. There is an important element missing from that statement, however: The data type of the variable also must have been previously defined.

In C and C++, a number of data types are predefined, such as *int*, *float*, and *long*, so there is no problem with the definition restriction. But if you want to declare a variable object of a structure, you cannot do so until you tell the compiler what that structure contains.

The definition is where you set up the members of a data type. In the case of a structure, union, or class, you specify the names and types of variables that it contains. It would also be a simple *typedef* statement. This is like saying, "I want the word Stuff to mean the collection of objects in my junk box." From then on, anyone who knows the definition knows that when you use the word "Stuff" you are referring to the members of your junk box, whether they are transistors, vacuum tubes, or tuning coils.

Defining an object or data type does not reserve any storage. That part of the operation is left to the declaration.

A declaration is when you specifically tell the compiler you want to create an object of a certain data type. The compiler then adds code to reserve space for the object.

In C and C++, you must define something (such as a structure, a class, or a data type name) before you can declare a variable using that type. For example, you cannot define a structure at the bottom of a source code file, then attempt to declare a variable of that structure at an earlier point in the file. This is why programmers usually place such definitions in header files, then include the file at the top of a source file.

44. Understanding Declarations: Declaring Variables

A "declaration" is a directive to set aside storage space for a variable or object. Ordinarily, the position of the declaration determines where the storage is allocated. A global variable is placed in the program's data segment when the execution unit is loaded.

If the object is contained within a function or in a function call, the stack pointer is altered to accommodate the space required for the object; if it is a global variable, space is set aside in the program's data segment.

In these cases, the storage class is implied, but you can modify it by using one of the keyword modifiers, static or automatic. The keyword "register" often is taken to refer to a storage class, but according to the language definition it is a special case of the automatic storage class.

45. Understanding Declarations: Declaring Variables in a Function Call

Although a variable in a function call must have been previously declared, another declaration takes place automatically in the function call itself. The data type is specified in the function prototype. When you include a variable as a parameter to a function call, the compiler checks the data type in the prototype against the data type of the variable and generates an error if they do not match.

If the data types match, space is reserved on the stack and the variable's contents are copied into that space. If the parameter is an expression, the expression is evaluated and the result is placed in the storage space. For this reason, variables passed to functions are always automatic variables and cannot be subclassed as register variables.

When a function uses or modifies a parameter variable, it actually is using a copy of the original variable, and any changes are not reflected in the original variable. When the function returns to the caller, the variable is destroyed and its contents are permanently lost.

46. Understanding Declarations: Prototyping Functions

As mentioned earlier, you must declare or define functions before they can be used in a program. In practice, programmers always declare the functions through a process called prototyping. A function prototype essentially is a pattern.

The function prototype specifies its return type and the number and data types of its parameters. When you compile the program, the compiler checks your function calls against the prototype to make sure the parameter counts match and the parameters are of the proper data type.

A prototype can set default values for parameters. If your program calls the function without a value for that parameter, the compiler substitutes the default value:

```
void ThisFunction (int x = 0);
```

After the prototype you can call the function without any parameters and the compiler will substitute *0* for *x*.

Some special rules apply for prototyping functions with default values and for calling these functions.

Default parameters work their way inward from the right. After you set a default value for a parameter, all the parameters to the right of it must have default values. You can't write something like the following and expect the compiler to understand it:

```
void ThisFunction (int x = 0, int y, int z = 0);
```

Instead, you would have to place the *y* parameter first in the list.

When you call a function with default parameters, you need not include the parameter in the function call. If you do include a value, all parameters to the left of it must have values, but parameters to the right can still use the default values.

47. Understanding the #define Compiler Directive: Defining Constants

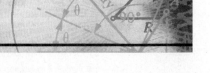

You can create new identifiers and give them values that cannot be changed—called constants—by using the *#define* compiler directive. A constant is the antithesis of a variable. Although the value of a variable can change throughout the program code, you cannot modify the value of a constant.

To declare a constant, type the *#define* directive at the "beginning" of the line (leading white space is allowed), followed by the name of the new identifier, and then the value you want the constant to contain. The name must conform to the rules for variable names or other identifiers: It cannot duplicate a keyword or contain illegal characters such as spaces or an operator. In practice, constants are named using all uppercase letters, but that is not a requirement of C or C++.

The compiler reads all text after the identifier name until the end of the line or a comment marker is encountered, and then strips leading and trailing white space. The result is the definition of the identifier, and all unquoted occurrences of the identifier are replaced by the definition. After defining *PI* in the following line, you can use the name anywhere you need the value 3.141593.

```
#define    PI    3.141593
```

You can't assign the identifier another value using, say, *PI = 3.141592653589793238*. To do so, you need to undefine the constant and redefine it, as shown in the following:

```
#ifdef PI
#undef PI
#endif
#define    PI 3.141592653589793238
```

> *Note: The definition does not include a terminating semicolon. The compiler simply stores the definition for later use. Error checking is performed when it is used, and if the semicolon is included, it might abruptly terminate an expression.*

A constant definition can be an expression and can contain constants previously defined, as in the following example:

```
#define    TWO_PI    (2.0 * PI)
```

48. *Understanding the #define Compiler Directive: Defining Macros*

Defining a macro is the same as defining a constant, except immediately after the identifier name you attach an opening parenthesis. There must be no space between the identifier name and the opening parenthesis. Otherwise, the same rules apply as if you were defining a constant.

After the macro is defined, you can use it as you would use any function call.

Macros are expressions and can include other expressions and defined constants. Given the definitions of *PI* and *TWO_PI* from the preceding tip, you can write a macro to find the circumference of a circle:

```
#define    CIRCUM(float Diameter)    TWO_PI * Diameter
```

When you want to find the circumference of a circle with a radius of say, 4, write the following line:

```
float Circumference = CIRCUM (8.0);
```

Beyond this simple example, macros start getting complex, involved, and well, just plain weird. There are some very good arguments to be made against using macros, and when you look at the following constructions, you'll see why.

Macros can contain the special preprocessor operators # (replacement) and ## (concatenation). When the # is encountered, the matching parameter is quoted and inserted in place of the #. The parameter is not evaluated before the replacement takes place:

```
#define   PRINT(val)   printf(#val " = %d", val)
```

After defining the preceding macro, you might write something like this:

```
int x = 2, y = 4;
PRINT(x+y);
```

The unevaluated *x+y* is substituted for *#val* and placed within double quotes. In the second occurrence of *val*, the expression is evaluated and replaced with the actual value. The macro expands to the following line:

```
printf("x+y" " = ", 6);
```

When one string follows another with no operators in between, the compiler concatenates them into a single string. The net effect of the macro is to produce the following line:

```
printf("x+y = ", 6);
```

When the ## is encountered in a macro definition, the operator and all leading and trailing white spaces are removed and the two matching parameter names are joined to produce a new identifier.

```
#define AVERAGE(First,Second) (First ## Second / 2)
int One = 4, Two = 8;
int OneTwo = One + Two;
cout << "The average of ";
cout << One << " and " << Two << " is ";
cout << AVERAGE(One, Two) << endl;
```

The preprocessor concatenated the variable names *One* and *Two* to form a new variable, *OneTwo*, and substituted it in the macro call, resulting in the following output:

```
The average of 4 and 8 is 6
```

Of course, the variable *OneTwo* must be declared and evaluated prior to the macro substitution. The preprocessor does not test whether the passed parameters have been declared, however, so a compile error will result if you have not already declared the concatenated name.

You should avoid macros such as these. They only make your code more obscure and almost certainly will confuse anyone who doesn't follow your train of thought. You should be aware of their constructions, however, so that you will recognize them in other programmers' code.

49. *Understanding Variable Storage Classes: The Automatic Variable*

Automatic variables are so named because they are created and destroyed as needed and the programmer does nothing more than declare them. They are identified with the keyword *auto*. This is the default storage class for variables declared in a function or compound statement, and the *auto* keyword is assumed.

Variables of this type are created on the stack and are destroyed when the function or compound statement ends. Except for variables declared in a function call, automatic variables are never initialized, and you must give them values before using them. If you don't, their initial value will be whatever residual data remains in their storage location. Usually, the compiler will warn you when you attempt to use an automatic variable without initializing it; ignoring the warning could produce some undesired results.

Variables used in a function call are always automatic. When you use a variable in a function call, the compiler inserts code to create new variables on the stack and then copies in the values of the original variables. This mechanism is part of the "call by value" used in C and C++, and prevents a function from modifying variables in another block of code.

50. *Understanding Variable Storage Classes: The Register Variable*

Although it often is referred to as a distinct storage class, the register class is a subclass of the automatic storage class. You declare a variable of this class by using the keyword *register* before the data type:

```
register int RegVar;
```

This is a request to the compiler to place the variable's value into one of the processor's arithmetic registers. One might do this because the variable will be used often and CPU registers provide quick access. More often than not, the request is wishful thinking, and only serves to limit the use of the variable. For example, you cannot take the address of a register variable. Usually, when you compile your program with optimization turned on, the compiler makes its own choices of what variables it will place in the registers.

Only function parameters and local variables can be declared with the register storage class. You cannot specify the register type in a function argument because the compiler creates space for arguments in the function call. Register variables persist only until the end of the block in which they are declared.

Because of the limited number of registers, only a few register variables can be declared, and their types are limited to the implementation on the particular machine. In addition, in C you cannot use the address operator on a register class variable (it is allowed in C++, however). Theoretically at least, the variable has no memory storage and thus no address.

51. *Understanding Variable Storage Classes: The Static Variable*

Persistent data storage in C and C++ is implemented with the static storage class. A variable with this storage class is declared by using the *static* keyword before the data type; static variables are guaranteed to be initialized to 0 unless another value is specified (there are special rules for static variables declared in a C++ class definition):

```
static int StaticVar = 4;
```

The preceding declaration sets aside storage for *StaticVar* and gives it an initial value of 4.

Variables with this storage class are created when the program is run and persist until the program ends. Only one copy of a static variable is ever created, and its value must be shared by all function calls using it.

A function parameter can never be declared static, but static variables can be used in function calls. In a function call, a variable with the *auto* storage class is created and the value is copied into it, so the storage class in a function call parameter is automatically converted. In this case, modifying the parameter has no effect on the static variable's value.

This is the default storage class for global variables. If a global variable is declared static, the effect is to limit its access to the execution unit. A global declared static in one source file cannot be accessed by a function defined in another source file.

Static variables are useful for maintaining values that need to be retained throughout function calls. The following code modifies the values of *Counter* each time *Count()* is called and thus keeps track of the calls to the function.

```
void Count ();
main ()
{
    Count ();
    Count ();
    Count ();
}
void Count ()
{
static int Counter;
    ++Counter;
    cout << "Count () has been called " << Counter;
    cout << (Counter == 1 ? " time" : " times") << endl;
}
```

Running the preceding snippet produces the following output:

```
Count () has been called 1 time.

Count () has been called 2 times.

Count () has been called 3 times.
```

52. Understanding Variable Storage Classes: The Static Variable in a Class

Variables declared as members of a class require special rules. Only one instance of a static class is ever created, and no initialization is guaranteed. Just defining a class doesn't create an instance, so how do you initialize something that doesn't exist yet? You have to give it an initial value in global scope. First, lets define a class:

```
class CmyClass
{
    CMyClass ();
    ~CMyClass ();
    static int    Counter;
}
```

In the file containing your source code, usually near the top but definitely *outside* any function definition (in other words, in global scope), you need to initialize the variable:

```
int CMyClass::Counter = 0;
```

In the initialization, notice that you have to specify the data type, but you do not repeat the *static* storage class keyword.

53. *Introduction to Recursion*

An important side effect of the way C and C++ deal with automatic variables is that recursive routines are easier to write. Because new variables are created each time your program calls a function, even from within the function itself, successive calls will not modify the values from previous calls.

Recursion is the capability of a function to call itself. Recursion can be used to implement complex algorithms in a small, compact function, but it might not be efficient or fast. In fact, recursion can be downright dangerous in some cases, causing the program to run out of stack space and terminate abnormally. Recursive functions rely on decision-making statements such as an *if* statement or a loop statement. You must provide some method to terminate the call or the program will run out of stack space. (You will learn more about the *if* statement in the section on "Writing Conditional Statements" beginning with Tip 162; you will learn about loop in the section, "Program Loops," beginning with Tip 173.)

54. *Understanding Recursion: A Sorting Problem*

Sorting is a particularly good subject for recursion. Sort loops can be built without recursion, but a great deal of care must be taken to ensure that one iteration of the loop does not modify already calculated values.

The following implementation of the *Quicksort* algorithm demonstrates the use of recursion. You pass it an array of integers to sort, the index of the beginning number (usually 0 to encompass the entire array), and the number of elements to sort (usually the size of the array). When additional elements need to be sorted, the function calls itself. When it finally emerges, the array is sorted.

```
void QuickSort (int Nums[], int begin, int elems)
{
int    val, i, j, temp, part;
    if (elems > begin)
        {
        part = elems - 1;
        val = Nums[part];
        i = begin;
        j = part - 1;
        for (;;)
            {
            while (Nums[i] < val)
                ++i;
            while (Nums[j] > val)
                --j;
```

```
            if (i >= j)
                break;
            temp = Nums[i];
            Nums[i] = Nums[j];
            Nums[j] = temp;
            }
        temp = Nums[i];
        Nums[i] = Nums[part];
        Nums[part] = temp;
        QuickSort (Nums, begin, i);
        QuickSort (Nums, i + 1, elems);
        }
}
```

Quicksort is an efficient algorithm and one that is particularly easy with recursion. It can be implemented without recursion, but it gets very complicated very quickly. The algorithm uses a "divide and conquer" method of sorting, and calls itself at least twice with each iteration until the array is sorted. With each call, the array is partitioned and the elements within it are sorted. By the time the function gets back to the original call, the array is sorted.

55. *Understanding Recursion: A Math Problem*

Many mathematical operations are good candidates for recursion. Computing number sequences such as the Fibonacci sequence requires repeated calculations using the same algorithm.

Another good candidate is the factorial of a number, that is, multiplying all the positive integers (except 0) below and including a number. The code for finding a factorial can be implemented in a loop, but recursion reduces it to only a few lines:

```
#include    <stdio.h>
#include    <iostream.h>
#include    <stdlib.h>

unsigned long factor (unsigned long Num);

void main (int argc, char *argv[])
{
    if (argc < 2)
        return;
    unsigned long factorial = factor (atol (argv[1]));
    cout << " = " << factorial << endl;
}

unsigned long factor (unsigned long Num)
{
    cout << Num;
    if (Num > 1)
    {
        cout << " x ";
        return (Num * factor (Num - 1));
    }
    return (1);
}
```

The parameter to the function is repeatedly reduced by 1 until it is equal to 1, at which time the function returns without calling itself.

Running the program with a parameter of 10 results in the following output:

```
10 x 9 x 8 x 7 x 6 x 5 x 4 x 3 x 2 x 1 = 3628800
```

56. *Understanding Pointers*

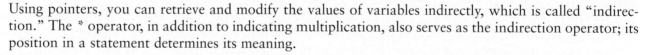

Each piece of information in a computer's memory, whether code or data, has a specific address. When you run a program and create a variable, the program assigns it a specific address and the value you assign to the variable moves in. You also know that the address occupies a certain number of bytes that you can determine by using the *sizeof* operator. Generally, in high-level languages, you aren't concerned with the variable address; there's no way for you to know the address unless you are using a debugger and interrupt the code to look it up.

In C and C++, you can use the address operator (&) to look up the memory location of a variable. This capability, usually associated with assembly language programming, is one of the features that give C a low-level quality. A reference to the location of a variable, or any object, is called a "pointer" to the variable.

C contains a derived data type called a pointer to contain the addresses of variables and objects. Technically, a pointer to each data type, including the pointer and user-defined data types, has its own data type (an important fact in performing arithmetic on pointers), giving C and C++ a virtually unlimited number of pointer types. In practice, however, all pointers are unsigned values as large as a word on a particular computer. To assign the value of one pointer type to another, you must use the cast operator.

57. *Understanding Pointers: Indirection*

Using pointers, you can retrieve and modify the values of variables indirectly, which is called "indirection." The * operator, in addition to indicating multiplication, also serves as the indirection operator; its position in a statement determines its meaning.

Pointers themselves are variables. To get the address of a variable or object, you use the & operator on the variable itself; to refer to the contents of an object pointed to by a pointer, you use the indirection (*) operator on the pointer variable. Using the indirection operator to get the value is called "dereferencing" the variable.

The preceding paragraph implies that you can take the pointer to a pointer, and indeed this is common practice. As you will see later, an array variable is a pointer variable, as is a string variable (an array of type *char*). So an array of string variables is a pointer to a pointer, and the first character of a member can be accessed by doubling the indirection operator (**). It isn't common, but neither is it rare, to see programs that use up to three levels of indirection (***); anything beyond that, however, is unusual.

The following snippet shows how the address and indirection operators are used:

```
int     x;    // Declare an int variable
int     *px;  // Declare a pointer variable
// using the indirection operator
```

```
px = &x;  // Set the value of px to the address of x
*px = 4;  // Set the value of x indirectly
cout << "The address of x is " << &x << endl;
cout << "The value of x is " << x << endl;
cout << "The value of px is " << px << endl;
cout << "The value of the variable pointed to ";
cout << "by px is " << *px << endl;
```

In the expression *px = 4, the variable x wasn't set directly. Instead, I placed the value 4 into the memory location pointed to by px, which is the address of x. So I set the value indirectly. In the last line of the snippet, I use the indirection operator again to get the value in the memory location pointed to by px.

Pointer operations can seem confusing to new programmers. For convenience, think of an address as the location of a house. You put the address of the house in the variable px. But someone (x in this case) lives in that house and that person has a name (x). You refer to the house using px and the *name* (value) of the person living there as *px. It's like getting mail addressed to "Occupant." It's really you, but the sender doesn't know your name (x).

Pointers also have their own arithmetic, which will be discussed in the section, "C++ Arrays and Pointers," beginning with Tip 368.

C++ contains a special data type, *reference*, that allows you to use pointers as you would any other variable. A reference is a variable that holds the address of an object but behaves syntactically like that object. A reference variable lets you use pointers without having to use the indirection operator. In addition, you must initialize a reference when you declare the reference variable. When you use a reference as a function parameter, C++ automatically initializes the variable when you call the function containing the reference as a parameter.

The following snippet shows us an interesting and important property of a reference variable:

```
int    x;        // Declare an int variable
int&   rx = x;   // Declare and initialize a reference
    rx = 4;  // Set the value of x through reference
    cout << "The address of x is " << &x <<endl;
    cout << "The value of x is " << x << endl;
    cout << "The address of rx is " << &rx << endl;
    cout << "The value of rx is " << rx << endl;
```

When you run this code snippet, you find the address of x and rx are the same. Despite the appearance, no operator ever causes an operation on a reference. Instead, the operation, including the address operation, is performed on the object of the reference, the original variable. C++ will not enable you to get the address of a reference, because then you would be able to modify its contents indirectly.

C and C++ use "call by value" functions, but the reference data type in C++ extends the possibility of "call by reference," the type used by many languages such as FORTRAN. When you pass a reference and the called function modifies the reference, the variable in the calling function is modified.

A reference is declared by using the address operator. The syntax of the expression determines whether C++ will evaluate it as an address or reference operator. In the following, if you mean to pass a pointer to x, you have to declare the function as *FunctionTwo (int *x);* thus, the & operator must mean you intend to declare a reference.

```
void FunctionOne (void);
void FunctionTwo (int &x);
void FunctionOne ()
{
int x = 4;
    cout << "Before FunctionTwo x = " << x << endl;
```

```
    FunctionTwo (x);
    cout << "After FunctionTwo x = " << x << endl;
}

FunctionTwo (int &x)
{
    x = 5;
}
```

58. *Understanding Arrays*

An *array* is a group of data values that is all of the same type and can be referenced by an expression that equates to an index number. In C and C++, the elements of an array are contiguous, that is, their memory locations are not separated by any other data.

Arrays can be declared of any of the fundamental data types available in C or C++ except type *void*. From the derived data types, you can declare arrays of any type except function and reference, but you can declare an array of function pointers and declare a reference to an array.

You declare an array by using the data type, the name of the array, and the array operator [ ], with the number of elements you want in the array between the brackets:

```
int    AnArray[10];
```

The preceding example declares an array of 10 integers named *AnArray*. The name of the array becomes a pointer to the first element in the array.

The first element in an array is element 0 and the last element is element *n-1*, where *n* is the number you used to declare the array. Unlike BASIC, there is no *OPTION BASE* statement that lets you set the array base to 0 or 1.

There are two methods of accessing elements in the array.

First, you can use the address operator and include the index of the element you want to access. Writing *AnArray[5]* means you want to access the sixth element in the array (remember, indexing begins at 0).

Second, because the array name is a pointer to the first element in the array, you can add the index to the array name and dereference the expression: Writing **(AnArray + 5)* also means you want the value in the sixth element of the array. C and C++ automatically take the size of the array elements into account. An *int* is four bytes, so the sixth element actually is in the 24th to 27th bytes of the array. The language understands this and translates the + to adjust the operation by the size of an *int*.

Using multiple array operators in an array declaration creates a multidimensional array. Declaring *int AnArray[10][10];* creates a 10-by-10 two-dimensional array. The first element is at *AnArray[0][0]* and the last is at *AnArray[9][9]*. You'll look at multidimensional arrays in Tip 199, "Declaring Multidimensional Arrays."

Although C and C++ place no limit on the number of dimensions in an array, the memory used increases rapidly so that the operating system and available memory might impose limits. *AnArray[10]* uses 40 bytes (the size of an *int* times the number of elements), *AnArray[10][10]* uses 400 bytes, and *AnArray[10][10][10]* uses 4,000 bytes.

Neither C nor C++ sets any limits on the size of an array (other than the maximum value the index can hold) nor do they perform array bounds checking. Using an array with 10 elements, you could easily access element 11 or element –11. Placing a value in those locations might step on another variable, however, or even the function's return address (automatic variables are created on the stack, which is also where the return address is stored). It is up to your program to keep your array access within bounds.

Within a function, Visual C++ creates arrays on the stack, but no size checking takes place. For most applications, the default stack size in Visual C++ is one megabyte. If you declare an array that exceeds the stack memory (remember you already might have other automatic variables and function return addresses on the stack), you'll get a stack overflow error when the program enters the function where the stack is declared. An *int* array of 250,000 or more elements is almost certain to produce a stack overflow. If you need a large array, allocate memory for it or use one of the Visual C++ global allocation functions.

You also can declare an array with an unspecified number of elements by omitting the number from the array operator. You must initialize it at the same time so that the compiler knows how many elements to create space for.

```
int    AnArray[] = {42, 6, 12, 23, 18, 20};
```

The preceding line declares and initializes an array of six elements. *AnArray[0]* contains 42 and *AnArray[5]* contains 20.

Using an array of unspecified size introduces a bounds problem, particularly if you later change your code and modify the size. How does your program know how many elements are in the array? Well, you could count them and remember to limit your access to that many, but if you change the code, you would have to find every reference to the last element and modify that code. Programmers use the *sizeof* operator to set a constant to the size of the array.

```
#define    ELEMENTS    (sizeof(AnArray)/sizeof(int))
```

The constant *ELEMENTS* is 6, the number of elements in the example. *sizeof(AnArray)* returns 24 (six elements times 4, the size of an *int*) and *sizeof(int)* returns 4. This definition must be declared after the array, of course, but C and C++ place very few restrictions on where you can use the *#define* directive.

```
int    AnArray[] = {42, 6, 12, 23, 18, 20};
#define    ELEMENTS    (sizeof(AnArray)/sizeof(int))
    int x = 0;
    for (int a = 0; a < ELEMENTS; ++a)
      x += AnArray[a];
```

The previous snippet calculates the sum of the array elements using the *ELEMENTS* constant as the upper boundary of the array (actually *ELEMENTS-1* because the test statement specified the index variable *a* must be less than *ELEMENTS*). If you later add more elements to your array, the preprocessor will adjust the constant; you don't have to search for and modify any other code.

59. *Understanding Strings as an Array of Type* char

Within the standard namespace, neither C nor C++ contains any support for strings. Instead, you use an array of data type *char* to store a string. Because there is no array bounds checking, you need to keep track of where the string ends. Library functions use a value of 0 to indicate the size of a string, and when you declare and initialize a string, the compiler automatically adds one element to the *char* array and places a 0 there.

The following example declares an array of type *char* that contains 10 elements, the number of characters in the string plus one for the ending 0:

```
char    MyString[] = "My String";
```

You also can declare and initialize a string pointer and the compiler will set aside enough space to contain the string and set the pointer to the string itself:

```
char    *MyString;
```

The preceding example only declares a string pointer; it neither initializes the pointer nor sets aside any memory for a string. In contrast, the following declaration sets aside storage space for the string (and a terminating 0) and initializes the pointer:

```
char    *MyString = "My String";
```

There are some significant differences in the declarations, and the operations you can perform on the variables are determined by how you declare them. You'll take a much closer look in the section on strings beginning with Tip 239, "Understanding Strings and the User Interface."

60. *Commenting Your Code*

Standard C provides only one method of inserting comments into source code: You must declare the start of the comment with the /* characters and end the block using the reverse sequence, */. The compiler will ignore everything it encounters between those character sequences. Commented areas cannot be nested.

C++ provides a more convenient method. Any time the C++ compiler encounters an unquoted double slash (//), it ignores the rest of the line. Unlike the Standard C method, if your comment spans more than one line, you must include the // on every line. As a general rule, you should use the // method whenever possible for two very good reasons.

The first reason is compiler efficiency. If you include a comment using the // method, the compiler simply ignores the rest of the line. If you use the /* */ method, the compiler must search through the text for the ending sequence. The search doesn't take long for a single comment, but every programming text stresses that you should profusely comment your code. In a large program, the search time could be noticeable with a large number of commented areas.

Secondly, the /* */ comment method cannot be nested, but you can include // comments within it. If, for testing purposes, you need to comment out a large block of code, you can use the first method and not have to worry about encountering a */ sequence.

```
/* Comment Test */
    x = Something;          /* Set x to Something */
    y = SomethingElse;      /* Set y to SomethingElse */
```

In the preceding code, if you want to comment out the entire section to isolate it for debugging, you would have to search through all the comment markers and change them. If, however, you use the // method as shown in the following:

```
// Comment Test
    x = Something;          // Set x to Something
    y = SomethingElse;      // Set y to SomethingElse
```

Here, if you need to remove the code temporarily, say for debugging, you could use the standard C method:

```
/*
// Comment Test
  x = Something  ;            // Set x to Something
  y = SomethingElse;         // Set y to SomethingElse
*/
```

The nested // markers have no effect and the entire block of source code is removed from the compiled code. Remove the /* and */ markers and the code is restored.

61. *File Types Used by the Visual C++ IDE*

When you create a project or workspace in the Visual C++ Integrated Development Environment, a number of files will be generated depending on the project type you select.

All workspaces include at least three files:

- **The workspace file used in the IDE.** This file has an extension of .DSW and is an ordinary text file. A message at the top warns you not to edit or delete the file, but there are times when you might want to modify it. For example, if you add a class to your project or give it the wrong name, there's no way from the IDE to remove it from your project. Instead, you will need to edit this file along with the ClassWizard file.

- **A "No Compile Browser" file with an extension of .NCB.** This file is generated by the parser and is used by the ClassView, the Wizard Bar, and the Component Gallery. It is a binary file and, if deleted, is automatically regenerated.

- **A workspace options file.** This file is binary and has an extension of .OPT. It contains the workspace options you have set for this particular workspace, such as which toolbars you want displayed. If you close and reopen the workspace, the IDE reads this file to provide the look and feel you set.

Other application types might generate other files. An MFC application includes a ClassWizard file with an extension of .CLW that contains class information for your project. You should edit this file only when you need to make corrections in class declarations or if you remove a class from your project.

A *README.TXT* is generated with most projects. This is a standard, boilerplate file describing your project. You can read it when you create your first project, or the first project of a particular type, but after that it contains little information you don't already know. Deleting it has no effect other than to free up a few sectors on your disk.

The IDE also might create a RES directory in which it places the icons for your project, any toolbar images, and a resource file with an extension of .RC2. The last file is not maintained by the IDE, and you are free to edit it and create your own resources. It is included in the main resource file at compile time.

Other file types used by the IDE can include:

- **Output Description Language file with an extension of .ODL.** This file is used to generate a type library for controls; it also exposes the controls interface to the outside world. When you begin creating your own controls with ActiveX or DCOM, you might have to edit this file, but by then you should understand the definition process. Otherwise, it is best to let the IDE maintain it.

- **An Interface Description Language file with an extension of .IDL.** This file is used by the IDL compiler (in Visual C++, the MIDL compiler) and contains the interface specification along with a table of data types and functions that can be executed remotely. Unless you understand the IDL compiler (you're an ex-UNIX hacker, eh), let the IDE maintain this file for you.

- **A Resource Control file.** This file has an extension of .RC and contains definitions for resources (menus, dialog boxes, string tables, etc.) used in your project. It is updated any time you modify objects in the ResourceView panel of the workspace window.

- **A definition file with an extension of .DEF.** This file is needed by control and DLL projects. For a DLL it is the module definition file; for a control it contains the name and description of the control and the size of the runtime heap.

- **A registry file with an extension of .REG.** Registers any project in which you have selected any automation option or a document extension that requires an entry in the registry. The file might be used by your setup program to set entries in the registry.

For a number of the project types, the wizards create a number of .C, .CPP, and .H source code files, including a skeleton Windows program file if you select one of the Win32 types. For a project using the Microsoft Foundation Class library, your application, view, and window frame files are created for you. Using these is encouraged unless you want to perform a lot of tedious, repetitious tasks.

You also might generate a makefile from the IDE so that the project can be compiled from the command line. Select the Project menu, and then choose Export Makefile.

If you are new to the IDE, creating a project of each type and then examining the source files for each will give you a good idea of how much work the IDE actually does for you and an idea of how to use the different project types.

62. Understanding Text Files and Document Files

In Windows, text files contain only ordinary text and control characters that are defined by the American Standard Code for Information Interchange (ASCII). There are other characters and character sets available, but the C language specification sets the range of characters to seven-bit ASCII.

Text files in Windows are created using NotePad or the DOS *EDIT.COM* program. The editor program integrated into the Developers Studio reads and saves source code files as plain text. Although for display purposes it does show them in different colors and attributes, these are not saved as part of the source file.

A document file, on the other hand, can store text colors and attributes, along with other formatting information, as part of the document file. None of this information is usable by language compilers, and in fact tends to produce quite a mess on the screen when you try to run it through a compiler. Document files are created and used by word processor programs such as WordPerfect or Microsoft Word.

Document or word programs also tend to be large and cumbersome for writing source files (*WIN-WORD.EXE*, the main executable for Microsoft Word, is more than 5MB). A plain-text editor usually is of the "short and sweet" variety because it doesn't have to interpret and maintain complicated pattern and formatting information. *NotePad.exe* is only about 45KB and *EDIT.COM* is about 70KB (on Windows NT it is only 413 bytes, but it invokes the QBASIC editor; *QBASIC.EXE* is about 255KB).

63. Creating and Using Source Files

Create and edit your source files using the Developers Studio editor or one of the smaller text editing programs available in Windows. If you use a document or word processing program, you run the risk of saving your file in the wrong format.

For quick editing and creating brief test programs, I keep a copy of the old DOS program Norton Commander around. It has limited capabilities, tabs are fixed at eight spaces, and the file size is limited to about 32KB, but it makes easy-to-navigate directories and editing is a matter of point and shoot. You make your changes, save the file, and exit with relatively few keystrokes.

With *EDIT.COM*, when you enter without naming a file you get a silly welcome screen that you must dispatch before you can do anything. After that, you can write your source code and save it with a .c or .cpp extension. After you create the file, you can name it on the command line (*EDIT MyFile.cpp*, for example) and bypass the welcome window. To create the file, you can name it from the command line and go right into editing it and then save it, bypassing everything. Unfortunately, it doesn't give you cut and paste capability between Windows programs.

NotePad.exe has its own set of peculiarities. When you create a file, you have to name it from the command line (*notepad myfile.cpp*, for example). Then it says it doesn't exist and you have to dispatch the message with a "Yes," you really do want to create a file by this name. If you don't name a new source file from the command line and try to save it with, say, a *.cpp* extension, you wind up with something like *myfile.cpp.txt*, which is not acceptable to the compiler. *NotePad* does, however, give you cut and paste capability between programs.

Of the two, *EDIT* probably is preferable unless you need the cut and paste. Eventually you might want to create your own text file editor using the tools available in the Developers Studio. *NotePad* and *EDIT* can invoke only one file at a time, but your own editor could use a multidocument interface.

In a few pages, when you start exploring the Visual C++ environment, you'll create a simple, multi-document program editor that you can use to try out the code samples. All the snippets and sample programs in this book were written using this editor. It not only gives us a common tool, but it will introduce you to the Visual C++ Integrated Development Environment.

64. *Creating and Using Header Files*

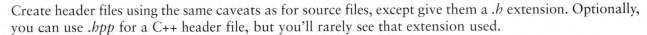

Create header files using the same caveats as for source files, except give them a *.h* extension. Optionally, you can use *.hpp* for a C++ header file, but you'll rarely see that extension used.

Actually, you can use just about any extension for a file read in with the *#include* directive as long as it's a plain-text file. Common practice is to use the .h extension, although there are a few standard *include* files that have no extension.

It is common practice to place a comment at the top of the file describing why you created it and how it is used. It doesn't have to be more than a couple of lines, and if you are so inclined you can put your copyright notice in the comment field.

As you create and use header files, you might find the declarations in one header file need the definitions in another. A header file can include other files by using the *#include* directive.

The *#include* directive reads files in one of two ways:

- If you write the name of the file between angle brackets (<>), the preprocessor looks for the file in the paths specified in the /I compiler runtime option, then in the path specified in the *INCLUDE* environment variable. (In Tip 130, "Compiler Command-Line Options," you will look at this compiler option more closely.)

- If you write the file name between double quote marks (""), the preprocessor first looks in the same directory as the file containing the *#include* directive, then the path specified in the /I option, and finally in the path specified in the *INCLUDE* environment variable.

In addition, if you specify a complete path for the header file between the double quote marks, the preprocessor will search only that path, ignoring the standard include paths.

For standard header files such as *stdio.h*, always place them between angle brackets. That will shorten the search time for the file, and you know it won't be in the local directory.

On the other hand, header files you create almost always will be in the current directory. If the preprocessor is to find them, you must put the name between double quote marks.

65. Using a Guardian to Protect Against Including a Header File More Than Once

As one header file includes another, and source files then include them, you run the risk of including a header file more than once in your compilation. A simple guardian or sentry directive in the header file will allow it to be included only once.

A guardian directive is nothing more than an *#ifndef* statement followed by a unique definition to identify the header file. The application wizards use a sentry built from "AFX" followed by the file name, then a UUID (Universally Unique Identifier), and finally the word "INCLUDED," all in uppercase. That's a long guardian directive, but there's a pretty good chance it is going to be unique.

You don't have to be as exact as the application wizards. You might, for example, use two underscores, the name of the file minus the extension, an underscore, the letter "H," and end it with two underscores. That's less likely to be unique in a system environment than the application wizard method, but within the local directory it should not cause any problems.

Follow the *#ifndef* on the next line with a *#define* directive, and then give it the same identifier you did in the *#ifndef* directive. Move to the bottom of the file and enter *#endif* followed by an optional comment. (It's always a good idea to match lengthy condition compilations with a comment line showing the corresponding *#if* directive.) For a header file called *proto.h*, the sequence might look something like this:

```
/*
proto.h - Function prototypes for MYPROJECT.EXE.
          Function definitions are in utility.cpp.
*/
#ifndef __PROTO_H__
#define __PROTO_H__
// Some declaration and definitions
// needed by the program files.
#endif        // __PROTO_H__
```

The first time you include the file in your source code, the *#ifndef* is true (the sentry definition has not been defined), so the preprocessor reads the file normally. The next statement defines the sentry definition. At the end of the file, you end the conditional block with the *#endif* directive. All the definitions and declarations are contained in the conditional block.

If you include the file a second time, the *#ifndef* condition is false because the first include defined the sentry, so the preprocessor jumps to the matching *#endif* at the bottom of the page. The body of the header file is skipped.

You'll look into sentry statement in more detail later. Right now I want to give you enough C++ background to get you started.

66. *Understanding Makefiles*

Before integrated environments such as the Developers Studio were available, creating program files from source files meant compiling them from the command line. If the program consisted of several source files, each file had to be compiled to produce object files, which contained the binary code and link information to put them together with other object files. Then the object files had to be linked to create the final program file.

To automate the process, a program called *make* was devised. The program operates on a file called a *makefile*, which contains statements naming the various components of a program, commands to generate the components, and how to put them together into a program.

The make program then looks at the component to see if any of the files the program depends on have been modified since the last time the program was created. If any file has been modified, it will recompile the component. If any of a program's components change during the make process, *make* will invoke the compiler or linker as necessary to regenerate the program's executable file.

The IDE handles all those tasks for you. Simply click a build button and the IDE program performs all the tasks once assigned to make and builds a new program file. Make remains a valuable tool for command-line builds, however, and virtually all IDEs include some form of it. In the Developers Studio, the make program is *NMAKE.EXE*. In fact, the studio has a menu option that allows you to create a makefile for your project. Select the Project menu and then choose Export Makefile. The exported makefile contains all the information required to build the project from the command line. The makefile specifies the same project build settings you set in the Developers Studio.

Eventually, make became a very sophisticated program. Entire books have been written about it, and I couldn't hope to cover all aspects of it in the space I have here, but I will cover the basics of setting up environment variables, setting dependencies, and creating the eventual program file. I'll give you enough information to build simple makefiles to use from the command line. If you prefer, you can just skip the next few tips and use the makefiles you generate from within the IDE.

67. *Understanding Makefiles: Defining Environment Variables*

The make program inherits all the environment variables set at the system level before you run the program. From within the makefile, you can redefine any of these environment variables or create new ones. Any changes or new variables are lost when the make program exits.

By convention, environment variables usually are entered in all uppercase letters to distinguish them from other makefile commands. Set a variable by declaring it with the equals sign, followed by the value. To create a variable that contains the name of the Visual C++ compiler command along with the flag to generate only an object file, write it on a line by itself:

```
CC=cl.exe -c
```

In many environments the linker is a separate program. In Visual C++, the linker is *LINK.EXE*. Usually, you don't see the linker command because the compiler invokes it automatically. To define an environment variable for the linker:

```
LINK=link.exe
```

If the command extends to more than one line, use the backslash character to join the lines. If my project contains a number of object files that must be linked to produce the executable file, for example, they can be named in a single environment variable:

```
OBJ=adventure.obj database.obj english.obj itverb.obj \
    turn.obj verb.obj say.obj pspeak.obj rspeak.obj
```

Access the environment variable using a dollar sign followed by the environment variable in parentheses. Combining the preceding variables, the following command would execute the linker to generate an executable:

```
$(LINK) $(OBJ)
```

When it encounters the line, make expands the variables and issues the following command:

```
link.exe adventure.obj database.obj english.obj itverb.obj turn.obj verb.obj say.obj
pspeak.obj rspeak.obj
```

68. *Understanding Makefiles: Setting Dependencies*

A dependency statement tells make that a given file is dependent on other files, and if the modified time of those files is later than the dependent file, the dependency must be updated.

You create a dependency statement by naming the target file in the first column, following it with a colon, and then naming the dependent files to check. If the list continues to the next line, join them with a backslash. On a line by itself and indented (the indent is important), enter the command you want the make program to execute to build the target file. If my *database.cpp* file contains the directives to include the header files *database.h* and *proto.h*, the following line makes *database.obj* dependent on the source file and the two headers, and then instructs make to run *cl.exe* to build *database.obj*:

```
database.obj:   database.cpp database.h proto.h
                cl.exe -c database.cpp
```

You can specify multiple targets by separating them with a colon.

After all your object file dependencies are declared, make your executable file dependent on the object files.

```
myprog.exe:   $(OBJ)
              link.exe /o myprog.exe $(OBJ)
```

The preceding lines tell make to check the last modified times of all the files you specify in the OBJ variable. If any of them are later than *myprog.exe*, perform the command on the following line, which is to link the files into the executable.

69. *Using* **NMAKE.EXE**

The *NMAKE* program looks in the current directory called simply "makefile" with no extension. When you export a makefile from the IDE, however, it is given the project name with a .mak extension. You can rename that file to "makefile" or specify it on the command line when you run make:

```
C:>NMAKE /f myprog.mak
```

When the preceding command is run from the DOS prompt, it will cause *NMAKE* to use *myprog.mak* instead of *makefile*.

70. *Understanding Executable Files*

The primary executable file type on Windows is the *EXE* file (it has an extension of *.EXE)*. The extension is a flag to the operating system telling it what to expect when it reads a program and loads it into memory to be run.

There are other types of executables, such as *COM*, which is rapidly disappearing from Windows. The multitasking environment of Windows and modern processor chips require more information in the executable file than is available in a *COM* program. When Windows loads and runs a *COM* file, it must emulate an older processor, which increases the processing overhead.

Visual C++ tools produce *EXE* files. This type of file contains an extensive header section that gives Windows the information it needs to set up the various segments needed to run the program, including minimum sizes required for the data segments and the size of the stack.

It also contains a relocation map containing information needed to move the code in memory or to run the program in different memory locations. The actual code segment, called the program image, in an *EXE* file contains relocatable code. When you run an *EXE* program, the Windows loader reads the header and uses the information to manage the program while it is executing.

A running program isn't necessarily loaded into memory all the time. Depending on the available memory and the number of other programs you have running, Windows can force the program into a dormant state and write its current state to a disk file, freeing up memory for other programs. When your program needs to execute part of its code, another program might be swapped to disk and your program again loaded into memory.

71. *Understanding Characters: The ASCII Character Set*

Until the late 1960s there was no standard method of representing characters on the various models of computers. Each manufacturer had its own way of representing characters, numbers, and symbols. As the sun began to rise on the digital age, it was clear that computers "speaking in tongues" was not workable.

The development of the American Standard Code for Information Interchange in 1968 went a long way toward relieving the situation, but it was not a cure-all. Machines still used their Tower of Babel characters, but at least ASCII gave them a means of translating data and sending it to other computers. Other character codes persisted for some time. The Extended Binary Coded Decimal Interchange Code (EBCDIC) developed by IBM is still being used even today.

ASCII defines 128 characters using seven bits. Because the unit used by most computers to represent characters was eight bits (the object now considered a byte was not always eight bits), that left plenty of room for proprietary characters. Virtually all minicomputers and personal computers use the ASCII character set today, and an Extended ASCII set using the full eight bits of a byte has been defined to represent international characters. The extended set has not been standardized.

The order of characters in the ASCII is far from random. The first 32 characters, those that can be represented using only the four least significant bits, are used as control characters. Although the names of many of them seem like names from a fairy tale, the printers and other devices used in the 1960s and 1970s needed them for such things as advancing the paper, sounding a bell, returning the carriage to its home position, and so on.

Punctuation characters fill the next 16 bytes, and the numerical digits start at 48, or 30 hexadecimal. The alphabetical characters begin with capital letters at 65 (41 hex), and are arranged so that there is only one bit difference between upper- and lowercase values of the same character. This means an uppercase letter set can be made lowercase by the simple operation of ORing it with the hex value 20, the value of a spaceband. Conversely, lowercase letters can be made uppercase by ANDing them with the 1's complement of a spaceband, DF hexadecimal.

The character set for the keywords and data types in the C and C++ languages is limited to the seven-bit ASCII sequence.

72. Understanding Characters: The Trans-ASCII or Extended Character Set

The representation of international characters is limited in the ASCII character set; a number of these characters have been assigned unofficial positions in the character values above 127 (the limit of the seven-bit ASCII sequence) and below 256 (the limit for an eight-bit character value is 255). Fonts might vary, but generally you'll find typesetting and currency symbols in the range from 128 to 191 and accented characters from 192 to 255.

It is clear that the standard codes for representing characters will be undergoing changes in the near future. Computers, even personal computers, today are international devices, and the eight bits used to represent ASCII and extended ASCII characters cannot represent all the characters in use throughout the world.

Between 1988 and 1991, the Unicode Consortium developed a 16-bit system to represent the full range of international characters. The Unicode scheme can contain 65,536 possible characters, and about 40,000 have been defined so far. Some 21,000 of these are Chinese ideographs. Most of the symbols represented in the extended ASCII set retain their unofficial positions in the Unicode set.

Unicode, sometimes called a *wide* character set, is supported in C++ using the *wchar_t* type. Although *wchar_t* is a keyword in C++, it actually is implemented in Visual C++ as a *typedef* of unsigned short *int*. Alternatively, you can implement a character as a wide character by prefixing it with "L." Thus, *'e'* is an eight-bit representation of the letter "e," but *L'e'* and *wchar_t 'e'* are 16-bit representations. Strings also can be declared using the *L* modifier. *L"A string"* defines a string of wide characters, and the compiler automatically tacks on a 16-bit null terminator.

Many of the standard library functions that deal with characters and strings have wide character equivalents, generally named by prefixing the eight-bit function with a "w." The 16-bit version of *printf* is *wprintf*, for example.

In Visual C++, additional macros and *typedefs* provide conditional support for wide characters. The *TCHAR* type can be used in place of *char*, *LPTSTR* in place of *char **, and *LPCTSTR* in place of *const char **. You can define and declare strings using the *_T* or *_TEXT* macro, as in *_T("My String")* or *_TEXT("My String")*. Using these identifiers, your program can be recompiled for Unicode by adding the following line:

```
#define    _UNICODE
```

With *_UNICODE* defined, Visual C++ replaces the *_T()* with *L*. Otherwise it simply removes the *_T()* before compilation.

Another identifier, *_MBCS* (for *multibyte character set*), is used to compile non-Unicode wide-character sequences. *_UNICODE* and *_MBCS* are like the *_STDC* and *_cplusplus* definitions: They cannot both be defined in the same program file. Without either being defined, the default is to use the single byte character set used by ASCII.

Eventually, there will be some official standards for wide characters. If you practice using these macros and definitions, it's almost certain Microsoft will modify them to reflect the changing standards and porting your code will be simplified.

73. C/C++ Escape Sequences: Embedding Unprintable Characters

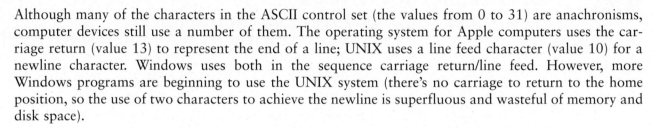

Although many of the characters in the ASCII control set (the values from 0 to 31) are anachronisms, computer devices still use a number of them. The operating system for Apple computers uses the carriage return (value 13) to represent the end of a line; UNIX uses a line feed character (value 10) for a newline character. Windows uses both in the sequence carriage return/line feed. However, more Windows programs are beginning to use the UNIX system (there's no carriage to return to the home position, so the use of two characters to achieve the newline is superfluous and wasteful of memory and disk space).

Generally, the control characters are unprintable and cannot be displayed on monitors, and most of them cannot be entered directly from the keyboard. The C and C++ languages define a set of character constants, or escape sequences, to represent most of the control characters. The escape sequences combine a backslash with another character, and the combination is translated by the compiler into the proper control character.

Usually, the escaped character is representative of the original name of the control character; the form feed character (0C in hexadecimal) was used to move the paper in a printer to the top of the next page and to clear the screen on terminals. It is represented by a \f as a mnemonic for form feed.

The newline character, \n, is of particular interest because its interpretation depends on the operating system, and can be a carriage return, a line feed, or both. Visual C++ translates it to a carriage return/line feed combination.

Character constants defined by C and C++ are shown in Table 73.

Name	Character	Hex Value	Escape Sequence
Newline	NL or LF	0A*	\n
Horizontal tab	HT	09	\t
Vertical tab	VT	0B	\v
Backspace	BS	08	\b
Carriage return	CR	0D	\r
Form feed	FF	0C	\f
Audible alert (bell)	BEL	07	\a

Table 73   C and C++ escape sequences (continued on following page)

Name	Character	Hex Value	Escape Sequence
Backslash	\	5C	\\
Question mark	?	3F	\?
Single quote	'	27	\'
Double quote	"	22	\"

Table 73   C and C++ escape sequences (continued from previous page)

The backslash is escaped to represent itself and the question mark is escaped to support a reduced character set. The double and single quote marks are escaped because they are used in the language to delimit single characters and strings.

74.   C/C++ Escape Sequences: Using the Backslash

The backslash character is a special character in C and C++. Its use is carried over from the UNIX operating system, where it is used in command-line sequences to embed control characters. It was only natural for C to use the backslash, because C was the predominant language on UNIX long before it became available for personal computers.

If you are new to C and C++, you'll probably get dinged by the compiler for having an "illegal escape sequence" when misusing the backslash. You'll quickly get used to it, however.

In addition to the character constants, the backslash is used to define numerical constants in a character or to embed a constant in a string. Even if a character cannot be represented in the ASCII or extended ASCII character sets, it can be represented as a numerical constant.

The backslash character followed by three digits is used to enter a character value in octal (base 8). When followed by a lowercase x and two hexadecimal (base 16) digits, it is used to enter a value in hexadecimal. Octal \177 or Hex \x7F is used to enter the DEL character, which normally cannot be displayed on a monitor, in octal or hexadecimal. If the octal value is less than three digits, you must zero fill on the left. A carriage return is represented as "\015"; just "\15" would generate an illegal escape sequence on most compilers. Although it is acceptable to Visual C++, avoid using octal values with less than three digits for portability. No method has been established for entering constants as decimals.

The backslash method of representing constants has meaning only within single or double quote marks. You cannot enter \012 or \n, for example, on a line and expect the compiler to recognize that as the end of a line. To set the value of a variable or to represent a numerical constant using an octal number, precede the number with a 0 ("012" is 10 in decimal, but "12" is 12). To represent a hexadecimal value, precede it with 0x ("0x0a" is 12 in decimal).

Be careful entering decimal values in C and C++. If you enter them with a leading 0, most languages will ignore it. But C and C++ compilers will interpret that as an octal value and results might not be what you expect. Also, make it a practice, for portability, to always use an even number of digits when entering a hexadecimal value (0x0a instead of just 0xa).

75.

C/C++ Escape Sequences:
Using the Percent Character to Format Text

Standard library functions such as *scanf* and *printf* use the percent sign (%) as an escape character to signify a value to be decoded on input or encoded on output. These sequences are not a part of the C or C++ languages but are defined as part of the standard library. "%d" or "%i" is used to signify a decimal value, "%o" an octal value, and "%x" or "%X" a hexadecimal number.

Argument types used with the percent character are listed in Table 75. Other than the three exceptions noted in the table, all sequences are entered in lowercase.

Character	Argument Type	Conversion
d,i	int	Signed decimal.
o	int	Unsigned octal. Used without a leading 0.
x,X	int	Unsigned hexadecimal. Used with a leading 0X. Uppercase X is used to output hex characters in uppercase.
u	int	Unsigned decimal.
c	int	Single character (after conversion to unsigned *char*).
s	char pointer	The characters in the location identified by the pointer are printed until a terminating \0 is encountered or the precision limit is reached.
f	double	Decimal floating point.
e,E	double	Decimal exponential. The precision determines the number of decimal places printed.
g,G	double	Decimal floating pint or decimal exponential. If the exponent is less than −4 or greater than or equal to the precision, %e or %E is used. Otherwise %f is used.
p	void pointer	Prints the value of the pointer. Not available with all compilers.
n	int	*printf* maintains a count of the number of characters output during the current call. The %n sequence causes *printf* to write the value at the point specified into a variable. The parameter is a pointer to a type int variable.
%	none	None. %% causes a single % to be printed.

Table 75   Formatted text escape sequences

The *d*, *i*, *o*, *u*, and *x* can be preceded by an *h* to indicate a short *int* value, or by the letter *l* to indicate a long *int* value. Used before the *e*, *f*, and *g* conversion characters, the lowercase *l* indicates a *double* (rather than float) value and the uppercase *L* indicates a *long* double.

76. *Using* printf: *Formatting Output*

The standard library function *printf ()* is used to produce formatted output to the standard output device. It requires at least a format string as a parameter, followed by optional parameters of any data type. The string is printed with any escape sequences converted. If more than one string is passed as the format parameter (without intervening commas), the strings are concatenated to form a single string.

Neither the compiler nor the *printf* function performs any type checking to make sure the conversion sequences match the data types of the parameters. Mismatches can produce some unexpected results.

To insert a value into a format string, use the percent sign (%) escape character followed by the conversion character. A "%d" in the string causes the function to get the corresponding parameter and print it as a decimal value. To print "The number 10" followed by a newline using *printf*, you would write

```
printf ("The number %d.\n", 10);
```

If a character following a percent sign is not recognized as a conversion character, it is output without the percent sign. To output a percent sign, enter "%%" in the format string.

Where a character can be used in the formatting (such as the *x*, *e*, and *g* conversions), the case of the conversion character determines the case of the output. To print the line "The number 10 in hex is a (or A).", you would enter

```
printf("The number %d in hex is %x (or %X).\n",10,10,10);
```

A parameter can be a constant value, an expression, or a function call, but note that you cannot use a call to a void function.

77. *Using* printf: *Setting the Field Width*

There are times when you want the output of a parameter to fill a fixed number of spaces, such as in tabular columns to maintain alignment. The minimum field width can be set by entering a number between the percent sign and the conversion character. Entering a positive value causes the output to be aligned to the right of the field; a negative number aligns the output to the left of the field.

```
printf ("The number %4d.\n", 10);
printf ("The number %-4d.\n", 10);
```

The preceding lines produce the following output:

```
The number   10.
The number 10  .
```

If the number is too wide to fit into the field width, the width argument is ignored and the entire number is printed.

78. *Using* printf: *Setting the Precision*

Normally, when printing a decimal value, *printf* displays six digits to the right of the decimal point. You can set the number of digits to display by using a decimal point and an optional precision value, which can be combined with a field width value.

```
printf ("This is a fraction: %f.\n", 1.0 / 7);
printf ("This is a fraction: %.10f.\n", 1.0 / 7);
printf ("This is a fraction: %20.10f.\n", 1.0 / 7);
printf ("This is a fraction: %-20.10f.\n", 1.0 / 7);
```

Running the preceding code produces the following output:

```
This is a fraction: 0.142857.
This is a fraction: 0.1428571429.
This is a fraction:         0.1428571429.
This is a fraction: 0.1428571429         .
```

Notice in the preceding example that I use 1.0/7 to cast the constant to a floating type. Simply using 1/7 would equate to the integer value of the fraction, or zero. In some cases, the sample lines above would cause a runtime error. To optimize code, Visual C++ links the floating-point library only if it detects a floating-point operation in the compiled code. The *%f* sequence is not detected as a floating point—there's no type checking, remember—and when the code is run you get "runtime error R6002 – floating point not loaded." Simply declaring a float variable and assigning it a value—such as *float dummy = 1.0;*—would cause the floating-point code to be linked.

For a string, the precision specifies the maximum number of characters to print from the argument. If the string is longer than the precision, it is truncated, as shown in the following example:

```
char *str = "This is a string.";
printf ("String example: \"%.10s.\"\n", str);
```

Instead of printing the entire string, the *printf* writes only the first 10 characters; the rest of the string is ignored:

```
String example: "This is a . "
```

79. *Using* printf: *Zero and Space Filling the Field*

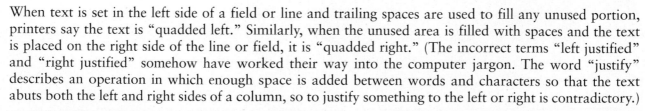

When text is set in the left side of a field or line and trailing spaces are used to fill any unused portion, printers say the text is "quadded left." Similarly, when the unused area is filled with spaces and the text is placed on the right side of the line or field, it is "quadded right." (The incorrect terms "left justified" and "right justified" somehow have worked their way into the computer jargon. The word "justify" describes an operation in which enough space is added between words and characters so that the text abuts both the left and right sides of a column, so to justify something to the left or right is contradictory.)

The *printf* function can be used to force text to the left or right, producing aligned columnar output. Consider the following code and output:

```
int Sales = 12484;
int Returns = 123;
```

```
printf ("Sales %d\n", Sales);
printf ("Returns %d\n", Returns);
printf ("Net turnover %d\n", Sales - Returns);
```

On output, all the information is there, but the staggered numbers look awkward:

```
Sales 12484
Returns 123
Net turnover 12361
```

Wouldn't it look better if you could insert enough spaces so that the text aligned to the left of the column and the numbers to the right? Flags used with the width and precision values produce that result. Say you want the label to fit in the left 12 spaces of the line and the number in the right 8 spaces.

Normally, a string is printed in the right of a field, but you can force it to the left by specifying a negative field width. Numbers normally are set at the left of a column, so you need only specify the field width.

```
printf ("%12s %8d\n", "Sales", Sales);
printf ("%-12s %8d\n", "Returns", Returns);
printf ("%-12s %8d\n", "Net turnover",Sales-Returns);
```

The result is a nicely aligned table (the text is said to be "quadded in the middle" or simply "quad mid"):

```
Sales          12484
Returns          123
Net turnover   12361
```

If you use a 0 instead of a space preceding the width, the field is padded to the left with leading 0s:

```
printf ("%-12s %08d\n", "Sales", Sales);
printf ("%-12s %08d\n", "Returns", Returns);
printf ("%-12s %08d\n", "Net turnover",Sales-Returns);
```

In this case, you still have the numbers aligned, but all the spaces in the number fields now contain zeros.

```
Sales        0012484
Returns      0000123
Net turnover 0012361
```

The following list summarizes the sequence and meaning of the various components of a format:

- **The percent character symbolizes a formatting sequence to follow.** If it is followed by another percent character, no formatting is performed and a single percent character is output.

- **One or more flags, in any order:**

  A minus sign (–) to specify the argument is to be placed in the left of the field.

  A plus sign (+) to indicate a number is to be printed with a sign, even if positive.

  A space. If the first character is not a sign (+ or –), a space is output to preserve column alignment.

  The digit *0* to pad the spaces in a number field with leading 0s.

  The poundal (#) to specify alternate output for octal, hexadecimal, and exponential output. For an octal argument, a leading 0 will be output. For hexadecimal, a *0x* or *0X* will be output if the argument is non-zero. For exponential and floating-point numbers, the output will always have a decimal point. For the double g or G, trailing 0s will not be stripped.

- **Any number specifying a minimum field width.** If the space required to print the number is less than this value, a wider field will be used.

- **A period if precision value is specified.**

- **An optional precision value.** For a string, this number specifies the maximum number of characters to print. For an integer, this number specifies the maximum number of characters to print, including leading 0s. For floating-point or exponential numbers, it specifies the maximum digits to print after the decimal point. For the g or G conversion, it specifies the number of significant digits to print.

- **A length modifier.** A lowercase h indicates the argument is to be printed as a short or unsigned short. A lowercase l indicates a long or unsigned long and an uppercase L indicates a long double.

- **The conversion character itself from Table 75.**

80. *C++ I/O Streams:* cout, cin, cerr

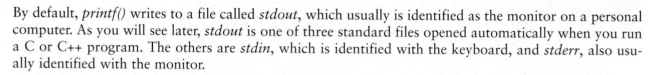

By default, *printf()* writes to a file called *stdout*, which usually is identified as the monitor on a personal computer. As you will see later, *stdout* is one of three standard files opened automatically when you run a C or C++ program. The others are *stdin*, which is identified with the keyboard, and *stderr*, also usually identified with the monitor.

When you run a C++ program, you can use byte stream classes for these standard files. Byte streams, derived from a class named *iostream*, treat files as a sequence of bytes, and in many cases are easier to use than the standard files. C++ identifies these streams as *cin* for *stdin*, *cout* for *stdout*, and *cerr* for *stderr*. C++ also defines another standard output device called *clog*, which is similar to *cerr* but provides more buffering capability. To use the *iostream* operators, you must include the standard header file *iostream.h* in your source file.

To use *cout* and *cerr*, name the stream, use the shift left operator, and follow it with the text to be output:

```
cout << "This is text to standard output";
```

To include a variable or number in your output, place it in the output stream using another shift left operator. You don't have to include a format string or identifier.

```
cout << "This is the number 10: " << 10;
```

In the section "Getting Started with Programming," you'll look at some of the differences between the standard files and iostreams.

81. *Creating a Project*

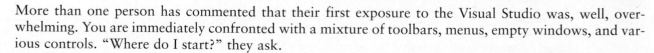

More than one person has commented that their first exposure to the Visual Studio was, well, overwhelming. You are immediately confronted with a mixture of toolbars, menus, empty windows, and various controls. "Where do I start?" they ask.

When you first start Visual Studio, you are greeted with a Tip of the Day dialog. You might want to keep this function, perhaps even go through the tips using the Next Tip button, but eventually you probably will find it troublesome to dispatch every time. Just uncheck the Show Tips at Startup box and the dialog will not reappear. To re-enable it, select Tip of the Day from the Help menu and check the box again.

Right now, the Studio is an empty room, ready for you to add the classes, source file, and resources that make up a program. In fact, many of the features of the Studio don't come to life until you load a project. So now you'll create a simple text-editing project to demonstrate the features of Visual Studio. Later you'll use the resulting program from the command line to create and edit your own source files. I'll skip a fully detailed explanation of the wizard options for now and get back to them later.

Call your first project *ProgramEditor*. Select New from the File menu. The New dialog should appear. This dialog is the starting point for the project wizards you invoke when creating projects.

Select the Projects tab and click the MFC AppWizard (exe) item. On the right side of the dialog, select the location for your project. I place all my C and C++ projects in a directory called CFiles; under that, I have subdirectories for projects in the various C++ development environments I use: BC5 for Borland C++, Builder for Borland Builder, Warrior for CodeWarrior, and VisualC++ for the Visual Studio. For the location, I would enter "C:\CFiles\VisualC++." Enter the location where you want to keep your files; if the directory doesn't exist, the Studio program will create it.

Enter "Program Editor" in the Project Name field. Notice the name has been added to the location field. The Studio program will create a subdirectory folder to hold the various files you will use in your project.

Press the OK button to enter the MFC AppWizard. There are six pages in the wizard that enable you to select various options for your project; you can use the Next and Back buttons to step forward or backward to refine your project options. On the first page, select Multiple Documents for application type and make sure the Document/View Architecture Support box is checked. The Resource Language box should have your default language selected.

Click the Next> button to move to the second page. Leave the database options set to none and then click the Next> button again to move to page 3. If you select any compound document support on this page, the wizard will add code to your project to enable OLE (Object Linking and Embedding). Later, if you select the rich edit view for your project, you'll have to select at least Container Support. For now, leave the selection set to None. For other support, leave the ActiveX box checked; you won't use ActiveX or automation in this project, but checking ActiveX will allow you to include any of the ActiveX controls shipped with Visual Studio later. Click the Next> button to move on to page 4, the Features page.

The default features will be enough for your first project. Click the Advanced button to set up your initial document template. Enter "cpp" in the File Extension field and then change the Filter Name field to read C/C++ Source Files (*.cpp). At the end of this section, you'll change the template string to include standard C, header, and resource files (a resource file, usually with an extension of .rc, is where you define the menus, strings, dialog boxes, etc., for your program). Leave the defaults for the other fields and close the Advanced dialog box with the Close button. Move on to page 5. Leave the defaults as they are and click the Next> button to move to page 6.

The wizard displays a list of the classes it will create for your project. These include the application class, the window frame classes, the document manager, and the view class. You can change the class name or the implementation and header file names by selecting the default class name and altering the names in the fields at the bottom of the box. The default names are fine for now, but select the view class, CProgramEditorView, in the list window. In the Base Class box at the bottom, select CEditView rather than the default CView class.

Click the Finish button. A final dialog box will list the type of application you are creating, the classes the wizard will create, and the features you selected for the project. Click the OK button to create the new project.

The first thing you will notice is that several of the previously inactive controls in the Visual Studio have become available. Notice the Workspace window at the left of the studio frame. Instead of a large, grayed area, it now contains information about your project. At the bottom of the Workspace window, three tabs have appeared. You can use the windows revealed by these tabs to navigate through your project.

Quickly looking around the studio, you see a menu bar and a collection of toolbars at the top. The toolbars are all "dockable," you can grab them using the mouse and move them to other locations, or hide and show them as needed. The menu bar is dockable as well, but you might not hide it. (The menu bar can be hidden when working in full-screen mode, but that's another topic altogether.)

The large gray area to the right of the Workspace window is the Editing window. This is the "client" area for the studio. When you open your source code files to edit them, this is where they will appear.

At the bottom and stretching across the screen is the Output window, which contains a number of tabs. The number and labels on the tabs vary according to the Visual Studio edition you installed, but generally you will find tabs for Build and Debug and at least two Find in Files tabs and a Results tab. You'll learn the purposes of these tabs later.

At the end of this section, you'll modify the project to set the Editor window font, modify the document template, and generally make the editor useful as a tool to create and edit sample programs from the command line. Later, as you learn more about Visual C++ and Windows programming, you can expand it to include features you want in a command-line editor.

For now, you have one last task. By default, the IDE creates executable files that have the same name as your project. You don't want to have to type "Program Editor" every time you want to run your program, so call it simply PE.EXE. Select the Project menu and then the Settings ... item, or simply type Alt+F7, to summon the Project Settings dialog box. The combo box at the upper left of the box should show Win32 Debug. If not, click the box's down arrow and select the debug version. Next, select the Link tab from the tab control that fills the right portion of the dialog. In the Output File Name field, change it to read Debug\PE.exe. Next, select Win32 Release in the combo box at the upper left and change the output file to Release\PE.exe. Click the OK button to save the settings.

82. *Visual Studio Menus*

The Visual Studio is full of menus. In addition to the standard menu bar at the top, there are numerous pop-up, or context, menus that change in response to what you are doing and where the mouse cursor is when you right-click the mouse. With a project open, most of the menu items have been enabled, allowing you to explore them.

83. *Visual Studio Menus: The File Menu*

The File menu contains standard file operations, including the New item you saw already. Other menu items allow you to open, close, and save individual files or entire workspaces and to set up and use your printer. Toward the bottom of the menu, the Most Recently Used (MRU) list is split into two items: Recent Files and Recent Workspace. By default, the last four files opened with the Open menu item and the last four workspaces you opened are included in this list. You can change the number in the Options dialog, which I'll cover later.

84. *Visual Studio Menus: The Edit Menu*

The Edit menu contains some interesting and useful entries in addition to the usual search and replace and cut and copy functions. Under Advanced ... you'll find options for incremental searching, "tabifying" and "untabifying" text, changing the case of text, and viewing the white space in a file.

Incremental searching involves searching for text while you type the search string. Select Incremental Search on the menu (or type Ctrl+I) and the cursor moves to the status bar at the bottom of the screen. Type the first character of the search and the editor will highlight it in the text. Type the next character and the editor will search for the combination. Continue until you find the first occurrence of your search string. After that, typing Ctrl+I will find the next occurrence.

Revealing white space causes the tab characters in your file to show as "»." In typesetting, this character is called a "guillemotright." Ordinary spacebands show as a small bullet (·).

Also on the Edit menu is an option to list the members of the current class. If you want to type a variable name but are not sure of its spelling, select this option and begin typing the name. With each character, the pop-up list will move closer to the item you want; you can use the up and down arrow keys to select an item. When you find the item, press the Return key and the editor will finish typing the name for you. The Complete Word item works much the same way, but if it finds the sequence you have typed to match a full word in the list, the editor will complete the word. Otherwise, it will show you the same list as the List Members item.

Next, place the cursor over a variable or function name in your source code file and select the Type Info item, or type Ctrl+T. The data type of the variable, and parameter types for a function name, are displayed in a ToolTip window. The Parameter Info item does the same thing but for function names only.

The Bookmarks item allows you to edit, name, or jump to a bookmark you have set in your file. Bookmarks are a handy tool used to mark your place in text so that you can return to it later. If you type Ctrl+F2 in an editing window, a cyan box appears in the selection margin (the vertical gray strip along the left side of the editing window). This bookmark is a temporary marker in the text. You can return to it by typing F2. If you have multiple bookmarks in the file, F2 will advance toward the end of the file to the next bookmark and Shift+F2 will advance toward the top of the file. Ctrl+Shift+F2 on a line with a bookmark will remove the bookmark.

When you close the file, the bookmarks are lost. To save a bookmark, move the cursor in the editing window to the line you want to bookmark and select the Bookmarks menu item (or type Alt+F9). In the dialog box that appears, type a label for the bookmark and then click the Add button. There is no bookmark indicator for a named bookmark, but the keyboard commands to move to the next or previous bookmark work the same.

Named bookmarks have two characteristics not shared with unnamed bookmarks. When you delete the line containing an unnamed bookmark, the bookmark itself is removed. With a named bookmark, it moves to the beginning of the next undeleted line and you still can continue to use it. Also, when you move to an unnamed bookmark, the cursor moves to the beginning of the marked line. Named bookmarks also save the column position in the line, so moving to a named bookmark will return you to the exact character where you created it. If you remove characters around a named bookmark, it retains its relative position in the line.

"Breakpoints" are used to set points in your code where the debugger will stop executing the program so that you can inspect program variables, memory state, and so on. I'll cover breakpoints extensively in Tip 676, "Setting and Using Breakpoints," in the section on debugging.

85. *Visual Studio Menus: The View Menu*

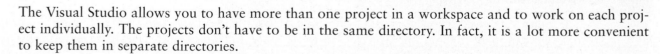

The ClassWizard, the first item on the View menu, is used to summon a dialog to add messages and resource variables to a class. The ClassWizard isn't a wizard in the programming sense, and you'll learn more about this handy tool later.

Resource Symbols lists the constants that are defined in your resource header file, *resource.h*. The Resource Includes item on the View menu lists the files that are included using the *#include* directive in *resource.h*. The fields are editable, and you can modify their contents.

The Full Screen item expands the client area (the portion of the workshop that holds the editing windows) to fill the full screen and places a small, single-item toolbar in the upper-left corner. Click the toolbar item to restore the workshop

The Output and Workspace items unhide the Output and Workspace windows, respectively. They are not toggles and do not hide the windows; for that you must use one of the context menus.

Debug Windows displays a submenu in which you can select items to view the current CPU state, memory, the call stack, and other programming events. These items are disabled unless you are in debug mode.

Properties calls up a small property sheet to display information about the currently selected item. For files, it displays the complete path and file type; for resource items, you can set the features and styles on the property page.

86. *Visual Studio Menus: The Insert Menu*

From the Insert menu, you select options to add a new class to your project (this is not the Class Wizard), add a new form (dialog box), or a new resource object. These items are a bit clumsy from the main menu and are better handled from their workspace pop-up menus.

The File as Text item allows you to open another file and read its contents into the currently selected editing window.

New ATL Object item allows you to insert an Active Template Library item into your project. If you did not select ATL support when you created your project, this menu item will allow you to add it. Adding an ATL object will insert a new support class into your project.

87. *Visual Studio Menus: The Project Menu*

The Visual Studio allows you to have more than one project in a workspace and to work on each project individually. The projects don't have to be in the same directory. In fact, it is a lot more convenient to keep them in separate directories.

All the projects in the workspace and their components are displayed in the Workspace window with the currently active project's name displayed in bold text. Use the Set Active Project item on the Project menu to switch between them. Visual Studio commands such as Build or Start Debug always operate on the active project. The "Insert Project into Workspace" item at the bottom of the Project menu enables you to add other projects, even those in other directories, to the current workspace.

From the submenu displayed with the Add to Project item, you can add individual files, directories, or registered ActiveX and COM controls to your project. ActiveX is a programming standard that allows components of programs, even on different operating systems, to interact with each other. COM is the "Component Object Model" specification for Windows that serves as the basis for Windows ActiveX controls. If it is a database project, the Data Connection item summons the ODBC manager to allow you to select a data source name. (ODBC stands for Open Database Connectivity, a specification for accessing databases over a network.)

The Source Control item provides a connection between the Visual Studio and a source code archival system. Visual SourceSafe is included with the Enterprise Edition of the Developers Studio, but you can use third-party systems.

With multiple projects, you can mark one as being dependent on another by using the Dependencies item. For example, if you have one project that is used to set the configuration of another, you might make the second project dependent on the configuration project. When the configuration project is modified, the other project is marked as needing a rebuild. The dialog box will allow you to select a project and then list the other projects in the workspace. To create a dependency, check the box next to a project name.

The Settings item allows you to alter project settings. This line summons a fairly complicated dialog box, which I will cover in a later section.

Export Makefile creates a makefile that permits you to build the project from the command line.

88. Visual Studio Menus: The Build and Tools Menus

The Build menu contains items that enable you to compile individual source files, build an entire project, and start and stop the debugger. The Clean item removes the object and linker files for the current object and forces the compiler to rebuild them from scratch. The IDE uses incremental linking that sometimes gets confused after major changes to the project, and a periodic "clean" might help if you are getting erratic and confusing errors when you run your program.

The Program Wizards create at least two versions of your project: Release and Debug. You can add your own version and set its options independently of the others. For example, suppose you have a client that has paid for some particular features in your program that you don't want to distribute to all purchasers. You can create a special build for that client and set options to include those features.

The Tools menu contains a listing of external programs you can run from within the IDE (you can include your own; I will show you how shortly). In addition, the Tools menu provides access to the source code browser (but you must have browsing enabled for the project).

The Tools menu also contains selections to allow you to customize menus and toolbars and customize the IDE, which are covered in the next couple of Tips.

The Tools menu also contains access to the macro functions. In this case, "macro" is not the same as I used in the #*define* directive. Instead, it is a sequence of recorded keystrokes that you can replay to perform repetitious tasks. You also can write macros in Visual BASIC. The Visual Studio includes a collection of macros in a file called *SAMPLE.DSM* that includes several useful items. To explore it, select the Macro item on the Project menu. A dialog explaining how to start and stop macros might appear; dispatch it with the OK button. In the Macro dialog box, select SAMPLE from the combo box labeled Macro File, select a macro from the list, and press the Edit button. The file will appear in an editing window.

Visual BASIC is a topic for a book in itself, so I won't even attempt to show you how to write macros here. If you are not familiar with VB, a good tutorial on the language will be useful.

The sample file does contain some useful macros that you can use, however. For example, adding revision marks to a program file is an easy chore to neglect, but the AddRevisionMarks macro makes the task a bit easier. Place the cursor in the source file where you want a revision comment to appear. Select Macro from the Tools menu, choose AddRevisionMarks from the SAMPLE macro file, and press "Run." The macro inserts the following text into your file:

```
/**********************************
  REVISION LOG ENTRY
  Revision By: ...
  Revised on 3/25/00 5:12:13 AM
  Comments: ...
  **********************************/
```

The date and time is when you ran the macro. You need only replace the ellipses with your name and comments.

89. Customizing Visual Studio Menus

Selecting Customize from the Tools menu puts the Visual Studio into a sort of maintenance mode. While on the Command or Toolbar tab of the Customize dialog box, you can pull down the menus but clicking an item does not invoke it. Instead, the menus are editable; you can rearrange the items on the menu bar by grabbing them with the left mouse button and dragging to a new position. For example, grab the Edit menu and drag it to the right until a bar appears between the Tools and Windows menus. Release the mouse button and the Edit menu appears in a new position. (Go ahead and try; at the end just click the Reset All Menus button to undo your changes.)

Individual menus also are editable. On the Edit menu, grab the Undo item with the left mouse button and drag it down until a black line appears before the Go To item. Release the mouse button and the item appears in the new position. You can move an item from one menu to another. Grab the item with the mouse, move the mouse along the menu bar until the new menu is selected, and then down to the new location. Release the mouse button to drop the item. You can even drop an individual item onto the main menu bar.

Remove a menu item by grabbing it with the mouse and dragging it into any area not occupied by a menu. Release the mouse button and the item disappears.

With a menu or a menu item selected, press the Modify Selection button. From here you can undo changes made to an individual menu, add icons to the menus and items, or build your own menu groups.

Practice moving and changing menu items. When you are finished, press the Reset All Menus button and the menus are restored to their original state. Later, as you get more experience with the IDE, you might want to keep your changes.

90. Adding Commands to the Tools Menu

The Tools menu contains a group of external commands you can run from within the IDE. The commands are identified by the golden pick symbol. You can edit or delete any of these items, change their order on the menu, or add your own custom tools.

Select the Customize option on the Tools menu and then select the Tools tab on the dialog box. You'll see a list of commands and external programs labeled Menu Contents. To the right are four icons representing, in order, New, Delete, Move Up, and Move Down. (Be careful with the delete icon; once you delete an item it is gone, and the Restore All Menus button on the Commands page will not bring it back.)

To move an item up or down the list, select it in the list and then press the Move Up or Move Down icons.

To add an item, press the New icon or move to the bottom of the list and select the empty entry. Enter the description as you want it to appear on the Tools menu (the & symbol creates a quick key for the letter following). Press the Return key and the set of edit controls at the bottom of the page will be enabled. From the edit controls, you specify the command to run by entering the full path (you must include the file extension even if it is an executable file). The button with an asterisk to the right of the Command box summons a Browse dialog box from which you can find and select the program to execute.

Below that is a line on which you can enter arguments to be passed to the program when it is started. There are a number of predefined macro values available. Press the arrow key to the right of the Arguments box to see a list of them.

Under the Arguments box is an Initial Directory box. Windows will change the directory to this argument before running the program. Some predefined constants are available for this box as well. Just click the arrow key to the right.

At the bottom of the Tools page are three check boxes of interest. The first is Use Output Window. If you check this box, Visual Studio will add a tab for your tool to the Output window (the window stretching across the bottom; if it is not visible, select Output on the View menu to display it). This window becomes your tool's standard output device and anything you write using *printf()* or *cout* will appear in this window. The tab panel is erased every time the tool is invoked, so don't expect to scroll up and see what was there in a previous invocation.

If you are running a command-line program, this is a good option to check. Notice that if you check this box, the last box, Close Window on Exiting, is disabled. You can't close the Output window. For a command-line program, you should have one of these two boxes checked. If neither is checked, Visual Studio will run the command-line program and close the window right away; you won't have a chance to check the program's output.

Finally, if you check Prompt for Arguments, Visual Studio will prompt you for arguments (with a dialog very similar to the Arguments edit field and button) before running the program. Anything you enter will be passed on to your tool as a command-line argument.

91. *The Visual Studio Pop-Up (Context) Menus*

I mentioned that the Visual Studio has a lot of menus. Well, that might have been an understatement. If you thought the main menu bar has lots of options, you've only begun to explore the Studio. Virtually everything in the Studio has some form of pop-up, or context, menu, that you can summon by right-clicking somewhere in the studio's boundaries. Even the window frame has a pop-up menu that lets you hide and show toolbars and various window components. Many of these are difficult to describe because they change according to what you are doing and which window has the focus.

I'll try to cover these briefly so that you will be familiar with them, but more detailed discussion of the menus will appear in Tips about that particular component.

First, open a workspace. (You did the ProgramEditor project, right?) The Visual Studio will not display many of the menus without project components in the studio. To open a workspace, select the Open Workspace item on the File menu and then use the dialog box to move to your project and select it.

When the workspace is loaded, open one or more source files using the following sequence:

1. Select the FileView panel of the Workspace window on the left side of the Studio.

2. Expand the tree by clicking the "+" sign, and then expand either the Source Files or Header Files branch by clicking the "+" sign next to it.

3. Double-click a file name and that file will open in the Edit window.

4. Right-click an open area away from any text. The pop-up menus are mostly a collection of items that can be found on the Main menu. Now, move the mouse over a function or variable name and right-click again. About two-thirds of the way down are two additional items: Go To Definition Of and Go To Reference To whatever variable or function you selected. (If you do not have browsing selected for the project and you click the Go To Reference, you'll be asked if you want rebuild with browser references. Answer Yes and do it again.)

Move to the FileView panel of the Workspace window and repeat the mouse clicks. Try it on the workspace name line and each branch of the tree. In each case, items are deleted and added to the menu to reflect the object under the cursor.

The Visual Studio program is tracking your keyboard and mouse movements and adjusting the menu contents to reflect the "context" of what you are doing. If you are new to the Visual Studio, it is worth your while to spend some time exploring the different context menus and how they can speed up your work.

92. *Exploring Visual Studio Windows: The Editing Window*

The Editing window is the large gray area that fills most of the middle area of the screen. This is the client area of the Visual Studio and contains what is known as a multidocument interface. Everything else you see in the studio is a part of the window frame.

When you open a source file, the Editing window is where the file is displayed. For a large project, it can get cramped and confusing quickly; there are tools available for managing the window. Open several files (double-click file names in the FileView panel to the left) and select the Windows menu (on the main menu bar) and successively select Cascade, Tile Horizontally, and Tile Vertically to see how the Studio arranges the windows for you. Tiling is an effective way of arranging windows so that you can work on several at once. The more windows you have open, however, the smaller the individual windows become when you tile them, even though there might be only two or three you need active at once. Fortunately, there is a way around this.

With large projects, you'll find window management in the Editing window quickly becomes a problem. The Windows item on the Window menu (on the menu bar) brings up a dialog box that helps you manage the editor windows. An asterisk next to a window name indicates the file has been modified, and the Save button writes it to disk. You can activate or close windows from this dialog.

From the Window dialog box, you can select two or more windows to tile. Select the first window you want to tile by clicking it with the left mouse button. While holding the control key down, select the second window by left-clicking it. With the second selection, the Tile Horizontally and Tile Vertically buttons will become active. Continue selecting windows using the Control key and the left mouse button until all the windows you need are selected. Press one of the tile buttons and only the selected windows will be tiled. The others are reduced to icons at the bottom of the Editing window.

With several source files open in the Editing window, you can switch between them by pressing the Ctrl+Tab keys. The Window menu lists up to 10 open windows in the editing area. Select one of the menu items to move to that window.

The more toolbars you have open in the Studio, the smaller the Editing window. If you find you need more room to manipulate source files in the area, try hiding some of the toolbars you don't need. Closing the Output or Workspace windows when they aren't needed can give you a lot of room. The Standard toolbar contains buttons for toggling these windows on and off.

You can also switch to a full screen view of the Editing window. Select the View menu and then choose Full Screen. The full screen view covers the Windows taskbar, however, and you will have to use the Alt+Tab key to switch between another Windows task. To return to a normal view, select the Full Screen icon in the small toolbar at the upper left of the full screen view. There are some tricks for using the full screen view, which I'll cover in a later tip.

93. *Exploring Visual Studio Windows: The Output Window*

The Output window normally occupies the bottom of the Studio area and stretches the full width of the screen. If it isn't visible, right-click in a blank area of the main window frame and select Output.

At the bottom of the Output window you'll find a number of tabs that open different panes of the window. The panes available vary depending on the Visual Studio edition you installed and whether you added any tools to your menu. Generally, however, you'll find at least four tabs: Build, Debug, Find In Files 1, and Find In Files 2. The last two are used with the Find In Files tool, which I'll cover later. If you installed the Enterprise edition, you'll also find an SQL Debugging tab.

The Build pane is where the compiler writes while it is compiling a file or building a project. Look for any error messages in this pane. To move to the point in the source code where the error occurred, double-click on the line containing the error and the source file will open. If you don't understand an error, click once on the line to select it and then press the F1 key to invoke the Developers Network help file where, hopefully, the purpose of the error is explained.

The Studio automatically switches the Output window to the Build pane when you start a compile or build.

When you run your program in the debugger, the Studio switches to the Debug pane. As your program starts, you'll see a list of all the DLLs it invokes as they are loaded into memory. In addition, you'll see debug trace messages throughout the course of your program.

When you stop your program, you'll see the thread exit messages and return code and the final return code from your program. This pane is where you'll see any runtime problems such as memory leaks the debugger detected during the test run. Double-click on the line containing the debug message and the source location will open. For memory leaks, the Studio will move to the line where the offending object was created, which often will contain a *new* statement; you'll have to find the proper place and then destroy the object.

Your program can write to the Debug pane using the *TRACE* macro. This macro uses the same arguments as *printf* except it writes to the Output window rather than *stdout*. Remember to place a \n at the end of your format string, otherwise the next line output by the Studio debugger will be tacked onto the end, making it difficult to find your message.

In a scroll view, for example, you might want to confirm the initial scroll area you set for a window. Enter the following code in the *OnInitialUpdate* function:

```
    CSize sizeTotal;
//  TODO: calculate the total size of this view
    sizeTotal.cx = sizeTotal.cy = 200;
    SetScrollSizes(MM_TEXT, sizeTotal);
    TRACE("In OnInitialUpdate. cx = %d, cy = %d\n",
            sizeTotal.cx, sizeTotal.cy);
```

When you run your program, as soon as you open a Scroll View window you see the following line added to the Output window:

```
In OnInitialUpdate. cx = 100, cy = 200
```

Older versions of Visual Studio used *TRACE* macros that required a fixed set of parameters rather than using the *printf* scheme. You might see *TRACE0*, *TRACE1*, *TRACE2*, and *TRACE3* macros in older code, but any new code you write should use *TRACE*. These macros do nothing in the release version of your code, so you do not have to remove them in your final build.

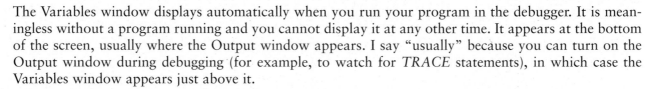

94. Exploring Visual Studio Windows: The Variables Window

The Variables window displays automatically when you run your program in the debugger. It is meaningless without a program running and you cannot display it at any other time. It appears at the bottom of the screen, usually where the Output window appears. I say "usually" because you can turn on the Output window during debugging (for example, to watch for *TRACE* statements), in which case the Variables window appears just above it.

When you stop your program by using a breakpoint or by choosing the Break item on the Debug menu, the Variables window displays variables in the current context of the program in a spreadsheet format, enabling you to examine variables in the function in which you placed the breakpoint. The window also is updated when an exception occurs. You cannot look at variables in another function because they have no meaning in the current context.

The Variables window has three panes, and as you get deeper into programming you will become very familiar with them. Select one of the following panes by using the tab at the bottom of the window:

- **The Auto pane displays variables in the current and previous statement.** When you step out of or over a function call, the return value of the function is displayed in this pane.

- **The Local pane displays variables in the current function *and* current block.** I emphasize the "and" because sub-blocks in a function can present some curious results. For example, suppose the function declares and sets a variable, then, in a block, declares another variable of the same name. When you step into the block, the Local pane will display two variables with the same name but possibly with different values. The variable in the current block is higher in the list than the variable outside the block; it is up to you to determine that you are inspecting the correct variable.

- **The *this* pane displays variables in the *this* object.** In C++, each class inherits a pointer to itself called this. Use the pane to display member variables in the class and member variables of parent classes.

If a variable is an object that contains members, a "+" will appear to the left of its name. Click this character to examine the member variables.

You can alter the contents of a variable while the program is paused, something that comes in very handy during the debugging phase. Double-click the variable's value in the window and it will turn into an editable field. Type the new value and press Enter when you're done. When you resume the program, the variable will have the new value you gave it.

While the debugger is running, you can hide the Variables window. Right-click a blank area of the frame and select Variables. Repeating the selection toggles the window on and off.

95. *Exploring Visual Studio Windows: The Watch Window*

Like the Variables window, the Watch window has meaning only while a program is running, you cannot display it otherwise. It is toggled on and off by choosing the Watch selection on the Shortcut menu (right-click a blank area of the frame to display the Shortcut menu) and normally appears to the right of the Variables window.

The Watch windows are updated only when the program is stopped with a breakpoint, a break command, or an exception. The Watch window contains four panes labeled Watch1 to Watch4, enabling you to separate code segments to examine. Select them using the tabs at the bottom of the window.

Place variables you want to examine at a breakpoint in one of the panes. Highlight the window by clicking it with the mouse and type the variable name (when you start typing, the field turns into an editable field). Unlike the Variables window, you are not limited to variables only; you can enter any valid expression in the field and use program variables in the current context. If a variable is out of context, say it is from another function or in a block that has gone out of scope, the result field will display an error message saying the variable was not found.

You also can place CPU registers in the Watch window (CPU stands for Central Processing Unit and in modern personal computers is the main computing chip; historically, this acronym has had other meanings). Prefix the register name with an at sign (for example, *@EAX*). The register name can be upper- or lowercase. As you step through the program in debug mode, you can keep track of the state of important registers through the Watch window.

96. *Exploring Visual Studio Windows: Hiding, Showing, and Docking Windows*

There's a lot going on in the Visual Studio. Some of the windows might seem confusing or unnecessary, or placed in awkward positions, or the Studio just might seem too busy for your tastes.

Everything in the studio except the title bar at the top and the status bar at the bottom can be rearranged. In addition, everything except the title bar, the status bar, the menu bar, and the editing (client) area can be hidden or displayed at your command.

Some objects can be displayed by choosing items on the View menu, others can be turned on and off by using the "shortcut menu," a context-sensitive menu that only appears when you right-click a blank area of the window frame or editing area. The menu will change according to what you are doing. For example, the Variables and Watch options will not appear unless you run your program from within the Studio, so you cannot display them otherwise.

Toggle an item—such as a toolbar or a window—on and off by selecting it in the shortcut menu. When it is displayed, a check mark will appear to the right of its name in the menu.

If you turn everything off, you'll see that the Studio appears as any other Windows application.

The "furniture" in the studio is all "dockable," meaning you can detach an item from the frame and move it to another location. For example, by default the Workspace window appears to the left and middle of the screen, next to the editing area. You might prefer it on the right side. Using the mouse, click and hold the left button on any place on the window's frame and start moving it. You'll see a rectangular area following the mouse cursor. When you have found the new location for the window, release the mouse button.

If the window position is in an open area, it will be left "floating." If you drop it on the main window frame, it will dock itself at the new location.

Many of the windows can be resized, some only vertically and some only horizontally. To change the width of a window, move the mouse cursor to the left or right side until the cursor changes into a double bar with lines jutting from either side. Hold the left mouse button down and move the mouse left or right to stretch or compress the window size. To change the height, move the cursor to the top or bottom, grab the window when the cursor changes, and move the mouse up or down. If the cursor does not change, it probably means the window cannot be resized from that side.

The locations and sizes of the windows are saved when you exit the Visual Studio, and that's how they will appear the next time you run Visual Studio.

97. Exploring the Workspace Window: The ClassView Panel

The Workspace window, normally located on the left-center area of the main window frame, contains project information maintained by the Visual Studio. It contains three panels: the ClassView, ResourceView, and FileView (older versions of Visual Studio included a fourth panel, InfoView, which was used to access the help system). If you have the Enterprise Edition and installed the Visual Database Tools, you will also see a DataView panel.

Create or open a project in the Visual Studio. Without an active project, the Workspace window appears as a blank gray area. If the Workspace window is not visible, right-click an empty area of the main window frame and select the Workspace item. If there is a check mark next to the item, it already is visible. Toggling the window on and off will help you to identify it. The Workspace Window with the ClassView pane selected is shown in Figure 97.

After you display and identify the Workspace window, select the ClassView panel by clicking the tab at the bottom. (The labels on the tabs probably don't completely display because of the width of the window. You might see something like "Clas . . . ," but the full text on the tab is ClassView.)

If the view includes only one line, click the "+" symbol next to it to expand the tree and display the classes in your project. Each class is displayed by name with a symbol before it consisting of blue, magenta, and cyan blocks. (For the record, yes, cyan, magenta, and yellow, not blue, are the primary subtractive colors; I don't know why Microsoft chose blue instead of yellow.) Program globals are listed in the item marked Globals with a file folder next to it.

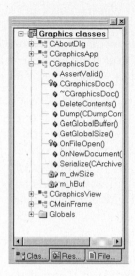

Figure 97   The ClassView panel in this view of the Workspace window shows the classes in your project

Click the "+" symbol next to a class to display its members. In the list, functions are represented by a magenta block and variables are represented by a cyan block. If the block appears by itself, the object is a public member of the class. If a small key appears next to the block, the object is a protected member. A small lock next to the block indicates a private member. Other symbols might appear depending on the project type. A key by itself represents an interface, a green block with some lines next to it (even blowing it up in a graphics program I couldn't make out its exact form) indicates a COM method, a finger pointing to a sheet of paper indicates a COM property, and a sheet of paper by itself is a dialog.

That's all very fine, you say, to have a central point where the objects of a program are listed. Okay, but ClassView is more than just a list of your program objects in a tree; it's a navigation terminus from which you can get to the point in your code where objects are declared or used. If you are a Star Trek fan, it's the transporter room. If you are a model railroader, it's the roundhouse. You can even add functions and variables from this window.

Double-click a class name and the header file containing the class definition is opened in the editing area. Double-click a variable name and the cursor moves to the point in the code where the variable is declared. Double-click a function name and the source code file containing the function definition is opened and the cursor is moved to the function.

So much for double-clicking. Now right-click a class name. From the pop-up menu you can add functions, variables, and message handlers to the class. You can find all the other points in your program containing references to the class. You can look up parent and derived classes, walk through the hierarchy, and examine variables and functions in those classes. You can copy an entire class definition and declaration into the Gallery (more on the Gallery later) and include it in other projects.

Next, right-click a function member of a class. You can move to its declaration (prototype) or its definition (the place containing the actual code) or delete it (the operation will remove the declaration and comment out the definition so that you won't lose any work).

Now right-click a variable. From the menu, you can move to its declaration or find references to it in your code. Select the References item and a dialog will appear. On the right you will see a list containing the point where it was declared and all references to the variable in your program. Double-click any of these to open the source code and move to that point.

If I could give you only one tip on how to use the Visual Studio, it would be to spend some time with ClassView and learn how to use it efficiently. It can speed up your programming efforts.

About the only thing relating to classes you can't do from ClassView is delete a class or rename it. Suppose you made a typo when creating a class name and you want to fix the error. Perhaps the purposes of one class have been absorbed by other objects and you need to remove the class altogether. Maybe you've removed a dialog box from your project and you want to get rid of the class that implemented it. So far I haven't found any easy way to do this, but later I'll show you how it can be done.

The Gallery mentioned a few paragraphs back deserves some attention. Before you add anything to the Gallery, look at it to see what it contains. From the Project menu select Add to Project and then Components and Controls. The Components and Controls Gallery dialog box should appear. Notice that it contains only two folders: Registered ActiveX Controls and Visual C++ Components. (You also might see a file named *mscreate.dir* depending on your operating system settings. Ignore this file.) The contents of these folders are shipped with the Visual Studio, and other programs can add to the ActiveX folder. You're not concerned with these folders right now. Instead, click the Close button to dispatch the dialog box.

Go back to the ClassView panel and right-click a class name. Move down and select Add to Gallery. For grins, select another class and add it to the Gallery. You won't see anything happen. Now repeat the process of opening the Components and Controls Gallery using the Project menu, Add to Project, and Components and Controls. There's a new folder bearing the name of the project from which you added the two classes. Double-click the folder to open it and you will see a file (with an extension of *.ogx*) for each of the classes you added to the Gallery. These classes—their definitions and code—are contained in these files, and you can select and include them in any other project just as you would any component shipped by Microsoft or any other vendor.

If the class you placed in the Gallery implements a dialog box that was created using ClassWizard, the entire dialog, along with its controls, class, and definitions, is imported into the Gallery object. Add it to another project and you've got an instant dialog box.

The Components and Control Gallery dialog box essentially is a File Open dialog, and you can delete the components by selecting them and pressing the Delete key. Answer Yes to move them to the Recycle Bin (the Recycle Bin is an OLE container in which Windows places deleted items until you clean it out using the Empty Recycle Bin command).

If anything, ClassView is a tough act to follow. I've used Visual C++ through all its revisions (except 3.0, which was never released), and I'm not sure I have discovered everything about this wonderful panel.

98. Exploring the Workspace Window: The ResourceView Panel

ResourceView does for your program's resource file what ClassView does for classes. To display ResourceView, click the tab at the bottom of the Workspace window. Figure 98 shows the ResourceView panel of the Workspace window.

Resources are an important component to any Windows program. Almost everything you see in a window is a control: menus, toolbars, and icons. Even the client area contains a control of some sort. In your ProgramEditor project, each source file window contains an underlying Edit control.

In addition, Windows doesn't really use *stdin*, *stdout*, and *stderr* as defined in the C language. Resources are the means through which your program gets input from users and displays information and results back to them. Well-designed resources can make using a program a pleasurable experience; poorly designed resources can make it something a user tolerates only grudgingly.

Figure 98   The ResourceView panel of the Workspace window shows the resource types available in your project

If the tree on the ResourceView is collapsed, expand it by clicking the "+" symbol. The list now contains all the resource types in the project. For most projects, this should include Accelerator, Dialog, Icon, Menu, String Table, Toolbar, and Version. You can add resource types and even create your own. To see the standard resource types, right-click any item in the tree and select Insert from the pop-up menu. In the Insert Resource dialog box, you should see Bitmap, Cursor, and HTML, in addition to the types already mentioned. The Expanding the Cursor item shows three standard cursors you can include in your project. Expanding the Dialog item reveals several different types of dialog boxes you can use. For now, press the Cancel button (you don't want to insert anything yet).

Right-click the tree root (the very top item) and select Resource Includes. The dialog box shows your resource include file (be careful, you can rename it from this dialog), any files that are included in it, and a list of compiler directives in the resource include file. You can edit any of these items, or add your own, from this dialog box.

Press the Cancel button on the dialog box and again right-click the tree root. Select Resource Symbols from the menu. The dialog box that appears lists the name and integer value of symbols defined in your program. If the symbols have been assigned to a resource, the In Use column will contain a check mark. Select an item that is in use (for a new project, they all should be in use) and a list of the resources that use that identifier is listed in the Used By box at the bottom. Click the View Use button to edit the resource item that uses the symbol.

In some cases, the symbol might be used by more than one resource. The *IDR_MAINFRAME*, which was added when the project was created, is used by several resources. Select *IDR_MAINFRAME* in the Name list and then select a resource in the Used By list. Click View Use and that resource will be open for editing.

You can create a new symbol by clicking the New button. The next available integer value is assigned to it by default, but you can change it, even if it duplicates another value. Go ahead and add a new symbol and call it *IDC_TESTSTUFF*.

A symbol's name and value can be changed if it is not being used. Double-click the symbol name, or select it and press the Change button. If the symbol is in use, the dialog will display where it is being used and enable you to open the resource for editing. Select the symbol you added, *IDC_TESTSTUFF*, and press the Change button. The dialog box is the same as the one you used to create the symbol, but now you are changing the name or value of the identifier.

Some resource symbols are used by the operating system and should not be changed. Normally they are hidden, but checking Show Read-Only Symbols box will include them in the list with the text dimmed a bit to distinguish them from editable symbols.

Close the Resource Symbols dialog box and right-click again on the root item. The Save listing, which includes your resource file name, writes the resource file and any changes you have made to disk. The Check Out item might not appear if you haven't installed a source code archiving system such as SourceSafe. If you have, the item enables you to "check out" a copy of a file. Insert enables you to add a blank resource to your list, and Import is used to include an outside file (a cursor, icon, or WAV file, for example). You'll use Import later in the section, "Common Controls Introduced in Windows 95 (and Later)," to create resource types that are not listed, such as animation objects.

The next two items—Docking View and Hide—appear on all the ResourceView menus and are used to control the Workspace window.

Now right-click the Accelerator item. The Resource Includes and Resource Symbols items have been removed from the menu, but a new item, Insert Accelerator, has been added. Right-clicking any other primary branches of the tree (a branch that is directly connected to the root) reveals the same menu, except each contains an option to insert a resource of that type.

Expand the Dialog branch by clicking the "+" symbol next to it. A list of dialog boxes in your project should appear. For a new project, the only one is the *IDD_ABOUTBOX* dialog. Right-click *IDD_ABOUTBOX*.

Two new items have been added to the top of the menu: Open and Open Binary. Selecting Open starts the Resource Editor and displays the dialog box, ready for you to customize. The Controls toolbar should appear as well. Close the dialog box window and the toolbar should disappear as well. Open Binary opens the resource item in binary form as it appears in the compiled resource file. You can edit the binary code, but unless you know what you are doing and this is the only way to make the changes you need, don't attempt to edit this binary code.

The new item, Insert Copy, enables you to copy the selected resource using the same symbol. To avoid conflicts, however, only one of the resources is included at compile time, and you must specify the condition by which the selection is made. Go ahead and select Insert Copy. In the Insert Resource Copy dialog, you can select an alternate language for the condition or enter an identifier (one that can be defined using the #*define* directive) in the Condition box. Select a language from the list and click OK. Visual Studio will not translate anything for you; that's your job. But a condition copy of the dialog has been added to the resource file.

To compile using an alternate language, you must select Project from the main menu bar and then choose Settings. From the Project Settings dialog box, select the Resources tab and then in the Language combo box select the same language you chose in the previous step. Until you provide the translation by editing the dialog box, it will appear the same as the original. If you are using another condition, follow the same steps to open the Resource page in the Settings dialog and add your condition to the Preprocessor Definitions box.

The final new item on the menu is Export, and it is grayed out for dialog boxes. Expand the Icon branch and select *IDR_MAINFRAME*. Export is no longer grayed out. Select it and the Export Resource dialog appears. You can save an individual resource into a file to include it in a different project. Just name the file and press the Export button. This dialog is a File Save dialog and you can change the directory by using the Save In: control at the top.

99. *Exploring the Workspace Window: The FileView Panel*

The FileView panel of the Workplace window provides file and project access and menu items that enable you to manage a project. Select the FileView tab at the bottom of the Workspace window. Unless you have previously expanded the tree, you should have two lines visible: The first line identifies the workspace and the number of projects in it (such as "Workspace 'Program Editor', 1 project(s)"); the second line is the root item for a file tree for a particular project. If you have more than one project in the workspace, there will be one root item for each project. Figure 99 shows the FileView panel of the Workspace window.

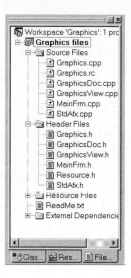

Figure 99   The FileView panel of the Workspace window with the source
and header files items expanded shows the files used in your project

Right-click the first line. The first item, Add New Project to Workspace, opens the New dialog (from the File menu) and positions it on the Projects page. Notice, however, that the Add to Current Workspace button has been selected and the Dependency of box is enabled. You can change these items, but the intent when entering the dialog from FileView is to add a new project to the workspace. From here, the wizard steps are the same as creating any new project. When you are finished and the project is added to the workspace, it will appear as a root item in FileView. In addition, it is added to the list when you select the Project menu (on the main menu bar) and Sct Active Project.

The next menu item, Insert Project into Workspace, creates a File Open dialog from which you can select another project and add it to the workspace. The result is the same as Add New Project except the project must already exist.

Add to Source Control gives you access to a source control archival system if one has been installed.

At the bottom of the menu is the Properties item. Selecting it displays a one-page property sheet showing the workspace name and the path to the workspace file. It also shows the status in any source code archival system that has been installed.

Now, right-click a project name line. The Build and Rebuild (Selection Only) items cause the appropriate projects to be rebuilt (the Selection Only refers to the currently selected configuration [e.g., Debug or Release] in the selected project). Clean (Selection Only) removes the object and other intermediate files in the currently selected configuration. After these files are removed, issuing a Build command will recompile the entire project.

Add Files to Project allows you to import files created elsewhere, even in another directory, and include them in the file list. Set As Active Project is the same as selecting the highlighted project from the Project menu on the main menu bar and then selecting Set Active Project.

Unload Project removes the project from memory; it does not remove it from the workspace. Use this option if you are low on memory and need to improve the performance of Visual Studio. You can reload a project by right-clicking its name and then selecting Load Project from the menu. While a project is unloaded, the files are not listed and you cannot open or perform any other functions on them from FileView.

The Settings item opens the project settings dialog box. Add to Source Control works the same as in the workspace menu.

Open a project branch by clicking the "+" symbol next to it. This should display a list of folders containing the various file types and a list of files at the bottom that don't quite fit into the other categories. The "folder" here does not refer to a Windows directory; all the file locations default to the project directory. In this case, the folder is a category under which the files are kept in the Visual Studio.

New Folder creates a new subfolder to hold files you want to segregate from the other files, and Add Files to Folder allows you to import additional files. Settings takes you to a Project Settings dialog box from which you can set options for *all* files of this type.

Next, expand a file folder by clicking the "+" symbol next to it. A list of all the files in the folder will be displayed. Right-click one of the file names to call up the context menu.

Open creates an editing window and reads the file into it. You also can open a file simply by double-clicking the name. Compile <filename> compiles the selected file without rebuilding the entire project. Changes in the compiled file will not be included in the executable until the project is rebuilt, however.

Settings takes you to a Project Settings dialog box where you can set options for this file only. In the previous Settings selection, remember you set options for all files in the folder. Any options you set here are applied only to the selected file.

You can move a file from one folder to another by grabbing it with the left or right mouse button, dragging it to the other folder, and then releasing the mouse button. It doesn't make much sense to move a .cpp file to the Header Files folder, but you can create something like a "Dead Files" folder, use Project Settings to exclude it from the build, and then move files you no longer use to that folder. You can still open and manipulate them from FileView.

100. *Exploring Visual Studio Toolbars*

Like menus, the Visual Studio is full of toolbars. There's a toolbar for editing, two for building, and still another for debugging. Fortunately, not all the toolbars are open at the same time or there would be little room for anything else in the Studio.

Technically, items such as the Workspace window and the Output, Variables, and Watch windows are toolbars. They just contain single controls that make them appear as ordinary windows (there more than one control in these windows, but they are subordinate to the primary control).

Most of the controls on the toolbars duplicate menu items or keystroke commands. Some toolbars have controls that even duplicate those on other toolbars! You can hide or display and position the toolbars to suit your fancy.

101. *Exploring Visual Studio Toolbars: What They Do*

During the editing phase of a project, as many as 11 toolbars are available to you depending on the edition and options you installed: Standard, Build, Build Minibar, ATL, Resource, Edit, Debug, Browse, Database, Source Control, and the WizardBar. This list doesn't include the Workspace and Output windows, which are covered separately. The WizardBar has special powers over your project and is covered in a separate section.

While a program is paused in the Debugging phase, another five are available: the Variables, Watch, Registers, Memory, and Call Stack windows. I covered the Variables and Watch windows earlier, the others will be covered in the section, "Debugging Techniques," (Tips 673–686).

If this weren't confusing enough, none of the toolbars are static. You can customize them to fit your needs and add or remove controls. If there aren't enough toolbars to suit your needs, you can create your own. Instead of taking a lot of space detailing each toolbar, I'll give you a picture of each toolbar to help you identify it and describe its purpose in general. Hovering the mouse cursor over a toolbar button for a second will bring up a ToolTip window telling you what it does. (A "ToolTip" is a small window that that contains a short description of a control. It normally is displayed with toolbars, but it can be used anywhere in a Windows program.)

Figure 101a   The Standard toolbar

The Standard toolbar (Figure 101a) contains buttons for general file editing and displaying and hiding the Workspace and Output windows. It also contains a context-sensitive combo box used in conjunction with the Find In Files command. A Search button gives you access to the Visual Studio help.

Figure 101b   The full Build toolbar, top, and the Build Minibar, bottom

The full Build toolbar (Figure 101b, top) contains controls to select the active project, select the active configuration, and compile individual files or the entire project. Other buttons include breakpoint toggle, abort compile or build, run program, and start/resume debugging. The combo boxes on the toolbar require so much real estate on the frame that it normally is hidden in favor of the Build Minibar (Figure 101b, bottom), which contains only the buttons from the full toolbar.

Figure 101c   The ATL toolbar

The ATL toolbar contains a single button: New ATL Object. Don't be fooled by its single button; it summons a complex dialog box for selecting and inserting an object from the Active Template Library. The ATL is a collection of C++ templates intended to ease the construction of Component Object Model objects.

Figure 101d   The Edit toolbar

The Edit toolbar (Figure 101d) contains buttons to set and remove bookmarks and to move forward or backward to them. It also contains a search button, indenting buttons, and a button to toggle white space display. (White space is any character that produces a space on the screen but does not display a character. This includes the space character itself, the tab character, and other control characters. The white space button displays alternate characters for the space and tab characters.)

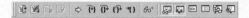

Figure 101e   The Debug toolbar

The Debug toolbar (Figure 101e) gives you control over the program while it is running in debug mode. The buttons allow you to break and restart execution, recompile code on-the-fly, examine statements and variables, and display the debugging windows. You also can summon the QuickWatch dialog from this toolbar. (The QuickWatch dialog enables you to quickly examine and modify variables and expressions or add them to the Watch window.)

Figure 101f   The Browse toolbar

On the Browse toolbar (Figure 101f), you find buttons to use in conjunction with the browse database. To use it, you must enable browsing for the project. The buttons let you navigate to functions and variables, display information about a function (what it calls and what calls it), display a chart showing the functions in a file, and display the parent and derived classes. To use these buttons, place the cursor in or at the identifier name in the source code and press the appropriate button.

Figure 101g   The Resource toolbar

The Resource toolbar (Figure 101g) appears automatically when you create or edit a dialog box in your project. Normally, it is left floating, but it can be attached to any side of the window frame. It contains buttons to select the various Windows controls and draw them on the dialog box being edited. Custom controls, ActiveX controls, and COM controls can be added to this toolbar.

Figure 101h   The Database toolbar

The Database Toolbar (Figure 101h) controls give access to the ODBC manager and simplifies the addition of database connections to your project.

Figure 101i   The Source Control toolbar

If you installed a source code archiving system such as SourceSafe (which is included with the Enterprise Edition), the Source Control toolbar (Figure 101i) offers access to it. You can log in to the source control database, archive existing code, check out previously archived versions of a project, and perform other source control functions.

102. *Exploring Visual Studio Toolbars: Hiding and Showing Toolbars*

Depending on the task at hand, you might want to hide certain toolbars to reduce the busy window frame in the Visual Studio or to clean up clutter. This is akin to tucking a magazine away when you are finished with an article, or placing the TV's remote control in a pouch when you turn to more productive activity. Alternately hiding and showing toolbars also will help you to identify them.

To display a list of available toolbars, right-click any empty area of the Studio's window frame. The context menu displayed is called the shortcut menu. If a toolbar already is displayed, it will have a check mark next to the name and selecting it will hide it. Otherwise, selecting it will display it.

A word of caution is in order when displaying long toolbars such as the Standard toolbar. Toolbars "remember" their last position, even after you've left and restarted Visual Studio. The Studio attempts to place them in the same location when they are unhidden. If you move things around in the meantime, other toolbars will be pushed out of the way, sometimes nearly off the screen, and you can spend a lot of time rearranging the "furniture." It's best to float the seldom-used toolbars and then arrange the toolbars you use most often. That way, when you reveal another toolbar it won't clutter up your Studio.

103. *Exploring Visual Studio Toolbars: Customizing Toolbars*

Now that I've described most of the toolbars, it's time to confuse the issue even more. You can customize the toolbars by adding or deleting buttons through the Customize dialog box. There are two ways to get to this dialog:

- Select the Tools menu from the main menu bar and then select the Customize item.

- Right-click an empty part of the main window frame to display the Shortcut menu, and then select Customize at the bottom of the menu.

After you display the dialog box, select the tab marked Toolbars. Actually, toolbar editing can be done any time the Customize dialog box is displayed. The Toolbars tab just gives you some extra information and options.

The list shows available toolbars, the ones with check marks are currently displayed in the Studio. To edit a toolbar, it must be displayed. If the toolbar you want to customize is not displayed, check the box next to its name to unhide it.

Select the Command tab and then select the tool category you want for your customized toolbar. As you go through the categories, you'll find a lot of buttons that aren't on any of the toolbars, so choose carefully; one button might not do exactly what you want, but another will. To see what a button does, click it in the Buttons area and a short description will appear just below the Category box.

To add an item to a toolbar, grab the button icon in the Buttons area with the left mouse button and drag it across and to the toolbar where you want to place it. When you are over the toolbar, a dark black line will appear; this is where the control will be placed when you drop it. Make sure the black line appears; if you drop it without a position, you'll create a new toolbar.

If you drop it into the wrong place, simply grab it from the toolbar and move it. Existing buttons can be moved in the same way.

To remove a tool from a toolbar, grab it with the left mouse button and drag it away from any other toolbar and drop it. In this case, instead of creating a new toolbar, the tool just disappears. If you make a serious mistake and want to restore the toolbar to the way it was, move back to the Toolbars tab, select it in the list, and press the Reset button. Pressing Reset All does just that, so make sure to select the right button.

On the Toolbars tab, the three check boxes enable you to select options. If you check Show ToolTips, a small window will appear when you hover the mouse cursor over a tool. The window contains a short description of the tool. The descriptions were predetermined when the Visual Studio was created and you cannot change them.

You can, however, choose whether to display the corresponding shortcut key in the tooltip window by checking or unchecking the With Shortcut Keys box. If this box is unchecked, the tooltip for the tool to set a bookmark, for example, will display Toggle Bookmark. With the box checked, it displays Toggle Bookmark (Ctrl+F2). Checking or unchecking this box applies to all the toolbars in the Studio; you cannot set the option for a single toolbar.

Finally, you can choose to display large images for the buttons. The large images are, shall I say, large, and you'll find the workspace getting more crowded with fewer toolbars showing. It's great for bleary-eyed, 2 a.m. debugging sessions, though.

104. Exploring Visual Studio Toolbars: Creating Your Own Toolbars

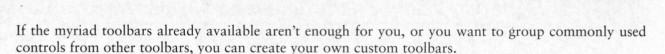

If the myriad toolbars already available aren't enough for you, or you want to group commonly used controls from other toolbars, you can create your own custom toolbars.

Open the Customize dialog box as described in the previous tip. Select the category from which you want to select controls. You can mix categories on the same toolbar. As you change categories, the available buttons in the Buttons area will change.

When you find the button to start your new toolbar, grab it and drag it out of the dialog box. Drop it in an open area of the Visual Studio away from other toolbars. This simple act adds to the toolbar madness of Visual Studio by creating a new one. Notice the tool you just dragged out is not removed from the Buttons display; it still is available for other toolbars.

Continue adding to your toolbar until all the buttons you want are placed on it. Rearrange them in the sequence you want by dragging them around the toolbar. Create a toolbar separator (the dull gray line between controls) by moving a tool slightly further from the adjacent tool, and remove a separator by moving the tool closer.

After you build your toolbar, you'll notice that it has been given a ho-hum name such as "Toolbar1." That's not very descriptive, and you want to be able to identify your toolbars easily. Select the Toolbars tab on the Customize dialog box. Move to the bottom of the list of toolbars until you find "Toolbar1" and select it. The Toolbar Name box goes from inactive to active, and you can rename the toolbar in it. (This implies, of course, that the names of standard toolbars cannot be changed, which is indeed the case.)

To eliminate a toolbar you created previously, select it in the toolbar list and press the Delete button. Here, too, the Delete button is disabled for standard toolbars, meaning you can't delete them.

Check that the new toolbar is available by summoning the shortcut menu (right-click a blank area of the Studio). It should be displayed at the bottom of the list. Close the dialog box and go about using your new toolbar.

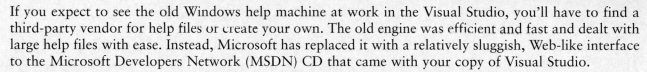

105. *Getting Help in Visual Studio*

If you expect to see the old Windows help machine at work in the Visual Studio, you'll have to find a third-party vendor for help files or create your own. The old engine was efficient and fast and dealt with large help files with ease. Instead, Microsoft has replaced it with a relatively sluggish, Web-like interface to the Microsoft Developers Network (MSDN) CD that came with your copy of Visual Studio.

The Help menu contains an item, Use Extension Help, that connects to a third-party help file using the old help engine. Without the additional help file, however, it only contains help on how to set up the help file. You might as well ignore it for now.

On the Help menu (assuming you have Use Extension Help unchecked), the first three items start or bring to the top the MSDN help file. The Contents item starts with the Contents tab selected, the Search item with the Search tab selected, and the Index item with the, you guessed it, the Index tab selected.

The Keyboard Map brings up a dialog listing the various commands and quick keys available in the Studio editors, along with a short description of each. You can't edit or add to this list, but you can print it or copy items from it using the Clipboard.

The next item, Tip of the Day, summons the familiar dialog box that displays each time you start Visual Studio. If you previously unchecked the Show Tips at Startup box and want to re-enable it, you can do so from this menu item.

Technical Support brings up help on how to submit help requests and incident reports to Microsoft. Good luck!

Microsoft on the Web is a handy item. From here you can access MSDN and search the Knowledge Base (affectionately called the "KB") for information regarding your problem. The KB contains a number of articles on Windows programming, using Visual Studio, and sample programs that might contain snippets of code that duplicate what you are trying to do. It's worth exploring.

With the Help menu out of the way, let's explore the MSDN library that came with Visual Studio. Summon it by selecting one of the first three items on the Help menu, or by pressing the Search button on the Standard toolbar.

The Contents page looks much like the old search engine, and is just as responsive. There are pointers to a lot of information here, even on non-C++ topics, but you'll have to wade through a lot of tree branches to get to it. You can limit the display by selecting one of the Visual C++ entries in the Active Subset box in the upper-right corner. When you find a topic, simply select it with the mouse to display it in the window next door.

Help on specific topics can be found more quickly by selecting the Index tab and then typing the name of the function, control, class, or object in the Keyword field. As you type, the list below moves downward toward the topic. When you find the topic, double-click it or press the Display button to call it up in the adjacent window.

If you find yourself repeatedly searching for the same topic, you can add it to a favorites list. Find and display the topic you want to add to the favorites list. Select the Favorites tab in the MSDN window. Right-click in the Topics window and select Add from the menu. (Alternatively, you can press the Add button at the bottom of the window.) Any time you want to return to the topic, select the Favorites tab and select the topic. You can double-click the topic to display it, right-click on the topic and select Display from the menu, or press the Display button at the bottom of the window.

To create your own search subset, select the View menu in MSDN and then Define Subset. Find the topics you want to include in the subset and add them to your list. For this example, assume you want to define a subset that searches only the Microsoft Foundation Class library. Open the tree root, move down to Visual C++ Documentation, and open it by double-clicking the book symbol. Next, open the

Reference book and select Microsoft Foundation Class Library and Templates. Click the Add button to move it to the selection box at the right. At the bottom right is a box labeled Save New Subset as. Enter a name such as "Microsoft Foundation Class" and press the Save button. Press Close to get rid of the Define Subset dialog box. Move up to the Active Subset control and you should find your new set at the bottom of the list.

106. *Using the Find In Files Command*

The Find command on the Edit menu is a useful tool for searching through a file to find a word or string. Unfortunately, it is limited to just one file at a time, and often the phrase you want to find might be in another file and you don't know which. To find the string, you would have to open each file and search through it. Visual Studio has implemented a useful tool, the Find In Files command, to search several files for a string. The command not only will search your project files, but can also be expanded to include files in another directory.

To access the Find In Files command, select the Edit menu and then the Find In Files item. Alternatively, you can press the Find In Files button on the Standard toolbar. Use it the same as you would the Find command; if you define a string or set your cursor on a word, the search box will be prefilled. The Find In Files dialog box is shown in Figure 106.

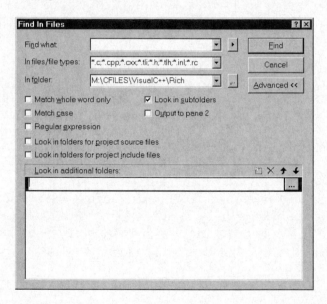

Figure 106   The fully expanded Find In Files dialog box provides options for searching other directories

If you've ever used the UNIX *grep* program, you'll appreciate the utility of the Find In Files dialog box. *grep* gets its name from "get regular expression," and to the right of the Find What: box you'll find a button labeled with a right-pointing arrow. Pressing the button reveals a number of *grep*-like terms. Selecting one of them inserts the *grep* syntax into the Find What: box. After the *grep* syntax characters have been inserted, you must fill in the blanks. To use the regular expression syntax, you must check the Regular Expression box at the bottom of the dialog box. There are far too many variations of the regular expression syntax to list here, but you'll find a complete list in MSDN under "regular expressions."

The Find in Files command saves the last 16 searches, so to repeat a search you need only select it from the Find What: box.

Next, select the names or extensions of the files you want to search. You can enter your own set of extensions or select a preset collection from the In Files/File Types box.

Select the directory you want to search. Use the button just to the right labeled with an ellipsis to select a directory or type it in yourself. The In Folder: box can hold the name of only one directory, but if you press the Advanced button you get an expanded dialog box that includes space for other directories.

When I discussed the Output window, I noted that there are two Find In Files tabs. By default, the command writes to the Find In Files 1 pane, and each new search erases the previous search results. You can select the alternate pane and save the first search results by checking the Output to Pane 2 box.

After you enter the search expression, select the directory, and choose the options, press Enter or press the Find button and watch the Output window panel for the results.

As you sift through the results and you find an occurrence you want to edit or inspect, double-click the line and the Studio will open the file and move the cursor to the proper line. (When I say "double-click the line," I also imply that you can select the line with a single click and then press the Enter key. Windows and the Visual Studio are full of such shortcuts.)

107. *Context Tracking in the Visual Studio*

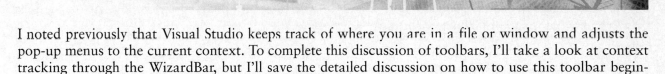

I noted previously that Visual Studio keeps track of where you are in a file or window and adjusts the pop-up menus to the current context. To complete this discussion of toolbars, I'll take a look at context tracking through the WizardBar, but I'll save the detailed discussion on how to use this toolbar beginning in Tip 585, "Understanding the Wizard Bar."

Make sure the WizardBar is visible and locate it on the Visual Studio frame. Generally you'll find it just below the Standard toolbar on the left side of the studio. The Wizard bar is shown in Figure 107.

Figure 107   The Visual Studio WizardBar uses context tracking to display project information

Context tracking takes place passively in the background and the results are reflected in the WizardBar. The controls on the toolbar attempt to display relevant information about the current location of the cursor in a source file.

Context tracking results are always 100 percent accurate, and sometimes the display lags behind your actual cursor movements. It doesn't take long for it to catch up, though, and it is accurate enough to be a useful tool.

With a project open, select and edit a source file, preferably a .cpp file containing class functions. The class name is displayed in the first box in the WizardBar, called the Class box. You can select another class name for this box, but as soon as you return to editing the file, the class name from the current file will be redisplayed.

The next control in the toolbar is the Filter box, which works in conjunction with the next control, the Members box. The filter contains a list of the resource IDs associated with the current class. This control is not always accurate and it is wise to recheck an ID before acting on it. For now, leave it on (All class members).

Using the down arrow key, move the cursor downward in the file to the first line before the first function. The function name in the Class box is slightly grayed. The context tracking is aware of the first function, but I have not yet entered it. Move down one more line and the Class box brightens up, with the name of the function and a magenta class box next to it.

Context tracking is active only in the source editor and the resource editor. In other editors (the bitmap editor or icon editor, for example) the WizardBar controls go dim, indicating context tracking is no longer taking place.

108. *Using the Full Screen Editor*

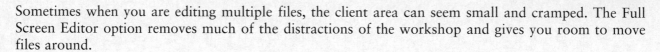

Sometimes when you are editing multiple files, the client area can seem small and cramped. The Full Screen Editor option removes much of the distractions of the workshop and gives you room to move files around.

Move to the View menu and select Full Screen. The client area is expanded to fill the entire screen. Right-click a blank area away from a file window and select Menu Bar to reveal the main menu. Using the pop-up context menu, you can redisplay any of the Studio components individually. Again select one of the tile options from the Windows menu to see its effect.

The Visual Studio "remembers" the menu and toolbars you open in Full Screen mode, so the next time you invoke the full screen, the tools will be in place. Be careful not to open too many or the Full Screen mode will seem just as cramped as the normal mode.

Select the Full Screen object in the small toolbar at the upper left of the screen. If you closed it, right-click a blank area and select Full Screen to redisplay it.

109. *Using the Split Panel to View Two Locations in the Same File*

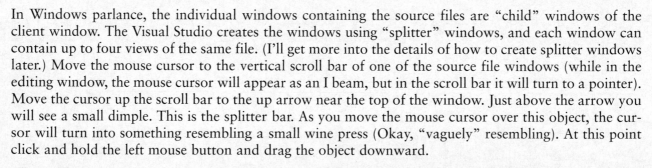

In Windows parlance, the individual windows containing the source files are "child" windows of the client window. The Visual Studio creates the windows using "splitter" windows, and each window can contain up to four views of the same file. (I'll get more into the details of how to create splitter windows later.) Move the mouse cursor to the vertical scroll bar of one of the source file windows (while in the editing window, the mouse cursor will appear as an I beam, but in the scroll bar it will turn to a pointer). Move the cursor up the scroll bar to the up arrow near the top of the window. Just above the arrow you will see a small dimple. This is the splitter bar. As you move the mouse cursor over this object, the cursor will turn into something resembling a small wine press (Okay, "vaguely" resembling). At this point click and hold the left mouse button and drag the object downward.

The window is split and you now have two views of the same file. The vertical scroll bar has duplicated itself for each view and you can scroll the contents of either window individually. You can edit the file in two different locations and each change you make will be reflected in the other window (the different components of a splitter window are called "panes").

You can do the same thing with the horizontal scroll bar to produce four views of the same file. You'll find the horizontal splitter bar just to the left of the left arrow on the horizontal scroll bar.

In practice, because of the nature of splitter windows and the fact that some panes have to share scroll bars, a four-way split of an editing window doesn't add much utility. If you keep your splits to either horizontal or vertical, you'll find them extremely handy, however.

To undo a split window, simply drag the splitter bar to the top or bottom (or left or right) of its scroll bar.

110. *Using the Debug Windows*

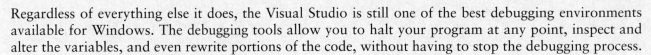

Regardless of everything else it does, the Visual Studio is still one of the best debugging environments available for Windows. The debugging tools allow you to halt your program at any point, inspect and alter the variables, and even rewrite portions of the code, without having to stop the debugging process.

The Studio contains a number of utility debugging windows that allow you to examine and alter memory, look at and modify the CPU registers, and examine the sequence of function calls that brought you to the current position. A detailed examination of the debugging windows must wait until I start discussing debugging techniques, but to complete this discussion of Visual C++, you need to be aware of the windows and how to access them. The other debugging windows are the Call Stack window, the Registers window, the Memory window, and the Disassembly window.

The debugging windows can be activated in one of several ways. In any case, you must be running your program and pause it at any point (a pause can be caused by a breakpoint, issuing a break command from the Debug menu or toolbar, or by a program error that causes an exception). Start your program in the debugger and pause it using a breakpoint or a break command (hopefully, at this stage, you won't have paused it with an exception).

The debugging windows can also be activated from the shortcut menu. Right-click an open area of the Visual Studio frame and select the window you want to view from the list. The debugging windows appear in this menu only when the program is running.

Alternatively, select the View menu and then select Debugging Windows. A submenu will pop up listing the debugging windows. Select the one you want to view.

Third, you can use shortcut keys to view the windows. This is by far the easiest way to use the windows. The shortcut keys are not toggles and only make the windows visible. Using them while a window is displayed gives that window the focus (generally, the window with focus is the one that is capturing the keyboard). Use the following keystrokes to turn on individual windows:

Alt +3—Watch window

Alt +4—Variables window

Alt +5—Registers window

Alt +6—Memory window

Alt +7—Call Stack window

Alt +8—Disassembly window

The Variables and Watch windows get a lot of use, especially during the early stages of debugging, and I have covered them already.

The Registers window displays the contents of the CPU. Windows is a 32-bit operating system, so the primary registers display 32-bit values (eight hexadecimal digits). You'll also see some 16-bit registers with names from the past (CS for Code Segment, DS for Data Segment, etc). Registers that changed in the last statement are shown in red. From the Registers window you can alter the contents of a register. The actual registers that are available depend on the CPU being used (Windows runs on 80386 through the latest Pentium processor chips). Consult a data manual or Assembly language book on your CPU for register names and usage. Unless you are familiar with the workings of a CPU, altering a register can have some serious side effects. The important registers to examine are EAX, the accumulator register, which is where the return value of a function is placed, and EFL, the flags register. The EIP register is the Instruction Pointer, which indicates the current memory location being executed. The flags register is broken down into its bit components in the Registers window. For example, after executing a conditional statement, you might want to examine the Zero flag, which is listed as ZF in the window. A 0 here indicates the result was non-zero and a one indicates a 0 result (the logic might seem backward, but it is called the "zero" flag because it indicates true if the zero test was successful and false otherwise).

Now that I've covered the dangerous territory, the Memory window displays a snapshot of the computer's memory when the program was paused. The Address field at the top allows you to specify the location in memory you want to examine. You can use register names here. Entering ESP and pressing Return will allow you to examine the stack memory. Used in conjunction with the Variables and Watch windows, the Memory window is a handy tool. The Variables window will indicate the value of a pointer variable, for example, and then you can go to the Memory window to inspect that address. You can cut and paste between the windows. The Address field also accepts identifier names from your program such as variables or classes. To inspect the memory where the current class is stored, type "this" in the Address field and press Enter. To inspect the memory of a variable just enter it in the Address field; depending on the size of the variable, the first few bytes in the memory dump will show the value. Pointer variables show the address value they contain, but dereferencing them with an asterisk displays the value to which it points. For example, if you have a variable x that contains the value 42 and a pointer variable that you set to the address of x, dumping px will show the address of x, but dumping *px will show 42, the value in x.

The Call Stack is handy for determining why your program caused an exception or assertion. An *exception* is a hardware or software event that disrupts the program and makes it impossible to continue. It can be caused by an illegal memory operation or an attempt to divide by zero, among other things. An *assertion* is an artificial debugging event; you will only get assertions while running the debug code. An assertion is raised when a checkpoint fails, such as an incorrect value passed to a library routine. An assertion helps you to find problems before you compile the release (non-debugging) code for your program, where it most likely would cause an exception, or at least some very unexpected results. When you get one of these errors, press the Retry button on the error dialog box to enter debugging. More than likely the error was caused deep within some library code and you have no idea how your program got there. Invoke the Call Stack window to show the path your program took to the problem code. Walk back through the calls until you find a function call in your code, double-click it, and your program file will open with the cursor on the line *after* the function call.

A simple C++ statement can contain any number of instructions for the CPU. When you dump the contents of the instruction pointer in the Memory window, you are confronted with a maze of numbers that indicate these instructions, the object code. Because you don't understand object code, you have no idea what these instructions mean. Invoke the Disassembly window and you'll see the instructions translated back to assembly code. Of course, you will need some understanding of assembly to fully appreciate the window contents, but you can see how the CPU treats a C++ statement such as *for (x = 0; x < 10; ++x)*. This is a single statement in C++, but it breaks down into seven assembly statements. Without the Assembly window displayed, single stepping moves through this line with a single press of the F10 key. In the Assembly window, you see each instruction as it is executed.

111. *Finishing the Program Editor*

Before leaving the Visual C++ environment, you need to add some code to the ProgramEditor project you started at the beginning of the section. This code will turn the program into a usable, minimal editor for creating and editing source code for the samples I present throughout this book.

First, remove any test code you entered while checking out the tips in this section. Then compile and run the program. Notice that it creates a blank edit window on start. The first thing you want to do is keep that from happening. You're going to open files with different extensions, so you don't want the program to assume everything is .cpp.

Open the application source file (if you followed the steps, the source file name should be *ProgramEditor.cpp*). Scroll down to the line in the *InitInstance* function that reads *ParseCommandLine(cmdInfo)*. After that line, add the following code:

```
if (cmdInfo.m_nShellCommand == CCommandLineInfo::FileNew)

    cmdInfo.m_nShellCommand =
CCommandLineInfo::FileNothing;
```

Setting *cmdInfo.m_nShellCommand* to *FileNothing* keeps the program from opening the blank window, but still allows you to specify a file name when running it from the command line. Recompile the program and run it.

Next, you want to add other extensions to your file template. In addition to .cpp, you want the file list on an Open command to include .c, .h, .hpp, and .rc files. Unfortunately, when you register the document template in *InitInstance()*, it will accept only one extension. You need to override the message handler to open a file. Select the ClassView pane of the Workspace window and right-click the *CProgramEditorApp* class name. Select Add Windows Message Handler. In the dialog box, scroll down to the *ID_FILE_OPEN* item and select it. The upper-right window should have *COMMAND* highlighted. Press the Add and Edit button and accept the default function name, *OnFileOpen*. Add the following code to the body of the function:

```
CString Filter;
Filter = "All Source files (*.c, *.cpp, *.h *.hpp, "
        " *.rc)|*.c;*.cpp;*.h;*.hpp;*.rc|";
Filter += "Header Files (*.h;*.hpp)|*.h;*.hpp|";
Filter += "Source Files (*.c;*.cpp)|*.c;*.cpp|";
Filter += "Resource Files (*.rc)|*.rc|";
Filter += "Text Files (*.txt)|*.txt|";
Filter += "All Files (*.*)|*.*||";
CFileDialog   cfd(true, NULL, NULL, OFN_HIDEREADONLY
                    | OFN_OVERWRITEPROMPT, Filter);
if (cfd.DoModal () == IDCANCEL)
    return;
OpenDocumentFile (cfd.m_ofn.lpstrFile);
```

Return to the ClassView pane and right-click the *CProgramEditorView* class. Select Add Windows Message Handler. In the dialog, scroll down to *ID_FILE_SAVE* and again COMMAND should be highlighted in the upper-right panel. Select the Add Handler button, accept the default function name, and exit.

Repeat the previous step, but this time select the *ID_FILE_SAVEAS* message and press the Add and Edit button.

In the *OnFileSaveAs* handler you just added, erase any contents and replace with it the following code:

```
CString Filter;
Filter = "All Source files (*.c, *.cpp, *.h *.hpp, "
        " *.rc)|*.c;*.cpp;*.h;*.hpp;*.rc|";
Filter += "Header Files (*.h;*.hpp)|*.h;*.hpp|";
Filter += "Source Files (*.c;*.cpp)|*.c;*.cpp|";
Filter += "Resource Files (*.rc)|*.rc|";
Filter += "Text Files (*.txt)|*.txt|";
Filter += "All Files (*.*)|*.*||";
CfileDialog   cfd(false, NULL, NULL, OFN_HIDEREADONLY |
```

```
                               OFN_OVERWRITEPROMPT, Filter);
      if (cfd.DoModal () == IDCANCEL)
          return;
      GetDocument()->OnSaveDocument (cfd.m_ofn.lpstrFile);
      GetDocument()->SetPathName(cfd.m_ofn.lpstrFile, TRUE);
```

Notice the first parameter to the *CFileDialog* constructor is false, indicating this is a save dialog.

Change the code in the *OnFileSave* handler to the following:

```
      if (GetDocument()->GetPathName().IsEmpty ())
      {
          OnFileSaveAs ();
          return;
      }
GetDocument()->OnSaveDocument(GetDocument()->GetPathName());
```

In the first line, you check to see whether there is a file name in the document object. If not, it is a new file and you want to call the *OnFileSaveAs* function. Otherwise, you use the file name and save the document.

Run the program to check the results. When you open a file, the editing window uses the default system font, which doesn't enable your characters to line up. For program editing, you want to use a fixed pitch font such as Courier New Bold. Also, the tab stops default to eight spaces, and you really would prefer four in C++.

In ClassView, right-click the *CProgramEditorView* class again, but this time select Add Member Variable. In the dialog box, enter "static CFont" for the variable type and "m_Font" for the variable name. Check the Private button and then click the OK button. Remember that only one instance of a static class member is created. All the views can use the same font, so you don't need to clutter your resources with a lot of copies of the font. You can use a static member instead and initialize it only once.

Right-click the *CProgramEditorView* class in ClassView again. Select Add Windows Message Handler. In the dialog, select *WM_CREATE* and then click the Add Handler button. Accept the default function name and exit the dialog box.

Open the *ProgramEditorView.cpp* file and move to the top. Just before the beginning of code, add the following line (remember, you have to declare static class members in global scope):

```
CFont CProgramEditorView::m_Font;
```

Move to the class constructor, which should be empty at this point, and add the following code to it:

```
CProgramEditorView::CProgramEditorView()
{
    if (m_Font.m_hObject == NULL)
        {
        m_Font.CreatePointFont (100, "Courier New Bold");
        }
}
```

The CFont constructor sets its *m_hObject* to NULL. You can initialize a font only once, and if this value is not NULL, you don't want to repeat the step.

Scroll down a few lines to the *PreCreateWindow* function and remove the line that is commented *Enable word wrapping*. For a program editor, you don't want automatic word wrapping.

You're almost done. Move to the bottom of the file and find the *OnCreate* message handler you added a few paragraphs ago. Change the body of the code to read

```
int  bResult = CEditView::OnCreate(lpCreateStruct);
if (bResult == -1)
    return (bResult);
CEdit& edit = GetEditCtrl ();
if (m_Font.m_hObject != NULL)
    edit.SetFont  (&m_Font);
edit.SetTabStops (16);
return (bResult);
```

In the first line, you save the result of the *CEditView::OnCreate* call; if the result is –1, the creation failed and just return with it; you aren't going to have a window if it fails.

Then you get a reference to the view's edit control. You use that in the next statement to set the font if it was created successfully. Otherwise, just let the window default to the system font.

The default tab stops are set at 32 dialog units (a relative measure based on the screen resolution, font size, etc.), which equates to 8 characters. Set it to 16 to get your 4-character tab indent.

Test the program with the debugger. If it works, compile a release version of it. Select the Build menu, Set Active Configuration, and in the dialog select the release configuration. Click the OK button and recompile the program. From a Windows command line prompt, copy the program file *pe.exe* from the Release directory to a directory in your path, say the Windows\System folder. That way you can start it simply by typing *pe* rather than having to enter the full path.

There still are a few things to be done to make it into a really good editing program, but they are beyond the scope of this section. As it is, the program will fit the purpose of creating and editing multiple source files. The ProgramEditor project is included in the sample code on the enclosed disk.

112. *Running the Compiler from the Command Line*

In Visual C++, the compiler program is *CL.EXE* and is invoked using *cl* on the command line. This is the same compiler that is used when Visual Studio is invoked to compile a program. Actually, *cl* performs no compilation; it is only an executive program that runs other programs called a preprocessor, the actual compiler, and a linker program (in Visual C++ the preprocessor and compiler are implemented using DLLs, or dynamic link libraries).

The preprocessor reads through the source files prior to compilation. Any constant definitions and macros are substituted and include files are placed in the compilation stream. Only then is the compiler itself invoked.

The compiler generates an object file. In Windows and DOS, these files have an extension of *.obj*. The *cl* program then invokes a linker, *LINK.EXE*, to put the object files together into a single executable file with an extension of *.exe*. If the compiler detects an error in the source code, the linker step is skipped because no executable can be formed.

If you run the compiler with no flags, the assumption is that it should produce an executable file. *C:>cl tester.cpp* would result in an object file, *TESTER.OBJ*, and an executable file, *TESTER.EXE*, being created. If you give the compiler a */c* flag, the link stage is omitted and you have only the object file. In the next few examples, you'll run the compiler with no flags.

113. *Creating a Source File*

From a Windows command line (press the Start button, select Programs, and then Command Prompt), change to a directory you want to use for sample programming (I generally use \CFiles\Tester for scratch testing programs). Start an editing program of your choice, perhaps the *PE.EXE* program you created in the last section. The editing program must permit you to save files as plain text because rich text and document type files cannot be used by the Visual C++ compiler.

For a command-line program, the first thing you should do is enter a line to include the standard header file *stdio.h*. This file declares the basic functions and macros that you associate with programming. Without it, you can't even use the *printf()* function to write text to the screen. Enter the following line:

```
#include        <stdio.h>
```

The brackets around the file name (<>) tell the compiler to look in the standard include directories for the file. In Visual C++, it wouldn't be an error to place the file name in double quotes, but on some operating systems that syntax limits the search to the current directory. In Visual C++, the double quotes cause the compiler to look first in the current directory and then in the standard include directories. For portability, you should make it a practice to place the names of all standard header files inside the brackets.

114. *The* main() *Function*

If you try to compile the program at this point, you will get an error from the linker declaring the entry point function must be declared. In C and C++, all programs must include at least one function, *main()*, which is the entry point function. Add the following code to the program:

```
int main ()
{
}
```

Save the file like it is as something like *tester.c.* You're not going to compile it until it does something. First, you're going to add a local header file to the program to declare some constants, and then go back and write some code that does something. If you've shelled out the bucks for a program such as Visual C++, I assume you are serious about learning C and C++ and want to get beyond the baby steps quickly. It's rare that you will write any significant program without header files, so get used to them as an integral part of programming in C and C++.

115. *Adding a Header File to the Program*

If you are using a program such as NotePad, you have to save your first file before creating a header file. With a program such as *PE.EXE*, which has a multidocument interface, you can have several files open at the same time; just select New from the File menu.

Create a blank document in your editor. At the top of the document enter the following lines:

```
/*
    tester.h - header file for testing
               command line programming.
 */
```

Make it a practice the first time you create a header file to include a description of how it is used. If you don't do it first thing, you're likely to forget it during the pangs of programming. When you look at it six months later, you won't have to decipher its purpose.

Now add a couple of definitions to the header file:

```
#define    HELLO          "Hello, world!\n"
#define    ANOTHER_HELLO  "Hello to the world!\n"
```

Save the file as *tester.h* and return to *tester.c*. After the line including the *stdio.h* file, add an include for *tester.h*:

```
#include        "tester.h"
```

This time I placed the include file in double quotes, which tells the compiler (actually the preprocessor, which handles the task of reading include files) to look first in the local directory for the file.

116. *Using printf to Output Text*

You can compile the program without error at this point, but it doesn't do anything except return a zero exit code. The classic C example is to have your first program print something like "Hello, world," so let's do that, but let's also add a line to demonstrate the fact that the constants in your header file are available. Add the following lines to the *main()* function between the curly braces (remember to indent):

```
printf ("Hello, world\n");
printf (HELLO);
```

Save the program and return to the command line. Compile it with the following command:

```
C:>cl tester.c
```

The *.c* extension tells the compiler to invoke the rules for Standard C, and you should not get any warnings or errors. In the next tip, you'll rename the program file to *tester.cpp* and recompile it under C++ rules. For now, run the program with the following command:

```
C:>tester
```

You should see something on the screen like the following:

```
Hello, world
Hello, world!
```

The bang (printer's jargon for exclamation point) after the second line proves that the include file constant was used. Now return to *tester.c* and change the second *printf* statement as follows:

```
printf (HELLO ANOTHER_HELLO);
```

Recompile and run the program again to see the effect of the change. When the compiler sees two strings one right after the other with no intervening operator, it concatenates them into a single string. This is not the same as writing *string1 + string2*, however, which would attempt to add two pointer values and would generate a compiler error.

Okay, enough of that. Change the program line back to *printf(HELLO);* and save the file as *tester.cpp*. Now I'm going to show you a fundamental difference between C and C++.

117. *"Hello, World": A Simple Command-Line C++ Program*

Using the same file but with a *.cpp* extension, you tell the compiler to change the rules, this time compile under the stricter C++ rules. Compile the C++ file using the following command line:

```
C:>cl tester.cpp
```

The program compiled and linked, but now you see a warning: *tester.cpp(7) : warning C4508: 'main' : function should return a value; 'void' return type assumed.*

In C++, all functions must be declared (prototyped) or defined before they are used. The automatic definition of a function is of type *int*, so an undeclared function is assumed to return an integer value. One way to get rid of the warning message is to add the following as the last line to *main()*:

```
return (0);
```

You also could get rid of the warning by writing the following definition for *main()*:

```
void main (void)
```

Returning zero is a convention carried over from the UNIX operating system. Having *main()* return a value of zero indicates success; non-zero means something went wrong and the return value usually indicates an error code. This practice enables programs in UNIX to be used in shell scripts, where the return value can be tested and used for conditional branching.

In this case, not returning a value simply generates a warning. When you get into Windows programming and use the Microsoft Foundation Class library, this would result in a genuine error message and the program wouldn't be linked. In C++, even if you return a dummy value, always return something unless the function is not declared as type *void*.

118. *The Formatted Output Family*

The *printf()* function is one of a family of formatted output functions that use the same format string and variable argument sequence. Other members of the group are *fprintf()*, which writes formatted output to a file, and *sprintf()*, which writes formatted output to a string. The syntax and formatting are the same as described earlier for *printf()*, except *fprintf()* takes a file pointer as its first argument and *sprintf()* requires a string pointer.

By default, *printf()* writes to a file called *stdout*, which usually is the monitor on a personal computer. Thus, the following two lines produce the same output:

```
printf("This is output text.\n");
fprintf(stdout, "This is output text\n");
```

sprintf() writes formatted text into a string pointed to by its first argument. No size checking is performed to make sure the string is large enough to accept the formatted output, and overwriting the string's boundaries can cause some disastrous results. It is the programmer's responsibility to make sure the string does not overflow. After the formatted text is written, a terminating '\0' is added to the string. The following code results in "*This is output text\n\0*" being written to the string:

```
char str[128];
fprintf(str, "This is output text\n");
```

In the section called, "The Microsoft Foundation Class library," you'll learn how to use the class *CString* to avoid overwriting a string's boundaries.

119. *Formatted Input*

C and C++ also accept formatted input using the *scanf()* function. Unlike the formatted output family, the arguments to *scanf()* must be pointers to variables that will hold the converted values. No type checking is performed, and *scanf()* is particularly prone to error when used as a user input function. It is more useful in its file form, *fscanf()*, and string form, *sscanf()*, where the input is more predictable. Consider the following code:

```
int x, y;
scanf("%d, %d", &x, &y);
printf("x = %d, y = %d\n", x, y);
```

This code waits for the user to enter a number separated by a comma and one or more spaces, such as "10, 20," and prints the result. But suppose the user types "10 20" (without the comma)? The variable x is assigned the value 10, but y gets something unexpected, 4201238. When taking input from the keyboard, it's better to accept a raw string and have your program parse it for the correct syntax. First, include the *string.h* header file by using the following line:

```
#include    <string.h>      // declares strchr()
```

Use the following code in place of the *scanf()* function:

```
int x, y;
char str[128];
fgets(str, 128, stdin);
if ((char *s = strchr(str, ',')) == NULL)
    sscanf (str, "%d %d", &x, &y);
else
    sscanf (str, "%d, %d", &x, &y);
printf("x = %d, y = %d\n", x, y);
```

There's a little more coding involved, but you've got a far better chance of getting the right value for the second variable.

120. *The Three Standard Files:* stdin, stdout, *and* stderr

When you run a C or C++ program, three files are opened for you automatically. The first is the standard input, usually the keyboard, which is identified by the file pointer *stdin*. The second is the standard output, usually the monitor or terminal screen, identified by the pointer *stdout*. The third file is the standard error device, *stderr*, which also is usually the screen. You can read from *stdin* or write to *stdout* or *stderr* without having to open or close them. The standard error device is separated from the standard output so that error messages written to it can be redirected to a file or printer for examination later. Windows and the DOS command processor are not very good at redirection, and this practice is mostly useful on UNIX systems.

Many of the standard library's input and output functions have corresponding file functions that can be used to direct I/O to or from a file. For *printf*, there is a corresponding function called *fprintf*, which requires a file pointer as its first argument. If the pointer is not to standard output or standard error, the file must have been opened with the *fopen()* function. The following line prints to the screen or redirected standard error device:

```
fprintf(stderr, "This is a test of standard error\n");
```

All formatting functions available in *printf()* are available in *fprintf()*.

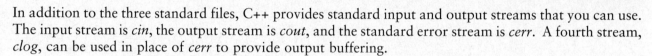

121. *Using the C++ Streams* cout, cin, *and* cerr

In addition to the three standard files, C++ provides standard input and output streams that you can use. The input stream is *cin*, the output stream is *cout*, and the standard error stream is *cerr*. A fourth stream, *clog*, can be used in place of *cerr* to provide output buffering.

The output stream understands certain word arguments. The word *endl* indicates the end of a line. Inserting *dec*, *oct*, or *hex* into the stream converts the following number argument to decimal, octal, or hexadecimal:

```
cout << "The number 10 in octal is ";
cout << oct << 10 << endl;
cout << "The number 10 in hex is ";
cout << hex << 10 << endl;
cout << "Hex 20 in decimal is ";
cout << dec << 0x20 << endl;
```

Reading from the keyboard involves using the right shift operator (these operators are redefined by the iostream class using a process known as *operator overloading* to represent new operations).

```
int x;
cout << "Enter a value for x: ";
cin >> x;
cout << "You entered " << x << endl;
```

When you run this snippet, the program outputs the prompt "Enter a value for x: " and then waits for you to enter a number. When you press the Return key, the value you entered is converted to a number (if the conversion fails, the value is 0).

You won't use the *cin*, *cout*, or *cerr* much for the rest of this book because you are primarily concerned with programming for Windows rather than the command line. For more detailed information on the iostream and its uses, see *Jamsa's C++ Programmer's Bible*.

122. *Redirecting* stdout *to a File*

Sometimes you need to capture the output of a program to a file for use by another program or later analysis. If the program was written using *printf()*, you might go through the process of opening a file and then searching through the source code to find all occurrences of *printf* and change it to *fprintf*. On a large program, this can be a tedious job, at best.

One of the reasons for standardizing file pointers for the keyboard and screen was to support a concept called *redirection*. Redirection is useful from the command line to capture output to *stdout* to another file. Type the command followed by ">" and the name of the file to which the output is to be sent. The following command takes the output from the *dir* command and saves it in a file called *dir.txt*:

```
C:>dir > dir.txt
```

You won't see anything printed on the screen. Instead, the directory command will be written to *dir.txt*.

The preceding command always empties *dir.txt* before writing to it. Output can be appended (added at the end) to a file by using the >> symbols. If the file doesn't already exist, it will be created. By appending the output, previously saved information is not lost.

The standard input also can be redirected to take input from a file by using the < symbol. The *scanf* example I used before could take its input from a file instead of the keyboard. Make the file *tester.cpp* code read as follows:

```
#include    <stdio.h>

void main(void)
{
int x, y;
    scanf("%d, %d", &x, &y);
    printf("x = %d, y = %d\n", x, y);
}
```

Now create a simple text file called *nums.txt*, enter "10, 20", and then press the Enter key (the return signals to *scanf()* that input is finished). Enter the following command from the DOS prompt:

```
C:>tester < nums.txt
```

You should see the expected output:

```
x = 10, y = 20
```

123. *Arguments to* main(): argc *and* argv

When you run a C or C++ program, the program loader passes two arguments to it, which are passed to *main()*. The first argument is an *int* type and contains the number of arguments that are found on the command line. The second is an array of type *char* * and contains the arguments themselves. Usually you'll see the integer argument declared as *int argc* for "argument count" and the second argument as *char *argv[]* or *char **argv*. The value of *argc* is always greater than 0; the first entry in the *argv* array is always the name of the program, so the count can never be less than 1. Command-line arguments are passed as strings, so your program must do any conversions before it can use any of them as numerical arguments.

Enter the following code into *tester.c* and run it against a varying number of arguments.

```c
#include        <stdio.h>

void main(int argc, char *argv[])
{
int x;

    printf("Your argument list:\n");
    for (x = 0; x < argc; ++x)
        printf("    %s\n", argv[x]);
}
```

If you enter a number, say 10, the argument is the string "10" and you must use the *atoi()* function to get the integer value.

```c
    int y = atoi(argv[x]);
```

124. *Using an* if *Statement to Control Output*

The preceding example always prints the argument list, even if you don't give any arguments when you run the program. At the very least, it would print *argv[0]*, which points to the name of the program.

If *argc* is less than 2 (it can't be less than 1), you know you didn't enter any arguments. In this case, you can use an *if* statement to detect that condition and print the string "You didn't enter any arguments." In the following code, you start at *argv[1]* and skip the program name:

```c
#include        <stdio.h>
void main(int argc, char *argv[])
{
int x;

    if (argc < 2)
        {
        printf("You didn't enter any arguments\n");
        }
    else
        {
        printf("Your argument list:\n");
        for (x = 1; x < argc; ++x)
            {
            printf("    %s\n", argv[x]);
            }
        }
}
```

Notice that I use braces around the statement immediately after the line containing the *if*. I could have gotten along without them, but it's a good idea to use them even for a single statement line to encapsulate the code and make it more readable. In the code following the *else*, the braces are required because it is a compound statement.

125. *Opening a File*

C and C++ provide low-level file functions in the form of *open()* and *close()*. These functions return an integer file descriptor that can be used by other low-level seek, read, and write functions.

The formatted functions, however, operate on streams and do not understand the file descriptors. The standard files *stdin*, *stdout*, and *stderr* are stream identifiers that are also identified by file descriptors 0, 1, and 2. The standard library contains file functions that operate on streams. The file open function, *fopen()*, returns a pointer to a structure that contains information about the file such as the current position in the file, how many characters have been buffered, and whether any errors have occurred. To use the formatted output functions on a file, you must open the file with *fopen()* to obtain a file pointer. The open function also takes a string description of how the file is to be opened. The following statement opens the file *file.txt* in the current directory for reading and writing. If the file does not exist, the call fails and a NULL pointer is returned.

```
FILE *fp = fopen ("./file.txt", "r+");
```

The mode descriptors and their meanings are listed in Table 125. If Windows detects a line feed character in a file stream, it replaces it with the carriage return/line feed combination. In addition, Windows and DOS interpret the Ctrl+Z character as the end of a file. That's not always desirable when writing binary data in which the line feed character doesn't necessarily indicate the end of a line nor a Ctrl+Z as the end of the file. To accommodate this, Windows and DOS support a binary form of each mode description by adding a "b" after the character. A file opened for binary reading and writing, for example, would be opened with the "rb+" mode.

Mode	Access	Constraint
"r"	Read only	The call fails if the file does not exist or cannot be opened.
"r+"	Read/write	The call fails if the file does not exist or cannot be opened.
"w"	Write only	If the file already exists, its contents are emptied. Otherwise, the file is created.
"w+"	Read/write	If the file already exists, its contents are emptied. Otherwise, it is created.
"a"	Append	Data can only be written at the end of the file. If the file does not exist, it is created.
"a+"	Read/append	The file can be read at any location, but data can be written only at the end of the file. If the file does not exist, it is created.

Table 125 Stream mode access types

To be safe and for portability, you should include the "b" identifier in the mode for all open commands and your program should read and write the file in binary mode. The binary mode is the default on most operating systems, and the "b" is simply ignored.

126. *Using the File I/O Functions*

C and C++ provide considerable support for file streaming. In many cases, the stream functions are more robust and easier to use than the low-level functions. In "The Microsoft Foundation Class Library" section, you'll see how to use the *CFile* class for even easier access.

The *fopen()* function returns a file pointer that is used in all the stream operations. After a file has been opened, it should be closed using the *fclose(FILE *fp)* command, which takes the file pointer as its only parameter.

Always check for a successful open before issuing any of the other file commands. The test should be for NULL and not simply 0; on some operating systems, NULL is not necessarily 0 and might point to some safe place in memory where accidental reads and writes won't interfere with the system.

```
// WRONG! May not be portable.
if ((FILE *fp = fopen ("filename", "r")) == 0)
   {
   // Abort statements
   }


// RIGHT! Binary mode and NULL are used
if ((FILE *fp = fopen ("filename", "rb")) == NULL)
   {
   // Abort statements
   }
```

After the file has been opened successfully, other operations can be made on it using the file pointer obtained from the *fopen()* call. The following list summarizes some of the operations you may perform on a file pointer.

- *ftell(FILE *fp)* returns a long giving the current file position.

- *fseek(FILE *fp, long offset, int origin)* sets the file position to *offset* in relation to *origin*, the beginning or end of the file, or some arbitrary position. Standard descriptors can be used for *origin*: *SEEK_SET* to set the origin to the beginning of the file, *SEEK_END* at the end of the file, and *SEEK_CUR* to indicate that the seek is relative to the current file position. It is possible to seek and write beyond the end of a file, in which case the unwritten contents of the file will be undefined (this is often done to reserve file space). If *fseek()* is successful, a 0 is returned; otherwise, a non-zero result is returned.

- *fread(void *buffer, size_t size, size_t count, FILE *fp)* reads *count* items of size *size* from the current file position into buffer *buffer*. The return value is of type *size_t* indicating the actual number of bytes read, which can be 0 if a read error occurs or a read beyond the end of the file is attempted. If the return value is 0 or less than *count*, use *feof(FILE *fp)* or *ferror(FILE *fp)* to check for an end-of-file or error condition.

- *fwrite(void *buffer, size_t size, size_t count, FILE *fp)* writes *count* items of size *size* at the current file position from buffer *buffer*. The return value is the number of items actually written. If the return value is less than *count*, use *ferror(FILE *fp)* to determine the error.

- *fgets(char *buffer, int count, FILE *fp)* reads a string into *buffer* from the current file position until an end of line or *count* characters have been read. The return value is *buffer* on success or NULL if the call fails.

- *fputs(char *buffer, FILE *fp)* writes *buffer* at the current file position. A non-negative number is returned on success, or the constant EOF on failure.

- *fgetc(FILE *fp)* reads a single character from the current file position. The return value is the character read or EOF on failure. If EOF is returned, use *feof(FILE *fp)* or *ferror(FILE *fp)* to distinguish between a read failure and a valid character with a value equal to EOF.

- *fputc(char ch, FILE *fp)* writes character *ch* at the current file position. The return value is the character written and error checking should be performed the same as for *fgetc()*.

In the following example, I use *argc* to make sure a file name has been passed to the program and report an error if it has not. Then I take the second argument to the *main()* and assume it is a file name. If I can't open a file, I report the error and end the program. If the file can be opened, I read it line by line and print it to the screen.

```cpp
/*
    print.cpp - Read a file and print it to the screen.
*/
#include        <stdio.h>
#include        <string.h>


main(int argc, char *argv[])
{
char *ProgName;
FILE *fp;

    if ((ProgName = strrchr (argv[0], '\\')) != NULL ||
        (ProgName = strrchr (argv[0], '/')) != 0)
        {
        ++ProgName;
        }
    else
        {
        ProgName = argv[0];
        }
    if (argc < 2)
        {
        fprintf (stderr, "%s: Please enter a file name\n",
                        ProgName);
        return (-1);
        }
    if ((fp = fopen (argv[1], "rb")) == NULL)
        {
        fprintf (stderr, "%s: Cannot open %s\n", ProgName,
                        argv[1]);
        return (-1);
        }
    char Line[256];
ReadIn:
    if (fgets(Line, sizeof(Line), fp) != NULL)
        {
        fputs (Line, stdout);
        goto ReadIn;
        }
    if (!feof(fp))
        {
        fprintf (stderr, "%s: Error %d reading %s\n",
                ProgName, ferror (fp), argv[1]);
        }
```

```
    fclose (fp);
    return (0);
}
```

In this example, I introduce the concept of *error checking*. First, you get the name of the program using some string manipulation and the *strrchr()* function to use to report errors. This might not seem important when running the program from the command line, but if you put it in a batch (or a shell script on UNIX) that might contain a number of commands, knowing the name of the program reporting the error can be handy. Suppose you have 10 commands in a batch file operating on different files and one of them reports simply "Cannot open file." Which file? Which program?

Using *argv[0]* to get the program name ensures you will get the correct name even if the user has renamed the program. Windows and DOS always pass the full path name, so you extract only the last part of the name. By checking for a NULL after the extraction and rechecking for a forward slash, you make it portable to UNIX, which uses the forward slash as a path delimiter and only passes the name as entered on the command line.

Next, you check to make sure an argument has been entered. If not, you report the error to *stderr* and exit. Obviously, without a file name you can't continue. After that, you try to open the file. If the call fails, *fp* is NULL so you report the error to *stderr* and exit. In both cases, you return a non-zero to indicate something went wrong.

By the time you start reading the file, you know everything is correct, so you read it line by line and write it out to *stdout* using the *puts()* function. When the read is finished, check to make sure the NULL return was caused because you had reached the end of the file. If it wasn't, get the file's error code from *ferror()* and report it to *stderr*.

127. *Adding a* while *Loop*

In the previous example, you have no idea how many lines are in the file, so when you actually read a line from the file, you test the return value from the *fgets()* function, which returns a pointer to the line read if it succeeded or a NULL otherwise. Again, check NULL rather than for a value of 0 to maintain portability.

If the return value is not NULL, execute the following compound statement. You write the line to the screen and jump back to read another line, repeating the process until *fgets()* reports a failure.

In this section, the program is *looping* through the code, repeating the same process over and over until a certain condition is met. This is common in programming, and most languages provide some loop control statements. In this case, the syntax of your loop is almost identical to what takes place in a C *while* loop. You could improve your code by using a *while* loop:

```
/*
    print2.cpp - Read a file and print it to the screen
    using a while loop.
 */
#include     <stdio.h>
#include     <string.h>

main(int argc, char *argv[])
{
char *ProgName;
FILE *fp;
```

```
    if ((ProgName = strrchr (argv[0], '\\')) != NULL ||
        (ProgName = strrchr (argv[0], '/')) != 0)
        {
        ++ProgName;
        }
    else
        {
        ProgName = argv[0];
        }
    if (argc < 2)
        {
        fprintf (stderr, "%s: Please enter a file name\n",
                          ProgName);
        return (-1);
        }
    if ((fp = fopen (argv[1], "rb")) == NULL)
        {
        fprintf (stderr, "%s: Cannot open %s\n",
                          ProgName, argv[1]);
        return (-1);
        }
    char Line[256];
    while (fgets(Line, sizeof(Line), fp) != NULL)
        {
        fputs (Line, stdout);
        }
    if (!feof(fp))
        {
        fprintf (stderr, "%s: Error %d reading %s\n",
                          ProgName, ferror (fp), argv[1]);
        }
    fclose (fp);
    return (0);
}
```

I won't go so far as to say the *while* loop is any more efficient than the *goto* loop; basically, the two constructions generate the same code. The *while* loop is more compact and easier to read, however. There are few places in C or C++ where a *goto* statement cannot be replaced by one of the C or C++ loop statements.

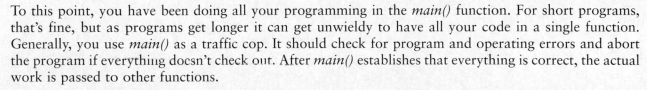

128. *Adding a Function to the Program*

To this point, you have been doing all your programming in the *main()* function. For short programs, that's fine, but as programs get longer it can get unwieldy to have all your code in a single function. Generally, you use *main()* as a traffic cop. It should check for program and operating errors and abort the program if everything doesn't check out. After *main()* establishes that everything is correct, the actual work is passed to other functions.

In the following example, you will add two functions to your program. The first will extract the program name. The second will do the actual file reading and screen writing. To make the second function even more useful (for what you will see later), let's pass it both a pointer to the file to read and a pointer to the file to write.

```cpp
/*
    print3.cpp - Read a file and print it to the screen
    using functions.
 */
#include        <stdio.h>
#include        <string.h>
// Prototype our functions.
char *GetProgName (char *);

void ReadIn (FILE *ifp, FILE *ofp);

main(int argc, char *argv[])
{
char *ProgName;
FILE *fp;

    ProgName = GetProgName (argv[0]);
    if (argc < 2)
        {
        fprintf (stderr, "%s: Please enter a file name\n",
                        ProgName);
        return (-1);
        }
    if ((fp = fopen (argv[1], "rb")) == NULL)
        {
        fprintf (stderr, "%s: Cannot open %s\n",
                        ProgName, argv[1]);
        return (-1);
        }
    ReadIn (fp, stdout);
    fclose (fp);
    return (0);
}

char *GetProgName (char *Path)
{
char *s;

    if ((s = strrchr (Path, '\\')) != NULL ||
        (s = strrchr (Path, '/')) != 0)
        {
        return (s + 1);
        }
    else
        {
        return (Path);
        }
}

void ReadIn (FILE *ifp, FILE *ofp)
{
char Line[256];
```

```
    while (fgets(Line, sizeof(Line), ifp) != NULL)
        {
        fputs (Line, ofp);
        }
    if (!feof(ifp))
        {
        fprintf (stderr, "%s: Error %d reading %s\n",
                        ProgName, ferror (ifp), argv[1]);
        }
}
```

The program is a little longer, but the code is more compact. In the next section, you'll see how to reuse the code in the function to read multiple files.

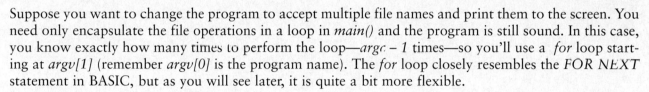

129. _Using a **for** Loop_

Suppose you want to change the program to accept multiple file names and print them to the screen. You need only encapsulate the file operations in a loop in _main()_ and the program is still sound. In this case, you know exactly how many times to perform the loop—_argc_ – 1 times—so you'll use a _for_ loop starting at _argv[1]_ (remember _argv[0]_ is the program name). The _for_ loop closely resembles the _FOR NEXT_ statement in BASIC, but as you will see later, it is quite a bit more flexible.

```
/*
    print4.cpp - Read multiple files and print
                 them to the screen using a for loop.
 */
#include    <stdio.h>
#include    <string.h>

char *GetProgName (char *);
void ReadIn (FILE *ifp, FILE *ofp);

main(int argc, char *argv[])
{
char *ProgName;
FILE *fp;

    ProgName = GetProgName (argv[0]);
    if (argc < 2)
        {
        fprintf (stderr, "%s: Please enter a file name\n",
                        ProgName);
        return (-1);
        }
    for (int x = 1; x < argc; ++x)
        {
        if ((fp = fopen (argv[x], "rb")) == NULL)
            {
            fprintf(stderr, "%s: Cannot open %s\n",
                            ProgName, argv[x]);
            }
        else
```

```
            {
            ReadIn (fp, stdout);
            fclose (fp);
            }
        }
    return (0);
}
```

Rather than returning when a file cannot be opened, you report the error to *stderr* and let the loop repeat itself. Otherwise, you call *ReadIn* to print the file to the screen. You try to open each file in sequence until all the parameter names have been used.

You could encapsulate the code even further by modifying *ReadIn* to accept a file name as its argument rather than a file pointer and let it perform the *open* and *close* operations.

130. *Compiler Command-Line Options*

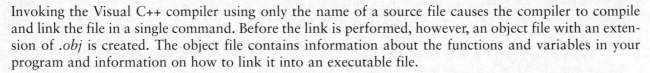

Invoking the Visual C++ compiler using only the name of a source file causes the compiler to compile and link the file in a single command. Before the link is performed, however, an object file with an extension of *.obj* is created. The object file contains information about the functions and variables in your program and information on how to link it into an executable file.

There are times, however, when you don't want to generate an executable file. When you have multiple files in your program, for example, you might want to compile them individually, and then use the linker to combine the resulting object files into a single executable. That's exactly what you accomplish when you add a simple makefile to your project.

To do this, you need to invoke a command-line option when you run the compiler. The Visual Studio invokes a number of compiler options when it compiles your program, and there are many available. The following command will list the compiler command-line options:

```
C:>cl -?
```

Although the options are all prefixed with a slash, you can use a hyphen. The compiler accepts either to maintain compatibility with UNIX compilers. Thus, *cl -?* is equivalent to *cl /?*.

The compiler pages through the option list. Press Ctrl+C to abort the listing, or press Enter to move to the next page. Right now, you are concerned only with the */c* option, "compile only, no link."

In the previous example, erase the object and executable files (they're easy to re-create as long as you don't erase the source file) and confirm they are erased by using the *dir* command.

```
C:>erase print4.obj print4.exe
C:>dir print4.*
Volume in drive C is System-P
 Volume Serial Number is A8EB-2911

 Directory of C:\CFILES\VisualC++\Tester

03/27/00  08:37p                    1,144 Print4.cpp
              1 File(s)             1,144 bytes
                          4,544,364,544 bytes free
```

Now invoke the compiler with the *−c* option and again use the directory command to see the result:

```
C:>cl -c print4.cpp
C:>dir print4.*
 Volume in drive C is System-P
 Volume Serial Number is A8EB-2911

 Directory of C:\CFILES\VisualC++\Tester

03/27/00  08:37p               1,144 Print4.cpp
03/27/00  09:15p               1,153 print4.obj
               2 File(s)        2,297 bytes
                       4,544,360,448 bytes free
```

Notice that only the object file has been produced. There is no *print4.exe*. There are two ways to link *print4.obj* into an executable file. First, you could invoke the linker directly by using the command *link print4.obj*. The linker has its own set of command-line options that you can see by using *link -? | more*. You *pipe* the command through *more* because the linker doesn't page its options. (A *pipe* is an inter-process communication technique; I'll cover it later.)

Second, you could invoke the compiler again, this time using the object file rather than the source file. The compiler will invoke the linker and produce the executable. Use the following command:

```
C:>cl print4.obj
```

Issue the *dir print4.** command again to see the result.

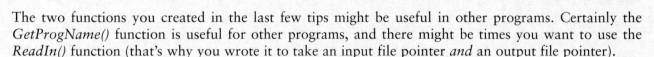

131. *Adding a Second Source File*

The two functions you created in the last few tips might be useful in other programs. Certainly the *GetProgName()* function is useful for other programs, and there might be times you want to use the *ReadIn()* function (that's why you wrote it to take an input file pointer *and* an output file pointer).

The problem is that the functions are contained in the same file as *main()*, and you can't include the file in another program; there can be only one *main()* function in any program.

To get around this, you must move the functions into a separate file and compile it by itself. I use a file called *utility.cpp* to hold general purpose programs that have not yet made it to my personal library file, so let's use the same name.

Using the ProgramEditor (if you are using NotePad or EDIT, you'll have to take some extra steps because, unlike the ProgramEditor, these programs can have only one file open at a time), edit the *print4.cpp* file. Also create a new file. You should have two editing windows open in the program.

Place the cursor on the line before the definition of the *GetProgName()* function. While holding the shift key down, use the Cursor Down key to select everything to the bottom of the file. Now place the defined functions into the Clipboard by pressing Shift+Del. Move to the new, and still blank, window and insert the contents of the Clipboard into it by pressing Shift+Ins. At the top of the file add the following lines:

```
/*
    utility.cpp. A collection of general purpose
            routines for C++
 */
#include   <stdio.h>
#include   <string.h>
```

Save this file as *utility.cpp*. Move back to the *print4.cpp* file. Open the File menu, select Save As, and save it as *print5.cpp*.

Return to the command prompt. Now you're ready to build a program file using two source files, but first let's look at the error message that results from compiling *print5.cpp* only. Enter the following command:

```
C:>cl print5.cpp
```

The compiler reports it can't find the two functions even through you prototyped them in *print5.cpp*. Enter the following command:

```
C:>cl print5.cpp utility.cpp
```

Everything is well with the world again. The compiler is happy and you're on your way to building your own personal library.

132. *Adding a Header File*
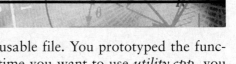

There is one remaining issue before *utility.cpp* becomes a truly reusable file. You prototyped the functions in your main program so that you can use them there. Anytime you want to use *utility.cpp*, you will need to prototype the functions.

Instead, let's lift the prototypes out of *print5.cpp* and place them in a header file, which, surprisingly, you will call *utility.h*.

In the editor, open *print5.cpp*. You no longer need the *#include <string.h>* because the code that uses the string functions has been moved to *utility.cpp*. Replace it with *#include "utility.h"*, being careful to use the double quotes rather than the < and > symbols. Now delete the function prototypes at the top of the file and place them in the Clipboard (define the two lines by holding the Shift key down and pressing the down arrow key, and then pressing Shift+Del to put them into the Clipboard). Save this file as *print6.cpp*.

Create another file by opening the File menu and selecting New. Move to the file and put the following text at the top:

```
/*
    utility.h -- Definitions and function prototypes
            for use with utility.cpp.
 */
#ifndef __UTILITY_H__    // Two leading underscores
                         // and two following
#define __UTILITY_H__    // Define the sentry
```

The sentry statement prevents the file from being included more than once. After the line containing the *#define* statement, insert the two lines you placed in the Clipboard by pressing Shift+Ins. Leave a blank line after them and enter the following line:

```
#endif    // __UTILITY_H__
```

Save this file as *utility.h*. Finally, open *utility.cpp* and add *#include "utility.h"* after the last *#include* line (it's customary, though not required, to place local includes after system includes). Return to the command line and compile the files:

```
C:>cl print6.cpp utility.cpp
```

Now, anytime you need to reuse the functions in *utility.cpp*, just remember to use the include file *utility.h* to prototype the functions. Keep building the utility file and you'll find you use it often. Place any definitions in *utility.h* to make sure other programs have them available.

133. *Creating a Makefile*

Compiling and linking two short C++ files from the command line is not a big deal, but suppose your program keeps growing and you have three, four, five, or even more larger files. You don't really want to type the resulting command every time you make a change in your program, and you really don't want to waste time compiling files that haven't changed.

What you need is a program that looks at the modified times of your source files, the object files, and the executable. If any of the object files were modified since the executable was last linked, or any of the source files were modified since the object files were generated, it should rebuild any files necessary.

Such a program maintenance utility does exist in most C and C++ development environments. It is called *make* on UNIX and most other environments. In Visual C++ it is implemented as *NMAKE.EXE*. It is called *nmake* as opposed to *make* to distinguish it from its 16-bit predecessors.

The make program operates on a file called a *makefile*, in which you declare the relationships between the various elements of a program. Usually this file is called simply *makefile* but you can specify a different name by using the *–f* command-line option when you run *nmake*. Like the compiler and linker, you can get a list of the various options by using *nmake -?*.

Now you'll make a simple makefile for your *print6.exe* program to demonstrate the basics of writing dependencies. Create a new edit window in the program editor or use NotePad or EDIT.COM. In a makefile, you can enter a comment by using the # symbol in the first column of a line, so enter the following text:

```
#
#  Sample makefile for print6.exe
#
```

The reasons for commenting makefiles are the same as for source code files. Because makefile lines tend to be more cryptic than source files, the comments are even more important.

In a makefile, you can define environment variables for the make program or redefine existing environment variables. Set or reset a variable using its identifier, an equals sign, and the value you want to assign to it. *NAME=value* sets the environment variable *NAME* to *value*. (In DOS and Windows, you have to use the *set* command.) Environment variables exist only for the time the make program is processing the makefile; if you redefine an existing variable, its value reverts to the old value when the processing ends.

DOS and Windows don't care whether case of the environment variable is upper or lower; they treat them the same. UNIX, however, is a case-sensitive operating system, and the custom is to name environment variables in uppercase.

Set the variable CC to the program file for the compiler. You know that in Visual C++ it is *cl.exe*, but you set it anyway. If you have 20 lines where you specify *cl.exe* and want to use the makefile with another compiler, you would have to seek out every instance and change it. The Borland compiler for Windows is *bcc.exe*, on UNIX the compiler is simply cc, and if you want to use the Gnu C++ compiler, it is gcc on UNIX and *gcc.exe* for Windows. By setting the variable, you need only change it in one place. It's common practice to use CC for Standard C and CPP for C++ when defining variables. On the next line of the file, enter the following:

```
CPP=cl.exe
```

In the makefile syntax, you now can invoke the compiler by referring to it as *$(CPP)*. Now you add any compiler options. Again, *CFLAGS* usually is used for Standard C and *CPPFLAGS* for C++. You want to compile only:

```
CPPFLAGS=-c
```

Next, you set the objects variable by using the following line:

```
OBJ=print6.obj utility.obj
```

Again, if you add object files to your program, you need only modify the one line. If the file list extends over more than one line, join them by using a backslash at the end of each line except the last.

Now set a variable for the header files. Include only the local header files that all (or most of) your source files need. If a local header file is referenced by only one or two source files, you can add it in the dependency line. Set the HDR variable using the following:

```
HDR=utility.h
```

Finally, add a variable for the link command. Include any command-line options:

```
LINK=link.exe
```

You also can define a variable for any additional libraries you want to link into the file. For now, the standard libraries are all you need, so set the variable to nothing (be careful not to use *LIB* or you will overwrite an important existing variable):

```
LIBS=
```

Before you start building dependencies, save the file under the name *makefile*. At this point it should look like the following:

```
#
#  Sample makefile for print6.exe
#
CPP=cl.exe
CPPFLAGS=-c
OBJ=print6.obj utility.obj
HDR=utility.h
LINK=link.exe
LIBS=
```

As I pointed out earlier, whole books have been written about the make program. It contains a wealth of internal macros and predefined sequences. For the sake of brevity (and because it's a lot easier to understand), I'm going to use the straightforward approach.

Press the Enter key to produce a blank line. Always include a blank line between dependencies. Enter the following lines:

```
print6.exe:     $(OBJ)
                $(LINK) /OUT:$(EXE) $(LIBS) $(OBJ)
```

These lines tell the make program that the file *print6.exe* is dependent on the OBJ environment variable. If any of the files in OBJ are newer than *print.exe*, perform the command on the next line. (LIBS is empty, so it inserts nothing into the command string.)

Enter another blank line and then the following lines:

```
print6.obj:      print6.cpp $(HDR)
                    $(CPP) $(CPPFLAGS) print6.cpp

utility.obj:    utility.cpp $(HDR)
                    $(CPP) $(CPPFLAGS) utility.cpp
```

These lines inform the make program that *print6.obj* is dependent on *print6.cpp* and the header files. The command to make *print6.obj* is indented on the next line. Similarly, *utility.obj* is dependent on *utility.cpp* and the header files and the make program uses the command on the next line to make it.

134. *Running nmake.exe to Compile a Program*

Invoke the 32-bit program maintenance utility *NMAKE.EXE* by typing the name on the command line by itself:

```
C:>nmake
```

The program looks in the current directory for a file named *makefile* and acts on the instructions it finds there. Alternatively, you can specify a file by naming it on the command line using the */f* option:

```
C:>nmake /f  FileName.mak
```

To see the effects of the makefile, try making a change in one of the two source files, either *print6.cpp* or *utility.cpp*. (NMAKE has a resolution of only one minute, so if you make the changes too soon, the program might not detect them. Use the */u* option to force the resolution down to two seconds.)

Next make a change in the header file *utility.h* and run NMAKE again. Both object files are dependent on this one file, so both should be recompiled.

135. *Understanding Operator Types*

Operators are the punctuation marks of a computer language and are used to indicate that an evaluation is to take place. C and C++ operators fall into three general categories: unary (or monadic, which require only one operand), binary (or diadic, which require two operands), and ternary (which require three operands). Within these three categories, there are arithmetic, relational, bitwise, logical, and assignment operators.

You've already seen the operators used in C and C++ and you have used a few of them without really explaining how the operations are performed. In this section, you'll look at the operators and see examples for each.

In the ASCII character set, there just aren't enough symbols to go around, so several of them are reused, and the compiler sorts out their exact meaning from the syntax of the statement. Often operator symbols are combined to produce new operator symbols. For example, the vertical bar (|) is used as the bitwise OR operator, but used in a pair (||) it is a logical OR symbol. The descriptions might be similar, but the operations are far different.

136. *Understanding Unary Operators: The Indirection Operator (*)*

Used in a declaration, the indirection operator (*) indicates that the variable being declared is a pointer type. Used in an expression, the indirection operator *dereferences* the variable, that is, the value in the address pointed to by the variable is to be used rather than the value of the variable itself. It gets its name from the way values are assigned and obtained *indirectly* by using an address rather than the value itself.

The effects of this operator are cumulative, and you can have several levels of indirection. For example, *int *x* declares a pointer variable to type *int*. The declaration *int **x* indicates that the variable holds a pointer to a type *int* pointer. And *int ***x* declares a variable to contain a pointer to a pointer to a pointer to a variable of type *int*. This could go on, but it can (and does!) quickly get very confusing. In practice, you often see two levels of indirection, but rarely three or more.

After a pointer variable has been assigned the address of another variable, the value is taken using the indirection operator. During assignment, the indirection operator can be used in the *lvalue* to place a value indirectly into the address contained in a pointer variable. In the following code, the value 42 is placed into the variable *x* indirectly:

```
int x;
int *px = &x;   // The address operator is
                // covered in the next tip
*px = 42;       // x contains 42 after this statement
```

The following example accomplishes the same result by using two levels of indirection, and then resets the value of *x* using three levels of indirection:

```
int x;
int *px = &x;        // a pointer to an int variable
int **ppx = &px;     // value must be pointer to pointer
int ***pppx = &ppx;  // pointer to pointer to pointer
x = 92;              // x contains 92 after this
*px = 86;            // x contains 86 after this
**ppx = 42;          // x contains 42 after this
***pppx = 160;       // x contains 160 after this
```

By now, the compiler must be getting as confused as you are, so let's stop here. This could go on until you run out of paper or you run out of patience. Pointers to pointers are fairly common (an array of strings is an example).

Indirection is useful in pointer arithmetic to get the value of a calculated element in an array. It also allows you to modify a variable in another function when the address of the variable is passed as a parameter.

If you declare a variable to be a pointer to one type, then you cannot assign it the address of a variable of another type. For example, if you have an *int* pointer variable, you cannot assign it the address of a string or the address of a *long* variable. This would violate the strict typing rules in the language. The following code would produce an assignment error during compilation:

```
float y;
int *py = &y
```

137. *Understanding Unary Operators: The Address Operator (&)*

In an assignment statement, the address operator (&) means "use the address of the operand rather than its value." You use the address operator to assign values to a variable declared to be a pointer.

The address operator can only be applied to objects in memory. You cannot get the address of an expression or a constant. When you declare a variable as a register type, more often than not it actually is given a memory location. The compiler, however, has no way of knowing whether the variable is in memory or in a register at a given time, so you can't take the address of a register type variable. Also, you can't use the address operator when a variable is declared (you can, but it has a different meaning).

The address operator always appears on the right side of an assignment operation. An *lvalue* can never be modified with the address operator.

To take the address of a variable, use the address operator immediately in front of the variable's name. The variable or expression that will hold the address must be declared or cast as a pointer to the variable type.

Taking the address of a variable gives you a pointer to the variable, which is a handy way of passing large objects to other functions. If you have a large structure, for example, with 10 or so members, you don't have to place each member on the stack to pass it. Instead, you pass a pointer to the structure (its address), which in Windows is only a four-byte value. The called function then can access and modify members of the structure using the "pointer to member" operator (->).

138. *Understanding Unary Operators: The Increment and Decrement Operators (++ and – –)*

These operators are C shorthand for a common practice of incrementing and decrementing variables, such as when they are used in loop control statements. In the simplest form, you initialize the variable and then increment it or decrement it each time the loop executes. At some predefined value, you say "That's it! Enough," and cause the loop to exit. The following code increments a variable, *x*, using the increment operator:

```
    int x = 0;
label:
    // Statements within the loop
    ++x;    // increment x
    if (x < 10)
        goto label;
```

You could just as easily set the initial value of *x* to 10 and then decrement it by using – –*x*. You would then leave the loop when *x* reaches 0.

The increment and decrement operators come in two flavors: prefix and postfix. In the prefix version, the operator is placed before the variable identifier (such as ++*x or* – –x), and the operation is performed before the variable is used in the expression. As a postfix (as in *x*++ or *x*– –), the operator is placed after the variable identifier and the variable is used in the expression *before* the operation is performed.

In the preceding example, it wouldn't make any difference whether you use *++x* or *x++*. The result would be the same because the statement is an expression in itself. If, instead, you place the operation in the loop control statement (a very common practice in C++ programming), the order becomes significant:

```
    int x = 0;
label:
    // Statements within the loop
    if (++x < 10)
        goto label;
```

In the preceding code, the first time you test the value of *x*, it is 1 because the increment is performed before the test. The tenth time you test it, it is 10 and the *x<0* test fails and you exit the loop. Thus, the loop executes a total of nine times. Now change the loop control statement to use a postfix operator in the following line:

```
    (x++ < 0)
```

Here, the value of *x* is tested before it is incremented. For the first test, the value is 0 instead of 1. On the tenth test, the value is 9, the *x<10* test succeeds, and the loop executes one more time for a total of 10 iterations.

139. Understanding Unary Operators: The Negation and Complement Operators (! and ~)

The negation operator (!) is a logical operator and thus can have only two values, 0 or 1. It is 1 when the operand is 0, and 0 when the operand is not 0.

You use the negation operator to test whether something contains a non-zero value. For example, the test *if (!var)* is semantically equivalent to saying "if *var* is equal to 0," "if not var" or, in C syntax, *if (var == 0)*. You want the result to be true if *var* is equal to 0 and false otherwise.

The complement operator (~) is sometimes called the *bitwise not* operator and should not be confused with the negation operator because of its nickname. Programmers tend to use the word "not" when reading both symbols, but this operator takes the bitwise complement of the operand, operating at a bit level. If a bit is 1, it is turned to a 0; similarly, if a bit is 0, it is turned to a 1.

The complement operator often is used as a mask to remove a bit in a flag set. For example, if you get the style of a window and want to remove the WS_VSCROLL bit, you take the complement of WS_VSCROLL and perform a bitwise AND operation on the style. In Windows, WS_VSCROLL is defined as hexadecimal (base 16) 00200000, or, in binary 00000000001000000000000000000000. If you take the complement ~WS_VSCROLL, you have 11111111110111111111111111111111. If you then do a bitwise AND on the style flags, only the WS_VSCROLL bit is changed (AND'ing two bits yields a 1 only if both are 1). The code to perform this operation would look like the following:

```
    DWORD dwStyle = GetStyle ();
    dwStyle &= ~WS_VSCROLL;
```

140. Understanding Unary Operators: The Plus and Minus Operators (+ and –)

Here's a change: an operator that does nothing and is not needed. The unary plus operator was added to the language just to maintain symmetry with the unary minus operator. In the old C it was a sin to say $x = +3$, but perfectly fine to say $x = -3$. Now they're both kosher.

The unary minus operator, on the other hand, returns the negative value of the operand. If it is a positive value, a negative value is returned. If negative, a positive value is returned. The negative value is obtained by subtracting 1 from the operand and then toggling all the bits, a process known as "taking the nine's complement" of the number (actually, on a computer it's a binary operation, so it would be the "two's complement"). If you start out with 1 and subtract 1, you have 0, which has none of the bits set. So you toggle all the bits and wind up with a value that has all the bits set, or -1. That's why in some definitions you'll see a negative 1 defined as something like 0xFFFF.

141. Understanding Arithmetic Operators: The Multiplicative Operators (*, /, and %)

Bertrand Russell and Alfred Whitehead might have had some trouble with it, but most of us with a less philosophical bent "know" from first-year algebra that division is really the reverse of multiplication. In the C language, the division operators are grouped with the multiplication operator to form the "multiplicative" group, a mouthful even for Russell and Whitehead. Each of the operators in this group requires two operands.

The multiply operator is symbolized by an asterisk (*). The operands are called the *multiplicand* and the *multiplier* and the result is the *product* of the two. To us, it doesn't matter which is the multiplicand and which is the multiplier; *4 * 6* is the same as *6 * 4*. We know from memorizing the times table in elementary school that both are equal to 24. Computers, however, do things the hard way. Multiplication of this sort is done by a series of addition, and *4 * 6* means "add four six times" and *6 * 4* means "add six four times."

The division operator is the slash mark (/). To a computer, division really is the reverse of multiplication. The operands of a division are called the *numerator* and the *denominator*, and in this case, it really does matter which is which. The number is the identifier to the left of the operator (/) and the denominator is the identifier to the right. Computers perform division by a series of subtraction. The denominator is subtracted from the numerator until the numerator is less than the denominator. The number of times the subtraction was performed is the *product* and anything left over is called the *remainder*. The operation *25 / 4* means "subtract 4 from 25 until the result is less than 4." The subtraction is performed six times before the numerator is less than 4 (in this case, it equals 1), so you have a product of 6 and a remainder of 1. In an integer division, the remainder is discarded.

Obviously, if you start with a denominator of 0, you are never going to get to the point where the first number is less than the denominator. In mathematics, division by 0 is *undefined* (no, it isn't infinity; if it were, our number system wouldn't work). On a computer, subtracting 0 from a number results in the number, so the process would just continue until the end of time. It's an error condition. On the Intel processors and their derivatives used in personal computers, division by zero causes a hardware interrupt, a physical signal in the processor that is caught by the operating system. The operating system then stops the program.

If you mix data types in a multiplication or division, the operands and the result of the expression are cast to the larger precision. The expression *25 / 4.3* results in 25 being cast to a float and the entire expression returns a float.

There are times when you are more interested in the remainder of an integer division than the actual product. In this case, the modulo division operator (%) discards the product and returns the remainder. If you want to know whether a particular year is a leap year, you can modulo divide the year by 4 and get the remainder. If it is 0, the year is a leap year. (Well, you still have the 400 year test, but that's simply a couple more modulo divisions.)

```
bool IsLeapYear (int Year)
{
    if (Year % 4)
        return (false);    // Not divisible by 4 so not a
                           // leap year
    if (Year % 100)        // A century year?
        {
        if (Year % 400)
            return (false); // Not divisible by 400
                           // so not a leap year
        }
    return (true);         // The only remaining possibility
}
```

If you are printing the page number for a book or newspaper (the folio), you want to print the odd numbered pages with the page number on the right and the even numbered pages on the left. To determine which side to print on, use the page number and do a modulo 2 division. The result is 1 (it's an odd numbered page) or 0 (it's an even numbered page):

```
void DoFolio (int PageNo)
{
    int Odd = PageNo % 2;   // modulo 2 returns 1
                           // if the number is odd
    if (Odd)
        DoOddFolio (PageNo);
    else
        DoEvenFolio (PageNo);
}
```

Modulo division can only be performed on integer data types. The C and C++ languages don't define the sign of the returned value, and it is dependent on the machine and the implementation. The expression *25 % -3* can return 1 or –1. In Visual C++ it returns a positive value, but don't rely on it.

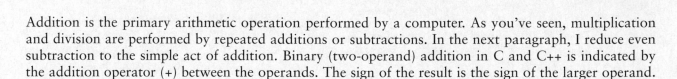

142. *Understanding Arithmetic Operators: The Additive Operators (+ and –)*

Addition is the primary arithmetic operation performed by a computer. As you've seen, multiplication and division are performed by repeated additions or subtractions. In the next paragraph, I reduce even subtraction to the simple act of addition. Binary (two-operand) addition in C and C++ is indicated by the addition operator (+) between the operands. The sign of the result is the sign of the larger operand.

Subtraction is indicated by a minus sign between the operands. When a computer subtracts one number from another, it converts the negative operand (or both operands if both are negative) to the two's complement and then adds the result. For the sake of simplicity (and so you don't wear out the 1 and 0 keys) assume you have a four-bit processor, so 7 is stored as 0111 and 3 as 0011. You write the expression 7 – 3. The computer converts the –3 to the two's complement by subtracting 1 and toggling all the bits. So –3 becomes 1101, which the computer adds to 0111, yielding 10100. The high bit is discarded (it *is* a four-bit processor) and the answer is 0100, which is binary for 4.

When addition or subtraction is performed on mixed types (a double and an integer, for example), the operands are promoted to the type with the higher precision and the expression is cast to that type. In the expression 27 – 8.3, the first operand is cast to 27.0 before the operation, and the expression yields a float result of 18.7. (You often use this notation to distinguish between integral and non-integral data types. The compiler interprets the number 27 as an integer type, but you can change that interpretation by adding one or more zeros after the decimal point.)

143. Understanding Relational Operators: The Equality Operators (== and !=)

In mathematics, you know that you can compare two quantities by subtracting one from the other. If the result is 0, you know they are equal to each other. Such comparisons are common in programming and all languages provide an operator to perform the test. In C and C++, the operator is formed by doubling the equals sign to form ==. The resulting symbol is read as "is equal to."

The result of an equality test is Boolean. The result is 1 if the two quantities are equal to each other and 0 otherwise. The test is linear with respect to the number scale. By linear I mean that if you start at some arbitrary number greater than 0 and proceed in one direction (the positive direction), the numbers get larger. If you go in the other direction, the numbers get smaller until you pass through 0 and into the negative numbers, where they begin getting larger again. The journey along the number line didn't change direction, so by convention you say the negative numbers are "less than" the positive numbers even though their scalar quantities might be larger. A larger negative number is "less than" a smaller negative number. (The word *scalar* is used to indicate magnitude without respect to direction. You use the words "larger" and "smaller" when comparing scalar (absolute) values and "greater" and "less" when comparing linear values.)

C and C++ also provide an operator to test the reverse logic by combining the negation operator and the equals sign to form !=. In words, you read this combination to mean "is not equal to" and the result is Boolean.

The equality operators obey the laws of logic, so you can extract the negation operator by changing the sense of the test and apply the negation operator to the entire test. Thus, x != y is syntactically the same as saying !(x == y).

When two operator symbols are combined to produce a new one, there is no space between them. The "is equal to" operator must be written as "==" instead of as "= =".

144. Understanding Relational Operators: The Less Than and Greater Than Operators (< and >)

The relative value of an expression is an important concept in programming. Often, you are not concerned with the actual value as much as you care whether one expression is numerically larger or smaller than another. You use these relative values to control program flow and execute alternating sets of statements.

To test whether one expression is not as great as another, use the less than operator, symbolized in C and C++ with the < symbol. The test is sign-dependent and linear, and by convention –5 is less than +4, although the "quantity" (the absolute value) of –5 is more than 4. Similarly, to test whether one expression is greater than another, you use the > symbol.

Both operators require two operands, and the left operand is compared to the right operand. The result of the expression is logical and returns 0 if the comparison is false and 1 if the comparison is true. The symbols are interchangeable if the order of operands is changed as well.

Normally, these operators are used in a test containing an *if* statement, as shown in the following code:

```
if (x < y)
{
    // First statement set
}
else
{
    // Second statement set
}
```

Reversing the order of operands and using the operator with the opposite meaning gives you the same result, and in logic *(x < y)* is described as "materially equivalent" to *(y > x)*.

In both cases, *First statement set* will be executed if *y* is greater than *x* and *Second statement set* otherwise.

Expressions containing these operators can be used as stand-alone statements, and often are used to return Boolean values, as in the following code:

```
bool Compare (int x, int y)
{
    return (x < y);
}
```

This function returns the Boolean relationship between the first argument and the second.

145. *Understanding Relational Operators: The Less Than or Equals and Greater Than or Equals Operators (<= and >=)*

C and C++ provide a number of shorthand symbols to reduce the number of keystrokes in writing a program. Sometimes you need to test whether an expression is less than *or equal to* another expression. You could write it as *if ((x < y) || (x ==y))*. By combining the less than symbol (<) with the equals sign, the languages provide a shorter method of writing this common test: *if (x <= y)*. Similarly, to write a statement that tests whether one expression is greater than or equal to another, you combine the greater than and equals symbols: *if (x >= y)*.

There is no space between the combined operator symbols. The compiler reads something like "> =" as two operators and generates an error.

146. *Understanding Bitwise Operators: The Shift Operators (<< and >>)*

Of the six bitwise operators in the C language, the shift operators are the most curious. Their presence belies the low-level heritage of the language. Most programming languages provide some bitwise operators, but the bitwise shift usually is something that is left to low-level languages such as Assembly.

The shift left operator, noted by the << symbols (notice there is no space between them), shifts the individual bits in the left operand to the left the number of bits specified in the expression to the right of the operator. As the bits are shifted, a 0 is shifted into the rightmost bit with each shift. Shifting one bit to the left is equivalent to multiplying by 2.

The expression *x* << *1* shifts the bits in *x* one to the left, and *x* << *4* shifts them to the left four times. The left operand must evaluate to a positive quantity and both operands must be integer values.

When a left shift is performed on a signed value, the sign of the result depends on the bit shifted into the most significant bit, referred to as the *sign bit*. If the sign bit is set, the result is negative; otherwise, it is positive. This can produce some unexpected results. Consider the following snippet:

```
short x = 14285;
while (x > 0)
{
    x <<= 1;
    printf ("x = %d\n", x);
}
```

You would think this loop would continue until a 0 has been shifted into all the bits and the *x > 0* test fails, in other words, for 16 shifts. When you run the code, however, you get the following results:

```
x = 28570
x = -8396
```

Oops and double oops! Not only did you get just two shifts instead of the expected 16, but the second shift resulted in a negative number. If you look at the binary value of 14285, you see that it is 0011011111001101. The next shift moves everything to the left and the result is positive because the sign bit is still 0. But on the second shift, a 1 is moved into the sign bit, *x* becomes negative, and the *x > 0* test fails, stopping the loop.

If you cast *x* to an *unsigned short*, you do indeed get the expected 16 shifts because *x* can never be negative, even with the sign bit set.

The shift right operator, indicated by the >> symbol, also presents some curious behavior when the sign bit is set. The operation shifts the left operand to the right the number of times indicated in the right expression.

If you write *x* >> *1*, the bits in *x* are shifted to the right one place. Writing *x* >> *4* causes them to be shifted right four times. As with the left shift operator, the left operand must evaluate to a positive quantity and both operands must be integer values.

Right shifting an unsigned value always places a 0 in the sign bit. But for signed values the result is unpredictable. If the sign bit is reset (that is, 0), a zero is shifted into the bit and the remaining bits are shifted to the right. But neither C nor C++ specify any behavior for the sign bit if it is set (1). The operating system and the compiler creator are free to set it to 1 or 0.

In Visual C++, right shifting a signed negative value (a signed value with the sign bit set) moves a 1 into the sign bit. If you start out with a value of *–1* (all the bits including the sign bit are set), no matter how many times you right shift it the result will always be *−1*. The following code snippet produces a loop that will never exit:

```
short x = -1;
while (x < 0)
{
    x >>= 1;    // Don't try this. It will
}               // result in an endless loop
```

Obviously, to be safe and to obtain predicable, portable results, it is best to limit shift operations to unsigned values. If you need to shift a signed value to the left, multiply it once by 2 for each shift required or cast it to an unsigned type first.

Use care shifting a signed value to the right. If you divide it by 2, the result will leave the sign bit set and produce some unexpected results as well. Dividing −1 by a positive or negative 2 is equal to 0 in integer arithmetic. It's best to simply cast it to an unsigned type before performing a right shift.

147. Understanding Bitwise Operators: The AND Operator (&)

The bitwise AND operator (&) logically ANDs the bits in the left operand with the corresponding bits in the right operand. To help you understand this tip, the truth table for an AND operation is shown in Table 147. The result of the expression is not assigned to either operand.

Bit1	Bit2	Bit1 AND Bit2
1	1	1
1	0	0
0	1	0
0	0	0

Table 147   The bitwise AND truth table

The AND operator works on a bit-by-bit basis, and the results of one bit operation do not affect the next. From the truth table, you can see that a bit is set if and only if the corresponding bits in both operands are 1. In any other case, the resulting bit is 0. This fact is useful when the operator is used to clear a bit (set it to 0) in a flag field. (See Tip 139, "Understanding Unary Operators: The Negation and Complement Operators (! and ~)," for an example of clearing a bit.)

To see an example, use the unsigned short values 8142 and 3671 and write their binary equivalents one above the other (as you would for addition):

```
      8142 = 0001111111001110
      3671 = 0000111001010111
8142 AND 3671 = 0000111001000110
```

Checking the result with a calculator shows it is 3654.

148. *Understanding Bitwise Operators: The OR Operator (|)*

The ASCII vertical bar (|) is used to indicate a bitwise OR operation. Depending on the font you use, this symbol might be a solid vertical line or it might be a broken vertical line. The ASCII value is the same. The bitwise OR operator logically ORs the bits in the left operand with the corresponding bits in the right operand. Neither operand is assigned the result. Table 148 illustrates the use of the bitwise OR operator.

Bit 1	Bit 2	Bit 1 OR Bit 2
1	1	1
1	0	1
0	1	1
0	0	0

Table 148   The bitwise OR truth table

Using the truth table, you can see that the result of a bit operation is 1 if either or both of the bits is 1. The result is 0 only if both bits are 0.

Using the same numbers you used for the AND operations, apply the logical OR statement:

```
         8142 = 0001111111001110
         3671 = 0000111001010111
8142 OR  3671 = 0001111111010111
```

The result, 8151, shows a very different result, reflecting the addition bits that were set in the operation.

149. *Understanding Bitwise Operators: The Exclusive OR Operator (^)*

The exclusive OR operator, signified by (^), has some curious and interesting properties. The operation is performed the same as a bitwise AND or a bitwise OR: The bits of one operand are XOR'ed with the corresponding bits of the second operand. The result is the value of the expression, but it is not assigned to either operand.

From the truth table shown in Table 149, you can see that the operation results in a bit being set to 1 *if and only if* one of the bits is 1. If both bits are 1 or both are 0, the result is false, or 0. Table 149 illustrates the use of the bitwise XOR operator.

Bit 1	Bit 2	Bit 1 XOR Bit2
1	1	0
1	0	1
0	1	1
0	0	0

Table 149   The bitwise XOR truth table

Hardware designers use this property to control the level of logic signals. An XOR gate (sort of an electronic switch) has two input lines that might be high (1) or low (0) and a single output, which is the result of XORing the two input signals. If one input is tied high and a logic signal is sent through the other, the output is always the reverse of the input. But if the first line is tied low, the output follows the input. Designing with an XOR gate enables you to put a jumper on the circuit board to invert the state of a logic signal.

If you XOR something with itself, the result is always 0. Assembly programmers use this property to quickly "zero out" a CPU register. Setting a register to 0 requires many clock cycles to fetch the value 0 from a memory location and move it into the register. The XOR operation, however, is usually built into the CPU's hardware, and XORing a register with itself requires only a few clock cycles at most. Apply the truth table to your test values to XOR a value with itself:

```
        8142 = 0001111111001110
        8142 = 0001111111001110
8142 XOR 8142 = 0000000000000000
```

If you XOR something (a byte, a word, a CPU register) with all 0s, the result is the value of the original something. To test whether a register contains 0, assembly programmers would XOR it with 0. The operation wouldn't change the value in the register, but it would set or clear the CPU's zero flag depending on the result. The operation is much more efficient than the time-consuming compare instructions. Using the same value 8142, XOR it with 0:

```
     8142 = 0001111111001110
        0 = 0000000000000000
8142 XOR 0 = 0001111111001110
```

Finally, if you XOR something with all 1s (remember, a –1 is all 1s), the result is the logical complement of the original value. This property is what gives the XOR operator its nickname of the "toggle" operator. If you want to change the value of a bit (say to turn a lamp on or off), you don't have to know or even test for the original value. Simply XOR it with 1, and the value toggles.

```
      8142 = 0001111111001110
        -1 = 1111111111111111
8142 XOR -1 = 1110000000110001
```

An ActiveX control I wrote recently for a project involved blinking an LED (not a real LED, just one drawn on a dialog box) when a certain condition existed. The initial state of the LED was set to 0 (off) using a class member variable and the LED was drawn on or off based on this member. The timer routine that causes it to blink every half second contains only two statements:

```
void CLEDCtrl::OnTimer(UINT nIDEvent)
{
    m_bLEDIsOn ^= 1;
    InvalidateControl ();
}
```

The current state of the LED is irrelevant. Whatever it is, you want it to be the opposite for the next cycle, so you toggle it using the XOR operator.

150. *Understanding Logical Operators: The AND Operator (&&)*

The logical AND symbol is formed by doubling the ampersand (&&). This operator compares the Boolean values of two operands. The first expression is evaluated, and if it is non-zero, it is given a

Boolean value of 1, or a 0 otherwise. The second expression is evaluated and similarly assigned a Boolean value.

A logical AND is then performed on the two Boolean values and the result of the comparison is the result of the AND.

If you did a bitwise AND on the two operands, you might get the wrong results, so the Boolean (true or false) value is taken first. If the first operand is 0x83 and the second operand equates to 0x74, you want the result to be true because neither result is 0. The value 0x83 is *10000011* in binary and 0x74 is *01110100*. Performing a bitwise AND would produce an incorrect result of 0 (false).

151. Understanding Logical Operators: The OR Operator (||)

The logical OR (||) requires two operands and performs a Boolean OR operation after first taking the Boolean result of the expressions in the operands. If one or both of the expressions evaluate to non-zero, the result of the operation is 1 (Boolean true). If both are 0, the result is 0 (Boolean false). The operands are expressions and thus are not assigned any value as the result of the operation.

A bitwise OR operation will produce a similar Boolean result if used instead, although the numerical value of the results will not be the same. The expression *83 ||74* yields a Boolean 1 result, and *83 | 74* yields 91, which is still a non-zero value. For consistency, however, use the logical || operation when you intend to perform a Boolean test.

152. Understanding Assignment Operators: The Equals Operator (=)

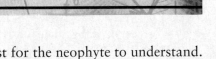

Of all the operators, the assignment operator (=) probably is the easiest for the neophyte to understand. This symbol means "set the left operand to the result of the expression in the right operand." There are some rules, however.

The left operand in an assignment operation is called the *lvalue*, a name taken from the fact that it is on the left side of the operator and the requirement that it be something whose value can be set, usually a variable. The *lvalue* can never be an expression. The *lvalue* also should be the same data type as the result of the expression on the right of the operator. Data typing isn't so strong in C, and you can set an *int* variable to a pointer. The compiler might warn you that the operands differ in "levels of indirection," but it isn't an error. In C++, however, the same assignment will produce an error message because the *int* and pointer to *int* types are strongly cast.

In an assignment operation, the expression to the right is fully evaluated before the value is assigned to the *lvalue*. In addition, a statement containing an assignment is itself an expression and the result is the value assigned to the *lvalue*, which means you can use an expression containing another equals sign in the right expression. Suppose you want to initialize three integer variables to 0. The following code does just that:

```
int x, y, z;
x = 0;
y = 0;
z = 0;
```

But you can use the evaluation clue to compress these statements, as shown in the following code:

```
int x, y, z;
x = y = z = 0;
```

To set the value of *x*, the compiler evaluates the right side, *y = z = 0*, first. But there's another assignment operator, so the compiler evaluates the right side of it, *z = 0*, before assigning a value to *y*. There it finds a third assignment operator, so it evaluates the right side first. Here the result is 0 (there are no further assignment operators), and it assigns the value to *z*. The expression *z = 0* evaluates to 0, so it then sets the value of *y* to 0. Finally, the result of *y = z = 0* is 0, and it gives that value to *x*. All three variables have been set to the same value in a single line.

There's no limit to how far you can carry this. The variables must be declared first and be of the same data type, and the final expression, the one after the last equals sign, must evaluate to a value of the same data type.

153. Understanding Other Assignment Operators (+=, -=, *=, /=, %=, >>=, <<=, &=, ^=, |=)

Hopefully, you didn't really believe the assignment operator was as simple as I led you to think in the previous tip. It really is, but C is not going to let you off the hook that easily. Programmers can be "temporally frugal" at times (some people say "lazy"). Why write two lines of code when you can combine it into one? In writing a paper, you want to be as concise as possible, yet still get your meaning across, right? Why not apply the same technique to a language?

The architects of C and C++ considered this when building the languages, and the result is that you can combine an arithmetic or logical operation with an assignment. You first enter the name of the variable as the *lvalue*, the logical or arithmetic operation you want performed on it, and then the equals operator (no spaces between the operators). You then enter the expression to use on the right side of the combined operator. The expression will be evaluated, the result applied to the *lvalue* using the first operator, and the *lvalue* given the result. The first operator can be an arithmetic operation (+, -, *, /, or %), a logical operation (&, ^, or |), or a shift operation (<< or >>).

The expression *n = n + 1* is a common operation in any programming language to increment the value of a variable. In C and C++, you can replace that with *n += 1* and achieve the same result. If *n* contains 4, for example, the right side of the expression is evaluated first, in this case it is 1. The + operator is then applied, using the *lvalue* as the left operand and the result of the expression as the right operand. The result is then assigned to the *lvalue*, and *n* is assigned a value of 5.

Now you probably are asking yourself whether multiple combined operations can be performed on the same line. Can you write *x += y += z += 1* the same as you would write an ordinary assignment, *a = y = z = 0*? The answer is yes, the syntax of the languages enables it, but you're not sure how helpful that information will be. As the evaluation walks from right to left, you have to be certain the right value is being applied to each variable. Consider the following code:

```
int x, y, z;
x = y = z = 0;
x += y += z += 1;
printf ("x = %d, y = %d, z = %d\n", x, y, z)
x += y += z += 1;
printf ("x = %d, y = %d, z = %d\n", x, y, z)
```

The variables are declared in the first line and initialized to 0 in the second line. In the third line, the combined operation is performed on *z* first, so it becomes 1. Then the combined operations are performed on *y* and finally on *x*. All are assigned the value of 1, as the *printf* will show.

The next line, however, might not produce the result (incrementing the variables) that you expect. The operations are performed on *z* first, which becomes 2. Next comes *y*, but the result of the previous expression is 2, so it is added to *y*, which becomes 3, and finally that result is added to *x*, which becomes 4.

Mixing operators on the same line is allowed, but I'll leave it to you to experiment.

154. *Other Operators: The Conditional Operator (? ... :)*

Of the C and C++ operators, the conditional is the only *ternary* operator, meaning it requires three operands. All the operands in the conditional are expressions, and no values are assigned as the result of the operation (although one or more of the expressions can assign a value). The conditional can be, and usually is, the right expression in an assignment operator and the result saved in an *lvalue*.

You build the conditional statement by placing a question mark (?) between the first and second expressions and then a colon (:). If the first expression is non-zero, the second expression is executed and the third is ignored. Otherwise, the second expression is ignored and the third is executed.

The conditional operator is a convenient shorthand for another common programming construction. Often you want to set a variable to one value or another based on the result of an expression. You could write the code the traditional way, as shown in the following:

```
int FunctionOne (bool bParm)
{
int nVal;
    if (bParm)
        nVal = 15
    else
        nVal = 42;
    return (nVal);
}
```

The conditional operator enables you to skip all that typing and assign a value to *nVal* when you test *bParm*. The following example achieves the same result:

```
int FunctionOne (bool bParm)
{
int nVal;
    nVal = bParm ? 1 : 0;
    return (nVal);
}
```

If *bParm* is non-zero, *nVal* is given the value of 1. Otherwise, the value is 0.

I'll revisit the conditional operator in more detail in the section "Writing Conditional Statements."

155. *Other Operators: The Comma Operator*

"It was the best of times, it was the worst of times, . . ." Now isn't that a perfectly ridiculous statement? Two contradictory declarations separated only by a comma. And the sentence is so long and full of commas.

A comma is the symbolic equivalent of a linguistic conjunction (such as the *word* "and") as so dramatically demonstrated by the opening sentence of Dickens' *A Tale of Two Cities*. It's widely misused, but creatively so in the hands of a wordsmith. In C and C++, it serves the same purpose.

The comma operator is used to separate two or more complete statements when they appear on the same line, or when you need more than one statement where the syntax of the language will allow you to enter only one. The latter condition happens quite often in setting up *for* loops. If the first statement is a declaration statement, all the statements until the semicolon are assumed to be declaration statements. The following code demonstrates the long (wordy) method of declaring and initializing variables:

```
int x;
int y;
int z;
x = 0;
y = 4;
z = 9;
```

For a large number of variables this could consume a lot of paper when printed. Using the comma to combine multiple statements, you can shorten it to two lines:

```
int x, y, z;
x = 0, y = 4, z = 9;
```

In the first line, you declare the variable *x* of type *int and* the variable *y* of type *int and* the variable *z* of type *int*. In the second line, the English equivalent would be to "set *x* equal to 0 *and* set y equal to 4 *and* set *z* equal to 9." I'm using the word "and" as a conjunction here rather than an operation. (No, you can't program in journalese and drop the second comma!)

If you really want to be a concise programmer, an assignment can be made when a variable is declared, so you can shorten everything to one line:

```
int x = 0, y = 4, z = 9;
```

When multiple statements are separated by a comma, they are evaluated in order from left to right, just as though you had written them on separate lines and ended each with a semicolon.

When building a *for* loop, you are allowed three statements. The first statement is the initializing statement, the second is the control or test statement, and the third is executed each time the loop completes one cycle. Suppose you want to initialize and modify two variables in the *for* statement? You could use just one in the loop statement. The other could be initialized outside the loop and modified in the body of the loop:

```
int x = 0;
for (int y = 10; y > 0; --y)
{
    // Do something in the loop
    ++x;
}
```

You could, on the other hand, use the comma operator to include everything within the controlling parentheses:

```
for (int y = 10, x = 0; y < 10; --y, ++x)
{
    // Do something in the loop
}
```

Be careful not to assume that you can use the comma operator in the middle statement, which is your control statement. Suppose you write $y > 0, x < 10$ for the control. When performing the test, the first statement would be evaluated, then the second. The result would be the second statement only, and the first statement would have no effect on the loop. If you really need to test both variables in the control statement, you would have to join them with the OR symbol: *(y > 0) || (x < 10)*.

In some uses, the comma may be a mere separator. Remember that C++ ignores white space except to separate tokens. In a function call, for example, you use the comma to separate the arguments. Otherwise, the compiler would read all the arguments as a single argument.

When you use the comma as a separator, the C++ language does not specify the order in which expressions will be evaluated. In a function call, the C++ rules about evaluating the expressions from left to right do not apply. In fact, Visual C++ usually evaluates the argument expressions in a function call from right to left, and other compilers might use a different order. Look what happens in the preceding program when you place the expressions $x = 3, y = x * 4$ in a function call:

```
#include    <iostream.h>

void MyFunction (int, int);

void main (void)
{
    int x;
    int y;
    MyFunction (x = 3, y = x * 4);
}

void MyFunction (int x, int y)
{
    cout << "x = " << x << endl;
    cout << "y = " << y << endl;
}
```

In this program, the order of evaluation in the function call is from right to left, so in the expression $y = x * 4$, the variable *x* does not yet have a value. When you compile and run the code, you will see output similar to the following:

```
x = 3
y = 16829624
```

That may not be the value you had in mind for *y*. To help you avoid this situation, the Visual C++ compiler will warn you when you use a variable without initializing the variable's value. You should see the following warning when you compile the code:

```
local variable 'x' used without having been initialized
```

The distinction between the uses of the comma may seem as thin, but you should realize how C++ treats this symbol in the different uses and recognize the warning the compiler will print to your screen.

156. *Other Operators: The Parentheses*

Parentheses are used to group expressions and to encapsulate subexpressions to change the order in which they are evaluated. In the *for* loop sample, you saw how the compiler uses the parentheses to mark the beginning and end of the three statements.

Operators have a certain order in which they are evaluated, which I will cover shortly. Multiplication is evaluated before addition. Parentheses have a very high priority, and expressions within parentheses are evaluated before any other arithmetic is performed. You can force addition to take place first by placing the addition operands within parentheses. To convert degrees Fahrenheit to degrees Celsius, for example, subtract 32 from the Fahrenheit temperature, multiply the difference by 5, and divide by 9. To make sure the subtraction occurs before the multiplication or division, place it in parentheses as shown in the following code:

```
double F2C (double DegreesF)
{
    double DegreesC = 5 * (DegreesF - 32) / 9;
    return (DegreesC);
}
```

First, the expression inside the parentheses is evaluated and then the result is multiplied by 5. Finally, the result of the multiplication is divided by 9.

You can also use the parentheses as the *casting* operator. The following code assigns a *double* variable and then tries to assign the result to an *int* variable:

```
double y = 5.3;
int x = y;
```

The compiler rejects the operation because the types differ. You could temporarily cast the type of *y* to an *int* by writing *int x = (int) y;* and the compiler is happy. The variable *x* is set to the integer equivalent of the value of *y*. Of course, *x* contains only 5 (the integer portion of 5.3), but *y* retains the complete value.

Parentheses also make your code more readable by making it clear which expressions are evaluated first. If you write *y > 0 || x < 10*, you know from the order of evaluation that the > and < will be evaluated before the ||, but in a debugging situation it is easy to misread the sequence of operations. If you instead write *(y > 0) || (x < 10)*, the meaning is quickly clear.

Be careful not to overuse parentheses, however. Earlier you saw what happened when you wrap the parameters of a function call with an extra set of parentheses. If you prototype a function with default values such as *void ThisFunc (int x = 0, int y = 0);* and then call it with an extra set of parentheses, the compiler won't generate an error, but you won't get the results you expect:

```
void ThisFunc (int x = 0, int y = 0);
void ThatFunc ()
{
    int x = 1, y = 2;
    ThisFunc((x, y));
}
```

You might have every reason to expect the function call to have parameters of *1* and *2*, but this is not what happens. The extra set of parentheses causes the *(x, y)* to be evaluated as a single expression and the first parameter is given the value of *y*. There is no second parameter, so it is given the default value of *0*.

157. *Other Operators: The Reference Operator*

The reference operator is sometimes called the "copy" operator because variables declared as a reference give the appearance of being a duplicate of another operator. The reference operator is the ampersand symbol (&), the same symbol used as the address operator.

In fact, the result of declaring a reference operator is the same as taking the address of another variable. Nothing is actually copied, but you use the reference variable as though it is a separate variable. The reference operator is available in C++ only.

Except in a function declaration and as the member of a class, a reference variable must be initialized when it is declared. You declare it by giving it a data type and an identifier. Somewhere between the type and the identifier you must include the & symbol. So *int& var*, *int &var*, and *int & var* are all equivalent. Immediately after the identifier, you must assign it to another variable. The following statements declare an integer variable *m* and a reference variable *n*:

```
int m;
int& m = n;
```

From this point, anytime you use the variable *m*, you actually are referring to *n*. After the declaration and assignment, no operation can ever be performed on a reference variable; the operation instead is performed on the variable to which it refers.

Reference variables allow you to pass parameters by reference rather than value. To modify a variable in one function from another in the C language, you have to write something like the following:

```
void FuncOne();
void FuncTwo(int *var);

void FuncOne()
{
    int  x;
    FuncTwo(&x);      // Pass a pointer to x
}

void FuncTwo(int *var)
{
    *var = 2;         // Dereference the pointer and set x to 2
}
```

This code uses a pointer to set the value in the first function. In C++, you can pass a reference:

```
void FuncOne();
void FuncTwo(int &var);

void FuncOne()
{
    int  x;
    FuncTwo(x);       // Pass reference to x
}

void FuncTwo(int &var)
{
    var = 2;          // No dereferencing needed
}
```

This code sets the value of *x* in the first function as though it were declared in the second function.

Used as the member of a class, a reference variable does not have to be initialized when it is declared. However, it must be initialized in all constructors:

```
class MyClass
{
    // The constructor
    MyClass (int &var);
    // Some other declarations
    int& m_var;
};

// Define the constructor

MyClass::MyClass (int &var) : m_var (var)
{
}
```

158. Beware of the & Symbol

With a limited number of symbols in the ASCII table, it isn't possible to represent all the C and C++ operators with unique symbols. Rather than find word substitutes (such as FORTRAN's ".GE." to represent "is greater or equal to"), C and C++ recycle symbols, combining them to produce new operators.

In some cases, the same operator can have different meanings. In this case, the syntax of the language determines the operation. The ampersand (&) is a good example of symbol reuse. As a unary operator it takes only one operand and is the address operator. Used with two identifiers, it becomes the bitwise AND operator. Used as a pair (&&) it becomes the logical AND operator. C++ adds yet another use for the ampersand: the reference operator.

The compiler resolves any operator ambiguity; if it can't, you get a compile error, so you should recognize the various incarnations of the operators to fix such errors.

159. Understanding How C++ Evaluates Expressions

Two considerations determine the eventual outcome of an expression: The precedence of the operators and the direction in which subexpressions are evaluated. In Tip 34, I presented a table listing the precedence and direction of the operators.

That table doesn't tell all, however. To use the table, you need to understand how the operators and identifiers group together in an expression and how the automatic type conversions occur. In the following code, you get the correct result, but not because of the cast operator:

```
int x = 25;
double y = (double) x / 4.0;
```

You might think you are casting the expression to a double, but the cast operator applies to the variable *x* only, rather than the entire expression, because of the grouping. In reality, the cast does nothing. In an expression containing mixed types, all variables are automatically cast to the type with the greatest precision. In the preceding example, *4.0* is a double by definition, and you can achieve the same answer, *6.25*, by writing *x / 4.0* or *(double) x / 4.*

If you add parentheses to the expression, the outcome might change altogether. If you write the statement as *double y = (double) (x / 4);* you get *6.0* rather than *6.25* as the result. The expression within the parentheses is evaluated first. All the operands within the parentheses are of type *int,* so the result of the expression is type *int* and the value is 6. By the time you cast it to a double, you've lost the fractional portion of the division.

Sometimes you can rewrite an expression to avoid casting problems. In the following code, your only variable is placed in such a position that you have to cast one of the constants to a double to force the entire expression to evaluate as a *double,* so you write *5.0* instead of just *5:*

```
double DegreesF = 68;
double DegreesC = 5.0 / 9 * (DegreesF - 32);
```

If you did not cast either constant to a double, the division would have been done on integer types, and the result would be 0. If you rearrange the formula a bit, you can get the correct result without having to worry about the types:

```
double DegreesC = 5 * (DegreesF - 32) / 9;
```

Here, the expression in parentheses is evaluated first and cast to a *double* because *DegreesF* is declared as a *double*. Then the multiplication is done and cast to a double to match the type of the parenthetical expression. Finally, you have a *double* result being divided by an integer 9, so the final result of the expression is cast to a *double* and you have the correct answer, a nice, balmy 20.0 degrees Celsius.

Identifiers are evaluated first. These include the structure or class member (names containing a period), the pointer to structure or class member (name containing the -> symbol), and scope resolution (names containing ::). Next come the unary operators, the multiplicative operators, and the additive operators, in that order.

The shift operators (<< and >>) are applied *after* any arithmetic operators, so the shift would group with the expression. If you intend the shift to be applied to only one identifier, you must group it using parentheses.

The relational operators are applied next, and are a potential source of bugs. The equality operators (== and !=) have a lower priority. It's best to group relational expressions using parentheses even if the parentheses are not needed. In addition to avoiding any evaluation accidents, it helps to make the code more readable.

Bitwise operators are applied before any logical comparisons are performed, but after the relational operators. In the code below, the additions are performed first, then the equality operator, and the test result is *true*. This might lead you to believe (erroneously) that the second test would return a *false* result.

```
int a = 7, b = 4;
int c = 9, d = 19;
if (a + b == c + d)
    printf ("First expression is true\n");
if (a & b == c | d)
    printf ("Second expression is true\n");
```

In the second test, the expression *a & b* gives you *4,* and *c | d* equates to *27,* which obviously are not equal, so you should expect the expression to return *false.* Surprisingly, the second test is true! In this case, the equality operator is applied first. Because *4* is not equal to *9,* the test is false and is assigned a Boolean 0. It is automatically promoted to an *int* and a bitwise *AND* performed with 7. The result so far is *0,* or Boolean false. The next operation does a bitwise OR with *d,* giving you the final result of *19.*

That's non-zero, so the expression is assigned a Boolean value of *true*. To get the *false* result you expect, you have to write the test as *if ((a & b) == (c | d))*.

If you had written the code using parentheses as in the following code, you never would have encountered this problem. In the first test, the extra parentheses serve no purpose other than to make the code more readable, but they cause no harm either:

```
if ((a + b) == (c + d))
    printf ("First expression is true\n");
if ((a & b) == (c | d))
    printf ("Second expression is true\n");
```

The conditional operator is evaluated next, followed by the assignment operators. The comma operator has the lowest evaluation priority.

160. *Beware of Complex Expressions*

Because of the way C and C++ evaluate expressions and the latitude allowed in combining them, it is possible to construct complex statements that neither you nor anyone else can understand later. The architects of C, Brian Kernighan and Dennis Ritchie, warn about this type of "impenetrable code."

You want your code to be short and compact for efficiency, but code must be maintained. When you think you have found all the bugs in a program, give it to a user. A user will discover bugs in places you didn't even consider.

If you choose to build complex expressions, comment profusely. In the comments, break the code down and explain how you think the expression will be evaluated. If you run into problems months down the road, at least you will have a reminder of your thought processes at the time.

161. *Writing Statements in C/C++*

The simplest statement is the empty statement, consisting of only a semicolon. You use it where the syntax of the language requires a statement but you have no code to execute. For example, suppose you have a function that pours an ounce of coffee into a cup. It returns a 0 to indicate the cup is full and non-zero to indicate the cup can take more coffee. If you want to call it repeatedly until you get a zero return, you can write it in the following way:

```
while (PourCoffee(ONE_OUNCE))
    ;
```

The statement is required by the language syntax, but you have nothing you need to execute while the coffee is pouring. In this case, use an empty statement as the object of the loop.

There are six types of statements in C, and C++ adds two more:

- **Label *statements* are prefixed by an identifier, which is followed by a colon (:). The label and semicolon don't comprise a statement by themselves and they do not alter the flow of execution. Labels join with the following expression statement to form a label statement. The *case* statement in a *switch* is an example of a label statement. A label statement also can be the object of a *goto* operation. Labels are contained in their own namespace and can duplicate identifiers.

- **Expression statements** are a complete execution unit and all effects of this type of statement are evaluated before the next statement is executed. An expression statement can have zero or more expressions.

- **Compound statements** are formed by enclosing zero or more statements with curly braces. A compound statement can be used where only one statement is expected. The type of statement is often called a "block" and can contain its own declarations.

- **Selection statements** are used to control program flow by evaluating an arithmetic or pointer expression and then directing the program to alternate statements. They are used to form conditionals in programming. The *if*, *if...else*, and *switch* statements are selection statements.

- **Iteration statements** cause the repetitive execution of an object statement and are used to control program loops. This type of statement acts on an expression, which is fully evaluated before the object statement is executed. The *for*, *while*, and *do ... while* statements are iteration statements.

- **Jump statements** transfer control unconditionally to another part of the program. The *goto*, *return*, *break*, and *continue* are jump statements.

- **Declaration statements** are used to declare an identifier and optionally set its value. Technically, a declaration statement is not a part of C syntax, and a declaration can be made only at the beginning of a block or in global scope. In C++, a property called *locality of execution* enables declaration statements to appear within the body of a block rather than just at the beginning.

- **Try-block statements** are used to encapsulate statements to process exceptions. The *try*, *catch*, and *throw* are try-block statements.

162. *Introduction to Flow Control*

Ordinarily, statements are executed in the order they are entered in the program, and the contents of a statement are fully evaluated and acted on before the next statement is executed. The selection, iteration, and jump statement types can be used to interrupt the normal sequential flow and transfer control to another point in the program.

The jump statements always transfer control. The *goto* is used only with a label statement and control is transferred unconditionally to the label statement. The *continue* statement is used only with an iteration statement, and transfers control to it. The *break* statement is used in iteration statements and in the *switch* selection statement. It terminates the current block and transfers control to the statement immediately following the block. The *return* statement can be used only in the body of a function and transfers control back to the point where the function was called.

Iteration statements cause a statement or block to be executed repeatedly. The control expression must be arithmetic or pointer type. With each execution, the program transfers to the iteration statement where the control expression is re-evaluated. In a *while* loop, the expression is evaluated before the statements are executed. In a *do ... while* loop, the expression is evaluated after each cycle of the loop. In the *for* statement, the first expression in the control is evaluated only once. The second expression is evaluated before each execution of the object statement or block and the loop is terminated if it equates to 0. The third expression in a *for* statement is executed after each cycle.

Selection statements also are used with a control expression enclosed in parentheses and are followed by an object statement or block. With the *if* statement, execution is transferred to the object only if the expression equates to non-zero. In the *if ... else* statement, control is transferred to the *else* statement if the conditional equates to zero. The *switch* statement transfers control to one of several *case* statements depending on the result of the controlling expression, or to an optional *default* statement if no *case* statement matches the result. The expression must return an integral data type, and each *case* statement must contain an integral constant.

163. *Using the* if *Keyword*

The *if* statement is always used with a controlling expression enclosed in parentheses. The expression usually is written on the same line as the *if* statement, but it doesn't have to be. However, it must follow without any intervening characters other than white space. There is no terminating semicolon after the control expression.

The *object* of an *if* statement is the next statement in the program sequence, which can be a compound statement enclosed by curly braces. The object can appear on the same line as the *if* statement, but for readability it often is placed on the following line and indented with respect to the *if* statement. The following examples of an *if* statement are syntactically equivalent:

```
if (expression) statement;
    if (expression)
        statement;
    if (expression)
    {
        statement;
    }
```

The control expression must evaluate to an arithmetic or pointer data type. If the expression evaluates to a non-zero result, program control is transferred to the object. Otherwise, the object is ignored.

164. *Using the* else *Keyword*

An *else* statement is used as an alternate object for an *if* statement. It can never be used without an *if* statement, and it must be the first statement after the *if* object. When the compiler encounters an *else* statement, it attempts to pair it with the first previous *if* statement (which can be a problem, as you will see in the next tip). If there are intervening statements, an error is generated.

The object of an *else* statement is the next statement in the program, and it is of the same form as the object of an *if* statement. A simple *if else* statement can be written on a single line. The following statements produce the same results:

```
if (expression) statement1 else statement2;

if (expression)
    statement1;
else
    statement2

if (expression)
{
    statement1;
}
```

```
else
    statement2

if (expression)
{
    statement1;
}
    else
{
    statement2
}
```

165. *Executing a Single Statement*

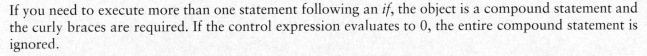

When executing a single statement as the object of an *if* statement, you can write it on the same line. Commonly, however, the statement is written on the next line and indented in relation to the *if* statement. The single statement can be an ordinary statement, another *if* statement, or even a loop. Even if the object statement executes multiple statements, the block still is not required.

```
if (expression1)
    if (expression2)
        for (x = x; x < 10; ++x)
        {
            // Statements executed in the for loop
        }
```

Obviously, curly braces around the code for each *if* statement would make this construction more readable.

166. *Executing Multiple Statements as the Object of an if Operator*

If you need to execute more than one statement following an *if*, the object is a compound statement and the curly braces are required. If the control expression evaluates to 0, the entire compound statement is ignored.

The compound statement is also a block, and thus follows the rules for blocks in C and C++. You can, for example, declare variables within it, but the variables only have meaning within the compound statement.

```
if (expression)
{
    int x = 0;
    statements;
}
```

167. *Combining the* if *and* else *Keywords*

Neither C nor C++ has an *elseif* statement, but an *if* statement can serve as the object of another *if* statement or an *else* statement, giving it the appearance and functionality of an *elseif*.

When using another *if* statement as the object of an *if*, it's good practice to enclose it in braces to isolate its meaning.

```
if (expression1)
{
    if (expression2)
        statements;
}
```

If the control expression of an *if* statement evaluates to zero, control can be passed to an optional *else* statement. If the *else* statement is present, it must be the first statement after the *if* statement's object.

```
if (expression1)
{
    if (expression2)
        statement1;
}
else
    statement2;
```

Now you see the value of the block as the conditional's object. In this case, if you did not use the braces, the *else* statement would pair with the second *if*.

168. *Using Multiple* if *Conditions*

When using an *else if* form of the statement, it's important to remember that the *if* statement is the object of the *else* and not a part of it. In the previous tip I pointed out that the compiler attempts to pair an *else* statement with the nearest previous *if*. The following examples show a common error:

```
if (expresssion1)
    statement1;
else if (expression2)
    statement2
else
    statement3;
```

The code works as expected. Only one of the statements will be executed. However, let's replace *statement1 and statement2* with a conditional as their objects:

```
if (expresssion1)
    if (expression1a)statement1;
else if (expression2)
    if (expresssion2a) statement2;
else
    statement3;
```

Now it's not so clear which *else* statement pairs with which *if* statement. Rewriting them with braces and indents will show how the compiler sees this construction:

```
if (expresssion1)
{
    if (expression1a)
    {
        statement1;
    }
    else if (expression2)
    {
        if (expresssion2a)
        {
            statement2;
        }
        else
        {
            statement3;
        }
    }
}
```

It's clear now that the final *else* no longer pairs with the first *if*; in fact, the first *if* statement has no alternate block.

169. *Using the Conditional Operator*

C provides you with a shorthand method of setting the value of a variable based on the value of an expression. You don't need to go through the usual *if ... else* statements. Instead, you can use the *conditional* operator.

The conditional operator doesn't actually set a variable. It is composed of three expressions—a control expression and two alternate expressions—only one of which is evaluated. If the control expression is non-zero, the second expression is evaluated and the third is ignored. If the control expression is 0, the second expression is ignored and third is evaluated.

You write a conditional statement by writing the control expression followed by a question mark, then the second expression, a colon, and then the third expression:

```
control_expr ? expr_if_true : expr_if_false;
```

If you want to assign a variable a value based on the control expression, you use an assignment operator:

```
int x = control_expr ? value_if_true : value_if_false;
```

This is similar to writing an *if else* statement:

```
if (control_expr)
    x = value_if_true;
else
    x = value_if_false;
```

If the data types of the expressions differ, they are all promoted to the data type with the highest precision, and that must be the data type of the *lvalue* in an assignment. This isn't true of the *if else* construction in which the result of the expression must be specifically cast to the proper data type.

The conditional can be used as a stand-alone statement and used to alter the program flow. The page folio snippet from an earlier tip can be reduced from five lines to a single line of code:

```
void DoFolio (int PageNo)
{
    PageNo % 2 ? DoOddFolio (PageNo) : DoEvenFolio (PageNo);
}
```

If the modulo 2 division of the page number is 1 (that is, the page number is odd), the *DoOddFolio()* function is called. Otherwise the *DoEvenFolio()* function is called.

170. Introduction to Scope

A few paragraphs ago I hinted that you can declare variables within a compound statement following an *if* statement but the variables would be usable only within the compound statement. I was alluding to the scope of the variables.

Scope is the extent of code in which a variable exists and can be referenced. The scope of a variable can be *global* or *local*. If a variable is declared outside a function, it has global scope. Otherwise, it has local scope. When you speak of a variable as being global or local, you actually are referring to its scope. The local scope is what interests us.

The statements within a function definition are contained in the function's *block*. If a variable is declared within a block, its scope is the block from the point it is declared to the end of the block. In C, a variable can be declared only at the beginning of a block, so its scope is the block itself. In C++, variables can be declared anywhere within a block, so their scope is from the point of declaration to the end of the block. That's a fancy way of saying you can't use a variable until you declare it.

If you declare a variable within a function block and give it the same name as a global variable, the global variable becomes invisible to the function. The local variable is said to *mask* the global declaration. The two variables are *not* identical: Changing the value of a local variable does not affect a global variable, as shown in the following code:

```
int x = 5;       // declare x in global scope
void FunctionOne()
{
    int x = 3;       // declare another x in local scope
                     // The global x is invisible but
                     // retains its value
    // some function statements
}
```

A block can contain other blocks as well, as is the case of the *if* statement with a compound statement. The compound statement is a block, and variables can be declared within a block. In this case, they are local to the block. After the block ends with the closing brace, the variable is destroyed and its value is lost. Even if it is declared again outside the block, it won't be the same variable nor will it have the same value.

Similarly, if you declare a variable within a sub-block with the same name as a variable that is local to a function, the variable in the sub-block hides the function variable. To see the effects, try the following short program:

```
#include    <stdio.h>

int x = 1;              // declare a global instance of x
void FunctionOne();    // Prototype our function

main ()
{
    printf ("The global x is %d\n", x);
    FunctionOne ();
    printf ("The global x is still %d\n", x);
}

void FunctionOne ()
{
int x = 2;
    printf ("The local x in the function is %d\n", x);
    {
    int x = 3;
        printf ("The local x in a block is %d\n", x);
    }
    printf ("Block has ended. x = %d\n", x);
}
```

Generally, the rule is that when variable identifiers are identical, C and C++ always use the variable with the smallest scope.

If a variable is declared within a container such as a class or structure, it doesn't exist until an instance of the container has been declared. In that case it has the same scope as the container instance.

171. *Understanding Scope Within a Conditional*

A compound statement that serves as the object of an *if* statement is a block, and you can declare local variables within it. If you duplicate a variable identifier with a larger scope, it is masked and the identifier with the smallest scope is used.

Inside the conditional block, you can access and modify variables with a larger scope.

If both the *if* and *else* have compound statements as their objects, variables declared within one are not in scope in the other compound statement. In the following code, each *x* is declared local to its own block. The fact that *x* is initialized in the first block does not initialize it in the other block.

```
if (control_statement)
{
   int x = 2;   // x local to this block only
}
   else
{
   int x;       // x local to this block only
   {
```

172. *Some Common Errors with Conditional Statements*

Unlike many other languages, C does not contain a keyword to mark the end of a conditional block. You cannot execute more than one statement after a conditional statement unless you encapsulate them into a compound statement. Although the *else* statement can be used to provide an alternate statement, it does not mark the end of a conditional block. The following code will generate errors on compile:

```
if (expression)
    statement1;
    statement2;
else
    statement3;
```

The line *statement1* is the only line under the control of the conditional statement. The line after that is always executed and the *else* has no matching *if* statement, so it will cause an error when compiled.

Another error commonly made even by experienced programmers is to place a semicolon after the conditional statement. Ending a line with a semicolon gets to be a natural action, and it's easy to accidentally place one in the wrong place. The compiler sees a terminating semicolon as an empty statement, which is a valid statement in C and C++, and will not generate an error:

```
if (expression);
{
    int x;
    statement1;
    statement2;
}
```

The preceding code will not generate a compile error, but the code within the block will always execute, regardless of the result of the expression. The compiler sees the semicolon at the end as a valid statement that is the object of the *if* statement.

173. *Introduction to Loops*

When humans are asked to perform a tedious job repeatedly—say sort stacks of coins, put the dimes here, the nickels there, and the pennies in that pile—eventually they are going to make mistakes. Computers, on the other hand, excel at the tedious and happily repeat tasks over and over. It seems they always are looking for a loop to fall into, as many late-night debugging sessions have taught you.

Nearly every language provides some form of loop control. Even in those rare languages that don't, there is always some form of conditional and transfer statements that make it possible to build loops.

In C and C++, you can build a loop using a label statement and a *goto*, or you can use one of the iteration statements available in the language. As you will see in this section, C loop devices are powerful and flexible tools in the hands of a programmer.

174. Constructing a Loop with a Conditional Statement and a goto

The simplest form of a loop requires a jump statement and a statement to which control can be transferred, a label statement in C. The following is a valid statement in C and provides the basic means of looping. Granted this statement doesn't do anything, but it doesn't do anything very fast, and it will do nothing for a very long time (please don't try to execute this line):

```
here:    goto here;
```

To construct a useful loop, you need a control statement that will enable you to perform the jump or not, giving you some way to exit the loop. Ideally, the statements between the control statement and the jump point should modify a memory location used by the control statement. The following code initializes a control variable before entering the loop section. The code within the loop modifies it and the control statement provides a means of exiting:

```
    int x = 20;
here:
    x -= 1
    if (x > 0)
        goto here;
```

Other statements between the label and the control statements can be used to perform some useful work, such as read a record from a file, modify it, and write it back to the file.

175. Introducing the while Loop

Fortunately, C and C++ provide more eloquent means of building loops. The simplest form of a loop is the *while* loop. Don't let the word *simplest* fool you; a lot of work can be done in a very limited amount of code with the *while* statement.

The iterative statement for a *while* loop is formed by using the *while* keyword followed by a control expression in parentheses. The *while* statement takes a single statement as its object, or the object can be a compound statement enclosed in curly braces.

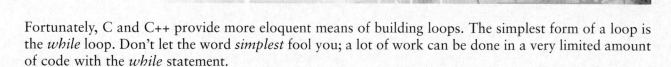

```
while (control_expression)
    object_statement;
```

The control expression must evaluate to an arithmetic or pointer data type. The *while* loop contains no provision for initializing or modifying the loop condition, so any variables used in the control expression should be initialized before the *while* statement is encountered. The code in the control expression or object statement should modify the control statement to provide some means of exiting the loop.

The control expression is evaluated *before* each iteration, including the first. If it evaluates to 0, the loop is not executed and control passes to the first statement after the object. After each iteration of the loop, control is passed back to the *while* statement and the expression is re-evaluated. If the control statement is 0 when the loop is first encountered, it is not executed at all and control immediately is passed to the next statement. The following are examples of valid *while* loops. Notice there is no semicolon after the control expression.

```
while (x) statement;

while (x)
    statement;

while (x)
{
    statement1;
    statement2;
}
```

The control expression can modify itself. If you set x equal to 10 and write *while (x--)*, the loop will execute 10 times. (The rules for postfix and prefix operators apply here. If you instead write *while (--x)*, the loop will execute only nine times.)

176. Using the continue and break Statements

At certain points in a loop you might discover conditions that make it impossible or undesirable to continue with the rest of the loop statements. The *break* statement gives you the ability to abort the loop altogether, and the *continue* statement enables you to abort only the current iteration of the loop.

When the *break* statement is encountered, the loop terminates and control passes to the first statement following the loop object. The control expression is not re-evaluated.

The *continue* statement transfers control to the iteration statement. The control expression is re-evaluated and the next iteration begins if the result is non-zero.

The *break* and *continue* are complete statements and take no operands. Each statement must be followed by a semicolon.

The *continue* statement can be used only within a compound statement that is the object of a loop statement. The *break* statement is used in the *switch* statement as well as loops.

177. Introducing the do while Loop

In the *do while* form of the loop, the *while* statement is placed at the end of the loop section. The loop is entered at the *do* statement and the control statement is evaluated at the *while* statement. Unlike the *while* loop, the *do while* loop is guaranteed to execute at least once. Also unlike the *while* loop, a semicolon must be used after the control expression.

In its simplest form, the *do while* loop can be written on a single line, as shown in the following. It might look odd, but the semicolon after the object statement is required:

```
do object_statement; while (control_expression);
```

More complicated *do while* loops can be constructed using a compound statement as the object. The following program uses the *FindFirstFile()* and *FindNextFile()* functions to list the DOS and Windows names of files in a directory. In this case, if the *FindFirstFile()* function succeeds, you know it is safe to execute the loop at least once, and you use a different function to find the next file. When *FindNextFile()* returns 0, you are finished.

```cpp
/*
    ListDir.cpp - - lists the DOS and Windows file name of
                    files in a specified directory.
 */
#include    <stdio.h>
#include    <windows.h>
#include    <windef.h>
#include    <winbase.h>
#include    "utility.h"

bool ListFiles (char *pszDir);

main (int argc, char *argv[])
{
    char *pszProgName = GetProgName (argv[0]);
    if (argc < 2)
        {
        fprintf (stderr, "%s: Enter a directory path\n",
                pszProgName);
        return (-1);
        }
    if (!ListFiles (argv[1]))
        {
        fprintf (stderr, "%s: Cannot open path\n",
                pszProgName);
        return (-1);
        }
    return (0);
}

bool ListFiles (char *pszDir)
{
char    Path[MAX_PATH];
HANDLE  hFile;
WIN32_FIND_DATA    fileData;

    strcpy (Path, pszDir);
    if ((Path[strlen(Path) - 1] == '\\') ||
        (Path[strlen(Path) - 1] == '/'))
        strcat (Path, "*.*");
    else
        strcat (Path, "\\*.*");

// If we can't find the first file, we can't continue
    if ((hFile = FindFirstFile(Path, &fileData))
            == INVALID_HANDLE_VALUE)
    {
        return (false);
    }
    do
    {
// Don't list directories
        if (fileData.dwFileAttributes &
                FILE_ATTRIBUTE_DIRECTORY)
            continue;
// If no DOS name, it's same as Windows name
```

```
            if (!strlen (fileData.cAlternateFileName))
            {
                 strncpy (fileData.cAlternateFileName,
                          fileData.cFileName, 13);
// DOS name is always caps
                 _strupr (fileData.cAlternateFileName);
            }
// List the file names
            printf ("%-16s%s\n", fileData.cAlternateFileName,
                                 fileData.cFileName);
       } while (FindNextFile (hFile, &fileData));
// Close the find functions
       FindClose (hFile);
       return (true);
}
```

For this sample, you'll want to use the *utility.cpp* and *utility.h* files you prepared in Tip 132, "Adding a Header File."

178. *Introducing the* for *Loop*

Neither the *while* loop nor the *do while* loop provides any mechanism for initializing or modifying the variables contained in the loop control statement. C contains an eloquent *for* loop that incorporates these capabilities. You might see a vague resemblance between the C *for* loop and the BASIC *for next* statement, but the resemblance is all they have in common.

The *for* statement contains three expressions, each separated by semicolons, contained within parentheses. An expression can be omitted, but the semicolon must be included. The object of the loop can be a single statement or a compound statement enclosed by curly braces.

The first expression is the initializing expression. It is executed before any statement in the loop object and before the control expression is evaluated. There are no restrictions on its data type.

The second is the control expression. It is executed before any object statements and terminates the loop if the expression is 0. If it is 0 on the first iteration, the loop is never executed. The data type must evaluate to an arithmetic or pointer type.

The third and final expression is the re-initialization expression, and it is evaluated at the end of each iteration of the loop. With each iteration, it is executed before the control statement is re-evaluated for the next iteration. There are no restrictions on its data type.

Multiple expressions can be used in any of the three expressions by separating them with a comma operator. If multiple expressions are used in the control expression, however, only the last will have any effect on loop control; the others will be evaluated and ignored, but the results can be used in the loop object statements.

To build a *for* loop, type the keyword *for* followed by an open parenthesis. There can be intervening white space but no other characters. After the parenthesis, type the initialization expression followed by a semicolon. If the initialization is omitted, the semicolon must be entered anyway. Next, enter the control expression followed by a semicolon. Again, if the expression is omitted, the semicolon must be entered. Finally, enter the re-initialization expression followed by a close parenthesis. No semicolon is used in the re-initialization expression, and the expression can be omitted.

The following example shows the *for* loop in its simplest form and in a more typical form:

```
for (x = 0; x < 10; ++x) object_statement;

for (x = 0; x < 10; __x)
    {
    object_statements;
    }
```

The following code uses a *for* statement to reverse the characters in a string:

```
/*
    elba.cpp - Reverse the characters in a string.
 */
#include    <stdio.h>
#include    <string.h>

main ()
{

char    *pszElba = "Able was I ere I saw Elba";
int     x;
char    ch;

    int max = strlen (pszElba);
    printf ("%s\n", pszElba);
    for (x = 0; x < max / 2; ++x)
    {
        ch = pszElba[x];
        pszElba[x] = pszElba[max - x - 1];
        pszElba[max - x - 1] = ch;
    }
    printf ("%s\n", pszElba);
    return (0);
}
```

The original string is a palindrome, but you know it was reversed in the preceding code by the position of capital letters in the *printf* statements.

179. *Understanding Scope Within a Loop*

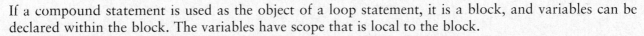

If a compound statement is used as the object of a loop statement, it is a block, and variables can be declared within the block. The variables have scope that is local to the block.

The variables come into scope when they are declared and go out of scope at the end of each iteration of the loop. Thus, they are destroyed and their values are permanently lost every time the loop completes a cycle. On the next iteration, new variables are created. Don't expect them to retain the values of the variables from a previous cycle, however. They must be initialized on each repetition of the loop.

180. *Understanding the* switch *Statement*

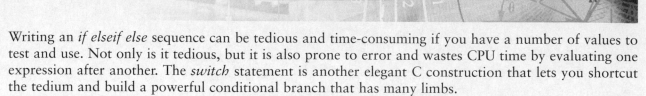

Writing an *if elseif else* sequence can be tedious and time-consuming if you have a number of values to test and use. Not only is it tedious, but it is also prone to error and wastes CPU time by evaluating one expression after another. The *switch* statement is another elegant C construction that lets you shortcut the tedium and build a powerful conditional branch that has many limbs.

Write a *switch* statement using the keyword *switch* followed by an open parenthesis, an expression, and a close parenthesis. Because of the nature of its use, the *switch* statement almost always takes a compound statement as its object. It is possible to build a *switch* statement using a single object statement, but, as a friend of mine pointed out, it's also possible to drink milk through your nose with a straw; neither has any practical application.

The expression is akin to a loop control expression except it must be an integral data type. If it isn't, you can't use the *switch* statement and must resort to the *if elseif else* construction.

Within the compound object statement are a series of label statements using the keywords *case* and *default*. Each case is associated with an integral constant and the program control is transferred to a *case* label if its constant matches the expression evaluation. If none of the case statements match, control is transferred to the optional *default* label. Each *case* and *default* is a label and requires a colon.

After the control has been transferred, the statements are executed sequentially until the end of the compound statement or a *break* statement is encountered. It is possible to let one *case* "fall through" to another by omitting the *break* statement.

181. *Using* case *and* default *Statements*

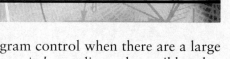

Switches are excellent mechanisms for evaluating and directing program control when there are a large number of possibilities. Within the compound object statement of the *switch*, you list each possible value your evaluation can take in separate *case* statements. Then you write the code to handle that possibility.

The identifier for a *case* label must be an integral constant. You can't use a variable as a *case* identifier. Also, you cannot duplicate cases; you can have one and only one *case 10:*, for example.

The following message handler responds to the *LVN_GETDISPINFO* Windows message to draw the items in a list control using *LPSTR_TEXTCALLBACK*. This is an efficient method of managing a large number of items in a list control, and I'll show you how to use it in the section on Windows Resources. For now, the list control has six columns of mixed data types, so each has to be handled separately. The message includes a pointer to a structure containing information about the line in the list control. In setting up the control, you place a pointer to your own structure in the *lParam* member for this item. Now you retrieve the information from the Windows structure and your own structure:

```cpp
void CAdList::OnGetdispinfo(NMHDR *pNMHDR, LRESULT *pResult)
{
CString    string;

    LV_DISPINFO* pDispInfo = (LV_DISPINFO*)pNMHDR;
//  Make sure the call is for text
    if (pDispInfo->item.mask & LVIF_TEXT)
    {
        *pResult = 0;    // No further processing needed
```

```cpp
        return;
    }
//  Retrieve point to our ad data structure for this item
    ADITEM *pItem = (ADITEM *) pDispInfo->item.lParam;
//  The iSubItem member contains the column to be displayed
    switch (pDispInfo->item.iSubItem)
    {
        case 0:              // Needs Ad Number
            string.Format ("%08d", pItem->AdNumber);
            ::lstrcpy(pDispInfo->item.pszText,
                            (LPCSTR) string);

            break;
        case 1:              // Needs Account
            ::lstrcpy (pDispInfo->item.pszText,
                            pItem->Account);

            break;
//  Pub Date is stored as Unix time. Put it into
//  a CTime object and extract the month, day and year.
        case 2:              // Needs Pub Date
            if (pItem->PubDate)
            {
                CTime PubDate = pItem->PubDate;
                string.Format ("%02d/%02d/%04d",
                            PubDate.GetMonth(),
                            PubDate.GetDay,
                            PubDate.GetYear);
                ::lstrcpy(pDispInfo->item.pszText,
                            (LPCSTR)string);

            }
            break;
        case 3:              // Needs Ad Tag Line
            ::lstrcpy (pDispInfo->item.pszText
                        (LPCSTR) pItem->AdTagLine);

            break;
        case 4:              // Needs Columns
            string.Format ("%d", (int)pItem->Columns);
            ::lstrcpy (pDispInfo->item.pszText,
                            (LPCSTR) string);

            break;
//  Depth and Linage are stored as
//  integers containing hundredths.
//  Separate the integral part from the fraction
        case 5:              // Needs Depth
            string.Format ("%d.%02d",(int) pItem->Depth/100
                                (int) pItem->Depth % 100);
            ::lstrcpy (pDispInfo->item.pszText,
                                (LPCSTR) string);

            break;
        case 6:              // Needs Total Linage
            string.Format("%d.%02d",
                        (int)pItem->TotalLinage/100,
                        (int)pItem->TotalLinage%100);
            ::lstrcpy (pDispInfo->item.pszText,
                            (LPCSTR) string);

            break;
//  The only columns we need have been processed.
```

```
// default does nothing
      default:
         break;
   }
   *pResult = 0;      // No further processing needed
}
```

Notice that a *break* statement is used at the end of each item. The *break* terminates the *switch,* and without it an item would "fall through" to the next item. There might be times when you want to do this. This makes it possible to "stack" cases and let the same code process them. In the following snippet, cases 2, 7, and 16 would be handled by the same code:

```
switch (expression)
{
    case 2:
    case 7:
    case 16:
       // statements cases 2, 7 and 16
       break;
    case 1:
       // statements to handle case 1
       break;
    case 3:
       // statements to handle case 3
       break;
    default:
       // statements to handle the default
       break;
}
```

The *case* statements were not placed in order. There's no requirement that you do so, and in fact that would limit your ability to stack cases. There can be only one *default* case in a *switch* statement.

182. Declaring Variables Within the Scope of a switch Statement

Variables used only in the *switch* statement can be declared inside the compound statement block following the *switch* statement. In C++, you also can declare variables at the bottom of the block, but, of course, they wouldn't be much use there. Declaring a variable within a *case* label requires some special attention, which I cover in the next tip.

In the message handler in the previous tip, the *pItem* variable is used only within the *switch* statement, so you could have declared it differently:

```
switch (pDispInfo->item.iSubItem)
{
    ADITEM *pItem = (ADITEM *) pDispInfo->item.lParam;
    case 0:            // Needs Ad Number
```

In this case, the scope of the variable is the braces in the compound statement.

183. *Declaring Variables Within a case*

You can declare variables within a *case* statement in C++ but not in C. However, you cannot initialize a variable in the declaration statement except in the last *case* statement. Trying to compile the following snippet results in "error C2360: initialization of 'x' is skipped by 'case' label":

```
switch (expr)
{
    case 0:
        // statements for case 0
        break;
    case 3:
        int x = 0;
        // statements for case 3
        break;
    case 0:
        // statements for case 0
        break;
    default:
        // statements for default
        break;
}
```

The idea is that the variable is available to the rest of the code (until the end of the block) but the initialization is not. To avoid the error, simply declare the variable and then initialize it in a separate statement:

```
case 3:
    int x;
    x = 0;
    // statements for case 3
    break;
```

Of course, if you need the initialization in other *case* statements that use x, you have to repeat the $x = 0$ in each of them. If you need to declare and initialize a variable within a *case*, you can declare a block in the *case* statement. This way, the variable's scope is the block only, and it has no effect on the other cases.

```
case 3:
    {          // Establish a block
        int x = 0; // Declare and initialize x
        // statements for case 3
    }          // End of block. x is destroyed
    break;     // break may go inside or outside block
```

184. *A Brief History of C*

The C programming language was developed at Bell Laboratories in 1972 by Dennis M. Ritchie. It takes its name from the fact that it was derived from the B programming language, which itself was derived from BCPL developed by Martin Richards. Unlike C, B and BCPL are "typeless," but many of the languages' other concepts have worked their way into C.

C was developed on a DEC PDP-7 computer where it was used to write the first UNIX operating system. Over the years, implementations were developed for other operating systems, and it became very popular on personal computers because of the concise nature of the language and some of its assembly-like qualities. Despite the fact it technically is a high-level language, it produced compact executable code in memory-starved personal computers. Versions of C were available even on the eight-bit CP/M operating system that predated the personal computer and PC-DOS.

Ritchie and Brian W. Kernighan gave the language a formal definition in their book *The C Programming Language*, which has been revised in the second edition to include the more formal definitions developed by a committee of the American National Standards Institute (ANSI). The manual still is the definitive resource for C, and programmers refer to it simply as "K and R."

185. *Making the Transition to C++*

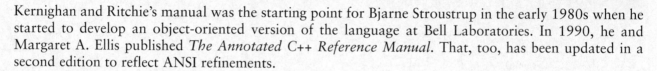

Kernighan and Ritchie's manual was the starting point for Bjarne Stroustrup in the early 1980s when he started to develop an object-oriented version of the language at Bell Laboratories. In 1990, he and Margaret A. Ellis published *The Annotated C++ Reference Manual*. That, too, has been updated in a second edition to reflect ANSI refinements.

Moving over to C++ can be an unnerving experience for a hard-core C programmer. I began using C in the late 1970s on a UNIX system running on a PDP-11 computer. Although I kept up with the trade articles and the development of C++, many of the object-oriented concepts seemed foreign to the programming style I was used to. The newspaper industry in which I work was using personal computers more and more, so about 10 years ago I purchased a copy of Turbo C++ (later to become Borland C++) and soon afterward Microsoft C++ (later to become Visual C++). Many expletives and late nights later, I had "morphed" into a C++ programmer and couldn't go back. (For the record, Borland's C++ is still my favorite. Microsoft could learn a lot from studying it and Borland's Object Windows Library [OWL], which in my opinion is far superior to the Microsoft Foundation Class [MFC] library.)

For the most part, C code is portable to C++, but the reverse isn't true. You'll still find some of the old C-style function definitions around, such as the following example:

```
int main (argc, argv)
int argc;
char *argv[];
{
}
```

Visual C++ will accept that syntax using the C rules, but it's not acceptable in C++. Both C and C++ now use the following style for function definitions:

```
int main (int argc, char *argv[])
{
}
```

Except for that (just break down and rewrite the function definitions) I've had little trouble porting my old C code to C++.

186. *Understanding Structures in C*

The *structure* is a handy C device that enables you to encapsulate related data, even of different types, and treat the collection as a single object. Other languages have structure-like constructions, but they use different names, such as "record," to describe them. Although the structure is an example of object-oriented devices, its primary purpose is to treat the encapsulated data as a single unit.

This is particularly useful in C, in which function calls use values for parameters rather than references. If you have, say, 10 data items you want to pass to a function, you have to declare every one of them as function parameters. In C, you can enclose them in a structure definition, declare an instance of the structure, and then simply pass a pointer to it as a single parameter.

Structures are widely used in C and C++, and are the basis for the C++ *class* object. The most common way to define a structure is to use the *struct* keyword followed by an identifier for the structure. The identifier does not declare an instance of the structure, but rather C creates a data type by that name and you can use it to create variables of the structure. Continue building the structure by entering an open brace, which can be on the same line. Declare variables in the structure the same as you would a function call. You cannot initialize any variables here because they don't exist until you create a variable of the structure. Adjacent variables of the same type can be included in a single declaration, but for readability each variable is placed on a single line. End the definition with a close brace. A structure definition must be terminated with a semicolon. Here's how you might create a simple structure describing an employee record:

```
#define   MAXNAMELEN    24

struct EMPLOYEEDATA
{
    long    EmployeeID;
    char    FirstName[MAXNAMELEN];
    char    MiddleInitial;
    char    LastName[MAXNAMELEN];
    int     Department;
    long    Flags;
};
```

You can now create an instance of the structure. The members can be initialized at the time they are declared by entering the values in the same order between braces. The first line below simply declares a variable; the second declares and initializes a variable.

```
struct EMPLOYEEDATA  ed;
struct EMPLOYEEDATA  ED = {1641, "Thomas ", 'A ',
                    "Jefferson ", 3527, 0};
```

More often than not, structures are used to hold dynamic data and are rarely initialized when they are declared.

You also can declare an instance of the structure when you define it. Make the last line of your definition above read "*} ed;*" and you have a variable *ed* of the type *struct EMPLOYEEDATA*. You can initialize the declaration at the same time:

```
struct EMPLOYEEDATA
{
    long    EmployeeID;
    char    FirstName[MAXNAMELEN];
    char    MiddleInitial;
```

```
    char    LastName[MAXNAMELEN];
    int     Department;
    long    Flags;
} ED = {1641, "Thomas", 'A ', "Jefferson", 3527, 0};
```

The elements in a structure are called *members*, and you reference them by using the variable name, a period, and the member name. *ED.EmployeeID* gives you access to the first member of your structure.

You use pointers to structures to pass them around to various functions. In this case, you use the symbol -> to access a member through a pointer, as shown in the following code:

```
void FunctionOne ()
{
struct EMPLOYEEDATA  ED = {1641, "Thomas", 'A',
                     "Jefferson", 3527, 0};
struct EMPLOYEEDATA *pED = &ED;

    printf ("%s %c. %s's employee number is %d\n",
               pEmpl.FirstName, pEmpl.MiddleInitial,
               pEmpl.LastName, pEmpl.EmployeeID);

    FunctionTwo (pED);  // Or, we could use FunctionTwo (&ED);
}

void FunctionTwo (struct EMPLOYEEDATA *pEmpl)
{
    printf ("%s %c. %s's employee number is %d\n",
               pEmpl->FirstName, pEmpl->MiddleInitial,
               pEmpl->LastName, pEmpl->EmployeeID);
}
```

The *sizeof* operator returns the size of the structure, so in using it for file I/O you never need to count the number of bytes it uses. (The compiler will align the data elements on convenient memory boundaries, so chances are your count would be incorrect anyway.)

```
    fwrite (&ED, 1, sizeof (struct EMPLOYEEDATA), fp);
```

For simplicity, you can *typedef* the structure and drop the use of *struct* when referring to it (in C++ you don't have to *typedef* it for reasons you will examine a bit later). Use a unique identifier for the *typedef* name. In the example below, I've added an underscore to the structure name so that I can reuse the original name in the *typedef*:

```
struct EMPLOYEE_DATA
{
    // structure member declarations
} EMPLOYEEDATA;
```

Now *EMPLOYEEDATA* is synonymous with *struct EMPLOYEE_DATA*.

Structures also can be assigned to another by using the equals sign. The old C wouldn't let you do that; you had to use the *memcpy()* function. But now the equals sign causes the members of the structure on the right to be copied into the corresponding members of the structure on the right.

187. Introduction to the Class in C++

The C structure was Bjarne Stroustrup's model when he began developing the C++ class definition. It's not exactly true to say a class is a specific type of structure, but as you'll see in the next tip, the two have a lot in common.

Virtually everything you have learned about structures can be applied to classes. You don't have to *typedef* a class to use its name, but in C++ you no longer have to *typedef* structures either. (It is not an error to *typedef* a class or structure, however.) C places the names of structures, unions, and enumerated types in a separate namespace. C++ maintains them in the same namespace as user-defined data types, so once a class or structure is defined, its name becomes a user-defined data type and can be used the same as any other data type.

A class can contain member functions that can be used by other class members or by external functions. Two functions are required in any C++ class: a constructor and a destructor. The *constructor* is called automatically anytime a variable of the class is declared so that it can be used to initialize members of the class. The *destructor* is called automatically when a variable goes out of scope or is destroyed, so it can be used to clean up any memory allocations or close any files. The constructor function has the same name as the class; the destructor has the same name but is prefixed by a tilde. Neither the constructor nor the destructor has any data type and cannot return any values.

Class members are distinguished by their *access* level: *public*, *private*, or *protected*. I'll discuss access in detail in the section titled "The C++ Class" beginning with Tip 332, but by default all members of a class are private and can be accessed only by members of the class. This presents a problem, because declaring a variable usually requires access to the constructor, so constructors usually are declared in a *public* section of the class definition.

Private members are accessible only by members of the class. *Protected* members are accessible by derived class, friend classes, and friend classes of friends. *Public* access enables the member to be changed or executed by any outside function.

Define a class the same way you would a structure, except use the keyword *class* rather than *struct*. In the body of the class, enter the keyword *public* followed by a colon and enter the constructor function. If your constructor is going to do a lot of work, you might want to define it outside the class definition, but for now let's define it *inline*. (When a function is declared inline, the compiler substitutes the actual code for the function call. This results in slightly larger code modules, but it speeds up execution time. Inline functions should be kept as short as possible. Any function defined in the class definition is automatically made inline.) Assume your class name is *CEmployee*. The constructor should be written as follows (a trailing semicolon is not needed for an inline definition), and add a destructor.

```
CEmployee () {}
~CEmployee () {}
```

As you enter your class members, you can use *public*, *private*, and *protected* as often as you like. Once entered, all members declared after that point have that access until another access keyword is encountered. At this point your class definition should look like the following:

```
class CEmployee
{
public:
    CEmployee () { };
    ~CEmployee () { };
};
```

Now add some functions and variables. In the *public* section, add the following inline functions. Note the location of the semicolons in the functions.

```
    int GetID () {return (m_EmployeeID);}
    void SetID(int ID) {m_EmployeeID = ID;}
```

On a line by itself, enter *private:* and on the next line declare an *int* called *m_EmployeeID*. Your class definition should look like the following:

```
class CEmployee
{
public:
    CEmployee () { };
    ~CEmployee () { };
    int GetID () {return (m_EmployeeID);}
    void SetID(int ID) {m_EmployeeID = ID;}
private:
    int     m_EmployeeID;
};
```

Now enter some code to test your class and call the program *employ.cpp*. The entire program should look line this:

```
#include    <stdio.h>

class CEmployee
{
public:
    CEmployee () { };
    ~CEmployee () { };
    int GetID () {return (m_EmployeeID);}
    void SetID(int ID) {m_EmployeeID = ID;}
private:
    int     m_EmployeeID;
};

int main ()
{
CEmployee emp;

    emp.SetID (1641);
    printf ("The employee ID is %d\n", emp.GetID());
    return (0);
}
```

The only way you can access the *m_EmployeeID* member is through the two member functions. Try writing code to access it in a different way and see what errors the compiler gives you.

Now let's require that the employee's ID must be entered when the instance is declared. Remove the function *SetID* in the class definition and change the constructor to read as follows:

```
    CEmployee (int ID) {m_EmployeeID = ID;}
```

Change the declaration in *main()* to read *CEmployee emp(1641)* and delete the call to *emp.SetID*. Recompile the program and run it. Now you not only can't access the *m_EmployeeID* member, but you can't set it to anything else. The declaration automatically sets the member and it will stay that way until the variable is destroyed. You can declare other instances of the class, but you can't change *m_EmployeeID* after they are created.

For more detailed discussion on the C++ class, jump ahead to the sections titled, "Object-Oriented Programming" and "The C++ Class." For now, though, you should know enough about classes to write them and understand the following tips.

188. Understanding Similarities and Differences Between Classes and Structures

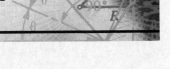

The C++ structure has undergone a lot of remodeling to the point that it provides a great deal more functionality than the C structure. The structure and class are so similar that it is difficult to distinguish between them. In fact, if you define a structure in a Visual Studio project and then look at the ClassView pane of the Workspace window, you'll see the structure listed there among the class names.

C++ structures can contain functions, but in C they cannot (but they can contain *pointers to functions*). The function can include constructors and a destructor that operate the same as the class counterparts.

C++ structures (but not C structures) can be derived from another structure or from a class. This isn't a well-known property of C++ structures, so let's examine how it works. First, declare a structure called *Struct1*:

```
struct Struct1
{
    int    x;
    int    y;
};
```

Now define a second structure, but derive it from the first. (Until you read the section on inheritance beginning with Tip 327, "Understanding Inheritance," just accept the following as the syntax for deriving one object from another.)

```
struct Struct2 : Struct1
{
    int    z;
};
```

Next, write a quick program to test the inheritance. (This brings up a fundamental *difference* between structures and classes: By default, all class members are *private*, but structure members are *public* by default.) You now can access and use the members declared in *Struct1* as though they were part of your *Struct2* definition:

```
int main()
{
Struct2    s;

    printf ("sizeof (Struct1) is %d\n", sizeof(Struct1));
    printf ("sizeof (Struct2) is %d\n", sizeof (Struct2));
    s.x = 1;
    s.y = 2;
    s.z = 3;
    printf ("Structure member values are %d, %d and %d\n",
            s.x, s.y, s.z);
    return (0);
}
```

You get the following output from the preceding code:

```
sizeof (Struct1) is 8
sizeof (Struct2) is 12
Structure member values are 1, 2 and 3
```

This gives your "record" object (the structure) the capability to leap tall buildings in a single bound.

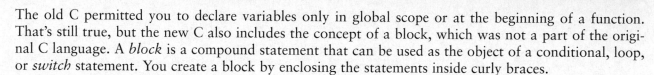

189. *Declaring Variables in C and C++*

The old C permitted you to declare variables only in global scope or at the beginning of a function. That's still true, but the new C also includes the concept of a block, which was not a part of the original C language. A *block* is a compound statement that can be used as the object of a conditional, loop, or *switch* statement. You create a block by enclosing the statements inside curly braces.

You can declare a block at any point in a function, even without the condition, loop, or *switch* statements. You can declare variables at the beginning of the block, but they lose scope and are destroyed when the program flow exits the block.

If the name of a variable inside a block duplicates a name outside the block, the variable masks or hides the variable with larger scope. Try the following code to see how this works:

```
#include    <stdio.h>

int main ()
{
int x;
    x = 2;
    printf ("x prior to the block is %d\n ", x);
    {
    int x;
        x = 3;
        printf ("x inside the block is %d\n", x);
    }
    printf ("x after the block is %d\n", x);
    return (0);
}
```

In C++, you can declare variables and blocks anywhere you would in C, but C++ also allows you to define variables at any point of a function. The same rules apply, but by placing the declaration of a variable near where it is first used, the readability of program code improves.

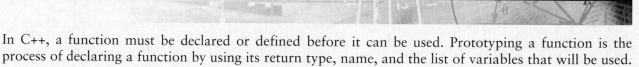

190. *Understanding Function Prototyping*

In C++, a function must be declared or defined before it can be used. Prototyping a function is the process of declaring a function by using its return type, name, and the list of variables that will be used.

Function prototyping does more than just declare the function for later use. It gives the compiler a pattern against which it compares all calls to the function. Using the prototype as a template, it compares the variable that will hold the return value against the function type, and then checks to make sure the number, order, and data types of any parameters match the prototype. If the comparison fails, an error is generated.

In C there is no such comparison. All functions by default are type *int*, and the only time you need to declare them is when the return type is other than *int*. Even if you declare them, there is no parameter checking, so it is possible to pass an integer value when you really mean to pass a pointer value. The following code generates several errors in C++, but compiles without even a warning in C:

```
#include    <stdio.h>

int FunctionOne ();

int main ()
{
int x;
    x = 3;
    FunctionOne (x, &x, "Test");
    return (0);
}

FunctionOne (int x)
{
    return (0);
}
```

C++ has much stricter rules on data typing and declarations. If you are going to program in C, you will have to be more careful. The compiler is not going to give you as much help as it will using C++ rules.

191. *Understanding Arrays*

Webster's defines an *array* as "a regular and imposing arrangement" or "an imposing series of things."

That's cool, because that's exactly what an array is in C++. What kind of things? Well, just about anything you can declare in C++, you can build an array of. For programming purposes, an array is one of the fundamental concepts of data structures. To programmers, an array is a collection of objects of all the same type arranged so that any element can be referenced using an identifier and an index expression.

C and C++ add a condition to that definition: The array elements must occupy contiguous locations in memory. Otherwise, they are just a collection of data objects.

When you declare an array in C (and in C++ as well), you are setting aside a contiguous block of memory that is large enough to hold as many elements as you select. The declaration doesn't necessarily initialize any of the elements; you still have to do that in your program's code. The next few tips will help you understand this concept.

Now for the exception of the day: One thing you can't build an array of in C++ is reference objects.

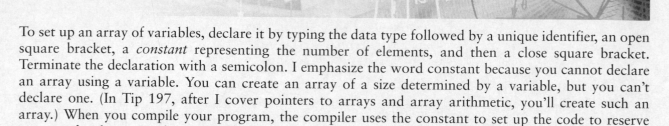

192. *Declaring Arrays of Variables*

To set up an array of variables, declare it by typing the data type followed by a unique identifier, an open square bracket, a *constant* representing the number of elements, and then a close square bracket. Terminate the declaration with a semicolon. I emphasize the word constant because you cannot declare an array using a variable. You can create an array of a size determined by a variable, but you can't declare one. (In Tip 197, after I cover pointers to arrays and array arithmetic, you'll create such an array.) When you compile your program, the compiler uses the constant to set up the code to reserve memory for the array. If the number is variable, it can't do that, so it gives you an error.

The following statement sets up an array of 10 items of type double:

```
double AnArray [10];
```

You can initialize an array at the time it is created. Use an equals sign followed by the list of initial values inside a set of braces:

```
Double AnArray[10] = {2.5, 6.8, 12.4, 3.2, 100.45,
                      10.1, 8, 25.6, 32.7, 86.0};
```

I purposely threw the integer 8 into the list to show you what happens. The compiler takes each initializing value and places it into the corresponding element, casting each to the array data type. If you change the example to an array of type *int*, the compiler will cast the values to *int*, stripping away the fractional part, without so much as a warning. In the example above, the compiler automatically promoted the integer 8 in the list to a *double*.

Some data types can't be cast to other types. If you enter a string in the initializer list, you'll get an error at compile time.

When declaring and initializing an array at the same time, you don't need to include the number of elements. The compiler will count the items in the initializer list and create an array large enough to hold them. The array of doubles could have been written as shown in the following code:

```
Double AnArray[] = {2.5, 6.8, 12.4, 3.2, 100.45,
                    10.1, 8, 25.6, 32.7, 86.0};
```

You don't have to count the values and use a hard-coded value in your program. You can programmatically get the number of elements by getting the number of bytes the array occupies and dividing it by the size of the data type. The following line shows an example. Don't forget that C arrays begin at element 0, so the size you get is one more than the maximum index value you can use.

```
int ArraySize = sizeof (AnArray) / sizeof(double);
```

In the example above, *ArraySize* will contain 10, but the maximum indexing value is 9.

Declaring an array in global scope creates it in the program's data segment of memory. Declaring it in a function creates it "on the stack." The default stack size for a program compiled with Visual C++ is one megabyte, so if you create a very large array (a double uses eight bytes for each element), you run the risk of depleting your stack space (C uses the stack to store other variables and function return addresses). Use the */F* compiler option or the */STACK linker* option to increase the stack size. Alternatively, you can create the array "in the heap" (I'll show you how shortly) or use one of Windows' global allocation functions.

193. *Using the String Array*

Neither C nor C++ has a string data type (C++ does have a *string* class in the Standard Template Library). Instead, you create arrays of type *char* and use them for strings. This sometimes makes string processing a bit awkward compared with other languages, but considering everything else you get in C, it's worth the trade-off. Most class libraries, including MFC, contain one or more string classes that ease the burden of string processing.

Most C library functions use the character constant '\0' to signify the end of a string; this is called a *null terminated string*. When you declare an array for a string, don't forget to add an extra byte for the terminator, which usually goes unseen in most programs. The compiler automatically adds the extra byte when you initialize a string when it is declared. The following lines show three ways to declare and initialize a string. In the third line, notice that the compiler initializes only the elements you give it and does not automatically provide a null terminator. You must include it in your list.

```
char *String1 = "This is String1";
char String2[] = "This is String2";
char String3[] = {'T', 'h', 'i', 's', ' ', 'i', 's', ' ',
                  'S', 't', 'r', 'i', 'n', 'g', '3', '\0'};
```

When using the *sizeof* operator on these various types of declarations, the size returned for *String1* is 4 because it is declared as a *char pointer*. The size of the other two is 16 because they are declared as arrays of type *char*. Use the *strlen()* library function to get the length of the first string (and remember *sizeof()* counts the null terminator, but *strlen()* does not).

194. *Using Arrays of Objects*

The array operator doesn't really care what the data type is. A basic type such as *int* or a user-defined type such as a class or structure is all the same to it. The array operator simply takes the size of the data type and the number of elements you want, multiplies them, and sets aside that much memory.

When initializing an array such as a class that has a constructor, the list of initializers is a list of variables required by the constructor. Using the employee sample, you can declare and initialize 10 objects using the following line:

```
CEmployee emp[] = {1641, 1802, 1732, 1752, 2401};
```

Now do it in a program and see what you have. The following code uses the class you examined in Tip 187, "Introduction to the Class in C++":

```
#include    <stdio.h>

class CEmployee
{
public:
    CEmployee (int ID) {m_EmployeeID = ID;}
    ~CEmployee () { };
    int GetID () {return (m_EmployeeID);}
private:
    int     m_EmployeeID;
```

```
};

int main ()
{
CEmployee emp[] = {1641, 1802, 1732, 1752, 2401};

    for (int x = 0; x < sizeof(emp)/sizeof (CEmployee); ++x)
        printf ("Employee ID No. %d is %d\n",
                   x, emp[x].GetID());
    return (0);
}
```

When you run the program, you should see the following output:

```
Employee ID No. 0 is 1641
Employee ID No. 1 is 1802
Employee ID No. 2 is 1732
Employee ID No. 3 is 1752
Employee ID No. 4 is 2401
```

Initializing for a constructor that requires more than one parameter is a bit trickier. With just one argument, you can pass it in a list, but for multiple arguments, you must supply the full constructor syntax. Change the class definition to include arrays for the first and last names, and then change the constructor to include *char* pointers in the parameter list. Add functions to access the first and last name members. Change the declaration of the array and *printf* statements in the function body to print the additional information. The resulting code should look like this:

```
/*
    array.cpp -- Initializing array of class with multiple
                 arguments in the constructor.
 */
#include    <stdio.h>
#include    <string.h>

class CEmployee
{
public:
    CEmployee (int ID, char *First, char *Last)
    {
        m_EmployeeID = ID;
        strcpy (m_EmployeeFirst, First);
        strcpy (m_EmployeeLast, Last);
    }
    int GetID () {return (m_EmployeeID);}
    char *GetFirstName () {return (m_EmployeeFirst);}
    char *GetLastName () {return (m_EmployeeLast);}
private:
    int     m_EmployeeID;
    char    m_EmployeeFirst[24];
    char    m_EmployeeLast[24];
};

int main ()
{
CEmployee emp[] = {
                CEmployee (1641, "Thomas", "Jefferson"),
```

```
                    CEmployee (1802, "George", "Washington"),
                    CEmployee (1732, "John", "Adams"),
                    CEmployee (1752, "Andrew", "Jackson"),
                    CEmployee (2401, "Elsie", "Smith")
                    };

    for (int x = 0; x < sizeof(emp)/sizeof (CEmployee); ++x)
        printf ("%s %s's Employee ID is %d\n",
                        emp[x].GetFirstName(),
                        emp[x].GetLastName(),
                        emp[x].GetID());
    return (0);
}
```

When you run this code, you should see the following output (okay, so this firm hires some influential people):

```
Thomas Jefferson's Employee ID is 1641
George Washington's Employee ID is 1802
John Adams's Employee ID is 1732
Andrew Jackson's Employee ID is 1752
Elsie Smith's Employee ID is 2401
```

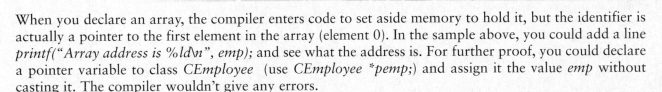

195. *Understanding Pointers to Arrays*

When you declare an array, the compiler enters code to set aside memory to hold it, but the identifier is actually a pointer to the first element in the array (element 0). In the sample above, you could add a line *printf("Array address is %ld\n", emp);* and see what the address is. For further proof, you could declare a pointer variable to class *CEmployee* (use *CEmployee *pemp;*) and assign it the value *emp* without casting it. The compiler wouldn't give any errors.

There is no actual variable that holds the array. The actual data is tucked away in memory and referenced through your pointer. This fact is the reason you can declare your arrays in Tip 193 in three different ways and get the result. In the next tip, you'll learn some other ways to access array elements.

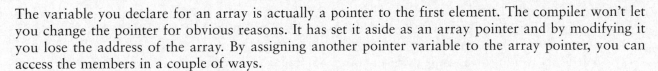

196. *Accessing Array Elements*

The variable you declare for an array is actually a pointer to the first element. The compiler won't let you change the pointer for obvious reasons. It has set it aside as an array pointer and by modifying it you lose the address of the array. By assigning another pointer variable to the array pointer, you can access the members in a couple of ways.

First, you could use the subscript method but use your pointer variable instead. The compiler won't gripe about a thing.

```
CEmployee *pemp = emp;

    printf("Array address is %ld\n", pemp);
```

```
    for (int x=0; x<sizeof(emp)/sizeof(CEmployee); ++x)
        printf ("%s %s's Employee ID is %d\n",
                    pemp[x].GetFirstName(),
                    pemp[x].GetLastName(),
                    pemp[x].GetID());
```

Second, you could use the pointer variable to point to the element you want to access, incrementing it each time through the loop. This time, however, you use the member pointer operator instead of the subscript:

```
CEmployee *pemp = emp;

    for (int x=0;x<sizeof(emp)/sizeof(CEmployee);++x,++pemp)
        printf ("%s %s's Employee ID is %d\n",
                    pemp->GetFirstName(),
                    pemp->GetLastName(),
                    pemp->GetID());
```

Both of these methods give you exactly the same output you got in the original program.

197. *Understanding Array Arithmetic*

You can increment the array pointer to access the next element because of the way C and C++ do arithmetic on array pointers. It's also the reason you can't assign a pointer of one data type to a pointer of another.

With each iteration of the loop, you increment *pemp*. The runtime code adds *sizeof(CEmployee)* to the pointer value, so you are pointing to the next element in the array. The same is true of any data type. If the array is of type *char*, the compiler adds *sizeof(char)*, if type *double* the compiler adds *sizeof(double)*, and so on.

Similarly, when you decrement a pointer, C uses the size of the data type and subtracts it from the array pointer. If you were able to assign one pointer to another of a different data type, the increment and decrement operations might not point to the beginning of array elements.

You can override this restriction by specifically casting one pointer to a pointer to the other data type. In the following code, the compiler tells you it is wrong to assign an *int* pointer to a *long* pointer:

```
long l;
int m;
long *lp = &m;
```

The compiler tells you the "types pointed to are unrelated" and refuses to do the assignment. However, you know that in Windows the *long* and *int* data types are the same size, four bytes, so you can safely change the third line to read *long *lp = (long *) &m;* to override the compiler's objections. This type of operation is highly non-portable, however. On Windows 3.1, an *int* data type is only two bytes, and the cast likely would cause some problems.

In Tip 192 I told you that you can create an array of a size determined by a variable, but you can't declare one. Now that I've covered pointers to arrays and touched on array arithmetic, I'll go over how to create an array with a computed size.

Simply create the array "on the heap," meaning you'll use the *new* operator. Assuming the integer variables *x* and *y* have been initialized to, say, 3 and 5 respectively, you can create the array with the following line:

```
double *DoubleArray = new double [x * y];
```

The expression inside the brackets must equate to an integer value. In this case, the result is 15, so an array of 15 doubles has been created. They can be accessed as any other array by using subscripting such as *DoubleArray[4]* or by using array arithmetic.

The actual array is on the heap and the pointer to it is a local variable. Before the variable goes out of scope and the pointer is lost permanently, you must free up the memory by using the *delete* operator:

```
delete [] DoubleArray;
```

198. Incrementing and Decrementing Array Variables

If incrementing and decrementing a pointer adjust the pointer by the size of the data element, how, you ask yourself, can you access the array element and increment or decrement it?

You do this by *dereferencing* the pointer after you adjust it to point to the array element. If you have an array of 10 *long* elements, and you assign another pointer variable to point to it, you add to the pointer the number of the element *minus* one (remember that the first element is element 0). You then dereference the pointer using the *indirection operator*, which is the asterisk (*). Suppose you want to access the third element of your long array. Simply add 2 to the pointer, as shown in the following snippet:

```
long LongArray[] = {96, 1024, 562, 89, 263, 10860,
                    42, 390, 235, 3247};
long *lp = LongArray;

   lp += 2;
   printf("The third element in the array is %ld\n",*lp);
```

Any operation you perform on the dereferenced pointer is performed on the array element instead. To increment the element, you use the increment operator ++ (or any other method to add 1 to the element, such as +=) together with the indirection operator. The following code shows three different methods:

```
lp += 2;
printf("The third element in the array is %ld\n",*lp);
++*lp;
printf("The third element in the array is %ld\n",*lp);
*lp += 1;
printf("The third element in the array is %ld\n",*lp);
*lp = *lp + 1;
printf("The third element in the array is %ld\n",*lp);
```

With each *printf* you see that the element has been incremented, although the pointer variable remains pointed to the third element.

Subscripting has the same effect as dereferencing the pointer. In this case, *LongArray[2]* describes the same data element as *(lp + 2)*. When do you use one or the other? There are times when array arithmetic will be more natural than subscripting; at other times subscripting might be the better way. C merely provides you with the option of doing it either way.

When using pointers to array elements, remember that neither the compiler nor the runtime code does any boundary checking to make sure you are actually pointing to an array element. A pointer can be decremented before the beginning of the array or incremented beyond the end.

The same is true with subscripted operations. Neither the compiler nor the runtime code gives you an error or even warns you when you try to access an element outside the array. *LongArray[-8]* is a valid operation in C and C++, although it might produce some unexpected results.

199. *Declaring Multidimensional Arrays*

C and C++ treat multidimensional arrays as "arrays of arrays." There is no limit to the number of dimensions an array can contain, but multidimensional arrays consume lots of memory very fast, and a practical limit is the amount of memory you have available.

Declare a multidimensional array by declaring its data type, the array identifier, and the size of each dimension, each enclosed in its own set of brackets. For example, *LongArray[2][3]* declares a two-dimensional array. The declaration *LongArray[2,3]*, such as you might find in most other languages, is a valid statement in C and C++, but it won't produce a two-dimensional array. Instead, the comma operator is used and the result of the expression is *3*, so you'll get a one-dimensional array with three elements. And you won't get a compiler error either.

If you declare a two-dimensional array such as *LongArray[2][3]*, you are telling the compiler you want a two-element array of three element arrays. The arrays must all be of the same data type; you can't have one of them be an array of *long*, another of *int*, and the third of type *char*. For that you would have to create three distinct arrays. Okay, because you're so insistent, you can build an array of pointers to those arrays (which is almost as good), even though they are of different data types. I'll show you how at the end of this tip.

When your program declares and creates your 2-by-3 array, the first array of three elements is laid out in memory, one right after the other, and then the next array is laid out right after it. If you have more than two such arrays, this head-to-tail construction will continue until they have all been laid out in continuous memory.

To access a single element, you have to say which array you want and then which element you want in that array, in that order. To get to the second element in the first array of three in *LongArray*, you write *LongArray[0][1]*. Once again, neither the compiler nor the runtime code provides any boundary checking, and it is easy to step outside a multidimensional array.

Now you turn to that array of arrays of different data types. It's sort of a two-dimensional array (but the arrays are continuous in memory), so it fits right into this tip. Remember when I told you about the *void* data type and the fact that you can't declare any variables of that type (it's used as a function return type)? You can, however, declare a *pointer to void*, and you can put a pointer to any data type in that pointer. On top of that, you can create an array of pointer to *void*. Let's declare and initialize three arrays: an array of four *int*s, an array of three *double*s, and a *char* array. Then declare an array of three pointers to *void* and initialize it with your other three arrays:

```
int IntArray[] = {4, 8, 22, 12};
double DoubleArray[] = { 2.5, 6.8, 12.4};
char CharArray[] = "This here's a string";
void *Voids[] = {IntArray, DoubleArray, CharArray};
```

Great, you can pass around an array that has all kinds of information in it. Now for the bad news: Declaring it was the easy part. You can't simply say *Voids[1][2]* and expect to get 12.4 in return. Not without a fight, anyway. The compiler and runtime modules have absolutely no idea how large the data elements are (the arrays are type *pointer to void*, remember). In addition, it isn't really a two-dimensional array; it just looks that way. To get to the individual arrays, you first have to cast the element in *voids* to a pointer of the proper type. To get to the first element in the first array (*IntArray* in this case), you write *((int *) voids[0])[0]*. That tells the compiler what size data element is being returned, and it's happy. Now that you've declared it, print it out to make sure this thing works:

```
/*
    voids.cpp - A test of an array of different types.
 */

#include    <stdio.h>

int main ()
{
int IntArray[] = {4, 8, 22, 12};
double DoubleArray[] = { 2.5, 6.8, 12.4};
char CharArray[] = "This here's a string";
void *Voids[] = {IntArray, DoubleArray, CharArray};

    printf ("IntArray is %d %d %d %d\n",
            ((int *) Voids[0])[0],
            ((int *) Voids[0])[1],
            ((int *) Voids[0])[2],
            ((int *) Voids[0])[3]);

    printf ("DoubleArray array is %f %f %f\n",
            ((double *) Voids[1])[0],
            ((double *) Voids[1])[1],
            ((double *) Voids[1])[2]);

    printf ("The string array is \"%s\"\n", Voids[2]);
    return (0);
}
```

You should see the following output:

```
IntArray is 4 8 22 12
DoubleArray array is 2.500000 6.800000 12.400000
The string array is "This here's a string"
```

You could have accessed the string elements one by one, but all you needed was a pointer to the string to print it in its entirety. Because *Voids[2]* merely gets a *pointer to void* without trying to access any other data, the compiler doesn't object.

I'll stress it one more time: This isn't really a two-dimensional array as defined by the C and C++ language. Functionally, however, it operates the same, and you can pass it as a single argument in a function call. Of course, a structure would be a lot easier to use. I don't necessarily encourage this type of programming, but it points out the lack of prohibition in the C and C++ languages. Often, you need to look at what the language doesn't *disallow* as much as what it allows, because sometimes you just might have to do something creative in your programming.

200. *Understanding Constants*

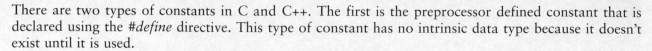

There are two types of constants in C and C++. The first is the preprocessor defined constant that is declared using the *#define* directive. This type of constant has no intrinsic data type because it doesn't exist until it is used.

There also is the *const* modifier that can be used with any data type to create a constant identifier. This type of constant must be initialized when it is declared, and it cannot be modified later (at least, not directly).

201. *Using the #define Preprocessor Command*

Constants created by the preprocessor are declared using the *#define* preprocessor directive. The directive doesn't create a constant; it simply sets aside a value that will be used when the compiler sees the identifier in the program code. Data typing is done when the identifier is used.

Case is significant when you define a preprocessor constant, and by convention this type of constant is declared in all uppercase to distinguish it from program constants. You declare a preprocessor constant by entering *#define* (you can indent the directive, but the # symbol must be the first non-white character in the line). Follow with one or more spaces or tabs and the identifier for the constant. The identifier must conform to the rules for any C or C++ variable. Next, enter one or more spaces or tabs and then enter the value for the constant. At this point, everything you enter up to the end of the line or a comment marker is assumed to be a part of the constant's value. If you need to continue the definition on another line, terminate the first line with a backslash (\).

After a preprocessor constant is defined, you can't redefine it using another *#define* directive. As long as the definition is exactly the same, you can repeat it. The following two lines are acceptable because the definitions are the same:

```
#define    TABSTOPS    4
#define    TABSTOPS    4
```

Of course, you don't gain anything, but if you accidentally repeat a definition, it won't do any harm.

You also can pass a preprocessor definition from the command line. Instead of defining *TABSTOPS* in your program code, you can use the compiler option *-D* on the command line to define it. From the command line, the definition can be quoted to. The following two lines are equivalent:

```
C:>cl -DTABSTOPS=4 myprog.cpp  <ENTER>
C:>cl -D"TABSTOPS=4" myprog.cpp  <ENTER>
```

202. *Beware of the Semicolon in #define Statements*

Putting a semicolon at the end of a line becomes so natural that eventually you are certain to include one in the constant definition. The preprocessor isn't creating any values or doing any type checking. It's simply picking up a group of characters that will be substituted into the code when the identifier is encountered. If you place a semicolon after the definition, it will be included in the substitution string. The following line defines the identifier *TABSTOPS* and links it with the characters *4;*:

```
#define    TABSTOPS        4;
```

If you subsequently use *TABSTOPS* in your code, the compiler will see the string *4;*. In a statement such as *int x = TABSTOPS;*, the compiler sees *int x = 4;;* but the extra semicolon doesn't cause an error (it's simply an empty statement). But if you declare *int tabs[TABSTOPS] = {4, 8, 12, 16};*, the compiler will have plenty to gripe about, and will display the following error messages:

```
voids.cpp(17) : error C2143: syntax error : missing ']' before ';'
voids.cpp(17) : error C2143: syntax error : missing ';' before ']'
voids.cpp(17) : error C2143: syntax error : missing ';' before '{'
voids.cpp(17) : error C2143: syntax error : missing ';' before '}'
```

Errors such as this can be tough to track down. You'll look at the code repeatedly and never see the offending semicolon. Just remember that if a preprocessor constant is in the line, that's a good place to check.

203. *Declaring Constant Values*

Often, you may need to use numbers that do not change when you run your program. There are values that should remain *constant* from the time you start your program until the time you exit the program. For example, the value of the mathematical constant *pi* never changes, so it would not be wise to let your program accidentally increment its value, or add another value to it.

Visual C++ provides two methods of using constants. The first is a *literal constant* using the preprocessor's *#define* command. The preprocessor substitutes all occurrences of the constant you define with the value you give it in the definition:

```
#define    PI                3.14159
```

The second method is to declare an ordinary variable and assign it the value you want. Then you use the *const* keyword to tell the compiler that the variable should not change during the course of your program. If you attempt to change it in a statement, the compiler will generate an error and display it on your screen:

```
const double Pi = 3.14159;
```

Many C++ programmers shun using the *#define* statement to declare constants. However, both methods have advantages and disadvantages.

204. *Declaring Constants Without Values*

Because the preprocessor simply copies the identifier and its value, it is possible to define an empty constant. When the preprocessor sees the identifier in your code, it substitutes nothing in its place. Such definitions usually are used as flags and sentries to provide conditional compilation.

In the Microsoft Visual Studio, when the application wizard creates a debug version of your program, it uses the command-line option to define _DEBUG as an empty constant, and some sections of wizard-generated code are conditionally compiled. In the release version, the constant isn't defined.

Empty constants often are used as sentries in header files to prevent accidental inclusion of the code multiple times, as shown in the following example:

```
/*
    MyHeader.h - a test header file.
 */
#ifndef __MYHEADER_H__
#define __MYHEADER_H__
//
// declarations/definitions appear here
//
#endif        // use this to end the conditional assembly at
              // the bottom of the header file
```

The first time through, __MYHEADER_H__ is not defined, so the code is included. If the file is included a second time, __MYHEADER_H__ is defined and the preprocessor ignores everything to the matching #endif directive.

205. Understanding String Constants

Preprocessor string constants are defined using the #define directive, an identifier, and the string enclosed in double quotes. The double quotes are included in the replacement string when the identifier is encountered in the program. The following line defines a string constant:

```
#define   STRINGDEF      "This here's a string"
```

Whenever STRINGDEF appears in your program, the compiler substitutes "This here's a string" in its place. If you write char MyString[] = STRINGDEF;, the compiler sees the following line when the program is compiled:

```
char MyString[] = "This here's a string";
```

You can rewrite your short string reversion program to define the original string as a constant, this time using a while loop to perform the reversal:

```
/*
    elba1.cpp - Reverse the characters in a string
             using a string constant and while loop.
 */
#include   <stdio.h>
#include   <string.h>

#define    ELBA    "Able was I ere I saw Elba"

int main ()
{

char *pszElba = ELBA;
char    ch;
```

```
    int x = 0;
    int max = strlen (pszElba);
    printf ("%s\n", pszElba);
    while (x < max / 2)
    {
        ch = pszElba[x];
        pszElba[x] = pszElba[max - x - 1];
        pszElba[max - x - 1] = ch;
        ++x;
    }
    printf ("%s\n", pszElba);
    return (0);
}
```

String constants can be defined from the command line, but they must be enclosed in quotes, and an inner set of quote marks enclosing the string itself must be escaped using backslashes. Remove or comment out (put // in front of it) the *#define* statement in the program and recompile with the following command:

```
C:>cl -D"ELBA=\"Able was I ere I saw Elba\"" elba1.cpp
```

The result is the same as when you wrote *#define ELBA "Able was I ere I saw Elba"* in the source file. You can change the string to try other possibilities from the command line without changing the source file.

206. *Defining Numerical Constants*

Numerical constants defined using the preprocessor directive can be literal constants or expressions. A *literal constant* is a number that is expressed as itself rather than as an expression or a variable. The number *42* is a literal constant, but *2*21* is not. The latter would produce a constant equal to 42, but it is not literal. Both, however, would be legitimate constants for a *#define* statement.

Constants also can contain other constants that have been defined previously, but there are some cautions in doing so. First, be careful what you write and how you use the constant. Suppose you define two constants as shown in the following:

```
#define    FORTYTWO        42
#define    SIXTYSIX          FORTYTWO + 24
```

You later use it in an expression such as the following line and get an unexpected and incorrect result:

```
int ThrityThree = SIXTYSIX / 2;
```

It *looks* right, so why did your program give a result of 54 instead of 33? The preprocessor substituted exactly what you entered for the definition, and the resulting expression as seen by the compiler is *int ThirtyThree = 42 + 24 / 2;*, which evaluates to 54. First, the division is performed and then the addition. To be safe, when using operators in a preprocessor definition, always enclose the definition in parentheses, as shown in the following. The extra parentheses won't do any harm but they might prevent a bug.

```
#define    SIXTYSIX           (FORTYTWO + 24)
```

If you use a previously defined constant in a preprocessor *define*, and then later undefine it (undefining is covered below) and give it a new definition, the preprocessor will substitute whatever definition is in effect at the time.

```
#define      FORTYTWO       42
#define      SIXTYSIX            (FORTYTWO + 24)


// some program code
#undef FORTYTWO
#define      FORTYTWO    0x42


// More program code
int ThrityThree = SIXTYSIX / 2;
```

Even though you used the parentheses to isolate the constant, you got 45 as the result. The most recent definition of *FORTYTWO* is hexadecimal *0x42*, which is 66 in decimal. The expression *(66 + 24) / 2* equates to 45, which is the result you got.

207. Defining a Constant Using Variables

The preprocessor does no type or error checking when you define a constant, so you can use a variable identifier in a definition. When the substitution is made, the identifier will be placed in the code stream. If it hasn't been declared or is out of scope, the compiler will issue an error. The following code, for example, will generate *"error C2065: 'x' : undeclared identifier"*:

```
#include     <stdio.h>


#define      FORTYTWO          (23*x)


int main()
{
    printf ("FORTYTWO = %d", FORTYTWO);
    return (0);
}
```

To make it work, you must include a declaration and initialization for the variable *x*. Variables in preprocessor definitions are used commonly with macros and, along with the *sizeof* operator, to get the size of an array.

208. Undefining a Constant

You can undefine a preprocessor defined constant by using the direction *#undef*. When you undefine a constant, the preprocessor conveniently "forgets" it completely. If you try to use it later in a program, the preprocessor won't do any substitutions and the compiler will give you an *"undeclared identifier"* error. Undefining doesn't affect any substitutions already made, however.

Undefine a constant by entering the poundal as the first non-white character on a line, followed by the contant's name. There can be one or more spaces between the "#" and "undef." The following lines define and then remove the definition for *FORTYTWO*:

```
#define    FORTYTWO          0x42
#undef     FORTYTWO
```

Identifiers can be undefined at any point, even if they haven't been defined yet. If you are not sure whether an identifier has been defined, it's safe to undefine it before writing your new definition.

Two other preprocessor directives work with the *#define* and *#undef* directives. The *#ifdef* tests whether an identifier has been defined already, and returns 1 if it has, otherwise 0. The *#ifndef* reverses the sense of the test, and returns 0 if the identifier has been defined, 1 otherwise. The latest revision of C lets you write *#if (defined)* in place of *#ifdef* and *#if !(defined)* in place of *#ifndef*.

209. *Understanding the* sizeof *Operator*

The *sizeof* operator returns a *size_t* value containing the size of its operand in bytes. If the operand is a data type, the value returned is the size required to store an object of that type. The *size_t* type is implementation-dependent, but usually (and in Visual C++) it is *typedef*'ed in *stdio.h* as an unsigned integer.

The operand can be an expression, in which case it is typed only and *not* evaluated. If you enter something like *sizeof (x++);*, the expression is not evaluated, so *x* will not be incremented. The operator returns *4*, the size of the *type* (integer) of the expression.

You can use *sizeof* in a *#define* directive, or you can use a preprocessor defined constant as a *sizeof* operand. In the following snippet, you use *sizeof* to obtain the number of elements in your array and use it in a *for* loop. The first *sizeof* returns the number of *bytes* in the array, and then you divide by the size of the array type and get the number of elements in the array.

```
int IntArray[] = {4, 8, 22, 12, 42, 24};
#define    ARRAYSIZE    ((sizeof(IntArray)/sizeof(int))
for (int x = 0; x < ARRAYSIZE; ++x)
    ;
```

You can use the *sizeof* operator to get the number of bytes you need to store a string constant using the constant as the object of the operator. In the following, the first line returns *26*, the number of bytes in the string plus the null terminator. The second line, however, returns only *4* because *Elba* is declared as a *char pointer*.

```
#define    ELBA    "Able was I ere I saw Elba"
    char *pszElba = ELBA;
    printf("sizeof (ELBA) = %d\n", sizeof (ELBA));
    printf("sizeof(Elba) = %d\n", sizeof (pszElba));
```

210. *Understanding the const Keyword*

The idea of a "constant variable" is one of the oxymora we've gotten used to in the computer industry. When you modify a variable declaration with the keyword *const*, the object takes on the properties of a constant, but still has the scope of a variable. It becomes a constant declaration rather than a variable declaration.

Any of the C and C++ data types, and any derived or user-defined types, can be modified with the *const* keyword. Enter *const*, followed by the data type, and the identifier name. Unless it has an external storage class, you must initialize a constant when it is declared. Theoretically, at least, a constant is immutable and your program code can't modify its value after the declaration statement. The real world is always theoretical, however, and there are ways to change the value of a constant.

The following line declares a constant integer, and then declares an array of constants, and finally a string constant using the *const* keyword:

```
const int x = 4;
const int IntArray[] = {4, 8, 22, 12, 42, 24};
const char *pszElba = "Able was I ere I saw Elba";
```

If you later try to modify using something like *x = 3 or IntArray[3] = 14*, you'll get a compile error saying the *"l-value specifies const object."* Remember that part of the definition of an *lvalue* is that it must be modifiable. If you try to use an increment or decrement operator on it, such as *x++* or *++IntArray[3]*, you're told that *"++ needs l-value."*

211. *Understanding When to Use const and #define*

Now that you know two methods of setting up constants—#*define* and *const*—which one do you use and when? Understanding how each of them works will give you some idea of how and where you should select one over the other.

When you use the #*define* directive, you don't set aside any storage for a constant. That's done when you actually use the constant in an expression. #*define* is merely a text substitution mechanism used by the preprocessor. Every time you use it, memory is allocated for the constant's value.

The *const* modifier, on the other hand, is used with an identifier name and storage is set aside for it *once*. When you use a *const* in an expression, the value used in that memory location is retrieved. No additional storage is allocated.

The *preferred* method in C++ is to avoid the #*define* directive whenever possible. If you're using a literal constant, such as an integer value, it doesn't make much difference in code size or speed which method you use. You can't, however, define a *const* using an expression and expect the expression to be used whenever you invoke it. You can use an expression to set the value of a *const*, however, and it is evaluated only once. When you use an expression with the #*define* directive, the expression is evaluated each time you use it.

For strings, the #*define* method is particularly inefficient. When you define a string constant using the #*define* directive, you set aside a new block of storage for the entire string each time you use it. For long string constants used many times, this could burn up a lot of memory and increase the resulting executable file size, which translates to longer load times when you run the program.

In the following three lines, you define a string constant, and then use it to set the value for two string pointer declarations. For each declaration, you are setting aside memory for duplicate strings. If you truly intend it to be a constant, you've wasted memory.

```
#define    NETWORK    "A network can be loosely defined "\
                      "as the hardware and software that "\
                      "allow two entities to communicate.";
char *str1 = NETWORK;
char *str2 = NETWORK;
```

If you drop this code into a program, compile it, and do a hex dump, you'll see two identical strings.

A *const*, however, needs storage only once. It's actually a variable that has had a non-modifiable constraint placed on it. When you use it, you are invoking the value that was stored when it was initialized. If you replace the preceding code using a *const*, compile it, and once again do a hex dump of the program, you see only one copy of the string:

```
const char *Network ="A network can be loosely defined "\
                      "as the hardware and software that "\
                      "allow two entities to communicate. ";
char *str1 = (char *) Network;
char *str2 = (char *) Network;
```

To make the assignment, you have to cast the *const char* * type back to a *char* *, but the two new variables, *str1* and *str2*, use only four bytes, the size of a *char* pointer in Windows. There are some problems here, as you will see in the next tip.

Although you can use *#define* constants in a header file, you should avoid that practice using *const* declarations. Each source file that includes the header file will declare its own instance of the constant, and when you link the object files, the linker will object to multiple defined identifiers.

When using a *const* in a header, you could declare it *static* as described in the section, "Functions and Variables." Then you would be setting up separate storage for each instance, which might gain you little ground over the *#include* method.

Instead, you would have to declare and initialize the *const* identifier in one source file, and then declare it *extern* in the other source files where you intend to use it.

There are advantages and problems with each method, and you have to weigh them for each program you create. Academicians and pundits will avow that you should always use one method and never the other, but your program will dictate your choice.

212. *Using a Pointer to Modify a const Value*

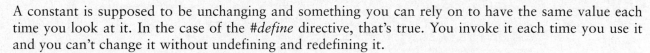

A constant is supposed to be unchanging and something you can rely on to have the same value each time you look at it. In the case of the *#define* directive, that's true. You invoke it each time you use it and you can't change it without undefining and redefining it.

In the case of the *const* modifier, however, its constancy is relative. Its value can be changed by assigning its address to a non-*const* variable, and then changing the value indirectly. You can't do that with the *#include* method.

First, try the following code:

```
#include    <stdio.h>
#include    <iostream.h>
```

```
#include    <string.h>
#define    NETWORK   "A network can be loosely defined "\
                     "as the hardware and software that "\
                     "allow two entities to communicate.";
char *str1 = NETWORK;
char *str2 = NETWORK;

int main ()
{
    char *s = strstr (str1, " two");
    if (s != NULL)
        strcpy (s, " 2 entities to communicate");
    cout << str1 << endl;
    cout << str2 << endl;
    return (0);
}
```

When you run this code, you see that each string is independent, further proof that you have actually set up two separate memory locations for each string. If, however, you use the *const* method, modifying one string modifies them both (actually, there is only one string).

```
#include    <stdio.h>
#include    <iostream.h>
#include    <string.h>

const char *Network = "A network can be loosely defined "\
                      "as the hardware and software that "\
                      "allow two entities to communicate.";
char *str1 = (char *) Network;
char *str2 = (char *) Network;

int main ()
{
    char *s = strstr (str1, " two");
    if (s != NULL)
        strcpy (s, " 2 entities to communicate");
    cout << str1 << endl;
    cout << str2 << endl;
    return (0);
}
```

When you run this code, you see that *str1* and *str2* have both been modified. Because they both point to the same string, which you modified by casting the *const char ** to *char **, modifying one changed the value of both. The "constant" turns out to be not so constant after all.

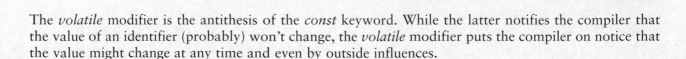

213. *Understanding the* volatile *Keyword*

The *volatile* modifier is the antithesis of the *const* keyword. While the latter notifies the compiler that the value of an identifier (probably) won't change, the *volatile* modifier puts the compiler on notice that the value might change at any time and even by outside influences.

When the *volatile* modifier is used, the compiler won't try to optimize the use of the variable. Often, when a variable isn't used for several statements, the compiler might tuck it away in a register or internal buffer and retrieve it when it is needed. If the value changes suddenly (say the computer's clock system changes the value of a variable holding the current time), the value will no longer be valid, but the runtime code will have no way of knowing about the possible change.

In addition, when the program changes the value of a *volatile* variable, its value is written into memory immediately even if the next statement in the program modifies it again.

With the programming technologies in use today—ActiveX and the Component Object Model, for example—such events are entirely possible. With DCOM, where parts of the program can run on other computers, the source of the change can be from another computer altogether.

Even without the advanced technologies, it is possible in a multithreaded program for one thread to modify a variable in another thread. In most single-threaded applications you won't have much need for this modifier, but you find more and more times when it is needed.

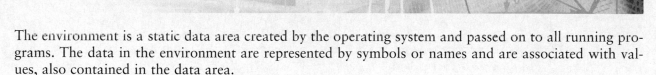

214. *Understanding Environment Variables*

The environment is a static data area created by the operating system and passed on to all running programs. The data in the environment are represented by symbols or names and are associated with values, also contained in the data area.

You can see the contents of the environment by typing "set" from the DOS command line and pressing Enter. On UNIX, you type "env" and press Enter. On some operating systems, such as Windows NT and UNIX, the environment might be too large to view on one screen. If so, type "set | more" and press Enter to page through it.

The operating system uses the environment to store and pass on to programs important operating-system and user-defined data. By convention, the names of environment variables are uppercase, but on Windows systems the case is not significant.

Environment variable processing on Windows is not nearly as robust as it is on other operating systems like UNIX where there are specialized commands and syntax to display and set environment variables. To see the contents of an individual environment variable on Windows (by "Windows," I mean Windows 95 or later), from a DOS command line you type "ECHO" followed by the name of the variable enclosed between two percent characters and press Enter. To see the value of *PROMPT*, enter the following line, and the command processor will respond with the second line below:

```
C:>echo %PROMPT%    <Enter>
$p$g
```

If Windows responds with something like *%PROMPT%*, it means that the variable has not been set. On Windows NT, you can type "SET" followed by the environment variable name to get the entire syntax of the variable:

```
C:>set PROMPT    <Enter>
PROMPT=$p$g
```

To set an environment variable from the command line, type "SET" followed by the variable name, an equals sign, and the new value. For now, don't change any existing variables. Create a new one using the same syntax:

```
C:>set MYVAR=A new environment variable    <Enter>
```

Now display the new variable by typing the next line, and the command processor will respond with the contents of the new variable:

```
C:>echo %MYVAR%    <Enter>
A new environment variable
```

To delete an environment variable, repeat the *set* command, but give the variable an empty value:

```
C:>set MYVAR=   <Enter>
```

Using operating-system interface functions, you program your *read* and *set* environment variables. The changes will be reflected in the environment that is passed on to new programs started by your program, but not from other programs. The environment thus becomes a form of interprocess communications.

To set permanent environment variables, on Windows 95 enter them in the *AUTOEXEC.BAT* file using the preceding syntax. On Windows NT, use the System icon from the Control Panel, and select the Environment tab.

215. *Getting the Size of an Environment Variable*

Visual C++ has two sets of functions to read and set environment variables. The first set includes the *getenv()* and *putenv()* functions and is compatible with UNIX and other operating systems. If you want to maintain portability, you should use these functions. The *getenv()* function returns a pointer to the environment string, and *putenv()* takes a pointer to a string in your program to set the variable. For these functions, you don't need to know the size of the environment string beforehand.

The second set of functions are Windows-specific and include the *GetEnvironmentVariable()* and *SetEnvironmentVariable()* functions. Getting a variable involves copying it to a string local to your program, and you must know the size of the variable first. To use these from a command-prompt program, you have to include the *windows.h* and *winbase.h* header files in your source code.

If you already know the approximate length of an environment variable (for example, it's one you set from your program), you can declare a *char* array large enough to hold it. More often than not, you will be looking at system and preset variables, and you will need to know their size to create strings large enough to hold them. Some of these variables, such as *PATH*, vary widely in length from machine to machine.

The *GetEnvironmentVariable()* function requires as arguments the name of the environment variable, a buffer to hold the copied value, and the size of the buffer. It returns the number of characters copied into your local string. If you pass it a *NULL* pointer for the buffer and a 0 for the length, the function will return the number of characters in the value. If it returns 0, the variable was not found. You may use the result to create a buffer large enough to hold the variable. To get the size of *PATH*, try the following code and save it as *env.cpp*:

```
/*
    env.cpp -- Get the size of an environment string.
 */


#include    <stdio.h>
#include    <windows.h>
#include    <winbase.h>


int main ()
{
```

```
    int x = GetEnvironmentVariable ("PATH", NULL, 0);
    printf ("PATH variable contains %d characters\n", x);
}
```

When you compile and run your program, you will see a line similar to the following. The exact number depends on your environment. The number is the length of the variable, *not including* the terminating null character.

```
PATH variable contains 473 characters
```

You will use this value in the next tip to read the value of the variable.

216. *Getting the Value of an Environment Variable*

First, you use the portable *getenv()* function to display the contents of *PATH*. Then, you use the Windows *GetEnvironmentVariable()* function. Last, you modify your program to accept any environment variable name and display it.

The *getenv()* function returns a pointer to the environment variable's value. You may use this pointer directly to examine and print its contents. Change the *main()* function in *env.cpp* to read as follows:

```
printf ("Using getenv():\n");
char *env = getenv ("PATH");
if (env == NULL)
{
    fprintf (stderr, "Cannot find PATH variable\n");
    return (-1);
}
printf ("PATH = %s\n", env);
getenv("PATH");
return (0);
```

When you run the program, it will display something similar to the following:

```
Using getenv():
PATH=C:\WINNT\system32;C:\WINNT;C:\MSSQL\BINN;C:\PROGRA~1\MTS;D:\Program Files\Microsoft
Visual Studio\Common\Tools\WinNT;D:\Program Files\Microsoft Visual
Studio\Common\MSDev98\Bin;D:\Program Files\Microsoft Visual Studio\Common\Tools;
D:\Program Files\Microsoft Visual Studio\VC98\bin;D:\DevTools\BC5\BIN;C:\bin
```

Not very easy to read, but now your program knows where the system is looking for program files when you enter them on the command line. In Tip 221, "Understanding the *INCLUDE* Path Environment Variable," you will learn how to use the *strtok()* function to read these path elements one by one. When using *getenv()*, don't modify the string directly. Make a copy of it before you change anything; then, use *putenv()* to modify the actual environment variable.

Now it's time to add the Windows function to get the environment string. I suspect that Microsoft added this function because modifying the environment value directly in the environment block can have disastrous effects. Add the following lines to *env.cpp* before the *return (0)* statement:

```
int x = GetEnvironmentVariable ("PATH", NULL, 0);
if (!x)
{
    fprintf (stderr, "Cannot find PATH variable\n");
```

```
        return (-1);
}
char *WinEnv = new char [x + 1];  // Need room for the '\0'
if (WinEnv == NULL)
{
    fprintf (stderr, "Memory error allocating string\n");
    return (-1);
}
if (!GetEnvironmentVariable ("PATH", WinEnv, x+1))
{
    fprintf (stderr, "Error getting PATH\n");
    return (-1);
}
printf ("\nUsing GetEnvironmentVariable:\n");
printf ("PATH=%s\n", WinEnv);
delete [] WinEnv;        // Clean up after ourselves
```

When you run the program, you will see the *PATH* variable repeated.

Finally, because you have a copy of the variable's value, you can modify it without worrying about the real environment. The path delimiter is a semicolon, so use the *strchr()* function to put some newline characters in its place. Add the following three lines to your code before the *printf()* statement:

```
char *s;
while ((s = strchr (WinEnv, ';')) != NULL)
    *s = 0x0a;
```

Recompile and run the program again, and the second listing will appear as follows:

```
C:\WINNT\system32
C:\WINNT
C:\MSSQL\BINN
C:\PROGRA~1\MTS
D:\Program Files\Microsoft Visual Studio\Common\Tools\WinNT
D:\Program Files\Microsoft Visual Studio\Common\MSDev98\Bin
D:\Program Files\Microsoft Visual Studio\Common\Tools
D:\Program Files\Microsoft Visual Studio\VC98\bin
D:\DevTools\BC5\BIN
C:\bin
D:\DEVTOOLS\BC5\BIN
```

That's much easier to read than the "packed" version.

As an exercise, use *argc* and *argv* to enter an environment variable name from the command line and display it or to print an error saying that it wasn't found.

217. Getting a Pointer to Environment Strings

In addition to getting an individual environment variable, the Windows function *GetEnvironmentStrings()* returns the memory address of your program's environment block. This is a sequence of null-terminated strings, and the last string ends with two null terminators. This block was never intended to be used directly. Instead, it is used to pass the block on to other programs your program may start by using the *CreateProcess()* function. After stepping over some housekeeping data, you can examine all your environment variables. After getting the environment block, you should free it using the *FreeEnvironment Strings()* function.

Enter the following program and save it as *getenv.cpp*:

```
/*
    env.cpp - Get the size of an environment string.
 */


#include    <stdio.h>
#include    <windows.h>
#include    <winbase.h>

int main ()
{
    char *Block = GetEnvironmentStrings ();
    char *s = Block;
    while (*s)
    {
        if (*s != '=')        // Skip housekeeping stuff
            printf ("%s\n", s);
        s += strlen (s) + 1;  // To the next string
    }
    FreeEnvironmentStrings (Block);    // Free the block
    return (0);
}
```

When you compile and run this program, you will see the same listing as when you run the *SET* command from the command line.

The program first gets the environment block and then copies the pointer *Block* into *s*. You don't want to lose the value of *Block* because you will need it to free the block when you are done. You then enter a loop to print the variables. If the first character is an equals sign, you skip it because it is housekeeping data; otherwise, you print the string pointed to by *s*. You then add the length of the string plus one, to step over the string and the terminating null. When you get to the end of the block, *s* will point to a null terminator, and you will know that you are finished.

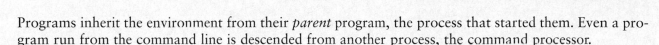

218. *Setting Environment Variables*

Programs inherit the environment from their *parent* program, the process that started them. Even a program run from the command line is descended from another process, the command processor.

Although the environment may be hereditary, it doesn't work in reverse. Changes a program makes in its own environment are not reflected in the parent process's environment or any programs started by an unrelated process. Thus, a program is free to modify its own environment, to delete variables, and to add new ones without affecting any programs other than those it spawns.

The portable function to set an environment variable is *putenv()*. It takes a single string pointer as the argument to specify the variable name, an equals sign, and the new value for the variable. As is typical of UNIX programs, it returns 0 if successful and -1 if an error occurs.

Specify the string for *putenv()* exactly as you want the variable to appear. For example, *putenv ("MYVAR=value for myvar")*; would set the environment variable *MYVAR* to *value for myvar*. To delete an environment variable, enter the variable name, followed by an equals sign, but give it no value.

putenv("MYVAR="); would remove *MYVAR* from the environment. Always remember to enter a double backslash in a character string when you want a single backslash, as in a path.

The Windows version to set an environment variable is *SetEnvironmentVariable()* and takes two arguments: a pointer to a string containing the name of the variable and a pointer to a string containing the value to be set. There is no equals sign in either argument. If you pass a *NULL* as the second argument, the variable is removed from the environment. *SetEnvironmentVariable ("MYVAR", "value for myvar");* would set the variable, and *SetEnvironmentVariable ("MYVAR", NULL);* would remove it.

If successful, *SetEnvironmentVariable()* returns a non-zero *BOOL* value and a 0 on failure.

A word of caution is in order concerning the Visual Studio–cast *BOOL* type. It is not the same as the C++ *bool* variable type, which takes a value of either 1 for *true* or 0 for *false*. The *BOOL* type is cast as an integer and may return something other than 1 to indicate success. Unfortunately, the Visual Studio–cast *TRUE* is 1, the same as the *bool* value for *true*. If your test is something like *if (RetVal == TRUE),* you quite probably could get a false indication of failure. When using the Microsoft *BOOL*, *TRUE*, and *FALSE*, always test for a zero or non-zero value. Simply say *if (RetVal)* to test for a non-zero result or *if (!RetVal)* to test for a zero result. Unfortunately this Microsoft-defined data type is spread throughout the Windows and MFC libraries, so you have to learn to deal with it. In your original code, where possible, try to use the standard *bool* type for portability.

219. An Example: Finding the Windows Directory

You've already seen how to retrieve a value from the environment, so now you will use the information to retrieve the location of the Windows directory. Many setup programs place their initialization file (with an extension of *.ini*) in the Windows directory, so it's a handy environment variable to know.

The environment variable containing the Windows directory is *WINDIR*. From the command line, you find the location by typing "echo %WINDIR%" and pressing Enter. For Windows 95, you will see something like "C:\WINDOWS," and on Windows NT it might be "C:\WINNT." Normally, they have different directory names because both operating systems may be installed on the same machine.

When you get an important environment variable such as the Windows directory, always make a copy of it. In fact, it's a good rule never to operate directly on an environment string. Always retrieve it, copy it, modify the copy, and put the modified version back in the environment. Remember that *getenv()* returns a pointer to the variable, so if you modify the value it points to, you will be modifying the environment strings directly. *GetEnvironmentVariable()*, on the other hand, gives you a copy of the string.

The following short program gets the Windows directory using both methods. With *getenv()*, you get the pointer, create a string long enough to hold a copy, and then copy it into the string. With *GetEnvironmentVariable()*, you first get the length, create a string, and then pass the new string as the argument. The function copies the variable value for you.

```
/*
    windir.cpp - get the setting for the Windows
            Directory.
 */
#include    <stdio.h>
#include    <windows.h>
#include    <winbase.h>


#define    WINDIR          "WINDIR"
```

```
int main ()
{
char *pWinDir, *pWinDirCopy;

// First using getenv()
    pWinDir = getenv (WINDIR);
    if (pWinDir == NULL)
    {
        fprintf(stderr, "getenv() failed\n");
    }
    else
    {
        pWinDirCopy = new char [strlen (pWinDir) + 1];
        strcpy (pWinDirCopy, pWinDir);
    printf("Windows Directory = %s\n",pWinDirCopy);
        delete [] pWinDirCopy;    // Delete old string
    }
// Now using GetEnvironmentVariable()
    int len = GetEnvironmentVariable (WINDIR, NULL, 0);
    if (!len)
    {
    fprintf(stderr, "GetEnvironmentVariable failed");
    }
    else
    {
        pWinDirCopy = new char [len + 1];
        len=GetEnvironmentVariable(WINDIR,
                              pWinDirCopy,len+1);
    printf("Windows Directory = %s\n",pWinDirCopy);
        delete [] pWinDirCopy;
    }
    return (0);
}
```

(Some versions of Windows NT do not use the *windir* environment variable and this program might display an error that it failed to get the environment string.)

220. *Understanding the #include Preprocessor Command*

Now that you've learned about environment variables, it might be a good idea to revisit the *#include* preprocessor command briefly. You will look at how the preprocessor finds that *stdio.h* file even though it's buried several directories deep in the Program Files folder.

When you specify a header file in your program, you may include it in one of two ways: using the less than and greater than symbols or placing it in double quotes. Your selection determines how the preprocessor uses the *PATH* environment variables.

You also will return to the makefile to show how it sets and uses environment variables in the process of building your program files.

221. *Understanding the* **INCLUDE** *Path Environment Variable*

When you compiled and ran the *getenv.cpp* sample program, you may have noticed a long string following a variable named *INCLUDE*. The value of the *INCLUDE* variable is named the *include path*, and the preprocessor uses this path to search through directories to find your include files according to a preset pattern. Now you will write a program to look for a file in the include path using a string function named *strtok()*:

```
/*
    findfile.cpp - search the include path for a specified
                   file. */
#include     <stdio.h>
#include     <io.h>
#include     <errno.h>
#include     <windows.h>
#include     <winbase.h>


#define   INCLUDEPATH        "INCLUDE"
#define   EXISTS             0

bool exist (char *pszFileName);

int main (int argc, char *argv[])
{
char *pszInclude;

    if (argc < 2)
    {
        fprintf (stderr, "Please name a file to find\n");
        return (-1);
    }
    char *pszFile = argv[1];
    int len = GetEnvironmentVariable (INCLUDEPATH, NULL, 0);
    if (!len)
    {
        fprintf (stderr, "Could not find include path\n");
        return (-1);
    }
    pszInclude = new char [len + 1];
    if (pszInclude == NULL)
    {
        fprintf (stderr, "Memory error\n");
        return (-1);
    }
    GetEnvironmentVariable (INCLUDEPATH, pszInclude, len + 1);
    char *s = strtok (pszInclude, ";");
    if (s == NULL)
    {
        fprintf (stderr, "Include path is empty\n");
        delete [] pszInclude;
        return (0);
    }
    do
```

```
    {
        char *str = new char [strlen(s)+strlen(pszFile)+2];
        if (str == NULL)
            continue;
        sprintf (str, "%s\\%s", s, pszFile);
        if (exist(str))
        {
            printf ("FOUND IT!!!\n%s\n", str);
            delete [] str;
            break;
        }
        printf ("%s was not found\n", str);
        delete [] str;
    } while ((s = strtok (NULL, ";")) != NULL);
    delete [] pszInclude;
    return (0);
}

bool exist (char *pszFile)
{
    int nExists = access ((const char *) pszFile, EXISTS);
    if (!nExists)
        return (true);
// Is it there and we just can't get to it?
    if (errno == EACCES)
        return (true);
    return (false);
}
```

The *strtok()* function divides your copy of the include path into sections delimited by the semicolon (which you specified in the second argument). You will take a look at this function in the *second on* string functions, but for now remember *never* to use *strtok()* directly on an environment variable. Always use a copy of the variable.

The *exist()* function is a general-purpose routine you use to check whether a file exists before trying to use it. In this case, I didn't want to open the file anyway, so the Boolean return value is all I needed. This function might be a good candidate for your personal library.

Running this program will demonstrate the steps the preprocessor takes to find a header file. Try it with *stdio.h* and a few other header files in different directories. If this program doesn't find it, the preprocessor won't find it in the include path either.

222. *Understanding the Difference Between #include <file.h> and #include file.h*

If you specify a header file using the *#include* directive and place the file name between the < and > symbols, the preprocessor will first look in the paths specified by any /I compiler options, then in the include path. For simplicity, your program didn't include the possibility of another path identifier.

If, however, you place the file name between double quotation marks, the preprocessor will first look in the same directory as your source file (the file that contains the *#include* directive), then along the path specified by any /I compiler options, and finally down the include path.

If you could have a local file named *stdio.h* in addition to the system file, including it in your program inside double quotes would cause the preprocessor to find it before the system include file. Then, including *<stdio.h>* would find the system file before the local file, so the following two lines would include both files:

```
#include    <stdio.h>       // Would find system file first
#include    "stdio.h"       // Would find local file first
```

223. Using a Guardian Definition in Your Header Files

Preprocessor directives named "sentry" or "guardian" definitions are used in header files to prevent them from being included more than once in a program file compilation. In larger projects, header files often include other header files, and it is possible (likely?) that at some point a file is going to be included more than once in the same source file.

A *guardian* (or *sentry*) statement is nothing more than one line containing the preprocessor *#ifndef* statement and another line defining the guardian value. It usually is placed at the top of the include file, and the entire file is selectively included or not included in the compilation. At the bottom of the header file, an *#endif* directive ends the conditional compilation:

```
/*
    tester.h - Test header file for simple programs.
 */
#ifndef __TESTER_H__
#define __TESTER_H__

// The body of the include file goes here.

#endif    // __TESTER_H__  (place this line at the
          // bottom of the header file)
```

The first time through, *__TESTER_H__* is not defined, so the code is included. If the file is included a second time, *__TESTER_H__* is defined, and the preprocessor ignores everything to the matching *#endif* directive. Even if you accidentally include *tester.h* from within *tester.h*, the include loop will stop the first time through.

If you use an application wizard in the Developers Studio to generate your project, you will set a guardian statement at the top of each header file. The statement is a combination of the header file name and a large, strange-looking hexadecimal number called a *globally unique identifier*, or GUID. This number is created using a combination of the current time and the network address of any LAN card in your computer. If you don't have a LAN card, the number generated is a UUID *(universally unique ID)*. A GUID is guaranteed to be unique; neither your machine nor anyone else's will generate that ID number again. UUIDs are unique only on your machine.

Using a GUID virtually ensures a unique sentry, but generally you don't have to be that elaborate. If you do choose to use a GUID, use the same number throughout your project.

Along with Visual Studio, you have a program named *guidgen.exe*, which you can use to create these 10-character numbers. Run *guidgen* from the DOS command line or from the Run selection on the Start menu. Select option 4, Registry Format, and click the Copy button. Click the Exit button and return to your program. Press Shift+Insert to retrieve the GUID. Add it to your guardian statement. Remove the enclosing braces and change the hyphens to underscores. You have a guardian statement that is virtually guaranteed not to be duplicated:

```
#ifndef __TESTER_H__F93DCBEE_0C72_11d4_85B1_76CD12000000
```

224. Using Common Header Files for a Large Program

In the short sample programs so far, guardian definitions haven't served much purpose. In a large project, however, you will probably want to keep constant and structure definitions in a common header file to be included in the various source files in your program. Unless you are very, very careful, duplicate includes are very likely to happen. Redefining constants isn't a problem; the language lets you do that as long as you don't change the definition in any way.

Other definitions, such as structures, are a different story. You can't redefine them in any way, even if the definitions are identical. Attempting to do so causes a compile error.

Create a simple header file that has only one constant definition and one structure definition:

```
/*
    GuardTst.h -- Test include file for
                guardian definitions.
 */

#define   NAMESIZE    20

struct RECORD
{
    char    FirstName[NAMESIZE];
    char    MiddleName[NAMESIZE];
    char    LastName[NAMESIZE];
    char    IDNumber;
};
```

Next, create a simple program file. It doesn't have to do anything. You're just going to include the header file twice to see what happens:

```
#include    <stdio.h>
#include    "GuardTst.h"
#include    "GuardTst.h"

int main ()
{
    return (0);
}
```

The *NAMESIZE* redefinition didn't cause any problems, but the compiler didn't like seeing the structure definition a second time. Now, add the guardian or sentry statements:

```
/*
    GuardTst.h -- Test include file for
                guardian definitions.
 */

#ifndef __GUARDTST_H__
#define __GUARDTST_H__

#define   NAMESIZE 20

struct RECORD
{
```

```
    char    FirstName[NAMESIZE];
    char    MiddleName[NAMESIZE];
    char    LastName[NAMESIZE];
    char    IDNumber;
};
#endif      // __GUARDTST_H__
```

The sentry statements caused the definitions to be omitted on the second include. When you see errors such as "struct type redefinition," it means that you are attempting to redefine an object. Check your header files for sentry statements; trying to track down the source of the second include may be time-consuming, and chances are that you can't do much about it anyway.

If you look in the system header files, and even the MFC header files, you will find that they invariably include sentry statements.

225. *Adding a Header File to the Dependencies in a Makefile*

In Tip 133, you created a simple makefile for your *Print6* program. As part of that, you created a make variable called *HDR*. You can name the variable anything you want, but try to make it descriptive and do not duplicate other variables. *HEADERS*, *HDR*, or *HDRS* is plain enough that you know its purpose without having to read through the makefile. You call the variables created with the *NAME=* syntax *environment* variables because you use them the same as environment variables, but *NMAKE.EXE* doesn't actually add them to the environment.

If a new header is a general-purpose header, add its name to the list after the variable is defined. If the list continues on to another, use a backslash to join lines. The following definition of *HDR* is equivalent to writing both header file names on a single line:

```
HDR=utility.h \
    Header2.h
```

You can then enter the entire list of header files in a dependency using only the environment variable name, as in the following:

```
print6.obj:     print6.cpp $(HDR)
                $(CPP) $(CPPFLAGS) print6.cpp
```

The make variable is your shortcut to avoid typing a long list of file names, and you generally place files used by all your modules in it. If the header file is included in only one or two source files in your project, you don't have to place it in the make variable (in fact, you probably don't want to, as you will see in the next tip). Instead, you may specify it individually on a dependency line:

```
print6.obj:     print6.cpp $(HDR) print6.h
                $(CPP) $(CPPFLAGS) print6.cpp
```

In this case, the *print6.obj* file is dependent on *print6.cpp*, *print6.h*, and all the header files you have named in the *HDR* make variable.

226. Understanding What Happens When a Header File Is Changed

When you run *NMAKE.EXE*, it uses your dependency lists to determine which modules need to be rebuilt. It gets the last modified time of the module file and checks it against the modified times of all the files in the dependency list. If any of the files in the list are later than the module's time, the module is rebuilt by running the command specified on the next line. The module's name is specified in the left margin and followed by a colon and one or more white-space characters:

```
print6.obj:     print6.cpp $(HDR) print6.h
                $(CPP) $(CPPFLAGS) print6.cpp
```

In this dependency, *print6.obj* is the module. *NMAKE* will get its modified time and compare it with *print6.cpp*, all the files listed in the *HDR* variable, and *print6.h*. To bring the module up to date, *NMAKE* executes the second line, first substituting variable contents for variable names. For your *Print6* program, the preceding command line expands to the following:

```
cl.exe -c print6.cpp
```

You may have multiple commands to execute. Just enter them on separate lines below the dependency list, and indent them (*NMAKE* sees a nonindented line as the beginning of a new dependency list).

227. Understanding the #if Preprocessor Directive

Lest you think by now that the only preprocessor conditionals are *#ifdef* and *#ifndef*, there is also a plain old *#if* conditional. The *#ifdef* and *#ifndef* conditions simply test whether an identifier has been defined previously, but the *#if* condition may contain an expression.

The preprocessor evaluates the expression and tests it for a zero or non-zero result. If it is zero, the block of code following is ignored until a matching *#endif* or *#elseif* directive is encountered. The expression must be an integral type and contain only integer constants, character constants, and the *defined* operator. It may not contain any casts or the *sizeof* operator or use any enumeration data types. The evaluation is performed during preprocessing, so none of your actual C or C++ code values may be used in an *#if* directive. The actual data type resulting from the expression is considered an *unsigned long*.

In most compilers, some predefined variables are passed to the preprocessor. In Visual C++, when compiling on a computer using an Intel processor, the preprocessor is passed a variable named *_M_IX86* to identify the target processor. By default, the value was set for the dominant processor at the time Visual C++ was released. At this writing, the default value is 500 to indicate a Pentium processor. Other values it can take are 300 for an 80386, 400 for an 80486, and 600 for a Pentium Pro (32-bit Windows won't run on a processor prior to the 80386). The preprocessor and compiler use this value to optimize code for the target processor. For values other than the default, you may set the value using a compiler flag: *-G3* for an 80386, *-G4* for an 80486, *-G5* for a Pentium, and *-G6* for a Pentium Pro.

You can test this variable to make sure that the proper platform is being used. Suppose that you want to ensure that your program can run on 80386 and above processors. You might write the following preprocessor code:

```
#if !defined _M_IX86
#error Intel platform is required for this program
#endif
#if _M_IX86 > 300
#error Incorrect platform specified. Use /G3 compiler
option
#endif
```

Notice that you first check whether the _M_IX86 constant was actually defined. Other similar constants are available for the MacIntosh, Alpha, and MIPS platforms, so you first want to ensure that you are using an Intel platform before performing this test.

If you add this code to one of the sample programs and try to compile using only the *cl.exe* command, you get an error such as the following, and the compilation will stop:

```
Incorrect platform specified. Use /G3 compiler option.
```

Now try recompiling it using *cl.exe /G3*, and the program will compile.

228. Understanding the #endif *Preprocessor Directive*

Unlike the C *if* statement, there is no default target for the *#if* directive. Conditional compilation blocks must *always* be ended with the preprocessor *#endif* directive, even if the object of the *#if* directive is the entire file and regardless of whether the following expression is *true* or *false*.

When you specify a condition, you are telling the preprocessor to include or exclude code from your program, and it continues looking for an end to the conditional block until the end of the file. If the *#endif* directive has not been found by the end of the file, you will get the following error message:

```
fatal error C1004: unexpected end of file found.
```

The preprocessor can't continue, and the compiler program exits. The compilation stage never starts.

229. Understanding the #ifdef *Preprocessor Directive*

The *#ifdef* and *#ifndef* preprocessor directives are special forms of the *#if* directive and are beginning to lose favor. They are kept in the language for compatibility with older code.

The *#ifdef* directive tests whether an identifier has been defined, and the *#ifndef* tests whether it has not yet been defined. In both cases, the result is 1 if *true* and 0 if *false*.

The latest revision of the C and C++ languages includes a new preprocessor operator using the keyword *defined* to replace these directives. Writing *#if defined IDENTIFIER* is the same as writing *#ifdef IDEN-TIFIER*. Conversely, for *#ifndef*, you now may write *#if !defined IDENTIFIER* using the C *NOT* operator to reverse the sense of the test.

It isn't likely that the *#ifdef* and *#ifndef* directives will be removed from the language specification any time soon, but the stage has been set. Use either form at your discretion—even mix them—but be aware that sometime in the future you might have to remove the older directives.

230. *Using the #else and #elif Preprocessor Directives*

You can specify an alternative compilation block using the *#else* directive or multiple blocks using the *#elif* directive (*#elif* is a combination of the words "else" and "if"). If you use one of these directives, the *#endif* should be moved to the end of the last block, and only one *#endif* should be used.

The following short program shows the effect of the *#if . . . #else . . . #endif* combination:

```
#include    <stdio.h>

int main ()
{
#if _M_IX86 == 300
    printf ("This program was compiled for 80386\n");
#else
    printf ("Program was compiled for 80486 and later\n");
#endif
    return (0);
}
```

First, compile the program using no compiler options, run it, and see what the output is. Then compile it using the */G3* option *(cl -G3 progname.cpp)* to see the difference. Only one of the *printf()* statements is ever compiled.

The *#elif* provides an alternative condition for the preprocessor. You may use it in addition to (but before) the *#else* directive. Change your test program to look like the following code:

```
#include    <stdio.h>

int main ()
{
#if _M_IX86 == 300
    printf ("This program was compiled for 80386\n");
#elif _M_IX86 == 400
    printf ("Program was compiled for 80486\n");
#else
    printf ("Program compiled for Pentium and later\n");
#endif
    return (0);
}
```

Recompile the program first using no compiler options and then using the *-G3* option. Then compile one more time using the *-G4* option to see the difference.

Finally, you may stack the *#elif* directives until you run out of options for your expression:

```
#include    <stdio.h>

int main ()
{
#if _M_IX86 == 300
    printf ("This program was compiled for 80386\n");
#elif _M_IX86 == 400
    printf ("Program was compiled for 80486\n");
#elif _M_IX86 == 500
```

```
    printf ("Program was compiled for Pentium\n");
#elif _M_IX86 == 600
    printf ("Program was compiled for Pentium Pro\n");
#else
#error Unknown processor type specified
#endif
    return (0);
}
```

Try the program using the *-G3*, *-G4*, *-G5*, and *-G6* options. The *#else* section handles any unknown processor types, but you should not be able to enter any other values from the command line. If you do use a line such as *cl -D_M_IX86=700 progname.cpp*, you will get an error from the preprocessor (unless you have a much later version of Visual C++ than I do).

231. *Defining a Constant on the Command Line*

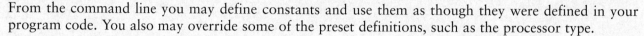

From the command line you may define constants and use them as though they were defined in your program code. You also may override some of the preset definitions, such as the processor type.

To define a constant, use the *-D* compiler option followed by the identifier of the constant, an equals sign, and the value for the constant. You may define an empty constant by leaving off the equals sign and value.

(You also may specify the option by typing "/D." DOS grew up accepting only the / for a program flag, but UNIX systems generally use the hyphen syntax. For compatibility, Microsoft made the syntax optional for most of its programs, so you may type "-D" or "/D." My recommendation is to use the hyphen syntax when possible.)

Try the following simple program, which requires a constant *TESTVAR* to compile:

```
#include    <stdio.h>

#if !defined TESTVAR
#error TESTVAR not defined
#endif
int main ()
{
    return (0);
}
```

First, compile it simply using *cl.exe*. You will get an error, and the preprocessor will abort the compilation. Next, use the command *cl -DTESTVAR testprog.cpp*, and the program will compile without error.

String constants require special attention. You must enclose the definition and value within separate sets of double quotation marks and escape the inner quotes using the backslash character. The following three lines generate compile errors:

```
C:>cl -DELBA="Able was I ere I saw Elba" myprog.cpp   <Enter>
C:>cl -D"ELBA="Able was I ere I saw Elba" " myprog.cpp   <Enter>
C:>cl -DELBA=\"Able was I ere I saw Elba\" myprog.cpp   <Enter>
```

Instead, you have to quote the definition *and* the string, as in the following line:

```
C:>cl -D"ELBA=\"Able was I ere I saw Elba \"" myprog.cpp   <Enter>
```

The last line is equivalent to writing the following in your program code:

```
#define  ELBA  "Able was I ere I saw Elba"
```

232. Understanding Macros in C/C++

As you finish this discussion on the preprocessor, you need to return to macros. There are some important points to remember when writing macros, and some strange quirks about using them.

Although macros serve important purposes in C, they have much less value in C++ and should be avoided, if possible. In essence, you are designing your own subset of the programming language and making it harder to read, both for yourself later on and for other programmers who might have to maintain your code. The best admonition about C++ macros comes from Bjarne Stroustrup himself: "The first rule about macros is: Don't use them unless you have to. Almost every macro demonstrates a flaw in the programming language, in the program, or in the programmer."

That's a bit presumptuous and a very sweeping indictment of macros. At times macros can *improve* readability and accuracy in programming. Strostrup holds up the following as an example of a "completely unnecessary" macro:

```
#define  PI  3.141593
```

In this case, the definition makes the code more readable and introduces only one place where you could accidentally enter an incorrect value. The compiler doesn't care whether you enter 3.141593 or 3.145193 as a constant. All the compiler sees is a double constant, and it won't ask you, "Do you really mean 3.141593?" In this case, you've improved readability and accuracy with a "completely unnecessary" macro. There are other methods, but they aren't necessarily portable between C and C++.

C++ contains constructs that are intended as alternatives to macros, such as *const, enum, inline, namespace,* and *template*. Certainly, you could have written something like *const double PI = 3.141593;* in global memory, but the result is the same. When you view the line in a debugger, you're going to see "PI" in both cases. When you learn about these alternative mechanisms, you might actually prefer them, but for now, try to keep your macros as simple as possible.

233. Defining a Macro—The #define Directive Again

Boiled down to basics, virtually every constant definition in a program is a macro. You use definitions, for the most part, to avoid errors in retyping values or identifiers that you use several times. In this case, you try to make the identifier descriptive to avoid confusion as to its meaning later on.

Generally, though, when most programmers speak of macros, they are referring to the special form of the *#define* statement that lets you specify variable replacements, as well as identifier replacements.

You form a macro by typing the directive *#define* followed by white space, the name of the macros followed by an opening parenthesis (with no intervening white space), a variable list, and finally a closing parenthesis. More white space follows and then the operation you want performed using the variables you listed. Macros may use previously defined constants, but be careful that you don't make them so involved that they are impossible to decipher.

The following line defines a macro without arguments, generally called a *constant*:

```
#define    PI       3.141593
```

Certainly, you could get along without it, but you're less likely to make a typo entering "PI" than entering a string of numbers.

The following line uses a variable and is of the form most programmers mean by "macro":

```
#define    CIRCUMFERENCE(x)         x * 3.141593
```

Thereafter, to use the macro, you use the identifier and pass it the variable you want. To get the circumference of a circle with a diameter of 4 inches, you enter the following line:

```
    int diameter = 4;
    double Circum = CIRCUMFERENCE(diameter);
```

By the time the code is compiled, the preprocessor has replaced the macro with the following code:

```
double Circum = diameter * 3.141593;
```

The compiler automatically casts *diameter* to the highest precision in the statement, which is a *double*, so the result of the assignment is a *double* variable.

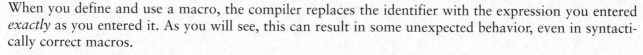

234. *Understanding Macro Substitution*

When you define and use a macro, the compiler replaces the identifier with the expression you entered *exactly* as you entered it. As you will see, this can result in some unexpected behavior, even in syntactically correct macros.

If you make a mistake in your definition, say, a wayward semicolon, every invocation of the macro will contain the same error. Sometimes these errors can be insidious because the mistake itself might not appear in your code. The preprocessor does no syntax checking when it substitutes; it merely performs a text replacement. Only when it gets to the compile stage do the errors show up.

Sometimes you will stare for many minutes at the line containing the error without realizing that you need to go back to the macro definition itself to find the source of the problem. Don't assume that because the preprocessor accepted it, the macro is free of errors.

You can see the results of macro substitution by writing the preprocessor output to the screen with the -*E* compiler directive. Don't try this with a program file containing many #*include* directives because it will show you every line in every included file. Just *stdio.h* will take some time to page through.

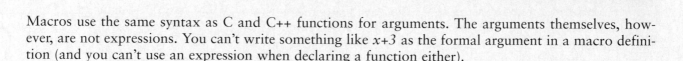

235. *Defining a Macro Using Variables*

Macros use the same syntax as C and C++ functions for arguments. The arguments themselves, however, are not expressions. You can't write something like *x+3* as the formal argument in a macro definition (and you can't use an expression when declaring a function either).

In the substitution, however, the argument becomes an expression, and you can pass any expression as the argument. The preprocessor does no checking on whether the expression is correct or even of the proper data type.

The expression you pass is simply dropped into the macro definition and is not evaluated until the compiler gets to it. This can cause unexpected results. Let's return to your macro to compute the circumference of a circle:

```
#define    CIRCUMFERENCE(x)        x * 3.141593
```

You got the correct result when you passed it a simple expression, but what happens if you pass it *diameter + 2*? You get 10.283186, which is smaller than the value you got when you passed *diameter* by itself. Obviously, something is awry. By the time the compiler handled the macro, it already had been expanded, and the compiled statement was *diameter + 2 * 3.141593*. The multiplication is evaluated first; then, the result is added to the value of *diameter*, giving you the incorrect result.

There are a couple of ways to handle this. First, you can enclose your expression in a double set of parentheses, thus ensuring that it is evaluated before being passed as a parameter:

```
double Circum = CIRCUMFERENCE((diameter + 2));
```

Obviously, this is fraught with peril because you are not always going to remember the double set of parentheses, and neither the preprocessor nor the compiler is going to raise any objections. The better method is to return to your macro definition and enclose the variable in parentheses:

```
#define    CIRCUMFERENCE(x)        (x) * 3.141593
```

This might look strange, but you will see most macros defined this way to handle the possibility of an expression being passed instead of a simple value. When the compiler runs into the code, it sees *(diameter + 2) * 3.141593*, so the addition is performed first. In fact, it's not a bad idea to enclose the entire macro in an extra set of parentheses:

```
#define    CIRCUMFERENCE(x)        ((x) * 3.141593)
```

Even better, avoid the macro altogether and write a short function to handle the computation. You could declare it *inline* and achieve the same functionality as a macro:

```
// Declare the function
double Circumference (int diameter);
// Define the function
inline double Circumference (int diameter)
{
    return (diameter * 3.141593);
}
```

In this case, the parameter is *always* evaluated before it is used in the calculation. The *inline* declaration causes the compiler to substitute the function code in place of the function call, which is what you are trying to do with macros. In this case, however, you avoid many of the pitfalls, and you get type checking to go along with it.

With many compilers, including Visual C++, the *inline* modifier simply indicates your preference, but the compiler is free to ignore it if inline expansion is not practical, such as in recursive functions.

Another alternative to macros is to use *template functions*, which are covered in Tip 287, "Understanding Function Templates."

236. *Understanding How the Compiler Interprets Macros*

Another area where you run into problems with macros is the use of unary operators that modify the variable's value. These include the increment (++) and decrement (−−) operators. If the parameter uses an argument more than once, it is evaluated each time it is used, and the operator is applied to it each time. Now you will write a macro to get the area instead of the circumference of a circle so that you use the same argument twice. Then you call it twice, incrementing the variable outside the macro substitution:

```
#include   <stdio.h>

#define   AREA(x)      ((x)*(x)*3.141593)

int main()
{
    int radius = 3;
    printf ("Area = %f\n", AREA(radius));
     ++radius;
    printf ("Area = %f\n", AREA(radius));
}
```

When you compile and run it, you get 28.274337 and 50.265488, which you would expect if you work out the values on a calculator.

Now for some of the C shorthand magic that proves what a great programmer you are. You will increment the radius after you use it to get ready for the next call:

```
#include   <stdio.h>

#define   AREA(x)      ((x)*(x)*3.141593)

int main()
{
    int radius = 3;
    printf ("Area = %f\n", AREA(radius++));
    printf ("Area = %f\n", AREA(radius));
}
```

Hmmmm. The second value is 78.539825. What happened? Run it through the preprocessor using the -*E* compiler option to see what happened. Here's what you see after the actual substitution has taken place:

```
printf ("Area = %f\n", ((radius++)*(radius++)*3.141593));
printf ("Area = %f\n", ((radius)*(radius)*3.141593));
```

Although the correct *value* was applied properly in both substitutions in the first macro call, the increment operator was applied with each evaluation. This resulted in a value of 5 when you invoke the second call, giving you the unexpected result.

There's no way around this one, folks. It's a fact of life when using macros. In this case, or any time a parameter is used more than once, an inline or template function definitely would be preferable.

237. *Understanding Macros in the Runtime Library*

Like it or not, the C heritage of the C++ language leaves you with the possibility of macros, and the standard header files include a number of them. They've gone through a lengthy process of debugging and have been written to avoid most of the macro dangers, but they still are macros.

Looking in *stdio.h*, you can see some of these macros. In particular, look closely at the file-handling macros:

```
#define getc(_stream)      (--(_stream)->_cnt >= 0 \
         ? 0xff & *(_stream)->_ptr++ : _filbuf(_stream))
#define putc(_c,_stream)  (--(_stream)->_cnt >= 0 \
            ? 0xff & (*(_stream)->_ptr++ = \
            (char)(_c)) : _flsbuf((_c),(_stream)))
#define getchar()          getc(stdin)
#define putchar(_c)        putc((_c),stdout)
```

These are safe macros, and generally you can use them without any problems. However, you should be aware of them if you are browsing through preprocessor output looking for bugs. In a couple of cases, *getchar()* and *putchar()* are macros that actually invoke other macros. The substitution for a simple, unassuming statement such as *char ch = getchar();* would appear like this in the preprocessor output:

```
char ch = (--((&_iob[0]))->_cnt >= 0 ? 0xff &
*((&_iob[0]))->_ptr++ : _filbuf((&_iob[0])));
```

You know that you didn't write it, but that's what the compiler sees when it processes your code.

238. *An Example: Getting the Square of a Number*

Before you decide that macros are the devil's own handiwork and you will never, ever use them, remember: Macros are simply a part of the C toolkit. There are alternatives, but despite what the textbooks and the high priests have to say about them, in the end it is your choice.

Properly named and invoked, a macro is a useful tool. Macro names don't have to be any particular case, but the practice of using all uppercase to distinguish them helps to remind you when you use them to take extra care.

Inline functions are not without their problems as well. They are useful when they are short, but making functions with more than a couple of statements in them inline can significantly increase the size of your finished code. On the other hand, the speed of your finished code is improved because inline functions don't have the overhead of a function call.

In their favor, macros are untyped. You can write a macro to take the square of a number such as the following:

```
#define    SQUARE(x)        (x)*(x)
```

If you pass it an *int* type, you are going to get an *int* result. If you pass it a *double, long,* or even a *float*, the expression will be evaluated as that type.

Using inline functions, you have a problem with data types. Whatever you pass it will be cast automatically to the data type expected by the function. To ensure that you get back the proper type, you have to declare the function and its arguments as that type, say, a type *float*:

```
float Square(float x);
```

Now, if you pass it an integer value, say, 12, you have to specifically cast the return type to ensure accuracy. The following code compiles without error, but the two *printf()* statements give entirely different results:

```
#include     <stdio.h>

#define   SQUARE(x)     ((x)*(x))

float Square (float x);

int main ()
{
    int x = 12;
    printf ("x * x = %d\n", Square(x));
    printf ("x * x = %d\n", SQUARE(x));
    return (0);
}

inline float Square (float x)
{
    return (x * x);
}
```

The inline function prints a value of 0, but the macro yields the proper 144. To get the proper result with the function, you would have to write the following:

```
printf ("x * x = %d\n", (int) Square(x));
```

Too, there is the problem with precision. You know that *float* types store values in an exponential fashion. After the result has been optimized, passed around in a couple of registers, and whatever else the operating system and compiler do with it, it is conceivable (but not likely—Visual C++ is a good compiler) that you could wind up with a return value of 143.9999999999. That's particularly true if you do any other arithmetic on it. For all intents and purposes, that's 144.0, but casting it to *int* gives you 143 as the square of 12. That's not desirable unless you want to invent a new number system.

In this case, the macro and inline functions come out fairly even, with the macro winning in a push. Despite the precautions you had to take, the macro did deliver the goods in the end. Before you say that macros are all bad, examine the alternatives to see whether macros provide the flexibility and result you want.

239. Understanding Strings and the User Interface

An episode of *Star Trek: The Next Generation* featured a species called "Binars" that communicated in a binary language not unlike computers. If you were a Binar and could understand binary numbers at the speed computers use them, the computer probably wouldn't have been invented—or, at best, that invention would be somewhere in our distant future.

As intelligent as I think my dog is, he still can't read this. Therefore, it's safe to assume that all who read this book are human. Right now the most efficient way for humans to put data into, and get data out of, a computer is through the collection of characters combined into compound objects called words and sentences—or *strings*.

Even when you write something like *12 * 12*, your universal translator (the compiler) turns it into a series of bits that the computer can use. The computer, in return, gives you back a series of bits that are turned into another string, "144".

240. Understanding the Relationship Between Uppercase and Lowercase in the ASCII Table

Until the ASCII *(American Standard Code of Information Interchange)* table was developed, about the closest anyone got to a standardized character set was the five-bit code developed by Jean-Maurice Emile Baudot. The code was not a very widely accepted alternative to the Morse code, but the *baud*, a unit of code speed, survives today. Baudot died before the ultimate application of his code by E.E. Kleinschmidt and Howard Krum, when they invented the first practical teleprinter in the mid-1920s. (In 1910, Howard Krum invented the synchronization technology that gave us the "start" and "stop" bits still used in serial communications today.)

With only 32 choices, it was impossible to represent all the characters used in the English language, so the Baudot code used one for a shift and another for an unshift to represent different characters with the same codes. Still, the lowercase alphabet was beyond the reach of the Baudot code.

By the 1960s, every computer maker had its own way of representing the lowercase alphabet (and in many cases, the uppercase alphabet as well). In 1968, the seven-bit ASCII character set was introduced, with the uppercase and lowercase characters arranged in such a way that there was only a one-bit difference between their representation in binary code. An uppercase *A* was given the code 01000001, and the lowercase equivalent was assigned 01100001. The assignments were more than accidental and meant that computers could represent all the letters by toggling one bit for uppercase or lowercase.

241. Using Bitwise AND and Bitwise OR to Change the Case of a Character

The ASCII character set can be divided into four general categories:

- **Control characters.** These are all the values below 32 plus the DEL character (value 127).

- **Numerical digits.** These have sequential positions from 0 (value 48) to 9 (value 57).

- **Alpha characters.** Uppercase *A* (value 65) to uppercase *Z* (value 90) and lowercase *a* (value 97) to lowercase *z* (value 122).

- **Punctuation characters.** All the remaining characters except the spaceband (value 32).

This leaves out a single character, the spaceband (value 32, commonly called a *space*), which doesn't really fit into any of the categories. In its own way, it is a member of all four groups.

If you examine the alpha characters, you will see that their values are all consecutive, with uppercases and lowercases in separate blocks. This wasn't always true with other character sets, and it allows you to do logical comparisons and arithmetic operations on characters. The position of the uppercase and lowercase blocks also is significant. The difference between a character's uppercase and lowercase values is 32, or 0x20 in hexadecimal, the value of a spaceband. Their position in the character set arranges them so that the fifth bit in an alpha character's value determines whether it is uppercase or lowercase.

This difference allows you to manipulate the case of a character using only bitwise logical operations. You may change any character to lowercase by logically *OR*'ing it with a space (0x20). You may change any character to uppercase by logically *AND*'ing it with the complement of a space (the same as ~0x20). Finally, you may *toggle* the case of the character (change lowercase to uppercase, and vice versa) by *XOR*'ing it with a space. The following program first changes all the characters in a string to uppercase, then changes them to lowercase, and finally, toggles all the characters:

```c
#include    <stdio.h>
#include    <string.h>

#define    SPACEBAND    0x20
bool IsAlphaChar(char ch);

int main()
{
    char *s;
char str[] = "Able was I ere I saw Elba";
    char *dup = new char [sizeof (str)];
    if (dup == NULL)
        {
        fprintf (stderr, "Memory error\n");
        return (-1);
        }
    strcpy (dup, str);
printf ("Original string is \"%s\"\n", str);
    for (s = dup; *s; ++s)
        {
        if (IsAlphaChar (*s))
            *s &= ~SPACEBAND;
        }
printf ("Uppercase string is \"%s\"\n", dup);
    strcpy (dup, str);
    for (s = dup; *s; ++s)
        {
        if (IsAlphaChar (*s))
            *s |= SPACEBAND;
        }
printf ("Lowercase string is \"%s\"\n", dup);
    strcpy (dup, str);
    for (s = dup; *s; ++s)
        {
        if (IsAlphaChar (*s))
            *s ^= SPACEBAND;
        }
printf ("Toggled case string is \"%s\"\n", dup);
    delete [] dup;
    return (0);
}
```

```
bool IsAlphaChar(char ch)
{
    ch &= ~SPACEBAND;
    if ((ch > 0x40) && (ch < 0x5b))
        return (true);
    return (false);
}
```

The *IsAlphaChar()* function uses the relationship to convert the character to uppercase first, simplifying the test for an alpha character. You could have omitted that operation and written this test as *if (((ch > 0x40) && (ch < 0x5b)) || ((ch > 0x60) && (ch < 0x7b)))*.

242. *Understanding Punctuation Marks*

The punctuation characters don't categorize themselves logically. In fact, not all the punctuation characters in the ASCII set are truly punctuation marks. The tilde (~) and caret (^), for example, are *diacritical* or *accent* marks. Others are mathematical symbols, and the at sign (@) is a symbol used in commerce. Rather than have many groups containing only one or two characters, you categorize all these as punctuation marks in the C and C++ languages.

The control characters are assigned values below 32 (and the DEL character). The digits are arranged so that you may logically *OR* a binary digit with 0x30 to produce the ASCII digit. The punctuation group occupies all other positions that are not alpha characters or the space.

243. *Understanding Control Characters*

In the early years of computing, the most common I/O device was some sort of printer. Even after the microcomputing hobby sprang up in the 1970s, printers remained the primary source of entering data into and retrieving data from a computer. Terminals featuring a cathode ray tube (picture tube) were very expensive, often costing well over $1,000, but a good Teletype machine could be picked up on the used market for a couple of hundred dollars.

These machines required special characters to perform mechanical operations. One character returned the type carriage to the home position, another advanced the paper, and yet another advanced the paper to the top of the next page or form. The ASCII table had to deal with these command characters, so a set of *control* characters was created and given the first 32 positions in the table. Over the years, the original purpose of many of these characters has disappeared, and they have assumed new functions. The ESC character was used to signal the beginning of a control sequence for a printer, but today Windows uses Esc to manipulate menus and as a cancel key.

The DEL control character was given the special position of 127 to accommodate tape and punch devices. Essentially, it's a "non-operation" character. In the seven-bit code, its value contains all 1s. A bit value of 1 (a *mark*) on a paper tape was represented as a hole punched in the tape, and a 0 (a *space*) was the absence of a hole. If you made a mistake, it was difficult to put the *chads* (the little round pieces of paper that came from the holes) back on the tape. You had to move the tape back to the mistake and enter the DEL character, which filled all seven positions with holes. When the reader device encountered this character, it simply ignored it. Today, of course, we don't have a lot of use for paper tape or the DEL character, but it remains on the ASCII table. (And its position well outside the block of control characters can give programmers fits sometimes).

244. *Understanding the* char *Variable Type*

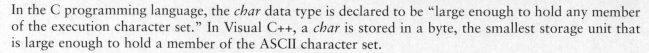

In the C programming language, the *char* data type is declared to be "large enough to hold any member of the execution character set." In Visual C++, a *char* is stored in a byte, the smallest storage unit that is large enough to hold a member of the ASCII character set.

It would be a serious programming error, however, to assume that a *char* is synonymous with a byte. Various computer platforms may use a larger value for a *char*, and even among different versions of the same operating system, the size of *char* may vary. C also contains a derived type, *wchar_t*, which represents a character in an *unsigned short*. With the growing influence of the Unicode character set to represent international characters, you're likely to see this type used more often than *char*.

A character may be promoted automatically to an integer in arithmetic operations. Writing the expression *int x = 2 * 'A'* generates neither an error nor a warning. The 'A' is automatically promoted to its integer value and used in the assignment.

245. *Understanding How C and C++ Store Strings*

Don't look for much support from C or C++ when it comes to handling strings. There are a number of functions in the standard library for manipulating strings, but the language itself doesn't support a string data type.

Instead, a string is stored in an array of type *char*, which means that strings inherit all the weaknesses of arrays. When a string is created, the size is fixed, and it's the programmer's responsibility to make sure that the string fits into the array. The following statements are allowed in C, but almost certainly they will cause problems:

```
char str[4];    // An array of type char
strcpy (str, "This here's a string");
```

The library function *strcpy()* will dutifully copy the entire string into the four-character array, overwriting any other data that might be there, including function return addresses.

On the positive side, the Standard Template Library (STL) in C++ does contain a class for handling strings. It greatly simplifies many of the string operations, but it is not available in C. The Microsoft Foundation Class also contains a *CString* class that offers BASIC-style string handling without using the STL. You will look at both when you get to object-oriented programming (OOP) beginning with Tip 317, "Introduction to Object-Oriented Programming."

246. *Understanding the NUL character (\0)*

The NUL character is the first entry in the ASCII character set and has a value of 0. You use it in C and C++ to represent the end of a string and represent it with \0. Strings represented this way are called ASCIIZ strings, although they don't have to contain only ASCII characters.

Note: You use the word "NUL," instead of "NULL," to indicate the 0 character. In C and C++, NULL is used to represent an invalid pointer value. In most implementations, NULL is 0, but it doesn't have to be. Its size varies according to the operating system and compiler. NUL is the ASCII name for the first element in the table. Its value is always 0, and its size is always the size of a character.

In many cases, you don't have to include the terminating null when you create strings. When you define a string constant, the compiler automatically adds a terminating NUL to the string. You do, however, have to take it into account when manipulating strings. The standard library functions look for this character to mark the end of a string.

247. Understanding and Using Pointers to Strings

When you declare an array, the return value is a pointer to the first element in the array. The same is true with strings, and the return value is a pointer to type *char* and points to the first character in the string.

The operations you can perform on the resulting pointer are determined by how you declare and initialize the string, either as a *char* pointer or as a *char* array. Declare a variable as a string pointer using the keyword *char* followed by the pointer operator and the identifier for the variable. If you declare and initialize it as follows, you can change the value of the pointer to move through the string:

```
char *str = "This here's a string";
```

In this case, the variable is declared to be a string pointer instead of an array, but the resulting string is an array. You can step through the string using a loop:

```
while (*str)
{
    putchar (*str++);
}
```

In declaring the string, the compiler added the NUL terminator for you. In the loop statement you *dereference* the pointer to get the single character pointed to. In the *putchar()* statement, you again dereference the pointer to put the character on the screen and then increment the pointer. When the pointer advances to point to the NUL character, the expression *s is 0, so the loop terminates.

In this case, the pointer to the first character is lost. Unless you saved it either by counting the number of increments or assigning it to another *char* pointer, there's no way to get back to the beginning of the string.

The length of the string is fixed. If you know the size, or length, of the string, you can copy other strings of equal or shorter length into its storage space. However, if you try to copy a longer string, you will overwrite some potentially important data.

String pointers can be assigned other values. To preserve the pointer to your original string in the previous code, you can declare another string pointer and set its value to *str*:

```
char *str = "This here's a string";
char *s = str;
```

In this case, you would use *s* to step through the string and leave *str* pointing to the first character.

248. *Getting the Size of a String*

The standard library contains a function, *strlen()*, to return the length of a string. The function stops counting the characters in a string when it encounters a NUL character, and the returned count doesn't include the terminator.

If you want to imbed a NUL character in the string, *strlen()* will count characters only up to the first NUL. There are several places in Windows programming where you will want to do this, such as templates for the File Open dialog box:

```
char *Template="Text Files\0*.txt\0C++ Files\0*.cpp\0\0";
```

In this case, *strlen(Template)* will return 10, the length up to but not including the first \0.

If you use the *sizeof* operator on a string declared and initialized this way, the return value is the size of a *char* pointer, not of the string. Try the following snippet to see the results:

```
char *Template="Text Files\0*.txt\0C++ Files\0*.cpp\0\0";
printf ("strlen(Template) = %d\n", strlen(Template));
printf ("sizeof(Template) = %d\n", sizeof (Template));
```

249. *Declaring a Variable as a Type* char

A character variable is declared using the type *char* and may be assigned a character constant enclosed in single quotation marks. *char ch = 'A'* declares a variable *ch* and assigns it the value of A. A *char* type also may be assigned an integer value if the value is not too large to fit into the size of a *char* type. *char ch = 0x41* assigns the hexadecimal value 41 to the variable *ch*. Trying to assign it a value of 0x141 will result in a warning from the compiler, and the character will be truncated to its lowest byte.

250. *Declaring a Variable as an Array of Type* char

Declaring a variable as a string array gives you some additional capability, but you lose a little in return. Declare a character array using the keyword *char* followed by the variable identifier, an opening bracket, an integer value specifying the size of the array, and a closing bracket. If the array is being initialized at the same time, the size is optional and the compiler will calculate it for you. The following lines declare character arrays:

```
char str[16];              // Uninitialized string array.
char str[16]= "String array"; // Initialized string array.
```

In the first declaration, space is set aside for 16 characters, and its contents are whatever happens to be in the memory location at the time. In the second example, space is set aside and the array contents initialized to the string constant. If the size is less than the length of the string constant, the compiler fills the rest of the array with the last character, a NUL.

If the size of the array is included in the declaration, the value must be large enough to hold the string *plus* the NUL terminator. The following declaration results in an "array bounds overflow" error:

```
char str[12]= "String array"; // Initialized string array.
```

The string length is 12, and you need one more for the NUL character, so you would have to increase the length by one. However, if you are declaring and initializing in the same statement, you can leave out the size and let the compiler calculate it:

```
char str[]="String array"; // Initialized string array.
```

From appearances, you might think that there is little difference between declaring and initializing a *char* pointer and a *char* array. The compiler, however, sees thing differently. For one, you can no longer modify *str* to point to another character in the string. The sample loop from earlier now gives a compile error saying, "++ requires lvalue":

```
while (*str)
{
    putchar (*str++);
}
```

To do this, you would have to assign a string pointer the value of *str* and use it to step through the array.

For another difference, the *sizeof* operator no longer returns just the size of a *char* pointer. Instead, you get the size of the array, including any elements initialized to NUL. Now you will declare the template from earlier using an array instead of a pointer:

```
char Template[]="Text Files\0*.txt\0C++ Files\0*.cpp\0\0";
printf ("strlen(Template) = %d\n", strlen(Template));
printf ("sizeof(Template) = %d\n", sizeof (Template));
```

The *strlen()* function still says the length is 10, but the *sizeof* operator returns 35, the actual size of the array plus an additional element for the NUL terminator. The compiler didn't recognize the NUL characters in your initialization string, so you now have three NUL characters at the end of the line. You need only two, so you could remove one in the initialization.

251. *Declaring an Array of Strings*

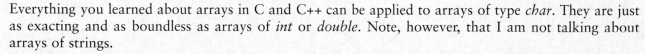

Everything you learned about arrays in C and C++ can be applied to arrays of type *char*. They are just as exacting and as boundless as arrays of *int* or *double*. Note, however, that I am not talking about arrays of strings.

You can think of a string array as a two-dimensional character array, but don't carry the analogy too far. It's more proper to think of string arrays as array "doublets." A true two-dimensional array contains all its data in contiguous memory. The string array, however, contains only pointers to the strings, which themselves are arrays but can be stored elsewhere in memory.

You know that a string is an array of type *char*, so you will begin by creating a two-dimensional array of *char*. As with any array, you must declare the number of elements when you declare it, or initialize it at the same time and let the compiler figure out the number of elements. If you choose the latter, you still must give the second dimension a size, as you learned in Tip 199, "Declaring Multidimensional Arrays"; the compiler will compute only the number of elements in the first dimension. Your *char* array then would have to have its second dimension large enough to hold the longest string plus the NUL terminator. You would declare it along these lines:

```
char chArray[][32] = {
                       {"First String\n"},
                       {"Second String\n"},
                       {"The Third String is a long one\n"}
                       };
```

You've set aside an array large enough to hold 96 characters, but you're using only 61 of the elements. You're wasting more than a third of the memory in the array. With more and longer strings, it could add up to a lot of memory.

C and C++ enable you to resolve this potential memory waste by permitting you to declare and initialize an array of strings. The strings themselves are only as long as they need to be, and the array contains pointers to them. To do this, you declare the array variable to be a pointer to *char* and remove the second dimension from the declaration:

```
char *strArray[] = {
                     {"First String\n"},
                     {"Second String\n"},
                     {"The Third String is a long one\n"}
                     };
```

Your memory usage has dropped to 73 bytes: 61 for the strings themselves and 12 bytes to hold the pointers to the strings. You are "wasting" only about 16 percent of the memory.

This comes at a slight increase in complexity. The variable *strArray* is a pointer to a pointer of type *char*, but you still may use the array elements as individual strings. In fact, there are two ways you can access the strings. First, you can use direct indexing, as in the following code:

```
for (int x = 0; x < 3; ++x)
{
    printf (strArray[x]);
}
```

Second, you can declare another variable as a pointer to a *char* pointer, set it equal to the first element in the array, and increment it to get to the individual strings:

```
char **pstrArray = strArray;
for (int x = 0; x < 3; ++x, ++strArray)
{
    printf (*pstrArray);
}
```

You had to dereference the pointer to pointer once to get to the string pointer, but the result is the same as the direct indexing.

252. *Understanding Dynamic Strings: The new Operator*

For the most part, you have been creating variables "on the stack," and they are destroyed automatically when the function or block containing them exits. Sometimes, however, you need to create variables that survive the function. In the case of arrays, you don't always know how large they have to be until you do some calculations, and you can't declare an array of indeterminate size.

C++ provides an operator to create variables in dynamic memory ("in the heap"), and thus, the variables are not destroyed by the stack adjustments made when a function exits. In the earlier discussion on environment variables, I introduced you to the *new* operator, which you use to allocate heap memory. The *new* operator is available only in C++; in standard C, the library contains functions to accomplish the same purpose.

The *new* operator always returns a pointer to the newly created object, whether it is a single variable or an array. You can use the *new* operator to create any data type in the heap, but you must reference it through the pointer variable.

The *new* operator doesn't require you to assign the return value to a pointer variable. However, if you don't, you can't access the newly reserved memory, nor can you destroy it when it is no longer needed. In Windows, you've created a stranded section of memory that can't be used until you reboot your computers. Some operating systems have "garbage collectors," programs that look for such items and automatically delete them.

To create an item on the stack, use a pointer variable to catch the return value. Then enter the keyword *new* followed by the data type you want to create. The following three lines create a *char*, an *int*, and a *double* on the heap:

```
char *pch = new char;
char *pInt = new int;
char *pDouble = new double;
```

You can initialize the new memory object by enclosing the value in parentheses after the data type: *char *pch = new char ('A');* creates a *char* in the heap and initializes it to *A*.

The picture is not so nice for arrays, however. You may create them using brackets after the data type, but you must include the size of the array. There is no way to initialize them at the time they are created. The following operation creates an array to hold 48 characters:

```
char *pch = new char [48];
```

Unlike arrays created on the stack, the size of an array created with *new* may be the result of an expression. If you are going to copy a string, you specify the size of the new string using the *sizeof* operator on the original string:

```
char str1[] = "This here's a string";
char *str2 = new char [sizeof (str1)];
```

Objects created on the heap not only survive the function but also can linger around after the program has ended. However, the variable holding the pointer to the object is subject to normal scope. If it is not saved before the block or function ends, it will be destroyed, and the allocated memory block will be stranded. If you don't destroy the object before the pointer goes out of scope, save the pointer in a global variable or as a member variable of a class.

253. *Understanding Dynamic Strings: The* delete *Operator*

Objects created with the *new* operator are in the *heap*, an area sometimes referred to as the "free store" on some operating systems. Depending on the operating system, if you don't destroy the object before your program exits, the memory may be stranded until the system is rebooted. This is true in Windows, and the resulting loss of memory is called a "memory leak."

C++ also provides a *delete* operator to destroy heap objects created with the *new* operator. In standard C, heap objects are destroyed by the *free()* function.

To destroy a heap object, type the keyword "delete" followed by the address of the object to be deleted. The address may be (and usually is) the pointer variable you used to save the address when you created the object. The following line would delete your previously allocated *pch* * (a single *char* item) from the heap:

```
delete pch;
```

To destroy an array created by the *new* operator, follow the *delete* keyword with a pair of empty brackets. You don't have to enter the size. Assuming that *pch* is an array instead of a single character, the following will delete it:

```
delete [] pch;
```

When an array is created in the heap, an extra allocation is made for strategic information such as its size. When you enter "delete[]," you are notifying the operator that it should delete the entire array.

254. *Understanding the Library String Functions*

Your favorite programming language, be it C or C++, might be shy on string support, but the standard library provides a number of functions to make up for that shortcoming. Although you have to be careful assigning and moving strings, the library offers most of the functionality you could expect from any language.

The functions let you copy strings from one to another, duplicate them without worrying about the length, search a string for a single character or a substring, and loop through a string picking out substrings delimited by token characters.

255. *Using String-Loading Functions*

String-loading functions are those that initialize or set the contents of a string or add to the contents. The functions normally place a NUL terminator at the end of the string being operated on, and no size or bounds checking is performed.

The *sprintf()* function writes formatted data into a string using the same syntax and escape characters as *printf()*. The arguments are a pointer to the string into which the formatted data is written, a pointer to a format string, and a variable number of arguments of any type. It returns the number of characters written to the string, not including the NUL terminator.

```
char buf[124], str[] = "Able was I ere I saw Elba";
int x = 24;
float pi = 3.141593
sprintf (buf, "string = %s\n   int = %d\n float = %f\n",
             str, x, pi);
```

strcpy() copies the contents of one string into another. Required arguments are a pointer to the destination string and a pointer to the source string. The previous contents of the destination string are lost, and the function returns a pointer to the destination string.

```
char buf[64];
```

```
char *src = "This here's a string. ";
    strcpy (buf, src);
```

The *strcat()* function adds one string to the end of another. Arguments are a pointer to the target string and a pointer to the source string. The function returns a pointer to the target string. The sample first copies the first 12 characters of *src1* into the buffer and then appends *src2*. After the *strcat*, the buffer contains "*This here's a real string.*"

```
char buf[64] = "";          // Initialize string to NULs
char *src1 = "This here's a string. ";
char *src2 = "a real string. ";
    strncpy (buf, src1, 12);
    strcat (buf, src2);
```

You will meet *strncpy()* in Tip 257, "Using String Functions to Copy a Specified Number of Characters." In this example, the statement copies 12 characters from *src1* to *buf*.

The *strdup()* function creates a copy of a source string using the C function *malloc()*. The return value is a pointer to the copy or *NULL* if the string could not be allocated. The string must be destroyed using a call to the C function *free()*. DO NOT use the *delete* operator to free the string. The following example duplicates *src*, prints it, and then deletes the duplicate string:

```
char src[] = "Able was I ere I saw Elba\n";
    char *dup = strdup (src);
    if (dup != NULL)
        {
        printf (dup);
        free (dup);
        }
```

strset() sets all the characters in the string to a specified character up to the NUL terminator. The arguments are a pointer to the target string and the character to use. The function returns a pointer to the string. Be careful with this one. It is *not* an initialization function. If the string is not NUL-terminated already, *strset()* will overrun the bounds of the string until it encounters a NUL or an exception is thrown. Another function, *strnset()*, initializes a certain number of characters to a given value. In addition to the arguments required by *strset()*, this function requires an integer count value of the number of characters to set. *strnset()* also stops at a NUL character even if *count* has not been reached.

```
char str[] = "Able was I ere I saw Elba\n";
    strset (src, 'X');     // Sets the string to X
    strnset(src, '.', sizeof(str)-1); // same as strset
                                      // because count is
                                      // more than strlen
```

256. *Using String Information Functions*

A number of standard library functions return information about a string or compare one string to another. None of them load or change any characters in the strings.

The *strcmp()* function compares one string with another and returns the lexical relationship of the two: a negative number if the first string is less than the second, a positive number if the first string is greater than the second, and 0 if they are equal. This function is case sensitive.

strncmp() compares two strings up to a given length. The return value is the same as for *strcmp()*. In addition to pointers to two strings, an integer count parameter is required.

The *strlen()* function returns the length of the string, not including the terminating NUL. The only argument is a pointer to the string to count.

257. Using String Functions to Copy a Specified Number of Characters

Two library functions enable you to restrict the number of characters that are copied from one string to another.

strncpy() copies a specified number of characters from a source string into a destination string, overwriting the contents of the destination. Required arguments are a pointer to the destination string, a pointer to the source string, and an integer specifying the count of characters to copy. A NUL is not automatically appended if the count does not encompass the NUL character in the source string. If a NUL is encountered in the source before the count, the copy is terminated and a NUL is appended. The function returns a pointer to the destination string. In the example, the destination buffer is initialized to NULs and the first 12 characters of the source are copied into it. This results in the buffer containing *"This here's "*.

```
char buf[64] = "";          // Initialize string to NULs
char *src = "This here's a string. ";
    strncpy (buf, src, 12);
```

strncat() adds a specified number of characters from a source string to the end of a destination string, returning a pointer to the destination string. The arguments are a pointer to the destination string, a pointer to the source string, and a count of the number of characters to copy. Unlike *strncpy()*, this function appends a NUL terminator. If the source string is shorter than the count, the concatenation stops at the NUL character. At the end of the sample code, *buf* contains *"This here's almost a strin"*.

```
char buf[64] = "" ;         // Initialize string to NULs
char *src1 = "This here's a string. ";
char *src2 = "almost a string. ";
    strncpy (buf, src1, 12);
    strncat (buf, src2, 14);
```

258. Finding a Character Within a String

Two library functions search a string to find a specified character. The first function, *strchr()*, searches from the beginning of the string, and the other, *strrchr()*, searches from the end of the string backward.

Each requires two arguments, a pointer to the string to be searched and the search character, and both return a *char* pointer to the character. If the character wasn't found, a *NULL* is returned.

```
char str[] = "The Ring Nebula in the constellation Vega";
char *s = str;
int count = 0;
```

```
    while ((s = strchr(s, ' ' )) != NULL)
        {
        ++s;            // move past character
        ++count;    // increment counter
        }
    printf ("%d spaces found\n", count);
```

The preceding example won't work with *strrchr()* because the loop will find only the last spaceband and then exit. *strrchr()* is useful for isolating the last item in a delimited list, such as getting the file name from a full path:

```
char str[] = "C:\\dev\\ati\\nt40\\ati.dll";
char *s = str;
    if ((s = strrchr (str, '\\')) == NULL)
        s = str;        // If file name only
    else
        ++s;                // Move past the backslash
    printf ("The file name is %s\n", s);
```

259. *Finding a Substring Within a String*

Use the *strstr()* function to look for a substring within a longer string. As arguments, the function takes a pointer to the string to be searched and a pointer to the substring to find. It returns a pointer to the location in the first string where the substring occurs or a *NULL* if the substring was not found. The search is case sensitive.

```
char str[] = "A network can be loosely defined as the "
             "hardware and software that allow two "
             "entities to communicate. ";
char *s;

    if ((s = strstr (str, "the")) != NULL)
        printf ("Found: %s\n", s);
    else
        printf ("Search string not found\n");
```

This is a useful search mechanism, especially for long strings. Unfortunately, a matching version of the function that is not case sensitive is unavailable. If you need a version that is not case sensitive, the following function works:

```
char *strstri (char *s1, char *s2)
{
char    *s, *t, *u;

    if ((s1 == NULL) || (s2 == NULL))
            return (NULL);

    s = new char [strlen (s1) + 1];
    if (s == NULL)
        return (NULL);
    t = new char [strlen (s2) + 1];
    if (t == NULL)
```

```
    {
        delete [] s;
        return (NULL);
    }
    strcpy (s, s1);      // Copy the strings
    strcpy (t, s2);
    strupr (s);          // Convert copies to uppercase
    strupr (t);

    if ((u = strstr (s, t)) != NULL)    // Do the search
    {
        u = s1 + (u - s);   // Adjust pointer to real string
    }
    delete [] s;         // Delete the copies
    delete [] t;
    return (u);          // Return the pointer or NULL
}
```

260. *Finding a Token in a String*

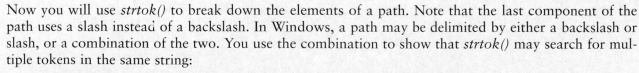

A tokenized string, such as a path or a delimited string, may be repeatedly searched for tokens and substrings extracted using the *strtok()*. Each successive call finds the next token and returns the substring.

The *strtok()* function modifies the original string by placing NUL characters in place of the tokens. If you need to preserve the original string, make a copy of it and use the copy for the call to *strtok()*. Also, *strtok()* uses static variables in the search. If you call the function using a different string, the original search pattern will be lost. Finish all your searches through the first string before invoking *strtok()* for another string. The function is thread-safe, so it is possible to call it using two different strings from different threads.

strtok() requires two arguments: a pointer to the string to be searched and a pointer to a string containing the tokens. On the second and successive calls, use *NULL* as the first argument. A pointer to the substring is returned on success or *NULL* if no tokenized substring could be found. Successive calls to *strtok()* may use different tokens.

261. *Using* strtok *to Parse a String*

Now you will use *strtok()* to break down the elements of a path. Note that the last component of the path uses a slash instead of a backslash. In Windows, a path may be delimited by either a backslash or slash, or a combination of the two. You use the combination to show that *strtok()* may search for multiple tokens in the same string:

```
char str[] = "C:\\dev\\ati\\nt40/ati.dll";
char *s = str;
//
// Initialize strtok. A path may be delimited by
// backslashes or slashes. The first call uses the
// string as the first argument.
```

```
        s = strtok (str, "\\/");
        if (s == NULL)
            return;
        printf ("Path components are:\n");
        do
        {
            printf ("\t%s\n", s);
        } while ((s = strtok (NULL, "\\/")) != NULL);
// Successive calls to strtok use NULL as the
// first argument
```

When you run this snippet, you will see the following output:

```
Path components are:
        C:
        dev
        ati
        nt40
        ati.dll
```

262. Extending strtok to Parse for Empty Tokens

One of the problems with *strtok()* is that it has a nasty habit of skipping over empty tokens without your knowing it. You're not likely to run into that problem parsing path names, but suppose that you had something like the following line:

```
doe:147::/usr/doe::John Doe
```

Now you want to parse the data in the string and pick out the individual entries. *strtok()*, unfortunately, will skip over the double colons as though they were one token. I'm often faced with having to parse strings with empty fields in them. A typical comma-delimited account record transferred from the business system has three fields for the account address. Likely, one or more of them may be empty, as well as the extended ZIP code field and one of the two phone number fields. It's important to me to know when *strtok()* skips empty fields and how many it skips.

You don't want to change *strtok()*'s behavior. It's defined this way, and you want to keep it for portability.

Fortunately, it's easy to modify this behavior and make *strtok()* return empty fields when they are encountered.

Assuming that you installed Visual Studio in the *C:\Program Files* directory, look in the subdirectory *Microsoft Visual Studio\VC98\CRT\SRC*, and find a file named *strtok.c*. (If you didn't install the C runtime source code, you can do it at any time, or you can find the file on the CD. If you are getting the files off the CD, you will also need *cruntime.h*, and if you want to build a multithreaded version, *mtdll.h*.). *Copy* this file (please *copy* it rather than work on it directly) into a working directory. You may keep the same name or rename it something like *strtokex.c* for clarity.

Edit this copy of the file, and change all references to *strtok* to *strtokex*. The function name on line 47 is the only important place. Move down to and comment out lines 88 and 89. They should read as follows:

```
while ( (map[*str >> 3] & (1 << (*str & 7))) && *str )
            str++;
```

Remember, this is a C file, so you have to use the /* and */ comment markers. These are the two lines that cause *strtok()* to skip empty fields. By commenting them out, the function will respond to the empty fields in the next few lines.

You're done. Save the file (it is a *copy*, right?). Next, create the following makefile and call it *strtokex.mak*:

```
#
#  Makefile for strtokex.c
#
CC=cl.exe
CFLAGS=-c -D_CRTBLD
#
# Put your source code path in the following line
INCDIR=-I"D:/DevTools/Microsoft Visual Studio/VC98/CRT/SRC"
strtokex.obj:    strtokex.c
                  $(CC) $(CFLAGS) $(INCDIR) strtokex.c
```

The makefile makes it much easier to compile the function. You don't really want to be typing all that every time you want to rebuild the file. (Actually, you should have to build it only once, but you could add other functions to the makefile and even set it up to build your own personal library of custom functions).

The *-c* option causes the compiler to create only the *.obj* file. The *-D_CRTBLD* defines *_CRTBLD*, which the source file needs in order to include *cruntime.h* and *mtdll.h*.

When you write your program to use it, declare it as follows:

```
extern "C" char * __cdecl strtokex (char * string,
                                    const char * control);
```

Until you get around to adding it to your personal library, you may add it to your programs by specifying the object file on the command line, instead of specifying the C file:

```
C:>cl tester.cpp strtokex.obj
```

Try it using the following parsing code:

```
char str[] = "accountno,name2,address1,,,city,"
             "state,zip,,phone1,phone2";
char *s = str;

    s = strtokex (str, ",");
    if (s == NULL)
        return;
    printf ("Components are:\n");
    do
    {
        printf ("\t%s\n", s);
    } while ((s = strtokex (NULL, ",")) != NULL);
```

Run your tester program and the empty fields for address2, address3, and the ZIP+4 fields will show up as empty lines. *strtokex()* returns an empty string (not *NULL*) for an empty field. Now you know when and how many times the function skips empty fields.

Of course, the pundits would say that you should never do something like this, that you should work within the framework of *strtok()* for portability. To do that, you would have to find the empty tokens, make your code "remember" them, and adjust your loop dynamically to accommodate them (remember, the next record through might not have empty fields, or some other fields might be empty). Maintaining portability is an admirable goal, and you should attempt to do so when possible.

263. *Understanding Functions That Are Not Case Sensitive*

Some systems have versions of the string information functions that are not case sensitive, but on Visual C++ you have only *stricmp()* and *strnicmp()*. Functions that are not case sensitive are not part of the standard library, and their names may appear differently on other systems, such as *strcmpi()* instead of *stricmp()*.

Obviously, these functions are not very portable, and you should avoid using them if you can. Instead, you can write your own functions within your programs or build your own library of functions. If you need to port the code to another operating system, at least you have the source code to the functions as a starting point.

Here's how you might build a version of *strstr()* that is not case sensitive:

```
/*
    strstri.c - case-insensitive version of strstr.
 */
#include    <stdlib.h>

char *strstri (char *s1, char *s2)
{
char    s, t, u;

    if ((s1 == NULL) || (s2 == NULL))
        return (NULL);
/*
    Copy the strings so we can upper case them
 */    s = strdup (s1));
    if (s == NULL)
        return (NULL);
    t = strdup (s2);
    if (t == NULL)
        {
        free (s);
        return (NULL);
        }
    strupr (s);
    strupr (t);
/
    Call strstr on the strings. If not NULL, take the
    difference between s and u and apply it to s1. Then
    set u to s1 for the return.
 */
    if ((u = strstr (s, t)) != NULL)
        u = s1 + (u - s);
    free (s);
    free (t);
    return (u);
}
```

Notice that I used the *free()* function from C instead of the C++ operator *delete*. *strdup()* creates the duplicate strings using *malloc()*, so you must use *free()*. This is primarily for portability. Most UNIX systems have a C compiler; not all have a C++ compiler.

264. *Understanding the sizeof Operator*

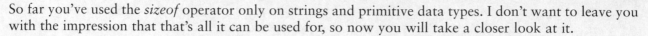

So far you've used the *sizeof* operator only on strings and primitive data types. I don't want to leave you with the impression that that's all it can be used for, so now you will take a closer look at it.

This is a handy operator to have around. Virtually any expression or identifier you use may be used as the object of the *sizeof* operator. This means, for example, that you don't have to know the size of a structure to read and write blocks from and to files. In fact, simply adding up the sizes of individual elements in a structure won't necessarily give you the proper size. An optimizing compiler adjusts the position of members on convenient memory boundaries for efficiency. Try the following structure definition and program to print the size of the structure:

```
#include <stdio.h>

struct ACCOUNT
{
    long    Number;
    char    Name[33];
    char    Address[16];
    char    City[13];
    char    State[3];
    char    Zip[6];
    char    ZipPlus[5];
};

int main ()
{
    printf ("sizeof (ACCOUNT) = %d\n", sizeof (ACCOUNT));
}
```

When you run the program, you see that the structure size is 80, which is what you would get by adding up the sizes of all the members. Now change the *Name* field so that it is 34 instead of 33. Recompile and run the program. The tally of the individual members is now 81, but instead, the actual size of the structure jumps to 84. The compiler has optimized the arrangement of the members to make it more efficient. You don't know where this adjustment took place, but the compiler keeps track of the relative positions of all the members.

Always use the *sizeof* operator to get the size of any object. You may be a whiz at addition, but the compiler is a real whiz at memory management.

265. *Using sizeof to Determine the Available Length for a String*

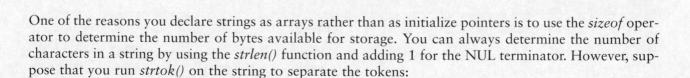

One of the reasons you declare strings as arrays rather than as initialize pointers is to use the *sizeof* operator to determine the number of bytes available for storage. You can always determine the number of characters in a string by using the *strlen()* function and adding 1 for the NUL terminator. However, suppose that you run *strtok()* on the string to separate the tokens:

```
char str[] = "accountno,name2,address1,city,"
             "state,zip,phone1,phone2";
char *s = str;
//
    printf ("strlen (str) = %d\n", strlen (str));
    printf ("sizeof (str) = %d\n", sizeof (str));
    s = strtok (str, ",");
    if (s == NULL)
        return;
    printf ("Components are:\n");
    do
    {
        printf ("\t%s\n", s);
    } while ((s = strtok (NULL, ",")) != NULL);
    printf ("strlen (str) = %d\n", strlen (str));
    printf ("sizeof (str) = %d\n", sizeof (str));
```

Using *strlen()*, you see that the length of the string first is 56. Adding 1 for the NUL terminator gives you 57, the same length shown by *sizeof*. At the end of the snippet, however, *strlen()* shows you a length of only 9, but the return from *sizeof* remains unchanged.

Had I declared this string as *char *str* instead of *char str[]*, the *sizeof* operator in both cases would have returned 4, the size of a *char* pointer in Visual C++. Syntactically, there's little difference in the declarations, but practically, if you want to reuse the string's storage space, you must be able to determine its actual size.

266. *Using* sizeof *to Determine the Number of Strings in an Array*

Often, you need to use arrays of strings to manipulate them in a loop. In this case, you have no choice. When you declare an array of strings, you are creating an array of string pointers, and the actual value of the strings, the characters within them, is stored elsewhere in memory.

You declare an array of string pointers by writing the definition with the pointer operator in front of the identifier and the array operator at the end of the identifier. You don't have to specify the number of array elements if you are initializing the array at the same time, which usually is the case.

Consider the following code to initialize the header bar on a list control:

```
LV_COLUMN    lc;
CListCtrl&   cc = GetListCtrl();
char         *Titles[] = {"Account", "Account Name", "City",
                          "State", "Zip Code", "Ad Rep",
                          "Ad Type", "Ad Class"};
int   Widths[] = {90, 200, 90, 50, 80, 80, 50, 50};

    FreeItemMemory ();
    as.m_strSort = "AccountNumber ASC";
    as.m_strFilter.Empty();

    for (int x = 0; x < 8; ++x)
    {
        lc.mask = LVCF_FMT | LVCF_TEXT | LVCF_WIDTH |
```

```
                LVCF_SUBITEM;
        lc.fmt = LVCFMT_LEFT;
        lc.pszText = Titles[x];
        lc.cx = Widths[x];
        lc.iSubItem = x;
        cc.InsertColumn (x, &lc);
    }
```

When you finish a program and everything is working, you like to think of it as a "done deal." You don't want to fix it if it isn't broken. In reality, however, programs are dynamic and are constantly changing to reflect the company's business model and needs. Suppose that the boss comes to you and says, "We dropped the *Ad Type* from the database, and we don't want to show it in the list control anymore." You dutifully remove the string from the array, but your code still is initializing the header with eight subitems. Worse, somewhere later in the function you are filling the list control with "8" data items. Now you have to search through the code and change these to "7."

There's no requirement that a *#define* be placed at the top of a program file. Actually, you may use the directive anywhere in your program, so you use the *sizeof* operator to determine the actual number of strings in the array:

```
#define   TITLES   (sizeof(Titles)/sizeof(char *))
```

Now you have a constant identifier, *TITLES*, that calculates the size of the array dynamically. You change your *for* loop to use the macro definition:

```
for (int x = 0; x < TITLES; ++x)
```

Now, just the simple act of removing the string adjusts the rest of the program. The boss is happy because you were able to do it so quickly, and he gives you a healthy raise.

267. Accessing Individual Characters in a String

You've seen some benefits of declaring a string as an array rather than as a pointer. However, don't discount the benefits of character pointers. By far, the fastest way to access elements in any array—whether it's a string, an array of numerical items, or an array of classes or structures—is through pointers.

By accessing an array using subscripting, you are giving the compiler an expression it has to evaluate before accessing the element itself. Using a pointer, it has direct access to the element without any further evaluation.

With the tools at hand now, I would be hard pressed to show you any quantitative results on Windows. Also, a good optimizing compiler such as Visual C++ can handle indexing with ease. I can, however, give you a quick sample of what the difference is. Enter the following code and name it *ttest.cpp*:

```
#include   <stdio.h>
#include   <time.h>

void   TimeTestIndex();
void   TimeTestPointer();

int main()
{
time_t tStart, tEnd;
long y;
```

```
    time (&tStart);
    for (y = 0; y < 10000000; ++y)
        TimeTestIndex();
    time (&tEnd);
    printf ("Time elapsed = %ld\n", tEnd - tStart);

    time (&tStart);
    for (y = 0; y < 10000000; ++y)
        TimeTestPointer();
    time (&tEnd);
    printf ("Time elapsed = %ld\n", tEnd - tStart);
    return (0);
}

void TimeTestIndex()
{
char str1[] = "The quick red fox jumps over the "
              "lazy dog's back. RY Testing";
char str2[124];
int    i = 0;
int    j = sizeof (str1);

    do
        {
        str2[i] = str1[i];
        } while (i++ < j);
}

void TimeTestPointer()
{
char str1[] = "The quick red fox jumps over the "
              "lazy dog's back. RY Testing";
char str2[124];
char *pstr1 = str1;
char *pstr2 = str2;

    do
        {
        *pstr2++ = *pstr1++;
        } while (*pstr1);
}
```

Run on a Windows NT machine with two 400MHz processors, the indexing took 25 seconds to complete, and the pointer copy took only 18 seconds, about a third faster. (For grins, on the same machine compiled for 16-bit code by the Borland 5.0 C++ compiler, the times turned in at 13 and 9 seconds, respectively—nearly twice as fast as the Visual C++ code!)

Certainly, some of that is the cost of indexing, and incrementing the index variable, but that's part of the cost of using the indexing method.

If your program handles only an occasional string, it probably doesn't make any difference. For a character-intensive program, however, the pointer method comes out far ahead. Fortunately, by declaring the array and then declaring a separate pointer to it, you can have it both ways at the expense of a little more code space.

268. *Dynamically Allocating Strings*

With C++, you have two methods of dynamically allocating memory (in Windows, there also is a *GlobalAlloc()* function, but that isn't part of the language). You've already seen the *new* and *delete* operators that are available only in C++. Standard C originally used functions to allocate and deallocate memory, and they still are available in C++.

The basic C function for allocating memory from the heap is *malloc()*. For compatibility, this function is used by the standard library functions that allocate memory. This function returns a *void* pointer and takes as its only argument the number of bytes you want to allocate. The number may be the result of an integer expression, such as the value returned by the *sizeof* operator. To use these functions, you must include either *malloc.h* or *stdlib.h* in your program.

Because it returns a void pointer, you must cast it to the specific data type you want. *malloc()* only sets aside memory; it doesn't type it. If the allocation fails, a *NULL* pointer is returned. I've been a little lax so far for the sake of brevity, but with *malloc()* and the C++ *new* operator, always test for a *NULL* return before performing any operation using the pointer.

Like the *new* operator, you need to release the memory before the pointer variable you used to capture the return value goes out of scope. DO NOT use the *delete* operator to release memory allocated by *malloc()*. Always use the *free()* function, which takes the pointer as its argument. The following example shows how to use *malloc()* and *free()*:

```
#include    <stdio.h>
#include    <stdlib.h>    /* Or malloc.h */

int main ()
{
    char str1[] = "This here's a string";
    char *str2 = (char *) malloc (sizeof (str1));
    if (str2 == NULL)
        return (-1);
    strcpy (str2, str1);
    free (str2);
    return (0);
}
```

Notice that you had to cast *malloc()* to a *char* pointer using *(char *)*. Unlike *new*, *malloc()* does not do an automatic cast. If you want to use the memory for a numerical array, you have to use *(int *)*, *(double *)*, and so on, to get the right pointer.

You shouldn't try to use *free()* with a *NULL* pointer. Under the new C, as with the C++ *delete* operator, the *NULL* argument causes the function to return without doing anything, so you won't cause any damage. However, if your code is ever compiled with a pre-ANSI version of C, it could cause some problems.

Another C function, *calloc()*, is used to allocate space for arrays and initialize the memory to 0 in the same operation. *calloc()* takes two arguments: the number of array elements and the size of each element. Either or both may be an expression, and the return value is a *void* pointer to the memory block or a *NULL* on error.

The *realloc()* function is used to expand or contract a previously allocated memory block. The reallocated block may be moved in memory, and the return value is a pointer to its location. If the block is moved, the original block is copied to the new location. It takes as arguments a pointer to the original block of memory and the new size in bytes and returns a void pointer or *NULL* if no reallocation was done. If the reallocation was unsuccessful, the original block is left unchanged.

If their parameters are 0, both *malloc()* and *calloc()* still return pointers to memory blocks on success. *realloc()*, however, returns a *NULL* to indicate that no reallocation was performed. When calling *realloc()*, always save the pointer to the original memory block; if *realloc()* is *NULL*, you will still need the original block to call *free()*.

The following code shows how you can use *realloc()* to increase the length of a string:

```
#include    <stdio.h>
#include    <stdlib.h>      /* Or malloc.h */
#include    <string.h>


int main ()
{
char str1[] = "This here's a string";
    char str2[] = " and another string appended";
    char *str3;
    char *str4=(char *)calloc(sizeof (str1), sizeof(char));
    if (str4 == NULL)
        {
        fprintf (stderr, "Memory allocation failed\n");
        return (-1);
        }
    strcpy (str4, str1);
    str3=(char *)realloc(str4,sizeof(str1) + strlen(str2));
    if (str3 == NULL)
    {
        printf ("No reallocation was done\n");
        str3 = str4;
    }
    else
        {
        strcat (str3, str2);
        }
    printf ("string = \"%s\"\n", str3);
    free (str3);
    return (0);
}
```

In this example, you use a different pointer to receive the return from *realloc()*. If the call does not reallocate any memory, you use the old pointer to the block. If it succeeds, you use the new pointer and append the second string to the first, giving you a concatenated string. Notice that I used *sizeof(str1) + strlen(str2)* as the expression to get the size for the reallocated block. You need only one NUL terminator, which is given to you with the *sizeof* operator. If I had used *sizeof(str2)*, I would have gained an extra byte in the reallocation. There's nothing wrong with that, but by keeping your allocation requests as small as possible, you improve your chance of success.

269. *An Example: Reversing the Characters in a String*

Now that you've learned about dynamic memory allocation and you know that string operations using pointers are faster than the indexing method, take another look at the string-reversing program to see how you can use these notions:

```
/*
    elba1.cpp - Reverse the characters in a string using
    pointers and dynamically allocated memory.
*/

#include    <stdio.h>
#include    <string.h>

main ()
{
char    pszElba[] = "Able was I ere I saw Elba";
char    *pszAble = new char [sizeof(pszElba)];
char    *s1, *s2;

    if (pszAble == NULL)
        {
        fprintf (stderr, "Memory allocation error\n");
        return (-1);
        }
    memset (pszAble, '\Ø', sizeof (pszElba));
    s1 = pszElba + strlen (pszElba) - 1;
    s2 = pszAble;
    printf ("%s\n", pszElba);
    while (s1 >= pszElba)
        {
        *s2++ = *s1--;
        }
    strcpy (pszElba, pszAble);
    delete [] pszAble;
    printf ("%s\n", pszElba);
    return (Ø);
}
```

Using pointers and a dynamically allocated string, you don't have to save the character in between trans-positions. You simply store it in the other string. When you're done, you copy the reverse string into the original and delete your temporary string.

270. *Understanding Functions*

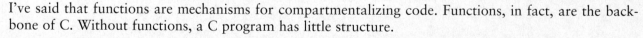

I've said that functions are mechanisms for compartmentalizing code. Functions, in fact, are the backbone of C. Without functions, a C program has little structure.

You can write code outside a function. So long as it is in the form of a declaration, the code outside a function is evaluated before the program starts, and it can act on previously declared variables and even call functions. There's not much structure in it, however, and the sequence of evaluation will depend on how you write declarations.

There's only one required function in C and C++, the *main()* function. It has been said that the program enters through *main()*, but that's only because we are conditioned to think linearly. The program *will* include *main()*, but only because Brian Kernighan and Dennis Ritchie said so when they defined the language. The program doesn't even have to execute *main()*. You could actually write a program with dozens or hundreds of functions and set it up so that *main()* is the last function executed, or you could call a function named *exit()* before the program even gets to *main()*. Examine the following program. It's valid C++ code. Although it's not good code, maybe it will help you to understand how C evaluates variables and functions.

```
/*
    NoMain.cpp. A short program to demonstrate an
                alternate starting point for a program.
 */
#include    <stdio.h>

int PrintSomething();
int x = PrintSomething ();

int main()
{
    printf ("x = %d\n", x);
    return (x);
}
int PrintSomething()
{
    printf ("Contrary to common belief, our program\n");
    printf ("is actually beginning in this function.\n");
    return (25);
}
```

You could call other functions from within your starting function and, in fact, let it perform everything you need before even releasing the code to *main()*. I'm not sure what good this knowledge is, nor have I found a practical application for it, but the idea is to get you thinking outside the textbooks and the lines of the ordinary. If we all wrote programs according to the textbooks, we all would write the same program, and the world really doesn't need another million *NotePad.exe*s. Would Henry David Thoreau have written *Walden* had he simply followed in Ralph Waldo Emerson's footsteps? Would Author Dickens have written his masterful but wordy opening to *A Tale of Two Cities* had he been concerned with the Fog Index?

Not that I've thoroughly digressed, my point is that the function call is what started things happening in this program, even though it was outside the expected operation of the program. By building on this one function and adding more functions, you build a program.

In an ideal world, you try to keep your functions as short as possible. That makes it easier for you to reuse them as building blocks for your program.

271. *Understanding Function Declarations in C and C++*

A function *declaration* puts the C++ compiler on notice that you have an idea for a function and this is how you would use it. It doesn't commit you to writing the function, but you can't call it until you do write it. It's like declaring a variable; you don't *have* to use a variable, but you can't use it until it is declared. Declaring a function and not giving it a body of code is not an error in C++; calling a function without a body of code is an error.

You write programs to solve problems or accomplish a task at hand. Going into a project, you often have no idea how you will reach the goal. Just sitting down and thinking through the program flow and then declaring a sequence of functions with descriptive names helps you to organize the project. It's like writing the outline for a term paper before you write the paper.

You declare a function by writing its return data type followed by the name of the function. The name should be descriptive and preferably short, but if you need to be wordy in your naming convention, there's nothing stopping you. Just don't ask me to go over it. Function names are case sensitive. Changing the case of only one character in the name makes it a different name. There is a library function named *strtok()*, but you could write a function named *Strtok()* or even one named *strtoK()*. They don't have to be related or use the same return type or the same variable types, as in the following set of declarations:

```
_CRTIMP char * __cdecl strtok(char *, const char *);
int *Strtok (double, int);
float strtoK (void);
```

The compiler sees all these as declarations of different functions. It has an orderly method of setting aside the names and never gets confused, but you probably would if you habitually declared functions this way.

Following the name, you type an opening parenthesis. That's what distinguishes a function call from an ordinary variable declaration. The set of parentheses after the name tells the compiler that this is a function and it isn't necessary to evaluate it. After the opening parenthesis, you write the data types of the arguments you will use when calling the function. You only need the data types; naming the variables is unnecessary and, in fact, will be ignored by the compiler. When you write the code for the function, you can give the arguments different names as long as they are of the same type and in the same order as the declaration. The C language doesn't require you even to include the data types in a declaration, but C++ does.

Finally, you end your declaration with a closing parenthesis and a semicolon. The semicolon notifies the compiler that this is a declaration only and that nothing has to be done with it now. Without the semicolon, the compiler would look for a compound statement that forms the body of the function, and it would become a function *definition*.

Function declarations are subject to the same scope constraints as variables. They may be declared inside or outside function definitions. If declared within a function, its declaration is available to that function only; if you declare it in a block, you may use it only in that block. You can't use a function until it has been declared or defined.

Declarations give the compiler a forward resolution on function names. If you define the body of the function first, you don't have to declare it because the name already has been resolved. If you're not careful, you can get into a round-robin function declaration/definition cycle. This function calls an earlier function, so you don't have to declare it, but it calls a later one, which must be declared. Soon, you're the one going in circles. It never causes any problems to declare functions, and it's a good idea to do so at the top of your source file or in a separate header file.

272. *Understanding Function Definitions*

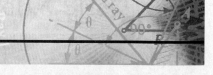

When someone throws a new word out, you have to know what it means before it is of any use to you. The same is true of functions. You can declare a new function, but until you give it a definition, you can't use it.

The process of defining a function involves giving it a body of code. All functions take a compound statement as their definition. It can be an empty compound statement, consisting only of opening and closing braces, but it must be a compound statement.

You define a function by writing it the same as you would for a declaration, except that you omit the semicolon at the end. Instead, you enter an opening brace, usually on the beginning of the next line. Except for lines containing preprocessor directives, line enders are not required in C or C++. They are for your reading convenience only, so you use them to make the code more readable and place the opening brace at the beginning of the line after the function name.

Next you write the statements you want performed when the function is called. Except for functions of type *void*, the very minimum a function may contain is a *return* statement containing the value to be returned as a result of the function call. Void functions don't return values, so the *return* statement is implied. If a function contains no statements, it is an *empty* function. Empty functions are valid definitions and may be required in some cases, such as class constructors and destructors.

Finish the definition with a closing brace. Again for readability, you normally place the brace at the beginning of the line and on a line by itself. Any code or variable declarations written after the closing brace are in global scope, even if they are on the same line as the closing brace. A semicolon after the brace is not required but causes no harm if you include it. Programmers normally omit it.

After you have declared your functions, the order in which you define them makes no difference. They must be defined in global space, however, and defined separately. A function defined within the body of another function, such as the following, is a *local* function definition and is not allowed in C or C++:

```
int main()            // Defines main()
{
int Hey(int y)        // Local function definition is
{                     // illegal in C and C++
    y = 0;
    return (y)
}
    printf ("x = %d\n", x);
    return (x);
};
```

You may arrange the functions alphabetically or by their purpose. Ordinarily, you place a comment at the top of your source file to explain the purpose of the file. Many programmers like to list the functions in the file and their purpose in this comment area. At the very least, you should include a comment just before the definition, describing how the arguments are used and the purpose of the function.

273. *Understanding Function Prototypes*

The idea of prototyping something is to build a working model of the object being prototyped. In that sense, the word "prototype" is misapplied in the C and C++ languages, but then, many words are misused in the programming world. In programming, to prototype a function is to create a "template" of it. However, the word "template" is used differently in C++, so we call this practice "function prototyping." (Strangely, in C++, what you call "templates" are more like prototypes.)

When you prototype a function, you give the compiler a pattern of the function, which it uses to compare calls to the function and the function definition itself. The pattern declares the return type, the name, and the data types of the arguments. If you think that this sounds a lot like a function declaration, you are correct. Many writers scrupulously avoid the word "prototype" and stick with "declaration" altogether, but you will hear the process described using either word or both words at some time.

When you call a function, the C++ compiler compares the call against the patterns it has in memory and generates an "undeclared identifier" error if none of them match. The return type is not considered in the comparison, and it isn't an error to assign the return value of a double function to an integer variable. Some compilers issue a warning that truncation may occur.

The name and the sequence and type of arguments, however, must match exactly. In C++, the same name for more than one function, but using a different argument type sequence, is legal and is called "overloading."

274. Declaring and Defining Functions That Return a Value

Every function has a return type, which is not to say that every function must return a value. A function declared or defined as *void* is not permitted to return a value, and the C++ compiler will generate an error if you try it. C compilers are more forgiving; they ignore the return statement and the return value.

If a function is not given a return type, a type of *int* is assumed. If you later define it using another return type, the compiler will gripe that the "overloaded function differs only by return type." If you should get that error, check your function declaration. It's probably due to mismatched return types.

Declare a function as described in Tip 271, "Understanding Function Declarations in C and C++," and Tip 273, "Understanding Function Prototypes." Elsewhere in your program, write the body of code using the same syntax as the declaration to name it. Write the code within a set of braces. At any point in the code, you may use the *return* statement followed by an expression or a variable of that data type. It isn't necessary to enclose the return expression or variable in parentheses, and there doesn't seem to be any consensus on whether to use them as standard practice. Personally, I prefer the parentheses because they visually isolate the return expression.

Functions may return pointers, and they may return references. In the case of references, be careful not to misunderstand the data type. What is being returned is an *address*, but you use it as though it were the actual value being returned; the compiler takes care of the details for you. If, however, you return a reference to a variable that was local to the function being called, you will get whatever is in the address pointed to by the reference at the time of the assignment. More likely than not, the value is going to be invalid. The local variable was destroyed when the function ended.

Usually, the compiler will give you a warning when you return a reference to a local variable, but it won't stop your program from compiling. The following program is fairly trivial, but it shows you the warning message:

```
#include    <stdio.h>

int& RefTest(void);   // Declare function

int main()
{
    int a = RefTest();  // Call function
    printf ("a = %d\n", a);
    return (0);
}

int& RefTest ()
{
    int x = 4;
    return (x);        // Return reference to local x
}
```

When you compile this program, you are warned about "returning address of local variable or temporary." When you run it, it may or may not work. The result is unreliable. In some instances, I did get the correct result, and other times I got something else.

In this case, of course, I should have just returned the value of the variable, avoiding any complications. References are most useful when returning references to larger objects such as classes or structures.

275. *Declaring and Defining Functions That Use Arguments*

When you declare a function in C, you are giving the compiler a forward reference for the name of the function. In C++, however, you also are giving the compiler a pattern to compare calls to the function to make sure that the arguments are of the correct data type and in the correct order. You will see what happens if the patterns don't match, when you get to function overloading in Tip 286, "Understanding Function Overloading."

So far I've used the words "parameter" and "argument" almost interchangeably. A *parameter* is a value that might be assigned to a variable or used in some other operation. An *argument* is a variable that might be modified independently of its original or current value. You may pass a parameter in a function call. However, when the called function receives it, it is always an argument, and the function is free to modify it unless you declare it using the *const* modifier. You can't declare a function to use a value directly in its argument list.

A function that uses arguments when called is declared with an *argument list* inside the parentheses of its declaration. If the function takes no arguments, you may write the word "void" as its argument to make that clear, but its use is optional.

In declaring a function with an argument list, you must declare the data types of the arguments in the order in which they will be passed. The declaration may contain optional identifiers for arguments, but the identifier names are not binding and are discarded by the compiler. All it's interested in are the data types. The following two declarations are identical to the compiler:

```
int FunctionOne (int& x, char c, struct tm *TheTime);
int FunctionOne (int &, char, struct tm *);
```

Unlike variables, declaring identical functions does not create an error. The reason for this is that you can *overload* functions (use more than one function with the same name), but you can't overload variables. Like variables, you are not committed to using the function, and if you make no calls to a declared function, you don't have to write a definition for it.

When you define a function, you must use the same syntax and the same data types in the same order. In the definition, identifiers for the arguments, again, are optional unless you plan on using them in the function, which usually is the case. To define your *FunctionOne()*, you use the same syntax but don't follow it with a semicolon. Instead, you give the function a body that contains zero or more statements within braces. If the function returns a value, you must have a return statement at the end:

```
int FunctionOne (int &, char, struct tm *)
{
    return (0);
}
```

The preceding definition is legal because you didn't use any of the arguments in your functions. That makes them perfectly useless, of course, so you want to define it using identifiers for the arguments:

```
int FunctionOne (int &hour, char ch, struct tm *TheTime)
{
    time_t now = time(NULL);
    TheTime = localtime(&now);
    hour = TheTime->tm_hour;
    if (hour < 12)
        ch = 'A';
    else
        ch = 'P';
    return (0);
}
```

Often, in developing a program you find that you declared a function with a certain argument list, but you no longer need one or more of the arguments in your function. Each time you compile the program, you get warnings about an argument never being used. You have many calls to the function spread throughout the program, and finding and changing all of them might take more time than you want. Of course, you always want to see no errors and no warnings when you compile your programs, so you may omit the identifier of any unused arguments:

```
int FunctionOne (int &hour, char, struct tm *TheTime)
{
    time_t now = time(NULL);
    TheTime = localtime(&now);
    hour = TheTime->tm_hour;
    return (0);
}
```

Here you no longer use the second argument, so you simply removed the *ch* identifier and you stop getting the warnings from the compiler.

If the pattern doesn't match, the compiler will look for another function by that name.

276. *Understanding Default Values for Arguments*

Many times, you want to assume a certain value for an argument, but each time you call the function, you have to enter a parameter for the call to give it that value. In this case, you may give one or more of the parameter's default values and then omit them from the function call itself. The compiler will include the defaults in the statement making the function call.

To use default values, simply assign them to the identifiers at the time the function is declared or defined.

You may assign default values in the declaration or the definition of a function, but not both, even if you use the same default values—and there are some gotcha's.

First, if you put the default values in the definition rather than in the declaration, you must define the function before you call it with default values. Remember that the declaration is a forward resolution device used by the compiler to identify functions before they are defined. If the function is defined toward the bottom of the source file, the compiler doesn't know about default variables until it gets to that point. If you try to call it using defaults before the definition, the compiler will tell you that you have the wrong number of arguments in the call. Default arguments usually are placed in the declaration for this reason.

Second, you can't assign a value to a reference argument. You may assign a variable as the default for a reference argument, but it must be one that has already been declared. This means that it must be in global scope. In the following two declarations, the first is an error, but the second is acceptable:

```
int x = 4;     // Declare in global scope
int FunctionOne (int &intvar = 4);
int FunctionOne (int &intvar = x);
```

You may, however, use a *static* member of a class or structure, using the scope resolution operator (::) before an instance of the object has been declared. Remember that static members are created when they are declared, so the reference has an object. The following is an example:

```
struct INTS
{
    static int    x;
    int     y;
    int     z;
};
int FunctionTwo (int &intvar = INTS::x);
```

If an instance of a class or structure already has been declared, you may use a member of it using the "member of" operator, as in the following:

```
struct INTS
{
    int    x;
    int    y;
    int    z;
};
INTS    MyInts;
int FunctionTwo (int &intvar = MyInts.x);
```

Third, when you assign a default value to an argument, all the arguments that follow it in the list must have default parameters. If it were otherwise, the compiler would have no way of knowing whether an argument had been left out in a call. In the following two declarations, the third argument is assigned a default parameter, but not the fourth, so the compiler will complain about "missing default parameter for parameter 4." In the second line, you include a default for the fourth argument, and all is well with the compiler:

```
int FunctionTwo (int count, int x, int y = 0, int z);
int FunctionTwo (int count, int x, int y = 0, int z = 10);
```

Fourth, when you call a function that uses default parameters and you assign a parameter to an argument with a default value, all the arguments *to the left* in the function call must have parameters. This is only reasonable. Let's declare another function:

```
int FunctionThree (int x = 0, int y = 0, int z = 0);
```

Later in your code, you want to call *FunctionThree()* and assign *y* a value of, say, 10:

```
int a = FunctionThree(10);
```

To the compiler, you are assigning the first argument, *x*, the value of 10, and the second and third will be given default values. To put the parameter into the correct position, you must use a placeholder in your call:

```
int a = FunctionThree(0, 10);
```

Now the first argument is assigned the value 0, and *y* gets the value 10, which is what you wanted.

277. Understanding Inline Functions

A certain amount of overhead code is involved in calling a function and returning from it. Any parameters, along with the return address in the calling function, must be pushed onto the stack, and the CPU's instruction pointer is changed to point to the beginning of the called function.

When the function returns, the return address has to be retrieved and the stack register changed to destroy the variables used in the call.

For very short functions, the time, code, and memory involved may be greater than performing the operation directly in the calling functions. We're programmers, though, and we really like functions. They isolate code and objects for us, and they perform the same operations repeatedly without our having to retype them, not to mention the fact that we can reuse them in other functions. We are loath to give up a function call just to save a few bytes of memory or a few instruction cycles.

Fortunately, in C++ you can have it both ways by modifying your function declaration with the *inline* keyword. This keyword instructs the compiler to perform a cost/benefit analysis of the code and to replace the call with the actual function code if it will save enough time or memory. If it fails the analysis, the function is compiled and linked as a regular function, but the compiler won't tell you about it. In computer jargon, you give the word verb qualities and speak of this process as *inlining*. Declare a function inline by adding the modifier to its declaration line, as in the following:

```
inline int FunctionTwo (int x, int y, int z);
```

At times, the compiler will flatly refuse to inline a function (but you're never told about it during the compilation). It won't place a recursive function inline (in Visual C++, you have a compiler option you can set to allow inline expansion of recursive functions to a certain depth), nor will it inline a function referenced by a pointer. Functions that use a variable argument list also are rejected. Programs compiled with the debug flag automatically have inlining turned off.

In Visual C++, you have another keyword, *__forceinline*, that you can use to replace the *inline* modifier. This instructs the compiler to bypass the usual ROI analysis (*Return on Investment*—as a programmer, you will hear that acronym frequently) and place the code inline anyway. Still, there are times a program will refuse to inline a function, but with this keyword, you will be told about it through a compiler warning.

278. Understanding Call by Reference Versus Call by Value

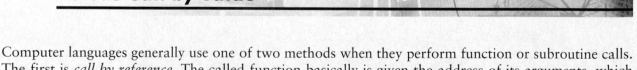

Computer languages generally use one of two methods when they perform function or subroutine calls. The first is *call by reference*. The called function basically is given the address of its arguments, which are then given the title *reference parameters*. This is the method used by most application languages, such as COBOL or FORTRAN.

The second method is *call by value*, in which the actual value of a parameter is passed to the called function. In this case, the arguments are called simply *parameters*. Systems-level and low-level languages such as C and C++ use this method of calling functions.

Both methods have their advantages and disadvantages, and it is possible to mix the two methods in a language. In C++, the default calling method is by value, but provision is made to use reference variables in a function call.

279. Advantages and Disadvantages of Reference Calling Versus Value Calling

When calling a function by reference, a called function is told where in memory the value of a variable is located. When the function modifies an argument, it modifies the variable itself, and the calling function may use the new value.

To its advantage, calling by reference allows the called function to modify more than one variable. A function or subroutine can have only one return value. If the caller needs to calculate new values for more than one variable, the call by reference simplifies the overhead involved.

On the other hand, calling by reference makes it difficult to encapsulate data. As you read through a program, that a variable might have been modified by a subroutine call is not immediately obvious without examining the subroutine itself.

Call by reference systems tend to use stack space more efficiently. Because there's only one instance of a variable, it usually is placed in a data segment of memory, and the subroutines manipulate it by address. There's no need to push temporary values on the stack because the language compiler already knows where the variable is located.

Such behavior is despicable to low-level language users and to us as C and C++ programmers. We believe in keeping things compact and independent, and we don't want a called function willy-nilly changing a value we've set. We might as well be using BASIC, right?

Using call by value, as in C and C++, the value of a variable is used as the parameter. The function is free to bounce the value around and change it to whatever suits its fancy, but it can never get back to the original variable and modify it. This keeps your data encapsulated, and only the enclosing function can modify its own variables. You're cozy inside while the blizzard rages all around.

This does pose some problems. Suppose that you want to get the x and y coordinates of a point by calling a function. You need to modify two variables, but you have only one return value available to you. You can get around this by packing the two values in the single return, placing the x value in the upper bits and the y in the lower bits. (This used to be common practice in the 16-bit days of PCs, and you will still see the macros HIWORD and LOWORD used a lot.) This works for smaller values, but eventually you are going to run into values that are too large to pack.

To get around this, you can pass argument *pointers* to the original variables and let the called function alter them by dereferencing the pointers. This is similar to passing a parameter by reference, but you have to write code specifically intended to dereference the pointers.

In C++, you also have the reference operator, which allows you to pass a variable as a reference parameter and modify it directly without any specific dereferencing instructions.

280. Understanding Function Calls in C/C++

Because you pass parameters by value in C and C++, you need some way to separate the variable from its actual value. You could duplicate the variable in your data segment, but as function calls get deeper, you would wind up with a fragmented data area, and parts of it might become unusable.

What you need is some way to progressively create new variables to give the functions as they are called and then remove them in the reverse order—a last-in, first-out data structure. That's how the program stack works. The stack is a segment of memory that is set aside for use by the CPU to save return addresses when functions or subroutines are called. Each time a value is added to the stack, a register called the *stack pointer* is adjusted so that the next addition to the stack is placed in a different memory location. When something is removed from the stack, the register is adjusted in the opposite direction. The stack pointer allows you to access not only the last item placed on the stack but also additional items by using an offset from the register value.

Virtually all CPUs contain at least two instructions to enable programmers to use the stack for purposes other than return addresses. These are the PUSH instruction and the POP instruction. The PUSH instruction places a register or memory value onto the stack and adjusts the stack pointer. The POP instruction reads an item from the stack and places it into a register or memory location, adjusting the stack pointer in the reverse direction.

C and C++ use the stack almost to the point of its being an affliction. Everything that isn't nailed down gets put on the stack. I don't mean to make it sound like a bad thing, because it's a very efficient use of resources. The language enlists the help of the CPU in making room for objects and then cleaning up after itself.

When your program calls a function, the parameters to the called function are placed on the stack along with the return address, the point in the code where the program flow will resume when the called function returns. Then all the variables that are local to the called function are put onto the stack. If you have a block within the function that declares local variables, they are pushed onto the stack. When you call another function from within the called function, its parameters and a new return address, along with its local variables, are put on the stack.

When a function finishes, the return expression, if any, is evaluated and the result placed in another CPU register, called the *Accumulator*. (I'm generalizing here; a particular compiler could use another register or a memory location if its creator so desires. The Accumulator usually is used because that's where Assembly routines place and usually expect to find C++ return values.) The code returns to the calling point, the stack pointer is readjusted, and *>POOF<*! The local variables, the arguments, all residue of the called function except the return value are gone. The caller retrieves the return value from the Accumulator and goes on its way.

281. *Understanding the Scope of a Function*

Functions take on a scope depending on where they are declared or defined. To understand the scope of a function, you must look at the various modules that make up a C/C++ program.

Programs are rarely built with just one source file. Usually, multiple source files are used, and the functions within them perform related operations. Perhaps one source file defines all the functions that are members of a single class. Another may contain file-related operations.

A function is always defined in global scope and is available in the source file after the point of definition. It also may be declared in global scope and may be used at any point in the source file after the declaration point. If it isn't subsequently defined in the same module or even in another, the linker will issue an error about an "unresolved external symbol."

Among all the modules in your program, you cannot declare duplicate functions with the same return type. *Duplicate* functions have the same name and same sequence and type of parameters. Within the *same* module, you cannot have identical functions if they differ only by return type. In different modules, however, you may have identical functions that differ only in return type, and the linker will process them as different functions. In this case, from within a module, you can only declare the function that is defined in the same module.

A function also may be declared within a function (but it can't be *defined* within a function) or a block of code. In this case, its declaration is valid only for the scope of the function or block. To use it elsewhere, it must be redeclared.

If you've followed me so far, maybe I haven't done a good enough job of confusing the issue. Let's create a couple of source files. The first you will name *first.cpp*, and you enter the following code:

```
/*
    first.cpp. A test of function scope
             use with second.cpp
 */
#include  <stdio.h>

int main ()
{
void Stuff ();
    Stuff ();
    {
    int Stuff ();
       Stuff ();
    }
    return (Ø);
}
void Stuff ()
{
    printf ("In first module\n");
}
```

Now create another source file, call it *second.cpp*, and enter the following code:

```
/*
    second.cpp. A test of function scope
             use with first.cpp
 */
#include    <stdio.h>
int Stuff ()
{
    printf ("In second module\n");
             return (Ø);
}
```

Now compile the source files together using *cl first.cpp second.cpp*. The resulting executable will be named *first.exe*. Run it and you will see that the first call to *Stuff()* was to the function in the first module, and the second call was to the *Stuff()* function in the second module. Because the declarations had different scope, they didn't conflict with each other.

You can limit a function's scope to the current source file, or code module, by declaring or defining it as *static*. It doesn't matter whether you put the *static* modifier on the declaration, the definition, or both; its scope is still limited to the one module. Each module can have identical functions with the same return type and not conflict with the others.

Function scope can be a difficult topic for beginners. If you are thoroughly confused, do like the rest of us: Make sure that your function definitions are unique, even in different modules.

282. *Using Pointers in a Function Call*

When you must modify a variable that is outside the scope of a function, you pass the function a pointer to the variable. A *pointer* is an ordinary parameter that represents a special value. It contains the memory address of another object. Because it's a variable independent of the original variable, it can be in the scope of a function while the original variable is not. By knowing the address of a variable, you can modify it indirectly.

The function's argument list must contain a variable that is a pointer to the data type of the original variable. You designate the pointer using an asterisk before the parameter name. If you want to send an *int* pointer to a function, you declare it like the following:

```
void Function (int *pInt);
```

Programmers often use the lowercase "p" in front of a pointer variable to designate it as such, but it isn't required.

When you call the function, you can either pass it another pointer variable or take the address of the original variable in the function call itself. To take the address, use the ampersand in front of the variable's name in the function call. The following snippet shows two calls to a function that pass an address:

```
void Function (int *pVar);   // Declare the function
int x = 3;                   // Declare and set the variable
int *px = &x;                // Declare a pointer variable
    Function (px);           // Call with pointer variable
    Function (&x);           // Call taking the address
                             // of the variable.
```

Both calls have the same effect of calling the function with an address parameter. To modify the variable in *Function()*, you use the indirection operator (also an asterisk) to dereference the pointer:

```
void Function (int *pVar)    // Define the function
{
    *pVar = 5;               // Set a new value for the
}                            // original variable.
```

When you examine the code, you can see that *pVar* is within the scope of *Function()*, but the variable *x* is not. You're not violating the scope of the variable; you're simply using an indirect route to access it.

283. *Understanding the Reference Operator (&)*

Another way you can modify a variable in the calling function is to pass a reference to the variable to the called function. A *reference* works exactly like an address, but syntactically you use it as though it were a local variable. You declare a variable to be a reference by using the ampersand in its declaration. In a function call, you use the ampersand with the identifier in the argument list:

```
void Function (int &Var);
```

When you call the function, you either pass it a reference variable or use the reference operator on the original variable name when you include it as a parameter, as in the following snippet:

```
void Function (int &Var);    // Declare the function
int x = 3;                   // Declare and set the variable
int &rx = x;                 // Declare a reference variable
   Function (rx);            // Call with reference variable
   Function (&x);            // Call it by using reference
                             // operator on the variable.
```

You've reversed the role of the ampersand in using it as the reference operator, and you no longer need the indirection operator (*) to use the variable:

```
void Function (int &Var)    // Define the function
{
   Var = 5;                 // Set a new value for the
}                           // original variable.
```

The change is reflected in the variable in the calling function.

Other than in a function declaration, you have to initialize it at the same time you declare it. You can't use a reference variable on a constant, or on a variable that was declared with the *const* modifier. The following declarations result in errors:

```
const int x = 3;       // Declare and set the variable
int &rx = x;           // Error. x is const
int &rx = 3;           // Error. 3 is a constant
```

After a reference variable is declared and initialized, all operations that are performed using it are performed on the original variable.

You may have heard the reference operation referred to as the "copy" operator, which describes the illusion it produces. As C++ programmers, we are so used to "values" being placed on the stack as parameters, it appears that the operator copies the object onto the stack so that you can modify it directly. In fact, the opposite is true: *Not* using the reference operator on an object causes it to be copied onto the stack. Knowing that in a function call C++ pushes variables onto the stack from right to left, you can write a function call using a structure with and without the reference operator and compare the addresses of parameters on either side of it. In the following, you declare a structure and use it with and without the reference operator in function calls:

```
/*
   reftst.cpp. Testing the reference operator
 */
#include    <stdio.h>

// Define the structure
struct TESTER
{
   int    x;
   char   ch;
   char   str[27];
};
// Declare our functions
void FuncOne(int x, TESTER t, int y);
void FuncTwo(int x, TESTER &t, int y);

int main()
{
int a = 2, b = 3;
TESTER test = {1, 'X', "This is a string"};
```

```
    printf ("sizeof (TESTER) = %d\n", sizeof (TESTER));
    FuncOne (a, test, b);      // Using variable
    printf ("test.x = %d\n", test.x);
    FuncTwo (a, test, b);      // Using reference
    printf ("test.x = %d\n", test.x);
    return (0);
}

void FuncOne(int x, TESTER t, int y)
{
    printf ("Using normal variable call:\n");
    printf ("\tAddress of x = %ld\n", &x);
    printf ("\tAddress of y = %ld\n", &y);
    printf ("\tDifference is %d\n", (int) &y -
            (int)(&x+1));
    t.x = sizeof (TESTER);
}

void FuncTwo(int x, TESTER &t, int y)
{
    printf ("Using reference variable call:\n");
    printf ("\tAddress of x = %ld\n", &x);
    printf ("\tAddress of y = %ld\n", &y);
    printf ("\tDifference is %d\n", (int) &y -
            (int)(&x+1));
    t.x = sizeof (TESTER);
}
```

When you run this program, you see that the space between the end parameters is 32 bytes in the call to *FuncOne()*, the same size as the structure. That's exactly what you would expect if the structure were copied onto the stack.

However, in the call to *FuncTwo()*, where you used the reference operator, the difference is only 4, the size of a pointer to the structure. Not only did the reference operator *not* copy the structure, but it also gave you more compact code.

Notice also in your code that when you changed the *x* member of the structure in the functions, the first change was not reflected in the original structure, but the second, using the reference operator, was.

284. *Using the Reference Operator to Modify Variables*

In the example in Tip 283, "Understanding the Reference Operator (&)," you could modify the structure in the first function using the normal structure member operator, represented by a period. However, you would be modifying the copy on the stack only, and when the function returns, the copy would be destroyed and the changes lost. To modify the original structure, you would have to pass it as a pointer and use the pointer-to-member operator, represented by ->.

Now go back to the example and change the code to pass a pointer to the structure for *FuncOne()* and to print the structure values after returning. I'm also going to introduce you to function overloading, which I cover in the next two tips, by having you give both your functions the same name:

```cpp
/*
    reftst2.cpp. Testing the reference operator
 */
#include    <stdio.h>
#include    <string.h>
// Define the structure
struct TESTER
{
    int    x;
    char   ch;
    char   str[27];
};
// Declare our functions
void FuncOne(int x, TESTER *t, int y);
void FuncOne(int x, TESTER &t, int y);

int main()
{
int a = 2, b = 3;
TESTER test = {1, 'X', "This is a string"};

    FuncOne (a, &test, b);     // Using pointer
    printf ("\ttest.x = %d\n", test.x);
    printf ("\ttest.ch = %c\n", test.ch);
    printf ("\ttest.str = %s\n", test.str);

    FuncOne (a, test, b);      // Using reference
    printf ("\ttest.x = %d\n", test.x);
    printf ("\ttest.ch = %c\n", test.ch);
    printf ("\ttest.str = %s\n", test.str);
    return (0);
}

void FuncOne(int x, TESTER *t, int y)
{
    printf ("Using normal variable call:\n");
    t->x = sizeof (TESTER);
    t->ch = 'B';
    strcpy (t->str, "Modified String");
}

void FuncOne(int x, TESTER &t, int y)
{
    printf ("Using reference variable call:\n");
    t.x = 2 * sizeof (TESTER);
    t.ch = 'C';
    strcpy (t.str, "Changed again, eh?");
}
```

In both functions, you can modify the original structure. In the call to the first function using the pointer to the structure, you use the pointer-to-structure member operator, but in the call using the reference operator, you use the normal structure member operator as though the structure were a local variable.

285. *Introducing Overloading*

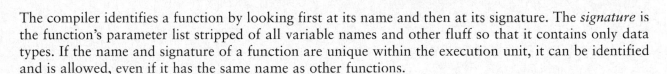

If you are just moving over to C++ from standard C or from another programming language, you might be wondering how you were able to give both your functions the same name in the preceding example and have the compiler distinguish between them.

As long as a function can be uniquely identified, you may have multiple functions with the same name through a process known as "function overloading." The key is the word "uniquely." What you find unique might not be unique to the compiler.

In addition, structures and classes may redefine the C++ operators to perform new operations through operator overloading. You've already seen some examples of *operator overloading* when you used the stream classes *cin*, *cout*, and *cerr* to read and write to *stdin*, *stdout*, and *stderr* by using the shift left and shift right operators. Instead of their normal operations, these operators perform an action defined by the stream classes. You will see more of operator overloading in Tip 356, "Understanding Operator Overloading."

286. *Understanding Function Overloading*

The compiler identifies a function by looking first at its name and then at its signature. The *signature* is the function's parameter list stripped of all variable names and other fluff so that it contains only data types. If the name and signature of a function are unique within the execution unit, it can be identified and is allowed, even if it has the same name as other functions.

This process of overloading function names enables you to have functions that perform similar operations but on different data types to share the same name. The functions don't *have* to perform similar operations, but it makes your programming efforts and maintaining programs easier if you keep it that way. Overloading has no counterpart in C.

The return data type is not part of the function identification process because C++ lets you discard the return value. If you have two functions that differ only in return type and you call one without capturing the return value in a variable, the compiler has no way of identifying the correct function.

The key to uniqueness is in the call to a function. If the name and signature of the call can be uniquely matched to the name and signature of a function declaration or definition, the call is allowed. Otherwise, the compiler flags the call as "ambiguous" and issues an error.

In the *reftst.cpp* example in Tip 283, you could have declared your functions as follows, and the compiler would have allowed the declarations and even the definitions of both functions:

```
void FuncOne(int x, TESTER t, int y);
void FuncOne(int x, TESTER &t, int y);
```

When you try to call one of these functions, however, the syntax and data types are the same. Assuming that you want to call the function that uses the reference operator, the call would look like the following:

```
TESTER test = {1, 'X', "This is a string"};
FuncOne(25, test, 30);
```

Later you want to call the function that doesn't use the reference operator, so you issue the following call:

```
TESTER test = {1, 'X', "This is a string"};
FuncOne(25, test, 30);
```

The two calls are identical. The compiler has no way of distinguishing which function you want to call, even though it allowed you to declare and define both functions. Therefore, it flags the calls as ambiguous and doesn't let you do it.

In Tip 284, "Using the Reference Operator to Modify Variables," however, you changed one of the functions to take a pointer to a structure and the other, a reference to a structure. In this case, the function calls differ enough that the compiler could distinguish the correct function. In the first call in the following, it is obvious that you want the function containing a pointer, and the second call is to the function using a reference:

```
TESTER test = {1, 'X', "This is a string"};
FuncOne(25, &test, 30);
FuncOne(25, test, 30);
```

In addition to the data types, functions may differ in the number of parameters and have unique signatures. You could have dropped the *int y* portion of your declaration for one of the functions, and the compiler would be able to identify the proper function from the calling syntax. Be careful in assigning default parameters in this case because you still could produce an ambiguous call. In the following snippet, the compiler can't distinguish the calls because you might want to call the function that assigns a default value of 0 to the *y* parameter:

```
void FuncOne(int x, TESTER t);
void FuncOne(int x, TESTER &t, int y = 0);

FuncOne (25, test);
```

Functions may also differ in the order of data types and still be unique. In the preceding example, had you declared and defined your second function as *void FuncOne (int x, int y, TESTER t):*, the call would have been unique and the compiler would have allowed it.

This can and does propose some interesting problems. First, it is possible to write, compile, and use code that has the potential for ambiguous calls. When the compiler checks the declarations and definitions of functions, it doesn't look at the calls that might cause confusion. Six months later, you return to your code to make some changes, and suddenly you begin getting errors about ambiguous calls and start scratching your head. It's up to you to examine the possibility of ambiguous calls and avoid them.

Too, you have the problem with data type promotion. You know that when you mix data types in an arithmetic operation, the compiler automatically promotes the operands to the type with the highest precision. For example, adding an integer to a double results in the integer operand being promoted to a double, and the result of the operation is a double.

Suppose, for the sake of demonstration, that you write two functions with the same name, one that multiplies two integers and another that multiplies two doubles:

```
int Product (int x, int y);
double Product (double x, double y);

int Product (int x, int y)
{
    return (x * y);
}
double Product (double x, double y)
{
    return (x * y);
}
```

When you call these functions with *Product(2, 3)* and *Product(2.4, 3.6)*, there's no problem. You know exactly which function is being called because of the data types in the signature. Now, suppose that you call a function with mixed data types: *Product(2.3.6)*. How do you know which function the compiler will use or whether it will give you an ambiguous call error?

Actually, the promotion of the integer in the call to a *double* is legal for the function that returns a *double* type, and the demotion to integer from *double* is legal for the function returning an integer type. In this case, the compiler issues an error that both functions have similar conversions and refuses to allow the call. If you never call the function using mixed types, the compiler never sees a conflict.

This does, however, show you the two rules the compiler uses in converting data types and deciding which function to call. In it's testing, both of the following must be true for the compiler to select an overloaded function. If either test fails, the compiler can't select a proper function:

- The conversions applied to the arguments can be no worse than the conversions applied to call other possible functions. In other words, the conversion cannot result in a lower precision than another function call.

- The conversion on at least one of the arguments must be better than the conversion required when another possible function is called.

In your mismatched parameter call, the conversions for both possibilities met the first rule, but neither was better than the other, so the compiler wants *you* to decide which to use.

The problem with function overloading is that the process of resolving which function to call is very complex, perhaps one of the most complex aspects of C++. The compiler cannot always anticipate all the possibilities when you declare and define overloaded functions. Although they might appear to be unique, down the road the uniqueness test might fail.

Function overloading is a powerful and useful tool in programming and can hide much of the data conversion process from the programmer. When using function overloading, it's the compiler's responsibility to distinguish unique calls and select the proper function. It's the programmer's responsibility to make sure that all the calls to the functions are unique.

287. *Understanding Function Templates*

One of the tedious parts of function overloading is that to be safe, you must declare functions that perform the same operation on different data types. You don't have to define the functions until you actually use them, but to be safe, you should define them and give the code a body. In your *Product()* example, if you anticipate ever calling it with, say, *int*, *double*, and *long* types, you must write a function body for each type returning the proper value.

Wouldn't it be easier to write just one function and let the compiler sort out the details? Function templates let you do exactly that. They don't solve all your problems with function overloading, but they do ease the burden. In addition, they provide a solution to your mismatched parameter dilemma.

A set of overloaded functions is a good candidate for a template if the code remains the same in all definitions, but the data types differ. You declare a function template by using the keyword *template* followed by the less than symbol, a template parameter list (which cannot be empty—this requires more explanation), and the greater than symbol. You then write the return data type of the function, the function name, and a parameter list. The last part is very similar to declaring an ordinary function, but other options are available.

A member of the template parameter list can be a *template type parameter* or a *template nontype parameter*. The type parameter consists of the keyword *class* or *typename* (they are interchangeable) followed by a unique identifier. A nontype parameter is an ordinary declaration using one of the C++ data types and a unique identifier.

When you declare the return type, you may use any of the C++ data types or one of the types identified in the template parameter list with the keywords *class* or *typename*. In addition, any of the arguments in the function parameter list may be of a C++ data type or a type from the template parameter list.

Before the explanations become too complicated, you will start out with a simple template that uses only one type and one parameter. Then you will deal with the other options. Now you declare a template for a trivial function that simply returns half of the value that it is passed:

```
template <class T> T Half (T x);
```

This statement tells the compiler to set the undefined data type *class T* to the type of *x* and set the return data type to that type.

The definition is similar to the declaration, only you omit the semicolon and include the body of code that makes up the function:

```
template <class T> T Half (T x)
{
    return (x / 2);
}
```

When an instance of the function is created, the compiler matches the type of the first function parameter, and that becomes the type for *class*. Each time you call the function using a different data type than before, the compiler creates a new instance of the function using the new data type. Now try some examples and look at the output. You're going to cast your returns to a higher precision to show that the called function returned the proper data type:

```
/*
    template.cpp - A program to test trivial templates.
 */
#include    <stdio.h>

template <class T> T Half (T x);;

int main ()
{
    printf ("Return for int is %f\n", (float) Half (7));
    printf ("Return for long is %f\n", (float) Half (7L));
    printf ("Return for double is %f\n", Half (7.0));
    return (0);
}

template <class T> T Half (T x)
{
    return (x / 2);
}
```

When you compile and run this program, you see the following output:

```
Return for int is 3.000000
Return for long is 3.000000
Return for double 3.500000
```

You can see by the truncation that the function did indeed perform integer arithmetic on the *int* and *long* data types, but floating arithmetic when you passed it a floating data type.

In fact, you can pass it any data type—fundamental, derived, or user-defined—and if an instance for that data type has not been created, the compiler will create it. It's sort of like automatic function overloading.

This has its dangers, however. If you have a structure named *STUFF* and you pass the template a variable of type *STUFF*, the compiler will dutifully create a new instance and try to compile it. You get error messages like the following:

```
template.cpp(25) : error C2676: binary '/' : 'struct STUFF' does not define this operator
or a conversion to a type acceptable to the predefined operator
        template.cpp(19) : see reference to function template instantiation 'struct STUFF
__cdecl Half(struct STUFF)' being compiled
```

You are being told respectfully to look at your template; the first error message contains a hint that you can define a division operation for *STUFF* that would be acceptable to the compiler. You will do that when you get to operator overloading in Tip 356, "Understanding Operator Overloading."

Speaking of overloading, now would be a good time to pour a cup or glass of your favorite beverage. Things are going to get a little hairy.

Now, use more than one argument in the template list, and apply it to your mismatched data type call from the last tip. First, you declare your function in template form:

```
template <class T, class U> T Product(T x, U y);
```

Your function now is going to accept two unknown data types that you name *T* and *U* (these can be any unique identifiers, but for simplicity they usually are given single-character names). *T* will be of the first data type and *U*, of the second data type in the argument. Now you define the function in template form:

```
template <typename T, typename U> T Product (T x, U y)
{
    return (x * y);
}
```

Put it all in a short program so that you can test the results:

```
/*
   templ2. Testing template with two arguments
 */
#include    <stdio.h>

template <class T, class U> T Product (T x, U y);

int main ()
{

    printf ("Return for int, double is %f\n",
                        (float) Product (2, 3.6));
    printf ("Return for double,int is %f\n",
                        (float) Product (3.6, 2));
    printf ("Return for int,int is %f\n",
                        (float) Product (2, 3));
    printf ("Return for double,double is %f\n",
                        (float) Product (3.6, 2.4));
    return (0);
}
```

```
template <typename T, typename Y> T Product (T x, Y y)
{
    return (x * y);
}
```

When you examine the test run, you see that the compiler created an instance for each call using the first data type in the parameter list as the return type:

```
Return for int, double is 7.000000
Return for double,int is 7.200000
Return for int,int is 6.000000
Return for double,double is 8.640000
```

In calling the function, if you want an integer result, you need only use an *int* as the first parameter. If you want double, then use a *double* as the first parameter. You've eliminated your error message with the overloaded functions and reduced considerably the amount of code you have to write.

288. Determining When to Use Templates and Overloaded Functions

Like function overloading, function template use is a complex issue in C++. Unless you're very lucky, you're going to get a lot of error messages from the compiler when you start writing your own particular template functions. I can't possibly go over all the error messages the compiler might issue, but use them to guide your way through constructing your templates. The compiler is trying to tell you what to do; it just has a limited number of messages it can deliver.

Obviously, templates work only where the code for each instantiation can be identical. The compiler can't rewrite your code to provide different statements for different data types. If you must perform different operations for the various data types, you have to resort to function overloading.

289. Understanding Pointers to Functions

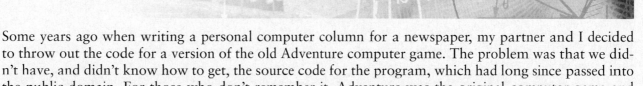

Some years ago when writing a personal computer column for a newspaper, my partner and I decided to throw out the code for a version of the old Adventure computer game. The problem was that we didn't have, and didn't know how to get, the source code for the program, which had long since passed into the public domain. For those who don't remember it, Adventure was the original computer game and was written in FORTRAN. We had a number of programmers among our readership, and we hoped that they would come up with some interesting twists on the game (and did they ever).

We set out by dissecting a version we had on an HP3000, hoping to decipher enough so that we could write our own C version of it. To simplify our code, we built a table of function pointers that let the program calculate the results of a player's move, rather than try to determine it through a series of switch and conditional statements. A move returned an integer value based on the current room the player was in and the current conditions, and that was used as an index into the function table. By the time we finished, we had a C version of it, and every move in our program matched the HP3000 version.

Function pointers look strange when you first encounter them. To declare a function pointer variable, you use the return data type, an opening parenthesis, the pointer operator, the variable identifier, a closing parenthesis, and finally, the parameter list enclosed in another set of parentheses. In its simplest form, a pointer to a void function that has no parameters, the declaration would look like the following:

```
void    (*FunctionName)(void);
```

Carefully note that you place the pointer operator and the function name inside a set of parentheses to set them apart. If you don't, the declaration will be nothing more than a declaration of a function that returns a void pointer. Using the parentheses, the declaration is a variable identifier to which you may assign a function. Afterwards, you may call the function using the variable name instead of the function name itself. Trivially, such a program might look like this:

```
/*
    func.cpp -- A program demonstrating function pointers.
 */
#include    <stdio.h>

void TestFunc ();

int main ()
{
void (*FunctionName)(void);

    FunctionName = TestFunc;
    FunctionName ();
    return (0);
}

void TestFunc ()
{
    printf ("Test function called\n");
}
```

Of course, that's not very useful. It would have been easier to call the function directly rather than assign it a variable and then call it. Let's develop something more useful. You will build a table of commands to your dog and a table of functions that might be called when one of the commands is entered. You will use a binary search to speed up the process:

```
/*
    dog.cpp -- A program demonstrating function pointers.
 */
#include    <stdio.h>
#include    <iostream.h>
#include    <string.h>

const char *Commands[] =
    {
    "come", "done", "fetch", "heel",
    "sit", "speak", "stay"
    };
#define COMMANDS    (sizeof (Commands) / sizeof (char *))

// Declare our functions
void Come(), Done(), Fetch(), Heel();
void Sit(), Speak(), Stay();
```

```cpp
// Put the functions in an array of functions
void (*Command[])(void) =
    {Come, Done, Fetch, Heel, Sit, Speak, Stay};

// Binary search function
int Binary (char *In);

int main ()
{
int Action = 0;
int Done;

    Done = Binary ("done");
    if (Done < 0)
    {
        cerr << "Cannot find exit command" << endl;
        return (-1);
    }
//
// Make sure the function table isn't too small. Jumping
// to an undefined spot can be dangerous.
    if (COMMANDS > (sizeof(Command)/sizeof(void(*)(void))))
    {
        cerr << "Function table is too short" << endl;
        return (-1);
    }
    do
    {
        char In[128];
        cout << "Please enter a command: ";
        cin >> In;
        Action = Binary (In);
        if (Action < 0)
        {
            cout << "Valid commands are" << endl;
            for (int x = 0; x < COMMANDS; ++x)
                cout << '\t' << Commands[x] << endl;
            continue;
        }
        Command[Action]();
    } while (Action != Done);
    return (0);
}

int Binary (char *In)
{
int low = 0;
int high = COMMANDS - 1;
int mid, check;

    strlwr (In);
    while (low <= high)
    {
        mid = (low + high) / 2;
        if (!(check = strcmp (In, Commands[mid])))
            return (mid);
```

```
            if (check < 0)
                high = mid - 1;
            else
                low = mid + 1;
        }
    return (-1);
}

void Done ()
{
    cout << "Your dog licks your face in enormous ";
    cout << "gratitude" << endl;
}

void Sit()
{
    cout << "Your dog is now sitting" << endl;
}

void Stay()
{
  cout << "Your dog stays put (good dog!)" << endl;
}

void Come()
{
    cout << "Your dog is running toward you" << endl;
}

void Fetch()
{
    cout << "You toss a stick and your dog runs after it";
    cout << endl;
}

void Heel()
{
    cout << "Your dog walking by your side" << endl;
}
void Speak()
{
    cout << "\"Arf!\" says Sandy" << endl;
}
```

Notice particularly where you test the size of the function table using *(void(*)(void)*. A function doesn't have a data type you can test, such as *sizeof (char *)*. It is defined by parentheses and its return type. You use the asterisk because you want a function pointer.

You call the function simply by getting its address out of the function table, *Command[Action]()*, and tacking the set of parentheses on the end. You don't have to dereference the pointer variable because you can only call a function or get its address. The compiler has no trouble with not dereferencing it, but you could write *(*Command[Action])()* and achieve the same result.

This program could have been done by a long series of *switch* and *strcmp()* statements, but expanding it would entail much more coding. Using the binary search and a function table, you need only add new commands to the string list (in alphabetical order), write the appropriate function, and add a pointer to it in the table.

You didn't have to use a binary search, but parsers such as this typically have many more than seven commands, and the binary search is an efficient method of looking through a long list of strings. The trade-off, of course, is that everything has to be kept in lexical (alphabetical) order for it to work, which translates to a little more work for the programmer.

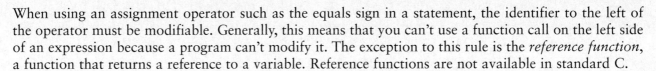

290. *Getting the Address of an Overloaded Function*

In declaring a function pointer variable, you must include the parameter data types just as if you were declaring the function itself. Only a function containing the same data type in its argument list can be assigned to the variable. The return type for the function also must match the data type for the variable.

This exact specification requirement means that you can take the address of an overloaded function without worrying about ambiguity. Using your *Product()* functions as examples, you can take the address of them even if they are defined in a different source file:

```
int Product (int x, int y);
double Product (double x, double y);
int (*IntPointer)(int, int) = Product;
double (*DoublePointer)(double, double) = Product;
```

Even though the assignment in both cases is the generic name *Product*, the compiler knows from the return type and argument list which pointer to use. The functions then may be called using the variable names:

```
IntPointer (1, 1);
DoublePointer (1.0, 1.0);
```

291. *Understanding Reference Functions*

When using an assignment operator such as the equals sign in a statement, the identifier to the left of the operator must be modifiable. Generally, this means that you can't use a function call on the left side of an expression because a program can't modify it. The exception to this rule is the *reference function*, a function that returns a reference to a variable. Reference functions are not available in standard C.

You declare a reference function by following its return type with the reference operator, the ampersand. The rest of the declaration is the same as for any other function. The following code shows a sample of using a reference function:

```
/*
    reffunc.cpp. An example of using reference
                functions as lvalues.
 */
#include    <stdio.h>
#include    <iostream.h>

int IntArray[] = {1, 2, 3};
#define    SIZE    (sizeof(IntArray)/sizeof(int))
```

```
int& RefFunc(int x);

int main ()
{
int x;

    cout << "Before Reference Function: " << endl;
    for (x = 0; x < SIZE; ++x)
    {
        cout << "IntArray[" << x << "] = ";
        cout << IntArray[x] << endl;
    }
    for (x = 0; x < SIZE; ++x)
        RefFunc(x) = x * 42;

    cout << endl << "After Reference Function: " << endl;
    for (x = 0; x < SIZE; ++x)
    {
        cout << "IntArray[" << x << "] = ";
        cout << IntArray[x] << endl;
    }
    return (0);
}
//
// Return a reference to the array member indexed by
// parameter.
int& RefFunc (int x)
{
    return (IntArray[x]);
}
```

After you declare and initialize a reference variable, no operation can be performed on it. Instead, the operation is transferred to the object of reference. The same is true of reference functions, and none of the rules of C++ are being violated. It only appears that the function is being assigned a value, but the assignment is actually on the object being returned, the integer member of *IntArray*.

A word of caution is in order here. Be sure that the variable referenced in the *return* statement does not go out of scope when the reference function exits. In this case, *IntArray* is a global array, and thus remains in scope. However, if it were a local variable in the reference function, it would go out of scope and be destroyed. Your statement then would be assigning a value to a variable that no longer exists.

292. *Understanding the Difference Between Functions and Macros*

Macros are similar to inline functions. Each time a macro is invoked in your code, the statement you defined in the macro is substituted in the code. This offers some speed advantage over functions by not introducing the time required to create new variables and call a function. However, the trade-off is increased difficulty in debugging.

You can't trace into a macro using a debugger. The compiler knows nothing about the original macro. When the program is compiled, the preprocessor inserts the text of the macro into the code before it is compiled. So the compiler, when inserting debug information in the code, knows only of the replacement text. Your source code, however, contains only the macro name. When stepping through the code with a debugger, your trace will step over the macro code without showing you what's going on inside it.

When a function is called, the compiler generates code to produce what is referred to as a *function activation record*. This is the stack space used by the function for variable and argument storage and remains with the function until the function terminates.

This requires a slight amount of overhead, of course, while the runtime code initializes the activation record, evaluates the arguments, and sets their values. The edge over macros is so slight as to be negligible. In return, you get more readable code that can be traced into during debugging.

Inline functions give you the advantages of both. Inline expansion can be turned off when producing debug code, so you can trace into it and locate any bugs. When the finished code is compiled, the expansion can be turned on, and the function code placed inline.

293. *Determining When to Use Functions or Macros*

Macros are handy to have for making code more readable. When you are defining an unwieldy number such as pi or a value that occurs often in your code, using a short and easy-to-remember name makes it easier to find occurrences of typos and eliminates the danger of making a typographical error in the value when you enter it.

Macros, however, are not suitable for much more than simple definitions and limited arithmetic operations. Arithmetic expressions and arguments are evaluated each time you use them in your macro and can actually be more time consuming than a function call. If your macro requires more than one argument or performs more than one arithmetic operation, it is a good candidate to become an inline function.

At times, macros yield some odd results. More often than not, you can trace this to the fact that the passed expression is evaluated each time it is used. For example, if you define the following macro and use it with an increment or decrement operator on the argument, the operator is applied twice to the argument:

```
#define SQUARE(x) (x)*(x)
    int x = 1;
    int square = SQUARE(x++);
```

After the line containing the macro has been executed, you find that *x* contains the value 3 because the argument was evaluated twice. Compare this with an inline function that accomplishes the same result:

```
inline SQUARE (int x)
{
    return (x * x);
}
    int x = 1;
    int square = SQUARE(x++);
```

The variable is passed to the function, its square calculated and captured by the variable *square*, and then the argument is incremented. Because the argument is evaluated only once, it is incremented only once.

294. *Understanding Variables*

A *variable* is a named storage location that is large enough to hold a unit of its data type. The size may differ on various operating systems and with different implementations of the C and C++ compilers. When you declare a variable, the compiler sets aside storage to hold it, and you use the declared name to access the memory location in which its value is stored.

Depending on their storage class, variables have different lifetimes. Variables declared outside a function are in global memory and exist for the duration of the program. Most variables declared within a function survive only while the function is in scope and are re-created each time the function is called. I say "most" because variables with a storage class of *static* are created outside the function activation record, usually in the program's data memory segment, and survive the destruction of the record. Static variables are created only once, and repeated calls to a function containing a static variable reference the one variable location.

295. *Understanding Variable Typing*

That a variable identifies storage large enough to hold a unit of its data type implies that every variable declared must be of a type. In C and C++, this is true. In some languages, enough storage is set aside for a variable to hold the largest data type, and you may assign any value to it. This is true of BASIC, especially older implementations of BASIC. C, C++, and most object-oriented programming *(OOP)* languages use strong variable typing, and you can't declare a variable without declaring its type along with it.

C and C++ have a limited number of fundamental data types and a large number of derived types. In addition, the programmer is free to create new data types using structures, unions, classes, and other mechanisms. User-defined variable types are on a per program basis and are not available to programs that are not aware of the data types.

296. *Modifying Variable Types*

In C and C++, the *fundamental* data types include the *char*, integer, and floating arithmetic types. In addition, "adjective" keywords may be used to modify these data types. All other data types are derived and user-defined types.

Integer data types come in three flavors and sizes. An integer type may be *short* or *long* in addition to its basic type. Integer data types, and the *char* type, also may be modified as being *signed* or *unsigned* in addition to their basic types.

Floating types come in three sizes and are always *signed*: *float* for single precision, *double* for double precision, and *long* for extended precision calculations.

Data types may be cast to another data type for assignment to a different data type. In this case, the programmer must be careful to use assignment properly, especially when pointer types are being recast.

297. *Understanding Local Variables*

Variables declared within a function or block are considered to be *local* variables. With the exception of the *static* storage class, local variables are destroyed when the function or enclosing blocks (the nearest set of opening and closing braces) end. Non-static local variables are created in the function activation record on the stack when the enclosing scope begins, and this record is destroyed when the enclosing scope terminates.

Local variables almost never are initialized. The programmer must provide an initial value for them when they are declared, or the resulting operations using it can produce some unexpected results. Never assume that a newly created variable has a value of 0; more likely than not, it contains some other value.

The arguments passed to a function also are considered local arguments within the scope of the function. They are created and initialized when the function is called and are destroyed when the function terminates.

298. *Understanding Global Variables*

There are two types of global variables: semi-global and global. You refer to both types as simply "global."

Global variables are those that are declared outside a function and usually are placed in the program's data memory segment. They may be used from the point of declaration to the end of the module in which they are contained, and they can be accessed from other modules where they are declared to have an *extern* storage class. For example, suppose you have the following global variable declaration in one source file:

```
int g_iValue;
```

You could use this same variable in another source file by declaring it as follows:

```
extern int g_iValue
```

Global variables that are subclassified as *semi-global* are those that are declared in global memory but have limited access. This type would include all static variables, whether declared inside or outside a function. A semi-global variable may not be accessed by other code modules. Even within the same code module, they may have limited access.

299. *C++ Allows Variables to Be Declared in the Body of a Function*

A property of C++, *locality of execution* allows variables to be declared within a function near the point where they are first used. This helps to improve readability of the code, especially for functions with a large number of statements. Older versions of standard C did not include locality of execution as a property, and variables had to be declared at the beginning of a function.

Locality of execution also makes it possible to declare temporary variables in a block of code within a function. The scope of these temporary variables is the nearest set of enclosing braces. The block of code might be the compound statement for a conditional or loop, or you can just declare a block as shown below:

```
void Func()
{
    int x = 2
    x *= 4;
    {
        int iNewVar;
        iNewVar = 6;
    }
}
```

In the above code, you can use and access the *iNewVar* variable only within the block, the code within the set of braces.

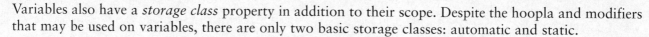

300. *Understanding Storage Classes*

Variables also have a *storage class* property in addition to their scope. Despite the hoopla and modifiers that may be used on variables, there are only two basic storage classes: automatic and static.

Automatic variables are those that are created within a function or block of code and survive only to the end of the function or block.

A local variable may be given a "storage class" of *register*. This is not a separate storage class. *Register* variables are automatic variables that are intended to be stored in and used from one of the central processing unit's registers. The compiler is free to ignore the request, and it is possible to declare more register variables than there are registers. Usually, the register variable request is used for variables that you use often, such as loop control variables.

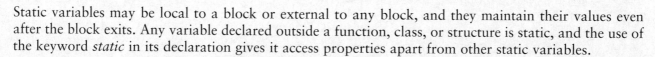

301. *Understanding Static Variables*

Static variables may be local to a block or external to any block, and they maintain their values even after the block exits. Any variable declared outside a function, class, or structure is static, and the use of the keyword *static* in its declaration gives it access properties apart from other static variables.

A program creates only one instance of a static variable. The following snippet declares and initializes a static variable inside a function:

```
void Func()
{
    static int x = 1;
}
```

The program creates the static variable when you run the program and performs the initialization only once. The static variable persists until the end of the program. If you assign it a new value during a call to the function, it will retain that new value through successive function calls, or until you give it a different value.

The following function initializes the static variable *Counter* to *0*, then increments the variable each time you call the function.

```
void Func()
{
    static int Counter = 0;
    ++Counter;
    printf ("This function has been called %d times", Counter);
}
```

Because a program performs the initialization only once, the value of *Counter* increases by one each time you call the function, as the *printf()* function will show.

302. *Defining a Global Static Variable*

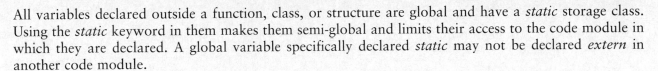

All variables declared outside a function, class, or structure are global and have a *static* storage class. Using the *static* keyword in them makes them semi-global and limits their access to the code module in which they are declared. A global variable specifically declared *static* may not be declared *extern* in another code module.

There may be only one instance of a global variable in a program unless it is declared with the *static* keyword. A global variable declared *static* may be declared in other modules, but they are separate variables local to the one module.

A global static variable is initialized to 0 when a program creates the variable unless the programmer assigns it a different value.

A static member variable of a class or structure must also be declared in global space, in addition to its declaration within the class or structure definition. These variables are created when the program is loaded into memory.

303. *Defining Static Variables Within a Program Block*

When you declare a static variable within a function or program block, the program actually creates the variable in global memory. However, the variable is visible only to statements in the function or block in which you declared the variable. The following sample declares a static variable within a block in a function:

```
void Func()
{
    Statement1;
    {
        static int var - 1;
        Statement2;
    }
}
```

Only *Statement2* (and any other statements in the block) may access *var*. Any statements outside the block such as *Statement1* are completely unaware that *var* exists, and attempting to access the variable outside the block will cause the compiler to generate an error.

Your program automatically initializes the value of a static variable to 0, but you may assign the variable a different value when you declare it, as in the preceding example.

304. *Creating Your Own Variable Types: The* typedef *Keyword*

In addition to the fundamental and derived data types, users may create their own data types. A class or structure is a user-defined data type created when the class or structure is defined.

In addition, programmers may declare other data types using the *typedef* keyword. The syntax is to use the *typedef* keyword followed by the existing data type and the name for the new type followed by a semicolon:

```
typedef   unsigned int   UINT;
```

The *typedef* mechanism doesn't actually create a new data type but assigns an additional programmer-defined keyword (an "alias") to the existing data type.

Variables declared using a *typedef*'ed data type may not be modified with one of the "adjective" modifiers such as *signed*, *unsigned*, or *short*. The following code snippet defines a new keyword, *INT*, for the *int* data type, then attempts to declare an unsigned variable of *INT*:

```
typedef    int   UINT;
unsigned INT var;
```

This will cause the compiler to generate an error message because you cannot combine unsigned and INT in a declaration.

305. *Understanding the Scope of a Variable*

The *scope* of a variable is the extent to which a program may access the variable. The scope does not affect the lifetime of a variable within a program. A static variable within a function or block, for example, persists even after the program exits the function or block, but the scope of the static variable is the function or block. Statements outside the function or block cannot access the variable.

Your program creates an automatic variable when it enters the function or block in which you declare the variable. Your program destroys the variable when it leaves the function or block, so the scope of the variable is the function or block in which you declared the variable.

A program creates global variables when the program is loaded into memory. The scope of a global variable is the current module from the point where you declare the variable. A global variable can't be accessed until it is declared. You may declare a global variable *extern* in another module to extend its scope, but the extended scope takes on the properties of the *extern* declaration. If declared *extern* within a function or block, the extended scope ends with the function or block. If declared *extern* in global space in another module, the extended scope is from the point of declaration to the end of the module in which the *extern* declaration is made.

306. *Understanding lvalues*

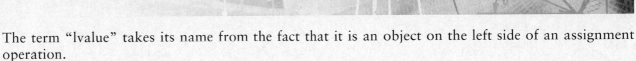

The term "lvalue" takes its name from the fact that it is an object on the left side of an assignment operation.

An lvalue must be a modifiable object. Functions, *const*, reference variables, and preprocessor defines can't be used as lvalues because they can't be modified.

A *reference function*, a function that returns a reference to a data object, may be used as an lvalue provided that the reference object is modifiable. The modification is performed on the reference object in this case and not on the function itself.

307. *Understanding NULL*

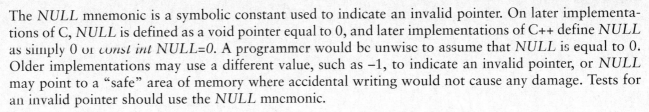

The *NULL* mnemonic is a symbolic constant used to indicate an invalid pointer. On later implementations of C, *NULL* is defined as a void pointer equal to 0, and later implementations of C++ define *NULL* as simply 0 or *const int NULL=0*. A programmer would be unwise to assume that *NULL* is equal to 0. Older implementations may use a different value, such as –1, to indicate an invalid pointer, or *NULL* may point to a "safe" area of memory where accidental writing would not cause any damage. Tests for an invalid pointer should use the *NULL* mnemonic.

The standard header file, *stdio.h*, defines *NULL*.

308. *Understanding the void Type*

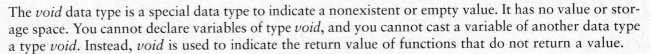

The *void* data type is a special data type to indicate a nonexistent or empty value. It has no value or storage space. You cannot declare variables of type *void*, and you cannot cast a variable of another data type a type *void*. Instead, *void* is used to indicate the return value of functions that do not return a value.

An *expression* may be cast to type *void* to indicate that the value is being discarded. A void expression is commonly used to indicate an empty argument list for a function.

Programmers may, however, declare pointer variables of type *pointer to void*, in which case the data type indicates the pointer variable may hold a pointer to a variable of any data type. The following snippet declares a *void* pointer variable, then assigns the address of other variables of different data types to the *void* pointer variable:

```
void *pVoid;
int iVar;
long lVar;

pVoid = &iVar;
pVoid = &lVar;
pVoid = "This here's a string";
```

None of these statements causes the compiler to generate an error.

309. Understanding Pointers to Variables

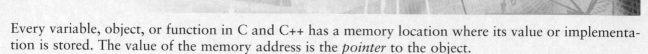

Every variable, object, or function in C and C++ has a memory location where its value or implementation is stored. The value of the memory address is the *pointer* to the object.

You get the pointer to an object or variable by using the address operator, an ampersand, in front of its identifier. If you have a variable *x*, you can get the address of the variable using *&x*. Pointers often are used to pass the address of large objects in function calls and are the only method of accessing an object created in heap, or free-store, memory.

Pointers to objects may be stored in special *pointer variables*. Pointer variables themselves have a memory location, and scope and pointers may be obtained for them. To declare a pointer variable, declare the variable using the *indirection* operator. The following snippet declares an *int* pointer variable, then assigns the address of an *int* variable to the pointer variable:

```
int *pVar;
int iVal;
pVar = &iVal;
```

You cannot assign the address of a variable of one data type to a pointer variable for another data type. For example, the following causes a compiler error:

```
int *pVar;
float fVal;
pVar = &fVal;
```

Different data types require different amounts of memory to store their values. An *int*, for example, needs four bytes of memory, but a float requires eight bytes. In the above example, if the compiler allowed the assignment, then when you try to get the value in the memory addressed by *pVar*, you would read only four bytes, which would not contain the full value of a *float*.

Programmers often prefix the name of a pointer variable with a "p" to indicate the variable is a pointer variable.

310. Declaring and Initializing Pointers to Variables

If you want to get a pointer to a single data item, you declare the pointer variable using the pointer operator, the asterisk, which also serves as the indirection operator that you later will use to get the data from storage. You then take the address of the "ordinary" variable using the address operator (&) and assign it to the pointer variable:

```
int SomeInt = 42;
int *pSomeInt = &SomeInt;
```

Pointers don't have to be initialized at the time they are declared. You may assign new values to them at any time, even the address of another variable of the same data type. The only restriction is that the pointer data type and the data type of the variable being pointed to should be the same. As you will see, there are ways around that.

You also may take the address of a variable when you pass it to a function. In that case, the argument to the function becomes a pointer:

```
void SomeFunc (int *);
int SomeInt = 42;
    SomeFunc  (&SomeInt);
```

Of course, unless you need the pointer to the integer variable, it's just as easy to pass the variable itself to the function. Pointers *really* come in handy when you are dealing with objects.

Pointers are the fastest method of getting to elements in an array. When you create an array, the name of the array is a pointer to the first element in the array. Unfortunately, you can't use it to point to other members of the array because the compiler won't let you use it as an lvalue.

To get around that compiler restriction, you declare another variable as a pointer to the data type of the array and set it equal to the array's first member. Then you can do pointer arithmetic and get to any individual member of the array as in the following code:

```
int iArray[6] = {1, 2, 3, 4, 5, 6};
int *pArray = iArray;
for (int x = 0; x < 6; ++x)
{
    printf ("iArray[%d] = %d\n", x, *pArray);
    ++pArray;     // or pArray += 1;
}
```

You're about to get into object-oriented programming. In the following example, you declare a different kind of structure, one that initializes itself. (Remember, I said earlier that in C++ a structure may contain functions. You can't do this in standard C.) Then you declare and initialize an array of these structures. Finally, you declare a pointer to the array itself:

```
#define    BAUDLEN    8

struct BAUDTABLE
{
    BAUDTABLE(DWORD Speed)
    {
        Rate = Speed;
        sprintf (Text, "%d", Speed);
    }
    DWORD  Rate;          // Baud rate as a number
    char   Text[BAUDLEN]; // Baud rate as a string.
};

BAUDTABLE   Bauds[] = {300,   600,  1200,  1800,  2400,
                       4800,  9600, 19200, 38400, 56000};
#define   BAUDS   (sizeof(Bauds)/sizeof(BAUDTABLE))
BAUDTABLE *pBauds = Bauds;
```

A self-initializing table like this is handy if you want to list the items in a list box or combo box control in Windows. You already have both the *DWORD* to set the item data and the text to set the display in a compact structure without having to do additional conversions. The function you embed in the structure is called a *constructor*. You could omit the constructor and initialize the array by giving it both the *DWORD* and the string:

```
BAUDTABLE Bauds[]   = {
                  {300,   "300"},
                  {600,   "600"},
                  {1200,  "1200"},
                  {1800,  "1800"},
                  {2400,  "2400"},
```

```
            {4800,  "4800"},
            {9600,  "9600"},
            {19200, "19200},
            {38400, "38400"},
            {56000, "56000"}
            };
```

Oops! Left out the ending quote on the "*19200* entry. Compile errors will be forthcoming. You can see how using a constructor is much faster to code and much less prone to errors.

You declare your pointer *pBauds* to the array using the pointer operator, an asterisk; then, you assign the contents of *Bauds* to it. *Bauds* is a pointer to the first element that you *may not* modify; *pBauds* is a pointer to the first element that you *may* modify.

311. *Understanding Indirection: Getting the Value Pointed to by a Pointer*

In the case of a single value, you get the value pointed to by a pointer variable by using the indirection operator, an asterisk, which is convenient because the syntax is very nearly the same as declaring the pointer variable. The operator gets its name from the fact that you are getting the value indirectly through the pointer.

```
int  SomeInt = 42;
int *pSomeInt = &SomeInt;
int AnotherInt = *pSomeInt;
```

Both *SomeInt* and *AnotherInt* are ordinary integer variables that now contain the same value, 42, but you got it through an *indirect* route, thus the term "indirection."

Arithmetic operations may be performed on pointers, but the compiler has its own way of doing it. The reason you may assign pointers only to variables of the same data type is that the compiler will know the size of the data type when it performs arithmetic on a pointer. You may use only integers in doing pointer arithmetic, and when you add a number to a pointer, the compiler adds the number *times* the size of the data type. If you have an array of integers, which in Visual C++ have a size of 4 bytes, and a pointer to the array, you can step through the array simply by incrementing the pointer:

```
int IntArray[] = {4, 12, 36, 42};
int *pInt = IntArray;
    for (int x = 0; x < 4; ++x)
    {
        printf ("pInt = %d; IntArray[%d] = %d\n",
                pInt, x, *pInt);
        ++pInt;
    }
```

When you run this snippet, you can see that, with each iteration of the loop, *pInt* is incremented by 4 to point to the next element in the table. Instead of *++pInt*, you could write *pInt += 1;* or even *pInt = pInt + 1;* and get the same result.

Whatever the size of the data type, the compiler adds (or subtracts, in the case of decrementing) that much to the pointer value when it is incremented.

When accessing a member of a structure or class using a pointer, you have to use the pointer-to-member operator (->). Try it on your baud rate table. You've already declared the pointer. (By the way, if you try to compile this in a test program, you will need to include *windows.h*. DWORD is a Windows *typedef*.):

```
printf("sizeof(BAUDTABLE) = %d\n", sizeof(BAUDTABLE));
printf ("\n\n\t  Baud Rate Table\n");
printf ("\tAs DWORD  As string\n");
for (int x = 0; x < BAUDS; ++x)
{
    printf ("\t%6ld      %6s\n",
            pBauds->Rate, pBauds->Text);
    ++pBauds;
}
```

Because you use the pointer-to-member operator, the compiler knows that you are using a pointer, so you don't have to dereference the pointer. From the first line, you see that the structure size is 12 (the constructor didn't add to the size), so each time through the loop the compiler adds 12 to the value of *pBauds*.

312. *Understanding Arrays of Pointers: Pointers to Pointers*

The difference between a two-dimensional array and an array of pointers can be subtle, and programmers new to C and C++ can easily be confused by the difference.

If you declare and initialize a two-dimensional array of integers *int IntArray[15][20]*, you are reserving memory for 15 times 20 integers, or a total of 1,800 bytes of memory in Visual C++. Even if you don't need 20 elements in each of your 15 subarrays, you still have to declare it that way because the memory for a multidimensional array must be contiguous. If only one array needs 20 elements and the others need variously 5 to 10, you've wasted a lot of memory. The compiler simply fills the empty elements of a subarray with the value of its last element:

```
int IntArray[15][20] = {
            int *x1 ={1, 2, 3, 4, 5, 6, 7, 8,
                      9, 0, 11},
            {42, 18, 3, 92, 21},
            {86, 85, 84, 83},
            . . .
            };
```

Regardless of whether each subarray contains 20 members, it still has space for them. To get the fourth element of the second subarray, you would write *IntArray[1][3]* (remembering, of course, that 0 is your first element in each case).

If, instead, you declare your array as an array of pointers, each subarray will contain only as many elements as it needs:

```
int *pIntArray[15];
```

You have set aside a single-dimensional array of pointers to *int*, but syntactically you may address them the same as your two-dimension array. Assuming that the array of pointers has been initialized, you still may access the fourth element of the second array by writing *pInt[1][3]*. Next, you initialize the array.

313. Initializing an Array of Pointers

Unlike a multidimensional array, the arrays pointed to by an array of pointers need not be the same size. It's the programmer's responsibility to make sure that the member arrays are addressed properly and that the array boundaries are honored.

To initialize an array of pointers, first declare the arrays that are to be members. As you have seen, the identifier for an array is a pointer to the first element of an array, so it may be assigned to the array of pointers:

```
int x0[] = {1, 2, 3, 4, 5, 6, 7, 8, 9, 10, 11};
int x1[] = {42, 18, 3, 92, 21};
int x2[] = {86, 85, 84, 83};
. . .
```

After the arrays have been declared, declare the array of pointers and assign the subarrays to it:

```
int *pIntArray[3] = {x0, x1, x2};
```

To get a pointer to the first element of the second array, you would declare a pointer to a pointer of type *int*. You do this by using two pointer operators in your declaration:

```
int **ppInt = pIntArray;
```

When you work with pointer-to-pointer variables, it's important to remember what is being dereferenced when you try to access member elements. *ppInt[0]*, for example, dereferences the first element of the first member of the array of pointers, so the value of that expression is *1*. You might expect *ppInt[1]* to point to the second member of the first array, but actually it points to the first member of the second array. The order of evaluation for pointers and array expressions is right to left. The expression first evaluates the *[1]* to point to the second array and then dereferences it to use the first integer in the second array.

To get the value of the first integer in the second array, you first have to dereference *ppInt* and then use the index operator: *(*ppInt)[0]*. Alternatively, you could use two index operators and skip the dereferencing altogether: *ppint[1][0]*. Here, the use of two index operators provides you with implied dereferencing.

314. Understanding Casting: Temporarily Modifying the Variable Type

A property of a C and C++ data type is its size, how many bytes it takes to hold the value of a datum of a particular type. When you try to assign the value of one variable to one of another data type, the compiler objects because of the possibility of underwriting or overwriting the memory location, which may not be the same size as the object of the assignment.

Sometimes, however, you must temporarily change the data type of a variable. If you need to use a *double* as an index into an array, for example, the index value must equate to an integer expression, so the compiler objects. The following, for example, generates a compiler error:

```
double x = DoubleFunc();       // Returns, say, 1.2
int y = IntArray[x];
```

To change the data type temporarily, you use the cast operator, which is simply the new data type enclosed in a set of parentheses written before the expression you want to cast. When you cast to another data type, the expression being cast is given a temporary size of the cast, and any extra precision is lost. To cast the preceding index expression temporarily to an integer, you would write *int y = IntArray[(int) x]*, which would be acceptable to the compiler. Any fractional part of the double is stripped, and the expression gives you the integer result.

A cast affects only the value of an expression. The variable itself is left unchanged. Because of the danger of overwriting memory, you can't cast an lvalue to another type in an assignment operation if the result of the cast would overwrite memory. If you have a variable *x* declared as a *double* and another variable *y* declared as an *int*, the first line of the following will cause the compiler to issue an error, but the second will be acceptable:

```
(double) y = x;
x = (int) y;
```

In the first line, casting an *int* to a *double* would require a larger memory allocation. In the second line, the memory required for a *double* is larger than an *int*, so the compiler allows you to do it. In fact, you would write just *x = y;* and let the compiler perform an automatic cast. In this case, the compiler would warn you of a possible loss of data from the assignment, but it would allow the assignment. (From the command line, Visual C++ uses a default warning level of 1, which will not issue a warning in this case. If you set the warning level to 2 using –W2 in the command line, you will see the warning.)

The compiler is pickier about casing pointers. You can't assign a pointer of one data type to a pointer of another type, with one exception: You can assign a pointer of any type to a variable of *pointer to void*.

The compiler uses the data type size to make sure that assignments don't write to larger portions of memory than is allotted for the data type. When you assign one pointer to another type, the compiler loses the size information and the ability to control mismatched assignments.

At times, however, you must assign pointers of different types. The *malloc()* function, for example, returns a *pointer to void* for the newly allocated memory. Although you may assign a pointer of any type to *pointer to void*, the reverse isn't true. That requires an explicit cast. If you allocate space for 40 *int*s, you have to cast the return value to *pointer to int*, as in the following:

```
int *Ints = (int *) malloc (40 * sizeof (int));
```

315. *Automatic Casting: Mixing Variables of Type* int *and* char

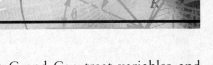

The type *char* is considered an *integral* data type, which means that C and C++ treat variables and expressions of that type as just small integers. Because of this, the types *int* and *char* may be used almost interchangeably.

You may use a *char* type in any expression where you can use an *int*. The value of the *char* expression is automatically promoted to the size of *int*. When you use an *int* in place of a *char*, it is automatically demoted, and any higher-order bits are stripped off before an expression is evaluated or an assignment is made.

The automatic demotion of an *int* to a *char* might, in some cases, cause a loss of bits, and certain compilers might issue a warning about it. However, unlike trying to assign a *double* to an *int*, the compiler will permit the operation, making the conversion in the process as though you had explicitly cast the *int* to a *char*. In Visual C++, you need to raise the warning level to its limit and use the *–W4* command-line option to see the warning message.

This indifference to *char* and *int* doesn't carry over to pointers, however. The compiler still will issue an error if you try to assign a *pointer to int* to a *pointer to char* variable without an explicit cast, and vice versa.

316. *Casting Pointers: Some Danger Signs*

This taboo against assigning pointer variables values of another pointer type is not without reason. It's inherently dangerous. When you cross-assign pointer types, the compiler no longer can keep track of the data size in any future assignments. If you aren't careful, you can overwrite some important memory, such as your function's return address.

Consider the following example of reckless abandon:

```
char MyArray[] = {'A', 'B', 'C', 'D', '\0'};
#define  ARRAYSIZE  (sizeof(MyArray)/sizeof(char))
    double *MyDouble = (double *) MyArray;
    for (int x = 0; x < ARRAYSIZE; ++x)
    {
        *MyDouble = x * 42.3;
        ++MyDouble;
    }
```

Put this into your code and you will be lucky if your program survives it. When the loop terminates (if your program runs that long), you will have written five times the size of a *double* (8 bytes in Visual C++) or 40 bytes into an array that was only 5 bytes in size. In fact, just the first time through the loop, you overwrite the size of the array—and quite legally; the compiler won't object a bit to this code.

317. *Introduction to Object-Oriented Programming*

If you remember *Byte* Magazine, you probably recognize the name *Robert Tinney*. He's the guy who used to draw those great covers. One of my favorites (along with the Model Railroad cover, of course) is one depicting a broad, green valley with mountains. You're looking at it from hills on the other side from the mountains. Beginning where you are, winding through the valley, and disappearing through a gap in the mountains is a floating path whose interlocking tiles are made of sheets from programs.

Whether this path is a personal journey through programming or one that our culture and technology are taking is up to the viewer. You have to take this path one step at a time, and each step builds on the next. Somewhere along this path, you come to something known as *object-oriented programming*, or *OOP*.

Whether we realize it or not, we treat our world as a collection of objects. We look at an automobile as an object rather than as an engine, some tires, various sheet metal parts, and so on. We see a bird flying through the air, instead of a bunch of feathers wrapping a bunch of bird bones and body parts. The bird is an instance of a species, which, in turn, is one object of a broader genus, and so on, down the biological tree.

The idea behind object orientation is to treat your programming the same way. In procedure-oriented programming, you might call a function, declare all the variables you need in order to deal with something, and write functions to deal with it. Then you return from the function. Basically, you deal with one object, one variable, or one function call at a time.

You take all the variables that go into building something and all the functions that describe its behavior and wrap them up into a single definition. When you need an object of that type, you declare an instance of it, using a single identifier to encompass all these variables and functions you need. If you need more than one instance of an object, you simply declare another instance of it. Each of these objects shares the same attributes and functionality while maintaining its individuality.

318. *C++: The Next Step in the Evolution of C*

Standard C took us a long way down the path toward object-oriented programming by giving us the concept of structures and unions. With these mechanisms, you could encapsulate all the variables related to a particular operation into a single object and pass it around in your program using a single identifier. Although a C structure could contain pointers to functions, it didn't allow you to declare certain operations or procedures specific to the structure. It fell short of one of the goals of object orientation, that an object contains the mechanism to describe its own behavior. This is one way you distinguish between an object and an ordinary variable. A variable contains only value information; an object also contains state information that describes how a variable gets its value.

Although C++ brought a number of other changes, if you had to identify one single concept as the most important difference between C and C++, it would have to be the introduction of functions instead of simply function pointers within the C structure. The C++ class is built on the concept of a structure, and despite some very important differences, it's difficult to distinguish between a class and a structure. You might look upon C++ itself as a model of object orientation: It inherits and encapsulates the properties of the C language and modifies them to produce a new language, but not one with which you are totally unfamiliar. With only a few changes to accommodate stricter data typing and such, you can still write standard C code in a C++ program.

319. *Three Principles of OOP*

Object-oriented programming encompasses three basic principles. An object-oriented language must provide the mechanism for *encapsulating* all the information about an object within the object itself. Standard C did this with the structure.

The language must provide a means of letting the programmer use the definition of an object to create new objects. The C structure did not provide this mechanism of *inheritance*, but as you have seen, a C++ structure may inherit properties from another structure definition.

Finally, you have to have a method of modifying a new object's behavior even if it is derived from an existing object definition. This is the principle of *polymorphism*, the idea that an object may inherit the characteristics of a parent but also may take on properties and methods of its own and even change the behavior of a parent.

320. *Understanding Encapsulation*

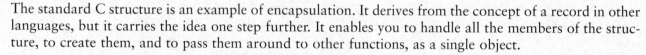

Encapsulation allows you to define and treat the individual elements—the variables and functions—of an object as a whole without having to deal with its internal structure. In fact, by using methods or member functions of the object, you need never know even the identifiers of an object's properties, or variables.

You've seen many examples of encapsulation in the way you deal with the real world. If you need to replace the transmission in your car, you don't walk into the auto parts store with a detailed list of all the components of the transmission. You might not even know the individual components or what they are called. Instead, you just say, "Gimme a transmission." The details, or definition, of the transmission might be contained in the parts manual.

Using class libraries such as the Microsoft Foundation Class (MFC), you see many examples of encapsulation. The particular details of, say, an edit control are embedded in the definition of the control itself, and the various properties and methods are detailed in the *CEdit* class of MFC. You need only declare an instance of *CEdit* to display text to a user and accept user input.

321. *Understanding the Structure as an Encapsulation Device*

The standard C structure is an example of encapsulation. It derives from the concept of a record in other languages, but it carries the idea one step further. It enables you to handle all the members of the structure, to create them, and to pass them around to other functions, as a single object.

The definition of a structure may contain instances of other previously defined structures, thus encapsulating multiple objects into a single definition. In the following structure definitions, for example, you define space to hold a sequence of characters you might want to assign to a particular keystroke based on the condition of the Shift and Alt keys. These definitions are independent of the font in use or whatever you chose to call your keyboard table. Next, you define a structure that is your actual keyboard table, and one member of it is an array containing your key definitions. You needn't create 103 different variable names for these keystrokes. When you define an instance of *KEYTABLE*, you also define 103 instances of *KEYDEF*:

```
#define   MAXKEYS   103
typedef struct _KeyDef
{
    char    Base[16];
    char    Shift[16];
    char    Alt[16];
    char    ShiftAlt[16];
} KEYDEF, *PKEYDEF;

typedef struct _KEYTABLE
{
    char    TableName[16];
    char    FontName[32];
    KEYDEF  Key[MAXKEYS];
} KEYTABLE, *PKEYTABLE;
```

That's about as far as the C structure goes, however. It doesn't demonstrate the principles of inheritance or polymorphism, which, as you will learn, C++ does.

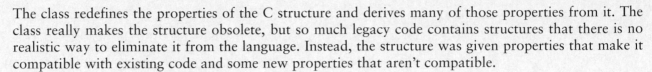

322. *Understanding the Class in C++*

The class redefines the properties of the C structure and derives many of those properties from it. The class really makes the structure obsolete, but so much legacy code contains structures that there is no realistic way to eliminate it from the language. Instead, the structure was given properties that make it compatible with existing code and some new properties that aren't compatible.

The class didn't have all that baggage, so it was free to inherit the structure properties and change them to become a programming element itself. Both classes and structures may inherit from other structures and classes and from each other. A structure may be derived from a class or another structure, and a class may be derived from a structure or another class.

The C++ class also gives us the notion of access privileges to its members. Variables and functions declared as members of a class or structure may be declared as being *private* to the structure, *protected* and available to friend and derived classes, or *public* and open to all. To make it compatible with legacy code, members of a structure are public by default, but members of a class are private by default.

The class allows you to define not only the properties of an object but also its behavior. Special function calls to constructors to initialize the class and destructors to clean up afterward execute automatically when an object is created or destroyed. Properties may be exposed outside the class on a need-to-know basis only.

The declaration of a class is the same as a structure, except that you use the *class* keyword instead of *struct* as in the following sample:

```
class CMyClass
{
// Class member declarations
};
```

That's very much like defining a structure. To derive a new class from another class, follow the name with a colon and the name of the parent class. Your new class then will have all the properties of the parent class, plus any other properties you give the new class:

```
class CBaseClass
{
// Base class member declarations
};

class CMyClass : CBaseClass
{
// Class member declarations
};
```

Although the colon is not listed as a separate operator, you use the colon after the class name to indicate that it is being derived from another class or structure.

323. *Understanding Polymorphism*

You define base classes with the distinct purpose of having them serve as ancestors to derived classes, but that doesn't always have to be the case. A programmer can declare an instance of a base class (except in certain cases, as you will see later). To accomplish this, you make the base class independent and give it all the properties and functions it needs in order to serve as a class that may be declared.

You may not want this basic behavior in your derived classes, however, so you use polymorphism to displace certain properties and functions of a base class and redefine them for your derived class.

In object-oriented programming, *polymorphism* is the ability to redefine an existing data structure, which in C++ means a class or a structure. C structures do not exhibit polymorphism because you can't derive descendents from them. The programmer needn't know or even care about the data types of variables and return types of functions in the base class to redefine the variables and functions. A variable declared in a base class as *double m_Number;* may be redeclared with the same name, using a different data type in a derived class. In this case, the base class variable is inaccessible unless you use the scope resolution operator (::).

324. *Polymorphism in the Real World*

Numerous examples of polymorphism exist in the world around us. Take the dog, for example. Pomeranians and Dalmatians clearly evolve from a common ancestor, but they exhibit distinctly different traits. They look different and have different statures, and they even act different. (Dalmatians actually act like dogs.) If it weren't for their common traits, they might even be classified as different species.

In fact, polymorphism is an important principle in genetics, and sometimes nature can carry it to extremes. Who can explain, for example, how the duck-billed platypus descended from the anteater? For more than 80 years after its discovery, scientists refused to believe that such a creature could exist and thought it a joke.

You see other examples of polymorphism at work in nature. Minerals can exhibit it. Calcite, aragonite, and vaterite are all different states of calcium carbonate, called "polymorphs." Coal and diamonds are different states of carbon; one you burn for heat and fuel, and the other, well, you wouldn't want to burn it even if you could.

Among man-made examples of polymorphism, you need only look as far as the driveway. The car is derived from what we call an "automobile." A property of an automobile is that it is self-propelled, and it may crawl, float, fly, or roll, among other methods, on zero or more wheels. The car derives those properties, but it redefines the method of propulsion and declares that it must have four wheels to accomplish the motion.

325. *Understanding Function Overloading as an Example of Polymorphism*

Functions don't "inherit" from other functions and, therefore, don't exhibit the type of polymorphism we think of when we speak of a class inheriting from a parent and changing the properties and methods in the resulting new class. In its strictest sense, however, polymorphism doesn't require inheritance and only describes alternative states and conditions of something. Minerals, for example, don't inherit traits but can exist as polymorphs.

With this, you can view overloaded functions as exhibiting basic traits of polymorphs. Normally, you define overloaded functions to perform similar operations but on different data types. This doesn't have to be the case, however, and you may, in fact, construct overloads to perform entirely different actions, depending on the data types passed.

This is especially true when you start dealing with objects. Polymorphism enables you to manipulate many different objects without worrying about what each one is. Overloaded functions don't have to be associated with a class or other object; you may overload a general-purpose function, pass it different objects, and write different code for each object. Take the simple act of writing to a log file. You may pass one object and write code to log certain properties of that object. When you pass it a different object, though, those properties might be meaningless, so you write a different function with the same name that logs the appropriate properties of the alternative object. You write your code as though you were calling a single function, but using different object types, and let the compiler select the appropriate function to call.

326. Using the Class as an Object of Polymorphism

Usually, when you think of polymorphism, you think of classes and generations of classes built down from one base class. The one base class defines the general behavior of objects, and you derive other classes from it and define the specific behavior, perhaps in terms of the general class object.

The primary mechanism through which classes support polymorphism is the *virtual function*. You use a virtual function to allow a base class to call a member function by the same name in a derived class, even though the derived class may not even exist at the time you define the base class. This concept may be difficult for newcomers to object-oriented programming to understand, but it's well worth the effort.

You declare a virtual function by placing the keyword *virtual* in front of the function declaration. Virtual functions have meaning only within classes, so you can't declare one outside a class definition.

Let's define some shape classes as an example. Your base class will be named *Shape* and will contain a function named *Draw()* to draw itself. It also will contain a function, named *Show()* that you can invoke to cause the shape to draw itself. Then you will define two other classes, *Circle* and *Square*, that inherit from *Shape* and themselves contain *Draw()* functions that draw only a circle and a square, respectively:

```
#include    <stdio.h>

class Shape
{
public:
    void Draw();
    void Show();
};

class Circle : public Shape
{
public:
    void Draw();
};
```

```
class Square : public Shape
{
public:
    void Draw();
};

void main (void)
{
Circle circle;
Square square;

    circle.Show();
    square.Show();
}

void Shape::Show()
{
    printf ("Shape::Show is used to set up the ");
    printf ("output device for drawing,\n ");
    printf ("then calls Draw()\n");
    Draw();
}

void Shape::Draw()
{
    printf ("Shape::Draw ");
    printf ("draws a circle within a square\n");
}

void Circle::Draw()
{
    printf ("Circle::Draw ");
    printf ("draws only the circle\n");
}

void Square::Draw()
{
    printf ("Square::Draw ");
    printf ("draws only the square\n");
}
```

The class *Circle* inherits *Show()* from its base class, so you don't have to redefine it. You would use the function perhaps to set up the output device for drawing and then put the actual drawing code in *Draw()*. What you intend here is to call the *Draw()* in the *Circle* and *Square* classes. However, when you run the code, you see the following output:

```
Shape::Show is used to set up the output device for drawing,
then calls Draw()
Shape::Draw draws a circle within a square
Shape::Show is used to set up the output device for drawing,
then calls Draw()
Shape::Draw draws a circle within a square
```

Clearly, that's not what you intended. The *Shape::Draw()* is a generic function you wrote as a place-holder so that you could call it from the *Shape::Show()* function.

How do you get *Show()* in the parent class to call the *Draw()* function in the derived classes? You could copy *Show()* into the derived classes, but it would be silly to have a separate copy of an identical function in all your derived classes. One of the goals of object-oriented programming is to avoid that very thing. You want to be able to define a generic function only once and then use it as necessary.

One method is to make the declaration of *Draw()* in the base class a virtual function. When you declare a function *virtual*, the compiler doesn't bind its address when the source file is compiled. You declare a function *virtual* by using that keyword in front of the name, so make that change:

```
class Shape
{
public:
    virtual void Draw();
    void Show();
};
```

Now, when you compile and run the program, you see the following output, which is exactly what you want:

```
Shape::Show is used to set up the output device for drawing,
then calls Draw()
Circle::Draw draws only the circle
Shape::Show is used to set up the output device for drawing,
then calls Draw()
Square::Draw draws only the square
```

With a single word, by using a *virtual* declaration in the base class, you are able to modify its behavior in a derived class without modifying the base class function.

327. *Understanding Inheritance*

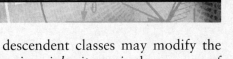

I've mentioned inheritance in describing polymorphism and how descendent classes may modify the behavior of their parent or base classes. In object-oriented programming, *inheritance* is the process of transferring the characteristics of an object to objects that are derived, or descended, from it.

When you define a class, particularly if you intend it to serve as a base, or ancestor, class, you include functions and variables to describe your object generally. You aren't concerned with specific instances of the class; you let the programmer take care of that. Instead, you try to generalize.

In a drawing program, for example, you might want to have a class to describe a shape. You would want to include functions and variables for such things as line width and fill color, but it would be inappropriate to assign it a property describing the number of sides. What, then, of the circle, ellipse, or oval?

In this case, you might want to derive another class from your shape class that describes shapes with corners and sides and another that describes rounded shapes. Both would inherit the line width and fill color properties, and you would then include only properties and methods that are specific to these types of shapes. From the rounded shapes class, you may then derive specific classes to describe a circle, an oval, or an ellipse and include properties such as radius and major and minor axes.

In the other branch of the tree, the one describing shapes with sides, you then might derive a polygon class where the concepts of radius and major and minor axes are meaningless, but in which the number and length of sides is important.

In both trees, neither derived sequence is burdened with properties that have no meaning for it, and when you declare an instance of a specific class, you need not be concerned with which branch of the tree spawned it. You wouldn't, for example, have need for a *DrawCorner()* function in a rounded shape class, nor would you call a *DrawArc()* function for a square or rectangle shape.

328. *Building Down from the Top Using Inheritance*

As in genetics, inheritance doesn't work backward. You can't give an ancestor class a property or characteristic of a derived class. Even the virtual function doesn't do that; the ancestor class had the trait when you declared the function *virtual*. It's more like a time capsule—you put the function in a time capsule by declaring it *virtual* and then unseal the capsule when you declare new functions.

Thus, you work your way downward in the class hierarchy. Like an evolving species, each descendant is given only the characteristics it needs, becoming more specific as you work toward the class you actually will use. This way, you can branch off at any point and work your way toward a new descendent, inheriting only the properties and functions you need.

In the example in Tip 327, " Understanding Inheritance," you could just as easily declare a rounded shapes class between *Shape* and *Circle*. You would again declare the *Draw()* function *virtual* and perhaps make it draw a circle, an oval, and an ellipse with the same center, or you might choose not to include a *Draw()* function at all in the intermediate descendent because you don't intend to use it. You would let the descendents all inherit the grandfather function and let only the individuals override it.

329. *Using Objects*

The advantage of using objects is that they encapsulate all the properties and functions of an object into a single identifier. You then may use that identifier, the variable, to access and manipulate the object, even pass it to other functions.

A function receiving an object, whether as a pointer or as a reference, is like subscribing to a magazine. The publisher doesn't have to send you every photo, every article, and every ad separately. Instead, you get a single publication with all these wrapped neatly in a single package.

More importantly, when you pass an object to a function, you are giving that function not only the current instance of an object but also its entire ancestry. If you were to pass the instance of your *Circle* class to a function, that function would be able to call *Show()* as the base class just as easily as the passing function could.

330. *Dividing a Program into Objects*

After you become accustomed to using objects in your programming, you begin looking at your code differently. I've written a lot of C code in the past 20 or so years. Each time I have reason to revisit some of it, I can't help but think how much easier it would have been to accomplish a task using objects.

First, you begin by looking for common variables that are used in your code to achieve a given result repeatedly. In your C code, any time you use a function, there is a very good possibility that you could use a class instead, or at least some of the extended capabilities of the structure in C++. In your baud rate structure from Tip 310, "Declaring and Initializing Pointers to Variables," for example, in the old C you would have to declare an instance for each baud rate, then assign the *long* member, and then assign the *char* member, or at least go through an exhaustive initializing list at the declaration. It was so much easier just to give it the numerical value and let the constructor handle the assignments.

You also look for common functions that are used to manipulate these common variables. If you read or write a sequence of values to and from a file, would it not be better to create a class function to handle the details? Then when you need to output the data to your file, you call the class's *Read()* or *Write()* member functions in a single statement.

After you get used to programming with objects, it's difficult to go back. Something bigger and better than object-oriented programming might be down the programming path, but for now it removes a lot of the drudgery from programming and from maintaining programs.

331. An Example of Object-Oriented Programming

Now you will put this object-oriented idea into a simple program. Soon you will be writing Windows programs, so let's take the shapes example from Tip 326, "Using the Class as an Object of Polymorphism," and put it into a program that actually draws. Don't worry about the Windows part of it yet; I'll be explaining that soon enough. What concerns you here is the use and manipulation of objects. The code on the CD-ROM is a Visual Studio project, so you can open it as a project and trace through it.

You're going to have to add some variables to your classes, and a couple of them might be unfamiliar to you. The *HWND* type is a pointer (handle) to an internal Windows structure that defines the window in which you are drawing. The *HDC* type is a pointer to another internal Windows structure, the device context, which describes the surface on which you will be drawing.

You're also going to add a couple of classes, *CArc* and *CLine*, to your shapes example and use these to draw your circle and square. Now, there are far easier ways to draw rectangles (a square is a special case of the rectangle), but the objective here is to show you how you can create an object and manipulate it to produce different results.

The *CShape* is much as you defined it in Tip 326, except that you put some real variables and drawing code in it. You store the *HWND* and *HDC* objects in this class, and each derived class simply passes them up to *CShape*:

```
class CShape
{
public:
    CShape(HWND hWnd, HDC hdc);
    virtual ~CShape();
    virtual void Draw ();
    virtual void Show();
protected:
    virtual HWND GetWindowHandle();
    virtual HDC GetDeviceContext();
    HDC m_hDC;
    HWND m_hWnd;
};
```

```
// Shape.cpp: implementation of the shape classes.
//
//////////////////////////////////////////////////////////
// CShape Class
//////////////////////////////////////////////////////////


CShape::CShape(HWND hWnd, HDC hdc)
{
    m_hWnd = hWnd;
    m_hDC = hdc;
}

CShape::~CShape()
{
}

void CShape::Show()
{
HPEN   hPen, hOldPen;

    hPen = CreatePen (PS_SOLID, 2, RGB(0x0, 0x0, 0x0));
    hOldPen = (HPEN) SelectObject (m_hDC, hPen);
    Draw ();
    SelectObject (m_hDC, hOldPen);
    DeleteObject (hPen);
}

void CShape::Draw()
{
RECT   rc;
SIZE   size;

    GetClientRect (m_hWnd, &rc);
    size.cx = rc.right / 3;
    size.cy = rc.bottom / 3;
    Rectangle (m_hDC, rc.right / 2 -
                      size.cy, rc.bottom / 2 - size.cy,
                      rc.right / 2 + size.cy,
                      rc.bottom / 2 + size.cy);
    Ellipse (m_hDC, rc.right / 2 - size.cy,
                    rc.bottom / 2 - size.cy,
                    rc.right / 2 + size.cy,
                    rc.bottom / 2 + size.cy);
}
```

The *Show()* function creates a pen for you and then calls *Draw()*, a virtual function that is intended to be overridden by derived classes. When you get more into Windows programming, you can elect to create the pen in your derived class, especially if you want to use different colors. For now, though, this suits your purpose. The *Draw()* function is simply a placeholder, and if you don't override it, a large square with a circle inside will appear on the screen.

You draw the square by starting with a line, a *CLine* object, and then rotating it about its end point. The advantage of doing it this way is that the image always remains a square, even if your points are not aligned. In the Windows API, the function to draw a rectangle will draw a different-shaped rectangle;

using your objects, the shape will retain its form but just be tilted on the screen. In addition, by giving it a "squash" value, the square becomes a rhombus.

The *CLine* class definition and code follow. The definitions for all the classes you use are in the *shape.h* file, and the code is in *shape.cpp*:

```cpp
/////////////////////////////////////////////////////////////////

//     CLine class definition

class CLine : virtual public Cshape
{
public:
    CLine(HWND hWnd, HDC hdc, POINT & ptStart,
          POINT ptEnd);
    virtual ~CLine();
    void Rotate (int nDegrees, int nWhichEnd);
protected:
    POINT m_ptEnd;
    POINT m_ptStart;
    void Draw();
private:
    double m_fRadius;
    double m_fCurAngle;
};


/////////////////////////////////////////////////////////////////
// CLine Class implementation
/////////////////////////////////////////////////////////////////
CLine::CLine(HWND hWnd, HDC hdc, POINT & ptStart,
                                  POINT ptEnd)
                                  : CShape (hWnd, hdc)
{
    m_ptStart = ptStart;
    m_ptEnd = ptEnd;
//
// Calculate the radius and current angle of the line
    int cx = m_ptEnd.x - m_ptStart.x;
    int cy = m_ptEnd.y - m_ptStart.y;
    m_fRadius = sqrt (abs(cx * cx + cy * cy));
    m_fCurAngle = asin((m_ptStart.y-m_ptEnd.y) /
                       m_fRadius);
}

CLine::~CLine()
{
}

void CLine::Draw()
{
    MoveToEx (m_hDC, m_ptStart.x, m_ptStart.y, NULL);
    LineTo (m_hDC, m_ptEnd.x, m_ptEnd.y);
}

void CLine::Rotate(int nDegrees, int nWhichEnd)
{
```

```
double fAngle;

    POINT ptTemp;
    GetCurrentPositionEx (m_hDC, &ptTemp);

    if (!m_fRadius)
        return;

    fAngle = (double) nDegrees / (10.0 * RADIAN);
    fAngle += m_fCurAngle;
    if (!nWhichEnd)     // Rotate the begin point
    {
        m_ptEnd.x = m_ptStart.x +
                (int) ((cos (fAngle) * m_fRadius));
        m_ptEnd.y = m_ptStart.y -
                (int) ((sin (fAngle) * m_fRadius));
    }
    else                // Rotate the end point
    {
//
//  New start point is the old end point.
//  Calculate the new end point. Rotate the angle
//  180 degrees to indicate that we are going from
//  end to start points.
        fAngle += PI;
        m_ptStart = m_ptEnd;
        m_ptEnd.x = m_ptEnd.x -
                (int) ((cos (fAngle) * m_fRadius));
        m_ptEnd.y = m_ptEnd.y +
                (int) ((sin (fAngle) * m_fRadius));
    }
    m_fCurAngle = fAngle;
}
```

If you don't understand the trigonometric functions, don't worry about it for now. I'll try to explain them when you get into more Windows programming. Meanwhile, hide yourself out and get a good crib sheet on elementary math such as trigonometry and calculus.

Your starting line doesn't have to be exactly horizontal or vertical. The constructor calculates the starting line as though it were a circle radius and stores the results, along with the start and end points, in class data members. The *Draw()* function, which overrides the base class function, simply moves to the beginning point and draws a line to the ending point.

The real magic of *CLine* is in the *Rotate()* function. The parameters tell it how much to rotate the line and from which end to perform the rotation. The Windows drawing function usually operates in terms of radians. However, humans find it more convenient to work in degrees, so the angle argument to the function is in tenths of degrees (300 equals 30.0 degrees). A zero means to rotate the line around the starting point, and a non-zero to rotate it around the end point. A positive value is a counterclockwise rotation around the rotation point, and a negative value is a clockwise rotation. Depending on how you choose your rotations, the reference point may be any corner of the square.

The *CSquare* class declares a *CLine* object and uses that to draw the edges of the square, as shown in the code. In the example, I've purposely made the initial line slightly skewed to show you how that tilts the square, but its basic shape remains unchanged. The *CSquare* class definition and implementation are shown here:

```
class CSquare : virtual public CShape
{
public:
    CSquare(HWND hWnd, HDC hdc, POINT & ptStart,
                        POINT & ptEnd, int nSquash = 0);
    virtual ~CSquare();
    virtual void Draw();

protected:
    int m_nSquash;
    POINT m_ptEnd;
    POINT m_ptStart;
};
/////////////////////////////////////////////////////////////
// CSquare Class
/////////////////////////////////////////////////////////////

CSquare::CSquare(HWND hWnd, HDC hdc,
                POINT & ptStart, POINT & ptEnd,
                int nSquash)
                : CShape (hWnd, hdc)
{
    m_ptStart = ptStart;
    m_ptEnd - ptEnd;
    m_nSquash = nSquash;
}

CSquare::~CSquare()
{
}

void CSquare::Draw()
{
    CLine line (m_hWnd, m_hDC, m_ptStart, m_ptEnd);
    line.Show ();
    line.Rotate (-900 + m_nSquash, 1);
    line.Show ();
    line.Rotate (900 - m_nSquash, 1);
    line.Show ();
    line.Rotate (900 + m_nSquash, 1);
    line.Show ();
}
```

After drawing the initial line, you rotate the line –90 degrees from the end point and then two positive 90-degree rotations from the end point. After three rotations, the line segments join, and you have a square that is independent of the screen axis. A rhombic effect is generated by alternately adding and subtracting a "squash" angle to and from the rotation angles. In fact, the rhombus generated by the menu item is drawn by the same function that draws the square.

Carefully designing and using a simple object makes all this possible, and in relatively few lines of code.

If you've ever used the *Arc()* function in the Windows API, you will appreciate the *CArc* class. The *Arc()* function takes nine parameters, including the handle to the device context. The constructor takes six parameters (five really; the only reason you need the *HWND* parameter is for the default drawing code in *CShape*, which could be eliminated). The parameters are the window handle, the device context handle, a *POINT* marking the center of rotation, a start angle in tenths of degrees, and the angle to draw, again in tenths of degrees, which may be positive or negative. The *CArc* class is remarkably simple; most of the complexity is contained in the *Rotate()* function and in the *Draw()* function, which calls the Windows API. The class definition stores the variables necessary to iterate calls to a class object:

```cpp
/////////////////////////////////////////////////////////
// CArc class definition
/////////////////////////////////////////////////////////
class CArc : public CShape
{
public:
    void Rotate (int nDegrees);
    CArc(HWND hWnd, HDC hdc, POINT& ptCenter,
            int nRadius=0, int nStart = 0,
            int nSubtend = 0);
    virtual ~CArc();
    virtual void Draw();
private:
    POINT   m_ptCenter;
    POINT   m_ptStart;
    POINT   m_ptEnd;
    double  m_fRadius;
    double  m_fStart;
    double  m_fEnd;
};
/////////////////////////////////////////////////////////
// CArc Class Implementation
/////////////////////////////////////////////////////////

CArc::CArc(HWND hWnd, HDC hdc, POINT & ptCenter,
              int nRadius, int nStart, int nSubtend)
              : CShape (hWnd, hdc)
{
    m_fRadius = (double) nRadius;
    m_ptCenter = ptCenter;
    m_fStart = ((double) nStart / 10.0) / RADIAN;
    m_fEnd = m_fStart + ((double) nSubtend / 10.0) / RADIAN;
    Rotate (0);
}

CArc::~CArc()
{
}

void CArc::Draw()
{
    Arc (m_hDC, m_ptCenter.x - (int) m_fRadius,
                m_ptCenter.y - (int) m_fRadius,
                m_ptCenter.x + (int) m_fRadius,
                m_ptCenter.y + (int) m_fRadius,
                m_ptStart.x, m_ptStart.y,
                m_ptEnd.x, m_ptEnd.y);
}

void CArc::Rotate(int nDegrees)
{
    m_fStart += ((double) nDegrees / 10.0) / RADIAN;
    m_fEnd += ((double) nDegrees / 10.0) / RADIAN;
```

```
        m_ptStart.x = m_ptCenter.x +
                        (int) ((cos (m_fStart) * m_fRadius));
        m_ptStart.y = m_ptCenter.y -
                        (int) ((sin (m_fStart) * m_fRadius));
      m_ptEnd.x = m_ptCenter.x -
                        (int) ((cos (m_fEnd) * m_fRadius));
      m_ptEnd.y = m_ptCenter.y +
                        (int) ((sin (m_fEnd) * m_fRadius));
}
```

The constructor initializes the variables for the radius, the center point, and the initial angle and then calls *Rotate()* with a 0-degree angle to initialize the other variables.

The *Rotate()* function converts the passed angle from tenths of degrees to radians and then adds it to both the start and end angles. The actual screen points are then calculated and stored in member variables.

You draw the circle using *CArc* segments. In the example, you set the angle to 90 degrees and rotate it three times to complete the circle.

```
/////////////////////////////////////////////////////////
// CCircle Class
/////////////////////////////////////////////////////////
class CCircle : virtual public CShape
{
public:
    CCircle(HWND hWnd, HDC hdc, POINT & ptCenter, int
            nRadius);
    virtual ~CCircle();

private:
    POINT m_ptCenter;
    int m_nRadius;
    int m_nSide;
protected:
    virtual void Draw ();
};
/////////////////////////////////////////////////////////
// CCircle implementation
/////////////////////////////////////////////////////////

CCircle::CCircle(HWND hWnd, HDC hdc,
                POINT & ptCenter, int nRadius)
                : CShape (hWnd, hdc)
{
    m_ptCenter = ptCenter;
    m_nRadius = nRadius;
}

CCircle::~CCircle()
{
}

void CCircle::Draw()
{
    CArc arc (m_hWnd, m_hDC, m_ptCenter,
            m_nRadius, 900, 900);
```

```
    for (int i = 0; i < 4; ++i)
    {
        arc.Draw ();
        arc.Rotate (900);
    }
}
```

If all you need to draw is a circle, the Windows API function might be easier. If you need to draw an arc, though, the *CArc* function brings the operation down to degrees, which are more understandable to humans. You could, for example, draw a dashed circle of your own design by drawing an arc of, say, 10 degrees, incrementing the arc 15 degrees to leave a slight gap, and continue until the circle is complete.

Like the *CLine* class, it's a simple object that can do a lot of work for you.

332. *Understanding the Elements of a Class*

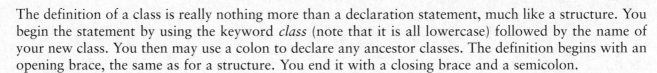

The definition of a class is really nothing more than a declaration statement, much like a structure. You begin the statement by using the keyword *class* (note that it is all lowercase) followed by the name of your new class. You then may use a colon to declare any ancestor classes. The definition begins with an opening brace, the same as for a structure. You end it with a closing brace and a semicolon.

Everything within the braces is local to, or a member of, the class. There is no immigration authority for classes, so nothing declared outside the braces may become a member of the class.

Static variables declared within the class must also be redeclared outside the class and in global memory, but the effect is to limit access to them as though they were ordinary members. There is no class object until an instance is declared within your program, but static variables and functions may be accessed before any such declaration. Hence, that is why there is the need to declare the variables again outside the class definition.

It doesn't matter in what order you declare variables and functions. As you will see shortly, by default, all the members are considered private and may be accessed only by other member functions of the class. The exceptions are a default constructor and destructor. If you don't specifically declare a constructor, a public constructor and destructor are implied. If, however, you declare either of these functions, it is your responsibility to make them public. Without a public constructor, you can't declare an instance of the class because there is no way from outside the class to access the constructor, which must be done at the time an object is declared. Without a public destructor, you can't destroy an object because the destructor function can't be accessed from outside the class. In the examples in Tip 326, "Using the Class as an Object of Polymorphism," you don't declare any constructors or destructors, so the compiler generates them for you. Try declaring them with different access levels—private and protected—to see what compiler errors you get.

You don't have to go outside the class declaration to define the member functions. The code for the functions may be written at the time they are declared, and any function defined this way is considered to be *inline*. For short functions, this is no problem. However, for longer functions, having them inline might cause your code to grow considerably, so you usually define the functions outside the class definition. The declaration of a function is the same as you would write for any function, but when you define it, you have to tell the compiler to what class this function belongs. You do that by using the scope resolution operator (::). If you have a class named *Shape* that contains a member function *Draw()*, you declare and define it as follows:

```
class Shape
{
```

```
public:
    void Draw();
};

void Shape::Draw()
{
    printf ("Shape::Draw ");
    printf ("draws a circle within a square\n");
}
```

The definition is much the same as defining any other function except you use the class name, the scope resolution operator, and the function name to tell the compiler that this is the function you declare in the class. Without it, the function becomes just any other utility function.

333. *Understanding Constructors*

Objects of a class are created like any other variables—on the stack as a variable within a function, in global space, or on the heap using the *new* operator. After objects are created, you might have to go through a sequence of function calls to initialize the variables to prepare the class.

C++ gives you a way to do that automatically through a special function, a *constructor*. Even if you don't declare one in the class definition, the compiler generates an empty constructor that essentially does nothing. A constructor has no return type, not even *void*, and attempting to give it one will cause an error from the compiler.

A default constructor takes no parameters, but you may declare a constructor that does. If you do, you must pass the arguments at the time an instance of the class is declared. A constructor should be *public* if you intend to declare any instances of the class. A base class constructor may be *protected*, however, preventing you from declaring instances of the base class but still giving access to its descendents.

If your class is a derived class, the constructor for each base class in the hierarchy is executed when you declare an instance of the class. The constructor for the most distant relative is called first, then the second most distant, and on down the line until you come to the class being declared; its constructor is called last. In the case of multiple inheritance, the constructors and those of any ancestors are called in the order they are inherited. There's no way to control the order of construction, so you're not allowed to call a constructor after the declaration, and you can't declare constructors *virtual*.

Declaring a pointer to a class does not create an instance of the class, so no constructor is called. Creating an instance on the heap does create an object, however, and the constructor is called. Every class instance inherits a pointer to itself, named *this*, so it always knows where in memory it is located, whether it is on the stack, global, or on the heap. The *this* pointer is discussed in more detail in Tip 370, "Introducing the *this* Pointer."

334. *Passing Parameters to a Constructor*

A constructor executes only when the class object is created, and there is no way to call it after the declaration statement. If you need to pass one or more parameters to a constructor, you have to declare it with parameters and pass the parameters as an argument in the statement where you declare or create the class instance. If you declare a constructor with arguments, the compiler does not create a default constructor, and you get an error if you try to declare an instance without values for the parameters.

If you declare a class with a constructor having one parameter as follows, you then create an instance of the class by declaring it and putting the parameter in parentheses:

```
class Shape
{
public:
    Shape (int x) {m_x = x;}
    void Draw();
private
    int    m_x;
};

Shape shape (1);
```

It's the same as calling any other function except that you do it at the time of declaration. If you have multiple parameters, enter them separated by commas just as you would for any other function.

If a base class needs a parameter for its constructor, you must declare a constructor and pass it to the base class, even if your class doesn't use it. You can pass it a default argument or accept one at the time the instance is declared. In the following example, the base class requires a parameter, but the class being created doesn't:

```
class Shape
{
public:
    Shape (int x) {m_x = x;}   // Inline constructor
private
    int    m_x;
};
class Circle : public Shape
{
public:
    Circle ();
    Circle (int x);
    void Draw();
};
```

To handle this situation, you define your constructors for *Circle* so that they pass a value up to *Shape*, even though you don't need them in *Circle*. In the first constructor, which doesn't take a parameter, you pass it a default value:

```
Circle::Circle () : Shape (0)    // Pass default value
{
}
```

In the second case, the declaration accepts the parameter on behalf of the base class and simply passes it along:

```
Circle::Circle (int x) : Shape (x)    // Pass parameter up
{
}
```

Initializing an array of a class requiring a parameter is as simple as initializing any array; you enclose the comma-separated parameters inside braces after the declaration. If, however, your constructor requires more than one parameter, the declaration can be trickier. You must include the complete syntax of the constructor in your declaration. Look back in Tip 194, "Using Arrays of Objects," for an example of how this is done.

335. Using Multiple Constructors in a Class

Constructors can be overloaded. That is, you may declare multiple constructors as long as they differ in the number or type of parameters being passed. As with any other overloaded function, the compiler will select the proper constructor depending on the number or type of arguments you specify in the declaration.

The compiler knows that a function is a constructor because it has the same name as the class. You can declare it inline, or you can define it outside the class definition. The following code sets up both an inline constructor and one that is defined outside the class:

```
class Shape
{
public:
    Shape (int x) {m_x = x;}    // Inline constructor
    Shape (int x, int y);       // Normal constructor
    void Draw();
private
    int     m_x;
    int     m_y;
};
Shape::Shape (int x, int y)
{
    m_x = x;
    m_y = y;
}
```

The external constructor was defined using the same scope resolution operator you use for other class functions. Neither in the declaration within the class nor in its definition do you give it a return type. The declaration itself determines which constructor is called:

```
Shape shape1;       // Illegal. No default constructor
Shape shape2(1);    // The inline constructor is called
Shape shape3(1,2);  // The external constructor is called
```

One, and only one, of the constructors is executed, however.

336. Understanding Destructors

Suppose that your class constructor—or any other member function, for that matter—allocates memory using the *new* operator without deleting it, as in the following code:

```
class Baud
{
public:
```

```
    Baud (long speed);
private:
    int     m_nSpeed;
    char    *m_pszSpeed;
};
Baud::Baud (int speed)
{
    m_nSpeed = speed;
    m_pszSpeed = new char [10];
    if (m_pszSpeed != NULL)
        sprintf (m_pszSpeed, "%ld", speed);
}
```

You have a problem here. The constructor has allocated some heap memory and assigned its address to a private variable. The class has no idea when it will go out of scope and, therefore, when to delete the memory. You can't delete it from your code because it is a private member. If it isn't deleted before the class declaration goes out of scope, you will be left with stranded memory (a "memory leak").

Like constructors, every class has a destructor that is called automatically when the class object is destroyed. Its purpose is to clean up after the class in situations such as I just described. Even if you don't declare it, the compiler will generate a default constructor. It has no return type, and it's an error to try to assign it one.

Unlike constructors, a class may have one, and only one, destructor, and you can't pass it parameters. You also may call a destructor from within your code, which can cause you some problems.

You declare the destructor the same as a constructor except that you prefix its name with the *not* operator, a tilde. In your class (in the preceding example), you would simply declare it as *~Baud()* and define it as follows:

```
Baud::~Baud ()
{
    delete [] m_pszSpeed;
}
```

The allocation for *m_pszSpeed* was made in the constructor, so you know that it will either be *NULL* (the allocation failed) or point to a valid heap memory block. You needn't worry about the *NULL* case because the definition of *delete* states that it will do nothing with a *NULL* pointer.

You can call a destructor at any time in your code, and this presents some potential problems of its own. Suppose in this example that you call the destructor and delete the heap memory. The constructor is going to be called again when the class object is destroyed, and there's no way to stop it. As a safeguard, it's a good idea to add a line—*m_pszSpeed = NULL;*—to the destructor after the memory has been deleted as shown below:

```
Baud::~Baud ()
{
    delete [] m_pszSpeed;
    m_pszSpeed = NULL;
}
```

It's a better idea never to call the destructor and to let it do its work at the proper time.

Why does C++ do this to you, let you perform an operation that you shouldn't? Well, C++ lets you do many things you shouldn't, but in this case you need to be able to call destructors in base classes to shut down a class instance properly.

When a derived class object is destroyed, the destructors are called in the reverse order the constructors were called, with the destructor of the most distant ancestor being called last.

337. Understanding the Access Keywords in a Class

One aspect of encapsulation is that you be able to keep data elements in a secure place and away from accidental modification. The class enables you to do that by allowing you to set access levels for your data and function members.

You set the access level of class members by specifying one of the security keywords *(public, protected, or private)* followed by a colon. After the access level has been set, all members declared after that point are given that access. You may change it at any point and even have several blocks with the same access level. It's common practice among some programmers to declare their functions in one part of the definition and their variables separately. In this case, they would use multiple declarations of the access keywords.

The *public access* level grants unrestricted access to a function or variable. Any member or non-member function that has access to the object's instance, or scope, may read or modify a public variable. Similarly, public functions may be called at any time an instance of the object is in scope.

Protected access is stricter. Only member functions of the class, those of derived classes, and those of special classes called "friends," may access protected variables or execute protected functions. The protected status allows you to nestle your functions and variables behind a wall of safety, yet open them up for those special classes. Without it, inheritance would, at best, be difficult.

The *private access* level gives the greatest protection for variables and functions. Only member functions may modify private variables or execute private functions. These functions may be public or protected, but they must be members of the class.

338. Using Access Keywords to Enforce Encapsulation

Declaring private variables and then using public functions helps you to control the range and content of your member variables by writing rules into the functions.

The class object gives you a safe place to store data. Using a *public* function, for example, gives your program a chance to perform value and range checking before setting the value of a *private* variable as shown in the following sample, which assures *iValue* is never less than 0:

```
class MyClass
{
private:
    int    iValue;
public:
    void SetValue(int Value)
    {
        if (Value < 0)
            iValue = -Value;
        else
            iValue = Value;
    }
};
```

The *SetValue()* function will check the value each time you call it, so you don't have to perform the check every time you want to set the value of *iValue*. This greatly reduces the risk of programming errors.

Another benefit is that you may change the internal makeup of your class without having to worry about the effect on other parts of the program that use the class.

339. Keep Your Powder Dry (and Your Data Members Private)

Ordinarily, in designing a class you try to keep the variables private, or at the very least, protected. In this way, you isolate them from the outside world, and you are free to change their behavior and content from within the class itself. From outside the class, you can continue to make them appear as they did.

In your *Circle* class, you might want to store the center point of the circle in terms of its x and y coordinates and provide a public function to return them on request:

```
class Circle : public Shape
{
public:
    void Draw();
    void GetCenter (int& x, int& y)
        {
            x = m_x;
            y = m_y;
        }
private:
    int   m_x;
    int   m_y;
};
```

Later, when you get into Windows programming, you find a convenient structure named *POINT* for storing such information. You return to your class and give it a new function to take advantage of this newly discovered structure:

```
void GetCenter (POINT& point)
{
    point.x = m_x;
    point.y = m_y;
}
```

You need not modify your class, nor do you need to find all the places in past code where you have used the old function. Your code, after all, isn't concerned with the internal data structure of the class, but with the values returned.

You also may provide some value checking to avoid programming errors. In a statistical class, you may store the number of occurrences of two or more events and then provide a function to return their average. The constructor initializes the member variables to 0:

```
class Stat
{
public:
    Stat () {m_e1 = m_e2 = m_Total = 0;}
    int GetEvent1Average ()
    {
        return (((double) e1 / (double) m_Total) / 100);
```

```
    }
private:
    int  m_e1;
    int  m_e2;
    int  m_Total
};
```

The intent is that your function return the integer average of the first event as compared to the total events. What happens if you happen to call *GetEvent1Average()* before any events have been recorded? You get a "divide by zero" error and your program bombs. Every time you call it, you have to test and not call the function if the total is zero. Why not simply rewrite the function to perform the test for you, as follows:

```
int GetEvent1Average ()
{
    if (m_total == 0)
        return (-1);
    return (((double) e1 / (double) m_Total) / 100);
}
```

You know that your average is supposed to be a positive value, so if you get a negative value in return, you know that there have been no events and your program is safe from the dreaded "divide by zero" error.

340. Understanding Base Classes

If you examine any class library, you will find any number of classes that are never intended to be used directly. Rather, they are intended to serve as base classes for other classes that you will declare in your code. In many cases, you might go through several descendants before you finally arrive at a class you intend to use in your code.

If you wanted to write a program about ships, for example, you might start out with a very basic class named *Ship* that describes the basic nature of ships. You wouldn't intend to use the class directly, but from there you could derive any number of branches. There would be sailing ships and powered ships. Under powered ships, you might have steam-powered ships, oil-powered ships, nuclear-powered ships, and so forth. Again, these would be base classes for further derived classes. Perhaps under nuclear-powered ships, you would have submarines and aircraft carriers. It's at this point that you would begin using the classes.

You can protect your base classes from being used in a couple of ways. First, you can make the constructor protected, thus preventing an instance of it from being declared. Second, you can make it an abstract class by having it contain one or more pure virtual functions. I discuss the latter shortly.

A top-level base class should provide the most general properties and functions for the class structure you are working toward. The idea is to build an interface that will remain stable as you build down toward your most specific classes. By the time you reach the bottom, you might be surprised at how little additional code you need to write.

341. *Deriving a New Class from a Base Class*

You make one class a descendant of another when it is defined by following its identifier with a colon and then naming the base class. You may give the base class an access level of public, protected, or private in the declaration. As you might suspect, the access keywords function much the same as they do for members of the class.

The *public* access inherits members of the base class with their existing access levels. Public members are still public, protected members are protected, and private members are still invited to the best parties. Generally, this is the access you will use in deriving one class from another. If the class structure is well designed, it will provide all the protection you need.

The *protected* level makes all public members of the base class protected members of the derived class, and the *private* level makes all the base class members private to the derived class.

To derive one class from another, you first need a base class. Then, you define your derived class using the definition of the base class, as in the following code. From here on, you are going to start using the capital "C" as part of the name to indicate a class; when you get to the Microsoft Foundation Class, you will see a lot of that:

```
class CShips
{
 protected:
    CShips() { }   // Protected to use only as base class
public:
    // Functions to support the ship class
private:
    // Data members (properties) of ships
}
class CPoweredShips : public CShips
{
protected:          // Again for use as base class only
    CPoweredShips () { }
public:
    // Functions to support the powered ship class
private:
    // Data members (properties) of powered ships
}
class CNuclearShips : public CPoweredShips
{
public:            // This class we will use in our code
                   //  or we may want to derive yet another
                   //  class for submarines and carriers
    CNuclearShips () { }
public:
    // Functions to support the nuclear-powered ship class
private:
    // Data members (properties) of nuclear-powered ships
}
```

With each successive class definition, you inherit the properties and functions of the parent class and all the properties and functions of its parent, if any.

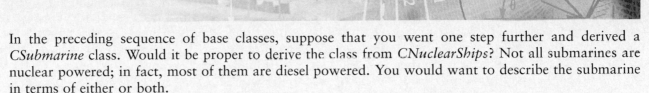

342. *Understanding Multiple Inheritance*

In the preceding sequence of base classes, suppose that you went one step further and derived a *CSubmarine* class. Would it be proper to derive the class from *CNuclearShips*? Not all submarines are nuclear powered; in fact, most of them are diesel powered. You would want to describe the submarine in terms of either or both.

You could derive another series of classes and finally wind up with *CDieselShips* and then derive your submarine class from both *CNuclearShips* and *CDieselShips*. To do this, you would add a comma after the name of the first base class, then an access level, and then the name of the second base class. If you don't use another access level, the access of the first base class is used. You then would write your identifier for the submarine class like the following:

```
class CSubmarine : public CNuclearShips, CDieselShips
```

Your submarine class then would inherit the properties and functions of both the base classes, and you could describe an object in terms of either type.

The order in which you add base classes determines the order in which the constructors and destructors are called. When an object is declared, the most distant relative of the first base class is constructed first; then the constructors work their way down the branch. When that branch is constructed, the most distant relative of the second base class is called, and the constructors again work their way down the branch. Only when all the branches have been constructed is the derived class constructor called.

When a class object is destroyed, the destructors are called in the reverse order of the constructors, with the derived class's constructor being called first.

Multiple inheritance also introduces the potential problem that somewhere along the tree, more than one base class is going to inherit from a single parent. Your *CSubmarine* class readily lends itself to serving as an example of what happens. Although both branches are distinct, eventually they both are going to derive from *CPoweredShips* and *CShips*. This means that your instance of *CSubmarine* is going to inherit two copies of each of these base classes.

This isn't always undesirable. Perhaps you need separate copies of base classes. Usually, though, it's a waste of good memory and resources. You can prevent this from happening by declaring your inheritance *virtual* when you come to a point where the tree splits into two branches. In this case, the tree splits where *CDieselShips* and *CNuclearShips* both use *CPoweredShips* as their base class. At this point, you would declare your base classes as *public virtual* instead of simply *public*:

```
class CNuclearShips : public virtual CPoweredShips
class CDieselShips : public virtual CPoweredShips
```

The declaration causes both branches to converge at the split, and you inherit only one copy of the base classes *CPoweredShips* and *CShips*.

343. *Laying the First Brick: Using a Base Class*

Any class may serve as a base class. Some are designed specifically to be used as base classes. However, if at any time you need to add functionality or new properties to a class, you are free to inherit from it and build a new class.

Class libraries such as the Microsoft Foundation Class or the C++ standard iostream library, both of which are included with Visual C++, use tree-like structures in which a single class serves as the base for several branches in the tree.

You've seen how using a *protected* constructor can prevent you from declaring an instance of a class, thereby limiting its use to serving as a base class. Another method is to create the base class as a *virtual* class by declaring one of the member functions as *pure virtual* (by declaring it *virtual* and setting its address to 0). When you do this, you don't write a definition for the pure virtual function; you leave it to the derived class to provide the code. The compiler won't let you create an instance of the class, and you can't use it as a base class unless you provide the code for the function. In Tip 346, "Understanding Friend Functions," you have an example of declaring a pure virtual function.

If your base class inherits from another base class, it's a good idea to declare the inheritance *virtual* unless your base class needs its own private copy of the parent class. This allows multiple inheritance later down the branch.

344. *Understanding Member Functions*

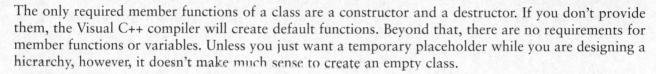

The only required member functions of a class are a constructor and a destructor. If you don't provide them, the Visual C++ compiler will create default functions. Beyond that, there are no requirements for member functions or variables. Unless you just want a temporary placeholder while you are designing a hierarchy, however, it doesn't make much sense to create an empty class.

Member functions, sometimes referred to as "methods," are used to support class operations and to provide controlled access to protected and private functions and data. They may be given any one of the access levels of public, protected, or private. You declare a function in a class definition the same as you would outside a class, using its return type and parameter list. It is possible, and probable, that more than one class may contain functions with the same name. Therefore, when you define the body of the function, you identify it as a member of the class, using the class name and the scope resolution operator (::). If you declared an *int* function named *GetEngineType* within your *CPoweredShips* class, you write the definition as shown here. You then follow with the function's code enclosed in braces:

```
int CPoweredShips::GetEngineType ()
{
    return (m_EngineType);
}
```

Functions also may be defined within the class definition at the time they are declared. In this case, the compiler treats them as *inline* functions:

```
class CPoweredShips : public CShips
{
protected:          // Again for use as base class only
    CPoweredShips () { }
public:
    int GetEngineType ()
    {
        return (m_EngineType);
    }
private:
    int  m_EngineType;
}
```

To call a class function, you use the member operator, a period, just as you would to access a variable member of a class or structure. When you call the function using a pointer to the class, you must use the pointer-to-member operator:

```
void RefFunction (CPoweredShips& Natilus)
{
    int Engine = Nautilus.GetEngineType ();
}

void PointerFunction (CPoweredShips *Natilus)
{
    int Engine = Nautilus->GetEngineType ();
}
```

From within the class, member functions may call other member functions by using the functions' name. This sometimes presents a resolution problem when external functions have the same name as member functions. The compiler will treat the call as a call to the member function unless you use the scope resolution operator to indicate that you want the external function.

This is particularly true in Windows programming. For example, the *CWnd* class, from which most of the Windows controls and application windows are derived, contains a *MessageBox()* function that takes only three parameters, the first of which is the text for the message box. There also is a global *MessageBox()* function that requires a window handle as its first parameter. The compiler doesn't treat these as overloaded functions and will issue an error if you try to call the global function with a handle from within a *CWnd*-derived class. In this case, you must specify the global function using the scope resolution operator:

```
// Call the CWnd Message box function:
MessageBox("Hello, World!", "Howdy", MB_OK);

// Call the global MessageBox function:
::MessageBox (this->m_hWnd, "Hello,  World!",
                            "Howdy",MB_OK);
```

The MFC *CWnd* class contains a public member variable, *m_hWnd*, that contains the handle of its window.

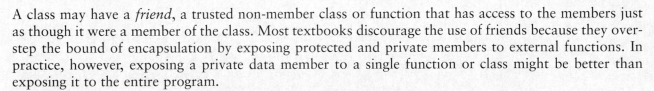

345. *Understanding Friend Classes*

A class may have a *friend*, a trusted non-member class or function that has access to the members just as though it were a member of the class. Most textbooks discourage the use of friends because they overstep the bound of encapsulation by exposing protected and private members to external functions. In practice, however, exposing a private data member to a single function or class might be better than exposing it to the entire program.

You declare a friend class using the keyword *friend* and identifying the class by name. This, in effect, makes the friend a member of the class with all the privileges associated with that honor. A function in a friend class may access data members without regard to their access level. Let's redefine your *CSubmarine* class slightly, add another class, and declare it a friend:

```
#include    <stdio.h>
#include    <string.h>
```

```
class CSubmarine;    // Forward reference declaration

class CFirstClass
{
public:
    char *GetEngineType (CSubmarine & sub);
};

class CSubmarine
{
public:
    CSubmarine (char *Engine);
    ~CSubmarine ();
private:
    char   *m_EngineType;
    friend CFirstClass;
};

int main ()
{
CSubmarine sub("Nuclear");
CFirstClass first;

    printf ("Engine type is %s\n",
                      first.GetEngineType(sub));
    return (0);
}

CSubmarine::CSubmarine (char *Engine)
{
    m_EngineType = new char [strlen (Engine) + 1];
    strcpy (m_EngineType, Engine);
}
CSubmarine::~CSubmarine ()
{
    delete [] m_EngineType;
}

char *CFirstClass::GetEngineType (CSubmarine & sub)
{
    return (sub.m_EngineType);
}
```

Note the forward declaration of *CSubmarine*. The function in *CFirstClass* requires an argument of type *CSubmarine*, but you haven't defined the class. To get away from the need for a forward reference, you would have to define *CSubmarine* before *CFirstClass*, in which case your *friend* declaration wouldn't work. Usually, in *friend* declarations, this is the case, and some sort of forward reference is necessary.

If you leave out the *friend* declaration in *CSubmarine*, the compiler gives you an error that it can't access the private member of the class. By including it, *CFirstClass* essentially becomes a member of *CSubmarine*.

346. *Understanding Friend Functions*

A friend doesn't have to be an entire class. You could have given just the one function friend access to your class. You would name the function using the scope resolution operator and its return type. In your *friend* class definition from the preceding example, if you wanted to give access only to the *GetEngineType()* function, your declaration would look like the following:

```
friend char *CFirstClass::GetEngineType (CSubmarine & sub);
```

Although friends might be necessary in some cases, specifying only certain functions limits the exposure to the outside world.

Friend functions don't have to be members of another class. This fact will be important when I start discussing streams. You can define a function in global scope to access a private data member and then declare it a friend of the class:

```
#include    <stdio.h>
#include    <string.h>

class CSubmarine;    // Forward reference declaration
char *GetEngineType (CSubmarine & sub);
class CSubmarine
{
public:
    CSubmarine (char *Engine)
    {
        m_EngineType = new char [strlen (Engine) + 1];
        strcpy (m_EngineType, Engine);
    }
    ~CSubmarine () {delete [] m_EngineType;}
private:
    char   *m_EngineType;
    friend char *GetEngineType (CSubmarine &sub);
};

int main ()
{
CSubmarine sub("Nuclear");

    printf ("Engine type is %s\n", GetEngineType(sub));
    return (0);
}

char *GetEngineType (CSubmarine & sub)
{
    return (sub.m_EngineType);
}
```

If you *absolutely* need access to a private data member, the best way is to include a public member function in your class. The second best way is to use a friend declaration. The worst way is to make the data member itself public.

347. *Understanding Virtual Functions*

During compilation, a function is defined by its address. When the compiler comes across a call to a function, it substitutes the address of a function.

Earlier, however, you saw with virtual functions that the address might not be known at compile time. Using the *virtual* keyword on a function declaration in a base class means that you might want to override it in a later, derived class.

When the compiler encounters a virtual function, it creates a table of virtual function addresses, and at runtime the table is consulted to decide which function to call. Even if the virtual function is in a library file and you don't have the source code to it, you still can override it by declaring a similar function in your derived class. This process is known as *dynamic* or *late* binding. Obviously, the addition of a virtual function address table requires more file space, and loading it takes more time because of the binding, so you shouldn't overuse virtual declarations.

If you had a series of derived classes that used the same function, you could declare them *virtual* as well. The runtime code would search the virtual function table until it came to one that was not virtual or to the end of the inheritance chain.

A function also may be declared as a pure virtual function by declaring it *virtual* and setting its address to 0:

```
virtual int SomeFunction() = 0;
```

Essentially, you are telling the compiler that you want to declare this function for whatever reason, but you expect it to be overridden (required, in fact), so you aren't going to define it. It becomes the responsibility of a derived class to provide a definition of the function.

348. *Understanding Abstract Classes*

A class that contains a *pure virtual* function declaration is an *abstract* class. You can't call it "virtual" because that word has a different meaning when applied to classes in the inheritance process.

You can't declare an instance of an abstract class because the member function has no address. An abstract class may be used only as a base class to derive other classes, and at some point in the inheritance chain the pure virtual function must be defined. I pointed out that one way of ensuring that a class can be used only as a base class is to make its constructor protected. Using *friend* declarations, it is possible to get around that condition. However, there is *no* way around an abstract declaration; you must derive a class from it and provide a definition for the pure virtual function.

Using your *Shape* class example from Tip 326, "Using the Class as an Object of Polymorphism," you can ensure that each derived class will have its own *Draw()* function by declaring your class with a pure virtual function:

```
class Shape
{
public:
    virtual void Draw() = 0;
    void Show();
};
```

You know that the function is going to be overridden by a derived class, and this saves you the work of having to provide a body for the function.

349. *Understanding Nested Data Types*

Classes don't have to be defined globally. C++ allows you to define classes, structures, and unions within a class, effectively nesting the definitions. When you do this, the definitions are available only within the enclosing class, and any references to them must include the enclosing class name.

Often in Visual C++ samples, you will see references to a *CData* class. You won't find this class defined anywhere in the Microsoft Foundation Class. Rather, it's a common identifier used when you need to provide encapsulated data that you pass to and from a class. Usually, *CData* (it can have any other name so long as it doesn't conflict with the C++ keyword) is defined within another class, and a public instance of it declared within the class. It's also common to see it passed as a reference. Outside functions then use the *CData* instance to communicate with the class itself.

Using a separate data structure enables you to pass around only the data necessary for a class, instead of the class instance itself. Let's use your submarine class again and see how it can benefit from a nested class. You will name the nested class *CData*, and you will use a reference to it in the constructor. In the following code, before you can declare an instance of *CSubmarine*, you must prepare a *CData* instance. That's what you're using to provide the class with its initial information:

```
#include    <stdio.h>
//
class CSubmarine
{
public:
    void ShowData ();
    class CData
    {
    public:
        char    m_EngineType[32];
        int     m_Range;
        int     m_Displacement;
        int     m_MaxSpeed;
    };
    CSubmarine (CData& data);
    CData&  m_Data;
private:
    char    m_EngineType[32];
    int     m_Range;
    int     m_Displacement;
    int     m_MaxSpeed;
};

CSubmarine::CSubmarine (CData &sub) : m_Data (sub)
{
    strcpy (m_EngineType, sub.m_EngineType);
    m_Range = sub.m_Range;
    m_Displacement = sub.m_Displacement;
    m_MaxSpeed = sub.m_MaxSpeed;
}
```

```
void CSubmarine::ShowData()
{
    printf ("Engine Type: %s\n", m_Data.m_EngineType);
    printf ("Range: %d miles\n", m_Data.m_Range);
    printf ("Displacement: %d tons\n",
                          m_Data.m_Displacement);
    printf ("Maximum speed: %d knots\n", m_Data.m_MaxSpeed);
}
//
void CheckData (CSubmarine::CData& data);

int main ()
{
CSubmarine::CData data;
    strcpy (data.m_EngineType, "Nuclear");
    data.m_Range = 400000;
    data.m_Displacement = 22000;
    data.m_MaxSpeed = 23;

    CheckData (data);
    return (0);
}

void CheckData (CSubmarine::CData& data)
{
CSubmarine Nautilus (data);
    Nautilus.ShowData();
}
```

It's a little burdensome, but you've neatly encapsulated your data so that you can have both private and public copies of it. Later, you will see how you can use operator overloading to improve on this concept.

350. Understanding Static Members

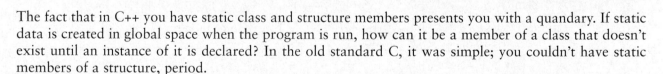

The fact that in C++ you have static class and structure members presents you with a quandary. If static data is created in global space when the program is run, how can it be a member of a class that doesn't exist until an instance of it is declared? In the old standard C, it was simple; you couldn't have static members of a structure, period.

C++ treats static data members as external data elements, and you have to declare them outside the class, as well as in the class definition. The following class declares a static data member:

```
class CSomeClass
{
public:
    // Some declarations
    static int m_SomeVar;
}
```

Then, somewhere in your source file (usually at or near the top), you make the following declaration. Notice that you do not have to repeat the *static* keyword:

```
int CSomeClass::m_SomeVar;
```

Normally, when you declare and define a member function in a class, you cannot call it until you actually create an instance of the class. Static member functions get special treatment, however. Although you declare a static function as a member of a class, you may call it even before you create an instance of a class. The special treatment also imposes some special limits on static member functions, as you will see in the next tip.

351. *Understanding Static Functions*

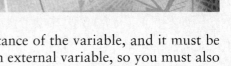

Sometimes you need to fix the address of certain functions that you use in Windows programming, such as *callback* functions. For example, the list control class, *CListCtrl* in the Microsoft Foundation Class, provides you with a function to direct the control to sort its list, but you must provide the sort function. In addition, you have to pass the function address to the control when you call *CListCtrl::SortItems()*. To get the address of a member function for these situations, you declare the function *static*.

You declare a static member function by using the keyword *static* in front of its declaration in the class definition. However, when you write the definition of the function, you have to omit the *static* keyword.

Static member functions may be called the same as any other member function using the member or pointer to member operator. In addition, they may be called even though no instance of the class has been declared, by using the class name, the scope resolution operator, and the function name.

The last property presents some problems with static functions. Because you may call a static function even before you declare an instance of the class, the compiler has no way of establishing the addresses of member variables. Therefore, static functions are not allowed to access anything in the class other than static member variables and other static functions, nor do they have access to the *this* pointer inherited by a class instance. (Accessing a non-static member implies access to the *this* pointer.)

You will have some samples of static member functions when you start looking at Windows callback routines and the MFC controls classes.

352. *Understanding Static Data Members*

When you declare a class data member *static*, you get only one instance of the variable, and it must be shared between all instances of the class. The compiler treats it as an external variable, so you must also declare it outside the class (in global space) using the data type, the class name, the scope resolution operator, and the variable name.

The following code adds a static property to your *CSubmarine* class:

```
class CSubmarine
{
public:
    CSubmarine (char *Engine);
    ~CSubmarine ();
private:
    static int m_TypeOfShip;
    char   *m_EngineType;
};
```

To complete the declaration, in one of your source files you add the following declaration as well. Without it, the linker would complain about an "unresolved external symbol."

```
int CSubmarine::m_TypeOfShip;
```

Although it must be declared in global space, the variable takes on the access level given it in the class declaration. In this example, you have declared it *private*, so only member functions of *CSubmarine* may access or modify it.

353. *Using Static Members*

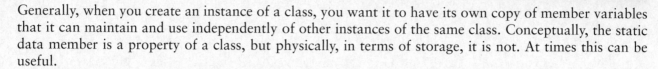

Generally, when you create an instance of a class, you want it to have its own copy of member variables that it can maintain and use independently of other instances of the same class. Conceptually, the static data member is a property of a class, but physically, in terms of storage, it is not. At times this can be useful.

If your class is one that creates or is a member of a linked list, it can use a static member variable to maintain a pointer to the head of the list and, perhaps, another pointer to the tail of the list. When you create a new instance, the static members tell it where to start looking to link itself into the list.

You also can use a static variable to share error information between instances of a class, alerting all instances of an error condition, such as a failed file open. It can also be used as a "set and forget" variable that has to be initialized only once for every instance of a class. In the latter case, you set it using a static member function before any instances of the class are declared.

In a recursive function, you can use it to keep track of the number of instances a class is declared at any particular time. After the variable is initialized to 0, the class's constructor can increment it and the destructor can decrement it.

Although it seems to violate the encapsulation principle of object-oriented programming, there are times when using a static member variable is faster and cleaner than the alternatives. A static variable may be almost any data type, even a structure or another class if complex data sharing is required.

354. *Understanding Scope Resolution*

The scope resolution operator uniquely identifies variables or functions where the use of the identifier alone might produce ambiguous or erroneous results. Earlier you saw how to use the operator to distinguish between the MFC *CWnd* class *MessageBox()* and the general-purpose Windows *MessageBox()* functions.

It's also used to identify a particular class, for example, when you define your member functions. You can use it to access base class functions that you have overridden in your derived classes. If you have a virtual function *Draw()* in class *CBase* that you have overridden and for some reason you need to call the base class function instead of your own, you call it using *CBase::Draw()* (declaring a function *virtual* and overriding it in a derived class doesn't remove it from memory).

Identifiers in other *namespaces* may be accessed using the operator. If you have a variable *int Stuff;* in namespace *Other* and you currently are using the *std* namespace, you may access the variable by specifying *Other::Stuff*.

You also may use it in functions to access a global identifier that is hidden or masked by an identifier in the function. In the following code, you use it to show the difference in values between the global and local variables:

```
int x;
void SomeFunc ()
{
    int x = 24;
    ::x = 42;
    printf ("Global x = %d\n", ::x);
    printf ("Local x = %d\n", x);
}
```

355. *Understanding Callback Functions*

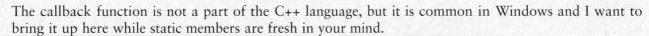

The callback function is not a part of the C++ language, but it is common in Windows and I want to bring it up here while static members are fresh in your mind.

Often in Windows programming you have occasion to pass a Windows procedure a request. Along with this request, you must provide the address of a function that will be used to deliver the results of your request. This function is referred to as a "callback" function. In a standard Win32 application, the name of the procedure you pass in the *lpfnWndProc* member of the *WNDCLASSEX* structure is a callback function. The function you pass to process a dialog box is a callback function.

They're much less common when you start building programs using the Microsoft Foundation Class. The MFC framework handles much of the callback details for your main windows and dialogs, but several of the Windows controls use callback functions. Invariably, the controls that are capable of sorting their content on demand—the tree and list controls, for example—require that you pass the address of a callback routine when you call the sort function. You must supply the sorting code in this callback routine.

When using MFC, you usually create separate classes to contain the code to process dialog boxes. If you need a callback function in one of these classes, it must be declared as a *static* member function. You can't pass the address of any other type of class member function as the callback procedure. When you do this, remember that the *static* function, although a member of the class, cannot access any variables or functions that are not declared *static*. The use of a callback function thus can affect the way you design and write your class functions and declarations.

356. *Understanding Operator Overloading*

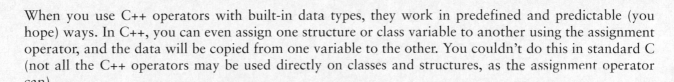

When you use C++ operators with built-in data types, they work in predefined and predictable (you hope) ways. In C++, you can even assign one structure or class variable to another using the assignment operator, and the data will be copied from one variable to the other. You couldn't do this in standard C (not all the C++ operators may be used directly on classes and structures, as the assignment operator can).

The assignment is great as long as the structure or class definition doesn't contain any pointers and the functions don't dynamically allocate memory. In this case, the pointer values themselves are copied in the assignment and no new memory is allocated. If the destructor cleans up the heap memory when the class is destroyed, the other variable still contains a pointer to the destroyed data. When it is destroyed, its destructor tries to clean up memory that already has been freed. It's almost guaranteed that an exception will be thrown at that point and your program will die.

C++ allows you to redefine how the operators function on your user-defined data types, classes, and structures through a process called "operator overloading." The overloaded operators work normally on the built-in data types and affect only the classes or structures for which they are defined. Most, but not all, operators may be overloaded. The following list summarizes those that may be overloaded:

```
+    -    *    /    %    &    |    ^    !    ~
<    >    <<   >>   =    +=   -=   *=   /=   %=
^=   &=   |=   <<=  >>=  ==   !=   <=   >=   &&
||   ++   --   ,    ->   ()   []   new  delete
```

You must use a structure or class member function to overload an operator. The overloading does not affect the precedence table. In fact, the overloaded operators go to the bottom of the table.

357. Overloading an Operator

Let's retrieve your *CEmployee* class and make some modifications to it. As it stands, the assignment operator works just fine, but in terms of memory use, it's not efficient. Using 24 elements for the character array for the first and last names provides enough storage, you hope, for the longest names you might encounter, but it's possible that some might be longer. In addition, most names are considerably shorter, and for a large number of instances, the wasted memory might be considerable. It would be much more efficient to allocate the memory for the name when you create an instance of the class.

You will change it to dynamically allocate the memory it needs and then free it up in the destructor when the object is destroyed (DON'T try to run this code just yet! It will compile, but it contains some serious errors):

```cpp
/*
    Employ2.cpp -- Testing operator overloading.
 */
#include    <stdio.h>
#include    <iostream.h>
#include    <string.h>

class CEmployee
{
public:
    CEmployee (int ID, char *First, char *Last);
    CEmployee ()
    {
        m_EmployeeFirst = NULL;
        m_EmployeeLast = NULL;
    }
    ~CEmployee ();

    int GetID () {return (m_EmployeeID);}
    char *GetFirstName () {return (m_EmployeeFirst);}
    char *GetLastName () {return (m_EmployeeLast);}
    void PutNewData (int NewID = 0,
```

```
                            char *NewFirst = NULL,
                            char *NewLast = NULL);
private:
    int     m_EmployeeID;
    char    *m_EmployeeFirst;
    char    *m_EmployeeLast;
};


int main ()
{
CEmployee emp[] =  {
                       CEmployee (1641, "Thomas", "Jefferson"),
                       CEmployee (1802, "George", "Washington"),
                       CEmployee (1732, "John", "Adams"),
                       CEmployee (1752, "Andrew", "Jackson"),
                       CEmployee (2401, "Elsie", "Smith")
                   };
//
// Thomas Jefferson got married and wants to change his
// last name to "Skelton. " We need to save the old record,
// so create a new one
    CEmployee NewEmp;
// Copy the data in emp[0] to NewEmp
    NewEmp = emp[0];
    NewEmp.PutNewData(0, NULL, "Skelton");
// Print the results
    printf ("%s %s employee ID is %d (emp[0])\n",
            emp[0].GetFirstName(),
            emp[0].GetLastName(), emp[0].GetID());
    printf ("%s %s employee ID is %d (NewEmp)\n"
            NewEmp.GetFirstName(),
            NewEmp. GetLastName(), NewEmp.GetID());
    return (0);
}


CEmployee::CEmployee (int ID, char *First, char *Last)
{
    m_EmployeeID = ID;
    m_EmployeeFirst = new char [strlen (First) + 1];
    strcpy (m_EmployeeFirst, First);
    m_EmployeeLast = new char [strlen (Last) + 1];
    strcpy (m_EmployeeLast, Last);
}


CEmployee::~CEmployee ()
{
    delete [] m_EmployeeFirst;
    delete [] m_EmployeeLast;
}


void CEmployee::PutNewData (int NewID, char *NewFirst,
                                char *NewLasl)
{
    if (NewID)
        m_EmployeeID = NewID;
    if (NewFirst != NULL)
```

```
    {
        delete [] m_EmployeeFirst;
        m_EmployeeFirst = new char [strlen (NewFirst) + 1];
        strcpy (m_EmployeeFirst, NewFirst);
    }
    if (NewLast != NULL)
    {
        delete [] m_EmployeeLast;
        m_EmployeeLast = new char [strlen (NewLast) + 1];
        strcpy (m_EmployeeLast, NewLast);
    }
}
```

If you try to run this code, you're almost certain to get an exception error. Let's examine why. When you used the assignment operator to copy one class instance to another, only the pointers to the strings were copied, and no new strings were created. Then you gave the new instance a different last name, which means that it deleted the old memory allocation and created a new one. However, the original instance still points to the now invalid memory location. When the function exits and the variables are destroyed, one or both of them is going to try to delete memory that already has been deleted, and an exception will be thrown.

What you must do is overload the assignment operator for the *CEmployee* class and make it allocate new memory in the assignment, leaving the old allocation alone. Add the following declaration in the *public* section of *CEmployee*:

```
const CEmployee& operator= (const CEmployee &);
```

The declaration says that you are going to return a reference to a *CEmployee* instance, which will be the instance on the left side of the equals sign. You passed the instance on the right as a reference, but you could just as easily have passed a pointer and taken the address of the right variable. The reference is just easier to work with. (You could define both overloads if you so desired. The code on the CD-ROM contains both.)

You must implement the operator overload code in your source file. Add the following function to the file:

```
const CEmployee& CEmployee::operator=(const CEmployee &Old)
{
    delete [] m_EmployeeFirst;
    delete [] m_EmployeeLast;
    m_EmployeeFirst = new char
                        [strlen (Old.m_EmployeeFirst) + 1];
     m_EmployeeLast = new char
                        [strlen (Old.m_EmployeeLast) + 1];
    strcpy (m_EmployeeFirst, Old.m_EmployeeFirst);
    strcpy (m_EmployeeLast, Old.m_EmployeeLast);
    m_EmployeeID = Old.m_EmployeeID;
    return (*this);
}
```

In case this instance already had been assigned values, you delete the memory for the first and last names and create new allocations. Then, you copy the names into the new memory and assign the same ID number. You then dereference your *this* pointer and return it as a reference.

This will work as long as you first declare the instance and then assign it in a different statement, such as in the following:

```
CEmployee NewEmp;
```

```
NewEmp = emp[0];
```

It won't work if you declare and assign the instance at the same time, as in *CEmployee NewEmp =
emp[0]*, because it's an *assignment declaration* and the operator overload is never called. This doesn't
have anything to do with overloaded operators, but let's finish this off by adding a copy constructor to
your class. You really should include a copy constructor when you overload the assignment operator.
Add the following declaration to your code:

```
CEmployee (const CEmployee &);        // Copy constructor
```

Now implement the copy constructor code with the following function:

```
CEmployee::CEmployee (const CEmployee &Old)
{
    m_EmployeeFirst = new char
                      [strlen (Old.m_EmployeeFirst) + 1];
    m_EmployeeLast = new char
                      [strlen (Old.m_EmployeeLast) + 1];
    strcpy (m_EmployeeFirst, Old.m_EmployeeFirst);
    strcpy (m_EmployeeLast, Old.m_EmployeeLast);
    m_EmployeeID = Old.m_EmployeeID;
}
```

Now modify the code in *main()* to read *CEmployee NewEmp = emp[0];* so that the declaration and
assignment take place on the same line.

358. *Using* cin, cout, *and* cerr

In this example of the *this* pointer, you've used the C++ streams *cin*, *cout*, and *cerr* alternately with the
stdin, *stdout*, and *stderr* standard file descriptors. Your use of the C++ streams, however, has been limited to outputting to the screen and getting input from the keyboard. Although C supports streams, the
cin, *cout*, and *cerr* streams are distinctly C++. They are implemented through classes and are capable of
much more than just console I/O, as you have used them. The *stdin*, *stdout*, and *stderr* are streams as
well, but they are carryovers from C.

To use the C++ stream classes, you must include the standard header file *iostream.h* in your program.
Like C, no built-in I/O capability exists in C++. That capability is achieved through an object-oriented
package that includes the standard streams. The classes also contain functions to set the precision and
field width of the streams, just as you did using the C function *printf()*. They also support output to
memory strings, as you did with *sprintf()*.

You set the field width of a stream by calling the member function *width()*. To set the width for *cout* to
5 spaces, you would call *cout.width(5)*. You output to the left or right of the field by setting flags in the
class using the *flag()* member function. Unlike the C streams, you may set your fill character by calling
the *fill()* member function, passing as an argument the character you would like to use to occupy the
spaces used to pad the field to the width you set. Each of these functions returns the old value, so you
may restore it after you're done. The following snippet changes the field width and fill character, sets the
field alignment to print on the left, outputs a string, and then restores the old values:

```
char chFill = cout.fill ('.');
int nWidth = cout.width(10);
int nFlags = cout.flags(ios::left);
cout << "Stuff" << endl;
```

```
cout.fill (chFill);
cout.width (nWidth);
cout.flags (nFlags);
```

A basic rule of programming is that when you use a resource, you leave it the way you found it. In the case of iostreams, changing the parameter doesn't affect other programs, but by restoring the original values you know what to expect when you use it again. You also may use the class's *setf()* function to set flags, in which case you could use the *unsetf()* function to clear the flags you had set. Flags also may be combined using the C++ *OR* operator. The following code sets the text to the left in the field and then restores the flags after output:

```
int nWidth = cout.width(10);
cout.setf(ios::left);
cout << "stuff" << endl;
cout.width (nWidth);
cout.unsetf (ios::left);
```

This method relieves you of the burden of having to save the old flags, but you have no idea what the original flags were. If another function has set the *ios::left* flag and its output is still pending, you have just reset the flag for it as well. It's best in most cases to save the flags and restore them to their original values as you did in the previous example.

359. *Understanding Inserters*

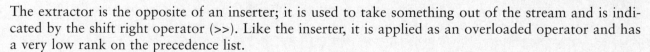

When applied to the C++ streams classes, the shift left operator (<<) is taken to mean an *inserter*, an operation that is intended to insert something into the stream. The inserter is applied as an overloaded operator, and just about any other operator could have been used. The shift operations, however, conveniently show the direction of the stream transfer.

The inserter operator has a very low rank on the precedence list, so arithmetic expressions may be used as an operand without using many parentheses.

Inserters operate from left to right, and each expression following an inserter is fully evaluated before the next operation is performed.

There are operator overloads in the stream classes for the C++ built-in and derived data types, but if you want to use them on your own user-defined types, such as structures and classes, you yourself must provide them, as you will do in Tip 366, "Creating Your Own Inserters."

360. *Understanding Extractors*

The extractor is the opposite of an inserter; it is used to take something out of the stream and is indicated by the shift right operator (>>). Like the inserter, it is applied as an overloaded operator and has a very low rank on the precedence list.

Extractors also operate from left to right, and there are operator overloads for the C++ data types. Again, to use them on your own classes, you yourself must write them. You will get into creating your own inserters and extractors in Tip 367, "Creating Your Own Extractors."

361. *Understanding File Streaming*

A *stream* is a sequence of data flowing from one part of the computer to another, whether it is from keyboard to screen, file to file, or file to hardware port. Actually, the hardware destinations are programs called "drivers," and streams don't write to or read from a hardware device directly. Data written by a user process or driver travels downstream to its destination, and data read travels upstream from its source. These directions are relative, or course, because what is upstream at one end will be downstream at the other.

From a practical standpoint, both ends of the streams are processes, and C++ defines several stream types to handle various types of I/O. The *istream* class is used for input from *cin*, the standard input device. The *ifstream* is used to read from a file, and the *istrstream* is used to read buffered input from a string.

I'll explain enough about streams here to enable you to open, read and write, and then close them, but your primary focus will be on Windows programming. For a more complete explanation of stream operations, I recommend *Jamsa's C++ Programmer's Bible*.

For output streams, C++ provides you with the *ostream* for output to the standard file devices *cout*, *cerr*, and *clog*. The *ofstream* is used for writing to a file, and *ostrstream* for buffered output to a string.

The *fstream* class combines both the *istream* and *ostream* functionality for reading and writing of files. Use the header file *fstream.h*.

If you include the name of a file when you declare an *ifstream* or *ofstream* object, the file is opened automatically, or you may delay opening the file by not giving it a name and later using the *open()* member function. The file streams have four overloaded constructors:

```
ifstream();
ifstream( const char* szName, int nMode = ios::in,
                    int nProt = filebuf::openprot );
ifstream( filedesc fd);
ifstream( filedesc fd, char* pch, int nLength );
```

The first constructor lets you open a generic class instance without specifying a file name or any other specific information. The second allows you to open a new stream giving it the file name, the mode, and a specification as to whether you want to share the open file or have exclusive access to it. This is the same syntax and sequence of parameters you would use if you called the *open()* member function instead. The default mode for *ifstream* is *ios::in*, meaning that the file is opened for read-only. The Windows default is to open the file in text mode, but you should get accustomed to using the binary open, which is the default on most operating systems. To open a file for input in binary mode, use *ios::in\ios::binary*. Eventually, as Windows evolves into a real operating system, it probably will assume the default most other operating systems use. You also may use *ios::nocreate* to indicate that you don't want the file to be created if it doesn't already exist; in this case, the call to the *nProt* argument allows you exclusive or shared access to a file. The default *filebuf::openprot* gives read and write shared access, *filebuf::sh_none* opens the file in exclusive mode, *filebuf::sh_read* allows other programs to read the file while you have it open, and *filebuf::sh_write* allows other programs to write to the file while you have it open.

The *ostream* class also offers additional flags for the *nMode* parameter. You may specify *ios::app* to indicate that all writes to the file are to be made at the end (append mode), but that you may read from any position in the file. *ios::ate* is another append mode, except that after the first write you may change the file pointer to another location for future writes. The *ios::in* value specifies that you *don't* want to truncate a file on open if it already exists, but the *ios::trunc* value erases the old contents of the file on open (*ios::trunc* is the default if *ios::ate*, *ios::in*, or *ios::app* are not specified). Finally, you may specify *ios::noreplace*, which specifies that you want to create a new file and that the open will fail if the file already exists.

You combine modes using the *OR* operator (¦). The mode *ios::app | ios::noreplace* specifies that you want to create a new file (not overwrite an existing file), but that all writes are to be made at the end of the file, regardless of where the file pointer may be.

The third form of the constructor associates a file descriptor obtained with the low-level *open()* function with the stream. The low-level open function was the original file open operation used by C on the UNIX operating system; very seldom in Windows programming do you use this function. You can get this file descriptor value, an integer, using the *fd()* member function if you already have the stream open.

The fourth form of the constructor performs the same job but also allows you to specify an area of memory to use as a buffer. A *NULL* for the *pch* parameter or a 0 for the *nLength* parameter indicates that no buffering is to take place.

A stream is closed automatically when the stream object goes out of scope and is destroyed. You also may close it using the *close()* member function. If you close the file, you may reuse the stream object to open another file.

362. *Understanding Sequential Streaming Functions*

C++ gives you two sequential streaming operations in the form of the *write()* and *read()* member functions. When you use one of these functions, the file pointer (the position in which the next read or write operation will take place) is moved automatically to the position *after* the point where the last byte of the read or write was performed.

Disk files are *random access objects*, meaning that you may move to any point in the file to perform an operation. Sequential streaming allows you to read and write multiple records without your having to position the file pointer.

363. *Understanding Random Streaming Functions*

Often you need to move the file pointer around in the file to access records in a non-sequential manner, or *randomly*. If you read a record, for example, the file pointer is moved to the point after the record you read. If you make a change to the record and subsequently write it back to the file, you overwrite the record following the one you just read. Two functions allow you to manipulate the file pointer and overcome this possibility: *tellg()* and *seekg()*.

The *tellg()* member function gives you the current position of the file pointer. It returns a value of type *streampos*, which is *typedef*'ed as a *long* data type.

You use the *seekg()* member function to move the pointer to a random position in the file for your read or write operations. If you read an object or value from the file, modify it, and subsequently rewrite it, the *write()* operation is performed at the point *after* your record of value. The *seekg()* allows you to move back to where you want to rewrite the record.

The *seekg()* function takes as its parameters the position where you want to move the pointer, which you may obtain with a call to *tellg()*. Optionally, you may specify the position as a *streamoff* value specifying the relative position where you want to move the pointer. You then specify as the second parameter the starting point for the relative movement. You may specify *ios::beg* for the beginning of the file, *ios::end* for the end of the file, or *ios::cur* for the current position in the file. The value for *ios::beg* and *ios::end* should be a positive value, but the *ios:cur* may be positive or negative, depending on the direction you want to move the pointer.

The following snippet shows how you might use the *read()*, *write()*, and *seekg()* functions to read and modify a record and then write it back to the file. Assume that the file contains many records of a structure named *EMPLOYEE* and you want to get to the 20th record:

```
#include      <iostream.h>

int main ()
{
    fstream f("employee.dat", ios::in | ios::out
                               | ios::binary
                               | ios::nocreate);
    EMPLOYEE emp;
    if (f)
      {
        f.seekg (0, ios::end);
        long lSize = f.tellg();
        f.seekg (19 * sizeof (EMPLOYEE));
        if (f.tellg() < lSize)
            {
                f.read ((char *) &emp, sizeof (EMPLOYEE));
// Code here to modify the record
                f.seekg (-(sizeof (EMPLOYEE)), ios::cur);
                f.write ((char *) &emp, sizeof (EMPLOYEE));
            }
        else
          {
            cerr << "ERROR: end of file reached" << endl;
          }
        f.close();
      }
    else
      {
        cerr  << "ERROR: Cannot open data file" << endl;
      }
    return (0);
}
```

First, you open the file and test whether the open succeeded. If it did, you seek to the 20th record. (The first is 0, so you use 19 times the size of the structure; a value of 20 would give you the 21st record.) You read the record, modify it, move back the number of bytes equal to the size of the structure relative to your current position, and rewrite the record.

Truthfully, as one who has used both, when it comes to binary file I/O, I find that the C++ streams classes offer little to recommend them over the standard C streams. The standard C routines provide the same functionality, are easier to use, and have the advantage of a longer evolutionary lifetime.

364. *Understanding* width(), precision(), *and* fill()

For tabular and scientific notation output, the streams classes provide you with functions to set the field width, the precision for the numerical output, and the fill character that is used in place of blanks (spaces). Each function comes in two flavors. With no parameters, the functions return the current value but do not change it. If you pass a parameter, the value is set to the new value and the old is returned.

The *width()* member function lets you set the minimum field width to be used when outputting to the stream, using inserters. The default or starting value is 0, and the inserters output only the number of characters to represent the inserted value. When the width is non-zero, the inserters expand the field to the width value using the stream's fill character. The *width()* function applies to the next output operation only.

The *precision()* function sets the stream's floating-point precision variable. The starting value is 6. If the display format is *ios::scientific* or *ios::fixed*, the precision is the number of decimal digits to display after the decimal point. Otherwise, the precision specifies the number of significant digits in the output.

The *fill()* member function sets the stream's internal fill character, the character used as padding between fields. In the *printf()* function from standard C, you had no choice in the fill character; it was always a space. Using C++ streams, you may set it to any character you want. The default character is a space.

365. *Understanding I/O Manipulators*

The standard library provides you with functions to modify the stream without having to deal with flags. An example would be *endl* to produce a newline in the stream. These functions are known as *manipulators*. Their purpose is to modify the state of the stream between objects being read or written, in some cases temporarily and in others persistently.

Most of the standard library's manipulators apply to output streams, but a number may be applied to input streams as well. To use manipulators that require arguments, you include the standard header *iomanip.h* in your source file. The output-only manipulators include:

- *endl*. Outputs a newline character to the stream and flushes the stream.
- *ends*. Outputs a *NULL* to the stream.
- *flush*. Causes the contents of the stream's buffer to be written.
- *setbase(base)*. Sets the number base of the next output to the new value base.
- *setprecision(precis)*. Sets the precision to the new value. The value remains set until changed again.
- *setfill(char)*. Sets the fill (padding) character to the parameter.
- *setw(width)*. Sets the field width to *width*.

The following manipulators may be used on input and output streams:

- *dec*, *hex*, and *oct*. Set the input and output conversion bases to decimal, hexadecimal, or octal, respectively
- *setioflags(flags)*. Turns on the flags specified in the argument
- *resetioflags(flags)*. Turns off the flags specified in the argument

A single manipulator, *ws*, applies only to input streams and instructs the stream to skip over leading white space.

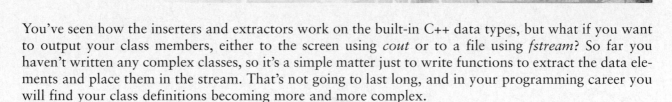

366. Creating Your Own Inserters

You've seen how the inserters and extractors work on the built-in C++ data types, but what if you want to output your class members, either to the screen using *cout* or to a file using *fstream*? So far you haven't written any complex classes, so it's a simple matter just to write functions to extract the data elements and place them in the stream. That's not going to last long, and in your programming career you will find your class definitions becoming more and more complex.

C++ provides an inserter class template that lets you define inserters for your own classes. If you use your class for file I/O, as well as screen output, you must define inserters for both the *ostream* and the *ofstream* class. This isn't usually a problem, because the way you display the information is likely to be different from the way you store it in a file.

An inserter returns a reference to a stream object, so you declare it using the stream object reference as the first parameter and a reference to your class as the second parameter. Using your *CEmployee* class from Tip 357, "Overloading an Operator," the following first line declares an inserter for console output, and the second for a file stream. The inserters need access to private data members of your class, so declare them as *friend* functions within the class definition:

```
friend ostream& operator<<(ostream& stream, CEmployee& c);
friend ofstream& operator<<(ofstream& stream, CEmployee& c);
```

Now you must provide a body for the inserters. They are not members of your class, so don't include the scope resolution in the definition:

```
ostream& operator<<(ostream& stream, CEmployee& c)
{
    stream << "First Name: ";
    stream << c.m_EmployeeFirst << endl;
    stream << "Last Name: ";
    stream << c.m_EmployeeLast << endl;
    stream << "ID Number: " << c.m_EmployeeID << endl;
    return (stream);
}
```

When you define the file inserter, you don't need the descriptive text that you used in the display inserter. You separate the variables with a comma so that you can distinguish them when you read the file (be sure to use the *fstream.h* include file):

```
ofstream& operator<<(ofstream& stream, CEmployee& c)
{
    stream << c.m_EmployeeFirst << ',';
    stream << c.m_EmployeeLast << ',';
    stream << c.m_EmployeeID << endl;
    return (stream);
}
```

To display the record, you need only insert the class in the stream where you used the *printf()* statement. You should see the following output:

```
cout << emp[0];
First Name: Thomas
Last Name: Jefferson
ID Number: 1641
```

To write the record to a file, you first open the stream file and use the inserter the same as you do for *cout*:

```
ofstream f("employ3.dat", ios::in | ios::out | ios::binary);
f << Emp;
f.close ();
```

When you look in the file, you see the following data, followed by a line-feed character (you specified *binary* when you opened the file, so Windows didn't do its silly translation):

```
Thomas,Jefferson,1641
```

To write all six of your records to the file, you use the same syntax, but in a loop:

```
for (int x = 0; x < 6; ++x)
    f << emp[x];
```

The extractor handled all the details, so all you have to do is put each class instance in succession into the stream.

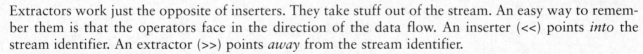

367. *Creating Your Own Extractors*

Extractors work just the opposite of inserters. They take stuff out of the stream. An easy way to remember them is that the operators face in the direction of the data flow. An inserter (<<) points *into* the stream identifier. An extractor (>>) points *away* from the stream identifier.

If the extractors will need access to private members of the class, declare them as *friend* in your class definition. In your extractors, you will take advantage of the assignment operator overload you wrote so that they don't have to be friends of the class. It won't hurt to declare them as friends, however, so include the following declarations in your class definition:

```
friend istream& operator>>(istream& stream, CEmployee& c);
friend ifstream& operator>>(ifstream& stream, CEmployee& c);
istream& operator>>(istream& stream, CEmployee& c)
{
char First[128], Last[128], ID[128];
    cout << "Employee's First Name: ";
    stream >> First;
    cout << "Employee's Last Name: ";
    stream >> Last;
    cout << "Employee's ID Number: ";
    CEmployee temp(atoi (ID), First, Last);
    c = temp;
    return (stream);
}
```

For the file extractor, you know that the data was written into your file using commas as field delimiters, so you read one line of the file and use *strtok()* to parse the individual fields:

```
ifstream& operator>>(ifstream& stream, CEmployee& c)
{
char buf[128];
      stream >> buf;
      char *First = strtok (buf, ",");
      char *Last = strtok (NULL, ",");
      char *ID = strtok (NULL, ",");
      CEmployee temp(atoi (ID), First, Last);
      c = temp;
      return (stream);
}
```

To use the extractor, you open a stream file and place your class instance in the stream, just as you did with the *cin* extractor:

```
CEmployee NewEmp;
ifstream f("employ3.dat", ios::in | ios::out
                                 | ios::binary);
f >> NewEmp;
f.close();
cout << NewEmp;
```

These file inserters and extractors don't use fixed-length records, so reading, modifying, and rewriting the records could cause some data corruption. If you want to be able to modify the records, you must put some field widths in the inserter and use the same widths in the extractor to retrieve the data.

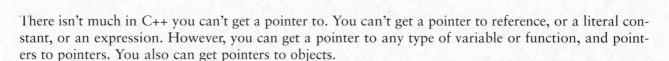

368. *Understanding Pointers to Objects*

There isn't much in C++ you can't get a pointer to. You can't get a pointer to reference, or a literal constant, or an expression. However, you can get a pointer to any type of variable or function, and pointers to pointers. You also can get pointers to objects.

When you declare or create an object, memory is set aside for it. The compiler keeps track of the relative memory location internally, and the runtime code inherits that memory location when you load your program. When you ask for a pointer to the object, you get the address of this memory. You take the pointer to an object using the address unary operator, the ampersand.

Normally, when you reference members of objects, you use the member-of operator, separating the name of the object and its member with a period. With a pointer, however, you must use the pointer-to-member-of operator, which, with a little imagination, even resembles a pointer. It's the hyphen followed by the greater than symbol (->). When you use it, the effect is the same as dereferencing the pointer and getting the member directly. If you have a pointer to an object named *Pointer* and a member of it named *Member*, you address the member as *Pointer->Member*. You yourself could just as easily dereference the pointer and write **Pointer.Member*.

Together with the reference, which, itself, is a pointer, pointers make it easy for you to pass large objects efficiently to functions, and they let you modify variables that are outside the scope of a function.

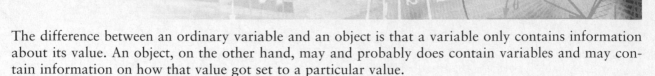

369. *Understanding Pointers to Classes*

The difference between an ordinary variable and an object is that a variable only contains information about its value. An object, on the other hand, may and probably does contain variables and may contain information on how that value got set to a particular value.

The class is the epitome of objects. An instance of a class is a "smart" object; it can tie its own tie, so to speak.

You can take a pointer to a class object the same as any other object. Syntactically, it is the same as taking and using a pointer to a structure. You also can assign a pointer to a class to the address of one of its base classes, as long as the reference is unambiguous. Remember (in Tip 342, "Understanding Multiple Inheritance") when I talked about using the *virtual* keyword when you derive a new class? That prevented you from inheriting more than one copy of a base class, thus making references to a parent class ambiguous.

In Tip 342, you derived a class, *CSubmarine*, using multiple inheritance, and both trees led back to the same ultimate ancestor, a *CShips* class. So long as you declare your inheritance *virtual*, you can write a declaration such as the following:

```
int main ()
{
    CSubmarine sub;
    CShips *ship = &sub;
}
```

The assignment of one pointer to another is legal even though they are of different classes because *CSubmarine* is derived from *CShips* and only one copy of the parent class is inherited. However, if you remove the *virtual* declaration from the inheritance and recompile, you get the following error message:

```
ships.cpp(54) : error C2594: 'initializing' : ambiguous conversions from
'class CSubmarine *' to 'class CShips *'
```

Two copies of the *CShips* class were inherited in this case, and the compiler didn't know which to use.

370. *Introducing the* this *Pointer*

In the old Smalltalk language developed by Xerox's Palo Alto Research Center, objects have a strange property called "self." One instance of an object can always distinguish itself from another by referring to this construct.

C++ classes have a similar construct, a pointer to the class instance called *this*. The pointer is created for each instance of a class, and non-static member functions may refer to the instance itself using the keyword *this*. Static member functions, you will recall, may be executed even when no instance of a class has been declared, so they are not given the *this* pointer.

However, if a member function needs to call a static member function, or any function declared outside the class itself, it may pass the pointer as a reference to itself. The keyword may be used only within member functions and must be given a different identifier in the called function.

You saw an example of *this* when you wrote your operator overloads in Tip 357, "Overloading an Operator." The overload function had to return a reference to the calling class instance, but how could the function "know" exactly which instance made the call? You couldn't possibly write an overload for each instance; that wouldn't make much sense and wouldn't make your programming any easier.

The overload function is a member of the class, so it inherits the *this* pointer. You dereference it and return the reference. It doesn't matter which instance of the class calls it; *this* always points to the current instance.

371. *Using* malloc() *and* free()

The standard C functions *malloc()* and *free()* may be used to create dynamic instances of classes and to release the memory when it is no longer needed. Originally, *malloc()* returned a pointer to type *char*, and the allocated memory had to be cast to a pointer of the type desired. In newer implementations, the function returns a pointer to type *void*, but the allocation still must be cast, and the call still must be passed the size of the object being created.

The *free()* function requires a pointer to *void* as a parameter. Any pointer type may be assigned to a *void* pointer, so no cast is necessary when freeing memory.

Suppose that you wanted to create a dynamic instance of your class *CSubmarine*. Your call to *malloc()* and *free()* would look something like the following:

```
CSubmarine *Sub = (CSubmarine *) malloc(sizeof(CSubmarine));
// Some program statements using the Sub pointer
free (Sub);
```

That's a wordy function call and requires you to use the *sizeof* operator within the call to *malloc()*. If you were allocating an array of 10 classes, you would have to pass it *10 * sizeof (CSubmarine)* as the size to allocate. In C++ there is an easier way, the *new* operator, which is covered in the next tip.

372. *Using the* new *Operator*

The *new* operator serves the same function in C++ as the C function *malloc()*, but it operates more intelligently. *new* allocates and casts the memory to the data type being allocated, and it uses the operand's size as the amount of memory to allocate. Thus, you don't have to state these explicitly. Like *malloc()*, the *new* operator allocates space in the heap, or free store, memory.

In Tip 252, "Understanding Dynamic Strings: The *new* Operator," you saw how to use *new* to allocate memory for strings. You also may use the operator for your own user-defined data types. To dynamically allocate memory for your *CSubmarine* class, you would simply write the following:

```
CSubmarine *Sub = new CSubmarine;
```

The operand gives *new* the data type, and the compiler already knows the size of your class, so you don't have to specify either. To allocate an array of 10 class instances, you need only indicate the size of the array:

```
CSubmarine *Sub = new CSubmarine[10];
```

There are a couple of rules to remember when using the *new* operator. First, an expression can't be used as the operand, and you must not use parentheses around the operand. However, an expression, including one with parentheses, may be used within the *[]* to indicate the number of array elements. Second, as is the case with *malloc()*, you can't initialize a class or variable at the time it is allocated, so a class must have a default constructor, one that requires no parameters.

373. *Using the delete Operator*

Using the *delete* operator is just as easy as using the *new* operator. You need only specify the object being deleted as the operand. Unseen by the programmer, the allocation structure includes the size of the memory block allocated, and *delete* retrieves the block size in performing the operation.

If, however, you need to release a block that contains an array, you specify that fact in your call to *delete* using the array operator *[]*. You didn't need to do this in the call to *free()*. The first line in the following frees a single instance of *CSubmarine*, and the second frees your array of the class:

```
delete Sub;
delete [] Sub
```

Notice that you didn't have to pass the size of the array. Just indicating it is an array using the *[]* is sufficient.

You can't use *free()* and *delete* interchangeably. Any memory allocated using *malloc()* must be released using the *free()* function, and any memory allocated with *new* must be freed using *delete*.

You must not call *delete* on any memory not allocated with *new*. The following declaration and *delete* are legal operations, but they might produce some unexpected, and unwanted, results:

```
CSubmarine Sub[10];    // Returns a pointer to the array
delete [] Sub;
```

Because the array was created on the stack, its allocation doesn't contain the free store structure information, so the subsequent call to *delete* will produce unpredictable results. Most compilers warn you about it, but the operation is permitted.

The specification for the *delete* operator assures you that calling it with a *NULL* pointer as the operand will do nothing. A failed allocation using *new* returns a *NULL* pointer, so it is safe to call it after a *new* operation without testing it. If you are not allocating memory at the time a pointer variable is declared, it's a good idea to initialize it to *NULL* as protection against calling *delete* on a block that hasn't been allocated.

> **Note:** *Actually, according to the C++ specification, a failed allocation is supposed to throw a* bad_alloc *exception, which you can catch and process. The MSDN documentation for Visual C++, however, says that "if there is insufficient memory for the allocation request, by default operator new returns NULL." You will get into C++ exceptions and exception handling later.)*

374. *Understanding Memory Leaks*

A *memory leak* is caused by a stranded block of memory, allocated with *malloc()* or *new*, that you have neglected to release. Class instances may allocate memory that, if not freed at the time of their destruction, results in memory leaks. When designing your classes, take care to delete any memory they allocate. If you allocate memory in the constructor, make sure you delete it in the destructor.

When you allocate memory, the value returned is a pointer to the memory. You store it in a pointer variable that has a certain scope, and you must use it to free the memory before the pointer variable goes out of scope. After it is destroyed, you have no way of accessing the memory to free it, and you wind up with a memory leak. The only way to recover the lost memory is by rebooting your computer.

375. *Using Pointers to Derived Classes*

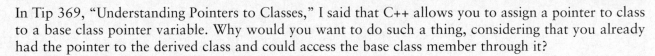

In Tip 369, "Understanding Pointers to Classes," I said that C++ allows you to assign a pointer to class to a base class pointer variable. Why would you want to do such a thing, considering that you already had the pointer to the derived class and could access the base class member through it?

Using your *CShips* class again, you created an instance of *CSubmarine* and then assigned its address to a pointer to class *CShips*.

Suppose that you had a function that dealt with a pointer to *CShips* and you need to call it with your *CSubmarine* pointer. The compiler will automatically cast it to a pointer to *CShips*, just as it accepted your pointer assignment.

It's true that you might never have occasion to use a pointer to a base class in such a way that you need to create a second pointer in the same function. It does, however, show that the assignment is legal and you can cast it when you pass it to another function.

Of course, the called function would have access only to the members of *CShips* and its base classes, if any. The function couldn't cast it back to a *CSubmarine* pointer. Any changes made in the *CShips* class would be reflected in the *CSubmarine* instance in the original function, of course.

Try the following code to see how it works. You don't need anything in the body of the classes other than a variable in the base class, so you will just take the compiler defaults:

```
#include    <stdio.h>

class CShips
{
public:
    int Stuff;
};
class CSubmarine : virtual public CShips
{
};

void Stuffn (CShips *ships);

int main ()
{
CSubmarine sub;

    sub.Stuff = 12;
    printf ("sub.Stuff = %d\n", sub.Stuff);
    CShips *ships = &sub;
    Stuffn (ships);
    printf ("sub.Stuff = %d\n", sub.Stuff);
```

```
    return (0);
}
void Stuffn (CShips *ships)
{
    ships->Stuff = 42;
}
```

When you call the function, the member variable is 12. When you return, it is 42, so the operation did take place on the *CSubmarine* instance.

This is an example of why you declare *virtual* inheritance. If you had multiple lines through which you inherited the base class, the pointer assignment would be ambiguous and you wouldn't be able to perform an operation such as this.

376. *Understanding Pointer Arithmetic on Objects*

Part of the information the compiler stores about your classes is the size of each one. In Tip 197, "Understanding Array Arithmetic," you saw how the compiler automatically adds multiples of the size of the operand when you do pointer arithmetic. Objects are no exception. The compiler retrieves the size information for your class and treats it the same as a built-in data type.

You have to be careful, however, when taking a pointer to a base class and performing arithmetic on it. The size information stored when you make the assignment is the size of the base class. Examine the following code:

```
CSubmarine sub[10];

    sub[0].Stuff = 12;
    printf ("sub[0].Stuff = %d\n", sub[0].Stuff);
    CShips *ships = &sub[0];
    Stuffn (ships);
    printf ("sub[0].Stuff = %d\n", sub[0].Stuff);
    printf ("sub[1].Stuff = %d\n", sub[1].Stuff);
// this is a NO NO!
    ++ships;
    Stuffn (ships, 23);
    printf ("sub[0].Stuff = %d\n", sub[0].Stuff);
    printf ("sub[1].Stuff = %d\n", sub[1].Stuff);
```

When you increment *ships*, you are incrementing it by the size of the class *CShips*, but you are operating on an array of type *CSubmarine*. The second call to *Stuffn()* is going to produce some unexpected results, at best. It's all legal as far as the compiler is concerned, but by the time the call gets down to the function, there is no way to determine the true size of the parameter.

377. *Understanding Procedure-Driven Programming*

Your programming so far—all these little test programs and class examples—has been based on *procedure-driven* programming. One thing follows another in this type of programming. Your code has determined what happens next in the program, and the sequence in which the instructions are executed is predictable

Even your dog-training exercise from Tip 289, "Understanding Pointers to Functions," is predictable. You don't know with each iteration of the loop what command the user will enter, but the range of acceptable commands is limited. You could look at each keystroke and anticipate the command when you have enough letters for it to be unique. Then you could execute the command automatically without requiring the user to press the Enter key (you've all seen programs that show this nasty behavior). While the program is getting the command, however, nothing else is happening in the program. It's still one program line at a time.

Processing of this type is *synchronous*. The events in the program must happen one after the other. Of course, all programs must execute this way when it comes right down to the basics. You couldn't have the computer executing a line that uses a variable before it executes the line that sets the variable. There are cases, however, where other programs can interject themselves into the processing stream, thus interrupting the sequential chain of instructions.

378. *Understanding Event-Driven Programming*

Technically, C++ is a procedure-driven language. Some Windows and DOS device drivers are used to handling I/O to and from a hardware port on the computer. When the port is ready to accept data or requires attention, it signals the operating system through a control line, causing an *interrupt*. The signal causes the operating system to interrupt the code it is processing and to respond to the request.

The events are *asynchronous* with respect to the operating system, whether it is Windows, DOS, UNIX, or MacOS. The operating system can't know when or why the hardware interrupted its normal sequence. The operating system transfers control to the interrupt routine, which usually saves the current machine state, processes the data, restores the machine state, and then transfers control back to the operating system. Usually, this happens so quickly that the computer user doesn't even know it; the events appear to happen transparently.

The execution sequence is controlled by the events happening in the computer. It's still procedural—you can't get away from the design principles of C++—but now the procedures are being driven by events.

In Windows programming, you use event-driven programming in a different way. You can process your code sequentially, but when the program isn't performing a specific task, it waits in a loop for Windows to send it a *message* containing a request from the user or operating system to perform some task. This might be a simple movement of the mouse cursor or a complex request that results from the user pressing a key sequence.

The program may set up a timer so that it is interrupted from the message loop periodically to perform tasks that need to be done.

Neither the program nor the operating system has any notion of when or what type of a message will be sent to the Windows program.

379. *Introducing Controls*

When you run a Windows program, virtually everything you see in a window, and many things you don't see, is a *control*. A menu and each menu item are separate controls, a pushbutton is a control, and the title bar and its associated buttons and icons are all separate controls. Even the window in which you edit text probably has one or more controls behind it. In essence, a control is an object the user interacts with to control or manipulate data.

Controls are Windows resources. They are how a program interacts with a user. They are used to accept input, such as a button click or a menu selection that the operating system passes on to the program, or they are used to display output to the user, such as in a list box, a combo box, or an edit window.

Controls usually are associated with dialog boxes, but even the main frame of an ordinary window contains many controls. Typically, a frame includes at least a menu, one or more toolbars, and a status bar. Each of these objects may contain a number of other controls.

Although you may design your own controls, Windows has a set of *common controls* that are available to the programmer without his or her having to code them individually. The controls in 32-bit Windows are provided through a *dynamic link library*, or DLL. A dynamic link library is a library file the operating system can load into memory on demand rather than have the functions in it link into the program at compile time, a process known as *static linking*. The advantage of using a DLL instead of static linking is smaller program code size and more efficient use of memory. When the DLL functions are no longer needed, they may be unloaded from memory. DLLs also may be updated to repair bugs and introduce new features without requiring all programs that use them to be recompiled.

Many objects in a Windows program are controls, even though the user may never see them. The image list that contains icons for a list or tree control, for example, is a new control that was introduced with Windows 95. The user never sees the image list, but its effects are readily apparent in the appearance of an application.

The controls send messages to their parent windows, typically messages containing information about a user event, such as a key being pressed, a button being clicked, or a mouse movement.

The simplest of Windows programs may be written with a single function, *WinMain()*, and a single statement to call the Windows *MessageBox()* library function. Windows has no concept of *stdin*, *stdout*, or *stderr*, so the only reason you need the standard header *stdio.h* is for the *sprintf()* function. You use the Windows standard header file *windows.h*. Enter the following code in a new source code file:

```
/*
    first.cpp. Our first Windows program
 */
#include <windows.h>
#include <stdio.h>

int WinMain(HINSTANCE hInst,
                    HINSTANCE hPrevInst,
                    LPSTR    lpCmdLine,
                    int      nCmdShow)
{
char szStr[128];
    sprintf (szStr, "hInst = %ld\nhPrevInst = %ld\n"
                 "lpCmdline = %s\nnCmdShow = %d",
                 hInst, hPrevInst,
                 lpCmdLine, nCmdShow);
    return (MessageBox (NULL, szStr,
                 "Howdy", MB_OK |
                 MB_ICONINFORMATION));
}
```

Compile this program with the following command line to link it with the *user32.lib* module:

```
cl first.cpp user32.lib
```

You can see at least five controls when you run this program. The title bar and the disabled box with an × in its right side are separate controls. The static field that holds the balloon image is a control, as are the text field and the OK pushbutton.

380. Understanding How Windows Interacts with Programs

Windows "talks" to applications by sending them a series of messages. Unlike programming under DOS, programs don't directly access the hardware devices. Instead, they "open" them using calls to the operating system, and Windows responds to requests from the ports by sending the application program messages containing the information about the port request. Other devices, such as the mouse and keyboard, don't even have to be opened by the program. Windows automatically sends mouse messages to the window under the mouse cursor. Keystrokes are automatically sent to the window that has the current "focus." The program is free to act on these messages or ignore them altogether.

381. Introducing the Windows Message Pump

In your programming so far, you've made calls to the operating system to perform certain operations. Through library functions, you have written to the screen, opened and read files, and taken input from the keyboard. In a manner of speaking, the operating system, Windows, has been waiting for you to call it with your requests.

In a Windows program, you still call the operating system to perform certain tasks, and Windows also may call your program when it has data or information for it. However, in a multi-tasking environment, the operating system can't wait until you get around to responding to its call, so Windows calls your program through messages and then goes about its task of tending to other processes.

Windows provides you with functions to watch this message queue even while your program is busy performing other tasks. The *PeekMessage()* function allows you to look at messages on the queue without removing them. You can retrieve the messages and remove them from the queue by calling *GetMessage()*, which returns a zero when the user or operating system has posted a quit message to the application or returns a non-zero value otherwise.

When you use the Microsoft Foundation Class, a function in *CWinThread* named *PumpMessage()* does exactly that. It implements a message loop within the main message loop and processes the next message when you call it. If it returns 0, you know that the *WM_QUIT* message has been posted, so you wrap up your processing to get ready to exit.

382. Responding to Windows Messages

A message to a window contains an integer that identifies it and usually one or two parameters describing the event that caused the message. You can retrieve messages from the queue by calling the Windows *GetMessage()* function. Before you can create a real Windows program (something that displays more than a simple message box), you need to look at Windows resources. You will examine the *GetMessage()* function closer in Tip 384, "Understanding Resources."

In an ordinary Windows program, you may use the integer identifier in a *switch* statement to select the messages to which you want to respond. In an MFC application, you use a message map macro to establish the message response table. In either case, the program usually is directed to a specific function that you write to handle the message, and you call the function a *message handler*.

Typically, a message handler in an MFC application is a *void* type and doesn't return any information to the operating system. Some, however, do require you to return a value or set a flag to indicate your program handled the message. The message handler may require no parameters or up to three parameters, depending on how you have defined them. In MFC, a number of the message handler functions are predefined in the message map, and you must use the same name and parameter list as the message map definition. Fortunately, the Visual Studio has wizards to handle these details for you.

383. *Using the Module Definition File*

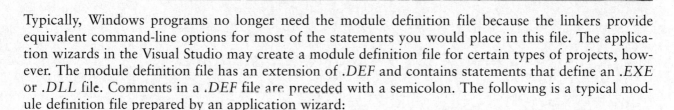

Typically, Windows programs no longer need the module definition file because the linkers provide equivalent command-line options for most of the statements you would place in this file. The application wizards in the Visual Studio may create a module definition file for certain types of projects, however. The module definition file has an extension of *.DEF* and contains statements that define an *.EXE* or *.DLL* file. Comments in a *.DEF* file are preceded with a semicolon. The following is a typical module definition file prepared by an application wizard:

```
LIBRARY        "rtimedPS"

DESCRIPTION  'Proxy/Stub DLL'

EXPORTS
        DllGetClassObject       @1    PRIVATE
        DllCanUnloadNow         @2    PRIVATE
        GetProxyDllInfo         @3    PRIVATE
        DllRegisterServer       @4    PRIVATE
        DllUnregisterServer         @5    PRIVATE

IMPORTS
        WSACleanup          @0
```

If the *NAME* statement is used in a definition file, it must be the first statement in the file and specify the output file name. This is the same as the linker */OUT* option. Alternatively, you may use the *LIBRARY* statement to identify a dynamic link library.

The *DESCRIPTION* statement writes a string into the data section of the program. The string must be enclosed in single or double quote marks if the string contains no quote marks. If the string contains double quotes, enclose it in single quote marks. If the string contains no quote marks or single quote marks, enclose it in double quotes.

The *STACKSIZE* statement sets the size of the program's stack. The default for a Visual C++ program is 1MB. The equivalent linker option is */STACK*.

The *SECTIONS* or *SEGMENTS* statement sets the attributes for the data, stack, and code segments of the output file. You may use more than one of these statements in a *.DEF* file.

The *EXPORTS* statement makes one or more statements (variables or functions) available to outside programs. The name of the statement being exported is case sensitive.

The *VERSION* statement causes the linker to place two integers in the output file's header identifying the major and minor version numbers of the program. The default is version 0.0.

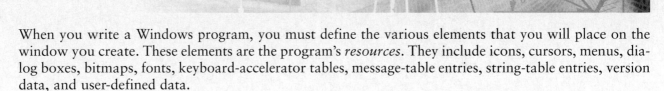

384. *Understanding Resources*

When you write a Windows program, you must define the various elements that you will place on the window you create. These elements are the program's *resources*. They include icons, cursors, menus, dialog boxes, bitmaps, fonts, keyboard-accelerator tables, message-table entries, string-table entries, version data, and user-defined data.

Although you could write them directly in binary format, it's much easier to use a resource file and compile it using the resource compiler, *RC.EXE*, provided with the Visual Studio. Normally, you write a resource file using the same name as your program but with an extension of *.RC*. The resulting binary file is included in your program when you link your project.

When you use the Visual Studio IDE, you have the advantage of various resource editors for creating and editing resources. In the end, though, it creates a single resource file, and you might have occasion to edit this file, particularly if you need to add resources that can't be created directly in the IDE (these would include such things as Registry information and the messages you might want to log in the Windows NT events viewer).

Let's create a minimum Windows program that will include a single menu with a single item allowing you to exit the program.

First, you need a couple of icons. You can draw them, get them from the various graphics files in the Visual Studio directory, or use those on the enclosed CD-ROM. Also, you can purchase commercial icon libraries. My drawing ability doesn't extend beyond stick figures, so I tend to use icons from a commercial library. You will need a small icon, one that is 16 by 16 pixels, and a large icon, one that is 32 by 32 pixels. However you get the icon files, copy them into your program directory. Name the small icon file *small.ico* and the large icon file *second.ico*. A Windows directory contains four views; Windows uses the large icon for the large icon view and the small icon for the other three views.

Second, create a file named *resource.h* to hold your resource definitions. This program will not have a lot of resource defines, so you really don't need this file, but it's a good practice to keep them in a separate header file. That's the way the Visual Studio wizards handle resource definitions:

```
/*
    resource.h - resource definitions for
              second.cpp
 */
#ifndef __RESOURCE_H__
#define __RESOURCE_H__

#define IDC_SMALLICON      100
#define IDC_SECONDICON     101
#define IDC_SECOND         102
#define IDM_EXIT           103

#endif    //  __RESOURCE_H__
```

Next, create the resource file and name it *second.rc*. The file will contain only the large and small icons and the single-item menu:

```
#include "resource.h"


IDI_SECONDICON ICON    DISCARDABLE      "SECOND.ICO"
IDI_SMALLICON  ICON    DISCARDABLE      "SMALL.ICO"


IDC_SECOND MENU DISCARDABLE
BEGIN
    POPUP "&File"
    BEGIN
        MENUITEM "E&xit", IDM_EXIT
    END
END
```

Finally, you create the source file, *second.cpp*. When you start using the Visual Studio IDE, Windows programming will become much easier, but this is the way programmers used to have to create Windows programs. Most programmers kept a skeleton program that they just copied into their working directory as a starting point, and that's essentially what the Visual Studio does.

You will add some stock functions to your program in addition to *WinMain()*. These will be used to initialize the program, register the window, and your callback function, which traditionally is named *WndProc()*:

```
/*
    second.cpp. - Our second Windows program.
 */


#include <windows.h>
#include "resource.h"


#define MAX_STRING 124


// Global Variables:
HINSTANCE    hInst;  // The current instance
TCHAR        szTitle[MAX_STRING]; // Title bar text
TCHAR        szWindowClass[MAX_STRING]; // The name
                    // used to register the window
HWND         hWnd;   // Handle to our window


// Declare functions
ATOM    RegisterWindowClass(HINSTANCE hInstance);
BOOL    InitInstance(HINSTANCE, int);
LRESULT CALLBACK WndProc(HWND,UINT,WPARAM,LPARAM);


int APIENTRY WinMain(HINSTANCE hInstance,
                     HINSTANCE hPrevInstance,
                     LPSTR     lpCmdLine,
                     int       nCmdShow)
{
    MSG msg;
// Initialize strings
    strcpy (szTitle, "Second Program");
    strcpy (szWindowClass, "SecondProgram");
    RegisterWindowClass(hInstance);
    hInst = hInstance;
```

```
// Initialize application
   if (!InitInstance (hInstance, nCmdShow))
   {
       return FALSE;
   }
// Main message loop:
   while (GetMessage(&msg, NULL, 0, 0))
   {
       TranslateMessage(&msg);
       DispatchMessage(&msg);
   }
return msg.wParam;
}


//  Register the window class.
//
ATOM RegisterWindowClass(HINSTANCE hInstance)
{

   WNDCLASSEX wcex;

   wcex.cbSize = sizeof(WNDCLASSEX);
   wcex.style        = CS_HREDRAW | CS_VREDRAW;
   wcex.lpfnWndProc = (WNDPROC)WndProc;
   wcex.cbClsExtra  = 0;
   wcex.cbWndExtra  = 0;
   wcex.hInstance   = hInstance;
   wcex.hIcon       = LoadIcon(hInstance,
                     (LPCTSTR)IDI_SECONDICON);
   wcex.hCursor       = LoadCursor(NULL,
                          IDC_ARROW);
   wcex.hbrBackground = (HBRUSH)(COLOR_WINDOW+1);
   wcex.lpszMenuName  = (LPCSTR)IDC_SECOND;
   wcex.lpszClassName = szWindowClass;
   wcex.hIconSm       = LoadIcon(wcex.hInstance,
                     (LPCTSTR)IDI_SMALLICON);

   return (RegisterClassEx(&wcex));
}


//  Create the main window
//
BOOL InitInstance(HINSTANCE hInstance,
                  int nCmdShow)
{
  hWnd = CreateWindow(szWindowClass, szTitle,
                      WS_OVERLAPPEDWINDOW,
                      CW_USEDEFAULT, 0,
                      CW_USEDEFAULT, 0, NULL,
                      NULL, hInstance, NULL);

   if (!hWnd)
   {
     return FALSE;
   }
```

```
      ShowWindow(hWnd, nCmdShow);
      UpdateWindow(hWnd);

      return TRUE;
}

//  Message processor.
//

LRESULT CALLBACK WndProc(HWND hWnd,
                         UINT message,
                         WPARAM wParam,
                         LPARAM lParam)
{
    switch (message)
    {
    int wmId, wmEvent;
       case WM_COMMAND:
           wmId    = LOWORD(wParam);
           wmEvent = HIWORD(wParam);
// Parse the menu selections:
           switch (wmId)
           {
               case IDM_EXIT:
                   MessageBox(hWnd,"Exit Called",
                         "Bye Bye", MB_OK);
                     DestroyWindow(hWnd);
                   break;
               default:
                   return DefWindowProc(hWnd,
                                        message,
                                        wParam,
                                        lParam);
           }
           break;
       case WM_DESTROY:
           PostQuitMessage(0);
           break;
    default:
       return DefWindowProc(hWnd, message,
                            wParam, lParam);
    }
    return 0;
}
```

Compile the resource file with the resource compiler. Then compile and link the source file with the resource file and the USER32.LIB library file using the following commands:

```
C:>rc second.rc  <Enter>
C:>cl second.cpp second.res user32.lib  <Enter>
```

I will discuss the *WNDCLASS* and *WNDCLASSEX* structures and the reasons for registering window classes shortly. After the window class is registered, you call the *InitInstance()* function to create and show the window. Then you return to *WinMain()* and enter a message loop, waiting for Windows to call you with data for your application.

Notice that you never call the *WndProc()* function directly. When you call Windows through the *DispatchMessage()* library function, Windows looks up the procedure you used when you registered your window and calls this procedure; hence, the *CALLBACK* function type.

385. *Using the Makefile for a Windows Program*

Now that you've added the resource compiler to your list of tools, the idea of a makefile to build your program sounds good. You can add environment variables to invoke the compiler. Right now, you aren't using any resource compiler flags, but you will add an environment variable for them anyway.

Enter the following code and save it as *makefile* in the same directory as *Second.cpp*. By default, *NMAKE.EXE* looks in the current directory for a file called *makefile* (notice there is no extension).

```
#
# Makefile for second.exe
#
HDR=resource.h

CPP=cl.exe
CPPFLAGS=-c
OBJ=second.obj

RES=second.res
RC=rc.exe
RCFLAGS=

LINK=link.exe
LINKFLAGS=

LIBS=user32.lib

second.exe: second.obj second.res
            $(LINK) $(LINKFLAGS) $(OBJ) \
            $(RES) $(LIBS)

second.obj: second.cpp $(HDR)
            $(CC) $(CPPFLAGS) second.cpp

second.res: second.rc resource.h
            $(RC) $(RCFLAGS) second.rc
```

Notice that you use the file name *resource.h* for the .*RES* target instead of *$(HDR)*. You may add other header files to your program later, but *second.res* depends only on the resource file (*second.rc* in this program) and the file containing the resource definitions (*resource.h*).

Build the program by simply typing *nmake* on the command line.

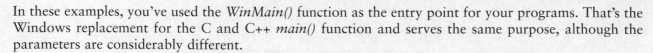

386. *Understanding the* WinMain() *Function*

In these examples, you've used the *WinMain()* function as the entry point for your programs. That's the Windows replacement for the C and C++ *main()* function and serves the same purpose, although the parameters are considerably different.

The *APIENTRY* is a calling type declaration that may be redefined for different platforms, such as Windows or the Apple operating system. By changing command-line definitions when the library is compiled, the same code may be built using different calling sequences, such as for Pascal or C.

The first parameter to the function, *hInst*, is a handle—a pointer—to the current program, the one you are running when you view the message box. If more than one instance of the programming is running, the second parameter, *hPrevInst*, is a handle to the most recently started instance of the program. This parameter is a legacy from older Windows and is always *NULL* in 32-bit Windows.

The *lpCmdLine* is the input command line *without* the program name. If you run your program from the command line and include arguments, this parameter will contain the arguments. This is a single string and Windows does not parse the string to break them into individual arguments. If you intend to use command-line arguments, you will have to provide your own parsing code.

Finally, *nCmdShow* is the Windows suggestion of how to display the window. Normally, this is 1 or *SW_NORMAL*, but you may override it when you display your window. In this program, you are displaying only a stock message box, so you don't use it.

387. *Using Command-Line Arguments in* WinMain()

When you use the standard C++ function *main()*, the command processor parses the input line into separate strings and passes *main()* an integer giving the total number of arguments and an array of strings containing the actual arguments. The argument count is always at least one, and the first parameter is the program name itself.

In a Windows program, however, you get the entire command line stripped of the program name as a single argument. It's up to you to parse it if you are expecting more than one argument.

Try running the *FIRST.EXE* sample program from Tip 379, "Introducing Controls," with various command-line arguments. It's a simple matter to use *strtok()* to parse the space-delimited elements of the command line. When using the standard C++ entry function *main()*, you learned that the first argument was the name of the program. In a Windows program, the argument string does not include the program name. If you need your own program's name, you must call a function, *GetModuleFileName()*, to retrieve it using the instance handle passed to you:

```
char szFileName[_MAX_PATH];
GetModuleFileName (hInstance,
                   szFileName, _MAX_PATH);
```

The function parameters are the instance handle (the *HINSTANCE parameter* to *WinMain()*), a character buffer, and a 32-bit integer containing the size of the character buffer.

388. *Understanding the nCmdShow Parameter*

The fourth parameter to *WinMain()* function is *nCmdShow*. This is the Windows suggestion on how to display the window when you create it. Normally, you simply pass this parameter to the *ShowWindow()*, but you are free to override it and pass another value to the function.

The *nCmdShow* parameter uses an integer value and normally is 1, the value of *SW_SHOWNORMAL* to display a normally sized window (one that doesn't fill the entire screen). When you create and initially display a window, you usually use one of four values in your call to *ShowWindow()*: *SW_HIDE*, *SW_SHOWNORMAL*, *SW_SHOWMAXIMIZED*, or *SW_SHOWMINIMIZED*.

Even after the window is initially created, you may call *ShowWindow()* repeatedly to change the display mode. The function may pass any of the following flags:

- *SW_HIDE* (value 0) creates a hidden window that shows on neither the screen nor the Taskbar. If you use this value, you have to call up the Task Manager window (Ctrl+Alt+Del on Windows 95 and 98; right-click on the taskbar and select Task Manager in Windows NT) to stop the program. If you need to run a program in the background and never have to interact with it, something such as a monitor or daemon process would be run in this mode. Several Windows programs run this way; on Windows 95 and 98, when you press Ctrl+Alt+Delete, you see a list of running programs, most of which don't show up on the Taskbar.

- *SW_SHOWNORMAL* or *SW_NORMAL* (1) produces an intermediate-size window. It initially displays a window on the screen, but it doesn't fill the entire screen. This is the mode normally passed in the *nCmdShow* parameter.

- *SW_SHOWMINIMIZED* (2) creates the window but does not display it. Windows displays an icon for the program on the Taskbar, and you may click on this icon to show the window and close it. The numerical value is 2. A program would use this mode if it normally runs in the background and only occasionally needs user interaction. The popular remote-control program *pcAnywhere* is an example of a program that runs in this mode.

- *SW_SHOWMAXIMIZED* (3) activates and shows a full-screen window that covers everything else on the screen except the Taskbar. Windows that are created this way normally can't be resized by the user without using the resize box in the title bar.

- *SW_MAXIMIZE* (also 3) sizes the window so that it fills the entire screen.

- *SW_SHOWNOACTIVE* (4) shows the window in its most recent size and position but does not change the active window.

- *SW_SHOW* (value 5) causes an inactive window to become the active window but doesn't change its size or position.

- *SW_MINIMIZE* (value 6) minimizes the window and the role of active window passes to another window.

- *SW_SHOWMINNOACTIVE* (7) minimizes the window but does not change the active window.

- *SW_SHOWNA* (8) displays the window in its current state but does not change the active window.

- *SW_RESTORE* (9) activates and displays the window. If the window is maximized or minimized, it is restored to its original size and position. This is the value to use when restoring a minimized window.

- *SW_SHOWDEFAULT* (10) sets the size to the default that was specified when the process that created the window was started.

389. *Understanding Program Instances*

In C++ you use an instance to describe an object created from a definition of something. Defining a structure, union, or class doesn't create an object, and thus, no instance is created by the definition. When you declare a variable based on the definition, however, and an object is created, you call the object an "instance" of the structure, union, or class.

An instance of a program is created when a copy of the program file is loaded into memory and runs. It becomes the object created from the definition, the program file.

A handle is an indirect pointer to a memory location. In early versions of Windows when computers had limited memory, Windows had to manage memory a little more carefully. Sometimes memory management involved moving objects around in memory, which meant any pointer to this memory in the program might become invalid at any time. To get around this, Microsoft came up with handles. The operating system maintains the memory and lets the program access it through an identifier, the handle, regardless of the exact location in memory. When your program needs the exact memory address, it may obtain the address from the operating system using the handle. You will run across handles often as you program in Windows.

An *HINSTANCE* is a handle the operating system assigns to keep track of a program. In older versions of Windows, a program used the handle to a previous instance of itself to share resources. In 32-bit Windows, all instances of a program are given the same handle, and the previous instance handle passed to a program is no longer used.

390. *Understanding Window Classes*

Windows requires you to register your window class so that it knows the callback procedure and other characteristics of the window. Once registered, you can create more windows of the same class without having to register them again.

The window class uniquely identifies characteristics of the window type, and all objects that create windows create them using a windows class. The combobox control, for example, uses one window class, a button control uses another, and an edit control uses yet another class. However, all instances of the same control type use the same window class.

391. *Understanding the* **WNDCLASS** *and* **WNDCLASSEX** *Structures*

When you register your window classes, you pass the function a pointer to a structure that contains members describing the characteristics of your window. You can't create a window unless its class is registered.

The *WNDCLASS* structure was used with older versions of Windows and may still be used, but the *WNDCLASSEX* structure used with 32-bit windows is preferred. The extended structure contains a *cbSize* member and a handle to a small icon; otherwise, the two structures are identical.

The *WNDCLASSEX* structure is defined as follows. If you remove the *dbSize* and *hIconSm* members, the definition is the same as the *WNDCLASS* structure:

```
typedef struct _WNDCLASSEX
{
    UINT cbSize;
    UINT style;
    WNDPROC lpfnWndProc;
    int cbClsExtra;
    int cbWndExtra;
    HANDLE hInstance;
    HICON hIcon;
    HCURSOR hCursor;
    HBRUSH hbrBackground;
    LPCTSTR lpszMenuName;
    LPCTSTR lpszClassName;
    HICON hIconSm;
} WNDCLASSEX;
```

The *style* member describes how the window will appear and how it will draw itself. It is a 32-bit number built by combining a number of style flags.

The *lpfnWndProc* member specifies the function Windows will use to call your program when it needs to send messages for the window. You should never call the window procedure directly. If you need to call it, you may use the Windows API function *CallWindowsProc()* using the address of the procedure, the instance handle, a message identifier, and any parameters needed by the message.

When you register a window class, Windows allocates memory for the structure. You may specify extra memory to allocate using the *cbClsExtra*, and your program may use this extra memory to store additional information. Similarly, extra memory for each instance of the class may be specified in the *cbWndExtra* member. Normally, you set these members to 0, but if you are going to create a dialog box using the window class, you must set the *cbWndExtra* value to *DLGWINDOWEXTRA*. The amount of extra memory reserved for dialog boxes differs according to the platform you are using, so you should always use the value defined by *DLGWINDOWEXTRA*.

The *hIcon* member specifies the icon used to represent the window when it is minimized. You get this handle when you call the *LoadIcon()* function. If you set this member to *NULL*, your program must draw the icon when a user minimizes a window. For Windows 95/98 and Windows NT, this member is the large icon.

When a user moves the mouse pointer into your window arrow, the handle in the *hCursor* member is used to draw the cursor. You can get a handle to the standard arrow cursor by calling *LoadCursor (NULL, IDC_ARROW)*. If you set this member to *NULL*, Windows will call your *WndProc* function to draw the cursor when the user moves the mouse over your window.

The window background is drawn using the *hbrBackground* member, which is the handle to a brush object. You also may specify a color value by adding 1 to a standard system color and casting it to an *HBRUSH* data type. If you set this member to *NULL*, your program must draw the background whenever requested by Windows.

The *lpszMenuName* specifies the default menu to use when Windows creates a window of this class. You can set this member to *NULL* and no default menu will be used. This member value is used only when a window is first created, and you may change the menu in your program code.

One of the most important members of the class is the *lpszClassName* member. This is a null-terminated string specifying the name used to identify the window class. After the class is registered, you may use this name at any time to create a window of this class.

The *hIconSm* member is used only by Windows 95 and later versions of Windows. It specifies the small icon to be used in certain Windows procedures. For example, in a list control, one of the options is to display the list elements using small icons, in which case the control would use this value to represent your window.

392. Registering Window Classes

Use the Windows functions *RegisterClass()* or *RegisterClassEx()* to register your window class. The first function is the older Windows version and takes a pointer to a *WNDCLASS* structure; the second requires a pointer to a *WNDCLASSEX* structure. If you don't need to set a small icon for your window, you may use the *RegisterClass()* function.

If you use the *WNDCLASSEX* structure, you must set the size member. If your structure variable is named *wcex*, you can set the *cbSize* member with the following simple statement:

```
wcex.cbSize = sizeof(WNDCLASSEX);
```

Set the small icon handle by calling the *LoadIcon()* Windows function using your program instance handle and the small icon name you used in your resource file.

393. Understanding the Components of a Window

When you speak of a "window," you often refer to the object you see on the screen that displays a frame, a title bar, some icons to minimize, maximize, and close the window, and perhaps a menu.

Although the term may not be inaccurate, this single window really is a complex structure built using a number of smaller windows. The title bar is a window, which, in turn, contains several other smaller windows, the icon, and the minimize, maximize, and close buttons. Each menu is another window, each containing more elemental windows to hold the individual menu items. The same is true of a toolbar, which is a window built to hold several buttons, which are also individual windows.

A window may contain scroll bars, which, again, are windows designed for a special purpose.

By dividing your larger window into smaller windows, you give them some common properties, and you can control them by calling common functions. You may use the *ShowWindow()* function, for example, display or hide only to a menu, a toolbar, or an individual button.

394. Understanding the Windows Client Area

When you run your *SECOND.EXE* program from Tip 384, "Understanding Resources," you see a large empty white area surrounded by the window frame on the top, left, and right, and by the menu and title bar on the bottom.

This is the part of the window where an application displays output such as text or graphics and is commonly referred to as the "client" area. This is your working area, and you are free to do just about anything you want in this window.

The client area may be given special attributes and may be used to contain other smaller windows, such as in a multiple-document interface. The client window has its own coordinate system, and Windows contains functions to map screen coordinates to the client area, and back again.

Normally white, the color of this client area can be changed by specifying a different value in the *hbrBackground* member of the *WNDCLASSEX* structure. *COLOR_WINDOW+1* sets it to white, but try changing the brush to some other color, such as *COLOR_BACKGROUND+1* or *COLOR_APP-WORKSPACE+1*, to see the effects (remember that adding 1 to a system color gives you the brush equivalent when using this structure member).

395. *Understanding Overlapped Windows*

A window on a personal computer is overlapping by its nature. It may be covered completely or partially by another window, or it may cover part or all of other windows. In Windows programming, however, the term "overlapped window" has a slightly different context.

An *overlapped* window usually has at least a title bar and a frame and is intended to serve as an application's main window. It's the top-level window in your structure of smaller windows that creates the display your application shows on the screen.

The overlapped style, designated by the constant *WS_OVERLAPPED*, is the default mode for creating a window. A window created using only this style has a title bar, a thin frame, and a client area, and it cannot be resized. To make things easier, the *windows.h* header file defines another constant, *WS_OVERLAPPEDWINDOW*, which includes the *WS_OVERLAPPED* style, along with the *WS_CAPTION*, *WS_SYSMENU*, *WS_THICKFRAME*, *WS_MINIMIZEBOX*, and *WS_MAXIMIZE-BOX* styles.

Most of the main windows you will see for applications are overlapped windows, but many of their component windows are non-overlapped. A control, for example, often creates a non-overlapped window; it has no title bar and no system menu, and it can't be resized.

Creating an overlapped window allows you to place it in the Windows *Z order*. This is the display sequence of windows on the screen and takes its name from the fact that windows appear deeper or higher on the screen, or in the z-axis of the display. A window at the top of the Z order is fully displayed, whereas one at the bottom of the Z order may be only partially visible, if at all.

396. *Understanding Pop-Up Windows*

Often your application may need to create secondary windows. Normally, these windows are limited to the boundary of the main window, and in the case of the multiple-document interface, they are limited to the client area as well. If you try to move these secondary windows beyond the main window boundary, Windows will "clip" them so they display only partially.

It is possible, however, to create a window that is not bound by these limits, using the *pop-up* style. This is a special type of overlapped window typically used for dialog boxes, message boxes, and other temporary windows, and it may appear outside an application's main window.

In your *SECOND.EXE* program, you placed a message box in the *IDM_EXIT* case in the *WndProc()* function. Run the program and then exit. When the message box appears, it normally is created in the middle of your screen and within the confines of your main application window. Grab it with the mouse cursor and move it around the screen. It freely moves outside your window area.

This is an example of a pop-up window. It is created within the screen coordinate system and is bound by the screen rather than by your window system.

You may create a pop-up window using the *WS_POPUP* style when it is created. In the next tip, you will create a child window; then you will change it to a pop-up style to demonstrate the difference.

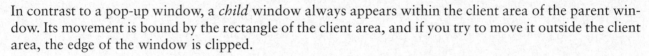

397. *Understanding Child Windows*

In contrast to a pop-up window, a *child* window always appears within the client area of the parent window. Its movement is bound by the rectangle of the client area, and if you try to move it outside the client area, the edge of the window is clipped.

You create a child window using the *WS_CHILD* style. This style cannot be used with the *WS_POPUP*. To show the difference, let's create another Windows program, named *THIRD.EXE*. First, create the following makefile and name it *makefile*. As with the preceding program, you should create the files in a separate directory.

```
#
# Makefile for third.exe
#
HDR=resource.h

CPP=cl.exe
CPPFLAGS=-c
OBJ=third.obj

RES=third.res
RC=rc.exe
RCFLAGS=

LINK=link.exe
LINKFLAGS=

LIBS=user32.lib

third.exe:   third.obj third.res
             $(LINK) $(LINKFLAGS) $(OBJ)\
                $(RES) $(LIBS)

third.obj:   third.cpp $(HDR)
             $(CC) $(CPPFLAGS) third.cpp

third.res:   third.rc resource.h
             $(RC) $(RCFLAGS) third.rc
```

Create the resource header file and name it *resource.h*:

```
/*
    resource.h - resource definitions for
                 third.cpp
 */
#ifndef __RESOURCE_H__
#define __RESOURCE_H__

#define IDI_THIRDICON      100
#define IDI_SMALLICON      101
#define IDC_THIRD          102
#define IDM_EXIT           103
#define IDM_CREATECHILD    104

#endif   // __RESOURCE_H
```

In the resource file, you will add an item to the menu to create a child window. In your code, you will limit it to a single child window, however. Create the following resource file and name it *third.rc*:

```
#include "resource.h"

IDI_THIRDICON  ICON  DISCARDABLE    "THIRD.ICO"
IDI_SMALLICON  ICON  DISCARDABLE    "SMALL.ICO"

IDC_THIRD MENU DISCARDABLE
BEGIN
    POPUP "&File"
    BEGIN
        MENUITEM "E&xit", IDM_EXIT
        MENUITEM "&Create Child", IDM_CREATECHILD
    END
END
```

Finally, create the program source file and name it *third.cpp*. In this file, you will add code to register your child window type and a default window procedure for handling messages:

```
/*
    third.cpp.
 */

#include    <windows.h>
#include    "resource.h"
#include    <stdio.h>

#define MAX_STRING 100
#define CHILD_STYLE (WS_CHILDWINDOW | WS_VISIBLE \
                      | WS_CAPTION | WS_SYSMENU)

// Global Variables:
HINSTANCE   hInst;        // current instance
TCHAR  szTitle[MAX_STRING] = "Third Program";
TCHAR  szWindowClass[MAX_STRING] = "ThirdProgram";
TCHAR  szChildClass[MAX_STRING] = "ThirdPgmChild";
HWND   hMainWnd, hChildWnd;

// Declare functions
```

```
ATOM    RegisterWindowClass(HINSTANCE hInstance);
BOOL    InitInstance(HINSTANCE, int);
LRESULT CALLBACK WndProc(HWND, UINT, WPARAM,
                         LPARAM);
LRESULT CALLBACK ChildWndProc(HWND, UINT, WPARAM,
                         LPARAM);
int APIENTRY WinMain(HINSTANCE hInstance,
                     HINSTANCE hPrevInstance,
                     LPSTR     lpCmdLine,
                     int       nCmdShow)
{
    MSG msg;
    // Initialize global strings
    RegisterWindowClass(hInstance);
    hInst = hInstance;

// Initialize application
    if (!InitInstance (hInstance, nCmdShow))
    {
        return FALSE;
    }
// Main message loop:
    while (GetMessage(&msg, NULL, 0, 0))
    {
        TranslateMessage(&msg);
        DispatchMessage(&msg);
    }
    return msg.wParam;
}


ATOM RegisterWindowClass(HINSTANCE hInstance)
{
WNDCLASSEX wcex;

    wcex.cbSize         = sizeof(WNDCLASSEX);
    wcex.style          = CS_HREDRAW | CS_VREDRAW;
    wcex.lpfnWndProc    = (WNDPROC)WndProc;
    wcex.cbClsExtra     = 0;
    wcex.cbWndExtra     = 0;
    wcex.hInstance      = hInstance;
    wcex.hIcon          = LoadIcon(hInstance,
                        (LPCTSTR)IDI_THIRDICON);
    wcex.hCursor        = LoadCursor(NULL,
                                IDC_ARROW);
    wcex.hbrBackground  =
                (HBRUSH)(COLOR_APPWORKSPACE+1);
    wcex.lpszMenuName   = (LPCSTR)IDC_THIRD;
    wcex.lpszClassName  = szWindowClass;
    wcex.hIconSm        = LoadIcon(wcex.hInstance,
                        (LPCTSTR)IDI_SMALLICON);

    if (!RegisterClassEx(&wcex))
    {
        return (0);
    }
//
```

```
// Register child window class
    wcex.lpfnWndProc    = (WNDPROC)ChildWndProc;
    wcex.lpszClassName  = szChildClass;
    wcex.lpszMenuName   = NULL
    wcex.hbrBackground  =
                        (HBRUSH)(COLOR_WINDOW+1);
    wcex.hIconSm        = NULL;


    return RegisterClassEx(&wcex);
}

BOOL InitInstance(HINSTANCE hInstance,
                  int nCmdShow)
{
    hChildWnd = NULL;
    hMainWnd = CreateWindow(szWindowClass,
              szTitle, WS_OVERLAPPEDWINDOW,
              CW_USEDEFAULT, 0, CW_USEDEFAULT,
              0, NULL, NULL, hInstance, NULL);

    if (!hMainWnd)
    {
        return FALSE;
    }

    ShowWindow(hMainWnd, nCmdShow);
    UpdateWindow(hMainWnd);

   return TRUE;
}


//
//  Window procedure for main window
LRESULT CALLBACK WndProc(HWND hWnd,
                         UINT message,
                         WPARAM wParam,
                         LPARAM lParam)
{
PAINTSTRUCT ps;
HDC hdc;
char szText[MAX_STRING]="Main Window Client Area";

    switch (message)

int APIENTRY WinMain(HINSTANCE hInstance,
                     HINSTANCE hPrevInstance,
                     LPSTR     lpCmdLine,
                     int       nCmdShow)
{
    MSG msg;
    // Initialize global strings
    RegisterWindowClass(hInstance);
    hInst = hInstance;

// Initialize application
    if (!InitInstance (hInstance, nCmdShow))
```

```
        {
            return FALSE;
        }
// Main message loop:
    while (GetMessage(&msg, NULL, 0, 0))
    {
        TranslateMessage(&msg);
        DispatchMessage(&msg);
    }
    return msg.wParam;
}


ATOM RegisterWindowClass(HINSTANCE hInstance)
{
WNDCLASSEX wcex;

// Register the main window class
    wcex.cbSize         = sizeof(WNDCLASSEX);
    wcex.style          = CS_HREDRAW | CS_VREDRAW;
    wcex.lpfnWndProc    = (WNDPROC)WndProc;
    wcex.cbClsExtra     = 0;
    wcex.cbWndExtra     = 0;
    wcex.hInstance      = hInstance;
    wcex.hIcon          = LoadIcon(hInstance,
                          (LPCTSTR)IDI_THIRDICON);
    wcex.hCursor        = LoadCursor(NULL,
                                IDC_ARROW);
    wcex.hbrBackground  =
                (HBRUSH)(COLOR_APPWORKSPACE+1);
    wcex.lpszMenuName   = (LPCSTR)IDC_THIRD;
    wcex.lpszClassName  = szWindowClass;
    wcex.hIconSm        = LoadIcon(wcex.hInstance,
                          (LPCTSTR)IDI_SMALLICON);

    if (!RegisterClassEx(&wcex))
    {
        return (0);
    }
//
// Register child window class
    wcex.lpfnWndProc    = (WNDPROC)ChildWndProc;
    wcex.lpszClassName  = szChildClass;
    wcex.lpszMenuName   = NULL
    wcex.hbrBackground  =
                        (HBRUSH)(COLOR_WINDOW+1);
    wcex.hIconSm        = NULL;

    return RegisterClassEx(&wcex);
}


BOOL InitInstance(HINSTANCE hInstance,
                  int nCmdShow)
{
    hChildWnd = NULL;
    hMainWnd = CreateWindow(szWindowClass,
            szTitle, WS_OVERLAPPEDWINDOW,
```

```
                       CW_USEDEFAULT, 0, CW_USEDEFAULT,
                  0, NULL, NULL, hInstance, NULL);

    if (!hMainWnd)
    {
        return FALSE;
    }

    ShowWindow(hMainWnd, nCmdShow);
    UpdateWindow(hMainWnd);

    return TRUE;
}


//
//  Window procedure for main window
LRESULT CALLBACK WndProc(HWND hWnd,
                            UINT message,
                            WPARAM wParam,
                            LPARAM lParam)
{
PAINTSTRUCT ps;
HDC hdc;
// Declare a string to display in the main window
char szText[MAX_STRING]="Main Window Client Area";

    switch (message)
    {
    int wmId, wmEvent;
        case WM_COMMAND:
            wmId    = LOWORD(wParam);
            wmEvent = HIWORD(wParam);
            // Parse the menu selections:
            switch (wmId)
            {
                case IDM_EXIT:
                    SendMessage (hWnd,
                            IDM_EXIT, 0, 0);
                    DestroyWindow(hWnd);
                    break;
// Handle the menu item to create a child window. Testing for
// a NULL value limits the program to only one instance of the
// child window
                case IDM_CREATECHILD:
                    if (hChildWnd == NULL)
                    {
                        RECT rt;
                        GetClientRect(hWnd, &rt);
                        hChildWnd = CreateWindow(
                                szChildClass,
                                szTitle,
                                CHILD_STYLE,
                                10, 10,
                                3 * rt.right / 4,
                                3 * rt.bottom / 4,
                                hWnd, NULL,
```

```
                                           hInst, NULL);
                             break;
                       }
                       return (DefWindowProc(hWnd,
                                                message,
                                                wParam,
                                                lParam));
                  default:
                     return DefWindowProc(hWnd,
                                             message,
                                             wParam,
                                             lParam);
              }
            break;
        case WM_PAINT:
// Handle the paint message. Draw the string at the top
// of the main window client area.
            hdc = BeginPaint(hWnd, &ps);
            RECT rt;
            GetClientRect(hWnd, &rt);
            rt.top += 15;
            DrawText(hdc, szText, strlen(szText),
                    &rt, DT_CENTER);
            EndPaint(hWnd, &ps);
            break;
        case WM_DESTROY:
            PostQuitMessage(0);
            break;
        default:
            return DefWindowProc(hWnd, message,
                                    wParam, lParam);
    }
    return 0;
}


//
//  Window procedure for child window
LRESULT CALLBACK ChildWndProc(HWND hWnd,
                                UINT message,
                                WPARAM wParam,
                                LPARAM lParam)

{
PAINTSTRUCT ps;
HDC hdc;
TCHAR szText[MAX_STRING] = "Child Window";

    switch (message)
    {
    int wmId, wmEvent;
        case WM_COMMAND:
            wmId    = LOWORD(wParam);
            wmEvent = HIWORD(wParam);
            // Parse the menu selections:
            switch (wmId)
            {
                default:
```

```
                         return DefWindowProc(hWnd,
                                              message,
                                              wParam,
                                              lParam);
            }
            break;
// Draw the "Child window" string in the child window
        case WM_PAINT:
            hdc = BeginPaint(hWnd, &ps);
            RECT rt;
            GetClientRect(hWnd, &rt);
            DrawText(hdc, szText, strlen(szText),
                     &rt, DT_CENTER | DT_VCENTER |
                          DT_SINGLELINE);
            EndPaint(hWnd, &ps);
            break;
        case WM_DESTROY:
            hChildWnd = NULL;
            break;
        default:
            return DefWindowProc(hWnd, message,
                                 wParam, lParam);
    }
    return 0;
}
```

Build the program by running *NMAKE.EXE*. Create the child window by selecting Create Child from the File menu. Move the child window around in the client area to see how it is clipped at the edge of the client area.

To see the difference between child and pop-up windows, change the *CHILD_STYLE* definition on line 10 from *WS_CHILDWINDOW* to *WS_POPUPWINDOW*. Rebuild the program and run it. Create the child window and move it around. The window no longer is bound by the client area, and you can move it anywhere on the screen. It's still dependent on the main window. It remains on top of your main window, hides with it when you use the minimize button, and returns to the screen when you restore the main window. It is destroyed with the main window when you exit the program. By giving it the pop-up style, however, you allow it to go outside the client area.

398. *Understanding the Title Bar*

You can give a window a title bar by specifying *WS_CAPTION* in its style. At its least, the title bar not only gives you a place to label the window but also provides a drag point so that you can move it around the screen using the mouse. The dragging capability is a Windows function built in to the title bar properties.

A window doesn't have to have a title bar. In the program from the preceding tip, try removing the *WS_CAPTION* style from the child window style. You can create the child window, but you no longer can move it around with the mouse. Even using the *WS POPUPWINDOW* style, you can move the main window, but the child window remains fixed.

The title bar enables the Move item when you add the system menu to it. It also gives you a place to keep the minimize, maximize, and close buttons. When you give it a system menu using the *WS_SYSMENU* style, you also give it a close button by default. Adding the *WS_MAXIMIZEBOX* adds a maximize button to the title bar and enables the Maximize item on the system menu. (The maximize button becomes a restore button when the window is maximized; a minimize button also is added to the title bar but is disabled.) You add or enable the minimize function on the system menu and the minimize button by specifying the *WS_MINIMIZEBOX*.

Add the *WS_MAXIMIZEBOX* and *WS_MINIMIZEBOX* styles to the child window style in the program in Tip 387, "Using Command-Line Arguments in *WinMain()*." Then build and run the program. When you click the minimize button or select it from the system menu, the window is minimized within the client area of the main window. You will see this behavior in Tip 504, "Using the *CFrameWnd* Classes: The Multiple-Document Interface" when you examine child windows in the multiple-document interface.

Now change the style from *WS_CHILDWINDOW* to *WS_POPUPWINDOW*, and build and run the program again. Click the minimize button or select it from the system menu, and Windows minimizes the pop-up window on the desktop. The minimized window hides when you minimize your main window, however, demonstrating that it still is a descendant of your program's window.

399. *Understanding the System Menu*

When you use the *WS_SYSMENU* style to create your window, the operating system creates a pop-up menu that contains commands to set the window size and position and to close the window. Although most of the menu items are defined by Windows, it is possible to place items in it from your program. To see the system menu, click on the icon at the far left of the title bar in any Windows application.

The system menu contains keyboard equivalents for common mouse operations. If you select the Move item, for example, the cursor changes to a four-way arrow, and you can use the cursor keys to reposition the window. The Size item produces a similar cursor, and the window may be resized without the mouse.

Many applications don't need complicated and involved menus. If that's the case with your program, you can place a few items on the system menu. The only requirement is that the resource IDs be less than 0xF000 so that they don't interfere with Windows functions. The two items on your meager menu in the program from Tip 397, "Understanding Child Windows," fit the bill, so let's change your program slightly to move them to the system menu. In fact, the system menu already contains a Close item, so you can do away with your Exit item and add just the Create Child item.

In the *RegisterWindowClass()* function, set the *lpszMenuName* member of *wcex* to *NULL*. In the *InitInstance()* function, just before the call to *ShowWindow()*, add the following lines of code:

```
HMENU hMenu = GetSystemMenu (hMainWnd, NULL);
AppendMenu (hMenu, MF_STRING, IDM_CREATECHILD,
            "Create Child");
```

Finally, messages from the system menu are *WM_SYSCOMMAND* messages, so in the *WndProc()* function you change *WM_COMMAND* to *WM_SYSCOMMAND*.

Build the program again using *NMAKE* and select the system menu. Below the Close item, you should see a menu separator and your Create Child item, which should function the same as it did when you had it in your own menu.

400. *Understanding the Minimize, Maximize, and Close Window Buttons*

Button controls give you mouse-clickable icons that represent items on a menu. The minimize, maximize, and close window buttons on the title bar represent the same items on the system menu. These buttons, represented as small boxes on the right side of the title bar, generate the same Windows messages as their menu counterparts, and you don't have to add cases in your window procedure to handle them.

When you click one of these buttons, Windows generates a *WM_SYSCOMMAND* message with the button's resource identifier in the lower 16 bits of the first message parameter, the *wParam* parameter in your sample programs. You can extract it using the *LOWORD* macro, which masks off the upper 16 bits and returns only the lower portion of the parameter. Windows uses resource identifiers of 0xF000 (61440 decimal) and higher to represent system functions.

Unless you keep track of mouse positions and events, you don't know whether the user invoked the system commands using the system menu or by clicking on one of the buttons. Windows does send a *WM_SYSCOMMAND* message with 0xF093 in *wParam* when the system menu is opened, but this still doesn't tell you whether the user moved the mouse to a button and clicked it instead of the menu item.

The close window button, represented by the button with a bold **X**, corresponds to the Close item on the system menu. System commands usually are identified with the *SC_* prefix, and the close window button message contains *SC_CLOSE* (0xF060) in the *wParam* value. If you pass this value on to the default window procedure, Windows will shut down your program and destroy the window. If you need to do any processing, such as save file information, you can intercept the message and process it before allowing Windows to shut down the program.

When you use the *WS_SYSMENU* style to create your window, Windows automatically adds the close window button to the title bar. There is no additional style flag to set in order to obtain this button control.

The minimize window button, the button with a bold underscore, places the *SC_MINIMIZE* (0xf020) value in *wParam*, and Windows uses the message as a signal to reduce the program window to an icon on the Taskbar. In the case of a child window in which the window is reduced to an icon in the workspace area, the minimize button changes to a restore window button when minimized and sends the *SC_RESTORE* (0xF120) in *wParam* when clicked.

You can add the minimize window button to your title bar by specifying the *WS_MINIMIZEBOX* style when creating your window. The maximize window button also is added to the title bar, but it is disabled unless you also specify the *WS_MAXIMIZEBOX* style.

The maximize window button—the middle of the three buttons, containing a pictograph of a window— places the *SC_MAXIMIZE* (0xF030) value in *wParam*. Like the minimize window button, it doubles as a restore window button when the window is maximized.

Add the maximize window button to your window by specifying the *WS_MAXIMIZEBOX* flag in your style when you create the window. The minimize window button also is added to the title bar, but it is inactive unless you also specify the *WS_MINIMIZEBOX* style.

It's usually easier to let Windows process these buttons rather than write your own code. However, if you need to do any special processing before the commands are executed, you can intercept the *WM_SYSCOMMAND* messages in your window procedure and use them before passing them on to Windows.

401. *Understanding Menus and Toolbars*

Menus provide a mechanism for the user to send commands to an application and to interact with the program. In pre-Windows programming, applications often gave users a command line on which they could enter their requests to the program and perform actions. There always was the problem of misspelled commands and parsing the line typed by the user. Too, the user had to remember the proper commands or keep a cheat sheet near the computer. Alternatively, programs might have used the function keys for user input, but their number was limited and not always the same on all keyboards.

Menus provide you with a way around the command-line and function key problems and parsing errors from trying to interpret the user's command. A typical menu item contains two elements: a text string that tells the user the purpose of the item and a number identifier used by the application to act on the request. The number of menus and menu items a program may contain is limited only by the range of numbers that can be used and the size of the screen. You can change menus programmatically depending on the needs of your program and can insert or delete menu items as needed.

In Windows, you place menus on a *menu bar* that normally is inserted below the title bar. The menu bar may contain menus—that appear when you select their title either by using the mouse or a keyboard command—or it may contain individual menu commands. Usually, however, you reserve the menu bar for menus, placing the actual menu items in the pop-up menu, even if there is only one item.

Menu commands usually are grouped according to their function. For example, you place all the operations dealing with opening, writing, and closing files on a menu you call the "File" menu. The label is arbitrary; you can call it anything you want, but usually you make it describe the items that will be found in the menu. You then place editing functions—the cut, copy, and paste commands, for example—in another menu and name it "Edit." You also may provide *context* menus, which can be summoned in place without the user resorting to the menu bar.

The menu items are Windows controls and contain only one event, the click event, which is invoked when the user selects the item. Windows then sends your application a WM_COMMAND message with parameters to identify the specific event. You will look at how to define menus in your resource file in Tip 407, "Using Menus in a Resource File."

Toolbars are button representations of menus that can be selected primarily by a mouse click event. Although it is possible to create and use a toolbar that doesn't correspond to menu items, it's normal to have the most commonly used menu items appear on toolbars.

You can make toolbar buttons act like buttons, check boxes, or radio buttons. Most implementations of toolbars, such as that in the Microsoft Foundation Class, allow toolbars to be *dockable*—the user may place them on any side of the frame or leave them floating—or fixed in one position, or even left floating as a tool window.

You will get into building your own toolbars in the section on Windows Controls and "The Microsoft Foundation Class Library" in Tips 486 to 542 and "Common Controls Introduced in Windows 95 (and Later)" in Tips 853 to 941.

402. *Understanding Scroll Bars*

Very often, a window isn't large enough to display its entire contents at once. When this is the case, you may create windows with scroll bars, or you may add the scroll bars to the window dynamically as needed. A vertical scroll bar is used for up and down movement, and a horizontal scroll bar is used for side-to-side movement of the window contents. Vertical and horizontal scroll bars may be created, enabled, and used individually.

Scroll bars are among the oldest of Windows devices and are used in other windowing systems, such as the Apple operating system and the X Window system on UNIX (believe it or not, windowing predates Windows, and very little about the Microsoft operating system is original).

The scroll bar allows a user to move horizontally or vertically through the window's contents using the mouse. Properly designed and programmed, however, the scroll bar is an indicator device as much as it is a movement device.

Normally, a vertical scroll bar is placed on the right side of the window, and a horizontal scroll bar along the bottom of the window. A scroll bar is a slightly grayed area with pushbuttons at each end; the push-buttons normally contain arrows pointing in the direction of window movement when they are clicked. A small box called a "thumb" floats along the grayed area between the arrow buttons.

The user may click the scroll buttons, or the grayed area between them, or grab and hold the thumb with the mouse. These actions don't produce any movement of the window contents. Instead, Windows sends messages to your program containing information about the scroll bar action, and it's up to your program to provide the scrolling action, if any.

The thumb should be sized to represent the ratio of the total size of your data area to the amount that is displayed. This gives the user a visual indication of the relative size of the scroll area. In addition, it should be positioned along the scroll bar so that it represents the current section of data being displayed. You can get the current values using the *SCROLLINFO* structure and calling *GetScrollInfo()*, or you can set them with the *SCROLLINFO* structure by calling the *SetScrollInfo()* function.

403. *Using the Resource File*

An application's resources include the menus, toolbars, cursors, icons, bitmaps, and dialog boxes it uses while it is running. It also includes elements that are never seen directly by the user, such as a string table, version control, and accelerator tables.

You define these resources in a *resource file* using an extension of *.RC*. The resource file is compiled sep-arately and linked into the program's executable file as any other binary file. Each resource is given a unique number known as its *resource ID*, and your program uses this number to access the resources. Rather than deal with raw numbers, you normally give the resources descriptive names using a *#define* directive. The C++ compiler can't understand resource syntax, and the resource compiler can't under-stand C++ syntax; they both, however, understand preprocessor directives. To make the same identifiers available to the resource and C++ compilers, these *#define* statements should be placed in a separate header file—normally, *resource.h*—and added to the resource and source code files using the *#include* directive.

When you define a resource in the resource file, you may give it a name or use the resource ID. How you declare it in the resource file determines how you use it in your source file. For example, you may declare a cursor in the resource file in one of two ways, as shown in the following:

```
IDC_CURSOR1  CURSOR DISCARDABLE "BRUSH.CUR"
Cursor1  CURSOR DISCARDABLE BRUSH.CUR
```

Notice that when you use the resource ID, the ID must be previously defined, and you quote the file name. However, if you use a text name, you do not quote the file name. The text name of the cursor must not have been previously defined (the cursor statement is its definition). In the following, the first statement loads the cursor using the resource ID, and the second loads it from the second definition:

```
LoadCursor(hInst, MAKEINTRESOURCE(IDC_CURSOR1));
LoadCursor(hInst, "Cursor1");
```

The Visual Studio IDE uses the first method, with resource IDs, and in the following samples, that is the method you will use. There's nothing wrong with either method, and the choice is a matter of programmer preference.

404. Using the Resource Compiler

The resource compiler reads your text-based resource file and creates a binary file containing the compiled resources used in your program. The binary file, identified by a *.RES* extension, is linked into the program file by the linker.

The Visual C++ resource compiler is *RC.EXE*. Normally, you run it without any command-line flags, but it has very few anyway. You can see them by typing "RC -?" (without the quotes) on the command line. Some useful flags are *-v* for verbose output if you want to see the progress of the compile, *-d* to define a resource symbol (similar to the *-D* flag for the C++ compiler), *-i* to specify an include file path, and *-fo* to specify the name of the *.RES* file (the output file normally defaults to the input file name with the extension changed).

405. Understanding Cursors and Icons

In a non-Windows application and in command-line operations, the cursor is the indicator, sometimes blinking, that tells you where the next character typed will appear on the screen. In a Windows application, however, not all events take place at that position, and the text indicator is called the "caret." The name "cursor" is reserved for the symbol that indicates the position of the mouse.

Windows contains a number of predefined cursors your program can use simply by loading them with the *LoadCursor()* function. In your *THIRD.EXE* program, you load the standard cursor identified by *IDC_ARROW* when you register your window class, and you pass that as the name of the cursor to be used when the mouse pointer is over your window. Try substituting some of the standard cursor names listed in Table 404. Use a *NULL* for the *HINSTANCE* parameter when loading standard Windows cursors. To load the *IDC_APPSTARTING* cursor (this is a good one to put as the very first line of your code in the *WinMain()* function), you would write *LoadCursor(NULL, IDC_APPSTARTING)*. When the operating system creates the window, it replaces the cursor with the one you specified in the *WND-CLASSEX* structure. Table 404 lists the standard Windows cursor constants.

Resource ID	Description
IDC_APPSTARTING	Standard arrow and small hourglass
IDC_ARROW	Standard arrow
IDC_CROSS	Crosshair
IDC_HELP	Arrow and question mark
IDC_IBEAM	I-beam

Table 404   Standard Windows cursors (continued on following page)

Resource ID	Description
IDC_NO	Slashed circle
IDC_SIZEALL	Four-pointed arrow pointing north, south, east, and west
IDC_SIZENESW	Double-pointed arrow pointing northeast and southwest
IDC_SIZENS	Double-pointed arrow pointing north and south
IDC_SIZENWSE	Double-pointed arrow pointing northwest and southeast
IDC_SIZEWE	Double-pointed arrow pointing west and east
IDC_UPARROW	Vertical arrow
IDC_WAIT	Hourglass

Table 404   Standard Windows cursors (continued from previous page)

You also may draw your own cursors. They are 32×32 pixel bitmaps (a *pixel* is a picture element and represents one image dot on your screen or printer) saved in a file with an extension of *.CUR*, but you will need a cursor editor to save the file with cursor information needed by Windows. Conveniently, one is built in to the Visual Studio IDE, and a number of them are available in the public domain on the World Wide Web. There also is an *IMAGEDIT* project in the samples directory on the Microsoft Developers Network disk that came with your copy of Visual C++. Just copy the *SAMPLES\VC98\ SDK\SDKTOOLS\IMAGEDIT* directory from the CD-ROM to your hard drive. The directory includes a makefile, so just run *NMAKE* from the directory to build the *IMAGEDIT.EXE* program. Don't worry about the warnings on compile; it's an older application, but it should compile and link without any problems. The *RES* subdirectory contains a number of cursor samples to start you out. Do not be concerned with changing them; you always can copy them back from the CD-ROM.

When you've prepared your new cursor, save it in a *.CUR* file and move it to your program directory. Give it a resource ID in the *resource.h* file, and declare it as an icon in your resource *(.RC)* file using a line similar to the following. You may eliminate the *DISCARDABLE* declaration. The last entry on the line is the name of the file containing the icon image:

```
IDC_CURSOR1   CURSOR   DISCARDABLE  "BRUSH.CUR"
```

In the *WNDCLASSEX* structure instance *wcex*, change the *LoadCursor()* function for the *hCursor* member to load your cursor instead of the standard Windows cursor. Use the *hInstance* parameter passed to *WinMain* as the first parameter for the *LoadCursor()* call. To specify your cursor ID, you must use the *MAKEINTRESOURCE* macro. Your call should look like the following:

```
wcex.hCursor = LoadCursor(hInstance,
              MAKEINTRESOURCE(IDC_CURSOR1));
```

When the mouse moves over your application window, the cursor changes to your *IDC_CUSROR1*, but when it moves over a Windows area, such as the title bar, menu bar, or an area outside your application, Windows displays its own cursor.

Icons also are bitmap files. Windows uses the icon to represent your program in directory lists and to give you a graphic identification of your program when it is minimized. Beginning with Windows 95, icons may be small or "normal," 16×16 pixels. Icons also may large, 64×64 pixels. You can use the *IMAGEDIT.EXE* program to create and edit them. Unfortunately, because it is an older application, it can handle only the 32×32 pixel icons that 32-bit Windows now considers "normal icons." That's all you will need for most of your applications, but eventually with more extensive projects you might want to create icons of other sizes. The icon editor in the Visual Studio IDE lets you build both icons in several different sizes.

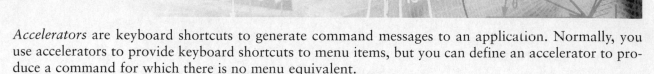

406. *Understanding Accelerators*

Accelerators are keyboard shortcuts to generate command messages to an application. Normally, you use accelerators to provide keyboard shortcuts to menu items, but you can define an accelerator to produce a command for which there is no menu equivalent.

When typed in an application, accelerators generate *WM_COMMAND* or *WM_SYSCOMMAND* messages with the command identifier passed to the message-processing function as a parameter.

An accelerator table has a resource ID, but it may share the same ID as a menu, icon, or cursor. You define an accelerator table in your resource file by using the resource ID followed by the keyword *ACCELERATORS*. On a line by itself, use the keyword *BEGIN*. The accelerators themselves are defined, one per line, following the *BEGIN* statement. When the table is complete, use the keyword *END* on a line by itself. Indenting is optional but makes for easier reading.

The syntax for defining an accelerator is the key within double quotes, a comma, and the resource ID of the command it is to invoke, another comma, and any key modifiers, each separated by a comma. Modifiers are *CONTROL* to indicate that the control key must be pressed, *ALT* to indicate that the alternate key must be pressed, and SHIFT to indicate that the shift key must be pressed. You also may use *VIRTKEY* for a keystroke that can't be typed or a mouse button. If you use *VIRTKEY* you must use the virtual key name for the key (such as *VK_F5* for the F5 key) as the name of the key.

For example, to make your *THIRD.EXE* program respond to Ctrl+W to create the child window, you would enter the following accelerator table in your resource file (you define it twice so that you may use uppercase or lowercase Ctrl+W):

```
IDC_THIRD ACCELERATORS
   BEGIN
        "w", IDM_CREATECHILD, CONTROL, VIRTKEY
        "w", IDM_CREATECHILD, CONTROL,SHIFT, VIRTKEY
   END
```

In your source code you need to load the accelerator table with the following statement:

```
HACCEL hAccel = LoadAccelerators (hInstance,
                 MAKEINTRESOURCE(IDC_THIRD));
```

You're not done. Windows doesn't automatically handle accelerators for use. In your message loop, you must call another function to deal with the accelerator key. The *TranslateAccelerator()* function returns 0 if it did not translate and handle the message as an accelerator, or non-zero if it did. If the message was handled, you don't want to process it a second time, so you modify your message loops as follows:

```
while (GetMessage(&msg, NULL, 0, 0))
    {
      if (TranslateAccelerator(hMainWnd,
                         hAccel, &msg))
        continue;
      TranslateMessage(&msg);
      DispatchMessage(&msg);
    }
```

If the accelerator translation is non-zero, the translation succeeded and the message (*IDM_CREATE-CHILD* for this example) was sent to the window procedure. The *continue* statement causes the loop to jump back to the top, and the *TranslateMessage()* and *DispatchMessage()* functions are not executed.

You also can define accelerators on-the-fly in your source code. I'll save that discussion for Tip 697, "Adding Accelerator Tables to Your Resources," when you get into more advanced programming.

407. Using Menus in a Resource File

You define menus in the resource file using a unique identifying number and the resource keyword *MENU*. The menu definition starts with the *BEGIN* keyword and finishes with the *END* keyword. In between, you create any submenus using the *POPUP* keyword and another set of *BEGIN/END* keywords and define your menu items using the keyword *MENUITEM*.

The following definition of a menu creates a single item on the menu bar that is acted on when it is selected. There is no drop-down menu.

```
IDC_THIRD MENU DISCARDABLE
BEGIN
        MENUITEM "&Create", IDM_CREATECHILD
END
```

If, however, you wanted to create a drop-down menu that contains the *Create* item, you would define a menu list using the *POPUP* keyword and another set of *BEGIN/END* keywords, as in the following sample. The indenting is optional, but as with all your source files, you should use indents to make the code readable.

```
IDC_THIRD MENU DISCARDABLE
BEGIN
    POPUP "&File"
    BEGIN
        MENUITEM "&Create", IDM_CREATECHILD
    END
END
```

> *Note: The* DISCARDABLE *keyword informs Windows that this item may be removed from memory, if necessary, to obtain more free memory. If it is discarded, Windows reloads it automatically on demand.* DISCARDABLE *is the default in 32-bit Windows and doesn't have to be specified, but old habits are hard to break, and you will see it frequently in menu definitions. Even the Visual Studio resource editor includes it.*

Each top-level pop-up menu appears on the menu bar itself. However, pop-up menus themselves may contain other pop-up menus. The lower level pop-up will appear to the side of the main pop-up menu. Pop-up menus may be nested as deeply as necessary. The following code shows how to nest a pop-up menu:

```
IDC_THIRD MENU DISCARDABLE
BEGIN
    POPUP "&File"
    BEGIN
        POPUP "Create Windows"
        BEGIN
            MENUITEM "&Create Child", IDM_CREATECHILD
        END
    END
END
```

Resource files may contain any number of menus that may be loaded and unloaded by your program code.

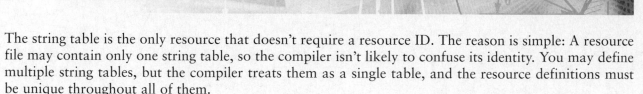

408. Understanding the String Table

The string table is the only resource that doesn't require a resource ID. The reason is simple: A resource file may contain only one string table, so the compiler isn't likely to confuse its identity. You may define multiple string tables, but the compiler treats them as a single table, and the resource definitions must be unique throughout all of them.

The string table lets you define character sequences in your resource file that may be loaded into a character array at any time using the *LoadString()* function.

Declare a string table in the resource file simply using the keyword *STRINGTABLE*. You don't need any resource ID or modifiers, but you may use the *DISCARDABLE* keyword if you enjoy typing. The string table requires a *BEGIN* and *END* block, just like the menu and accelerator tables. Define the strings within the block by entering the resource ID for the string, a comma, and the string itself enclosed in double quotes. Don't place a semicolon at the end.

You will use the preceding code to create another program to demonstrate the use of string tables and, in the next tip, bitmaps. Create another program, *FOURTH.EXE*. You will use your program name and window class strings as resources and load them into the variables using the *LoadString()* function. The string table is defined as shown here:

```
STRINGTABLE
    BEGIN
        IDS_PROGNAME, "Fourth Program"
        IDS_WINDOWCLASS, "FourthProgram"
        IDS_CHILDCLASS, "FourthPgmChild"
    END
```

In *WinMain()*, you load the strings into the variables using the following code:

```
LoadString (hInstance, IDS_PROGNAME,
            szTitle, MAX_STRING);
LoadString (hInstance, IDS_WINDOWCLASS,
            szWindowClass, MAX_STRING);
LoadString (hInstance, IDS_CHILDCLASS,
            szChildClass, MAX_STRING);
```

The code and makefile are on the companion CD-ROM. Copy them to your hard drive and use *NMAKE.EXE* to build the executable.

The string table allows you to compile alternative tables, say, for different languages, in the resource file using conditionals and then to load them into your program without modifying the source code.

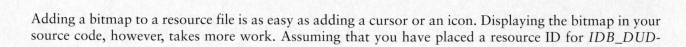

409. Adding Bitmaps to a Resource File

Adding a bitmap to a resource file is as easy as adding a cursor or an icon. Displaying the bitmap in your source code, however, takes more work. Assuming that you have placed a resource ID for *IDB_DUD-*

LEY in your *resource.h* file and that you have a bitmap in a file named *DUDLEY.BMP* (as luck would have it, there is one on the enclosed CD-ROM), you declare your bitmap in the resource file as follows:

```
IDB_DUDLEY   BITMAP DISCARDABLE  "DUDLEY.BMP"
```

In your source code file, you add a global variable to hold the bitmap handle and load the bitmap:

```
HBITMAP hBmp;


   hBmp = LoadBitmap (hInstance,
                      MAKEINTRESOURCE(IDB_DUDLEY));
```

You will display the bitmap in your child window. In the *ChildWndProc()* function, you change the code for the *WM_PAINT* message as follows:

```
hdc = BeginPaint(hWnd, &ps);
RECT rt;
GetClientRect(hWnd, &rt);
HDC BmpDC;
BmpDC = CreateCompatibleDC(hdc);
SelectObject (BmpDC, hBmp);
BitBlt (hdc, 0, 0, rt.right, rt.bottom,
        BmpDC, 0, 0, SRCCOPY);
DeleteDC (BmpDC);
EndPaint(hWnd, &ps);
break;
```

You begin the code as before, by getting the device context from the *BeginPaint()* function and getting the client rectangle. Next, though, you create a compatible memory device context and select the bitmap object. The *BitBlt()* function copies the image from the memory device context to the window device context. When you create the child window, you get to see your bitmap. Say "Hello" to Dudley.

After the bitmap is drawn, you no longer need the memory device context, so you free up the resource by calling *DeleteDC()*.

410. *Understanding Dialog Boxes*

Useful as they may be, menus and toolbars can accomplish only so much when it comes to user input, and they're almost useless for displaying additional information to the user. For this purpose, you resort to the *dialog box* resource, a pop-up window that may contain a number of child window controls. You specify the placement of the dialog box on the screen and the type and placement of the child controls on the dialog box using a *dialog box template*.

Defining a dialog box template in the resource file is one of the more complicated resource definitions. Dialog boxes come in two flavors: modal and modeless. A *modal* dialog box requires the user to dispatch the dialog box before returning to work in the application. *Modeless* dialog boxes may remain visible and available to the user while he or she is working in the application. The typical Find and Replace dialogs are examples of modeless dialogs.

Modal dialog boxes are the most common, and the type I will discuss here. Modeless dialog boxes are covered in Tip 707, "Creating a Dialog Box," when you are using the Resource Workshop.

To define a dialog template, you use a resource ID followed by the keyword *DIALOG*. Following that and on the same line, you enter four comma-delimited integers specifying the x and y coordinates of the upper-left corner of the box (relative to the client area of the window creating the dialog) and its width and height. These numbers are not screen coordinates, but rather a relative measurement called "dialog units." I'll cover dialog units soon, but first you must complete the template declaration.

On the next line you use the keyword *STYLE* and define the style of the window. Normally, a dialog box is a pop-up window, so you specify *WS_POPUP*. In addition, for a modal dialog box you use *DS_MODALFRAME*. Use the *WS_SYSMENU* style to place the Close button on the upper right of the title bar (a system menu isn't actually added to a modal frame dialog box, but it does enable the buttons).

If you want to put a caption on the dialog box, you use the keyword *CAPTION* at the beginning of the next line followed by the caption in double quotes. You don't need to specify a caption, nor is it set in stone if you do. You always can change the caption in your dialog box procedure using the *SetWindowText()* function.

Also, on a line by itself you use the keyword *FONT* to set the font you will use for the dialog box controls and text. Follow the keyword with an integer representing the point size, a comma, and a quoted string identifying the font. To get the names of fonts available to you, select Settings from the Start menu and then Control Panel, and double-click on the Fonts icon. Change the view to Details, and the names of the fonts will be displayed in the first column. The name in your *FONT* statement must match the name of a font listed here. When selecting a font, remember that your application might be used on other computers that do not have the same fonts installed. A good beginning font is MS Sans Serif, which is on nearly all Windows installations. You will learn about fonts and their families, styles, and point sizes beginning with Tip 431, "Understanding the Graphics Device Interface."

Next comes the body of the dialog box template, starting with a *BEGIN* keyword and finishing with an *END* keyword, each on lines by themselves. Within the body you define the various controls you will use on the dialog box.

Before you define any controls, you need to step back to dialog units. In Tip 111, "Finishing the Program Editor," you may remember that you changed the tab stops from 32 to 16 dialog units to set your tabs at every fourth character (using a fixed pitch font). A *dialog unit* is a relative measurement based on the current font size. Horizontally, one dialog unit is one-fourth the width of an average character in the font. Vertically, a dialog unit is one-eighth the character cell height. You use dialog units to set the position and size of controls on your dialog boxes.

The syntax of a control definition is the type of control, the text for the control in double quotes, and the resource ID of the control. The *FIFTH.EXE* program on the companion CD-ROM contains an About box for your program, so let's examine it:

```
IDD_ABOUTBOX DIALOG 40, 40, 180, 100
STYLE DS_MODALFRAME | WS_POPUP | WS_SYSMENU
FONT 8, "MS Sans Serif"
CAPTION "About Fifth Program"
BEGIN
    DEFPUSHBUTTON    "OK", IDOK, 65, 80, 50, 14
    ICON             IDI_FIFTHICON, IDC_STATIC,
                                    7, 7, 21, 20
    CTEXT            "Fifth Program", IDC_STATIC,
                                    7, 30, 160, 8
    CTEXT            "Fifth Program to demonstrate dialog boxes",
                     IDC_STATIC, 7, 48, 160, 8
END
```

You have only one button on this dialog box, so you use the *DEFPUSHBUTTON* identifier to set it to the default pushbutton. That's the button that is invoked if the user presses the Enter key instead of clicking a button with a mouse. If you had more than one button, only one could be the default, and the others would have to be defined using *PUSHBUTTON*. Next, you have the text for the button, followed by the resource ID. The first two numbers following are the position of the upper-left corner of the button in dialog units relative to the dialog box client area. The next number is the width of the button, and the last number is the depth, both in dialog units. You could specify additional styles at the end, but you will get into that when you learn about the Resource Workshop beginning with Tip 687, "Understanding Windows Resources."

The static text fields are declared using *CTEXT*, which causes the text to be centered in the field. You could have used *LTEXT* to set the text to the left of the static control or *RTEXT* to set it to the right. The next parameters for the text fields are the same as for the buttons.

Although you may change the contents programmatically, a static field is intended to remain constant throughout the life of the dialog box. Its background is the same as the dialog box background, so it appears as though no control is present and the text or object is sitting on the dialog box itself.

The control types, window classes, and the default styles for dialog controls are listed in Table 410.

Control	Window Class	Default Style
CTEXT	static	SS_CENTER	WS_GROUP
LTEXT	static	SS_LEFT	WS_GROUP
RTEXT	static	SS_RIGHT	WS_GROUP
EDITTEXT	edit	ES_LEFT	WS_BORDER	WS_TABSTOP
CHECKBOX	button	BS_CHECKBOX	WS_TABSTOP
COMBOBOX	combobox	CBS_SIMPLE	WS_TABSTOP
GROUPBOX	button	BS_GROUPBOX	WS_TABSTOP
LISTBOX	listbox	LBS_NOTIFY|WS_BORDER|WS_VSCROLL
PUSHBUTTON	button	BS_PUSHBUTTON	WS_TABSTOP
DEFPUSHBUTTON	button	BS_DEFPUSHBUTTON	WS_TABSTOP
RADIOBUTTON	button	BS_RADIOBUTTON	WS_TABSTOP
SCROLLBAR	scrollbar	SBS_HORZ
ICON	static	SS_ICON
CONTROL	None	None

Table 410   Dialog controls and default styles

The general syntax for declaring a control in a dialog template is to enter the control type, the text for the control in double quotes, the resource ID, the x and y positions of the upper-left corner, the width and depth, and any addition styles you want to add to it.

The *EDITTEXT, SCROLLBAR, COMBOBOX,* and *LISTBOX* controls require no text, so you omit them from the declaration.

The last item in the table requires some extra comment. This is a general control statement, and in fact, you could use it to declare any of the other types. Instead of using *CTEXT* in your About box, you could have declared the following line:

```
CONTROL    "Fifth Program", IDC_STATIC, "static",
           SS_CENTER | WS_GROUP, 10, 30, 160, 8
```

The syntax for the generalized form is *CONTROL*, text, resource ID, class, style, x, y, width, height. If you don't want to memorize the entire table, memorize this one. Knowing the window class of the other controls, you can build any of them from it. In fact, if you want to prefill text, such as for an edit control, you have to use this form because the *EDITTEXT* form won't take an initialization string. For an edit control, you would write the following:

```
CONTROL   "Enter text here", IDC_FIFTHEDIT,"edit",
                ES_LEFT | WS_BORDER | WS_TABSTOP,
                10, 25, 160, 12
```

This statement would set up the edit control and prefill it with "Enter text here."

To activate your About box, you add the following case to the *switch* statement under the *WM_COMMAND* case in your *WndProc()* function:

```
case IDM_ABOUT:
    DialogBox (hInst,MAKEINTRESOURCE(IDD_ABOUTBOX),
            hMainWnd, AboutWndProc);
    break;
```

Finally, you add your dialog procedure (yes, each dialog box needs its own procedure) to the code (that's the *AboutWndProc* in the preceding declaration). First, declare it at the top of the source file:

```
int CALLBACK AboutWndProc(HWND, UINT,WPARAM,LPARAM
```

Notice that the main window procedure and the child window procedures from the previous programs use *LRESULT* as the return type, but a dialog procedure returns an *int*. You add the following procedure to your code:

```
//
//  Window procedure for the about box
BOOL CALLBACK AboutWndProc(HWND hAboutWnd,
                           UINT message,
                           WPARAM wParam,
                           LPARAM lParam)
{
    switch (message)
    {
        case WM_INITDIALOG:
            return (TRUE);
        case WM_COMMAND:
            switch (LOWORD(wParam))
            {
                case IDCANCEL:
                case IDOK:
                    EndDialog (hAboutWnd, 0);
                    return (TRUE);
                default:
                    break;
            }
            break;
        default:
            break;
    }
    return (FALSE);
}
```

Okay, About boxes are easy. They don't require any input from the user. How do you retrieve information the user entered in the dialog box and use it before the dialog is destroyed? If you use the *DialogBox()* function as you did for the About box, you can't, without declaring global variables and saving them before the dialog is destroyed. Loading up your program with a lot of global variables usually isn't considered a good idea, but you can pass the dialog box a pointer to an object to hold the information, such as a structure or string.

For this, you use the *DialogBoxParam()*, which takes an extra parameter to hold the pointer. Let's first define a dialog box that contains an edit control:

```
IDD_FIFTHBOX DIALOG 40, 40, 180, 100
STYLE DS_MODALFRAME | WS_POPUP | WS_SYSMENU
FONT 8, "MS Sans Serif"
CAPTION "Take the Fifth"
BEGIN
    DEFPUSHBUTTON "OK", IDOK, 35, 80, 50, 14
    PUSHBUTTON    "Cancel", IDCANCEL,95, 80, 50, 14
    EDITTEXT      IDC_FIFTHEDIT, 10, 25, 160, 12
END
```

You change your menu to add *IDM FIFTH* to the Files menu. You next add a dialog procedure *FifthDlgProc()* to your program to handle this new dialog box and change the declaration for *szText* in *WndProc()* to *static*. Next, you add a case in the *WM_COMMAND switch* statement to handle the call to the new dialog box procedure. To make the dialog do something useful, you also change the *WM_PAINT* case to write the text message in the client area. The code for the entire program, including the About box and your new dialog procedure, is listed next.

The key to using the *DialogBoxParam()* function is to catch the passed parameter in your dialog-handling function. The parameter is valid *only* during the *WM_INITDIALOG* message call and is contained in the *lParam* argument. If you don't catch it during this call, the pointer is lost to your dialog procedure. You declare a *static* pointer to your object in the dialog box procedure and set it once, during the *WM_INITDIALOG* message call.

If the user clicks the OK button, you get the text out of the edit control and copy it into the string using *GetDlgItemText()*. You're dealing with only one string, but your pointer could be to a structure in which you could store multiple strings or other values.

When the dialog procedure ends, you invalidate the client area and let the *WM_PAINT* message redraw the window.

```
/*
   fifth.cpp.
 */


#include    <windows.h>
#include    "resource.h"
#include    <stdio.h>


#define MAX_STRING 100
#define CHILD_STYLE (WS_CHILDWINDOW | WS_VISIBLE \
               | WS_CAPTION | WS_SYSMENU \
               | WS_MAXIMIZEBOX | WS_MINIMIZEBOX \
               | WS_OVERLAPPED)


// Global Variables:
HINSTANCE   hInst;      // current instance
TCHAR  szTitle[MAX_STRING];
TCHAR  szWindowClass[MAX_STRING];
TCHAR  szChildClass[MAX_STRING];
HWND   hMainWnd, hChildWnd;
HBITMAP hBmp;
```

```cpp
// Declare functions
ATOM        RegisterWindowClass(HINSTANCE hInstance);
BOOL        InitInstance(HINSTANCE, int);
LRESULT CALLBACK WndProc(HWND, UINT, WPARAM,
                         LPARAM);
LRESULT CALLBACK ChildWndProc(HWND, UINT, WPARAM,
                         LPARAM);
int CALLBACK AboutWndProc(HWND, UINT, WPARAM,
                         LPARAM);
int CALLBACK FifthDlgProc(HWND, UINT, WPARAM,
                         LPARAM);


int APIENTRY WinMain(HINSTANCE hInstance,
                    HINSTANCE hPrevInstance,
                    LPSTR     lpCmdLine,
                    int       nCmdShow)
{
MSG msg;
    LoadCursor (NULL, IDC_APPSTARTING);
    LoadString (hInstance, IDS_PROGNAME,
                  szTitle, MAX_STRING);
    LoadString (hInstance, IDS_WINDOWCLASS,
                  szWindowClass, MAX_STRING);
    LoadString (hInstance, IDS_CHILDCLASS,
                  szChildClass, MAX_STRING);
    // Initialize global strings
    RegisterWindowClass(hInstance);
    hInst = hInstance;

// Initialize application
    hBmp = LoadBitmap (hInstance,
                MAKEINTRESOURCE(IDB_DUDLEY));
    if (!InitInstance (hInstance, nCmdShow))
    {
        return FALSE;
    }
// Main message loop:
    HACCEL hAccel = LoadAccelerators (hInstance,
                MAKEINTRESOURCE(IDC_FIFTH));
    while (GetMessage(&msg, NULL, 0, 0))
    {
        if (TranslateAccelerator(hMainWnd,
                                    hAccel, &msg))
            continue;
        TranslateMessage(&msg);
        DispatchMessage(&msg);
    }
    return msg.wParam;
}

ATOM RegisterWindowClass(HINSTANCE hInstance)
{
WNDCLASSEX wcex;

    wcex.cbSize            = sizeof(WNDCLASSEX);
    wcex.style             = CS_HREDRAW | CS_VREDRAW;
```

```
    wcex.lpfnWndProc   = (WNDPROC)WndProc;
    wcex.cbClsExtra    = 0;
    wcex.cbWndExtra    = 0;
    wcex.hInstance     = hInstance;
    wcex.hIcon         = LoadIcon(hInstance,
                       (LPCTSTR)IDI_FIFTHICON);
    wcex.hCursor       = LoadCursor(NULL,
                                   IDC_ARROW);
    wcex.hbrBackground =
                (HBRUSH)(COLOR_APPWORKSPACE+1);
    wcex.lpszMenuName  = (LPCSTR)IDC_FIFTH;
    wcex.lpszClassName = szWindowClass;
    wcex.hIconSm       = LoadIcon(wcex.hInstance,
                       (LPCTSTR)IDI_SMALLICON);

    if (!RegisterClassEx(&wcex))
    {
        return (0);
    }
//
// Register child window class
    wcex.lpfnWndProc   = (WNDPROC)ChildWndProc;
    wcex.lpszClassName = szChildClass;
    wcex.lpszMenuName  = NULL;
    wcex.hbrBackground =
                       (HBRUSH)(COLOR_WINDOW+1);
    wcex.hIconSm       = NULL;
    wcex.hIcon         = LoadIcon(hInstance,
                       (LPCTSTR)IDI_FIFTHICON);

    return RegisterClassEx(&wcex);
}

BOOL InitInstance(HINSTANCE hInstance,
                  int nCmdShow)
{
    hChildWnd = NULL;
    hMainWnd = CreateWindow(szWindowClass,
            szTitle, WS_OVERLAPPEDWINDOW,
            CW_USEDEFAULT, 0, CW_USEDEFAULT,
            0, NULL, NULL, hInstance, NULL);

    if (!hMainWnd)
    {
        return (FALSE);
    }
    ShowWindow(hMainWnd, nCmdShow);
    UpdateWindow(hMainWnd);
    return TRUE;
}

//
//  Window procedure for main window
LRESULT CALLBACK WndProc(HWND hWnd,
                         UINT message,
                         WPARAM wParam,
```

```
                            LPARAM lParam)
{
PAINTSTRUCT ps;
HDC hdc;
static char szText[MAX_STRING]="";

    switch (message)
    {
    int wmId, wmEvent;
        case WM_COMMAND:
            wmId    = LOWORD(wParam);
            wmEvent = HIWORD(wParam);
            // Parse the menu selections:
            switch (wmId)
            {
                case IDM_EXIT:
                    SendMessage (hWnd,
                                    IDM_EXIT, 0, 0);
                    DestroyWindow(hWnd);
                    break;
                case IDM_CREATECHILD:
                    if (hChildWnd == NULL)
                    {
                        RECT rt;
                        GetClientRect(hWnd, &rt);
                        hChildWnd = CreateWindow(
                                szChildClass,
                                szTitle,
                                CHILD_STYLE,
                                10, 10,
                                3 * rt.right / 4,
                                3 * rt.bottom / 4,
                                hWnd, NULL,
                                hInst, NULL);
                        break;
                    }
                    return (DefWindowProc(hWnd,
                                            message,
                                            wParam,
                                            lParam));
                case IDM_ABOUT:
                    DialogBox (hInst,
                        MAKEINTRESOURCE(IDD_ABOUTBOX),
                        hMainWnd, AboutWndProc);
                    break;
                case IDM_FIFTH:
                    if (DialogBoxParam(hInst,
                        MAKEINTRESOURCE(IDD_FIFTHBOX),
                        hMainWnd, FifthDlgProc,
                       (long) szText) != IDCANCEL)
                    {
                        RECT rt;
                        GetClientRect(hMainWnd, &rt);
                        InvalidateRect (hMainWnd,
                                    &rt, TRUE);
                    }
```

```
                break;
            default:
                return DefWindowProc(hWnd,
                        message, wParam, lParam);
        }
        break;
    case WM_PAINT:
        hdc = BeginPaint(hWnd, &ps);
        RECT rt;
        GetClientRect(hWnd, &rt);
        rt.top = 15;
        if (!strlen (szText))
          strcpy (szText, "Main Window Client Area");
          DrawText(hdc, szText, strlen(szText),
                    &rt, DT_CENTER);
          EndPaint(hWnd, &ps);
          break;
      case WM_DESTROY:
          PostQuitMessage(0);
          break;
      default:
          return DefWindowProc(hWnd, message,
                               wParam, lParam);
    }
    return 0;
}

//
//  Window procedure for child window
LRESULT CALLBACK ChildWndProc(HWND hWnd,
                              UINT message,
                              WPARAM wParam,
                              LPARAM lParam)
{
PAINTSTRUCT ps;
HDC hdc;
TCHAR szText[MAX_STRING] = "Child Window";

    switch (message)
    {
    int wmId, wmEvent;
        case WM_SYSCOMMAND:
        case WM_COMMAND:
            wmId    = LOWORD(wParam);
            wmEvent = HIWORD(wParam);
            // Parse the menu selections:
            switch (wmId)
            {
                default:
                    return DefWindowProc(hWnd,
                        message, wParam, lParam);
            }
            break;
        case WM_PAINT:
            hdc = BeginPaint(hWnd, &ps);
            RECT rt;
```

```
                GetClientRect(hWnd, &rt);
                HDC BmpDC;
                BmpDC = CreateCompatibleDC(hdc);
                SelectObject (BmpDC, hBmp);
                BitBlt (hdc, 0, 0, rt.right,
                        rt.bottom, BmpDC,
                        0, 0, SRCCOPY);
                DeleteDC (BmpDC);
                EndPaint(hWnd, &ps);
                break;
        case WM_DESTROY:
                hChildWnd = NULL;
                break;
        default:
                return DefWindowProc(hWnd, message,
                                       wParam, lParam);
    }
    return 0;
}


//
//  Window procedure for the about box
BOOL CALLBACK AboutWndProc(HWND hAboutWnd,
                               UINT message,
                               WPARAM wParam,
                               lPARAM lParam)
{
    switch (message)
    {
        case WM_INITDIALOG:
            return (TRUE);
        case WM_COMMAND:
            switch (LOWORD(wParam))
            {
                case IDCANCEL:
                case IDOK:
                    EndDialog (hAboutWnd, 0);
                    return (TRUE);
                default:
                    break;
            }
            break;
        default:
            break;
    }
    return (FALSE);
}

int CALLBACK FifthDlgProc (HWND hFifthWnd,
                               UINT message,
                               WPARAM wParam,
                               LPARAM lParam)
{
static char *szText;


    switch (message)
```

```
{
    case WM_INITDIALOG:
        szText = (char *) lParam;
        return (TRUE);
    case WM_COMMAND:
        switch (LOWORD(wParam))
        {
            case IDCANCEL:
                EndDialog (hFifthWnd, 0);
                return (IDCANCEL);
            case IDOK:
                GetDlgItemText (hFifthWnd,
                        IDC_FIFTHEDIT,
                        szText, MAX_STRING);
                EndDialog (hFifthWnd, 0);
                return (IDOK);
            default:
                break;
        }
        break;
    default:
        break;
    }
    return (FALSE);
}
```

411. *Understanding Keyboard Input in Windows*

Once upon a time on a computer far, far away, your programs read the keyboard directly. You read the keyboard flag from the BIOS data area to determine which combination of the Shift, Ctrl, or Alt keys were being held down and had your programs act accordingly.

In multi-tasking and multi-user operating systems, you rarely have that advantage. To protect other programs and users, usually one or more software layers—driver programs—exist between applications and the hardware.

In Windows, the operating system sends the window that has the *focus* (the currently active window) keyboard information through messages. Windows first translates the message and ships it to the application through one of four message types. In addition, four other messages tell you when a key is pressed and released. If you want to process all keyboard messages, you must include cases for each of them in your window procedure, or you can elect to process only one or two of the message types. The messages and their meanings are listed in Table 411.

Message	When Sent
WM_KEYDOWN	When a key is pressed and the Alt key is not being held down.
WM_SYSKEYDOWN	When the F10 key is pressed or the Alt key is held down when another key is pressed.
WM_KEYUP	When a key is released that was pressed when the Alt key was not pressed.

Table 411   Windows character messages (continued on following page)

Message	When Sent
WM_SYSKEYUP	When a key is released that was pressed when the Alt key was held down.
WM_CHAR	When the *TranslateMessage()* function has processed a *WM_KEYDOWN* message.
WM_SYSCHAR	When the *TranslateMessage()* function has processed a *WM_SYSKEYDOWN* message.
WM_DEADCHAR	When the *TranslateMessage()* function translates a *WM_KEYUP* message. A dead character is one that is combined with another character to produce a composite character, such as an accented character.
WM_SYSDEADCHAR	When the *TranslateMessage()* has processed a *WM_SYSKEYDOWN* message and a dead key was pressed while the Alt key was held down.

Table 411 Windows character messages (continued from previous page)

For the key down and key up messages, the *wParam* argument contains the virtual key code for the key being pressed or released. For character messages, it contains the character code of the key or dead key.

The *lParam* argument is a set of bit flags. The lower 16 bits contain the repeat count for the key, which may be greater than 1 if the key presses or typematic action (the feature that causes a character to repeat when the key is held down) send characters faster than Windows can process them. The next eight bits contain the scan code that the documentation warns can vary according to keyboard manufacturer (in reality, keyboard makers tend to stick to the same scan codes so that they don't have to provide special driver code for their keyboards).

Bit 24 of *lParam* is 1 if the key is an extended key, such as the right Ctrl or Alt key. Otherwise, it is 0. Bits 25 to 28 are "reserved."

Bit 29 is the context code. It is always 0 for the *WM_KEYDOWN* and *WM_KEYUP* messages, but for the other messages it is an indicator of how the character was generated. If no window has the keyboard focus, Windows sets this bit to 0 and sends the message to the active window. If the Alt key was down when the key was pressed, Windows sets this bit to 1.

Bit 30 is the previous key state. It is always 1 for a key up message. For other messages, it is 1 if the key is still down when the message is sent; otherwise, it is 0.

Bit 31 is the transition state. It is always 0 for a key down message and always 1 for a key up message. For other messages, it is 1 if the key is being pressed or 0 if it is being released.

Most keystrokes come to you through the *WM_CHAR* message. If the Alt key is being held down when a character key is pressed, the message is delivered through the *WM_SYSCHAR* message.

412. Understanding the WM_KEYDOWN and WM_KEYUP Messages

When you press a key without the Alt key being held down, Windows sends the *WM_KEYDOWN* message to the window that has the keyboard focus. When the key is released, Windows sends the *WM_KEYUP* message.

In text processing, you have to process the *WM_KEYDOWN* message to catch the cursor key presses and other keys that don't produce printable characters. No *WM_CHAR* message is generated for non-printing characters other than control characters.

The information contained in the *WM_KEYDOWN* message parameters, however, doesn't tell you the actual character that will be sent in an eventual *WM_CHAR* message. The *wParam* argument tells you only the value of the virtual key. The *A* key, for example, generates a *wParam* value of 65 on either message, regardless of whether the shift key is up or down and without regard to the Caps Lock state.

If you are using the keyboard in a game or drawing program, you might not care about the actual character, however. You might want an action to be performed continuously while a certain key is down and to stop it when the key is released. In this case, you would want to process these messages and ignore the *WM_CHAR* messages. In a text processing program, however, you might want to ignore these messages and wait for the actual *WM_CHAR* message.

413. *Understanding the* WM_CHAR *Message*

The *WM_CHAR* message delivers the actual character to the window with the keyboard focus after the *WM_KEYDOWN* message has been processed by the *TranslateMessage()* function. The character in the *wParam* argument reflects the current state of the keyboard, including the Caps Lock, Shift, Ctrl, and Alt keys.

By the time the message progresses to this point, the information in the *lParam* argument generally isn't of much use. You can determine the actual keypress by examining the low-order half of the argument, but you already know that because of the character. The high-order half of the argument applies only to the last *WM_KEYDOWN* message and not necessarily to this message.

A single *WM_KEYDOWN* message may be followed by one or more *WM_CHAR* messages. If the user holds down a key, for example, there will be only one *WM_KEYDOWN* message, but the key will begin to repeat and you might receive several *WM_CHAR* messages.

414. *Understanding the* WM_SYSKEYDOWN, WM_SYSKEYUP, *and* WM_SYSCHAR *Messages*

The system character messages operate in much the same way as the character messages except that they are posted when the Alt key is held down and another key is pressed.

In addition, Windows posts the *WM_SYSKEYDOWN* message whenever the user presses the F10 key. Windows uses the F10 key to activate the menu bar. Pressing this key allows a user to maneuver through the menus using the cursor movement keys.

When you release a key that was pressed while the Alt key was held down, Windows sends a *WM_SYSKEYUP* message. In between, Windows posts a *WM_SYSCHAR* message for printable and control characters to the window with the keyboard focus.

In programming with MFC in the Visual Studio, the ClassWizard does not list the system key messages in its message map, but you may include them manually. I'll cover that in the section called "The ClassWizard" (Tips 565–584).

415. *Understanding the Caret*

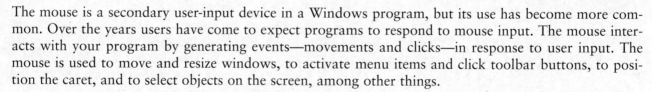

In Windows, the *caret* is used to describe the marker that indicates the next insertion point in a window's client area, whether it is a character or graphic object. The caret usually is represented by a flashing line or block or by a user-defined bitmap.

There is only one caret, regardless of how many windows are open, and the caret can appear in only one window at a time. A 32-bit Windows application may create its own caret, change the blink time, and move it around in the client area. Each window that accepts keyboard input should create the caret when it receives the keyboard focus and destroy it when it loses the focus.

The *SIXTH.EXE* program on the CD-ROM contains examples of caret and character message processing. When the window is created, you select a fixed pitch font and get the character widths and heights. You use that information to set your caret size and move it about the screen. You also save the old blink rate so that you can restore it when your window loses focus.

When the window gets the focus, it creates a caret as high as your character cell and one pixel wide. You change the blink rate to 0.2 second, which is a fast blink rate but different enough from the normal 0.5-second rate that you can tell the difference.

As you process characters, you constantly update the caret position so that it keeps in front of the last character typed, or when you move it with the cursor keys so that it is behind the next character, which will be replaced when the next *WM_CHAR* message is processed.

When your window loses focus, you restore the old blink rate and destroy your caret. You also restore the blink rate and destroy the caret when your window is destroyed.

416. *Using Mouse Input in Windows*

The mouse is a secondary user-input device in a Windows program, but its use has become more common. Over the years users have come to expect programs to respond to mouse input. The mouse interacts with your program by generating events—movements and clicks—in response to user input. The mouse is used to move and resize windows, to activate menu items and click toolbar buttons, to position the caret, and to select objects on the screen, among other things.

The *cursor* is the mouse position indicator, and in Tip 405, "Understanding Cursors and Icons," you saw how to change the cursor for your program. The cursor is an ambiguous indicator, however. It often is large enough to span more than one object—a menu item or a toolbar button—when the user clicks a mouse button. To resolve this, the cursor is assigned a *hot spot*, the pixel in a cursor that marks the exact screen location affected by a mouse action, such as a button click. Mouse messages include the coordinates of this hot spot. Most cursor editing programs, such as the one in the Visual Studio or the *IMAGEDIT.EXE* program on the MSDN disk (see Tip 405), allow you to set the hot spot to any location within the cursor image. By default, the hot spot is the upper-left corner of the cursor at coordinates 0, 0, but for cursors that appear as crosshairs, brushes, or pens, it's common to set the hot spot at a more intuitive location.

You will use mouse events to create lines in the section called, "The Graphics Device Interface" (Tips 431–485).

417. *Understanding Mouse Messages*

As the user moves the mouse across an application, Windows sends the application window a series of *WM_MOUSEMOVE* messages. In all mouse messages, the *wParam* argument contains a set of flags indicating whether any keyboard or mouse keys are down at the time the message was sent.

The content of messages Windows sends the application depends on the mouse features, which vary widely. The *wParam* argument contains a set of flags indicating the current state of the mouse buttons and the keyboard Ctrl and Shift keys. The *lParam* value contains the x coordinate of the hot spot in the lower 16 bits and the y coordinate in the upper 16 bits.

The mouse—that started out as a simple and elegant pointer device—is becoming very sophisticated and may have more than three buttons, a "wheel," and other indicator devices.

Windows sends a message whenever one of the mouse buttons—left, middle, or right—is depressed in a window's client area (*WM_LBUTTONDOWN*, *WM_MBUTTONDOWN*, and *WM_RBUTTON-DOWN*) and another when a button is released (*WM_LBUTTONUP*, *WM_MBUTTONUP*, and *WM_RBUTTONUP*). If a button is pressed and released twice rapidly, a double-click event message is sent (*WM_LBUTTONDBLCLK*, *WM_MBUTTONDBLCLK*, or *WM_RBUTTONDBLCLK*).

Another set of messages is sent when a mouse event occurs in the non-client area of a window, the window frame area. These messages are prefixed by an *NC* to indicate a non-client area event, such as *WM_NCLBUTTONDOWN* to indicate that the left mouse button was pressed.

418. *Responding to Mouse Events*

You can distinguish between the client area clicks and those outside the client area so that you can make them perform different functions. You can use the client area events to move your caret around your text window and the non-client clicks to pop up a message box. Add the following cases to the *SIXTH.EXE* program in *\SAMPLES\TIP415*:

```
case WM_LBUTTONDOWN:
   nCaretPosX = (LOWORD(lParam)
                + nCharX / 2) / nCharX;
   nCaretPosY = (HIWORD(lParam)
                + nCharY / 2) / nCharY;
   SetCaretPos (nCaretPosX * nCharX,
                nCaretPosY * nCharY);
   break;
case WM_NCLBUTTONDOWN:
   char str[128];
   sprintf (str,
       "Non-client area click at\nx = %d, y = %d",
       HIWORD(lParam), LOWORD(lParam));
   MessageBox (hWnd, str, "Mouse", MB_OK);
   break;
```

The caret now tracks the left button clicks from the mouse. You add half the size of a character to the parameter so that when you do integer division on the coordinate, you effectively round off to the nearest character boundary.

When you click on a non-client area, you get a message box telling you the location of the click event. Of course, now you can't activate any of the menus or click the Close button, but you may use the standard Windows exit key, Alt+F4, to exit the program.

419. Determining Whether a Mouse Button Is Down

You used the client area left mouse button to set the new caret position when the button is clicked, but what happens if the user moves the mouse before releasing the button? You might want to use the movement information to perform another action, such as set a selection area in reverse video. In a graphics program you might want to draw a line from the point where the button was clicked to the point where the button was released.

Each client area mouse event message contains information about the current state of the mouse buttons and the keyboard's Ctrl and Shift keys in the *wParam* argument. The flags may be any combination of the values listed in Table 419.

Flag	Key
MK_CONTROL	The Ctrl key is down.
MK_SHIFT	The Shift key is down.
MK_LBUTTON	The left mouse button is down.
MK_MBUTTON	The middle mouse button is down.
MK_RBUTTON	The right mouse button is down.

Table 419   Flags for mouse messages

Some of these flags may be irrelevant for certain messages. For example, *MK_LBUTTON* will be meaningless for a left-click event because the left mouse button was clicked and released in rapid succession.

To determine whether a key is down, use a bitwise *AND* to mask off all but the bits you want to test. The following statement tests whether the left mouse button is down when the message was sent:

```
int nLButton = wParam & MK_LBUTTON;
```

The *nLButton* variable will be 0 if the left mouse button was not clicked when the message was sent, or non-zero if it was clicked. You may combine flags to test multiple key states. The following statement returns a non-zero result if either the left or right mouse buttons were clicked when the message was sent:

```
int nButtons = wParam & (MK_LBUTTON | MK_RBUTTON)
```

420. Developing a Windows Program

So far, you haven't done much with your simple Windows programs except make them display a graphic and some text, but already the window procedures, particularly *WndProc()*, are starting to get long and unmanageable. When you get to the Microsoft Foundation Class, you will see how a class library can make life much easier. Before you go too far with this program, though, you must start organizing it before it runs away from you.

First, you can take your static variables in *WndProc()* and place them in a structure so that they can be passed to functions as a single item. Windows delivers the messages to the *WndProc()* function; there's not much you can do about that. However, you can move the *WM_COMMAND* processing to another function. The paint code can be placed in a function as well.

In a procedure-oriented programming environment, it's possible to build a substantial application starting with a general idea of what you want the program to do and then coding around the idea. A Windows program takes more planning, however, and you should have a good understanding of the program flow before you start coding.

In the following tips, you will go over the basic elements of a Windows program, what these elements do, and how to make the best use of functions.

421. *Writing the* WinMain() *Function*

The *WinMain()* function is responsible for starting the application and delivering the result code to the operating system when the application terminates. In Windows NT, it is possible to have an entry point other than *WinMain()*, but in other versions of windows, this function must be the entry point. For portability, you should stick with *WinMain()* as the entry point.

Whether directly or in function calls, *WinMain()* is responsible for initializing the application, registering the window class, creating and showing the main window, and processing messages. When message processing is finished, *WinMain()* is responsible for cleaning up after the application, such as deleting any objects allocated on the heap, and returning an exit code to the operating system.

The return value for the application is contained in the *wParam* argument when the *WM_QUIT* message is processed. If the message loop is moved to another function, that function should return this value to *WinMain()* so that it can be passed back to the operating system.

422. *Creating the Main Window*

After *WinMain()* registers the window class, it should create the application's main window as soon as possible. The create function returns a handle to the new window. You should store the handle in a variable that other functions may access, such as a global variable or class member, which will remain in scope until the application exits. The handle, of type *HWND*, is used in a number of Windows functions.

Two functions are available for creating the main window: *CreateWindow()* and *CreateWindowEx()*. The latter contains an extended style parameter that is used with 32-bit Windows and should be used for new programs.

The call to the create function specifies the window class, the title bar text, the parent window (*NULL* for the application's main window), the program instance, and the menu to be used on the menu bar. Optionally, it may contain a pointer to a structure or data area containing information about the window. In a multiple-document interface, the pointer must point to a *CREATECLIENTSTRUCT* structure. The application may specify the initial size and position of the main window in the call to *CreateWindowEx()* but normally uses the *CW_USEDEFAULT* constant for these parameters.

A typical application creates its main window using the *WS_OVERLAPPEDWINDOW* style. This style includes a flag to give the window a title bar, a system menu, a sizing border, and minimize and maximize boxes. If the main window needs scroll bars, you can add them by *OR*'ing in the values *WS_VSCROLL* and *WS_HSCROLL*.

423. *Making the Main Window Visible*

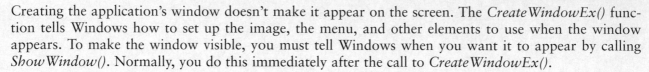

Creating the application's window doesn't make it appear on the screen. The *CreateWindowEx()* function tells Windows how to set up the image, the menu, and other elements to use when the window appears. To make the window visible, you must tell Windows when you want it to appear by calling *ShowWindow()*. Normally, you do this immediately after the call to *CreateWindowEx()*.

Windows passes an integer to *WinMain()* in the fourth *(nCmdShow)* parameter to *WinMain()* that can be used as the flag in the call to *ShowWindow()*. If the application is being started by another program, the flag should be set to *SW_SHOWDEFAULT* to display the window as directed by the calling program.

An application doesn't have to display a window, and it isn't always desirable to call *ShowWindow()*. Often you will want an application to process information in the background. As long as you create the window, Windows will create message queue, and an application can receive and process messages without ever having to call *ShowWindow()*.

424. *Entering the Message Loop*

An application must process and remove messages posted to its message queue. Typically, an application enters and uses a message loop in its *WinMain()* function after initializing the application, registering the window class, and creating at least one window. Applications may have more than one thread, and each thread that creates a window may have its own message loop. A *thread* is an execution point within a process and has its own stack space and execution sequence. A *multithreaded* application has multiple execution points within the same program space, and each has access to the global data and system resources available to the process.

Windows routes messages through a system message queue. When an event occurs—a keyboard key is pressed, or the user moves or clicks the mouse, for example—the message is placed on the system queue first. Windows removes and examines the messages one at a time, determining the destination window and posting them to the message queue of the thread that created the window. The thread then routes the messages to the proper window procedure.

This system/thread queue method allows windows to pass messages to each other, and one application may pass messages to an instance of another application. Each message is time-stamped and contains the position of the mouse pointer when the message was queued. These two elements are not normally a part of the message parameters, but an application may get the time by calling the *GetMessageTime()* function and get the mouse position by calling the *GetMessagePos()* function before calling the *DispatchMessage()* function.

Windows also handles certain messages outside the queue, in which case they are sent to the destination window ahead of the system and thread message queues. These messages require immediate handling, such as messages to activate a window or to set the focus to another window.

425. *Writing Code to Respond to Messages*

A minimum message loop includes a call to *GetMessage()*, *TranslateMessage()*, and *DispatchMessage()*. The *GetMessage()* function contains logic to limit and filter the messages it returns.

The call to *GetMessage()* includes a pointer to a message structure, a handle to the window for which the function is to return messages, and a lower and an upper bound for message IDs. The MSG structure pointer must not be *NULL*, but you may pass a *NULL* for the window handle indicating that you want to receive all messages for the thread. The upper and lower bounds usually are set to 0, indicating that all messages are to be processed, but you may use these parameters to set a range of messages, to *filter* the message list. Filtering is inherently dangerous because the programmer must ensure that the range includes messages that will be received by the application. If the range is too restrictive, the function may never return with a message, thus "hanging" the application.

GetMessage() is a *blocking* function. When called, it does not return until a message is available. It returns zero when the *WM_QUIT* message is received and non-zero otherwise. If your application must perform processing between messages and you don't want the function to block, you call the *PeekMessage()* function instead. *PeekMessage()* takes the same parameters as *GetMessage()* but also includes a fifth parameter, a flag indicating whether you want to remove a message from the queue. This parameter should be set to *PM_REMOVE* to remove the message from the queue or *PM_NOREMOVE* to leave it in the queue for later retrieval by the *GetMessage()* or *PeekMessage()* function.

The *PeekMessage()* function returns immediately with zero if no message is waiting or non-zero if a message is in the queue. If your code removes the message and does not subsequently call the *GetMessage()* function, your code should detect and exit the message loop when your program receives the *WM_QUIT* message. *GetMessage()* returns *0* when it receives the *WM_QUIT* message, but *PeekMessage()* does not give *WM_QUIT* any special treatment, so you should check for it.

The following snippet shows how a message loop can be constructed to perform background processing when the message queue is empty:

```
HWND hWnd;
bool bDone;
MSG msg;
   bDone = false;
   while (!bDone)
   {
      bDone = DoBackgroundTask();
      while (PeekMessage(&msg,NULL,0,0,PM_REMOVE))
      {
         switch (msg.message)
         {
            case WM_QUIT:
               // Cleanup code
               bDone = true;
               break;
            case: ( . . . process other messages)
         }
      }
   }
```

Unless your background task includes code to check the message queue, it will effectively lock up the program while it is executing. However, when it returns, the message loop will process all pending messages before returning to the background task.

426. *Using the Microsoft Linker*

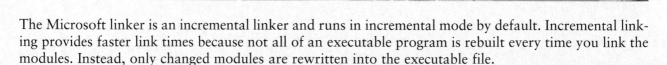

The process of linking brings together all the compiled object modules for your project and combines them to produce an executable program, either a program file or a dynamic link library. The object files include any files with an extension of *.OBJ* that were created by the compiler using the *-c* option and library files.

As implemented in Visual C++, the linker is *LINK.EXE* and is a 32-bit linker. It may be used only with 32-bit object files and produces only 32-bit executable program files. You can't use it to create a program for 16-bit Windows (versions prior to Windows 95) or 16-bit DOS. the Visual C++ linker also cannot use library files generated by the earlier, 16-bit versions of the library manager, even if the modules are 32-bit libraries. If you have older libraries you would like to use, you must first extract the object modules using a 16-bit version of the library manager and rebuild the library with the 32-bit version provided with Visual C++.

Normally, unless you specify the *-c* option to compile only, the compiler will invoke the linker as the last step of compiling a program. You may invoke the linker from the command line, as in the following:

```
C:>LINK ObjFile1.obj ObjFile2.obj LibFile1.lib LibFile2.lib
```

The above command links the object and library files and generates an executable file.

From within the Visual Studio development environment, the build commands will invoke the linker as necessary, including whatever flags you need to generate your program.

Unlike earlier versions, the linker provided with Visual C++ 6.0 makes no assumptions about an input file based on its extension. Instead, it examines the object file to decide what type of file it is. Thus, an object file can have any extension, and the linker will still link it properly (assuming, of course, that it is a valid object file).

The linker uses object files in the Common Object File Format (COFF) by default. (COFF files are the default object file type created by the Visual C++ compiler.) There are other object file formats around, particularly the older Object Module Format (OMF). The linker may use OMF files, but it first converts them to COFF.

427. *Understanding Incremental Linking*

The Microsoft linker is an incremental linker and runs in incremental mode by default. Incremental linking provides faster link times because not all of an executable program is rebuilt every time you link the modules. Instead, only changed modules are rewritten into the executable file.

Incremental linking provides faster build times, but it does have its cost. Functionally, an executable linked incrementally is the same as one created by a full link. However, to provide room in the executable for modified functions, the linker pads the address after a function with extra bytes to provide room for writing modified functions. It also contains "thunks" to allow relocating the function when it outgrows the padded space. Both of these result in larger executable files, so after testing your finished program, it should be linked again with incremental linking turned off (use the *–INCREMENTAL:NO* option) to reduce the file size.

Incremental linking also causes some subtle problems in building a program. If you change a define or a flag in one module that can affect another but do not subsequently recompile the affected module, the linker has no way of knowing that the other module needs to be relinked. If you start experiencing strange behavior in a module that you know works, delete the executable and all object files and rebuild the entire project. From within Visual Studio, you can remove these files by using the following steps:

1. With the project open in the Visual Studio, select the FileView pane of the Workspace window.

2. Right-click the item that includes the files. For example, if your project is called *Graphics*, right-click the line that reads "Graphics files."

3. Select the Clean option on the menu that pops up when you right-click the item.

4. Rebuild the project using one of the build commands from a toolbar or the main menu.

The linker generates an incremental link information file that it uses to update the executable. The file has an extension of *.ILK* and you do not have to specify it in the linker command. The linker builds the name from the program file name and updates it automatically.

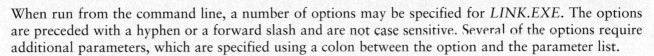

428. *Understanding Linker Options*

When run from the command line, a number of options may be specified for *LINK.EXE*. The options are preceded with a hyphen or a forward slash and are not case sensitive. Several of the options require additional parameters, which are specified using a colon between the option and the parameter list.

You can get a list of the linker flags by typing *LINK -?* on the command line. The list probably will scroll off your screen, so you should pipe it through the *more* program to pause it between pages, as in the following command:

```
C:>link -? | more  <Enter>
```

Each time the output pauses, you'll have "-- MORE --" displayed at the bottom of the screen. Press the Enter key to move to the next page.

To set the alignment for program sections to 8192, for example, the command line would read like the following:

```
C:>link -ALIGN:8192 myprog.obj  <Enter>
```

Unless you specify one of the non-link options (such as *-c* for compile only), the Visual C++ compiler automatically will start the linker when the source files have been compiled. Options specified for the compiler are translated into linker options, but you can override them and specify additional linker options using the compiler flag *-link*. For example, specifying the compiler option *-Zi* (compiler options are case sensitive) causes the compiler to run the debugger with the *-debug* flag.

429. *Invoking the Linker in a Make File*

From the command line, it's more convenient to let the compiler spawn the linker; using separate compile and link statements requires you to type two command lines.

From within a make file, however, only source files that have changed will be compiled. Invoking the linker separately is common practice and lets you use the native linker flags. You can, however, use the compiler for linking as well. If you had a couple of object files and a library, you would write the following line as the command in the make file:

```
cl File1.obj File2.obj Lib1.lib
```

The compiler would pass the file names directly to the linker. (The compiler operates only on files with extensions of .C, .CPP, .CXX, and .DEF.)

430. *Using* DUMPBIN.EXE *and* EDITBIN.EXE

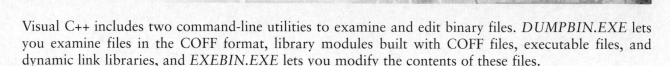

Visual C++ includes two command-line utilities to examine and edit binary files. *DUMPBIN.EXE* lets you examine files in the COFF format, library modules built with COFF files, executable files, and dynamic link libraries, and *EXEBIN.EXE* lets you modify the contents of these files.

When used to examine an object file, *DUMPBIN* lists the symbols in the file and the sections of the file. Specifying the /DISASM flag will cause *DUMPBIN* to disassemble the file and give you an Assembly listing:

```
C:>dumpbin /DISASM ProgFile.exe
```

EDITBIN allows you to modify sections of the file and realign data without having to recompile a file and specify the new alignments. You also may use it to convert an OMF format file to a COFF file.

431. *Understanding the Graphics Device Interface*

Graphics on a personal computer used to be an arduous task. If you were serious about it, you either wrote or purchased a graphics library to perform primitive tasks such as drawing lines or geometric shapes. Still, graphics meant many hours of "bumming" code (the process of tweaking code so that it runs a wee bit faster) and fine-tuning your program. Most of the programming was in Assembly because that was the only way you could realize any decent speed for your program.

Then there was the problem of multiple display adapters. There was the very low resolution Color Graphics Adapter, the Enhanced Graphics Adapter, and eventually the Video Graphics Array, the VGA that most of us now use in one form or another. More often than not, the interface to the graphics device was your program, and supporting all these devices meant either a large program to contain all the code (megabyte-size programs simply were not possible) or maintaining different versions of your code for each device. Too, there was the problem of supporting a myriad of printers, each with its own peculiarities.

One of the most pleasing aspects of Windows programming is that you no longer have to worry about such things. The Windows Graphics Device Interface (GDI) lets you draw, say, an ellipse with an eccentricity of 1.5 and be confident that when the program is run, on whatever machine, the proper ellipse will be drawn. Also, it will be drawn properly on whatever printer the image is sent to, regardless of that printer's oddities.

The GDI doesn't do any drawing for you. Instead, it provides device-independent arbitration, translates the graphics call, and ships it on to the proper driver. You no longer have to worry about the underlying hardware and can concentrate on developing your program.

The graphics services are provided by a system library, *GDI32.DLL*, for 32-bit applications. To support older applications, another program, *GDI.EXE*, serves as the interface for 16-bit graphics calls. To access the functions in the system modules, you link your programs with a graphics library, *GDI32.LIB*. There is no corresponding library for 16-bit graphics applications because Visual C++ 6.0 doesn't support 16-bit program development.

432. *Understanding the Device Context*

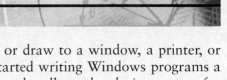

In Windows everything is graphics, even text, and when you write or draw to a window, a printer, or another device, you do it in the context of the device. When you started writing Windows programs a few tips back, you used an object named an *HDC*. That's a Windows handle to the *device context* for the device to which you were writing—in the samples, the screen. A device context, or DC, is an object that contains information about the attributes of a device such as a display or a printer.

You also used another object, a font, to write your text. You will get into fonts shortly, but the idea of using the GDI is that you get the DC and then create and select an object you will use for drawing in the DC. If you want to set text, you use a font. If you want to draw a line, you create and select a pen. Similarly, if you want to color an area, you create and select a brush.

Every time you create a GDI object, you should delete it before the variable identifying it goes out of scope. In the older Windows versions, if you didn't delete the object, it remained in memory until you rebooted your machine, and future incarnations of the program would continue to eat away at system resources. Since Windows 95, however, the operating system keeps track of GDI objects created by a program and automatically deletes them when the program terminates. Still, if you don't delete them, they will remain in memory for the life of your program. For example, if you make a few thousand calls to create a pen (not unreasonable in a graphics program) and don't delete the pen, eventually your program will run out of memory and stop. In addition, deleting an object while it is still selected in the device context is not considered good practice. The DC should always be left in a state where the current pen font and brush point to valid objects. If you delete an object that is still selected and your program subsequently makes a call that uses this attribute, it will be pointing to a nonexistent object.

There are two methods of setting a device context attribute before you delete an object. First, you select a stock object, one that is maintained by Windows and won't be deleted. Usually, this is the default attribute. For the pen, it is *BLACK_PEN*; for the brush, it is *WHITE_BRUSH*; and for the font, it is *SYSTEM_FONT*. The following snippet shows how to create an object (in this case, a pen), use it, and restore the default before deleting the object you created:

```
HPEN hPen = CreatePen (PS_SOLID, 1, RGB(0x77, 0xff, 0x00));
SelectObject (hPen);
// Use the pen in your drawing
SelectObject (BLACK_PEN);
DeleteObject (hPen);
```

The other method involves saving the old object and restoring it before you delete your object. This is the preferred method and adheres to the programming practice of "Leave it as you found it." The *SelectObject()* function returns the old object as type *HGIDOBJ*, so you must cast the function to the type of object you are selecting. The following snippet shows how:

```
HPEN hPen = CreatePen (PS_SOLID, 1, RGB(0x77, 0xff, 0x00));
HPEN hOldPen = (HPEN) SelectObject (hPen);
// Use the pen in your drawing
SelectObject (hOldPen);
DeleteObject (hPen);
```

Some objects you already have met may be used directly in a DC. The bitmap, for example, is a collection of pixels that you can transfer directly to the DC, which you did in Tip 409, "Adding Bitmaps to a Resource File," using the *bitblt()* function ("bitblt" is short for "bit block transfer," but programmers often refer to it as "bit blast").

433. *The Device Context and the Output Device*

In essence, your drawing is done on a logical display surface provided by the DC, which translates your drawing and passes it on to the actual device. The DC determines what type of operations you can perform on a device. A window and a printed page share many attributes but also have other characteristics that are unique. It wouldn't make much sense, for example, to erase a printed page, but it's a perfectly good operation when dealing with a display.

Unlike DOS programs, you never draw directly to the device itself. In fact, most of the graphics functions don't care what the eventual output device will be and leave the translation of the graphic up to the device driver. That makes sense. When you can describe a circle in a few command bytes on a PostScript printer, why be concerned with placing the pixels? You don't know at the time whether the output will be PostScript or a bit stream.

The device context stores the attributes that describe how you draw on the output device. The attributes, defaults, and related functions are summarized in Table 433.

DC Attribute	Default Value	Retrieve By	Modify By
Background Color	White	*GetBkColor()*	*SetBkColor()*
Background Mode	OPAQUE	*GetBkMode()*	*SetBkMode()*
Bitmap	NULL	*SelectObject()*	*SelectObject()*
Brush	WHITE_BRUSH	*SelectObject()*	*SelectObject()*
Brush Origin	0, 0	*GetBrushOrgEx()*	*SetBrushOrgEx()*
Character Spacing	0	*GetTextCharacterExtra()*	*SetTextCharacterExtra()*
Clipping Region	NULL	*GetClipBox()*	*SelectClipPath()* *SelectClipRgn()* *OffsetClipRgn()* *IntersectClipRgn()* *ExcludeClipRgn()* *SelectObject()*
Current Position	0, 0	*GetCurrentPositionEx()*	*MoveToEx()*
Drawing Mode	R2_COPYPEN	*GetROP2()*	*SetROP2()*
Font	SYSTEM_FONT	*SelectObject()*	*SelectObject()*
Mapping Mode	MM_TEXT	*GetMapMode()*	*SetMapMode()*
Pen	BLACK_PEN	*SelectObject()*	*SelectObject()*
Polygon Fill Mode	ALTERNATE	*GetPolyFillMode()*	*SetPolyFillMode()*

Table 433   Windows device context attributes and defaults (continued on following page)

DC Attribute	Default Value	Retrieve By	Modify By
Region	None	*SelectObject()*	*SelectObject()*
Stretching Mode	*BLACKONWHITE*	*GetStretchBltMode()*	*SetStretchBltMode()*
Text Color	White	*GetTextColor()*	*SetTextColor*
Viewport Extents	1, 1	*GetWindowExtEx()*	*SetViewportExtEx()* *ScaleViewportExtEx()* *SetMapMode()*
Viewport Origin	0, 0	*GetViewportOrgEx()*	*SetViewportOrgEx()* *OffsetWindowOrgEx()*
Window Extents	1, 1	*GetWindowExtEx()*	*SetWindowExtEx()* *ScaleWindowExtEx()* *SetMapMode()*
Window Origin	0, 0	*GetWindowOrgEx()*	*SetWindowOrgEx()* *OffsetWindowOrgEx()*

Table 433   Windows device context attributes and defaults (continued from previous page)

Most of these attributes and the functions to retrieve and set them will become more obvious as you read the following text. The device context is one of the most important objects you encounter in Windows programming, and it's well worth the time to learn about it.

434. Using Microsoft Foundation Class Device Context Classes

The Microsoft Foundation Class library provides classes for drawing in a device context. The base class for these is *CDC*, which may be used directly to access the entire display or to access non-display contexts, such as a printer.

Table 434 summarizes the various MFC device context classes and their uses.

Class	Purpose
CDC	The top level or base class for the MFC device context classes. May be used to access the full display.
CClientDC	A device context for the client area only of a window.
CMetaFileDC	A Windows metafile device context. A metafile contains GDI commands that may be used to reconstruct an image.
CPaintDC	A general device context class used when responding to a *WM_PAINT* message. The *CPaintDC* class calls *BeginPaint()* in its constructor and *EndPaint()* in its destructor.
CWindowDC	A device context for an entire window, including both client and non-client areas.

Table 434   MFC device context classes

When responding to a *WM_PAINT* message, a program must call the *BeginPaint()* function before doing any output to the device and must call the *EndPaint()* function when the output is complete. If you don't call these functions, Windows will reissue the *WM_PAINT* message repeatedly. The *CPaintDC* class handles these functions and should be used only in response to a *WM_PAINT* message.

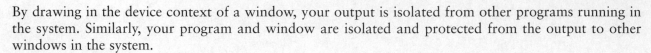

435. *Drawing with the GDI*

By drawing in the device context of a window, your output is isolated from other programs running in the system. Similarly, your program and window are isolated and protected from the output to other windows in the system.

Drawing in a device context is called "painting," whether you are using a brush object, a font, or a pen object.

The device context restricts your display to the window for which the DC is valid. You can draw a line that is 20 inches long, but if your window is only 5 inches wide, the DC will "clip" anything that falls outside the window boundary. This also is one of the reasons Windows provides you with a separate DC for the client area. If you used the full-window device context, you might accidentally paint on the window frame itself.

Every window has a device context, which is obtained by calling the Windows API function *GetDC()* with a handle to the window. When a program is finished with the DC, it should call *ReleaseDC()*. Windows has a limited number of common device contexts available, and failing to release the DC can prevent other windows from accessing a device context. In an MFC program, the DC is held by the *CWnd* class from which window objects are created. You obtain the DC by calling the parent class's *GetDC()* without any parameters. For the *CWnd* class, it is not necessary to release the DC when finished.

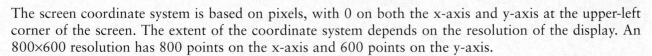

436. *Understanding Screen Coordinates*

The screen coordinate system is based on pixels, with 0 on both the x-axis and y-axis at the upper-left corner of the screen. The extent of the coordinate system depends on the resolution of the display. An 800×600 resolution has 800 points on the x-axis and 600 points on the y-axis.

When you have the device context for your window, you can get the overall screen resolution by calling *GetDeviceCaps()*, as in the following code:

```
HDC hdc = GetDC(hWnd);
int x = GetDeviceCaps (hdc, HORZRES);
int y = GetDeviceCaps (hdc, VERTRES);
ReleaseDC (NULL, hdc);
char str[512];
sprintf(str,"Horizontal = %d\nVertical = %d\n", x, y);
MessageBox (NULL, str, "Hello", MB_OK);
```

When you get the rectangle for your window, the coordinates are based on the screen coordinate system, and you can modify the size and position of your window based on the screen coordinates. The following snippet shows you the screen coordinates of the upper-left corner of your window:

```
RECT rc;
GetWindowRect (hWnd, &rc);
sprintf(str,"Rect x = %d\nRect y = %d\n", rc.left, rc.y);
MessageBox (NULL, str, "Hello", MB_OK);
```

Using this information, you can move your window using the *MoveWindow()* function. The following line moves the window 30 pixels to the right and 20 pixels down without changing the size:

```
MoveWindow( hWnd, rc.left + 30, rc.top + 20,
           rc.right - rc.left, rc.bottom - rc.top, TRUE);
```

You also may use the *SetWindowPos()* Windows API function to move a window. This function has the advantage of forcing the window to re-read its style and other information. If you have changed any of the window parameters using the *SetWindowLong()* function, you should call *SetWindowPos()* to activate the changes even if you do not actually move the window.

Be careful when moving and resizing a window. It is possible to move your window off the screen and make it inaccessible. If you move just the title bar off the screen, there's no way to grab the window and move it back into the screen area. If that happens and you cannot access the menus, use the Alt+F4 key to exit the application. Alt+F4 is a standard Windows accelerator to terminate an application and most programs use it. If it doesn't work, use the Windows taskbar to close the application. Right-click on the taskbar item and select Close from the pop-up menu that appears.

437. *Understanding Client Coordinates*

Whereas your main window frame must deal with the entire screen coordinate system, the client area remains constant with respect to the frame. If you had to deal with screen coordinates, you could spend a lot of time adjusting your variables to fit within the client area.

Because the client area is relative to the frame, Windows gives you an easier coordinate system for client windows. In the client coordinate system, the upper-left corner is 0 on the x-axis and 0 on the y-axis. Your code must deal only with the size of the window and does not have to adjust for the absolute position on the screen. Drawing functions use the client coordinate system.

You can get the client window size by calling *GetClientRect()*. If you want to draw a line diagonally from the upper-left to lower-right corners, you use the values returned in the rectangle. You need not concern yourself with the actual position of the corners:

```
RECT rc;
GetClientRect(hWnd, &rc);
HPEN hPen;
hPen = CreatePen (PS_SOLID, 1, 0x00FFFFFF);
SelectObject (hdc, hPen);
MoveToEx (hdc, 0, 0, NULL);
LineTo (hdc, rt.right, rt.bottom);
DeleteObject(hPen);
```

In programming with MFC, the *CClientDC* and *CPaintDC* functions operate using the client coordinate system.

438. *Understanding the Printer Device Context*

Generally, you need not concern yourself with the actual device that is the target of your drawing operations. The printer, however, presents you with some interesting problems and capabilities. With the device context, you do not need to worry about the actual printer type. The printer manufacturer supplies a driver program that translates the Windows API function calls into the actual commands to write to the printer. A laser printer, dot-matrix or inkjet printer all use the same functions in the device context.

Before painting to the screen, you have to call *BeginPaint()* and end the drawing with a call to *EndPaint()*. You're done with it until the next *WM_PAINT* message is sent to your window. With the printer, however, it's not always that simple. Part of your painting might be done on one page and extend into the next page or multiple pages.

In a multi-tasking operating system, you can't write directly to the port because you might step into the middle of another process's printing operation. Instead, the device context sends the output to a *spool* file, and the Windows print spooler outputs it to the printer when your turn comes. To start the spooling operation, you call *StartDoc()* before you do any painting and *EndDoc()* when you finish writing to the printer. These are the printer equivalents to *BeginPaint()* and *EndPaint()*, but you must deal with individual pages between these calls.

To delimit a page for your painting operations, you must call *StartPage()* before beginning your paint operation and call *EndPage()* when you are done with the page. Because you might be dealing with multiple pages, you call these functions (in pairs, of course) to draw on each page. Only when the last page is done do you call *EndDoc()* to commit the document to the printer.

In a non-MFC application, setting up and using a printer requires considerable maneuvering to allocate global memory space. Your concern here is with the Graphics Device Interface, not printers. The program in *\SAMPLES\Tip438* on the CD-ROM contains a commented non-MFC program that selects a printer, prepares the device context, and outputs a couple of boxes in opposite corners.

439. *GDI Objects: Fonts*

A "font" is a lead or stone basin used to hold baptismal water, but with the advent of printing and moveable type, the name came to be applied to the lead object that held the ink for transfer to paper. Thus, a font is a set of characters that share a common design. In modern printing, the font has little to do with holding ink, but the name persists to describe a set of characters with the same typeface. In computing, a *font* is a collection of graphics objects that describe a set of characters with a common typeface, style, and weight.

The concept of fonts comes to us from an industry that was born even before Charles Babbage, so a peculiar jargon is attached to it. Many aspects of fonts have been badly mangled by the font gurus at Microsoft and Apple to the point that they don't make much sense.

A font *face* is a single set of characters with the same characteristics, and a font *family* is the collection of faces sharing the same style of construction. Fonts are *serif*, meaning that they have serifs, or *sans serif*, having no serifs. *Serifs* are the short, angled lines at the ends of a character's upper and lower strokes ("serif" is the Latin word for "foot") and were intended to make one character flow into another. Inherently, serif fonts are more readable than sans-serif fonts; you rarely see a book or newspaper that uses a san-serif font for body type.

440. *Understanding Font Families*

A font *family* is the collection of typefaces that share the same design characteristics and have similar names. A font takes its name from its family (such as Garamond), its weight (such as bold, regular, or light), and its style (such as italic or oblique).

For example, Clarendon is a font face, but Clarendon Italic, Clarendon Bold, and Clarendon Bold Italic, are typefaces in the Clarendon family. Some families are large; the popular Helvetica family, for example, has about four-dozen members. With five centuries of type design in our history, there are a large number of font families, and most of the "modern" typefaces we use today were designed in the nineteenth century.

A serif font is *roman* if its characters are built vertically. An *italic* font is a serif font built with a slanting aspect (slanting sans-serif fonts are called *oblique*; the word "italic" is applied only to serif fonts). An italic font is not simply a slanted serif font. If you examine certain roman and italic characters closely, such as the lowercase "f," in the same family you will see that they are distinctly different characters. You can approximate an italic font by slanting it, but if the italic face is available, it should be used.

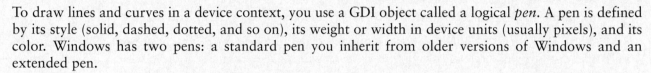

441. *GDI Objects: The Pen*

To draw lines and curves in a device context, you use a GDI object called a logical *pen*. A pen is defined by its style (solid, dashed, dotted, and so on), its weight or width in device units (usually pixels), and its color. Windows has two pens: a standard pen you inherit from older versions of Windows and an extended pen.

There are seven predefined pen styles in Windows, as shown in Table 441. To use a pen, you first create it using *CreatePen()* or *CreatePenIndirect()*, select it into the device context, and name it in your line-drawing functions. When you are finished with a pen, it must be destroyed using the *DeleteObject()* function to free up the resources it uses.

Pen Style	Description
PS_DASH	Used to draw a dashed line
PS_DASHDOT	Used to draw a line with alternating dashes and dots
PS_DASHDOTDOT	Used to draw a line with a dash alternating with two dots
PS_DOT	Used to draw a dotted line
PS_NULL	An invisible pen
PS_SOLID	Used to draw a solid line
PS_USERSTYLE	Used only with the extended pen (see text)
PS_INSIDEFRAME	A solid pen used to shrink a figure so that it fits into a bounding rectangle (see text)

Table 441   *Windows pen styles*

The *CreatePen()* function takes the style, width, and color as parameters and returns an *HPEN* handle to the object. The *CreatePenIndirect()* takes a pointer to a *LOGPEN* structure as its only argument and returns an *HPEN* handle. The *LOGPEN* structure is defined as follows:

```
typedef struct tagLOGPEN
{
    UINT lopnStyle;      // The predefined Windows pen style
    POINT lopnWidth;     // Width in device units in the x member
    COLORREF lopnColor;  // The RGB value of the pen color
} LOGPEN;
```

The *x* member of the *POINT* structure contains the pen's width, and the *y* member is ignored. The *COLORREF* is a *long*, with the red, green, and blue components of the color contained in the lowest three bytes. The value 0x00000000 describes black and 0x00FFFFFF describes white; 0x00FF0000 is blue, 0x0000FF00 is green, and 0x000000FF is red. A color value can be anywhere between 0 and 0xFF. Normally, you create this color value using the RGB macro with the red, green, and blue components as parameters.

The following snippet creates two identical, solid-green pens one unit wide using both *CreatePen()* and *CreatePenIndirect()*:

```
LOGPEN lp;
HPEN hPen;
lp.lopnStyle = PS_SOLID;
lp.lopnWidth.x = 1;
lp.lopnColor = RGB(0x0, 0xFF, 0x0);
hPen = CreatePenIndirect (&lp);
hPen = CreatePen (PS_SOLID, 1, RGB(0x0, 0xFF, 0x0));
```

Before you can draw using the pen, you must select it into the device context. The snippet in Tip 437, "Understanding Client Coordinates," gives an example of selecting and using a pen object to draw a line.

The *PS_INSIDEFRAME* style is used to keep the drawing inside the bounding rectangle. If, for example, you draw a circle with a radius of 50 using a wide brush, say, 5 units wide, the circle inside the line is a circle with a radius of 50, but the width of the pen extends outside the area bounded by the circle. This makes an outer circle with a radius of 55. If you use *PS_INSIDEFRAME*, the line is kept within the radius of 50 (within a rectangle 50 units on each side), so the circle inside the line has a radius of 45. Tip 462, "Drawing Circles and Ellipses," shows how this works.

The extended pen is created by calling *ExtCreatePen()*; there is no indirect method to create it. The extended pen gives you more control over the appearance and allows you to set a custom style for the pen. There also are some added restrictions, and, of course, some additional work to set it up. The syntax of the call is shown in the following code:

```
HPEN ExtCreatePen(
  DWORD dwPenStyle,      // pen style
  DWORD dwWidth,         // pen width
  CONST LOGBRUSH *lplb,  // pointer to brush attributes
  DWORD dwStyleCount,    // length of lpStyle array
  CONST DWORD *lpStyle   // array of custom style bits
);
```

The pen style parameter is considerably more complicated than the standard pen. In addition to the pen styles listed, you may include *PS_GEOMETRIC* or *PS_COSMETIC* by logically *OR*'ing them into the style parameter. The dimensions of a *cosmetic* pen are specified in device units; those for a geometric pen are in the new *world coordinate system*. You won't get into transformations here, but the MSDN CD-ROM has a good sample program that shows various coordinate systems in *\SAMPLES\VC98\ SDK\GRAPHICS\GDI\WINNT\WXFORM*.

If you use a geometric pen, you may include an end cap and join style by logically *OR*'ing them into the *dwPenStyle* parameter. If you've used PostScript, the terms used for these styles probably will be familiar to you. Only one of the following end cap styles may be used:

- *PS_ENDCAP_ROUND.* The ends of the lines are drawn using a semicircle. The rounded end is added to the end of the line.

- *PS_ENDCAP_SQUARE.* The ends of the line are drawn using a square shape. The side of the square is the width of the pen and is added onto the line.

- *PS_ENDCAP_FLAT.* The ends of the lines are drawn flat with no protruding end.

When your line takes a sharp turn, as in a graph line, you specify the way the lines join in the *dwPenStyle* parameter:

- ***PS_JOIN_BEVEL.*** The line joins are beveled.
- ***PS_JOIN_MITER.*** The joins are mitered within the limits set by a call to *SetMiterLimits()*. Otherwise, they are beveled.
- ***PS_JOIN_ROUND.*** The line joins are rounded. This gives a smooth transition and looks best on wide lines.

The *dwWidth* parameter specifies the width of the pen in logical units if the pen is geometric. If the pen is cosmetic, the width must be 1.

Figure 441a shows the various drawing styles for Windows pens. Figures 441b and 441c show the effects produced by the end cap and join styles. These figures, and the other GDI images, were programmatically generated; the code for them is on the CD-ROM. This program, *PATTERNS.EXE*, is a Visual Studio project, so you can open in the IDE. Feel free to experiment with the code. From this point, you will be dealing mostly with Windows rather than command-line programs, and the sample code will be in the form of Visual Studio projects.

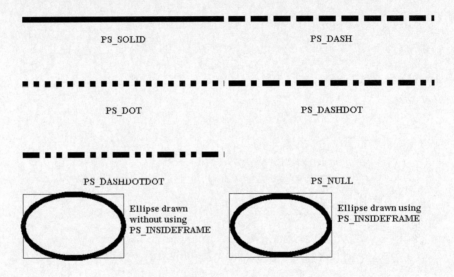

Figure 441a   Pen drawing styles

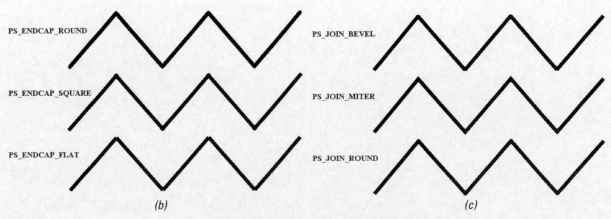

Figure 441b   End cap styles for Windows pens
Figure 441c   Join styles for Windows pens

One thing you will notice about the code that draws the join images: Windows doesn't let you use the join styles unless you draw the lines as part of a path and subsequently render them with the *StrokePath()* function. You begin the drawing with a call to *StartPath()*. When all the lines have been drawn, you call *EndPath()*; then, you call *StrokePath()* to display the lines. Later you will look at paths more closely.

The *lplb* argument points to a *LOGBRUSH* structure (the structure is described in Tip 442, "GDI Objects: The Brush"). For a cosmetic pen, the *lbColor* member specifies the color of the pen, and the *lbStyle* member must be *BS_SOLID*.

The last two parameters, *dwStyleCount* and *lpStyle*, let you set the style of a dashed line to the lengths you specify. To use it, you must include the *PS_USERSTYLE* in the *dwPenStyle* parameter. Set *dwStyleCount* to the number of elements in the array and *lpStyle* to the address of the array. The first element is the length of the first dash, the second element is the length of the first space, and so forth. When the array is exhausted, the GDI will loop back to the first element and continue drawing the line.

Well, I did say that it would be more work to set up the extended pen, but the results are worth it. The following snippet draws a bold dashed line with two different dash lengths (defined in the *dashes* array) across the middle of your client window:

```
hdc = BeginPaint(hWnd, &ps);   // hWnd and PAINTSTRUCT are
RECT rc;                       // passed to us by Windows
GetClientRect(hWnd, &rc);
HPEN hPen;
LOGBRUSH lb;
lb.lbStyle = BS_SOLID;      // Use a solid line
lb.lbColor = 0x00FF00FF;    // Magenta
lb.lbHatch = 0;             // A plain line
DWORD dashes[] = {10, 5, 20, 5};
hPen = ExtCreatePen (PS_GEOMETRIC | PS_USERSTYLE,
                   3, &lb, 4, dashes);
SelectObject (hdc, hPen);
MoveToEx (hdc, 0, rc.bottom / 2, NULL);
LineTo (hdc, rc.right, rc.bottom / 2);
DeleteObject(hPen);
EndPaint (hWnd, &ps);
```

Try the snippet using the various end cap styles to see the difference. In MFC, the pen is encapsulated in the *CPen* class. The *CPen* class contains functions to encapsulate a standard or extended pen. You can create the pen in the constructor or call the member function *CreatePen()*. Both the constructor and the member functions are overloaded and may be used with the same parameters as the global functions *CreatePen()* and *ExtCreatePen()*.

The following code shows how you would draw the same line using a *CPen* object:

```
DWORD dashes[] = {10, 5, 20, 5};
CPaintDC dc(this); // device context for painting
CPen Pen;
Pen.CreatePen (PS_GEOMETRIC | PS_USERSTYLE,
              10, &lb, 4, dashes);
RECT rc;
GetClientRect(&rc);
dc.SelectObject (&Pen);
dc.MoveTo (0, rc.bottom / 2);
dc.LineTo (rc.right, rc.bottom / 2);
```

You could construct your *CPen* object with the following declaration and omit the call to *Pen. CreatePen()* altogether:

```
CPen Pen(PS_GEOMETRIC | PS_USERSTYLE, 10, &lb, 4, dashes);
```

442. *GDI Objects: The Brush*

A *brush* is a bitmap used to fill the insides of shapes such as polygons, ellipses, and paths. You create a brush indirectly by filling out a *LOGBRUSH* structure and calling *CreateBrushIndirect()* or by calling *CreateSolidBrush()*. The brush is used in applications to fill areas such as pie chart sections or the indicators on bar graphs.

Normally, you use the *CreateSolidBrush()* function for most applications that use a brush. However, the *CreateBrushIndirect()* may be used to create patterned brushes that contain hatch patterns. You specify the pattern in the *LOGBRUSH* structure, which is defined as follows:

```
typedef struct tagLOGBRUSH
{
    UINT lbStyle;
    COLORREF lbColor;
    LONG lbHatch;
} LOGBRUSH;
```

The *lbStyle* member may be any one of the constants shown in Table 442. The pattern styles involve allocating global memory to create a device-independent bitmap (DIB) and are beyond the scope of this discussion.

Brush Style	Description
BS_DIBPATTERN	A pattern brush defined by a DIB. The *lbHatch* member must contain a handle to a packed DIB.
BS_DIBPATTERN8X8	Same as *BS_DIBPATTERN*.
BS_DIBPATTERNPT	A pattern brush defined by a DIB. The *lbHatch* member must point to a packed DIB.
BS_HATCHED	A hatched brush pattern.
BS_HOLLOW	Same as *BS_NULL*.
BS_NULL	An empty brush.
BS_PATTERN	A pattern brush defined by a memory bitmap.
BS_PATTERN8X8	Same as *BS_PATTERN*.
BS_SOLID	A solid brush. Creates the same brush type as a simple call to *CreateSolidBrush()*.

Table 442   Brush styles for CreateBrushIndirect()

The *lbColor* member is the same as for a pen. Normally, you create it using the RGB macro.

If the style is *BS_HATCHED*, the *lbHatch* member may contain any one of six predefined hatch patterns. Figure 442 shows the pattern constants and the image each produces.

When using the hatched brushes, Windows uses an 8×8–pixel tile pattern to draw the hatch lines. By default, the *brush origin*, the point where this tile pattern begins, is the upper-left corner of the window, not the area being filled by the brush. Thus, the apparent origin of the hatch marks changes according to the position of the image in the window. This can be a real problem when you are doing something like a crossword puzzle program. You correct this by resetting the brush origin. In the *PATTERNS.CPP* file, the following lines in the *DrawHatch()* function reset the origin:

```
POINT point;
point.x = rc[i].left;
point.y = rc[i].top;
DPtoLP (hdc, &point, 1);
point.x %= 8;
point.y %= 8;
UnrealizeObject (hBrush);
SetBrushOrgEx (hdc, point.x, point.y, NULL);
```

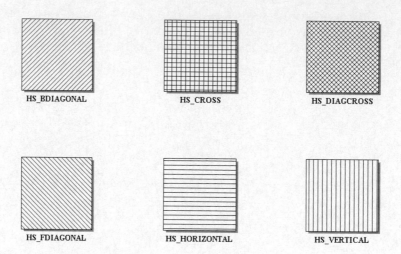

Figure 442   Crosshatch patterns used by Windows brushes

First, you save the device coordinates of the upper left of your rectangle and call *DPtoLP()*, which converts device coordinates into logical coordinates. Next, you do a modulo 8 division on the translated coordinates. You don't have to do this modulo division, but to get used to it, you should do it anyway. Later, when you start using MFC, the values you send to the device context class object's *SetBrushOrg()* function *must* be in the range of 0–7. The *SetBrushOrgEx()* function does the modulo division for you if you send it a value larger than 7. If you're not consistent, however, you will forget at the wrong time and wind up scratching your head and wondering what went wrong. The *UnrealizeObject()* resets the object's palette, and finally, you call *SetBrushOrgEx()* to reset the brush origin.

You must include these calls *before* you select the brush into the device context. Try commenting out these lines and resizing the window so that the images move on the screen. You should see the starting points for the crosshatch marks move in the image.

You can use a solid brush to fill in backgrounds. In the images in Figure 442, I created the hatch patterns in a *shadow box* similar to what you see in many newspapers and books. You achieve this by first filling a slightly offset rectangle with a solid brush and then setting your images on top of it. The code in *PATTERNS.CPP* shows how it is done. If you don't exaggerate the size of the shadow—three or four logical units usually is enough—the shadow gives a 3-D effect to the graphic, as though it were floating slightly above the page.

A lightly shaded brush on a text box also gives emphasis to the text. This creates what is called a *benday box* (it's named after Benjamin Day, the founder of the *New York Sun*). The shading should be very light so that it doesn't obscure the text. Combined with a shadow box, it gives a particularly pleasing effect, as well as emphasis. Run the *PATTERNS.EXE* program from Tip 441, "GDI Objects: The Pen," and select Benday from the Pattern menu. Resize the window to force the box to change shape, and see how the effect remains, regardless of the size of the box. Try various combinations of color for the background and text to create different effects. The code is in the *DrawBenDay()* function in *PATTERNS.CPP*.

Notice that the benday box is always just large enough to hold the text without giving you a gaping empty spot when you resize it. If the window becomes too small, you pop up a message box and refuse to draw the box. You will look at how you do this when you get to the text functions of the GDI beginning with Tip 476, "Understanding Text Output Functions."

443. GDI Objects: The Bitmap

A *bit map* is a method of representing information as a collection of bits, either on disk or in memory. For graphics, you usually put the two words together and refer to a *bitmap* as a collection of bits that represent the individual pixels in an image. This may be color, gray scale, or simply black-and-white information. Actually, by the time you see anything on the screen or on a printer, it has been converted to a bitmap image, whether it is text, an icon, or a graphic in any format.

Graphics stored in a bitmap format file have an extension of *.BMP*. In Tip 409, "Adding Bitmaps to a Resource File," you saw how to add a bitmap file to your program, load it, and display it on the screen using a bit transfer function. The *PATTERNS.EXE* program from Tip 441 also includes a bitmap that is painted to the screen using the *BitBlt()* function. Select the *BitBlock* Transfer item from the Bitmaps menu.

A bitmap is a Graphics Device Interface object. As such, you must select it into the device context using *SelectObject()*, use it, and then destroy it with a call to *DeleteObject()* when you are finished, to free up the resources it uses. This is the same sequence you use for a pen or brush object. Unlike other objects, however, you first create a compatible device context in memory and select the bitmap into it. This gives you a memory buffer to use as the source for a bit transfer.

You can include bitmap images in your program in the resource file, assigning them an identifier, which you then use in the *LoadBitmap()* function to create a handle to the image. Using the handle, you then can manipulate the image and transfer it to the screen.

The *BitBlt()* function simply copies the bit pattern to your window, another area of memory, a metafile, or a printer, depending on the device context. At times, you might want to increase or reduce the image size to fit a particular object, such as your display window. One way to accomplish this is to use the *StretchBlt()* function, which stretches or compresses the bitmap to fit the dimensions of the destination rectangle. In *PATTERNS.EXE*, you stretch and copy the bitmap to the screen using the following statement:

```
StretchBlt(hdc, 0, 0, rc.right, rc.bottom,
        BmpDC, 0, 0, 320, 274, SRCCOPY);
```

The arguments specify the destination device context for your transfer, the x and y positions of the upper-left corner where you want to display the graphic, and the x and y positions of the lower-right corner of the rectangle you want to fill. Next, you have the source device context into which you have selected the image, the x and y positions in the file where you want to start reading the bitmap, the x and y positions in the file to stop reading the image, and finally the transfer mode.

The problem with *StretchBlt()* is that you must know the original size of the bitmap. If you are reading it from a file, that's not much of a problem, but it can be difficult to obtain the size of a resource image. Assuming you have a bitmap in your resource file identified by *IDB_DUDLEY*, the following code will get the bitmap information into the *BITMAP* structure:

```
hBmp = LoadBitmap (hInst, MAKEINTRESOURCE (IDB_DUDLEY));
BITMAP bmp;
GetObject (hBmp, sizeof (BITMAP), &bmp);
```

The width of the bitmap is in the *bmWidth* member of the *BITMAP* structure, and the depth of the bitmap is in the *bmHeight* member.

Later versions of Windows have a generic function, *LoadImage()* that allows you to load and stretch the image at the same time. This function works with Windows 95 and later and Windows NT 4.0 and later (it does *not* work with Windows NT 3.5). The function allows you to load icons and cursors as well, and you may load the image from a file, as well as from a resource. It returns a generic handle to the resource, which you then must cast to the handle type you are using.

To load and stretch (or compress) your bitmap image to fit a particular boundary, such as your client window, you pass the function the desired image size. Then you select it into your memory device context and use *BitBlt()* to copy it to the screen without ever knowing the original size of the image. The following code loads the bitmap, selects it into the memory DC, and copies it to the screen:

```
HBITMAP hBmp;
RECT    rc;
HDC     BmpDC;


GetClientRect(hWnd, &rc);
hBmp=(HBITMAP) LoadImage (hInst,MAKEINTRESOURCE(IDB_DUDLEY),
                    IMAGE_BITMAP, rc.right, rc.bottom,
                    LR_DEFAULTCOLOR);
BmpDC = CreateCompatibleDC(hdc);
SelectObject (BmpDC, hBmp);
BitBlt (hdc, 0, 0, rc.right, rc.bottom,
        BmpDC, 0, 0, SRCCOPY);
DeleteObject (hBmp);
DeleteDC (BmpDC);
```

A bitmap has three dimensions. It has the width on the x-axis and the depth on the y-axis, and it also has a *color depth*, sometimes called the *bits per pixel*. Mouse cursors are an example of a bitmap that is only one bit deep, but that is the rare case. Originally, the bitmap was intended for use on monochrome displays and the Enhanced Graphics Adapter (EGA), which had four bit planes for color: intensity, red, green, and blue. The bitmap is stored with these planes separate so that they can be block-transferred to the graphics device. You can examine the number of planes using the *GetObject()* function and examining the *bmPlanes* member of the *BITMAP* structure.

Today, however, we aren't that concerned with the EGA, and it's a rare PC that still contains one. Also, the bit plane method isn't usable by many modern graphics devices, such as color printers. A new format was defined beginning with Windows 3.0, called the *device-independent bitmap*, or DIB. The new format can be displayed on any raster output device, although the colors sometimes must be converted to colors the device can use. The DIB format specifies the color format and resolution of the device on which it was created.

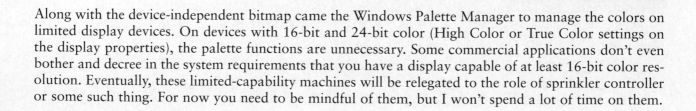

444. *GDI Objects: The Palette*

Along with the device-independent bitmap came the Windows Palette Manager to manage the colors on limited display devices. On devices with 16-bit and 24-bit color (High Color or True Color settings on the display properties), the palette functions are unnecessary. Some commercial applications don't even bother and decree in the system requirements that you have a display capable of at least 16-bit color resolution. Eventually, these limited-capability machines will be relegated to the role of sprinkler controller or some such thing. For now you need to be mindful of them, but I won't spend a lot of time on them.

When the colors are carefully selected, most images can be displayed using 256 colors (8 bits of color information). Originally, the palette referred to a lookup table on the graphics device, and programmers called palette-loading functions to load their color values into it. In a multi-tasking system such as 32-bit Windows, however, programs can't be allowed to manipulate the hardware directly because they might change the settings for other running programs. A program never knows when it loses its time slice in the operating system. If programs could manipulate hardware, each application would have to check constantly to make sure that the hardware settings haven't changed. That would leave little time available to perform the program's primary tasks.

Through the Palette Manager, programs can change 236 of the 256 colors available; Windows reserves 20 of the colors for system use. Windows maintains a system palette containing these 20 *static* colors, and applications can create and define *logical* palettes containing their own colors. When an application's window is at the top of the Z order (the topmost visible window), its logical palette is applied, and windows in the background can experience some color changes as a result. When another window comes to the top, its logical palette is applied, and its colors appear.

You create a logical palette by calling the *CreatePallete()* function with a pointer to a *LOGPALETTE* structure. The *LOGPALETTE* structure contains a pointer to an array of *PALETTEENTRY* structures that define the colors. The structures are defined as shown here:

```
typedef struct tagLOGPALETTE
{
    WORD palVersion;
    WORD palNumEntries;
    PALETTEENTRY palPalEntry[1];
} LOGPALETTE;

typedef struct tagPALETTEENTRY
{
    BYTE peRed;
    BYTE peGreen;
    BYTE peBlue;
    BYTE peFlags;
} PALETTEENTRY;
```

The *palVersion* member contains the major version of the system in the upper eight bits and the minor number in the lower eight bits. It should always be set to 0x0300, indicating that it is compatible with Windows 3.0. The *palNumEntries* holds the number of entries in your palette table, and the *palPalEntry* points to the actual palette table, an array of *PALETTEENTRY* structures.

The first three members of the *PALETTEENTRY* structure contain eight-bit entries for the red, green, and blue components of the color. This gives you some 16 million colors from which to choose (but, of course, you can't use more than 236). Normally, you should set the *peFlags* member to 0, but it can take one of three other values.

PC_EXPLICIT indicates that the low-order word (effectively, the *peRed* member) contains an index into the hardware palette; use this value to display the current palette.

PC_NOCOLLAPSE is a request to place the entry into an unused position in the palette. Normally, when you enter a color, Windows tries to match it with an existing color instead of duplicate entries. If no empty positions are available, the color is matched normally.

PC_RESERVED puts the system on notice that the color may be used for *palette animation* and can change frequently. Palette animation involves changing the contents of the palette colors to simulate animation. By drawing a single image with various colors representing different positions, the programmer can manipulate the palette, making some colors invisible while changing others, so that the object appears to move. Palette animation can be very fast but sometimes difficult to realize. Also, it won't work unless the video is in 256-color mode, and the new animation control introduced with Windows 95 makes it virtually obsolete.

445. *GDI Objects: The Region*

A *region* is a continuous area on a graphics device. Beyond that, it's almost impossible to describe a region; it has no particular shape or position. Regions are used to provide clipping boundaries for drawing functions. In its simplest form, the rectangle, represented by the *RECT* structure, is a region. You use it to describe the client area of a window, and it serves as a clipping boundary for your window paint functions. You also can use it to capture mouse events within the area.

The Windows API has functions for creating regions of common shapes, as well as a complex one for creating regions from a collection of *RGNDATA* structures and an *XFORM* structure. In addition, there are functions to manipulate and use regions.

The region is represented in the Graphics Device Interface as a handle, *HRGN*, which is returned by the functions that create regions. As with any GDI object, it is selected into the device context for use with the *SelectObject()* function, and it should be deleted by calling *DeleteObject()* when your program is finished using it.

CreateRectRgn() creates a rectangular region and returns a handle to it. The parameters are the x coordinate of the rectangles upper-left corner, the y coordinate of the upper-left corner, the x coordinate of the lower-right corner, and the y coordinate of the lower-right corner. The *CreateRectRgnIndirect()* function is functionally the same but takes a single argument, a pointer to a *RECT* structure that describes the rectangle.

CreateRoundRectRgn() creates a rectangular region with rounded corners. It takes the same four parameters used by *CreateRectRgn()*, plus the width and height of the ellipse used to draw the rounded corners.

CreateEllipticRgn() creates an elliptical-shaped region whose major and minor axes are described by a bounding rectangle. The parameters are the same as for the *CreateRectRgn()* function, and the resulting region is described by an ellipse that will fit into the rectangle. An ellipse described within a square boundary is a circle and has equal major and minor axes. The *CreateEllipticRgnIndirect()* function takes a pointer to a *RECT* structure that describes the bounding rectangle.

CreatePolyRgn() function creates a polygon region described by an array of points. The parameters are a pointer to the array of points, the number of points in the array, and the fill mode. To demonstrate the fill mode, the sample program *REGIONS.EXE* on the companion CD-ROM draws a star using both the *ALTERNATE* and *WINDING* modes. If the fill mode is *ALTERNATE*, the GDI fills every other closed area in the polygon with your drawing commands (in this program, lines); if it is *WINDING*, all closed areas in the region are filled. Select Star from the Regions menu to see the difference.

After you create a region, you can perform several operations on it. You can fill it or paint it with a brush color, you can frame it with a brush color, or you can invert the pixels in it. Figure 445 shows a normal polygon region and an inverted one. *REGIONS.EXE* contains examples of many of the commands that operate on regions.

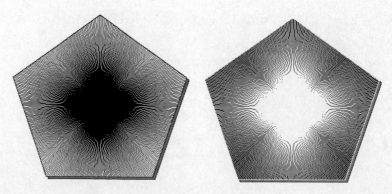

Figure 445   Normal and inverted regions

The examples in *REGION.EXE* use the shadow boxes like the *PATTERNS.EXE* example, but it's much easier with regions. You simply shift the region the amount of your shadow, fill it with a gray brush, then shift it back to the original position, and fill it with a white brush. When you set the clipping region, the shadow will be outside and won't be affected by your drawing.

The Star and Clover samples also demonstrate how to combine regions. Be forewarned, however, that combined regions are getting into the realm of the complex for the GDI and might take a few seconds to draw, even on fast machines.

The Windows API call also has a handy function to create a region from a drawing path. You will look at it in Tip 453, "Using the *BeginPath()* and *EndPath()* Functions," when I start discussing graphics paths.

In the Microsoft Foundation Class library, the region functions are encapsulated in the *CRgn* class.

446. *Understanding Mapping*

I've mentioned "logical" and "device" coordinates in previous tips, but I haven't explained how one gets translated into another. When you specify a position in a Graphics Device Interface call, you give it the position in logical coordinates. The GDI translates them into device coordinates depending on the device for which the device context was prepared.

To do this, the GDI uses its current mapping mode. Windows has six predefined mapping modes, as shown in Table 446. In addition, two other modes are available for the programmer to define.

Mapping Mode	y-Axis Orientation	Description
MM_TEXT	Down	Each logical unit is mapped to a device unit.
MM_LOENGLISH	Up	Each logical unit is mapped to 0.01 inch.
MM_HIENGLISH	Up	Each logical unit is mapped to 0.001 inch.
MM_LOMETRIC	Up	Each logical unit is mapped to 0.1 millimeter.
MM_HIMETRIC	Up	Each logical unit is mapped to 0.01 millimeter.
MM_TWIPS	Up	Each logical unit is mapped to approximately 1/20 of a point, or about 1/1440 of an Old French inch. This unit is called a *twip*.
MM_ANISOTROPIC	User defined	Logical units are mapped to arbitrary units with arbitrarily scaled axes. The programmer specifies the units, orientation, and scaling in the *SetWindowExtEx()* and *SetViewportExtEx()* functions.
MM_ISOTROPIC	User defined	Logical units are mapped to arbitrarily scaled units with equally scaled axes. The units, orientation, and scaling are set the same as for *MM_ANISOTROPIC*, and the GDI makes adjustments to make sure that x and y units remain the same.

Table 446   Graphics Device Interface mapping modes

Mapping seems much more complicated than it is. The important point to remember is that when you change mapping modes, the size of your graphics objects that you subsequently draw will change, and if you change from *MM_TEXT* to another mode, the direction of the y-axis will change.

447. *Understanding Mapping Modes*

So far, you've been using the default graphics mapping mode to draw your images. The default mode is *MM_TEXT*, or 1, in which each logical unit is mapped to a pixel with the origin at the upper-left corner of the window. Positive values on the x-axis move you to the right, and positive values on the y-axis move you down. Negative values move you in the opposite direction. Normally, the GDI handles the aspect ratio difference and compensates so that when you draw a circle, you see a circle on the screen.

The *mapping mode* is the mechanism (or attribute) by which the GDI converts logical coordinates (the values you pass to the GDI functions) into device coordinates (the corresponding pixels on the output device—the screen or printer). The GDI has eight mapping modes, two of which are defined by the programmer. When you switch to one of the other modes, the y-axis flips, so the positive values move up from the top of the client area and negative values move down. If you change to a mode other than *MM_TEXT* and suddenly your drawings are not visible, check the sign on the y-axis. If it's positive, the graphic will be drawn off the top of the window, outside the window's clipping region.

Select Mapping and then Modes in the *REGION.EXE* program in Tip 445, "GDI Objects: The Region." I've drawn six squares with the value for a side in each of the six preset mapping modes and each in a different color. You can see how the mode affects the size and position of your drawings.

448. *Understanding Device Coordinates*

Device coordinates don't change. A logical unit is the same no matter what mapping mode you are using. If you want to draw a square 100 units on a side, you set the values in your *RECT* structure to reflect the position and size of the square and call *Rectangle (hdc, &RECT)*. It doesn't matter whether you are using a 10-inch or 12-inch screen.

When you pass a GDI function a value, you are giving the *logical* dimension or position. Windows translates that into a size or position on the output device. The device context determines the actual size or position that results from your GDI call. When you draw a circle using the call *Ellipse (100, 100, 300, 300)*, you're telling the GDI to draw a circle with a radius of 100 *units* centered at 300 on the horizontal axis and 300 on the vertical axis. It just so happens that in the default *MM_TEXT* mode 1 unit translates into 1 pixel. That might not be the case on an output device, where the horizontal and vertical resolutions might not be the same.

449. *Understanding Logical Coordinates*

Not all devices are created equal. A monitor screen, for example, can contain as many as 1024×768 pixels or more, but the actual width in inches of screen varies considerably. A screen that is 12 inches wide has about 85 pixels per inch horizontally when set for 1024×768 resolution, but a screen 8 inches wide has about 102 pixels per inch. The situation gets even more confusing when it comes to output devices other than the screen—printers, plotters, and fax machines, for example.

If your program displays a form on the screen and lets the user send it to a printer or fax, you might want to change the mapping mode for the other device context to something other than text and leave the screen device context in *MM_TEXT* mode. It's then up to the device driver to translate the logical units into units the printer can use.

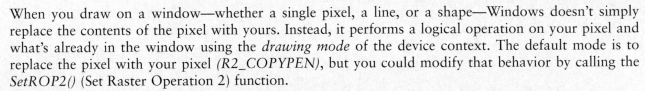

450. *Understanding Drawing Modes*

When you draw on a window—whether a single pixel, a line, or a shape—Windows doesn't simply replace the contents of the pixel with yours. Instead, it performs a logical operation on your pixel and what's already in the window using the *drawing mode* of the device context. The default mode is to replace the pixel with your pixel *(R2_COPYPEN)*, but you could modify that behavior by calling the *SetROP2()* (Set Raster Operation 2) function.

If you examine the *DoMappingModes()* function in *REGIONS.CPP* in Tip 445, you will notice that I set the mapping mode to *R2_NOTXORPRN*. If I hadn't changed the mode, the last rectangles I drew on the screen would have clipped those underneath, and you might not have been able to see one or more of them. Because the window background is white, I could have used several other modes to achieve the same result. The drawing modes and their meanings are listed in Table 450.

Drawing Mode	Meaning (Operation on Pixel Being Drawn)
R2_NOP	The pixel remains unchanged.
R2_BLACK	The pixel is always black.
R2_WHITE	The pixel is always white.
R2_NOT	The pixel is the reverse of the screen color.
R2_COPYPEN	The pixel is the same color as the selected pen color. This is the default mode.
R2_NOTCOPYPEN	The pixel is the inverse of the selected pen color.
R2_XORPEN	The pen color is *XOR*'ed with the screen color and the pixel set to the result.
R2_NOTXORPEN	The pixel is the inverse of the *R2_XORPEN* operation.
R2_MERGEPEN	The pen color is combined with the screen color and the pixel set to the result.
R2_NOTMERGEPEN	The pixel is the inverse of the *R2_MERGEPEN* operation.
R2_MERGEPENNOT	The pixel is a combination of the pen color and the inverse of the screen color.
R2_MERGENOTPEN	The pixel is the combination of the screen color and the inverse of the pen color.
R2_MASKPEN	The pixel is the combination of the color common to both the pen and the screen.

Table 450   Windows drawing modes (continued on following page)

Drawing Mode	Meaning (Operation on Pixel Being Drawn)
R2_NOTMASKPEN	The pixel is the inverse of the R2_MASKPEN operation.
R2_MASKPENNOT	The pixel is the combination of the colors common to the pen and the inverse of the screen color.
R2_MASKNOTPEN	The pixel is the combination of the color common to the screen and the inverse of the pen.

Table 450   Windows drawing modes (continued from previous page)

The *DoMouseLine()* function in *REGIONS.EXE* shows how you can use the *R2_NOT* mode to alternately draw and erase a line between mouse moves while the left button is held down. Using this mode, the line is contrasted against the background, even if you already have an object in the window. When the mouse moves, you redraw the line using the *R2_NOT* mode again to erase the old line and restore the background. Then you draw the new line.

First, add the following function prototypes at the top of *REGIONS.CPP*:

```
void DoMouseEvent (HWND hWnd, UINT message,
                   UINT nFlags, POINT & point);
void DoMouseLine (HDC hdc, POINT & ptLineStart,
                  POINT & ptLineEnd);
```

Next, add the following cases to the *WndProc()* function:

```
case WM_LBUTTONDOWN:
case WM_LBUTTONUP:
case WM_MOUSEMOVE:
    POINT point;
    UINT nFlags;
    point.x = LOWORD(lParam);
    point.y = HIWORD(lParam);
    nFlags = wParam;
    DoMouseEvent (hWnd, message, wParam, point);
    break;
```

Finally, add the following functions to the program:

```
void DoMouseEvent (HWND hWnd, UINT message,
                   UINT nFlags, POINT & point)
{
static bool   bTracking = false;
static POINT  ptLineStart = {0, 0};
static POINT  ptLineEnd = {0, 0};

    switch (message)
    {
        case WM_LBUTTONDOWN:
            ptLineStart = point;
            break;
        case WM_LBUTTONUP:
            bTracking = false;
            ptLineStart.x = 0;
            ptLineStart.y = 0;
            break;
        case WM_MOUSEMOVE:
            if (!(nFlags & MK_LBUTTON))
```

```
            return;
        if (bTracking)
        {
        HDC hdc;
            POINT pt;
            pt = point;
            hdc = GetDC (hWnd);
            DoMouseLine (hdc, ptLineStart, ptLineEnd);
            DoMouseLine (hdc, ptLineStart, pt);
            ReleaseDC (hWnd, hdc);
        }
        ptLineEnd = point;
        bTracking = true;
        break;
    }
}

void DoMouseLine (HDC hdc, POINT & ptLineStart,
                POINT & ptLineEnd)
{
    HPEN hPen = CreatePen (PS_SOLID, 2, 0);
    int nOldMode = SetROP2 (hdc, R2_NOT);
    MoveToEx (hdc, ptLineStart.x, ptLineStart.y, NULL);
    SelectObject (hdc, hPen);
    LineTo (hdc, ptLineEnd.x, ptLineEnd.y);
    SetROP2 (hdc, nOldMode);
    DeleteObject (hPen);
}
```

To draw a mouse line in *REGIONS.EXE*, move the mouse cursor to the point in the window where you want the line to start. Then click and hold the left mouse button and move to the end point of the line. As you move the mouse around, the program erases any old line and redraws a new line to the current mouse position. Try creating an image on the screen by, say, selecting Ellipse from the Regions menu. Then drag the mouse line through it to see what happens. There's not a lot of error checking in these routines, so if you move the mouse out of the window while the left button is down, you lose the line tracking.

451. *Understanding Graphics and Points*

In Windows, everything you see on the screen is a *graphic*. A graphic is anything from a single point to a bitmapped image that fills the entire screen. In between, you have graphics objects such as fonts, windows, icons, and the like.

A graphics object on the screen is composed of *points*. In mathematics, a point has no dimension, so you would have an infinite number of points from one side of your screen to the other, and it would take forever, literally, to draw a line across the screen. In computers, however, you deal with discrete units, and in Windows a point on the screen is the size of 1 pixel. A character on the screen, for example, is composed of pixels; which ones are visible and which ones are not determine the shape of the graphic and thus the character being displayed.

It can take from 1 bit to 3 or 4 bytes to describe a pixel, depending on the color resolution of the display. A black-and-white display can define 8 pixels in a single byte—a pixel is either on or off and needs only 1 bit to represent it. A screen using True Color needs 3 bytes to describe the same pixel, and some of the newer displays need 4 bytes. If all the bits are turned on, you get a white pixel; if all are turned off, you get a black pixel. In between are all the other colors.

452. Understanding Paths

In the earlier discussion on fonts, I mentioned that TrueType fonts are scalable to virtually any size because they consist of paths and not a pixel map (a bitmap). A *path* is the collection of line segments you generate when you call the GDI drawing functions. Normally, the path is drawn as you call individual functions, but it is possible to define a path first and then generate the entire drawing with a single command. A path can be composed of more than one figure, but a device context can define only one path at a time.

453. Using the BeginPath() and EndPath() Functions

You define a path in the device context by calling the *BeginPath()* function, drawing the lines and shapes that you want in the path, and to finish, calling the *EndPath()* function. In between, none of the GDI drawing calls is rendered to the output device or screen. Instead, they are stored and later rendered using the *StrokePath()* or *StrokeAndFillPath()* function.

The *DrawJoins()* function in the *PATTERNS.EXE* program uses a path to draw the lines with the join style. The GDI draws line joins only as part of a path.

In the discussion on regions in Tip 445, "GDI Objects: The Region," I mentioned an API function to create a region from a path. This is particularly useful in creating special effects with text. The *TextOut()* and *TextOutEx()* functions may be used within a path. When the path is closed, you call *PathToRegion()* to convert the path into a region. If you simply show the region at this point, you get a rectangular region filled with white text.

The problem is that the path describes the character cells instead of the characters themselves, which are outside the path but within the cells. You could invert the path, of course, but that would be more complicated than just putting the text out to the screen. You want to be able to use the region for special effects, such as shadow text.

If you get the region's rectangle and create another region from it, you can then logically *XOR* the two regions in a *CombineRgn()* statement to reverse the sense of the region. You can set the shadow text by offsetting it slightly and filling it with a gray brush. You then move the region back to its original position and fill it with a black brush.

You can see the result by selecting Text from the Paths menu in the *REGIONS.EXE* program. You could accomplish this same effect using text output functions, but the intent here is to show you how to modify and use a region created from a path. The code is in the *DoTextPath()* function in the *Region.cpp* source code file.

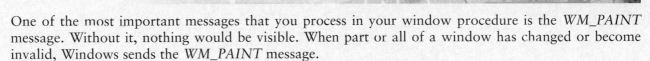

454. *Interpreting the* WM_PAINT *Message*

One of the most important messages that you process in your window procedure is the *WM_PAINT* message. Without it, nothing would be visible. When part or all of a window has changed or become invalid, Windows sends the *WM_PAINT* message.

The window is invalid, of course, when it is first created, so Windows sends you the message. If you resize the window, you again get a *WM_PAINT* message. You also may invalidate the window by getting the client area and calling *InvalidateRect()*, which you do when processing your menu commands.

Painting in the window when responding to the *WM_PAINT* message always begins with a call to *BeginPaint()* and finishes with a call to *EndPaint()*. You should never call these functions at any time other than in response to a paint message.

BeginPaint() does a couple of things for you. First, it gives you the device context for the window, which you need for most of the GDI drawing functions. You could get the DC by calling *GetDC()* just as easily, but *BeginPaint()* also fills out your *PAINTSTRUCT* structure.

```
typedef struct tagPAINTSTRUCT
{
    HDC  hdc;
    BOOL fErase;
    RECT rcPaint;
    BOOL fRestore;
    BOOL fIncUpdate;
    BYTE rgbReserved[16];
} PAINTSTRUCT;
```

The *hdc* member is the device context, which you got by calling the *BeginPaint()* function. The second member, *fErase*, is the erase background flag you used when you called *InvalidateRect()*. If only part of the window needs repainting, Windows will fill in the members of the *rcPaint* structure; otherwise, they will be 0. The last three members are reserved for use by the operating system.

If you don't call *BeginPaint()* and *EndPaint()*, Windows will continually reissue the *WM_PAINT* message, and your program will have little time to do anything but repaint itself. The functions signal Windows that you have processed the message and it doesn't have to reissue it.

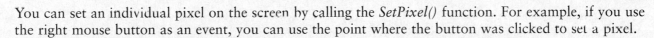

455. *Using the* SetPixel() *Function*

You can set an individual pixel on the screen by calling the *SetPixel()* function. For example, if you use the right mouse button as an event, you can use the point where the button was clicked to set a pixel.

The *SetPixel()* function requires a point in logical coordinate space—relative to your window—that is the coordinate space used by the mouse message. The parameters to the function are a handle to the device context, the x coordinate of the pixel, the y coordinate of the pixel, and the color of the pixel. You can set a black pixel using the following message handler for the right-mouse button down event:

```
case WM_RBUTTONDOWN:
    hdc = GetDC (hWnd);
    SetPixel (hdc, LOWORD(lParam), HIWORD(lParam), 0);
    ReleaseDC(hWnd, hdc);
    break;
```

The function returns the actual color used to set the pixel. If your screen is using 24-bit or higher colors (True Color), the return should be the same color you passed to the function. For 16-bit color, the return should be a very close approximation, and for 256-color, it is the palette entry closest to the color you specified.

A companion function, *GetPixel()*, returns the color of the pixel at a specified point. Its arguments are the handle to the device context, the x coordinate of the pixel, and the y coordinate. The coordinates are logical, and 0, 0 represents the upper-left corner of the client area.

The program *LINES.EXE* on the CD-ROM contains the code to draw a line using the right mouse button, which you will develop in the next few tips.

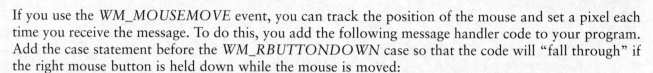

456. *Drawing a Series of Points*

If you use the *WM_MOUSEMOVE* event, you can track the position of the mouse and set a pixel each time you receive the message. To do this, you add the following message handler code to your program. Add the case statement before the *WM_RBUTTONDOWN* case so that the code will "fall through" if the right mouse button is held down while the mouse is moved:

```
case WM_MOUSEMOVE:
if (!(wParam & MK_RBUTTON))
    break;
// Fall through to the RBUTTONDOWN event
```

If you hold down the right mouse button while moving the mouse, you should see a distinct pattern of dots being created along the path of the mouse cursor. It's not a very good trace because you don't necessarily get a *WM_MOUSEMOVE* message for every point on the screen. The faster you move the mouse, the points get farther apart and the coarser the line becomes.

Actually, however, if you examine the points, they are a good approximation of the mouse path. If you could somehow connect them, you would have a good-looking trace.

457. *Drawing Lines*

You can connect the dots by drawing lines from one to another. First, you have to create a pen for the device context, move to either the current point or the previous point you received, and draw the line from one to the other.

You first must save the previous point in a static variable. You will initialize it to –1 in both axes, so you will know not to draw a line on the first button down event. Add the following variable declaration to the *WndProc()* function:

```
static POINT ptLast = {-1, -1};
```

Change the *WM_RBUTTONDOWN* handler so that it reads like the following. Notice the peculiar construction 0^0x00FFFFFF in the call to create the pen. This will produce a solid white pen, but you are *XOR*'ing your line on the screen, so the result will be a solid black trace. You could just use 0x00FFFFFF to specify a white pen, but soon you are going to replace the 0 with a color. You also need to add a handler for the *WM_RBUTTONUP* event so that you can reset your static point to −1 as a flag not to connect points that were not generated during previous mouse events:

```
case WM_RBUTTONDOWN:
    hdc = GetDC (hWnd);
    SetPixel (hdc, LOWORD(lParam), HIWORD(lParam), 0);
    if (ptLast.x >= 0)
    {
        HPEN hPen = CreatePen (PS_SOLID, 2, 0 ^ 0x00ffffff);
        int nOldMode = SetROP2 (hdc, R2_XORPEN);// R2_NOT);
        MoveToEx(hdc, LOWORD(lParam), HIWORD(lParam), NULL);
        SelectObject (hdc, hPen);
        LineTo (hdc, ptLast.x, ptLast.y);
        SetROP2 (hdc, nOldMode);
        DeleteObject (hPen);
    }
    ptLast.x = LOWORD(lParam);
    ptLast.y = HIWORD(lParam);
    ReleaseDC(hWnd, hdc);
    break;
case WM_RBUTTONUP:
    ptLast.x = -1;
    ptLast.y = -1;
    break;
```

Click and hold the right mouse button while you move the mouse around the client area. You should see a smooth line describing the mouse movements.

458. *Using the MoveToEx() Function*

In the last tip, you called an API function, *MoveToEx()*, to move to a particular point on the screen. This is a replacement function for the old *MoveTo()* function. The old function cannot be used in 32-bit versions of Windows because the return value is a 32-bit packed value representing the current position, the location just before the move was executed, in two 16-bit values. In 32-bit Windows, however, coordinates are 32-bit values, so there is no way to represent both the x and y points in the return value.

Instead, the new *MoveToEx()* function requires a pointer to a *POINT* structure where it returns the old point value. If you don't need the old position, you can use *NULL* in its place. The function returns a non-zero value if it was successful and 0 if the call failed. The following statement moves the current position of the device context *hdc* to 150 on the horizontal axis and 75 on the vertical axis, then fills in the *POINT* structure with the values before updating the current position:

```
POINT point;
MoveToEx (hdc, 150, 75, &point);
```

The point you specify in the function call is a logical coordinate in the device context and has nothing to do with the mouse pointer. It is the starting position for the next GDI line-drawing command. Actually, it updates the *Current Position* attribute of the device context. The current position also is updated by the line-drawing functions.

459. *Using the* **LineTo()** *Function*

A *line* is a series of pixels or dots (depending on the output device) from a starting point to an ending point. It may be straight or curved. The device context maintains the current position where your drawing functions will start. You can change this position with the *MoveToEx()* function, specifying the new position. You then can draw a straight line from the current position attribute of the device context to another point using the currently selected pen using the *LineTo()* function. When complete, the current position is updated to the end point of the line.

Obviously, a line drawn with points having a finite size can't be truly straight unless it's exactly vertical or horizontal. The Graphics Device Interface uses a digital differential analyzer algorithm to examine the points on the line and decide which pixel or dot on the output device most closely matches its position. In the old 16-bit Windows, the algorithm rounded off interim values to 16-bit integers, so the line drawn didn't match the requested line. Later versions of Windows use a non-rounding system, so the line more closely approximates the true line requested by the function call.

460. *Drawing a Curve Using a Series of Straight Lines*

For shapes that are more complex than a straight line, the Windows API provides a *Polyline()* function and for even more complex shapes, a *PolyPolyline()* function. You can use either to represent a curve by drawing a series of short, straight lines. Using the right mouse button, you already have seen that a series of straight lines can be made to resemble a curve.

The *Polyline()* function takes as parameters a handle to the device context, a pointer to an array of *POINT* structures, and a count of the number of points in the array. Let's first use it to draw a line in the center of the screen and then extend it to a triangle, a square, a pentagon, and so on, until you have something resembling a circle.

The *DoPolyline()* function in *LINES.CPP* (from Tip 455, "Using the *SetPixel()* Function") starts out with a vertical line and then recalculates the lines for a rectangle, then a square, and on up to 50 sides. By then, the shape has formed a nice circle. Best just to run it and watch the sides build out into the curve of a circle. To start the drawing, select Polyline from the Line Menu. There's a 300-millisecond delay between iterations of the loop, so you can speed it up or slow it down by changing the call to the *Sleep()* function.

After setting up your pen, brush, and font, the body of the loop looks like this:

```
for (int cSides = 2; cSides < 51; ++cSides)
{
    Sleep (300);
    FillRect (hdc, &newClient, hBrush);
    fAngle = PI / 2;
    pPoint = new POINT[cSides + 1];
    for (int i = 0; i < cSides; ++i)
    {
        pPoint[i].x = (int) fRadius * cos (fAngle) + 0.5;
        pPoint[i].y = (int) -fRadius * sin (fAngle) + 0.5;
        fAngle += 2 * PI / cSides;
    }
    pPoint[cSides] = pPoint[0];
```

```
        Polyline (hdc, pPoint, cSides + 1);
        delete [] pPoint;
        if (i > 2)
    {
            char strText [_MAX_PATH];
            sprintf (strText, "Side = %d", i);
            DrawText (hdc, strText, strlen (strText),
                    &rcText, TEXT_FORMAT);
    }
}
```

Starting with two sides (a straight line), the angle on the circumference for the end points starts at 90 degrees (pi/2—that makes your triangle stand up rather than take an awkward twist). The end points define a *chord* on the circle. You begin computing successively shorter chords until you reach 50, and the circle is well formed. Notice, too, that you change the viewport origin to the center of the screen. You could choose any arbitrary point on the screen, but the idea is to have the center of the circle at (0, 0). It's much easier to do these types of computations with a convenient origin. You can waste a lot of time and burn up a lot of code trying to calculate the chords as offsets from the upper left. If you intend to perform other drawing on the screen, you can always change it when needed. In fact, your drawing function should restore it before exiting, leaving it in a known state.

461. *Drawing an Arc*

In addition to straight lines, the Windows API contains functions for drawing curved lines. An example is *Arc()*, which draws a portion of a circle between two specified points. Drawing curved lines is considerably more complicated than drawing straight lines, and you must pass *Arc()* more arguments than you used for *LineTo()*.

Arc() requires nine arguments, one of which is the device context. The other eight arguments describe the arc. First, you must give it the rectangle that contains the circle (actually an ellipse). Then you must specify the starting point on the circle or ellipse to start drawing the arc. Finally, you must specify the point at which to stop drawing the arc. If the start and endpoints are the same, *Arc()* will draw the entire ellipse or circle.

The following *DoArc()* function in *LINES.CPP* (from Tip 455, "Using the *SetPixel()* Function") draws a circle using five distinct arcs:

```
void DoArc (HWND hWnd, HDC hdc)
{
POINT   ptOldOrigin;
POINT   ptStart, ptEnd;
HPEN    hPen, hOldPen;
HBRUSH  hBrush, hOldBrush;
RECT    rcClient;
double  fAngle, fRadius;

    hBrush = CreateSolidBrush (0x00ffffff);
    hOldBrush = (HBRUSH) SelectObject (hdc, hBrush);
    hPen = CreatePen (PS_SOLID, 2, 0x0);
    hOldPen = (HPEN) SelectObject (hdc, hPen);
    GetClientRect (hWnd, &rcClient);
    SetViewportOrgEx (hdc, rcClient.right / 2,
```

```
                    rcClient.bottom / 2, &ptOldOrigin);
    ptEnd.x = 150;
    ptEnd.y = 0;
    fAngle = (2 * PI) / 5;
    fRadius = 150.0;
    RECT rcCircle = {-150, -150, 150, 150};
    for (int i = 0; i < 10; ++i)
    {
        if (i == 5)
        {
            ptEnd.x = 150;
            ptEnd.y = 0;
            fAngle = (2 * PI) / 5;
        }
        ptStart = ptEnd;
        ptEnd.x = (long) (fRadius * cos (fAngle) + 0.5);
        ptEnd.y = (long) (-fRadius * sin (fAngle) + 0.5);
        Arc (hdc, -150, -150, 150, 150, ptStart.x, ptStart.y,
             ptEnd.x, ptEnd.y);
        fAngle += (2 * PI) / 5;
        if (i < 5)
        {
            Sleep (300);
            FillRect (hdc, &rcCircle, hBrush);
        }
    }
    SetViewportOrgEx (hdc, ptOldOrigin.x, ptOldOrigin.y, NULL);
    SelectObject (hdc, hOldPen);
    SelectObject (hdc, hOldBrush);
}
```

After setting the viewport to the middle of the screen, the program specifies a starting point at the far-right edge of the circle and calculates the angle as one-fifth of the full circle, *(2*PI)/5* or 60 degrees.

The code actually draws the circle twice. The first time through, it erases the previous arc and then draws the next so you can see the distinct parts of the circle. The second time around, it leaves the previous arc to complete the full circle.

462. *Drawing Circles and Ellipses*

The algorithm you used to construct a circle from straight lines is fast enough that you could use it to draw circles using just the inner loop and granularity you want. Fortunately, however, you don't have to go to all this trouble. The Windows API provides you with curve- and line-drawing functions.

A circle is a special instance of an *ellipse* in which the major and minor axes are equal. The Windows function to draw an ellipse is *Ellipse()* and takes as its arguments a handle to the device context and the two opposite corners of the rectangle that bound it. To draw your circle in the preceding two tips, you could have called *Ellipse(hdc, -r, -r, r, r)* after setting your viewport to the center of the desired circle, where *r* is the radius of the circle. To stretch the circle into an ellipse, you stretch the sides of the bounding rectangle, either the top and bottom or the left and right sides, depending on how you want the ellipse to look.

463. *Drawing Closed Areas*

The *Arc()* function from Tip 461, "Drawing an Arc," has some interesting possibilities if you examine it. You don't have to draw an entire circle. The *Arc()* function lets you specify the beginning and end points of a chord, in addition to the bounding rectangle. Let's say that in your circle calculations the chord in which you are interested begins at (–154, –94) and ends at (–49, 132). For convenience, let's call the points *X1*, *X2*, *Y1*, and *Y2*. You could draw just that section of the circle with the following statement:

```
Arc (hdc, (int) -fRadius, (int) -fRadius,
        (int) fRadius,  (int) fRadius,
      X1, Y1, X2, Y2);
```

Looks like the start of a pie chart, doesn't it? Surprisingly, you can change the single line to a pie chart section just by changing the function call from *Arc()* to *Pie()*. The arguments are identical. Just for grins, let's bracket the call with a path statement. Then you will create a brush and fill it:

```
hbrCyan = CreateSolidBrush (0x00ffff00);
BeginPath (hdc);
// Select the cyan brush. That will be the fill color for the
// pie section.
SelectObject (hdc, hbrCyan);
Pie (hdc, (int) -fRadius, (int) -fRadius,
        (int) fRadius, (int) fRadius,
          X1, Y1, X2, Y2);
EndPath (hdc);
StrokeAndFillPath (hdc);
```

Nice. You have a good cyan pie section. Let's see if you can create a complete pie chart; it's not that difficult. You need some numbers to work with first. Say that you have five units of something and whatever those five units did produced the following five numbers: 72, 276, 156, 108, and 84. (Hey! A pie chart doesn't care what the numbers represent.) Try the following function (the code is in *TEXT.CPP* in the project from Tip 477, "Using the *DrawText()* Function"):

```
void DoPieChart (HWND hWnd, HDC hdc)
{
RECT    rcClient;
POINT   pOldOrigin;
POINT   pPoint[6];
int nVals[] = {72, 156, 108, 84, 276};
int     nSum, i;
HBRUSH  hBrush[5], hOldBrush;
HPEN    hPen, hOldPen;
double  fAngle, fRadius;
COLORREF crColors[] = {0x00ffff00, 0x00ff00ff, 0x001111ff,
                    0x0000ffff, 0x0011ff11};

    GetClientRect (hWnd, &rcClient);
    fRadius = rcClient.bottom / 3;
    fAngle = PI / 4;
    hBrush[0] = CreateSolidBrush (0x0);
    SetViewportOrgEx (hdc, rcClient.right / 4 + 6,
                    rcClient.bottom / 2 + 6, &pOldOrigin);
    hOldBrush = (HBRUSH) SelectObject (hdc, hBrush[0]);
```

```
    hPen = CreatePen (PS_SOLID, 2, 0);
    hOldPen = (HPEN) SelectObject (hdc, hPen);
    Ellipse (hdc, (int) -fRadius, (int) -fRadius,
                (int) fRadius, (int) fRadius);
    SelectObject (hdc, hOldBrush);
    DeleteObject (hBrush[0]);
    SetViewportOrgEx (hdc, rcClient.right / 4,
                        rcClient.bottom / 2, NULL);


    nSum = 0;
    for (i = 0; i < 5; ++i)
    {
        hBrush[i] = CreateSolidBrush (crColors[i]);
        nSum += nVals[i];
    }
    hPen = CreatePen (PS_SOLID, 2, 0);
    hOldPen = (HPEN) SelectObject (hdc, hPen);
    hOldBrush = (HBRUSH) SelectObject (hdc, hBrush[0]);
    for (i = 0; i < 5; ++i)
    {
        pPoint[i].x = (long)(fRadius * cos (fAngle) + 0.5);
        pPoint[i].y = (long)(-fRadius * sin (fAngle) + 0.5);
        fAngle += (nVals[i] * 2.0 * PI) / nSum;
    }
    pPoint[5] = pPoint[0];
    for (i = 0; i < 5; ++i)
    {

        SelectObject (hdc, hBrush[i]);
        Pie (hdc, (int) -fRadius, (int) -fRadius,
                (int) fRadius, (int) fRadius,
                pPoint[i].x, pPoint[i].y,
                pPoint[i+1].x, pPoint[i+1].y);
        SelectObject (hdc, hOldBrush);
        DeleteObject (hBrush[i]);
    }
    SelectObject (hdc, hOldPen);
    DeleteObject (hPen);
    SetViewportOrgEx(hdc, pOldOrigin.x, pOldOrigin.y, NULL);
}
```

Voilà! Instant pie chart. Not a great one, but a good start. Let's go over what the code does. First, notice that your point array is six *POINT* structures for only five wedges; you need the extra to avoid additional calculations for the last slice. After getting the client rectangle, you set the values for the radius of the chart to one third of the vertical height of your window by *fRadius = rcClient.bottom / 3*. This is where you adjust the size to fit your own needs. The beginning angle is *PI/4*, or 45 degrees. Change this value to rotate the slices to suit your needs.

You then set the viewport to the center of your pie chart, plus six logical points to the right and down for the shadow effect; then, you draw your shadow. The *Ellipse()* function fills it in with the current pen. After drawing the shadow, you move the viewport back and up six logical points. Setting the viewport to the center of your chart makes the calculations easier.

Next, you have a short loop to create the brushes of the various colors for the pie chart and sum the items. The sum will be used to calculate the angular portion of the pie that an element will use.

In the *for* loop, you calculate the chord points just as you did when you drew the circle from straight lines. This time you're going to use them to specify arc segments, however. Then you calculate the angle for the next slice. The total of your data items is 696, so you know that a slice is going to get *360 * n/696* angles in the total circle. The *Arc()* and *Pie()* functions use radians, however, so you multiply the result by *2 * PI/360* to get radians. The 360 degrees in the numerator and denominator cancel each other, so you can remove them, leaving *(nVals[i] * 2.0 * PI) / nSum* as the delta angle for this slice, and you add it to the preceding angle so that you step around the circle. By the time you use all your data, you should have stepped around *2*PI* radians.

For ease of creating the paths, you use your extra *POINT* array member to duplicate the first. You then go through another loop to draw each slice. The *Pie()* function draws the lines in the current pen (black) and fills the section with the current brush, which differs for each slice. You then select your old brush for safety and delete the one you just used; you won't need it again.

After five loops (or however many data elements you have), you return your viewport to the original position, clean up any objects you created, and you're done.

For a real experience, try exploding the pie chart. You can do it by shifting the viewport for each path. You have to bisect the angle of each wedge to find the direction to move. Finally, try putting some shadows under the slices to give the chart a 3-D effect.

In Tip 482, "Rotating Text," after you have learned more about fonts and drawing text, you will return to this pie chart and actually set text in the sections.

464. *Using the Pen*

When you create an object such as a pie chart, using the logical pen to draw lines gives it emphasis. In the example, you use a two-point (in logical sizes) pen to draw the lines between the slices and around the arc (it was done with the *StrokeAndFillPath()* statement). Nobody really notices the lines; you could use a one-point line just as well. But you can be sure that they notice when the lines are missing.

Try changing the *StrokeAndFillPath()* statement to just *FillPath()*. With a shadow, it doesn't look too bad, but it definitely looks unfinished without the pen strokes.

465. *Using the Brush*

Colors give life to visual objects. Periodical publishers spend millions of dollars on color-rendering equipment just to have color photos on a few pages of the publication—and it's becoming very difficult to find a black-and-white computer monitor these days.

The brush is the main tool you use to give color to your projects. It paints the background and fills the regions and paths you create. The pen augments the effects created by the brush. Your pie chart in gray scales drawn with a magenta pen, for example, would look, well, funny. But color sections surrounded by a black stroke (black is 100-percent gray) look good.

466. *Filling a Closed Area*

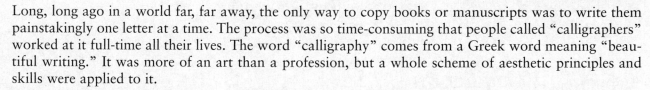

Perhaps the subject of this tip should be how *not* to fill a closed area. Most of the Graphics Display Interface functions that draw closed areas—such as *Ellipse(), Rectangle(), Pie(),* and *Polygon()*—automatically fill the areas with the default brush. At times, however, you want to draw the shape but still have any objects below it visible. If you call the functions within a *BeginPath()/EndPath()* bracket, they aren't automatically filled; you have to do it when you render the path to the screen with the *StrokeAndFillPath()* function. You can avoid filling the shapes by calling *StrokePath()* instead, and objects below the shape will appear through it.

Still, having to bracket calls is tedious. There are two other ways around the automatic fill. If you examine the GDI drawing modes, you will see that the *R2_MASKPEN* mode produces a pixel that is the combination of the colors common to both the pen and the screen. If the background is white (all colors) and you are filling with a white brush, the object underneath will be visible because all the brush colors that are not a part of it are masked out. This method affects other GDI objects as well.

You also can create a null brush that fills with nothing. To create a null brush, you fill in a *LOGBRUSH* structure with 0 in the *lbColor* and *lbHatch* members and *BS_NULL* in the *lbStyle* member. Then you create the brush with a call to *CreateBrushIndirect()*.

There also is a null brush among the Windows stock objects. You can get it by using the following statement:

```
HBRUSH hNullBrush = (HBRUSH) GetStockObject (NULL_BRUSH);
```

If you use the stock object, be sure not to delete it when you clean up your function before returning.

467. *Introduction to Text Metrics*

Long, long ago in a world far, far away, the only way to copy books or manuscripts was to write them painstakingly one letter at a time. The process was so time-consuming that people called "calligraphers" worked at it full-time all their lives. The word "calligraphy" comes from a Greek word meaning "beautiful writing." It was more of an art than a profession, but a whole scheme of aesthetic principles and skills were applied to it.

About 1440, a German named Johann Gutenberg began working on a scheme to create type that could be moved about so that books could be reproduced more quickly. His background as a goldsmith (some people erroneously claim that he was a priest because his first production was the Bible) obviously influenced the method by which he created type and the new industry and profession that followed. His *replicating* process involved engraving a character in relief and then punching it into a brass slab to produce a matrix from which many copies of the character could be made by casting with molten metal.

For a pre-industrial world, this was terribly complicated. Errors could creep in at any point and would multiply as the character made its way from the engraving to the casting. Also, errors would be replicated each time the character was cast. Accuracy means careful measuring and calculation, and the world got *text metrics*. Now, we don't know for sure that the name was born with the industry, but it was text metrics nonetheless.

Letters had to be a specific height then, which later came to be known as *typehigh*. (No, the point size is *not* the height of a character.) Even a slight discrepancy would render them darker or lighter on the printed page. They had to have certain dimensions and certain escapements around the character elements. Measurement systems evolved to cope with these new ideas, and when you have measurements, you have *metrics*.

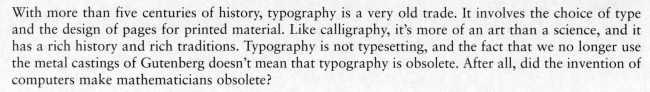

468. *Understanding Typography*

With more than five centuries of history, typography is a very old trade. It involves the choice of type and the design of pages for printed material. Like calligraphy, it's more of an art than a science, and it has a rich history and rich traditions. Typography is not typesetting, and the fact that we no longer use the metal castings of Gutenberg doesn't mean that typography is obsolete. After all, did the invention of computers make mathematicians obsolete?

The tools of the typographer have been evolving rapidly over the past 40 to 50 years. Much of what we know about typesetting has been developed since the middle of the twentieth century. As a copy boy at a great metropolitan newspaper in the early 1960s, I was awed watching the industry work. It was amazing how a story fresh out of a reporter's typewriter could be set in type and dropped into a page in a matter of 2 to 3 minutes. Today, with computerized typesetting and high-speed typesetters, you can do it in, well, 10 minutes.

Part of the art of typography is knowing the characteristics and visual effects of the various character sets available today. When is a bold typeface required, and when is a lighter face called for?

As you explore the typefaces available in Windows (there are many, and many applications add their own to your collection), study them for visual effect. The correct selection of type is a valuable asset to a computer application.

469. *Understanding Windows Font Types*

In computerland, we have seen a number of font types come and go, but generally they now fall into the bitmapped and TrueType categories. A *bitmapped* font contains a matrix of square cells that form the character, depending on whether the cells are light or dark. As you increase the size of a bitmapped font, you have to shift to a finer matrix, or the curves and slanted lines of a character will show a stair-step effect. Bitmap font files, with an extension of *.FON*, contain several *glyphs* of the font, each designed to be used within a specified point range. Bitmapped fonts sometimes are called *raster* fonts.

TrueType is a type technology first introduced to computers by Apple in 1991. Microsoft quickly followed suit and introduced it to Windows the following year. TrueType font files, with an extension of *.TTF*, contain glyphs that describe characters in terms of lines and hints that are used by the Graphics Device Interface to paint the characters. These fonts retain their shape regardless of their size or the device on which they are drawn and are considered device-independent fonts.

470. *Understanding Point Sizes*

Type and fonts have their own units of measurement, the most common of which is the *point*. Before I go any further, I want to dispel a nasty notion. The point size of a font is *not* a measure of its height.

The idea apparently came about because we tend to think two-dimensionally. We see the characters on the screen and they are standing upright, so we think of the point size as the height of the characters. Try dumping some text from your screen to the printer; take the paper and lay it flat on your desk. How high is the character now?

Type is measured in both dimensions of its face in points. In much of Europe, type is measured in *ciceros* and *didots*. There are 72.27 points in an inch, or 0.01383 inch in a point. The font gurus have told us that the 0.27 is negligible and you can approximate by using 72 points to the inch. Let's see how negligible the fractional part is.

A typical newspaper page is 21 inches deep. In real points that's about 1518.4. In font guru points, it's 1512, so you've come up short by 6.4 points already. Newspapers charge for advertising by the line, and there is slightly more than a line in 6.4 points, depending on the newspaper. With an average cost of $15 per line and a 30-page classified advertising section with 11 columns per page, the "negligible" factor amounts to about $5,600 a day or about $2 million a year. Most publishers don't consider that "negligible." If you program for a company that buys advertising space, you also are paying for space that you aren't using.

Modern typesetting equipment and most good printers use 72.27 points to the inch and will continue to do so. You can truncate the value for screen display, but when you prepare your text for type, do us all a favor and adjust it accordingly.

A *didot* (often capitalized) is the European equivalent of a point, but it is slightly larger in scale and you probably won't find it in many American dictionaries. A didot is about .038 millimeter, and a U.S. point is about .35 millimeter. Twelve points make up a *pica* and 12 didot points make up a *cicero*.

In the Windows *LOGFONT* structure, the point size of a font is entered in logical units in the *lfHeight* member. In the default MM_TEXT mapping mode of the device context, you can convert points to logical units using the following formula:

```
lfHeight = -MulDiv(PointSize, GetDeviceCaps(hdc, LOGPIXELSY), 72);
```

471. *Understanding Character Widths*

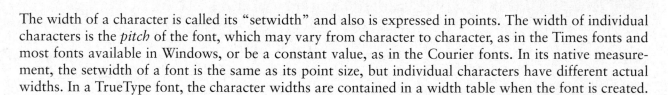

The width of a character is called its "setwidth" and also is expressed in points. The width of individual characters is the *pitch* of the font, which may vary from character to character, as in the Times fonts and most fonts available in Windows, or be a constant value, as in the Courier fonts. In its native measurement, the setwidth of a font is the same as its point size, but individual characters have different actual widths. In a TrueType font, the character widths are contained in a width table when the font is created.

You can get the widths of characters in a font by calling *GetCharWidth32()* to get just the character widths themselves or *GetCharABCWidths()* for more detailed information. Both yield the widths in logical units and take as parameters a handle to the device context, the first character in a group of *consecutive* characters, and the last character in the group. The fourth parameter for *GetCharWidth32()* is a pointer to an array of type *int*. The array should be large enough to hold the width information. The following snippet gets the widths of the capital letters of the currently selected font:

```
int *nWidths[26];
GetCharWidth32 (hdc, 'A', 'Z', nWidths);
```

The fourth parameter to *GetCharABCWidths()* is a pointer to an array of *ABC* structures. This structure holds three members. The *abcA* member contains the amount of spacing that will be added to the current position before drawing the character. The *abcB* member is the actual width of the character glyph. The *abcC* member is the amount of space that will be added to the current position after the glyph has been drawn. The sum of these three members should be what you obtain using the *GetCharWidth32()* function.

Characters also have a built-in horizontal escapement called the *kern* that adds to their width and provides some intercharacter spacing. Portions of a character may actually exceed the character cell that contains them, and many italic characters extend into the next character's cell when they are set. The kerning may be adjusted to provide a closer fit between characters and often is changed for certain pairs of characters to get a better look to the font. For example, a capital "T" and a lowercase letter such as "a" or "o" can be placed closer together by adjusting the kern so that the lowercase letter fits under the wing of the "T."

With modern typesetting equipment, the setwidth of a font can be changed, particularly with TrueType fonts. For example, you could specify a setwidth of 10 for a 12-point font, in which case the characters would be slightly compressed. None of this was possible until the advent of computerized typesetting. The width and kern of a character was determined when it was stamped on the matrix, and every character poured from the matrix was identical.

The *lfWidth* member of the *LOGFONT* structure is used to specify the *average* width of the characters of a font in logical units. For most practical purposes, the average character width of a font is a useless piece of information, and you should set this member to 0 when you create a font.

472. *Understanding Character Attributes*

Fonts also are defined by the attributes of their characters. These include the weight (normal, bold, light, and so on), whether a character is slanted or italic, and for programming purposes, whether it is underlined or has a horizontal strikethrough line through it.

Computerized fonts generally don't have underlines and strikethrough lines. These are added by the Graphics Display Interface when you create the font.

In may cases, the GDI also can embolden a normal or light font and can slant it to produce *oblique* type in sans-serif fonts or to approximate italic in serif fonts.

473. *Understanding Text Alignment*

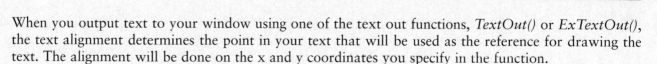

When you output text to your window using one of the text out functions, *TextOut()* or *ExTextOut()*, the text alignment determines the point in your text that will be used as the reference for drawing the text. The alignment will be done on the x and y coordinates you specify in the function.

The default is to set the text using the x coordinate as the left starting point for drawing the text, or *TA_LEFT*, and the y coordinate as the top starting point, or *TA_TOP*. The output functions create a bounding rectangle based on the size of the character cells and the width of the text.

You get the current text alignment by calling *GetTextAlign()*, and you set it using the *SetTextAlign()* function. The *SetTextAlign()* function returns the old settings, so you can restore it to its previous value after you output your text. When you set the alignment flags, you may specify only one of the flags that set the horizontal position, one of the flags that set the vertical position, and one of the flags that alter the Current Position attribute of the device context. If you specify more than one of these, the call will return *GDI_ERROR* (-1) and the alignment won't be changed.

The *TA_CENTER* flag affects the horizontal alignment. The text will be centered in the width of the bounding rectangle.

Other flags that affect the horizontal alignment are *TA_LEFT* (the text will be set using the x coordinate in the text out function as the left side of the bounding box) and *TA_RIGHT* (the x coordinate will be used as the right side of the bounding box).

Other vertical alignment flags are *TA_TOP* (the y coordinate will be used as the top of the bounding box) and *TA_BOTTOM* (the y coordinate will be the bottom of the bounding box).

You also may specify *TA_BASELINE* to indicate that you want the box alignment made with reference to the baseline of the current font instead of the top of the characters. You have to be careful with this one. If you specify this flag and set text at 0, 0 in your window, the text will be set above the client area. The top of the bounding rectangle is the bottom of the text.

You also may specify *TA_NOUPDATECP* (the default) or *TA_UPDATECP* to indicate whether you want the text output to update the current position attribute of the device context. If you use *TA_NOUPDATECP* and repeatedly output text to, say, 100, 100, the text will be drawn in the same position each time. If you set it to *TA_UPDATECP*, the function will use the current position as the point at which text will be output, and the position will be updated according to the vertical and horizontal alignment flags.

The update flag is an interesting one. If you are using *TA_LEFT* with *TA_UPDATECP*, the text from each *TextOut()* statement using the same x and y coordinates appears one right after the other. If you use *TA_RIGHT*, each output appears to the left of the preceding. If you use *TA_CENTER*, each block of type is set on top of the preceding.

474. Using the MFC CFont Class

The Microsoft Foundation Class library's *CFont* class encapsulates the *HFONT* object of the Graphics Device Interface and contains the functions for manipulating and using the font object. If you've mastered the *HFONT* object, you will have no problems using the *CFont* class.

After you create a font using the MFC class, you generally don't have to worry about deleting it to free system resources. The object will be destroyed when the class object goes out of scope and is destroyed. If you create a *CFont* object on the heap, you still have to destroy it using the *delete* statement, of course.

475. Understanding CFont Functions to Create Fonts

The *CFont* class incorporates its own functions to create fonts. The functions return *TRUE* or *FALSE* to indicate whether the operation was successful. In the global function *CreateFont()*, the function returned an *HFONT* handle. The *CFont* functions retain the handle, and you never have to specify it in your programs. You can retrieve it simply by casting the *CFont* object to *HFONT*.

The *CFont::CreateFont()* and *CFont::CreateFontIndirect()* functions are no easier to use than the global functions. You still have to fill out a *LOGFONT* structure for the *CFont::CreateFontIndirect()* function or pass the parameters for the structure in the *CFont::CreateFont()* function. The class does, however, have a couple of very useful functions named *CreatePointFont()* and *CreatePointFontIndirect()*.

In the examples, you've filled in a *LOGFONT* structure to specify your font size and used a formula for converting the point size to logical points. The *CFont* class includes a *CreatePointFont()* function that lets you do that without any calculations. You specify the point size in tenths and the face name of the font you want to use. Suppose that you wanted to create a 12-point font using Times New Roman Bold. Rather than waste code filling out a *LOGFONT* structure, you would let the class function handle it, as in the following snippet:

```
CFont cFont;
cFont.CreatePointFont (120, "Times New Roman Bold");
```

The *CFont::CreateFontIndirect()* function is not quite as handy. It still requires a pointer to a *LOGFONT* structure, but instead of specifying the *lfHeight* member in logical units, you specify it in tenths of a point.

The following snippet produces a 12-point font similar to the preceding but using the indirect method:

```
CFont cFont;
LOGFONT lf;
lf.lfHeight = 120;
strcpy (lfHeight, "Times New Roman Bold");
// fill out the rest of the logfont members
cFont.CreatePointFontIndirect (&lf);
```

Both these functions include an optional pointer to a *CDC* object as the last parameter. It defaults to *NULL* if you don't specify it, in which case the functions use the screen device context for converting logical points to font points. The *CDC* class in MFC encapsulates a device context object. You will look at it later.

476. *Understanding Text Output Functions*

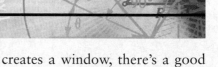

No matter what type of application you are writing, if the program creates a window, there's a good chance you will be doing text output. By far, text is the most common output used by Windows applications. Text output is not limited just to windows, and if you use a printer in your application, chances are, you will need to output text to it.

The Windows API contains functions you can use to format and draw text. The text output functions can be used to draw individual characters or strings of text on the screen, giving you control over their placement and appearance. The formatting functions allow you to measure and align text and set the text colors, among other attributes.

Text output has several characteristics. Among these are its alignment (where it is placed in the drawing rectangle), background and foreground colors, word spacing, and character spacing. Character spacing is most common in *justified* lines, which require the text to extend from one side of the rectangle to the other.

In commercial printing, limits usually are placed on how much space can exist between words in a justified line. When that limit is reached, character spacing is used.

In addition to setting text attributes, the API contains functions for retrieving and testing the attributes.

Windows has four basic text output functions, some of which have extended versions named with a preceding or trailing *Ex*.

477. *Using the* **DrawText()** *Function*

The *DrawText()* and *DrawTextEx()* functions provide many of the capabilities of a Windows edit control. They are part of the Window Manager API and not the Graphics Device Interface. Along with the *TabbedTextOut()* function, the *DrawText()* and *DrawTextEx()* functions serve as a programmer's interface to the *TextOut()* and *ExtTextOut()* functions.

DrawText() is the function used by many Windows controls, such as menus. It processes the ampersand character and removes it from the string, replacing the character immediately after it with an underlined character. You have to use the *DT_NOPREFIX* style to turn off this behavior.

When you call the *DrawText()* function, the operating system passes the call along to the GDI, which in turn sends it to the device driver for the selected device. The driver then calls into its own *TextOut()* or *ExtTextOut()* functions. Thus, there is somewhat more overhead in using the *DrawText()* and *DrawTextEx()* functions, but you would have to write extra code anyway to perform much of the work done by these functions.

In the *PATTERNS.CPP* file from the program in Tip 441, "GDI Objects: The Pen," you'll find a function called *DrawBenDay()*. This function calls the *DrawText()* function to "trial set" the text and measure the depth of the rectangle you would need to set your text. For this, you used the *DT_EDITCONTROL, DT_WORDBREAK*, and *DT_CALCRECT* styles.

The *DT_EDITCONTROL* mimics many of the text-handling capabilities of a multi-line edit control. With this style, a partial line of text is not displayed if the entire string won't fit into the rectangle.

The *DT_WORDBREAK* style causes the line to be broken at the space before a word if it would extend beyond the right edge of the bounding rectangle. A carriage return/line feed combination also causes a line break.

When you use the *DT_CALCRECT* flag, the *DrawText()* function does not draw any text to the screen. The flag provides the capability to trial set the text to determine how large a rectangle will be needed to contain the entire text. When *DrawText()* returns, it has adjusted the bottom of the rectangle so that all the text will fit. You then can use the rectangle to produce special effects such as a shadow or screen before actually setting the text.

Multi-line text handling is the default for *DrawText()*. It can be converted to single-line display using the *DT_SINGLELINE* style. In this case, only the text that fits on one line is displayed, and carriage return/line feed combinations won't break the line. This style does give you some added capability, however, that is worth noting.

In the single-line mode you can position the text to the top or bottom of the rectangle using the *DT_TOP* or *DT_BOTTOM* styles. You can align the text to the right in the rectangle using the *DT_RIGHT* and to the left using the *DT_LEFT* style (the default) or center it horizontally with the *DT_CENTER* style.

Also in single-line mode, you can use *DT_END_ELLIPSIS* to insert an ellipsis at the end of a line if the line won't fit in the rectangle. The title bar of a window uses this style when the title is too long to fit on a single line. You also may use the *DT_PATH_ELLIPSIS* style to insert an ellipsis in the middle of the text to show both the beginning and end of the text. This is handy when you have a long file path name to display. It will show the first part of the path, an ellipsis, and the last part of the path. The function will try to preserve as much of the text after the last backslash (which would be the file name) as possible.

You can specify the tab spacing by placing it in bits 8–15 of the style parameter; then, use the *DT_TABSTOPS* style to set them. *DT_EXPANDTABS* is used to expand the tabs on output. The default is 8 spaces for a tab, but if you wanted to set it to 4 spaces, you would use something like the following snippet:

```
DrawText (hdc,szText,strlen(szText), rc, (4 << 8) |
          DT_TABSTOP | DT_EXPANDTABS);
```

The expression *(4 << 8)* shifts the value 4 to the right by 8 bits and thus places it in bits 8–15 of the style parameter.

In the sample *TEXT.CPP* program on the CD-ROM, the *DoJustify()* function shows how you can use *TextOut()* to produce text justified to fit a line. I've also included my version of *CreatePointFont()* to make it easier to play around with different fonts when using these samples. This is a Visual Studio project, so you can open it in the IDE and trace through the code.

In *DoJustify()*, you set your line width to about the size of a standard newspaper column and draw a rule alongside for reference. In real life, you would display the rule a bit to the right to allow some white space after the text, but you want it to abut the characters to show the quality of justification.

Then, also for reference, you use *DrawText()* to display the text using the edit control styles after first measuring it with a call to *DrawText()* with the *DT_CALCRECT* style.

The call to *GetTextExtentExPoint()* measures how many characters fit on the line. Of course, you want to break at a spaceband, not just any character, and you don't want to justify the last line. Therefore, you look at the return, copying it into a temporary string. If it's the last line, you output the text and you're done. If, however, the next character is a spaceband, you want to use all the characters that will fit on the line. Otherwise, you back up to the previous space using *strrchr(str, ' ')*. If there is no space, you handle it as best as you can, but the Windows functions don't negotiate this situation well.

When you've settled on the text for the line, you call the *JustifyLine()* function, also in *TEXT.CPP*, which outputs the line. Here you count the number of spacebands in the line; then, you measure the unjustified line using *GetTextExtentPoint32()*. The deficit is the difference between the desired line width and the actual line width, so you distribute it among the spacebands by calling the *SetTextJustification()* function, and you draw the text.

A word of caution about *SetTextJustification()*. The amount you specify to add to the width of the spacebands is cumulative. If you add 5 points on one call, then 3 points on another, the total distribution will be 8 points. Rather than keep track of the amount, you call the function again, after the text has been output, with the negative value of the deficit to remove your change.

When you compile the project, you can see the results in *TEXT.EXE*. Select Justify from the Text menu.

478. *Using the* TextOut() *and* ExtTextOut() *Functions*

In your justification program, you could just as easily use *TextOut()* or *ExtTextOut()* functions and achieve the same result. In fact, because you are not using any of the special styles of *DrawText()*, it probably would be faster to use *ExtTextOut()*.

That's exactly what you do when you can't get the Windows functions to handle a line with no spaces in it. In the *DoJustify()* function of *TEXT.CPP*, you take advantage of the character-spacing array that you can pass to *ExtTextOut()*. You couldn't do that with other functions. The code to do that is shown here:

```
int *lpDx = new int [strlen (szText)];
memset (lpDx, 0, sizeof (int) * strlen (szText));
int nWidths[256];
GetCharWidth32 (hdc, 0, 255, nWidths);
for (unsigned int i = 0; i < strlen (szText); ++i)
    lpDx[i] = nWidths[szText[i]];
```

```
for (i = 0; i < (unsigned int)(nWidth - sz.cx); ++i)
    lpDx[i] += 1;
ExtTextOut (hdc, rc->left, rc->top, 0, NULL,
            szText, strlen (szText), lpDx);
delete [] lpDx;
```

First, you allocate an integer array for each character in the string. This array specifies the actual space that will be used by the individual characters. You declare a width array for every possible character, 256, and get the widths by calling *GetCharWidth32()*. Then you add your deficit to the first characters in the string, stopping when you reach the deficit limit. This means that the first characters in the line will have slightly more space between them, but the difference is barely noticeable.

To see how this works, go back to the *DoJustify()* function and change the first two statements in the function to use *TESTSTRING1* instead of *TESTSTRING*. This is an alternate string in which I've removed the first eight spacebands to force you to get to the preceding code.

479. *Using* TabbedTextOut

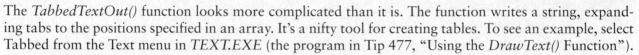

The *TabbedTextOut()* function looks more complicated than it is. The function writes a string, expanding tabs to the positions specified in an array. It's a nifty tool for creating tables. To see an example, select Tabbed from the Text menu in *TEXT.EXE* (the program in Tip 477, "Using the *DrawText()* Function").

```
void DoTabbedText (HDC hdc, HWND hWnd)
{
HFONT hFont, hOldFont;
int nTabs[2], nLineWidth, i;
SIZE    sz;
const char *szText[] =
    {
    "Division\tSales\tReturns",
    "Widgets\t12654\t345",
    "Wombats\t96734\t3829",
    "Weasels\t4583\t485"
    };

    hFont = CreatePointFont (120, "Times New Roman", hdc);
    hOldFont = (HFONT) SelectObject (hdc, hFont);
    GetTextExtentPoint32 (hdc, szText[0],
                          strlen (szText[0]), &sz);

    nLineWidth = GetSizeInPicas (180, hdc);
    nTabs[0] = nTabs[1] = nLineWidth / 3;
    MoveToEx (hdc, 0, sz.cy, NULL);
    LineTo (hdc, nLineWidth, sz.cy);
    TabbedTextOut (hdc, 0, 0, szText[0],
                   strlen (szText[0]), 2, nTabs, 0);
    int nPoints = sz.cy;
    sz.cy += 3;
    for (i = 1; i < (sizeof(szText)/sizeof (char *)); ++i)
    {
        TabbedTextOut (hdc, 0, sz.cy, szText[i],
                       strlen (szText[i]), 2, nTabs, 0);
```

```
        sz.cy += nPoints;
    }
    SelectObject (hdc, hOldFont);
    DeleteObject (hFont);
}
```

After a few lines of declaring your variables and creating and selecting the font, you call *GetTextExtentPoint32()* to get the width and depth of a line of text. You split the line evenly, setting each element in your tab stop array *nTabs* to one-third of the line width.

To separate the first line, the header, from the rest of the table, you draw a line just below where the first line of text will appear; then, output the line with *TabbedTextOut()*. To avoid overwriting the line you drew with text, you add a few logical points to the *SIZE* array's *cy* member.

The *for* loop outputs the remaining lines in the character array.

480. *Understanding the* **GrayString()** *Function*

The *GrayString()* function outputs text to the device indirectly. First, it creates a bitmap image of the string using *TextOut()* and the currently selected font. It then grays the text using the stock gray brush or one specified in the function call and copies the bitmap to the screen or output device.

This function isn't useful for drawing text to the client area unless you are using the same brush for the window background color. If you specify a brush, it draws the text and the background in the same color.

You use this function to draw inactive menu items if you decide to use the *OWNERDRAW* menu style. You may specify your own function to gray the text, however, but you yourself also have to copy it to the screen.

You may specify a bitmap in the text parameter, but, again, you have to provide your own function to gray the bitmap and copy it to the screen.

There are nine parameters to *GrayString()*. The handle to the device context is the first parameter. The second is the brush to use to gray the text, which may be *NULL* to use the same brush that was used to draw the window text.

The third parameter is the *CALLBACK* function to gray and output the text to the screen. If it is null, *DrawText()* is used. If you provide your own function, it must be in the form *BOOL CALLBACK FunctionName (HDC, WPARAM, LPARAM)*. You can pass a pointer to a structure containing a pointer to the string and position information by casting it to *(WPARAM)*. If you use this method, your function is responsible for graying the text and outputting it.

The fourth parameter is the length of the string to output. If you are using the callback method, this value is placed in the *lParam* parameter to the function.

The last four parameters are the x and y coordinates to output the string and the width and depth of the bounding rectangle.

481. *Understanding Background Modes in Text Output*

In *PATTERNS.EXE* (from Tip 441, "GDI Objects: The Pen"), you drew a benday box by placing black text on a grayed background. The function you used to achieve this effect was *SetBkMode()*. The "background mode" you set with this function determines whether the text or drawing you produce will overwrite the background shapes or color.

The mode has only two possibilities:

- *OPAQUE.* The background is filled with the current brush before text, hatch marks, or shapes are drawn.

- *TRANSPARENT.* The background remains unchanged and the text, hatch marks, or shapes are drawn over it.

The default mode is *OPAQUE.* Try commenting out the *SetBkMode(TRANSPARENT)* statement in *PATTERN.EXE* to see the effect of an opaque output.

482. *Rotating Text*

Sometimes you need to set text at an angle, such as in the header for a table, or vertically, such as an index tab on a page. Rotating text is simple, but you must create a separate *HFONT* object for each angle and font you intend to use.

Before you get started, you should have a basic understanding of trigonometric functions. If you were told that there would be no math in programming, somebody lied to you. Programming is about 33-percent math, 33-percent inspiration, and 33-percent perspiration. The other 1 percent is for all those other esoteric things programmers do while they drink pop and eat munchies.

If you start with a right triangle, the side away from the right angle is the *hypotenuse.* You know that one angle is 90 degrees, and the trigonometric functions let you find the lengths of the sides and the size of the other angles, provided that you have some limited information. Starting with one of the angles (not the right angle, however), if you divide the length of the side farthest from the angle by the hypotenuse, you get the *sine* of the angle, which you call *theta* (θ), so you say that *sine* θ = *opposite/hypotenuse.* The adjacent side divided by the hypotenuse is the *cosine*, abbreviated *cos.* The opposite side divided by the adjacent side is the *tangent*, or *tan.* The sine and cosine vary between 1 and −1, and the tangent ranges to nearly infinity in both directions. The sine starts at 0 for an angle of 0, the cosine starts at 1, and the tangent at 0. There are some other ratios in trigonometry (the secant, cosecant, and cotangent), but *sin*, *cos*, and *tan* are the primary ratios. The C++ functions are *sin()*, *cos()*, and *tan()*.

If you know the value of one of the ratios, you can find the corresponding angle using an inverse function known as the *arc* function. Knowing the sine of an angle, you can find the angle using the *arcsine* function, which in C++ is *asin()*. The *arccosine* function is *acos()* and the *arctangent* function is *atan()*.

These functions all deal in *radians.* If you take the radius of a circle and lay it along the circumference, the length of the arc it spans is one radian, or about 57.29578 degrees. The ratio of the circumference to the radius of a circle is *pi* (π), and there are exactly 2π radians in the circumference of a circle. There are well-known formulas that let you covert between radians and degrees easily. An angle of π is 180 degrees, one-half of a rotation, so $\pi/2$ is 90 degrees, and $3\pi/2$ is 270 degrees, three-fourths of a rotation. The zero angle, 0π, is the same as 360 degrees, 2π.

The text angle for a font is entered in the *lf.lfOrientation* and *lf.lfEscapment* members of a *LOGFONT* structure. You should make both these members the same. On Windows NT it is possible to specify the members independently by setting the graphics mode to *ADVANCED*, but it doesn't work on Windows 95 and 98. The angle is given in tenths of degrees, so if you want a 45-degree rotation, you put 450 in these members.

The classic example for demonstrating text rotation is to set a string with the first character centered on the screen and then rotate the string around the center, giving you radials of the string. Let's do it a bit differently, using the *SetViewportOrgEx()* and *SetROP2()* along with rotated text to give a spinning effect. You will set the viewport origin to the center of the screen so that you don't even have to do any calculations. Then you will set the drawing mode to *R2_XORPEN* so that you can erase the text on the screen simply by writing it again. The code is listed here:

```c
void DoRotateText (HDC hdc, HWND hWnd)
{
RECT    rcClient;
POINT   ptOrigin;
HFONT   hFont, hOldFont;
LOGFONT lf;
char    *szText = "  Hey! to the world  ";
int     nOldR2;
int     nOldAlign;

    GetClientRect (hWnd, &rcClient);
    SetViewportOrgEx (hdc, rcClient.right / 2,
                         rcClient.bottom / 2, &ptOrigin);
    memset (&lf, '\0', sizeof (LOGFONT));
    lf.lfCharSet = DEFAULT_CHARSET;
    lf.lfClipPrecision = OUT_TT_PRECIS;
    lf.lfQuality = DEFAULT_QUALITY;
    lf.lfPitchAndFamily = DEFAULT_PITCH | FF_ROMAN;
    strcpy (lf.lfFaceName, "Times New Roman Bold");
    lf.lfHeight = 240;
    nOldAlign = SetTextAlign (hdc, TA_CENTER | TA_BOTTOM);
    hOldFont = (HFONT) GetStockObject (SYSTEM_FONT);
    nOldR2 = SetROP2(hdc, R2_XORPEN);
    for (int i = 0; i < 3610; i += 10)
    {
        lf.lfEscapement = i;
        lf.lfOrientation = i;
        lf.lfHeight = 240;
        hFont = CreatePointFontIndirect (&lf, hdc);
        SelectObject (hdc, hFont);
        TextOut (hdc, 0, 0, szText, strlen (szText));
        Sleep (25);
        TextOut (hdc, 0, 0, szText, strlen (szText));
        SelectObject (hdc, hOldFont);
        DeleteObject (hFont);
    }
    SetROP2(hdc, nOldR2);
    SetTextAlign (hdc, nOldAlign);
    SetViewportOrgEx (hdc, ptOrigin.x, ptOrigin.y, NULL);
    SelectObject (hdc, hOldFont);
  DeleteObject (hFont);
}
```

When you run this code, the text "spins" around the center of the screen. You have to create a new font with a new angle each time through the loop, so you destroy the old font just before the loop ends to keep from tying up too many Windows resources.

The *CreatePointFontIndirect()* is your own version of a function to create a font based on a point size, rather than have to calculate the *lfHeight* member of the *LOGFONT* structure.

Well, enough fun. Now let's do something useful, such as labeling the sections on a pie chart. You are going to resurrect your pie chart function from the previous examples. A new version is in the *TEXT* project in the SAMPLES\0482 directory on the companion CD-ROM.

You have two major problems to solve in positioning the text on the pie slices. First, simply rotating the text around the center of the pie works for the right side of the circle, but the text on the left side of the circle will appear upside down, or nearly so, depending on the angle. You have to devise a way to reverse the text output to put it right side up. On a real typesetter, you could just specify a negative point size and adjust your angle, and that's how you would do it if you were writing for real type output. However, that's not possible using the device context in Windows, which uses the sign of the *lfHeight* member of *LOGFONT* to set the origin of the type at the top or bottom of the character cell.

Second, you need to position the text so that it lives midway between the radials of the pie chart sections. In the loop where you figure the points for the pie sections, you can bisect the angle and save it as the text angle. To output the text, you have two choices, each of which has its benefits and disadvantages.

The *DrawText()* function is the easier option, but this means that you have to calculate four points on a rotated rectangle, which could require some involved floating-point calculations. When these are calculated, you can center the text both horizontally and vertically in the rectangle.

The *TextOut()* function, on the other hand, requires that you calculate only the starting point for the text. Because you already know the angle, you need only select a convenient distance from the origin for the text. Unfortunately, with *TextOut()*, you can't center the text on the radial line. For large sections of the pie, the offset would be barely noticeable, but for small slices the error would stand out and perhaps make the text overwrite the radial on the side of the slice. You have to correct the text angle to account for the size of the type.

The correction, it turns out, is simple, so you will use the *TextOut()* function to write your text. Before you draw the pie, you use *GetTextExtentPoint32()* to measure the text in your selected point size. Then use the *y* member of the *SIZE* structure to calculate the sine of the angle subtended by a line of text, and use one-half of that angle as your correction. The angle can be found from the sine, which is the *y* member of the SIZE structure in your function call divided by the radius, which you established based on your window dimensions. You then use the *asin()* function to find the angle and convert it to degrees as required by the *LOGFONT* structure.

To see the results of this code, select Pie Chart from the Text menu in the *TEXT.EXE* program. The code is listed here. I've included one narrow wedge to show you how tightly the text can fit:

```
#define    PI         3.14159

void DoPieChart (HWND hWnd, HDC hdc)
{
RECT    rcClient;
POINT   pOldOrigin;
POINT   ptPoint[6];
SIZE    sizeText;
int nVals[] = {72, 22, 108, 84, 276};
int     nSum, i;
int     nOldBkMode;
HBRUSH  hBrush[5], hOldBrush;
HPEN    hPen, hOldPen;
double  fAngle, fRadius, fTextAngle[5];
```

```c
COLORREF crColors[] = {0x00ffff00, 0x00ff00ff, 0x001111ff,
                       0x0000ffff, 0x0011ff11};
HFONT   hFont, hOldFont;
LOGFONT     lf;
char *szText[] =
    {
    "Widgets",
    "Wombats",
    "Weasels",
    "Wiseguys",
    "Wallabies"
    };

    GetClientRect (hWnd, &rcClient);
    if (rcClient.right > rcClient.bottom)
        fRadius = rcClient.bottom / 3;
    else
        fRadius = rcClient.right / 3;
    fAngle = PI / 4;            // Start at 45 degrees
    hBrush[0] = CreateSolidBrush (0x0);
    SetViewportOrgEx (hdc, rcClient.right / 2 + 6,
                      rcClient.bottom / 2 + 6, &pOldOrigin);
    hOldBrush = (HBRUSH) SelectObject (hdc, hBrush[0]);
    hPen = CreatePen (PS_SOLID, 2, 0);
    hOldPen = (HPEN) SelectObject (hdc, hPen);
//
//  Draw the shadow.
//
    Ellipse (hdc, (int) -fRadius, (int) -fRadius,
                  (int) fRadius, (int) fRadius);
    SelectObject (hdc, hOldBrush);
    DeleteObject (hBrush[0]);
    SetViewportOrgEx (hdc, rcClient.right / 2,
                      rcClient.bottom / 2, NULL);

    memset (&lf, '\0', sizeof (LOGFONT));
    lf.lfCharSet = DEFAULT_CHARSET;
    lf.lfClipPrecision = OUT_TT_PRECIS;
    lf.lfQuality = DEFAULT_QUALITY;
    lf.lfPitchAndFamily = DEFAULT_PITCH | FF_ROMAN;
    strcpy (lf.lfFaceName, "Times New Roman Bold");
    nSum = 0;
    for (i = 0; i < 5; ++i)
    {
        hBrush[i] = CreateSolidBrush (crColors[i]);
        nSum += nVals[i];
    }
    hPen = CreatePen (PS_SOLID, 2, 0);
    hOldPen = (HPEN) SelectObject (hdc, hPen);
    hOldBrush = (HBRUSH) SelectObject (hdc, hBrush[0]);
    lf.lfHeight = 90;
    hFont = CreatePointFontIndirect (&lf, hdc);
    hOldFont = (HFONT) SelectObject (hdc, hFont);
    GetTextExtentPoint32 (hdc, szText[0],
                          strlen (szText[0]), &sizeText);
    SelectObject (hdc, hOldFont);
```

```
DeleteObject (hFont);
double fTextOffset = asin (((double)sizeText.cy )/
                                    fRadius);
fTextOffset *= 10.0 * 57.28578;
for (i = 0; i < 5; ++i)
{
    ptPoint[i].x = (long)(fRadius * cos (fAngle)+0.5);
    ptPoint[i].y = (long)(-fRadius * sin (fAngle)+0.5);
    fTextAngle[i] = fAngle;
    fAngle += (nVals[i] * 2.0 * PI) / nSum;
    fTextAngle[i] += (fAngle - fTextAngle[i]) / 2;
    fTextAngle[i] *= 57.29578;
    fTextAngle[i] *= 10;
    fTextAngle[i] += fTextOffset;
}
ptPoint[5] = ptPoint[0];
for (i = 0; i < 5; ++i)
{
    SelectObject (hdc, hBrush[i]);
    Pie (hdc, (int) -fRadius, (int) -fRadius,
              (int) fRadius, (int) fRadius,
            ptPoint[i].x, ptPoint[i].y,
            ptPoint[i+1].x, ptPoint[i+1].y);
    SelectObject (hdc, hOldBrush);
    DeleteObject (hBrush[i]);
}
nOldBkMode = SetBkMode (hdc, TRANSPARENT);
for (i = 0; i < 5; ++i)
{
    if ((fTextAngle[i] > 899) && (fTextAngle[i] < 2700))
    {
        lf.lfEscapement = (int) fTextAngle[i] + 1800;
        lf.lfOrientation = (int) fTextAngle[i] + 1800;
    }
    else
    {
        lf.lfEscapement = (int) fTextAngle[i];
        lf.lfOrientation = (int) fTextAngle[i];
    }
    lf.lfHeight = 90;
    hFont = CreatePointFontIndirect (&lf, hdc);
    SelectObject (hdc, hFont);
    SIZE size;
    GetTextExtentPoint32 (hdc, szText[i],
                              strlen (szText[i]), &size);
    POINT ptText;
    ptText.x = (long)((fRadius * .9 - size.cx)
                * cos (fTextAngle[i]/572.9578) + 0.5);
    ptText.y = (long)(-(fRadius * .9 - size.cx)
                * sin (fTextAngle[i]/572.9578) + 0.5);
    if ((fTextAngle[i] > 899) && (fTextAngle[i] < 2700))
    {
        SetTextAlign (hdc, TA_RIGHT | TA_BOTTOM);
        TextOut (hdc, ptText.x, ptText.y,
                    szText[i], strlen (szText[i]));
    }
```

```
        else
        {
            SetTextAlign (hdc, TA_LEFT);
            TextOut (hdc, ptText.x, ptText.y,
                        szText[i], strlen (szText[i]));
        }
        SelectObject (hdc, hOldFont);
        DeleteObject (hFont);
    }
    SetBkMode (hdc, nOldBkMode);
    SelectObject (hdc, hOldPen);
    DeleteObject (hPen);
    SetViewportOrgEx(hdc, pOldOrigin.x, pOldOrigin.y, NULL);
}
```

After declaring your variables and constants, you get the client rectangle and set your radius to one-third of the shorter side. This ensures that the pie chart will fit in the window. You then set your viewport to the middle of the screen plus six logical points to the right and down for the shadow. Then you create a black brush and draw the shadow. You then reset the viewport to the center of the screen to make the calculations easier.

Next, you set the constant member of the *LOGFONT* structure. The *lfOrientation* and *lfEscapement* members will hold your angle, and the *lfHeight* will hold the font point size, which will be modified by the *CreatePointFontIndirect()* function (the code for this function is listed later).

After creating a temporary font, you measure the size of one of your strings. The measurement is returned in the *sizeText* variable, which you then use to calculate your text correction angle using the *asin()* function. The statement *fTextOffset *= 10.0 * 57.28578;* converts the angle from radians to tenths of degrees. You use half this angle to correct your text position.

The first *for* loop calculates the points on the circle for the pie slices using trig functions. Then the *for* loop bisects the subtended angle and converts it to degrees, saving the result in the *fTextAngle* array.

The sixth member of the *ptPoint* array is initialized to the first, so your next loop will work correctly. The extra space required for one more member is more than offset by the extra code it would take to reference the first member at the end of the loop.

You now set the pie slices in a *for* loop, selecting the brush for the slice color and deleting it after the slice is drawn. You won't need the brushes again, so here's a good place to delete them.

To set the text, you change the background mode to *TRANSPARENT*. If you didn't, the text would be written in a block using the current brush. This might not be a bad thing and sometimes can produce a pleasing effect. You might try commenting out this line using different brushes for the text background to see the results.

Now the big day has arrived. You set the text on the pie slices in a *for* loop. First, you test the text angle to see whether the direction places it on the left side of the circle. If it does, you spin it around another 180 degrees so that the text is upright; otherwise, you use the text angle as is.

The next few lines create the rotated font and measure the string you are going to set. The reference point to set your string is 9/10ths of the length of a radius minus the string length along the text angle. The resulting point is saved in *ptText*.

If the angle places the text on the left of the circle, you align the text to the right and bottom of the point (remember, the angle at which you created your font is 180 degrees out of phase). If it's on the right side, you align the text to the left and bottom of the point. Safely select the old font and delete the font you just created; you won't need it again, either.

With a few lines of cleanup, you reset your viewport and the pie chart is drawn and labeled.

The *CreatePointFontIndirect()* function is based on the MFC function in the device context classes. It works well if your map mode is *MM_TEXT*, but if you use one of the other modes *and* the viewport origin is not (0,0), the MFC function won't work properly. The function here sets the viewport origin to (0,0) before measuring the font points and then resets it to the original value before returning. I mention this here to remind you to use a viewport origin of (0,0) when using the MFC function in modes other than *MM_TEXT*.

The code for *CreatePointFontIndirect()* and *CreatePointFont()* is shown next. You should place the *HDC* argument at the beginning of the parameter list to be consistent with other device context functions. The MFC classes place it at the end so that it can default to *NULL*. I believe that being consistent with MFC makes it easier to remember.

```
HFONT CreatePointFont (int nPoints, char *szFace, HDC hdc)
{
LOGFONT lf;

    memset (&lf, '\Ø', sizeof (LOGFONT));
    lf.lfCharSet = DEFAULT_CHARSET;
    lf.lfClipPrecision = OUT_TT_PRECIS;
    lf.lfQuality = DEFAULT_QUALITY;
    lf.lfPitchAndFamily = DEFAULT_PITCH | FF_ROMAN;
    lf.lfHeight = nPoints;
    strcpy (lf.lfFaceName, szFace);
    return (CreatePointFontIndirect (&lf, hdc));
}


HFONT CreatePointFontIndirect (LOGFONT *lf, HDC hdc)
{
POINT ptView;

    SetViewportOrgEx (hdc, Ø, Ø, &ptView);
    POINT pt;
    pt.y = ::GetDeviceCaps(hdc, LOGPIXELSY) * lf->lfHeight;
    pt.y /= 720;
    DPtoLP(hdc, &pt, 1);
    POINT ptOrg = {Ø, Ø};
    DPtoLP(hdc, &ptOrg, 1);
    lf->lfHeight = -abs(pt.y - ptOrg.y);
    SetViewportOrgEx (hdc, ptView.x, ptView.y, NULL);
    return (CreateFontIndirect (lf));
}
```

483. *Setting Text and Background Colors*

The Graphics Device Interface provides a single function for setting the color of text, *SetTextColor()*. The function sets only foreground color, that is, the color of the character itself. The background is filled in with the currently selected brush.

The window background itself may be set by calling *SetBkColor()*, but if you want the text background to be a different color from the window background, you create and select a brush of the proper color first.

As with other GDI manipulation functions, *SetTextColor()* returns the old value, so you can use it to restore the previous state. On error, the return value is the constant *CLR_INVALID*.

In the Microsoft Foundation Class, the *CWnd* class handles color differently as you will see in the next tip.

484. *Deriving Classes from* CEdit *and* CStatic *to Set Text Attributes*

Very soon you're going to get into using the Microsoft Foundation Class library, so the samples in this and the next tip will be built using MFC classes. MFC *CEdit* and *CStatic* encapsulate the functions of Windows edit and static text controls. These controls provide rectangular areas where text can be displayed, usually on a dialog box. The edit control may be used to allow the user to enter or modify text.

Both classes are derived from *CWnd*, and the font and point size may be changed by creating the font and calling the *SetFont()* member function of the base class. Neither class, however, has provision for changing the background or text colors, which could be handy in some applications. For example, when you make a *CEdit* window read-only on a dialog box, the background color turns gray. It's easy to confuse it with a static text control, and it sometimes blends into the background.

Both the text and background colors of a dialog box control may be changed using *message reflection*, a feature that was introduced in MFC version 4.0 (the version that comes with Visual C++ 6.0 is version 4.2).

Message reflection works like this: Controls send their parent windows—in the case of a dialog control, the parent is the dialog box window—messages informing the parent that they need something or an action needs to be taken. These messages are *WM_NOTIFY*, and prior to version 4.0 the parent window had to handle the message, by either a base class message handler or one in the derived class.

In the newer versions of MFC, however, the message is *reflected* to the control itself. If the control doesn't handle the message, the parent gets the message back and handles it. This allows certain messages to be handled in the control itself, and if you derived your own classes from the control classes, you can add the *WM_NOTIFY* message handlers.

One of these reflected messages is *WM_CTLCOLOR*, which is reflected back to the control that sent it as *WM_CTLCOLOR_REFLECT*. The *WM_CTLCOLOR* message is a request by the control for the parent window to provide a brush to paint its background. If you set up a message handler in your control class to catch and process this message, you must return a non-*NULL* brush, or the message will be handled by the parent window.

You also can take advantage of this message to set the text color. Just be sure that your message handler returns a non-*NULL* brush.

Let's start out by deriving your own control classes from *CStatic* and *CEdit*. You will use these in the next tip when you create a dialog-based program to view the characters in a font. First, you will need a project. Start the Visual Studio and create a dialog-based project called "Derived" using the following steps:

1. Select New from the File menu, then select the Project tab when the New dialog box appears.

2. From the project list on the left side of the dialog box, select the "MFC AppWizard (exe)" item.

3. In the Location box at the right side of the dialog box, select the directory where you want to place your project.

4. In the Project Name field, enter "Derived." Press the OK button to start the wizard.

5. On Page 1 of the wizard, select "Dialog-based" as the application type.

6. Press the Next button to move to Page 2. On this page, uncheck the About Box item. The wizard doesn't handle About boxes in dialog-based applications very well, and later it would just confuse the ClassWizard. For now, it's best not to use an About box.

7. Press the Next button to move to Page 3. You don't need to change anything on this page, so just press the Next button again to move to Page 4.

8. On Page 4, you can accept the defaults and press the Finish button.

9. When the New Project Information dialog box appears, press the OK button. The AppWizard will respond by creating your project.

Enter the ClassWizard by typing Ctrl+W. You also may select ClassWizard from the View menu. From the ClassWizard dialog box, select the Add Class at the upper right.

When the New Class dialog box appears, enter *CStaticEx* in the Name field. Notice that "staticex.cpp" has appeared in the File Name. You can put this control and the one you will derive from *CEdit* in the same file, but I prefer to have them separate, and I have placed them in the gallery as separate files. That way I only have to add the one I need for the current project.

From the Base Class list (it's a drop-down box), select *CStatic*. Click the OK button; the class will be added and you will return to the Class Wizard. Repeat the process, except this time make the name of the new class *CEditEx* and select *CEdit* as the base class. The default file name will be "editex.cpp." Click the OK button to return to the ClassWizard.

If you look in the Class Name list, you should see *CEditEx* and *CStaticEx*. (If these don't appear, try exiting the Class Wizard and compiling the code.) Select one of these; then, click on the Message Maps tab. Scroll down past the virtual function, and just before the usual list of messages you will see a group of them beginning with an equals sign (*CStaticEx* has only three, but *CEditEx* has quite a few more). These are the messages the control sends to the parent window, and they are reflected back to the control. You may set up your own message handlers for these, but if you don't, the parent window will handle them.

Select *=WM_CTRLCOLOR* and click the Add Function button. Do this for both *CStaticEx* and *CEditEx*. Click OK to exit the ClassWizard. You need to add some member functions and variables, but you can do that from the ClassView pane of the Workspace Window.

On the ClassView pane, right-click the *CEditEx* class and select Add Member Variable. In the dialog box, enter *COLORREF* as the variable type and *m_clrText* as the variable name. Make it a *private* variable. Do the same and add a *COLORREF* variable for *m_clrBkgnd* and a *CBrush*-type variable named *m_brBkgnd*. Add the same three variables to *CStaticEx* by right-clicking on it and then on Add Member Variable.

You need to add four functions to each class as listed here. Add these for both *CStaticEx* and *CEditEx*:

- *COLORREF GetTextColor()*
- *COLORREF GetBackColor()*
- *COLORREF SetTextColor(COLORREF cr)*
- *COLORREF SetBackColor(COLORREF cr)*

To add these functions, right-click on the *CEditEx* class in the ClassView pane just as you did to add variables. Select Add Member Function. Type "COLORREF" in the Function Type box, then the function name in the Function Declaration Box. Leave the access set to "Public" and do not check either the Static or Virtual boxes. Click on the OK button and the ClassWizard will add the function to your class.

Now you add the code. Assuming that you entered the functions and variables in the same order, both *staticex.h* and *editex.h* should be identical except for the class names. You list the header file for *CStaticEx*:

```cpp
#if _MSC_VER > 1000
#pragma once
#endif // _MSC_VER > 1000
// StaticEx.h : header file
//


/////////////////////////////////////////////////////////////////
// CStaticEx window

class CStaticEx : public CStatic
{
// Construction
public:
    CStaticEx();

// Attributes
public:

// Operations
public:

// Overrides
    // ClassWizard generated virtual function overrides
    //{{AFX_VIRTUAL(CStaticEx)
    //}}AFX_VIRTUAL

// Implementation
public:
    virtual ~CStaticEx();

    virtual COLORREF SetBackColor (COLORREF cr);
    virtual COLORREF SetTextColor (COLORREF cr);
    virtual COLORREF GetBackColor ();
    virtual COLORREF GetTextColor ();

    // Generated message map functions
protected:
    //{{AFX_MSG(CStaticEx)
    afx_msg HBRUSH CtlColor(CDC* pDC, UINT nCtlColor);
    //}}AFX_MSG

    COLORREF  m_clrText;
    COLORREF  m_clrBkgnd;
    CBrush    m_brBkgnd;

    DECLARE_MESSAGE_MAP()
};
/////////////////////////////////////////////////////////////////

//{{AFX_INSERT_LOCATION}}
// Microsoft Visual C++ will insert additional declarations
// immediately before the previous line.
```

You should have four functions, one message map entry, and three variables in the class definition.

You now have to enter the code for the functions you added. The dialogs simply set up the functions; they don't write the code for you. The *staticex.cpp* file is listed here. The constructor in *editex.cpp* will be a little different, and I will show it after the following listing:

```cpp
// StaticEx.cpp : implementation file
//

#include "stdafx.h"
#include "StaticEx.h"

#ifdef _DEBUG
#define new DEBUG_NEW
#undef THIS_FILE
static char THIS_FILE[] = __FILE__;
#endif

/////////////////////////////////////////////////////////////////
// CStaticEx

CStaticEx::CStaticEx()
{
    m_clrText = GetSysColor (COLOR_WINDOWTEXT);
    m_clrBkgnd = GetSysColor (COLOR_ACTIVEBORDER);
    m_brBkgnd.CreateSolidBrush (m_clrBkgnd);
}

CStaticEx::~CStaticEx()
{
}

BEGIN_MESSAGE_MAP(CStaticEx, CStatic)
    //{{AFX_MSG_MAP(CStaticEx)
    ON_WM_CTLCOLOR_REFLECT()
    //}}AFX_MSG_MAP
END_MESSAGE_MAP()

/////////////////////////////////////////////////////////////////
// CStaticEx message handlers

HBRUSH CStaticEx::CtlColor(CDC* pDC, UINT nCtlColor)
{
    pDC->SetTextColor (m_clrText);     // text
    pDC->SetBkColor (m_clrBkgnd);      // text bkgnd
    return m_brBkgnd;                  // ctl bkgnd
//  return NULL;        // Be sure to remove this line
}

COLORREF CStaticEx::SetBackColor (COLORREF cr)
{
    COLORREF clrOld = m_clrBkgnd;
    m_clrBkgnd = cr;
    m_brBkgnd.DeleteObject ();
    m_brBkgnd.CreateSolidBrush (m_clrBkgnd);
    Invalidate();
```

```
        return (clrOld);
}

COLORREF CStaticEx::SetTextColor (COLORREF cr)
{
    COLORREF clrOld = m_clrText;
    m_clrText = cr;
    return (clrOld);
}

COLORREF CStaticEx::GetTextColor ()
{
    return (m_clrText);
}

COLORREF CStaticEx::GetBackColor ()
{
    return (m_clrBkgnd);
}
```

The constructor initializes your colors to the current system colors. Obviously, these are not going to be the same for both *CStaticEx* and *CEditEx*, so make the constructor for *CEditEx* read as follows:

```
CEditEx::CEditEx()
{
    m_clrText = GetSysColor (COLOR_WINDOWTEXT);
    m_clrBkgnd = GetSysColor (COLOR_WINDOW);
    m_brBkgnd.CreateSolidBrush (m_clrBkgnd);
}
```

After you finish with these classes, close the editing windows containing the files. Build the project by pressing the F7 key. The project's dialog box should be left on the screen. If it is not, open it by using the following steps:

1. Select the ResourceView pane on the Workspace Window.

2. If the tree on the ResourceView pane is not expanded, expand it now. Click the "+" symbol next to the item labeled "Derived resources." The control should respond by listing three items under the top item.

3. Click on the "+" symbol next to the "Dialog" item. The control should list one item, *IDD_DERIVED_DIALOG* under the "Dialog" item.

4. Double-click on *IDD_DERIVED_DIALOG* to open the dialog box in an editing window.

Draw one or more static and edit text controls on this dialog box. Use the Controls toolbar to select the control type, "Static Text" or "Edit Box," then move the mouse cursor to the dialog box, press and hold the left mouse button, then move the cursor to draw the control in the size you want. Give these controls unique resource IDs by right-clicking on each one. When you right-click on a control, a pop-up menu will appear. Select Properties from this menu to display the control's properties. Enter the unique resource ID in the ID box on this Properties dialog box. Create at least one static text control with the ID of *IDC_STATIC_TEST* and one edit box with the ID of *IDC_EDIT_TEST*.

Start the ClassWizard again and select the Member Variables tab at the top of the ClassWizard dialog box. You should see *IDC_STATIC_TEST* and *IDC_EDIT_TEST* in the list of control IDs. Click on *IDC_EDIT_TEST* to select it, then press the Add Variable button. The Add Member Variable dialog box should appear. On this dialog box, type "m_Edit" in the Member Variable Name box. In the Category box, select Control. In the Variable Type box, select CEditEx. Press the OK button and the ClassWizard will warn you that you need to add the proper header file to the dialog box class's header file. Press the OK button to dispatch the message for now.

Add a member variable for *IDC_STATIC_TEST*, except call the variable *m_Static* and select CStaticEx as the variable type.

Open the dialog class header file *DerivedDlg.h* and put the following lines near the top (just before the class definition is a good place):

```
#include   "staticex.h"
#include   "editex.h"
```

Build the program to make sure there are no errors to this point. Press F7 or select the Build button to build the project.

Assuming that you named the edit control *m_Edit*, you can change the text and background colors of the controls using the following examples:

```
m_Edit.SetTextColor(NewTextColor);
m_Edit.SetBackColor(NewBackgroundColor);
```

In my installation of Visual Studio, I added these control classes to the Gallery. To add them to a project, you select the Project menu, then Add to Project, and Components and Controls and select them from the list.

Changing the control's font and point size requires no extra coding in your derived classes and may be handled entirely from the application using *CWnd* functions. In your application's dialog box class definition, add a private *CFont* data member:

```
CFont   m_Font;
```

Find the *OnInitDialog()* function in the *DerivedDlg.cpp* source file. If the AppWizard did not include this function, add a message handler for the *WM_INITDIALOG* message by selecting the Message Maps tab from ClassWizard. Then select *WM_INITDIALOG* from the Messages list and click Add Function. You set the font and colors in *OnInitDialog()*:

```
BOOL CTestDlg::OnInitDialog()
{
    CDialog::OnInitDialog();
    // TODO: Add extra initialization here
    m_Font.CreatePointFont (120, "Comic Sans MS");
    m_Edit.SetFont (&m_Font);
    m_Edit.SetBackColor (0x00ffff00);
    m_Edit.SetTextColor (0x00ff00ff);
    m_Static.SetBackColor (0x0000ffff);
    m_Static.SetTextColor (0x00c0c0ff);
    return (TRUE);
}
```

This code sets the *m_Edit* control's font to 12-point Comic Sans MS, the background color to cyan, and the text color to magenta. It's a weird-looking edit control, but it stands out. Make sure that you draw your control in the Resource Editor big enough to accept the size of font you are creating.

Build the project again and run the program by pressing F5 or by pressing the Go button on the Build toolbar. Notice the changes to the controls. Try experimenting with the colors and font to see the results.

Also, notice the call to *CDialog::OnInitDialog()* at the very top of your *OnInitDialog()* function. Don't remove this call, and add any initialization *after* this point. This function creates the dialog box and the controls. You can't change the attributes of any of the controls until after the call to *CDialog::OnInitDialog()* because they don't exist yet.

You should also note that the text background color does not have to be the same as the background brush. In your *CtlColor()* function, you specifically set the text background to be the same as the brush color, but you could just as easily have used a different color. In an edit control, having the text color different from the control's background makes a strange-looking control. However, you might find this fact handy when you derive classes to modify the behavior of other controls. To do this, you might add another variable, *m_TextBackColor*, and another function, *SetTextBackColor()*, to handle a separate color.

485. A GDI Example: Drawing a Character Map

Nearly every Windows programming book has some sample program to show you different fonts. Typically, the sample lists a line of text in the various fonts on your computer, or you can select one for display.

Your entry is the *FONTVIEW.EXE* program contained in the *0485* subdirectory on the CD-ROM. After more than 35 years in the newspaper business, about half of that dealing with computers, I'm not particularly interested in the *appearance* of fonts. Over the years I've seen most of them at one time or another and can well distinguish one font from another. My concern, and yours as a Windows programmer, is with the *metrics* of fonts, and that's the center of focus for *FONTVIEW*. The *FontView* program is a dialog-based project. The dialog box is shown in Figure 485.

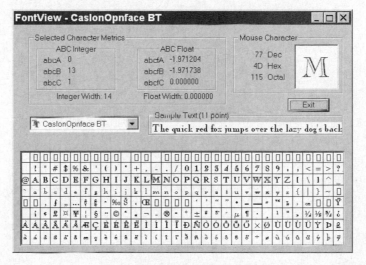

Figure 485   The FontView window

The dialog box is pretty busy, but it does give you a lot of information about the characters in a font. It also demonstrates a number of aspects of Windows programming—using the GDI to intermix fonts and drawing functions, sending messages from a control window to the parent window, using different fonts on a single dialog box, and using a callback function to enumerate the available fonts. It also uses the new extended combo box, which is one of the few good things to come out of Microsoft's obsession with the Internet.

You start with a simple dialog-based application. Create a new project as you did in the last tip, but name your dialog window class *CFontViewDlg*. The code for this project is on the companion CD-ROM. There are several new items in this project that you might not be familiar with right now. such as image lists and the extended combobox. As you progress through this book, you will learn about each of these.

During creation, you resize the static control to fit the space at the bottom of the window, taking care that the dimensions match an integral multiple of the width and height of the individual cells that will hold the characters.

```cpp
// FontViewDlg.cpp : implementation file
//

#include "stdafx.h"
#include "FontView.h"
#include "FontViewDlg.h"

#ifdef _DEBUG
#define new DEBUG_NEW
#undef THIS_FILE
static char THIS_FILE[] = __FILE__;
#endif

struct FONTDATA
    {
    CString        strFont;
    CComboBoxEx*   FontBox;
    };

/////////////////////////////////////////////////////////////
// CFontViewDlg dialog

CFontViewDlg::CFontViewDlg(CWnd* pParent /*=NULL*/)
    : CDialog(CFontViewDlg::IDD, pParent)
{
    //{{AFX_DATA_INIT(CFontViewDlg)
    m_FontViewChar = _T("");
    m_FontList = _T("");
    m_MouseDecimal = _T("");
    m_MouseHex = _T("");
    m_MouseOctal = _T("");
    m_AbcA = _T("");
    m_AbcB = _T("");
    m_AbcC = _T("");
    m_AbcfA = _T("");
    m_AbcfB = _T("");
    m_AbcfC = _T("");
    m_FloatWidth = _T("");
    m_IntWidth = _T("");
    //}}AFX_DATA_INIT
    m_strFont = _T("Times New Roman");
    m_Title.Empty ();
    m_chCurrent = 0;
}

CFontViewDlg::~CFontViewDlg()
{
}

void CFontViewDlg::DoDataExchange(CDataExchange* pDX)
{
    CDialog::DoDataExchange(pDX);
```

```
    //{{AFX_DATA_MAP(CFontViewDlg)
    DDX_Control(pDX, IDC_STATIC_SAMPLETEXT, m_SampleText);
    DDX_Control(pDX, IDC_COMBO_FONTS, m_FontBox);
    DDX_Control(pDX, IDC_EDIT_FONTVIEW, m_FontView);
    DDX_Control(pDX, IDC_STATIC_FONTVIEWCHAR,m_MouseSelWin);
    DDX_Text(pDX, IDC_STATIC_FONTVIEWCHAR, m_FontViewChar);
    DDX_CBString(pDX, IDC_COMBO_FONTS, m_FontList);
    DDX_Text(pDX, IDC_STATIC_MOUSEDECIMAL, m_MouseDecimal);
    DDX_Text(pDX, IDC_STATIC_MOUSEHEX, m_MouseHex);
    DDX_Text(pDX, IDC_STATIC_MOUSEOCTAL, m_MouseOctal);
    DDX_Text(pDX, IDC_METRIC_ABCA, m_AbcA);
    DDX_Text(pDX, IDC_METRIC_ABCB, m_AbcB);
    DDX_Text(pDX, IDC_METRIC_ABCC, m_AbcC);
    DDX_Text(pDX, IDC_METRIC_ABCFA, m_AbcfA);
    DDX_Text(pDX, IDC_METRIC_ABCFB, m_AbcfB);
    DDX_Text(pDX, IDC_METRIC_ABCFC, m_AbcfC);
    DDX_Text(pDX, IDC_METRIC_FLOATWIDTH, m_FloatWidth);
    DDX_Text(pDX, IDC_METRIC_INTEGERWIDTH, m_IntWidth);
    //}}AFX_DATA_MAP
}


BEGIN_MESSAGE_MAP(CFontViewDlg, CDialog)
    //{{AFX_MSG_MAP(CFontViewDlg)
    ON_WM_LBUTTONDOWN()
    ON_WM_MOUSEMOVE()
    ON_CBN_SELCHANGE(IDC_COMBO_FONTS, OnSelchangeComboFonts)
    //}}AFX_MSG_MAP
    ON_MESSAGE(WM_USER+40, OnUser)
END_MESSAGE_MAP()


/////////////////////////////////////////////////////////
// CFontViewDlg message handlers

BOOL CFontViewDlg::OnInitDialog()
{
    CDialog::OnInitDialog();
    CClientDC dc (this);
//
//  Set up the image list
    m_pImages.Create (16, 16, ILC_COLOR, 2, 2);
    HICON hIcon = AfxGetApp()->LoadIcon (IDI_ICON_TRUETYPE);
    m_pImages.Add (hIcon);
    hIcon = AfxGetApp()->LoadIcon (IDI_ICON_BITFONT);
    m_pImages.Add (hIcon);
    m_FontBox.SetImageList (&m_pImages);

    FONTDATA fd;
    fd.FontBox = &m_FontBox;
    fd.strFont = m_strFont;
    ::EnumFontFamilies ((HDC) dc, NULL,
                        (FONTENUMPROC) AddFontName,
                        (LPARAM) &fd);

    m_MouseSelWin.SetBkgndColor (0x00ffffff);
    GetWindowText (m_Title);
    RECT rcFontView = {0, 0, 0, 0};
```

```cpp
        RECT rcClient = {0, 0, 0, 0};
        CWnd *cwFontView;
        if ((cwFontView = GetDlgItem(IDC_EDIT_FONTVIEW))!= NULL)
        {

            cwFontView->GetWindowRect(&rcFontView);
        }
        GetClientRect (&rcClient);
        m_FontView.SetWindowRect (rcClient, rcFontView);
        m_FontView.SetBkgndColor (0x00ffffff);
        m_SampleText.SetWindowText(_T("The quick red fox jumps"
                                      " over the lazy dog's "
                                      "back. RY testing"));
        SetFont (m_strFont);
        return (TRUE);
}

void CFontViewDlg::SetCurrentSel (UINT sel)
{
    m_FontView.SetCharSelection(sel);
}

void CFontViewDlg::SetMouseChar(UINT ch)
{
    if (!ch)
    {
        m_FontViewChar.Empty ();
    }
    else
    {
        m_MouseOctal.Format ("%o", ch);
        m_MouseDecimal.Format ("%d", ch);
        m_MouseHex.Format ("%X", ch);
        m_FontViewChar = ch;
        if (ch == '&')
            m_FontViewChar += ch;
    }
    UpdateData (false);
}

void CFontViewDlg::OnLButtonDown(UINT nFlags, CPoint point)
{
RECT    r;
POINT   ptPoint;

    m_FontView.GetWindowRect (&r);
    ptPoint.x = point.x;
    ptPoint.y = point.y;
    ClientToScreen(&ptPoint);
    CPoint vPoint (ptPoint);
    ptPoint.x -= r.left;
    ptPoint.y -= r.top;
    CPoint clientPoint (ptPoint);
    CRect cr (r);
    if (cr.PtInRect (vPoint))
        m_FontView.OnLButtonDown (nFlags, clientPoint);
```

```
        else
            CDialog::OnLButtonDown(nFlags, point);
}

void CFontViewDlg::OnMouseMove(UINT nFlags, CPoint point)
{
RECT    r;
POINT   ptPoint;

    m_FontView.GetWindowRect (&r);
    ptPoint.x = point.x;
    ptPoint.y = point.y;
    ClientToScreen(&ptPoint);
    CPoint vPoint (ptPoint);
    ptPoint.x -= r.left;
    ptPoint.y -= r.top;
    CPoint clientPoint (ptPoint);
    CRect cr (r);
    if (cr.PtInRect (vPoint))
        m_FontView.OnMouseMove (nFlags, clientPoint);
    else
    {
        m_FontViewChar = '\0';
        UpdateData (false);
        m_FontView.m_uiMouseSelection = 0;
        CDialog::OnMouseMove(nFlags, point);
    }
}

void CFontViewDlg::SetFont(CString &strFont)
{
    m_fontMouse.DeleteObject ();
    m_fontMouse.CreatePointFont (300, strFont);
    m_fontSample.DeleteObject ();
    m_fontSample.CreatePointFont (110, strFont);
    m_MouseSelWin.SetFont (&m_fontMouse, true);
    m_SampleText.SetFont (&m_fontSample, true);
    CString Title = m_Title + " - " + strFont;
    SetWindowText (Title);
    m_FontView.SetFont (strFont);
    OnUser ((WPARAM) WM_USER+41, (LPARAM) m_chCurrent);
}

void CFontViewDlg::OnUser (WPARAM wparam, LPARAM lparam)
{
    switch (wparam)
    {
        case WM_USER + 40:
            m_FontViewChar = (char) lparam;
            SetMouseChar (lparam);
            UpdateData (false);
            m_MouseSelWin.Invalidate ();
            break;
        case WM_USER + 41:
            if (!lparam)
                break;
```

```
            m_AbcA.Format ("%d",
                        m_FontView.m_abc[lparam].abcA);
            m_AbcB.Format ("%d",
                        m_FontView.m_abc[lparam].abcB);
            m_AbcC.Format ("%d",
                        m_FontView.m_abc[lparam].abcC);
            m_AbcfA.Format ("%f",
                        m_FontView.m_abcf[lparam].abcfA);
            m_AbcfB.Format ("%f",
                        m_FontView.m_abcf[lparam].abcfB);
            m_AbcfC.Format ("%f",
                        m_FontView.m_abcf[lparam].abcfC);
            m_FloatWidth.Format ("Float Width: %f",
                        m_FontView.m_fWidths[lparam]);
            m_IntWidth.Format ("Integer Width: %d",
                        m_FontView.m_nWidths[lparam]);
            UpdateData (false);
            break;
        }
}

 int CALLBACK CFontViewDlg::AddFontName (
                        ENUMLOGFONT *lpelfe,
                        NEWTEXTMETRIC *lpntme,
                        int FontType, LPARAM lParam)

{
static int nItem = 0;

    FONTDATA *fd = (FONTDATA *) lParam;
    CComboBoxEx *FontBox = fd->FontBox;
    COMBOBOXEXITEM cbi;
    memset (&cbi, '\0', sizeof (COMBOBOXEXITEM));
    cbi.iItem = nItem++;
    cbi.mask = CBEIF_IMAGE | CBEIF_TEXT
            | CBEIF_SELECTEDIMAGE;
    switch (FontType)
    {
        case TRUETYPE_FONTTYPE:
            cbi.iImage = 0;
            cbi.iSelectedImage = 0;
            break;
        default:
            cbi.iImage = 1;
            cbi.iSelectedImage = 1;
            break;
    }
    cbi.pszText = lpelfe->elfLogFont.lfFaceName;
    FontBox->InsertItem (&cbi);
    if (fd->strFont == lpelfe->elfLogFont.lfFaceName)
        FontBox->SetCurSel (nItem - 1);
    return (TRUE);
}

void CFontViewDlg::OnSelchangeComboFonts()
{
    CString strNewFont;
```

```
    int nIndex = m_FontBox.GetCurSel ();
    m_FontBox.GetLBText (nIndex, strNewFont);
    if (strNewFont == m_strFont)
        return;
    m_strFont = strNewFont;
    SetFont (strNewFont);
    PrevDlgCtrl();
}
```

In the *OnInitDialog()* function, you let the framework create the dialog box for you. Generally, don't try to modify any controls or initialize any display on the dialog box until the *CDialog::OnInitDialog()* function completes. The controls simply don't exist until this function creates them. Next, load a couple of icons that you prepared to represent TrueType and other fonts in the combo box. The icons are added to a *CImageList* object, which is then assigned to the combo box.

The structure passed to *:EnumFontFamilies()* contains the address of your combo box, so you may add the font name to it and the name of your current font, which will be selected when the combo box first appears. You could have made these global variables, but encapsulating them into a structure allows you to pass them both in the function call and still hide them from the outside world.

Next, you retrieve the main window title; you will use it to add the selected font name as different fonts are selected.

The next few lines set the stage to resize the static control in which you will display the individual characters. The control will resize itself the first time its *OnPaint()* member function is called, so you set the initial size of 0 in both dimensions. You have to get the position of the control here because the control can't find itself in the client area.

The *SetMouseChar()* function sets the large character in the mouse window at the upper right and modifies the decimal, octal, and hex values displayed next to it. Notice that if the character is an ampersand (&), you put another ampersand after it. The *DrawText()* function Windows uses to draw the controls interprets an ampersand as an escape character and draws a line under the next character. If the next character is an ampersand, it draws the ampersand without an underline.

The *OnLButtonDown()* message handler gets the window of the font view control, maps it to the screen, and then tests whether the mouse button was clicked in the control itself. If so, it passes the click event to the font view window so that it can draw a rectangle around the selected character. Otherwise, the function defaults to the *CDialog* message handler.

The *OnMouseMove()* handler does the same thing for mouse movements except that simply defaulting to the *CDialog* handler, it clears the mouse character window if the point is outside the font view window.

SetFont() reuses your *CFont* objects to display the characters in the newly selected font. The character under the mouse window is 30 points and the sample text window is 11 points. You prepare and set the new fonts and then adjust your window title to reflect the current font.

The *OnUser()* message handler intercepts the user message sent from the font view window. In *OnLButtonDown()*, we didn't even try to determine which character in the font view window was clicked. The click might not even have occurred in the control. Instead, you pass the point of the click on to the control and let it determine which character was selected. It needs that information anyway. After it has determined the character, the control sends it back to the dialog box using a *WM_USER* message. You use the character to get the font metric data (also kept by the control because it needs portions of it to display the characters in the correct place) and display the values on the screen. As a programmer, I am concerned with the integral widths of the characters for display purposes. As one who deals with type, I am concerned with the *float* widths because that's how you calculate text positions on real typesetters. The *float* widths weren't available on older versions of Windows. (If you're running Windows 95, the *float* values might always show 0.)

The two remaining functions handle the extended combo box. The *AddFontName()* function is the call-back function you pass to *::EnumFontFamilies()* in the *OnInitDialog()* function. Each time Windows gets a font name, it calls you back through this function. A callback function must be a static member function or declared in global space. In either case, it doesn't have access to the combo box control or the selected font name. That's why you passed them in the *FONTDATA* structure, which Windows also gives you in the *lParam* argument. You cast that back to a *FONTDATA* pointer, and you have access to the member variables. I discuss setting the combo box data in Tip 861, "Adding Items to an Extended Combo Box."

Finally, when the user changes the selection in the combo box, you have Windows notify you through this message handler. You get the new font name; if it's the same as the old one, you do nothing. Otherwise, you set the new font. The *PrevDlgCtrl()* call is a little trick to keep the combo box text from always being highlighted. It's the only user-modifiable control on the dialog box, so the focus never leaves it until the Exit button is clicked. You don't really want that because it's easier to read the text on a white background. This function shifts the focus back to the previous control on the dialog box.

Now you look at the *CFontView* class, the one you derived from the control class to perform the actual drawing of the font character in the font view window. The *OnPaint()* message handler is the primary concern here, and that's where most of the action takes place.

```cpp
// FontWindow.cpp : implementation file
//

#include "stdafx.h"
#include "FontView.h"
#include "FontWindow.h"

#ifdef _DEBUG
#define new DEBUG_NEW
#undef THIS_FILE
static char THIS_FILE[] = __FILE__;
#endif

/////////////////////////////////////////////////////////////////
// CFontWindow

CFontWindow::CFontWindow()
{
    memset ((char *) m_abc, '\0', 256 * sizeof (ABC));
    memset ((char *) m_abcf, '\0', 256 * sizeof (ABCFLOAT));
    memset ((char *) m_nWidths, '\0', 256 * sizeof (int));
    memset ((char *) m_fWidths, '\0', 256 * sizeof (float));
    memset ((char *) &m_TM, '\0', sizeof (TEXTMETRIC));
    memset ((char *) &m_rcSelect, '\0', sizeof (RECT));
    m_uiSelection = 0;
    m_uiMouseSelection = 0;
}

CFontWindow::~CFontWindow()
{
}


BEGIN_MESSAGE_MAP(CFontWindow, CStaticEx)
    //{{AFX_MSG_MAP(CFontWindow)
    ON_WM_PAINT()
```

```
    //}}AFX_MSG_MAP
END_MESSAGE_MAP()

///////////////////////////////////////////////////////////
// CFontWindow message handlers

void CFontWindow::OnPaint()
{
int nWidth, nCellWidth;
int nHeight, nCellHeight;
int     i, j;

    CPaintDC dc(this); // device context for painting
    dc.SelectObject (&m_Font);
    if (m_rcPosition.right == 0)
    {
        nWidth = m_rcClient.right - m_rcClient.left - 20;
        nWidth -= nWidth % 32;
        m_rcPosition.left = (m_rcClient.right - nWidth) / 2;
        m_rcPosition.right = m_rcPosition.left + nWidth;
        m_rcPosition.top = m_rcOriginal.top;
        m_rcPosition.bottom = m_rcClient.bottom - 10;
        m_rcPosition.bottom -= (m_rcPosition.bottom-14) % 8;
        MoveWindow (&m_rcPosition, FALSE);
    }
    nWidth = m_rcPosition.right - m_rcPosition.left;
    nCellWidth = nWidth / 32 - 2;
    nHeight = m_rcPosition.bottom - m_rcPosition.top;
    nCellHeight = nHeight / 8 - 2;

    CBrush blackBrush ((COLORREF) 0x00000000);
    CBrush whiteBrush ((COLORREF) 0x00ffffff);
    CPen blackPen;
    blackPen.CreatePen(PS_SOLID, 2, RGB(0x00,0x00,0x00));
    dc.SelectObject (blackPen);
    dc.Rectangle (0, 0, nWidth, nHeight);
    for (j = 0; j < 8; ++j)
    {
        for (i = 0; i < 32; ++i)
        {
            if (!(i + j))
                continue;
            RECT rcChar;
            char ch = i + j * 32;
            rcChar.top = 2 + j * (nCellHeight + 2);
            rcChar.bottom = rcChar.top + nCellHeight;
            rcChar.left = i * (nCellWidth + 2);
            rcChar.right = rcChar.left + nCellWidth;
            dc.DrawText (&ch, 1, &rcChar,
                    DT_VCENTER | DT_CENTER | DT_NOPREFIX);
        }
    }
    RECT rc = {0, 0, nWidth, nHeight};
    dc.DrawEdge (&rc, EDGE_SUNKEN, BF_TOPLEFT);
    dc.DrawEdge (&rc, EDGE_ETCHED, BF_BOTTOMRIGHT);
    blackPen.DeleteObject ();
```

```
        blackPen.CreatePen (PS_SOLID, 1, RGB(0x00, 0x00, 0x00));
        dc.SelectObject (blackPen);
        for (i = 1; i < 32; ++i)
        {
            POINT ptTop = {(2 + nCellWidth) * i - 2, 1};
            POINT ptBottom = {ptTop.x, nHeight - 1};
            dc.MoveTo (ptTop);
            dc.LineTo (ptBottom);
        }
        for (i = 1; i < 8; ++i)
        {
            POINT ptLeft = {1, (2 + nCellHeight) * i - 1};
            POINT ptRight = {nWidth - 1, ptLeft.y};
            dc.MoveTo (ptLeft);
            dc.LineTo (ptRight);
        }
        HighlightSelection ((CWindowDC *) &dc);
}

void CFontWindow::HighlightSelection(CWindowDC* dc)
{
RECT    r, rc;
CPoint  Boundary[5];

        CWindowDC *pDC;
        if (dc == NULL)
            pDC = new CWindowDC (this);
        else
            pDC = dc;
        rc.left = 0;
        rc.right = m_rcPosition.right - m_rcPosition.left;
        rc.top = 0;
        rc.bottom = m_rcPosition.bottom - m_rcPosition.top;
        r = rc;

        int iPenWidth = 2;
        CPen blackPen;
        blackPen.CreatePen (PS_SOLID | PS_GEOMETRIC, 2,
                        RGB(0x00, 0x00, 0xff));
        dc->SelectObject (&blackPen);
        CBrush blackBrush ((COLORREF) 0x00ff0000);
        dc->SelectObject (&blackBrush);
        int iInterval = (r.right) / 31;
        int jInterval = (r.bottom) / 8;
        int iObjectX = m_uiSelection % 32;
        int iObjectY = m_uiSelection / 32;
        int Left = iInterval * iObjectX - 1;
        int Top = jInterval * iObjectY - 1;

        m_rcSelect.left = Left;
        m_rcSelect.right = Left + iInterval;
        m_rcSelect.top = Top;
        m_rcSelect.bottom = Top + jInterval;

        Boundary[0].x = m_rcSelect.left + 1;
        Boundary[0].y = m_rcSelect.top + 1;
```

```
        Boundary[1].x = m_rcSelect.right;
        Boundary[1].y = m_rcSelect.top;
        Boundary[2].x = m_rcSelect.right;
        Boundary[2].y = m_rcSelect.bottom;
        Boundary[3].x = m_rcSelect.left;
        Boundary[3].y = m_rcSelect.bottom;
        Boundary[4] = Boundary[0];
        dc->Polyline (Boundary, 5);
        if (dc == NULL)
            delete pDC;
}

void CFontWindow::SetFont(CString &FontName)
{
    m_Font.DeleteObject ();
    m_Font.CreatePointFont (85, FontName);
    Invalidate ();
    CWindowDC dc(this);
    dc.SelectObject (&m_Font);
    GetTextMetrics (dc.GetSafeHdc (), &m_TM);
    dc.GetCharWidth (0, 255, m_nWidths);
    dc.GetCharWidth (0, 255, m_fWidths);
    dc.GetCharABCWidths (0, 255, m_abc);
    dc.GetCharABCWidths (0, 255, m_abcf);
}

void CFontWindow::SetCharSelection(UINT sel)
{
    m_uiSelection = sel;
    Invalidate ();
}

void CFontWindow::OnLButtonDown(UINT nFlags, CPoint point)
{
RECT    r;
int     x, y, sel;

    r = m_rcPosition;
    int iInterval = (r.right - r.left) / 31;
    int yInterval = (r.bottom - r.top) / 8;
    x = point.x / iInterval;
    y = point.y / yInterval;
    sel = 0;
    for (int i = 0; i < y; ++ i)
        sel += 32;
    sel += x;
    if (!sel)
        return;
    SetCharSelection (sel);
    ::SendMessage (GetParent()->m_hWnd, WM_USER+40,
                (WPARAM) (WM_USER+41), (LPARAM) sel);
    CStatic::OnLButtonDown(nFlags, point);
}

void CFontWindow::OnMouseMove(UINT nFlags, CPoint point)
{
```

```
RECT    r;
int     x, y;
UINT    sel;

    GetClientRect (&r);
    int iInterval = (r.right) / 31;
    int yInterval = (r.bottom) / 8;
    x = point.x / iInterval;
    y = point.y / yInterval;
    sel = 0;
    for (int i = 0; i < y; ++ i)
        sel += 32;
    sel += x;
    if (m_uiMouseSelection != sel)
    {
        m_uiMouseSelection = sel;
        ::SendMessage (GetParent()->m_hWnd, WM_USER+40,
                        (WPARAM) (WM_USER+40), (LPARAM) sel);
    }
    else
        CStaticEx::OnMouseMove(nFlags, point);
}

void CFontWindow::SetWindowRect(RECT &rcClient, RECT &rcFontView)
{
    m_rcClient = rcClient;
    m_rcOriginal = rcFontView;
    m_rcPosition.top = 0;
    m_rcPosition.left = 0;
    m_rcPosition.bottom = 0;
    m_rcPosition.right = 0;
}
```

If the control's window hasn't been resized yet (the *right* member of the rectangle is 0), the first call to *OnPaint()* will resize it to fit the window. The width is calculated so that 10 logical points exist between the control window and the right and left sides of the dialog box. Then you subtract the result of a modulo 32 division to make sure that the width is evenly divisible by 32, the number of character cells across the window. You then subtract half of the resulting width from the width of the dialog box and set your left side to that value (the coordinates are relative to the dialog box's client area). Then add the width and the left margin to get the right side. The top and bottom are figured in much the same way. You start out with the original position of the control (if you look at it in the dialog editor, you will see that we weren't concerned with the original size but positioned it so that the top was correct). Then you figure how deep it has to be to hold 8 character cells and put the bottom there, allowing at least 10 logical points for a bottom margin.

You figure the width and height of a character cell, allowing two points for the pen width. That describes the area in which the character will be drawn after adding the values to a rectangle. First, you draw a rectangle around the control. That fills the area with your default color, which in the *CStaticEx* control is white. The first loop draws the characters themselves, adjusting the rectangle each time around. You use *DrawText()* because you can center the character vertically and horizontally in the rectangle, but you also specify the *DT_NOPREFIX* style to keep the function from converting the ampersand character.

With that done, draw the edge so that it appears slightly sunken in the dialog box. Then you draw the horizontal and vertical lines that define the character cells. You highlight the selection, if any, and you're done with the *OnPaint()* call.

The *HighlightSelection()* function draws a rectangle around the selected area using the *PolyLine()* function so that you don't overwrite the character itself.

SetFont() deletes any old font and creates a new one. It then invalidates the control window, so Windows will call you with a *WM_PAINT* message. Then you get the text metrics that are used to display information about the selected character.

The *OnLButtonDown()* function is never called by Windows because you don't have an entry for it in the message map. You named it such to remind you that it performs the same function as a message handler, but it's called only from the parent dialog box. The function calculates the selected character from the *point* argument and then sends a message back to the parent dialog box informing it of the character.

OnMouseMove() does the same thing, calculating the character under the cursor, and then sends a message back to the parent.

This dialog box originally was part of another program that is used to prepare width and recode tables for translation of text between a screen display (the *softsetter*) and an output device (the *typesetter*). It has seen a lot of use in that capacity, and you might find some remnants of that code left over from the conversion to a stand-alone program. They obviously aren't doing any harm, but you can remove them if you want. The code has served me well, and I fully expect you to morph this program into something *you* can use.

486. *Understanding Class Libraries*

A *class library* is a collection of C++ classes designed to implement a particular task. Usually, they encapsulate the objects and code that are particular to the task at hand.

The Microsoft Foundation Class library is an example of a class library that was designed to program for Windows. Among its classes you find the code to create windows, classes for device contexts, and other objects peculiar to Windows. In your non-MFC applications from earlier tips, you had to go through the process of registering your window classes and creating the windows in your own code. This is all encapsulated in the MFC functions.

A class library can make some programming tasks much easier, but an extensive library such as MFC can require much additional learning. If you've mastered your basic Windows applications and the use of the device context, you should have no problems learning MFC; many of the encapsulated functions have the same names as the API functions.

MFC is not the only Windows-based class library. A number are available. Some are free by downloading them on the World Wide Web, and others are provided as part of integrated development environments. Borland's Object Windows Library (OWL), for example, is an excellent class library that goes several steps further than MFC but is available only with the Borland IDE.

Class libraries don't have to be all-encompassing. Remember, they are designed to facilitate the task at hand. In the case of MFC and OWL, that means programming Windows applications. You can build your own class libraries using Visual C++ (or even Visual Basic) to meet particular needs.

Typically, class libraries are contained in a dynamic link library (DLL), which holds the implementation code for the library. Thus, you don't have to compile an entire library to use it; you just load the dynamic link library when you run your program. In most extensive Windows class libraries such as MFC and OWL, even that code is encapsulated in the library.

487. *Building a Program Using a Class Library*

Most comprehensive Windows programming class libraries typically contain an application class from which you derive your own application. In MFC, it's *CWinApp*. Normally, the application class is intended for use as a base class, and you don't create class objects from it directly. Instead, you derive your own class from it containing code specific to your application and inherit the properties and functions of the application class.

The Visual Studio has application wizards that prepare a lot of basic code for you. You used them in some of the previous samples, including the *FontView* program in Tip 485, "A GDI Example: Drawing a Character Map," which was built using MFC. The MFC AppWizard in Visual Studio will prepare a *CApplication*-derived class that basically starts your program. From there it creates the document/view architecture (more on this later) if you so choose, or a beginning dialog class if you elect to build a dialog-based application, as was the case with *FontView*.

Not all programs can benefit from a class library. For one, the class library approach locks you into a particular architecture that might not be appropriate for your needs, and the coding around it might be more difficult than not using a class library. Or, you might choose to use a class library for a portion of your project and strike out on your own when your particular needs differ from the approach taken in the library. Just because there's a dialog class in a library doesn't mean that you *have* to use it.

488. *Introducing the Microsoft Foundation Class Library*

The Microsoft Foundation Class is Microsoft's offering of a class library for programming for Windows in C++. The library contains about 200 classes, many of which you may use directly, but some are abstract classes intended to serve only as base classes.

Some of these classes are utility classes intended to make programming simpler. The *CString* class, for example, has no base class and encapsulates many of the string-handling capabilities of BASIC. It may even include embedded NUL characters, making it useful for building file filters and such.

Others are simple types. The *CRect* class very closely resembles the *RECT* structure and, in fact, may be cast to type *RECT* for calling API functions that don't recognize MFC objects.

The device context (DC) is one of the primary concepts of Windows programming, and MFC encapsulates the DC in several ways, including a *CPaintDC* class intended to be used when Windows sends a *WM_PAINT* message. In many cases, the device context is transparent to you, and the MFC classes take care of many of the details.

The *CWnd* class encapsulates the functionality of a window, and you don't have to worry about setting up a *WNDCLASS* structure and registering the window class. You don't have to create it, either, with the lengthy *CreateWindow()* function call. All you need to do after declaring an object of *CWnd* or one of its descendent classes is to call the *ShowWindow()* member function. In some cases, such as in the *CDialog* class, even that is handled for you.

If you mastered programming in the Windows API, MFC *eventually* will come easily to you. I stress "eventually" because there is a learning process and you will have to become familiar with some new terms and concepts.

489. *How MFC Is Implemented in Visual Studio*

The Visual Studio includes wizards for creating applications using the Microsoft Foundation Class. You will look at the wizards and their options for doing that in the next tip.

When you create an MFC-based application, normally the application loads MFC as a dynamic link library. The Visual Studio comes with four versions of the DLL. There's the standard *MFC42.DLL* and its debug version, *MFC42D.DLL*. There also are Unicode versions, *MFC42U.DLL* and *MFC42UD.DLL*. You find these in the Windows System or System32 directory, depending on the version of Windows you are running.

If you purchased the professional or enterprise editions of Visual C++, the Developers Studio also includes a static link library for MFC. The static linking process embeds the necessary MFC code into the application's runtime module, and thus, you don't have to worry about installing the proper version of a dynamic link library. Static linking is handy in a number of cases, such as a Windows NT service program or any other program where you don't want to create a setup program.

If you are using the standard or learning edition of Visual C++, you don't have the option of using the static library.

For applications that you write, the MFC code is *redistributable*, meaning that you may include it in your setup programs without having to pay a royalty fee to Microsoft. The terms of redistribution are in your license agreement.

> *Note:* I should point out that there is a C runtime library, MSVCRTXX.DLL—the XX indicates the revision level—that you may have to distribute with your code. This library also has redistribution rights, which are spelled out in your license agreement. Several versions of it might already be installed in your Windows System or System32 directory from other applications.

In the following tips, I'll discuss the general classifications of MFC classes and after that get down to specifics with some examples. Understanding how some of the classes are implemented in an application requires at least an exposure to other groups of classes. For example, in discussing shared memory files, you should have some notion of how the synchronization classes work.

490. *Invoking the Visual Studio Wizard to Create an MFC-Based Program*

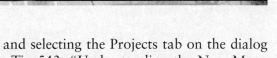

You create a project by selecting New from the Files menu and selecting the Projects tab on the dialog box. I'll go over the various options for this dialog box in Tip 543, "Understanding the New Menu Command," but for now you are concerned with creating a project.

If you have a project open in the Visual Studio, close it by selecting Close Workspace from the Files menu. Next, select the New item on the Files menu to summon the dialog box. With no workspace open, it should appear with the Projects tab selected.

Select the project type you want to create. The options depend on the Visual Studio edition you are using and the options you chose when you installed it. They all should have MFC AppWizard (exe), so select that type now.

To the right of the dialog box are several controls where you specify how to create your project. The first is the Project Name box, which the wizard uses to create the executable file name for your program. Just below it is the Location box, and just to the right of that is a button labeled with an asterisk. The path you enter here is the directory in which your project will be created. If it doesn't exist, the appropriate directories will be created for you.

It's generally easier to specify the location before naming the project. When you enter the project name, the studio adds it to the path name. If you've already specified a base path, the resulting path name will be ready for you. If you enter the project name first, you might need to edit the path name before creating the project. By default, Visual Studio enters the last path you used in this field, but you can select another by clicking the button to the right. This brings up a "Choose Directory" prompt (this dialog is not available in the current selection of common dialogs, but later I'll show you how to build one that looks similar to this).

With no workspace open, the Create New Workspace will be checked, and the Add to Current Workspace will be disabled. You have no other choice right now.

Finally, at the bottom right is a list of platforms. Visual C++ 6.0 does not support 16-bit Windows applications, so the only choice you should have is Win32, and that option should be checked. You can uncheck it, but you can't go any further until you check it again.

After you've entered all the required data, click the OK button to start the wizard. The first page allows you to select single- or multiple-document support (I'll cover these later). It's easier if you select the proper one now, but you can convert later (it does take some work). You also may select a dialog-based application, in which case, the document/view option will be disabled. An example of a dialog-based application is the properties sheet you see when you right-click on the desktop and select Properties from the menu. On this page you also select whether you want the document/view support. If you choose this option, the wizard will prepare a view class and a document class for your project and link them together. Select the language for your project. The language will determine how the wizard prepares its default resource, but you will have to translate everything else if you don't select the default language, which was determined when you installed the Visual Studio.

The second page allows you to select your database options and set a data source for the project. Some of the options available here may not appear or may be disabled. Database programming is a topic for an entire book, and I won't be covering it here. For now, leave it set to None and click the Next button.

You now get into compound-document support. If you didn't select document/view support on the first page, all these options will be disabled. A *compound document* may contain information in different formats. It may, for example, contain some text, a graphic in one of several formats (say, a bitmap-tagged image format), and some sound and video clips. If you select *CRichEditView* as the base class for your view, you must select at least Container support because the rich edit control won't work unless the Windows Object Linking and Embedding (OLE) functions are enabled. In addition to None, you have the following options:

- **Container** lets your program contain embedded objects and links to objects in other files.

- **Mini-Server** is a program that is used to view, edit, or play objects embedded in a file. This type of program can't be run stand-alone but is invoked from other programs when the user selects an embedded object.

- **Full-Server** applications can be run stand-alone and used to create and edit objects embedded in another program's document. It may be invoked from other applications to view, edit, or run embedded objects.

- **Both Container and Server** gives your application the capabilities of a server and a container. You may create documents that contain embedded objects, and your application may be started or manipulated by other programs to support embedded objects. Select whether you want your application to be an Active Document server or container. An *active document* server is an application that runs in the background when an active document container opens one of its documents. The server actually controls the display of data in the container application. For example, Internet Explorer is an active document container and can open Microsoft Word files. When it does, Word runs in the background, providing the display information for Internet Explorer.

Along with databases, programming for embedded objects and active documents isn't covered in this book. I tried, but there's not enough room to cover them adequately and still cover the basic programming information.

Compound File Support determines how your program will manage embedded objects. If you select yes, your application will be able to store the object information in its document file but still access the individual files containing the embedded objects. Objects are loaded into memory "on demand." You also may incrementally save individual objects. If you select no, all objects in a compound document will be loaded into memory when the document is opened. If one object changes, all the objects are saved again.

Automation is the ability of one program to execute code in another program. If you choose automation support, you may include "methods" by which other programs can access your program code.

ActiveX support is the ability to use ActiveX controls in your program. This option should be checked. Again, I don't cover ActiveX programming in this book, but I've included the source code for an ActiveX control on the CD-ROM so that you can manipulate it in the Visual Studio Resource Editor and experiment with the code.

Page 4 of the wizard contains appearance and support options for your application. Most of these are self-explanatory. MAPI is the Windows messaging interface and allows your program to send its documents through an email system by menu command. Sockets enables the WinSock programming options so that your program can communicate with programs on other machines over a network. The number you enter in the recent files list option at the bottom determines how many file names will appear on the Files menu of your program after you have opened or created the files. Select 0 to have no Most Recently Used (MRU) on your menu.

The Advanced page contains options for file names and file operations on the Document Template Strings page and window appearance options on the Window Styles page (if you didn't select view/document support, you won't see this page). Two items are not prefilled here and are worth mentioning. The File Extension field is used to identify documents created by your program to other programs, including Windows. If you enter a unique extension here (don't include the period), Windows will launch your program automatically when a user double-clicks an icon for your file type. In addition, Windows Explorer can automatically print a document of your type without opening your application when the user drags an icon over a printer icon. The Filter Name field is how your program will be identified in filters for the FileOpen and FileSave dialogs. If your file extension is, say, *.hey*, you might want to make this field read "Hey day files (*.hey)".

Clicking the Window Styles page displays options for the appearance of your main window and child windows (in multiple-document programs, that is; if you selected single-document support, the bottom half of this page will be disabled). You already saw most of these options in your earlier Windows programming, so they should be self-explanatory. The Use Split Window option causes your document windows to be created with a splitter bar to provide different views for your document. I usually ignore this option because the wizard provides only a single split and usually won't support the view/split combination I want. You will manually create a split window application later.

Page 5 contains more appearance options, along with code options. You can select the Windows Explorer type of window frame only if you selected document/view support. Generally, I prefer to stick with the MFC standard frame. If you leave the source comment selection set to Yes, the wizard will insert comments in the code it creates. This is a handy option and very recommended, even for seasoned programmers who need a memory jog from time to time. If you have the professional or enterprise editions of Visual C++, you may select whether to use MFC in a DLL or statically link it to your program. If you have the standard edition, your only option is to use the DLL.

Finally, you're at the end. Page 6 lists the classes the wizard will prepare for you when you click the Finish button. Assuming that you selected document/view support, you may change the view class information at this point. Select another name for the class or a different name for the files containing it. The base class may be changed in the combo box at the bottom, but the wizard may place some restrictions on your selection. For example, if you didn't select at least Container for compound-document support, the wizard won't create an application using *CRichEditView* as the view base class.

Click Finish and the wizard will summarize your application options and the classes it will create for you. If you want to change anything, click Cancel and go back through the wizard steps. Otherwise, click OK and the wizard will create your project and open it in the Visual Studio.

491. Introducing CObject

The MFC *CObject* class is an example of the ultimate ancestor abstract class. It has no ancestors, and you can't create an object of this class directly. It contains basic runtime class information and serialization support. It has a protected constructor and, thus, must be initialized from a derived class. A derived class inherits only four functions (not including operator overloads) and a runtime class object. It doesn't support multiple inheritance, so derived classes cannot have more than one *CObject* class in their tree.

CObject is the base class for most of the application and window classes in MFC, such as the generic window class *CWnd*, the device context class *CDC* and its derivatives, and the file services classes.

Generally, in MFC programming you never deal with *CObject* directly unless you want to derive your own classes from it. Usually, you inherit from and use descendent classes to create and manipulate objects. At times, however, you will want to derive directly from *CObject*, as discussed in Tip 493, "User Object Classes."

492. Application Architecture Classes

A number of classes are used to create objects that are at the center of your program. These are the application architecture classes and include *CWinThread*, *CWinApp*, and *CDocument* among those that you will meet frequently.

CWinApp actually is derived from *CWinThread*, which creates and processes the message loop for your application. All programs have at least one thread, but you may use *CWinThread* to create multiple threads in your application.

The *CWinApp* is the base class the application wizards use to create your project application class. You can have only one instance of an application class in a program, and it should be declared in global space. When it is destroyed, the program ends.

Applications normally override the *InitInstance()* member of *CWinApp* to initialize their own objects and data. Four global functions are provided in MFC for dealing with the *CWinApp* object. The return values from these functions will remind you of programming in the Windows API. The *AfxGetInstanceHandle()* gives you the familiar *HINSTANCE* handle to your program. *AfxGetResourceHandle()* also returns an *HINSTANCE*, which may be cast to *HMODULE* for use in API functions that need that type of handle. *AfxGetAppName()* returns a pointer to the string that was used as the *szTitle* parameter in your call to the API's *CreateWindow()* function. Finally, the global *AfxGetApp()* function returns a pointer to the application class instance so that at any point in your program you may access public members of the application.

493. User Object Classes

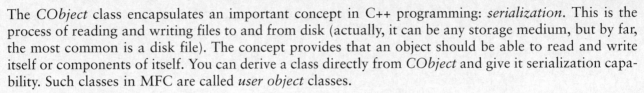

The *CObject* class encapsulates an important concept in C++ programming: *serialization*. This is the process of reading and writing files to and from disk (actually, it can be any storage medium, but by far, the most common is a disk file). The concept provides that an object should be able to read and write itself or components of itself. You can derive a class directly from *CObject* and give it serialization capability. Such classes in MFC are called *user object* classes.

For example, in a drawing program your code might capture a line drawn with the mouse. The points returned in the *WM_MOUSEMOVE* messages would be stored in an array in a class object that could serialize them directly to disk. When they are read back from disk, the original stroke could be reconstructed. This is how the Visual Studio sample program *SCRIBBLE.EXE* captures, stores, and reconstructs mouse strokes.

In a text-editing program, you could store a line of text in a *CObject*-derived object capable of writing it to disk and restoring it. Such an object could include the font used for the line of text, and you could read the text back and display it in the font you originally used to create it.

Serialization using *CObject*-derived classes is implemented using the *DECLARE_SERIAL* macro in the class definition and *IMPLEMENT_SERIAL* macro in the implementation file. You will find more on serialization in Tips 622, "Understanding *CView*," and 623, "Overriding the *OnPaint* Message Handler," including how to implement an object capable of reading and writing itself.

CObject also supports runtime class information and dynamic creation support. When you derive a class from *CObject* (or any class derived from *CObject*), you can implement the runtime class information using the *DECLARE_DYNAMIC* macro in the definition and the *IMPLEMENT_DYNAMIC* macro in the source code file. Using these macros enables you to query an object to determine whether it was derived from a particular class using the *IsKindOf()* function. If the function returns *TRUE*, it is safe to cast a pointer to it to the base class (remember in the C++ discussion that the language permits you to cast a pointer of a derived class to its base class). If the function returns *FALSE*, your code knows to avoid an illegal cast.

Dynamic creation support is provided using the *DECLARE_DYNACREATE* and *IMPLEMENT_DYNACREATE* macros. Dynamic creation causes an object of the class to be created at runtime without your having to create it as a class object in your code. When you use the document/view support in the MFC AppWizard, the wizard includes dynamic creation in the document and view classes it creates for you.

494. File Services Classes

The *CFile* class and its derivatives compose the *file services classes*. This set of classes not only encapsulates C++ streaming functions but also allows you to treat many non-file objects as if they were files.

The base *CFile* class may be instantiated in your code, or you may derive your own class from it. The class functions open and close files, read and write files, and seek to move the file pointer to positions within a file, just as you did with the C++ streams classes. In addition, you can perform Windows-specific operations on files, such as read and set file attributes and rename or delete files.

The files used with derivatives of *CFile* don't have to be physical files on the disk. The *CMemoryFile* class creates a file in memory and allows you to perform operations on it just as though it were a disk file. This can speed up operations when intensive I/O is being done on a file; you read the physical file into a memory file, perform your operations on it then, and when finished, write it back to disk. The memory file can be used to share data between active applications

The *CSharedFile* class is a memory file that implements the shared memory operations of UNIX. If you've ever had to deal with UNIX shared memory, you will find the *CSharedFile* class functions much easier to use.

I'll present an example of memory and shared files in Tip 518, "Using Memory Files," after you've had a chance to look at synchronization objects.

495. *Using the Device Context Classes*

The MFC device context classes encapsulate access to the Graphics Device Interface through member functions. The base device context class, *CDC*, may be used directly, but it is more common to use one of the derived classes, which are written for specific purposes.

Through the device context classes, you may access the drawing surface of printers and displays, as well as a Windows metafile. A *metafile* contains a sequence of GDI operations that you may read and "replay" to re-create an image in a window.

To demonstrate the metafile function, let's create an MFC application. Go through the steps in Tip 490, "Invoking the Visual Studio Wizard to Create an MFC-Based Program," to create an application. On Page 1, select Single document, and then uncheck the View/Document box. Accept the defaults through the rest of the pages.

In the ResourceView, select the only menu item on the list and add a pop-up named "MetaFile." Under this menu, add the items Record, Stop, Play Metafile, and Clear. The resource IDs should be *IDM_METAFILE_RECORD*, *IDM_METAFILE_STOP*, *IDM_METAFILE_PLAY*, and *IDM_METAFILE_CLEAR*, respectively.

Open the *ChildView.cpp* file that the wizard created for you. From this file, open the Class Wizard and add message map functions for *WM_MOUSEMOVE*, *WM_LBUTTONUP*, *WM_LBUTTONDOWN*, *WM_RBUTTONUP*, and *WM_RBUTTONDOWN*.

In the Object IDs box, select and add command message handlers for the four menu items you added. Close the Class Wizard (click OK, not Cancel, or else the functions won't be added).

Using the ClassView pane, add the following member variables:

```
bool    m_bTracking;
POINT   m_ptLineStart;
POINT   m_ptLineEnd;
POINT   m_ptLast;
CMetaFileDC  m_mdc;
HMETAFILE    m_hm;
bool    m_bSave;
```

You can see the results by opening the project on the CD-ROM and running the program. You are primarily interested in the *CChildView* class the wizard created because that's where all the action happens for a simple program. The code is listed here:

```cpp
// ChildView.cpp : implementation of the CChildView class
//

#include "stdafx.h"
#include "Meta.h"
#include "ChildView.h"

#ifdef _DEBUG
#define new DEBUG_NEW
#undef THIS_FILE
static char THIS_FILE[] = __FILE__;
#endif

/////////////////////////////////////////////////////////////
// CChildView

CChildView::CChildView()
{
    m_bTracking = false;
    m_ptLineStart.x  = m_ptLineStart.y  = 0;
    m_ptLineEnd.x = m_ptLineEnd.y = 0;
    m_ptLast.x = m_ptLast.y = -1;
    m_bSave = false;
    m_hm = NULL;
}

CChildView::~CChildView()
{
}

BEGIN_MESSAGE_MAP(CChildView,CWnd )
    //{{AFX_MSG_MAP(CChildView)
    ON_WM_PAINT()
    ON_WM_MOUSEMOVE()
    ON_WM_LBUTTONDOWN()
    ON_WM_RBUTTONDOWN()
    ON_WM_LBUTTONUP()
    ON_WM_RBUTTONUP()
    ON_COMMAND(IDM_METAFILE_PLAY, OnFilePlaymetafile)
    ON_COMMAND(IDM_METAFILE_RECORD, OnMetafileRecord)
    ON_COMMAND(IDM_METAFILE_STOP, OnMetafileStop)
    ON_COMMAND(IDM_METAFILE_CLEAR, OnMetafileClear)
    //}}AFX_MSG_MAP
END_MESSAGE_MAP()

/////////////////////////////////////////////////////////////
// CChildView message handlers

BOOL CChildView::PreCreateWindow(CREATESTRUCT& cs)
{
    if (!CWnd::PreCreateWindow(cs))
        return FALSE;
```

```cpp
            cs.dwExStyle |= WS_EX_CLIENTEDGE;
            cs.style &= ~WS_BORDER;
            cs.lpszClass = AfxRegisterWndClass (CS_HREDRAW |
                                  CS_VREDRAW | CS_DBLCLKS,
                                  ::LoadCursor(NULL, IDC_ARROW),
                                  HBRUSH(COLOR_WINDOW+1), NULL);
        return TRUE;
}


void CChildView::OnPaint()
{
    CPaintDC dc(this); // device context for painting

    // TODO: Add your message handler code here

    // Do not call CWnd::OnPaint() for painting messages
}


void CChildView::DoMouseEvent (UINT message,
                                  UINT nFlags, POINT & point)
{
CWindowDC        dc (this);

    switch (message)
    {
        case WM_LBUTTONDOWN:
            m_ptLineStart = point;
            break;
        case WM_LBUTTONUP:
            m_bTracking = false;
            m_ptLineStart.x = -1;
            m_ptLineStart.y = -1;
            break;
        case WM_RBUTTONUP:
            m_ptLast.x = -1;
            m_ptLast.y = -1;
            break;
        case WM_RBUTTONDOWN:
            dc.SetPixel (point, 0);
            if (m_bSave)
                m_mdc.SetPixel (point, 0);
            if (m_ptLast.x >= 0)
            {
                DoMouseLine (dc, m_ptLast, point);
            }
            m_ptLast = point;
            break;
        case WM_MOUSEMOVE:
            if (nFlags & MK_RBUTTON)
            {
                DoMouseEvent (WM_RBUTTONDOWN,
                                  nFlags, point);
                break;
            }
            if (!(nFlags & MK_LBUTTON))
                return;
```

```
            if (m_bTracking)
            {
                POINT pt;
                pt = point;
                if (m_ptLineStart.x >= 0)
                {
                    DoMouseLine (dc, m_ptLineStart,
                                     m_ptLineEnd);
                    DoMouseLine (dc, m_ptLineStart, pt);
                }
            }
            m_ptLineEnd = point;
            m_bTracking = true;
            break;
    }
}

void CChildView::DoMouseLine (CWindowDC& dc,
                              POINT & ptLineStart,
                              POINT & ptLineEnd)
{
CPen    *penOld, *penMetaOld, Pen;

    Pen.CreatePen (PS_SOLID, 2, (COLORREF) 0x00ffffff);
    int nOldMode = dc.SetROP2 (R2_XORPEN);// R2_NOT);
    dc.MoveTo (ptLineStart);
    penOld = dc.SelectObject (&Pen);
    dc.LineTo (ptLineEnd);
    dc.SetROP2 (nOldMode);
    dc.SelectObject (penOld);
    if (m_bSave)
    {
        int nOldMetaMode = m_mdc.SetROP2 (R2_XORPEN);
        m_mdc.MoveTo (ptLineStart);
        penMetaOld = m_mdc.SelectObject (&Pen);
        m_mdc.LineTo (ptLineEnd);
        m_mdc.SetROP2 (nOldMetaMode);
        m_mdc.SelectObject (penMetaOld);
    }
    Pen.DeleteObject ();
}

void CChildView::OnMouseMove(UINT nFlags, CPoint point)
{
    DoMouseEvent (WM_MOUSEMOVE, nFlags, point);
}

void CChildView::OnLButtonDown(UINT nFlags, CPoint point)
{
    DoMouseEvent (WM_LBUTTONDOWN, nFlags, point);
}

void CChildView::OnRButtonDown(UINT nFlags, CPoint point)
{
    DoMouseEvent (WM_LBUTTONDOWN, nFlags, point);
}
```

```
void CChildView::OnLButtonUp(UINT nFlags, CPoint point)
{
    DoMouseEvent (WM_LBUTTONDOWN, nFlags, point);
}

void CChildView::OnRButtonUp(UINT nFlags, CPoint point)
{
    DoMouseEvent (WM_LBUTTONDOWN, nFlags, point);
}

void CChildView::OnFilePlaymetafile()
{
    if (m_hm == NULL)
        return;
    CWindowDC   dc(this);
    dc.PlayMetaFile (m_hm);
}

void CChildView::OnMetafileRecord()
{
    m_mdc.Create ();
    m_bSave = true;
}

void CChildView::OnMetafileStop()
{
    m_hm = m_mdc.Close ();
    m_bSave = false;
}

void CChildView::OnMetafileClear()
{
    Invalidate ();
}
```

If a lot of this looks familiar, it should. The drawing steps are very similar to the statements you used earlier in *LINES.EXE*. I mentioned that if you have mastered the device context functions in the Windows API, you won't have any problem with them in MFC. The function names are the same, but you don't have to use the *HDC* as a parameter in the calls. The *HDC* is a member variable, *m_hDC*, in the class and the class functions retrieve it before calling the API function.

Run the program and select the Record item on the MetaFile menu. Use the left and right mouse buttons to draw some lines on the screen, and then select Stop from the menu. Clear the screen by selecting Clear from the MetaFile menu.

When you select Play MetaFile from the menu, all the mouse strokes you entered while in the record mode will reappear on the screen.

496. *Graphical Drawing Object Classes*

The Graphics Device Interface objects you have used to draw on and write text to the screen are all represented in the Microsoft Foundation Class library. The member functions closely resemble the Windows API functions, so if you have become used to the API, switching to the MFC classes won't be much of a bother.

The GDI objects and their MFC classes are summarized in Table 496. Using them is much the same as using the objects in the Windows API. If the objects are created on the stack as function variables or class members, you don't have to delete them before they go out of scope. The class destructors take care of that for you.

GDI Object	Handle	MFC Class
Pen	HPEN	CPen
Brush	HBRUSH	CBrush
Font	HFONT	CFont
Region	HRGN	CRgn
Bitmap	HBITMAP	CBitmap
Palette	HPALETTE	CPalette

Table 496   GDI objects and their MFC classes

In addition, the class objects are *reusable*. You don't need a separate *CPen* object for every pen you plan to use. You may use the class member functions to create the pen. When you are finished, use the object's *DeleteObject()* member function to remove it from memory, and then call one of the create functions again to build a new pen. If you reuse an object, you *must* delete it between successive calls to the create functions, or an exception will be thrown.

The following code shows how you can reuse one *CPen* object to draw three rectangles—a blue rectangle enclosing a green one, which in turn encloses a red rectangle:

```
void CChildView::OnFileRectangles()
{
    CWindowDC dc(this);
    CPen  pen;
    RECT rcBlue = {20, 20, 120, 200};
    RECT rcGreen = {22, 22, 118, 198};
    RECT rcRed = {24, 24, 116, 196};
    pen.CreatePen (PS_SOLID, 2,  RGB(0x00, 0x00, 0xFF));
    dc.SelectObject (&pen);
    dc.Rectangle (&rcBlue);
    pen.DeleteObject();
    pen.CreatePen (PS_SOLID, 2,  RGB(0x00, 0xFF, 0x00));
    dc.SelectObject (&pen);
    dc.Rectangle (&rcGreen);
    pen.DeleteObject();
    pen.CreatePen (PS_SOLID, 2,  RGB(0xFF, 0x00, 0x00));
    dc.SelectObject (&pen);
    dc.Rectangle (&rcRed);
}
```

This code is fairly simple and is included in the *METAFILE.EXE* program from the previous tip. Select Rectangles from the File menu to see the rectangles.

Well, it is a nice-looking rectangle. You may create a GDI object when you declare it, but you run the risk of throwing an exception if the constructor fails. (More on exception handling later, but if you want to see an example of catching an exception, look no further than Tip 499, "Internet Services Classes.") You could have declared your *CPen* object and created a blue pen at the same time with the following declaration:

```
CPen pen(PS_SOLID, 2, RGB(0x00, 0x00, 0xFF));
```

The default constructor will not throw an exception, however, as will the *CreatePen()* member function, so you usually opt to create the GDI object in a separate statement.

497. Control, Support, Database, Menu, Command-Line, Synchronization, and Sockets Classes

All the Windows common controls are represented by MFC classes, including some that have been introduced very recently, such as the extended combo box. In the Windows API, you usually communicated with controls using messages. For example, to find out how many characters are in an edit control, you would send it a *WM_GETTEXTLENGTH* message.

The MFC *control classes* isolate the programmer from the message process, and you only need to call member functions to get information where once you used the message system. You will look at the control classes and see examples on how to use each one beginning with Tip 807, "Understanding Controls in the Windows Environment."

The *support classes* include the command enablers—one of the weaker aspects of MFC—and the data, field, and property exchange classes. The *CWaitCursor* class also is listed among the support classes. Tip 540, "Understanding the *CWaitCursor* Class," contains an example of using the wait cursor.

Using the *database classes* requires understanding database operations and how the Open Database Connectivity (ODBC) system works, which could fill a book in itself. I won't try to get into database programming here.

The *CMenu* is a single class that encapsulates the Windows API's *HMENU* object. Using *CMenu*, you may create a menu, assign it to a window, and detach and destroy the *CMenu* object without destroying the *HMENU* object. Thus, the *CMenu* class may be used in local function scope and does not have to remain in memory for the life of a program or window.

Using the *CCommandLineInfo* class makes it easier to parse command-line information. To use it, you declare an instance and then call the *CWinApp* class's *ParseCommandLine()* function. When the function returns, the *CCommandLineInfo* object contains a value to indicate what action the application should perform. For example, if you start a program using something like */p filename*, the *CCommandLineInfo* contains a *FilePrint* value in its *m_nShellCommand* member variable. The purpose of this is not to make life easier for the programmer but to support Windows automation. If you need to process flags of your own making, you can derive your own class from *CCommandLineInfo* and parse the line yourself.

Synchronization between programs or the threads in a single program is achieved using the *synchronization classes*. The *CSemaphore* encapsulates some of the properties of the UNIX semaphore interprocess communications device. You will examine semaphores and other synchronization classes in the section on interprocess communications, beginning with Tip 979, "Understanding Interprocess Communications."

The *sockets classes* encapsulate Microsoft's version of Berkeley sockets. A *socket* is an end point for a network connection based on Internet protocols. The *CAsyncSocket* class encapsulates the WinSock programming interface and is derived from *CObject*. The *CSocket* class is derived from *CAsyncSocket* and is further removed from the underlying protocols. You will use *CSocket* in Tip 519, "Using Socket Files," when you explore the *CSocketFile* class.

The Berkeley sockets scheme is a well-designed communication procedure, and the MFC classes only serve to isolate you from its functions. Often, it's far easier—and more flexible—to deal with the sockets interface (WinSock on Windows) than to use the MFC classes.

498. *Array, List, and Map Classes*

Three class groups that often are overlooked in discussions on MFC are the *CArray*, *CList*, and *CMap* classes and their derivatives. Probably, this is because most of their functionality is included in the C++ Standard Template Library.

Together, these classes make up the *collection* classes in MFC. If you've ever had to dynamically allocate and initialize an array or build a linked list in the heap, you will appreciate the MFC collection classes.

THE *CARRAY* CLASS AND DERIVATIVES

The first group is *CArray* and its derivatives. These classes give you the functionality of unbounded arrays (within memory limits, of course) as you might find in a language such as BASIC. One of the characteristics of C++ is that it provides no bounds checking on arrays, and if your code doesn't keep track of the bounds, you can overwrite the array. If the array is created on the stack, you likely will overwrite other data elements or, drastically, return addresses. If the array was created in the heap, you will get an access violation, and your program will come to a screeching halt. This isn't necessarily a weakness of the language; because it gives you so much control over the programming environment, C++ imposes more responsibility on you.

The *CArray*-derived classes and the sizes and data types they store are listed in Table 498a.

Class Name	Data Size	Data Type Stored
CByteArray	8	BYTE (unsigned byte)
CDWordArray	32	DWORD
CObjArray	32	Pointers to CObject objects
CPtrArray	32	void type pointers
CStringArray	Varies	CString objects
CUIntArray	32	UINT (unsigned int)
CWordArray	16	WORD

Table 498a CArray-derived classes and storage objects

What makes these classes easy to use is that they all share common function names to insert, extract, and manipulate elements. When you learn to use one member of a group, you will have learned to use all of them. In addition, *CArray* itself is a template class, so you may define a storage object for virtually any data type.

As an example, you will calculate the five points of a star and use a *CArray* object to store the points, which you will place in *CPoint* object.

```cpp
// ChildView.cpp : implementation of the CChildView class
//

#include "stdafx.h"
#include "Array.h"
#include "ChildView.h"
#include <math.h>
#include <afxtempl.h>

#ifdef _DEBUG
#define new DEBUG_NEW
#undef THIS_FILE
static char THIS_FILE[] = __FILE__;
#endif

#define PI        3.14159


/////////////////////////////////////////////////////////////////
// CChildView

CChildView::CChildView()
{
}


CChildView::~CChildView()
{
}

BEGIN_MESSAGE_MAP(CChildView,CWnd )
    //{{AFX_MSG_MAP(CChildView)
    ON_WM_PAINT()
    //}}AFX_MSG_MAP
END_MESSAGE_MAP()


/////////////////////////////////////////////////////////////////
// CChildView message handlers

BOOL CChildView::PreCreateWindow(CREATESTRUCT& cs)
{
    if (!CWnd::PreCreateWindow(cs))
        return FALSE;

    cs.dwExStyle |= WS_EX_CLIENTEDGE;
    cs.style &= ~WS_BORDER;
    cs.lpszClass = AfxRegisterWndClass (CS_HREDRAW | CS_VREDRAW |
                      CS_DBLCLKS, ::LoadCursor(NULL, IDC_ARROW),
                      HBRUSH(COLOR_WINDOW+1), NULL);
```

```
    return TRUE;
}

void CChildView::OnPaint()
{
RECT     rcClient;
CPoint   ptOrg;
CPoint   point;
CArray<CPoint, CPoint&> points;
double   fAngle, fRadius;
int      i;
CPen     pen, penOld;

    CPaintDC dc(this); // device context for painting
    pen.CreatePen (PS_SOLID, 2, (COLORREF) 0);
    penOld = (CPen *) dc.SelectObject (&pen);
    GetClientRect (&rcClient);
    fRadius = rcClient.bottom / 3.0;
    ptOrg = dc.SetViewportOrg (rcClient.right / 2,
                               rcClient.bottom / 2);
    for (i = 0, fAngle = PI/2; i < 5; ++i, fAngle += 6 * PI/5.0)
    {
        point.x = (long)(fRadius * cos (fAngle) + 0.5);
        point.y = (long)(-fRadius * sin (fAngle) + 0.5);
        points.Add (CPoint (point.x, point.y));
    }
    points.Add (CPoint (points[0].x, points[0].y));
    dc.MoveTo (points[0].x, points[0].y);
    for (i = 1; i < 6; ++i)
        dc.LineTo (points[i].x, points[i].y);
    dc.SelectObject (penOld);
    dc.SetViewportOrg (ptOrg);
}
```

Unlike a dynamic array you create on the heap, you don't have to worry about deleting the *CArray* object before it goes out of scope. When the object is destroyed, the constructor deletes any memory it has allocated to hold your objects.

THE *CLIST* CLASS AND DERIVATIVES

We've all had the task of creating a linked list at some time in our programming past. After a few of them, you usually create your own generic functions or class to implement such lists. A *linked list* is a collection of data elements that contain a pointer to the next or previous object. If the pointers go only in one direction, say, from the first to the last, the list is *singly* linked; if it contains pointers so that you can go in either direction from any point in the list, it is *doubly* linked. Such lists generally are created on the heap, with each being created and inserted as needed.

The MFC *CList* class creates just such a list for you. The class and its derivatives are doubly linked, which provides for fast traversal of the list. To get to the item preceding the one you are using, you don't have to return to the beginning of the list and count back down. Instead, you use the class function *GetPrev()*. The classes derived from *CList* are summarized in Table 498b.

Class Name	Data Size	Data Type Stored
CObjList	32	Pointers to *CObject* objects
CPtrList	32	*void* pointers
CStringList	Varies	*CString* objects

Table 498b   CList-*derived classes and storage objects*

Like *CArray*, the *CList* class is a template, and you may define your own data type when you declare an object. The functions to access and manipulate the elements of the list are the same for all the derived classes, so, again, when you learn one, you will have learned them all. To demonstrate how the list works, you will define a data structure that contains the names of states and their capitals. You won't put them in alphabetical order, but you will insert them into the list in alphabetical order. Most samples you have seen of this class start with a sorted list, but that's not typically how your data are arranged when you need a linked list. More often than not, the data come at you randomly, and it's your job to put them into some sort of order. If you always start out with neatly sorted data, the linked list has only limited usefulness. You won't list every state, but just enough to give you an idea how the list works.

```cpp
// ChildView.h : interface of the CChildView class
//
/////////////////////////////////////////////////////////////

#include    <afxtempl.h>

struct CAPITOL
    {
    char *State;
    char *Capitol;
    };


/////////////////////////////////////////////////////////////
// CChildView window

class CChildView : public CWnd
{
// Construction
public:
    CChildView();

// Attributes
public:

// Operations
public:

// Overrides
    // ClassWizard generated virtual function overrides
    //{{AFX_VIRTUAL(CChildView)
    protected:
    virtual BOOL PreCreateWindow(CREATESTRUCT& cs);
    //}}AFX_VIRTUAL

// Implementation
public:
    virtual ~CChildView();
```

```
    // Generated message map functions
protected:
    int CompareStrings (CAPITOL & c1, CAPITOL & c2);
    void SortArray();
    //{{AFX_MSG(CChildView)
    afx_msg void OnPaint();
    afx_msg void OnSortBycapitol();
    afx_msg void OnSortBystate();
    //}}AFX_MSG

    CList<CAPITOL, CAPITOL&> m_States;
    int m_nSortBy;

    DECLARE_MESSAGE_MAP()
};

/////////////////////////////////////////////////////////////
```

After defining a simple structure, you declare the *CList* template class to be of that type. The *OnSortBycapitol()* and *OnSortBystate()* functions are the message handlers for the menu items. *CompareStrings()* is the function that actually sorts the data before inserting a structure into the list. The *m_nSortBy* is your sort flag. You set it to 0 to sort the list by state name and to 1 to sort by the capital city name.

In the code that follows, one of the problems with sorting the data is that you have no way of directly setting a variable of type *POSITION*. The only way to give it a value is to pass it to one of the *CList* functions. In the *SortList()* function, when you get the next member of the list using your *POSITION* variable, the function alters the variable to point to the next element. There is a chance that the last comparison, based on the test in your *for* loop, won't be performed, so you have to do an additional test after you exit the loop. If *pos* (the *POSITION* variable) is *NULL*, you check again to make sure that the order is correct. The list *probably* would sort correctly without this additional test; try commenting it out and shuffling the order of the entries in the *States* array, and you might find some combination where two elements are not in order.

```
// ChildView.cpp : implementation of the CChildView class
//

#include "stdafx.h"
#include "List.h"
#include "ChildView.h"

#ifdef _DEBUG
#define new DEBUG_NEW
#undef THIS_FILE
static char THIS_FILE[] = __FILE__;
#endif

CAPITOL States[] =
    {
    "Colorado", "Denver",
    "Texas", "Austin",
    "Alabama", "Montgomery",
    "Alaska", "Juneau",
    "Oregon", "Salem",
    "New Hampshire", "Montpelier",
```

```
        "Virginia", "Roanoke",
        "Arizona", "Tucson",
        "Idaho", "Boise",
        "Minnesota", "St. Paul"
        };

/////////////////////////////////////////////////////////////
// CChildView

CChildView::CChildView()
{
    SortArray ();
}

CChildView::~CChildView()
{
}

BEGIN_MESSAGE_MAP(CChildView,CWnd )
    //{{AFX_MSG_MAP(CChildView)
    ON_WM_PAINT()
    //}}AFX_MSG_MAP
END_MESSAGE_MAP()

/////////////////////////////////////////////////////////////
// CChildView message handlers

BOOL CChildView::PreCreateWindow(CREATESTRUCT& cs)
{
    if (!CWnd::PreCreateWindow(cs))
        return FALSE;

    cs.dwExStyle |= WS_EX_CLIENTEDGE;
    cs.style &= ~WS_BORDER;
    cs.lpszClass = AfxRegisterWndClass (CS_HREDRAW |
                        CS_VREDRAW | CS_DBLCLKS,
                        ::LoadCursor(NULL, IDC_ARROW),
                        HBRUSH(COLOR_WINDOW+1), NULL);
    return TRUE;
}

void CChildView::OnPaint()
{
CFont font;
CPoint point(0, 0);
int    tabs = 130;
char   szText[_MAX_PATH];

    CPaintDC dc(this); // device context for painting
    font.CreatePointFont (100, "Times New Roman Bold");
    dc.SelectObject (&font);

    LOGFONT lf;
    memset (&lf, '\0', sizeof (LOGFONT));
    font.GetLogFont (&lf);
    CAPITOL state = m_States.GetHead ();
```

```
        POSITION pos = m_States.GetHeadPosition ();
        while (pos != NULL)
        {
            state = m_States.GetNext (pos);
            sprintf (szText, "%s\t%s", state.State,
                                    state.Capital);
            dc.TabbedTextOut (point.x, point.y, szText,
                            1, &tabs, 0);
            point.y += abs(lf.lfHeight);
        }
        // Do not call CWnd::OnPaint() for painting messages
}

void CChildView::SortArray()
{
    for (int i = 0; i<(sizeof(States)/sizeof(CAPITOL)); ++i)
    {
        if (m_States.IsEmpty())
        {
            m_States.AddHead (States[i]);
            continue;
        }
        CAPITOL next;
        POSITION pos = m_States.GetHeadPosition ();
        next = m_States.GetTail ();
        for (next = m_States.GetHead();
                pos != NULL;
                next = m_States.GetNext (pos))
        {
            if (strcmp (next.State, States[i].State) > 0)
                break;
        }
        if (pos == NULL)
        {
            if (strcmp (States[i].State, next.State) < 0)
            {
                pos = m_States.GetTailPosition ();
                m_States.InsertBefore (pos, States[i]);
            }
            else
                m_States.AddTail (States[i]);
            continue;
        }
        m_States.GetPrev (pos);
        m_States.InsertBefore (pos, States[i]);
    }
}
```

In the last two lines, note that you move the position back one element before inserting the data. The statement *next = m_States.GetNext (pos)* in the loop control gets the next structure from the list and increments *pos* to point to the next member. Thus, *pos* is not correctly positioned for the insert operation. When I first ran across this, after using *CList* successfully in several other programs, I scratched my head for a long time before I realized that the list pointer was one step ahead of me.

THE *CMAP* CLASS AND DERIVATIVES

A *map* essentially is a translation table and sometimes is called a *dictionary*. The concept is familiar to Assembly programmers because maps provide very fast lookup performance. You start out with a unique identifier, a *key*, which may be a simple two- or three-letter value, and use a map to translate it to your actual data, which might be a complex structure.

The performance is achieved by *hashing* the key. Hashing converts the key into a number value, which is then used as an index into the map table. To understand how hashing works, you will take a list of the postal abbreviations for all 50 states and use that as your set of keys. The ASCII table is basically a numeric table of 128 elements, from 0 to 127, so you can set the hash table size to 127 (I'll explain how you got this number shortly). A single character, then, has a unique hash value. If you add the values of the individual characters in a key and divide by 127, you come up with the hash values in Table 498c.

State AK, Hash 13	State AL, Hash 14	State AR, Hash 20
State AZ, Hash 28	State CA, Hash 5	State CO, Hash 19
State CT, Hash 24	State DE, Hash 10	State FL, Hash 19
State GA, Hash 9	State HI, Hash 18	State IA, Hash 11
State ID, Hash 14	State IL, Hash 22	State IN, Hash 24
State KS, Hash 31	State KY, Hash 37	State LA, Hash 14
State MA, Hash 15	State MD, Hash 18	State ME, Hash 19
State MI, Hash 23	State MN, Hash 28	State MO, Hash 29
State MS, Hash 33	State MT, Hash 34	State NC, Hash 18
State ND, Hash 19	State NE, Hash 20	State NH, Hash 23
State NJ, Hash 25	State NM, Hash 28	State NV, Hash 37
State NY, Hash 40	State OH, Hash 24	State OK, Hash 27
State OR, Hash 34	State PA, Hash 18	State RI, Hash 28
State SC, Hash 23	State SD, Hash 24	State TE, Hash 26
State TX, Hash 45	State UT, Hash 42	State VA, Hash 24
State VT, Hash 43	State WA, Hash 25	State WI, Hash 33
State WY, Hash 49	State WV, Hash 46	

Table 498c   Hash values generated with a divisor of 127

The hash values were generated using the following loop. The algorithm to generate the values is simple and could be improved, but the idea is to show how a hash value is generated from a string:

```
for (int i = 0; i < 50; ++i)
{
    if (!(i % 3))
        printf ("\n");
    int Hash = 0;
    char *s = States[i];
    for (int j = 0; *s; ++s)
    {
        Hash += (int) *s;
    }
```

```
    printf ("State %s, Hash %2d   ", States[i], Hash % 127);
}
```

You then use these values as indexes into a table that contains information about the various states. Actually, you use the hash value to get a pointer into a table. Obviously, the values can't be unique. The two characters "TE" will produce the same hash value as "ET." When you get duplicate hash values, you build a linked list at the pointer location. If your key doesn't match the table value when you retrieve the data, you look at the *next* pointer for the linked list and move through the list until you get the proper key.

The efficiency depends on the size of the hash table (the default for *CMap* is 17) and the ability of the hash algorithm to produce a unique value. If you use the default hash table size with, say, 1,000 items, the retrieval process will involve looking at many linked lists and won't be very efficient. In this example, if you set the hash table size to 65,536 and then used the two characters to produce a hexadecimal number ("CO" would be 0x434F, or 17,231), every key would be unique. However, you would be wasting a lot of memory with a mostly empty hash table. You have to strike a balance between the size of the hash table and the number of keys you are going to store. Actually, you could improve the efficiency by subtracting 32 (the value of a space) from each character before getting its hash value; you know that you never will be storing keys with control characters in them.

You don't have to worry about the hash algorithm—that's handled by the *CMap* class—but you do have control over the size of the hash table. Generally, you figure the hash table to be about 20 percent larger than the number of items you are going to store. A prime number generally is preferred because it produces fewer duplicate hash values (that's why the default for *CMap* is 17 instead of 16). For the state abbreviations, 50 plus 20 percent is 60. You can look up prime number in many math reference books such as the *CRC Standard Math Tables*. There you will see that the closest prime number is 61, so that's the value you would use for the hash table size. Actually, that's a small hash table, and for efficiency it might be wise to double the value and use the nearest prime number, which would be 127.

The MFC classes derived from *CMap* are listed in Table 498d.

MFC Class	Storage
CMapWordToPtr	*void* pointers keyed by *WORD*s
CMapPtrToWord	*WORD*s keyed by *void* pointers
CMapPtrToPtr	*void* pointers keyed by *void* pointers
CMapWordToOb	*CObject* pointers keyed by *WORD*s
CMapStringToOb	*CObject* pointers keyed by strings
CMapStringToPtr	*void* pointers keyed by strings
CMapStringToString	*char* pointers keyed by strings

Table 498d   CMap-derived classes

If you had a structure containing information about each state, the example would use the *CMapStringToPtr* class. You would be storing the structure and using the two-letter abbreviation as the key. The *CMap* class is a template class, so you may define your own storage classes.

499. *Internet Services Classes*

To explore the Internet classes in MFC, you have to look in more than one branch of the hierarchy. The classes actually are grouped into the Internet Services classes, the Internet Server classes, and some in the File Services classes. The server classes are part of an application programming interface, and I won't cover them here.

It isn't surprising, with Microsoft's obsession with the Internet, to find a number of MFC classes to facilitate Internet access. The MFC Internet Services classes are *CInternetSession*, *CInternetConnection*, *CFileFind*, and *CGopherLocator*. In addition, *CInternetSession* is the base class for *CFtpConnection*, *CHttpConnection*, and *CGopherConnection*. The *CFileFind* class is the base class for *CFtpFileFind* and *CGopherFileFind*. The gopher classes have been largely made obsolete.

In the File Services classes, *CInternetFile* is the base class for *CGopherFile* and *CHttpFile*. FTP (*File Transfer Protocol*) files are handled using the *CInternetFile* class directly.

When you create the *CInternetSession* object, the session is established by the constructor. You may specify a proxy server and password if your connection to the Internet requires it.

The following program opens an Internet connection and prompts for a file name. When you select a file name, it is transferred to the host computer using FTP. The program is a command-line program, and you run it by specifying the host system as the command-line argument:

```cpp
// Internet.cpp
//

#include "stdafx.h"
#include "Internet.h"
#include <afxinet.h>

#ifdef _DEBUG
#define new DEBUG_NEW
#undef THIS_FILE
static char THIS_FILE[] = __FILE__;
#endif

/////////////////////////////////////////////////////////////////
// The one and only application object

CWinApp theApp;

using namespace std;

int _tmain(int argc, TCHAR* argv[], TCHAR* envp[])
{
    int nRetCode = 0;

    // initialize MFC and print an error on failure
    if (!AfxWinInit(::GetModuleHandle(NULL),
                    NULL, ::GetCommandLine(), 0))
    {
        // TODO: change error code to suit your needs
        cerr << _T("Fatal Error: MFC initialization failed")
             << endl;
```

```
        return (1);
    }
    if (argc < 2)
    {
        AfxMessageBox ("Enter the destination address",
                       MB_OK);
        return (1);
    }
    CFileDialog cfd (true);
    if (cfd.DoModal () == IDCANCEL)
        return (1);
    CString strSend = cfd.GetFileName();
//
// Make sure we can read the file
    FILE *fp;
    if ((fp = fopen (cfd.GetPathName (), "rb")) == NULL)
    {
        AfxMessageBox ("Cannot open FTP source file",
                       MB_OK);
        return (1);
    }
//
// OK. Close it
    fclose (fp);
    CInternetSession cis;
    CFtpConnection *cfc;
    TRY
    {
        cfc = cis.GetFtpConnection (argv[1],
                                    "anonymous",
                                    "your@email.com");
    }
    CATCH(CInternetException, e)
    {
        char errmsg [_MAX_PATH];
        memset (errmsg, '\0', MAXPATH);
        e->GetErrorMessage (errmsg, MAXPATH);
        AfxMessageBox (errmsg, MB_OK);
        return (1);
    }
    END_CATCH
    if (cfc->PutFile (strSend, strSend))
    {
        AfxMessageBox ("Could not write file to host",
                       MB_OK);
        nRetCode = 1;
    }
    cfc->Close ();
    return (nRetCode);
}
```

The code uses the File Open common dialog box to prompt for a file name. If a file is selected, it tries to open it in read-only mode. If unsuccessful, the error is reported and the program exits. If all is kosher, the Internet connection is established. You have no proxy server, so just declaring the class object is sufficient.

You then declare a *pointer* to a *CFtpConnection* and initialize it with a call to the *GetFtcConnection()* member of *CInternetConnection*.

If the call to *GetFtpConnection()* fails, an exception is thrown, and if you don't catch it, your program comes to an end. You will get into exception handling later, but the nature of this program requires an exception handler. If you catch an exception, you get the error message from the exception handler (an MFC class object) and display it. Then you exit; the connection's no good.

I've put in "anonymous" as the user and a dummy email address for the password. Normally, if a system allows anonymous logons, it expects an email address as the password, but little or no error checking is done. You might fill in your email address if the call fails. I've tried ftp'ing to several systems with this little program, and none has refused the connection. In the program on the CD-ROM, I've added a little dialog box to get a user name and password.

Now you have an FTP connection with the host. You put the file using the same file name to the host, where it will be written to the host's default directory for anonymous logons. A third parameter to *PutFile()* specifies the type of transfer and defaults to binary. You may use *FTP_TRANSFER_TYPE_ASCII* or *FTP_TRANSFER_TYPE_BINARY*. A fourth parameter allows a context ID, which is used to identify the connection in a status callback function.

In Tip 531, "Using *CFtpConnection*," I'll show you how to actually open a file on a remote system using an FTP connection and to read or write data to it dynamically.

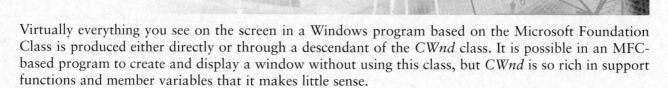

500. *Windows Classes: Introducing* CWnd

Virtually everything you see on the screen in a Windows program based on the Microsoft Foundation Class is produced either directly or through a descendant of the *CWnd* class. It is possible in an MFC-based program to create and display a window without using this class, but *CWnd* is so rich in support functions and member variables that it makes little sense.

The class contains a public member variable, *m_hWnd*, to hold the window handle (the *HWND* to which we grew accustomed in the Windows API) that you may use to call API functions directly. All dialog boxes you create using the *CDialog* class and all the common dialogs available to you in Windows are descendants of *CWnd*, as are the common controls (each control is actually one or more small windows) and the views you create in applications, whether you use the document/view support or just a view.

Generally, all the API functions you used outside MFC are available as member functions of *CWnd*. The major difference is that you don't have to specify the *HWND* in each call; the *CWnd* member functions handle that for you.

501. *Understanding Descendants of* CWnd

The *CWnd* class is derived from *CCmdTarget*, which is the base class for the MFC message map architecture. Thus, *CWnd* objects and objects created from *CWnd* descendant classes are capable of intercepting and directing Windows messages. (The *CWinApp* and *CDocument* classes also are derived from *CCmdTarget*.) By hiding the *WndProc()* function, *CWnd* is capable of forwarding messages directly to handler functions.

CWnd descendants fall into six general categories: the frame windows, the control bars, the property sheets, the dialog boxes, the view classes, and the controls.

It is important to remember that a *CWnd* object is not a Windows window, although it is convenient to think of it as such. A *window* is a structure internal to the Windows operating system, and it may be created and destroyed by *CWnd* member functions while the *CWnd* object persists. The *CWnd* object itself—but not the window—is created when the object comes into scope and is destroyed when the object goes out of scope.

The *CWnd* class encapsulates the window functions and assumes much of the complexity of handling window objects. A handle, a pointer to the internal window object, represents the Windows window. The *CWnd* object normally creates a window during its lifetime and destroys it before the class object goes out of scope. When it does create a window, the handle is stored in a *public* member variable, *m_hWnd*. You may use this variable in direct calls to the Windows API just as you would use an *HWND* identifier for a non-MFC operation.

All the classes that are derived from *CWnd*—*CFrameWnd*, *CToolBar*, *CMenu*, and most of the common controls, for example—inherit an *m_hWnd* member. The Windows API is very large, and even with 200 or so classes, the Microsoft Foundation Class doesn't encompass all the API calls you might need to make.

A couple of helper functions, which are declared in global space rather than as class members, take care of registering the window class. They are *AfxRegisterWndClass* and *AfxRegisterClass*. The first sets up a *WNDCLASS* structure and then calls the second, which takes a pointer to the structure as an argument. The actual call to the *CreateWindowEx()* API function is made in the *CWnd::Create()* function. If you look at it (it's in *wincore.cpp* if you installed the MFC source code), you will see that the sequence of registering and creating the window is virtually the same as with the Windows API, except that you don't have to do it anymore. You can call the functions to register your own window class and override the *CWnd::Create()* function to use your own window class, if you want to do things the hard way.

502. *Frame Window Classes*

The first group of *CWnd*-derived classes is the one responsible for creating the main window for an application—the *frame window* (a child window, such as one containing a multiple-document view, is also a frame window). By itself, *CFrameWnd*, the primary descendant, is capable of supporting a single-document interface (SDI), and descendant classes support the multiple-document interface (MDI).

CFrameWnd classes support control bars, menu bars, dialog bars, and status bars and contain the "harbors," where docking toolbars may be placed. Class objects are capable of intercepting Windows messages and directing them to child windows and controls. They perform the idle time processing to enable or disable the various menu commands and toolbar controls.

A *CFrameWnd* object also keeps track of the currently active view of a document and notifies the view windows when they come into focus.

Virtually every application you create using the document/view architecture has an object derived from *CFrameWnd*, whether it's a single-document or multiple-document interface project. The MFC AppWizard creates the class for you. When you create a multiple-document interface, the wizard derives the class indirectly from *CFrameWnd* through *CMDIFrameWnd*. In this case, a second frame class is created, a *child frame* class, from which the individual child windows will be created.

503. *Using the* **CFrameWnd** *Classes: The Single-Document Interface*

The Microsoft Foundation Class library uses frame windows to manage the user interface with a document. The frame window itself contains the client area and is charged with managing and maintaining the frame, such as positioning the toolbars, menu, and status bar. It contains the harbors where dockable toolbars may be placed.

A *view* is attached to the client area and manages the display of the document. Much of the programmer's work in a document/view MFC application is with the view class. In addition to displaying the document, this is where much of the Windows message processing takes place. Man messages sent to the frame window are passed on to the view. There are many forms of views, created from Windows controls. There also is a generalized view class, *CView*, which has almost no controls and must be built up by the programmer.

The *document* class is responsible for storing the data, writing the contents to disk, or reading from a disk file. A document doesn't have to operate on a disk file, however. It can use virtually any source, such as a disk file, a database, or even a Web connection, as in the case of *CHttpView*.

When you put these three elements together in a single MFC program, you have a single-document interface application. The division of responsibilities between the three elements greatly simplifies programming tasks. In the earlier examples using the Windows API, some of the code was becoming unwieldy even though it hadn't even begun to deal with storing and retrieving data. If you had gone much further, you would have had to break it down into something that resembles the MFC framework.

In a single-document application, the application class instance creates an instance of *CSingleDocTemplate*, which actually creates the frame window and the document. Because of this, the derived frame window class, the document class, and the view class definitions must include the *DECLARE_DYNACREATE* macro, and their implementations must include the *IMPLEMENT_DYNACREATE* macro. These macros are necessary for the RUNTIME_CLASS macro, which is used in the declaration of the document template, as in the following snippet:

```
pDocTemplate = new CSingleDocTemplate(
    IDR_MAINFRAME,
    RUNTIME_CLASS(CStuffDoc),
    RUNTIME_CLASS(CMainFrame),      // main SDI frame window
    RUNTIME_CLASS(CStuffView));
```

Once created, the frame window, in turn, creates the view and attaches it to the document object. When you close a document, none of these objects is destroyed unless you exit the program. They are recycled for the next document you open or create.

When the mainframe window is created, it handles the details of setting up the icon, the toolbar, and the menu, among other things, through its *LoadFrame()* member function. The *CFrameWnd* class, through the class derived for each project, can hold and manage many objects on the window frame, as shown in Figure 503. *LoadFrame* takes a single argument, a resource ID, and all frame elements that it sets up must have the same resource ID. (This is true in a multiple-document interface as well, but the application class object creates the main window.) If you look at the resource listing for a project created by the MFC AppWizard, you will see a menu, an icon, a toolbar, and an accelerator table with the same resource ID, typically IDR_MAINFRAME.

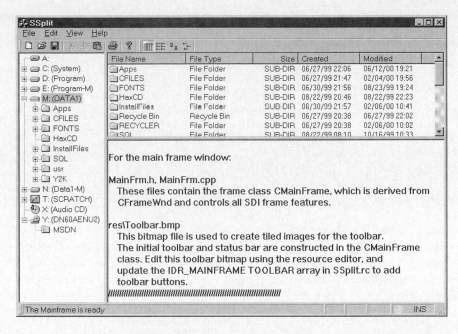

Figure 503   The CFrameWnd *class is capable of holding and managing numerous objects on the main window frame, such as this single-document interface application, which has two toolbars and three splitter windows with three different views, along with the standard window adornments.*

A curious aspect of the document object is that *CDocument* is not directly associated with a window, but it is derived from *CCmdTarget*, which means that it can receive messages. Typically, you use this functionality to send the document object user commands generated from menu items. The *CDocument* base class has message handlers to save and close files and to send a document through the Windows mail system.

504. Using the CFrameWnd *Classes:* The Multiple-Document Interface

By itself, *CFrameWnd* can manage only a single view/document in its client area. The view itself may be broken into several pieces, as in a splitter window (see Tip 505, "Using the *CSplitterWnd* Class"), but it expects only one document. Thus, *CFrameWnd* takes care of the single-document interface of MFC.

Some years ago, IBM developed a specification for a multiple-document interface (MDI) in which more than one child window can share the client area in the main window frame. The child windows have certain restrictions—they may not have menus, for example—but the specification allows a user to have many documents open and visible in the client workspace at the same time.

CFrameWnd can handle only single documents, but its immediate descendant, *CMDIFrameWnd*, is created specifically to handle the MDI, as its name implies.

The first difference you notice when you create an MDI application is in the call to create the document template in the application class's *InitInstance()* function. It is passed the runtime class of a child frame window instead of the mainframe:

```
CMultiDocTemplate* pDocTemplate;
pDocTemplate = new CMultiDocTemplate(
```

```
            IDR_GRAPHITYPE,
            RUNTIME_CLASS(CGraphicsDoc),
            RUNTIME_CLASS(CChildFrame), // custom MDI child frame
            RUNTIME_CLASS(CGraphicsView));
```

Rather than create the main window, the document template is responsible for creating the child windows that hold the MDI views. A couple of lines farther down in *InitInstance()* is a call to create the main window, which was missing in the single-document interface:

```
// create main MDI Frame window
CMainFrame* pMainFrame = new CMainFrame;
if (!pMainFrame->LoadFrame(IDR_MAINFRAME))
    return FALSE;
m_pMainWnd = pMainFrame;
```

The behavior of child windows is considerably different from the main window. Recall from Tips 396, "Understanding Pop-Up Windows," and 397, "Understanding Child Windows," that a child window can't leave the main window's client area, and the sides of it are "clipped" when you try to do so. Child windows also may not have their own menus but may respond to menu messages from the main window.

When you create a new document, the document template object creates a document object and the child frame window. The child frame, in turn, creates the view in an MDI child window and attaches itself to the client area of the child frame window. As in a single-document application, in an MDI application you may have multiple-document templates, along with multiple-document and view classes. The document/view type created depends on how you called the create function of the document template when you set it up. The MFC AppWizard creates only one document template for you, so to add more, you have to enter them manually.

To keep track of all these templates, views, and document objects, the MFC library includes a *CDocManager* class. You won't find any information about this class in the MSDN documentation, but you can look at its definition in the *afxwin.h* header file. (The document manager also is used in SDI applications to manage additional templates you define.) The application class creates the document manager and stores a pointer to it in its member variable, *m_pDocManager*. This is a *public* variable, so you may access it. If you are really into customization, there are a number of useful public functions as well. You can get the first document template using a *POSITION* variable much as in the *LIST.EXE* example from Tip 498, "Array, List, and Map Classes." After getting the position of the first template, you may access them sequentially:

```
CDocManager *pDocMan;
CDocTemplate *pTemplate;
if ((pDocMan = AfxGetApp()->m_pDocManager) == NULL)
    return;
POSITION pos = pDocMan->GetFirstDocTemplatePosition ();
while (pos != NULL)
{
    pTemplate = m_pDocMan->GetNextDocTemplate (pos);
}
```

What can you do with this? Well, for one, the document template object maintains a list of all documents that are open using that template. You can enumerate them just as you did to get the template pointer itself. Let's modify the preceding code to get a list of open documents. At the end, a message box will appear, listing the open documents:

```
CDocManager *pDocMan = AfxGetApp()->m_pDocManager;
if (pDocMan == NULL)
    return;
POSITION pos = pDocMan->GetFirstDocTemplatePosition ();
```

```
CString strDocs = "Documents currently open are:\n";
while (pos != NULL)
{
    CDocTemplate *pTempl = pDocMan->GetNextDocTemplate(pos);
    POSITION docpos = pTempl->GetFirstDocPosition();
    while (docpos != NULL)
    {
// Use your application document type for this template. Be
// sure to cast the function to that type.
        CAppDoc *doc =(CAppDoc *)pTempl->GetNextDoc(docpos);
// Do something here with the document object pointer
        strDocs += doc->GetTitle();   // or GetPathName()
        strDocs += '\n';
    }
}
AfxMessageBox (strDocs);
```

This code is on the companion CD-ROM as MDISample. To list the currently open documents, select Enumerate Files from the View menu. The code is in the *CMDISampleView* class.

The document object also maintains a list of views attached to it, which you can list using the same method. Just substitute the view class for the document class, and call *GetFirstViewPosition()* and *GetNextView(pos)*, casting the latter function to your view class, of course. I use a similar approach to let the user (usually a reporter) change the background and text colors of views on command. The lighting conditions at city hall vary considerably from, say, the dugout at a Rockies game, so the ability to adjust the colors sometimes can increase screen contrast on a laptop.

If you look at the code in Tip 505, "Using the *CSplitterWnd* Class," where the splitter windows are prepared, you will find just such a scheme in *explorerdoc.cpp* to look at the various views in the main window to find the editing view. Once found, you can load and save files using that view:

```
void CExplorerDoc::Serialize(CArchive& ar)
{
    POSITION pos;
    pos = GetFirstViewPosition ();
    while (pos != NULL)
    {
    CView *pView;
        pView = GetNextView (pos);
        if (pView->IsKindOf (RUNTIME_CLASS(CEditView)))
        {
// CEditView contains an edit control,
// which handles all serialization
            ((CEditView *)pView)->SerializeRaw(ar);
            break;
        }
    }
}
```

505. *Using the* **CSplitterWnd** *Class*

If you've used the editor in Visual Studio (of course you have by now), you've run across splitter windows, but you might not have noticed them. Each program source file window in the editor is split both horizontally and vertically. If you look at the vertical scroll bar just above the up arrow at the top, you will see a little bump. If you move the mouse cursor over this bump, the cursor will turn into something that resembles a wine press. Click and hold the left mouse button, and move the cursor downward.

You will see a second view of the window opening from the top. You can scroll and edit this file independently of the bottom view, but any changes you make to one will be reflected in the other.

The editing windows also are split vertically. At the left of the left arrow on the horizontal scroll bar, you will find another little bump. Click and hold it while dragging to the right, and a vertical split will appear in the window.

Each of these four windows is a view into the same document. When you edit one, you are editing all four. It's a convenient tool, though, because you can scroll either way in one view to look at another part of the text while keeping your place in the other. You close the split view simply by dragging the splitter bar all the way to the top or bottom (or the left or right, in the case of the vertical splitter).

You can create you own splitter window applications in one of three ways:

- On Page 5 of the MFC AppWizard (exe), you select Windows Explorer as the project type. With this option, the wizard always creates a tree control view for the left view. You can't change it (until after you create the application).

- On Page 4 you click the Advanced button; then, you select the Window Styles tab and check the Use Split Window box. The wizard will prepare a two-way splitter window application for you similar to what you saw in the Visual Studio editing windows. The only views you can select on the final page are *CHtmlView* (of course!), *CView*, and *CScrollView*.

- You "roll your own." The wizard creates only two types of splitter window styles and is picky about which views you put in them. This not only can be dull after a while but also all too often doesn't meet your needs. When you understand the splitter process, it's easy enough to create one that suits your purpose.

It's curious that the wizard is so picky about the view classes you can use. It's perfectly acceptable to use some of the seemingly *verboten* views, but you have to do it manually.

Actually, the easiest way is to let the wizard prepare a splitter window project and then edit it to change the views and/or orientation of the windows. Go ahead and create an Explorer-style splitter application (use the single-document interface; no sense complicating things at this point) and select the default views (*CTreeView* on the left and *CListView* on the right). Compile and run the application. You should have two panes in your window, the left pane about 100 logical units wide and the right filling the rest of the client area.

Now you can start fiddling around. Open *MainFrm.cpp* and scroll to about line 88 where it reads

```
if (!m_wndSplitter.CreateStatic(this, 1, 2))
```

The last two parameters in the function call are the number of rows and the number of columns to create in the splitter window. Change them around so that you have two rows and one column; then, move down four lines and change the *second* call to *CreateView* from 0, 1 to 1, 0. This creates the second view in the bottom row.

Last, move to the *GetRightPane()* function (about line 131) and reverse the order of the parameters so that they read 1, 0.

Recompile the application and run it. If you get an assertion, you forgot to change one or more of the parameters. You should again get two panes in your window, but this time one will be above the other.

Now, split the splitter. Each *CSplitterWnd* object is capable of handling only one split, so you must add a second splitter variable to the *CMainFrame* class. Right-click on the class name in the ClassView pane and select Add Member Variable from the menu. Enter *CSplitterWnd* as the variable type and *m_wndSplitter2* as the variable name. Make it *protected* and click OK.

The *CreateStatic* function takes five parameters. For a single split, you can specify the first three and just let the last two take default values. The fourth parameter is the window style, which defaults to *WS_CHILD | WS_VISIBLE*, and the fifth is the resource ID of the first window in the splitter, which defaults to *AFX_IDW_PANE_FIRST*. You can create the first split using the defaults, but you have to specify the parameters for the second split, so the second split is going to look more complicated. It really isn't; all you do is add *WS_BORDER* to the default style and get the ID from the first splitter by calling *IdFromRowCol()* using the position of the split. The *OnCreateClient()* function in *CMainFrm* should look like the following:

```
BOOL CMainFrame::OnCreateClient(LPCREATESTRUCT /*lpcs*/,
    CCreateContext* pContext)
{
    if (!m_wndSplitter.CreateStatic(this, 1, 2))
    return (FALSE);

    if (!m_wndSplitter2.CreateStatic(
        &m_wndSplitter,      // our parent window is the
                             // first splitter
        2, 1,                // new splitter is 2 rows, 1 col
        WS_CHILD | WS_VISIBLE | WS_BORDER,  // style,
                                            // need WS_BORDER
        m_wndSplitter.IdFromRowCol(0, 1)
// new splitter is in first row, 2nd column of first
        ))
    {
        TRACE0("Failed to create nested splitter\n");
        return FALSE;
    }

    if (!m_wndSplitter.CreateView(0, 0,
                        RUNTIME_CLASS(CLeftView),
                        CSize(100, 100), pContext))
    {
        m_wndSplitter.DestroyWindow();
        return FALSE;
    }
    if (!m_wndSplitter2.CreateView(0, 0,
                        RUNTIME_CLASS(CExplorerView),
                        CSize(150, 150), pContext))
    {
        m_wndSplitter.DestroyWindow();
        m_wndSplitter2.DestroyWindow();
        return FALSE;
    }
    if (!m_wndSplitter2.CreateView(1, 0,
                        RUNTIME_CLASS(CLeftView),
                        CSize(100, 100), pContext))
    {
        m_wndSplitter.DestroyWindow();
        m_wndSplitter2.DestroyWindow();
        return FALSE;
    }
    return TRUE;
}
```

Finally, the Explorer view (the list control) is now in the first split of the second splitter window, so change the first line in the *GetRightPane()* function to read as follows:

```
CWnd* pWnd = m_wndSplitter2.GetPane(0, 0);
```

Compile and run the program again, and you should have one vertical splitter pane on the left and two horizontal splitter panes on the right, similar to Figure 505.

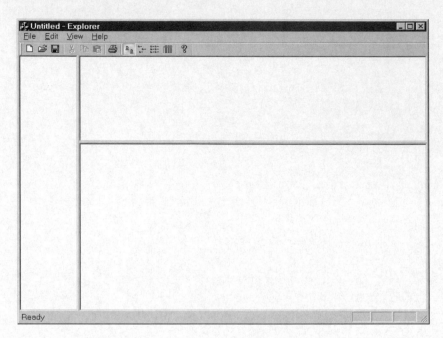

Figure 505   The client area split into three windows

The panes to the left and the lower right contain tree views, and the pane on the upper right is a list view. If you click the Report View button on the toolbar, a blank header bar should appear in the list view pane. If it doesn't or the toolbar buttons are inactive, you've incorrectly identified the pane in the *GetRightPane()* function.

You can continue this splitting process as far as you need. In my applications, the most I ever needed was six panes, and there was much pulling of hair on that project; it becomes complicated after the second split. Remember that for each split, you need another *CSplitterWnd* variable. You also need to create a window in each pane, or the framework won't accept it. The window can be a *CWnd*-derived object, but usually it is a view object. You can add more views to your project as needed. If necessary, map it out on paper, identifying the panes and the variable that holds them. You must also create member variables and functions to get to them (similar to *GetRightPane()*).

When you get to the section "Documents and Views" beginning with Tip 610, "Understanding the Document/View Architecture," you will use this program, or one similar to it, to build a directory tree on the left side and a directory list in the upper right and add an editing view in the lower right. The Visual Studio project for this program, such as it is, is on the CD-ROM.

Despite the wizard's reluctance to allow *CEditView* as a base view, *CEditView* did work in the sample program. Right now the topic is splitter windows, and an explanation of the modifications to use an editing view will have to come later.

506. Control Bar Classes

The control bar class *CControlBar* is the base class for the various control bars in the Microsoft Foundation Class library. The class is derived from *CWnd*, and thus, classes derived from it can be the target for Windows messages.

One of the most common classes derived from *CControlBar* is the *CToolBar* class, which is used to create and manipulate the docking control bar seen on many applications. A *toolbar* is a group of buttons with bitmapped images on them. Usually, the buttons are assigned the same function as menu items. When you click a button on a toolbar, it's the same as selecting a menu item; a Windows *ON_COMMAND* message is sent to the application's window containing the resource ID of the button that was clicked.

When you create an application in Visual Studio using the MFC AppWizard, the wizard creates and implements a basic toolbar for you containing buttons representing the options you selected when you set up the project. You may create your own using the toolbar editor in the Visual Studio package.

When used with the *CFrameWnd* class as a window mainframe, toolbars are "dockable" and may be placed at any position around the frame. The frame window contains the "harbors" where the toolbars dock. In addition, a toolbar may be made to "float" and not be attached to the window frame.

The toolbar is one of the Windows *common controls*, a set of controls implemented in a dynamic link library that is included with all releases of windows. A toolbar may be used by any application, not just MFC-based programs. The MFC *CToolbar* class encapsulates the functions of the toolbar control.

The next most common derivative of the *CControlBar* class is *CStatusBar*. This class, too, is based on a Windows common control. Along the bottom of many applications is a broad bar that may contain indicators for such things as CAPS LOCK, SCROLL LOCK, and NUM LOCK, as well as space for the programmer to write messages. This is the status bar, and the application wizards generally prepare it for you when you create your project.

The *CStatusBar* class isn't one of the Microsoft Foundation Class's strong points. It's difficult to work with, compared with those in other class libraries, and is limited. You would do well to derive your own class from it, but none of the member functions are *virtual*, and you can't override them to improve performance. Later, you will see how to derive your own class because you can at least intercept the messages to the status bar.

Your program may add additional indicators to the status bar and even insert icons in the indicator panes. For example, you might want to add an indicator for the insert text function. Most personal computer keyboards have status lights for Caps Lock, Shift, and Scroll Lk but none for the Insert key. Actually, it would be hard for the keyboard to track the insert because it's under software control.

Let's add a green light to the status bar that you can turn on when your program is in insert mode and turn off otherwise as shown in Figure 506. You can use the code in the *EXPLORER* project from the last tip. There are a couple of 16×16 icons for green LEDs (on and off), which you will load using *LoadImage()*, included with that project.

Figure 506   *The Insert pane used with a combination of text and an icon gives users a visual indication of the Insert key status*

First, create an entry in your string table by opening the String Table branch in the ResourceView of the Workspace window. Then double-click on String Table, and the application's string table list will appear. If you move down to the section of IDs starting with *ID_INDICATOR* and right-click on one of them, you can insert an ID at that point. I called mine *ID_INDICATOR_INSERT*. Close the string table and move to the *MainFrm.cpp* file.

At the top of the *CMainFrame* class, the wizard created for your application is a static array of unsigned *int*s. Add your new resource ID at the bottom so that the list looks like this:

```
static UINT indicators[] =
{
    ID_SEPARATOR,            // status line indicator
    ID_INDICATOR_CAPS,
    ID_INDICATOR_NUM,
    ID_INDICATOR_SCRL,
    ID_INDICATOR_INSERT
};
```

Add two member variables to the class definition, either *protected* or *private*:

```
HICON    m_iconGreenOn;
HICON    m_iconGreenOff;
```

Initialize these in the *CMainFrame* class constructor. Use the *LoadImage()* function. If you use the *LoadIcon()* function, the images will be exploded to 32×32 bits, which is too large for the status bar:

```
/////////////////////////////////////////////////////////////
// CMainFrame construction/destruction
CMainFrame::CMainFrame()
{
    m_iconGreenOn = (HICON) LoadImage (
            AfxGetInstanceHandle(),
            MAKEINTRESOURCE(IDI_LEDGREENON),
            IMAGE_ICON, 16, 16, LR_DEFAULTCOLOR);
    m_iconGreenOff = (HICON) LoadImage (
            AfxGetInstanceHandle(),
            MAKEINTRESOURCE(IDI_LEDGREENOFF),
            IMAGE_ICON, 16, 16, LR_DEFAULTCOLOR);
}
```

In the *OnCreate()* function of *CMainFrame*, after the status bar is created, you add some code to initialize the icon and text. If your application will start up with the insert off, change the call to *SetInsertLamp()* to *false*:

```
if (!m_wndStatusBar.Create(this) ||
    !m_wndStatusBar.SetIndicators(indicators,
      sizeof(indicators)/sizeof(UINT)))
{
    TRACE0("Failed to create status bar\n");
    return -1;      // fail to create
}
int nIndex;
nIndex = m_wndStatusBar.CommandToIndex(ID_INDICATOR_INSERT);
m_wndStatusBar.SetPaneInfo (nIndex, ID_INDICATOR_INSERT,
                            SBPS_NORMAL, 50);
SetInsertLamp (true);
```

Now you must add the *SetInsertLamp()* function that your view class will use to manipulate the lamp. A simple *true* or *false* function will work. When the user presses the Insert key (you can detect this in a *WM_SYSCHAR* message handler in the view or window frame classes), call the function with *true*; call it with *false* to turn off the lamp:

```
void CMainFrame::SetInsertLamp(bool bLampOn)
{
    int nIndex = m_wndStatusBar.CommandToIndex
                                (ID_INDICATOR_INSERT);
    if (bLampOn)
    {
        m_wndStatusBar.GetStatusBarCtrl().SetIcon (nIndex,
                                          m_iconGreenOn);
        m_wndStatusBar.GetStatusBarCtrl().SetText ("Ins",
                                          nIndex, 0);
    }
    else
    {
        m_wndStatusBar.GetStatusBarCtrl().SetIcon (nIndex,
                                          m_iconGreenOff);
```

```
            m_wndStatusBar.GetStatusBarCtrl().SetText ("Ovr",
                                        nIndex, 0);
        }
}
```

You can add a couple of menu items to test the function, as shown in the project on the CD-ROM.

One rather nasty habit of the *CStatusBar* class is that if you write a status message to the bar (it *is* a status bar, right?) and the user moves the mouse cursor over a toolbar or menu item, the frameworks writes the tool hint in the bar. When the user moves the mouse away from the item, the frameworks writes "Ready" to the status bar, and your status message goes somewhere to the west of Orion's belt. You've been running the application for several hours, and it says that it's "Ready." That's nice, but the message you put on the bar, informing the user of a change in the serial port status, has disappeared forever.

The Borland Object Windows Library handles this by placing a pane over your status text. When the user moves away from the object causing the message, the pane moves away and your status message reappears. In Tip 919, "Using the *CStatusBarCtrl* Class," you will derive your own class from *CStatusBar* and make it emulate The Borland Way.

Two other classes are derived from the *CControlBar* class. The *CDialogBar* class encapsulates a modeless dialog box inside a control bar. You can design the control bar as a dialog, which makes placing controls easier than attempting to insert them on the window frame.

The last of the *CControlBar* classes is the *CReBar* class. A *rebar* is similar to a toolbar except that it may contain virtually any Windows control and is separated into *bands*, which may be resized individually. Unlike the other three *CControlBar* classes, *CReBar* objects don't support docking on the window frame and must be attached permanently.

507. *Property Sheet Classes*

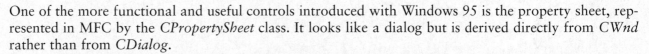

One of the more functional and useful controls introduced with Windows 95 is the property sheet, represented in MFC by the *CPropertySheet* class. It looks like a dialog but is derived directly from *CWnd* rather than from *CDialog*.

The property sheet incorporates a tab control and is designed to hold one or more property pages. It often is called a "tabbed dialog box," but don't confuse the property sheet with the tab control, which is a separate control. As you will see later, you can use a tab control on a property page or any other dialog box, for that matter. An example of a property sheet is shown in Figure 507.

You don't create a property sheet in the dialog editor. Instead, you create it in memory directly, and it allocates space for the property pages and the OK, Cancel, and Apply buttons. The only way to add other controls to the property sheet is to use the controls' create functions using the property sheet as the parent window. When the property sheet is created, the frameworks sizes it to fit the property pages, but you may resize it afterward to hold other controls.

You can see samples of property sheets throughout Windows. On the desktop, right-click any blank area of the screen and you will get the property sheet for the display.

The property sheet and property pages get an extensive workout in the section on the Windows common controls. Initially, you will create a property sheet application; then, as you look at the various controls, you will add a property page for each of them. When finished, you should have a program that shows the use of each control, and the code will contain samples you can lift out to use in your own applications.

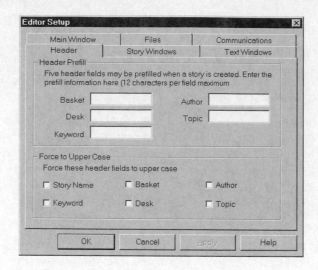

Figure 507   Property sheets enable you to group common items in a compact tabbed window rather than resort to a single, large dialog box.

The so-called "wizard" dialog is nothing more than a property sheet with a flag set. It does perform differently, however. With a property sheet, the user may go to any page at any time. With a wizard dialog, the page access is sequential, and you may prevent a user from going to the next page until some critical information is entered. The wizard dialog is common in installation and setup programs.

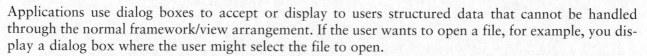

508. *Using the Dialog Classes*

Applications use dialog boxes to accept or display to users structured data that cannot be handled through the normal framework/view arrangement. If the user wants to open a file, for example, you display a dialog box where the user might select the file to open.

```
EXSTYLE WS_EX_APPWINDOW
CAPTION "Configure Time Service"
FONT 8, "MS Sans Serif"
BEGIN
    DEFPUSHBUTTON   "OK",IDOK,66,197,50,14
    PUSHBUTTON      "Cancel",IDCANCEL,157,197,50,14
    PUSHBUTTON      "&Help",ID_HELP,230,197,50,14
    CONTROL         "List1",IDC_SERVERLIST,"SysListView32",
                        LVS_REPORT | WS_BORDER |
                        WS_TABSTOP,28,32,228,115
    PUSHBUTTON      "Move Up",IDC_MOVEUP, 266,62,30,22,
                        BS_MULTILINE
    PUSHBUTTON      "Move Down",IDC_MOVEDOWN,266,97,30,22,
                        BS_MULTILINE
    PUSHBUTTON      "Add Server",IDC_ADDSERVER,266,31,30,22,
                        BS_MULTILINE
    EDITTEXT        IDC_INTERVAL,79,158,21,12,
                        ES_AUTOHSCROLL | ES_NUMBER
    RTEXT           "Check Time every",IDC_STATIC,19,160,55,9
    PUSHBUTTON      "Delete Server",IDC_DELETESERVER,
                        266,129,30,22, BS_MULTILINE
```

```
    LTEXT           "Hours",IDC_STATIC,103,160,21,9
    CONTROL         "Check and set time at service start",
                        IDC_CHECKATSTARTUP,
                    "Button",BS_AUTOCHECKBOX | WS_TABSTOP,
                        147,160,130,10
    LTEXT           "",IDC_STATICMESSAGE,26,7,228,25
    CONTROL         "DateTimePicker1",IDC_BEGINTIME,
                        "SysDateTimePick32",
                        DTS_RIGHTALIGN | DTS_UPDOWN |
                        WS_TABSTOP | 0x8,79,176,55,14
    RTEXT           "Beginning at",IDC_STATIC,22,178,54,9
    CTEXT           "On",IDC_STATIC,141,178,16,9
    CONTROL         "DateTimePicker2",IDC_BEGINDATE,
                        "SysDateTimePick32",
                        DTS_RIGHTALIGN | WS_TABSTOP,
                        164,176,58,14
END
```

*Figure 508a   The dialog box shown in Figure 508b as it appears in the application's resource file.
The resource editor generates this code for you.*

In MFC, most dialog boxes are derived from the *CDialog* class. Dialog boxes require a *dialog template* in the application's resource file. In Visual Studio, the resource editor creates this template for you as you build the dialog box. When you've finished laying out the dialog box, you right-click the mouse on it to summon the ClassWizard, which guides you through the process of deriving a class from *CDialog*.

Figure 508a shows the template for the same dialog box as it appears in the application's resource file.

In addition to the user-created dialogs, a set of dialog boxes is available in Windows, called the *common dialogs*, that are encapsulated in MFC classes derived from *CDialog*. Tip 509, "Understanding the Common Dialog Classes," summarizes the derived classes and the dialogs.

Property pages are dialogs, and classes for them are derived from *CDialog* (but not the property sheet class, which is derived directly from *CWnd*).

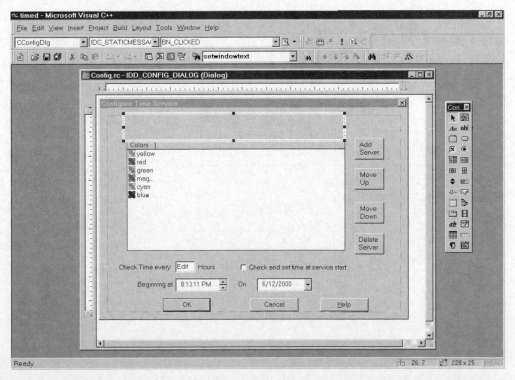

Figure 508b   A dialog box as it appears in the application's resource file. The resource editor generates this code for you.

509. *Understanding the Common Dialog Classes*

To provide a common look and feel for applications, Windows offers several dialog boxes for common operations. These are the common dialogs and are contained in the *commdlg.dll* file for 16-bit applications and *comdlg32.dll* for 32-bit Windows applications.

In MFC, the common dialog classes are derived from *CCommonDialog*, which, in turn, is derived from *CDialog*. Table 509 summarizes the common dialogs and their MFC classes.

Dialog	MFC Class	Purpose
Choose Color	CColorDialog	Incorporates a color selection dialog box using the CHOOSECOLOR Windows structure. The user may select and create custom colors, but the application is responsible for saving and storing the colors.
Choose Font	CFontDialog	Uses a CHOOSEFONT Windows structure to communicate with a font selection dialog. The user may select font families, faces, sizes, and colors, but the application is responsible for retrieving and using the font data.
File Open/Save	CFileDialog	Provides an open or save (depending on a flag supplied by the application) dialog box for files.
Find/Replace	CFindReplaceDialog	Provides a basic find string and replace function. The dialog communicates with the application using registered messages.
Print	CPrintDialog	Provides an interface to the printing process. In MFC, the printing functions use the data encapsulated in this class to access printers, even if the dialog is never displayed.

Table 509   Windows common dialogs and their MFC classes

The common dialogs are unadorned and barely meet the needs of most applications. They have remained basically unchanged since their introduction in Windows 3.1. The dialogs are not as common as their names imply because most application developers are opting to create their own.

510. *Understanding the Property Page Classes*

You've seen property pages used on property sheets. When Windows 95 was released, they were everywhere. The desktop uses them extensively. Right-click on any icon on the desktop, and you will get a property sheet, or a menu with a Properties item allowing you to display one. Right-click even on a blank area of the desktop, and you can get a property sheet for the system display.

You create the property sheet in memory, but you create the property pages in the Visual Studio dialog editor. A *property page* is nothing more than a dialog box containing a *PROPSHEETPAGE* structure that stores the characteristics of the page when it is placed on a property sheet. In fact, a property page often is called a "tab dialog."

You create a property page in the Resource Workshop by selecting one of the property page types under the dialog item on the Insert function, or you can create it as an ordinary dialog box. There are a few differences, however. You should give a property page dialog a thin border and make it a child window instead of a pop-up. It can have a title bar (the title is used as the default label for the tab), but it should not contain a system menu. On the More Styles page, you should mark it Disabled (the property sheet control will enable it, but failing to mark it disabled won't cause any problems). Figures 510a and 510b show a property sheet page under construction in the resource editor on the left, and as it appears on the screen on the right.

After creating the dialog box, right-click on any part of the dialog frame and select ClassWizard to create a control class for it. The base class must be *CPropertyPage* if you are going to put it on a property sheet. The *CPropertyPage* class itself is derived from *CDialog*.

In the section on Windows Common Controls, you will prepare a property page for each control or class of controls. When you're finished, you will have a number of pages on the property sheet and a good feel for how the individual pages can be used to encapsulate common types of data.

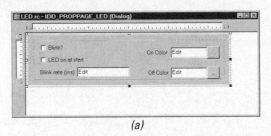
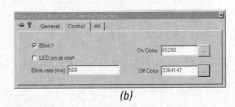

(a)   (b)

Figure 510a and 510b   You create a property page using the dialog editor, as shown for this ActiveX control (a).
You derive your class from CPropertyPage instead of CDialog.
The property sheet control adds the tab to it when you insert it on the property sheet (b).

511. *Understanding User Dialog Classes*

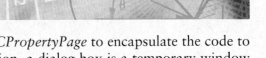

The user dialog classes are those you derive from *CDialog* or *CPropertyPage* to encapsulate the code to handle your own dialog boxes. When used within an application, a dialog box is a temporary window used to gather or present information to a user or to prompt for an action.

In MFC programming, you must create a unique class for every dialog box you build. The classes you create using the ClassWizard include a constructor, a destructor, and a data exchange function that allows you to exchange data between your class and the controls on the dialog. You may add your initialization code to the constructor and clean up code in the destructor, but you shouldn't edit this data exchange function, *DoDataExchange*, until you're familiar with what it does.

Dialog boxes come in two flavors: modal and modeless. The modal dialog is the most common. You create it simply by calling the *DoModal()* member function of *CDialog* or your own dialog class if you've overridden *DoModal()*. With a modal dialog, the user is prevented from continuing with the program until the dialog box has been closed. Typically, you override at least the *InitDialog()* to initialize the dialog controls and *OnOK* to retrieve data from the controls and send them back to your application. The most common way to do this is to create *public* variables that can be initialized in the application before the dialog is created and read before the dialog is destroyed. Another method is to override the *DoModal()* function and pass the data as arguments to it. I prefer to use a subclass in the dialog class, invariably named *CData* (which is *not* an MFC class). The application creates and initializes the *CData* object and passes a reference to it in the dialog class constructor. When the dialog exits, it writes the data back into the *CData* object. This way, it's possible to maintain the sanctity of data in both classes and exchange it through a common object.

You also may build a project using a dialog box as your main window, as in Tip 515, "Invoking the Visual Studio Wizard to Create a Dialog-Based Program." Dialog boxes normally get created in response to a user action, but in a dialog-based application, the dialog instance is created in the application's *InitInstance()* function, and the program terminates when the dialog box is closed.

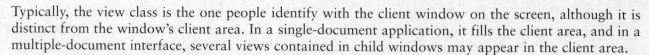

512. *Understanding View Classes*

Typically, the view class is the one people identify with the client window on the screen, although it is distinct from the window's client area. In a single-document application, it fills the client area, and in a multiple-document interface, several views contained in child windows may appear in the client area.

The view performs two important functions in Windows programming. First, it gives the user a visual presentation of the document. If the document is text, the view presents the characters in a chosen font in a predetermined way. If the document contains a graphic image, the view translates the graphics code into something that is meaningful to the user and displays it in the view. A view can be designed to present both text and graphics.

Second, the view accepts user input through the keyboard or mouse, or any other input device, and translates it for the document. Keyboard input is easy to imagine; you accept the keyboarded character, display it on the screen at the caret point, and ship the character's code to the document for insertion. A mouse stroke, on the other hand, might not be so easy. In this case, the view class might be responsible for capturing the mouse points sent to the window in an array and then packing them into an object the document can understand.

513. *Introducing the MFC View Classes*

In the class hierarchy, the Microsoft Foundation Class starts with a basic view class and builds into more specific purposes, incorporating controls and various features in the derived view classes.

The MFC library provides a number of view classes you may use to build your applications, as summarized in Table 513.

MFC View Class	Description
CView	A generic view class that may be used for graphic programming or to which you may attach a control. Only basic support is provided. This is the base class for all view classes in MFC.
CCtrlView	Another generic view class that may be used to build a view from virtually any control. It is derived from *CView* and is the base class for several MFC view classes.
CEditView	Embeds a *CEdit* control object into a view and provides basic text-editing support. Also provides basic printer support.
CRichEditView	Encapsulates a rich edit control into the view. This view may be used to display text in different fonts, colors, and point sizes and to display graphic objects simultaneously. Requires compound-document (OLE) support.

Table 513   MFC view classes and their uses (continued on following page)

MFC View Class	Description
CListView	Provides the functionality of a list control in a window view. The list control was introduced with Windows 95 and, itself, may provide several views, such as report, list, small icon, and large icon. In Windows Explorer, this is the view used on the right side of the window.
CPreviewView	Undocumented view. Used for print previewing. Works with undocumented device context class *CPreviewDC*, which contains two device contexts: one for the printer and one for the screen.
CTreeView	Encapsulates a tree control into a window view. In Windows Explorer, this is the view used on the left side of the application's window.
CScrollView	Another generic view class derived directly from *CView*. This is the class from which most user-defined views are derived. It controls the window display by controlling the viewport and mapping modes, and scrolls automatically in response to scroll bar messages.
CFormView	Incorporates a dialog template and lets you place various controls in the view. It is derived from *CScrollView* and supports the same viewport/mapping control features.
CHtmlView	This is a World Wide Web browser in a view control. This view presents a window in which the user may browse the Web and directories on the local machine. It supports hyperlinks and navigation and maintains a history list. Derived from *CFormView*.

Table 513   MFC view classes and their uses (continued from previous page)

Your application will determine what type view you use. A *CListView*-based application might be a good selection for a database program but is not suitable for a graphics application.

You may have more than one view in an application. A database program, for example, might benefit from a list view to present the database items in a scrollable list and from a form view to display the records and permit the user to modify the records. The intent of the *CSplitterWnd* class discussed earlier is to provide just this functionality.

514. *Invoking the Visual Studio Wizard to Create a View Class Program*

In the Visual Studio, you select the base class for your view as the sixth and last step in preparing a project using the MFC AppWizard. Before you get there, however, you have to make some decisions along the way that will affect your choice of views.

If you don't select Document/View Architecture Support on the first page of the wizard, you won't be able to select any of the view classes. Your "view" will be derived from *CWnd*.

On Page 3, if you don't select at least Container for the compound-document support, the wizard won't let you select *CRichEditView* as your base class. You may remove much of the OLE code from your application after it's created, but the wizard guru at Microsoft decided not to let you get past this point without it.

If you select Use Split Window from the advanced options on Page 4, the wizard imposes some curious restrictions. You can't, for example, select *CTreeView* or *CListView* as your base class; yet, those are exactly the views the wizard uses for a split window application when you select Windows Explorer for the project style on Page 5. Curiously, you may select *CHtmlView* as the base class, but not

CRichEditView, and *CEditView* isn't even listed as an option. Other than *CHtmlView*, your only options are *CView* and *CScrollView*.

Step back and remove the Use Split Window option and select Windows Explorer on Page 5, which is a splitter window application, and the only *verboten* view is *CRichEditView*. If, however, you choose *CEditView*, for example, your program will assert the first time you try to open a document. It is possible to use *CEditView* in a splitter window application, but you have to roll some of your own code. That's the approach taken later with the splitter window application from Tip 505, "Using the *CSplitterWnd* Class," when you start applying views to it in the section "Documents and Views" beginning with Tip 610, "Understanding the Document/View Architecture."

515. Invoking the Visual Studio Wizard to Create a Dialog-Based Program

If you create a dialog box–based application, you have only two pages of options. Obviously, the Windows Explorer–style application is disabled, but the other options are the same as for a document/view application.

Dialog-based applications can be complex programs containing a property sheet, or they can be a quick way to solve a programming problem. The first is adequately demonstrated in the section "Windows Common Controls Tips 807–817," so let's do the quick-hit program here, one to allow you to change the attributes of a disk file. The dialog uses a list box to show the contents of the current directory and four check boxes to show and to set or remove the file attributes.

Start out with the MFC AppWizard. You can call the project "Attributes" and select Dialog-Based on Page 1 of the wizard. On Pages 2 and 3, accept the defaults and go directly to Page 4. The wizard will prepare two classes for you. The first is the application class, *CAttributesApp*. The second is *CAttributesDlg*, which is the *CDialog*-based class from which you control and manipulate the dialog box. You can't change the base classes for either of these at this point (you can make changes after the application is created, however), so go ahead and create the application.

When the wizard creates the application, it prepares and displays a large dialog box. Using the resource editor, resize the dialog box to something more manageable. Grab the edge or corner of the dialog, and with the left mouse button, drag it inward to make the box smaller. The dialog box on the companion CD-ROM is 184 by 175 (the size of the dialog box is displayed at the far right of the Visual Studio status bar). The finished dialog box is shown in Figure 515.

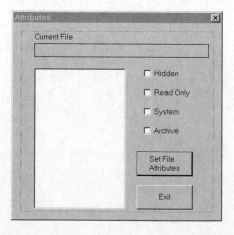

Figure 515   The File Attributes dialog box controls before coding starts

Right-click the OK button and select Properties from the menu. In the dialog that appears, change the caption on the General page to read "Set File Attributes." Select the Styles page and check the Multi-line check box. You don't need to change the resource ID. Do the same for the Cancel button, except make the caption read "Exit." While you're working on the dialog box, you might want to click on the push-pin on the properties dialog to keep it on the screen; if you don't, it will disappear each time you select another item, and you will have to go through the right-click and properties routine each time.

At the top of the dialog, add a static text field and set the caption to read "Current File." Select the static text icon on the toolbar; then, move to the dialog box and draw the control by holding down the left mouse button. Right below that, add another static text control and remove the caption. Use the *CStaticEx* class from Tip 484, "Deriving Classes from *CEdit* and *CStatic* to Set Text Attributes" because you will want to draw this field using the device context *TextOut()* function. Using this function, you can set the *DT_PATH_ELLIPSIS* flag so that a long path name, which otherwise would overrun the control, will be drawn with an ellipsis in the middle, keeping the file name visible. The static control doesn't have an owner draw style bit, but you can intercept the *WM_PAINT* message and draw over the object.

Select the list box icon and draw a list box on the dialog box, as shown in Figure 515a. Now add four check boxes by selecting the check box icon and drawing them on the dialog. You have to reselect the check box icon for each control you draw. Use the Layout menu on the main menu bar to align and size the controls so that they match. Make the captions for the four check boxes read "Hidden," "Read Only," "System," and "Archive." Select each control in order, and make sure that the ID fields contain the resource IDs shown in the figure.

Move to the *AttributesDlg.cpp* file. If you added *CStaticEx* to your gallery, add it to the project now. Otherwise, copy it from Tip 484. You will see shortly why this is important.

Right-click on the *AttributesDlg.cpp* file and select ClassWizard from the menu. Move to the Member Variables tab and add a *BOOL* variable for each of the check boxes. Make the variable names read *m_bHidden*, *m_bReadOnly*, *m_bSystem*, and *m_bArchive*. Add a member variable, *m_ctlCurrentFile*, for *IDC_CURRENT_FILE* as a static control type. Finally, add a member variable named *m_listDirectory* for the list box *IDC_LIST_DIRECTORY*.

Move to the Message Maps tabs and add a message handler for each of the check boxes. Select the check box ID in the Object ID field and *BN_CLICKED* in the Messages field, and click on the Add Function button. Accept the default function names for each. Now select *IDC_LIST_DIRECTORY*, and add message handlers for *LBN_SELCHANGE* and *LBN_DBLCLK*.

Select the ClassView pane on the Workshop window, and add two *CString* variables to the *CAttributesDlg* class. Name them *m_strCurrentFile* and *m_strCurrentPath*. Add a member function *LoadList()* of type *void* with no parameters. Open the *attributesdlg.h* file and change the control type for *m_ctlCurrentFile* to *CStaticEx*; add a line at the top of the file to include *staticex.h*. The *attributesdlg.h* file should look like this:

```
/////////////////////////////////////////////////////////////////
// CAttributesDlg dialog
#include   "StaticEx.h"

class CAttributesDlg : public CDialog
{
// Construction
public:
// standard constructor
    CAttributesDlg(CWnd* pParent = NULL);

// Dialog Data
    //{{AFX_DATA(CAttributesDlg)
    enum { IDD = IDD_ATTRIBUTES_DIALOG };
    CStaticEx m_ctlCurrentFile;
```

```
    CListBox    m_listDirectory;
    BOOL    m_bArchive;
    BOOL    m_bHidden;
    BOOL    m_bReadOnly;
    BOOL    m_bSystem;
    //}}AFX_DATA

    // ClassWizard generated virtual function overrides
    //{{AFX_VIRTUAL(CAttributesDlg)
    protected:
    virtual void DoDataExchange(CDataExchange* pDX);
    //}}AFX_VIRTUAL

// Implementation
protected:
    HICON m_hIcon;

    // Generated message map functions
    //{{AFX_MSG(CAttributesDlg)
    virtual BOOL OnInitDialog();
    afx_msg void OnSysCommand(UINT nID, LPARAM lParam);
    afx_msg void OnPaint();
    afx_msg HCURSOR OnQueryDragIcon();
    afx_msg void OnCheckArchive();
    afx_msg void OnCheckHidden();
    afx_msg void OnCheckReadonly();
    afx_msg void OnCheckSystem();
    afx_msg void OnSelchangeListDirectory();
    virtual void OnOK();
    afx_msg void OnDblclkListDirectory();
    //}}AFX_MSG
    DECLARE_MESSAGE_MAP()

    CString m_strCurrentPath;
    CString m_strCurrentFile;

private:
    void LoadList();
};
```

Before you start coding the dialog box controls, you must tend to a couple of housekeeping items. First, collapse the tree in the ResourceView pane of the Workshop window by clicking on the hyphen box just to the left of the entry Attribute Resources. This will close the resource editor. From the command line, move to the project directory and open *attributes.rc* in NotePad or another text editor.

Locate the list box entry in the dialog template. By default, the resource editor adds *LBS_SORT* to the list box styles, and you can't change it from the editor. You're going to be building a directory in this control, so you don't want to sort it. You want the drive entries at the top of the list, then the directories, and then the files themselves. Remove the characters *LBS_SORT |* from the following line. Save and close the file and return to Visual Studio.

```
LISTBOX        IDC_LIST_DIRECTORY,19,40,80,126,LBS_SORT |
                LBS_NOINTEGRALHEIGHT | WS_VSCROLL |
                WS_TABSTOP
```

Now move to *staticex.cpp* and add a message handler for the *WM_PAINT* message. The static control will draw the text for the control, so you must add this handler so that you can draw over the text with the *TextOut()* function. Depending on whether the ClassWizard picked up the class, you might have to do this by hand. I've found that sometimes the wizard doesn't recognize the control class until I add a couple of member variables to the dialog class that uses it. The message map and the *OnPaint()* function are shown here:

```
BEGIN_MESSAGE_MAP(CStaticEx, CStatic)
    //{{AFX_MSG_MAP(CStaticEx)
    ON_WM_CTLCOLOR_REFLECT()
    ON_WM_PAINT()
    //}}AFX_MSG_MAP
END_MESSAGE_MAP()

void CStaticEx::OnPaint()
{
    CPaintDC dc(this); // device context for painting
    CString strText;
    GetWindowText (strText);
//
// CStatic's OnPaint is called first and leaves some
// garbage in the window. Draw a rectangle to erase it.
    Rectangle (dc, m_ctlRect.left - 1, m_ctlRect.top - 1,
                m_ctlRect.right + 1, m_ctlRect.bottom + 1);
    dc.DrawText ((LPCSTR)strText, strText.GetLength(),
                &m_ctlRect, DT_PATH_ELLIPSIS |
                DT_VCENTER | DT_SINGLELINE);
}
```

When you get the program running, try removing the *DT_PATH_ELLIPSIS* flag from the *dc.DrawText()* function, and select a long path name. You will see why this extra trouble is more than worth the effort.

Now you're ready to start coding the dialog box functions. Note that the *about* box has been moved out of the file and its *include* file added at the top. Also, a few constants are at the top of the file to make the list box operations easier.

```
// AttributesDlg.cpp : implementation file
//

#include "stdafx.h"
#include "Attributes.h"
#include "AttributesDlg.h"
#include "about.h"

#ifdef _DEBUG
#define new DEBUG_NEW
#undef THIS_FILE
static char THIS_FILE[] = __FILE__;
#endif

#define    LB_DRIVEITEM    0x4000
#define    LB_DIRITEM      0x0010
#define    LB_FILEITEM     0x002f
#define    LB_EXCLUSIVE    0x8000
const char  *LB_WILDCARD = "*.*";

/////////////////////////////////////////////////////////
// CAttributesDlg dialog

CAttributesDlg::CAttributesDlg(CWnd* pParent /*=NULL*/)
```

```cpp
        : CDialog(CAttributesDlg::IDD, pParent)
{
    //{{AFX_DATA_INIT(CAttributesDlg)
    m_bArchive = FALSE;
    m_bHidden = FALSE;
    m_bReadOnly = FALSE;
    m_bSystem = FALSE;
    //}}AFX_DATA_INIT
// Note that LoadIcon does not require a subsequent
// DestroyIcon in Win32
    m_hIcon = AfxGetApp()->LoadIcon(IDR_MAINFRAME);
    m_strCurrentFile = _T("");
}

void CAttributesDlg::DoDataExchange(CDataExchange* pDX)
{
    CDialog::DoDataExchange(pDX);
    //{{AFX_DATA_MAP(CAttributesDlg)
    DDX_Control(pDX, IDC_CURRENT_FILE, m_ctlCurrentFile);
    DDX_Control(pDX, IDC_LIST_DIRECTORY, m_listDirectory);
    DDX_Check(pDX, IDC_CHECK_ARCHIVE, m_bArchive);
    DDX_Check(pDX, IDC_CHECK_HIDDEN, m_bHidden);
    DDX_Check(pDX, IDC_CHECK_READONLY, m_bReadOnly);
    DDX_Check(pDX, IDC_CHECK_SYSTEM, m_bSystem);
    //}}AFX_DATA_MAP
}

BEGIN_MESSAGE_MAP(CAttributesDlg, CDialog)
    //{{AFX_MSG_MAP(CAttributesDlg)
    ON_WM_SYSCOMMAND()
    ON_WM_PAINT()
    ON_WM_QUERYDRAGICON()
    ON_BN_CLICKED(IDC_CHECK_ARCHIVE, OnCheckArchive)
    ON_BN_CLICKED(IDC_CHECK_HIDDEN, OnCheckHidden)
    ON_BN_CLICKED(IDC_CHECK_READONLY, OnCheckReadonly)
    ON_BN_CLICKED(IDC_CHECK_SYSTEM, OnCheckSystem)
    ON_LBN_SELCHANGE(IDC_LIST_DIRECTORY,
                     OnSelchangeListDirectory)
    ON_LBN_DBLCLK(IDC_LIST_DIRECTORY, OnDblclkListDirectory)
    //}}AFX_MSG_MAP
END_MESSAGE_MAP()

/////////////////////////////////////////////////////////
// CAttributesDlg message handlers

BOOL CAttributesDlg::OnInitDialog()
{
    CDialog::OnInitDialog();

    // Add "About..." menu item to system menu.

    // IDM_ABOUTBOX must be in the system command range.
    ASSERT((IDM_ABOUTBOX & 0xFFF0) == IDM_ABOUTBOX);
    ASSERT(IDM_ABOUTBOX < 0xF000);

    CMenu* pSysMenu = GetSystemMenu(FALSE);
```

```
    if (pSysMenu != NULL)
    {
        CString strAboutMenu;
        strAboutMenu.LoadString(IDS_ABOUTBOX);
        if (!strAboutMenu.IsEmpty())
        {
            pSysMenu->AppendMenu(MF_SEPARATOR);
            pSysMenu->AppendMenu(MF_STRING, IDM_ABOUTBOX,
                                 strAboutMenu);
        }
    }

    // Set the icon for this dialog.  The framework does
    // this automatically when the application's main window
    // is not a dialog

    SetIcon(m_hIcon, TRUE);          // Set big icon
    SetIcon(m_hIcon, FALSE);         // Set small icon

    int nBytes = GetCurrentDirectory (0, NULL);
    char *szDir = new char [nBytes + 1];
    GetCurrentDirectory (nBytes + 1, szDir);
    m_strCurrentPath = szDir;
    delete [] szDir;
//
// Set the rectangle for the static control. We will
// draw it ourselves after MFC doinks with it.
    RECT rc;
    CWnd *cwStaticEx;
    cwStaticEx = GetDlgItem(IDC_CURRENT_FILE);
    cwStaticEx->GetWindowRect(&rc);
    rc.right = rc.right - rc.left;
    rc.bottom = rc.bottom - rc.top;
    rc.top = 0;
    rc.left = 0;
    m_ctlCurrentFile.m_ctlRect = rc;

// Load the directory info into the list box
    LoadList ();
    UpdateData(FALSE);
    return TRUE;  // return TRUE unless you set
                  // the focus to a control
}

void CAttributesDlg::OnSysCommand(UINT nID, LPARAM lParam)
{
    if ((nID & 0xFFF0) == IDM_ABOUTBOX)
    {
        CAboutDlg dlgAbout;
        dlgAbout.DoModal();
    }
    else
    {
        CDialog::OnSysCommand(nID, lParam);
    }
}
```

```cpp
// If you add a minimize button to your dialog, you will
// need the code below to draw the icon. For MFC applications
// using the document/view model, this is automatically done
// for you by the framework.

void CAttributesDlg::OnPaint()
{
    if (IsIconic())
    {
        CPaintDC dc(this); // device context for painting

        SendMessage(WM_ICONERASEBKGND,
                    (WPARAM) dc.GetSafeHdc(), 0);

        // Center icon in client rectangle
        int cxIcon = GetSystemMetrics(SM_CXICON);
        int cyIcon = GetSystemMetrics(SM_CYICON);
        CRect rect;
        GetClientRect(&rect);
        int x = (rect.Width() - cxIcon + 1) / 2;
        int y = (rect.Height() - cyIcon + 1) / 2;

        // Draw the icon
        dc.DrawIcon(x, y, m_hIcon);
    }
    else
    {
        CDialog::OnPaint();
    }
}

// The system calls this to obtain the cursor to display
// while the user drags the minimized window.
HCURSOR CAttributesDlg::OnQueryDragIcon()
{
    return (HCURSOR) m_hIcon;
}

// The following four functions are handlers for the check
// boxes. They simply reverse the variable's TRUE or FALSE
// value when a check box changes. You could achieve the
// same results simply by calling UpdateData(TRUE) in each
// message handler.
void CAttributesDlg::OnCheckArchive()
{
    m_bArchive = m_bArchive ? FALSE : TRUE;
}
void CAttributesDlg::OnCheckHidden()
{
    m_bHidden = m_bHidden ? FALSE : TRUE;
}

void CAttributesDlg::OnCheckReadonly()
{
    m_bReadOnly = m_bReadOnly ? FALSE : TRUE;
```

```
}

void CAttributesDlg::OnCheckSystem()
{
    m_bSystem = m_bSystem ? FALSE : TRUE;
}


//
// Message handler called when the user selects an item
//  in the list box.
void CAttributesDlg::OnSelchangeListDirectory()
{
CString strDir;
CFileStatus fs;

    int nIndex = m_listDirectory.GetCurSel ();
    m_listDirectory.GetText (nIndex, strDir);
    DWORD dwData = m_listDirectory.GetItemData (nIndex);
    switch (dwData)
    {
        case LB_DRIVEITEM:
            m_strCurrentFile.Empty ();
            m_ctlCurrentFile.SetWindowText (_T(""));
            fs.m_attribute = 0;
            break;
        case LB_DIRITEM:
            strDir.Delete (0);
            strDir.Delete (strDir.GetLength() - 1);
        default:
            CFile::GetStatus ((LPCTSTR) strDir, fs);
            m_strCurrentFile = fs.m_szFullName;
            m_ctlCurrentFile.SetWindowText
                            ((LPCSTR) m_strCurrentFile);
            break;
    }
    m_ctlCurrentFile.Invalidate (TRUE);
    m_bHidden = fs.m_attribute & FILE_ATTRIBUTE_HIDDEN ?
                                TRUE : FALSE;
    m_bArchive = fs.m_attribute & FILE_ATTRIBUTE_ARCHIVE ?
                                TRUE : FALSE;
    m_bSystem = fs.m_attribute & FILE_ATTRIBUTE_SYSTEM ?
                                TRUE : FALSE;
    m_bReadOnly = fs.m_attribute & FILE_ATTRIBUTE_READONLY ?
                                TRUE : FALSE;
    UpdateData (FALSE);
}

void CAttributesDlg::LoadList()
{
int nCount;
int i;

// Delete any old stuff in the list box.
    nCount = m_listDirectory.GetCount();
    while (nCount > 0)
    {
```

```
                nCount = m_listDirectory.DeleteString(nCount-1);
        }
// List the drive items first
    m_listDirectory.Dir (LB_DRIVEITEM | LB_EXCLUSIVE,
                         LB_WILDCARD);
// Next list the directories
    m_listDirectory.Dir (LB_DIRITEM | LB_EXCLUSIVE,
                         LB_WILDCARD);
// And finally list the files in the current directory
    m_listDirectory.Dir (LB_FILEITEM | LB_EXCLUSIVE,
                         LB_WILDCARD);
// Set the items data to the entry type
    nCount = m_listDirectory.GetCount ();
    for (i = 0; i < nCount; ++i)
    {
    CString strItem;

        m_listDirectory.GetText (i, strItem);
        if (strItem.GetAt(0) == '[')
        {
            if (strItem.GetAt(1) == '-') // It's a drive
                m_listDirectory.SetItemData(i,LB_DRIVEITEM);
            else                         // It's a directory
                m_listDirectory.SetItemData (i, LB_DIRITEM);
        }
        else                             // It's a file
        {
            m_listDirectory.SetItemData (i, 0x0000);
        }
    }
}


// Use the OK button to perform the operation. Don't call
// CDialog's OnOK function or you'll close the dialog.
void CAttributesDlg::OnOK()
{
CString strFileName;

    UpdateData (TRUE);
    int nIndex = m_listDirectory.GetCurSel ();
    if (nIndex < 0)
        return;
    DWORD dwData = m_listDirectory.GetItemData (nIndex);
    m_listDirectory.GetText (nIndex, strFileName);
    switch (dwData)
    {
        case LB_DRIVEITEM:
            AfxMessageBox (_T("Cannot change drive \
attributes"), MB_ICONSTOP);
            break;
        case LB_DIRITEM:
            strFileName.Delete (0);
            strFileName.Delete (strFileName.GetLength()-1);
            dwData = 0;
            dwData |= m_bHidden ?
                              FILE_ATTRIBUTE_HIDDEN : 0;
```

```
                    dwData |= m_bArchive ?
                                    FILE_ATTRIBUTE_ARCHIVE : 0;
                    dwData |= m_bSystem ?
                                    FILE_ATTRIBUTE_SYSTEM : 0;
                    dwData |= m_bReadOnly ?
                                    FILE_ATTRIBUTE_READONLY : 0;
                    if (!SetFileAttributes (strFileName, dwData))
                        AfxMessageBox (_T("Directory attribute \
change failed"), MB_ICONSTOP);
                    break;
            default:
                CFileStatus fs;
                CFile::GetStatus ((LPCTSTR) strFileName, fs);
// Mask out only the attributes under consideration
                fs.m_attribute &= ~(FILE_ATTRIBUTE_HIDDEN |
                            FILE_ATTRIBUTE_ARCHIVE |
                            FILE_ATTRIBUTE_SYSTEM |
                            FILE_ATTRIBUTE_READONLY);
                fs.m_attribute |= m_bHidden ?
                            FILE_ATTRIBUTE_HIDDEN : 0;
                fs.m_attribute |= m_bArchive ?
                            FILE_ATTRIBUTE_ARCHIVE : 0;
                fs.m_attribute |= m_bSystem ?
                            FILE_ATTRIBUTE_SYSTEM : 0;
                fs.m_attribute |= m_bReadOnly ?
                            FILE_ATTRIBUTE_READONLY : 0;
                TRY
                {
                    CFile::SetStatus (fs.m_szFullName, fs);
                }
                CATCH (CFileException, e)
                {
                    char errmes[_MAX_PATH];
                    memset (errmes, '\0', _MAX_PATH);
                    e->GetErrorMessage (errmes, _MAX_PATH);
                    CString Message =
                            _T("Set attribute call failed\n");
                    Message += errmes;
                    AfxMessageBox (Message, MB_ICONSTOP);
                }
                END_CATCH
                break;
    }
}

// Handle the double click on item event. If it's a drive,
// change to that drive. If it's a directory, change to
// that directory.
void CAttributesDlg::OnDblclkListDirectory()
{
CString strDir;

    int nIndex = m_listDirectory.GetCurSel ();
    DWORD dwData = m_listDirectory.GetItemData (nIndex);
    m_listDirectory.GetText (nIndex, strDir);
    switch (dwData)
```

```
{
    case LB_DRIVEITEM:
        strDir.Delete (0, 2);
        strDir.Delete (strDir.GetLength() - 2, 2);
        strDir += ':';
        if (!SetCurrentDirectory ((LPCSTR) strDir))
        {
            AfxMessageBox (_T("Drive change failed"),
                        MB_ICONSTOP);
            return;
        }
        break;
    case LB_DIRITEM:
        strDir.Delete (0);
        strDir.Delete (strDir.GetLength() - 1);
        if (!SetCurrentDirectory ((LPCSTR) strDir))
        {
            AfxMessageBox(_T("Directory change failed"),
                        MB_ICONSTOP);
            return;
        }
        break;
    default:
// If the double click is on a file item, treat it as
// a single click
        return;
}
// Rebuild the list box contents
    LoadList ();
// Reset the member variables
    int nBytes = GetCurrentDirectory (0, NULL);
    char *szDir = new char [nBytes + 1];
    GetCurrentDirectory (nBytes + 1, szDir);
    m_strCurrentPath = szDir;
    delete [] szDir;
// Unselect any selection
    m_listDirectory.SetCurSel (-1);
    m_bArchive = FALSE;
    m_bHidden = FALSE;
    m_bReadOnly = FALSE;
    m_bSystem = FALSE;
    UpdateData (FALSE);
}
```

Of primary interest is the *LoadList()* function. The list box class contains a handy function, *Dir()*, to get the contents of the current directory. Before the list control was added with Windows 95, this was a primary method of building a directory display for many applications. You call it first with the drive and exclusive flags set to list only the drives in the system. This places them at the top of the list box. Without the *LB_SORT* flag in the resource file, they will stay there.

Next, the subdirectories in the current directory are added to the list. Finally you list the files themselves. Using a value of *LB_FILEITEM (0x2f)* in the call lists *all* files, including hidden and system files. Microsoft surely would prefer that you not tinker with the attributes of these files, but it's your computer, right?

The code then loops through the items and sets the data for an item to its type. Each entry in the list box has a data item you can set either as a *DWORD* value or as a pointer. Often, you would use this to store a pointer to a structure containing more detailed information about the entry. You can set this value with *SetItemData()* or *SetItemDataPtr()*, but don't try to set both of them (they are the same object). The first function simply stores the value as a number, which can be negative. The second stores the value as a *void* pointer. You can retrieve the values by calling *GetItemData()* or *GetItemDataPtr()*. The latter returns a *void* pointer, so you will have to cast it to the type you stored. This simple program uses the item data to store the type of list entry.

The *OnDblclkListDirectory()* is called when the user double-clicks on an entry. If the entry is a drive, the code changes to that drive and accepts whatever is the current directory there. If it is a directory, it changes to that directory. In both cases, it reloads the list box to show the new contents. If the double-click is on a file item, the code does nothing and lets the operating system treat it as a selection change.

In the *OnOK()* message handler, there are two ways to set the attributes. The *CFile::SetStatus()* method works only on files, so it may be used to set file attributes. You can get the attributes of directories using *CFile::GetStatus()*, but you can't set them with *CFile::SetStatus()*, so you need to use *SetFileAttributes()* in the Windows API. You can't change the attributes of drives with either method, so just pop up a message box saying so.

The *CFile::SetStatus()* throws an exception if the call fails, but *SetFileAttributes()* simply returns an error code. For the file, you can catch the exception on failure and get the associated error message. Add this to your message lead-in and display it in a message box.

Your dialog-based application should be ready to go. To see the effects of custom-drawing the current selection window, select a directory/file combination that exceeds the width of the text in the window. You should see an ellipsis in the middle of it, but the file name itself at the end of the string should be intact.

516. *Introducing the File Services Classes*

The file services classes provide access to unbuffered file operations for binary, unformatted input and output. They are derived from *CObject* and thus provide serialization support for objects in conjunction with the *CArchive* class. The *CFile* class, which may be used directly, is the base class for all but one member of this group, the *CRecentFileList*, which, itself, is derived directly from *CObject*.

There are some points you should remember when you use the File Services classes:

- The descendant classes all inherit *CFile*'s polymorphic functions, so objects of any descendant class may be treated as disk files.

- *CFile* objects are intended for unformatted, binary data transfer. For text operations, the standard *iostreams* classes may be used.

- The *CRecentFileList*, provides direct access to the Registry or an initialization (*.INI*) file to store the most recently used (MRU) list of files opened by an application.

517. *Using* CFile *and Its Descendants*

CFile may be passed a file name and open flags in its constructor at the time the object is created, or it may be passed the handle of a file that already is open. A third constructor, the default constructor, takes no parameters. The first two methods, however, throw an exception if the file can't be opened. The default constructor always succeeds, and you can use the *Open()* member function to open the file. Except when *CFile* attaches to an already open file, the file is closed automatically when the *CFile* object is destroyed.

The default constructor is the preferred method of creating a *CFile* object. However, when using the other constructors, static member functions allow you to check the status of a file before creating the *CFile* object. The open flags consist of two or more items from Table 517. At least one access mode flag and one share flag are required.

Open Flag	Description
CFile::modeCreate	A new file is created. If the file already exists, it is truncated to 0 length.
CFile::modeNoTruncate	When combined with *modeCreate*, it does not truncate an existing file.
CFile::modeRead	Opens the file for reading only.
CFile::modeWrite	Opens the file for writing only.
CFile::modeReadWrite	Opens the file for reading and writing.
CFile::modeNoInherit	The open file is not inherited by child processes. Normally, a child will inherit open file handles.
CFile::shareDenyNone	Other processes may open the file for reading or writing. If combined with *modeCreate*, the creation will fail if the file already has been opened by another process.
CFile::shareDenyRead	Other processes may not open the file for reading. When combined with *modeCreate*, the creation will fail if the file already has been opened for reading by another process.
CFile::shareDenyWrite	Other processes may not open the file for writing. When combined with *modeCreate*, the creation will fail if the file already has been opened for writing by another process.
CFile::shareExclusive	Other processes may not open the file for reading or writing. The call will fail if the file already has been opened for reading or writing by another process or the same process.
CFile::typeText	The file is opened in DOS text mode. The end of a line is converted to a carriage return/line feed combination. This mode is intended for use by derived classes only.
CFile::typeBinary	The file is opened in binary. Data is written, as is, with no line ender conversion. *CFile* opens all files in binary, so this mode is intended for use by derived classes only.

Table 517 CFile *open flags*

CFile contains four static functions that you may call without creating a *CFile* object:

- **CFile::Rename(LPCTSTR OldFileName, LPCSTR NewFileName)**. Renames *OldFileName* to *NewFileName*. A file exception is thrown if the call fails.

- **CFile::Remove(LPCTSTR FileName)**. Deletes *FileName*. Throws a file exception if *FileName* is open or can't be deleted.

- **CFile::GetStatus(LPCTSTR FileName, CFileStatus& fs)**. Gets the attributes of the named file or directory.

- *CFile::SetStatus(LPCTSTR FileName, CFileStatus& fs)*. Sets the attributes of the named file. Throws an exception on error or if the *FileName* is a directory or drive.

When you need a file handle for calls to the Windows API, *CFile* stores the value in a *public* member variable, *m_hFile*, but its meaning may vary in derived classes.

518. *Using Memory Files*

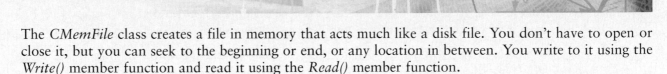

The *CMemFile* class creates a file in memory that acts much like a disk file. You don't have to open or close it, but you can seek to the beginning or end, or any location in between. You write to it using the *Write()* member function and read it using the *Read()* member function.

A *CMemFile* object is handy for a local process to store and retrieve data quickly, but there doesn't appear to be any way to share it between processes. You can't open it with a common name as you can shared memory files, and the file handle member of *CFile* isn't used, so there's no way to pass it to another process.

Using it, however, is simplicity itself. You include a *CMemFile* object in your class or program as something like *CMemFile m_sf*. At some point in your program, write to it as follows:

```
char stuff[] = "Now is the time for all good men "
               "to come to the aid of their teletype.";
m_sf.Write (stuff, sizeof (stuff));
```

Later, when you need the information you wrote to the file, execute the following code:

```
DWORD dwSize;
char stuff[4096];
memset (stuff, '\0', sizeof (stuff));
dwSize = m_sf.SeekToEnd ();
m_sf.SeekToBegin ();
m_sf.Read (stuff, dwSize);
Message = stuff;
AfxMessageBox (Message);
```

The class takes care of increasing the size of the allocated memory when you write too much into it, and the memory is deallocated when the *CMemFile* object goes out of scope.

Of even more curiosity is a descendant class, *CSharedFile*, which one would think from its name would implement a shared memory file that can be used by different processes. However, the following quote is from the MSDN documentation: "Please note that *CSharedFile* does not use memory-mapped files, and the data cannot be directly shared between processes." This apparently means that you yourself have to do the memory mapping, and the programming overhead thus becomes greater than the API it is supposed to encapsulate. For the purposes *CMemFile* and *CSharedFile* serve, there are more efficient and easier-to-use classes, such as *CArray* and *CList*.

Actually, implementing shared memory files is not that difficult. For those who want to see a sample, the code on the companion CD-ROM shows how to create a memory-mapped file and use it to pass data to another process. The first program, *DRAW.EXE*, starts the second program, *REDRAW.EXE*, and depends on a relative path. Be sure to open the workspace in the 01518\MemFile directory rather than the individual projects.

519. *Using Socket Files*

The MFC socket classes encapsulate the WinSock API. The low-level functions are wrapped in the *CAsyncSocket* class, and its descendant, *CSocket*, provides a more abstract level of sockets. The *CSocketFile* class is used with *CSocket* to achieve fill-like operations for sending and receiving data over a network using sockets.

Usually, *CSocketFile* is used with a *CArchive* class object to achieve serialization of data and objects across a network. ("Across a network" because that is the general purpose of the socket API, but socket functions also may be used between processes on the same computer without accessing a network.)

In the serialization model, you first construct the *CSocket* object and connect with the remote end point. Then you construct the *CSocketFile* object and attach to the *CSocket* object. After this is done, you create a *CArchive* object and serialize your data into the archive to send across the network, or you extract data from it to read from the network.

520. *Using* CStdioFile

The *CStdioFile* class wraps the C runtime stream functions into a class object. The file is opened as a stream, as you would with *fopen()*, and read, write, and seek operations are performed as you would on a stream. The *CFile* base class provides no file buffering, but using *CStdioFile* instead of *CFile* directly provides stream-type buffering.

If you've used the library stream functions, the *CStdioFile* operations will be familiar to you. However, *CStdioFile* objects usually throw an exception on failure where the stream function returns error codes, so operations on objects of this type should be used within a *try . . . catch* block or the Visual C++ macro equivalents, *TRY* and *CATCH*. The advantage of using the Visual C++ macros with MFC exception classes is that the class objects usually return string error messages, as well as error codes. The messages then may be displayed to the user or the error codes used by the program to decide a course of action.

```
CString strHello;
strHello = _T("Howdy, y'all in the world");
TRY
{
    CStdioFile sfFile ("Howdy.Txt", CFile::modeCreate |
                                    CFile::modeWrite |
                                    CFile::typeText);
    sfFile.WriteString ((LPCTSTR)strHello);
}
CATCH (CFileException, e)
{
    char errmes[_MAX_PATH];
    memset (errmes, '\0', sizeof (errmes));
    e->GetErrorMessage (errmes, _MAX_PATH);
    cerr << errmes << endl;
}
END_CATCH
```

Exceptions are a humane way of handling errors. Your code doesn't have to test and enter alternative code in case of an error. If the error is detected and an exception is thrown, the alternative code is entered normally, giving your program a chance to recover.

521. *Understanding the* CRecentFileList *Class*

With Windows 95 and later versions, Microsoft gave a system device called the *Registry*. This is a database where the operating system and applications store pertinent data and retrieve it on demand using an application-programming interface. Prior to that, most applications used an initialization file *(.INI)* to store persistent data that is used each time the program is run.

If the user moved the initialization file (or worse, deleted it), the application had no recourse but to use default values. If the *.INI* file contained critical data, it might require that the application be re-installed. With the Registry, there's no file for the user to move or delete (actually, the Registry data is kept in a hidden file in the Windows system directory).

One of the sections usually found in an *.INI* file is the *Most Recently Used* file list, or MRU, a list of files that were last opened by the application. Usually, the file names are displayed on the Files menu of most applications.

The *CRecentFileList* class encapsulates the tasks not only of saving the MRU in the Registry but also of updating the file list on the menu. To create a *CRecentFileList* object, you declare it on the stack or create it on the heap, passing it five parameters, the last having a default value. The first is the offset for the numbering in the MRU, which normally would be 0. The second is the section in the Registry (the key) or *.INI* file where the MRU is kept. For the Registry, this is Recent File List. Third is the format string for writing the entry into the Registry or *.INI* file and should contain a *%d* escape sequence to allow the class object to insert a number into the string. *File%d* would write the entries as *File0*, *File1*, *File2*, and so on. Fourth is the number of entries in the MRU. The fifth and last parameter is the maximum display length of an item on the file menu. Normally, you would use the default value, *AFX_ABBREV_FILENAME_LEN*.

In an application generated by the MFC AppWizard, the *CWinApp* object creates and maintains a *CRecentFileList* object for you, even though information about it is not included in the class documentation. The object is created on the heap when your program calls *LoadStdProfileSettings()* and is deleted when the *CWinApp* object exits. This function takes a single parameter, the number of MRU entries (the fourth parameter to the *CRecentFileList* constructor), and defaults to 4.

To access the *CWinApp* MRU object, you must include *afxadv.h* in your application class file or in *stdafx.h*. After *LoadStdProfileSettings()* has completed, the *CRecentFileList* object is identified as *m_pRecentFileList*, which is a pointer to the object.

You can add an item to the MRU by calling *m_pRecentFileList->Add("New Item Name")*. Items are added to the top of the list, and each time you open a file, the top item is pushed down one and the top spot filled with your new item.

Deleting an object takes a bit more code, however, because the *Delete()* operation is called with an index number, and the current directory name is added to an entry when it is inserted without a full path name. The following snippet adds and then removes an item from the MRU:

```
if (m_pRecentFileList != NULL)  // Always test this for NULL
{
    m_pRecentFileList->Add (_T("Howdy from us all"));
    int nCount = GetCurrentDirectory (0, NULL);
    ++nCount;
    char *dir = new char [nCount];
    GetCurrentDirectory (nCount, dir);
    CString strDir = dir;
    delete [] dir;
    strDir += '\\';
```

```
    strDir += _T("Howdy from us all");
    nCount = m_pRecentFileList->GetSize ();
    for (int i = 0; i < nCount; ++i)
    {
        if (strDir == m_pRecentFileList->m_arrNames[i])
        {
            m_pRecentFileList->Remove (i);
            break;
        }
    }
}
```

Actually, this was an easy one because you know the item is at the top of the list (index 0). If, however, you opened one or more files in between, the item would move down in the list until, when the maximum number is opened, the item is removed anyway.

522. *Understanding the Control Classes*

All the Windows common controls are encapsulated in MFC classes. In addition, MFC provides some controls that are not included in the common controls library, such as control bars.

The control classes fall into two categories. The first comprises the "old" controls, the ones that were around in 16-bit versions of Windows. These include such items as *CEdit* for the edit control, *CStatic* for the static text (or label) control, and *CListBox* for the list box.

The second group includes those introduced with Windows 95 or later versions of Windows. Generally, the names of the classes end with "Ctrl" so you can identify them readily. For example, *CListBox* is a carryover from 16-bit Windows, but *CListCtrl* is the new list control that allows different views of a list and supports the use of an image list for icons. You can't use this group in programs for 16-bit Windows, but then you can't write applications for 16-bit Windows using Visual C++ 6.0. Table 522 summarizes most of the useful Windows common controls.

Control	MFC Class	Description
Animation	*CAnimate*	Displays successive frames of an AVI video clip.
Button	*CButton*	Buttons such as OK or Cancel.
Combo box	*CComboBox*	An edit box and list box combination.
Edit box	*CEdit*	Boxes for entering text. Often used as the control in a document window.
Header	*CHeaderCtrl*	A button above a column of text. Controls the width of displayed text.
Hotkey	*CHotKeyCtrl*	Enables users to create a hotkey to perform an action quickly.
Image list	*CImageList*	Used to manage large sets of icons or bitmaps. (This is a support control, not a true common control.)
List	*CListCtrl*	Displays a list of items with or without icons.
List box	*CListBox*	Contains a list of strings.

Table 522   The common control classes in MFC (continued on following page)

Control	MFC Class	Description
Progress	*CProgressCtrl*	A bar that indicates the progress of an operation.
Rich edit	*CRichEditCtrl*	An edit control that allows multiple-character, paragraph, and color formatting. Often used as the control for a document view.
Scroll bar	*CScrollBar*	A scroll bar used inside a dialog box or on a view window.
Slider	*CSliderCtrl*	Similar to a sliding control used as a volume control on audio equipment.
Spin button	*CSpinButtonCtrl*	A pair of arrow buttons to increment or decrement a value.
Static text	*CStatic*	An edit control for labeling other controls.
Status bar	*CStatusBarCtrl*	A bar to display information, such as the state of the Insert or NumLk keys, or to write status or help messages.
Tab	*CTabCtrl*	Used in property sheets. Similar to notebook tabs.
Toolbar	*CToolBarCtrl*	Contains buttons to generate command messages.
ToolTip	*CToolTipCtrl*	A small pop-up window that describes the use of a button or tool.
Tree	*CTreeCtrl*	Displays a hierarchical list.

Table 522   The common control classes in MFC (continued from previous page)

Most of these classes provide minimum functionality, and almost all could benefit from deriving custom classes from them. Some of them support owner draw modes to some extent, and others contain only a limited number of overridable functions. The *CListCtrl* class, for example, supports owner draw but provides only one overridable function, *DrawItem()*, which is called only when the owner draw style flag is set. That's all it takes, though, to make some improvements to it.

Others don't give you any options, but in most cases, it is possible to derive a custom class and override the *OnPaint()* function of the *CWnd* parent, as you did with the static text control in *FONTVIEW.EXE* and *ATTRIBUTES.EXE*.

523. *Classes Not Derived from* CObject

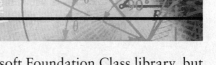

The *CObject* class is the ultimate ancestor of most classes in the Microsoft Foundation Class library, but a number of classes have no parent classes. They may be used as implemented, or you may use them as base classes for your own custom objects.

The group includes the classes created for the Internet server API, runtime support, synchronization, and simple data types, such as strings and structures.

Some of these contain only a single value but support enumerations and member functions that facilitate handling the value. If you check *sizeof(CTime)*, for example, it is the size of a *time_t* variable, but its member function makes manipulating time values much easier than the standard C library functions.

You can get a chart of how MFC is put together, including classes not derived from *CObject*, by looking up "hierarchy chart" in the MSDN help file.

524. *Understanding* CString

You've seen *CString* at work in some of the earlier samples. Sometimes string handling in C++ can be frustrating, especially when you constantly have to allocate, free, and reallocate string memory to account for varying sizes of strings you are using.

Some languages handle this by dynamically allocating string space, or allocating a large block to begin with, and then storing the length of the string as part of the data.

The *CString* class handles strings much the same way. The class contains only a *char* pointer, and you may cast it to a string at any time. If you assign a string to a *CString* object and cast it to a *char* pointer, you get a pointer to the string. Halt the program at this point and examine the memory area *before* the pointer is returned:

```
CString stuff = "This here's a string.";
003014D8  3E 00 00 00 FD FD FD FD  >.......
003014E0  01 00 00 00 15 00 00 00  ........
003014E8  15 00 00 00 54 68 69 73  ....This
003014F0  20 68 65 72 65 27 73 20   here's
003014F8  61 20 73 74 72 69 6E 67  a string
00301500  2E 00 FD FD FD FD 00 00  ........
```

There are 12 bytes in the memory allocation block that contain the string *before* the string itself. The *0xFDFDFDFD* value indicates the end of the block allocation table, so the string should begin immediately after it. In fact, if you allocate an ordinary string on the heap, that's where you will find the beginning of the string. However, this dump indicates that the class instance is setting aside 12 bytes for housekeeping information for the class.

If you use *strcat()* to add to the string outside the class's member function, these values remain unchanged. When you then use a member function or operator to add to the string, the allocation area changes, and only the original string—and none of those added with *strcat()*—is copied to the new location. (If you try this, be careful, and *never* do it in real code. You are writing into the heap space and likely will overwrite another allocation block and risk crashing the program. Oh, well, computers are cheap; knowledge isn't.)

The *CString* class has multiple overloads for the equals operator, along with the addition and += operators, so you may assign or add a single-character value, a string, or another *CString* object to it using only normal arithmetic-type notation.

The relational operators also are overloaded, so you may compare *CString* objects or strings and *CString* objects using the <, >, ==, <=, >=, and != operators, again normal arithmetic notation.

Member functions allow manipulation of the string object, such as converting it to all uppercase, all lowercase, reversing the string, emptying the string, and so on.

525. *Understanding* CPoint

The *CPoint* encapsulates the old *POINT* structure into a class object and overloads a number of operators to make it easier to manipulate the object. *POINT* is a very simple structure:

```
typedef struct  tagPOINT
     {
```

```
    LONG x;
    LONG y;
    } POINT;
```

It describes a single point, usually meant to be a point on the screen or output device in a device context environment. By encapsulating it, you get the advantage of operator overloads, but the original structure is left alone for standard C programming. In fact, in C++ you may use *POINT* and *CPoint* interchangeably. (Note that the member variables are of type *long*. In 16-bit Windows, the members are of type *int*. This is the case in the *RECT* and *SIZE* structures as well.)

Because it is a class object and not a structure, the initialization is different, but the equality operators used on a *CPoint* and a *POINT* act the same in both directions:

```
CPoint cpoint (24, 36);   // Constructor-type initialization
POINT point = {18, 30};   // Structure initialization
point = cpoint;     // Assigns cpoint.x and cpoint.y to point
cpoint = point;     // Assigns point.x and point.y to cpoint
```

Other than the default constructor and destructor, *CPoint* contains only one function, *Offset()*, which is overloaded, so you may pass it a *SIZE* or another *POINT* or separate *x* and *y* values.

The operator overloads are interesting. If you add a *CRect* object to a *CPoint* object, the return is a *CRect* object offset by *CPoint*. The result of the following snippet is a rectangle with the left at 124, the right at 224, the top at 136, and the bottom at 236—the *CPoint* was added to each corner of the original rectangle:

```
CPoint point (24, 36);
CRect rect (100, 100, 200, 200);
CRect rc = point + rect;
```

This might look strange because in C++ the compiler usually doesn't let you add variables of different data types, especially when they have different storage sizes. The preceding snippet shows the advantages of operator overloading.

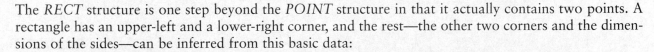

526. *Understanding CRect*

The *RECT* structure is one step beyond the *POINT* structure in that it actually contains two points. A rectangle has an upper-left and a lower-right corner, and the rest—the other two corners and the dimensions of the sides—can be inferred from this basic data:

```
typedef struct  tagRECT
{
    LONG left;
    LONG top;
    LONG right;
    LONG bottom;
} RECT;
```

The *CRect* class encapsulates the *RECT* structure, overloads some operators, and contains a wealth of member functions for manipulating the rectangle. You may use *CRect* and *RECT* objects interchangeably, except that *RECT* doesn't contain the member functions, which you will miss after you get used to them.

In Windows programming, it's accepted that a rectangle is defined by its upper-left and lower-right corners. In the previous samples, a rectangle always is drawn with the first point at the upper left, but that doesn't have to be the case. The following two declarations define the same rectangle:

```
CRect rc1 (100, 100, 200, 200);
CRect rc2 (200, 200, 100, 100);
```

The difference is that the sides on *rc1* are drawn in a positive direction along both axes, from the upper left to the lower right. The sides for *rc2*, however, are drawn from the lower right to the upper left in a negative direction along the axes. This compounds calculations when you try to determine, for example, whether a point is inside a rectangle. *CRect* contains a member function to determine this, *PtInRect()*. The following code returns *TRUE* for *rc1*, but *FALSE* for *rc2*, even though they describe the same rectangle:

```
CRect rc1 (100, 100, 200, 200);
CRect rc2 (200, 200, 100, 100);
CPoint pt (150, 150);
BOOL nResult;
nResult = rc1.PtInRect (pt);
nResult = rc2.PtInRect (pt);
```

Given the various operations and transformations that can be performed on a rectangle, this situation arises more often than you might think, especially when the rectangle coordinates are the result of calculations. To avoid this situation, *CRect* contains a member function, *NormalizeRect()* that swaps the top and bottom values if the height is negative and the left and right values if the width is negative. Adding this function to your code yields *TRUE* for both rectangles:

```
CRect rc1 (100, 100, 200, 200);
CRect rc2 (200, 200, 100, 100);
CPoint pt (150, 150);
rc1.NormalizeRect ();
rc2.NormalizeRect ();
BOOL nResult;
nResult = rc1.PtInRect (pt);
nResult = rc2.PtInRect (pt);
```

A number of the *CRect* member functions rely on normalized rectangles, and you should always perform this operation before using the other member functions. *NormalizeRect()* will alter the values, so if your rectangle is the result of calculations performed in a loop, it might be a good idea to call the function on a *copy* of the rectangle.

527. *Understanding CSize*

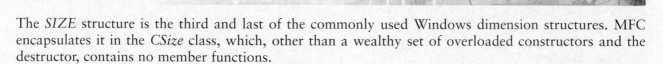

The *SIZE* structure is the third and last of the commonly used Windows dimension structures. MFC encapsulates it in the *CSize* class, which, other than a wealthy set of overloaded constructors and the destructor, contains no member functions.

Windows programmers commonly use the variables *cx* and *cy* to designate dimensions along the Cartesian coordinate system (you're right—they should use *dx* and *dy*). The *SIZE* structure includes variables with those names:

```
typedef struct tagSIZE
{
    LONG cx;
    LONG cy;
} SIZE;
```

You can construct a *CSize* object by giving it the width and height values and passing it a *SIZE* or *POINT* structure or by giving it a *DWORD* value with the *cx* value packed in the lower half of the *DWORD* and the *cy* value in the upper half. Alternatively, you can use the default constructor, which accepts no values, and you can initialize the members later.

The class definition overloads four relational operators—==, !=, >, and <—to compare two sizes, the addition operator and the subtraction operator. The overloaded operators work on combinations of *CSize, CPoint,* and *CRect* objects.

528. *Understanding Support Classes*

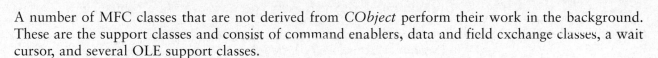

A number of MFC classes that are not derived from *CObject* perform their work in the background. These are the support classes and consist of command enablers, data and field exchange classes, a wait cursor, and several OLE support classes.

The command enablers are encased in the *CCmdUI* (for *Command User Interface*) class. They are, well, let's just say, adequate for the job they perform. In the MFC framework implementation, the command enabler class performs tasks around the main window frame, enabling and disabling menu and toolbar items. You can add functions to your program to enable or disable a control item based upon conditions in your program. Command enablers, unfortunately, are not implemented in MFC dialog classes. You can use them, but you will have to roll your own code, as shown in Tip 711, "Catching and Using Messages in a Dialog Box." Microsoft says, "This behavior is by design" (see the Knowledge Base article at *http://support.microsoft.com/support/kb/articles/Q242*).

Tip 539, "Understanding Command Enablers: The *CCmdUI* Class," contains an example of using *CCmdUI* objects for control objects on the window frame, including a range of objects.

The *CDataExchange* class is used with dialog boxes to exchange data between the dialog box controls and the program code. When you create a dialog class in Visual Studio, the ClassWizard adds a function named *DoDataExchange()*. Generally, you let the ClassWizard maintain this function for you, but if you choose to add items manually, be sure to add them outside the two lines containing *AFX_DATA_MAPI*. Anything between these two lines is subject to modification by the ClassWizard.

The *DoDataExchange()* function is where the program associates the class member variables with the actual dialog box controls. The data exchange works both ways, from the controls to the variables and the reverse. This function is called automatically when the dialog box is created to load the data into the dialog box controls and again when the user clicks the OK button to read the data into the member variables. You shouldn't call it directly, but you can force a call to it using the *UpdateData()* function. If you pass a *FALSE* value, the values of the member variables are placed in the controls. If you pass a *TRUE* value, the controls are read and the values placed in the member variables.

The *CFieldExchange* works much the same way, but it is used to exchange data between program variables and databases.

529. *Understanding the Synchronization (Lock) Classes*

The six synchronization classes are used to control access to resources or portions of code between threads of an application or between applications. A seventh class, *CSyncObject*, is a pure *virtual* class and you can't use it directly. It is the ancestor class for the four synchronization object classes, which are used to set up controlled access. The other two classes have no base class and are used to control access to the synchronization objects by creating synchronization access objects.

Some of these classes have overlapping uses, and the one you use depends on your application. In some cases, *CCriticalSection* and *CMutex* can achieve the same results. The classes and their uses are summarized in Table 529.

Class	Description
CCriticalSection	Used where only one thread at a time may be allowed to access resources, such as a linked list.
CEvent	Causes a thread or application to pause until some event has occurred, such as characters being read from a serial port or data being placed in a queue.
CMutex	Provides mutually exclusive access to a resource. Mutexes may be used with the synchronization access classes.
CSemaphore	Attempts to implement UNIX-like semaphores for Windows. Used to limit the number of threads or processes that may access a resource.
CSingleLock	Controls access to a single object. Must be used with one of the preceding classes.
CMultiLock	Controls access to multiple objects. Must be used with one of the first four classes.

Table 529   Synchronization and lock classes in MFC

The *CEvent*, *CSemaphore*, and *CMutex* are useful for operations between processes and are covered beginning with Tip 956, "Synchronizing Threads."

CCriticalSection is used when you want to permit only a single thread to access some resource, such as a *linked list* or *queue*. A *linked list* is a collection of data items with pointers to one another and generally are linked in some sort of order, such as alphabetically or by time. When you create a linked list without regard to order, it's a *queue*.

Suppose that you have a program that reads records sent across a network, perhaps the rate of widget production per hour from your 1,000 or so widget factories. The records might arrive once in a while or many in rapid succession. You don't have any way of predicting the frequency. The problem is, your program has to query a couple of other sources, databases on other servers, to get related information, correlate the information, and store it into a database. The second part takes time, probably so much that when records arrive quickly, you miss a few.

One solution to this is to split your program into a couple of threads. One thread reads the records from the network and stores them in a queue. The other thread reads the queue, indexes the data, and then removes the record from the queue. However, you can't have both threads changing pointers in the queue at the same time. Only one can have access at any given point.

The class that contains the queue information, in the example, *CSQLLink*, has a *CCriticalSection* member that is used to prevent simultaneous access to the queue by locking and unlocking the queue:

```
/////////////////////////////////////////////////////////////
// CSQLLink message handlers

bool CSQLLink::AddItemToQueue(WIDGETDATA *inWidget)
{
bool bResult;
    if (!m_csQueueLock.Lock ())
        return (false);
    {
        bResult = AddRecordToQueue (inWidget);
    }
    m_csQueueLock.Unlock ();
    return (bResult);
}

bool CSQLLink::DeleteItemFromQueue(PWIDGETQUEUE cur)
{
bool bResult;
    if (!m_csQueueLock.Lock ())
        return (false);
    {
        bResult = DeleteRecordFromQueue (cur);
    }
    m_csQueueLock.Unlock();
    return (bResult);
}

bool CSQLLink::AddRecordToQueue(WIDGETDATA *inWidget)
{
WIDGETQUEUE *pWidgetItem;

    pWidgetItem = new WIDGETQUEUE;
    if (pQueueItem == NULL)
    {
        return (false);
    }
    pQueueItem->data.Empty ();
    pQueueItem->next = pQueueItem->prev = NULL;
    memcpy(&pWidgetItem->Data,inWidget,sizeof (WIDGETDATA));
//
//  Zero the structure.
//
    memset (inWidget, '\0', sizeof (WIDGETDATA));
//
//  Add this item to the tail of the queue.
//
    if (m_pHead == NULL)
    {
        m_pHead = m_pTail = pQueueItem;
        return (true);
    }
    m_pTail->next = pQueueItem;
    pQueueItem->prev = m_pTail;
    m_pTail = pQueueItem;
//
//  Unlock the queue.
```

```
//
    return (true);
}

bool CSQLLink::DeleteRecordFromQueue(WIDGETQUEUE *cur)
{

    if (cur == NULL)
        return (false);
//
//  If there is a previous item, link it to the next.
//
    if (cur->prev != NULL)
    {
        cur->prev->next = cur->next;
    }
//
//  If there is a next item, link it to the previous.
//
    if (cur->next != NULL)
    {
        cur->next->prev = cur->prev;
    }
    if (cur == m_pHead)
        m_pHead = cur->next;
    if (cur == m_pTail)
        m_pTail = cur->prev;
    delete cur;
    return (true);
}
```

This code handles a real situation similar to the one described. The name was changed to "widget" to protect the real database. When one thread tries to add an item to the queue, it tries to lock the *CCriticalSection* object. If the object already is locked, it will wait until it becomes unlocked, then lock it again, and call *AddItemToQueue()*. When the second thread disposes of an item and tries to remove it from the queue, it encounters the same situation. If the first thread already has the *CCriticalSection* object locked, it must wait until it is unlocked before continuing.

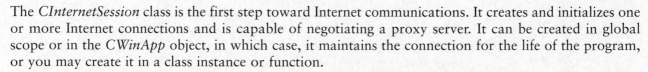

530. *Using* CInternetConnection

The *CInternetSession* class is the first step toward Internet communications. It creates and initializes one or more Internet connections and is capable of negotiating a proxy server. It can be created in global scope or in the *CWinApp* object, in which case, it maintains the connection for the life of the program, or you may create it in a class instance or function.

After the Internet session is established, you create a *CInternetConnection* to make the connection with an Internet server. The object may be a *CInternetConnection* class object or one of its derived classes, *CFtpConnection*, *CGopherConnection*, or *CHttpConnection*. You never create a *CInternetConnection* object on the stack. Instead, you call *CInternetSession* to create the connection and return a pointer to it.

The following snippets are from a Windows NT service program that receives information from a Tandem system, queries an account database on an HP3000, indexes the information in an SQL database running on a Windows NT system, and finally FTP's the information to an ad booking system running on a Sun Microsystems server.

Of course, you're not interested in the intricate details of how an ad gets into a newspaper, so the snippets show only the definitions and operator overloads that eventually enable the entire package to be sent to the booking system with a single statement: *arOut << cad*. First is the definition of the string class with the important overload of the << operator:

```
class CAdString : public CObject
{
DECLARE_SERIAL(CAdString)
public:
    CAdString ();
    CAdString (int Size);
    virtual ~CAdString ();
    int SetSize (int Size);
    char *GetData ();
    CAdString& operator=(char ch);
    CAdString& operator=(char *str);
    CAdString& operator=(long Var);
    CAdString& operator=(int Var);
    CAdString& operator=(CTime& Time);
    friend CArchive& operator<<(CArchive& o, CAdString& Ad);
private:
    int     m_Size;
    char    *m_Data;
};
```

The various operator overloads allow any of the data types used in the project to be assigned directly and converted into a fixed-length string (because the program deals with four operating systems running on four very different computers, a decision was made that all data would be transferred as strings). The one that should interest you involves the *CArchive*:

```
//
//  Stream inserters to write the strings through
//  a CArchive object.
//
CArchive& operator<<(CArchive& o, CAdString& Ad)
{
    char *Data = Ad.GetData ();
    o.Write(Data, strlen (Data));
    return (o);
}
```

The class describing the ad is composed of many *CAdString* objects (the resulting file is about 2,000 bytes):

```
class CCascadeAd : public CObject
{
DECLARE_SERIAL(CCascadeAd)
public:
    CCascadeAd ();
    CAdString       AdRecordType;
    CAdString       AdStatus;
    CAdString       AdNumber;
//  . . .
// Many more similar declarations
```

```
//  . . .
    CAdString  AdTillForbidFlag;
    CAdString  AdWebAdFlag;
    CAdString  AdCameraReadyFlag;
    friend CArchive& operator<<(CArchive& o,CCascadeAd& Ad);
};
//
//  Stream inserters to write the ad strings through
//  an CArchive object.
//
CArchive& operator<<(CArchive& o, CCascadeAd& Ad)
{
    o << Ad.AdRecordType;
    o << Ad.AdStatus;
    o << Ad.AdNumber;
//  . . .
//  Other data written here
//  . . .
    o << Ad.AdTillForbidFlag;
    o << Ad.AdWebAdFlag;
    o << Ad.AdCameraReadyFlag;
    o << '\x0a';
    return (o);
}
```

You could design classes using other data types or a combination of data types. *CArchive* has overloaded operators for most of the primitive data types—*int*, *long*, *DWORD*, and so on—but it doesn't handle strings well, so in the final analysis the string is written with the *CArchive::Write()* member function.

The following code enables the entire collection to be written using a single statement. In the *OpenFtpConnection()* function, *m_pcis* is the *CInternetSession* object. Normally, you can create an instance in the function itself. Because this is a Windows NT service program, that won't work, so it has to be created in the heap elsewhere in the program. The *m_FtpConn* is a class member of type *CFtpConnection*, and *m_ifFile* is an object of *CInternetFile*:

```
bool CSQLLink::FtpToCascade(NADDATA &ad)
{
CString strFileName;

    strFileName.Format ("%ld.sii", ad.AIMNumber);
    if (!OpenFtpConnection ())
        return (false);
    if (!OpenFtpFile ((LPCSTR) strFileName, GENERIC_WRITE))
    {
        CloseFtpConnection ();
        return (false);
    }
    WriteCascadeAd (ad);
    return (true);
}


bool CSQLLink::OpenFtpConnection()
{
    TRY
    {
            m_ftpConn = m_pcis->GetFtpConnection ("servername",
```

```
                                                   "username",
                                                   "password");
    }
    CATCH(CInternetException, e)
    {
        char errmsg [_MAX_PATH];
        memset (errmsg, '\Ø', _MAX_PATH);
        e->GetErrorMessage (errmsg, _MAX_PATH);
        LogMessage (errmsg);
        m_ftpConn = NULL;
        return (false);
    }
    END_CATCH

    TRY
    {
        m_ftpConn->SetCurrentDirectory
                        (_T("/usr/spoolers/ad_booking"));
    }
    CATCH(CInternetException, e)
    {
        CloseFtpConnection ();
        return (false);
    }
    END_CATCH

    return (true);
}

void CSQLLink::CloseFtpConnection()
{
    if (m_ftpConn == NULL)
        return;
    if (m_ifFile != NULL)
    {
        m_ifFile->Close ();
        m_ifFile = NULL;
    }
    m_ftpConn->Close ();
    m_ftpConn = NULL;
}

bool CSQLLink::OpenFtpFile(LPCTSTR strFileName, UINT uiMode)
{
    TRY
    {
            m_ifFile = m_ftpConn->OpenFile ((LPCTSTR)
                                strFileName, GENERIC_WRITE);
    }
    CATCH (CInternetException, e)
    {
        char errmsg [_MAX_PATH];
        memset (errmsg, '\Ø', _MAX_PATH);
        e->GetErrorMessage (errmsg, _MAX_PATH);
        LogMessage (errmsg);
        m_ifFile = NULL;
```

```
        return (false);
    }
    END_CATCH
    return (true);
}
```

All this is preliminary to the following function. The process is a little more involved than just opening an FTP connection and putting the information into a file. Error checking is done along the way.

```
bool CSQLLink::WriteCascadeAd(ADDATA &ad)
{
    CCascadeAd cad;
// Fill the class data members with the ad structure
    if (!GetCascadeData (cad, ad))
        return (false);
// Attach an archive to the ftp file
    CArchive arOut((CFile *) m_ifFile, CArchive::store);
    arOut << cad;
    return (true);
}
```

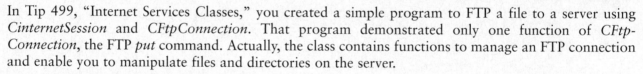

531. *Using* CFtpConnection

In Tip 499, "Internet Services Classes," you created a simple program to FTP a file to a server using *CinternetSession* and *CFtpConnection*. That program demonstrated only one function of *CFtp-Connection*, the FTP *put* command. Actually, the class contains functions to manage an FTP connection and enable you to manipulate files and directories on the server.

To use *CFtpConnection*, you first must establish an Internet session using *CInternetSession*. You don't declare a *CFtpConnection* object directly. You create a pointer variable and call the *CInternetSession* object to create the connection and return a pointer to it, as you saw in the code in Tip 499 and Tip 530, "Using *CInternetConnection*."

Of course, *CFtpConnection* by itself doesn't give you the command-line interface you're used to with most FTP programs. It does contain the member functions from which you can build either a command-line or graphic user interface.

The class contains commands for changing, creating, and removing directories on the remote server, as shown in Table 531, but none for the local machine. Presumably, in an FTP-type program you would use normal Windows API functions to manipulate the directory on your own machine.

CFtpConnection *Member Function*	Description
GetCurrentDirectory	Returns the current directory on the server in the *CString* object passed as a parameter.
GetCurrentDirectoryAsURL	Overloaded function. May use a string pointer or *CString* object as parameter. Returns the directory in URL format.
SetCurrentDirectory	Changes the current directory on the server if the user has permission.

Table 531   File and directory operations using CFtpConnection *(continued on following page)*

CFtpConnection *Member Function*	*Description*
CreateDirectory	Creates a new directory on the server.
RemoveDirectory	Deletes a directory on the server.
Rename	Renames an existing file on the server.
Remove	Deletes an existing file on the server.
PutFile	Transfers a file from the client machine to the server.
GetFile	Transfers a file from the server to the client machine.
OpenFile	Opens a file for reading or writing on the server. The open mode may be *GENERIC_READ* or *GENERIC_WRITE*, but not both.
Close	Closes the FTP connection with the server.

Table 531   File and directory operations using CFtpConnection *(continued from previous page)*

Similarly, *CFtpConnection* contains member functions to send and receive files and to open, rename, and delete files on the remote machine, but not on the local machine.

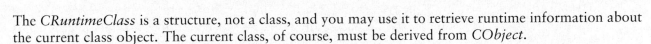

532. *Understanding CRuntimeClass*

The *CRuntimeClass* is a structure, not a class, and you may use it to retrieve runtime information about the current class object. The current class, of course, must be derived from *CObject*.

The *GetRuntimeClass()* member of *CObject* returns a pointer to a *CRuntimeClass* structure containing information about the current class, including the class name, the base class name, and the parent class.

The most common use of *CRuntimeClass* is to interrogate whether it is safe to cast a pointer to a class to a derived class (this is a legal operation in C++). The MFC view classes use this to get the document class, as in the following code:

```
CPEDoc* CPEView::GetDocument()// non-debug version is inline
{
    ASSERT(m_pDocument->IsKindOf(RUNTIME_CLASS(CPEDoc)));
    return (CPEDoc*)m_pDocument;
}
```

The code is used in Visual Studio debug compilations and causes the program to assert if the class cannot be cast. An *assertion* is an ANSI-defined debug function that causes the program to print a diagnostic message and terminate. In Visual C++, it is implemented with the *ASSERT* macro.

533. *Understanding the Document Classes*

The document classes are an integral part of the document/view architecture used by the Microsoft Foundation Class library. The document class contains the document's data, and the view class is used to display the data.

All the document classes, including those used in MFC applications, are derived from *CDocument*, which supports basic operations such as creating a document and loading and saving it. Your derived classes may provide more functionality.

Other classes derived from *CDocument* provide support for OLE *(Object Linking and Embedding)*, which permits them to contain other documents or objects or links to them. These include *COLEDocument* and its derived class, *CRichEditDoc*, which is used when you create an application using the rich edit view.

CDocument classes are derived from *CObject* through *CCmdTarget*, which means that they may receive messages even though they aren't windows.

An application may derive more than one class from *CDocument*, although it usually doesn't create them directly. Instead, the application code creates document templates, and these templates are used in the *File Open* command to create new *CDocument* objects.

534. *Understanding the Exception Classes*

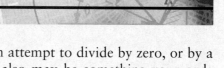

An *exception* is a runtime anomaly caused by faulty code, such as an attempt to divide by zero, or by a system condition, such as running out of memory on the heap. It also may be something your code detects, such as overwriting an array's boundaries, even before the problem is detected by the runtime code.

Rather than abruptly halt the program, the runtime code (or your own code) may *throw* or *raise* an exception. This gives your code a chance to handle and correct the problem before the code ultimately collapses and the program aborts. The program may *catch* the exception and take measures to correct the problem, or it may simply exit gracefully.

Exception handling is built in to the C++ runtime code through the *try*, *throw*, and *catch* statements. If it's possible that your code might throw an exception—such as when you use the *new* operator to allocate heap space—you may enclose the code in a *try* block, which is followed immediately by a *catch* block. If the statements within a *try* block cause an exception, control is transferred to the first statement in the *catch* block. It's much more elegant than the old method of just saying, "Yer outta memory, dummy. Bye!" and abruptly ending the program.

A *throw* statement may throw an exception of any legal data type, and you use that same data type to catch it. In some cases, such as those caused by hardware errors, a general exception is thrown and no information is conveyed as to what caused it. The following *will* cause your program to bomb (you can't just say 1000/0 because the compiler would catch it):

```
int zero = 0;
int stuff = 10000/zero;
```

Divide by zero is a hardware error, and the only way to catch it is with the generalized exception object, an ellipsis. The context of your code determines what type of error it is:

```
int zero = 0;
int stuff;
try
{
    stuff = 10000/zero;
```

```
}
catch (...)
{
    AfxMessageBox ("Divide by zero error");
// some code to adjust for the error
}
```

When your program executes this code, control is transferred to the first statement in the *catch* block.

C++ also provides structured exception handling (SEH), which is covered beginning with Tip 964, "Understanding Exceptions."

The Microsoft Foundation Class provides a set of exception-handling classes you may use. The base class for all the exception classes is *CException*, which you use as a generic exception handler by calling *CObject::IsKindOf()* to determine the exact exception type.

535. *Using the Exception Classes*

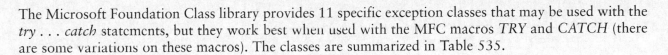

The Microsoft Foundation Class library provides 11 specific exception classes that may be used with the *try . . . catch* statements, but they work best when used with the MFC macros *TRY* and *CATCH* (there are some variations on these macros). The classes are summarized in Table 535.

Exception Class	Description
CArchiveException	An exception specific to a *CArchive* operation.
CDaoException	Exceptions from data access object classes.
CDBException	Exceptions from Open Database Connectivity (ODBC) operations.
CFileException	Exceptions thrown by *CFile* objects.
CInternetException	Exceptions specific to Internet classes.
CMemoryException	An attempt was made to allocate more heap memory than was available.
CNotSupportedException	An attempted operation is not supported. No further error information is available.
COleDispatchException	Exceptions thrown by an OLE dispatcher.
COleException	Exceptions thrown by an OLE operation.
CResourceException	Thrown when a requested resource can't be found or created.
CUserException	A general exception that can be used for end-user errors.

Table 535 MFC exception classes

The easiest way to use the exception classes is with the MFC macros. If it's possible that your code might generate more than one type of exception, you may stack the *CATCH* calls. You start out with the *TRY* macro:

```
TRY
{
    cfc = cis.GetFtpConnection (argv[1], (LPCSTR) strUser,
                                        (LPCSTR) strPass);
```

```
}
CATCH(CInternetException, e)
{
    char errmsg [256];
    memset (errmsg, '\0', 256);
    e->GetErrorMessage (errmsg, 256);
    AfxMessageBox (errmsg, MB_OK);
    e->Delete();
    return (1);
}
CATCH(CMemoryException, e)
{
    char errmsg [256];
    memset (errmsg, '\0', 256);
    e->GetErrorMessage (errmsg, 256);
    AfxMessageBox (errmsg, MB_OK);
    e->Delete();
    return (1);
}
END_CATCH
```

The variable *cis* is the *CInternetSession* object, and *cfc* is the *CFtpConnection* pointer variable. If the call to *cis.GetFtpConnection()* fails for any reason, it will throw a *CInternetException*. That's a known and is spelled out in the class documentation, so you set up the *CATCH* macro to handle that specific exception. The variable *e* is the exception object, and the macro takes care of casting it for you; this is a pointer type and is created by the macro. In the code, you use the member variable *Delete()* to remove the exception. If the object was created on the heap, the function will delete it; if it was created in global or local scope, it won't be deleted. This is a safe way to handle deleting exception objects.

If, however, you suspect that it might also throw a memory exception, you can add a second *CATCH* macro for that case. You can keep stacking them until you run out of exception classes. The exception code must start with the *TRY* macro, include at least one *CATCH* macro, and end with the *END_CATCH* macro.

Also, a *CATCH_ALL* macro can be used to catch all exception classes. The exception object pointer is all you need in the macro statement, and the block must end with an *END_CATCH_ALL* macro. You may use *CObject::IsKindOf()* to determine the exact exception class that was caught. The following example shows how you can use it to replace both *CATCH* macros in the preceding code:

```
TRY
{
    cfc = cis.GetFtpConnection (argv[1],
                    (LPCSTR) strUser, (LPCSTR) strPass);
}
CATCH_ALL (e)
{
    char errmsg [256];
    memset (errmsg, '\0', 256);
    e->GetErrorMessage (errmsg, 256);
    AfxMessageBox (errmsg, MB_OK);
    return (1);
}
END_CATCH_ALL
```

You also may nest *TRY* and *CATCH* macros. If you must allocate memory within the *TRY* block, for example, and you suspect that it might throw an exception, you can include exception code for it:

```
int nNumber = 0x0fffffff;
CString strUser = ftp.GetFtpUser ();
CString strPass = ftp.GetFtpPassword ();
TRY
{
    char *str;
    TRY
    {
        str = new char [nNumber];
    }
    CATCH(CMemoryException, e)
    {
        char errmsg [256];
        memset (errmsg, '\0', 256);
        e->GetErrorMessage (errmsg, 256);
        AfxMessageBox (errmsg, MB_OK);
        e->Delete();
    }
    END_CATCH
    cfc = cis.GetFtpConnection (argv[1], (LPCSTR) strUser,
                                         (LPCSTR) strPass);
}
CATCH(CInternetException, e)
{
    char errmsg [256];
    memset (errmsg, '\0', 256);
    e->GetErrorMessage (errmsg, 256);
    AfxMessageBox (errmsg, MB_OK);
    e->Delete();
    return (1);
}
END_CATCH
```

Generally, the MSDN documentation details when and what type of exception a class object can throw. Judicious use of exception handling can make your application much more immune to crashing.

536. *Using the Toolbar Classes*

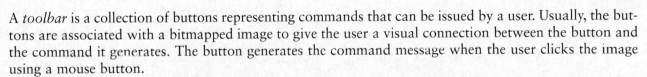

A *toolbar* is a collection of buttons representing commands that can be issued by a user. Usually, the buttons are associated with a bitmapped image to give the user a visual connection between the button and the command it generates. The button generates the command message when the user clicks the image using a mouse button.

Toolbars usually are associated with the main window frame, but they don't have to be. They may be permanently attached to the frame, "docking" (moveable to other parts of the frame), or "floating" (not attached to any part of the frame).

With the introduction of Windows 95, the toolbar control became a member of the Windows common controls and is represented in the Microsoft Foundation Class by the *CToolBarCtrl* class, which is derived from *CWnd*. A more commonly used class is the *CToolBar* class, which is derived from *CWnd* through the *CControlBar* class.

The easiest way to create and use a toolbar is to start with a bitmapped image and then use the toolbar editor in the Visual Studio to split it into individual images for the toolbar buttons, as shown in Figures 536a and 536b. You also may associate the Windows commands with the toolbar buttons in the toolbar editor.

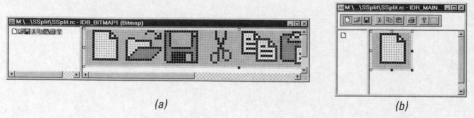

(a)   *(b)*

Figures 536a and 536b   Building a toolbar starts with a bitmapped image (a).
The toolbar editor separates the image into smaller images that will fit the toolbar buttons.

After you create the bitmap image, with the image selected in the Resource Workshop, select Toolbar Editor from the Image menu. A dialog box will ask you for the size of the toolbar buttons. Standard toolbars are 16 pixels wide by 15 pixels deep. The editor will split the image into sections and assign them to toolbar buttons. As you will see in Tip 541, "Using the *CImageList* Class," it's possible to create a toolbar with no images and then create an image list object to associate with the toolbar. Used this way, the images are assigned dynamically and may be changed by program code.

Toolbar buttons usually are associated with menu items, but they don't have to be. Programmers often create specialized toolbars for such things as drawing tools or font selection. Often, these types of toolbars are left floating rather than attached to the window frame.

When the buttons and images have been assigned a resource ID, a convenient place to construct a toolbar is in the window's mainframe, the *CMainFrame* class in projects created by the MFC AppWizard. The toolbars are easily accessed as members of the frame window class, the window frame object remains in scope for the duration of the program, and there's no danger of repeating the code that creates them.

The *CToolBar* class has two functions to create the toolbar. The old-style *Create()* builds a standard toolbar. The only toolbar possible with this function is the old style with raised buttons and no borders. Its parameters are the parent window (usually the main window frame), the window style, and a number the parent window can use to identify the toolbar.

The second function, *CreateEx()*, provides much more functionality and is intended for use with 32-bit Windows operating systems. In addition to a window style, you also may specify a control style and add a border around the toolbar.

The first parameter to both functions is the parent window, which usually is the main window frame. The second parameter to *CreateEx()* is the control style. The extensive list of toolbar control styles is listed in MSDN under "Toolbar Control and Button Styles." The most commonly used style is *TBSTYLE_FLAT*, which creates a toolbar with buttons that are flush with the window frame. When the mouse cursor moves over them, the frameworks redraws them to appear slightly above the frame and then redraws them flat when the cursor leaves the button. Another useful style, especially for toolbars containing many buttons, is *TBSTYLE_WRAPABLE*, which allows a toolbar to wrap to the next line if the user resizes the window so that the toolbar will not fit.

The third parameter to *CreateEx()* is the window style, the same as for *Create()*. The fourth parameter is a *CRect* object that specifies a border around the toolbar. The *CRect* doesn't actually specify a rectangle but is a convenient place to hold four *long* values. The four members specify the amount of extra space to leave around the left, top, right, and bottom edges, respectively, of the toolbar. Normally, these values are all 0 to create a borderless toolbar. Negative values are ignored but will cause an assertion in your debug code.

After you create the toolbar, you have to load it with the resource data you entered in the toolbar editor. The member function is simply *LoadToolbar()*, and the single parameter is the resource ID you gave the new toolbar. This assigns the specific command IDs to the individual buttons.

The create and load functions all return 0 on failure and non-zero on success. Your program should test the return values to ensure that the toolbar was properly created and loaded.

That's all pretty ho-hum. If you want to create a real toolbar that doesn't eat quiche, jump ahead to Tip 541, "Using the *CImageList* Class," where an image list gets attached to the toolbar.

537. *Printing and Print Previewing with MFC Classes*

Code generated by the MFC AppWizard contains extensive support for printing and print previewing. The MFC *CView* class includes printing and print previewing functions. Because this is the base class for all the control views in MFC, they all inherit the functionality. Some of them may modify it, however.

Print *previewing* is considerably different from printing, however. Rather than drawing on a printer surface, you are simulating a printer in a child window. Most of the work to perform this is contained in *CView*, but on those rare occasions when you need to modify it, you should know that there is an undocumented class in MFC named *CPreviewDC*, which is derived from *CDC*. The class definition for *CPreviewDC* is in the *afxpriv.h* file in the MFC source directory.

CDC and its derived classes all contain two device contexts. Except for *CPreviewDC*, these device contexts are identical. In *CPreviewDC*, however, one device context is used to simulate the target printer, and the other is used to draw on the preview window.

The *CPreviewDC* object is created in an undocumented view class, *CPreviewView*, which is the view used to display the document on the screen. The definition of this class is in *afxpriv.h* as well, and the implementation code is in *viewprev.cpp*. When you set the *m_bPreview* member of the print dialog's *CPrintInfo* member to *true*, you set the view's preview mode into operation.

538. *Understanding Thread Classes*

Windows NT and all versions of standard Windows since Windows 95 are *multithreaded* operating systems. A *thread* is an execution point in a program and describes the sequence of statement executions. All programs have at least one thread, the *primary* thread, but in multithreaded systems, they may have additional, *secondary*, threads.

A secondary thread has its own execution address, its own stack space, and its own set of CPU register state variables. It exists in the same program space as the primary thread and has access to all the global variables and functions and to the program's resources. Running under Windows, it has its own slot in the system scheduler.

Simple programs that perform one task and then exit without requiring user interaction have little need for more than the primary thread. Programs that display windows and perform time-consuming operations usually benefit from additional threads. There's no additional cost to adding threads to your program, and often this speeds it up.

The first place you might consider another thread is at startup. Does your program do anything that requires a lot of time before the window is finally displayed? Reporters at *The Denver Post* use an integrated editing and communications program when in the field. On the average laptop, it takes 2 or 3 seconds for the program to load and display. The communications section is initialized in a separate thread, so the windows can display long before the program is fully ready, and the user is happy. When I added a spell-checking library to it, the "load and show" time went up to about 12 seconds. I started another thread to initialize the spell checker, and the time went back to 2 to 3 seconds. By the time the user can begin issuing commands, the entire program is initialized.

Does your program do any time-consuming work during the course of its execution? If you're writing an editing program, for example, you might want to provide periodic writes to a temporary file from which you could recover if the computer or your program happens to crash. That can take several seconds and is noticeable to the user. When your backup timer goes off, you could use it to start another thread that would handle the backup. Intensive math calculations for a graphics or spreadsheet program might benefit from additional threads.

Visual C++ separates threads into two categories: *worker threads* and *user interface threads*. A worker thread often is used to perform background operations, such as those just described. User interface threads accept user input and respond to events independently of the main program. If a thread needs to receive Windows messages, it must be a user interface thread.

In an MFC-based program, you start both types of threads using *AfxBeginThread()*, an overloaded function that accepts the parameters needed by worker and user interface threads. For a user interface thread, you must derive a class from *CWinThread* and provide an *InitInstance()* function. You pass the runtime class as the first parameter to *AfxBeginThread()*. That's the only required parameter. The second parameter is the thread priority, and the third parameter sets the stack size. The fourth parameter determines whether the thread is created in a suspended state. The fourth parameter is the security attributes, which is meaningful only on Windows NT and usually is set to *NULL*. *AfxBeginThread()* creates an instance of your derived class and calls the *CreateThread()* member of *CWinThread* to start execution.

CWinThread is derived from *CCmdTarget* and thus can receive messages. The *Run()* member function provides a default message loop, and you may add message handler functions to your derived class. *Run()* should be overridden only to implement special behavior for the class.

Worker threads are even easier than user interface threads and, fortunately, are probably more useful. You declare a function to start the thread. The return type should be *AFX_THREADPROC* or *DWORD WINAPI*, and it must be static if it is declared as a member of a class. It also may be declared in global space. Call *AfxBeginThread()* with the function address and a pointer (which may be NULL) to any parameters the thread might need. You may pass it a *this* pointer. The rest of the parameters have default values, but you may include them in your call. They are the thread priority, the stack size, creation flags, and a pointer to a security attributes structure.

The *MemFile* project on the companion CD-ROM contains an example of a worker thread. The view class creates a thread to wait for another process to signal an event and then sends a message back to the view class, which reads the shared memory map and draws the lines from the other program on the screen.

```
DWORD AFX_THREADPROC CChildView::StartUpdateThread(
                                  void *pParam)
{
HANDLE  hWaitFor [2];
DWORD   dwSignal;
THREADPARMS parms;

    memcpy (&parms, (THREADPARMS *) pParam,
                   sizeof (THREADPARMS));
    hWaitFor [0] = parms.hevMemFile;
```

```
    hWaitFor [1] = parms.hevTerminate;
    if (hWaitFor[0] == NULL)
    {
        AfxMessageBox ("hevMemFile is null");
        return (-1);
    }
    if (hWaitFor[1] == NULL)
    {
        AfxMessageBox ("hevTerminate is null");
        return (-1);
    }
    for (;;)
    {
        dwSignal = WaitForMultipleObjects (2, hWaitFor,
                                FALSE, INFINITE);
        switch (dwSignal)
        {
            case WAIT_OBJECT_0:           // Memory file event
                ::SendMessage (parms.Papa->m_hWnd,
                                            WM_USER+40,
                        (WPARAM) (WM_USER+40), (LPARAM) 0);
                break;
            case WAIT_OBJECT_0 + 1:     // Terminate
                return (0);
            case WAIT_TIMEOUT:
                continue;
        }
    }
    return (0);
}
```

The thread function immediately makes a local copy of the thread parameters, which in this case is a parameters structure defined by the application. The structure members hold the handle to the event that will be signaled by another process after writing to the shared memory file, a handle to the terminate event, and a pointer to the parent window, where it will send messages.

The thread process then goes into a forever loop, waiting either for the remote process to set the event after writing to the shared memory file or for the parent window to set the terminate event. When it receives an event signal from the remote process, it notifies the parent window through a user message. The use of a thread here allows the parent window to continue receiving and processing messages. You could have accomplished the same thing by overriding the MFC-established message loop and using idle time processing to check the event.

539. *Understanding Command Enablers: The CCmdUI Class*

You use the command enablers with the *ON_COMMAND_UPDATE_UI* macro in the message map. When you invoke the ClassWizard and select a menu or toolbar item, you have two options in the Message list. One is for *COMMAND*, which inserts a message handler that is called when a user selects the menu item or clicks the toolbar button. The other option is *COMMAND_UPDATE_UI*, which inserts a command enabler function. When the function is called—during idle time processing or when the user opens the menu list—your code is supposed to look at existing conditions and determine whether the item should be enabled or disabled. The sole parameter to the function is a pointer to a *CCmdUI* object.

You may assign a command enabler function a range of items, but you yourself have to roll the code. The ClassWizard will add code for an update handler for a single command. If you have a number of related menu or toolbar items, you may use the *ON_UPDATE_COMMAND_UI_RANGE* macro and specify the lower and upper limits of the commands you want handled. The framework will call the update handler function with the item's resource ID and a pointer to a *CCmdUI* object.

First, edit the *resource.h* file to make sure that the items you want to handle are sequential. You have to do this from an editing program outside the Visual Studio. The resource editor assigns the IDs as they are created, so if you didn't create the items one right after another, you might have to shift some numbers around. The idea is to have all your IDs assigned sequential numbers. Note the first and last resource IDs and close the *resource.h* file.

In your view or frame class—wherever you want to handle the update commands—add a macro to the message map *outside* the section reserved for the ClassWizard. Anything you place between the lines containing *AFX_MSG_MAP* may be edited or even deleted by the ClassWizard. If you place something the wizard doesn't understand between these lines, it might give you an error when you try to start it. Add the macro, specifying the lowest number first and the highest number second, followed by the name of the message handler function, as shown here:

```
BEGIN_MESSAGE_MAP(CChildView,CWnd )
//{{AFX_MSG_MAP(CChildView)
ON_WM_PAINT()
//}}AFX_MSG_MAP
ON_UPDATE_COMMAND_UI_RANGE(ID_APP_FIRSTID,
                          ID_APP_LASTID, OnUpdateAppCmds)
END_MESSAGE_MAP()
```

Next, add the handler function itself. Right-click on the class name in the ClassView pane of the Workshop window, or use the WizardBar menu. The return type is *void* and the only parameter is a pointer to a *CCmdUI* object. Your code should handle each possible ID in a switch statement. Trying to do a mass enable or disable is just a waste of code. The function will be called once for each ID in the range.

With the command enabler object, you may enable or disable the item, set a check mark (for a toolbar item, setting the check mark puts the button in a down state), or set the text for a menu item.

Add a Test menu to an application and place four items on it. Make the resource IDs *ID_TEST_TESTITEM1* through *ID_TEST_TESTITEM4*. Add the following line to the message handler in the view class:

```
ON_UPDATE_COMMAND_UI_RANGE(ID_TEST_TESTITEM1,
                          ID_TEST_TESTITEM2, OnUpdateAppCmds)
```

Add the following function to your view class:

```
void CChildView::OnUpdateAppCmds(CCmdUI* pCmdUI)
{
static int nCount = 0;
CString strText;

    switch (pCmdUI->m_nID)
    {
        case ID_TEST_TESTITEM1:
            pCmdUI->Enable (TRUE);
            if (nCount % 2)
```

```
                        pCmdUI->SetCheck (FALSE);
                else
                        pCmdUI->SetCheck (TRUE);
                break;
        case ID_TEST_TESTITEM2:
            pCmdUI->Enable (TRUE);
            break;
        case ID_TEST_TESTITEM3:
            pCmdUI->Enable (TRUE);
            strText.Format ("Called %d times", ++nCount);
            pCmdUI->SetText ((LPCSTR) strText);
            if (nCount % 5)
                pCmdUI->SetCheck (FALSE);
            else
                pCmdUI->SetCheck (TRUE);
            break;
        case ID_TEST_TESTITEM4:
            if (nCount % 2)
                pCmdUI->Enable (FALSE);
            else
                pCmdUI->Enable (TRUE);
            break;
    }
}
```

When a menu item or a control within the range needs updating, the frameworks will call the *OnUpdateAppsCmd()* function with a pointer to a command enabler. Run the program and select the Test menu. Every other time you select the menu, the first item will have a check mark to the left of the text. The second item will always be enabled. The text for the third item will be updated each time through, and the fourth item will alternately be enabled or disabled.

540. *Understanding the* CWaitCursor *Class*

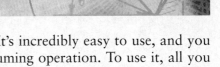

The *CWaitCursor* changes the mouse cursor to an hourglass shape. It's incredibly easy to use, and you should get used to using it when your program is doing a time-consuming operation. To use it, all you do is declare a *CWaitCursor* object. The cursor changes to an hourglass and remains that way until the object goes out of scope and is destroyed, at which time the old cursor reappears.

CWaitCursor has only one function, *Restore()*. During a block that uses a wait cursor object, the system may change the cursor if, say, you enter a dialog box. When that happens, you call the *Restore()* function when your code returns, and the hourglass appears again. Create a simple program named *CheckCursor* or use the code on the CD-ROM. You can use MFC AppWizard, but select Single Document and uncheck the Document/View Architecture Support. Accept the defaults on the rest of the pages.

First, open the *mainfrm.cpp* file, add a member function to write to the status bar message pane, and code it as shown here:

```
void CMainFrame::SetStatusMessage(CString &Msg)
{
    m_wndStatusBar.GetStatusBarCtrl().SetText ((LPCSTR) Msg,
                                      0, 0);
}
```

In the ResourceView pane, select the only menu available, and add an item named "Cursor" to the View menu. Make the resource ID *IDM_VIEW_CURSOR*. Close the menu and open the *childview.cpp* file. Right-click on the code someplace and select ClassWizard from the menu. On the ClassWizard's Message Maps page, find and select *IDM_VIEW_CURSOR* in the Object IDs list. In the Messages box, select COMMAND and then click the Add Function button. The default name for the function is *OnViewCursor()*, which is fine. Click OK, and select the Edit Code button to move to the function definition. Add the following code:

```
void CChildView::OnViewCursor()
{
CString Message;

    CMainFrame *frame=(CMainFrame *)AfxGetApp()->m_pMainWnd;
    Message = "Using wait cursor";
    frame->SetMessageText (Message);
    {
        CWaitCursor hey;
        Sleep (3000);
        Message = "System will change cursor";
        frame->SetMessageText (Message);
        ::SendMessage (frame->m_hWnd, WM_COMMAND,
                        (WPARAM) ID_APP_ABOUT, (LPARAM) 0);
        Message = "Restoring wait cursor";
        frame->SetMessageText (Message);
        hey.Restore();
        Sleep (3000);
    }
    Message = "Wait cursor out of scope";
    frame->SetMessageText (Message);
}
```

When you select Cursor from the View menu, the cursor changes to an hourglass, and the message appears on the status bar. After 3 seconds, the about dialog box opens, and the system sets the standard mouse cursor. (The *Sleep()* function causes the program to wait a number of milliseconds, so 3000 equates to a three-second wait.) When you click OK on the about box, the code restores the cursor and sleeps for another 3 seconds, and the cursor goes out of scope and is destroyed. The original cursor reappears.

541. *Using the CImageList Class*

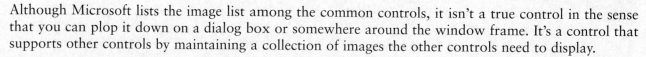

Although Microsoft lists the image list among the common controls, it isn't a true control in the sense that you can plop it down on a dialog box or somewhere around the window frame. It's a control that supports other controls by maintaining a collection of images the other controls need to display.

MFC encapsulates the image list in the *CImageList* class. Its member functions let you add, swap, move, and delete images to support operations of other classes. It is used by *CToolBar*, *CListCtrl*, *CTreeCtrl*, and *CComboBoxEx*.

The project on the CD-ROM uses *CImageList* with a *CToolBar* to customize a toolbar after the program has started running. The entire process is handled in the *CMainFrame* class, where the toolbar and image list are created.

First, you must create some images for your toolbar. You do this by creating a single bitmap image or by creating individual bitmaps for the buttons. You're going to do it the hard way, with individual images, because if you can handle putting together several images in code, you can handle the single image method easily. First, you collect all the images you need (they're in the *COMMON\GRAPHIC\BITMAPS\TlBr_W95* directory, where you installed Visual C++). You need nine images in all, and for your convenience, they are in the *RES* folder of the project on the companion CD-ROM. You make sure that these images are all 16 pixels wide by 15 pixels deep (that's why you copied them; the originals are 16 pixels deep). Each bitmap has its own resource ID, which you will use to load the images onto the toolbar.

Next, you add some variables to the *CMainFrame* class definition:

```
CImageList    m_Images;
CString       m_strExecProgram;
bool          m_bInserted;
```

The *m_Images* is the image list you will assign to the toolbar. *m_strExecProgram* is the program you are going to start; you don't know what that is yet. *m_bInserted* is a flag you use to determine whether a new toolbar button has been added. In the *CMainFrame* constructor, initialize the variable with the following line:

```
m_bInserted = false;
```

Add two member functions to the *CMainFrame* class as follows. You can either do this manually or use the ClassView pane of the Workshop window. You will be using a dummy resource ID for the *OnRunProgram()* function, so you will have to add the message map entry manually. You will be making some other changes to the message map, so that can wait.

```
void LoadImages(CImageList *Images);
afx_msg void OnRunProgram();
```

In the ResourceView pane, open the *IDR_MAINFRAME* menu and add a pop-up menu between the View and Help pop-ups. Add a single item to it named "Insert Button," and give it the resource ID of *IDM_IMAGES_INSERTBUTTON*. That's all you need; now that you've learned about command enablers, you can just change the text on it as necessary.

Right-click on the ImageList Resource tree in the ResourceView pane and select Resource Symbols. Add a new resource ID named *ID_FILE_RUNPROGRAM*. It doesn't matter what number the resource editor gives it; you just need to reserve an ID for the button you're going to add.

Open the toolbar and put an empty button between the print and the help icons. A print preview image is included in the image list, and you must leave space for it. Don't worry about copying the image to the toolbar; the program is going to override the images anyway. Just drag the blank button to the left into the proper position, and give it the resource ID *ID_FILE_PRINT_PREVIEW*. You also could create a blank toolbar (you've created one you can use in later projects), but make sure that it has the *IDR_MAINFRAME* resource ID.

Now, tend to the message map and the housekeeping chores will be done. Then you can start coding. Enter the ClassWizard and select the Message Maps page. Make sure that the *CMainFrame* class is selected. Find and select the *IDM_IMAGES_INSERTBUTTON* entry in the Object IDs list. Add handlers for *both* the COMMAND and UPDATE_COMMAND_UI entries. Exit the ClassWizard and manually add the handler for *OnRunProgram* to the message map. When you're done, the message map should look like the following code:

```
BEGIN_MESSAGE_MAP(CMainFrame, CFrameWnd)
    //{{AFX_MSG_MAP(CMainFrame)
    ON_WM_CREATE()
    ON_COMMAND(IDM_IMAGES_INSERTBUTTON, OnImagesInsertbutton)
```

```
    ON_UPDATE_COMMAND_UI(IDM_IMAGES_INSERTBUTTON,
                             OnUpdateImagesInsertbutton)
    //}}AFX_MSG_MAP
    ON_COMMAND(ID_FILE_RUNPROGRAM, OnRunProgram)
END_MESSAGE_MAP()
```

Finally, the housekeeping is done. You can start coding. When you see the action at the end of all this, you will appreciate the housekeeping chores. First, code the *LoadImages()* function:

```
void CMainFrame::LoadImages(CImageList *Images)
{
int x;
UINT    uiIndex[] =
    {
    IDB_FILE_NEW,
    IDB_FILE_OPEN,
    IDB_FILE_SAVE,
    IDB_FILE_CUT,
    IDB_FILE_COPY,
    IDB_FILE_PASTE,
    IDB_FILE_PRINT,
    IDB_FILE_PREVIEW,
    IDB_FILE_HELP
    };

    CBitmap bmp;
    COLORREF clrMask = GetSysColor (COLOR_BTNFACE);
    for (x = 0; x < (sizeof (uiIndex) / sizeof (UINT)); ++x)
    {
        bmp.LoadBitmap (MAKEINTRESOURCE(uiIndex[x]));
        Images->Add (&bmp, clrMask);
        bmp.DeleteObject ();
    }
}
```

The array of identifiers, *uiIndex*, is in the same order as the toolbar buttons, so you can assign them in a loop rather than in 30 lines of code. Note that they are the *bitmap* resource IDs, not the toolbar button IDs. The *clrMask* is the color value the system uses to mask the background when the button is inactive, and *COLOR_BTNFACE* is one of the 29 system colors maintained by Windows.

The loop first loads the bitmap and then places it in the image list. The last line in the loop deletes the bitmap object, so you can use the same *CBitmap* object to load the next image.

Code the message handlers next. The *OnUpdateImagesInsertbutton* is a long name for a function that simply changes the menu text. If the member variable *m_bInserted* is *true*, the text is changed to read "Delete Button." Otherwise, the new button isn't present and the text reads "Insert Button."

```
void CMainFrame::OnUpdateImagesInsertbutton(CCmdUI* pCmdUI)
{
    if (m_wndToolBar.CommandToIndex (ID_FILE_RUNPROGRAM) < 0)
        pCmdUI->SetText (_T("Insert Button"));
    else
        pCmdUI->SetText (_T("Delete Button"));
}
```

The code to insert and delete the new button is in the *OnImagesInsertbutton*, which is called when you select the Insert Button (or Delete Button) item on the Images menu. First, the code checks the *m_bInserted* member variable to determine whether the action is to insert or remove the button:

```
void CMainFrame::OnImagesInsertbutton()
{

    if (m_wndToolBar.CommandToIndex (ID_FILE_RUNPROGRAM) >= 0)
    {
        m_wndToolBar.GetToolBarCtrl().DeleteButton (8);
        m_Images.Remove (9);
RecalcLayout ();
        return;
    }
    CString Filter = _T("Executable files (*.exe)|*.exe||");
    CFileDialog fd(true, NULL, NULL, OFN_HIDEREADONLY
                             | OFN_OVERWRITEPROMPT, Filter);
    if (fd.DoModal () == IDCANCEL)
        return;
    HICON hIcon = ExtractIcon (NULL, fd.GetFileName(), 0);
    m_strExecProgram = fd.m_ofn.lpstrFile;
    m_Images.Add (hIcon);
    DeleteObject (hIcon);

    TBBUTTON tb;
    tb.iBitmap = 9;
    tb.idCommand = ID_FILE_RUNPROGRAM;
    tb.fsState = TBSTATE_ENABLED;
    tb.fsStyle = TBSTYLE_BUTTON;
    tb.dwData = 0;
    tb.iString = NULL;
    m_wndToolBar.GetToolBarCtrl().InsertButton (8, &tb);
RecalcLayout ();
}
```

If the button is present, the code removes it from the toolbar and the image from the image list, setting the flag to *false* so that the next time through it will be to add a button. The call to *RecalcLayout()* informs the window frame class that something has changed and that it should look over the layout and fix it if necessary. Without this function call, you would have a blank space in the toolbar when the button is deleted.

Next comes the *CFileDialog* common dialog to get the name of an executable file. This is where the magic comes in. When you select a file, the code extracts the icon from the executable and adds it to the image list. Nine images are already in the list, so you know that the zero-based index for the new image is 9 (unless you fiddled with something else). This image is an icon. The image list doesn't care. Bits is bits. The difference is that the call doesn't need a mask because that should be built in to the icon. After you've added the icon to the image list, you don't need to tie up unnecessary resources, so delete it.

When you have the name of the program and the icon, save the file path in the *m_strExecProgram* member variable.

The *TBBUTTON* structure is a Windows structure that describes a toolbar button. Set the image index to 9, the same as in the image list. The button itself, however, will be inserted before the Help button, so its zero-based index will be 8. The *idCommand* member in the Windows *ON_COMMAND* message the button will issue when clicked is *ID_FILE_RUNPROGRAM*, the bogus resource ID you added earlier. The button is enabled and the style is a toolbar button. No data is associated with it and no text. The *CToolBar* class doesn't have a member function to add a button, but the underlying control does.

Get the control and add the button; then, set the *m_bInserted* flag to *true*. Finally, call *RecalcLayout()* to resize everything. Here, if you don't recalculate the layout, you will lose the Help button because there's only room for nine buttons on the present toolbar.

The *OnRunProgram()* function is called when the user clicks the new button. If the *CreateProcess()* function fails, it returns *FALSE*, and you could add a message box here informing the user that something went wrong.

```
void CMainFrame::OnRunProgram()
{
PROCESS_INFORMATION pi;
STARTUPINFO          si;

    memset ((char *) &si, '\0', sizeof (STARTUPINFO));
    si.cb = sizeof (STARTUPINFO);

    CString ProgPath = m_strExecProgram;
    CString ProgParam = m_strExecProgram;
    CString StartPath = _T(".\\");
    BOOL bResult = CreateProcess((LPCTSTR) ProgPath,
                (char *) (LPCSTR) ProgParam,
                (LPSECURITY_ATTRIBUTES) NULL,
                (LPSECURITY_ATTRIBUTES) NULL,
                false,
                DETACHED_PROCESS,
                (LPVOID) NULL,
                (LPCTSTR) StartPath,
                (LPSTARTUPINFO) &si,
                (LPPROCESS_INFORMATION) &pi);
}
```

You're not quite done. Now you must add the essential piece of code that will make all this work. In the *OnCreate()* function in *CMainFrame*, you create and load the image list. The function should look like the following code:

```
int CMainFrame::OnCreate(LPCREATESTRUCT lpCreateStruct)
{
    if (CFrameWnd::OnCreate(lpCreateStruct) == -1)
        return -1;

    m_Images.Create (16, 15, ILC_MASK, 9, 5);
    LoadImages (&m_Images);

    if (!m_wndToolBar.CreateEx(this, TBSTYLE_FLAT, WS_CHILD
                    | WS_VISIBLE | CBRS_TOP | CBRS_GRIPPER
                    | CBRS_TOOLTIPS | CBRS_FLYBY
                    | CBRS_SIZE_DYNAMIC) ||
        !m_wndToolBar.LoadToolBar(IDR_MAINFRAME))
    {
        TRACE0("Failed to create toolbar\n");
        return -1;      // fail to create
    }
    m_wndToolBar.GetToolBarCtrl().SetImageList (&m_Images);
    m_wndToolBar.SetWindowText (_T("Edit"));

    if (!m_wndStatusBar.Create(this) ||
        !m_wndStatusBar.SetIndicators(indicators,
```

```
          sizeof(indicators)/sizeof(UINT)))
    {
        TRACE0("Failed to create status bar\n");
        return -1;       // fail to create
    }


    // TODO: Delete these three lines if you don't want the
    // toolbar to be dockable
    m_wndToolBar.EnableDocking(CBRS_ALIGN_ANY);
    EnableDocking(CBRS_ALIGN_ANY);
    DockControlBar(&m_wndToolBar);


    return 0;
}
```

After the window frame has been created, you create the image list, specifying that the images are 16 pixels wide by 15 deep and they use a mask. The initial size is 9, and the list may grow by 5 more images (this isn't a critical value). This is a dockable toolbar; give it a name such as "Edit" so that it has a title when the user leaves it floating.

It should all work now. Run the program and select the Images menu, then Insert Button (not that you have many choices on this menu). When the Open File dialog appears, try selecting something like *calc.exe* from your Windows system directory. Unless you click Cancel, when you see the toolbar again, it should have a new button with the icon for the program on it. Click the button and the program should run. The menu item under Images has now changed to Delete Button. Select it and you will have the old toolbar back.

You might want to add string table entries for *ID_FILE_RUNPROGRAM* and *IDM_IMAGES_ INSERTBUTTON* to give it some ToolTip text on the status bar.

Have fun with the code. Try adding buttons for other functions elsewhere in the toolbar. The important point is that your code is redesigning the toolbar on-the-fly. Also, there's not much error checking in this code, so you might want to add some in a real project. Oh yeah, try out the Print Preview button. You will probably want to add it to your other projects, and it doesn't cost anything.

The image list pops up quite often when you get to the section on "Windows Common Controls." In Tip 652, "Displaying the Various Views of the List Control," you will learn how to get the default icons from Windows.

542. *Deriving Your Own Classes from the MFC Library*

Nothing's perfect. In the world of commerce, no mass market product could ever hope to meet the needs of every potential buyer. The Microsoft Foundation Class library is no different. It was written for a mass audience according to the programming Microsoft expects of you. Of course, people have different expectations of themselves, so naturally you would want to make any class library reflect your needs.

That's part of the wonder of C++. You don't need to alter the MFC library code to customize it, and the authors of any class library should expect it.

Nearly all the MFC classes can benefit from customization. In reading this book, you will often derive new classes from the MFC base classes; you must do this just to claim some individuality in programming. Face it—the world doesn't need any more *NotePads* or *WordPads*.

Some of the classes are rich in virtual functions that you can override; others have none. In the *CStaticEx* and *CEditEx* classes, you've seen how you can impose your will on a class that won't let you draw it the way you want. You just draw over what it does.

In Tip 671, "Saving the Status Bar Message," you will learn how to derive a class from *CStatusBarEx* to get rid of some unfriendly behavior. The derived class has just one purpose—to override the *WM_SETTEXT* Windows message. Here's what the derived class definition looks like:

```
///////////////////////////////////////////////////////////
// CStatusBarEx window

class CStatusBarEx : public CStatusBar
{
// Construction
public:
    CStatusBarEx();

// Attributes
public:

// Operations
public:

// Overrides
    // ClassWizard generated virtual function overrides
    //{{AFX_VIRTUAL(CStatusBarEx)
    //}}AFX_VIRTUAL

// Implementation
public:
    virtual ~CStatusBarEx();

    // Generated message map functions
protected:
    //{{AFX_MSG(CStatusBarEx)
    //}}AFX_MSG
    afx_msg LRESULT OnSetText(WPARAM, LPARAM);

private:
    UINT    m_nWinId, m_nWinStyle;
    int     m_cxWinWidth;
    UINT    m_nId, m_nStyle;
    int     m_cxWidth;
    CString m_strStatusText;

    DECLARE_MESSAGE_MAP()
};
```

In this book, you will derive new classes from a number of the MFC classes. You can't break anything by deriving your own classes and trying some customization. MFC needs all the help you can give it. At the very least, you will learn more about the class itself.

543. *Understanding the New Menu Command*

When you select New from the Files menu in the Visual Studio, you aren't presented with the traditional dialog to create new files. Instead, you are presented with a dialog box that contains a tab control. The number of tabs depends on the Studio edition you are using, but they all contain Files, Projects, and Workspaces tabs.

The Files tab allows you to create the type of source files that are supported by the Visual Studio. Again, the list depends on the edition you are using. For example, if you installed the Enterprise edition, which is the only edition that supports SQL debugging, you will have an entry for SQL Script File. You won't find this entry on other editions.

On the Projects tab, you have a number of choices, again depending on the edition you installed. A project is a single application, library, Windows control, and so on, that you might want to create. Each of these project types invokes a different wizard or alternative steps for the same wizard. The ATL COM App Wizard and MFC AppWizard (dll) selections, for example, contain only a single page. The MFC AppWizard (exe), on the other hand, contains six pages with a couple of pop-up dialog boxes for additional information and options.

The Workspaces tab requires some explanation. It allows you to create an empty workspace. When you create a C++ program, you use one or more files, which you group together in the Visual Studio and place in a *project*. However, you often need more than one project to accomplish the task at hand. For example, you might be writing a dynamic link library to go along with your application program, so you might collect these projects and put them into a *workspace*. If you anticipate this, you can create an empty workspace and then create the various projects you need in the workspace. You may create other projects later and place them in your workspace. The *MemFile* application in the *SAMPLES\0518* on the CD-ROM is a sample of a workspace containing more than one project.

544. *Creating Files*

Select the Files tab of the New dialog to create files. If you have a workspace open, the box labeled Add to Project (upper right) will be checked, and the combo box directly below will contain a list of the projects in the current workspace.

If you add the file to your project, it will appear in one of the branches in the list of files on the FileView pane of the Workspace window and will become one of the project's dependents. As a dependent, the Visual C++ make process will check it for changes to determine whether, and which part of the program, to rebuild.

When you enter the file name, you don't have to include the extension. The IDE adds it according to the type of file you selected. The file by default is created in the current workspace's directory, but you may specify another direction by entering it in the Location field or by clicking the button to the right of this field to summon a "Choose Directory" prompt.

545. *Creating Workspaces*

As you saw earlier, a *workspace* is a collection of zero or more projects. You can use the Workspaces tab on the New dialog box to create an empty workspace, waiting for you to add projects, but you can't create a project without a workspace.

Usually, when you create a single project in a workspace, the workspace and project components live in the same directory. They don't have to, however. If you expect to have several projects for a single application, you may create an empty workspace here and then create the projects as you need them (see Figure 545).

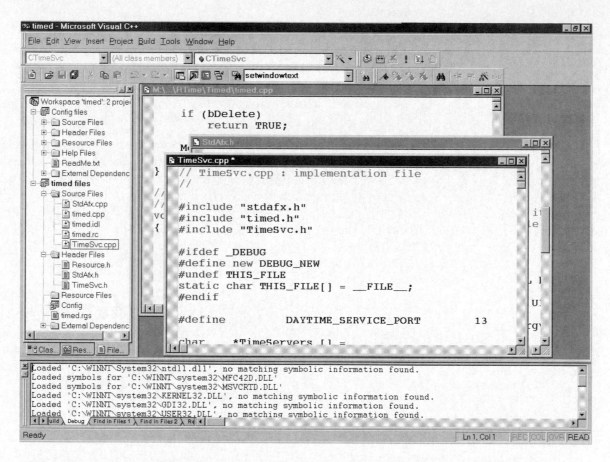

Figure 545 *This workspace contains two projects: a Windows NT service program, timed, that doesn't interact with the desktop and a dialog-based configuration program that is used to set the Registry values used by the service program. The contents of the workspace file appear in the text.*

Basic workspace information is kept in a file with the extension *.dsw*. This is an ordinary text file that you may open in any text-editing program, but be careful not to change anything unless you are familiar with the file contents. The following shows the contents of a workspace file that contains two projects:

```
Microsoft Developer Studio Workspace File, Format Version 6.00
# WARNING: DO NOT EDIT OR DELETE THIS WORKSPACE FILE!


###############################################################################

Project: "Config"=.\Config\Config.dsp - Package Owner=<4>
```

```
Package=<5>
{{{
}}}

Package=<4>
{{{
}}}


###################################################################

Project: "timed"=.\timed.dsp - Package Owner=<4>

Package=<5>
{{{
}}}

Package=<4>
{{{
    Begin Project Dependency
    Project_Dep_Name Config
    End Project Dependency
}}}


###################################################################

Global:

Package=<5>
{{{
}}}

Package=<3>
{{{
}}}


###################################################################
```

This workspace file lists the two projects in the workspace using the relative paths to the project files. Using relative instead of absolute paths enables you to move the project directory if necessary, even to a different drive. As long as you don't change the relative location of the two projects, the projects will open normally.

546. *Creating Other Documents*

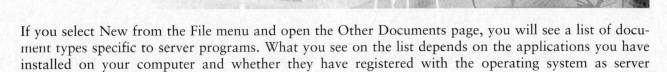

If you select New from the File menu and open the Other Documents page, you will see a list of document types specific to server programs. What you see on the list depends on the applications you have installed on your computer and whether they have registered with the operating system as server processes.

Document types listed on the Other Documents page are Active Documents. They are created by *COM* component programs such as Microsoft *Word*, *Excel*, or *Visual FoxPro* or by your own registered *COM* programs.

When you create a file on this tab, you select a *COM* component such as *Word*, give the document a name, and check whether you want to add it to a project. Select a location for the file—the default location is the current workspace directory—and click OK. The COM component program will start and the new document will open in it.

When you create a document from this page, the server process runs embedded in the Visual Studio, and your editing commands make calls to the server process. If you have *Word* installed, you should have an icon on this list for Microsoft Word Document. Create a file (it doesn't matter whether you add it to the project) and the toolbars will be replaced by *Word*'s toolbars. The menu will be a blend of *Word* and applicable items from the Visual Studio.

Don't use this page to create new source or header files. Instead, use the Files tab.

547. *Creating Projects*

By default, if you don't already have a workspace open, the wizards will create one for you. If you already have a workspace open in the Studio, the option to Add to Current Workspace will be enabled.

Project information is stored in a file with an extension of *.dsp* in the project directory. Again, this is an ordinary text file, but be careful not to modify it unless you know what you are doing.

Projects don't have to be in the same directory or even on the same disk drive, as the workspace. In fact, on a network you may create a project on a different machine and place it in your workspace.

548. *Understanding Utility Projects*

Occasionally, and for whatever reason, you might not want a project to result in an object module such as an executable or dynamic link library. You might just want a project to manage a group of related files, such as document, spreadsheet, or database files.

The *utility* project was intended for this purpose. It provides no compilation or linking rules, and no resulting output file type is expected. Like the empty workspace, this is an empty project. When you create a utility project, no files are added to it automatically.

You may include a utility project as part of a workspace. For example, as part of a larger project you could add a utility project to the workspace as a container for the documentation files. Then you could maintain these files from within the same IDE you use to develop your program.

549. *Understanding the MFC AppWizard*

For most of your projects, the MFC AppWizard will be your main wizard for creating projects. Using a class library has many advantages, one of which is code size. When you use a class library, much of the underlying program activity is contained in a dynamic link library containing the class library code. The MFC DLL is *redistributable*, meaning that you may include it with your program without paying an additional fee to Microsoft.

You may create an executable program, an *.EXE* file, using the MFC AppWizard (exe) entry in the project list. When you create a project using this wizard, it generates a complete set of program source files, header files, and resource files, including the common options, such as a toolbar and status bar. Not all the possibilities are covered in the AppWizard process, however. For example, you could create a "Win32 Application" and add MFC support to it manually; the wizard doesn't give you this option.

550. *Creating an MFC EXE Project*

After you establish a project name and a directory to contain it, start the AppWizard by clicking the OK button. On the first page, you set the course for the rest of the wizard steps. If you select single-document or multiple-document application on this page, the wizard will contain six steps. If you select a dialog-based application, only four steps are required.

The document/view support will determine your options on the last page. If you don't select this support, your view class will be derived directly from *CWnd* rather than through an MFC view class. In addition, you won't have the option of selecting a splitter window or creating an Explorer-type application. This doesn't mean that you can't use a splitter window; the wizard just won't add support for it, and you will have to roll your own code. The wizard also will not include any compound-document (OLE) support, and you won't have the advantage of the MFC print preview class.

In the following tips, you will go through the process of creating an AppWizard project, examining each of the options on each page. Remember that the more options you select the more specific the code generated by the wizard.

551. *Adding Multiple-Document Support to Your Project*

The default for the MFC AppWizard is to create a multiple-document interface program. MDI is a standardized interface developed by IBM that details how a single application may have more than one document open at the same time. These may be text documents, graphics images, Web interfaces, or any place that data may be stored, sent, or retrieved. There is no assumption that the data must be *persistent* (stored in some fashion for later retrieval). Figure 551 shows an example of an MDI application.

A single-document interface program, obviously, may have only one document open at a time. *NotePad* and *WordPad* are examples of a single-document interface application. *Word*, *PaintShop Pro*, and even the *Visual Studio* are examples of multiple-document interface applications.

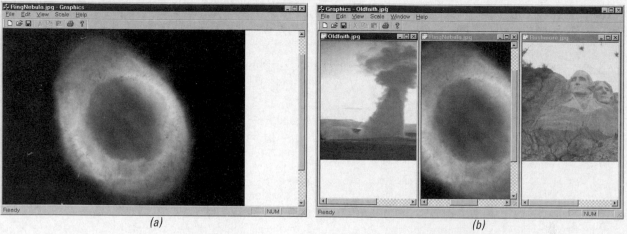

Figure 551   A single-document interface program (a), allows you to have only one file open at a time.
In a multiple-document interface (b), you may have many files open at the same time.

552. _Understanding Document/View Support_

The document/view architecture is at the heart of most MFC programs. It is possible to create and develop applications in MFC without the document part—in fact, many of the earlier samples up to this point have been view applications only. In the long haul, though, it's far easier to develop and maintain a Windows program with the document/view architecture than with the basic Windows API. The structure is already there, and it costs nothing more to use it.

In the document/view setup, an object called a "document template" is responsible for creating the document and the view, along with the window that holds the view. In a single-document interface, it creates the main window frame. In a multiple-document interface, the main frame is created in the application's _InitInstance()_ function, and the document template is responsible for creating the child windows.

Applications may use more than one view, and they may have more than one document template. The AppWizard, however, creates only one of each for you. It's a simple matter, however, to add views and document templates. Tip 616, "Adding Multiple Document Types to Your Project," shows you the process.

553. _Understanding Database Support_

Other than no database support, the wizard offers you three levels of database support options. The first, Header Files Only, adds the MFC database header files to your _stdafx.h_ file. Other than that, you are responsible for setting up the database connection and creating the recordset classes. The Database View without File Support option sets up the header files and the libraries your application must include, and the wizard will create a record view and one recordset class. It does not include the serialization support to read and write the data to a file. Ordinarily, you simply use the recordset's _Update()_ function to save the data to the database, and you don't need file serialization. The final option, Database View with File Support, includes file serialization support for those rare cases where you need it.

The last two options require that you select a data source, either ODBC, DAO, or OLE DB, and that you select a table for the single recordset class the wizard will set up for you. After the project is created, you may add recordset classes for other tables.

554. Adding Compound-Document Support, ActiveX, and Automation to the Project

Compound-document support determines whether and how your application will handle OLE objects. If you are planning to use the *CRichEditView* class as the base for your view, you have to select at least Container support here. A *container* is a program that can include embedded or linked items in its documents. The rich edit control won't initialize without OLE. Mini-Servers support compound documents in other applications but cannot run alone. Full Servers can create and support compound documents and may run alone. Both Container and Server support allows your application to include OLE objects or to support them in other applications.

ActiveX is a technology that allows components to interact over a network regardless of the programming language or platform. They don't *have* to operate over a network; they can operate on a single machine not connected to a network. Selecting this support lets your application use ActiveX controls.

If you select Automation support, you can let other applications use portions of your application's code, such as a dialog box control. This also makes it possible for your program to reach out and touch someone else's.

555. Selecting Features for Your Project

On the wizard's Page 4, you learned in the past few tips how to handle a docking toolbar, an initial status bar, and print preview and how to add print preview to the toolbar.

The next feature item is Context-Sensitive Help. With this support, the wizard includes a *HLP* directory in your project to support help files. As you build the project, help topic IDs are created and placed in a file bearing your project name and the extension *.HM* in this directory. Each compilation invokes the help workshop to recompile the help file if necessary. It doesn't write the help file for you; that's still your responsibility.

With context-sensitive help, additional code is added to your project to support the help file. For example, when the user presses the F1 key, the help file is opened directly, without your having to go through the menu item. The Shift+F1 key is used to place the application in *help mode*. In this mode, the mouse cursor changes to a pointer with a question mark, and the user can then click on any item to summon the help page for that item. A similar button is added to the toolbar to put the application in help mode.

The importance of a good help file and help system can't be overemphasized. You might know every facet of your application, but users might not be so sophisticated, and the first user you give it to is going to come up with questions you never knew could be asked. (A quick anecdote here: I once helped a user troubleshoot a problem with one of my communications programs over the phone. One of the things I wanted to know was whether she had an internal or external modem. With an external modem, the indicator lights might help diagnose the problem. When I asked the question, she replied, "Oh, it's internal. We keep it in the house.")

If you program internally for a company, a good help system keeps you off the phone and leaves your evenings free for something other than support. One of the problems is that there is very little literature on the market for writing help files. One good start is *Building Windows 95 Help* by Nancy Hickman, published by M&T Books. My copy was published in 1996, but most of the material is still relevant.

The 3-D Controls option is what gives the toolbar buttons that pop-up effect when the mouse moves over them in the case of a flat toolbar or the raised button effect on a standard toolbar. Three-dimensional controls produce only an aesthetic effect, but it gives the user some sense of interaction with the program.

MAPI is the Windows Messaging API. It accesses the Windows message system and lets you send documents to other users without resorting to the email. If you are planning on submitting your application to Microsoft as a Logo-qualified program, you must include this support, as well as some limited OLE support.

Windows Sockets makes the wizard insert a line into your application to initialize the Windows socket API. If you don't check this box and later want to use sockets to communicate over a TCP/IP network (such as the Internet), you simply add a call to *AfxSocketInit()* in your program before the sockets code is executed. In the *InitInstance()* function is a good place, and that's where the wizard places it.

The recent file list option allows you to specify how many menu items you would like to have for the recent file list. The default is 4, but if you want to change it later, you can add the number to the *LoadStdProfileSettings()* function call in *InitInstance*. Simply add the number as a parameter: *LoadStdProfileSettings(8)* would set the MRU item list to 8.

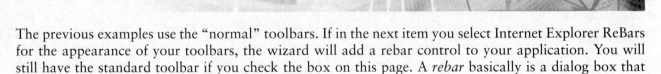

556. *Understanding the Toolbar Options*

The previous examples use the "normal" toolbars. If in the next item you select Internet Explorer ReBars for the appearance of your toolbars, the wizard will add a rebar control to your application. You will still have the standard toolbar if you check the box on this page. A *rebar* basically is a dialog box that acts like a toolbar and attaches itself to the frame. A rebar is *not* dockable.

A rebar allows you to create a toolbar-like window that accepts other controls, such as a combo box or edit control. Adding these to a standard toolbar in MFC is not an easy task, and the rebar control solves this problem. The only reason the rebar control is necessary is that MFC's support for toolbars is so weak and the rebar still falls short of being a good control. Other class libraries are capable of easily placing common controls on standard toolbars and still leaving them dockable. To read the Microsoft literature on the rebar control, you would think that it's the greatest thing since vanilla ice cream, but it's more hype than fact.

557. *Understanding Advanced Project Options*

Click the Advanced button to get to what Microsoft considers advanced window options. The Document Template Strings page is covered in Tip 490, "Invoking the Visual Studio Wizard to Create an MFC-Based Program," so click the Window Styles tab.

Use Split Window prepares a *CSplitterWnd* control in the window frame class. See Tip 505, "Using the *CSplitterWnd* Class," for an example of a splitter window.

The Main Frame Styles and MDI Child Frame Styles sections cover the same items, except that a child window may not have a system menu so that check box is not included there. The system menu is the pop-up menu that appears when you click on the application's icon in the upper-left corner of the window. It's rare to find a mouse-less user these days, and most users are unaware of the system menu anyway, so it gets little use. Still, it costs nothing to include it for the occasional user who expects a system menu.

AppWizard applications use a thick frame by default, both for the main window and for MDI child windows. If you unselect this option, the user will be unable to resize the window.

The Minimize Box and Maximize Box are the first two small boxes on the right side of the main title bar.

The last two check boxes (to the right) control the initial display of the window when it is created. In the case of the application's main window, the default is neither of these, and the window is displayed normally somewhere on the screen. If you select Maximized, the application will start up filling the entire display space; if you select Minimize, the application will start up as an icon on the Taskbar.

For MDI child windows, the Maximized option causes the window to fill the client area of the application's main window. Minimize causes it to appear initially as a quasi-icon in the lower-left portion of the client area.

558. *Other Project Options*

On the fifth page, if you select Windows Explorer as the application style, you will get a vertically split window with a tree view on the left side. You don't have any other choices. For the right side, you may choose any of the other views, but selecting *CEditView* as the base class will cause the program to assert when you try to open a file. Tracing the assertion reveals that apparently no edit control is attached to the view. This is curious because the *CRichEditView* option works. Even more curious is that if you select Splitter Window in the advanced options of Page 4, the wizard won't let you select *CRichEditView* as a base class.

For Source File Comments, you might as well leave Yes, Please checked. They're free and occasionally useful. After a lot of projects, you get to where they are markers for your searches.

Unless you have a need for statically linking MFC to your application, select As a Shared DLL in the final option on this page. If you are writing a Windows NT service program, you might want to statically link MFC, but then you probably would have chosen the ATL COM AppWizard instead of the MFC AppWizard. Using the MFC DLL results in smaller code size for your application, which translates to faster load and startup times.

559. *The Final Step: Naming Your Classes and Selecting a View Class*

On the AppWizard's final page, you select the base class for your view class. The other base classes are fixed. You may change the names of your derived classes, however.

To select a view base class, first click on the name of your view class in the list; then select a base class from the combo box at the bottom. The various MFC view classes and their uses are listed in Tip 513, "Introducing the MFC View Classes."

A non-splitter window application may use any of the base classes. If you selected an Explorer-type application, you also may select any of the view classes, with the caution that the *CEditView* selection will assert. This probably is a bug that will be fixed, but as of Service Pack 3, it is still there.

However, if you selected the splitter window option from the advanced options, you are limited to the non-editing base classes, which leaves out *CEditView* and *CRichEditView*. You may select *CView*, *CHtmlView*, or *CScrollView*.

560. *Creating a Dialog-Based Project*

Creating a full window application is only half the world of Windows programming. There are numerous useful applications that you may create using nothing more than a dialog box. You select the dialog-based application option from the first page of the AppWizard, as shown in Figure 560.

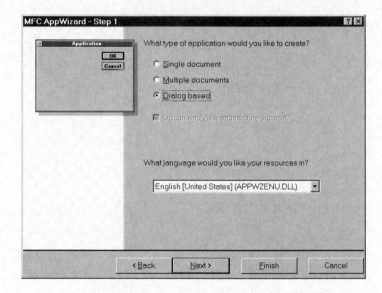

Figure 560   Select the dialog-based style application from the first page of the AppWizard. The image in the upper left shows how the program's window will appear.

MFC supports dialog box–based applications through the MFC AppWizard (exe). On the wizard's first page, select Dialog Based instead of a document-type interface. Your options are severely reduced, of course, because a dialog box application is not as complicated as a document/view application. This doesn't mean that you've lost all the options; you just can't select them all in the wizard.

The next tip explains some of the wizard options you have when you create a dialog box–based application, and Tip 562, "Selecting Dialog Box Options," discusses some that you have *after* the application is created.

561. Selecting Features and Support Options for Your Dialog-Based Project

After you select the dialog box–based option, you move on to Page 2 of the MFC AppWizard simply because there's not a lot left to choose from on Page 1.

If you select the About Box option, there's a little quirk with the way the wizard prepares about boxes in a dialog box application. The wizard places the class definition and implementation for the about box at the top of your main dialog class source file. When you summon the ClassWizard from this file (and you will, many times), it selects the about box class by default. You have to remember each time to select your dialog class before performing any operations. At best, the wizard placement is a real pain. The solution is to not select the about box option when you create the project or to move it to a file of its own. I prefer to opt out of the about box for dialog box applications, but then most of my programs are used internally and everybody knows who to blame.

Most of the rest of this page is similar to the document-based options, except that at the bottom you may enter the title for your dialog box. Don't worry about coming up with a descriptive name here; it's very easy to change after the application is created.

On Page 3, your only window style option is MFC Standard. So far you haven't seen anything even resembling an Explorer-type dialog application, but programmers can be innovative (if they don't work for Microsoft), so who knows.

On the last page, you have only the options to change the names of your classes and the implementation files.

562. Selecting Dialog Box Options

As soon as the MFC AppWizard creates your dialog box application, a nearly blank dialog appears in the Visual Studio's editing window. Right-click the mouse somewhere on a blank area of the dialog box, and select Properties from the menu.

You haven't given up quite as many style options as the AppWizard might have made you believe. On the properties dialog, you have four pages of options from which to choose.

On the first page, you can change the title, set the font, and even assign a menu to the dialog box. Of course, the wizard didn't prepare a menu for you because normally you don't use a dialog box with one. However, you can roll your own easily in the resource editor.

On the styles page, you can set the window style to pop-up, overlapped, or child. On a dialog box application, there's no parent window frame (other than the desktop), so the child window style really doesn't apply. You can also change the window frame to allow users to resize the dialog. If you do, you might want to make some provision for resizing your control dynamically to account for various window sizes.

563. *Creating Dynamic Link Library Projects Using MFC*

The code for an application doesn't have to be contained in a single file. You can create separate modules to be loaded at runtime that contain functions your program might need. These *dynamically* loaded modules go by different names on various operating systems, and on Windows they are called "dynamic link libraries" (DLLs).

You've seen them everywhere in Windows. They became much more common with the introduction of Windows 95 because memory management is much better than earlier versions of Windows. You can create your basic application code in a single project and then include specifics—such as graphics processing or document editing—in more specific DLLs.

The MFC AppWizard (dll) is used to create dynamic link libraries using the Microsoft Foundation Class library. If you installed the Professional or Enterprise edition of Visual C++, you have the option of statically linking your DLL with MFC (the applicable code from MFC is included in your finished DLL). Otherwise, you have only two options. You may create a regular DLL that makes calls to the MFC library as a shared DLL. With this type, you may create other MFC or non-MFC projects that can use your DLL. You also may create an MFC *extension* DLL, in which case, only MFC-based programs may use your DLL.

564. *Creating Win32 Libraries*

On the opposite side of the coin from dynamic link libraries are the *static link libraries*. DLLs are separate files that are loaded on demand when you run your application. They do not significantly add to the code size. With a static library, the code is included in your executable file.

Often you will find yourself including a number of functions in your applications on a regular basis. If you program for a particular industry or company, you will probably develop a number of industry-specific functions. Rather than rewrite or cut and paste them into your code, you can build a library containing them and add it to your application's settings.

In the static link library wizard, you have only two options. You may include a precompiled header, and you may include support for the Microsoft Foundation Class library. Unless you are using some MFC classes in your code, you don't need either of these.

Tip 262, "Extending *strtok* to Parse for Empty Tokens," includes a function named *strtokex()*, a customized version of the standard C function *strtok()*, that allows you to parse a string and find empty tokens, something the standard version can't do. It was suggested that you might want to put it into a personal library. Here's where you would do that.

First, create your library project. Name it *stringsex*. Create a source file named *strtokex.c* and a header file named *stringsex.h*. The header file will contain function declarations for all the functions in your library. You will have to include it in any project that uses your library. I prefer to keep each library function in its own source file and declare them all in a common header file.

Follow the steps in Tip 262 to create the *strtokex.c* file. The basic code is from the Microsoft runtime library and is copyrighted, so you won't include it here. Put the resulting code in the *strtokex.c* file you just created. Add the declaration to the header file, which should look like the following listing. Remember to use the C-style comment markers so that you may include it in C programs, as well as C++ code.

```
/*
    stringsex.h -- Function declarations for stringsex.lib */

/* Standard sentry */
#ifndef __STRINGSEX_H__
#define __STRINGSEX_H__

#include    <string.h>

#ifdef __cplusplus
extern "C"
#endif
char * __cdecl strtokex(char * string,const char * control);

#endif    /* __STRINGSEX_H__ */
```

You added the *extern "C"* as a conditional. If you are linking this function from a C++ program, you will need it, but you don't want it for a standard C program. The *string.h* file is included because it contains other definitions that make the library work.

Enter the Settings dialog from the Project menu. Note that there are settings for the debug and release versions of your library. You must add the following flag in both versions, but generally, you may select all Configurations.

Select the C/C++ tab and make sure that the General category is selected in the combo box. Add *_CRT-BLD* to the preprocessor defines field, which should look like the following after you add it. This flag lets you use the C runtime header files that come with Visual C++.

```
WIN32,_DEBUG,_MBCS,_LIB,_CRTBLD
```

Next, select Preprocessor from the category box. Either select All Configurations from the Settings For box, or do the following step for both the debug and release versions. Add the directory of the C runtime source code that you installed along with Visual C++. Add this to the field marked Additional include Directories. The actual directory depends on your installation, but it should look something like the following:

```
D:/DevTools/Microsoft Visual Studio/VC98/CRT/SRC
```

Close the Settings dialog box. You're ready to build your library. Build both release and debug versions. Move the libraries into a convenient place. I keep mine in \USR\LIB on the same drive as the runtime libraries, and the header files in the \USR\INCLUDE directory (you don't see any UNIX bias there, do you?). In the Visual Studio, you have to include these in the Settings dialog for any projects that use them.

565. *Introducing the ClassWizard*

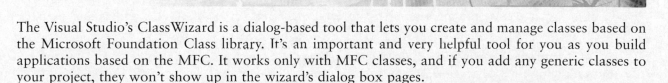

The Visual Studio's ClassWizard is a dialog-based tool that lets you create and manage classes based on the Microsoft Foundation Class library. It's an important and very helpful tool for you as you build applications based on the MFC. It works only with MFC classes, and if you add any generic classes to your project, they won't show up in the wizard's dialog box pages.

Although the MSDN literature stresses that you should derive classes from *CObject* to support serialization, the ClassWizard doesn't support this. That's a serious deficiency in a tool that is supposed to support MFC, but you still can derive classes from *CObject* using the generic class tool. You just can't maintain them using the ClassWizard.

In most projects, you will use the wizard to set up message handlers and add member variables associated with controls on a dialog box. If you are working with a database, the wizard takes a lot of work out of setting up the recordset classes. If you are using automation or creating an ActiveX control, the wizard can help with that, too. (There's just not enough room to cover ActiveX in this book and do it justice, but I've included one for you to study and play with. It's in the *\SAMPLES\ACTIVEX\LED* directory on the companion CD-ROM. It emulates a blinking LED of the sort you saw on the status bar earlier.)

566. *Invoking the ClassWizard*

Start up the ClassWizard by right-clicking anywhere on a program file. Select ClassWizard from the menu. The wizard also may be started (in the case of wizards, perhaps "invoke" or "summon" would be a better word) from the View menu. If you have a dialog box open in the resource editor and you right-click on it, you may select ClassWizard from the menu. If you haven't already created a class for the dialog box, you will get a check to do so when you start the wizard.

When you become used to the wizard, you might want to add it to one of your toolbars. The Edit toolbar is a good choice because you generally have it visible when editing source code.

To add it to a toolbar, make sure that the toolbar is visible. Then right-click on a blank area of the window frame. A menu of toolbars will appear with the entry "Customize" at the bottom. Select Customize. In the Category window, select All Commands; then, move to the Commands list and find ClassWizard (they are arranged alphabetically). Click and *hold* the ClassWizard list item and move the mouse cursor to the Edit toolbar (or whichever toolbar you choose); position it where you want it in the toolbar and release the mouse button.

> *Note: While you have the Customize window open, none of your toolbar buttons work. The window frame is in a maintenance mode, and at this time you may rearrange the toolbar buttons, add buttons to them, or delete buttons. To delete a button, grab it with the left mouse button, drag it to an empty spot, and drop it. When you close the Customize window, the window frame returns to normal.*

567. *Using the ClassWizard Dialogs*

The ClassWizard dialog box is a tab control with five tabs: Message Maps, Member Variables, Automation, ActiveX Events, and Class Info. From one of these windows, you may add member variables to your class, add message map handlers, add certain types of classes, and change the message filter for a class.

The Member Variables tab only creates variables that are mapped to a control ID, such as the control on a dialog box. The message map process only creates message map entries for the items listed in the Messages list. For many classes, the Messages list is incomplete, and for others the list might include messages that are never sent to a derived class. You might need to check the Message filter item on the Class

Info tab if your handlers are never called; the wizard sometimes picks the wrong filter when you create a class.

It's important to remember that most of the actions you take in the ClassWizard are not executed until you click the OK button. New classes are created when you close the New Class dialog box, but if you enter message map handlers or member variables and click the Cancel button to exit the wizard, none of them will be added to your project. To complete the transaction, you must click the OK button.

The ClassWizard only adds classes that are derived from the MFC classes or from a type library such as that created for an ActiveX or COM control. To add a generic class to your project, you must invoke the New Class dialog from the Insert menu or right-click on the class name in the ClassView pane of the Workspace window.

Every page has a Class Name combo box from which you may select the class you want to use for wizard operations.

568. *Understanding the Message Maps Page*

The Message Maps page has three large list areas that are of interest. The first is the Object IDs list. Here you find a list of the control IDs that apply to the currently selected class and usually the name of the class itself. The item you select in this list determines what appears in the second list, the Messages list.

Figure 568 shows the Message Maps page in the ClassWizard dialog box.

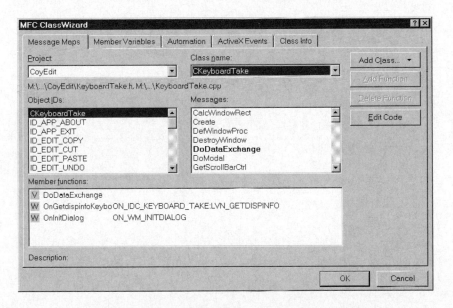

Figure 568   The ClassWizard Message Maps page

The items in the message list are the messages that might be generated by the object selected in the Object ID list and vary according to the function of the class. For example, a dialog box–based application has different message possibilities than a window frame–based application.

The dialog box class in an application has a list of the various control IDs in the Object IDs list. If you select, say, a button object, you get just two message possibilities, *BN_CLICKED* and *BN_DOU-BLECLICKED*, because these are the only two that will be sent to the dialog box window procedure.

The third list toward the bottom is the Member Function list, which is covered in Tip 570, "Understanding the Member Functions Window."

569. Adding a Message Handler Using the ClassWizard

Adding a message handler is a handy function built in to the ClassWizard. There are three steps you perform to add a message handler. First, you declare the function in the class definition, then you create a body for the function, and then you go to the message map and add an entry for the message. Typically, you will forget something like the order and type of parameters or the return type of the function when you go through this process. After two or three compiles with errors in them, you will get it right.

The ClassWizard takes the labor out of this, and if that's all it did, it would be worth having around.

Summon the wizard in your favorite way. Make sure that the class you want to work with is selected in the Class Name box. Select the class name or an object such as a menu item ID in the Object IDs box. Move to the Messages box and select the message you want to handle. For some of these, such as the main application window and some common control objects, the list might be long. Virtual functions are listed first, so you might have to scroll through the list to get to the messages.

After you select a message, move to the Add Function button and click it. Some functions will be added immediately because their message handler must conform to a naming convention. Others, such as a menu item, will open a dialog box with a default function name, which you may change. In this case, click OK after you settle on a name (the wizard-suggested name usually is descriptive enough that you don't need to change it).

If you click the Cancel button, none of these will be added. Be sure to click the OK button to seal the deal and actually add the functions to your application.

570. Understanding the Member Functions Window

At the bottom of the Message Maps page is a list labeled Member Functions. When you add a message handler to your class, the name of the function, along with the message macro that will implement it, is listed in this box.

The entry will contain a "W" in the left column to indicate that the entry is for a Windows message handler function. For a virtual function overridden by your class, the entry will have "V' in the left column. For each entry here, the corresponding entry in the Message box will be listed in bold type to remind you that the function already is a member of your class.

The ClassWizard is not the only one that can add member virtual functions. You also may add them manually or by clicking the action button on the Wizard Bar and selecting Add Virtual Function (Wizard Bar operations are covered in the next section, "The Wizard Bar"). The wizard maintains a section in the class definition where it places the virtual function declarations, identified by the words *AFX_VIR-TUAL*. An example is shown here:

```
// ClassWizard generated virtual function overrides
//{{AFX_VIRTUAL(CSplitter)
protected:
virtual void DoDataExchange(CDataExchange* pDX);
//}}AFX_VIRTUAL
```

If the virtual function name doesn't appear in this section, the wizard won't know that it already is a member of the class. It usually isn't polite to write in areas maintained by Visual Studio wizards, but if you do override a virtual function manually, make sure that its declaration is within this block.

571. Deleting a Message Handler Using the ClassWizard

Occasionally, some planned action on your part to handle a Windows message or to override a virtual function just doesn't pan out (naw, that never happens, does it?), and you might want to remove the function from your class. Rather than have people tinker with the wizard-maintained blocks of code, the ClassWizard contains a method to delete the function.

In the Messages box, select the message or virtual function name that you want to remove. The name should appear in boldface type; otherwise, it wasn't properly entered in the class using the ClassWizard or the Wizard Bar. When you select the item, the Delete Function button will be enabled and the Add Function button disabled. If you click the button, the wizard will remove the declaration from the class definition and any message map entry. Actually, the action isn't taken until you click the OK button, so you have the option of backing out. Be forewarned, however, that clicking the Cancel button cancels all the operations you have pending. It's a good idea not to stack up too many of them; exit the wizard using the OK button from time to time to flush out the pending operations.

For obvious reasons, the wizard will not delete the body of the function. You might have code in the function that you want to save and perhaps try elsewhere, so the wizard will leave it alone. You do, however, get a message box reminding you that the body of the function must be removed manually. That part of the operation is your responsibility. Either remove the code or comment it out. At any rate, make sure that the function no longer has a body, or you will get an error on the next compile.

572. Understanding the Member Variables Page

The Member Variables page of the ClassWizard is used to associate member variables with controls on a dialog box or control bar. It can be used only with resource IDs that map to control objects, such as on a dialog box. To add another type variable to a class, you may use the ClassView pane of the Workspace window or add it manually. Figure 572 shows the Member Variables page of the ClassWizard.

The large window in the center of the page contains a three-column list of all the objects that may be mapped to a class variable. The first column is the resource ID of the object. The second column is the variable type, and the third column lists the member variable names. If an object has not been associated with a variable yet, the second two columns will be empty for that object.

You're not limited to a single variable for resource objects. If a control returns a value or string, such as an edit box, you may assign variables of different types. For example, you might want a *CString* variable to set and retrieve the text from an edit box and a control variable so that you may access the object and set the text color or font. You can't have two variables of the same data type, however.

At the bottom of the page is a validation area. What appears in the area varies according to the variable type. A *CString* variable, for example, might be given a limit for the number of characters a user may enter. If you assign the same object a variable of type *int*, the validation area will contain two boxes, one for a minimum value and the other for a maximum value.

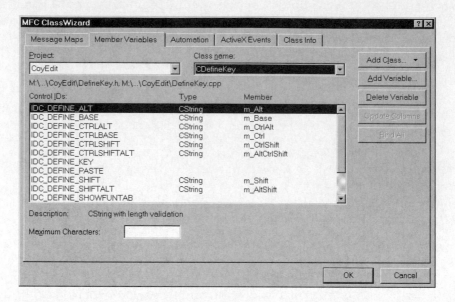

Figure 572   The Class Wizard Member Variables page

573. *Adding Variables to Your Program*

To add a member variable to your class and associate it with a control, select the resource ID of the item in the control list. The Add Variable button will be enabled, so click on it. You will get a dialog box prompting you for the name of the variable, and the leading *m_* to identify it as a class member will be entered for you. Finish the name and look at the Category box. Depending on the type of control, you will get one or two options here. A button object, for example, doesn't return any data, so the only option you have is Control, and the Variable Type box will show the type of control object. If you've derived a class from the control, the wizard may include the derived type in the list. You might use a control object to set the text on a button dynamically.

An edit window, on the other hand, might return any of several data types. Select an edit window resource ID and click Add Variable. In the category field, make sure that Value is selected. Move down to the Variable Type box and examine the options. You will see variable types ranging from a string, to a simple *int*, to a date and time value. Although this is an edit box and contains text, the data validation process will convert the text to your data type automatically.

Click OK and examine the data validation area at the bottom of the screen. If you entered a number type, you will have fields for minimum and maximum values the user will be permitted to enter in the edit box. If you don't enter a range here, there will be no range checking. Alternatively, you could enter just a minimum or just a maximum value.

The variable will be added to your class when you click the OK button to exit the ClassWizard. Now examine the code. The wizard has done three things for you.

The wizard added the variable to your class definition in an area bounded by the tag *AFX_DATA*. These are *public* variables, which isn't such a good idea, but you can change them to *protected* or *private* members; the ClassWizard really doesn't care. The idea behind making the dialog box items *public* is that they can be initialized from outside the class. This is common practice, but the C++ way is to make the data member's *private* and pass the initial values through the constructor or the *DoModal()* function.

Next, the wizard initialized the variables in your class constructor. These values are usually zeros or empty strings, depending on the variable type. You can change the initial values; the wizard won't mind a bit.

Last, in the *DoDataExchange()* the wizard has associated the variables with the dialog box controls using macros in the *AFX_DATA_MAP* section. Don't edit this section unless you know what you're doing. The slightest error can cause your program to throw an exception. The best bet here is to let the wizard do the housekeeping.

574. *Deleting Variables from Your Program*

Deleting a variable added by the ClassWizard is even easier than adding one. If you select a resource ID that has no associated variable, only the Add Variable button will be enabled. However, if you select one that has a variable, the wizard will enable the Delete Variable button. If you click on it, the variable is removed. No intermediate dialog boxes, no "really" messages—it's just gone. Of course, it isn't removed from your code until you click the wizard's OK button.

575. *Understanding the Update Columns and Bind All Buttons*

When you develop a database program, your code isn't the only thing that's likely to change. The structure of the database is going to change as the project evolves. Even after the code is finished and running, you might need to make some changes to the database, add a column to a table, add a new table, perhaps even restructure the whole database.

When this happens, your *CRecordSet*-derived classes are going to be out of sync with the database, and the database classes are really good at throwing exceptions when things don't match.

To correct this, you select the recordset class in the Class Name box. The Control IDs portion of the list on the Member Variables page changes to Column Names, and the name entries are bracketed. Also, when you click the Add Variable button, you don't have the option of creating more than one variable of different types for a single ID. There's one variable, and only one, for every column in the recordset, and it's always of type *value*.

To make the variables match the contents of the database, you click the Update Columns button. The wizard takes you back to the Database Options dialog, where you once again select the data source for your recordset. The number, type, and *order* of variables in your recordset class must match the database. By reselecting the data source, the wizard rereads it and makes any necessary changes in your recordset class.

There's no *DoDataExchange()* function in a recordset class. Instead, it's a *DoFieldExchange()*, which exchanges data between your recordset and the database when you call the member *Update()* function or one of the functions to get a new row from the database. The Bind All button updates the list in this function so that the class member variables exactly match the order and type of the database table.

576. *Understanding the Automation Page*

Automation is the process by which you expose portions of your program so that they can be accessed and manipulated by other programs. This may be through a class's member function, called a "method," or through a member variable, called a "property." You must add this support if you plan to use Visual Basic for Applications with your program, for example.

After you select automation support when you create your project, the wizard adds a global function call, *AfxEnableControlContainer()*, to the *InitInstance()* function in the application class. It also adds a number of items to the document class. The document class now has a dispatch map and an interface map, as well as an object called an *interface ID* (IID). Your application now becomes an automation *server*. In the ClassWizard, if you select a class that supports automation, you may use this page to add methods and properties to the class.

577. *Adding a Method to Your Automation Class*

Adding a method is about the same as adding a member function. The operation also involves placing an entry in the dispatch map to make it visible to the outside world.

When you select Add Method on the automation page, you get a dialog box that asks you for both an *internal* and an *external* name. The internal name is the one by which your code will access the function. The external name is entered in the dispatch map and is the name handed out when a client queries the interface.

You will also notice that the return type is limited. When adding a non-automation function to a class, you can give it any return type you want, even one that doesn't exist yet. Automation is different. A client process might have no idea what a return value of *pointer to class MyStuff* means. You are limited to standard variable types that both your application and the client application recognize. You will notice some new ones in there. *BSTR* is a BASIC-style string that is used to exchange strings with a Visual Basic application, and *VARIANT* is a typed union that is capable of handling virtually any of the predefined data types. In BASIC, you can use a variable without declaring, or *typing*, it. The variable becomes a type *VARIANT*. This doesn't work very well in C++, so the *VARIANT* union is used to contain the variable's data.

578. *Adding a Property to Your Automation Class*

When you add a property to an automation class, you are adding a class variable. The variable may have two names, the one your program uses internally and the name exposed to the automation clients that access the variable. The two are bound together, and a function is added to your class, which is called when an outside program modifies the property.

If you select the Get/Set Methods option when you add a property, the variable isn't directly exposed to the external clients. Instead, two functions are added: one for the client to get the value of the property and another to set its value. This is a safe, object-oriented method of accessing a class member variable. Your set function can include code to test for valid ranges and conditions.

579. *Understanding the ActiveX Page*

The ActiveX Events page is similar to the automation page, and the interface is implemented in much the same way. By their very nature, ActiveX controls are automation servers. It wouldn't make much sense to have a control that can't be manipulated by an application. ActiveX supports automation, and you may add methods and properties to a control using the automation page. Figure 579 shows the Add Event dialog from the ClassWizard's ActiveX Events page.

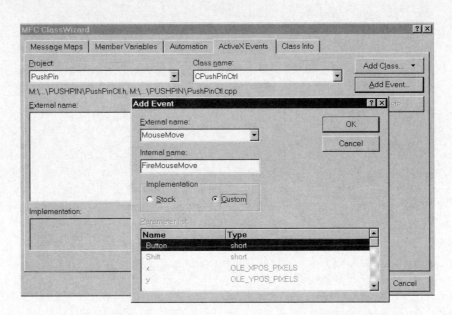

Figure 579   The ActiveX page is a convenient way to add events to your ActiveX control. This figure shows the page with the Add Event dialog box opened.

This page lets you add events—such as mouse movement or click or a keyboard event—to the ActiveX control. Events give the control the capability to respond to the external world.

580. *Understanding the Class Info Page*

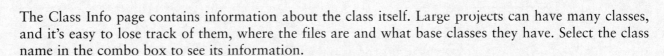

The Class Info page contains information about the class itself. Large projects can have many classes, and it's easy to lose track of them, where the files are and what base classes they have. Select the class name in the combo box to see its information.

A couple of items in the Advanced Option section are interesting. The message filter indicates the type of messages listed on the Message Map page. The messages are categorized by the window or dialog box type. You may change the filter here to change the list of messages from which you create handlers. Changing the filter, however, doesn't necessarily mean that the object is going to be sent the messages.

Usually, you don't need to change the message filter, but the ClassWizard occasionally sets the wrong filter when you use it to create a class. When it can't determine the proper filter, it usually sets the filter to "Not a window." If you know that your class should be receiving Windows messages and none are listed on the Message Maps page, check this control.

The Foreign Class combo box allows you to select another class and map the member variables of one class to those in another. For example, suppose that you have a dialog box that displays the contents of a rowset from a database. When users click a key that causes the record to change, you could go to the recordset class and fetch all the variables, load them into your dialog class, and redisplay the data. Alternatively, you could set the recordset class as a foreign class for the dialog box class and then map the control variables to the recordset variables. When the new rowset is fetched, the dialog's member variables are updated, and you need only call *UpdateData()* to display their new values.

581. *Adding a Class Using the ClassWizard*

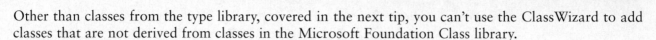

Other than classes from the type library, covered in the next tip, you can't use the ClassWizard to add classes that are not derived from classes in the Microsoft Foundation Class library.

To add an MFC-based class from the ClassWizard, click the Add Class button and select New from the menu that appears. You will be taken to the New Class dialog box.

In the dialog box, select a name for your new class. As you enter the class name, the wizard will build the names for the source code and header files as you type (only the name of the source file is shown on the dialog, but it is indeed building a header file name as well). In developing MFC programs, class names usually are prefixed by a capital "C." The wizard does not add this prefix to the file name. For example, if you enter *CStuff* as the class name, the wizard will build the file names as *Stuff.cpp* and *Stuff.h*.

If you don't like the wizard's suggestion or you want to place the class in an existing file, click the Change button on the dialog box. Here you will see both the header and source code file names, and you may change them. The Browse button next to each name summons a FileOpen dialog box, where you may select an existing file.

It's usually a good idea to accept the wizard's file names. The visual connection between the file and class names is simple enough, and in a large project it makes file handling easier. Also, it's a good idea to put only one class in an implementation and header file. If a file contains more than one class and you start the ClassWizard from the file, it's likely to accept the wrong class as the one to display, and you will have to check the Class Name box each time.

582. *Adding a Class from a Type Library Using ClassWizard*

In addition to their executable files, automation server projects generate a *type library* when you compile them. Usually, this is in a file with the extension *.tlb*, but the library can be included inside a DLL project's *.dll* file. Automation client programs then may build a member class by accessing this library and selecting one of the classes that support automation.

To add a class from a type library, click the New Class button and select the From a Type Library item on the menu. In the file dialog that appears, locate and select the file containing the type library.

A Confirm Classes dialog should appear. The names of the class objects from the type library to be added will be highlighted. If there's only one, its class name should appear in the Class Name field below. You may select individual classes and modify their names before they are added to your project. In many cases, such as type libraries generated by Visual Basic projects, the class name is preceded with an underscore, which you probably don't want. Also, common practice in Visual Basic is to name classes with a preceding "cls" designation, which you will probably want to change to the ClassWizard standard "C."

583. *Adding a Generic Class to Your Program*

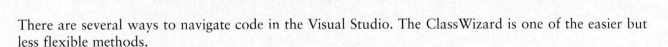

You can't add *generic* classes—those that are not derived from the Microsoft Foundation Class—using the ClassWizard. To add a generic class, you get to the dialog in one of three ways:

- Select the ClassView pane of the Workspace window, right-click on the tree root for the project (the one that says something like "MyProject classes"), and select New Class from the menu.

- From the Visual Studio's main menu bar, select the Insert menu and then select New Class.

- Click the Wizard Bar's Action button and select New Class from the drop-down menu.

You will get a dialog box similar to the New Class dialog you met in the ClassWizard. At the top, however, is a combo box labeled Class Type. Depending on the type of project, you will have up to four choices here. If this is a standard MFC project, you may select among an MFC-based class, a generic class, and a form-based class.

If yours is an ATL COM project, you may choose only between Generic and ATL Classes. If it's an ATL project that supports MFC, such as a Windows NT service program, you will have all four choices.

For an ATL class, the interface names will be built as you enter the new class name. For a generic class, you may specify which, if any, base class you want to use.

584. *Adding Code and Navigating to Code Using the ClassWizard*

There are several ways to navigate code in the Visual Studio. The ClassWizard is one of the easier but less flexible methods.

On the ClassWizard's Message Map page is a button labeled Edit Code. Generically, clicking this button will take you to the constructor for the selected class. If, however, you select the name of a virtual function or message handler that you've added to your class, clicking the button will take you directly to that function.

Suppose that you want to get to the *OnInitDialog()* message handler for a dialog box. Summon the ClassWizard and select the dialog box class. Select the class name in the Object IDs list, scroll through the Message list until you come to *WM_INITDIALOG*, and select it. Click the Edit Code button, and you will go directly to the function.

Alternatively, you may select the function from the Member Functions list at the bottom of the wizard's dialog and then click the Edit Code button. The result is the same.

In the next tip, you will learn other ways to navigate your project code using the Wizard Bar.

585. *Understanding the Wizard Bar*

If you were to ask programmers what the single, most distinguishing characteristic of Visual Studio is, most of them probably would say the Wizard Bar. Other IDEs have equivalents of the ClassWizard, resource editors, and integrated debugging. They're not necessarily better or worse; they're just different.

However, only the Visual Studio has the Wizard Bar. In the next few tips you will learn how to use this nifty tool. It moves you around code. It finds and opens files for you. It creates new functions and message handlers for you. For a large project, it's indispensable, and after you get used to it, you will want it even for the "quick and dirty" small projects. Figure 585 shows the WizardBar with the standard toolbar just below it.

Figure 585   The Wizard Bar (top) and the standard toolbar (bottom) join forces to provide code navigation for your projects

If you don't see the Wizard Bar when you start Visual Studio, see the next tip on how to make it visible. You don't want to miss it.

The Wizard Bar normally is placed right below the menu bar in the new installation of the Visual Studio. A companion, the standard toolbar, usually is placed right below it. The two work together to provide a real experience in code navigation. Together, they undoubtedly provide one of the most flexible and useful tools in the Visual Studio.

586. *Showing and Hiding Toolbars*

The Visual Studio is filled with toolbars. When you have a project open, you can make at least 11 toolbars visible. When you're in the process of debugging code, even more become available.

To see a list of the toolbars, click the right mouse button on a blank area of the window frame. Usually, off to the top right is a good place. At the top you should see the Output and Workspace windows listed, followed by a menu separator. After the separator are the dockable toolbars available to you. If there's a depressed check mark next to the toolbar name, the toolbar should be visible on the screen.

Select a toolbar with the left or right mouse button, or use the up and down arrow keys to step through the list and click return on a toolbar name. Either way will toggle the selected toolbar. If you don't know what a toolbar looks like, alternately turn it off and on to see which one disappears and reappears.

587. *Understanding the Wizard Bar Combo Controls*

The Wizard Bar itself contains only five items. The first three are combo boxes that give you some sense of where you are within your program, if you know how to interpret them.

The first combo box is the Class box. As you move around from file to file, this box shows the name of the class or structure containing the caret, even if the class or structure is empty. If the caret isn't in a class or structure, it should contain the name of the one nearest the caret. Its drop-down box contains all the classes, even those not derived from MFC, and all the structures you have defined in your application.

The next box, the center one, is the Message Filter box. Its list contains the resource IDs of message items the current class may handle. Don't select one just yet, but open the list box by clicking on the down arrow. If you have a view or window frame class open, the list should be extensive. This is the same list of messages you see in the ClassWizard when you sort through the Messages box.

The combo box to the far right on the Wizard Bar is the Members box. It contains a list of all the functions in the current class.

588. Understanding the Wizard Bar Action Control

Just to the right of the Members box on the Wizard Bar is the Action button. No matter where you are in the IDE, the wizard tries to interpret which of its commands you are most likely to need next. That command is executed when you click this button.

Of course, you don't necessarily know which command is going to be issued when you click the button. About 90 percent of the time, it will be to move to a function definition or declaration, depending on whether you are in the class definition header file or the source file.

To see which default action the wizard has selected, let the mouse cursor hover over the button for a second, and the pop-up ToolTip will tell you.

589. Understanding the Wizard Bar Action Menu

The Action control works in conjunction with the Action menu, which is a constantly changing menu. The wizard's not perfect and it is just a program, so the number of possibilities is limited. If you have the caret in a structure definition, it usually will select an option to add a member function. Structures can contain function declarations, but if you don't have any, the WizardBar will display a message stating that it can't find the implementation file.

If the wizard can't track what you are doing, the button icon will turn into something that looks like a firecracker with a short fuse. Still, it's right enough of the time that it's a useful tool. Even if you didn't intend to go to the function declaration, after you get there, the default action is to go back to the function definition, which is nearly where you were to begin with.

590. Summoning the Action Menu

You can see the contents of the Wizard Bar menu, the list from which it takes its default action, by clicking on the down arrow just to the right of the Action button. The default action is the menu item in boldface text.

This menu changes according to what you are doing and where the caret is located. If the caret is in a generic class that has no parent, it obviously doesn't make any sense to have message handler or virtual function options on the menu, so they will be removed.

Some items are constant, however. This is a good place to go, for example, to add a generic class to your project. It's always there, and you don't have to change any window panes to get to it.

591. Understanding Context Tracking

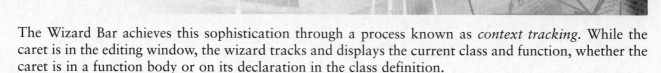

The Wizard Bar achieves this sophistication through a process known as *context tracking*. While the caret is in the editing window, the wizard tracks and displays the current class and function, whether the caret is in a function body or on its declaration in the class definition.

If the cursor is in an empty class, a structure, or a class that has no message filter, the center box will list All Class Members, and the Members box will say that there are no members. When you move into a comment area or between function definitions, the Members box will gray slightly.

There are places the wizard won't even try to track—when you enter the Workspace window or portions of the resource editor, for example. It will track in a dialog box in the resource editor if you already have created a class for the dialog box. As you select the various controls on the dialog box, the wizard combo boxes will change to reflect each control. If you select a button, for example, the Class box will contain the name of the class, the Message Filter box will show the resource ID for the button, and the Members box will show the message available for the button.

592. Adding a Class Using the Wizard Bar

To add a class with the Wizard Bar, summon the wizard's menu by clicking on the Action button's down arrow or by right-clicking on any of the boxes in the Wizard Bar. The menu that appears will contain a New Class selection toward the bottom. This is the generic class dialog, and you also may add MFC classes with this selection.

This is the same menu you get when you right-click on the project name in the ClassView pane of the Workshop window or select New Class from the Insert menu on the main menu bar. See Tip 583, "Adding a Generic Class to Your Program," for an explanation of the dialog box.

593. Adding a Message Handler Using the Wizard Bar

The Wizard Bar is particularly adept at adding message handlers to your class. There are a couple of ways to do it. The easiest way, if the message is from a resource item, is to select the message from in the Filter box and then press the Enter key. You will get a small dialog box with the suggested function name. You may change it, but the function will be added when you press the Enter key or click the OK button.

The other method is more complicated but much more flexible. Summon the Wizard Bar menu by right-clicking one of the combo boxes in the toolbar or by selecting the Action button's down arrow. If the class is capable of receiving messages, there will be an Add Windows Message Handler item on the menu. The dialog box that opens seems to be built upside down, but a lot of information is there. The dialog box is shown in Figure 593.

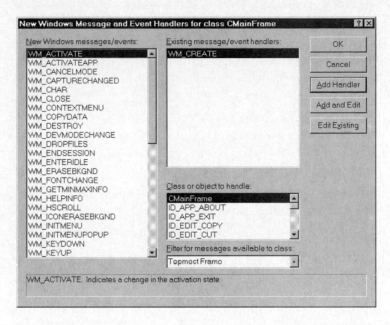

Figure 593   The message and event handler dialog box is a convenient place to add message handlers and virtual functions to a class

At the bottom right you will find a message filter selection box. This is the same as the filter you saw in the ClassWizard, and changing the filter will change the available messages. This should be left alone. Just above this box is a list of objects to be handled. Again, this is the same as the Object IDs list in the ClassWizard, except that the list to the left will not include any virtual functions (that's a separate menu item) and lists only available messages. The box just above the object ID box shows the messages that already have been added to the class.

The buttons to the right are self-explanatory, but you should be aware that clicking the OK button just gets you out of the dialog box. It doesn't add the selected handler. To do that, you must select the Add Handler or Add and Edit button.

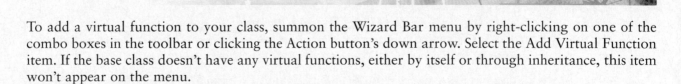

594. *Adding a Virtual Function*

To add a virtual function to your class, summon the Wizard Bar menu by right-clicking on one of the combo boxes in the toolbar or clicking the Action button's down arrow. Select the Add Virtual Function item. If the base class doesn't have any virtual functions, either by itself or through inheritance, this item won't appear on the menu.

The resulting dialog box is similar to the dialog box to add a message handler, except that you don't have the message filter box or the object ID list at the bottom. The list to the left of the pane contains the virtual functions that can be overridden, and the list to the right contains the virtual functions that already have been overridden.

Like the Message Handler dialog, clicking the OK button doesn't add the selected virtual function. You must add it by clicking one of the buttons.

595. *Adding a Member Function to a Class*

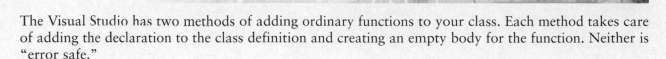

The Visual Studio has two methods of adding ordinary functions to your class. Each method takes care of adding the declaration to the class definition and creating an empty body for the function. Neither is "error safe."

In the first method, you call the Wizard Bar menu as before but this time select the Add Member Function item. In the second method, select the ClassView pane of the Workspace window, right-click the mouse on the name of the class to which you want to add a function, and select Add Member Function from that menu.

Both methods create the same dialog box. The first field is for the function return type. You may enter just about anything in this box, even return types that aren't defined in your program. Of course, if you enter a nonexistent return type, you will get an error on the next compile.

The next field in the dialog box is for the function declaration itself. Again, not much error checking is being done here. The program will check for syntax, but if you enter nonexistent data types, it won't warn you.

At the bottom of the box, select the access level for the function—*public*, *protected*, or *private*—and whether you want the function to be *static* or *virtual*. It doesn't have to be either, but it can't be both; when you select one box, the other is disabled.

When you finish, click the OK button and the function will be added.

596. *Adding a Form to Your Project*

Forms basically are nothing more than dialog boxes. Usually, the controls on the forms are associated with database information. A dialog box is a form, and a dialog-based application is a form application, but it doesn't have the advantage of being able to create new forms, as do the *CFormView* and *CRecordView* classes in MFC.

The process of adding a form through the Visual Studio menus is based on the document/view architecture. If you didn't select form support when you created your project, adding a form through the two Visual Studio methods will add it to your project.

There are three ways to access the form dialog box. To add a form other than a simple dialog box, you need a data source such as ODBC or DAO. The dialog may be accessed by selecting the New Form item on the Wizard Bar menu or from the Insert menu on the main menu bar. You also can right-click the project name in the ClassView pane and select the New Form item there.

Once in the dialog, you can select from a simple dialog box or one of three view classes: *CFormView*, *CRecordView*, or *CDaoRecordView*. With the view classes, if you summon the ClassWizard and look on the Class Info page, you will notice that the Visual Studio already has added the view class as a foreign class for the dialog controls.

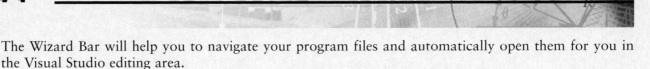

597. *Switching Between Source Files*

The Wizard Bar will help you to navigate your program files and automatically open them for you in the Visual Studio editing area.

To open a source file, select its class name in the Class combo box and press the Enter key, or right-click the control after selecting the class and click on the Go to Function Definition. In both cases, the wizard will open the file containing the constructor for the class and place the caret on it.

Another way is to summon the ClassWizard, select the virtual function or message handler function from the Member Functions box, and click the Edit Code button.

598. *Switching Between Function Definitions and Declarations*

After you land in the source code file, you can move directly to the header file by *double-click*ing on the Class combo box and pressing the Enter key. Alternatively, you may select the Go to Function Declaration from the Wizard Bar menu.

Clicking the Wizard Bar Action button will alternately switch you between a function declaration and the function definition.

You also may move to the body of a function by opening the tree item on the ClassView pane of the Workshop window and then double-clicking on the function name. Once at the function body, you can click the Wizard Bar Action button to go to the declaration.

599. *Moving Between Classes*

In a large project, it's easy to lose track of which files contain what classes. It's a good idea to make the class names and their source file names similar, and the ClassWizard tries to do this when it suggests file names for classes that you add. Still, navigating between a large number of classes can be a chore. The Visual Studio provides tools to make this task easier.

The first navigational method is through the ClassView pane of the Workspace Window. Click on the ClassView tab to display this pane. Expand the tree as necessary to find the class you want to select. If you double-click on the name of a class, the Visual Studio will open the header file containing the class definition and display it in an editing window.

If you expand the tree at the class name (click on the "+" symbol next to the class name), you'll get a list of all the functions and variables in the class. Double-click on a function name and the Visual Studio will open and display the source file and move to the first line of the function definition. Double-click on a variable name and the Visual Studio will move to the line in the class definition where you declared the variable.

The ClassView pane lists member functions and variables alphabetically. If you right-click on the class name and select Group by Access from the context menu that pops up, the Visual Studio will sort the items according to their access—public members first, then protected members, and finally private members.

A second method of moving between classes is to select the class name in the Wizard Bar class box at the far left of the Wizard Bar. Press the Enter key and the Visual Studio will open and display the source code file containing the class and place the caret at the class constructor.

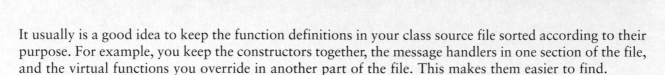

600. Moving from Function to Function Within the Wizard Bar

It usually is a good idea to keep the function definitions in your class source file sorted according to their purpose. For example, you keep the constructors together, the message handlers in one section of the file, and the virtual functions you override in another part of the file. This makes them easier to find.

Even with the best of intentions, this scheme often gets messed up. If you add functions using the Visual Studio tool, the new functions get tacked onto the end of the file. Unless you practice cutting and pasting the functions to their proper locations, functions with different purposes get interspersed with one another, and it gets more difficult to look for them.

When you select a class in the Wizard Bar class box, the members box (the combo box at the far right of the Wizard Bar) will display the names of the member functions. Select an item on this list and the Visual Studio will move to the definition of the member function.

The members box lists the functions in alphabetical order, making it easier to find them. Icons next to the function names indicate whether they are public, protected, or private.

To move quickly from a function in one class to a function in another class, select the new class name in the Wizard Bar's class box, then select the function name in the members box. The wizard will open the source file and move to the definition of the function.

601. Opening an #include File

The Wizard Bar will locate and open a header file that you have included in your program, even if the full path name is not specified. The wizard searches the path in the *INCLUDE* environment variable and any paths added in the project settings dialog to find the file.

Click the right mouse button on the line containing the *#include* statement, and you will find a line in the pop-up menu to open the file. This also will open any of the MFC header files, but the Wizard Bar won't track while the caret is in one of these files.

602. Using the Find in Files

The Find in Files command uses a *grep*-like syntax to search through one or more files for a variable expression. The *grep* program is a UNIX tool derived from the name *Get Regular Expression*. It is used to search through a file or group of files for an expression coded in the input string. The Visual Studio command uses a very similar syntax to search through your project files (and any others you specify) for a code expression.

The simplest form of a search expression is the string itself. Certain characters may be used to encode characters that can't be entered from the keyboard, to indicate wild cards, or to limit the characters that you want to match.

Much of the syntax is the same as the UNIX *grep* command. The nice part of it is that you can use regular expression searches and never have to learn the *grep* syntax (*now* they come up with something like this). When you use the Find in Files dialog box, you can enter your search string normally. When you come to some point in the string where you need to specify a *grep* expression, click the button to the right of the edit field (the button with the right-facing arrow), and a list of *grep*-type expressions will appear. Select one, and the syntax characters will be inserted into your search string. Enter any necessary values for the expression.

It's easier than you might think. Suppose that someplace in your file you used the word "Stuff" with an uppercase "T," and you suspect that someplace you even entered it as "SNuff." You want to search for it, ignoring the cases with a lowercase "t." Summon the Find in Files dialog box, either from the Edit menu or by clicking the button on the standard toolbar. Type "S" and then click the expression button. Select Character in Range, and the range syntax characters ([and]) will be inserted into your string. Enter "A-Z" in the range, then the rest of your word. It should look something like this: *S[A-Z]uff*.

Make sure that the Match Case box is checked. This apparently is a bug in the program. Checking the Regular Expression box to use *grep* syntax should force case matching, but it doesn't. Click the Find button to execute the search.

The Find in Files command has two panes on the Output window where it might write the search results (remember that Windows doesn't understand the *stdout* file). This enables you to conduct a second search without destroying the results of the first search. To write the results to the second pane, check the Output to Pane 2 box. When you execute your search, the results will be displayed in the Output window pane with the tab Find in Files 2.

The Advanced button allows you to specify additional directories to include in the search.

603. *Using the Window List Button*

Most applications have a Windows list, usually on the Help or Window menu, where you can select and move to an open window. In a large application, you can have many files open in the editing window at any given time. The menu list is limited necessarily. If you tried to list, say, 25 files here, the menu would go the full length of the screen. To overcome this, most IDEs list the open windows in a list box or list control on a separate dialog box and perhaps a limited number on the menu listing.

You summon this dialog in the Visual Studio by selecting the Windows item at the bottom of the Window menu or by clicking the Windows icon on the standard toolbar. From this dialog box, you may move directly to one of the listed windows, force the file in the window to be written to disk, close one or more windows, or tile all or a subgroup of the windows.

The tile buttons offer some interesting possibilities. Assume that you want to work on your source and header files for a class at the same time. With the windows list dialog open, select the first file with the mouse button. Hold down the Ctrl key and select the second file. The Tile Horizontally and Tile Vertically buttons should activate. Click one of them. Only the two selected windows are tiled, and the others are minimized at the bottom of the editing area (this method of minimizing windows in the client area is standard MDI behavior). If you selected Tile Vertically, the windows are displayed one next to the other; with Tile Horizontally, the windows are displayed one above the other.

604. *Using the Search Button*

The Search button, at the far-right end of the standard toolbar, gives you access to the Visual Studio help system, based on the Microsoft Developers Network library. If you're used to the old Windows help engine, you will definitely not be a fan of this. At its best, it's a sluggish help system, and if you are accessing it from the CD-ROM, you might as well get a 20-ounce bottle of Dr. Pepper for the wait time. If you run it on a fast machine, it's tolerable.

It is, however, an improvement over the mess we saw in Visual C++ 5.0, but it's far from being as snappy and responsive as the old Windows help system. You can use the old help engine, but you have to buy a third-party help file. Select Use Extension Help on the Help menu; then, click the Search button for details. (To get back the MSDN library, you unselect Use Extension Help.)

To access the MSDN help, click the Search button and you will be taken to the Search tab of the MSDN Library Viewer. To search for individual items—such as function, class, and structure names—click the Index tab. The viewer has its own set of help items, which you access by selecting MSDN Library Help from its Help menu.

605. *Using the Workspace and Output Window Buttons*

The standard toolbar has two buttons you may use to give yourself some breathing room if you find yourself working with many files. The Workspace and Output buttons are used to toggle the Workspace window and Output window on and off.

To gain more space quickly, you can use the Full Screen item on the view menu. This button hides *everything* on the desktop, including the Taskbar, and enables a single-button toolbar to get out of the full-screen mode. This is such a handy command that I've added a button for it to my standard toolbar.

You can add this full-screen capability to your own projects very easily. You have to create the one-button toolbar and then add a menu item and a message handler for the menu item. You also have to handle the *WM_GETMINMAXINFO* message. The *FULLSCREEN* project is on the companion CD-ROM.

First, create a project using your favorite view. For this project, I used a multiple-document interface project with the *CRichEditView* as the base class for the view. Add the following member variables to the *CMainFrame* class definition. You can make them *protected* or *private*:

```
CRect m_rectFullScreenWindow;   // Save Desktop rectangle
BOOL m_bFullScreen;             // Full-screen flag
CToolBar m_wndFSBar;            // One-button toolbar
WINDOWPLACEMENT m_wpOld;        // Save original placement
```

Now enter the resource editor and create a new toolbar. Call it *IDR_FULLSCREEN* and add a single button to it. You will need an image for it, but you can pick it up from the *FullScreen.bmp* file in the sample project. Give the single button the resource ID of *ID_VIEW_FULLSCREEN*. If you think that you will need additional buttons in full-screen mode, you can add them, but the purpose of the mode is to clear the screen of everything possible. It's like clearing the workbench for a special project; if you're going to leave a lot of idle tools on the bench, why bother? Add the same button to the original toolbar, *IDR_MAINFRAME*, and give it the same resource ID. You added it just before the Help button in your sample project. Open the menu list and add an item to the View menu. Give it the same resource ID as the toolbar button. You will also need the same menu item to the View Class menu, which, in this case, is *IDR_FULLSCREENTYPE*.

There's one last chore in the resource editor. Open the accelerator tables and add an accelerator key for the *ID_VIEW_FULLSCREEN* command. You can use Ctrl+Shift+F because it's mnemonic. If the user should happen to close the toolbar when in full-screen mode, there's no menu or other toolbar to get out of it. The only recourse would be to call up the Task Manager and kill the process. That's not a very nice thing to do, so the accelerator key gives a backup out.

Create the toolbar in the *OnCreate()* function of the *CMainFrame* source file. A good place is right after you give the default toolbar a title (you *do* that, don't you?):

```
m_wndToolBar.SetWindowText ('Edit');

if (!m_wndFSBar.CreateEx(this, TBSTYLE_FLAT, WS_CHILD |
                         WS_VISIBLE | CBRS_TOP |
                         CBRS_GRIPPER | CBRS_TOOLTIPS |
                         CBRS_FLYBY | CBRS_SIZE_DYNAMIC) ||
    !m_wndFSBar.LoadToolBar(IDR_FULLSCREEN))
{
    TRACE0('Failed to create full screen toolbar\n');
    return (-1);
}
```

At the bottom of the same *OnCreate()* function, add the following two lines of code. The first line will make the toolbar float and place it at the upper-left corner of your screen. The second line hides the toolbar initially (you won't need it until you go into full screen mode. You do this after the *EnableDocking()* call:

```
FloatControlBar (&m_wndFSBar, CPoint (0, 0));
ShowControlBar (&m_wndFSBar, FALSE, 0);
```

Using the ClassWizard or the Wizard Bar, add two message handlers, one for the menu item *ID_VIEW_FULLSCREEN* and another for the *WM_GETMINMAXINFO* Windows message. The body of the functions is shown here:

```
void CMainFrame::OnViewFullscreen()
{
RECT    rcDeskTop;
WINDOWPLACEMENT wpFullScreen;

    if (!m_bFullScreen)
    {
//
// Get the desktop window. If we can't get it, no
// sense doing this.
//
        CWnd *wndDeskTop = GetDesktopWindow ();
        if (wndDeskTop == NULL)
        {
            return;
        }
//
// Hide the normal toolbar and status bar; then
// make the full-screen toolbar visible.
//
        ShowControlBar (&m_wndToolBar, FALSE, 0);
```

```
            ShowControlBar (&m_wndStatusBar, FALSE, 0);
            ShowControlBar (&m_wndFSBar, TRUE, 0);
//
//  Get the current window display info and save it
//  in a member variable
//
            GetWindowPlacement (&m_wpPld);
            ::GetWindowRect (wndDeskTop->m_hWnd, &rcDeskTop);
            ::AdjustWindowRectEx (&rcDeskTop,
                            GetStyle (), TRUE, GetExStyle ());
            m_rectFullScreenWindow = rcDeskTop;
            wpFullScreen = m_wpOld;  // Set new to old
            wpFullScreen.showCmd = SW_SHOWNORMAL;
//
//  Set the rectangle for this window to the desktop
//  rectangle. This will make the client area fill the
//  entire screen.
            wpFullScreen.rcNormalPosition = rcDeskTop;
            m_bFullScreen = TRUE;
    }
    else
    {
        wpFullScreen = m_wpOld;
        ShowControlBar (&m_wndFSBar, FALSE, 0);
        ShowControlBar (&m_wndToolBar, TRUE, 0);
        ShowControlBar (&m_wndStatusBar, TRUE, 0);
        m_bFullScreen = FALSE;
    }
    SetWindowPlacement (&wpFullScreen);
}

void CMainFrame::OnGetMinMaxInfo(MINMAXINFO *lpMMI)
{
    if (m_bFullScreen)
    {
        lpMMI->ptMaxSize.y =m_rectFullScreenWindow.Height();
        lpMMI->ptMaxTrackSize.y = lpMMI->ptMaxSize.y;
        lpMMI->ptMaxSize.x = m_rectFullScreenWindow.Width();
        lpMMI->ptMaxTrackSize.y = lpMMI->ptMaxSize.x;
    }
    else
        CMDIFrameWnd::OnGetMinMaxInfo(lpMMI);
}
```

In the menu item message handler, if the window is not in full screen, the first block of code is executed. First, make sure that you can get to the desktop. That's a key element. Just return if it comes back false. Next, hide the default toolbar and the status bar by calling *ShowControlBar()* with the *bShow* parameter set to *FALSE*. The full-screen toolbar is not visible now, so call the same function for it with *bShow* set to *TRUE*.

Next, the program gets and saves the current window placement and rectangle. This will be used to restore everything to its original state when the user leaves full-screen mode. Then set the new window placement so that the client area fills the desktop area, including the Taskbar at the bottom of the screen. Set the class member variable, *m_bFullScreen*, to *TRUE* so that the next invocation will restore the screen.

The alternative block of code—if *m_bFullScreen* is *TRUE*—is executed to restore the window placement and window rectangles that were saved when the full-screen mode was being set. It then hides the full-screen toolbar and shows the default toolbar and the status bar. The window should bounce right back to its original size and position, with everything still in place.

The *WM_GETMINMAXINFO* message is sent the size or position of the window that is about to change. By capturing the message, you can override the default maximized size and position.

606. *Understanding the Workspace Panels*

The Workspace window is a multi-pane window usually attached to the left side of the frame directly below the toolbar area. It can be toggled on and off using the Toggle Workspace button on the standard toolbar. It also may be undocked and moved to another place or floated. In its docked state, you can resize it using the splitter bar on the side. In its floating state, it's not overly large, so if you need the space and still need to access the window, it's a good candidate for undocking. Figure 606a shows the Workspace window in its floating state and Figure 606b shows it docked.

Figure 606a   The Workspace window shown in its floating state

Figure 606b   The Workspace window shown in its docked state

The Workspace window normally contains three panes. The old InfoView pane from previous versions has been removed and replaced by tabs on the MSDN Library Viewer. The remaining panes contain information about objects in a project and convenient access to the tools of the Visual Studio. All the panes are built using tree controls, so you can expand only the branch you need at the time to get rid of some of the busyness of the window.

Select a pane from the window by clicking on the tab at the bottom.

Each pane gives you access to different tools. Double-clicking a file name in the FileView pane opens the file for editing in the Visual Studio editing area. Double-clicking an item in the ResourceView pane opens the object using one of the resource editors, such as the toolbar editor or the menu editor.

607. *Using the ClassView Pane*

The ClassView pane of the Workshop window, shown in Figure 607, lists all the classes and structures that have been defined in your project, even if they don't yet have source code.

Figure 607   The ClassView pane offers direct access to the classes in your project

From the tree control, you right-click on the branches to summon a changing menu that lets you navigate your code by moving directly to a class, definition, or function declaration.

The pane also offers access to the New Class dialog box for adding generic classes to your project. Right-click on the topmost item in the tree (the *root*), and select Add Class to summon the dialog box.

Opening a branch of the tree reveals the member functions and variables in a class. Items marked with a key next to them are *protected* members. If a member has a lock icon next to the identifier, the member is *private*. Member functions are marked by a magenta block next to them, and member variables have a cyan icon.

You can navigate your code from this pane. Double-click on an item, and you will go directly to the object. If it's a function, you will go to the body of the function in the source code file. To go to the declaration of a function, right-click on the function and select Go to Declaration from the context menu. Double-clicking a variable name will take you to the declaration. If you have browsing enabled for your project, right-clicking a variable and selecting References will take you to a dialog box that lists the files and location of every use of the variable. Double-click an entry in that dialog box, and you will go to the line where the variable is used.

Browsing is a nice feature of the Visual Studio.

608. *Using the ResourceView Pane*

The ResourceView pane contains a listing of the resources in a project and allows access to the resource editor simply by double-clicking on a resource item. You can create a new resource item by right-clicking on any item in the tree and selecting Insert to create a new object or Import to add a resource file such as a bitmap or cursor image to the project. The ResourceView pane is shown in Figure 608.

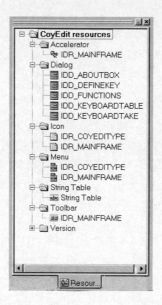

Figure 608   Resource objects and tools are accessed through the ResourceView pane

Only tree branches with objects associated with them are shown. If your project has no toolbar objects, for example, the Toolbar branch will be removed from the tree.

The tree grows according to the resource types in the project, and you can add resource types that are not included in the menu listing. For example, in Tip 910, "Adding an AVI Image File to Your Project," you will learn how to add an animation object to the resource file, in which case, the tree will sprout a new branch named "AVI."

To open a resource for editing, double-click on the item in the tree control. The proper editor will start and the resource object will be opened.

If any toolbars are necessary with the editor, they will be displayed as well. You can close the toolbars as you normally would, by right-clicking on a blank area of the main window frame and selecting it from the menu. Other toolbars may be displayed the same way.

609. *Using the FileView Pane*

Other than the header files in the *INCLUDE* path, every file even remotely connected with your project is listed in the FileView pane of the Workshop window. The tree branches are convenient categories for project files and greatly help to keep things sorted. Refer to Figure 606 to see the FileView pane.

You can move directly to a file by double-clicking on the tree entry. If the file already is open in the edit area, it will be brought to the top of the Z order. If not, it will be opened and the caret placed at the beginning of the window.

To remove a file from your project, select the tree entry and press the Delete key. This doesn't delete the file; it only removes the entry from the tree control.

The top item also contains a menu entry that comes in handy. Right-clicking on it opens a menu with a Clean entry. Use this often and wisely. The Visual C++ linker is an incremental linker, and just because a source file is recompiled doesn't always mean that all the code in the object file or executable is refreshed. Only sections where changes were *detected* are updated. The key here is "detected." If you are moving code around, adding and deleting files, and you go a long time between builds, the linker might become confused and some changed code might not be added to the executable file. If you start getting some weird and unexplainable results, or breakpoints seem to be winding up in strange places, try a clean. It can work miracles.

610. *Understanding the Document/View Architecture*

The document/view programming model is predicated on the principle of separating the data from its window interface. The window data is encapsulated in one object (the document), and another object (the view) handles displaying the data and accepting input from the user.

Using this model, you can define your document class to contain any type of data and then use more than one view to display it in different ways. Each of these views can alter the way the user sees and manipulates the data.

In the MFC version of the document/view architecture, there are four major players in the operation of a window display.

The *document template*, derived from the *CDocTemplate* class, is responsible for creating the document and view objects and the frame window that holds the view. In a single-document interface, the frame window is the main window. In a multiple-document interface, it is the child window.

The *document* itself, which is derived from the *CDocument* class, holds the data associated with the user interface. The derived class may be designed to hold any type of document information, such as text or drawing information. It encapsulates and controls access to that data and is closely associated with the views.

The *document manager*, which is basically undocumented in the MSDN literature, is instantiated from the *CDocManager* class. The application object creates the document manager object, which is responsible for coordinating the documents, the document templates, and the views. The document manager also contains the basic functions for opening documents and for closing the documents when the application exits.

The *view* is the interface between the document object and the user interface. The view design determines how the document's data is displayed on the screen, and what data is sent to the document object for storage. Although a document may be associated with several views, a view can be associated with only one document at a time.

Visual C++ supports two flavors of the document/view scheme: the single-document interface and the multiple-document interface. From reading the documentation and literature, you will discover that Microsoft discourages the multiple-document interface, although the AppWizard does select it as the default. Instead, Microsoft would prefer that you run a separate instance of the application for each document. Microsoft's own products—*Word*, *Excel*, and so on—are multiple-document applications, so

Microsoft doesn't seem to be following its own advice as to the single-document interface being a more document-centered way of doing things.

The more of the document/view architecture you use, the less code you have to write. Remember, however, that uniqueness, individuality, and functionality come with a price—hard work—and the more of the architecture you use, the more your program will look and perform like other programs. The document/view scheme has its restrictions, but you don't have to abide by them. Don't hesitate to override and add functions to your document class to step outside the "standard" programming model.

611. *Understanding the Document Object*

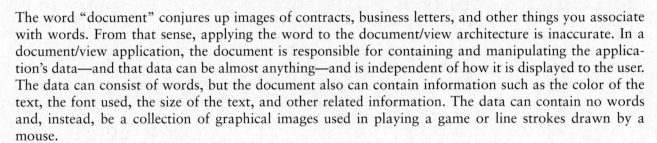

The word "document" conjures up images of contracts, business letters, and other things you associate with words. From that sense, applying the word to the document/view architecture is inaccurate. In a document/view application, the document is responsible for containing and manipulating the application's data—and that data can be almost anything—and is independent of how it is displayed to the user. The data can consist of words, but the document also can contain information such as the color of the text, the font used, the size of the text, and other related information. The data can contain no words and, instead, be a collection of graphical images used in playing a game or line strokes drawn by a mouse.

The point is that the information the user is working with is contained in the document portion of the document/view. The goal of your application determines how you design your document class and what type of data it manages.

The primary purpose is to store changes made in the views, to handle user requests relayed by the views, and to tell other views to update themselves when one view changes the data.

The document object is always derived from *CDocument*, which itself is derived from *CObject* through *CCmdTarget*, and thus, it is capable of receiving messages although it doesn't represent a window in itself. In a Windows API application, only actual windows may receive messages. In MFC, the *CCmdTarget* class is the base class for its message map architecture, and objects derived from it theoretically may receive messages. Although the ClassWizard Message Maps page does not contain any messages that it might handle, it does have a message map. You can add "command" messages to the document class. Command messages are menu, keyboard, or accelerator key messages (*WM_COMMAND*) or a control that sends a notification to its parent (*WM_NOTIFY*).

CDocument—and your derived class in turn—inherits an important function, *Serialize()* that makes it possible to store data objects in a file and retrieve them in the same state as when they were stored. Your class probably will override this function, and if you derive your own data classes from *CObject* as well and make them "serializable," they can be stored and retrieved in this function. You will get more exposure to serialization in the next few tips.

Your document class also inherits a number of other important functions from *CDocument*, as listed in Table 611. These include functions to interact with the attached view objects and to retrieve and modify document properties, such as the title and path of the associated file.

Document Operations	Purpose
GetFirstViewPosition	Returns a *POSITION* object representing the first view associated with the document. Call this function before calling *GetNextView()* to iterate the views.

Table 611   Document class functions inherited from CDocument *(continued on following page)*

Document Operations	Purpose
GetNextView	Returns a *CView* pointer (which may be cast to any other view type) to the view represented by the *POSITION* object and advances the *POSITION* object to the next view. Use this function to iterate through the views to find a particular one.
AddView	Attaches a view to the document. Adds the view to the view list and sets the view's document pointer to the current document.
RemoveView	Detaches a view from the document. Deletes the view from the view list and sets the view's document pointer to *NULL*.
UpdateAllViews	Notifies all views that the document's data has changed. Call *SetModifiedFlag()* before calling this function. Normally, this function would be called from the view in which the change was made. If a view object is included as a parameter, that view is *not* notified of the change.
GetDocTemplate	Returns a pointer to the document template from which this document was created. If the document is not managed by a document template, *NULL* is returned. When you have a pointer, you may use the *CDocTemplate* functions to iterate open documents of this type.
GetTitle	Gets the document's title, which by default is derived from the file name. This is the string that is added to the main frame's title bar when a view associated with the document has the focus. If you don't want the title added to the title bar, override the frame class *OnUpdateFrameTitle()* function.
SetTitle	Sets the document's title. Use this function to override the default method of deriving it from the file name.
GetPathName	Returns a *CString* reference containing the fully qualified path name of the associated file. The string will be empty if the document has not been associated with a file yet.
SetPathName	Sets or modifies the path of the associated file.
IsModified	Returns non-zero if the document's modified flag has been set since it was last saved. If it has not been set, the function will return 0.
SetModifiedFlag	Sets the state of the document's modified flag. The only parameter defaults to *TRUE*. Setting the flag ensures that the document will be saved before it is closed. You may unset the modified flag by passing a *FALSE* argument.

Table 611   Document class functions inherited from CDocument *(continued from previous page)*

The *CDocument* class also contains a number of virtual functions that can be overridden, including message handlers for the *ID_FILE_OPEN*, *ID_FILE_NEW*, and *ID_FILE_CLOSE* command messages.

The fact that the base class contains the message handlers and you may override them doesn't mean that your derived class will ever receive the messages, however. Generally, messages are sent to the main window frame, which handles them or directs them to other classes. Message routing is one of the key elements in the document/view architecture and is covered in Tip 613, "Understanding the Frame Window in the Document/View Architecture."

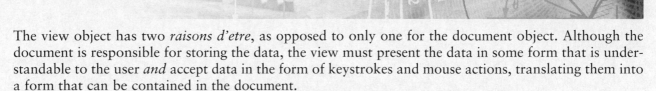

612. Understanding the View Object

The view object has two *raisons d'etre*, as opposed to only one for the document object. Although the document is responsible for storing the data, the view must present the data in some form that is understandable to the user *and* accept data in the form of keystrokes and mouse actions, translating them into a form that can be contained in the document.

If you took a line from a rich text file and dumped it onto the screen in a plain edit view, it probably wouldn't make much sense to the user. Consider the following three lines:

```
{\colortbl\red0\green0\blue0;}
\deflang1033\horzdoc{\*\fchars }{\*\lchars }\pard\plain\f2\fs24 This here be a test, eh.
\par \plain\f3\fs24\i And that was a test\plain\f3\fs24 .
\par \plain\f3\fs24\b Another test.\plain\f3\fs24
\par
```

There really are only three lines there, but unless you are familiar with rich text coding, it doesn't make much sense in an edit control.

Now take the same data and display it in a rich text control. You get the following:

```
This here be a test, eh.
And that was a test.
Another test.
```

The first line is normal type, the second is italic, and the third is bold. Now it makes much more sense. The selection of the view determines how the data is both stored and displayed.

Although a document object may have several views associated with it, a view is attached to one, and only one, document object. A member variable of the view, *m_pDocument*, points to the document object. Thus, the document, through its member functions, can always identify the views attached to it, and the view, through a member variable, can identify the document to which it is attached.

613. Understanding the Frame Window in the Document/View Architecture

The frame window is the physical workspace for the view. For a single-document interface application, the frame window is the same as the main window, but for a multiple-document project, the frame window is a child window inside the main window frame's client area. In both cases, however, the main window plays an important part in the document/view architecture. For right now, let's consider only the main window frame and look at the child windows later.

The frame window class, usually *CMainFrame* in applications created by the MFC AppWizard, contains member functions for identifying the currently active view and document. It is responsible for notifying the views when the user elects to close the application. If any documents have changed and not been saved, the *OnClose()* and *OnQueryEnding()* functions give the user a chance to save the modified documents before the application terminates.

The main frame also receives most of the Windows messages sent to the application. If it does not handle them, it is in charge of routing them to the proper object—the application class, the document, or a view—until one of them handles the message. In the case of a single-document interface, the main window frame also is in charge of resizing the view when the main frame is resized.

The multiple-document interface case is slightly different. The main window frame is capable of handling only one document at a time, although the frame may contain multiple views in a splitter window application. An MDI application, on the other hand, may have many document objects active in memory at any time, and each of these documents may have one or several views attached to it.

To accomplish this, MFC uses a derived class, *CMDIFrameWnd*, to handle the main window frame and another derived class, *CMDIChildFrame*, to support the individual documents and views. Each document has its own child frame instance, and to the document there is no difference between an SDI and an MDI application. The document is happily contained in a frame and can identify with its views, which also are contained in the same frame. There could be a hundred documents open in the MDI instance, and each would operate as though it were the only one around.

A single MDI document may have several views associated with it, and the child frame window may contain splitter windows, each containing a different view into a document. You also may have different MDI frame types, say, one with a splitter window and the other a normal, single-pane window. Let's go ahead and create such an animal, and you can use it in the following tip to understand the processes involved in setting up a complex project. Use the following steps.

Create an MDI project named "MultiView." Accept the defaults through the AppWizard steps until you come to the last page, where you name the classes. You're going to have at least two child frame classes, two types of documents, and three views, so if you accept the default names here, it will become confusing.

1. Change the view base class to *CHtmlView*.

2. Change the view class name to *CWebView*, the implementation file to *webview.cpp*, and the header file to *webview.h*.

3. Change the document class name to *CWebdoc*, the implementation file to *webdoc.cpp*, and the header file to *webdoc.h*.

4. Click Finish to create the project.

Open the *WebView.cpp* file and locate the *OnInitialUpdate()* function. Find the call to the *Navigate2()* function. The wizard sets it up to connect to the Microsoft Web site, and it should look like the following:

```
Navigate2(_T("http://www.microsoft.com/visualc/"),
          NULL,NULL);
```

You can leave this as it is if you are connected to the Internet. My development machine is not, and never will be, connected to the Internet, so I run the Internet Information Server just to test Web projects. You can change this to something more meaningful to you. In my case, it looks something like the following, where *hariseldon* is the machine running the IIS:

```
Navigate2(_T("http://hariseldon/"),NULL,NULL);
```

Compile and run the program. This time, however, don't use the normal steps. You want to enable browsing on this project, so instead of building it from the menu or toolbar button, open the ClassView panel and right-click on one of the classes. Select Base Class; the dialog box that appears will ask whether you want to enable browsing. Answer yes and the project will be compiled with browsing enabled. From this point, when you recompile the program, you can use the menu or toolbar items.

Run the program to test that it opens the Web link. The program should open a single child window and navigate to the URL you just entered. If not, it will display an error in the child window. Don't worry about whether it actually opens the Web site; right now you are concerned with whether it is working.

Now add a splitter window to the child window. You must create a view for the second pane. This can be a list or tree view that might eventually contain a collection of Web links, or a scroll view so that you can put virtually any information in it. For right now, make it a tree view.

Create a second view class. Name it "CLeftView" and derive it from *CTreeView*. Do this using the New Class dialog from the ClassWizard, or select New Class from the Insert menu. Now you meet your first problem. The AppWizard includes only the MFC header files you need when you originally create the project. Because you could have only one view, and you selected *CHtmlView*, it included only the MFC header file for that view. You must open the *stdafx.h* file and add the following header file:

```
#include <afxcview.h>          // MFC control view support
```

Save and close the *stdafx.h* file. Now add a *protected* member variable to the *CChildFrame* class. Right-click on the class name in the ClassView pane and select Add Member Variable. The variable type is *CSplitterWnd* and you name it "m_wndSplitter." Check the Protected box and click the OK button.

Open the *childfrm.cpp* file and override the virtual function *OnCreateClient()*. You can do this from the ClassWizard or from the Action button menu. Add the following code to the body of the function:

```
// create splitter window
if (!m_wndSplitter.CreateStatic(this, 1, 2))
    return FALSE;

if (!m_wndSplitter.CreateView(0, 0,RUNTIME_CLASS(CLeftView),
                         CSize(150, 150), pContext))
{
    m_wndSplitter.DestroyWindow();
    return FALSE;
}
if (!m_wndSplitter.CreateView(0, 1, RUNTIME_CLASS(CWebView),
                         CSize(150, 150), pContext))
{
    m_wndSplitter.DestroyWindow();
    return FALSE;
}
return (TRUE);
```

Remove the line shown below that calls the base class function. If you leave this line in, the normal window without splitters will be created, so remove it completely:

```
return CMDIChildWnd::OnCreateClient(lpcs, pContext);
```

Move to the top of the *childfrm.cpp* file and add the following header files to the include list. You need these to create the views you just added in the function.

```
#include "WebDoc.h"
#include "WebView.h"
#include "LeftView.h"
```

Compile and run the program again to test it. You should be able to open multiple windows, each with a Web browser in it. Each should be a splitter window with a blank area on the left side, as shown in Figure 613a. This is a tree view simply because you derived it from *CTreeView*, but you could use any other base class.

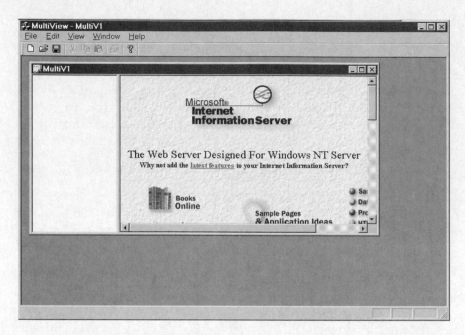

Figure 613a   The multiple-document interface application now opens a child window with a split view. You can use the left view to create a list of Web links or a list of objects found in the HTML view of the child window.

Use the ClassWizard or the menu item to add new classes to your project. Add another MDI frame class. Name it "CTextFrame" and derive it from *CMDIChildWnd*, the same as for your original child window class. Make the implementation file "TextFrm.cpp" and the header file "TextFrm.h."

Now, add a second document class named "CTextDoc" and derive it from *CDocument*. Also add a *third* view class, named "CTextView," and derive it from *CEditview*.

Open the *MultiView.cpp* file and add the header files "TextFrm.h," "TextDoc.h," and "TextView.h."

Now you add a document template for your new window frame and view class (the document template is explained in Tip 615, "Understanding the Document Template," using this project as an example). Locate the *InitInstance()* function. Near the middle of the code, the document template is declared, created, and registered. The code looks like the following:

```
CMultiDocTemplate* pDocTemplate;
pDocTemplate = new CMultiDocTemplate(
    IDR_MULTIVTYPE,
    RUNTIME_CLASS(CWebDoc),
    RUNTIME_CLASS(CChildFrame), // custom MDI child frame
    RUNTIME_CLASS(CWebView));
AddDocTemplate(pDocTemplate);
```

Immediately after this code, add your own document template using your new document, child frame, and view classes. For right now, just use the same resource ID. This will make the second template use the same string table entry, the same menu, and the same toolbar. This might make things confusing at first, but you want to make sure that everything works and then sort out the differences. Add a document template after the first one:

```
pDocTemplate = new CMultiDocTemplate(
    IDR_MULTIVTYPE,
    RUNTIME_CLASS(CTextDoc),
    RUNTIME_CLASS(CTextFrame), // custom MDI child frame
    RUNTIME_CLASS(CTextView));
AddDocTemplate(pDocTemplate);
```

Compile and run the program. The application should start with a New dialog box similar to Figure 613b. Note that the two entries are identical. That's because you used the same resource ID for both templates. In Tip 616, "Adding Multiple Document Types to Your Project," you will learn how to change the appearance and behavior of this dialog box. Right now, however, notice that the main window has not appeared yet, and it won't until you've selected a document type.

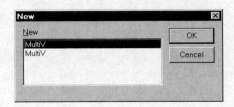

Figure 613b   The New dialog box prompts you to select a file type when you start your program

If you select the first item on the list, it should open a Web browser frame with a split window. If you select the second item, it should open an edit view for text documents without a splitter window.

To make the main window frame appear before the New dialog, look at the bottom of the *InitInstance()* function and you will find a couple of lines that are responsible for making the main window visible:

```
pMainFrame->ShowWindow(m_nCmdShow);
pMainFrame->UpdateWindow();
```

Move these two lines up to a point after the window is created and before the command line is processed. The section should look like the following:

```
// create main MDI Frame window
CMainFrame* pMainFrame = new CMainFrame;
if (!pMainFrame->LoadFrame(IDR_MAINFRAME))
    return FALSE;
m_pMainWnd = pMainFrame;
// The main window has been initialized, so show and update it.
pMainFrame->ShowWindow(m_nCmdShow);
pMainFrame->UpdateWindow();

// Parse command line for standard shell commands, DDE, file open
CCommandLineInfo cmdInfo;
ParseCommandLine(cmdInfo);
```

Recompile and run the program. The main window should appear before the New dialog box appears.

Up to this point, everything you've done, Microsoft would prefer that you didn't, but your program is starting to show some individuality. You can continue adding new document types and new views to your program following this same sequence. You don't have to create new child frame classes for each; they are reusable so long as their basic architecture is the same. For example, if you wanted to add a rich text view to your application, you could use the same child frame class as you used for the text view. If you created another document type that needs a splitter window, you could use the same splitter frame you used for the HTML view.

614. *Understanding the Document Manager*

The document manager, an object of class *CDocManager*, is an undocumented object in the Microsoft Foundation Class. The application class creates an instance of the document manager. The member variable, *m_pDocManager*, in the application class points to the instance.

Just as the frame window manages the views, this important object is responsible for managing the documents in the application and for maintaining the document templates. It also contains default message handlers for the File menu commands in case another class doesn't handle the messages.

There's no way to get to the document manager directly, but you may access its public functions using the application object's pointer variable. Through the document manager's *GetFirstDocTemplatePosition()* and *GetNextDocTemplatePosition()*, you can get to all the application's document templates and from there locate all the documents in the application. After you locate the documents, you may locate all the views attached to them. The document manager is a one-stop shop for all the objects in a document/view application.

In a single-document interface, you can have only one document open at a time, but the document manager is still at work. If you attempt to open a document when you already have one open, the document manager is responsible for closing the first and prompting you to save it if it has been modified.

615. *Understanding the Document Template*

In the division of labor in the document/view architecture, the document manager is responsible for maintaining the document templates, which in turn are responsible for managing the documents they create. The document template bears a special relationship to the application: It's the connection between the visible (the views) and the invisible (the documents).

The document template handles the creation of the document, the frame window, and the views. It manages documents of one particular type, and you can have multiple-document templates in your application to handle various document types. In the case of a single-document interface, the frame window it creates is the main window; in a multiple-document interface, the frame window is the child window that lives in the application's client area.

You build a document template by passing its constructor four parameters. The first is the resource ID of the frame objects that will be used when a document of this type is created or gets the keyboard focus. This includes the toolbar, the menu, the accelerator table, and the icon used to identify the document.

The other three parameters are pointers to *CRuntimeClass* structures of the document class, the frame window class, and the first view class used with the document. You get these structure pointers using the *RUNTIME_CLASS* macro. Only classes derived from *CObject* and declared using the *DECLARE_DYNAMIC*, *DECLARE_DYNCREATE*, or *DECLARE_SERIAL* macros return *CRuntimeClass* pointers. Thus, the document, view, and window frame classes must share a common ancestor, *CObject*.

In a normal application, you use two types of document templates, both derived from *CDocTemplate*. The first is *CSingleDocTemplate*, which is used for single-document applications and actually creates the main window frame. The second is *CMultiDocTemplate*, which creates the child windows for an MDI application.

If you look in the *InitInstance()* function of the application you created in Tip 613, "Understanding the Frame Window in the Document/View Architecture," you will see a few lines of code you didn't see in previous SDI applications:

```
// create main MDI Frame window
CMainFrame* pMainFrame = new CMainFrame;
if (!pMainFrame->LoadFrame(IDR_MAINFRAME))
    return FALSE;
m_pMainWnd = pMainFrame;
```

In this MDI application, the application class, not the document template, creates the main window frame.

The document template is how you use different frame classes for various file types. In the example in Tip 613 you know that you are using two different window styles because one has splitter panes and the other doesn't. You know that they are two different views because one gives you a mini-browser and the other a text editing window. In the next tip, I will show how to give each of these document templates other characteristics, including different toolbars and menus.

616. *Adding Multiple Document Types to Your Project*

In the application in Tip 613, "Understanding the Frame Window in the Document/View Architecture," the focus was on creating two different views using two different document types and window frames. Next, you need to give these templates their own characteristics, so first examine the string table entry for them. Both types used the same entry, *IDR_MULTIVTYPE*:

```
\nMultiV\nMultiV\n\n\nMultiView.Document\nMultiV Document
```

The elements of the string table entry are separated by newline characters, indicated by the \n. There are seven fields in this string entry, and if you don't use one, it still must have the newline character as a placeholder.

The first field is the main window title and is not used in MDI templates, so the string begins with a newline character (*always* in an MDI application, but it won't cause an error if you have an entry here). The second entry is the document name type and is used to build default names for new documents. You will notice that when you created new views, the title was MultiV1, MultiV2, and so on.

The third entry is the new file name and is the identifier used in the File New dialog box. Change this string to give the entry a more descriptive title in this dialog.

The next two entries are not used in your sample application, but this doesn't mean that they aren't important entries. The first of these two is the identifier string used in the File Open and Save dialogs. You will notice that in many applications these dialog boxes contain a drop-down box that has identifiers such as Web Documents (*.web). This is where you create that entry. The next unused entry is the extension type used in the filter for the Open and Save dialogs. In this case, you would enter "*.web" (without the quotes) to filter and save browser documents as *.web* type files.

The next entry is the registered file type to be placed in the registration database maintained by Windows. This field never contains spaces and usually consists of two words separated by a period. If you don't have this entry, the file type won't be registered.

The final entry is the registered file type name. This is the name used in the dialog boxes of applications that access the file type Registry. If you don't have an entry for the registered file type, you don't need an entry here (but you still must have the newline character).

The application in Tip 613 does not register file types, so you don't have to worry about the last two entries. It's not a bad idea to include them in case you later want to register them. To register file types, load the document templates you want to register; then, call the *RegisterShellFileTypes()* member function in *CWinApp* with a parameter of *TRUE*.

When you save a file using *CHtmlView*, nothing is actually saved. It just creates an empty file. If you want to save information from this file, you must modify the *Serialize()* function in the document class to write the information. Right now, however, you're only concerned with the document template, so you will create a set of resources for the Web browser type. Add a string table entry (right-click on any entry in the string table, and select New String from the menu), give it the resource ID of *IDR_WEBTYPE*, and enter the following string:

```
\nWeb\nWeb Browser\nWeb documents (*.web)\n.web\nMultiView.WebDocs\nMultiV Web Document
```

Create an icon using the same resource ID, *IDR_WEBTYPE*. You can copy and paste the *IDR_MULTIVTYPE* icon and modify it if you want. Notice that there are *two* icons, the small 16×16 pixel icon and the large 32×32 pixel icon. You need to copy them both. Right-click on the *IDR_MULTIVTYPE* icon in the ResourceView and select Insert Icon. Give the new icon the resource ID of *IDR_WEBTYPE* and either draw or copy the new icon.

Copy the *IDR_MULTIVTYPE* menu. Open the menu in the resource editor and, holding down the Shift key, click on each pop-up entry. This will select them all (the Select All entry on the main menu bar is disabled, so you have to roll your own here). Close the menu, then right-click on its entry in the ResourceView, and select Insert Menu. When the new, empty menu appears, just paste what you copied and you will have a copy of the original menu. You may customize this menu for Web-type documents. Give the new menu the resource ID of *IDR_WEBTYPE*.

Don't worry about copying the toolbar. The main window frame is going to load and use the one identified as *IDR_MAINFRAME*. If you want to use another, your view class will have to change the visible toolbar. You will learn how to do this in Tip 734, "Adding a Toolbar to Your Project," in the section on the Resource Workshop.

Now return to the *InitInstance()* function in the application class, and change the first document template to reflect the new resource ID. It should look like the following:

```
pDocTemplate = new CMultiDocTemplate(
    IDR_WEBTYPE,
    RUNTIME_CLASS(CWebDoc),
    RUNTIME_CLASS(CChildFrame), // custom MDI child frame
    RUNTIME_CLASS(CWebView));
AddDocTemplate(pDocTemplate);
```

Compile and run your program. The first entry in the New File dialog should be Web Browser, and when you select it, the application will open an HTML view.

You can use the *IDR_MULTIVIEW* resource ID for text files if you want, or you can repeat the process to create a new set of resources. You can change the string table entry to read like the following:

```
\nText\nText Document\nText documents (*.txt)
\n.txt\nMultiView.TextDocs\nMultiV Text Document
```

If you want to prove that the program is using separate resources, try making some changes in the menu. When you select or create different views, the menu will change to reflect the resource ID you entered in the call to create the document template.

617. Understanding Windows Message Routing in the Document/View

The construction of the document/view architecture makes it possible to route messages through the application so that they can be handled by the main window frame, the application class, a view, or a document. Most command messages and notification messages from controls are sent to the top-level window, as is normal in Windows programs. In an MFC application, this generally is the main window frame.

In a single-document interface application, the message handler is built in to the *CFrameWnd* base class in the *OnCmdMsg()* member function. Your frame window class may override this function if you want to provide a different message routing.

When the frame window receives a command message, it first pumps it through the current view. Actually, it calls the view object's own *OnCmdMsg()* function, which the object inherits from the base *CView* class. Again, your view class may override this function. If the view doesn't have a message handler, it then calls the associated document's *OnCmdMsg()* function. If the document object doesn't handle the message, it passes it up the line to the document template and the document manager. If any of them handle the message, the function returns *TRUE* and the routing is finished.

If, however, none of them handle the message (the return value through the sequence of function calls is *FALSE*), the frame window gets the message back and tries its own message handlers. If it doesn't have one to handle the message, it finally gets pumped back to the application class object.

If, by this point, none of the application's class objects have handled the message, it is passed on to the global *::DefWindowProc()*.

The routing in a multiple-document interface application is much the same, except that another window frame is involved, the child window frame that holds the view. If the view and document objects don't handle the message, the child window frame gets a shot at it before passing it back to the main window frame.

If you are letting the frameworks handle most of the messages, the order in which the objects' functions are called isn't really important. However, the sequence of events is important if you are writing your message handlers. If, for example, your view class handles a message such as *ID_FILE_SAVE* and you want the application class to handle it, the message is never going to get back to the application object until you remove the handler from your view class.

618. Understanding Default Messages

On the default menus provided by the MFC AppWizard, most of the items have default handlers built in to the calling sequence. The exception is the Edit menu. Only view classes capable of handling these messages, such as the cut, copy, and paste operations, have handlers for these messages. These include the *CEditView* and *CRichEditView* base classes. If, however, you derive your view class from one of the other bases, you have to roll your own message handlers for these menu items.

By default, the application class handles the *ID_FILE_NEW* and *ID_FILE_OPEN* messages, along with *ID_APP_EXIT* and *ID_FILE_PRINT_SETUP*.

The document object handles the *ID_FILE_SAVE* and *ID_FILE_SAVEAS* messages and the *ID_FILE_SEND_MAIL* message to send a document through the Windows message system.

The view class handles the *ID_FILE_PRINT* and *ID_FILE_PRINT_PREVIEW* messages.

Finally, the main window frame handles the messages to show or hide the toolbar and status bar, *ID_VIEW_TOOLBAR* and *ID_VIEW_STATUS_BAR*. If your application uses more than one toolbar and you need to show only one at a time depending on the view, these messages can be handled in the view objects, or you can override them in the window frame class.

For an MDI application, there also are messages to arrange, tile, and cascade the child windows. These are handled by the main window frame. The default tile message in projects created by the MFC AppWizard is *ID_WINDOW_TILE_VERT* to tile the windows vertically. You may add a menu item to tile horizontally using the message *ID_WINDOW_TILE_HORZ*. The message handler already is built in to the frameworks.

619. *Overriding the Frame Works Message Handlers*

In considering message handlers, remember, the active view gets the first shot at all messages. This makes sense. To Windows, the main window frame might be the main window, but to your application it's the active view that has the focus. By giving the active view the first option to handle a message, your application is mimicking the overall method by which Windows handles messages.

You have to remember the sequence of events when you write your own message handlers. Although the frame window class gets the message first, it is the last to get a chance to handle the message. As the message gets passed up through the hierarchy, any of the components may return *TRUE* and stop the message routing.

You really don't see this in your code. Many of your message handler functions will have a *void* return type. However, the message map macros that you add when you add message handlers take care of returning *TRUE* or *FALSE*. If a handler is in the message map, the controlling function, *OnCmdMessage()*, returns *TRUE*. Otherwise, it returns false. A typical message map may look like the following code:

```
BEGIN_MESSAGE_MAP(CMultiViewApp, CWinApp)
    //{{AFX_MSG_MAP(CMultiViewApp)
    ON_COMMAND(ID_APP_ABOUT, OnAppAbout)
    // NOTE - the ClassWizard will add and remove mapping
    // macros here.
    //    DO NOT EDIT what you see in these blocks of
    // generated code!
    //}}AFX_MSG_MAP
    // Standard file based document commands
    ON_COMMAND(ID_FILE_NEW, CWinApp::OnFileNew)
    ON_COMMAND(ID_FILE_OPEN, CWinApp::OnFileOpen)
    // Standard print setup command
    ON_COMMAND(ID_FILE_PRINT_SETUP, CWinApp::OnFilePrintSetup)
END_MESSAGE_MAP()
```

Notice the commented lines warn you about editing the code between the line beginning with "//{{AFX_MSG_MAP" and the line beginning "//}}AFX_MSG_MAP." This section is reserved for the Visual Studio wizards. If you add anything within this block, the ClassWizard likely will remove it.

620. *Understanding the CArchive Class*

One of the most arcane objects in the MFC document/view implementation is the *CArchive* class. It really isn't part of the document/view architecture, but it merits some consideration here because you will find it in virtually every MFC application you create using this architecture.

You can think of a *CArchive* object as being like a C++ stream but without all the goodies that make it useful. In MFC, classes derived from *CFile* provide no buffering other than the *CStdioFile* class, which is the same as a C++ stream. When you attach a *CArchive* object to the file object, however, *CArchive* provides the buffering.

The *CArchive* class allows you to save objects to disk in binary format and later read them back in and reconstruct them in their original format through the process of *serialization*. This isn't anything new, and programmers have been doing it since they started reading and writing records. *CArchive* gets a lot of ballyhooing in the Microsoft literature as the final answer to file I/O, but in real-life situations you might find that its design lacks the flexibility necessary to meet many applications.

Suppose that you want to read a text file into memory and display it in a view. Create a single-document interface project named "Text." Derive your view class from CView. You will use this project in Tip 624, "Displaying Text in *CView*," but right now the task is to design a line object to hold text. Don't worry that the program doesn't display anything yet. If you put a breakpoint in the overloaded >> operator at the point indicated in the code below, you can watch the text being read into the program line by line.

To this project, add a class named "CLine" and derive it from *CObject*. You have to do this from the generic class dialog because the ClassWizard doesn't list *CObject* as one of the MFC classes from which you may derive other classes. Right-click on the project name in the ClassView pane, and select New Class. Select Generic Class as the class type of the new class, *CLine*. Enter "CObject" in the Base class list. Click OK.

The class is very simple. The class is derived from *CObject*, so you must add the *DECLARE_SERIAL* macro and a *CString* variable to hold the line of text. Then write a few operator overloads to make it work. Leave the file names as *Line.cpp* and *Line.h*. The class definition should look like the following:

```
class CTextDoc;     // Forward reference

class CLine : public CObject
{
DECLARE_SERIAL(CLine)

public:
    CLine();
    virtual ~CLine();
protected:
    CString m_Line;
    friend CTextDoc;
public:
    BOOL bResult;
    CString& GetData();
    friend CArchive& operator<<(CArchive& ar, CLine& Line);
    friend CArchive& operator>>(CArchive& ar, CLine& Line);
    CLine& operator=(CLine &str);
};
```

The >> and << operator overloads let you read and write the class data through *CArchive* using the operators rather than calling the *ReadString()* and *WriteString()* functions. The = operator overload makes it easier for you to enter the data into an array when you read the file by letting you use the equals sign to set the contents of the *CString* object in the new object to that of the current object.

The *Line.cpp* implementation file is shown here:

```cpp
// Line.cpp: implementation of the CLine class.
//
//////////////////////////////////////////////////////////////

#include "stdafx.h"
#include "Text.h"
#include "Line.h"

#ifdef _DEBUG
#undef THIS_FILE
static char THIS_FILE[]=__FILE__;
#define new DEBUG_NEW
#endif


//////////////////////////////////////////////////////////////
// Construction/Destruction
//////////////////////////////////////////////////////////////

IMPLEMENT_SERIAL(CLine,CObject,0)

CLine::CLine()
{

}

CLine::~CLine()
{

}

//
//  Operator overload to set the data string.
//
CLine& CLine::operator=(CLine &Line)
{
    m_Line = Line.m_Line;
    return (*this);
}

//
//  Stream inserters to read and write the objects through
//  a CArchive object.
//
CArchive& operator<<(CArchive& ar, CLine& Line)
{
const char *nl = "\n";

    ar.WriteString((LPCSTR) Line.m_Line);
    ar.Write(nl, sizeof (nl));
    return (ar);
}
```

```
CArchive& operator>>(CArchive& ar, CLine& Line)
{
// Put a breakpoint on the following line to inspect
// the text as it is read.
    Line.m_bResult = ar.ReadString(Line.m_Line);
    Line.m_Line.FreeExtra();
    return (ar);
}


CString& CLine::GetData()
{
    return (m_Line);
}
```

The *CArchive::ReadString()* function reads a line up to a newline, but it does not include the newline in the returned data. You don't want the newline character anyway. Later, when you draw the text on the view, you would want to strip it out. The *m_bResult* flags the end of the file. When accessing a file through a *CArchive* object, there's no way of knowing when you've reached the end of the file, so you just continue reading until you get an error.

When you write the object back, you must add the newline character. *CArchive::WriteString()* doesn't do that. *CArchive::Write()*, which writes binary data, is used to add the newline to the archive, which probably will be a file.

Essentially, this gains you nothing. You could have accomplished the same thing using C++ stream functions, which are much more flexible than *CArchive*. You could, theoretically, change the file type to which the archive object is attached to something like a *CInternetFile* without changing your code.

621. *Using the* Serialize *Function*

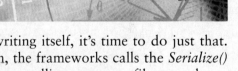

Now that you've created a class that is capable of reading and writing itself, it's time to do just that. When you save a file in a typical MFC document/view application, the frameworks calls the *Serialize()* function in the document object. Whether you're using serialization or rolling your own file procedures, this is your stopping point for file access in the document/view architecture.

Using the project from Tip 620, "Understanding the *CArchive* Class," open the *TextDoc.cpp* and *TextDoc.h* files. Add the following *protected* members to the class definition:

```
friend CTextView;
CArray<CLine, CLine&> m_Text;
```

This declares your view class as a friend so that it can get to the text to display it. The *m_Text* is an array containing your *CLine* objects, one for each line of text in the file.

Move to the *Serialize()* function in *TextDoc.cpp* and add the following code:

```
//////////////////////////////////////////////////////////////
// CTextDoc serialization

void CTextDoc::Serialize(CArchive& ar)
{
    if (ar.IsStoring())
    {
```

```
        int nCount = m_Text.GetSize ();
        for (int n = 0; n < nCount; ++n)
            ar << m_Text[n];
    }
    else
    {
        CLine Line;
        BOOL bReading = TRUE;
        while (bReading)
        {
            ar >> Line;
            bReading = Line.m_bResult;
            if (bReading)
                m_Text.Add (Line);
        }
    }
}
```

The *IsStoring()* condition is straightforward. It simply writes the data into the file using the overloaded operators provided in *CLine*.

When you are loading data, however, the situation is more complicated, and you will find out why you need the *m_bResult* flag in your *CLine* class.

Declare a flag that you are reading the file and set it to *TRUE*. Read the data from the archive and into the *CLine* object. This calls *CArchive::ReadString()*, which strips off line enders for you. You loop through until the *CLine* object reports a failure to read, and you exit the loop. Each line is added to the *m_Text* member array as the line is read.

CFile supposedly provides unbuffered access to a file, and *CArchive* provides the buffering for the reads and writes. When you link a file to a *CArchive* object, you lose some of the functionality of a stream. You can't determine when you are at the end of the file, for example. If you call *CFile::GetPosition()*, you might expect it to return the current file pointer. It does, but the pointer is not the position at which *you* are reading and writing the file. It's the position at which the archive object is operating, and there's no way to tell where you are in the scheme of things. As you will see throughout this section, this lack of a position property is a severe handicap for the *CArchive* class, and some of the MFC classes go to great pains to work around it.

For the typical MFC example showing you how to read and write class objects, this isn't a problem. The information you need is contained in the file when you write it. For files containing only text, however, this is a problem. Text files must be read and written back precisely, and you can't write size information in them. A compiler, for example, would have a field day with its error messages if you wrote size information about *CLine* in a *.cpp* file.

Microsoft gets around this by providing a special *SerializeRaw()* function in its *CEditView* class, and the document object calls it if the view is an ordinary edit type. This is a very un-C++ way out and obviates Microsoft's ballyhooing about how *CFile* and *CArchive* are the end-all for reading and writing files.

Of course, *CEditView* uses an edit common control. This *Text* project is going to do things the hard way, from the ground up, so that you will get some idea of how to build your own views without doing it the Microsoft way. Eventually, you could add color, font, point size, and other information to the *CLine* object and build your own version of the rich edit view.

Note: The rich edit control has some problems of its own, primarily stemming from the fact that it was designed to support an old DOS version of Microsoft Word. Even the 32-bit version, which certainly can't be used with DOS, exhibits the same problems.

---

622. *Understanding CView*

If you've used the Windows API, you will find *CView* very similar to the window you created in a standard Windows program. It's the unfettered window, waiting for your output. It does nothing for you. It won't display text or graphics; that's all up to your code, just as it was in the Windows API.

CView is the base class for all the views in MFC, including *CCtrlView*, which in turn serves as the base class for views based on Windows common controls. It provides the basic functionality for a view. All the other view classes build on this functionality. Generally, you derive your view classes from the other classes derived from *CView* to inherit their added functionality, but it is possible to use a class derived directly from *CView*.

You can't create an instance of *CView* directly. It's what is called an "abstract" class because the *OnDraw()* member function is a *pure virtual* function. *OnDraw()* is not implemented in *CView* and its address is set to *NULL*, so you must derive a class from *CView* and at least provide a body for *OnDraw()*.

When a view becomes invalid, Windows sends a *WM_PAINT* message, just as it sent your *WndProc()* function a *WM_PAINT* message in an application based on the Windows API. The *CView* class interprets this message and prepares a *CPaintDC* object; then, it calls your *OnDraw()* function with a pointer to it. The *CPaintDC* is used only in response to a *WM_PAINT* message because it calls *BeginPaint()* in the constructor and *EndPaint()* in the destructor.

Your derived class then uses the *OnDraw()* function to paint to the view surface, whether it is text, graphics, or other objects, such as control objects.

You can use *CView* as a white board and draw common controls on it. It's clear that Microsoft never intended it to be used this way because the ClassWizard provides no message handler options for the controls. However, it makes a good alternative to creating a dialog box–based application. You get the advantage of toolbars and full window menus, which you yourself have to implement in a dialog-based application.

Create an SDI application using *CView* as the base class. Call the project "Graphics." After selecting a single-document interface, accept the defaults through the MFC AppWizard and create the project. Open the view class, *CGraphicsView*, and override the virtual function *OnInitialUpdate()*. You can use the ClassWizard or the Wizard Bar's Action button to do this.

In the ResourceView, add two IDs, *IDC_LISTBOX* and *IDC_EDITBOX*. You don't need these just to create the controls, but if you want to get messages from them, you must assign them a resource ID. Add two member variables to the *CGraphicsView* class, a *CEdit* member and a *CListBox* member. Name them "m_Edit" and "m_ListBox," respectively. Add code to the *OnInitialUpdate()* function so that it looks like the following listing:

```
void CGraphicsView::OnInitialUpdate()
{
    CView::OnInitialUpdate();
    if (m_ListBox.m_hWnd != NULL)
        m_ListBox.DestroyWindow();
    if (m_Edit.m_hWnd != NULL)
        m_Edit.DestroyWindow();
    RECT rc;
    rc.top = 0;
    rc.bottom = 150;
    rc.left = 0;
    rc.right = 150;
    m_ListBox.Create (WS_BORDER | WS_VSCROLL | LBS_NOTIFY |
```

```
                        WS_VISIBLE, rc, this, IDC_LISTBOX);
    m_ListBox.AddString ("Stuff");
    m_ListBox.AddString ("More Stuff");
    m_ListBox.AddString ("Even more stuff");
    RECT rcList;
    m_ListBox.GetWindowRect (&rcList);
    rc.left = 150;
    rc.right = 300;
    rc.bottom = rcList.bottom - rcList.top;
    m_Edit.Create (WS_BORDER | WS_VSCROLL | ES_CENTER
                    | ES_MULTILINE | WS_VISIBLE, rc, this,
                    IDC_EDITBOX);
    m_Edit.ShowWindow (SW_SHOWNORMAL);
    m_Edit.SetWindowText ("This here's a string that will "
                        "be placed in the edit box in "
                        "the edit control on the view "
                        "window");
}
```

The code creates a list box in the upper-left corner of the view and adds three strings to it. The call to its *GetWindowRect()* is necessary to get the exact size of the control. The list box wants to size itself on a line boundary, so it might be slightly larger than what the code specifies. The resulting rectangle is used to figure the depth of the edit control. After creating the window, add some text to it.

The line right after the call to *CView::OnInitialUpdate()* protects the application against the controls' being created more than once. If you used the File New command, the *OnInitialUpdate()* function is called again, and the controls must be destroyed before their *Create()* member functions may be called again.

Compile and run the program. You can use the controls the same as you would a dialog box. You just don't have the advantage of wizard-assisted message handlers.

623. *Overriding the OnPaint Message Handler*

The *OnPaint()* member function of *CView* performs only a couple of actions. First, it initializes a *CPaintDC* device context and calls *OnPrepareDC()*. The *OnPrepareDC()* function is used to prepare the device context for rendering an image on the screen. It then calls your derived class's *OnDraw()* member function with a pointer to the device context.

Ordinarily, if you're just drawing to the screen, you don't need to override the function to handle the *WM_PAINT* message. However, if you are using *CView* to draw to a printer, or to both the screen and a printer, you can override it to prepare the device context using a *CPrintInfo* class object.

624. *Displaying Text in CView*

Now that you've created a class to store a line of text and can read it into your document, it's time to display the text. For now, you will display only as much text as fits on the screen. In a bit, when you get to the *CScrollView* class, you will see why it's just as well not to bother with it here. Revive the *TEXT* project from Tip 620, "Understanding the *CArchive* Class," for these code changes.

There's one more change to be made to the *CTextDoc* class. Open the *TextDoc.cpp* file and override the *DeleteContents()* virtual function. Add a line to dump the array containing the text objects. The function should look like the following code:

```
void CTextDoc::DeleteContents()
{
    m_Text.RemoveAll ();
    CDocument::DeleteContents();
}
```

When the document is cleared, such as on a File New or a File Open command, the frameworks calls this function. You can use it to dump the current contents of the *CLine* array and prepare yourself to read in a new file.

For now, this project won't try to create a caret, do any editing, or even try to scroll through the document. After you get the display under your belt, you will find that scrolling isn't difficult when you understand how the scroll bars work.

Close the document files and open the *CTextView* class files: *TextView.cpp* and *TextView.h*. Your document class already has done half the work by reading and storing the text you will display here.

Find the *OnDraw()* member function in the *CTextView* class source file. Right now all it does is get a pointer to the document class and check whether it's a valid object. After that, add some additional code so that the function looks like the following:

```
void CTextView::OnDraw(CDC* pDC)
{
    CTextDoc* pDoc = GetDocument();
    ASSERT_VALID(pDoc);

    int nLine;
    int nCount = pDoc->m_Text.GetSize ();
    if (!nCount)
        return;
    CLine clLine;
    CSize sz = pDC->GetTextExtent (" ", 1);
    RECT rc;
    GetClientRect (&rc);
    int nBottom = rc.bottom;
    rc.bottom = sz.cy;
    CFont *fontOld = pDC->SelectObject (&m_Font);
    for (nLine = 0; nLine < nCount; ++nLine)
    {
        clLine = pDoc->m_Text[nLine];
        pDC->DrawText (clLine.GetData(), &rc,
                   DT_EXPANDTABS | DT_SINGLELINE | DT_LEFT);
        rc.top += sz.cy;
        rc.bottom += sz.cy;
//
//    If we're out of the window, might as well bail out.
        if (rc.top > nBottom)
            break;
    }
    pDC->SelectObject (fontOld);
}
```

Compile and run the program. Simple, wasn't it? Of course, there's still a lot of work to go before you have a real text editor, and the display is pretty funky if you use the default system font. If you want to change the font, add a *CFont* member variable to the view class and name it "m_Font." Add the following line to the constructor:

```
m_Font.CreatePointFont (100, "Courier New");
```

You will need to select this font each time your program calls the *OnDraw()* function. When you have done this, *OnDraw()* should look like the following:

```
void CTextView::OnDraw(CDC* pDC)
{
    CTextDoc* pDoc = GetDocument();
    ASSERT_VALID(pDoc);

    int nLine;
    int nCount = pDoc->m_Text.GetSize ();
    if (!nCount)
        return;
    CLine clLine;
    CSize sz = pDC->GetTextExtent (" ", 1);
    RECT rc;
    GetClientRect (&rc);
    int nBottom = rc.bottom;
    rc.bottom = sz.cy;
    CFont *fontOld = pDC->SelectObject (&m_Font);
    for (nLine = 0; nLine < nCount; ++nLine)
    {
        clLine = pDoc->m_Text[nLine];
        pDC->DrawText (clLine.GetData(), &rc, DT_EXPANDTABS
                        | DT_SINGLELINE | DT_LEFT);
        rc.top += sz.cy;
        rc.bottom += sz.cy;
//
//  If we're out of the window viewport, might
//  as well bail out.
        if (rc.top > nBottom)
            break;
    }
    pDC->SelectObject (fontOld);
}
```

(Remember the old programming adage: "Leave it as you found it." In earlier projects, you learned to restore the original objects in the device context after you've changed them. The same is true in MFC programs. The last line in *OnDraw()* restores the old font.)

625. *Drawing Graphics Objects in* CView

Drawing graphics in a *CView* window is just as easy as drawing text, or drawing graphics in a standard Windows API function. For bitmaps, lines, and shapes, you can use the same code you used in the examples before you got to this section on documents and views. The only difference is that you don't need the *HWND* or the *HDC* variables. The view class encapsulates the *HWND* as a member variable, and *CView::OnPaint()* ships you a *CPaintDC* pointer when it calls your *OnDraw()* function.

Beyond bitmaps and lines, there are many graphics file formats, ranging from specific formats such as FITS (used by astronomers for telescope images) to the more general PCX format used by Windows *Paint*. Eventually, to be displayed on the screen, they have to be rendered into bitmaps, because that's the nature of a monitor. If graphics are your interest, you might look up *Graphics File Formats* by David C. Kay and John R. Levine, published by McGraw-Hill.

Some time ago on the Web, I came across a neat utility program named *loadpic.exe* that demonstrated the use of the OLE *IPicture* interface. This interface has a function to render a number of file formats to the screen, including JPEG, GIF, and Windows metafile formats. Unfortunately, none of the files that came with it included a copyright or any mention of the author's name. That's a shame because the programmer did an excellent job of presenting an example of the *IPicture* interface, and I certainly would give him or her credit here if I knew who that person is.

Also, unfortunately, it was written as a Windows API program. The bulk of my programming uses either Borland's Object Windows Library or the Microsoft Foundation Class, so I started about converting it to both. In the following project, I've cut and pasted the author's original code in some places and modified it for MFC; in other places, the code was completely rewritten to take advantage of class library functions. The scrolling calculations left much to be desired, even in unscaled mode. When I added scaling to the menu, the calculations didn't work at all, so the scrolling, for the most part, has been rewritten. An example of the result can be seen in Figure 625.

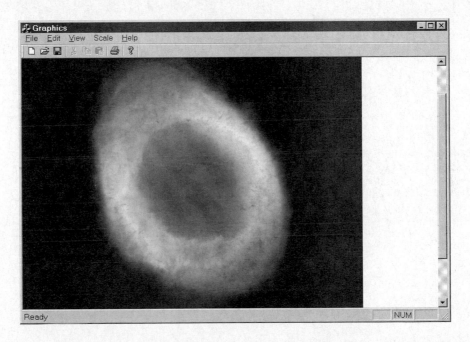

Figure 625   By using the IPicture interface, your application can display images in several formats

Create another MFC single-document interface project using *CView* as the base view class. The text project was named simply *Text*, so be original and name this one "Graphics." That will give you *CGraphicsDoc* and *CGraphicsView* classes, which are fairly descriptive. This will work just as well in an MDI application, by the way.

After you've created the project, open the *IDR_MAINFRAME* menu in the resource editor. Add a pop-up on the menu bar labeled "Scale." Add three items under it for 2:1, 1:1, and 1:2 scaling. Make the menu items read whatever you want, but the resource IDs should be *IDM_SCALE_21*, *IDM_SCALE_11*, and *IDM_SCALE_21*. Add ToolTips if you want them. Later you can add buttons to your toolbar to do the scaling.

Next, open the *graphicsdoc.cpp* and *graphicsdoc.h* files. Add two *protected* variables and two *public* functions as shown next. Also, use the ClassWizard to override the *ID_FILE_NEW* and *ID_FILE_OPEN* message handlers. In addition, override the *ID_FILE_OPEN* message handler. The *IPicture* interface can handle several file formats, but rather than register a template for each one, you yourself can handle it by calling the File Open dialog:

```
protected:
//{{AFX_MSG(CGraphicsDoc)
    afx_msg void OnFileOpen();
//}}AFX_MSG
DECLARE_MESSAGE_MAP()
    DWORD    m_dwSize;
    HGLOBAL  m_hBuf;
public:
    DWORD GetGlobalSize();
    HGLOBAL GetGlobalBuffer();
```

In the *GraphicsDoc.cpp* file, add the code to the *OnFileNew()* message handler. With so many file formats, the filter string for the *CFileDialog* box is involved, but this beats registering a template for each file type. If you develop any applications based on this code, the call is up to you. It might be preferable to use document templates. Also, add the following to the *GetGlobalBuffer()* and *GetGlobalSize()* functions. These allow the outside world to access the *protected* member variables you just added:

```
/////////////////////////////////////////////////////////////
// CGraphicsDoc commands

void CGraphicsDoc::OnFileOpen()
{
    CFileDialog cfd (TRUE);
//
// Set the filter string to a combined string, one
// string for each file type. This is a very long string.
// Notice that the individual filter types are separated
// by a \0.
    cfd.m_ofn.lpstrFilter   = _T("Supported Files Types"
                               "(*.bmp;*.gif;*.jpg;*.ico;"
                               "*.emf;*.wmf;)\0*.bmp;*.gif;"
                               "*.jpg;*.ico;*.emf;*.wmf;\0"
                               "Bitmaps (*.bmp)\0*.bmp\0GIF "
                               "Files (*.gif)\0*.gif\0JPEG "
                               "Files (*.jpg)\0*.jpg\0Icons "
                               "(*.ico)\0*.ico\0Enhanced "
                               "Metafiles (*.emf)\0*.emf\0"
                               "Windows Metafiles (*.wmf)\0"
                               "*.wmf\0\0");
    cfd.m_ofn.lpstrTitle   = _T("Open Picture File");
    cfd.m_ofn.nMaxFile = MAX_PATH;
    if (cfd.DoModal () == IDCANCEL)
        return;
    if (m_hBuf != NULL)
    {
        GlobalFree (m_hBuf);
        m_hBuf = NULL;
        m_dwSize = 0;
    }
    CDocument::OnNewDocument ();
```

```
        CString strPath = cfd.GetPathName();
        AfxGetApp()->OpenDocumentFile (strPath);
}


// Return the HGLOBAL pointer to the image memory
HGLOBAL CGraphicsDoc::GetGlobalBuffer()
{
    return (m_hBuf);
}


// Return the size of the globally allocated memory
DWORD CGraphicsDoc::GetGlobalSize()
{
    return (m_dwSize);
}
```

Now find the *Serialize()* function. You must add code to allocate the global memory, read the graphics file, and stuff it into the global memory. This program won't be concerned with writing the graphics file, so add code to the *Serialize()* function so that it looks like the following:

```
/////////////////////////////////////////////////////////////
// CGraphicsDoc serialization

void CGraphicsDoc::Serialize(CArchive& ar)
{
    if (ar.IsStoring())
    {
        // TODO: add storing code here
    }
    else
    {
        if (m_hBuf != NULL)
        {
            GlobalFree (m_hBuf);
            m_hBuf = NULL;
            m_dwSize = 0;
        }
        m_dwSize = ar.GetFile()->GetLength ();
        m_hBuf = GlobalAlloc(GMEM_MOVEABLE, m_dwSize);
        char *tmp = (char *) GlobalLock (m_hBuf);
        if (tmp == NULL)
            return;
        ar.Read (tmp, m_dwSize);
        GlobalUnlock (m_hBuf);
        POSITION pos = GetFirstViewPosition();
        while (pos != NULL)
        {
            CView* pView = GetNextView(pos);
            pView->UpdateWindow();
        }
    }
}
```

Now initialize the member variables in the constructor, and add code to free the global memory in case the user ends the application before closing the document:

```
// Initialize the global memory pointer to NULL and the
// size to 0.
CGraphicsDoc::CGraphicsDoc()
{
    // TODO: add one-time construction code here
    m_hBuf = NULL;
    m_dwSize = 0;
}


// If the global memory hasn't been released, do it in the
// destructor
CGraphicsDoc::~CGraphicsDoc()
{
    if (m_hBuf != NULL)
        GlobalFree (m_hBuf);
}
```

There's one last task in the *CGraphicsDoc* class. Override the *DeleteContents()* virtual function and add code to clear the view window. From here, the memory is freed and the picture is destroyed, so the pointer is set to *NULL*. The call to *UpdateAllViews()* ships a hint of 1 to indicate that the image is being deleted and the view should drop the scroll bars from the frame (the value of 1 is an arbitrary, application-defined value):

```
void CGraphicsDoc::DeleteContents()
{
    if (m_hBuf != NULL)
    {
        GlobalFree (m_hBuf);      // Free the global memory
        m_hBuf = NULL;            // Set the pointer to NULL
        m_dwSize = 0;             // And the size is 0
        UpdateAllViews (NULL, 1); // Tell the view about it
    }
    CDocument::DeleteContents();
}
```

Close the document class files for now and open the *CGraphicsView* class files. In the class definition, add the following variables in the *protected* section:

```
SCROLLINFO m_siVert;    // This program will need scrolling
SCROLLINFO m_siHorz;    // for sure
int m_nScale;           // Holds the current scale value
LPPICTURE m_pPix;       // Pointer to IPicture interface
```

Now you add the base class function overrides and the message handlers. This would be a good job for the ClassWizard. Override the *OnUpdate()* function. Then add message handlers for *WM_HSCROLL*, *WM_VSCROLL*, *WM_DESTROY* and the three menu items you added to the *IDR_MAINFRAME* menu, *IDM_SCALE_21*, *IDM_SCALE_11*, and *IDM_SCALE_12*. You should have the following functions in the class definition:

```
public:
    virtual void OnUpdate(CView* pSender, LPARAM lHint,
                          CObject* pHint);
private:
    afx_msg void OnHScroll(UINT nSBCode, UINT nPos,
                           CScrollBar* pScrollBar);
    afx_msg void OnVScroll(UINT nSBCode, UINT nPos,
                           CScrollBar* pScrollBar);
```

```
    afx_msg void OnScale11();
    afx_msg void OnScale12();
    afx_msg void OnScale21();
```

Move to the *GraphicsView.cpp* file. The scroll handlers and the menu messages to set the scale are nothing special, but two functions you should look closely at are *OnDraw()* and *OnUpdate()*. When you read a file in the document class, you will be calling the *OnUpdate()* function of the view to let it know that a new graphics file is in place. It takes care of invalidating the window and resetting the scroll bars.

The *OnDraw()* function is called by *CView::OnPaint()* when the view, or a portion of it, becomes invalid and needs repainting. It isn't necessary to override *OnPaint()* because all the work can be done in the *OnDraw()* function. This function calls the *IPicture* interface to render the image to the device context and thus display the image on the screen. After that, it resets the scroll bar information so that the scroll bars appear and have the right scrolling data for the size of the image.

The entire *GraphicsView.cpp* file appears here:

```
// GraphicsView.cpp : implementation of the
//                    CGraphicsView class
//

#include "stdafx.h"
#include "Graphics.h"

#include "GraphicsDoc.h"
#include "GraphicsView.h"

#ifdef _DEBUG
#define new DEBUG_NEW
#undef THIS_FILE
static char THIS_FILE[] = __FILE__;
#endif


/////////////////////////////////////////////////////////////
// CGraphicsView

IMPLEMENT_DYNCREATE(CGraphicsView, CView)

BEGIN_MESSAGE_MAP(CGraphicsView, CView)
    //{{AFX_MSG_MAP(CGraphicsView)
    ON_WM_HSCROLL()
    ON_WM_VSCROLL()
    ON_COMMAND(IDM_SCALE_11, OnScale11)
    ON_COMMAND(IDM_SCALE_12, OnScale12)
    ON_COMMAND(IDM_SCALE_21, OnScale21)
    //}}AFX_MSG_MAP
    // Standard printing commands
    ON_COMMAND(ID_FILE_PRINT, CView::OnFilePrint)
    ON_COMMAND(ID_FILE_PRINT_DIRECT, CView::OnFilePrint)
    ON_COMMAND(ID_FILE_PRINT_PREVIEW,
                           CView::OnFilePrintPreview)
END_MESSAGE_MAP()


/////////////////////////////////////////////////////////////
// CGraphicsView construction/destruction


CGraphicsView::CGraphicsView()
```

```cpp
{
    m_nScale = 100;
    m_pPix = NULL;
}


CGraphicsView::~CGraphicsView()
{
}


BOOL CGraphicsView::PreCreateWindow(CREATESTRUCT& cs)
{
    // TODO: Modify the Window class or styles here
    // by modifying the CREATESTRUCT cs

    return CView::PreCreateWindow(cs);
}

/////////////////////////////////////////////////////////////////
// CGraphicsView drawing

void CGraphicsView::OnDraw(CDC* pDC)
{
    CGraphicsDoc* pDoc = GetDocument();
    ASSERT_VALID(pDoc);

    if (!m_pPix)
        return;
// get width and height of picture
    long hmWidth;
    long hmHeight;
    m_pPix->get_Width(&hmWidth);
    m_pPix->get_Height(&hmHeight);
// Let the DC convert himetric to pixels
    SIZE sz;
    sz.cx = hmWidth;
    sz.cy = hmHeight;
    pDC->HIMETRICtoDP (&sz);
    int nWidth = (sz.cx * m_nScale) / 100;
    int nHeight = (sz.cy * m_nScale) / 100;
    RECT rc;
    GetClientRect(&rc);

    if ((rc.right - rc.left) > nWidth)
    {
        ShowScrollBar(SB_HORZ, FALSE);
        EnableScrollBar (SB_HORZ, ESB_DISABLE_BOTH);
        SetScrollRange (SB_HORZ, 0, nWidth, TRUE);
    }
    else
    {
        ShowScrollBar(SB_HORZ, TRUE);
        m_siHorz.cbSize = sizeof (SCROLLINFO);
        m_siHorz.nMin = 0;
        m_siHorz.fMask = SIF_ALL;
        m_siHorz.nMax = nWidth;
        m_siHorz.nPage = rc.right - rc.left;
```

```
        SetScrollInfo (SB_HORZ, &m_siHorz, true);
        EnableScrollBar (SB_HORZ, ESB_ENABLE_BOTH);
        SetScrollRange (SB_HORZ, 0, nWidth, TRUE);
    }
    if ((rc.bottom - rc.top) > nHeight)
    {
        ShowScrollBar(SB_VERT, FALSE);
        EnableScrollBar (SB_VERT, ESB_DISABLE_BOTH);
    }
    else
    {
        ShowScrollBar(SB_VERT, TRUE);
        m_siVert.cbSize = sizeof (SCROLLINFO);
        m_siVert.nMin = 0;
        m_siVert.fMask = SIF_ALL;
        m_siVert.nMax = nHeight;
        m_siVert.nPage = rc.bottom - rc.top;
        SetScrollInfo (SB_VERT, &m_siVert, true);
        EnableScrollBar (SB_VERT, ESB_ENABLE_BOTH);
        SetScrollRange (SB_VERT, 0, nHeight, TRUE);
    }

    sz.cx = m_siHorz.nPos;
    sz.cy = m_siVert.nPos;
    pDC->DPtoHIMETRIC (&sz);
    sz.cx = (sz.cx * 100) / m_nScale;
    sz.cy = (sz.cy * 100) / m_nScale;

// display the picture
    m_pPix->Render(pDC->m_hDC,
        0,              //  Horizontal position of image
                        //  in the device context
        0,              //  Vertical position of image in
                        //  the device context
        nWidth,         //  Destination rectangle width
        nHeight,        //  Destination rectangle depth
        sz.cx,          //  Horizontal offset in source
        hmHeight - sz.cy, //  Vertical offset in source
        hmWidth,        //  Amount to copy horizontally in
                        //  source picture
        -hmHeight,      //  Amount to copy vertically in
                        //  source picture
        &rc);           //  Pointer destination rectangle
    }
}

/////////////////////////////////////////////////////////
// CGraphicsView printing

BOOL CGraphicsView::OnPreparePrinting(CPrintInfo* pInfo)
{
    // default preparation
    return DoPreparePrinting(pInfo);
}


void CGraphicsView::OnBeginPrinting(CDC* /*pDC*/,
```

```
                                          CPrintInfo* /*pInfo*/)
{
    // TODO: add extra initialization before printing
}


void CGraphicsView::OnEndPrinting(CDC* /*pDC*/,
                                    CPrintInfo* /*pInfo*/)
{
    // TODO: add cleanup after printing
}


/////////////////////////////////////////////////////////////
// CGraphicsView diagnostics

#ifdef _DEBUG
void CGraphicsView::AssertValid() const
{
    CView::AssertValid();
}


void CGraphicsView::Dump(CDumpContext& dc) const
{
    CView::Dump(dc);
}


CGraphicsDoc* CGraphicsView::GetDocument() // non-debug version
                                          // is inline
{
 ASSERT(m_pDocument->IsKindOf(RUNTIME_CLASS(CGraphicsDoc)));
    return (CGraphicsDoc*)m_pDocument;
}
#endif //_DEBUG


/////////////////////////////////////////////////////////////
// CGraphicsView message handlers

void CGraphicsView::OnHScroll(UINT nSBCode, UINT nPos,
                         CScrollBar* pScrollBar)
{
    RECT    rClip;
    GetClientRect (&rClip);
    switch (nSBCode)
    {
        case SB_BOTTOM:         //  Scrolls to lower right.
        case SB_ENDSCROLL:      //  Ends scroll.
            return;
        case SB_LINEDOWN:       //  Scrolls one line down.
            if ((m_siHorz.nPos + (int) m_siHorz.nPage) >=
                                      m_siHorz.nMax)
                return;
            ++m_siHorz.nPos;
            ScrollWindowEx (-1, 0, NULL, &rClip, NULL,
                        NULL, SW_ERASE | SW_INVALIDATE);
            break;
        case SB_LINEUP:          //  Scrolls one line right.
            if (m_siHorz.nPos <= 0)
```

```
            return
        --m_siHorz.nPos;
        ScrollWindowEx (1, 0, NULL, &rClip, NULL,
                        NULL, SW_ERASE | SW_INVALIDATE);
        break;
    case SB_PAGEDOWN:        // Scrolls one page right.
        if (m_siHorz.nPos >= m_siHorz.nMax)
            return;
        Pos = m_siHorz.nPos;
        m_siHorz.nPos += m_siHorz.nPage / 2;
        if ((m_siHorz.nPos + (int) m_siHorz.nPage) >
                                        m_siHorz.nMax)
        {
            m_siHorz.nPos = m_siHorz.nMax -
                                        m_siHorz.nPage;
            Scroll=m_siHorz.nMax - m_siHorz.nPage - Pos;
        }
        else
            Scroll = m_siHorz.nPage / 2;
        ScrollWindowEx (-Scroll, 0, NULL, &rClip, NULL,
                        NULL, SW_ERASE | SW_INVALIDATE);
        break;
    case SB_PAGEUP:          // Scrolls one page left.
        if (m_siHorz.nPos == 0)
            return;
        Pos = m_siHorz.nPos;
        m_siHorz.nPos -= m_siHorz.nPage / 2;
        if (m_siHorz.nPos < 0)
        {
            m_siHorz.nPos = 0;
            Scroll = Pos;
        }
        else
            Scroll = m_siHorz.nPage / 2;
        ScrollWindowEx (Scroll, 0, NULL,
                        &rClip, NULL, NULL,
                        SW_ERASE | SW_INVALIDATE);
        break;
    case SB_THUMBPOSITION:   //  The user has dragged the
                             //  thumb and released the
                             //  mouse button. The nPos
                             //  parameter indicates the
                             //  position of the thumb at
                             //  the end of the end
    case SB_THUMBTRACK:      //  The user is dragging the
                             //  thumb. This message is
                             //  sent repeatedly until
                             //  the user releases the
                             //  mouse button. The nPos
                             //  parameter indicates the
                             //  final thumb position.
        ScrollWindowEx (m_siHorz.nPos - nPos, 0, NULL,
                        &rClip, NULL, NULL,
                        SW_ERASE | SW_INVALIDATE);
        m_siHorz.nPos = nPos;// HIWORD(wParam);
        break;
```

```
        case SB_TOP:            //  Scrolls to upper left.
            return;
            break;
    }
    SetScrollInfo (SB_HORZ, &m_siHorz, true);
}

void CGraphicsView::OnVScroll(UINT nSBCode, UINT nPos,
                              CScrollBar* pScrollBar)
{
    RECT    rClip;
    GetClientRect (&rClip);
    switch (nSBCode)
    {
    int     Pos, Scroll;
        case SB_BOTTOM:         //  Scrolls to lower right.
        case SB_ENDSCROLL:      //  Ends scroll.
            return;
        case SB_LINEDOWN:       //  Scrolls one line down.
            if ((m_siVert.nPos + (int) m_siVert.nPage) >=
                                            m_siVert.nMax)
                return;
            ScrollWindowEx (0, -1, NULL, &rClip, NULL,
                        NULL, SW_ERASE | SW_INVALIDATE);
            m_siVert.nPos += 1;
            break;
        case SB_LINEUP:         //  Scrolls one line up.
            if (m_siVert.nPos == 0)
                return;
            ScrollWindowEx (0, 1, NULL, &rClip, NULL,
                        NULL, SW_ERASE | SW_INVALIDATE);
            m_siVert.nPos -= 1;
            break;
        case SB_PAGEDOWN:       //  Scrolls one page down.
            if (m_siVert.nPos >= m_siVert.nMax)
                return;
            Pos = m_siVert.nPos;
            m_siVert.nPos += m_siVert.nPage / 2;
            if (m_siVert.nPos > m_siVert.nMax)
            {
                m_siVert.nPos = m_siVert.nMax;
                Scroll = Pos;
            }
            else
                Scroll = m_siVert.nPage / 2;
            ScrollWindowEx (0, -Scroll,
                        NULL, &rClip, NULL, NULL,
                        SW_ERASE | SW_INVALIDATE);
            break;
        case SB_PAGEUP:         //  Scrolls one page up.
            if (m_siVert.nPos == 0)
                return;
            Pos = m_siVert.nPos;
            m_siVert.nPos -= m_siVert.nPage / 2;
            if (m_siVert.nPos < 0)
            {
```

```
                m_siVert.nPos = 0;
                Scroll = Pos;
            }
            else
                Scroll = m_siVert.nPage / 2;
            ScrollWindowEx (0, Scroll, NULL,
                            &rClip, NULL, NULL,
                            SW_ERASE | SW_INVALIDATE);
            break;
        case SB_THUMBPOSITION:  //  The user has dragged the
                                //  thumb and released the
                                //  mouse button. The nPos
                                //  parameter indicates the
                                //  position of the thumb at
                                //  the end
        case SB_THUMBTRACK:     //  The user is dragging the
                                //  thumb. This message is
                                //  sent repeatedly until
                                //  the user releases the
                                //  mouse button. The nPos
                                //  parameter indicates the
                                //  position that the thumb
                                //  has been dragged to.
            ScrollWindowEx (0, m_siVert.nPos - nPos, NULL,
                            &rClip, NULL, NULL,
                            SW_ERASE | SW_INVALIDATE);
            m_siVert.nPos = nPos;
            break;
        case SB_TOP:            //  Scrolls to upper left.
            return;
    }
    SetScrollInfo (SB_VERT, &m_siVert, true);
}

void CGraphicsView::OnUpdate(CView* pSender,
                             LPARAM lHint, CObject* pHint)
{
    if (pSender == this)
        return;
//
//  If the screen is being cleared, hide the scroll bars.
//
    if (lHint == 1)
    {
        ShowScrollBar(SB_HORZ, FALSE);
        ShowScrollBar(SB_VERT, FALSE);
    }
    LPSTREAM pStream = NULL;
    DWORD dwSize = GetDocument()->GetGlobalSize();
    HGLOBAL hGlobal = GetDocument()->GetGlobalBuffer();
//
//  If there's already a picture, dump it
//
    if (m_pPix)
    {
        m_pPix->Release();
```

```cpp
        m_pPix = NULL;
        Invalidate ();
    }
    if (hGlobal == NULL)
        return;
// Create an IStream* from global memory
    HRESULT hr = CreateStreamOnHGlobal(hGlobal, TRUE,
                                       &pStream);
    _ASSERTE(SUCCEEDED(hr) && pStream);

// Create IPicture from image file
    hr = ::OleLoadPicture(pStream, dwSize, FALSE,
                          IID_IPicture, (LPVOID *)&m_pPix);
    _ASSERTE(SUCCEEDED(hr) && m_pPix);
    pStream->Release();
    m_nScale = 100;
    memset (&m_siVert, '\0', sizeof (SCROLLINFO));
    memset (&m_siHorz, '\0', sizeof (SCROLLINFO));
    m_siVert.cbSize = sizeof (SCROLLINFO);
    m_siHorz.cbSize = sizeof (SCROLLINFO);
    Invalidate ();
}


// Set the scale for normal image size
void CGraphicsView::OnScale11()
{
    if (m_nScale == 100)
        return;
    m_nScale = 100;
    memset (&m_siVert, '\0', sizeof (SCROLLINFO));
    memset (&m_siHorz, '\0', sizeof (SCROLLINFO));
    m_siVert.cbSize = sizeof (SCROLLINFO);
    m_siHorz.cbSize = sizeof (SCROLLINFO);
    Invalidate ();
}


// Set the scale for a half-size image
void CGraphicsView::OnScale12()
{
    if (m_nScale == 50)
        return;
    m_nScale = 50;
    memset (&m_siVert, '\0', sizeof (SCROLLINFO));
    memset (&m_siHorz, '\0', sizeof (SCROLLINFO));
    m_siVert.cbSize = sizeof (SCROLLINFO);
    m_siHorz.cbSize = sizeof (SCROLLINFO);
    Invalidate ();
}


// Set the scale to double the image size
void CGraphicsView::OnScale21()
{
    if (m_nScale == 200)
        return;
    m_nScale = 200;
    memset (&m_siVert, '\0', sizeof (SCROLLINFO));
```

```
    memset (&m_siHorz, '\Ø', sizeof (SCROLLINFO));
    m_siVert.cbSize = sizeof (SCROLLINFO);
    m_siHorz.cbSize = sizeof (SCROLLINFO);
    Invalidate ();
}
```

Next, code the scroll message handlers. The case statements in these functions tend to be long because there are so many cases to handle and each has to be duplicated for both the vertical and horizontal scroll bars.

In the project on the companion CD-ROM, I removed *FWS_ADDTOTITLE* from the frame window style in the *PreCreateWindow()* function to keep the file or "Untitled" from appearing in the frame title bar.

There are some images on the companion CD-ROM you can use to test and even improve this project. Sorry to put you through the details of scrolling an image, but it will make you appreciate the next tip.

626. *Using the CScrollView Class*

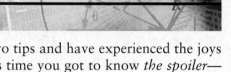

Now that you've been properly introduced to *CView* in the past two tips and have experienced the joys of scrolling in Tip 625, "Drawing Graphics Objects in *CView*," it's time you got to know *the spoiler*— the *CScrollView* class. This class is nothing but a *CView* with a couple of scroll bars attached, but that's enough for *CScrollView* to become your last stop when looking for a view class for your application.

CScrollView probably will be your most commonly used base class. It's plain enough that you can impose your own programming style on it but powerful enough that it can save you a lot of work. It manages both the windows viewport and mapping modes, adds or hides scroll bars as necessary, scrolls automatically in response to scroll messages, and supports the mouse wheel messages for scrolling. All you need to do is calculate how wide and how deep your application's overall display area is and notify the scroll controls.

First, apply *CScrollView* to the text display application from Tip 624, "Displaying Text in *CView*." Create a new application (the one on the companion CD-ROM is an SDI, but this works the same in an MDI application). Name this one "TextScroll," and when you get to the wizard's last page, select *CScrollView* as the base class for your view.

Before starting on the view, add the *CLine* class to the application and set up the *CTextScrollDoc* class the same as you did in the *Text* application in Tip 624. These will work the same as they did there; this application only applies the *CScrollView* to the view class.

In Tip 624 the code is a bit loose on tab expansion—it just sets the output rectangle to the width of the window and lets the *DrawText()* function expand the tabs—but for *CScrollView* you have to be more precise. Ordinarily, you could use the *MeasureText()* function to determine the line length, but it doesn't calculate the line length with expanded tabs. To figure the longest line (and hence, the width of your application) you yourself must expand the tabs. It's worth the effort because it gives your application control over the tab stops.

You will also add a left, right, top, and bottom margin to the text. This keeps the text from butting up against the window frame and makes it more readable. The margins will be initialized to 5 logical points each, but you very easily could let the user change them.

Other than these few variables, there's nothing to add to the basic class definition but the function to expand the tabs. The only message handlers and virtual function overrides you need already have been added by the MFC AppWizard. How much easier can this get?

Using the ClassView panel, add a member function to *CTextScrollView*. The return type is *void* and the only parameter is a reference to a *CString*. Name the function simply "ExpandTabs" and make it *protected* or *private*. Your class definition should look like the following code:

```
class CTextScrollView : public CScrollView
{
protected: // create from serialization only
    CTextScrollView();
    DECLARE_DYNCREATE(CTextScrollView)

// Attributes
public:
    CTextScrollDoc* GetDocument();

// Operations
public:

// Overrides
    // ClassWizard generated virtual function overrides
    //{{AFX_VIRTUAL(CTextScrollView)
    public:
    virtual void OnDraw(CDC* pDC);  // overridden to draw
                                    // this view
    virtual BOOL PreCreateWindow(CREATESTRUCT& cs);
    protected:
    virtual void OnInitialUpdate(); // called first time
                                    // after construct
  virtual BOOL OnPreparePrinting(CPrintInfo* pInfo);
  virtual void OnBeginPrinting(CDC* pDC, CPrintInfo* pInfo);
  virtual void OnEndPrinting(CDC* pDC, CPrintInfo* pInfo);
    //}}AFX_VIRTUAL

// Implementation
public:
    virtual ~CTextScrollView();
#ifdef _DEBUG
    virtual void AssertValid() const;
    virtual void Dump(CDumpContext& dc) const;
#endif

protected:

// Generated message map functions
protected:
    void ExpandTabs (CString &strText);
    //{{AFX_MSG(CTextScrollView)
        // NOTE - the ClassWizard will add and remove member functions here.
        //    DO NOT EDIT what you see in these blocks of
        //    generated code !
    //}}AFX_MSG
    DECLARE_MESSAGE_MAP()
private:
    CFont m_Font;
    int m_nTabStops;
    int m_nLeftMargin;
    int m_nRightMargin;
```

```
    int m_nTopMargin;
    int m_nBottomMargin;
};
```

If you are creating a multiple-document interface application and don't expect to need different fonts for each instance of the view, you might want to make *m_Font* a static variable and initialize it once, as shown in Tip 111, "Finishing the Program Editor." For an SDI application, of course, you reuse the same view.

With the preliminary work done, let's take a look at the coding. Be sure to add the *Line.h* file to the list of include files. Notice that in the *OnInitialUpdate()* function, the wizard has set the scroll sizes to 100×100 logical points. Before you can paint anything in a *CScrollView*, even a blank screen, you have to set these values. Your first call to *OnPaint()* will reset them.

The variables are initialized in the class constructor. The margin values used here are comfortable and keep the text away from the window frame, but you might want to adjust them to your own taste. There's nothing to clean up in the destructor:

```
#include    "Line.h"
/////////////////////////////////////////////////////////////
// CTextScrollView construction/destruction

CTextScrollView::CTextScrollView()
{
    m_Font.CreatePointFont (100, "Courier New");
    m_nTabStops = 4;
    m_nLeftMargin = m_nRightMargin = 5;
    m_nTopMargin = m_nBottomMargin = 5;
}


CTextScrollView::~CTextScrollView()
{
}
```

There are only two other functions you have to modify for this basic project. The first is the *OnDraw()* function that was added by the wizard. The second is the *ExpandTabs()* function you added. The code for the *OnDraw()* function is shown here:

```
/////////////////////////////////////////////////////////////
// CTextScrollView drawing

void CTextScrollView::OnDraw(CDC* pDC)
{
    CTextScrollDoc* pDoc = GetDocument();
    ASSERT_VALID(pDoc);

    int nLine;
    CSize sz;
    int nCount = pDoc->m_Text.GetSize ();
    if (!nCount)
        return;
    CString strText;
    CFont *fontOld = pDC->SelectObject (&m_Font);
    RECT rc;
//  Don't need these two lines with CScrollView
//  GetClientRect (&rc);
//  int nBottom = rc.bottom;
```

```
    rc.top = m_nTopMargin;
    rc.left = m_nLeftMargin;
    int nWidestLine = 0;
    int nRunningDepth = m_nTopMargin;
    for (nLine = 0; nLine < nCount; ++nLine)
    {
        strText = pDoc->m_Text[nLine].GetData();
        if (strText.IsEmpty ())
        {
            sz = pDC->GetTextExtent (" ", 1);
        }
        else if (strText.FindOneOf ("\t") < 0)
        {
            sz = pDC->GetTextExtent (strText);
        }
        else
        {
            ExpandTabs (strText);
            sz = pDC->GetTextExtent (strText);
        }
        if (sz.cx > nWidestLine)
            nWidestLine = sz.cx;
        rc.right = sz.cx + m_nRightMargin;
        rc.bottom = sz.cy;
        pDC->DrawText (strText, &rc,
                    DT_SINGLELINE | DT_LEFT | DT_NOPREFIX);
        rc.top += sz.cy;
        rc.bottom += sz.cy;
        nRunningDepth += sz.cy
//
//  This time we're not gonna bail out.
//      if (rc.top > nBottom)
//          break;
    }
// calculate the total size of this view
    sz.cx = nWidestLine + m_nLeftMargin + m_nRightMargin;
    sz.cy = nRunningDepth + m_nBottomMargin;
    SetScrollSizes(MM_TEXT, sz);

    pDC->SelectObject (fontOld);
}
```

After some housekeeping chores—setting up variables, getting the number of lines in the document, getting the default rectangle, and so on—the function enters the loop to set the text. Use a copy of the string; it may be modified, and you don't want the original string to change in case you later want to write it back to disk.

If the string is empty (it's a blank line), it measures the size of a single space. For an empty string, *GetTextExtent()* returns 0 for both members of *CSize*, but the spaces make it return the line depth. If you don't do this, the empty line just won't be apparent in the view. If there are no tabs in the line, measure the line and you're ready to set it. If there are tabs, it calls a function to expand the tabs. The function is shown next.

If the current line is the widest encountered so far, save it in a variable. You use it later to set the scroll extents. The next couple of lines set the text output rectangle and call *DrawText()*. Notice this time that the *DT_EXPANDTABS* isn't included in the flags. It wouldn't make any difference because at this point the output string shouldn't have any tabs.

After the text is output, you reset the rectangle for the next line and save the cumulative depth. You could have used a constant value for the line depth, but later on you might want to expand the function to output text of different sizes. Measuring it each time around prepares the function for that possibility.

Last comes the *CScrollView* magic. Add the margins to the widest line variable to get the horizontal size of your window, and use the running depth variable for the height of the window. Of course, not all of the window is going to be visible, but *CScrollView* will take care of setting the visible extent. Call *SetScrollSizes()*, notify *CScrollView* of the size of the text area, restore the old font, and the function is finished.

Now take a look at the *ExpandTabs()* function. The constructor set the tab stops to 4 (having programmed in C for so long, I've this unnatural fixation on 4 for the size of a tab; make it whatever value you like).

```
//////////////////////////////////////////////////////////////
// CTextScrollView message handlers

void CTextScrollView::ExpandTabs(CString &strText)
{
CString str;
LPCSTR  s;
int     n, nLen;
int     nPos;          // Position in converted line

    str.Empty();     // Make sure the copy is empty
    s = strText;     // Get a pointer to the text
    nLen = strText.GetLength ();   // And the length
    for (n = 0, nPos = 0; n < nLen; ++n)
    {
        if (*s == '\t')  // Tab encountered?
        {
            if (m_nTabStops > 0)   // Do this only for
            {                              // valid values
                int nSpaces=m_nTabStops-(nPos % m_nTabStops);
                for (int x = 0; x < nSpaces; ++x)
                {
                    str += ' ';    // Add requisite spaces
                    ++nPos;        // Increment current pos
                }
            }
        }
        else
        {
            str += *s;             // Transfer the character
            ++nPos;                // Increment current pos
        }
        ++s;                       // Increment pointer
    }
    strText = str;                 // Return the modified
                                   // string in CString
}
```

This function replaces the tab characters in the string with the necessary number of spaces to bring it up to an even tab stop. When a tab is encountered, figure the number of spaces by doing a modulo division on the position in the *expanded* line. Then subtract that number from the *m_nTabStops* variable. If it lands exactly on a tab stop, the number of spaces to be added is *m_nTabStops*, and the line jumps to the next tab position, which is what you want. If the character is one after the tab, *m_nTabStops* − *1* spaces are added, and so on.

If you don't want to expand tabs, set the *m_nTabStops* to 0 or a negative value. When the loop completes, the tabs will have been stripped out, leaving the bare string. Setting *m_nTabStops* to 1 causes all tabs to be replaced by a single space.

Before leaving *CScrollView*, converting the graphics application from Tip 625 to use this base class is even easier than converting the text program. Create a new project using *CScrollView* as the base class. You can call this one "Graphics" as well. (There are MDI and SDI versions of this application on the companion CD-ROM.) Set up everything as you did in Tip 625, except *don't* add message handlers for the vertical and horizontal scrolls. Let the base class handle them. The only function you need to modify is the *OnDraw()* virtual function. The code is shown here:

```
//////////////////////////////////////////////////////////
// CGraphicsView drawing

void CGraphicsView::OnDraw(CDC* pDC)
{
    if (!m_pPix)
        return;
    CGraphicsDoc* pDoc = GetDocument();
    ASSERT_VALID(pDoc);
// get width and height of picture
    long hmWidth;
    long hmHeight;
    m_pPix->get_Width(&hmWidth);
    m_pPix->get_Height(&hmHeight);
// Let the DC convert himetric to pixels
    SIZE sz;
    sz.cx = hmWidth;
    sz.cy = hmHeight;
    pDC->HIMETRICtoDP (&sz);
    sz.cx = (sz.cx * m_nScale) / 100;
    sz.cy = (sz.cy * m_nScale) / 100;
    RECT rc;
    GetClientRect(&rc);
    SetScrollSizes(MM_TEXT, sz);

// display the picture
    m_pPix->Render(pDC->m_hDC,
                0,         // Horizontal position of
                           // image in the device context
                0,         // Vertical position of image
                           // in the device context
                sz.cx,     // Horizontal dimension of
                           // destination rectangle
                sz.cy,     // Vertical dimension of
                           // destination rectangle
                0,         // Horizontal offset in source
                           // picture
                hmHeight, // Vertical offset in source
                           // picture
                hmWidth,  // Amount to copy horizontally
                           // in source picture
```

```
                -hmHeight,//  Amount to copy vertically
                          //  in source picture
                &rc);     //  Pointer to destination rect
    }
}
```

The only thing you have to calculate is the size of a rectangle to hold the entire image, even if it's larger than the window. Then set the scroll size to let *CScrollView* manage the window extent. The only remaining task is to render the image in the rectangle.

627. *Using the CEditView Class*

You've probably heard the story about why IBM invented the Personal Computer. Supposedly, it was designed around the worst available microprocessor of the time, the Intel 8088, and was intentionally limited by its design. By releasing the design specifications, IBM hoped to sidetrack the growing microcomputer industry enough that its sales of larger computers wouldn't be jeopardized.

Whether the story is true or just the computerland equivalent of an urban legend is irrelevant. What's relevant is that *CEditView* is the PC equivalent in that story. This view is the antithesis of the document/view architecture.

It's derived indirectly from *CView* through *CCtrlView*, which allows you to build a view class from virtually any of the Windows common controls. It's basically an old-style window with an edit control, the way editing windows used to be built before C++.

CEditView has a document attached to it apparently only to satisfy *CView*'s demand for one and to hold the modified flag. The latter is solely to force a call to the document's *Serialize()* function. Even so, the *Serialize()* function only calls *CEditView::SerializeRaw()* to accomplish the reading and writing of data. The document doesn't contain or manage the view's data, and it doesn't read or write it to disk. The actual data—the text being edited—is held in the edit control itself, and under Win32s *CEditView* maintains a copy of it in a *shadow* buffer. (The Win32s platform is a subset of Win32 used in earlier versions of Windows running under DOS; the shadow buffer isn't used in Win32 versions such as Window 95, Windows 98, or Windows NT.)

CEditView has all the functionality of a multi-line edit box that you would place on a dialog box, because that's basically all it is. You're limited to a single font, a single point size, a single text color, and a single background color. Its best feature is that it is so easy to implement. You can build a project based on *CEditView* and begin editing ASCII text files immediately after compiling it. It's there if you need to add a quick, text-only editing window to a project, but beyond that it has little to recommend itself.

628. *Inserting Text in the Edit View*

There is no function in *CEditView* for directly inserting text into the view. Normally, keystrokes and strings to be added to the view—and subsequently to the document—are passed on to the edit control. If you want to insert text from another source, for example, as the result of text entered through a dialog box, you have to resort to an indirect method. Too, you might want the Enter key to add an indent to the next paragraph automatically.

You could insert a string by emulating a series of keystrokes, repeatedly calling the *OnKeyDown()*, *OnChar()*, and *OnKeyUp()* functions for each character in the string, but that involves a lot of unnecessary overhead.

Text may be inserted into the edit control by sending it the *EM_REPLACESEL* message, along with a pointer to the string to be inserted. Any text currently selected in the control will be replaced by the string. If the text is really to be inserted, make sure that nothing is selected.

You can add an *Insert()* function to your *CEditView*-derived class that calls this message for you. You can overload it to accept a character pointer, a single character, or a *CString* object:

```
void CMyView::Insert (const char *szText)
{
    ASSERT(this->m_hWnd)
    SendMessage (EM_REPLACESEL,(WPARAM) 0,(LPARAM) szText);
}

void CMyView::Insert (CString &strText)
{
    Insert ((LPCSTR) strText);
}

void CMyView::Insert (char ch)
{
char szText[2];
    szText[0] = ch;
    szText[1] = '\0';
    Insert (szText);
}
```

If any text is selected in the edit control, it will be replaced by the string you send it. Otherwise, the text will be inserted at the caret position.

629. *Understanding Insert and Overstrike Modes*

You might have noticed in the Program Editor project from Tip 111, "Finishing the Program Editor," that the editing views always inserted the text you typed and there was no method of changing it so that one typed character replaced the next character in the window, an *overstrike* mode.

An *insert mode* would be used to add text to the document without overwriting any text. An *overstrike mode* would automatically replace the character immediately after the caret position with the new keystroke.

Although Windows intercepts and interprets Insert key depressions, inserting or overstriking text is not an operating system function. The Insert key does nothing but send a signal to the operating system that it has been pressed, and Windows then transfers that information to the window with the keyboard focus through a Windows message. It does set an internal flag for the key, which your program may query using the *GetKeyState()* function.

The Windows edit control is in perpetual insert mode, and you can't set it to an overstrike mode. Your program, however, can emulate an overstrike mode by intercepting the keystroke, checking whether the view is in insert or overstrike mode, and issuing the proper commands.

630. *Adding an Overstrike Mode to the Edit View*

You can use the system's internal flag to keep track of the state of the Insert key, but it's subject to change at any time. Other programs running on your machine can change it at any time, and you have to keep tracking it to make sure that your internal insert or overstrike functions match its state. You can get the Insert key's toggle state by calling *GetKeyState(VK_INSERT)*.

The overstrike mode, however, is just a state of mind, and I prefer to ignore the system's internal state and keep track of the insert mode within the views. This makes it immune to sudden changes, and in an MDI application, each view can maintain its own insert state. You also could maintain the insert flag in the *CMainFrame* class to make it common to all MDI views.

For starters, create a new project named "EditV." It can be an MDI or SDI. The program on the companion CD-ROM is an MDI application, so you can see how each instance of an edit view can track its own insert flag. Use *CEditView* as the base class for your view.

Start with the *CMainFrame* class. You can add a standard indicator where you can display "INS" or "OVR" for the insert status. You have to set the text in the indicator, however; Windows won't do that for you. Visual C++ has a predefined indicator ID, *ID_INDICATOR_OVR*, for the insert status. Alternatively, you can add the LED indicator from Tip 506, "Control Bar Classes." The LED will be used in this example, but the idea is the same: To go without it, you don't need to load the icons, but you do need to add the function to change the indicator text. Using the ClassView pane, add a member function to *CMainFrame* named "SetOverstrike" and give it a single parameter, a *bool* type named *bOverstrike*. At the top of the *FrameWnd.cpp* file, add *ID_INDICATOR_OVR* as the last member of the *indicators* array. Also add two *HICON* variables named "m_iconGreenOn" and "m_iconGreenOff."

Copy the LED icons from the project in Tip 506 into the *RES* directory, and import them into your project using the IDs *IDI_LEDGREENON* and *IDI_LEDGREENOFF*. Load the icons in the constructor by calling *LoadImage()*. Remember that *LoadIcon()* wants to load the images as 32×32 pixel icons, which is too large for the status bar. Increase the width of the overstrike pane. Note that by following Windows logic, you're going to set the *overstrike* mode, not the *insert* mode. When you're done, the *CMainFrame* class should look like the following code:

```cpp
static UINT indicators[] =
{
    ID_SEPARATOR,           // status line indicator
    ID_INDICATOR_CAPS,
    ID_INDICATOR_NUM,
    ID_INDICATOR_SCRL,
    ID_INDICATOR_OVR,
};


/////////////////////////////////////////////////////////////
// CMainFrame construction/destruction

CMainFrame::CMainFrame()
{
    m_iconGreenOn = (HICON) LoadImage(
                AfxGetInstanceHandle(),
                MAKEINTRESOURCE(IDI_LEDGREENON),
                IMAGE_ICON,
                16, 16, LR_DEFAULTCOLOR);
    m_iconGreenOff = (HICON) LoadImage(
```

```
                    AfxGetInstanceHandle(),
                    MAKEINTRESOURCE(IDI_LEDGREENOFF),
                    IMAGE_ICON,
                    16, 16, LR_DEFAULTCOLOR);
}

CMainFrame::~CMainFrame()
{
}

int CMainFrame::OnCreate(LPCREATESTRUCT lpCreateStruct)
{
    if (CMDIFrameWnd::OnCreate(lpCreateStruct) == -1)
        return -1;

    if (!m_wndToolBar.CreateEx(this, TBSTYLE_FLAT,
                        WS_CHILD | WS_VISIBLE | CBRS_TOP
                        | CBRS_GRIPPER | CBRS_TOOLTIPS
                        | CBRS_FLYBY | CBRS_SIZE_DYNAMIC) ||
        !m_wndToolBar.LoadToolBar(IDR_MAINFRAME))
    {
        TRACE0("Failed to create toolbar\n");
        return -1;      // fail to create
    }

    if (!m_wndStatusBar.Create(this) ||
        !m_wndStatusBar.SetIndicators(indicators,
          sizeof(indicators)/sizeof(UINT)))
    {
        TRACE0("Failed to create status bar\n");
        return -1;      // fail to create
    }

    int nIndex=m_wndStatusBar.CommandToIndex
                                (ID_INDICATOR_OVR);
    m_wndStatusBar.SetPaneInfo (nIndex,
                    ID_INDICATOR_OVR, SBPS_NORMAL, 60);
    SetOverstike (true);

    // TODO: Delete these three lines if you don't want the
    // toolbar to be dockable
    m_wndToolBar.EnableDocking(CBRS_ALIGN_ANY);
    EnableDocking(CBRS_ALIGN_ANY);
    DockControlBar(&m_wndToolBar);

    return 0;
}

BOOL CMainFrame::PreCreateWindow(CREATESTRUCT& cs)
{
    if( !CMDIFrameWnd::PreCreateWindow(cs) )
        return FALSE;
    // TODO: Modify the Window class or styles here by
    // modifying the CREATESTRUCT cs

    return TRUE;
```

```
}

///////////////////////////////////////////////////////////
// CMainFrame diagnostics

#ifdef _DEBUG
void CMainFrame::AssertValid() const
{
    CMDIFrameWnd::AssertValid();
}

void CMainFrame::Dump(CDumpContext& dc) const
{
    CMDIFrameWnd::Dump(dc);
}

#endif //_DEBUG

///////////////////////////////////////////////////////////
// CMainFrame message handlers

void CMainFrame::SetOverstrike(bool bOverstrike)
{
    int nIndex = m_wndStatusBar.CommandToIndex
                              (ID_INDICATOR_OVR);
    if (bOverstrike)
    {
        m_wndStatusBar.GetStatusBarCtrl().SetIcon (nIndex,
                                        m_iconGreenOff);
        m_wndStatusBar.GetStatusBarCtrl().SetText ("OVR",
                                        nIndex, 0);
    }
    else
    {
        m_wndStatusBar.GetStatusBarCtrl().SetIcon (nIndex,
                                        m_iconGreenOn);
        m_wndStatusBar.GetStatusBarCtrl().SetText ("INS",
                                        nIndex, 0);
    }
}
```

Move to the *CEditView* class, add a *private* variable of type *bool*, and name it "m_bOverstrike." Initialize it to *false* in the constructor if you want the views to start up in insert mode or to *true* for overstrike mode. Add three message handlers: *WM_CHAR*, *WM_KEYDOWN*, and *WM_SETFOCUS*. Windows does not send a *WM_CHAR* message when the Insert key is pressed, so you must intercept it in the message handler for *WM_KEYDOWN*. The code for that function is shown here (*VK_INSERT* is the predefined value for the Insert key):

```
void CEditVView::OnKeyDown(UINT nChar, UINT nRepCnt,
                                       UINT nFlags)
{
    CEditView::OnKeyDown(nChar, nRepCnt, nFlags);
    if (nChar == VK_INSERT)
    {
        m_bOverstrike = !m_bOverstrike;
        CMainFrame *frame =
```

```
                    (CMainFrame *) AfxGetApp()->GetMainWnd();
        frame->SetOverstrike (m_bOverstrike);
    }
}
```

The code for the *ON_CHAR* message handler is just as simple. As you develop an application, you will probably expand this function to handle special characters and such. Remember that the edit control inserts a character by replacing the current selection. If the internal values for the start and end of the selected text are the same, no text is selected, and the new text simply is inserted into the text. The secret to overstrike mode is to select the *next* character before inserting your new one.

```
void CEditVView::OnChar(UINT nChar, UINT nRepCnt, UINT nFlags)
{
    if (m_bOverstrike && (nChar >= ' '))
    {
        int nStart, nEnd;
        GetEditCtrl().GetSel (nStart, nEnd);
        if (nStart == nEnd)
            GetEditCtrl().SetSel (nStart, nStart + 1);
    }
    CEditView::OnChar(nChar, nRepCnt, nFlags);
}
```

If the overstrike mode is true *and* the new character isn't a control character, test to see whether any text is selected. If it is, the user is going to replace that text anyway, so you don't have to do anything. If, however, the beginning and end selection values are the same, set the selected text to one character after the start. Then let Windows handle the message normally.

Finally, when the view has the focus, you set the indicator on the main window frame to the proper value. Handle that in the *WM_SETFOCUS* message handler:

```
void CEditVView::OnSetfocus()
{
    CMainFrame *frame =
                    (CMainFrame *) AfxGetApp()->GetMainWnd();
    frame->SetOverstrike (m_bOverstrike);
}
```

Your application should now sport an overstrike mode. If it's an MDI application, try starting two edit windows and you will see the indicator change to match the state of each view.

631. *Saving and Retrieving a Text File with the Edit View*

Normally, when you read and write a plain text file using the edit view, the document object just calls a *SerializeRaw()* function in the *CEditView* base class. If your project works directly on program source files and the file data must be reproduced faithfully, this is the best method to use.

However, at times your project might have to store additional information in a plain text file. In this case, it becomes something more than just a plain text file. The file extension should reflect this so that it won't accidentally be opened by another program, such as *NotePad.exe*.

Assume that you have to write a simple office memo program. You don't need the whistles and bells of embedded HTML, and you don't want to get involved in a project that's akin to building the *Titanic*.

You do, however, need to save some basic information, such as who created the document, when it was created, the name of the last recipient, and the time it was sent. Perhaps even a topic and a reference field would be handy.

You can save all this information in the document object (it's not as though the document in a *CEditView* application has a lot to do) and store and retrieve it before the view's *SerializeRaw()* function gets hold of it.

Create a simple application named "MEMO." It can be a single-document interface, but make sure that *CEditView* is the base class for your view.

The first thing you do is edit the *IDR_MAINFRAME* entry in the string table to make it look like the following. You could have done this when you created the project, but you really don't need to register this file type.

```
Memo\n\nMemo\nMemo Files (*.mem)\n.mem\nMemo.Document
\nMemo Document
```

Create a dialog box similar to Figure 631. The figure shows the static fields with borders around them so that you can see their respective locations and sizes; you might not want the borders in the finished dialog box. Give the static edit fields with a border around them resource IDs; you will need them to create class variables.

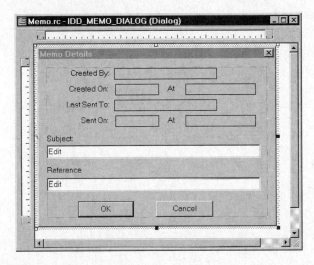

Figure 631   *The dialog box in Memo.exe gives the user a place to write and read memos in the file*

Create a class for the dialog box by right-clicking on it in the resource editor and selecting ClassWizard. Add member variables for the static boxes that have a border around them in Figure 631. While you are still in ClassWizard, add the *OnInitDialog()* virtual function and a message handler for *IDOK*, the OK button.

Make a subclass within the dialog class and name it "CData." Add a reference member variable for this class. Your dialog box class header should look like the following:

```
/////////////////////////////////////////////////////////////
// CMemoDlg dialogclass CMemoDlg : public CDialog
{
// Construction
public:

    class CData
    {
    public:
```

```
        CData ();
        CString m_dataCreatedBy;
        CTime   m_dataCreated;
        CString m_dataReference;
        CTime   m_dataSent;
        CString m_dataSentTo;
        CString m_dataSubject;
    friend CArchive& operator<<(CArchive& o, CData& data);
    friend CArchive& operator>>(CArchive& o, CData& data);
    };

// standard constructor
    CMemoDlg(CData &data, CWnd* pParent = NULL);

// Dialog Data
    //{{AFX_DATA(CMemoDlg)
    enum { IDD = IDD_MEMO_DIALOG };
    CString m_strCreatedBy;
    CString m_strCreatedDate;
    CString m_strCreatedTime;
    CString m_strReference;
    CString m_strSentDate;
    CString m_strSentTime;
    CString m_strSentTo;
    CString m_strSubject;
    //}}AFX_DATA


// Overrides
    // ClassWizard generated virtual function overrides
    //{{AFX_VIRTUAL(CMemoDlg)
    protected:
// DDX/DDV support
    virtual void DoDataExchange(CDataExchange* pDX);
    //}}AFX_VIRTUAL

// Implementation
protected:

    // Generated message map functions
    //{{AFX_MSG(CMemoDlg)
    virtual BOOL OnInitDialog();
    virtual void OnOK();
    //}}AFX_MSG
    DECLARE_MESSAGE_MAP()

    CData&  m_Data;
};
```

Notice that the constructor has been changed to include a reference to a *CData* object. This will help to link the container in the document class with the header itself. In the source file, make the *OnInitDialog()* and *OnOK()* functions look like the following (use whatever variable names you used):

```
BOOL CMemoDlg::OnInitDialog()
{
    CDialog::OnInitDialog();
```

```
    m_strCreatedBy = m_Data.m_dataCreatedBy;
    if (m_Data.m_dataCreated != 0)
    {
        m_strCreatedDate.Format ("%02d/%02d/%04d",
            m_Data.m_dataCreated.GetMonth(),
            m_Data.m_dataCreated.GetDay(),
            m_Data.m_dataCreated.GetYear());
        m_strCreatedTime.Format ("%02d:%02d:%02d",
            m_Data.m_dataCreated.GetHour(),
            m_Data.m_dataCreated.GetMinute(),
            m_Data.m_dataCreated.GetSecond());
    }
    if (m_Data.m_dataSent != 0)
    {
        m_strSentDate.Format ("%02d/%02d/%04d",
            m_Data.m_dataSent.GetMonth(),
            m_Data.m_dataSent.GetDay(),
            m_Data.m_dataSent.GetYear());
        m_strSentTime.Format ("%02d:%02d:%02d",
            m_Data.m_dataSent.GetHour(),
            m_Data.m_dataSent.GetMinute(),
            m_Data.m_dataSent.GetSecond());
    }
    m_strSentTo = m_Data.m_dataSentTo;
    m_strSubject = m_Data.m_dataSubject;
    m_strReference = m_Data.m_dataReference;
    UpdateData (FALSE);

// return TRUE unless you set the focus to a control
// EXCEPTION: OCX Property Pages should return FALSE
    return TRUE;
}


void CMemoDlg::OnOK()
{
    UpdateData(TRUE);
    m_Data.m_dataSubject = m_strSubject;
    m_Data.m_dataReference = m_strReference;
    CDialog::OnOK();
}
```

Now create the code for the *CData* class. You only need to initialize the variables in the constructor and define the overloaded operators. Because this is a class embedded in another class, you must address it as such: *CMemoDlg::CData*. Notice that in the operator to write to the archive, you keep a running total of the number of bytes written and then write it at the end. Actually, writing to the archive in a *CEditView* is no problem; reading it back is, and this extra work is for the benefit of reading the file. By writing the total bytes of your header information to the archive and reading it back, you can set the number of bytes to read for the edit control.

```
CMemoDlg::CData::CData ()
{
    m_dataCreatedBy = _T("");
    m_dataCreated = 0;
    m_dataReference = _T("");
    m_dataSent = 0;
```

```
        m_dataSentTo = _T("");
        m_dataSubject = _T("");
}

CArchive& operator<<(CArchive& ar, CMemoDlg::CData& data)
{
        DWORD nBytes;
        ar.WriteString (data.m_dataCreatedBy);
        nBytes = data.m_dataCreatedBy.GetLength();
// Remember that when you use ReadString to read back the
// data, it stops at a newline. Add the newline here and
// after each string. The other variables have fixed
// sizes and already have CArchive overloads.
        ar << '\n';
        nBytes += sizeof ('\n');
        ar.WriteString (data.m_dataSentTo);
        nBytes += data.m_dataSentTo.GetLength ();
        ar << '\n';
        nBytes += sizeof ('\n');
        ar << data.m_dataCreated;
        nBytes += sizeof (CTime);
        ar << data.m_dataSent;
        nBytes += sizeof (CTime);
        ar.WriteString (data.m_dataSubject);
        nBytes += data.m_dataSubject.GetLength();
        ar << '\n';
        nBytes += sizeof ('\n');
        ar.WriteString (data.m_dataReference);
        nBytes += data.m_dataReference.GetLength();
        ar << '\n';
        nBytes += sizeof ('\n');
        nBytes += sizeof (DWORD);
        ar << nBytes;
        return (ar);
}

CArchive& operator>>(CArchive& ar, CMemoDlg::CData& data)
{
        ar.ReadString (data.m_dataCreatedBy);
        ar.ReadString (data.m_dataSentTo);
        ar >> data.m_dataCreated;
        ar >> data.m_dataSent;
        ar.ReadString (data.m_dataSubject);
        ar.ReadString (data.m_dataReference);
        return (ar);
}
```

Open the document class header file. Add the dialog class header file to the list of *include* files at the top. Add a *public* function, *ShowHeader()*, with a *void* return type and no parameters. Add a *private* or *protected* data member, *CMemoDlg::CData m_MemoData*. When you create the dialog box in the *ShowHeader()* function, this will be linked to the reference variable in the dialog box class. Add the *ShowHeader()* function:

```
////////////////////////////////////////////////////////////
// CMemoDoc commands
```

```
void CMemoDoc::ShowHeader()
{
    if (m_MemoData.m_dataCreated == 0)
    {
        m_MemoData.m_dataCreated = CTime::GetCurrentTime ();
        char user[_MAX_PATH];
        DWORD dwSize = _MAX_PATH;
        GetUserName (user, &dwSize);
        m_MemoData.m_dataCreatedBy = user;
    }
    CMemoDlg    md (m_MemoData);
    md.DoModal ();
}
```

The wizard should have included the *OnNewDocument()* override in the document class for you. Use it to clean out the contents of the *m_MemoData* object:

```
BOOL CMemoDoc::OnNewDocument()
{

    if (!CDocument::OnNewDocument())
        return FALSE;

    ((CEditView*)m_viewList.GetHead())->SetWindowText(NULL);

    m_MemoData.m_dataCreated = 0;
    m_MemoData.m_dataCreatedBy.Empty ();
    m_MemoData.m_dataReference.Empty ();
    m_MemoData.m_dataSent = 0;
    m_MemoData.m_dataSentTo.Empty ();
    m_MemoData.m_dataSubject.Empty ();

    return TRUE;
}
```

Now comes the fun part: defining the *Serialize()* function. You get to do something that Microsoft apparently doesn't want, or doesn't expect, you to do. The Microsoft Magi have decreed in their implementation of the accursed *SerializeRaw()* function that you may write to the archive at any point, but you may read it *only* from the beginning of the file. This will cause you only temporary discomfort, really nothing more serious than a root canal. (Actually, they had to do it this way because someone apparently forgot to put a *position* property in *CArchive*).

First, you want to make sure that this is one of your memo files and has a *.mem* extension. If it doesn't, it's a plain text file. Just pass it on to the *SerializeRaw()* function and let it be. Otherwise, you want to read or write your header information first:

```
/////////////////////////////////////////////////////////
// CMemoDoc serialization

void CMemoDoc::Serialize(CArchive& ar)
{
    CString fn = ar.GetFile()->GetFileName();
    int pos;
    if ((pos = fn.FindOneOf(".")) >= 0)
    {
        pos = fn.GetLength() - pos;
        fn = fn.Right (pos);
```

```
            if (!fn.CompareNoCase (".mem"))
            {
                if (ar.IsStoring ())
                {
                    ar << m_MemoData;  // Read header info, then
                                       // drop through to
                                       // SerializeRaw().
                }
                else
                {
                    DWORD dwHeaderSize;
                    ar >> m_MemoData;
                    ar >> dwHeaderSize;
                    CFile* pFile = ar.GetFile();
                    DWORD nFileSize = pFile->GetPosition();
                    nFileSize = pFile->GetLength() -
                                             dwHeaderSize;
                    if (nFileSize/sizeof(TCHAR) >
                                        CEditView::nMaxSize)
                    {
                        AfxMessageBox(AFX_IDP_FILE_TOO_LARGE);
                        return;
                    }
// ReadFromArchive takes the number of
// characters as argument
                    ((CEditView*)m_viewList.GetHead())->
                                ReadFromArchive(ar,
                                (UINT)nFileSize/sizeof(TCHAR));
                    return;
                }
            }
        }
        // CEditView contains an edit control
        // which (sic) handles all serialization
        ((CEditView*)m_viewList.GetHead())->SerializeRaw(ar);
}
```

If this is a memo file, you can save it using the *ar << m_MemoData* operation; then, let the code drop to the *SerializeRaw()* function at the bottom to write the actual text.

Reading it is a bit different. First, read in your data using the *ar >> m_MemoData* operation. Then read the number of bytes taken up by the header. The rest of the code is much the same as in *CEditView::SerializeRaw()*, except that the number of bytes to read is being figured differently.

This seems like a lot of work to find a redeeming use for *CEditView*, but let's face it. After one or two text editors, how much more use can a class like *CEditView* be? Beyond basic text editing, the implementation of the class doesn't make it very flexible, so you have to apply some imagination to it.

632. *Using the CRichEditView Class*

Considering its heritage, you should not be surprised that the *CRichEditView* class suffers from many of the same defects as *CEditView*. It's basically an edit control imposed on a *CView* using the *CCtrlView* class. However, the control in this case is a rich edit control, and it does provide much more flexibility than *CEditView*.

The rich edit control—available only in Windows versions since Windows 95 and Windows NT 3.51—originally was written for DOS to support an older version of Microsoft Word. In its 32-bit incarnation, it provides text and paragraph formatting. If you've used this control in previous versions of Visual C++, you will notice some changes. You may use a variety of fonts, point sizes, text colors, and background colors. The MFC AppWizard doesn't include the code to access these control functions; you yourself have to write it.

In its default implementation, *CRichEditView* allows your application to embed OLE objects. This isn't always desirable, but it's a sanction imposed by the view class, not the control. Once again Microsoft has hobbled a potentially good thing by imposing its programming "wisdom" on the view. At times you could use the display capabilities of a rich edit control, but you don't necessarily want the user to be able to drop just any type file into the document. OLE support isn't a bad thing, but when and whether to use it should be up to the programmer. If you're shooting for a program that can sport the official Windows logo, you probably want to use this capability. However, the vast majority of programs are either in-house development projects or are never intended for a commercial market, and developing them as a Windows logo project is just extra work.

The rich edit control does require OLE. Whether it's on a dialog box or attached to a view, a rich edit control just won't create or initialize until you have initialized OLE. In MFC you do this by calling *AfxOleInit()*. Your application should include this call in the *InitInstance()* member of the application class.

Unlike the document class in a *CEditView* project, much of the work for a rich text editor is performed by the document class, which is derived from *CRichEditDoc*. This is an abstract class, and your derived class must provide the *CreateClientItem()* function, which is a pure virtual function in the base class. This function allows you to paste OLE objects into your document. The MFC AppWizard includes this function in the code it generates for you.

Also, unlike *CEditView*'s document, the rich edit document provides real serialization, and it can read and write OLE objects to a rich text document file.

In the next few tips, you will go through the process of creating a rich edit project, writing the code to format text and dealing with the OLE issues. The companion CD-ROM contains the special toolbars you will need, but if you want to strike off in another direction, you will find that the *WORDPAD* sample on the MSDN CD-ROM contains a number of toolbar images you can use with *CRichEditView*.

633. *Creating a Project Using* CRichEditView

Create a rich edit project by invoking the MFC AppWizard. You can select an MDI or SDI project. For simplicity, the project here will use a single-document interface, but the view class that develops from it will work just as well in an MDI application. Call the application simply "Rich." That will yield short file names for a change.

On Page 3, select Container for the compound document support. This is the minimum required for a rich edit project, and the wizard won't create the project without at least this level of support. Select No for the question "Would you like support for compound files?" If you select Yes, your documents will be stored in the OLE compound document format. If you intend to create and use rich text files, they should be saved in the unstructured, flat format and you should select No. If you do select Yes and later want to change it, this option places a call to *EnableCompoundFile()*, the document class constructor.

Either remove or change the parameter to *FALSE* (it defaults to *TRUE*) to disable compound file support, and use the flat format.

On Page 4, click the Advanced button and enter ".rtf" as the file extension. Close the Advanced dialog box. Continue to Page 6 and select *CRichEditView* as the base class for your view. Click Finish and create the project by clicking OK.

Before you add any code to it, you have a decent project going right now. As with the *CEditView* projects, you can start creating, reading, and writing rich text files as soon as you compile the program. The display won't *look* any different than the project you created using *CEditView*, and the wizard didn't create any menu or toolbar items to take advantage of the display capabilities of the rich text control.

You will, however, notice a few subtle differences in the display. Note that the text has margins around the window frame, just as you added margins in the earlier *CScrollView* project to keep the text from butting against the frame.

The Edit menu has a few new items on it, including Paste Special, in addition to the usual Paste item. This selection allows you to paste complex objects in to your file, including sound, graphics, Web links, even other program files.

Toward the bottom of the Edit menu are some items that might be unfamiliar to you. They are used in compound document support and allow you to embed objects from other programs into your file and edit them from within your program using the application that originally created them.

634. *Understanding Compound Document Support*

Compile the project from the previous tip and run the program. When the program is running, find an object to drop into it. A Microsoft Word document is a good choice. If you don't have Word, try an object created with the Windows Paint program. Both Word and Paint are *server* processes and can be summoned to create or edit a document in place from within your application. Many of the Corel Corporation's products, such as Corel WordPerfect, are server applications, as is Paint Shop Pro, so you also might try one of their files.

Figure 634a shows *rich.exe* with a Word document dropped into it. In Figure 634b, the same program is shown with the Word toolbars and menus attached. Word is running as a server program for your application.

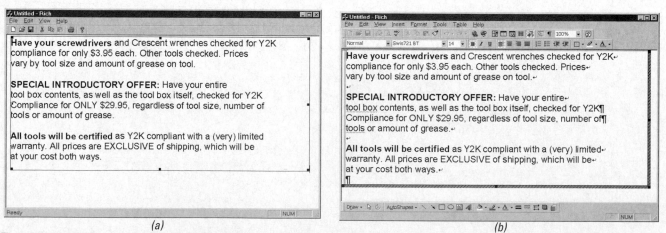

(a)   *(b)*

Figure 634a and 634b   The Rich program (a) after a Word document has been dropped into it. Double-clicking the object (b) opens Word as a server process in your application. Word has attached its toolbars and menu to your window's frame.

When you drop the Word (or other application) document into your window, it is opened and displayed in a border indicating that it is an embedded object. You can resize the object as you would any window by dragging on a corner or side, or you can reduce it to an icon by selecting Object Properties from the Edit menu and then View and checking the button labeled Display as Icon.

However, if you select Document Object and then Edit from the Edit menu, Microsoft Word will start up and the document will be displayed and ready for editing. If you select Document Object and then Open—or double-click on the object—Word will attach itself as a server process for your application. Its menu and toolbars will be merged to your window frame, and you truly can edit the object as a Word document.

This same technique is how programs such as Internet Exploder, uh, *Explorer*, are able to open these documents without leaving the browser or application. This is the *container* level of compound document support.

635. *Understanding OLE Container Support*

If you look at the list of files the MFC AppWizard created for your project, you will see a couple named *CntrItem.h* and *CntrItem.cpp*. These files implement the container class. Support for this class is provided through the *CreateClientItem()* function the wizard added to your document class. In the base class this is a *pure virtual* function, meaning that it was not implemented and any derived classes must provide a body of code for it. The wizard-generated code simply returns a pointer to a newly created object of this class (in the first line, *const* should immediately follow the parameter list):

```
CRichEditCntrItem* CRichDoc::CreateClientItem(REOBJECT* preo)
                                                    const
{
    return new CRichCntrItem(preo, (CRichDoc*) this);
}
```

The document's base class contains full support to serialize these objects, and they may be stored as part of your rich text file and read back when you later open the file for editing.

The object may be totally embedded in your document, or you may embed just a *link* to it. If you store a link, the object isn't copied into your file directly, and you may continue to edit and maintain it outside your program using the original application that created it. Any changes made to the original document will be reflected in your document.

If you choose to embed the object in your document, the entire contents of the file are copied into your file, and any changes made to the original will not be reflected in your document. Essentially, the embedded object is a new file contained as a subdocument in your file.

The embedded object contains information about the server process that should be called when you select the item and edit it.

636. *Understanding Server and Mini Server Support*

Had you chosen Both Container and Server support when you created the project, your program would have been able to work as a server process from within other applications, much as Word or Paint works with your rich text project. Projects created using the *CRichEditView* must use some sort of container support, so you can't select either Mini Server or Server alone. This doesn't mean that you can create such a project; you would have to use another base class for your view.

For your program to act as a server, you have to select and register a document type and a file extension, however. This is done from the Advanced dialog on Page 4 of the MFC AppWizard process.

When you create a server program, the wizard adds another class to your project, *CInPlaceFrame*, which is used to merge your project with the container program. The wizard adds an additional menu for in-place editing to the project. This menu contains only items that deal with the data and application-specific items such as the File and Window. The other drop-down menus are absent. This is the menu that is merged with the container program, which provides the other menu items.

Your server process also must provide an accelerator table, which is used when a document is edited in-place. This table is merged with the container program's accelerator table at runtime.

637. Adding Menu and Toolbar Items to Support Rich Text

Because it was created by the MFC AppWizard, your program is capable of displaying text in rich text format. If you create such a document using *WordPad* or another rich text editor and then open it with your program, you will see the various text sizes and attributes just as you created them in the other application.

Until you add formatting support to the menus and toolbar of your application, you have no way of invoking the commands that cause the rich edit control to set and alter these attributes.

To begin, add three new pop-up menus to the *IDR_MAINFRAME* menu: "Char," "Para," and "Font." You will be adding items to these pop-ups in the next few tips.

You will also create a toolbar similar to the one shown in Figure 637. You can copy the toolbar from the project on the companion CD-ROM. As your project develops, you might want to cut or add items to this toolbar or rearrange it to suit your tastes. Remember that every project is different, or there wouldn't be any need for new projects. Rather than try to make the program conform to the available toolbars, adjust the toolbars and menu items to meet the program's needs.

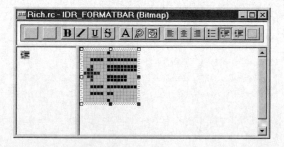

Figure 637   The format bar contains buttons for selecting the character attribute, paragraph alignment,
font and text color, and background color, as well as bulleting and paragraph indenting

Eventually, the format toolbar is going to handle a lot of traffic and will sport at least a couple of combo boxes. Rather than try to handle all of this in the *CMainFrame* class, you might want to create a separate class for the format toolbar. Using the ClassWizard or the ClassView panel of the Workspace Window, add a *CFormatBar* class to the project and derive it from *CToolBar*. Notice that the wizard doesn't list *CToolBar* as a base class, so select *CToolBarCtrl*. Then change all references to *CToolBarCtrl* (there are only two) in the header and source files to *CToolBar*. For now, just add the *OnCreate()* message handler function.

In the *CMainFrm* class, add a member variable, *m_wndFormatBar*, of type *CFormatBar*. Add the *FormatBar.h* header to the *mainfrm.h* file. Then add code to create the format bar in the *Create()* function in *mainfrm.cpp*:

```
if (!m_wndFormatBar.CreateEx(this, TBSTYLE_FLAT, WS_CHILD |
        WS_VISIBLE | CBRS_TOP | CBRS_GRIPPER |
        CBRS_TOOLTIPS | CBRS_FLYBY | CBRS_SIZE_DYNAMIC,
        CRect(0, 0, 0, 0), IDR_FORMATBAR))
{
    TRACE0("Failed to create toolbar\n");
    return -1;      // fail to create
}
```

When you are ready to add combo boxes for font selection and point sizes, you can do it all from the class definition rather than have to sort the functions between the two toolbars on the main window frame.

Add the following menu items, using the resource IDs, menu text, and ToolTip text indicated:

```
ID_COLOR_TEXT, "Text color," Select a text color\nText color
ID_COLOR_BACKGROUND, "Background," Select a background color\nBackground color
ID_PARA_LEFT, "Left," Left aligns the paragraph\nAlign Left
ID_PARA_CENTER, "Center," Horizontally centers the paragraph\nAlign center
ID_PARA_RIGHT, "Right," Right aligns the paragraph\nAlign Right
ID_PARA_BULLET, "Bullet," Inserts a bullet for this paragraph\nBullet
ID_PARA_INDENTMINUS, "Decrease Indent", Decrease the paragraph indenting\nDecrease Indent
ID_PARA_INDENTPLUS, "Increase Indent", Increase the paragraph indenting\nIncrease Indent
```

638. *Understanding Character Attributes in the Rich Edit Control*

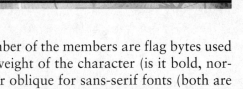

If you examine the *LOGFONT* structure, you will find that a number of the members are flag bytes used to determine the appearance of the character. These include the weight of the character (is it bold, normal, or lightface?), whether the character is italic for serif fonts or oblique for sans-serif fonts (both are set with the same attribute flag, *lfItalic*), whether the character is underlined, and whether it has a strikethrough line. The *lfHeight* member specifies the size of the character in logical points. The other members are used by the Windows font manager to select the closest matching font.

When you specify a font by name in Windows, there's a good chance that you will get that font if it is installed on the machine. However, that fact isn't guaranteed, and if the font you requested isn't found or doesn't match the criteria established in the other members of the *LOGFONT*, the font manager might just as well serve up a different font. The *LOGFONT* structure is shown here:

```
typedef struct tagLOGFONT
{ // lf
    LONG lfHeight;
    LONG lfWidth;
    LONG lfEscapement;
    LONG lfOrientation;
    LONG lfWeight;
```

```
    BYTE lfItalic;
    BYTE lfUnderline;
    BYTE lfStrikeOut;
    BYTE lfCharSet;
    BYTE lfOutPrecision;
    BYTE lfClipPrecision;
    BYTE lfQuality;
    BYTE lfPitchAndFamily;
    TCHAR lfFaceName[LF_FACESIZE];
} LOGFONT;
```

In drawing in the device context, if you want an italic version of the font you are using, you have to create a new font with that attribute and then select it into the device context. When you're done with it, you select the old font and delete the italic font, or save it for later use. Even with the *CEditView* class, to change the font, you still had to create the font using either the *CreateFont()* or *CreatePointFont()* members of *CFont*. (There are a couple of other functions you could use to create a font.)

With the rich text control, you don't have to create the fonts. The fonts and their appearance are controlled by a *CHARFORMAT* structure (or the *CHARFORMAT2* structure). You need only specify the font by name and set the *dwEffects* member to reflect the font attributes.

```
ID_CHAR_BOLD, "Bold," Makes the selection bold (toggle)\nBold
ID_CHAR_ITALIC, "Italic," Makes the selection italic (toggle)\nItalic
ID_CHAR_UNDERLINE, "Underline," Underlines the selection (toggle)\nUnderline
ID_CHAR_STRIKEOUT, "Strikeout," Makes the selection
                   strikeout text (toggle)\nStrikeout
```

639. *Understanding the* CHARFORMAT *and* CHARFORMAT2 *Structures*

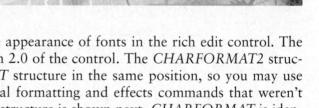

The *CHARFORMAT* structure is used to control the appearance of fonts in the rich edit control. The *CHARFORMAT2* structure may be used with version 2.0 of the control. The *CHARFORMAT2* structure contains all the members of the *CHARFORMAT* structure in the same position, so you may use either. However, the new structure contains additional formatting and effects commands that weren't available in the old structure. The *CHARFORMAT2* structure is shown next. *CHARFORMAT* is identical up to and including the *wPad2* member. The *CHARFORMAT* ends there, however. Not all the structure members are used by the rich edit control. The structure is shared with other Windows operations, such as the Microsoft Text Object Model.

```
typedef struct _charformat2
{
    UINT cbSize;     // Size of the structure in bytes
    _WPAD _wPad1;    // Padding member
    DWORD dwMask;    // Character effects mask
    DWORD dwEffects; // Flags for the character effects
    LONG yHeight;    // Height of the font in logical points
    LONG yOffset;    // Offset in twips from the baseline
    COLORREF crTextColor; // Character color
    BYTE bCharSet;   // Identical to LOGFONT
    BYTE bPitchAndFamily; // Identical to LOGFONT
    WCHAR szFaceName[LF_FACESIZE]; // Font name
```

```
    _WPAD _wPad2;    // Padding member
    WORD wWeight;    // Identical to LOGFONT
    SHORT sSpacing;  // Intercharacter spacing. Not used by
                     // the rich edit control
    COLORREF crBackColor; // Text background color. Has no
                          // effect on text display.
    LCID lcid;       // Language identifier. Not used by the
                     // rich edit control.
    DWORD dwReserved; // Must be 0.
    SHORT sStyle;    // Style handle. Has no effect on text
                     // display in the rich edit control
    WORD wKerning;   // Kerning value applied to font. Has
                     // no effect in rich edit control.
    BYTE bUnderlineType; // Underline style. Not all the
                         // possible values work with the rich
                         // edit control.
    BYTE bAnimation;// Animation flag. Has no effect in rich
                     // edit control.
    BYTE bRevAuthor;// Used to identify the person making
                     // changes to the file.
    BYTE bReserved1;// Must be 0.
} CHARFORMAT2;
```

To set an attribute, or *effect*, set the mask bit and the attribute member; then, call *SetCharFormat()*. For example, the following code would change the font to MS Comic Sans oblique underlined:

```
CHARFORMAT cf;
memset (&cf, '\0', sizeof (CHARFORMAT));
cf.cbSize = sizeof (CHARFORMAT);
cf.dwMask = CFM_FACE | CFM_ITALIC | CFM_UNDERLINE;
cf.dwEffects = CFE_ITALIC | CFE_UNDERLINE;
strcpy (cf.szFaceName, "MS Comic Sans");
SetCharFormat (cf);
```

Most of the *CRichEditView* functions still operate on the old *CHARFORMAT* structure, but in many cases calls directly to the rich edit control may be done using the new *CHARFORMAT2* structure. Alternatively, you could have used the *CHARFORMAT2* structure in the preceding code and made a call directly to the control:

```
GetRichEditCtrl().SetDefaultCharFormat (cf);
```

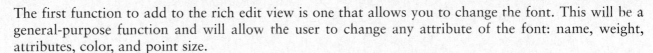

640. *Changing the Font*

The first function to add to the rich edit view is one that allows you to change the font. This will be a general-purpose function and will allow the user to change any attribute of the font: name, weight, attributes, color, and point size.

You can edit this function to remove those items you don't want the user to be able to change. Add a handler for the *ID_FONT_SELECT* message to the *CRichView* class. The code for this function is shown here:

```
void CRichView::OnFontSelect()
{
```

```
        LOGFONT lf;
        memset (&lf, '\0', sizeof (LOGFONT));
        CHARFORMAT cf = GetCharFormatSelection ();
        lf.lfItalic = cf.dwEffects & CFE_ITALIC ? TRUE : FALSE;
        lf.lfStrikeOut = cf.dwEffects & CFE_STRIKEOUT ? TRUE :
                                                        FALSE;
        lf.lfUnderline = cf.dwEffects & CFE_UNDERLINE ? TRUE :
                                                        FALSE;
        lf.lfCharSet = cf.bCharSet;

        lf.lfWeight = cf.dwEffects & CFE_BOLD ? FW_BOLD : 0;
        CWindowDC dc(this);
        lf.lfHeight = -MulDiv(cf.yHeight / 20,
                        GetDeviceCaps(dc.m_hDC, LOGPIXELSY), 72);
        strcpy (lf.lfFaceName, cf.szFaceName);

        CFontDialog cd;
        cd.m_cf.lpLogFont = &lf;
        cd.m_cf.Flags |= CF_INITTOLOGFONTSTRUCT;
        cd.m_cf.rgbColors = cf.crTextColor;

        if (cd.DoModal () == IDCANCEL)
            return;

        cf.dwMask = CFM_FACE | CFM_ITALIC | CFM_UNDERLINE |
                    CFM_STRIKEOUT | CFM_BOLD | CFM_COLOR |
                    CFM_SIZE | CFM_CHARSET;
        cf.dwEffects |= cd.IsItalic() ? CFE_ITALIC : 0;
        cf.dwEffects |= cd.IsBold() ? CFE_BOLD : 0;
        cf.dwEffects |= cd.IsUnderline() ? CFE_UNDERLINE : 0;
        cf.dwEffects |= cd.IsStrikeOut() ? CFE_STRIKEOUT : 0;
        cf.crTextColor = cd.GetColor();
        cf.yHeight = 20 * cd.GetSize () / 10;
        cf.bCharSet = lf.lfCharSet;
        strcpy (cf.szFaceName, lf.lfFaceName);
        SetCharFormat (cf);
}
```

First, initialize a *LOGFONT* structure to the information in the *CHARFORMAT* structure. The *CHOOSEFONT* structure used by the *CFontDialog* class and the *CHARFORMAT* don't share all the same font attributes, but the dialog box can be made to initialize from a *LOGFONT* structure.

The *CHARFORMAT* structure specifies type size in *twips*, which are about 1/20th of a printer's point, so there are about 1,440 twips in an inch. You need to convert this back to logical points for the *LOG-FONT* structure. When the dialog box returns, you can get the point size in tenths, which you can easily convert back to twips.

When the dialog box returns, you can set the character format mask to, well, just about everything. Include in the mask only those elements you want the user to change.

After the new values have been placed into the *CHARFORMAT* structure, call *SetCharFormat()* to set the new font for the view. If the user has selected text on the screen, the selection will be changed to the new format.

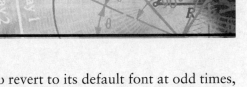

641. *Changing the Default Font in a Rich Edit View Document*

One common problem with the rich edit control is that it wants to revert to its default font at odd times, and that hasn't changed with the new release. Usually, the default font is the euglee (that's "ugly" for those of you who don't speak Texican) system font, and it's boldface on top of that. After you compile the program with the capability to change font, set the font to something other than System. Type a few words and press the Enter key. Use the Ctrl+Home key to go to the top of the window. Now use the Ctrl+End key to go to the end of the text you just typed. Enter some more text.

You can change the default font by setting up a *CHARFORMAT2* structure and calling the control's *SetDefaultCharFormat()* function. If your intent in Tip 640, "Changing the Font," is to change the default font, you can substitute the call to *GetCharFormatSelection()* with the following lines:

```
CHARFORMAT2 cf;
GetRichEditCtrl().GetDefaultCharFormat (cf);
```

The rest of the code would remain the same except that when you set the new font, you call the rich edit control function instead, as shown here. All the members of *CHARFORMAT* are in the *CHARFORMAT2* structure:

```
GetRichEditCtrl().SetDefaultCharFormat (cf);
```

This will change all the text in the control to the new selection. Usually, that isn't desirable because it destroys any formatting the user already has done.

Normally, I set the default font to something that is more readable than the system font in the view's *OnInitialUpdate()* function. This way, when the font changes unexpectedly, it's to one that I have selected. The code to set a new default font is shown here:

```
void CRichView::OnInitialUpdate()
{
    CRichEditView::OnInitialUpdate();

    // Set the printing margins (720 twips = 1/2 inch).
    SetMargins(CRect(720, 720, 720, 720));

    CHARFORMAT2 cf;
    memset (&cf, '\0', sizeof (CHARFORMAT2));
    cf.cbSize = sizeof (CHARFORMAT2);
    GetRichEditCtrl().GetDefaultCharFormat (cf);
    cf.dwMask = CFM_FACE | CFM_SIZE | CFM_UNDERLINE |
                CFM_COLOR | CFM_BOLD;
    cf.yHeight = 12 * 20;   // 12 points in twips
    cf.dwEffects &= ~(CFE_AUTOCOLOR | CFE_BOLD);
    cf.crTextColor = RGB(0xff, 0x00, 0x00);
    strcpy (cf.szFaceName, "Times New Roman");
    GetRichEditCtrl().SetDefaultCharFormat (cf);
    long lEventMask = GetRichEditCtrl().GetEventMask();
    lEventMask |= ENM_SELCHANGE;
    GetRichEditCtrl().SetEventMask(lEventMask);
}
```

Generally, in addition to turning off the bold effect, I turn off the autocolor bit in the effects flag. If autocolor is set, the text color automatically reverts to the system color *COLOR_WINDOWTEXT*, which usually is black. Setting the event mask to make sure that you get *EM_SELCHANGE* messages will come into play later when you make the format bar track the window contents.

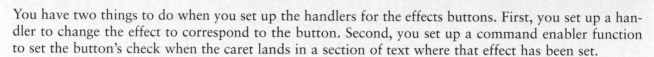

642. _Setting Text in Boldface_

You have two things to do when you set up the handlers for the effects buttons. First, you set up a handler to change the effect to correspond to the button. Second, you set up a command enabler function to set the button's check when the caret lands in a section of text where that effect has been set.

In addition, when the user selects text that spans bold and non-bold, you want the button to go into an indeterminate state, indicating that it's impossible to tell whether the selection is bold.

Start with the bold button. Add handlers for the *COMMAND* and *UPDATE_COMMAND_UI* messages using the ClassWizard.

To change the bold effect, you *XOR* the effect in the *CHARFORMAT* structure after first obtaining it with a call to *GetCharFormatSelection()*.

```
void CRichView::OnCharBold()
{
    CHARFORMAT cf = GetCharFormatSelection ();
    cf.dwMask |= CFM_BOLD;
    cf.dwEffects ^= CFE_BOLD;
    SetCharFormat (cf);
}
```

Setting the current button state couldn't be much easier. The *CRichEditView* class has a function to set the button for you. You need only pass it the pointer to the command enabler, a mask to tell it what effects to check, and the effects you want checked. The function then sets the button (and menu item) to checked, unchecked, or indeterminate:

```
void CRichView::OnUpdateCharBold(CCmdUI* pCmdUI)
{
    OnUpdateCharEffect (pCmdUI, CFE_BOLD, CFE_BOLD);
}
```

When you compile the code and run the program, notice that the bold button on the format toolbar has become active. The command enabler is working for you.

643. _Setting Italic, Underline, and Strikeout Text_

The same ideas apply when you set up the italic, underline, and strikeout buttons. You want them to reflect the state of the text at the caret position, or alternatively, the state of the text in a selection (in which case there is no caret).

Add handlers for the *ID_CHAR_ITALIC*, *ID_CHAR_UNDERLINE*, and *ID_CHAR_STRIKEOUT* messages. Add both the *COMMAND* and *UPDATE_COMMAND_UI* handlers. The code for these functions is shown here:

```
void CRichView::OnCharItalic()
{
    CHARFORMAT cf = GetCharFormatSelection ();
    cf.dwMask |= CFM_ITALIC;
    cf.dwEffects ^= CFE_ITALIC;
    SetCharFormat (cf);
}

void CRichView::OnUpdateCharItalic(CCmdUI* pCmdUI)
{
    OnUpdateCharEffect (pCmdUI, CFE_ITALIC, CFE_ITALIC);
}

void CRichView::OnCharStrikeout()
{
    CHARFORMAT cf = GetCharFormatSelection ();
    cf.dwMask |= CFM_STRIKEOUT;
    cf.dwEffects ^= CFE_STRIKEOUT;
    SetCharFormat (cf);
}

void CRichView::OnUpdateCharStrikeout(CCmdUI* pCmdUI)
{
    OnUpdateCharEffect (pCmdUI, CFE_STRIKEOUT,
                                CFE_STRIKEOUT);
}

void CRichView::OnCharUnderline()
{
    CHARFORMAT cf = GetCharFormatSelection ();
    cf.dwMask |= CFM_UNDERLINE;
    cf.dwEffects ^= CFE_UNDERLINE;
    SetCharFormat (cf);
}

void CRichView::OnUpdateCharUnderline(CCmdUI* pCmdUI)
{
    OnUpdateCharEffect (pCmdUI, CFE_UNDERLINE,
                                CFE_UNDERLINE);
}
```

Compile and run the program. All four effects buttons should now be enabled. You can set any or all of the effects at the same time, and the selection buttons should appear in their indeterminate state when a selection spans a particular effect.

644. *Setting the Font and Background Colors*

The font and background colors may be set independently. To do this, you either generate a menu of colors to limit the user's selection (how to do that is demonstrated in the section called, "The Resource Workshop," Tips 687–760) or use the Choose Color common dialog box. In this sample, the common dialog box will be used, and any custom colors the user creates will be saved, at least for the duration of the program.

In the ClassWizard or using the Wizard Bar, add message handlers for the *ID_FONT_COLOR* and *ID_FONT_BACKGROUND* messages. You won't need command enablers for these unless there are conditions during which you don't want the user to select them.

The code for these functions is similar. The basic difference is where the result from the Choose Color dialog is applied:

```cpp
void CRichView::OnFontColor()
{
static COLORREF clrCustom[16] = {
    RGB(0, 0, 0), RGB(0, 0, 0), RGB(0, 0, 0), RGB(0, 0, 0),
    RGB(0, 0, 0), RGB(0, 0, 0), RGB(0, 0, 0), RGB(0, 0, 0),
    RGB(0, 0, 0), RGB(0, 0, 0), RGB(0, 0, 0), RGB(0, 0, 0),
    RGB(0, 0, 0), RGB(0, 0, 0), RGB(0, 0, 0), RGB(0, 0, 0)
    };

    CColorDialog cd;
    cd.m_cc.lpCustColors = clrCustom;
    CHARFORMAT cf;
    cf = GetCharFormatSelection ();
    cd.m_cc.rgbResult = cf.crTextColor;
    cd.m_cc.Flags |= CC_RGBINIT;
    if (cd.DoModal () == IDCANCEL)
        return;
    cf.dwMask = CFM_COLOR;
    cf.crTextColor = cd.GetColor ();
    SetCharFormat (cf);
}

void CRichView::OnFontBackground()
{
static COLORREF clrCustom[16] = {
    RGB(0, 0, 0), RGB(0, 0, 0), RGB(0, 0, 0), RGB(0, 0, 0),
    RGB(0, 0, 0), RGB(0, 0, 0), RGB(0, 0, 0), RGB(0, 0, 0),
    RGB(0, 0, 0), RGB(0, 0, 0), RGB(0, 0, 0), RGB(0, 0, 0),
    RGB(0, 0, 0), RGB(0, 0, 0), RGB(0, 0, 0), RGB(0, 0, 0)
    };

    CColorDialog cd;
    cd.m_cc.lpCustColors = clrCustom;
    CHARFORMAT2 cf;
    GetRichEditCtrl().GetSelectionCharFormat (cf);
    cd.m_cc.rgbResult = cf.crTextColor;
    cd.m_cc.Flags |= CC_RGBINIT;
    if (cd.DoModal () == IDCANCEL)
        return;

    GetRichEditCtrl().SetBackgroundColor (FALSE,
                                cd.GetColor());
}
```

Unfortunately, there still doesn't seem to be any way to set the background color for the text only. Changing the background color requires changing the background of the entire window.

645. *Setting the Paragraph Alignment*

The rich edit control contains member functions for setting paragraph alignment and enabling and setting the button controls. Your code need only call these functions in the same manner you set the text attributes.

The bullet format is a little different. There's no built-in function to test and set this format, so it's a roll-your-own situation. Fortunately, it's not difficult.

In the ClassWizard, add message handlers for the *ID_PARA_LEFT*, *ID_PARA_RIGHT*, *ID_PARA_CENTER*, and *ID_PARA_BULLET* messages. Add the *COMMAND* message handlers and the *UPDATE_COMMAND_UI* handlers. The code for these functions is short and sweet, but pay particular attention to the bullet format:

```
void CRichView::OnParaLeft()
{
    OnParaAlign (PFA_LEFT);
}

void CRichView::OnUpdateParaLeft(CCmdUI* pCmdUI)
{
    OnUpdateParaAlign (pCmdUI, PFA_LEFT);
}

void CRichView::OnParaRight()
{
    OnParaAlign (PFA_RIGHT);
}

void CRichView::OnUpdateParaRight(CCmdUI* pCmdUI)
{
    OnUpdateParaAlign (pCmdUI, PFA_RIGHT);
}

void CRichView::OnParaCenter()
{
    OnParaAlign (PFA_CENTER);
}

void CRichView::OnUpdateParaCenter(CCmdUI* pCmdUI)
{
    OnUpdateParaAlign (pCmdUI, PFA_CENTER);
}

void CRichView::OnParaBullet()
{
PARAFORMAT    pf;
CHARFORMAT    cf;

    memset (&pf, '\0', sizeof (PARAFORMAT));
    pf.cbSize = sizeof (PARAFORMAT);
    pf = GetParaFormatSelection ();
    cf = GetCharFormatSelection ();
    pf.dwMask = PFM_NUMBERING | PFM_OFFSET;
```

```
        pf.wNumbering ^= PFN_BULLET;
        if (pf.wNumbering & PFN_BULLET)
        {
            pf.dxOffset = cf.yHeight;
        }
        else
        {
            pf.dwMask |= PFM_STARTINDENT | PFM_RIGHTINDENT;
            pf.dxOffset = 0;
            pf.dxStartIndent = 0;
            pf.dxRightIndent = 0;
        }
        SetParaFormat (pf);
}

void CRichView::OnUpdateParaBullet(CCmdUI* pCmdUI)
{
        memset (&pf, '\0', sizeof (PARAFORMAT));
        pf.cbSize = sizeof (PARAFORMAT);
        pf = GetParaFormatSelection ();
        if (pf.wNumbering & PFN_BULLET)
            pCmdUI->SetCheck (TRUE);
        else
            pCmdUI->SetCheck (FALSE);
}
```

Notice that in the bullet format, the code gets the character formatting, as well as the current formatting, and sets the *dxOffset* member equal to the size of the text. This makes the bulleted paragraphs indent and line up off to the side of the bullet. The control even provides the bullet. If you are turning off the bullet style, the *dxOffset* member is set to 0. The other two variables are set using the Increase Indent and Decrease Indent buttons. Turning off the bullet style cancels all indents for that paragraph.

The last two buttons deal with setting indents on the left and right sides of the paragraph. Generally, these are used to include something like a quotation, so the buttons work on both the left and right sides of the paragraph. If you would rather that they operate only on the left side, as in Microsoft Word, simply remove the *PFM_RIGHTINDENT* flag from the *pf.dwMask* variable. You don't have to remove the line where the indent is set; without the flag in the mask, the indent won't be changed. Alternatively, you could add another button that would cause the right indent to track the left indent when down or remain unchanged when up. You're the programmer; you decide.

The code for these two buttons is shown here:

```
void CRichView::OnParaIndentminus()
{
PARAFORMAT  pf;
CHARFORMAT  cf;

        memset (&pf, '\0', sizeof (PARAFORMAT));
        pf.cbSize = sizeof (PARAFORMAT);
        pf = GetParaFormatSelection ();
        cf = GetCharFormatSelection ();
        pf.dwMask = PFM_STARTINDENT | PFM_RIGHTINDENT;
        pf.dxRightIndent -= cf.yHeight;
        if (pf.dxRightIndent < 0)
            pf.dxRightIndent = 0;
        pf.dxStartIndent -= cf.yHeight;
        if (pf.dxStartIndent < 0)
```

```
        pf.dxStartIndent = 0;
    SetParaFormat (pf);
}

void CRichView::OnParaIndentplus()
{
PARAFORMAT  pf;
CHARFORMAT  cf;

    memset (&pf, '\0', sizeof (PARAFORMAT));
    pf.cbSize = sizeof (PARAFORMAT);
    pf = GetParaFormatSelection ();
    cf = GetCharFormatSelection ();
    pf.dwMask = PFM_STARTINDENT | PFM_RIGHTINDENT;
    pf.dxStartIndent += cf.yHeight;
    pf.dxRightIndent += cf.yHeight;
    SetParaFormat (pf);
}
```

You might want to set some indent limits in the *OnParaIndentplus()* function. When the left and right indents meet, repeated clicking of the button continues increasing the indents with some, well, interesting results. It's unlikely that these would cause any problems for a serious user. The *OnPara-Indentminus()* function prevents the indents from going negative, which produces some other interesting results.

646. *Adding Font and Point Size Boxes to the Format Bar*

Changing the font and point size is a common operation in a rich text editor, and asking the user to go through a font selection dialog every time he or she wants to change the font or point size puts too much of a burden on the user. It's customary to provide easier means to perform common operations.

In this tip, you will add combo boxes to the format toolbar to permit the user to set the font and size quickly. You will use an extended combo box for the fonts to take advantage of its image list capability and display icons next to the font names. You will use a plain combo box for the point sizes.

It's easy to add the combo boxes at the right end of the toolbar; you just create them and put them there. However, it's usually more convenient for the user if they are on the left side. Chances are, you will want to do things the hard way and make it easier on the user. Besides, eventually you're going to want to add controls in the middle of a toolbar, so you might as well learn now.

Open the format toolbar in the Resource Workshop. Add two empty buttons at the left end of the toolbar, as shown in Figure 646a. Make sure that the buttons have a separator between them and the first real button on the toolbar. To add the buttons here, grab the empty button at the end of the toolbar and drag it back to the left end. To make it stick, you give it a resource ID using the Properties dialog box. To get the Properties dialog box for a toolbar item, you right-click something in the ResourceView pane and select Properties, click the pushpin on the Properties dialog box to keep it visible, and then click the button. Give the first button the resource ID of *IDC_FONTLIST*. Do this again for the second blank button, making sure that there's a separator after it, and give it the resource ID of *IDC_POINTSIZE*. Actually, you don't care about the buttons; it's the separators you want, but you can't put two separators together in the toolbar editor, so you use blank buttons and just draw over the top of them.

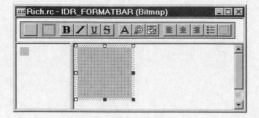

Figure 646a   Insert two blank buttons with separators on the left end of the toolbar

Open the *CFormatBar* header and source files you created earlier in this project. Add a couple of protected variables to the class definition. One is a *CComboBoxEx* named "m_FontList." The other is a *CComboBox* named "m_PointSize." Also add a *CFont* object named "m_Font" and a *CImageList* object named "m_Images."

You need a callback function to enumerate the font names so that you can add them to the extended combo box, and you need two *public* functions to access the selections in the combo box. The complete class definition for *CFormatBar* is shown here:

```cpp
#include <afxtempl.h>

/////////////////////////////////////////////////////////////
// CFormatBar window

class CFormatBar : public CToolBar
{
// Construction
public:
    CFormatBar();

// Attributes
public:
    class CFontData
    {
    public:
        CFontData () {
                    m_strName = _T("");
                    m_nIcon = 0;
                }
        ~CFontData () { }
        CString m_strName;
        int     m_nIcon;
    };

// Operations
public:

// Overrides
    // ClassWizard generated virtual function overrides
    //{{AFX_VIRTUAL(CFormatBar)
    //}}AFX_VIRTUAL

// Implementation
public:
    void SetPointSelection (int nPoints);
```

```
        void SetFontSelection (CString &strFontName);
        void GetSizeSelection (int &nSize);
        void GetFontSelection (CString &strFont);
        virtual ~CFormatBar();

        // Generated message map functions
protected:
        static int CALLBACK AddFontName (ENUMLOGFONT *lpelfe,
                                NEWTEXTMETRIC *lpntme,
                                int FontType, LPARAM lParam);
        //{{AFX_MSG(CFormatBar)
        afx_msg int OnCreate(LPCREATESTRUCT lpCreateStruct);
        //}}AFX_MSG

        CComboBoxEx m_FontList;
        CComboBox   m_PointSize;
        CFont       m_Font;
        CImageList  m_Images;

        CList <CFontData, CFontData&> m_FontData;

        DECLARE_MESSAGE_MAP()
};
```

For the image list, you can grab the *font.bmp* file from the *RES* directory of the *WORDPAD* sample project on the MSDN CD-ROM. You can build the image list directly from this bitmap, but icons have the advantage of being *maskable*, that is, the background can be made invisible. When you use an image list where a selection is possible, icons are the better choice. This project uses icons created from the bitmap images. You can copy and paste portions of the bitmap into a new icon resource. Make sure that the new icons are 16×16 pixels.

At the top of the *formatbar.cpp* file, define a structure that will contain the data sent to the function to enumerate the font names. This is similar to what you did in the *FONTVIEW* project from Tip 485, "A GDI Example: Drawing a Character Map." The *strFont* member will contain the font to select after the combo box is loaded. This is the font that will appear in the edit box of the combo box control when it first appears. If you set a default font for your view (see Tip 641, "Changing the Default Font in a Rich Edit View Document"), use the same font name here; otherwise, use the euglee system font. The *FontBox* member is a pointer to the extended combo box; the callback procedure is a static function, and it can't access non-static data members in the class.

```
struct FONTDATA
{
    CString     strFont;
    CFormatBar  *pPapa;
};
```

To size the combo boxes properly, you create a font. The default font for controls is 8-point MS Sans Serif, and you use the character height and average width from this font to set the control sizes. In the *OnCreate()* member function of *CFormatBar*, add the following code:

```
/////////////////////////////////////////////////////////////
// CFormatBar message handlers

int CFormatBar::OnCreate(LPCREATESTRUCT lpCreateStruct)
{
    if (CToolBar::OnCreate(lpCreateStruct) == -1)
        return -1;
```

```
    if (!LoadToolBar(IDR_FORMATBAR))
        return (-1);

    // TODO: Add your specialized creation code here
    CWindowDC dc(this);
    m_Font.CreatePointFont (80, _T("MS Sans Serif"));
    CFont *pOldFont = dc.SelectObject (&m_Font);
    TEXTMETRIC tm;
    dc.GetTextMetrics (&tm);
    int cxChar = tm.tmAveCharWidth;
    int cyChar = tm.tmHeight + tm.tmExternalLeading;
    dc.SelectObject (pOldFont);

    CRect rc;
//
//  The maximum size of a font name is 32 characters, and to
//  be sure that all names will fit, the value below should be
//  32*cxChar. That makes a very wide combo box that is
//  mostly open space. In reality, any font name longer
//  than 24 characters probably is a toy font and not very
//  useful.
    SetButtonInfo (0, IDC_FONTLIST, TBBS_SEPARATOR,
                              24 * cxChar);
    GetItemRect (0, &rc);
//
//  The rectangle bottom determines how far the drop-down
//  will appear. Sizing it properly will prevent a partial
//  line from appearing in the box.
//  Add 25 percent of the character height to the
//  overall depth of the list box. The baseline is above
//  the descenders, so that 25 percent of the type actually
//  is outside the rectangle.
    rc.bottom = rc.top + (cyChar * 16) + cyChar / 4;

    m_FontList.Create (WS_CHILD | WS_VISIBLE | WS_VSCROLL |
                       CBS_DROPDOWNLIST | CBS_SORT,
                       rc, this, IDC_FONTLIST);

//  Create the image list using the printer and TrueType
//  font icons.
    m_Images.Create (16, 16, ILC_MASK, 2, 2);
    HICON hIcon = AfxGetApp()->LoadIcon (IDI_TRUETYPEFONTS);
    m_Images.Add (hIcon);
    DeleteObject (hIcon);   // Don't need the icons after
                            // they have been added to the
                            // image list
    hIcon = AfxGetApp()->LoadIcon (IDI_PRINTERFONTS);
    m_Images.Add (hIcon);
    DeleteObject (hIcon);
//  Attach the image list to the extended combo box
    m_FontList.SetImageList (&m_Images);

    FONTDATA fd;
//  Use the view's default font here.
    CString strFont = _T("Times New Roman");
```

```
    fd.pPapa = this;
fd.strFont = strFont;
//  Enumerate the fonts and load the combo box
    ::EnumFontFamilies ((HDC) dc, NULL,
                        (FONTENUMPROC) AddFontName,
                        (LPARAM) &fd);
    int nCount = m_FontData.GetCount ();
    POSITION pos = m_FontData.GetHeadPosition ();
    CFontData font = m_FontData.GetHead ();
    for (int n = 0; pos != NULL; ++n)
    {
        font = m_FontData.GetNext (pos);
        COMBOBOXEXITEM cbi;
        memset (&cbi, '\0', sizeof (COMBOBOXEXITEM));
        cbi.iItem = n;
        cbi.mask = CBEIF_IMAGE | CBEIF_TEXT |
                   CBEIF_SELECTEDIMAGE | CBS_SORT;
        cbi.iImage = font.m_nIcon;
        cbi.iSelectedImage = font.m_nIcon;
        cbi.pszText = (char *) (LPCSTR) font.m_strName;
        m_FontList.InsertItem (&cbi);
        if (!font.m_strName.CompareNoCase (strFont))
            m_FontList.SetCurSel (n);
    }
    m_FontData.RemoveAll ();

//
//  Move on to the point size box.
    SetButtonInfo (1, IDC_POINTSIZE, TBBS_SEPARATOR,
                      5 * cxChar);
    GetItemRect (1, &rc);
//
//  Don't have to be so accurate with a plain combo box.
//  The list box will size itself on a line boundary.
    rc.bottom = rc.top + (cyChar * 10);
    rc.left += 2;
    rc.right = rc.left + 8 * cxChar;
//  Note that this combo box does not have the CBS_SORT style
    m_PointSize.Create (WS_CHILD | WS_VISIBLE |
                        WS_VSCROLL | CBS_DROPDOWNLIST,
                        rc, this, IDC_POINTSIZE);
    m_PointSize.SetFont (&m_Font);

//  List the common point sizes in the combo box
    int nPoints[] = { 8, 10, 11, 12, 14, 15, 18, 24,
                      32, 36, 42, 48, 54, 60, 72};
    for (int i=0; i < (sizeof (nPoints)/sizeof (int)); ++i)
    {
        CString str;
        str.Format ("%d", nPoints[i]);
        m_PointSize.AddString ((LPCSTR) str);
    }
//  Select the default size you set for the view
    m_PointSize.SelectString (-1, "12");

    return 0;
}
```

The function to enumerate the fonts and load the combo box is identical to the one you used in the *FONTVIEW* application. This is a standard way of loading combo boxes, and you might keep the code for it in your tool kit. Just modify it to meet your current needs.

```cpp
int CALLBACK CFormatBar::AddFontName(ENUMLOGFONT *lpelfe,
                    NEWTEXTMETRIC *lpntme, int FontType,
                    LPARAM lParam)
{

    FONTDATA *fd = (FONTDATA *) lParam;
    CFormatBar *bar = fd->pPapa;
    CFontData font;
    font.m_strName = lpelfe->elfLogFont.lfFaceName;
    switch (FontType)
    {
        case RASTER_FONTTYPE:
        case DEVICE_FONTTYPE:
            font.m_nIcon = 1;
            break;
        case TRUETYPE_FONTTYPE:
            font.m_nIcon = 0;
            break;
    }
    POSITION pos;
    if (bar->m_FontData.GetCount () == 0)
    {
        bar->m_FontData.AddHead (font);
        return (TRUE);
    }
    pos = bar->m_FontData.GetHeadPosition ();
    CFontData data;
    int nCount = bar->m_FontData.GetCount ();
    data = bar->m_FontData.GetHead ();
    for (int n = 0; n < nCount; ++n)
    {
        int nResult=data.m_strName.CompareNoCase(font.m_strName);
        if (nResult > 0)
            break;
        data = bar->m_FontData.GetNext (pos);
    }
    if (pos == NULL)
    {
        if (font.m_strName.CompareNoCase (data.m_strName) < 0)
        {
            pos = bar->m_FontData.GetTailPosition ();
            bar->m_FontData.InsertBefore (pos, font);
        }
        else
            bar->m_FontData.AddTail (font);
        return (TRUE);
    }
    bar->m_FontData.GetPrev (pos);
    bar->m_FontData.InsertBefore (pos, font);
    return (TRUE);
}
```

Finally, in the *formatbar.cpp* file, you need functions to retrieve the selected data from the combo boxes. It's convenient to return these values in reference variables. The font name is a *CString* object and the point size is an integer.

```
void CFormatBar::GetFontSelection(CString &strFont)
{
    int nIndex = m_FontList.GetCurSel ();
    m_FontList.GetLBText (nIndex, strFont);
}

void CFormatBar::GetSizeSelection(int &nSize)
{
    CString strSel;
    int nIndex = m_PointSize.GetCurSel ();
    m_PointSize.GetLBText (nIndex, strSel);
    nSize = atoi ((LPCSTR) strSel);
}
```

Close the format bar source and header files. The format bar was declared as a *protected* member of the *CMainFrame* class, so you must add functions to that class to access the functions you just added. Open the *mainfrm.cpp* and *mainfrm.h* files and add the following *public* functions. These are just pass-through functions so that you can keep your class data non-public:

```
/////////////////////////////////////////////////////////////
// CMainFrame message handlers


void CMainFrame::GetFontSelection(CString &strFont)
{
    m_wndFormatBar.GetFontSelection (strFont);
}

void CMainFrame::GetSizeSelection(int &nSize)
{
    m_wndFormatBar.GetSizeSelection (nSize);
}
```

Finally, you add message handlers to the view class to retrieve the new font or point size when the selection changes. The ClassWizard and Wizard Bar won't help you here. The combo boxes will send *CBN_SELCHANGED* messages when the selection changes, and the frameworks will dutifully deliver them to the view object in turn. The ClassWizard, however, has no idea that any combo boxes are around; to it, the associated resource IDs are toolbar buttons. Add the following two message map entries to the view class; make sure that they are outside the wizard's protected area:

```
ON_CBN_SELCHANGE(IDC_FONTLIST, OnSelchangeFontlist)
ON_CBN_SELCHANGE(IDC_POINTSIZE, OnSelchangePointsize)
```

Add the following protected entries to the view class definition. Again, make sure that they are outside the wizard's protected area in the class definition:

```
afx_msg void OnSelchangePointsize();
afx_msg void OnSelchangeFontlist();
```

Make sure that the *mainfrm.h* header file is among the list of *include* files in the view class source file. Really, this should be a standard way of setting up the view class, but the wizard doesn't do it for you. Now add function code:

```
void CRichView::OnSelchangeFontlist()
{
    CMainFrame *frame = DYNAMIC_DOWNCAST(CMainFrame,
                        AfxGetApp()->GetMainWnd());
    CString strFont;
    frame->GetFontSelection (strFont);
    CHARFORMAT cf = GetCharFormatSelection ();
    cf.dwMask |= CFM_FACE;
    strcpy (cf.szFaceName, (LPCSTR) strFont);
    SetCharFormat (cf);
    ::SetFocus (this->m_hWnd);
}

void CRichView::OnSelchangePointsize()
{
    CMainFrame *frame = DYNAMIC_DOWNCAST(CMainFrame,
                        AfxGetApp()->GetMainWnd());
    int nSize;
    frame->GetSizeSelection (nSize);
    CHARFORMAT cf = GetCharFormatSelection ();
    cf.dwMask |= CFM_SIZE;
    cf.yHeight = nSize * 20;
    SetCharFormat (cf);
    ::SetFocus (this->m_hWnd);
}
```

The functions are very similar. The difference is the information they retrieve. Use the *DYNAMIC_DOWNCAST* macro to cast the frame window to a pointer to your actual class. Then use that pointer to call the appropriate combo box function. Set the new information in the appropriate member of *CHARFROMAT*.

When this is done, the combo box has the focus, which means that the user must click on the view window to get back to the work at hand. If the click is away from the place where the font or point size was changed, the new information will be lost. You can recover from that by resetting the focus to the view window. You know that this window had the focus because it's the one that received the selection changed message. It's safe to yank the focus back using the global function *::SetFocus(this->m_hWnd)*, and the caret remains at the point where the change was made.

Before leaving the rich edit project, you should make one last tweak. When the user moves the caret around the window, it's a good idea to have the font and point size combo boxes track the movement, showing the values for the current position in the text.

The view keeps track of the current values to update the toolbar buttons while the caret is being moved around by way of a reflected notification message, *EN_SELCHANGE*, from the rich text control. You can intercept this message and use it to set the values in the combo boxes so long as you pass it along to the view when you are finished. The ClassWizard doesn't have entries for this message—in fact, it doesn't have entries for any of the notification messages from the rich text control—so you have to roll your own message handler. Add (outside the wizard's protected area in the message map) the following entry:

```
ON_NOTIFY_REFLECT(EN_SELCHANGE, OnSelChange)
```

Add a member function to the class. You can do this by hand, or you can use the ClassView pane on the Workspace Window:

```
void OnSelChange(NMHDR* pNMHDR, LRESULT* pResult);
```

Once again you have to be mindful that the format bar variable is a protected member of the *CMainFrame* class, and your code is going to have to call a function there, where it will be relayed to *CFormatBar*. There are other, less circuitous ways of doing this. For example, you could set up a command enabler message function in the *CFormatBar* class and call a function in the view class to get the current format. That would work well in a single-document interface application, but the route through the frame window is more direct if you want to convert the application to a multiple-document interface. The code for *OnSelChange()* is shown here:

```cpp
void CRichView::OnSelChange(NMHDR* pNMHDR, LRESULT* pResult)
{
    CString strFontName;
    int yHeight;
    CHARFORMAT cf;
    GetRichEditCtrl().GetSelectionCharFormat (cf);
    CMainFrame *frame = DYNAMIC_DOWNCAST(CMainFrame,
                     AfxGetApp()->GetMainWnd());
    if (cf.dwMask & CFM_FACE)
        strFontName = cf.szFaceName;
    else
        strFontName.Empty ();
    frame->SetFontSelection (strFontName);
    if (cf.dwMask & CFM_SIZE)
        yHeight = cf.yHeight / 20;
    else
        yHeight = -1;
    frame->SetPointSelection (yHeight);
    CRichEditView::OnSelChange (pNMHDR, pResult);
}
```

While you're at it, go ahead and add the two relay functions to the *CMainFrame* class:

```cpp
void CMainFrame::SetFontSelection(CString &strFontName)
{
    m_wndFormatBar.SetFontSelection (strFontName);
}

void CMainFrame::SetPointSelection(int nPoints)
{
    m_wndFormatBar.SetPointSelection (nPoints);
}
```

Finally, add the same functions to the *CFormatBar* class. This is where the work actually will be done:

```cpp
void CFormatBar::SetFontSelection(CString &strFontName)
{
    if (strFontName.IsEmpty())        // Is Selection valid?
    {
        m_FontList.SetCurSel (-1);  // Set to an empty
        return;                     // selection
    }
    COMBOBOXEXITEM boxitem;
    char szSelName[_MAX_PATH];
    memset (&boxitem, '\0', sizeof (COMBOBOXEXITEM));
    boxitem.iItem = m_FontList.GetCurSel ();
    boxitem.mask = CBEIF_TEXT;
    boxitem.pszText = szSelName;
    boxitem.cchTextMax = _MAX_PATH;
```

```
        m_FontList.GetItem (&boxitem);
        if (!strcmp (boxitem.pszText, (LPCSTR) strFontName))
          return;


        boxitem.mask = CBEIF_TEXT;
        boxitem.pszText = szSelName;
        boxitem.cchTextMax = _MAX_PATH;

        int nCount = m_FontList.GetComboBoxCtrl()->GetCount ();
        for (int nIndex = 0; nIndex < nCount; ++nIndex)
        {
            boxitem.iItem = nIndex;
            m_FontList.GetItem (&boxitem);
            if (!strcmp (szSelName, (LPCSTR) strFontName))
                break;
        }
        if (nCount != nIndex)
            m_FontList.SetCurSel (nIndex);
}

void CFormatBar::SetPointSelection(int nPoints)
{

    if (nPoints < 0)    // Is selection invalid?
    {
        m_PointSize.SetCurSel (nPoints);  // Set to empty
        return;                           // selection
    }
    CString strPoints;
    strPoints.Format ("%d", nPoints);
    int nIndex = m_PointSize.FindString (-1,
                                    (LPCSTR) strPoints);
    if (nIndex == CB_ERR)
    {
        nIndex = m_PointSize.AddString (strPoints);
        m_PointSize.SetCurSel (nIndex);
        return;
    }
    int nCurSel = m_PointSize.GetCurSel ();
    if (nCurSel == nIndex)
        return;
    m_PointSize.SetCurSel (nIndex);
}
```

Working with the plain combo box is easy. It has functions to get the current selection and find a string within the list box. The extended combo box is a very different story, however. The documentation on it is sparse and, like most Microsoft documentation, is totally accurate but tells you nothing you want to know.

To deal with the extended combo box, you have to work through a *COMBOBOXEXITEM* structure. Eventually, all Windows controls work through an item structure, so you might as well get used to it now. There must be an easier way to find a string in an extended combo box than searching each item, but I haven't found it yet. At any rate, this probably is how it would work, and it's quick and compact.

To reduce processing time, the code compares the format string with the string selected in the combo box. If they're the same, it just returns—no sense doing anything. This also keeps the controls from flickering.

If the character format contains a point size not in the list (perhaps the user got it from the full font dialog box), the code adds the string to the box and selects it.

Compile the program and mark up some text on the screen in different point sizes and fonts, as in Figure 646b. As you move the cursor through the text, the combo box controls should change to reflect the current character formatting at the caret position.

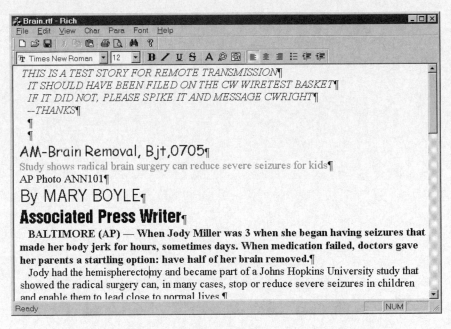

Figure 646b   The rich text editor is a good start on a text editing project

At this point, you should have a good, basic rich text editor. Someone once said that if you really want to learn about something, try changing it. You will find plenty to change and improve upon here. This should only be the beginning, and your own application will determine where you go from here.

647. *Adding User and File Information to the Rich Edit View*

Did you ever notice that word processors such as Corel *WordPerfect* and Microsoft *Word* keep some basic information with the document you created using them? This information can be as basic as what you used in the memo example using the dreaded *CEditView* class, or it can be more detailed, for example, when the document was modified and by whom.

In the memo sample, you used a class embedded within a dialog box class to contain the data. You don't have to do it that way. The *CRichEditDoc* class supports real serialization, not the bogus stuff you encountered with *CEditView*. This means that you can easily insert your own information into the file, as well as the data contained in the control itself.

For a rich edit version of *Memo*, define a couple of new classes to hold the modified data. There's a version on the companion CD-ROM that includes this code. You can expand on these classes to meet the needs of your application, but the basic process will be shown in the example. The first class will be a container for the modification data. Call it "CFileData." The second will hold the actual modification information. The class definition is shown here, along with the implementation, which uses operator overloads to write to the archive object:

```
#include    <afxtempl.h>

class CModified;

class CFileData : public CObject
{
    DECLARE_SERIAL(CFileData)

public:
    CFileData();
    virtual ~CFileData();

    CString   m_CreatedBy;
    CTime m_CreatedTime;

    CArray<CModified, CModified&>     m_History;

    friend CModified;
    friend CArchive& operator<<(CArchive& ar,
                                CFileData& history);
    friend CArchive& operator>>(CArchive& ar,
                                CFileData& history);
};


class CModified : public CObject
{
    DECLARE_SERIAL(CModified)
public:
    CModified();
    virtual ~CModified();

    CTime    m_ModTime;
    CString  m_ModUser;

    friend CFileData;
    CModified& operator=(CModified& data);
    friend CArchive& operator<<(CArchive& ar,
                                CModified& data);
    friend CArchive& operator>>(CArchive& ar,
                                CModified& data);
};


// FileData.cpp: implementation of the CFileData class.
//
//////////////////////////////////////////////////////////

#include "stdafx.h"
#include "Rich.h"
#include "FileData.h"

#ifdef _DEBUG
#undef THIS_FILE
static char THIS_FILE[]=__FILE__;
#define new DEBUG_NEW
```

```
#endif

///////////////////////////////////////////////////////
// Construction/Destruction
///////////////////////////////////////////////////////

IMPLEMENT_SERIAL(CFileData, CObject, 0)

CFileData::CFileData()
{
    m_CreatedBy = _T("");
    m_CreatedTime = 0;
}

CFileData::~CFileData()
{

}

CArchive& operator<<(CArchive& ar, CFileData& history)
{
    ar.WriteString (history.m_CreatedBy);
    ar << '\n';
    ar << history.m_CreatedTime;
    int nItems = history.m_History.GetSize ();
    ar << nItems;
    for (int i = 0; i < nItems; ++i)
        ar << history.m_History[i];
    return (ar);
}

CArchive& operator>>(CArchive& ar, CFileData& history)
{
    ar.ReadString (history.m_CreatedBy);
    ar >> history.m_CreatedTime;
    int nItems;
    ar >> nItems;
    for (int i = 0; i < nItems; ++i)
    {
    CModified cm;
        ar >> cm;
        history.m_History.Add (cm);
    }
    return (ar);
}

///////////////////////////////////////////////////////
// CModified Class
///////////////////////////////////////////////////////

///////////////////////////////////////////////////////
// Construction/Destruction
///////////////////////////////////////////////////////

IMPLEMENT_SERIAL(CModified, CObject, 0)
```

```
CModified::CModified()
{

}

CModified::~CModified()
{

}

CArchive& operator<<(CArchive& ar, CModified& data)
{
    ar.WriteString (data.m_ModUser);
    ar << '\n';
    ar << data.m_ModTime;
    return (ar);
}

CArchive& operator>>(CArchive& ar, CModified& data)
{
    ar.ReadString (data.m_ModUser);
    ar >> data.m_ModTime;
    return (ar);
}

CModified& CModified::operator=(CModified& data)
{
    m_ModUser = data.m_ModUser;
    m_ModTime = data.m_ModTime;
    return (*this);
}
```

The implementation is very similar to the *CEditView* version, except that you now are maintaining an array containing information on who modified the file and when. This array is kept in *CFileData* if of type *CModified*. Each time the file is saved, a new *CModified* object is created and added to the array and then written to disk as part of the file. When you read back the file, you have a chronological history of who changed the file. All the data for these objects is created in the *Serialize()* function of the *CRichDoc* class.

To implement, first change the *IDR_MAINFRAME* string table entry so that the program is looking for files with an extension of *.mem*:

```
Rich\n\nRich\nMemo Files (*.mem)\n.mem\nMemo.Document
                            \nMemo Document
```

In the *richdoc.h* file, add *FileData.h* to the list of include files and add a member variable, *m_History*, of type *CFileData*.

Now, create a dialog box similar to the one you created for the *CEditView* project. This time, however, include a list control on the dialog box, as shown in Figure 647. Instead of just the last modification, you may have many file changes to list, and the list control is where you do that. Don't worry about the code that implements the list control; that is covered in the section on "Windows Common Controls." When you add the list control to the dialog box, set the view to *Report* in the property sheet.

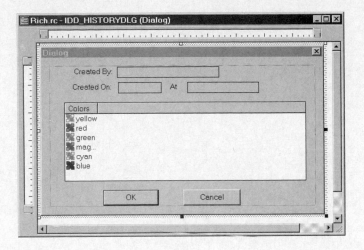

Figure 647   The file history dialog includes a list control, IDC_HISTORYLIST

Create a new class for the dialog box, *CHistoryDlg*, and add member variables for the static text fields shown with a border around them and for the list control. Add an override for the *OnInitDialog()* function. Also add a pointer for an object of type *CFileData*:

```cpp
// HistoryDlg.h : header file
//

/////////////////////////////////////////////////////////////
// CHistoryDlg dialog

#include    "FileData.h"

class CHistoryDlg : public CDialog
{
// Construction
public:
    CHistoryDlg(CWnd* pParent = NULL);//standard Constructor

    CFileData    *m_pData;

// Dialog Data
    //{{AFX_DATA(CHistoryDlg)
    enum { IDD = IDD_HISTORYDLG };
    CListCtrl   m_HistoryList;
    CString m_Creator;
    CString m_CreatedDate;
    CString m_CreatedTime;
    //}}AFX_DATA


// Overrides
    // ClassWizard generated virtual function overrides
    //{{AFX_VIRTUAL(CHistoryDlg)
    protected:
// DDX/DDV support
    virtual void DoDataExchange(CDataExchange* pDX);
    //}}AFX_VIRTUAL
```

```
// Implementation
protected:

    // Generated message map functions
    //{{AFX_MSG(CHistoryDlg)
    virtual BOOL OnInitDialog();
    afx_msg void OnGetdispinfoHistorylist(NMHDR* pNMHDR,
                                          LRESULT* pResult);
    //}}AFX_MSG
    DECLARE_MESSAGE_MAP()
};
```

The only unfamiliar item in the class definition probably is the *OnGetdispinfoHistorylist()* function. The list control will use *LPSTR_TEXTCALLBACK* and get its display information through this function. This is by far the easiest way to use a list control, and it's very memory efficient. To create the function, in the ClassWizard select the list box resource ID on the Message Maps page. Scroll through the messages until you find *LVN_GETDISPINFO*, and add it to the class. The implementation of this function is shown here. You will learn the details later, and you will agree that it's much easier than setting up the list control item by subitem.

```
// HistoryDlg.cpp : implementation file
//

#include "stdafx.h"
#include "Rich.h"
#include "HistoryDlg.h"

#ifdef _DEBUG
#define new DEBUG_NEW
#undef THIS_FILE
static char THIS_FILE[] = __FILE__;
#endif

/////////////////////////////////////////////////////////////////
// CHistoryDlg dialog

CHistoryDlg::CHistoryDlg(CWnd* pParent /*=NULL*/)
    : CDialog(CHistoryDlg::IDD, pParent)
{
    //{{AFX_DATA_INIT(CHistoryDlg)
    m_Creator = _T("");
    m_CreatedDate = _T("");
    m_CreatedTime = _T("");
    //}}AFX_DATA_INIT
    m_pData = NULL;
}


void CHistoryDlg::DoDataExchange(CDataExchange* pDX)
{
    CDialog::DoDataExchange(pDX);
    //{{AFX_DATA_MAP(CHistoryDlg)
    DDX_Control(pDX, IDC_HISTORYLIST, m_HistoryList);
    DDX_Text(pDX, IDC_CREATEDBY, m_Creator);
    DDX_Text(pDX, IDC_CREATEDDATE, m_CreatedDate);
    DDX_Text(pDX, IDC_CREATEDTIME, m_CreatedTime);
```

```
    //}}AFX_DATA_MAP
}


BEGIN_MESSAGE_MAP(CHistoryDlg, CDialog)
    //{{AFX_MSG_MAP(CHistoryDlg)
    ON_NOTIFY(LVN_GETDISPINFO, IDC_HISTORYLIST,
                              OnGetdispinfoHistorylist)
    //}}AFX_MSG_MAP
END_MESSAGE_MAP()

/////////////////////////////////////////////////////////////////
// CHistoryDlg message handlers

BOOL CHistoryDlg::OnInitDialog()
{
    CDialog::OnInitDialog();

char *Titles[] =
    {
    "Last User",
    "Date Modified",
    "Time Modified"
    };
int Widths [] = {125, 115, 115};
#define   LISTCOLUMNS   (sizeof (Titles) / sizeof (char *))


    for (int i = 0; i < LISTCOLUMNS; ++i)
    {
        LV_COLUMN   lvc;
        lvc.mask = LVCF_FMT | LVCF_SUBITEM |
                   LVCF_TEXT | LVCF_WIDTH;
        lvc.fmt = LVCFMT_LEFT;
        lvc.iSubItem = i;
        lvc.pszText = Titles [i];
        lvc.cx = Widths [i];
        m_HistoryList.InsertColumn (i, &lvc);
    }
    if (m_pData == NULL)
        return (TRUE);
//
// Fill in the static data fields
//
    m_Creator = m_pData->m_CreatedBy;
    if (m_pData->m_CreatedTime > 0)
    {
        m_CreatedDate.Format ("%02d/%02d/%04d",
            m_pData->m_CreatedTime.GetMonth(),
            m_pData->m_CreatedTime.GetDay(),
            m_pData->m_CreatedTime.GetYear());

        m_CreatedTime.Format ("%02d:%02d:%02d",
            m_pData->m_CreatedTime.GetHour(),
            m_pData->m_CreatedTime.GetMinute(),
            m_pData->m_CreatedTime.GetSecond());
```

```
        }
    int nCount = m_pData->m_History.GetSize ();
    if (nCount)
    {
    LV_ITEM    lvitem;
// Add any history records to the list control
        for (int i = 0; i < nCount; ++i)
        {
            CString strText;
            lvitem.mask = LVIF_TEXT;
            lvitem.iItem = i;
            lvitem.iSubItem = 0;
            lvitem.pszText = LPSTR_TEXTCALLBACK;
            m_HistoryList.InsertItem (&lvitem);
        }
    }
    UpdateData (FALSE);
    return TRUE;  // return TRUE unless you set focus to a
                  // control
                  // EXCEPTION: OCX Property Pages should
                  // return FALSE
}


//
// This function is called when the list control needs to
// draw an item. The item and subitem ids are in the
// pNMHDR parameter, which is really an LV_DISPINFO pointer
// in disguise.
//
void CHistoryDlg::OnGetdispinfoHistorylist(NMHDR* pNMHDR,
                                           LRESULT* pResult)
{
CString    string;

    LV_DISPINFO* pDispInfo = (LV_DISPINFO*)pNMHDR;
    int i = pDispInfo->item.iItem;
    if (pDispInfo->item.mask & LVIF_TEXT)
    {
        switch (pDispInfo->item.iSubItem)
        {
          case 0:
              ::lstrcpy (pDispInfo->item.pszText,
                  (LPCSTR) m_pData->m_History[i].m_ModUser);
              break;
          case 1:
            if (m_pData->m_History[i].m_ModTime <= 0)
                break;
            string.Format ("%02d/%02d/%04d",
                m_pData->m_History[i].m_ModTime.GetMonth(),
                m_pData->m_History[i].m_ModTime.GetDay(),
                m_pData->m_History[i].m_ModTime.GetYear());
            ::lstrcpy (pDispInfo->item.pszText,
                                        (LPCSTR) string);
            break;
          case 2:
            if (m_pData->m_History[i].m_ModTime <= 0)
```

```
          break;
        string.Format ("%02d:%02d:%02d",
          m_pData->m_History[i].m_ModTime.GetHour(),
          m_pData->m_History[i].m_ModTime.GetMinute(),
          m_pData->m_History[i].m_ModTime.GetSecond());
        ::lstrcpy (pDispInfo->item.pszText,
                                  (LPCSTR) string);
        break;
      }
    }
    *pResult = 0;        // Don't forget pResult!
}
```

Rather than insert every item and subitem in the list control, the code inserts only the first item using *LPSTR_TEXTCALLBACK*. This is the default mode for the subitems, so you don't even have to insert them. The list control desperately wants to use *LPSTR_TEXTCALLBACK*. When it must draw an item or subitem, it sends a message, *LVN_GETDISPINFO*, with pointers to structures containing the items it needs to paint. Your code then fills in the information and the list control is drawn.

648. *Using Serialize to Save and Retrieve User and File Information*

Now that the additional classes have been added to the project, move to the ResourceView pane and add an item to the View menu. Name it "Header" and give it the resource ID of *ID_VIEW_HEADER*. After this is done, the rest of the work will be in the document class.

In the document class header file, add *FileData.h* to the list of include files. Add a single member variable in the protected or private section:

```
CFileData    m_FileHistory;
```

Move on to the document class source code file and add a message handler for the *ID_VIEW_HEADER* message. Also add an override for the *OnNewDocument()* function. The code for these two functions is shown here:

```
BOOL CRichDoc::OnNewDocument()
{
    if (!CRichEditDoc::OnNewDocument())
        return FALSE;

    m_FileHistory.m_CreatedTime = 0;
    m_FileHistory.m_CreatedBy = _T("");
    m_FileHistory.m_History.RemoveAll ();
    return TRUE;
}


void CRichDoc::OnViewHistory()
{
    CHistoryDlg hd;
    hd.m_pData = &m_FileHistory;
    hd.DoModal ();
}
```

The code in *OnNewDocument()* clears out the variable contents when a new file is created or opened. Without it, the history of all previously opened files will be included in the next file saved. The *OnViewHistory()* function creates and displays the dialog box so that you can view the history elements.

The only thing left is the *Serialize()* function. The code checks to see whether the file has an extension of *.mem*. If so and if this is a new file, it sets up the creation information (there is no history yet). Otherwise, it adds a new element to the modification history and writes it to the file before calling the *CRichEditDoc::Serialize()* function. On a read, it first fills in the history variable before passing on the code to read the rest of the file.

```cpp
/////////////////////////////////////////////////////////////
// CRichDoc serialization

void CRichDoc::Serialize(CArchive& ar)
{

//  CString strPath = ar.m_pFile->m_strFileName;
    CString strPath = ar.GetFile()->GetFileName();
    int nPos;
    if ((nPos = strPath.ReverseFind ('\\')) >= 0)
    {
       strPath = strPath.Right (strPath.GetLength() - nPos);
    }
    if ((nPos = strPath.Find ('.')) >= 0)
    {
       strPath = strPath.Right (strPath.GetLength() - nPos);
    }
    if (!strPath.CompareNoCase (".mem"))
    {
        if (ar.IsStoring())
        {
            if (m_FileHistory.m_CreatedTime == 0)
            {
                m_FileHistory.m_CreatedTime =
                                    CTime::GetCurrentTime ();
                char user[_MAX_PATH];
                DWORD dwSize = _MAX_PATH;
                GetUserName (user, &dwSize);
                m_FileHistory.m_CreatedBy = user;
            }
            else
            {
                CModified cm;
                cm.m_ModTime = CTime::GetCurrentTime ();
                char user[_MAX_PATH];
                DWORD dwSize = _MAX_PATH;
                GetUserName (user, &dwSize);
                cm.m_ModUser = user;
                m_FileHistory.m_History.Add (cm);
            }
            ar << m_FileHistory;
        }
        else
        {
            ar >> m_FileHistory;
        }
```

```
    }
    // Calling the base class CRichEditDoc enables serialization
    // of the container document's COleClientItem objects.
    // TODO: set CRichEditDoc::m_bRTF = FALSE if you are
    // serializing as text
       CRichEditDoc::Serialize(ar);
}
```

By checking for the *.mem* file type, the program still can read and write ordinary text and rich text files.

The rich text format does have means to include simple information like this without resorting to this approach, and the revision history of the file itself might not be important to you. The key element here, however, is that you can store information related to the file—even complete class objects—with the file itself rather than have to set up a separate data file.

649. *Using the* CListView *Class*

The *CListView* class encapsulates a list control into a view. It is derived from *CCtrlView* and ultimately from *CView*. The list control was introduced with Windows 95 and is available only in 32-bit versions of Windows. Don't confuse it with the older list box control; the two are very, very different.

The *CListView* class actually adds very little other than to encapsulate the list control. Besides the standard constructor and destructor, it has only one function, *GetListCtrl()*, which is used to get a reference to the underlying list control. All the operations you perform with this view are from functions inherited from *CView* or included in the control itself.

That's not intended to cast any aspersions on *CListView*. It is, in fact, a workhorse class, just like its underlying control. You see it every time you use Windows. The window that appears when you open the My Computer icon is a list view, as are all the directory windows you open from it. After you become accustomed to using the list control, you will rarely go back to the old list box control (although sometimes the older control has some merit).

The list control, and consequently the view class, has four viewing modes. In *large icon* mode, it displays a 32×32 pixel icon and a label for an object. In *small icon* mode, it displays a 16×16 pixel icon and a label. In *list* mode, it generates a columnar output of its contents and a label.

The fourth view mode, *report*, is a virtual replacement for the old list box control. Using an optional header, the control can be programmed to display information about its contents in columns and an optional small icon. The items can be sorted by calling a user-supplied sort function, and the control's data can be kept in the application's memory, thus improving the memory utilization of programs using the control. The header can be used to generate messages to sort the items in the list control.

650. *Understanding the* CImageList *Class with* CListView

The icons for a list control are provided by an *image list*. Although it is listed among the Windows common controls, the image list is not a true control. It serves as a helper object by holding the collection of images used by other controls. You create an image list from icons or bitmap images and then assign items in the list control an image index into the image list. The image list is optional in the report mode, which makes it useful for displaying items such as database records where the icon would just add overhead. In the other three modes, however, the image list is a necessity. You don't *need* an image list; it's just that a collection of labels without icons is difficult for a user to decipher.

The list control can accept two image lists. One is for small images and the other for large images. The large image list is used only with the *LVS_ICON* style; all others use the small image list.

651. *Creating an Image List*

In the rich text editor project, you built an image list for the extended combo box, using two small icons to represent the printer fonts and the TrueType fonts. The process is similar for the list control. Usually, the image list is much larger, but you can use the same image list with the list control as well.

In fact, an image list doesn't have to be exclusive to one control. The list control, for example, has an *LVS_SHAREIMAGELISTS* style that prevents it from destroying the image list when the control is destroyed.

You can use the short font image list with the list control. Create a new project named "FONTS." Make it a single-document interface project, and accept the defaults through the MFC *(Microsoft Foundation Class)* AppWizard steps. In the last step, select *CListView* as the base class for your view.

Copy the font icons you used in the rich text editor project to this project. This time, however, create a large icon as well as the small icon. You can open the small, 16×16 pixel icon in the resource workshop, copy its contents to the Clipboard, and then paste them onto the large icon matrix. Resize the image by grabbing the lower-right corner and pulling it to fill the matrix. The icon editor is very good at this.

In *CFontsView*, add two member variables, *m_SmallImages* and *m_LargeImages*, of type *CImageList*. For this project, you will need only the large image list, but this gratuitous life of Riley will come to an end in the next tip, where you will need the small image list. Add a static callback function to enumerate the fonts:

```
int CALLBACK CFontsView::AddFontName(
                            ENUMLOGFONT *lpelfe,
                            NEWTEXTMETRIC *lpntme,
                            int FontType,
                            LPARAM lParam)
{
static int nItem = 0;

    CFontsView *fv = (CFontsView *) lParam;
    CListCtrl &FontList = fv->GetListCtrl();
    LV_ITEM lvi;
    memset (&lvi, '\0', sizeof (LV_ITEM));
    lvi.iItem = nItem++;
    lvi.mask = LVIF_IMAGE | LVIF_TEXT;
    switch (FontType)
    {
        case TRUETYPE_FONTTYPE:
            lvi.iImage = 0;
            break;
        default:
            lvi.iImage = 1;
            break;
    }
```

```
    lvi.pszText = lpelfe->elfLogFont.lfFaceName;
    FontList.InsertItem (&lvi);
    return (TRUE);
}
```

This time you are adding the font to a list view item structure instead of an extended combo box structure. The list control uses an *LV_ITEM* structure to access the list items, as shown next. To add an item, you first fill in the structure. Only the items identified in the *mask* member are used by the list control, and in the preceding code you are setting only the text and image members of the control. Later, when you use *LPSTR_TEXTCALLBACK* and *I_IMAGECALLBACK*, you will use the *lParam* member. This member may contain any user-defined *long* value and usually is used to point to a data structure containing the list information.

```
typedef struct _LVITEM {
    UINT   mask;
    int    iItem;
    int    iSubItem;
    UINT   state;
    UINT   stateMask;
    LPTSTR pszText;
    int    cchTextMax;
    int    iImage;
    LPARAM lParam;
#if (_WIN32_IE >= 0x0300)
    int iIndent;
#endif
} LVITEM, FAR *LPLVITEM;
```

Next, add the following code to the *PreCreateWindow()* function and the *OnInitialUpdate()* function, both of which should have been added when the wizard created your project:

```
BOOL CFontsView::PreCreateWindow(CREATESTRUCT& cs)
{
    cs.style &= ~LVS_TYPEMASK;
    cs.style |= LVS_ICON | LVS_SORTASCENDING;

    return CListView::PreCreateWindow(cs);
}
//
// Create the image lists and load the list control
// in OnInitialUpdate.
void CFontsView::OnInitialUpdate()
{
    CListView::OnInitialUpdate();

    if (m_SmallImages.m_hImageList == NULL)
        m_Images.Create (16, 16, ILC_MASK, 2, 2);
    if (m_LargeImages.m_hImageList == NULL)
        m_Images.Create (32, 32, ILC_MASK, 2, 2);
    HICON hIcon = AfxGetApp()->LoadIcon (IDI_TRUETYPEFONTS);
    m_SmallImages.Add (hIcon);
    m_LargeImages.Add (hIcon);
    DeleteObject (hIcon);
    hIcon = AfxGetApp()->LoadIcon (IDI_PRINTERFONTS);
    m_SmallImages.Add (hIcon);
    m_LargeImages.Add (hIcon);
```

```
    DeleteObject (hIcon);
    GetListCtrl().SetImageList(&m_SmallImages,LVSIL_SMALL);
    GetListCtrl().SetImageList(&m_LargeImages,LVSIL_NORMAL);
    CWindowDC dc (this);
    ::EnumFontFamilies ((HDC) dc, NULL,
            (FONTENUMPROC) AddFontName, (LPARAM) this);
}
```

This function creates two image lists, one for the large icon and the other for the small icons. As each icon is loaded into memory and placed in the lists, it is deleted because it no longer is needed. Afterward, the image lists are linked to the list control using *SetImageList()*. The small images are identified as *LVSIL_SMALL* and the large images by *LVSIL_NORMAL*.

Last, call the function to enumerate the fonts. This is where the items are added to the list control.

You should remove the Open, New, Save, and Save As items from the File menu. The default implementation of the document class doesn't do anything. If you don't, the only problem you will have is that the program will assert when you select one of the operations that causes the view to be reinitialized. To prevent that, override the *WM_DESTROY* message handler and add the following code:

```
void CFontsView::OnDestroy()
{
    CListView::OnDestroy();
    m_SmallImages.DeleteImageList ();
    m_LargeImages.DeleteImageList ();
}
```

This deletes the existing image list, which will be re-created when the frameworks again calls the *OnInitialUpdate()* function.

The *CImageList* class is covered in detail beginning with Tip 892, "Understanding the List Control." For now, you're more interested in the list control, so compile the program and run it. The window should display an array of large font icons labeled with the name of the font, similar to Figure 651. This is the normal icon view of the list control. The items are sorted alphabetically across the screen as the result of the *LVIS_SORTASCENDING* style applied in *PreCreateWindow()*.

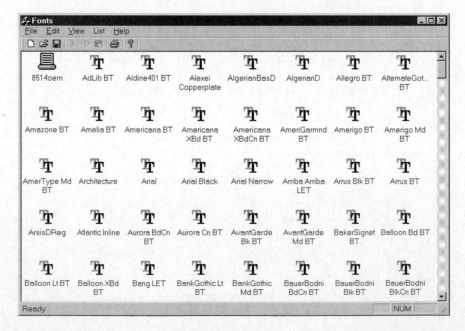

Figure 651   The large icon view is the normal display mode for the list control. Note that the items are listed in alphabetic order across the screen as the result of the sort style added to the control.

652. *Displaying the Various Views of the List Control*

Let's finish up the font list by adding menu items to see the various views available in a list. The report mode isn't very exciting because there's not much to show other than the icon to represent the font type and the name of the font. Therefore, you will create a similar list view that displays the contents of the directory and use the report mode to show the type of file, the file size, and the date the file was created and modified.

First, though, add a new pop-up named "List" to the *IDR_MAINFRAME* menu. Under this pop-up, add four items, "Large Icon," "Small Icon," "List," and "Report." The tool-generated resource IDs for these items are fine, so you will stick with them.

Move to the *FontsView.cpp* file and add message handlers for these menu items using the Class Wizard. Assuming that you used the default resource IDs and the default function names, add the following to the message handler functions. Each contains only a single line to change the mode of the list control to match the menu item. The first parameter to *ModifyStyle()* is a mask of the styles to remove, and the second is the styles to add. Remove the three list control styles (even though only one is in the style, you don't know which one, so remove them all). Then add the style you want:

```cpp
// Switch to large icon view
void CFontsView::OnListLargeicon()
{
    GetListCtrl().ModifyStyle (LVS_SMALLICON | LVS_LIST
                            | LVS_REPORT, LVS_ICON, TRUE);
}


// Switch to list mode
void CFontsView::OnListList()
{
    GetListCtrl().ModifyStyle (LVS_SMALLICON | LVS_REPORT
                            | LVS_ICON, LVS_LIST, TRUE);
}


// Switch to report mode
void CFontsView::OnListReport()
{
    GetListCtrl().ModifyStyle (LVS_SMALLICON | LVS_LIST
                            | LVS_ICON, LVS_REPORT, TRUE);
}


// Switch to small icon view.
void CFontsView::OnListSmallicon()
{
    GetListCtrl().ModifyStyle (LVS_REPORT | LVS_LIST
                            | LVS_ICON, LVS_SMALLICON, TRUE);
}
```

Recompile and run the program. Switch among the different views. At first, it's hard to tell the difference between the list mode and the small icon view. If you look more closely, though, you will see that in list mode the fonts are listed in columns, down the screen and then back to the top for the next column. In small icon view, the fonts are listed in rows, across the screen and then back to the left margin for the next row.

Another thing you will notice—actually, it's hard not to notice—is that the report mode generates a blank screen, other than an empty header at the top of the window. That's because you didn't add any columns to display the information. To cure this, add the following code to the *OnInitialUpdate()* function to create a single column across the window. You can add it anywhere in the function as long as it's after the call to *CListView::OnInitialUpdate()*:

```
LV_COLUMN lc;
CRect rc;
GetClientRect (&rc);
memset (&lc, '\0', sizeof (LV_COLUMN));
lc.mask = LVCF_WIDTH;
lc.cx = rc.right;
lc.iSubItem = 0;
GetListCtrl ().InsertColumn (0, &lc);
```

To get rid of the empty header at the top (you have only one column of data, so it doesn't make much sense to display it), add the *LVS_NOCOLUMNHEADER* to the style in the *PreCreateWindow()* function as shown below:

```
cs.style &= ~LVS_TYPEMASK;
cs.style |= LVS_ICON | LVS_SHOWSELALWAYS | LVS_SORTASCENDING
          | LVS_NOCOLUMNHEADER;
```

Recompile and run the program; then, select report mode. You should see a single column of fonts with the icon and the font name. Report mode probably is the most useful of the list control views, particularly if you are doing a database program, but report mode also is one of the pickiest modes when it comes to displaying columns.

Enough fonts. Now create another project named, say, "DirList." Add the same menu items that you used in *FontsView* to display the different modes. Don't worry about icons for the image list; this time, you can "borrow" the system's image list to display icons for the various file types. You will also use the image and text callback modes and see how they make adding and managing the list data more efficient.

After the project is created, remove the file items from the File menu. Add the List menu as you did for the *FontsView* project, but this time, add an "Arrange" item at the end of the List menu. Add message handlers to the view class for the menu items. Add the *PreCreateWindow()* and *OnInitialUpdate()* virtual functions.

Use the Class Wizard to add the following message handlers: *WM_DESTROY, =LVN_GETDISPINFO, WM_LBUTTONDBLCLK, =LVN_COLUMNCLICK, WM_KILLFOCUS,* and *WM_SETFOCUS.* When that's done, the list of message handlers in the *DirListView.h* file should look like the following:

```
afx_msg void OnDestroy();
afx_msg void OnGetdispinfo(NMHDR* pNMHDR, LRESULT* pResult);
afx_msg void OnLButtonDblClk(UINT nFlags, CPoint point);
afx_msg void OnColumnclick(NMHDR* pNMHDR, LRESULT* pResult);
afx_msg void OnKillfocus(NMHDR* pNMHDR, LRESULT* pResult);
afx_msg void OnSetfocus(NMHDR* pNMHDR, LRESULT* pResult);
```

Using the ClassView pane of the Workspace window, add the following functions and member variables with the proper access levels:

```
//  Protected member functions
protected:
    BOOL LoadSystemImageList (UINT uiImageList);
    CString & GetCurrentDirectory();
    static int CALLBACK CompareItems (LPARAM lParam1,
                    LPARAM lParam2, LPARAM lParamSort);
```

```
    void ListDirectory();
    void ListDirectory(CString & strDir);
    bool AddItem(int nIndex, WIN32_FIND_DATA * pfd);
    void FreeItemMemory();
    int  GetIconIndex (WIN32_FIND_DATA &fd, UINT uiOpen = 0);
    int  GetFileType (WIN32_FIND_DATA & fd,
                      CString &strFileType);


//  Public member functions
public:
    void SetDirectoryName (char *dir);


//  Private data members
private:
    int          m_SortItem;
    CString      m_DirectoryName;
    friend class CChildFrame;
    CImageList   m_SmallIcons;
    CImageList   m_LargeIcons;
    int          m_idxDirIcon;
```

Move to the *MainFrm.cpp* file and add message handlers for the *ID_LIST_LARGEICON*, *ID_LIST_SMALLICON*, *ID_LIST_LIST*, *ID_LIST_REPORT*, and *ID_LIST_ARRANGE* menu items. You might be wondering why they are being placed in the *CMainFrm* class rather than in the view class. Later you will split this window into two views to add a tree view on the left (*a la* Windows Explorer), and the reason for this will become more obvious.

Before you start coding the view and mainframe functions, you must add a few helper files to your projects. I generally use three such files:

- *Struct.h* is used to define the various structures used in a project. Keeping them here helps avoid having to search for their definitions.

- *Utility.cpp* is used to define global functions that don't fit into a class definition and may be needed in more than one class, in other words, utility functions.

- *Proto.h* keeps the function prototypes for the functions defined in *utility.cpp*. Add this file to the list of include files when you need to use one of the utility functions.

For this project, the *Struct.h* file contains the following structure definitions:

```
//
//    Struct.h — structures and declarations for DirView
//

#ifndef    __STRUCT_H__
#define    __STRUCT_H__

typedef struct tagITEMINFO
{
    int        nIcon;
    CString    strFileType;
    WIN32_FIND_DATA  fdFile;
} ITEMINFO, *PITEMINFO;


typedef struct tagLISTHEADER
{
    char  *Title;
```

```
   int   Width;
   UINT  Format;
} LISTHEADER;


#endif   // __STRUCT_H__
```

Depending on the project, *utility.h* might contain only a couple or very many utility functions. Sometimes I just copy it over from another project because it might contain functions that are potentially useful in the current project. To create the file, select New from the File menu; then, select the Files page and C++ Source File. Make sure that Add to Project is checked, and enter the file name in the box to the right. For now, the utility file contains the following functions:

```
//
//  utility.cpp -- general-purpose routines
//
//  Some utility routines. These should not be a part of a
//  class because they will be needed before the application
//  starts up or they may be called from routines in various
//  classes. Prototype them in PROTO.H
//
#include       "stdafx.h"
#include       "struct.h"
#include       "proto.h"
#include       <direct.h>
#include       <io.h>


//
// exist is a utility function that simply checks for the
// existence of a file. The mode defaults to
// ACCESS_READWRITE.
//
bool exist (char *path, int mode)
{
    if (!_access (path, mode))
        return (true);
    return (false);
}


//
// Unix time is a more transportable format than the Windows
// FILETIME structure. FileTimeToUnixTime converts the data
// in the structure to the long time_t variable used by Unix
// time functions. It could be made more generic by
// extracting the SYSTEMTIME operations and placing them
// in a separate function.
//
time_t FileTimeToUnixTime (FILETIME *ft)
{
SYSTEMTIME  st;
struct tm   NewTime, *DstTime;
time_t      theTime;

    tzset ();
    FileTimeToSystemTime(ft, &st);
    NewTime.tm_year = st.wYear % 100;
    if (NewTime.tm_year < 70)
```

```
        NewTime.tm_year += 100;

    NewTime.tm_mon = st.wMonth - 1;
    NewTime.tm_mday = st.wDay;
    NewTime.tm_hour = st.wHour;
    NewTime.tm_min = st.wMinute;
    NewTime.tm_sec = st.wSecond;
    theTime = mktime (&NewTime);
    theTime -= _timezone;
    DstTime = localtime (&theTime);
    if (DstTime->tm_isdst)
        theTime += 3600;
    return (theTime);
}
//
// FormatNumber takes a CString reference and an unsigned
// long and formats the number as a string, inserting a
// comma before every third digit. The result is returned
// in the CString. Passing 1234567 would return 1,234,567.
//
void FormatNumber (CString& strText, ULONG ulSize)
{
    TCHAR szBuf[32];

    strText.Empty();
    memset (szBuf, '\0', sizeof (szBuf));
    sprintf (szBuf + 1, "%ld", ulSize);
    TCHAR *psz = szBuf + strlen (szBuf + 1);
    for (int i = 1; *(psz - 1); ++i, --psz)
    {
        if (!(i%3))
            InsertChar (psz, ',');
    }
    strText = (szBuf + 1);
}
//
// InsertChar moves the string to the right one character
// and inserts the character in that position. The
// assumption is that the buffer is long enough to handle
// the extra character.
// The code was written for FormatNumber but has other
// potential uses.
//
void InsertChar (TCHAR *sz, TCHAR ch)
{
    char *s = sz + strlen (sz);
    while (s > sz)
    {
        *s = *(s-1);
        --s;
    }
    *s = ch;
}
```

Prototype these functions in *ptoto.h*. Any time your code needs to call one of these functions, include *proto.h* in the list of include files:

```
//
//  proto.h -- prototypes of generic functions.
//

#ifndef __PROTO_H__

#include   <time.h>

//
//     Modes used by the access command to test the
//     existence of a file
//
#define   ACCESS_EXIST      00  // Existence only
#define   ACCESS_WRITE      02  // Write permission
#define   ACCESS_READ       04  // Read permission
#define   ACCESS_READWRITE  06  // Read and write permission

bool      exist (char *path, int mode = ACCESS_READWRITE);
time_t    FileTimeToUnixTime (FILETIME *ft);
void      FormatNumber(CString& strText, ULONG ulSize);
void      InsertChar (TCHAR *sz, TCHAR ch);

#define __PROTO_H__
#endif        // __PROTO_H__
```

Now that the preliminaries are out of the way, you can start coding the *CDirListView* class. This project will use text and image callback for the list control. Basically, you will save all the information for the list display in memory and place a pointer to that data in the *lParam* member of the list item. When the control needs the information to draw the list item, it sends a reflected *ON_NOTIFY* message, *LVN_GETDISPINFO*, to the view, which will supply the information.

The view also provides for sorting the list according to the data in the various columns. The user clicks on a header column, and the control sorts the data accordingly. This view keeps the directories at the top in all the sorts.

Okay, what are you waiting for? Start coding. Add *proto.h* and *struct.h* to the list of include files in *DirListView.cpp*. Set up the list headers in the *OnInitialUpdate()* function:

```
void CDirListView::OnInitialUpdate()
{
CFont       font;
LV_COLUMN   lc;
int         n;
CListCtrl&  cc = GetListCtrl();
LISTHEADER Titles[] =
    {
    "File Name",   140,   LVCFMT_LEFT,
    "File Type",   120,   LVCFMT_LEFT,
    "Size",         80,   LVCFMT_RIGHT,
    "Created",     110,   LVCFMT_LEFT,
    "Modified",    110,   LVCFMT_LEFT
    };

#define    TITLES    (sizeof (Titles) / sizeof (LISTHEADER))

    CListView::OnInitialUpdate();
```

```
        while (cc.DeleteColumn(0))
            ;
        lc.mask = LVCF_FMT | LVCF_TEXT | LVCF_WIDTH
                            | LVCF_SUBITEM;
        for (n = 0; sub < TITLES; ++n)
        {
            lc.pszText = Titles[n].Title;
            lc.cx = Titles[n].Width;
            lc.fmt = Titles[sub].Format;
            lc.iSubItem = n;
            cc.InsertColumn (n, &lc);
        }
//
// The following tests protect us against the file
// commands on the File menu. They should have been
// removed, but if not...
        if (m_LargeIcons.m_hImageList != NULL)
            m_LargeIcons.Detach();
        LoadSystemImageList (SHGFI_LARGEICON);
        cc.SetImageList (&m_LargeIcons, LVSIL_NORMAL);
        if (m_SmallIcons.m_hImageList != NULL)
            m_SmallIcons.Detach ();
        LoadSystemImageList (SHGFI_SMALLICON);
        cc.SetImageList (&m_SmallIcons, LVSIL_SMALL);
        m_DirectoryName = GetCurrentDirectory ();
        ListDirectory ();
}
```

The *LoadSystemImageList()* function is where you borrow the system icons. You could hunt through the Registry for registered file types and get their icons that way. Then you could extract the icons from *.exe* and other executable files, but you would still come up short after doing a lot of work. The operating system already has done this, and it has included its own icons for drive types and a few other items. If you inquire of the shell to get the icon index for a known item, the shell will return the index along with a handle to its image list. You then can attach your *CImageList* objects to this image list. The system maintains large and small image lists, which are just what you need for this project.

```
BOOL CDirListView::LoadSystemImageList(UINT uiImageList)
{
    SHFILEINFO sfiInfo;
    memset(&sfiInfo, 0, sizeof(SHFILEINFO));
    HIMAGELIST hImages = (HIMAGELIST) (
        SHGetFileInfo (
            "C:\\",
            0,
            &sfiInfo,
            sizeof(sfiInfo),
            SHGFI_SYSICONINDEX | uiImageList)
    );
    if (hImages == NULL)
        return (FALSE);
    switch (uiImageList)
    {
        case SHGFI_LARGEICON:
            m_LargeIcons.Attach (hImages);
            break;
        case SHGFI_SMALLICON:
```

```
            m_SmallIcons.Attach (hImages);
            break;
    }
    return (TRUE);
}
```

The *OnInitialUpdate()* function then gets the current directory name and sets the class member variable. If this works, you will probably be doing this a lot, so it's worth wrapping the code up in its own function. Then *OnInitialUpdate()* calls *ListDirectory()* to load the current directory into the list control. *ListDirectory()* will be called each time the directory changes. It dumps any list control and memory contents and then sets up the new directory items in the list control.

```cpp
CString & CDirListView::GetCurrentDirectory()
{
static CString strCurrentPath;

    strCurrentPath.Empty ();
    int nBytes = ::GetCurrentDirectory (0, NULL);
    char *szDir = new char [nBytes + 1];
    ::GetCurrentDirectory (nBytes + 1, szDir);
    strCurrentPath = szDir;
    delete [] szDir;
    return (strCurrentPath);
}


//
// Overloaded member function to list the current
// directory.
void CDirectoryView::ListDirectory()
{
    ListDirectory (m_DirectoryName);
}


//
// Load the directory into the list control.
//
void CDirListView::ListDirectory(CString &strDir)
{
CListCtrl&  cc = GetListCtrl();
CString     OldDir, FindSpec;
WIN32_FIND_DATA fData;
HANDLE      hFind;
CString     FileName;
int         sub;

    m_DirectoryName = strDir;
    OldDir = GetCurrentDirectory ();
    if (strDir.IsEmpty())
        strDir = OldDir;

    FindSpec = strDir;
    sub = FindSpec.GetLength();
    if (sub)
    {
        if (FindSpec.GetAt (sub - 1) == '\\')
            FindSpec += "*.*";
```

```
        else
            FindSpec += "\\*.*";
    }
    FreeItemMemory();
    cc.DeleteAllItems ();
    hFind = FindFirstFile(FindSpec, &fData);
    if (hFind == INVALID_HANDLE_VALUE)
        return;

    int i = 0;
    do
    {
        if (!strcmp (fData.cFileName, "."))
            continue;
        if (!AddItem(i, &fData))
            break;
        ++i;
    } while (FindNextFile(hFind, &fData));
    FindClose (hFind);
    cc.SortItems (CompareItems, 0);
    cc.RedrawItems (0, cc.GetItemCount() - 1);
}
```

The two new functions called by *ListDirectory()* are *FreeItemMemory()*, which cleans up any objects created on the heap by previous calls to this function, and *AddItem()*, which creates the items on the heap and loads their addresses into the list control. In *AddItem()*, you allocate memory for a structure to contain the data and then copy the information into memory. Then you call a couple of functions to get the icon index for the file and a description if the file type is registered from the Windows shell. The address of the new structure is placed in the *lParam* member of the list view item structure. Using text and image callback, all you have to add to the list control item is the item number. *LPSTR_TEXTCALLBACK* is the default for subcolumns, so you don't need to bother loading them.

```
//
// Free up any heap structures. The list control data thus
// becomes invalid, so dump it, too.
//
void CDirListView::FreeItemMemory()
{
CListCtrl&  cc = GetListCtrl();

    int nCount = cc.GetItemCount ();
    for (int i = 0; i < nCount; ++i)
        delete (ITEMINFO *) cc.GetItemData (i);
    cc.DeleteAllItems ();
}


//
// Add an item to the list control. Get the icon index
// and the file type string from the shell and add that
// to the WIN32_FIND_DATA.
//
bool CDirListView::AddItem(int nIndex, WIN32_FIND_DATA *pfd)
{
ITEMINFO    *pItem;
LV_ITEM     lvitem;
```

```
// Allocate a new memory object for this item
    try
    {
        pItem = new ITEMINFO;
    }
    catch (CMemoryException *e)
    {
        e->Delete ();
        return (false);
    }
    memset ((char *) &lvitem, '\0', sizeof (LV_ITEM));
    memcpy (&pItem->fdFile, pfd, sizeof (WIN32_FIND_DATA));
    GetFileType (pItem->fdFile, pItem->strFileType);
    UINT uiOpen = 0;
    if (!strcmp (pItem->fdFile.cFileName, ".."))
        uiOpen = SHGFI_OPENICON;
    pItem->nIcon = GetIconIndex (pItem->fdFile, uiOpen);

//
// Set the state mask. This will allow us to do drag and
// drop operations later.
//
#undef STATEMASK
#define     STATEMASK   LVIS_CUT | LVIS_DROPHILITED\\
                        | LVIS_FOCUSED | LVIS_SELECTED

    lvitem.mask = LVIF_TEXT | LVIF_IMAGE | LVIF_PARAM
                            | LVIF_STATE;
    lvitem.stateMask = STATEMASK;
    lvitem.iItem = nIndex;
    lvitem.iSubItem = 0;
    lvitem.iImage = I_IMAGECALLBACK;
    lvitem.pszText = LPSTR_TEXTCALLBACK;
    lvitem.lParam = (LPARAM) pItem;

    if (GetListCtrl ().InsertItem (&lvitem) < 0)
        return (false);
    return (true);
}
```

Now that you've borrowed the system image list, the *AddItem()* function calls one routine to get the icon index from the shell and another to get the registered file type:

```
int CDirListView::GetIconIndex(WIN32_FIND_DATA &fd,
                                UINT uiOpen)
{
    SHFILEINFO sfi;
    memset(&sfi, 0, sizeof(sfi));
    CString strFilePath = m_DirectoryName;
//
// If the directory doesn't include a backslash at the end,
// add it before tacking on the file name.
//
    if (strFilePath.GetAt(strFilePath.GetLength()-1)!='\\')
        strFilePath += '\\';
    strFilePath += fd.cFileName;
```

```
//
// If a directory, get the proper icon. This will OR in
// any value passed in the uiOpen parameter.
//
    if (fd.dwFileAttributes & FILE_ATTRIBUTE_DIRECTORY)
    {
        SHGetFileInfo (strFilePath,
            FILE_ATTRIBUTE_DIRECTORY,
            &sfi, sizeof(sfi),
            SHGFI_SMALLICON | SHGFI_SYSICONINDEX |
            SHGFI_USEFILEATTRIBUTES | uiOpen);
        return (sfi.iIcon);
    }
    else
    {
        SHGetFileInfo (strFilePath, FILE_ATTRIBUTE_NORMAL,
            &sfi, sizeof(sfi),
            SHGFI_SMALLICON | SHGFI_SYSICONINDEX |
            SHGFI_USEFILEATTRIBUTES);
        return (sfi.iIcon);
    }
//
// return -1 on error
//
    return (-1);
}


//
// Get the string description for registered file types.
//
int CDirListView::GetFileType(WIN32_FIND_DATA &fd,
                                CString &strFileType)
{
    SHFILEINFO sfi;
    memset(&sfi, 0, sizeof(sfi));
    CString strFilePath = m_DirectoryName;
    strFilePath += '\\';
    strFilePath += fd.cFileName;
    SHGetFileInfo (
        strFilePath,
        FILE_ATTRIBUTE_NORMAL,
        &sfi,
        sizeof(sfi),
        SHGFI_TYPENAME);
    strFileType = sfi.szTypeName;
    return (0);
}
```

Just one more function and a few housekeeping statements and you will be ready for the first test of your program. Now that you've told the list control that you will hand-feed it the list information, you must provide a function to handle the message. The item and the subitem (column) numbers are in the structure passed with the message, so you must cast it to the proper type and then extract the necessary information. Retrieve the pointer to the data structure you created in the heap, and feed it back to the control:

```
void CDirListView::OnGetdispinfo(NMHDR* pNMHDR,
                                LRESULT* pResult)
```

```
{
CString     string;
PITEMINFO   pItem;
CTime       Now;
static int count = 0;

    LV_DISPINFO* pDispInfo = (LV_DISPINFO*)pNMHDR;
    pItem = (PITEMINFO) pDispInfo->item.lParam;

    if (pDispInfo->item.mask & LVIF_TEXT)
    {
        switch (pDispInfo->item.iSubItem)
        {
            case 0:         // Need file name
                if (!strcmp ((LPCSTR) pItem->fdFile.cFileName,
                                _T("..")))
                {
                    ::lstrcpy (pDispInfo->item.pszText,
                            (LPCSTR) _T("UP-DIR"));
                        break;
                }
                ::lstrcpy (pDispInfo->item.pszText,
                        (LPCSTR) pItem->fdFile.cFileName);
                break;
            case 1:          // Needs file type
                {
                    CString strFileType;
                    strFileType = pItem->strFileType;
                    if (strFileType.IsEmpty ())
                    {
                        if (pItem->fdFile.dwFileAttributes &
                                FILE_ATTRIBUTE_DIRECTORY)
                            strFileType = "File Folder";
                        else
                        {
                            char *s;
                            if ((s = strchr
                                (pItem->fdFile.cFileName,
                                '.')) != NULL)
                            {
                                ++s;
                                strFileType = s;
                                strFileType += ' ';
                            }
                            strFileType += "File";
                        }
                    }
                    ::lstrcpy (pDispInfo->item.pszText,
                            (LPCSTR) strFileType);
                }
                break;
            case 2:          // Needs file size;
                if (pItem->fdFile.dwFileAttributes &
                            FILE_ATTRIBUTE_DIRECTORY)
                {
                    if (!strcmp
```

```
                      ((LPCSTR) pItem->fdFile.cFileName,
                      ".."))
                  string = "UP-DIR";
              else
                  string = "SUB-DIR";
          }
          else
          {
              FormatNumber (string,
                          pItem->fdFile.nFileSizeLow);
          }
          ::lstrcpy (pDispInfo->item.pszText,
                      (LPCSTR) string);
          break;
      case 3:          // Needs created date
          Now = pItem->fdFile.ftCreationTime;
          string.Format ("%02d/%02d/%02d %02d:%02d",
              Now.GetMonth(), Now.GetDay(),
              Now.GetYear() % 100,
              Now.GetHour(), Now.GetMinute());
          ::lstrcpy (pDispInfo->item.pszText,
                      (LPCSTR) string);
          break;
      case 4:          // Needs modified time
          Now = pItem->fdFile.ftLastWriteTime;
          string.Format ("%02d/%02d/%02d %02d:%02d",
              Now.GetMonth(), Now.GetDay(),
              Now.GetYear() % 100,
              Now.GetHour(), Now.GetMinute());
          ::lstrcpy (pDispInfo->item.pszText,
                      (LPCSTR) string);
          break;
      }
  }

  if (pDispInfo->item.mask & LVIF_IMAGE)
  {
      pDispInfo->item.iImage = pItem->nIcon;
  }
  *pResult = 0;
}
```

Now for a couple of housekeeping statements and then you can compile and run your program. In the *OnDestroy()* virtual function, you must free any objects you created on the heap, namely, the data structures for the list display. You must do this in *OnDestroy()*. Don't try to do it in the destructor. By the time the destructor is called, the list control has been destroyed, and you no longer can get to the pointers. Also, detach the image list objects from the system image lists here. On Windows NT, it's no problem; the system won't let you delete the system image list. Windows 95, however, is like an idiot trying to figure out how he got a W&W in a package of M&Ms, and it will delete the image list. You wind up with a desktop full of labels without icons. Nothing is deleted physically, of course, and the next time the desktop restarts (usually with a reboot), the icons reappear.

Also, in the *PreCreateWindow()* function, set up the initial styles you need for the list control:

```
BOOL CDirListView::PreCreateWindow(CREATESTRUCT& cs)
{
```

```
//
// Set the list control for report view and
// add ownerdraw style.
   cs.style &= ~LVS_TYPEMASK;
   cs.style |= LVS_REPORT | LVS_SHOWSELALWAYS
                        | LVS_SHAREIMAGELISTS;
   return CListView::PreCreateWindow(cs);
}


void CDirListView::OnDestroy()
{

   FreeItemMemory();
   m_SmallIcons.Detach ();
   m_LargeIcons.Detach ();


   CListView::OnDestroy();
}
```

Add a dummy *return(0)* statement to *CompareItems()*; then, compile and run your program. If all went well, you should see a window that looks similar to Figure 652. Don't worry about that *res* directory being out of place. It will move up when you add your own sort function. Right now you can't change the view from the program, but try changing the style in *PreCreateWindow()*. Instead of *LVS_REPORT*, try *LVS_ICON*, *LVS_SMALLICON* or *LVS_LIST*.

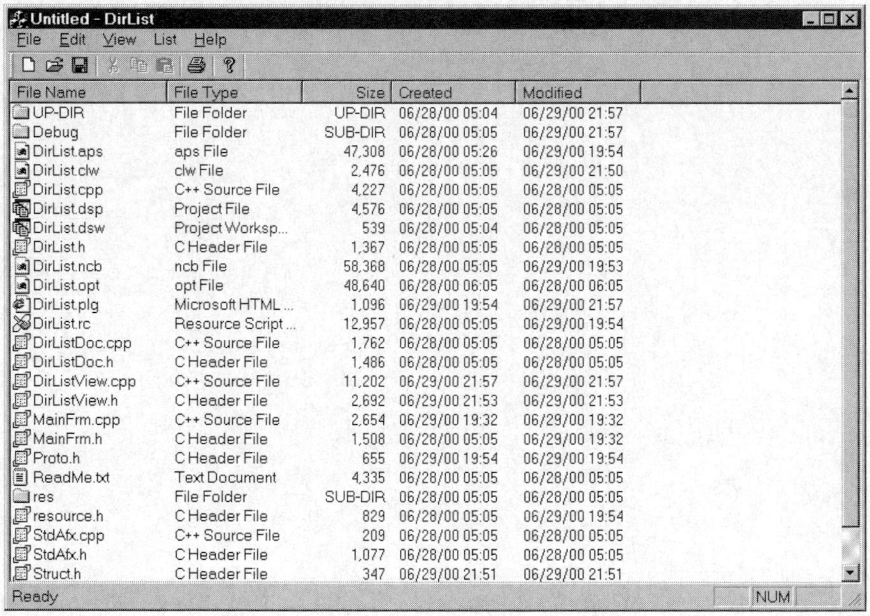

Figure 652   The current directory is listed in report view using system icons and descriptions for registered file types

Check the debug panel on the Output window for memory leaks. You've done a heap of heap operations, and you want to make sure that all the memory is deleted when the program exits. You will have either none or so many you can't find enough sticks to throw at them. If you do have memory leaks, check the *OnDestroy()* and *FreeItemMemory()* functions to make sure that the code in them is correct.

Add the code for the *CompareItems()*, *OnColumnClick()*, and *OnLButtonDblClick* functions. For the present, you won't have to worry about the *OnSetFocus()* and *OnKillFocus()* functions.

```
//
// Compare two items and return their difference. Use strcmp
```

```
// on strings. The name comparison (case Ø) forces the
// directory to stay on the top of the list. In the other
// cases, any time a directory is involved, recursively call
// the sort function to sort by name.
//
int CALLBACK CDirListView::CompareItems(LPARAM lParam1
                          LPARAM lParam2, LPARAM lParamSort)
{
int nResult;
time_t time1, time2;

    ITEMINFO *pItem1 = (ITEMINFO *) lParam1;
    ITEMINFO *pItem2 = (ITEMINFO *) lParam2;
    switch (lParamSort)
    {
        case Ø:              // Sort by name
//
//  The following tests force the UP-DIR item to always
//  land on top of the list.
//
            if (!strcmp ((LPCSTR) pItem1->fdFile.cFileName,
                                "..")) 
                return (-1);
            if (!strcmp ((LPCSTR) pItem2->fdFile.cFileName,
                                "..")) 
                return (1);
//
//  The following tests cause SUB-DIR items to always
//  stay above normal file items.
//
            if ((pItem1->fdFile.dwFileAttributes &
                        FILE_ATTRIBUTE_DIRECTORY) &&
                !(pItem2->fdFile.dwFileAttributes &
                        FILE_ATTRIBUTE_DIRECTORY))
                return (-1);
            if (!(pItem1->fdFile.dwFileAttributes &
                        FILE_ATTRIBUTE_DIRECTORY) &&
                (pItem2->fdFile.dwFileAttributes &
                        FILE_ATTRIBUTE_DIRECTORY))
                return (1);
//
//  The remaining tests compare directory/directory or
//  file/file names.
//
            nResult=strcmpi((LPCSTR)pItem1->fdFile.cFileName,
                        (LPCSTR) pItem2->fdFile.cFileName);
            break;
        case 1:              // Sort by file type
//
//  If a directory is involved, sort by name.
//
            if ((pItem1->fdFile.dwFileAttributes &
                        FILE_ATTRIBUTE_DIRECTORY) ||
                (pItem2->fdFile.dwFileAttributes &
                        FILE_ATTRIBUTE_DIRECTORY))
                return (CompareItems (lParam1, lParam2, Ø));
```

```
                    nResult = (int) (strcmp (
                                (LPCSTR) pItem1->strFileType,
                                (LPCSTR) pItem2->strFileType));
                break;
            case 2:              // Sort by size
//
//   If a directory is involved, sort by name.
//
                if ((pItem1->fdFile.dwFileAttributes &
                                FILE_ATTRIBUTE_DIRECTORY) ||
                    (pItem2->fdFile.dwFileAttributes &
                                FILE_ATTRIBUTE_DIRECTORY))
                    return (CompareItems (lParam1, lParam2, 0));
                nResult = (int) (pItem1->fdFile.nFileSizeLow
                                - pItem2->fdFile.nFileSizeLow);
                break;
            case 3:              // Sort by creation time
//
//   If a directory is involved, sort by name.
//
                if ((pItem1->fdFile.dwFileAttributes &
                                FILE_ATTRIBUTE_DIRECTORY) ||
                    (pItem2->fdFile.dwFileAttributes &
                                FILE_ATTRIBUTE_DIRECTORY))
                    return (CompareItems (lParam1, lParam2, 0));
                time1 = FileTimeToUnixTime (
                                &pItem1->fdFile.ftCreationTime);
                time2 = FileTimeToUnixTime (
                                &pItem2->fdFile.ftCreationTime);
                nResult = (int) (time1 - time2);
                break;
            case 4:              // Sort by modified time
//
//   If a directory is involved, sort by name.
//
                if ((pItem1->fdFile.dwFileAttributes &
                                FILE_ATTRIBUTE_DIRECTORY) ||
                    (pItem2->fdFile.dwFileAttributes &
                                FILE_ATTRIBUTE_DIRECTORY))
                    return (CompareItems (lParam1, lParam2, 0));
                time1 = FileTimeToUnixTime (
                                &pItem1->fdFile.ftLastWriteTime);
                time2 = FileTimeToUnixTime (
                                &pItem2->fdFile.ftLastWriteTime);
                nResult = (int) (time1 - time2);
                break;
    }
    return (nResult);
}


//
// OnColumnClick calls the list control to sort the list
// according to the subcolumn clicked.
//
void CDirListView::OnColumnclick(NMHDR* pNMHDR, LRESULT* pResult)
{
```

```
    NM_LISTVIEW* pNMListView = (NM_LISTVIEW*)pNMHDR;
    // TODO: Add your control notification handler code here
    GetListCtrl().SortItems (CompareItems,
                             pNMListView->iSubItem);


    *pResult = 0;
}


//
// OnLButtonDblClick right now works only on directory
// entries and causes the program to list the directory
// that was clicked.
//void CDirListView::OnLButtonDblClk(UINT nFlags,
                                      CPoint point)
{
ITEMINFO *pItem;
LV_ITEM lvItem;

    memset (&lvItem, '\0', sizeof (LV_ITEM));
    POSITION pos =
            GetListCtrl().GetFirstSelectedItemPosition();
    if (pos == NULL)
        return;
    int nItem = GetListCtrl().GetNextSelectedItem(pos);
    pItem = (ITEMINFO *)
                        (GetListCtrl().GetItemData (nItem));
    if (!(pItem->fdFile.dwFileAttributes &
                        FILE_ATTRIBUTE_DIRECTORY))
    {
        CListView::OnLButtonDblClk(nFlags, point);
        return;
    }
    CString OldDir = m_DirectoryName;
    CString strDir;
    if (!(strcmp(pItem->fdFile.cFileName, "..")))
    {
        int nIndex = OldDir.ReverseFind (_T('\\'));
        if (nIndex > 0)
        {
            strDir = OldDir.Left(nIndex);
//
//  Are we at the root? we need to add the backslash if so
//
            nIndex = strDir.Find (_T('\\'));
            if (nIndex < 0)
                strDir += '\\';
        }
    }
    else
    {
        strDir = OldDir;
//
//  Add a backslash only if the directory name doesn't
//  already end with a backslash (as at the root directory)
        if (strDir.GetAt (strDir.GetLength() - 1) != '\\')
            strDir += '\\';
```

```
            strDir += pItem->fdFile.cFileName;
        }
//
//  Save the new directory
    m_DirectoryName = strDir;
//  And change to it
    SetCurrentDirectory ((LPCSTR) m_DirectoryName);
//  Show it in the list control
    ListDirectory ();
}
```

Recompile and run your program. Amazingly, that stray *res* directory is in its proper place near the top of the list. Two things should be working now. You should be able to sort by any of the fields simply by clicking on the column header. Also, you should be able to maneuver through the directory structure by double-clicking on a directory icon. The UP-DIR icon should display as an open folder, and double-clicking on it will take you to the next higher directory in the current path. You could remove this item from the list and place it on the toolbar. With it in the list, you can negotiate only to the root directory of the current drive because at that point there is no UP-DIR. Placing it on the toolbar would let you negotiate up one more level to display the drives. Beyond that, you would have to explore the shell interface further, and you just don't have room to do that.

Finally, move over to the *MainFrm.cpp* file and add the code to the view functions. They're very simple, but they do make things look different. At this point, add a private member variable named *m_uiView* of type *UINT*. You will need it in the next tip to set the toolbar buttons. Make sure that the *DirListView.h* header file is among the list of include files.

```
/////////////////////////////////////////////////////////////
// CMainFrame message handlers


void CMainFrame::OnListLargeicon()
{
    CDirListView *view = DYNAMIC_DOWNCAST (CDirListView,
                                           GetActiveView());
    view->GetListCtrl().ModifyStyle (LVS_REPORT
                            | LVS_SMALLICON | LVS_LIST,
                            LVS_ICON, 0);
    m_uiView = ID_LIST_LARGEICON;
}


void CMainFrame::OnListSmallicon()
{
    CDirListView *view = DYNAMIC_DOWNCAST (CDirListView,
                                           GetActiveView());
    view->GetListCtrl().ModifyStyle (LVS_REPORT
                            | LVS_LIST | LVS_ICON,
                            LVS_SMALLICON, 0);
    m_uiView = ID_LIST_SMALLICON;
}


void CMainFrame::OnListReport()
{
    CDirListView *view = DYNAMIC_DOWNCAST (CDirListView,
                                           GetActiveView());
    view->GetListCtrl().ModifyStyle (LVS_LIST
                            | LVS_SMALLICON | LVS_ICON,
```

```
                                      LVS_REPORT, 0);
    m_uiView = ID_LIST_REPORT;
}


void CMainFrame::OnListList()
{
    CDirListView *view = DYNAMIC_DOWNCAST (CDirListView,
                                           GetActiveView());
    view->GetListCtrl().ModifyStyle (LVS_REPORT
                          | LVS_SMALLICON | LVS_ICON,
                          LVS_LIST, 0);
    m_uiView = ID_LIST_LIST;
}


void CMainFrame::OnListArrange()
{
    CDirListView *view = DYNAMIC_DOWNCAST (CDirListView,
                                           GetActiveView());
    view->GetListCtrl().Arrange(LVA_DEFAULT);
}
```

At this point, move to the *PreCreateWindow()* function in *MainFrm.cpp* and add the following line. This will keep "Untitled" from appearing on the title bar of the main window:

```
cs.style &= ~FWS_ADDTOTITLE;
```

Recompile and test your program. The menu items should take you through the four views of the directory. Occasionally, the large icon view will appear in a couple of columns rather than list across the window. If this happens, select the Arrange menu item to restore it to its default arrangement.

653. *Adding Toolbar Buttons to Change the View*

Changing the view of a list control is such a common operation that it's handy to have buttons on a toolbar to do this. You can add the buttons to the standard toolbar, or you can create a separate toolbar containing only buttons for the view and any other related operations, such as an UP-DIR function. In this sample, you will add a toolbar containing the four basic operations to switch between views.

Using the *DirList* project in Tip 652, "Displaying the Various Views of the List Control," create a new toolbar in the Resource Workshop and name it *IDR_VIEWBAR*. The toolbar should contain four buttons, as shown in Figure 653. You yourself can draw the images, or you can take them off the project on the companion CD-ROM.

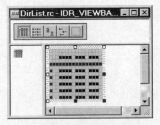

Figure 653   The list view toolbar

Give these buttons the same resource IDs as the menu items. Right-click on an item in the Resource View pane to get the properties page; then, click the push pin to keep the dialog box on top. Click one of the four buttons.

The first button is for the report view, and it should have the resource ID of *ID_LIST_REPORT*. The second is the list view, with a resource ID of *ID_LIST_LIST*. The third is the large icon view, which should have a resource ID of *ID_LIST_LARGEICON*. The fourth button is the small icon view, with a resource ID of *ID_LIST_SMALLICON*.

Add a member variable to *CMainFrame* named *m_wndViewBar* of type *CToolBar*. In the *OnCreate()* function, insert the following code after the main toolbar is created:

```
if (!m_wndViewBar.CreateEx(this, TBSTYLE_FLAT, WS_VISIBLE
                              | CBRS_TOP | CBRS_GRIPPER
                              | CBRS_TOOLTIPS | CBRS_FLYBY
                              | CBRS_SIZE_DYNAMIC,
                     CRect(0, 0, 0, 0),
                     IDR_VIEWBAR)
       || !m_wndViewBar.LoadToolBar(IDR_VIEWBAR))
{
    TRACE0("Failed to create view toolbar\n");
    return -1;      // fail to create
}
```

A few lines down, just before the return statement from *OnCreate()*, add the following two lines:

```
m_wndViewBar.EnableDocking(CBRS_ALIGN_ANY);
DockControlBar(&m_wndViewBar);
```

Recompile your program and test the buttons. They should produce the same views as the menu items. You will notice that when a button is clicked, the view changes and the button returns to its up state. You can stop here, but I prefer to have the buttons on this toolbar work as radio buttons. When a view is selected, the button stays down and any others pop back up. For this, all you must do is add command enablers for the four buttons and set the radio button check.

In the constructor for *CMainFrame*, initialize the *uiView* variable to the same mode you gave the view in the *PreCreateWindow()* function of *CDirListView*. If you set the initial mode to *LVS_REPORT*, initialize this variable to the resource ID of the report button: *uiView = ID_VIEW_REPORT*.

Using the Class Wizard, add command enablers to *CMainFrame* for the four buttons by selecting their resource IDs in the Messages window and *UPDATE_COMMAND_UI*. Then click the Add Function button. Do this for all four buttons. The code for each is a single line:

```
void CMainFrame::OnUpdateListLargeicon(CCmdUI* pCmdUI)
{
    pCmdUI->SetRadio (m_uiView == ID_LIST_LARGEICON);
}


void CMainFrame::OnUpdateListList(CCmdUI* pCmdUI)
{
    pCmdUI->SetRadio (m_uiView == ID_LIST_LIST);
}


void CMainFrame::OnUpdateListReport(CCmdUI* pCmdUI)
{
    pCmdUI->SetRadio (m_uiView == ID_LIST_REPORT);
}
```

```
void CMainFrame::OnUpdateListSmallicon(CCmdUI* pCmdUI)
{
    pCmdUI->SetRadio (m_uiView == ID_LIST_SMALLICON);
}
```

Recompile and test the program. The toolbar should have the proper view button depressed when the program starts, and the button should change as you select different views either by clicking a button or by selecting a menu item. Notice on the menu that the *SetRadio()* function adds a bullet next to the currently selected item.

Just a few tips down the road (Tip 657, "Combining *CTreeView*, *CListView*, and *CSplitterWnd* to Create an Explorer-Type Application"), you will add a splitter window to this application and place a tree view on the left side. You can stop here and develop this into whatever application you need. The project will be duplicated on the companion CD-ROM so that you will have a copy of the code up to this point.

654. *Using the LVS_OWNERDRAWFIXED Style*

The list control class *CListCtrl* doesn't have many virtual functions that you can override to improve performance. It's a good control as it stands, needing only your code to implement it.

One function that can be overridden, however, is the *OnDraw* function. This function is called any time you have the *LVS_OWNERDRAWFIXED* style set and the control has to draw an item in the window. If you set this style and don't override *OnDraw*, the program will assert because it expects you to provide the drawing code.

The list control and its MFC class are well done, and Microsoft deserves a compliment on this one. Except for the display of the current selection in report view, I haven't found much reason to implement the owner draw property.

Fortunately, this selection display problem is easy to fix by switching into owner draw mode when the report view is selected. The next tip shows you how to do that.

655. *Using the Owner Draw Property to Create a Full Line Selection*

One potential problem with the list control is that when you select an item, it highlights only the first column of the selection. Not only that, it selects only the text in the first column, so if you have a short item in the first column, the selection could be lost to the user.

When you add the *LVS_OWNERDRAWFIXED* style to the list view, or to the list control for that matter, you must override the *OnDraw()* member function and draw the list item in your own code on demand.

By selectively adding | *LVS_OWNERDRAWFIXED* when you switch to report view, you can provide the list view with the much-needed full line selection. You do this by placing a class derived form *CListView* between your view class and *CListView*. The intermediate class in this example is named *CListViewEx*. You might want to consider it for your gallery.

Add the *CListViewEx* class files to your project. Then add *ListViewEx.h* to the list of include files in your view class, *CDirListView* in this case. The code for the header file is shown here:

```cpp
/////////////////////////////////////////////////////////////
// CListViewEx view
#include   "afxcview.h"

class CListViewEx : public CListView
{
    DECLARE_DYNCREATE(CListViewEx)

// Construction
public:
    CListViewEx();

// Attributes

public:


// Overrides
protected:
   virtual void DrawItem(LPDRAWITEMSTRUCT lpDrawItemStruct);

    // Class Wizard-generated virtual function overrides
    //{{AFX_VIRTUAL(CListViewEx)
    public:
    protected:
    //}}AFX_VIRTUAL

// Implementation
public:
    virtual ~CListViewEx();
#ifdef _DEBUG
    virtual void Dump(CDumpContext& dc) const;
#endif

protected:

// Generated message map functions
protected:
    //{{AFX_MSG(CListViewEx)
    //}}AFX_MSG
    DECLARE_MESSAGE_MAP()

public:
    void      SetNormalTextColor (COLORREF newTextColor);
    void      SetNormalBkgndColor (COLORREF newBackColor);
    void      SetHiliteTextColor (COLORREF newTextColor);
    void      SetHiliteBkgndColor (COLORREF newBackColor);
    void      SetSelectedTextColor (COLORREF newTextColor);
    void      SetSelectedBkgndColor (COLORREF newBaclColor);

protected:
    COLORREF    m_NormalTextColor;
    COLORREF    m_NormalBackColor;
```

```
    COLORREF      m_HighlightTextColor;
    COLORREF      m_HighlightBackColor;
    COLORREF      m_SelectedTextColor;
    COLORREF      m_SelectedBackColor;

    CFont         m_NormalFont;
    CFont         m_BoldFont;

};
```

The color variables and functions were added to support a particular project that needed the color capability. You won't be using them for this project, and you can remove them if you don't plan on using custom colors.

You can add functions to the class all you want; the only base class function you can override, however, is the *OnDraw()* function. The code for *ListViewEx.cpp* is shown here, and after that you will see how to integrate it into your project:

```
// ListViewEx.cpp implementation file
//

#include "stdafx.h"
#include "DirList.h"
#include "ListViewEx.h"
#include "stdafx.h"
#include    "proto.h"

#ifdef _DEBUG
#define new DEBUG_NEW
#undef THIS_FILE
static char THIS_FILE[] = __FILE__;
#endif

// offsets for first and other columns
#define TEXT_OFFSET   6


/////////////////////////////////////////////////////////////
// CListViewEx

IMPLEMENT_DYNCREATE(CListViewEx, CListView)

BEGIN_MESSAGE_MAP(CListViewEx, CListView)
    //{{AFX_MSG_MAP(CListViewEx)
    //}}AFX_MSG_MAP
END_MESSAGE_MAP()


/////////////////////////////////////////////////////////////
// CListViewEx construction/destruction

CListViewEx::CListViewEx()
{

    m_NormalTextColor = ::GetSysColor(COLOR_WINDOWTEXT);
    m_NormalBackColor = ::GetSysColor(COLOR_WINDOW);
    m_HighlightTextColor=::GetSysColor(COLOR_HIGHLIGHTTEXT);
    m_HighlightBackColor = ::GetSysColor(COLOR_HIGHLIGHT);
    m_SelectedTextColor = ::GetSysColor(COLOR_INFOTEXT);
```

```
    m_SelectedBackColor=::GetSysColor(COLOR_INACTIVEBORDER);

    m_NormalFont.CreatePointFont (80, "MS Sans Serif");
    m_BoldFont.CreatePointFont (120, "Arial Bold");
}


CListViewEx::~CListViewEx()
{
}


////////////////////////////////////////////////////////////
// CListViewEx drawing

void CListViewEx::DrawItem(LPDRAWITEMSTRUCT
                                        lpDrawItemStruct)
{
    CListCtrl& lc=GetListCtrl();
    CDC* pDC = CDC::FromHandle(lpDrawItemStruct->hDC);
    CRect rcItem(lpDrawItemStruct->rcItem);
    UINT uiFlags;
    CImageList* pImageList;
    int nItem = lpDrawItemStruct->itemID;
    BOOL bFocus = (GetFocus() == this);
    COLORREF clrTextSave;
    COLORREF clrImage = m_NormalBackColor;
    CRect rcIcon;

    pImageList = lc.GetImageList (LVSIL_SMALL);
    CRect r;
    GetClientRect (r);
    rcItem.right = r.right;

    LV_ITEM lvi;
    lvi.mask = LVIF_IMAGE | LVIF_STATE;
    lvi.iItem = nItem;
    lvi.iSubItem = 0;
    lvi.stateMask = 0xFFFF;      // get all state flags
    lc.GetItem(&lvi);

    CRect rcFullRow;
    lc.GetItemRect(nItem, rcFullRow, LVIR_BOUNDS);

    CRect rcLabel;
    lc.GetItemRect(nItem, rcLabel, LVIR_LABEL);

    CRect rcSubLabels = rcFullRow;
    rcSubLabels.left = rcLabel.right;

//  Show the colors.
//
//  There are six cases.
//      The item is selected and the view has the focus
//      The item is selected and the view does not have
//       the focus
//      The item has the focus and is not selected and
//       the view has the focus
```

```
//      The item has the focus, is not selected and the
//        view does not have the focus
//      the item does not have the focus and is not
//        selected and the view has the focus
//      the item does not have the focus and is not
//        selected and the view does not have the focus
//

    lc.GetItemRect(nItem, rcIcon, LVIR_ICON);
    if (rcIcon.right > 2)
        rcFullRow.left += rcIcon.right + TEXT_OFFSET / 2;


    if (bFocus) // The view has the focus
    {
        if (lvi.state & LVIS_FOCUSED)
        {
            clrTextSave = pDC->SetTextColor(
                                      m_HighlightTextColor);
            pDC->FillRect(rcFullRow,
                            &CBrush(m_HighlightBackColor));
        }
        else if (lvi.state & LVIS_SELECTED)
        {
            clrTextSave = pDC->SetTextColor(
                                      m_HighlightTextColor);
            pDC->FillRect(rcFullRow,
                            &CBrush(m_HighlightBackColor));
        }
        else
        {
            clrTextSave = pDC->SetTextColor(
                                        m_NormalTextColor);
            pDC->FillRect(rcFullRow,
                            &CBrush(m_NormalBackColor));
        }
    }
    else
    {
        if ((lvi.state & LVIS_FOCUSED) &&
                        (GetStyle() & LVS_SHOWSELALWAYS))
        {
            pDC->Rectangle (rcFullRow);
            pDC->SetTextColor(m_NormalTextColor);
            pDC->FillRect(rcFullRow,
                            &CBrush(m_SelectedBackColor));
        }
        else if ((lvi.state & LVIS_SELECTED) &&
                        (GetStyle() & LVS_SHOWSELALWAYS))
        {
            pDC->SetTextColor(m_NormalTextColor);
            pDC->FillRect(rcFullRow,
                            &CBrush(m_SelectedBackColor));
        }
        else
        {
            clrTextSave = pDC->SetTextColor(
                                        m_NormalTextColor);
```

```
                    pDC->FillRect(rcFullRow,
                                &CBrush(m_NormalBackColor));
            }
    }
    BOOL bSelected = lvi.state &
                    (LVIS_DROPHILITED | LVIS_SELECTED);

//
// Set the color and mask for the icon.
// There are several values you can try:
//      ILD_BLEND25 -- Blends 25 percent of
//                      the system system color.
//      ILD_BLEND50 -- Blends 50 percent of
//                      the system system color.
//      ILD_NORMAL  -- Draws the image using the
//                      image list background color.
//
    if (lvi.state & LVIS_CUT)
    {
        clrImage = m_NormalBackColor;
        uiFlags |= ILD_SELECTED;
    }
    else if (bSelected)
    {
        clrImage = ::GetSysColor(COLOR_HIGHLIGHT);
        uiFlags |= ILD_FOCUS;
    }
    else
    {
        uiFlags = ILD_TRANSPARENT;
    }
//
// Draw the state icon if there is one
//
    UINT nStateImageMask = lvi.state & LVIS_STATEIMAGEMASK;
    if (nStateImageMask)
    {
        int nImage = (nStateImageMask>>12) - 1;
        pImageList = lc.GetImageList(LVSIL_STATE);
        if (pImageList)
        {
            pImageList->Draw(pDC, nImage,
                CPoint(rcItem.left, rcItem.top), uiFlags);
        }
    }
//
// Draw the icon if there is one
//
    pImageList = lc.GetImageList(LVSIL_SMALL);
    if (pImageList)
    {
        lc.GetItemRect(nItem, rcIcon, LVIR_ICON);
        UINT nOvlImageMask=lvi.state & LVIS_OVERLAYMASK;
        if (rcItem.left<rcItem.right-1)
        {
            ImageList_DrawEx(pImageList->m_hImageList,
```

```
                            lvi.iImage,
                            pDC->m_hDC,
                            rcIcon.left + 1,
                            rcIcon.top + 1,
                            16, 16,
                            GetSysColor (COLOR_WINDOW),
                            clrImage,
                            uiFlags | nOvlImageMask);
        }
    }

    UINT uiAlign;
    uiFlags = DT_SINGLELINE | DT_NOPREFIX | DT_NOCLIP
            | DT_VCENTER | DT_END_ELLIPSIS;
//
// Draw the text in the columns.
//
    LV_COLUMN lvc;
    lvc.mask = LVCF_FMT | LVCF_WIDTH;

    for(int nColumn = 0;
            lc.GetColumn(nColumn, &lvc);
            nColumn++)
    {
        CString strText;
        switch(lvc.fmt & LVCFMT_JUSTIFYMASK)
        {
            case LVCFMT_RIGHT:
                uiAlign = DT_RIGHT;
                break;
            case LVCFMT_CENTER:
                uiAlign = DT_CENTER;
                break;
            default:
                break;
        }
        if (!nColumn)
        {
            lc.GetItemRect(nItem, rcItem, LVIR_LABEL);
            rcLabel = rcItem;
// Override the switch statement. First column is always
// set to the left. (Doesn't have to be; change as needed)
            uiAlign = DT_LEFT;
        }
        else
        {
            rcItem.left = rcItem.right;
            rcItem.right += lvc.cx;
        }

        strText = lc.GetItemText(nItem, nColumn);
        if (strText.IsEmpty())
            continue;

        rcLabel = rcItem;
//
```

```cpp
//  Adjust the text rectangle so that the text doesn't butt
//  up against the edge of the column.
//
        rcLabel.left  += TEXT_OFFSET;
        rcLabel.right -= TEXT_OFFSET;

        pDC->DrawText(strText, rcLabel, uiAlign | uiFlags);
    }
//
// If the item has the focus, draw the focus rectangle
//
    if (lvi.state & LVIS_FOCUSED && bFocus)
        pDC->DrawFocusRect(rcFullRow);
//
// Restore original colors if item was selected
//
    if (bSelected)
    {
        pDC->SetTextColor(clrTextSave);
    }
}

/////////////////////////////////////////////////////////
// CListViewEx diagnostics

#ifdef _DEBUG

void CListViewEx::Dump(CDumpContext& dc) const
{
    CListView::Dump(dc);
}

#endif //_DEBUG

/////////////////////////////////////////////////////////////
// Some color functions. Not needed generally. Cut or modify
// as needed.

//  Sets the text color of an unselected, unhighlighted line
void CListViewEx::SetNormalTextColor (COLORREF newTextColor)
{
    m_NormalTextColor = newTextColor;
}

//  Sets the background color of an unselected,
//  unhighlighted line
void CListViewEx::SetNormalBkgndColor(COLORREF newBackColor)
{
    m_NormalBackColor = newBackColor;
//
//  This is the general background color of the control, so
//  set that now.
    GetListCtrl().SetBkColor (newBackColor);
}

//  Sets the text color of a highlighted line
```

```
void CListViewEx::SetHiliteTextColor (COLORREF newTextColor)
{
    m_HighlightTextColor = newTextColor;
}

//  Sets the background color of a highlighted line
void CListViewEx::SetHiliteBkgndColor(COLORREF newBackColor)
{
    m_HighlightBackColor = newBackColor;
}

//  Sets the text color of a selected line
void CListViewEx::SetSelectedTextColor(COLORREF newTxtColor)
{
    m_SelectedTextColor = newTxtColor;
}

//  Sets the background color of a selected line
void CListViewEx::SetSelectedBkgndColor(COLORREF newBkColor)
{
    m_SelectedBackColor = newBkColor;
}
```

This function first figures how far across the control the columns extend and then fills the rectangle with the proper color. This is necessary to wipe out the effects of any previous drawing. Other schemes I have seen do a full row selection tend to leave "droppings," remnants of the selection color either at the top or bottom as an item scrolls off the window or on the right when the columns don't quite fill the window. So far, I haven't found any instance of this function leaving droppings.

If the list contains icons and an item is selected, the system color for a selected item is blended into the icon color, giving the slightly tinted shade we've come to know and like.

After drawing the icons (you can have a user-defined state icon, as well as the normal icon), the function enters a loop to draw the text in the columns using the *DrawText()* function. This function saves you a lot of work by supplying an ellipsis on the end of the text if it is too wide for the column. The text is offset slightly from the left and right sides of the columns, so it doesn't tend to butt up against the text in the other columns. If the columns are full, they tend to read into each other, but the offset provides white space between them. Adjust this value to suit your needs. It's in a define statement at the top of the file.

Just before the colors are set, three lines of code add offset between the icon and the text:

```
lc.GetItemRect(nItem, rcIcon, LVIR_ICON);
if (rcIcon.right > 2)
    rcFullRow.left += rcIcon.right + TEXT_OFFSET / 2;
```

If you compare the full row select view with the small icon or list views (which are drawn by the control), you see the difference. It looks cleaner to have the text separated from the icon. If you want the list to appear similar to the other views, remove the *TEXT_OFFSET/2*. If you remove all three lines, the selected color rectangle will fill the icon area as well. Try all three and pick the style that suits you.

It's very easy to integrate this intermediate class into your list view. There's still some room for improvement, but over time (I have used it in a number of projects), it has become very stable and reliable.

656. *Using the* CTreeView *Class*

The *CTreeView* class is best used in a splitter window, where it better fits the size of the window. Unless you have some really long labels, it's rare that a tree view looks very good in a full window. You can, of course, resize the window to fit the text, and at times you might want to do this and have a tree view by itself in an application window.

The tree view can have an image list. You yourself can build it, or you can borrow the system image list if you're drawing a directory tree, which is a common use. In this example, you will build a directory tree. Then in the next tip you will put it with the directory list you created in the preceding tips to form an Explorer-type application.

This example will build the tree at its roots only, rather than spend a lot of time searching through all the directories and adding them. The only exception is the current directory. In the *OnInitialUpdate()* function, if you call *SetDirectoryName()* with a parameter of *true*, the current directory will be expanded and selected. To make sure that the plus sign (+) is added to the root nodes, if there are subitems, at least one will be added. When you expand an item, it then will search the directories and add the sublevels. Depending on the drives in your system and the operating system, it still might take a few seconds to start up. For some reason, the program seems to start more quickly on Windows 95 than on Windows NT.

Start off with a new application. The list application was named *DirList*, so maybe name this one "DirTree." Select a single-document interface, and accept the defaults until you get to the last page. There, select *CTreeView* as your view's base class.

Using Class Wizard, add message handlers for *WM_DESTROY*, *=TVN_ITEMEXPANDED*, and *=TVN_SELCHANGED* (these last two are reflected notify messages).

Using the Class View pane of the Workspace window, add the following member functions:

```
public:
    void SetDirectoryName (CString& dir,
                           bool Display = false);
private:
    CString & GetCurrentDirectory();
    void DeleteNode (CString& NodeName);
    void RefreshSelection();
    void BuildPath(CString& path, HTREEITEM node);
    void SelectStartDir(char * StartDir);
    HTREEITEM InsertChild (HTREEITEM parent, char *label,
                           int image, int selimage,
                           HTREEITEM SortType);
    void AddNode (const char * path, HTREEITEM node,
                  int type, int mode);
    void LoadTree();
    void InitializeTree();
    BOOL LoadSystemImageList (UINT uiImageList);
    int  GetIconIndex (WIN32_FIND_DATA fd);
```

In the class definition, add the following enumeration and member variables. The variables should have an access of *private*:

```
enum TreeModes
{
    tmShort = 0,
    tmDetail,
```

```
    tmExpanded
};
private:
    CImageList    m_Images;
    int           m_nLevel;
    CString       m_StartPath;
```

Actually, this is quite a bit simpler than the list view application. You only have to contend with one view. Adding the nodes can be tricky, but for the most part, they are deferred until the tree branch is opened. The code for *CDirTreeView* is shown here:

```cpp
// DirTreeView.cpp : implementation of the
// CDirTreeView class
//

#include "stdafx.h"
#include "DirTree.h"

#include "DirTreeDoc.h"
#include "DirTreeView.h"

#ifdef _DEBUG
#define new DEBUG_NEW
#undef THIS_FILE
static char THIS_FILE[] = __FILE__;
#endif

/////////////////////////////////////////////////////////////
// CDirTreeView

IMPLEMENT_DYNCREATE(CDirTreeView, CTreeView)

BEGIN_MESSAGE_MAP(CDirTreeView, CTreeView)
    //{{AFX_MSG_MAP(CDirTreeView)
    ON_WM_DESTROY()
    ON_NOTIFY_REFLECT(TVN_ITEMEXPANDED, OnItemexpanded)
    ON_NOTIFY_REFLECT(TVN_SELCHANGED, OnSelchanged)
    //}}AFX_MSG_MAP
    // Standard printing commands
    ON_COMMAND(ID_FILE_PRINT, CTreeView::OnFilePrint)
    ON_COMMAND(ID_FILE_PRINT_DIRECT, CTreeView::OnFilePrint)
    ON_COMMAND(ID_FILE_PRINT_PREVIEW,
                              CTreeView::OnFilePrintPreview)
END_MESSAGE_MAP()

/////////////////////////////////////////////////////////////
// CDirTreeView construction/destruction

CDirTreeView::CDirTreeView()
{
    m_nLevel = 0;
}


CDirTreeView::~CDirTreeView()
{
}
```

```
BOOL CDirTreeView::PreCreateWindow(CREATESTRUCT& cs)
{
    // TODO: Modify the Window class or styles here by
    // modifying the CREATESTRUCT cs
    cs.style |= TVS_HASBUTTONS | TVS_HASLINES
              | TVS_LINESATROOT | TVS_DISABLEDRAGDROP
              | TVS_SHOWSELALWAYS;
    return CTreeView::PreCreateWindow(cs);
}


/////////////////////////////////////////////////////////////
// CDirTreeView drawing

void CDirTreeView::OnDraw(CDC* pDC)
{
    CDirTreeDoc* pDoc = GetDocument();
    ASSERT_VALID(pDoc);
    // TODO: add draw code for native data here
}


void CDirTreeView::OnInitialUpdate()
{
    CTreeCtrl&  tc = GetTreeCtrl ();
    CTreeView::OnInitialUpdate();

    LoadSystemImageList (SHGFI_SMALLICON);
    tc.SetImageList (&m_Images, TVSIL_NORMAL);
    InitializeTree ();
}


/////////////////////////////////////////////////////////////
// CDirTreeView printing

BOOL CDirTreeView::OnPreparePrinting(CPrintInfo* pInfo)
{
    // default preparation
    return DoPreparePrinting(pInfo);
}

void CDirTreeView::OnBeginPrinting(CDC* /*pDC*/,
                                   CPrintInfo* /*pInfo*/)
{
    // TODO: add extra initialization before printing
}

void CDirTreeView::OnEndPrinting(CDC* /*pDC*/,
                                 CPrintInfo* /*pInfo*/)
{
    // TODO: add cleanup after printing
}


/////////////////////////////////////////////////////////////
// CDirTreeView diagnostics

#ifdef _DEBUG
```

```
void CDirTreeView::AssertValid() const
{
    CTreeView::AssertValid();
}


void CDirTreeView::Dump(CDumpContext& dc) const
{
    CTreeView::Dump(dc);
}


CDirTreeDoc* CDirTreeView::GetDocument() // non-debug version
                                         // is inline
{
    ASSERT(m_pDocument->IsKindOf(
                        RUNTIME_CLASS(CDirTreeDoc)));
    return (CDirTreeDoc*)m_pDocument;
}
#endif //_DEBUG

/////////////////////////////////////////////////////////////
// CDirTreeView message handlers

void CDirTreeView::SetDirectoryName(CString & dir,
                                    bool Display)
{
    if (!strcmp ((LPCSTR) dir, ".") || dir.IsEmpty())
    {
        m_StartPath = GetCurrentDirectory ();
    }
    else
    {
        m_StartPath = dir;
    }
    if (Display)
    {
        if (m_StartPath.GetLength())
            SelectStartDir ((char *) (LPCSTR)m_StartPath);
    }
}


void CDirTreeView::OnItemexpanded(NMHDR* pNMHDR,
                                  LRESULT* pResult)

{
    NM_TREEVIEW* pNMTreeView = (NM_TREEVIEW*)pNMHDR;


    CTreeCtrl&  tc = GetTreeCtrl ();
// get the node that was expanded or contracted
    HTREEITEM node = pNMTreeView->itemNew.hItem;

//  Get the Tree Item for the node. Zero out the new structure. //
     Tree control functions don't like stray data.
TV_ITEM item;
    memcpy ((char *) &item, (char *) &pNMTreeView->itemNew,
                                      sizeof (TV_ITEM));

//  if the node was contracted, then set the item data so
```

```cpp
//  that later we know not to rebuild the node.
    if (pNMTreeView->action == TVE_COLLAPSE)
    {
        item.mask = TVIF_PARAM;
        item.lParam = CDirTreeView::tmExpanded;
        tc.SetItem(&item);
        return;
    }

// If the node was already built once, then we don't need to
// do it again. If we do, we'll have duplicate entries
    if (item.lParam == CDirTreeView::tmExpanded)
        return;

// remove the first child because we're going to add it
// again. Remember that we have to have already added one
// child per node so that the plus sign gets added to
// the node
    HTREEITEM child = tc.GetChildItem(node);
    if (child)
        tc.DeleteItem(child);

// add this node and all subnodes
    AddNode(0, node, 0, CDirTreeView::tmDetail);

    *pResult = 0;
}

void CDirTreeView::OnSelchanged(NMHDR* pNMHDR,
                                LRESULT* pResult)
{
    NM_TREEVIEW* pNMTreeView = (NM_TREEVIEW*)pNMHDR;

    CTreeCtrl&  tc = GetTreeCtrl ();
    CWaitCursor waitcursor;

//  get the selected node
    HTREEITEM sel = tc.GetSelectedItem();
    CString s;
//  build the path name based on the selection
    BuildPath(s, sel);

//  m_List->ListDirectory (s);

    *pResult = 0;
}

void CDirTreeView::InitializeTree ()
{
    LoadTree ();
    if (m_StartPath.GetLength())
        SelectStartDir ((char *) (LPCSTR)m_StartPath);
}

void CDirTreeView::LoadTree()
{
```

```
char            drives [_MAX_PATH];
char *aDrive, *s;   // = drives;
CTreeCtrl&      tc = GetTreeCtrl ();
HTREEITEM       RootNode = tc.GetRootItem ();

//  Get the drive string. This is a double NUL terminated
//  list, with each item terminated with a NUL.
//
    if (::GetLogicalDriveStrings(_MAX_PATH, drives))
    {
    char    CurDrive[64];  // We need the copy because we
                           // are going to remove any
                           // trailing backslash, which
                           // would screw up our double
                           // NUL terminated list.

        aDrive = drives;
//  Parse the drives
        do
        {
        UINT    type;
//  Get a drive
            strcpy (CurDrive, aDrive);
            type = ::GetDriveType(CurDrive);

            if ((s = strchr (CurDrive, '\\')) != NULL)
                *s = '\0';
//  Make sure the drive letter is caps and add the
//  node for the drive.
            strupr (CurDrive);
            AddNode(CurDrive, RootNode, type,
                    CDirTreeView::tmShort);
                aDrive += strlen (aDrive) + 1;
        } while(strlen (aDrive));
    }
}

void CDirTreeView::RefreshSelection()
{
CString     strSelected;
CTreeCtrl&  tc = GetTreeCtrl ();
UINT        state;

//  Pop up a wait cursor
    CWaitCursor waitcursor;
//  get the selected node
    HTREEITEM sel = tc.GetSelectedItem();
    HTREEITEM parent = tc.GetParentItem(sel);
    state = tc.GetItemState (parent, TVIF_STATE);
    strSelected = tc.GetItemText (sel);
    tc.DeleteItem (sel);
    AddNode ((LPCSTR) strSelected, parent, 0,
            CDirTreeView::tmShort);
    BuildPath (strSelected, parent);
    SelectStartDir ((char *) (LPCSTR)strSelected);
    m_StartPath = strSelected;
    sel = tc.GetSelectedItem();
```

```
        if (state & TVIS_EXPANDED)
            tc.Expand (sel, TVE_EXPAND);          // Always expand
}


void CDirTreeView::DeleteNode(CString & NodeName)
{

}


// AddNode(). This function adds the nodes to the tree. The
// first time we display a node, we don't want to add each
// and every sub-directory to the tree. We only want to add
// nodes when necessary, or it will take forever for the
// program or dialog box to start the first time. At least
// one node is added to the + sign shows up, indicating that the
// node has subdirectories.
// up initially. But, we have to add at least one node so void
CDirTreeView::AddNode(const char * path,
                        HTREEITEM node,
                        int type, int mode)

{
WIN32_FIND_DATA fd;
HANDLE          hFind;
char            buff [_MAX_PATH];   //  temporary storage
HTREEITEM       newNode = node;     //  May be used to build
                                    //  pathname without
                                    //  adding any new nodes.
int             image1, image2; CString        dirPath;


//  If a node name was passed to us, then we will add the
//  node. Otherwise, we need to get a directory name first
//  and then recurse.
//
    if (path)
    {

//  if the mode indicates that we are adding a drive node,
//  then we need to
//      add the drive label in parens.
//      reset the mode to tmShort (actually, on fast
//      machines this doesn't really speed things up).
        if (type >= DRIVE_REMOVABLE)
        {
        char    VolName[24];
        char    RootName[10];
        DWORD   dwCompLen, dwFlags;

            memset (&fd, '\0', sizeof (WIN32_FIND_DATA));
            fd.dwFileAttributes = FILE_ATTRIBUTE_SYSTEM;
            sprintf (RootName, "%s\\", path);
            memset (VolName, '\0', sizeof (VolName));
            strcpy (fd.cFileName, RootName);
            GetVolumeInformation (RootName, VolName, 24,
                            NULL, &dwCompLen,
                            &dwFlags, NULL, 0);
            if (strlen (VolName))
```

```
            {
                wsprintf(buff, "%s (%s)", path, VolName);
            }
            else
                wsprintf (buff, "%s", path);
            image1 = image2 = GetIconIndex (fd);
            newNode = InsertChild (node, buff, image1,
                                   image2, TVI_LAST);
            mode = CDirTreeView::tmShort;
        }
// Otherwise, just use the node name passed
        else
        {
            strcpy(buff, path);

// Add the node as a child to the current node using the
// folder images. Use the sort flag to sort the tree as we
// go
            memset (&fd, '\0', sizeof (WIN32_FIND_DATA));
            strcpy (fd.cFileName, buff);
            fd.dwFileAttributes = FILE_ATTRIBUTE_DIRECTORY;
            image1 = GetIconIndex (fd);
            fd.dwFileAttributes = FILE_ATTRIBUTE_DIRECTORY |
                                  SHGFI_OPENICON;
            image2 = GetIconIndex (fd);
            newNode = InsertChild (node, buff, image1,
                                   image2, TVI_SORT);

        }
    }

// Build a path name based on the node.
    BuildPath(dirPath, newNode);
// Add wildcards
    dirPath += "*.*";
//
// Look for the first match. Return if none.
    if ((hFind = FindFirstFile(dirPath, &fd)) ==
                              INVALID_HANDLE_VALUE)
    {
        return;
    }
// add one to the level we're on
    m_nLevel++;
    do
    {
        if ((fd.dwFileAttributes & FILE_ATTRIBUTE_DIRECTORY)
              && (!(fd.dwFileAttributes &
                  FILE_ATTRIBUTE_HIDDEN)))
        {
            if (!strcmp (fd.cFileName, "."))
            {
                ;          // Current directory. Do nothing.
            }
            else if (!strcmp (fd.cFileName, ".."))
            {
                ;          // Parent directory. Do nothing.
```

```
            }
            else
            {

//  If we are building the initial tree structure
//  (tmShort) or we're expanding a level (tmDetail),
//  add the node by recursion.
                if (((mode == CDirTreeView::tmShort)
                        && (m_nLevel < 2))
                        || (mode == CDirTreeView::tmDetail))
                    AddNode(fd.cFileName, newNode, 0, mode);
//  If we're building the initial structure, we want to add
//  only one subnode to make the plus symbol appear.
                if (mode == CDirTreeView::tmShort)
                    break;

//  In the detail mode we need to fill this branch
//  completely but only one subnode per node under this
//  branch. Again, we have to do this so that the + sign shows up
//  next to the node.
                if ((mode == CDirTreeView::tmDetail) &&
                                    (m_nLevel > 1))
                {
                    break;
                }
            }
        }
    } while (::FindNextFile (hFind, &fd));  // Look for the
                                            // next match

    FindClose (hFind);

// decrement the level counter
    m_nLevel--;
}


//
//  InsertChild() inserts a new node into the tree as a
//  child of the node passed as the parent.Images default to
//  0 and SortType defaults to TVI_SORT
//
HTREEITEM CDirTreeView::InsertChild(HTREEITEM parent,
                                    char * label, int image,
                                    int selimage,
                                    HTREEITEM SortType)
{
CTreeCtrl&      tc = GetTreeCtrl ();
TV_INSERTSTRUCT TreeItem;

//
//  Zero out the new structure. CTreeCtrl doesn't like
//  stray data.
//
    memset ((char *) &TreeItem, '\0',
                    sizeof (TV_INSERTSTRUCT));
    TreeItem.hParent = parent == NULL ? TVI_ROOT : parent;
    TreeItem.hInsertAfter = SortType;
```

```
        TreeItem.item.mask = TVIF_TEXT | TVIF_PARAM | TVIF_IMAGE
                                     | TVIF_SELECTEDIMAGE;
    TreeItem.item.pszText = label;
    TreeItem.item.cchTextMax = strlen (label) + 1;
    TreeItem.item.lParam = 0;
    TreeItem.item.iImage = image;
    TreeItem.item.iSelectedImage = image;
    TreeItem.item.iSelectedImage = selimage;
    return (tc.InsertItem(&TreeItem));
}

void CDirTreeView::SelectStartDir(char * StartDir)
{
char    *startDir, Drive[32];
char    *s;
CTreeCtrl&  tc = GetTreeCtrl ();
HTREEITEM   RootNode, node, SelectedNode;

    if ((StartDir == NULL) || !strlen (StartDir))
        return;
//
//  Make a copy of the directory string.
//
    startDir = new char [strlen (StartDir) + 1];
    strcpy (startDir, StartDir);
//
//  Make sure the path contains no forward slashes.
//
    while ((s = strchr (startDir, '/')) != NULL)
        *s = '\\';

    s = strtok (startDir, "\\");
    if (s == NULL)
    {
        s = startDir;
    }
//
//  Make it all uppercase. Less confusion that way. Our
//  first node should be the device. Append the trailing
//  backslash, which is the way the node is returned from
//  BuildPath
//
//
    strupr (s);
    sprintf (Drive, "%s\\", s);


//  Get the root node
    RootNode = tc.GetRootItem ();
//  Get the first child item of the root node
    node = tc.GetNextItem(RootNode, TVGN_ROOT);
//
//  Loop through the siblings until we find our drive
//
    for (; node; node = tc.GetNextItem(node, TVGN_NEXT))
    {
        CString ItemText;
```

```
            BuildPath (ItemText, node);
//
//  If the root paths match, we've found it
//

        if (!strcmpi (Drive, (LPCSTR) ItemText))
            break;
    }
//
//  Did we find the start for the directory?
//

    if (node == NULL)
    {
        delete [] startDir;
        return;
    }
//
//  Select this item just in case the next strtok is NULL
//

    SelectedNode = node;
    s = strtok (NULL, "\\");    // Get the next part of
                                // the path
    if (s == NULL)              // If none, we are finished.
    {
        tc.Select (SelectedNode, TVGN_CARET);
        delete [] startDir;
        return;
    }
//
//  There's more to look for, so expand this item.
//

    tc.Expand (node, TVE_EXPAND);       // Always expand
    while (s != NULL)
    {
//      for (node = tc.GetNextItem(node, TVGN_CHILD);
        for (node = tc.GetNextItem(SelectedNode,
                               TVGN_CHILD);
             node;
             node = tc.GetNextItem(node, TVGN_NEXT))
        {
            CString ItemText = tc.GetItemText (node);
            if (!ItemText.CompareNoCase (s))
                break;
        }
//
//  If the node was not found, we can't continue. Leave the
//  current selection as it is.
//

        if (node == NULL)
            break;
//
//  Select the current item.
//

        SelectedNode = node;
        s = strtok (NULL, "\\");
//  If the next token is not null, expand the current item.
        if (s != NULL)
```

```
            tc.Expand (node, TVE_EXPAND);  // Always expand
    }
    tc.Select (SelectedNode, TVGN_CARET);
    delete [] startDir;
}


// BuildPath() builds the path name by recursing backward
// through the tree.
//
void CDirTreeView::BuildPath(CString & path, HTREEITEM node)
{
CTreeCtrl&  tc = GetTreeCtrl ();

// get the parent of the current node
    HTREEITEM parent = tc.GetParentItem(node);


// Get the text of the node. We'll use it to build the path
    CString buff = tc.GetItemText (node);


// add the backslash to the node
    buff += "\\";


// Add the current directory name to the path
//
    buff += path;
    path = buff;


// If this node has a parent, then we recurse until no
// parent is found. If there is no parent, then we are
// finished building the path.
//
    if (parent)
    {
        BuildPath(path, parent);
    }
    else
    {
// If the parent is found, strip the volume name from the
// string. It is enclosed in parentheses, so look for the
// first open paren and pick up the left side. Then find
// the first close paren and pick up the right part.
//
        CString dPath = path;
        int     Length = path.GetLength ();
        int pos = dPath.Find("(");
        if (pos > 0)
            path = dPath.Left (pos - 1);
        pos = dPath.Find (")");
        if (pos > 0)
            path += dPath.Right (Length - pos - 1);
    }
}


void CDirTreeView::OnDestroy()
{
    m_Images.Detach();
```

```
        CTreeView::OnDestroy ();
}

int CDirTreeView::GetIconIndex (WIN32_FIND_DATA fd)
{
    SHFILEINFO sfi;
    memset(&sfi, 0, sizeof(sfi));
    CString strFilePath = fd.cFileName;
    if (fd.dwFileAttributes & FILE_ATTRIBUTE_DIRECTORY)
    {
        SHGetFileInfo (
            strFilePath,
            FILE_ATTRIBUTE_DIRECTORY,
            &sfi,
            sizeof(sfi),
            SHGFI_SMALLICON |
                SHGFI_SYSICONINDEX |
                SHGFI_USEFILEATTRIBUTES |
                (fd.dwFileAttributes & SHGFI_OPENICON)
            );
        return (sfi.iIcon);
    }
    else
    {
        SHGetFileInfo (
            strFilePath,
            FILE_ATTRIBUTE_NORMAL,
&sfi,
            sizeof(sfi),
            SHGFI_SMALLICON | SHGFI_SYSICONINDEX
                        | (fd.dwFileAttributes & SHGFI_OPENICON)
        );
        return sfi.iIcon;
    }
    return (-1);
}

BOOL CDirTreeView::LoadSystemImageList(UINT uiImageList)
{
    SHFILEINFO sfiInfo;
    memset(&sfiInfo, 0, sizeof(SHFILEINFO));
    HIMAGELIST hImages = (HIMAGELIST) (
        SHGetFileInfo (
            "C:\\",
            0,
            &sfiInfo,
            sizeof(sfiInfo),
            SHGFI_SYSICONINDEX | uiImageList)
    );
    if (hImages == NULL)
        return (FALSE);
    switch (uiImageList)
    {
        case SHGFI_SMALLICON:
            if (m_Images.m_hImageList != NULL)
                m_Images.Detach ();
```

```
            m_Images.Attach (hImages);
            break;
        default:
            return (FALSE);
    }
    return (TRUE);
}


CString & CDirTreeView::GetCurrentDirectory()
{
static CString strCurrentPath;

    strCurrentPath.Empty ();
    int nBytes = ::GetCurrentDirectory (0, NULL);
    char *szDir = new char [nBytes + 1];
    ::GetCurrentDirectory (nBytes + 1, szDir);
    strCurrentPath = szDir;
    delete [] szDir;
    return (strCurrentPath);
}
```

Compile and run the program. It should start up with the drive containing the current directory expanded and the current directory selected, as shown in Figure 656. To prevent the initial expansion, call the *SetDirectoryName()* function with only the directory name, and let the *bDisplay* parameter default to *false*.

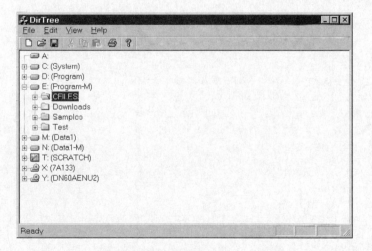

Figure 656   The DirTree application opens with the current directory selected.
The basic code can be used to create a directory selection in a dialog box.

To prevent "Untitled" from appearing in the window title bar, modify the *PreCreateWindow()* function in *CMainFrame* so that it looks like the following:

```
BOOL CMainFrame::PreCreateWindow(CREATESTRUCT& cs)
{
    cs.style &= ~FWS_ADDTOTITLE;
    if( !CFrameWnd::PreCreateWindow(cs) )
        return FALSE;

    return TRUE;
}
```

Much of this might look familiar to the *DirList* project. You are getting the node names by calling *FindFirstFile()*, getting the image list and icon index in the same manner, and initializing the current directory. In fact, that's the whole intent, as you will see in the next tip.

657. Combining CTreeView, CListView, and CSplitterWnd to Create an Explorer-Type Application

You've already done most of the work for this project, and the MFC AppWizard is going to take care of a lot that's left. If you create a new project and make sure that the view class names and the file names are exactly the same as in the last two projects, you can just copy the files over the new files and dress them up a bit.

Select New from the File menu, and create a new MFC AppWizard project. You can name it "Explorer," "Exploder," or whatever (during my residency in Minnesota, I learned that "whatever" is an acceptable reply to almost anything). Select a single-document interface, and select the defaults until you get to Page 5. On this page, select Windows Explorer as the style of project.

When you get to the final page, take care. Change your view class name from *CExplorerView* to *CDirListView*, and make sure that the header and implementation files are the same as you created in Tip 655, "Using the Owner Draw Property to Create a Full Line Selection." Change *CLeftView* to *CDirTreeView*, and make sure that the header and implementation files are the same as in Tip 656, "Using the *CTreeView* Class." Create the project.

You have three choices here:

- You can go over Tips 655 and 656 and re-create all the code in those sections. That's a lot of work.

- Being a lazy programmer, you can copy the view files from the projects in both tips and overwrite the existing files in the new project. Be sure to copy *ListViewEx.h, ListViewEx.cpp, struct.h, utility.cpp,* and *proto.h*. Edit the files and change all document class references from *CDirListDoc* and *CDirTreeDoc* to *CExplorerDoc*. Change all header references from *CDirList* and *CDirTree* to *CExplorer*. You should be able to compile and run the program. When it asserts, just click Ignore.

- Being even lazier, you can copy the files from the companion CD-ROM, where all the work already has been done.

You will notice a few things. First, notice that the wizard has created the toolbar for you and placed message handlers and command enabler functions in the *CMainFrame* class, just where you placed them in Tip 655. They're a little different, but they work just as well.

Also, the program probably asserted on startup (pretty hard not to notice that one). That's because you're trying to attach to the system image list twice within the same application. Both the list and tree controls need the small image list. You can take care of that by placing the image list variables in the main frame class.

Finally, the two views operate independently. You want them to stay together—when you change the directory in one, the other should reflect that change.

Let's tackle them one at a time. First, you want to get rid of the assertion when the program starts, so remove the *CImageList* variables from both the tree and list view classes. Add them to *CMainFrame*. Remove the *LoadSystemImageList()* function from both the views, and move it to the frame window class as well. Make the function get both image lists on a single call, and add another function, *GetImageList()*, to *CMainFrame*. Add a message handler for *WM_DESTROY*. The code for these functions is shown here:

```
void CMainFrame::LoadSystemImageLists()
{
    if (m_LargeIcons.m_hImageList != NULL)
        m_LargeIcons.Detach ();
    SHFILEINFO sfiInfo;
    memset(&sfiInfo, 0, sizeof(SHFILEINFO));
    HIMAGELIST hIcons = (HIMAGELIST) (
        SHGetFileInfo (
            "C:\\",
            0,
            &sfiInfo,
            sizeof(sfiInfo),
            SHGFI_SYSICONINDEX | SHGFI_LARGEICON)
    );
    m_LargeIcons.Attach (hIcons);
    if (m_SmallIcons.m_hImageList != NULL)
        m_SmallIcons.Detach ();
    hIcons = (HIMAGELIST) (
        SHGetFileInfo (
            "C:\\",
            0,
            &sfiInfo,
            sizeof(sfiInfo),
            SHGFI_SYSICONINDEX | SHGFI_SMALLICON)
    );
    m_SmallIcons.Attach (hIcons);
}

CImageList *CMainFrame::GetImageList(UINT uiImageList)
{
    switch (uiImageList)
    {
        case SHGFI_LARGEICON:
            if (m_LargeIcons.m_hImageList != NULL)
                return (&m_LargeIcons);
            break;
        case SHGFI_SMALLICON:
            if (m_SmallIcons.m_hImageList != NULL)
                return (&m_SmallIcons);
            break;
        default:
            break;
    }
    return (NULL);
}
void CMainFrame::OnDestroy()
{
    m_LargeIcons.Detach ();
    m_SmallIcons.Detach ();
    CFrameWnd::OnDestroy();
}
```

In the *OnCreate()* function, add a call to *GetImageList()*. This will make the image lists load and be ready before the view classes need them. While you're in the *CMainFrame* class, give the tree view more room by changing the *CSize* variables in *OnCreateClient()* from *CSize(100,100)* to *CSize(200,200)*. This sets the minimum size for both views to 200 logical units. It doesn't mean that you can't resize them to less than that; when they are created, they will be at least that size.

Go to the *DirListView.cpp* file and add *MainFrm.h* to the list of include files. In the *OnInitialUpdate()* function, remove all the lines dealing with loading and attaching the image lists, and replace them with the following four statements:

```
CMainFrame *frame = STATIC_DOWNCAST(CMainFrame,
                                     AfxGetMainWnd());
m_DirectoryName = GetCurrentDirectory ();
cc.SetImageList (frame->GetImageList (SHGFI_LARGEICON),
                                     LVSIL_NORMAL);
cc.SetImageList (frame->GetImageList (SHGFI_SMALLICON),
                                     LVSIL_SMALL);
```

Also remove the references to detaching the image lists from the *OnDestroy()* function. In the *DirListView.h* file, add *DirTreeView.h* to the list of include files. Remove the *CImageList* variables.

Do the same thing to the *CDirTreeView* class. You only need to set the small image list for the tree view, however.

Compile and run the program. It shouldn't assert this time. Try changing the list view using the toolbar buttons provided by the AppWizard to make sure that you are getting both large and small images.

Okay, 90 percent of the work is done. Let's make the two views track. Add a member variable, *m_bInitialized*, of type *bool* to both the *CDirListView* and *CDirTreeView* classes. These help speed up loading the program. What happens without them is that both views initialize and load the current directory. Then the tree view says, "Oh, I have a new directory. Better make the list view agree." It calls the list view function to load a new directory. In the meantime, the list view initializes and says, "Oh, I have a new directory. Better make the tree view agree." It calls the tree view and makes it reload the directory. They don't go into a loop, but in effect, the program is starting up twice. By setting a flag, you stop that from happening.

Initialize the *m_bInitialized* variable to *false* in the constructor for both classes. At the very end of the *OnInitialUpdate()* function of both classes, add another line setting them to *true*. Move to the *OnLButtonDblClk()* function in *DirListView.cpp*, and add the following lines at the bottom of the function:

```
if (m_bInitialized == true)
{
    CExplorerDoc *doc = GetDocument();
    pos = doc->GetFirstViewPosition ();
    while (pos != NULL)
    {
        CView *pView = doc->GetNextVicw (pos);
        if (pView->IsKindOf(RUNTIME_CLASS(CDirTreeView)))
        {
            ((CDirTreeView *)(pView))->SetDirectoryName
                            (m_DirectoryName, true);
        }
    }
}
```

Move to the *OnSelChanged()* message handler in *DirTreeView.cpp*, and add the following lines to the bottom of the function. Make sure that the **pResult = 0* statement stays at the bottom:

```
if (m_bInitialized == true)
{
    CExplorerDoc *doc = GetDocument();
```

```
    POSITION pos = doc->GetFirstViewPosition ();
    while (pos != NULL)
    {
        CView *pView = doc->GetNextView (pos);
        if (pView->IsKindOf(RUNTIME_CLASS(CDirListView)))
        {
//
//  Strip the trailing backslash off the directory name.
//  TreeView needs it, but ListView doesn't
            if (strDir.GetAt (strDir.GetLength() -1) == '\\')
                strDir = strDir.Left (strDir.GetLength() - 1);
            ((CDirListView *)(pView))->ListDirectory (strDir);
        }
    }
}
*pResult = 0;
```

Why, you ask, put in the *OnLButtonDblClk()* function in one view and the *OnSelChanged()* function in the other? You don't want the list view to change the directory in the tree view until a new directory has been double-clicked and the list view itself changes the directory. On the other hand, you want the tree view to change the list view *any* time a new selection is made.

While you're at it, you can get rid of the reference to the UP-DIR in the list view. You won't need it anymore (you can go up to another directory from the tree view). In the *ListDirectory()* function, add the following test within the *do . . . while* loop where you are getting file information:

```
if (!strcmp (fData.cFileName, ".."))
    continue;
```

Compile and run the program. The two views should track now and look like Figure 657. Try changing directories in the list view by double-clicking on a directory entry. Then try single-clicking on a branch in the tree view. If there are many subdirectories to list, it will take the tree view a couple or so seconds to respond. The *SHOWSELALWAYS* flag should be set for both views so that when one has the focus, the selection in the other will be a gray line.

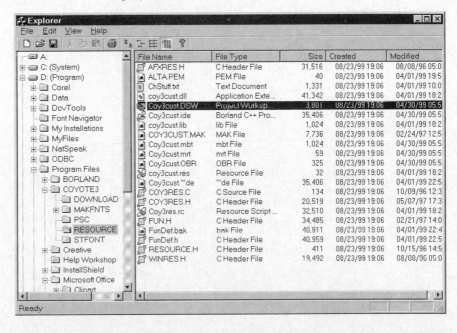

*Figure 657   The Explorer application features a tree view on the left and a list view on the right.
Both views track directory changes in the other.*

658. Using Alternate Views in the Right Panel in an Explorer-Type Application

No rule or Visual Studio condition says that the rightmost view in a Windows Explorer–type application must be a list view. That's the default, and when you select Windows Explorer as the application style, your left view *must* be a tree view. At least, that's how the MFC AppWizard sets it up. After the application is created, you can change it to whatever you want. It's just a lot of extra effort.

If you select the splitter window option from the Advanced dialog box on Page 4 of the AppWizard, the wizard will severely limit your choices of base classes for the right panel. That's not the case when you create a splitter window application using Windows Explorer style. You can choose from any of the base classes, although, as you have seen, the *CEditView* class will assert if you try to use it.

One of the problems with using different views is the document/view architecture itself. Each view must be attached to a document. *CView* won't grope around in the dark looking for a document; it must have one now. If your left view is a tree control and the left view is an editing window, the left view is going to be reinitialized when you open a new document.

The key is to create a dummy document that won't be reinitialized every time the right view is initialized and then attach the tree view to it.

Let's see how this works. In a single-document interface, after the main window is created and the views established, you must follow the chain of command from the document manager to get to the individual views. If the view is the left view, detach it from the document class and attach it to the dummy document. Create one of those demon Windows Explorer projects with *EditView* as the base class for the right view.

Now, add a new class to the application, *CDummyDoc*, and derive it from *CDocument*. Open its header file and change the constructor to *public*. Add the header file to the list of include files in the application class header file.

Add a member variable of type pointer to *CDocument* to the application class. Name it **m_pDummyDoc*. At the very bottom of the *InitInstance()* function, just before the *return TRUE* statement, add the following code:

```
m_pDummyDoc = new CDummyDoc;

POSITION pos;
pos = m_pDocManager->GetFirstDocTemplatePosition();
while (pos != NULL)
{
    CDocTemplate *pTempl =
                m_pDocManager->GetNextDocTemplate (pos);
    POSITION docpos;
    docpos = pTempl->GetFirstDocPosition ();
    while (docpos != NULL)
    {
        CDocument *pDoc = pTempl->GetNextDoc (docpos);
        POSITION viewpos;
        viewpos = pDoc->GetFirstViewPosition ();
        while (viewpos != NULL)
        {
            CView *pView = pDoc->GetNextView (viewpos);
            if (pView->IsKindOf (RUNTIME_CLASS(CLeftView)))
            {
```

```
                pDoc->RemoveView ((CLeftView *)pView);
                m_pDummyDoc->AddView ((CLeftView *)pView);
            }
        }
    }
}
```

In your left view class, change all references to the real document to *CDummyDoc*. Do this in the header and implementation.

Your left view is still a window, and it's going to respond to messages. You don't answer any of them, of course, unless they are intended for the control in your view. It's still a single-document interface, and the frameworks still calls *OnInitialUpdate()* when one of the file commands is issued. This, of course, will cause your view to reinitialize. To prevent this, in your left view class, add a member variable of type *bool* and name it *m_bInitialized*, similar to what you did in the Explorer project. Initialize it to *false* in the constructor, and then add the following lines at the top of the *OnInitialUpdate()* function:

```
if (m_bInitialized == true)
    return;
```

At the end of the *OnInitialUpdate()* function, add a line setting *m_bInitialized* to *true*.

And "viola"! The edit view—or any other view, for that matter—in the right panel will now function normally while you step off into space and do whatever you want with the left view. Your *CEditView* no longer asserts. The beauty of it is that the document self-destructs when you close the application. You don't have to worry about deleting it.

Some of this is contrary to the official documentation, and I'm sure that there are some traps waiting for this type of operation, but so far they haven't nailed me. The *Explorer* application on the companion CD-ROM shows how this is put together. Actually, attaching to the dummy document itself seems unnecessary. As long as the view makes no document-related calls and handles no-document related messages, it doesn't seem to make any difference in the preceding application whether the view is attached to the dummy document. It takes only about 50 bytes to create the dummy document, however, and that's cheap insurance.

659. *Using* CFormView

The MFC *CFormView* is a view that holds other controls and looks very similar to a dialog box contained in the client area of the main window. Although it appears as a dialog box and the view is laid out using a dialog template, a *CFormView* window is not a dialog box, nor is the view derived from *CDialog*.

CFormView is derived from *CView* through *CScrollView* and thus supports scrolling on demand if the form extends beyond the client area boundaries. It's a good view for database operations or any other application where fixed records need to be displayed, edited, and saved using the document/view architecture. A derived class, *CRecordView*, is directly connected to a *CRecordSet* object and can be used to automate the movement of data to and from a database. Figure 659 shows a program based on *CFormView* as the main window.

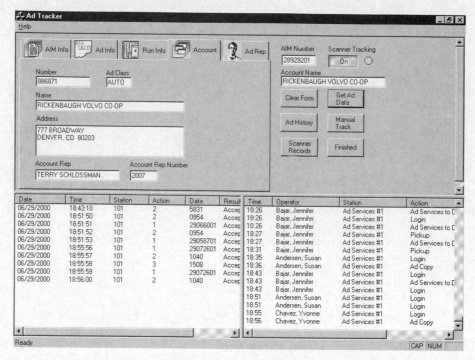

Figure 659   Views derived from CFormView *may support any number of controls and may be combined with other views. In this application, the database record is displayed on a tab control, and other controls provide the access to the data.*

Applications based on *CFormView* can support multiple form types, just as another view type can support different document types. For each form type, a document template is added to the application class's *InitInstance()* function.

Because *CFormView* is based on the document/view architecture, the data used in the controls may be serialized to and from a database or data file in the document class's *Serialize()* function.

At times when you might use a dialog-based application, consider *CFormView* as an alternative. Dialog box applications require extra programming effort to provide many of the features the document/view architecture provides as a minimum—menus, toolbars, printing, and print preview.

660. *Creating Forms-Based Applications*

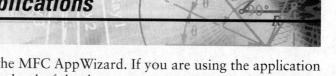

Create an application based on *CFormView* using the MFC AppWizard. If you are using the application with a database, you probably want to select some level of database support on Page 2 of the wizard and connect it to an ODBC or DAO recordset. When you do this, the wizard automatically selects *CFormView* as your base class on the final page and creates a *CRecordSet* object based on the record set you selected on Page 2. If you select none or header files only, you will have to select the base class manually on Page 6.

When you click Finish to create the project, you are presented with a dialog template just as you would in a dialog box–based application. If you examine the template, however, you will notice a number of differences between it and a normal dialog template.

First, most dialogs are pop-up windows with a dialog frame border. This one is a child window with no border. Beyond that, none of the style options is set, not even the Visible flag, nor should you set any of the style boxes. A form is created from a dialog template, but it is not a dialog box; the template is simply the medium for holding the controls you want to use with the form view. You lay out the controls you will use with the data the same as you would a normal dialog box.

When you compile and run the program, the frameworks tries to size the application window to match the size of the dialog template. It has the resize gripper, just like any other application, and if you size it below the size of the dialog template, scroll bars appear automatically. This is part of the support given by its heritage through *CScrollView*.

The toolbar and menu are different. Instead of the usual file commands, there are commands and toolbar buttons to move to the first and last records in the set and to the next or previous record.

661. *Inserting New Forms into an Application*

Adding new forms to a project is easier than adding new document templates. Essentially, that's what the wizard is doing—adding new document templates. As you build the project and add forms, the wizard adds a new document template to the *InitInstance()* function of the application class. When a form is added to a project, new documents are not created automatically when New is selected from the File menu. Instead, you go through the New dialog box, just as you would had you added document templates manually. Figure 661 shows the New Form dialog box.

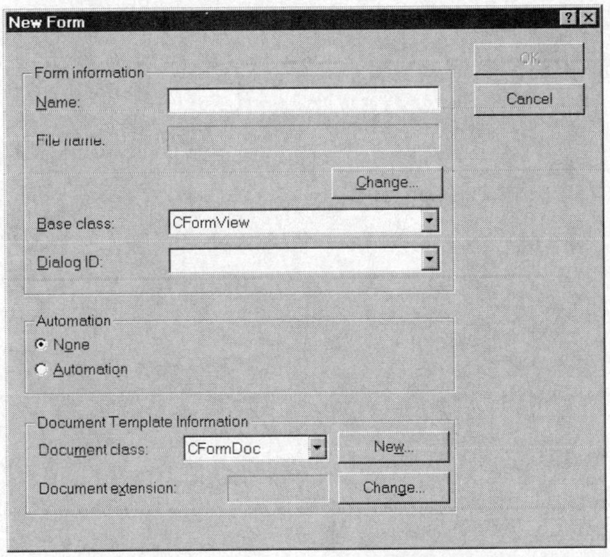

Figure 661   The New Form dialog

You can add forms manually by creating your own dialog template, setting the styles, and adding your own document template to the application class. However, the wizard does all that for you when you use the New Form dialog box. You access this dialog box in one of three ways: Select New Form from the Insert menu, select New Form from the wizard bar action menu, or right-click on the project name in the Class View pane of the Workspace window and select New Form.

The New Form dialog looks very similar to the New Class dialog. Essentially, you are adding a new class to your application. In this case, however, you may select as a base class only the form and record views available or *CDialog*. You also may create a new document class for the form, which the New Class dialog does not provide.

You can add forms to any application, not just those built using *CFormView*. If you didn't set up your application to support forms originally, that support will be added when you add the first form.

662. *Using Multiple Views in a Program*

You've already seen how to disconnect a view from a document and use it independently of any other views in a single-document application, as well as a few other ways to manipulate views. Generally, the same methods work with multiple-document applications as well. What you haven't seen yet is how to use multiple views normally.

The frameworks generally considers all the views contained in the same window to be connected to the same document. This is true of single-document applications, where the window is the main window client area, and of multiple-document applications, where the window is the client area of a child window frame created within the main window's client area.

When one of the views changes, you can call the document's *UpdateAllViews()* function, and the document will search through the list of views and call each view's *OnUpdate()* function. You can pass hints and objects (but only those derived from *CObject*) through the call to *UpdateAllViews()*. If the called view has implemented the *OnUpdate()* function, it can check the hint and decide what response to take, if any.

Create another of those accursed Windows Explorer–style applications. Name this one "Two," and select a single-document interface along with the Explorer style. On the last page, make the base class for the right view *CRichEditView*, the header file *RichView.h*, and the implementation file *RichView.cpp* (it will make life easier). The left view, of course, must be a tree view, but you will be changing that to *CScrollView*. It's too bad Microsoft makes this so difficult by limiting your options. You can't select *CRichEditView* as the base class if you use an ordinary splitter window, but you can with the Explorer style. However, with the Explorer style you can't opt for a different base class for the left view. It doesn't make much sense.

In this tip, you will create a program that displays a rich edit view on the right and an information panel on the left, similar to Figure 662.

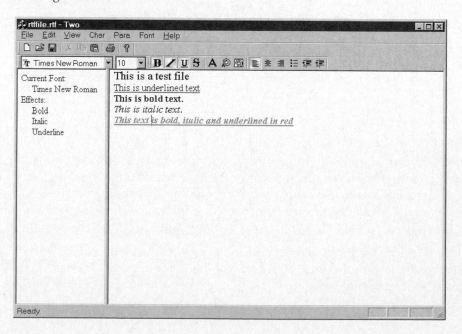

Figure 662   The left view in this application displays the character formatting for the selection in the rich text editor view

Open the left view class header and implementation file, and change all references to *CTreeView* to *CScrollView*. Initialize the scroll area in *OnInitialUpdate()* as shown in the following code:

```
void CLeftView::OnInitialUpdate()
{
    CScrollView::OnInitialUpdate();

    CSize sizeTotal;
    // TODO: calculate the total size of this view
    sizeTotal.cx = sizeTotal.cy = 100;
    SetScrollSizes(MM_TEXT, sizeTotal);
}
```

Copy the *RichView.cpp* and *RichView.h* files from Tip 633, "Creating a Project Using *CRichEditView*." The file names are the same as in the current project, so just copy and replace them. Change the header file references from *rich.h* to *two.h*. If you really want to do it right, as in the code on the companion CD-ROM, copy over the format bar and main window frame classes as well.

Open *RichView.cpp*. You should already have a message handler for the reflected notify message *EN_SELCHANGE*. At the end of the message handler function *OnSelChange()*, add the following statement. You don't really need the parameters, but the purpose of this project is to show you how to use them:

```
GetDocument()->UpdateAllViews (this, 1, NULL);
```

Close this file and return to *LeftView.cpp*. Add a 15-member array of type *CString* to the class and name it *m_FormatData*. Also, add type *int* variables for the margins and name them *m_TopMargin*, *m_BottomMargin*, *m_LeftMargin*, and *m_RightMargin*. Initialize them all to 6 in the constructor. Add the virtual function *OnUpdate()* and code it as shown here:

```
///////////////////////////////////////////////////////////////
// CLeftView message handlers

void CLeftView::OnUpdate(CView* pSender, LPARAM lHint,
                         CObject* pHint)
{
    if (pSender == NULL)
        return;
    if (pSender->IsKindOf (RUNTIME_CLASS(CRichView)))
    {
        CRichView *pView = (CRichView *) pSender;
        switch (lHint)
        {
            case 0:
                break;
            case 1:
                int x;
                for (x = 0; x < 15; ++x)
                    m_FormatData[x].Empty ();
                x = 0;
                m_cf = pView->GetCharFormatSelection ();
                m_pf = pView->GetParaFormatSelection ();
                m_FormatData[x++] = _T("Current Font:");
                m_FormatData[x++].Format ("    %s",
                                    m_cf.szFaceName);
                m_FormatData[x++] = _T("Effects:");
                if (!(m_cf.dwEffects &
```

```
                            (CFE_BOLD | CFE_STRIKEOUT
                         | CFE_UNDERLINE | CFE_ITALIC)))
                m_FormatData[x++] += _T("      Normal");
        else
        {
            if (m_cf.dwEffects & CFE_BOLD)
                m_FormatData[x++] +=_T("      Bold");
            if (m_cf.dwEffects & CFE_ITALIC)
                m_FormatData[x++] +=
                                _T("      Italic");
            if (m_cf.dwEffects & CFE_UNDERLINE)
                m_FormatData[x++] +=
                                _T("      Underline");
            if (m_cf.dwEffects & CFE_STRIKEOUT)
                m_FormatData[x++] +=
                                _T("      Strikeout");
        }
        Invalidate();
        break;
    default:
        break;
    }
  }
}
```

Move to the *OnPaint()* function and add code to draw the information you just got in the scroll view window:

```
////////////////////////////////////////////////////////////
// CLeftView drawing
void CLeftView::OnDraw(CDC* pDC)
{
    CRichDoc* pDoc = GetDocument();
    ASSERT_VALID(pDoc);

    int nLine;
    CSize sz;
    CString strText;
    sz = pDC->GetTextExtent (" ", 1);
    RECT rc;
    RECT rcClient;
    GetClientRect (&rcClient);
    rc.top = m_nTopMargin;
    rc.left = m_nLeftMargin;
    rc.bottom = sz.cy;
    CFont *fontOld = pDC->SelectObject (&m_Font);
    int nWidestLine = 0;
    int nRunningDepth = m_nTopMargin;
    for (nLine = 0; nLine < 15; ++nLine)
    {
        strText = m_FormatData[nLine];
        if (strText.IsEmpty ())
            continue;
        sz = pDC->GetTextExtent (strText);
        if (sz.cx > nWidestLine)
            nWidestLine = sz.cx;
```

```
        rc.right = sz.cx + m_nRightMargin;
        pDC->TextOut (rc.left, rc.top, strText);
        nRunningDepth += sz.cy;
        rc.top += sz.cy;
        rc.bottom += sz.cy;
}
// calculate the total size of this view
    sz.cx = nWidestLine + m_nLeftMargin + m_nRightMargin;
    sz.cy = nRunningDepth + m_nBottomMargin;
    SetScrollSizes(MM_TEXT, sz);

    pDC->SelectObject (fontOld);
}
```

Compile and run the program. Open a rich text file (one named *rtffile.rtf* is in the project folder on the companion CD-ROM). As soon as you give the rich text editor the focus, the character formatting will appear in the left view. Move the cursor around through the various fonts and attributes, and the formatting data should update with each cursor movement.

Although it isn't displayed, you could show the paragraph formatting information in the member variable *m_pf*. Go back and change the *lHint* parameter in *RichView.cpp* to something other than 1, and nothing will show in the scroll view window. Also, no attempt was made in this application to check the validity of the formatting. To use this properly, you check the *dwMask* variable to determine which effects are valid. For example, if *m_cf.dwMask & CFM_ITALIC* is false, don't bother to list the italic format.

663. *Adding a View to a Document*

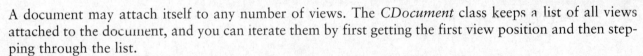

A document may attach itself to any number of views. The *CDocument* class keeps a list of all views attached to the document, and you can iterate them by first getting the first view position and then stepping through the list.

You can create views dynamically at any time, and a document may attach the view by calling the *CDocument::AddView()* function. This function also sets the view's document pointer to the current document. The frameworks calls this function to attach the view when a new document is opened or created. You normally don't have to call it unless you create a new view and want to attach it to the document.

To find a particular document, the view must start with the document manager in the application class object and then sort through the document templates until the correct document is found. Views themselves have no direct way of attaching themselves to a document object, but after the document is located, the view may call the document's *AddView()* function to attach itself.

664. *Deleting a View from a Document*

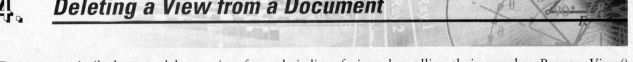

Documents similarly may delete a view from their list of views by calling their member *RemoveView()* function. This function also sets the view's document pointer to *NULL*. This function also is called by the frameworks whenever a window frame is closed—either the main window in a single-document application or a child frame in a multiple-document application.

As with the *AddView()* function, a view has no direct way to remove itself from a document's view list. Instead, it must locate the document and call that object's *RemoveView()* function. You saw how this is done in Tip 658, "Using Alternate Views in the Right Panel in an Explorer-Type Application." The view first got a pointer to the document manager from the application class object and then stepped through the document template pointers that it got from the document manager. Through the document templates, it looked through the documents to find a view with the same runtime class as itself. Then it removed itself from the document and attached itself to another document.

665. *Creating Other View Classes:* CCtrlView

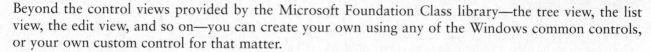

Beyond the control views provided by the Microsoft Foundation Class library—the tree view, the list view, the edit view, and so on—you can create your own using any of the Windows common controls, or your own custom control for that matter.

Of course, of the common controls left, the only one that lends itself to view-sized applications is the tab control. Can you imagine a full-window combo box view? It's possible; I've never tried it, but you might find some use for it.

Many books show you how to create a view based on the tab control, but that's as far as they go. That's because building a tab view is very, very easy. Implementing it, however, is a very different story. Even the MSDN documentation doesn't give you many clues as to how to implement a tab view. You didn't buy this book because you were interested in the easy way out, so in the following sample you will build a tab control and then implement it with some real controls and dialogs.

The important thing to remember is that the tab control is just that—it manages the tabs only. The actual pages associated with the tabs are your responsibility. After the tab control is built, you can create window-sized controls to fit on the tabs, or you can create a dialog box and place it on a tab. The tab control itself takes care of switching the tabs, but it doesn't handle switching what you place on the tabs.

The documentation doesn't help much when rolling your own view using *CCtrlView*, but you can go a long way by looking at *viewcmn.cpp* and *afxcview.h* in the MFC directory where you installed Visual C++.

Let's start with the basic tab control. The class definition is simple, and you need only three functions: a constructor, the *PreCreateWindow()* function, and a function to get the underlying tab control. The constructor is used to pass the window class for the control (this is the name used in the *WNDCLASS* structure in a Windows API application) and default style. The tab control window class is "SysTabControl32" (I can never remember where in the documentation these control class names are, so usually I just create a control on a dialog box and then look in the *.rc* file to find the name). The *PreCreateWindow()* function is used to initialize the common controls and to apply any style changes to the window. The function to get the underlying tab control is so simple that it's best implemented inline.

You can't use *CCtrlView* as a base class when you create your project; it just isn't among the choices offered by the MFC AppWizard. Your best bet is to select *CView* and then change the references to *CCtrlView* after the application is created.

The complete code to create a tab view is shown here, both header and implementation files:

```
//////////////////////////////////////////////////////////
// TabView.h : interface of the CTabView class
//
```

```
class CTabView : public CCtrlView
{
protected: // create from serialization only
    CTabView();
    DECLARE_DYNCREATE(CTabView)
public:
    virtual BOOL PreCreateWindow(CREATESTRUCT& cs);
    CTabCtrl& GetTabCtrl() const
            {
                return(*((CTabCtrl *) this));
            }

//////////////////////////////////////////////////////////////
// TabView.cpp : implementation of the CTabView class
//

#include "TabView.h"

//////////////////////////////////////////////////////////////
// CTabView

IMPLEMENT_DYNCREATE(CTabView, CCtrlView)

//////////////////////////////////////////////////////////////
// CTabView construction/destruction

CTabView::CTabView()
    : CCtrlView (_T("SysTabControl32"), AFX_WS_DEFAULT_VIEW)
{

    // TODO: add construction code here

}

BOOL CTabView::PreCreateWindow(CREATESTRUCT& cs)
{
    ::InitCommonControls ();
    // TODO: make any style changes here.
    return (CCtrlView::PreCreateWindow(cs));
}
```

That's it. When you build an application using just the preceding code, you get something that appears very much like *CFormView*, except that it doesn't support automatic scrolling. There aren't any tabs until you add them. Of course, when you use *CView* as the base class, you get a lot of other code along with it. Just make sure that you change all references to *CView* to *CCtrlView*.

Place any extra styles in the *PreCreateWindow()* function. For example, the tab control dynamically sizes the tabs themselves. If you want fixed-size tabs, add the statement *cs.style |= TCS_FIXEDWIDTH;* to this function.

Now to implement a project using the tab control. Create a single-document application named simply "Tab." Accept the defaults through the steps and accept *CView* as the base view class. After the project is created, search through *TabView.h* and *TabView.cpp*, and replace *CView* with *CCtrlView*.

You're going to need the virtual function *OnInitialUpdate()*, so go into the Class Wizard and add that function. You also will need two *WM_NOTIFY* message handlers to take care of messages reflected from the control. These are *TCN_SELCHANGE* and *TCN_SELCHANGING*. You use the first to hide any controls on the current tab and the second to show any controls on the newly activated tab. No, the tab control doesn't do this for you as a property sheet does; it's your responsibility.

Neither the Class Wizard nor the Wizard Bar is going to be any help to you in adding notification messages from the underlying tab control. The wizards have no idea that a tab control is present, so they won't list its messages among those available. Listed here are the message map entries you must enter manually and the basic functions for both:

```
ON_NOTIFY_REFLECT(TCN_SELCHANGE, OnSelchangeTab)
ON_NOTIFY_REFLECT(TCN_SELCHANGING, OnSelchangingTab)

void CTabView::OnSelchangingTab (NMHDR* pNMHDR,
                                 LRESULT* pResult)
{

    *pResult = 0;
}

void CTabView::OnSelchangeTab (NMHDR* pNMHDR,
                               LRESULT* pResult)
{

    *pResult = 0;
}
```

If you intend to use a tab view in an application, keep these in your toolbox so that you can drop them in when you need them.

Now let's continue with the implementation. When finished, the main window will look like Figure 665. You can create controls directly on a tab, or you can create a dialog box and place it on the tab. You handle the two cases differently, so this project will do one of each. If you place several controls on a tab, you have to hide them individually in the *OnSelChangingTab()* function and show them individually in the *OnSelChangeTab()* function. In this case, it's better to create a dialog box containing the controls; this lets you hide and show them all in one statement by manipulating the dialog box.

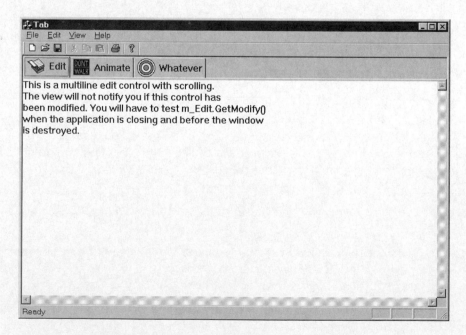

Figure 665   The newly created TabView has large icons

Add a message handler for the *WM_SIZE* message. The edit control is set up for scrolling, but the tab control doesn't provide any automatic scrolling, which *CScrollView* does provide. You will have to resize the edit control when the user resizes the application window.

Add an image list member variable, *m_Images*, to the class. Might as well add some icons to the tabs just because you can do it, and you might as well make the icon appear differently for a selected page and one that is not selected.

Set up a three-tab application. The first tab will hold an edit control, the second will hold the dialog box, and the third will be blank. Create the tabs in the *OnInitialUpdate()* function. Create a dialog box and place controls on it using the Resource Workshop. The sample on the companion CD-ROM borrows a dialog box from another application just for demonstration, and the class that goes along with it is *CAnimate*. Add member variables for a *CEdit* control *(m_Edit)* and the dialog box *(m_Animate)*. Also add a *bool* named *m_bInitialized*, and initialize it to *false* in the constructor. Each time you select an *Open* or *New* command on the File menu, the *OnInitialUpdate()* function will be called. You will use this variable to redirect the call to another function that performs any reinitialization you need.

The header file *TabView.h* is shown here:

```cpp
// TabView.h : interface of the CTabView class
//
/////////////////////////////////////////////////////////////////////
 #include    "Animate.h"

class CTabView : public CCtrlView
{
protected: // create from serialization only
    CTabView();
    DECLARE_DYNCREATE(CTabView)

// Attributes
public:
    CTabDoc* GetDocument();

// Operations
public:

// Overrides
    // Class Wizard-generated virtual function overrides
    //{{AFX_VIRTUAL(CTabView)
    public:
    virtual void OnDraw(CDC* pDC); // overridden to draw
                                   // this view (may remove)
    virtual BOOL PreCreateWindow(CREATESTRUCT& cs);
    virtual void OnInitialUpdate();
    virtual BOOL Create(LPCTSTR lpszClassName,
                LPCTSTR lpszWindowName, DWORD dwStyle,
                const RECT& rect, CWnd* pParentWnd,
                UINT nID,
                CCreateContext* pContext = NULL);
    protected:
    virtual BOOL OnPreparePrinting(CPrintInfo* pInfo);
    virtual void OnBeginPrinting(CDC* pDC,
                            CPrintInfo* pInfo);
    virtual void OnEndPrinting(CDC* pDC, CPrintInfo* pInfo);
    //}}AFX_VIRTUAL
```

```
// Implementation
public:
    virtual ~CTabView();
#ifdef _DEBUG
    virtual void AssertValid() const;
    virtual void Dump(CDumpContext& dc) const;
#endif

protected:

    CTabCtrl&   GetTabCtrl ();
// Generated message map functions
protected:
    void Reinitialize();
    //{{AFX_MSG(CTabView)
    afx_msg void OnSize(UINT nType, int cx, int cy);
    //}}AFX_MSG
    DECLARE_MESSAGE_MAP()
    CEdit       m_Edit;
    CAnimate    m_Animate;
    void OnSelchangingSampletab (NMHDR* pNMHDR,
                                 LRESULT* pResult);
    void OnSelchangeSampletab (NMHDR* pNMHDR,
                               LRESULT* pResult);
    CImageList  m_Images;
    bool        m_bInitialized;
};
```

You can remove the *OnDraw()* function, unless you want to use it. Also, unless you want to do the printing code, you can remove the three printing functions. They were added by the wizard because you had to use *CView* as the base class to create the project.

The six icons will be loaded into the image list so that the closed icon (the page is not selected) appears before the open icon. The tab control doesn't have a state image list, but you can select them just by changing the *iImage* member of the tab item structure. That's done in *OnSelChangedTab()* and *OnSelChangingTab()*. The code for the implementation file *TabView.cpp* follows:

```
// TabView.cpp : implementation of the CTabView class
//

#include "stdafx.h"
#include "Tab.h"

#include "TabDoc.h"
#include "TabView.h"

#ifdef _DEBUG
#define new DEBUG_NEW
#undef THIS_FILE
static char THIS_FILE[] = __FILE__;
#endif

CString g_strText = "This is a multiline edit control with"
                    " scrolling.\r\nThe view will not"
                    " notify you if this control has\r\n"
                    "been modified. You will have to test "
```

```
                        "m_Edit.GetModify()\r\nwhen the "
                        "application is closing and before the"
                        " window\r\nis destroyed.";

///////////////////////////////////////////////////////////
// CTabView

IMPLEMENT_DYNCREATE(CTabView, CCtrlView)

BEGIN_MESSAGE_MAP(CTabView, CCtrlView)
    //{{AFX_MSG_MAP(CTabView)
    ON_WM_SIZE()
    //}}AFX_MSG_MAP
    // Standard printing commands
    ON_NOTIFY_REFLECT(TCN_SELCHANGE, OnSelchangeSampletab)
    ON_NOTIFY_REFLECT(TCN_SELCHANGING,
                                    OnSelchangingSampletab)
    ON_COMMAND(ID_FILE_PRINT, CCtrlView::OnFilePrint)
    ON_COMMAND(ID_FILE_PRINT_DIRECT, CCtrlView::OnFilePrint)
    ON_COMMAND(ID_FILE_PRINT_PREVIEW,
                                    CCtrlView::OnFilePrintPreview)
END_MESSAGE_MAP()

///////////////////////////////////////////////////////////
// CTabView construction/destruction

CTabView::CTabView()
    : CCtrlView (_T("SysTabControl32"), AFX_WS_DEFAULT_VIEW)
{
    m_bInitialized = false;
}

CTabView::~CTabView()
{
}

BOOL CTabView::PreCreateWindow(CREATESTRUCT& cs)
{
    ::InitCommonControls ();
    CCtrlView::PreCreateWindow(cs);
    return (TRUE);
}

///////////////////////////////////////////////////////////
// CTabView drawing

void CTabView::OnDraw(CDC* pDC)
{
    CTabDoc* pDoc = GetDocument();
    ASSERT_VALID(pDoc);
    // TODO: add draw code for native data here
}

///////////////////////////////////////////////////////////
// CTabView printing
```

```cpp
BOOL CTabView::OnPreparePrinting(CPrintInfo* pInfo)
{
    // default preparation
    return DoPreparePrinting(pInfo);
}


void CTabView::OnBeginPrinting(CDC* /*pDC*/,
                               CPrintInfo* /*pInfo*/)
{
    // TODO: add extra initialization before printing
}


void CTabView::OnEndPrinting(CDC* /*pDC*/, CPrintInfo* /*pInfo*/)
{
    // TODO: add cleanup after printing
}


/////////////////////////////////////////////////////////
// CTabView diagnostics

#ifdef _DEBUG
void CTabView::AssertValid() const
{
    CCtrlView::AssertValid();
}


void CTabView::Dump(CDumpContext& dc) const
{
    CCtrlView::Dump(dc);
}


CTabDoc* CTabView::GetDocument() // non-debug
                                 // version is inline
{
    ASSERT(m_pDocument->IsKindOf(RUNTIME_CLASS(CTabDoc)));
    return (CTabDoc*)m_pDocument;
}
#endif //_DEBUG


/////////////////////////////////////////////////////////
// CTabView message handlers

CTabCtrl& CTabView::GetTabCtrl()
{
    return (*((CTabCtrl *) this));
}


void CTabView::OnInitialUpdate()
{
// Do NOT call the base class OnInitialUpdate
//   CCtrlView::OnInitialUpdate();

// If everything has been created, don't do it again.
// Go to a reinitialize function.
    if (m_bInitialized== true)
    {
```

```
            Reinitialize ();
            return;
        }
//
// Add the icons to the image list.
    if (m_Images.m hImageList == NULL)
    {
        HICON hIcon;
        m_Images.Create (32, 32, ILC_MASK, 6, 6);
        HINSTANCE hInst = AfxGetInstanceHandle ();
        hIcon = LoadIcon (hInst,
                    MAKEINTRESOURCE(IDI_PAGEONE_CLOSED));
        m_Images.Add (hIcon);
        hIcon = LoadIcon (hInst,
                    MAKEINTRESOURCE(IDI_PAGEONE_OPEN));
        m_Images.Add (hIcon);
        hIcon = LoadIcon (hInst,
                    MAKEINTRESOURCE(IDI_PAGETWO_CLOSED));
        m_Images.Add (hIcon);
        hIcon = LoadIcon (hInst,
                    MAKEINTRESOURCE(IDI_PAGETWO_OPEN));
        m_Images.Add (hIcon);
        hIcon = LoadIcon (hInst,
                    MAKEINTRESOURCE(IDI_PAGETHREE_CLOSED));
        m_Images.Add (hIcon);
        hIcon = LoadIcon (hInst,
                    MAKEINTRESOURCE(IDI_PAGETHREE_OPEN));
        m_Images.Add (hIcon);
        GetTabCtrl().SetImageList (&m_Images);
    }
//
// Create the edit control and dialog box.
//
    CRect rcItem, rc;
    m_Edit.Create (WS_VSCROLL| WS_HSCROLL | ES_MULTILINE
                | ES_WANTRETURN, CRect(10,10,100,100),
                this, 0);
    m_Animate.Create (IDD_TAB1_DLG, this);


//
// Create the three tab pages.
    TC_ITEM TabItem;
    memset (&TabItem, '\0', sizeof (TC_ITEM));
    TabItem.mask = TCIF_TEXT | TCIF_PARAM | TCIF_IMAGE;
    TabItem.iImage = 1;  // First page will be selected
    TabItem.lParam = (long) &m_Edit;
    TabItem.pszText = "Edit";
    GetTabCtrl().InsertItem (0, &TabItem);
    TabItem.pszText = "Animate";
    TabItem.lParam = (long) &m_Animate;
    TabItem.iImage = 2;  // Second page is not selected
    GetTabCtrl().InsertItem (1, &TabItem);
    TabItem.pszText = "Whatever";
    TabItem.lParam = 0;  // No controls here
    TabItem.iImage = 4;  // Not selected
    GetTabCtrl().InsertItem (2, &TabItem);
```

```cpp
    GetTabCtrl().ShowWindow (SW_NORMAL);

    GetTabCtrl().GetItemRect (0, rcItem);
    GetTabCtrl().GetClientRect (rc);
    rc.top = rcItem.bottom + 4;
    m_Edit.SetWindowText (g_strText);
    m_Edit.MoveWindow (rc, FALSE);
    m_Edit.ShowWindow (SW_NORMAL);
    m_Animate.MoveWindow (rc, FALSE);
    m_bInitialized = true;
}

void CTabView::Reinitialize()
{
    m_Edit.SetWindowText (_T(""));
}

BOOL CTabView::Create(LPCTSTR lpszClassName,
                      LPCTSTR lpszWindowName, DWORD dwStyle,
                      const RECT& rect, CWnd* pParentWnd,
                      UINT nID, CCreateContext* pContext)
{
    if (!CWnd::Create(lpszClassName, lpszWindowName, dwStyle,
                      rect, pParentWnd, nID, pContext))
        return (FALSE);
    return (TRUE);
}

void CTabView::OnSelchangingSampletab (NMHDR* pNMHDR,
                                       LRESULT* pResult)
{
TC_ITEM     ti;
CWnd*       cDlg;
int         result;

    // TODO: Add your control notification handler code here

    int sel = GetTabCtrl().GetCurSel();
    ti.mask = TCIF_PARAM | TCIF_IMAGE;
    result = GetTabCtrl().GetItem (sel, &ti);
    cDlg = (CWnd *) ti.lParam;
    if (cDlg)
        cDlg->ShowWindow (SW_HIDE);
    ti.mask = TCIF_IMAGE;
    ti.iImage -= 1;
    GetTabCtrl().SetItem (sel, &ti);
    *pResult = 0;
}

void CTabView::OnSelchangeSampletab (NMHDR* pNMHDR,
                                     LRESULT* pResult)
{
TC_ITEM     ti;
CWnd*       cDlg;
int         result;
```

```
    // TODO: Add your control notification handler code here

    int sel = GetTabCtrl().GetCurSel();
    ti.mask = TCIF_PARAM | TCIF_IMAGE;
    result = GetTabCtrl().GetItem (sel, &ti);
    cDlg = (CWnd *) ti.lParam;
    if (cDlg)
        cDlg->ShowWindow (SW_NORMAL);
    ti.mask = TCIF_IMAGE;
    ti.iImage += 1;
    GetTabCtrl().SetItem (sel, &ti);
    *pResult = 0;
}

void CTabView::OnSize(UINT nType, int cx, int cy)
{
    CCtrlView::OnSize(nType, cx, cy);
    if (!m_Edit.m_hWnd)
        return;
    CRect rcItem, rc;
    GetTabCtrl().GetItemRect (0, rcItem);
    GetTabCtrl().GetClientRect (rc);
    rc.top = rcItem.bottom + 4;
    m_Edit.MoveWindow (rc, FALSE);
    m_Animate.MoveWindow (rc, FALSE);
}
```

The address of the control or dialog box is stored in the item's *lParam* member. When the selection changes, it is retrieved and used to hide or show the page as necessary.

After you compile and test the program, try adding the statement *cs.style |= TCS_BUTTONS;* to the *PreCreateWindow()* function. This style produces button-like tabs that are depressed when selected. Also, try it with small icons and without an image list to see the difference. If you set a font for the tab control—*GetTabCtrl().SetFont (&Font);*—you can select a smaller type size for the tabs.

666. *Using CSplitterWnd for Multiple Views*

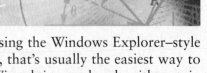

So far, your use of the splitter window has concentrated on projects using the Windows Explorer–style applications. Despite the restrictions placed on the views you may use, that's usually the easiest way to prepare an application with multiple-window panels. You let the AppWizard tie your hands with certain types of views. Then, when the wizard goes away, you untie yourself and change the views to what you want.

Even so, you've always let the MFC AppWizard prepare the splitter window for you. That's okay if you know beforehand that your application will use more than one view in a window, but sometimes you need to backtrack. Your application is mostly written, and you find that you must create a splitter window.

You can roll your own splitter window at any point during the development of your application, even break down a splitter window into other splitters. It isn't something that's fixed at the time the application is created.

You create the splitter window in the frame class. If it's a single-document application that means that you do it in the *CMainFrame* class; if it's a multiple-document application, you do it in the *CChildFrame* class. In this tip, you will go through the process of manually splitting a view window, and in the next you will break one of those splitter windows down into four other splitter windows, giving you a total of five window panes.

Create a new application named *Split*. It can be a single- or multiple-document interface; the same principles of splitting a main window frame apply to splitting a child frame. On the last page, select *CEditView* as the application, but change the name of the view class to *CFirstView* and the name of the files to *FirstView.h* and *FirstView.cpp*.

In the frame window class—*CChildFrame* for an MDI or *CMainFrame* for an SDI—add a *protected* member variable of type *CSplitterWnd*, and name it *m_wndSplitter*. Using the Class Wizard or the Wizard Bar, add the virtual function *OnCreateClient()*. That's where you will split the window. It's the client area you want to split, not the frame window itself. Remove the call to the base class *OnCreateClient()* function. This function is responsible for creating the view, so you yourself will have to do that work before you leave the overridden function.

There are two ways you can create a splitter window. You can use the *static* method, which is used by the AppWizard when you select an Explorer-style application, or you can use the *dynamic* method, which doesn't create the splitter window until the user opens it. The two display differently when they first appear. Using the static splitter, you have to create the views for each panel. MFC manages dynamic splitter windows and automatically creates the view and attaches it to the current document.

First, do the static split to see what it looks like. Add the following code to the *OnCreateClient()* function:

```
if (!m_wndSplitter.CreateStatic(this, 1, 2))
    return FALSE;

if (!m_wndSplitter.CreateView(0, 0,
                        RUNTIME_CLASS(CFirstView),
                        CSize(200, 200), pContext) ||
    !m_wndSplitter.CreateView(0, 1,
                        RUNTIME_CLASS(CFirstView),
                        CSize(200, 200), pContext))
{
    m_wndSplitter.DestroyWindow();
    return (FALSE);
}

return (TRUE);
```

This creates an editing view in both window panes. The pane is created and the main window frame is displayed. The split panel appears when the main window frame appears, as shown in Figure 666.

Notice that each pane has its own vertical scroll bar. These are provided by the *CEditView*. There are no horizontal scroll bars because the default editing view enables word wrapping.

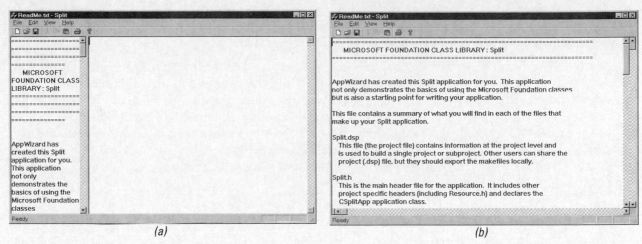

Figures 666a and 666b   Two splitter windows using a static split (a) using CreateStatic() *and (b) a dynamic split using* Create()

Now remove all that code and replace it with the following:

```
if (!m_wndSplitter.Create (this, 1, 2,
                           CSize(10,10), pContext))
    return (FALSE);

return (TRUE);
```

Compile and run the program. Notice that now there are two vertical scroll bars. The outer scroll bar is provided by the splitter window, the inner by the editing view. To remove the inner toolbar, you have to remove the *WS_VSCROLL* style from the *CFirstView::PreCreateWindow()* function by adding the statement *cs.style &= ~WS_VSCROLL*. The window will scroll, but you have to provide the splitter window with scroll information so that it can set the size and position of the scroll bar thumb.

More importantly, notice the little bump on the horizontal scroll bar just to the left of the thumb. That's for the splitter window, which hasn't been created yet. The new pane will be added when you grab this object and move it to the right. Although the object appears on the left of the scroll bar, the new splitter window will be created on the right. To prove this, open a file in the editing window (the *readme.txt* file in the current directory is a good one) and move the bump to the right. The file's text appears in the left pane, and the new pane is the one on the right.

Also notice that the new pane is blank. It's attached to the document, but it hasn't been updated to show the text. In the *CFirstView* class, add the *MainFrm.h* header file to the list of include files; then, add the virtual function *OnInitialUpdate()*. Place the following code in *OnInitialUpdate()*:

```
void CFirstView::OnInitialUpdate()
{
CMainFrame *frame = DYNAMIC_DOWNCAST(CMainFrame,
                           AfxGetApp()->GetMainWnd());
   CFirstView *pView = (CFirstView *)frame->GetActiveView();
   if (pView == this)
      return;
   CString strText;
   strText = pView->LockBuffer ();
   pView->UnlockBuffer ();
   SetWindowText (strText);
}
```

This code locates the active view. If this is the active view, it returns without doing anything. If, however, another view is active, the code retrieves the text from the active view and copies it to the current view, thus making it appear the same as the active view.

As you move the splitter window to the right, the new pane is destroyed when it reaches the far right side (or the left side if you move it the other way), and the splitter window now reappears on the left side of the horizontal scroll bar. The splitter window is being created *dynamically*, as opposed to the static method used previously. You can prove this by making a change in one of the panels. You are not yet updating the other views, so the changes won't appear in the other panel. Destroy the splitter window by moving it all the way to the right or left, and release the mouse button. Now reopen it. The text in the new pane will be identical to the text in the first pane.

In Tip 672, "Updating Multiple Views of the Same Document," you learn how to make changes in one panel appear in the other.

667. *Splitting a Splitter Window*

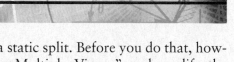

For this tip, you will split a splitter window into four panels using a static split. Before you do that, however, return to the project in Tip 666, "Using *CSplitterWnd* for Multiple Views," and modify the *OnCreateClient()* code to create both vertical and horizontal splitter windows.

Change the *m_wndSplitter.Create()* function to read as follows:

```
if (!m_wndSplitter.Create (this, 2, 2,
                    CSize(10,10), pContext))
    return (FALSE);
```

This is as far as you can go with a dynamic splitter window, a vertical split, and a horizontal split. Compile the code and examine the vertical scroll bar. You will see the same bump on it as you see on the horizontal scroll bar. Open the *readme.txt* file again, and drag each splitter bump to the center of the window so that it looks like Figure 667a.

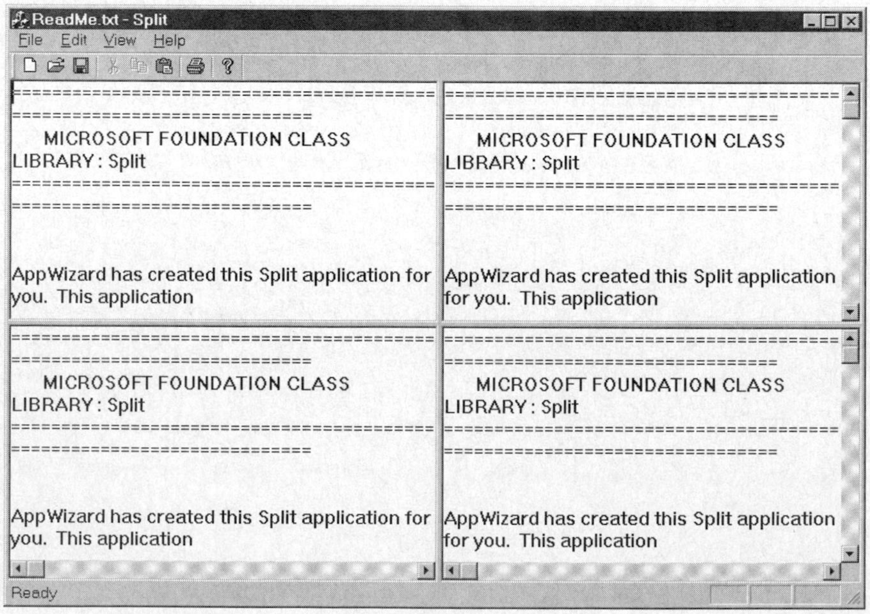

Figure 667a   The splitter window project with horizontal and vertical dynamic splits

Try scrolling. You will see that the two views at the same level vertically share the same vertical scroll bar and the vertical splits share the same horizontal scroll bars. As you scroll one window, the other window scrolls with it. There's nothing you can do about this using a dynamic split; that's the way the *CSplitterWnd* class works. If you examine the dynamic splits in the Visual Studio editing windows, you will see that they behave exactly this way. If you want separate scroll bars for each panel, you have to use the static method and put up with the additional work that goes with it.

Static creation lets you create up to 16 rows and 16 columns with a single splitter window. It's not likely that you will need that many. Also, there is so much interaction between the panes when you resize them that I like to keep splitter windows on a two-window basis, each splitter window variable contains only one split. It's much more work that way, but the result is that the windows tend to be more independent and you gain the flexibility of being able to do vertical or horizontal splits in any panel, as shown in Figure 667b.

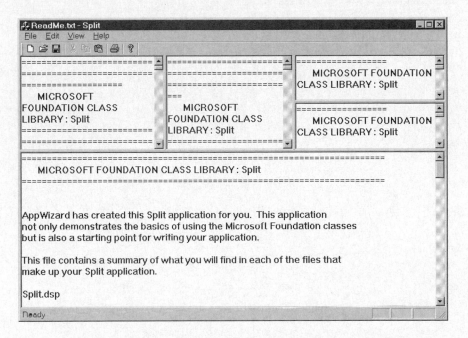

Figure 667b   The client area is split into two rows.
Then the top row is further subdivided into four smaller panels using static splitting.

You should try using a multiple split with one splitter window variable, if for no other reason than to see why you don't like it. Some alternative code built in to the project on the companion CD-ROM uses a single splitter window variable for the upper panel. At the top of the *MainFrm.cpp* file, include a definition, #*define FOUR_PANEL_TEST*, and recompile the program. It will create the same window as Figure 667b, but with four panels across the top. Try moving the far left or right splitter. When you release it, all four panels will be affected. It's not a pretty sight. Remove the definition and recompile. All the panels resize independently within the limits of the window frame. It's much more work to do it this way, and the logic gets tricky, but it's worth the effort.

If you removed the vertical scrolling style from the *CFirstView* class, change it back. The static splitters you are going to use now won't give you the automatic scroll bars. Figure 667b shows what the finished window will look like.

Add three new members to the *CMainFrame* class of type *CSplitterWnd*. Name them *m_wndSplitter2*, *m_wndSplitter3*, and *m_wndSplitter4*. Add a public member *m_Primary* of type pointer to *CFirstView*; then, add a forward reference to the class in *MainFrm.h*. (A *forward reference* is just a declaration that a class exists. It prevents loading down your file with unnecessary include files.) Near the top of the file, enter *class CFirstView;*. Be sure to include the semicolon.

Okay, get ready. Here's what the code in the *OnCreateClient()* function should look like. Numbering the splitter window variables should help you to keep track of what is happening:

```
BOOL CMainFrame::OnCreateClient(LPCREATESTRUCT lpcs,
                                CCreateContext* pContext)
{

// Create the first, basic splitter window. This will be
// a vertical split (two rows and one column).
//
    if (!m_wndSplitter.CreateStatic(this, 2, 1))
        return FALSE;

//****************************************************
//
//  Add the second splitter pane in the first row of the
//  first splitter. This new splitter window will have
//  two columns, each of which will be divided further.
//
//****************************************************
    if (!m_wndSplitter2.CreateStatic(
        &m_wndSplitter,    // parent window is first splitter
        1, 2,              // new splitter is 1 row, 2 cols
        WS_CHILD | WS_VISIBLE | WS_BORDER,  // WS_BORDER is
                                            // needed
        m_wndSplitter.IdFromRowCol(0, 0)
// new splitter is in the first row, first column of
// first splitter
        ))
    {
        TRACE0("Failed to create nested splitter\n");
        return FALSE;
    }

//****************************************************
//
//  Now split the left half of the second splitter into
//  another splitter window with two columns. This will be
//  the left directory listing, and the left pane will
//  contain the tree view and the right pane the list view.
//
//****************************************************
    if (!m_wndSplitter3.CreateStatic(
        &m_wndSplitter2, // parent window is second splitter
        1, 2,              // new splitter is 1 row, 2 columns
        WS_CHILD | WS_VISIBLE | WS_BORDER,  // WS_BORDER is
                                            // needed
        m_wndSplitter2.IdFromRowCol(0, 0)
// new splitter is in the first row, first column of
// second splitter
        ))
    {
        TRACE0("Failed to create nested splitter\n");
        return FALSE;
    }
//****************************************************
```

```
//
// Finally, split the right half of the second splitter into
// another splitter window, again with with two columns.
//
//*******************************************************
    if (!m_wndSplitter1.CreateStatic(
        &m_wndSplitter2, // parent window is second splitter
        2, 1,            // the new splitter is 2 rows,
                         // 1 column
        WS_CHILD | WS_VISIBLE | WS_BORDER,  // WS_BORDER is
                                            // needed
        m_wndSplitter2.IdFromRowCol(0, 1)
// new splitter is in the first row, 2nd columm
// of second splitter
        ))
    {
        TRACE0("Failed to create nested splitter\n");
        return FALSE;
    }


//*******************************************************
//
//   Now create the views inside the various panes.
//
//*******************************************************
//*******************************************************
//
//   Create a view in pane 0,0 of the upper left pane.
//
//*******************************************************
    if (!m_wndSplitter3.CreateView(0, 0,
        RUNTIME_CLASS(CFirstView), CSize(10, 10), NULL))
    {
        TRACE0("Failed to create view for upper pane 1\n");
        return FALSE;
    }
//*******************************************************
//
//   . . . and a view in pane 0,1 of the left pane.
//
//*******************************************************
    if (!m_wndSplitter3.CreateView(0, 1,
        RUNTIME_CLASS(CFirstView), CSize(10, 10), NULL))
    {
        TRACE0("Failed to create view for upper pane 2\n");
        return FALSE;
    }


//*******************************************************
//
//   Now create a view in pane 0,0 of the right pane.
//
//*******************************************************
    if (!m_wndSplitter4.CreateView(0, 0,
        RUNTIME_CLASS(CFirstView), CSize(10, 10), pContext))
    {
```

```
            TRACE0("Failed to create view for upper pane 3\n");
            return FALSE;
        }
//****************************************************
//
//  . . . and a view in pane 1,0 of the right pane.
//
//****************************************************
    if (!m_wndSplitter4.CreateView(1, 0,
        RUNTIME_CLASS(CFirstView), CSize(10, 10), pContext))
    {
        TRACE0("Failed to create view for upper pane 4\n");
        return FALSE;
    }
//****************************************************
//
//  Create the primary view. This will be the one the
//  document object uses to read and write the text file.
//  Put this view in the second row of the original
//  splitter window.
//
//****************************************************
    if (!m_wndSplitter.CreateView(1, 0,
        RUNTIME_CLASS(CFirstView), CSize(50, 0), pContext))
    {
        TRACE0("Failed to create lower pane view\n");
        return FALSE;
    }

//
//  Set the size information for the various panes. If you
//  don't, they'll all be crowded into the upper left
//  corner. Give the lower pane a bit more room.
//
    CRect rc;
    GetClientRect (rc);

    m_wndSplitter.SetRowInfo(0, rc.bottom / 3, 0);
    m_wndSplitter.SetRowInfo(1, rc.bottom / 2, 0);

    m_wndSplitter2.SetColumnInfo(0, rc.right / 2, 0);
    m_wndSplitter2.SetColumnInfo(1, rc.right / 2, 0);

    m_wndSplitter3.SetColumnInfo(0, rc.right / 4, 0);
    m_wndSplitter3.SetColumnInfo(1, rc.right / 4, 0);

    m_wndSplitter4.SetRowInfo(0, rc.bottom / 6, 0);
    m_wndSplitter4.SetRowInfo(0, rc.bottom / 6, 0);

//
//  Set the active pane and active view to the primary
//  view, which is the view at the bottom of the window.
//
    m_wndSplitter.SetActivePane (1, 0);
    m_Primary = (CFirstView *) m_wndSplitter.GetPane (1, 0);
    if (m_Primary != NULL)
```

```
// CSplitDoc commands

BOOL CSplitDoc::OnOpenDocument(LPCTSTR lpszPathName)
{
    CMainFrame *frame = DYNAMIC_DOWNCAST(CMainFrame,
                               AfxGetApp()->GetMainWnd());
    if (frame != NULL)
    {
        frame->SetActiveView ((CView *)frame->m_Primary);
    }

    if (!CDocument::OnOpenDocument(lpszPathName))
        return FALSE;

    // TODO: Add your specialized creation code here

    return TRUE;
}
```

These changes ensure that the document always works through the primary view. The *OnInitialUpdate()* function in *CFirstView* is written so that the primary view must be loaded first, or the text won't be spread to the other views.

You don't have to use the same view in all the splitter windows. In fact, that's not a common practice. The static splitter usually is used when you want to use different views in the various windows.

You can continue splitting the windows, even slice up the bottom panel if you want. Each splitter window variable accommodates only a single split, so be sure to add one variable for every split you perform. The logic can get a bit hairy after several splits, so try to perform all the operations on one splitter before moving on to the next. Managing this many splits can be quite a chore and makes you appreciate the MFC management of dynamic splits.

668. *Combining a Document View with CSplitterWnd*

Well, maybe it's time to do something more ordinary and use the static splitter windows the way they were intended. In this tip, you will reconstruct the *Explorer* application from Tip 657, "Combining *CTreeView*, *CListView*, and *CSplitterWnd* to Create an Explorer-Type Application." However, this time you will split the right panel again, place an editing view on the lower portion, and set it up so that when you double-click on a file, it opens in the editing view.

Create a new directory, say, *EditExplore*, and copy all the files from the *Explorer* application into it. No sense going through all the work again, and with only some slight changes, the same files can be used. (The directory name doesn't have to be the same as the project name; Visual Studio sets it up that way as a default.)

Add a *CEditView* class to the project and name it *CExploreView*. If you prefer, you could add a *CRichEditView* class instead, but you would have to manually set up the container class and initialize OLE. The edit view will do you just fine for now.

Also add a new document class and name it *CDummyDoc*. This is necessary because it will be the hub of communication between the list view and the tree view and keep them out of harm's way when the edit view is used to open or create a file.

```
        SetActiveView (m_Primary);
    return (TRUE);
}
```

Compile the application and run it to make sure that you get the five blank panels. You're not through with this crime against nature. You probably notice that when you try to open a file, it might or might not show up in the panels. *CEditView* and the document/view structure were not designed for this, and the frameworks becomes confused. The document object works through the view that is at the head of the list to put text into. I'm not sure how a view gets to the head of the list; I've tried changing the order of creation, and nothing seems to work consistently.

Open the document object. Assuming that you still are using the *Split* application from Tip 666, "Using *CSplitterWnd* for Multiple Views," that would be *SplitDoc.cpp*. This new code also is on the CD-ROM, however. Add *MainFrm.h* to the list of include files (a forward reference won't work here). The *OnNewDocument()* and *Serialize()* functions should have been added by the wizard when the project was created. You must modify these and add the virtual function *OnOpenDocument()*. The code for three functions is shown here:

```
BOOL CSplitDoc::OnNewDocument()
{
    if (!CDocument::OnNewDocument())
        return FALSE;

    CMainFrame *frame = DYNAMIC_DOWNCAST(CMainFrame,
                            AfxGetApp()->GetMainWnd());
    if (frame == NULL)
        ((CEditView*)m_viewList.GetHead())->SetWindowText(NULL);
    else
    {
        frame->SetActiveView ((CView *)frame->m_Primary);
        ((CEditView*)frame->m_Primary)->SetWindowText(NULL);
    }

    // TODO: add reinitialization code here
    // (SDI documents will reuse this document)

    return TRUE;
}

///////////////////////////////////////////////////////////
// CSplitDoc serialization

void CSplitDoc::Serialize(CArchive& ar)
{
    // CEditView contains an edit control that handles
    // all serialization
    CMainFrame *frame = DYNAMIC_DOWNCAST(CMainFrame,
                            AfxGetApp()->GetMainWnd());
    if (frame == NULL)
        ((CEditView*)m_viewList.GetHead())->SerializeRaw(ar);
    else
        ((CEditView*)frame->m_Primary)->SerializeRaw(ar);

}

///////////////////////////////////////////////////////////
```

Open the *Explorer.cpp* and *Explorer.h* files. In the header file, add a forward reference to the dummy document class (remember, *class CDummyDoc;*). Add a member variable of type *CDummyDoc* and name it *m_pDummyDoc*. In the implementation file, add *DummyDoc.h*, *DirTreeView.h*, and *DirListView.h* to the list of include files. Move to the end of the *InitInstance()* function and add the following code. This should look familiar to you, except that now you are detaching two view types from the real document and reattaching them to the dummy document:

```
m_pDummyDoc = new CDummyDoc;

POSITION pos;
pos = m_pDocManager->GetFirstDocTemplatePosition();
while (pos != NULL)
{
    CDocTemplate *pTempl =
                    m_pDocManager->GetNextDocTemplate (pos);
    POSITION docpos;
    docpos = pTempl->GetFirstDocPosition ();
    while (docpos != NULL)
    {
        CDocument *pDoc = pTempl->GetNextDoc (docpos);
        POSITION viewpos;
        viewpos = pDoc->GetFirstViewPosition ();
        while (viewpos != NULL)
        {
          CView *pView = pDoc->GetNextView (viewpos);
          if (pView->IsKindOf(RUNTIME_CLASS(CDirTreeView)))
          {
              pDoc->RemoveView ((CTreeView *)pView);
              m_pDummyDoc->AddView ((CTreeView *)pView);
          }
          if (pView->IsKindOf(RUNTIME_CLASS(CDirListView)))
          {
              pDoc->RemoveView ((CDirListView *)pView);
              m_pDummyDoc->AddView ((CDirListView *)pView);
          }
        }
    }
}
```

This is a brutish way of linking the two views through the document. There is a better, and easier, way using a *CCreateContext* structure, which you will see shortly. You should be aware of both methods, however, and choose the one that is more suitable to your application. The other method creates the document before the views are created and then attaches the views to the document when they are created. It's more elegant, but sometimes you need the more brutish method to change documents in the middle of a program.

Close the application class files. Open *MainFrm.cpp* and *MainFrm.h*. Add forward references in the header file for classes *CExploreView*, *CDirListView*, and *CDirTreeView*. Add *public* member variables of pointers to these classes. Add two *protected* variables of type *CSplitterWnd* named *m_wndSplitter* and *m_wndEditSplit*. Remove the *GetRightPane()* function altogether; it was added originally by the wizard and never was much use. To refresh your memory, the header is listed here:

```
class CDirListView;
class CDirTreeView;
class CExploreView;
```

```cpp
class CMainFrame : public CFrameWnd
{

protected: // create from serialization only
    CMainFrame();
    DECLARE_DYNCREATE(CMainFrame)

// Attributes
protected:
    CSplitterWnd m_wndSplitter;
    CSplitterWnd m_wndEditSplit;
public:

// Operations
public:

// Overrides
    // Class Wizard-generated virtual function overrides
    //{{AFX_VIRTUAL(CMainFrame)
    public:
    virtual BOOL OnCreateClient(LPCREATESTRUCT lpcs,
                                CCreateContext* pContext);
    virtual BOOL PreCreateWindow(CREATESTRUCT& cs);
    //}}AFX_VIRTUAL

// Implementation
public:
    CImageList *GetImageList (UINT uiImageList);
    virtual ~CMainFrame();
#ifdef _DEBUG
    virtual void AssertValid() const;
    virtual void Dump(CDumpContext& dc) const;
#endif

    CExploreView    *m_pEditView;
    CDirTreeView    *m_pTreeView;
    CDirListView    *m_pListView;

protected:  // control bar embedded members
    CStatusBar  m_wndStatusBar;
    CToolBar    m_wndToolBar;

// Generated message map functions
protected:
    void LoadSystemImageLists();
    //{{AFX_MSG(CMainFrame)
    afx_msg int OnCreate(LPCREATESTRUCT lpCreateStruct);
    afx_msg void OnDestroy();
    //}}AFX_MSG
    afx_msg void OnUpdateViewStyles(CCmdUI* pCmdUI);
    afx_msg void OnViewStyle(UINT nCommandID);
    DECLARE_MESSAGE_MAP()
private:
    CImageList m_SmallIcons;
    CImageList m_LargeIcons;
};
```

Close the header file. That should do it. Move to *MainFrm.cpp*. Remove the *GetRightPane()* function. There are two references to this function in the file, one in *OnUpdateViewStyles()* and again in *OnViewStyle()*. Change both these references to read as follows:

```
CDirListView* pView = m_pListView;
```

Finally in this file, add the virtual function *OnCreateClient()* and code it to read as follows. This creates the splitter windows and sets the edit view to the active window:

```
BOOL CMainFrame::OnCreateClient(LPCREATESTRUCT /*lpcs*/,
    CCreateContext* pContext)
{
    // create splitter window
    if (!m_wndSplitter.CreateStatic(this, 1, 2))
        return FALSE;

    if (!m_wndSplitter.CreateView(0, 0,
                            RUNTIME_CLASS(CDirTreeView),
                            CSize(200, 200), pContext))
    {
        m_wndSplitter.DestroyWindow();
        m_wndEditSplit.DestroyWindow();
        return FALSE;
    }

    if (!m_wndEditSplit.CreateStatic(
        &m_wndSplitter,   // parent window is first splitter
        2, 1,             // new splitter is 2 rows, 1 col
        WS_CHILD | WS_VISIBLE | WS_BORDER,  // WS_BORDER is
                                            // needed
        m_wndSplitter.IdFromRowCol(0, 1)
      ))
    {
        TRACE0("Failed to create nested splitter\n");
        return FALSE;
    }


    if (!m_wndEditSplit.CreateView(0, 0,
                            RUNTIME_CLASS(CDirListView),
                            CSize(150, 150), pContext))
    {
        m_wndSplitter.DestroyWindow();
        m_wndEditSplit.DestroyWindow();
        return FALSE;
    }
    if (!m_wndEditSplit.CreateView(1, 0,
                            RUNTIME_CLASS(CExploreView),
                            CSize(100, 100), pContext))
    {
        m_wndSplitter.DestroyWindow();
        m_wndEditSplit.DestroyWindow();
        return FALSE;
    }

    m_pTreeView=(CDirTreeView *)m_wndSplitter.GetPane(0,0);
```

```
    m_pListView=(CDirListView *)m_wndEditSplit.GetPane(0,0);
    m_pEditView=(CExploreView *)m_wndEditSplit.GetPane(1,0);

    SetActiveView (m_pEditView);

    return TRUE;
}
```

Open the header and implementation files for *CDirTreeView* and *CDirListView*. Search through all four files for occurrences of *CExploreDoc* and change them to *CDummyDoc*. That does it for the tree view files, so you can close them to keep your editing area clear. (It's a workshop, right? So keep it clean.)

You must add code to the *OnLButtonDblClk()* function to read a file into the editing view when the user selects a file. In the old *Explorer* application, the function just returned if the file was not a directory. Now you must replace that *return* with something useful. The new code for the function appears here:

```
void CDirListView::OnLButtonDblClk(UINT nFlags,
                                   CPoint point)
{
ITEMINFO *pItem;
LV_ITEM lvItem;

    memset (&lvItem, '\0', sizeof (LV_ITEM));
    POSITION pos =
            GetListCtrl().GetFirstSelectedItemPosition();
    if (pos == NULL)
        return;
    int nItem = GetListCtrl().GetNextSelectedItem(pos);
    pItem = (ITEMINFO *)(GetListCtrl().GetItemData (nItem));
    if (!(pItem->fdFile.dwFileAttributes &
                    FILE_ATTRIBUTE_DIRECTORY))
    {
        CString strPath = GetCurrentDirectory();
//
//  If there's no trailing backslash, add it.
//
        if (strPath.GetAt (strPath.GetLength() -1) != '\\')
            strPath += '\\';
        strPath += pItem->fdFile.cFileName;
        CMainFrame *frame = STATIC_DOWNCAST(CMainFrame,
                                    AfxGetMainWnd());
        if (frame->m_pEditView->GetDocument()->
                                OnOpenDocument (strPath))
            frame->m_pEditView->GetDocument()->SetPathName
                                            (strPath);

        return;
    }
    CString OldDir = GetCurrentDirectory ();
    CString strDir;
    if (!(strcmp(pItem->fdFile.cFileName, "..")))
    {
        int nIndex = OldDir.ReverseFind (_T('\\'));
        if (nIndex > 0)
        {
            strDir = OldDir.Left(nIndex);
```

```
//
//  Are we at the root? we need to add the backslash if so
//
        nIndex = strDir.Find (_T('\\'));
        if (nIndex < 0)
            strDir += '\\';
    }
}
else
{
    strDir = OldDir;
//
//  Add a backslash only if the directory name doesn't
//  already end with a backslash (as at the root directory)
    if (strDir.GetAt (strDir.GetLength() - 1) != '\\')
        strDir += '\\';
    strDir += pItem->fdFile.cFileName;
}
//
//  Save the new directory
    m_DirectoryName = strDir;
//  And change to it
    SetCurrentDirectory ((LPCSTR) m_DirectoryName);
//  Show it in the tree control
    if (m_bInitialized == true)
    {
        CDummyDoc *doc = GetDocument();
        pos = doc->GetFirstViewPosition ();
        while (pos != NULL)
        {
            CView *pView = doc->GetNextView (pos);
            if (pView->IsKindOf(RUNTIME_CLASS(CDirTreeView)))
            {
                ((CDirTreeView *)(pView))->SetDirectoryName
                                    (m_DirectoryName, true);
            }
        }
    }
//  And show it in the list control
    ListDirectory ();
}
```

At the very top of the *OnInitialUpdate()* function in both *DirTreeView.cpp* and *DirListView.cpp*, add the following statement. The variable already is in place. You just need to prevent the frameworks from reinitializing the controls whenever a file command is executed:

```
if (m_bInitialized == true)
    return;
```

There is light at the end of the tunnel. You must make the same modifications to the *CExploreDoc* class that you did with the *CSplitDoc* class in the preceding tip. Open the implementation file *ExploreDoc.cpp*. Add *MainFrm*.h to the list of include files. Add the virtual function *OnOpenDocument()*. You have to change this function, along with *Serialize()* and *OnNewDocument()*. The code for these functions is shown here:

```
BOOL CExplorerDoc::OnNewDocument()
{
    if (!CDocument::OnNewDocument())
        return FALSE;

    CMainFrame *frame = DYNAMIC_DOWNCAST(CMainFrame,
                                AfxGetApp()->GetMainWnd());
    if (frame == NULL)
        ((CEditView*)m_viewList.GetHead())->SetWindowText(NULL);
    else
    {
        frame->SetActiveView ((CView *)frame->m_pEditView);
        ((CEditView*)frame->m_pEditView)->SetWindowText(NULL);
    }
    // TODO: add reinitialization code here
    // (SDI documents will reuse this document)

    return TRUE;
}


/////////////////////////////////////////////////////////
// CExplorerDoc serialization

void CExplorerDoc::Serialize(CArchive& ar)
{
    // CEditView contains an edit control that handles
    // all serialization
    CMainFrame *frame = DYNAMIC_DOWNCAST(CMainFrame,
                                AfxGetApp()->GetMainWnd());
    if (frame == NULL)
        ((CEditView*)m_viewList.GetHead())->SerializeRaw(ar);
    else
        ((CEditView*)frame->m_pEditView)->SerializeRaw(ar);
}

BOOL CExplorerDoc::OnOpenDocument(LPCTSTR lpszPathName)
{
    CMainFrame *frame = DYNAMIC_DOWNCAST(CMainFrame,
                                AfxGetApp()->GetMainWnd());
    if (frame != NULL)
    {
        frame->SetActiveView ((CView *)frame->m_pEditView);
    }

    if (!CDocument::OnOpenDocument(lpszPathName))
        return FALSE;

    return TRUE;
}
```

If I didn't forget anything and you didn't skip any steps, the program should compile. Just in case, the complete code is on the companion CD-ROM. When you run the program, double-click on a file (the *readme.txt* again is a good candidate). It should appear similar to Figure 668.

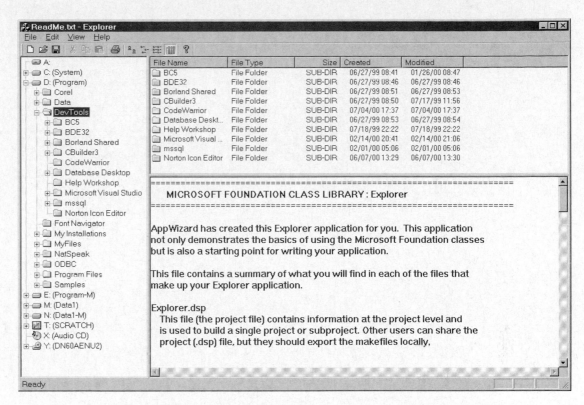

Figure 668   The new and improved Explorer application sports tree, list, and edit views. Double-clicking a file in the list view opens it in the editing view.

If you previously removed the *FWS_ADDTOTITLE* style from the main frame, you might consider restoring it at this point. Also, the font is the euglee system font, so you might want to change that. You have enough experience now, so that should be a piece of cake.

Unfortunately, I don't have room in this book to get into OLE drag-and-drop operations, but plenty of examples are on the Web and in the documentation. Try changing the program so that you can drag a file from the list view to the tree view and drop it into a directory. The code then should move the file from its original position to the new directory.

The other method of linking the views to the dummy document is done in the *CMainFrame* class (or *CChildFrame* class for an MDI application) when the views are created. Remove the *m_pDummyDoc* variable from the application class.

Add the *DummyDoc.h* header file to the list of include files in *MainFrm.cpp*. Locate the *OnCreateClient()* function and change the code to read as follows:

```
BOOL CMainFrame::OnCreateClient(LPCREATESTRUCT /*lpcs*/,
        CCreateContext* pContext)
{
    CDummyDoc *pDummyDoc =
                (CDummyDoc *) RUNTIME_CLASS
                (CDummyDoc)->CreateObject();

    CCreateContext Context;
    Context.m_pNewViewClass = RUNTIME_CLASS(CDirTreeView);
    Context.m_pCurrentDoc = pDummyDoc;

    // create splitter window
```

```
    if (!m_wndSplitter.CreateStatic(this, 1, 2))
        return FALSE;

    if (!m_wndSplitter.CreateView(0, 0,
                    RUNTIME_CLASS(CDirTreeView),
                    CSize(200, 200), &Context))
    {
        m_wndSplitter.DestroyWindow();
        m_wndEditSplit.DestroyWindow();
        return FALSE;
    }

    if (!m_wndEditSplit.CreateStatic(
        &m_wndSplitter,    // parent window is first splitter
        2, 1,              // new splitter is 1 row, 2 cols
        WS_CHILD | WS_VISIBLE | WS_BORDER,  // WS_BORDER is
                                            // needed
        m_wndSplitter.IdFromRowCol(0, 1)
      ))
    {
        TRACE0("Failed to create nested splitter\n");
        return FALSE;
    }

    Context.m_pNewViewClass = RUNTIME_CLASS(CDirListView);
    if (!m_wndEditSplit.CreateView(0, 0,
                    RUNTIME_CLASS(CDirListView),
                    CSize(150, 150), &Context))
    {
        m_wndSplitter.DestroyWindow();
        m_wndEditSplit.DestroyWindow();
        return FALSE;
    }
    if (!m_wndEditSplit.CreateView(1, 0,
                        RUNTIME_CLASS(CExploreView),
                        CSize(100, 100), pContext))
    {
        m_wndSplitter.DestroyWindow();
        m_wndEditSplit.DestroyWindow();
        return FALSE;
    }

    m_pTreeView=(CDirTreeView *)m_wndSplitter.GetPane(0, 0);
    m_pListView=(CDirListView *)m_wndEditSplit.GetPane(0,0);
    m_pEditView=(CExploreView *)m_wndEditSplit.GetPane(1,0);

    SetActiveView (m_pEditView);

    return TRUE;
}
```

CDummyDoc is defined using the macro *DECLARE_DYNCREATE*, so you can create an instance of it using the *RUNTIME_CLASS::CreateObject()* function. You don't have to worry about deleting the object. When the views attach to it, it goes into self-destruct mode and evaporates when the last view detaches from it or is destroyed.

The *CCreateContext* structure is used by the frameworks when it creates the frame windows and views associated with a document. The document must already exist, and you need only specify the members you intend to override. The default create context structure (a pointer to it was passed to *OnCreateClient()*) contains the document, view, and frame window classes that you specified when you created the document template in the application class's *InitInstance()* function. In this case, you are overriding the view and document, so that's all you need to load. The other members are initialized to *NULL*.

After you used the *CCreateContext* structure to create the tree view, you change the member variable to type *RUNTIME_CLASS(CDirListView)* and reuse the same structure to create the list view.

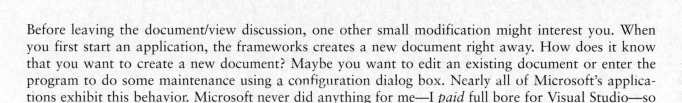

669. *Modifying* InitInstance *to Prevent the Initial Document from Being Created*

Before leaving the document/view discussion, one other small modification might interest you. When you first start an application, the frameworks creates a new document right away. How does it know that you want to create a new document? Maybe you want to edit an existing document or enter the program to do some maintenance using a configuration dialog box. Nearly all of Microsoft's applications exhibit this behavior. Microsoft never did anything for me—I *paid* full bore for Visual Studio—so I don't feel obliged to play the same game. I prefer to make my own selection at program startup.

If you are using the single-document interface, you don't have much choice. That's how the main window frame is created. With the multiple-document interface, however, the main frame is created independently of the document. Fortunately, it's easy to change the automatic create behavior.

Return to the *MultiView* application in Tip 613, "Understanding the Frame Window in the Document/View Architecture." In the *InitInstance()* function, locate the line that processes the command-line information. This should be a function call to *ProcessShellCommand()*. Add a couple of lines before that call so that the resulting code looks like the following:

```
// Parse command line for standard shell commands, DDE, file open
CCommandLineInfo cmdInfo;
ParseCommandLine(cmdInfo);

// Dispatch commands specified on the command line
if (cmdInfo.m_nShellCommand == CCommandLineInfo::FileNew)
    cmdInfo.m_nShellCommand = CCommandLineInfo::FileNothing;
if (!ProcessShellCommand(cmdInfo))
    return FALSE;
```

Recompile and run the application. The main window should appear minus the New dialog box. It won't appear now until you select the New command from the menu or use the accelerator key. In the preceding code, if nothing is entered on the command line, the *ParseCommandLine()* call defaults to the *FileNew* command. If that's the case, the next line changes it to *FileNothing* instead so that no files are opened. This method lets your program respond to drag-and-drop operations but assumes nothing more on startup.

If you do want the program to create a default document of a particular type without stopping on the File New dialog box, don't add these two lines. Instead, defer registering other templates until after the shell command executes. The following sequence creates a Web browser view when the program starts and registers the text document template so that you may create or open a text file:

```
// Register the application's document templates.
//  Document templates serve as the connection
//  between documents, frame windows, and views.

    CMultiDocTemplate* pDocTemplate;
    pDocTemplate = new CMultiDocTemplate(
        IDR_WEBTYPE,
        RUNTIME_CLASS(CWebDoc),
        RUNTIME_CLASS(CChildFrame), //custom MDI child frame
        RUNTIME_CLASS(CWebView));
    AddDocTemplate(pDocTemplate);

// create main MDI Frame window
    CMainFrame* pMainFrame = new CMainFrame;
    if (!pMainFrame->LoadFrame(IDR_MAINFRAME))
        return FALSE;
    m_pMainWnd = pMainFrame;
// The main window has been initialized, so show and update it.
    pMainFrame->ShowWindow(m_nCmdShow);
    pMainFrame->UpdateWindow();

// Parse command line for standard shell commands, DDE, file open
    CCommandLineInfo cmdInfo;
    ParseCommandLine(cmdInfo);

// Dispatch commands specified on the command line
    if (!ProcessShellCommand(cmdInfo))
        return FALSE;
    pDocTemplate = new CMultiDocTemplate(
        IDR_MULTIVTYPE,
        RUNTIME_CLASS(CTextDoc),
        RUNTIME_CLASS(CTextFrame), // custom MDI child frame
        RUNTIME_CLASS(CTextView));
    AddDocTemplate(pDocTemplate);
```

In the preceding code, you register only one document template to begin with. Document templates may be registered any time after this point, so you just defer registering the second template. Let the program process the *CCommandLineInfo::FileNew* command. At this point, it only knows about the Web document template, so it creates the default view. After that, you register your other templates to make them available on the Open, Save, and New commands.

Be careful with this one, though. If your program needs to respond to drag-and-drop operations for more than one file type, it might not work properly. In this case, you have to register all the templates and create the default view manually.

670. *Understanding Persistent Data*

If there's one thing Microsoft is persistent about (other than crushing Netscape), it's using the word "persistent" to describe data in the MSDN documentation. The idea of *persistent data* is that the data are saved between instances of an application and can be restored to their original state when the application is restarted.

The medium for the persistence might be a disk file, the system registry, a database, or any other device capable of storing data. In the Microsoft Foundation Class library, persistence of data in a document is achieved through the *Serialize()* function and the *DECLARE_SERIAL* and *IMPLEMENT_SERIAL* macros.

Persistent data doesn't have to be the result of editing a file or a data record, however. It can be the current state of an application's window and the arrangement of its views. Generally, this information would be stored in the system registry, which is the preferred method of data of less than 1KB, or in an initialization, or *.INI*, file.

You can add persistent data to the *Explorer* application by writing the information to the system registry. Add a configuration structure to the *struct.h* file similar to that shown here, adding any other information you would want to save:

```
struct CONFIG
{
    CRect    rcListPane;
    CRect    rcTreePane;
    int      cmdShow;
    CRect    rcWindow;
    CString  strDirectory;
    bool     bModified;
};
```

Open *Explorer.cpp* and add *struct.h* to the list of include files. At the top, add a global variable for the structure, *g_Config*. Configuration data often is made global so that it can be shared by other classes. Add the virtual function *ExitInstance()* to the application class, and then add two member functions of type void: *ReadRegistry()* and *WriteRegistry()*.

In the *InitInstance()* function, change the *SetRegistry()* value to whatever you are using for your company or personal registry information. Just above that line, add a call to *ReadRegistry()*. Move to the new *ExitInstance()* function and add a call to *WriteRegistry()*. The registry information will be read each time the application starts and written each time the application exits. In the meantime, any resizing of the splitter panels is saved in the global configuration structure, along with the last directory that was listed. The code for *WriteRegistry()* and *ReadRegistry()* is shown here:

```
//////////////////////////////////////////////////////////////
// CExplorerApp message handlers

void CExplorerApp::ReadRegistry()
{
CRegKey eKey;
long    lResult;
DWORD   dwValue;
TCHAR   szPath[1024];

    lResult = eKey.Open (HKEY_CURRENT_USER,
            "Software\\HAX Systems\\Explorer\\Settings");
    if (lResult != ERROR_SUCCESS)
    {
        g_Config.cmdShow = SW_SHOWNORMAL;
        g_Config.rcListPane.left = 2;
        g_Config.rcListPane.top = 2;
        g_Config.rcListPane.right = 152;
        g_Config.rcListPane.bottom = 152;
        g_Config.rcTreePane.left = 2;
        g_Config.rcTreePane.top = 2;
```

```
                g_Config.rcTreePane.right = 202;
                g_Config.rcTreePane.bottom = 202;
                g_Config.rcWindow.left = 0;
                g_Config.rcWindow.top = 0;
                g_Config.rcWindow.right = 0;
                g_Config.rcWindow.bottom = 0;
                g_Config.bModified = true;
                return;
        }
        eKey.QueryValue (dwValue, "TreeHoriz");
        g_Config.rcTreePane.left = dwValue >> 16;
        g_Config.rcTreePane.right = dwValue & 0xffff;
        eKey.QueryValue (dwValue, "TreeVert");
        g_Config.rcTreePane.top = dwValue >> 16;
        g_Config.rcTreePane.bottom = dwValue & 0xffff;

        eKey.QueryValue (dwValue, "ListHoriz");
        g_Config.rcListPane.left = dwValue >> 16;
        g_Config.rcListPane.right = dwValue & 0xffff;
        eKey.QueryValue (dwValue, "ListVert");
        g_Config.rcListPane.top = dwValue >> 16;
        g_Config.rcListPane.bottom = dwValue & 0xffff;

        eKey.QueryValue (dwValue, "WindowHoriz");
        g_Config.rcWindow.left = dwValue >> 16;
        g_Config.rcWindow.right = dwValue & 0xffff;
        eKey.QueryValue (dwValue, "WindowVert");
        g_Config.rcWindow.top = dwValue >> 16;
        g_Config.rcWindow.bottom = dwValue & 0xffff;

        DWORD dwSize = sizeof (szPath);
        memset (szPath, '\0', sizeof (szPath));
        eKey.QueryValue ((LPTSTR) szPath, "StartPath", &dwSize);
        g_Config.strDirectory = szPath;
}

void CExplorerApp::WriteRegistry()
{
CRegKey eKey;
long    lResult;
DWORD   dwValue;

        if (g_Config.bModified == false)
                return;

        lResult = eKey.Create (HKEY_CURRENT_USER,
                "Software\\HAX Systems\\Explorer\\Settings");
        if (lResult != ERROR_SUCCESS)
                return;
        dwValue = g_Config.rcTreePane.left << 16;
        dwValue |= g_Config.rcTreePane.right;
        eKey.SetValue (dwValue, "TreeHoriz");
        dwValue = g_Config.rcTreePane.top << 16;
        dwValue |= g_Config.rcTreePane.bottom;
        eKey.SetValue (dwValue, "TreeVert");
        dwValue = g_Config.rcListPane.left << 16;
```

```
        dwValue |= g_Config.rcListPane.right;
        eKey.SetValue (dwValue, "ListHoriz");
        dwValue = g_Config.rcListPane.top << 16;
        dwValue |= g_Config.rcListPane.bottom;
        eKey.SetValue (dwValue, "ListVert");
        dwValue = g_Config.rcWindow.left << 16;
        dwValue |= g_Config.rcWindow.right;
        eKey.SetValue (dwValue, "WindowHoriz");
        dwValue = g_Config.rcWindow.top << 16;
        dwValue |= g_Config.rcWindow.bottom;
        eKey.SetValue (dwValue, "WindowVert");
        eKey.SetValue (g_Config.strDirectory, "StartPath");
}

int CExplorerApp::ExitInstance()
{
        WriteRegistry ();
        return CWinApp::ExitInstance();
}
```

In the *ReadRegistry()* function, if the Registry key can't be opened, probably because it was never written, some default values are given to the structure members. Otherwise, the data is read from the Registry.

In the *MainFrm.cpp* file, add *struct.h* to the list of include files and at the top, an *extern* declaration for the configuration structure, as shown here:

```
extern CONFIG g_Config;
```

In the *OnCreateClient()* function, add some lines to recover the data from the structure, and make the list and tree view panels dependent on it:

```
int nTreeWidth = g_Config.rcTreePane.right
                - g_Config.rcTreePane.left;
int nListHeight = g_Config.rcListPane.bottom
                - g_Config.rcListPane.top;

if (!m_wndSplitter.CreateView(0, 0, RUNTIME_CLASS(CDirTreeView),
                            CSize(nTreeWidth, nTreeWidth),
                            pContext))
{
    m_wndSplitter.DestroyWindow();
    m_wndEditSplit.DestroyWindow();
    return FALSE;
}

if (!m_wndEditSplit.CreateView(0, 0,
                RUNTIME_CLASS(CDirListView),
                CSize(nListHeight, nListHeight), pContext))
{
    m_wndSplitter.DestroyWindow();
    m_wndEditSplit.DestroyWindow();
    return FALSE;
}
```

At the very top of the same function, resize the main window based on the information in the structure. This way, the window will be properly sized before the panes are created, and they can assume their old sizes:

```
if (g_Config.rcWindow.right)
    MoveWindow (g_Config.rcWindow, FALSE);
```

Add a message handler function for the *WM_SIZE* message using the Class Wizard. Let the window resize, and get the new size information in the structure. This information will give you the size of the window and its position on the screen:

```
void CMainFrame::OnSize(UINT nType, int cx, int cy)
{
    CFrameWnd::OnSize(nType, cx, cy);
    GetWindowRect (g_Config.rcWindow);
}
```

Close the *MainFrm.cpp* file and open the *DirListView.cpp* file. Add an *extern* statement for *g_Config* at the top of the file. Add a message handler for the *WM_SIZE* message and code it as follows. After you get the rectangle of the window (don't use *GetClientRect()* because that will get the entire client area), apply the *ScreenToClient()* function to make the coordinates relative to the main window client area:

```
void CDirListView::OnSize(UINT nType, int cx, int cy)
{
    CListView::OnSize(nType, cx, cy);
    if (m_bInitialized == false)
        return;
    GetWindowRect (g_Config.rcListPane);
    ScreenToClient (g_Config.rcListPane);
    g_Config.bModified = true;
}
```

In the *OnInitialUpdate()* function, rather than blindly get the current directory and list it, check first whether the structure member is empty, and use it if not:

```
if (g_Config.strDirectory.IsEmpty ())
{
    m_DirectoryName = GetCurrentDirectory ();
    g_Config.strDirectory = m_DirectoryName;
    g_Config.bModified = true;
}
else
    m_DirectoryName = g_Config.strDirectory;

ListDirectory ();
```

To save any new directory when it is selected, at the very bottom of the *OnLButtonDblClk()* function, add two lines of code:

```
g_Config.strDirectory = m_DirectoryName;
g_Config.bModified = true;
```

Placing it at the bottom won't cause it to change if a file is selected.

Now move to the *DirTreeView.cpp* file and add *struct.h* to the list of include files and an *extern* statement for *g_Config*. At the bottom of the *OnInitialUpdate()* function, change the directory statement to read as follows:

```
if (g_Config.strDirectory.IsEmpty ())
{
    SetDirectoryName (GetCurrentDirectory (), true);
    g_Config.strDirectory = GetCurrentDirectory ();
    g_Config.bModified = true;
}
else
    SetDirectoryName (g_Config.strDirectory, true);
```

In the *OnSelChanged()* message handler, add the following to the code where the new directory is passed to the list control:

```
if (pView->IsKindOf(RUNTIME_CLASS(CDirListView)))
{
//
// Strip the trailing backslash off the directory name.
// TreeView needs it, but ListView doesn't
    if (strDir.GetAt (strDir.GetLength() -1) == '\\')
        strDir = strDir.Left (strDir.GetLength() - 1);
    ((CDirListView *)(pView))->ListDirectory (strDir);
    g_Config.strDirectory = strDir;
    g_Config.bModified = true;
}
```

Recompile the application and run it. It should appear normal using the current directory. Change the size of the panels or the main frame, and select a new directory from either the list or tree views. Note how the window looks.

Exit the program and restart it. When the window reappears, it will be the same size and in the same position as when you last exited. The panels will retain their sizes, and the directory will be the last directory you listed.

Add to the *ReadRegistry()* and *WriteRegistry()* any other information you want saved. You might, for example, want to reopen any file that was in the editing panel.

671. *Saving the Status Bar Message*

You must make one more modification to the *Explorer* project and then leave it alone. You can take it wherever you want. Earlier, I pointed out that the frameworks' habit of writing that inane "Ready" message to the status bar does nothing but get in the way when you want to use the status bar to display real messages.

In this example, you will derive a new class from *CStatusBar*, capture the *WM_SETTEXT* message, and control its display. You can set up the message area so that it appears depressed in the status bar. When the frameworks sends a real message, a bar will appear to cover it for the duration of the message and then disappear, and your original message will show again.

You do this by creating an extra panel to the status bar to hold your messages. Then you dynamically resize it and the system message panel. When a message arrives from the frameworks, you can set the size of your message panel to 0 and increase the size of the system message panel. When the system message goes away, you do just the reverse. All the while you are looking for the "Ready" message and use it as a signal that the system message time has come and gone.

You can't really set the size of a status bar pane to 0. The way the panes are implemented imposes a minimum size of six device points, but that's small enough to be non-intrusive.

Start by adding a resource ID for the new status bar pane. Name it *ID_INDICATOR_DEFAULT* and give it a value of 59142. You will also use this ID in your messages to the status bar to differentiate them from system messages.

Derive a new class from *CStatusBar* named *CStatusBarEx*. The New Class dialog box doesn't list *CStatusBar* in the list of base classes, but it does have *CStatusBarCtrl*, so use it and then go through the new files and change it to *CStatusBar*. The base class doesn't have any virtual functions that can be overridden—Microsoft apparently thought that the status bar didn't stink—but you can capture messages to it. The first thing you want to do is add a message handler for the *WM_SETTEXT* message. The Class Wizard won't be much help beyond creating the new class, so you must enter the message handler manually. Also, add the member variables shown in the following *protected* section:

```cpp
/////////////////////////////////////////////////////////////////////
// CStatusBarEx window

class CStatusBarEx : public CStatusBar
{
// Construction
public:
    CStatusBarEx();

// Attributes
public:

// Operations
public:

// Overrides
    // Class Wizard-generated virtual function overrides
    //{{AFX_VIRTUAL(CStatusBarEx)
    //}}AFX_VIRTUAL

// Implementation
public:
    virtual ~CStatusBarEx();

    // Generated message map functions
protected:
    CString m_strStatusText;
    int     m_cxWidth;
    UINT    m_nId;
    UINT    m_nStyle;
    UINT    m_nWinId;
    UINT    m_nWinStyle;
    int     m_cxWinWidth;
    //{{AFX_MSG(CStatusBarEx)
        // NOTE - the Class Wizard will add and remove member functions here.
    //}}AFX_MSG
    afx_msg LRESULT OnSetText(WPARAM, LPARAM);

    DECLARE_MESSAGE_MAP()
};
```

In the implementation file, initialize the variables shown in the constructor. The only other function you have to worry about is the *OnSetText()* message handler. In this function, you check whether the incoming message has your ID (*ID_INDICATOR_DEFAULT*) and set the text in the window pane. Then save it in a member variable.

Most of the work is done when a message arrives from the frameworks. Here you check whether the message is "Ready." If so, you treat it justly and soundly pummel it to death, and restore your message to the status bar. If not, you resize your panel to 0 (well, actually 6) and set the system message panel style to *SBPS_POPOUT | SBPS_STRETCH*. This makes the panel seem to appear over your message panel. At least for the duration of the system message, you set your message panel to *SBPS_POPOUT* as well. That's esthetic; it seems to me that having a slight bump at the side looks better than a slight depression. Choose this one for yourself.

The code for the implementation file is listed here. Then you can move to the *CMainFrame* class and make some necessary changes there.

```cpp
// StatusBarEx.cpp : implementation file
//

#include "stdafx.h"
#include "Explorer.h"
#include "StatusBarEx.h"

#ifdef _DEBUG
#define new DEBUG_NEW
#undef THIS_FILE
static char THIS_FILE[] = __FILE__;
#endif

/////////////////////////////////////////////////////////////
// CStatusBarEx

CStatusBarEx::CStatusBarEx()
{
    m_nId = 0;
    m_nStyle = 0;
    m_cxWidth = 0;
    m_strStatusText = _T("");
}

CStatusBarEx::~CStatusBarEx()
{
}


BEGIN_MESSAGE_MAP(CStatusBarEx, CStatusBar)
    //{{AFX_MSG_MAP(CStatusBarEx)
    //}}AFX_MSG_MAP
    ON_MESSAGE(WM_SETTEXT, OnSetText)
END_MESSAGE_MAP()

/////////////////////////////////////////////////////////////
// CStatusBarEx message handlers

LRESULT CStatusBarEx::OnSetText(WPARAM wParam, LPARAM lParam)
{
char    *Message;
```

```
        Message = (char *) lParam;
        if (Message == NULL)
            return (0);

        if (m_nId == 0)
        {
            GetPaneInfo (1, m_nId, m_nStyle, m_cxWidth);
        }
        switch (wParam)
        {
            case ID_INDICATOR_DEFAULT:
                CStatusBar::SetPaneText (1, _T(Message), TRUE);
                m_strStatusText = _T(Message);
                break;
            default:
                if (!strcmp (Message, "Ready"))
                {
                    CStatusBar::SetPaneText (0, _T(""), TRUE);
                    GetPaneInfo (0, m_nWinId, m_nWinStyle,
                                            m_cxWinWidth);
                    SetPaneInfo (0, 0, SBPS_POPOUT, 0);
                    SetPaneInfo (1, m_nId, SBPS_STRETCH,
                                            m_cxWidth);
                    SetPaneText (1, (LPCSTR) m_strStatusText,
                                            TRUE);
                    break;
                }
                CStatusBar::SetPaneText (0, _T(Message), TRUE);
                SetPaneInfo (1, m_nId, SBPS_POPOUT, 0);
                SetPaneInfo (0, m_nWinId,
                                SBPS_POPOUT | SBPS_STRETCH,
                                m_cxWidth);
//
// Try the following style for a change
//              SetPaneInfo (1, m_nId, SBPS_NORMAL, 0);
//              SetPaneInfo (0, m_nWinId,
//                              SBPS_NORMAL | SBPS_STRETCH,
//                              m_cxWidth);
                SetPaneText (1, _T(""), TRUE);
                break;
        }
        return (0);
}
```

Close these files and open the *CMainFrame* files. In *MainFrm.h*, add the *CStatusBar.h* header file to the list of include files. Find the *m_wndStatusBar* member variable and change its type from *CStatusBar* to *CStatusBarEx*. Turn to the *MainFrm.cpp* file and add another separator to the top of the list of the *indicator* array at the top of the file:

```
static UINT indicators[] =
{
    ID_SEPARATOR,           // status line indicator
    ID_SEPARATOR,
    ID_INDICATOR_CAPS,
    ID_INDICATOR_NUM,
    ID_INDICATOR_SCRL,
};
```

That's all you have to do, but to make sure that things start up properly, move down to the *OnCreate()* function and locate the lines where the status bar is created. Immediately after this, add the following two lines. This will ensure that your message pane shows as the default. If you don't, the system message pane will hang around until you send your first message; then, the appearance of the status bar will change. I prefer to set this information so that the bar appears consistent from the start of the program.

```
m_wndStatusBar.SetPaneInfo(0,ID_SEPARATOR, 0, 0);
m_wndStatusBar.SetPaneInfo(1,ID_SEPARATOR,SBPS_STRETCH,100);
```

Okay, now let's find some information to put into the status bar. Close the *CMainFrame* files and open *DirListView.h*. Find the overloaded *ListDirectory()* function. The one you want is the one with all the code in it (the first overload simply calls the other with a default directory). Both the tree and list views operate through this function when the directory name is set. At the bottom of this function, add the following lines:

```
CMainFrame *frame = STATIC_DOWNCAST
                        (CMainFrame, AfxGetMainWnd());
::SendMessage (frame->GetMessageBar()->m_hWnd,
        WM_SETTEXT, (WPARAM) ID_INDICATOR_DEFAULT,
        (LPARAM) (LPCSTR) m_DirectoryName);
```

You've already included the *MainFrm.h* header file, so this code will work. In future projects, the *GetMessageBar()* function will be a member of the base class, so the *STATIC_DOWNCAST* in the first line can cast it either to *CFrameWnd* or to *CMDIFrameWnd*, whichever is appropriate. You are done. Compile and run your program. The first thing you should see is the current directory selected in the tree and list controls. Try moving the mouse cursor over a toolbar button or menu item that generates a ToolTip. The ToolTip text should appear to pop over the message line. When you move the mouse cursor away from the toolbar or menu, the original message with your selected directory should reappear.

Try changing the pane styles in *StatusBarEx.cpp*. For example, use *SBPS_NORMAL* instead of *SBPS_POPOUT* for the message panels to see which one you prefer.

Meanwhile, you've recovered a very, very valuable application resource that was being wasted by the frameworks.

672. *Updating Multiple Views of the Same Document*

Just because you've created a splitter window and built different views into the same document doesn't mean that the views are going to display the same information. If you change the text in one view, the other views don't automatically show the changes. You have to update them manually by calling the other views. Usually, this is done by calling the document object's *UpdateAllViews()* member function, which in turn calls the *OnUpdate()* member function of each view.

Before you start this tip, you should be aware that the edit control's scroll bars don't get along very well with those on the splitter window, which probably is one of the reasons Microsoft didn't allow it as one of the base classes permitted with a splitter window application.

The splitter windows work best with *CScrollView*-derived classes. There are several indications that the editing windows in the Developers Workshop are based on *CScrollView*. If you are hoping to get the same results with *CEditView*-based applications, it just isn't going to happen.

This example will use *CEditView*-derived classes anyway. The purpose is to show how to update other views so that you can dispense with the views' scroll bars. This doesn't mean that the views won't scroll. The scroll bars still will roll the text up and down and side to side, but the thumb won't be updated to reflect the new positions. To do any more, you must develop your own custom paint or draw code for *CScrollView*, which is beyond the scope of this book.

Static splitter windows are easier to handle than dynamic splitters. With static splitters, you know when and in what order the new views will be created. The user may create dynamic windows at any point in the program, however, and your code must deal with different scenarios. The code here will use dynamic splitters; if you can handle those, you can handle static splitters.

Re-create the *Split* project from Tip 666, "Using *CSplitterWnd* for Multiple Views," and set it up to handle a two-by-two dynamic split. It can be SDI or MDI—the same principles apply to child window frames as to the main window frame. When you create the project, don't select Use Splitter Window or Windows Explorer style applications; both these options create static splitter windows. Instead, create a normal project; on the final page change the base view class to *CEditView* and make your view class *CFirstView*, using *FirstView.h* as the header file and *FirstView.cpp* as the implementation file.

After the project is created, add a member variable to the *CMainFrame* class of type *CSplitterWnd* and name it *m_wndSplitter*. Add the virtual function *OnCreateClient* to the class. Make this function read as follows, noting that you completely remove the call to the base class function:

```
/////////////////////////////////////////////////////////////
// CMainFrame message handlers

BOOL CMainFrame::OnCreateClient(LPCREATESTRUCT lpcs,
                                CCreateContext* pContext)
{
//
// Create a dynamic splitter window with a single row
// and two columns (a vertical split).
//
    if (!m_wndSplitter.Create (this, 2, 2,
                               CSize(10,10), pContext))
        return (FALSE);
    return (TRUE);
}
```

To make the text from the first view appear in any new views, you must copy the text into it. Close the *CMainFrame* files and open the *CFirstView* files. Add *MainFrm.h* to the list of include files. Locate the *PreCreateWindow()* function, and remove the scroll bars by changing the style to *cs.style &= ~(WS_VSCROLL | WS_HSCROLL);* then, move to the *OnInitialUpdate()* function. Replace the code in this function with the following, again removing any call to the base class function:

```
/////////////////////////////////////////////////////////////
// CFirstView message handlers

void CFirstView::OnInitialUpdate()
{
    CMainFrame *frame = DYNAMIC_DOWNCAST(CMainFrame,
                             AfxGetApp()->GetMainWnd());
    if (frame == NULL)
        return;
    CFirstView *pView =
                 (CFirstView *)frame->GetActiveView();
    if ((pView == this) || (pView == NULL))
        return;
```

```
        CString strText;
        strText = pView->LockBuffer ();
        pView->UnlockBuffer ();
        SetWindowText (strText);
}
```

This copies the text from the active view into any new view when it is created. The first thing you will notice is that when a view is created with a dynamic splitter, the display always begins on the first line of the file, even if you have scrolled down in the original view. You want to make the new view appear the same as the original, so add the following code at the bottom of *OnInitialUpdate()*:

```
int nLine = pView->GetEditCtrl().GetFirstVisibleLine ();
GetEditCtrl().LineScroll (nLine);
```

Recompile the program and open a file. Scroll down a page or two and then open a splitter window. The first line of text in the new view should be the same as the first line of text in the original view.

If you type in one view, the changes are not made automatically to the other views. You yourself must do that by calling the document object's *UpdateAllViews()* function or by calling the *OnUpdate()* function in a particular view. You do this by adding message handlers for the *WM_CHAR* message, processing it in the current view, and then passing it on to the other views through the document object.

Add a structure like the following. At the top of the *FirstView.cpp* file is a good place. It will be used only by this class. Note that it is derived from *CObject*, so you can pass it in the *UpdateAllViews()* call without casting it:

```
struct    UPDATECHAR : CObject
{
    int     startSel;
    int     endSel;
    UINT    nChar;
    UINT    nRepCnt;
    UINT    nFlags;
};
```

For different types of updates, you can define a number of structures and derive them from *CObject*. When you get to the *OnUpdate()* function, you must cast them to the proper type.

In the *CFirstView* class, add a message handler for *WM_CHAR* and add the virtual function *OnUpdate()*. The code for these functions appears here:

```
void CFirstView::OnUpdate(CView* pSender, LPARAM lHint,
                                        CObject* pHint)
{
    if ((pSender == this) || (pHint == NULL))
        return;
    CEdit& edit = GetEditCtrl ();

    int startSel, endSel;
    switch (lHint)
    {
        case 1:
        {
            UPDATECHAR *puc = (UPDATECHAR *) pHint;
            edit.GetSel (startSel, endSel);
            edit.SetRedraw (FALSE);
            edit.SetSel (puc->startSel, puc->endSel);
            CEditView::OnChar(puc->nChar, puc->nRepCnt,
```

```
                                        puc->nFlags);
            edit.SetSel (startSel, endSel);
            edit.SetRedraw (TRUE);
            break;
        }
        default:
            break;
    }
}

void CFirstView::OnChar(UINT nChar,UINT nRepCnt,UINT nFlags)
{
UPDATECHAR  uc;

    GetEditCtrl ().GetSel (uc.startSel, uc.endSel);
    uc.nChar = nChar;
    uc.nRepCnt = nRepCnt;
    uc.nFlags = nFlags;
    CEditView::OnChar(nChar, nRepCnt, nFlags);
    GetDocument()->UpdateAllViews (this, (LPARAM) 1, &uc);
}
```

In the *OnChar()* function, get the current selection *before* you process the incoming character (or ship it off to *CEditView::OnChar()*). After the character is processed, it's likely that the selection will change, and you want the other views to be updated in the same position. Save the incoming parameters in the *UPDATECHAR* structure, and call *GetDocument()->UpdateAllViews()* to start the process in motion. Pass the *this* pointer in the first parameter. You can use the second parameter of this function as an integer constant for the *switch* statement in *OnUpdate()*.

In the *OnUpdate()* function, look at the *lHint* parameter to decide what action to take. Right now, there's only one possibility, but you will add more shortly. Save the current caret position in the window (even though the caret doesn't show) by calling the edit control's function. Then set the redraw flag to *false* to keep the text from jumping around. Set the selection to the members in the structure and call *CEditView::OnChar()*. The same character should appear in the same position in all the views almost simultaneously. Reset the old caret position and return.

Certain keystrokes don't work. For example, the DEL key isn't passed through the *OnChar()* function. For that, you must add a message handler for *WM_KEYDOWN*. Add the following code to the function:

```
void CFirstView::OnKeyDown(UINT nChar, UINT nRepCnt,
                                        UINT nFlags)
{
UPDATECHAR  uc;

    GetEditCtrl ().GetSel (uc.startSel, uc.endSel);
    uc.nChar = nChar;
    uc.nRepCnt = nRepCnt;
    uc.nFlags = nFlags;
    GetDocument()->UpdateAllViews (this, (LPARAM) 2, &uc);
    CEditView::OnKeyDown(nChar, nRepCnt, nFlags);
}
```

In the *switch* statement in *OnUpdate()*, add the code for *case 2*:

```
case 2:
{
    UPDATECHAR *puc = (UPDATECHAR *) pHint;
```

```
        edit.SetSel (puc->startSel, puc->endSel);
        CEditView::OnKeyDown(puc->nChar, puc->nRepCnt,
                                        puc->nFlags);
        break;
}
```

Notice two major changes. In the *OnKeyDown()* handler, the views are updated *before* the key is processed. This keeps the focus in the current window. If you processed it the other way around, a cursor movement key, for example, would cause the caret to jump between windows. If you need to process the key before calling *UpdateAllViews()*, you can retrieve the focus by calling *::SetFocus(this->m_hWnd);* at the end of the function.

Recompile and run the program. The DEL key should work now, along with the cursor keys and some other keys. Some keys are handled through the *WM_SYSCHAR* and *WM_SYSKEYDOWN* messages, and you probably won't need to worry about them. If you do have to add these message handlers, neither the Class Wizard nor the Wizard Bar has message map entries for them, so you will have to roll your own.

To add these message functions, add the message map entries *ON_WM_SYSCHAR* and *ON_WM_SYSKEYDOWN* at the top of the implementation file. Then add declarations to the header file for the functions:

```
Message Map Entries:
    ON_WM_SYSCHAR()
    ON_WM_SYSKEYDOWN()
Header file entries:
    afx_msg void OnSysChar(UINT nChar, UINT nRepCnt,
                                        UINT nFlags);
    afx_msg void OnSysKeyDown(UINT nChar, UINT nRepCnt,
                                            UINT nFlags);
```

Make the *lHint* parameters 3 and 4 for these two functions. The code for the functions follows:

```
void CFirstView::OnSysChar(UINT nChar, UINT nRepCnt,
                                        UINT nFlags)
{
UPDATECHAR  uc;

    GetEditCtrl ().GetSel (uc.startSel, uc.endSel);
    uc.nChar = nChar;
    uc.nRepCnt = nRepCnt;
    uc.nFlags = nFlags;
    CEditView::OnSysChar(nChar, nRepCnt, nFlags);
    GetDocument()->UpdateAllViews (this, (LPARAM) 3, &uc);
}

void CFirstView::OnSysKeyDown(UINT nChar, UINT nRepCnt,
                                            UINT nFlags)
{
UPDATECHAR  uc;

    GetEditCtrl ().GetSel (uc.startSel, uc.endSel);
    uc.nChar = nChar;
    uc.nRepCnt = nRepCnt;
    uc.nFlags = nFlags;
```

```
    CEditView::OnKeyDown(nChar, nRepCnt, nFlags);
    GetDocument()->UpdateAllViews (this, (LPARAM) 4, &uc);
}
```

Now add *case* statements for these two messages in the *OnUpdate()* function:

```
case 3:
{
    UPDATECHAR *puc = (UPDATECHAR *) pHint;
    edit.SetSel (puc->startSel, puc->endSel);
    CEditView::OnSysChar(puc->nChar, puc->nRepCnt,
                                     puc->nFlags);
    break;
}
case 4:
{
    UPDATECHAR *puc = (UPDATECHAR *) pHint;
    edit.SetSel (puc->startSel, puc->endSel);
    CEditView::OnSysKeyDown(puc->nChar, puc->nRepCnt,
                                         puc->nFlags);
    break;
}
```

You might want to provide some special handling for the cursor movement keys. For example, if it's a two-way split, you want the two windows to respond to these keys independently. If it's a four-way split, you might want to make the matching horizontal or vertical windows work together.

673. *Understanding the Visual Studio Debugger*

A *debugger* is a program that lets you run another program with some degree of supervision, enabling you to pause or stop the program at certain points and then examine or modify the contents of variables or CPU registers.

Every development environment has some sort of debugger, ranging from the very command-line-oriented *adb* on basic UNIX platforms to those on windowing platforms such as XWindow or Windows that offer a graphical user interface.

In Visual C++, the debugger is integrated into the Developers Studio, which provides editing and workshop tools in an integrated development environment (IDE). Although the appearance is quite different, the Visual C++ debugger has its heritage in the old *CodeView.exe* debugger from Microsoft, which itself grew out of *symdeb.exe*.

By default, the Visual C++ MFC AppWizard sets up two program configurations when you create a project. One is the *debug* version, which is compiled and linked with debug code in the object files, and a *release* version, which has all the debug code stripped from it. When a project is finished and all the bugs are worked out (dream on!), you should compile the release version for users. The code is more compact because it doesn't contain the debugging information; theoretically, at least, it should load faster.

You can set up other program configurations, depending upon your needs. Each has its own compiler/linker options and resources that you can modify using the Project Settings dialog box.

674. *Setting Project Options*

With the Project Settings dialog box, you control the construction of your program. The views, documents, code and all the other elements that you add to your program are the ingredients. The "mixing" and "baking" instructions are included in the project settings. To access the Project Settings dialog box, select Settings from the Project menu, or press Alt+F7. You'll get a dialog box that looks like the one in Figure 674.

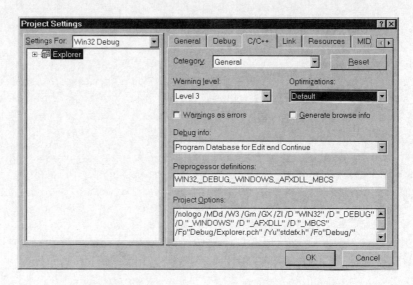

Figure 674   The Project Settings dialog box is where you select options for your project

The left side of the dialog box contains a tree control, where you can select all the configurations in your project, just a single configuration, a group of files, or just one file to configure.

The configuration is hierarchical, which explains the tree control. Changes made to one branch of the tree are applied to each subbranch. To change the setting for all the source files for the debug version, you select that configuration in the combo box just above the tree; then, you expand the tree and select the Source Files folder. This isn't a real folder in the sense of a directory; it's a "virtual" folder used to gather similar files. To set options for a single file, expand the tree one more level and select the file. The file-level settings override the more general folder settings.

On the right of the dialog box is a tab control where you actually administer the project settings. The tab control has scroll buttons to the far right, so what you see on the screen initially doesn't present all the possibilities. Don't let its appearance fool you; the pages on this tab control are much more involved than they first appear. Many of the tab pages have multiple sections that are selected using a combo box control on the tab page.

The General tab is where you set the directory for the output files. On this page, you can select whether you want to use the Microsoft Foundation Class library as a dynamic link library or whether you want to statically link it to your program (only the Professional and Enterprise editions allow static linking). When statically linked, all the required code from the MFC library is placed in the program's executable file, and it no longer needs the support of the system DLL.

The Debug tab is a two-section tab. The General section is where you set the executable to be run when you press either the Go button on the toolbar or the F5 key. Normally, this will be the program's executable file. However, if you are developing a project that can't be executed directly—a dynamic link library, custom control, or similar element—you should enter the name of the program that will test your project. Also set the working directory (the current directory for the program when it first starts) and any program arguments. The final box is for a remote debugging session, which will be discussed in Tip 681, "Understanding Remote Debugging."

The second section of the Debug page enables you to set any additional DLLs that need to be loaded before your program is run. You can list multiple DLLs and then select or disable them as needed. Select Additional DLLs in the combo box control to get to this section.

The C/C++ page is perhaps the most involved of all the pages. It has eight different sections selectable from the combo box control. At the General level, three controls are of particular interest. The first is the Warning Level, which is used to set the type of warning messages issued by the compiler. The None control turns off all warning messages, and the levels progress up to 4, where the compiler issues *beaucoup* messages, most of which you can ignore. This level is equivalent to the UNIX "lint" program listing and should be used only to perform a program cleanup. Normally, you will keep the warning levels set at 1, which limits them to "severe" warnings.

Also in this section is the Optimization box. Leave optimizations off for debugging; if you turn on any optimization, the line currently being executed in the debugger might not match the actual code line. The compiler alters the generated code to make it run faster or with less memory, whichever option you choose. If you select Custom optimization, you'll be able to select the optimization option in the Optimizations section of this tab page.

The Debug Info box enables you to set the level of debugging information that is placed in the object and executable files. Obviously, for the release version of your program, you should select None. The debugging levels are Line Numbers Only (for use with a command-line debugger—we've all experienced the joy of those), C7 Compatible (the CodeView type output used by the old Microsoft C Compiler product), Program Database (which produces a *.pdb* file used by the Visual C++ debugger—this should be your minimum setting for debugging programs), and Program Database for Edit and Continue (discussed in Tip 679, "Using Edit and Continue Debugging").

Choose the C++ Language option from the Category box to select language options. On this page, the Representation Method determines how the compiler points to class members. You might want to remember this option for future projects. The default, Best Case Always, requires that classes be defined before pointers to members are declared. This isn't always possible, and eventually you will encounter cases in which two or more classes reference each other. In this situation, you can't always define the class before declaring a pointer variable. If this is the case, select General-Purpose Always and select a representation method from the combo box just below.

The General Purpose Representation method is used only if you select General-Purpose Always in the Representation Method box. The Point to Any Class option is the default and requires the most code space, but it rarely, if ever, causes an error when referencing pointers to class members. It assumes virtual inheritance in class definitions. The Point to Single-Inheritance Classes method assumes that the class to which the pointer variable is a member has no inheritance or single inheritance. If the class actually has multiple or virtual inheritance, the compiler will generate an error. The option Point to Single- and Multiple-Inheritance Classes assumes multiple inheritance, and an error is generated if the class has virtual inheritance.

You should keep the Enable Exception Handling box checked. This allows the runtime code to call destructors automatically when an exception is handled. Run-Time Type Information is a recent addition to the C++ language that allows the type of an object to be determined at runtime. Checking this box enables the dynamic_cast, typeid, and type_info operators. Disable Construction Displacements requires a little explanation. When the constructor or destructor in a derived class calls a virtual member function that has been overridden by an earlier derived class, the function may be passed an incorrect *this* pointer. Checking this option enables a single construction displacement for each virtual base of a class. Say that you have a base class with a virtual function, and a derived class that overrides that virtual function. Then you have a third class, which is derived from the derived class, and its constructor calls the virtual function. You might have a potential problem. You won't encounter this situation often, and it's best to leave this box unchecked unless you know that the problem exists in your application.

Select the processor type from the Processor box in the Code Generation section. The default option is Blend, which blends the optimization code for the various processors but favors the Pentium processor. Note that as of Visual C++ 5.0, the 80386 and 80486 options are ignored.

Unless you know that your program will not use multiple threads, such as a single-threaded command-line option, you should leave the Use Run-Time Library set to one of the multi-threaded options, particularly for MFC programs. If you're building a DLL, selecting a single-thread option will limit your DLL to use with single-threaded programs.

The Calling Convention selection determines how parameters are passed to functions, how values are returned, and how the stack is cleaned up after a function returns. __cdecl is the default—if your program will use variable arguments (vararg), you will need this convention. This adds stack cleanup code with every function call and thus results in a slightly larger executable than the other options. Stack cleanup isn't that much of a penalty; if you study the assembly code for your functions in the Assembly window during a debug session, you'll see that usually this is nothing more than a single Assembly statement to adjust the stack pointer. __fastcall specifies that parameters are to be passed in registers, if possible, and __stdcall is a Microsoft-specific convention used to call Windows API functions—it is best avoided. If you need __stdcall functions, declare them as such when you write your code.

In the Customize section, select Disable Language Extensions to disable Microsoft-specific extensions to the language and force ANSI compliance. If you select this option, you likely will get some errors resulting from anonymous structures and unions, which are Microsoft extensions, when compiling programs for Windows. Enable Function-level Linking allows the compiler to package individual functions as needed by the linker. It is on by default, and you can't change it if you've selected Edit and Continue in Debug Info in the General section. Eliminate Duplicate Strings enables the compiler to put a single copy of duplicate strings in the executable file. If you #define a constant as a string and then use it in more than one place, normally the string would be duplicated for each use. This option causes the compiler to use a single string. If you select Enable Minimal Rebuild, the compiler will try to detect which source files need to be recompiled as a result of changing a header file. Visual C++ keeps dependency information on an .idb file that it creates on the first compilation. Enable Incremental Compilation allows the compiler to detect which functions in a source file have changed since the last compilation and then to recompile only those functions. This speeds up compilation but results in larger object files. The option Suppress Startup Banner and Information Messages turns off the verbose mode of the compiler. You can't see these messages from within the IDE anyway.

In the Listing Files section, select Generate Browse Info to build a browse database for your application. Browsing makes navigation faster within your project but increases compile time because the compiler must build an .sbr file for each object file. Listing File Type specifies how you want intermediate files to appear. Normally, you don't need these intermediate files, but sometimes they can be handy for finding problem areas related to optimization.

The Optimizations section contains a duplicate of the Optimizations combo box from the General section. If you selected Custom, the check list box below enables you to enable selected optimization methods. Just below the check list box, Inline Function Expansion, which is available only in the Professional and Enterprise editions, determines how the compiler treats inline functions.

The Precompiled Header section controls how and when the compiler will create and use precompiled header files. If necessary, you can turn off precompiled header use from this section.

Use the Preprocessor section to add command-line definitions or to specify additional include paths for the preprocessor to search while preparing source files for compilation. The Undefine Symbols option is used to undefine Microsoft specific macros. This option won't affect definitions in source files entered with the #define directive.

The other tab pages are considerably less involved than the C/C++ page. Next, click on the Linker tab to set or change options for the linker. If you need to link additional static libraries in your application, specify them in the Library/Object Modules box. The other options determine how the preprocessor hunts for include files and how library files are used in the project.

Set options for the resource compiler on the Resources tab page. You can specify the location of the compiled resource file (usually in the output directory) and include other resource files from this page.

The MIDL page is used with DLL projects and other applications that need an interface definition language file (the "M" is for the egocentric part of Microsoft—most other platforms call this simply IDL). Such projects would include Windows NT service programs, applications that use remote procedure calls, and ActiveX.

The Browse page controls browser options, including the location and name of the file containing the browse information.

The Custom Build page lets you specify additional commands to be run when a project is built and to set file dependencies for these commands.

The Pre-link Step page similarly enables you to specify commands that are executed before the object files are linked into your executable files.

Finally, you may specify commands to run after the build is complete on the Post-build Step. For example, if you want the executable or any intermediate files copied to another directory, you can specify the command to do that on this page.

675. *Using the Debug Windows*

To inspect and modify your program's variables, memory, CPU registers, and other program data, Visual C++ contains six special Debug windows that are available only while a program is executing and has been paused by an event such as a breakpoint, an exception, or an assertion.

The windows are Watch, Call Stack, Memory, Variables, Registers, and Disassembly. While the program is stopped, you can view these windows in one of four ways. You can right-click on any blank area of the Visual Studio window frame and select one from the pop-up menu (the Disassembly window doesn't appear on this menu). You can select Debug Windows from the View menu and select the one you want to view. Third, the Debug toolbar has buttons to toggle each of these windows on and off—just press the appropriate button. Finally, you can use the accelerator key as listed in Table 675.

Debug Window	Accelerator	Window Displays
Watch	Alt+3	Displays the value of selected variables or expressions.
Call Stack	Alt+7	Traces function calls to the pause point.
Memory	Alt+6	Displays or modifies the contents of a specific memory location. The location may be specified as an absolute address, an expression, or a variable name.
Variables	Alt+4	Displays variables in the current context (see the corresponding text in this tip).
Registers	Alt+5	Enables you to view and set the internal registers of the CPU.
Disassembly	Alt+8	Displays the current execution point in Assembly language. You may select an option to display the current C++ line as well.

Table 675   The Visual Studio Debug windows and their uses during debug sessions

The most common windows that you will encounter are the Watch and Variables windows, which are displayed automatically when the program is executed in the debug environment. Normally, these windows are at the bottom of the main frame, as shown in Figure 675a, but they are floatable and dockable, so you may change their appearance or location. The Call Stack window also will be a frequently used window.

Figure 675a   *The Variables window on the left and the Watch window on the right normally appear together at the bottom of the IDE when a program is running. Each is independently detachable, however, and a splitter bar between them allows them to share the same window area.*

The Variables window is a tabbed window. The Auto tab displays variables used in the current and previous statements, as well as the return value of any function when you step over or out of it. The Local tab displays variables local to the current function. The *this* displays member variables of the object pointed to by the *this* pointer, a structure or a class object. In each case, the last variable that changed is highlighted in red. You can change the value of a variable in this window by double-clicking on its value to display an edit control; then, enter the new value and press Enter.

The Watch window contains four tabs. Each tab is functionally the same, but you may list different variables to watch on different panels, enabling you to organize your variable collection by class or function. To enter a watch variable, select a blank line in one of the windows and begin typing. To modify the name of a watch variable, double-click on its name, and an edit control will appear. To modify the *contents* of a watch variable, double-click on its value. To delete a watch variable, select it with the mouse and press the Delete key. You can duplicate a watch variable by dragging the entry to a blank line and dropping it. You may want to do this, for example, to examine different areas of a large structure or class definition at the same time.

You also can enter variables or statements to the Watch window using the Quick Watch command. Place the caret on the variable that you want to add to the window, and then select Quick Watch from the Tools menu, press the Shift+F9 key, or press the Quick Watch button on the Debug toolbar (the button is the one that looks like a pair of glasses). In each case, you will be taken to the Quick Watch dialog box. You can force a recalculation of the variable's value or add it to the Watch window from this dialog box.

The Call Stack window, shown in Figure 675b, is useful for tracing backward in your code when your program encounters a fault, an exception, or an assertion. More often than not, the actual code displayed when one of these events happens will be Assembly code or will be somewhere in the MFC library code. To find the statement in your code that led to the event, display the Call Stack and look down the list until you find the first function call from your project. Double-click on it, and you'll go to the line that caused the error, or nearly so. In many cases, the pointer, a green triangle, actually will be on the line *after* the call that generated the error. You'll usually be able to tell from the syntax.

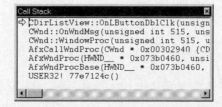

Figure 675b   *The Call Stack window*

The Memory window shown in Figure 675c can be used to display the contents of a memory location. The address may be the result of an expression, an absolute memory address, a variable name or event, or a CPU register. It's especially useful for examining large buffers or strings that don't display well in the Variables window. To use the window, display it and enter the address of the memory location or the name of the variable that you want to examine in the edit box; then, press Enter. You may enter an expression in this box, as long as it evaluates to a valid memory address. The memory at the address pointed to by the result will be displayed. You also may drag variable names from the Watch and Variables windows and drop them into the Memory window; the memory location will display immediately. You can move the first address displayed by double-clicking on another memory address so that it is highlighted. Then click and hold the left mouse button while dragging the address to another location. This doesn't rearrange the memory, however.

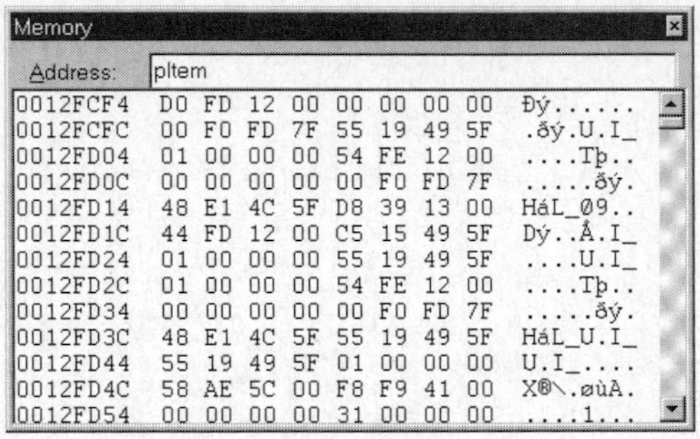

```
Memory                                              ×
 Address:  pItem
0012FCF4  D0 FD 12 00 00 00 00 00   Ðý......    ▲
0012FCFC  00 F0 FD 7F 55 19 49 5F   .ðý.U.I_
0012FD04  01 00 00 00 54 FE 12 00   ....Tþ..
0012FD0C  00 00 00 00 00 F0 FD 7F   .....ðý.
0012FD14  48 E1 4C 5F D8 39 13 00   HáL_Ø9..
0012FD1C  44 FD 12 00 C5 15 49 5F   Dý..Å.I_
0012FD24  01 00 00 00 55 19 49 5F   ....U.I_
0012FD2C  01 00 00 00 54 FE 12 00   ....Tþ..
0012FD34  00 00 00 00 00 F0 FD 7F   .....ðý.
0012FD3C  48 E1 4C 5F 55 19 49 5F   HáL_U.I_
0012FD44  55 19 49 5F 01 00 00 00   U.I_....
0012FD4C  58 AE 5C 00 F8 F9 41 00   X®\.øùA.
0012FD54  00 00 00 00 31 00 00 00   ....1...    ▼
```

Figure 675c   The Memory window

Use the Register window to examine the contents of the CPU register at the point at which the program stopped. Within certain limits, you can modify the contents of the registers. There are some registers that you can't modify; for example, the debugger won't let you violate the boundary of the protected memory space used by your program, or change the contents to point to another process. You can display the memory address pointed to by a register in the Memory window. With the program halted, display both the Register and Memory windows. Double-click on a register name or value, and then click and hold the left mouse button while you drag it to the Memory window. Drop it in the Memory window, and the address will be displayed. To change the value of a register, double-click on the register name or value, and drag it to the Watch window and drop it. Double-click on the value in the Watch window, modify the value, and press Enter; the Register window should display the new value. This can be handy for modifying the return values of a function. In C++, return values generally are passed back to the calling function in the CPU's Accumulator, the EAX register on later Intel processors. After the function's return statement has executed, but before the value is taken in the calling function, modify the Accumulator to reflect the new value. To change the value of a bit in the flags register (OV, UP, EI, PL, ZR, AC, PE, and CY in the Register window), simply double-click on one. Flag bits have only two possible values, 1 for set and 0 for reset; double-clicking will toggle a flag bit's state. For the record, however, it is ill-advised to change any CPU registers unless you know what you are doing. This doesn't mean that you shouldn't experiment; you'll learn by doing, even if you crash a program a few times.

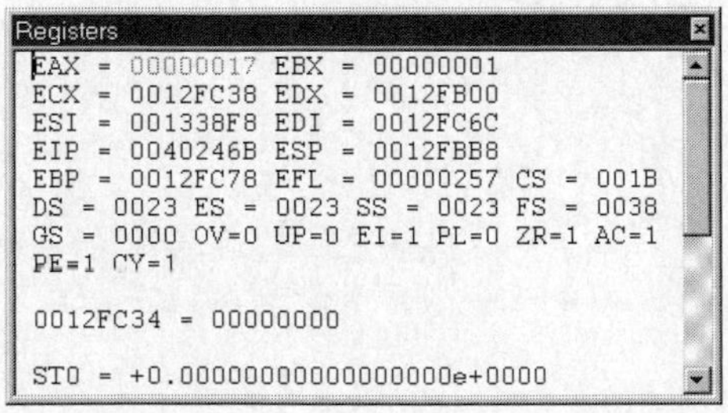

```
Registers                                           ×
EAX = 00000017 EBX = 00000001                  ▲
ECX = 0012FC38 EDX = 0012FB00
ESI = 001338F8 EDI = 0012FC6C
EIP = 0040246B ESP = 0012FBB8
EBP = 0012FC78 EFL = 00000257 CS = 001B
DS = 0023 ES = 0023 SS = 0023 FS = 0038
GS = 0000 OV=0 UP=0 EI=1 PL=0 ZR=1 AC=1
PE=1 CY=1

0012FC34 = 00000000

ST0 = +0.00000000000000000e+0000            ▼
```

Figure 675d   The Registers window

The Disassembly window, shown in Figure 675e, displays the current C++ source line along with the Assembly code that implements the C++ code. This helps to determine precisely which part of a C++

statement caused the program to halt, and a complex C++ statement may require many lines of Assembly code to implement. This window is slightly different than the other Debug windows. It is not dockable, but it displays as an MDI child window. The other debug windows are toolbars and remain on the top of the view, but the Disassembly window can be placed in the background and kept active without covering other work. You can view disassembly code at any point in the program using either the drag-and-drop method or the Go To dialog box. To use the drag-and-drop method, select any variable, expression, register, or function that evaluates to a valid memory address; then, drag it to the Debug window and drop it. The Assembly code for that address will be shown. To use the Go To command, select Go To from the Edit menu, or type Ctrl+G to summon the Go To dialog box. In the Go To What box, select Address; then, enter or paste any address or an expression that evaluates to an address, and press Enter.

```
Disassembly                                                    _ □ X
   263:         pItem = (ITEMINFO *) (GetListCtrl().GetItemData (nItem));
⇨ 0040246B    mov          edx,dword ptr [ebp-44h]
   0040246E    push         edx
   0040246F    mov          ecx,dword ptr [ebp-10h]
   00402472    call         CListView::GetListCtrl (00409428)
   00402477    mov          ecx,eax
   00402479    call         CListCtrl::GetItemData (004094dc)
   0040247E    mov          dword ptr [ebp-14h],eax
   264:         if (!(pItem->fdFile.dwFileAttributes & FILE_ATTRIBUTE_DIRECTOR
   00402481    mov          eax,dword ptr [ebp-14h]
   00402484    mov          ecx,dword ptr [eax+8]
   00402487    and          ecx,10h
   0040248A    test         ecx,ecx
   0040248C    jne          CDirListView::OnLButtonDblClk+179h (00402569)
   265:         {
   266:            CString strPath = m_DirectoryName;
```

Figure 675e   The Disassembly window shows C++ and Assembly source code

You can select what is displayed in the Assembly window by selecting Options from the Tools menu and then selecting the Debug tab and setting the options in the group marked Disassembly window.

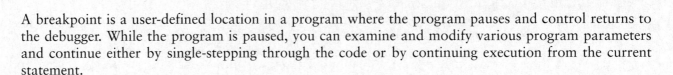

676. *Setting and Using Breakpoints*

A breakpoint is a user-defined location in a program where the program pauses and control returns to the debugger. While the program is paused, you can examine and modify various program parameters and continue either by single-stepping through the code or by continuing execution from the current statement.

Breakpoints are perhaps the single most important debugging tool you will use, and Visual C++ is very good with them. You can toggle a breakpoint on and off by pressing the Breakpoint button on the Build toolbar or the Build Minibar (the button is identified by an open hand with its palm facing you), or by pressing the F9 key. A breakpoint at the current line will be toggled on or off.

You can view, set, remove, edit, enable, and disable breakpoints using the Breakpoints dialog box. Breakpoints can be unconditional (they halt every time the execution point matches the breakpoint line), or they can be conditional (a user-defined condition must exist, or the breakpoint will be ignored). You also can specify that certain Windows messages cause a program break.

Enter the Breakpoints dialog box by selecting Breakpoints from the Edit menu, or press Alt+F9. This dialog box has a tab control containing three pages. The first enables you to set unconditional breakpoints. The second tab enables you to set breakpoints based on the content of variables or arrays, and the third sets breakpoints for Windows messages. At the bottom of each page is a check list box containing all the breakpoints in the project.

On the first page, enter the breakpoint in the edit box. This can be a line number, a function, a memory address, or a label (see, labels do have some use other than as the object of *goto* statements). Just to the right of this box is a button with a right-facing arrow. Pressing the button displays two options. The line number is the current caret line in the source file when you summoned the dialog box. The Advanced selection brings up the Advanced Breakpoint dialog box. From this dialog box, you can set a breakpoint in any function or at any line in any source file in the program. The Location field corresponds to the Break At field in the Breakpoint dialog box, and any changes that you make here will be reflected in the lower dialog box when you press the OK button.

When you've selected a breakpoint, either by entering a new one or by selecting one from the check-list box, the Condition button is enabled. Press this button to set conditions on the current breakpoint. In the Breakpoint Condition dialog box, you may enter an expression for the debugger to evaluate as a condition of the breakpoint. You also may enter the number of times that the breakpoint should be skipped before it halts the program. In the following snippet, you could set a breakpoint to stop when x = 5 at the first line in the loop in a couple of ways:

```
for (x = 0; x < 10; ++x)
{
    FirstExpression ();
    SecondExpression();
}
```

First, set an unconditional breakpoint on the line containing *FirstExpression()*, and then press Alt+F9 to edit the breakpoint. Select it in the check-list box, and press the Condition button. In the expression field, you could enter $x == 5$ (note the syntax is the same as in a C++ test). When the expression is false, the breakpoint will be ignored, but it will halt the program when x reaches 5. You also could enter 5 as the number of times to skip before stopping. The difference between the two methods is that the first will halt the program *only* when x is equal to 5; the second method will cause the program to halt the fifth time that the breakpoint is encountered and every time after that.

The Data page enables you to set breakpoints on data values, which implies a condition that you would enter as you did in the previous paragraph. This page also contains an Advance page, which you access by pressing the right-facing arrow to the right of the edit box.

On the Messages page, you can select a message from the second combo box, which does not contain all possible Windows messages, or enter one in the first box on the page.

To disable a breakpoint, remove the check mark from the front of it in the check-list box at the bottom of the dialog box. To remove a breakpoint, select it in the check-list box and either press the Delete key or press the Remove button to the right. Pressing Remove All deletes all breakpoints.

None of these changes take effect until you press the OK button, so if you make a drastic mistake, you can press Cancel to back out of all changes.

677. *Single-Stepping Through a Program*

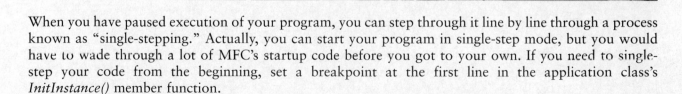

When you have paused execution of your program, you can step through it line by line through a process known as "single-stepping." Actually, you can start your program in single-step mode, but you would have to wade through a lot of MFC's startup code before you got to your own. If you need to single-step your code from the beginning, set a breakpoint at the first line in the application class's *InitInstance()* member function.

You single-step through a program using the F10 and F11 keys, abetted by the buttons on the Debug toolbar. With the program paused, the F10 key executes the current statement and moves the instruction pointer to the next statement. If the current pointer is on a function call, the call completes before the instruction pointer returns. This is called "stepping over" a function. To "step into" a function call, press the F11 key; the instruction pointer will move to the first statement of the called function. However, if there are any expressions in the argument list, they will be executed first. If there are embedded function calls in the parameter list, the instruction pointer will go to them in order before entering the called function. This also will happen if you create class objects in an argument list.

There are "step into" and "step over" buttons, along with a "step out" button on the Debug toolbar. The "step out" button is handy when you have entered a function or a loop and want to get out of it quickly. This button will complete the current function call or loop and return you to the next statement to be executed.

678. *Debugging a Command-Line Program*

If you are truly into self-abuse, you can debug a command-line program using the standard Windows debugging tool, *debug.exe*. If you've never experienced *debug* or its grown-up cousin, *symdeb.exe*, you might look up the documentation and try it once or twice. That's about all you'll want, and it will make you appreciate the benefits of an integrated development environment.

You can compile and run your command-line program from within the Visual Studio. If your program is not interactive—if it doesn't pause for user input—but simply writes to the screen, the command-line window will appear while the program is running and then close as soon as the program exits. You won't get a chance to view the program's output.

You can prevent this from happening by putting a breakpoint in the last line of your program. When the breakpoint is encountered, the program will pause, and you can select the DOS window from the Taskbar to examine the program output. You might have noticed that you can't do this with a Windows program. The difference is that a Windows program runs on its own, but a command-line program first spawns a command processor. When the program pauses and you examine the output, you actually are examining the command processor window rather than your program.

679. *Using Edit and Continue Debugging*

A new feature introduced with Visual C++ 6.0 is the Edit and Continue feature. While you are debugging a program, you can make changes to the code and apply those changes without having to stop and restart the program. This is a great advantage while debugging programs, especially if you've had to go through several menu or dialog steps to get to this point in the code you are debugging.

To use Edit and Continue, you must enable it by selecting Program Database for Edit and Continue on the C/C++ tab of the Options dialog box. You also must turn off all optimization. The selection box is on the General section of the Tab page. When you do this, the compiler builds a program database in a *.pdb* file that holds debugging and dependency information. The option is set by default when you create your project with the MFC AppWizard. After the option is set, you don't have to do anything else to use Edit and Continue.

While debugging an application, pause the program at a breakpoint and make a change in some nearby code. Press the F10 key to step to the next statement. The Output window will appear while the new code is being compiled. When the changes have been applied, you can hide the Output window by pressing the button on the main toolbar.

If errors occurred while the changes were being applied, you'll get a dialog box informing you of the errors and giving you the option to continue without applying the changes or to return to the code to fix the errors. If you opt to fix the errors, the errors will be displayed in the Output window and on the status bar.

You don't have to pause the program to make changes. At any time during the program's run, you can alter the code and press the Apply Code Changes button on the Debug toolbar, or press Alt+F10. The program will pause briefly while the changes are compiled and then will resume its normal execution.

There are some limits to Edit and Continue. Changes to resources can't be made using Edit and Continue, nor may changes be made to exception-handling blocks. You cannot change data types, such as make changes to a class or a structure definition, nor can you add new data types. Also, you can't delete functions or make changes to function prototypes or make changes to global or static code.

If any of these operations occur, you'll get a dialog box notifying you that the changes cannot be applied and giving you the option to continue.

Also, you can't alter a function while it is on the call stack. For example, if you modify a function that calls the function in which the instruction pointer is located, the changes won't be applied until the next time the function is called.

There is a 64-byte limit on new local function variables because of the limited space set aside on the stack for Edit and Continue. That's really very liberal, and it translates to 16 new pointer variables or the equivalent. If you do exceed the 64 bytes, the changes won't be applied until the next time the function is called.

When you terminate your program after performing Edit and Continue operations, the program is compiled automatically, and the new code is incorporated into the executable.

680. *Writing to the Output Window*

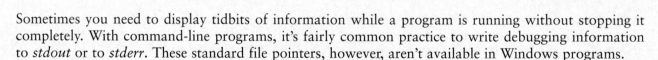

Sometimes you need to display tidbits of information while a program is running without stopping it completely. With command-line programs, it's fairly common practice to write debugging information to *stdout* or to *stderr*. These standard file pointers, however, aren't available in Windows programs.

Visual C++ provides macros that enable you to write to the Output window in a statement that mimics the C and C++ *printf()* function. The macros—*TRACE, TRACE0, TRACE1, TRACE2,* and *TRACE3*—are available only with MFC projects.

The *TRACE* macro can be used with a variable number of arguments, while the *TRACE0* macro cannot be used with arguments. The *TRACE1, TRACE2,* and *TRACE3* macros require one, two, and three arguments, respectively.

When you run an application in the debugger, you've probably noticed a number of lines in the Output window telling you that this or that DLL was loaded, and finally ending with a statement that some program has exited. It's convenient to think that these were written with the *TRACE* macros, but they weren't. However, when you use *TRACE*, your messages will appear intermixed with these.

Use *TRACE* the same as you would use *printf()*, using the same escape sequences and formatting characters. Suppose, for example, that you wanted to write the value of variable *x* and the contents of *CString* variable *strText* to the Output window. The line would look similar to the following:

```
TRACE("x = %d, strText = %s\n", x, (LPCSTR) strText);
```

Be sure to include the newline sequence at the end. If you don't, the next message written to the Output window will be appended to the end of your output.

If you are using *TRACE* in a Unicode program, you must include the *_T* macro for the formatting string. This isn't necessary with the other trace macros that require a fixed number of arguments.

681. *Understanding Remote Debugging*

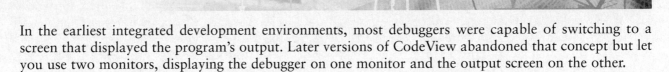

In the earliest integrated development environments, most debuggers were capable of switching to a screen that displayed the program's output. Later versions of CodeView abandoned that concept but let you use two monitors, displaying the debugger on one monitor and the output screen on the other.

You still can use a two-monitor setup, but without it you can't switch to the output screen and examine the state of the window while the program is paused. The remote debugging feature of Visual C++ lets you put the display for the program being debugged on one computer and then put the debugger itself on another. You should approach this topic with caution, particularly if you do your computing on a limited budget. Once you experience remote debugging, you probably won't want to go back to single-machine mode.

You'll need a second computer and a network connection to use remote debugging. The debugger communicates with the remote machine through a monitor program. The executable code for the program being debugged doesn't have to live on the remote machine, but the monitor module does. You can run the remote debug monitor on the same machine as the debugger using *localhost* as the network connection, but it won't gain you anything. While the program is paused, its paint code is never called, so you can't "switch" to its Output window.

When you start the remote debugging session, the monitor module loads and runs the executable from your project's *DEBUG* directory (or wherever you've placed the executable). The program still is under the control of the debugger, but you never lose sight of it because you've paused the program.

682. *Setting Up the Remote Debugger*

The easiest way to set up the remote debugger is to install the same version of Visual C++ on the remote machine as on the local machine. That way you know that all the DLLs are of the same revision level and in the operating system's PATH statement. However, if you have only one copy of Visual C++, that would violate your license agreement, and you would live the rest of your life in fear of midnight storm troopers from Redmond, or at least the software piracy dominion.

The remote debugger must be set up on an Intel-based platform. You can use Windows 95, Windows 98, or Windows NT Workstation or Server. The remote monitor program itself is *MSVCMON.EXE*, and you'll find it in the *COMMON\MSDEV98\BIN* subdirectory where you installed the Visual Studio. In addition, you'll need five DLLs: *MSVCRTD.DLL* (the MSDN documentation is incorrect—it says that you need *MSVCRT.DLL*, but you actually need the debug version), *MSVCP60.DLL*, *TLN0T.DLL*, *DM.DLL*, and *MSDIS110.DLL*. If the remote machine is running Windows NT, you'll also need *PSAPI.DLL*. You'll find the first two DLLs in the Windows\System32 directory and the others in the same directory where you found *MSVCMON.EXE*. Copy *MSVCRTD.DLL* to the Windows\System32 directory on the remote machine. Make a folder for the remote debugger, and copy the other files into it.

They aren't mentioned by the MSDN documentation, but you'll also need *MFC42D.DLL* and *MFCO42D.DLL*. You'll find these in your Windows\System32 directory, and you can copy them to the new folder for the remote debugger or to the System32 folder on the remote machine.

Make sure that the applicable directories are accessible from each machine. The remote machine will need access to the directory on the local machine where the executable is stored. The local machine will need access to the new Remote Debugger directory and the Windows\System32 directory. If the remote machine is running Windows 95, also make sure that the Windows\System directory is accessible.

On the local machine, enter the Settings dialog box for the Visual Studio by pressing Alt+F7. Select the Debug tab. For Remote Executable Path and File Name, enter the full path of the executable. This is the path *from* the remote machine. If you have network drives mounted, you can use them in the path; otherwise, you'll have to use the UNC path and the shared drive name. For example, the path back from my Windows 95 machine to the executable for the EditExplore program is \\JubalHarshaw\m$\CFILES\VisualC++\EditExplore\Debug\Explorer.exe. Close this dialog box and select Remote Debugger Connection from the Build menu. On this dialog box, select Network (TCP/IP) (or whatever network you are using), and then click the Settings button. Enter the network name or IP address of the remote machine. Close this dialog box and the connection dialog box.

On the remote machine, start *MSVCMON.EXE*. When the connection dialog box appears, press the Connect button. You'll get a smaller message box that says "Connecting . . . " and a Disconnect button. Leave it as it is for now and return to the local machine.

Start your program in the debugger. Each time you set up a project for remote debugging, you may be asked to locate a number of DLLs. Persevere—there are a lot of them. Locate the DLLs on the remote machine using either network drives or the UNC path. From my development machine back to the Windows 95 machine, if I need to locate *MPR.DLL*, I enter \\AdamSelene\C\Windows\System\MPR.DLL, where "AdamSelene" is the name of the remote machine and "C" is the share name of the drive.

Just when you think there is no end to locating DLLs, the application will pop up suddenly on the remote machine. As the debugging session progresses, you may be asked to locate a few more DLLs. Be patient; after you've located them, you won't need to do it in the next debugging session.

Try putting a breakpoint in the code on the local machine, and then operate the application on the remote machine so that it encounters the breakpoint. The application will appear to freeze when the debugger halts the program. As you single-step through the application, you can see the results of the new code on the remote machine.

You should be able to set up the remote debugger on any version of Windows. AdamSelene is an "original" Windows 95 machine, and the remote debugger has no problems with it.

683. *Switching Between Remote and Local Debugging*

Now that you've found an excuse to rush out and buy a second computer and network cards (don't forget to get a hub), sometimes you will want to return to local debugging. When you first set up remote debugging, the Visual Studio will set the option as the default.

To turn off remote debugging, select the Remote Debugger Connection item in the Build menu. In the Remote Connection dialog box that appears, select Local and then press the Enter key. The debugging will return to the local machine.

To switch back to remote debugging, follow the same process, except this time select Network (TCP/IP).

code, stepping over each function call. When the bug occurs, the function that was being executed is the likely candidate. Reset the cursor to this point, and rerun the program to the cursor. This time *step into* the problem function using the F11 key, and single-step through its code, again stepping over function calls.

The bug may be several function calls deep, but successively working your way into the function calls eventually will turn up the bug.

Another technique is to create a log file and write key information at certain places within the program to the file. In your utility file, create a function to log messages and overload it to make it easy to use; the easier it is to use, the more likely you are to use it. The following sequence of *LogMessage()* functions handles a number of calling possibilities, but eventually all the functions call one particular version that actually writes to the log file:

```cpp
//****************************************************

#define LOGFILE      "C:/Logs/MyApp.log"

void LogMessage (char *fmt, ...)
{
CString      msg, LogFile;
va_list      ap;
CTime        Today = CTime::GetCurrentTime();

    va_start (ap, fmt);
    msg.FormatV (fmt, ap);
    va_end (ap);
    msg += "\r\n";
    LogFile = LOGFILE;
    LogMessage (LogFile, msg);
}

void LogMessage (CString & str)
{
CString      LogFile;

    if (g_conf.LogPath.IsEmpty())
        return;
    str += "\r\n";
    LogFile = LOGFILE;
    LogMessage (LogFile, str);
}

//
//   This is the only LogMessage function that will actually
//   write to a log file. All others should boil down to
//   this calling sequence.
//
void LogMessage (CString & fn, CString & msg)
{
FILE         *fp;
CTime        Now = CTime::GetCurrentTime();

    fp = fopen ((LPCSTR) fn, "ab+");
    if (fp != NULL)
    {
        fprintf (fp, "%02d/%02d/%04d %02d:%02d:%02d ",
```

```
                Now.GetMonth(), Now.GetDay(), Now.GetYear(),
                Now.GetHour(), Now.GetMinute, Now.GetSecond());
            fprintf (fp, (LPCSTR) msg);
            fclose (fp);
        }
}


//
// Load a string from the string table using the passed
// ID, then format a string if necessary.
//
void LogMessage (UINT nID, ...)
{
CString Message;
char    str[512], *pszMessage;
va_list ap;

    if (!Message.LoadString (nID))
        return;
    pszMessage = new char [Message.GetLength() + 1];
    if (pszMessage == NULL)
        return;
    strcpy (pszMessage, (LPCSTR) Message);
    va_start (ap, pszMessage);
    vsprintf (str, pszMessage, ap);
    va_end (ap);
    delete pszMessage;
    Message = str;
    LogMessage (Message);
}
```

Add overloads as you need them, but keep it easy to use. You can exclude the code from release builds by placing it between *#ifdef _DEBUG* and *#endif* directives.

Finally, use the status bar to display current program state information. Add the status bar code from Tip 671, "Saving the Status Bar Message." This will prevent the inane "Ready" message from the frameworks from wiping out your debug messages.

686. *Using the CMemoryState Class to Detect Memory Leaks*

As you've seen, memory leaks occur when you allocate memory on the heap and then fail to free it. Steady memory leakage eventually will lead to an exhaustion of the heap, and your memory allocations will fail, particularly on limited memory systems.

Some C++ implementations provide *garbage collectors* to sniff out unreferenced memory and deallocate it; Visual C++ does not, and management of the heap memory used by your program is your responsibility. (Garbage collector programs are available for Windows systems, but don't assume that one will be present; your program may run on other machines that don't have such a utility.)

The MFC *CMemoryState* is a tool to help you find and eliminate memory leaks in your program. It is available only in debug versions of programs, and all object declaration references to its member functions should be wrapped between *#ifdef _DEBUG* and *#endif* directives. In addition, it will detect only memory that was allocated using the *new* operator. Thus, it is applicable only to C++ programs.

When developing in the Visual Studio, you have the advantage of its memory leak detection, and any stranded memory will be dumped and freed when you exit a program running under the Visual Studio debugger. If your program uses a lot of memory, or if your computer is short on memory, you can invoke your own *CMemoryState* sessions to locate memory leaks while your program is running.

Declare an object of *CMemoryState* where you want to monitor the memory. Use the member *CheckPoint()* function to get a snapshot of memory at any location. Thereafter, you can compare the current memory situation using the *Difference()* member, or you can dump it using the *DumpAllObjectsSince()* functions. When using the *DumpAllObjectsSince()* function, make sure that you have called the *CheckPoint()* function first, or it will dump all objects in memory. The dump goes to the *afxDump* device, which usually is the Output window of the Visual Studio.

You also can use *CMemoryState* as a debugging tool to examine memory during the course of a program. For example, in the *EditExplore* project from Tip 668, "Combining a Document View with *CSplitterWnd*," if you wanted to examine the contents of the memory used when the program starts, you could wrap the *ListDirectory()* call in the *InitInstance()* function around a *CMemoryState* object, as in the following code:

```
CMemoryState memState;
memState.Checkpoint ();
ListDirectory ();
memState.DumpAllObjectsSince ();
```

You don't have to halt the program to examine the memory. The addresses and first few bytes of all the items for which memory was allocated will be dumped to the Output window. Make the Output window visible to get the addresses, and then make the Memory window visible to dump those address and examine the memory contents.

687. *Understanding Windows Resources*

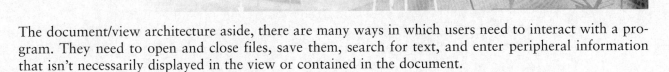

The document/view architecture aside, there are many ways in which users need to interact with a program. They need to open and close files, save them, search for text, and enter peripheral information that isn't necessarily displayed in the view or contained in the document.

You achieve this interaction through *resources*. Resources are the menus, toolbars, dialog boxes, and various controls that you use to present and receive user input. Technically, resources are binary data that is included in the programs executable, and the resource editor makes them visible so that you can work on them.

Creative use of resources and good design can make the difference between an application that is difficult to use and understand and one that a user takes to quickly. When you design a resource such as a dialog box, you should use it to make sure that the work pattern flows across the box. If the user constantly has to reach for the mouse or hit the Tab key many times to get from one field to another related field, it isn't going to be a pleasant experience. Carefully designing and testing your resources is just as important as the design and testing of your program code.

688. *Using the Resource Workshop*

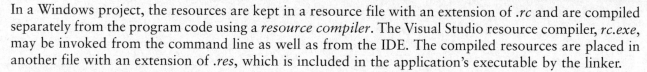

The Resource Workshop is part of the Visual Studio's integrated development environment. Actually, there is no part of the IDE named the Resource Workshop, and none of the MSDN documentation refers to it as such. Programmers, however, develop their own jargon, and the part of the IDE—any IDE, not just the Visual Studio—where you work with resources is commonly referred to as a resource workshop.

Visual studio has a number of tools that enable you to work with resources. There's a dialog box editor for creating and building dialog boxes, a cursor editor for creating custom cursors, and an icon editor for creating or modifying icons, among other tools.

Windows has a set of "standard" resources that you can draw upon. For most applications, these are all you need, but if you need to go beyond that, you can create your own custom resources. In Tip 690, "Understanding the ResourceView Panel of the Workspace Window," you'll go through the process of creating custom resources.

689. *Understanding the Resource Compiler*

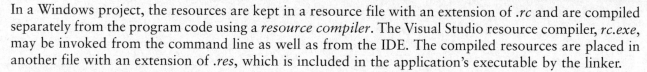

In a Windows project, the resources are kept in a resource file with an extension of *.rc* and are compiled separately from the program code using a *resource compiler*. The Visual Studio resource compiler, *rc.exe*, may be invoked from the command line as well as from the IDE. The compiled resources are placed in another file with an extension of *.res*, which is included in the application's executable by the linker.

The resource compile has its own language. Some of it may seem like C or C++. If you examine the resource file for any project, you'll see that it uses the same *#include* and *#define* preprocessor directives as C++, but the resemblance ends there. It's a specialized language designed just to manipulate resource data.

Fortunately, you don't have to learn this language. It won't hurt if you do have some familiarity with it, because there may be times when you want to edit the resource file directly or look at the file to glean some insight into why something is happening in your program. The various tools in the Visual Studio convert the graphical image that you create into the syntax required for the resource compiler.

690. *Understanding the ResourceView Panel of the Workspace Window*

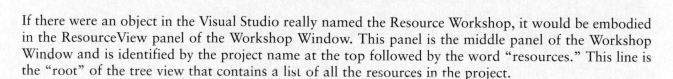

If there were an object in the Visual Studio really named the Resource Workshop, it would be embodied in the ResourceView panel of the Workshop Window. This panel is the middle panel of the Workshop Window and is identified by the project name at the top followed by the word "resources." This line is the "root" of the tree view that contains a list of all the resources in the project.

To open a branch of the tree, click on the "+" symbol next to the root or a branch. Under the root, you should see a branch for each of the standard resource types. If your project doesn't contain a certain resource type, it won't appear as a branch on the tree.

Click on the "+" symbol next to the name of a resource type to get a listing of the resources of that type in your project. These are the *resource IDs* of the objects in the resource file. A resource ID may be a quoted string or a number identified by a symbol such as *IDR_MAINFRAME*. By default, the Visual Studio uses numbers associated with symbols, but some programmers prefer to use quoted strings for the IDs. To get a list of resource IDs and their associated numbers, right-click on the root of the tree and select Resource Symbols from the pop-up menu.

If you double-click on one of these IDs, the object will be opened in the editing area using the proper editor for that resource type. Double-clicking on an icon resource, for example, will open the resource using the icon editor; double-clicking on a toolbar resource will open it using the Toolbar Editor.

To add a resource, right-click on any branch of the tree and select Insert from the menu. If you right-click on a resource type or a resource ID, the menu also will include an option to insert a resource of that type. For example, right-clicking on Dialog will include an item to Insert Dialog. The generic Insert command, however, will bring up a dialog box that will let you insert a resource of any type. Select a resource type from this dialog box and click on the New button. A new, blank resource will be created and given a generic name such as *IDI_ICON1* or *IDD_DIALOG1*. To change this ID, right-click on the item's name in the tree control, and select Properties from the menu, or type Alt+Enter. In the ID field of the Properties dialog box, enter the new resource ID, or select one from the drop-down list. If you enter a new identifier, a number will be assigned to it, and it will be added to the list of resource IDs.

You also can import resources from outside files. Select Import from the pop-up menu when you right-click on a resource. You'll get a File Open dialog box. Select the file type that you want to import, and then change to the directory in which the file is located and select it. Then press the Import button. Similarly, you can export files. If you right-click on the icon branch, you'll notice that you have the option of exporting it to a file. Select the option to get the File Save dialog box, give the new file a name, and press the Export button. This feature is handy for moving between applications; unfortunately, other resource types don't have this menu item enabled.

Notice also that if you right-click on a resource *item* rather than a resource *type*, you'll get an option to insert a copy of that resource. To insert a copy, you must change the language ID or give it a condition, such as a *#define* symbol, under which it will be included in the resource compile rather than the original item. You can't include them both in the same compilation.

When you change the language or set a condition for the new resource item, it will appear in the list with the same name as the original, but with the condition added to the name.

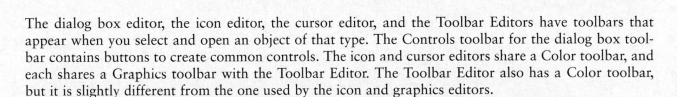

691. *Using the Resource Workshop Toolbars*

The dialog box editor, the icon editor, the cursor editor, and the Toolbar Editors have toolbars that appear when you select and open an object of that type. The Controls toolbar for the dialog box toolbar contains buttons to create common controls. The icon and cursor editors share a Color toolbar, and each shares a Graphics toolbar with the Toolbar Editor. The Toolbar Editor also has a Color toolbar, but it is slightly different from the one used by the icon and graphics editors.

In a project, either open a dialog box or create a new one. Most applications already have an IDD_ABOUT dialog box. Displaying the About box displays the toolbar as well. In its original state, the Controls toolbar has two columns of 13 buttons each. It may be resized for convenience, and it is capable of docking to the edge of the Visual Studio.

The upper-left button is a selection button. It is selected by default, and each time you draw a control on the dialog box, the selection reverts to the selection button. Use it to select objects on the dialog box by clicking on them, or select multiple items by holding down the Shift or Ctrl key while you click on them.

The lower-left button is for custom controls. The other buttons all represent common controls. To draw a control on a dialog box, select the control from the toolbar (let the mouse cursor hover over a button for a second, and a ToolTip will appear telling you what control the button represents—they're not all obvious). Move to the dialog box, and the mouse cursor should turn into a crosshair. Select a corner where you want the control to appear, and press and hold the left mouse button while you drag the crosshair to the opposite corner of the area where you want the control to appear. Set the resource ID and any text or styles for the new control by right-clicking on it and selecting Properties from the menu. Enter the data on the property pages (the property sheet is discussed in Tip 693, "Using the Resource Workshop Properties Dialog Box").

Close the dialog box editor by closing the dialog box itself. If necessary, you can delete the dialog box by selecting it in the tree control and pressing the Delete key. If you accidentally delete a dialog box, the Ctrl+Z undo sequence will restore it.

To preview a dialog box without opening it, right-click on any item in the tree control and select Properties from the menu. On the property sheet, press the push pin in the upper-left corner to keep the property sheet visible. Move to the dialog item on the tree control and select it. A small preview window will appear on the property sheet, giving you an image of the dialog box.

Similarly, you can preview icons, cursors, and toolbars the same way without opening them.

Select an icon or a cursor (in most projects, there probably are no cursors in the tree until you add them) from the tree control by double-clicking on it to start the appropriate editor. The graphics toolbar is about what you would expect to find with any graphics editor, but some of the icons are better done (it is a nice-looking air brush, isn't it). The Color toolbar has some interesting points. One of the key features of an icon or cursor is that both are maskable—that is, the background can be made transparent so that the image appears without a surrounding box. That's the result of the mask (transparent) color, which is indicated in the small monitor at the center top of the toolbar. Just below it is the inverse color, the mask color that is used with an inverse image. You can change these colors if needed by double-clicking on one of them and selecting a new color from the Choose Color dialog box.

For the icon editor, the other 16 boxes contain the colors in the current palette. You also can change these by double-clicking on a color and selecting a new one from the Choose Color dialog box. For the cursor editor, the other boxes contain crosshatch patterns that you can apply to areas of the cursor. When you select one by clicking on it, a preview appears at the bottom of the graphics toolbar.

692. *Understanding Resource Symbols*

Every resource item in your program must have a unique ID. The ID may be a number, an unsigned integer, or a quoted string. The default resources prepared by the MFC AppWizard use number identifiers and assign them a unique name using a #*define* statement. The definition that is associated with the number is the resource item's *resource symbol*.

You can view a list of the resource symbols and the numbers associated with them by right-clicking on the root of the tree control in the ResourceView panel and then selecting Resource Symbols from the menu.

The resource symbol doesn't have to be a number; you can assign the item a symbol consisting of a quoted string. When you create a new resource item, summon its property sheet by right-clicking on the item and tying its new name in the ID field. If you don't give it a symbol, either a string or a number, Visual Studio will assign it a number and give it a default resource symbol. For example, if you create an icon, it will be given a resource symbol of *IDI_ICON1*. The next icon will be *IDI_ICON2*, and so on.

You have no direct control over the number assigned to a resource symbol, but you can control it indirectly by creating the resource symbol, assigning it a number, and then assigning the symbol to the resource item. For example, let's say that you create a check box on a dialog box, and you want it to have a resource number of 2512 and a symbol of *IDC_CHECKBOXSTUFF*. The resource editor assigns it a symbol of *IDC_CHECK1* by default. Right-click on the root of the tree view in the ResourceView to summon the Resource Symbol dialog box. Click on the New button and enter "IDC_CHECK-BOXSTUFF" in the Name field and "2512" in the Value field. Click OK and close both dialog boxes. Get the property sheet for your check box control, and type the new symbol in the ID field. You also can select it from the drop-down box, but you'll have to find it first; there are a lot of system IDs in the box. Sometimes you have to assign resource numbers this way, making them consecutive so that you can use the *ON_COMMAND_RANGE* message map entry.

Many programmers, particularly those accustomed to programming in the Windows API, prefer to use quoted strings as resource symbols. You do this simply by quoting the symbol when you enter it in the ID box of the resource item's property sheet.

For example, you create an icon and give it the resource value of *IDI_LEDGREENON*. When you use the *LoadIcon()* function to create a handle to it, you would use the *MAKEINTRESOURCE* macro, as in the following line:

```
HICON hIcon = LoadIcon (AfxGetInstanceHandle(),
                 MAKEINTRESOURCE(IDI_LEDGREENON));
```

You could just as easily have given the icon a symbol of *LedGreenOn*. Then your call to *LoadIcon()* would look like the following:

```
HICON hIcon=LoadIcon (AfxGetInstanceHandle(),"LedGreenOn");
```

The icon will load the same, and you can use it the same. Sometimes, however, you need a resource number for some graphics functions. It's easy to convert from a number resource symbol to a string using *MAKEINTRESOURCE*. There's no macro to go the other way because there is no number associated with a string symbol.

693. *Using the Resource Workshop Properties Dialog Box*

Although the Properties dialog box is different for each resource type, there are some items in common. The push pin at the upper left is used to keep the property sheet visible; if it isn't pressed (push in), the sheet will disappear every time you select another item.

All the resource types have language settings, and most also have a condition setting that determines when they are included in the resource file. A few—the icon, toolbar, and cursor—have boxes to enter a file name that holds their binary data.

The dialog box item has the most involved property sheet. Open a dialog box (the *IDD_ABOUT* item on the tree control). On the first page, you set the caption for the title bar, the associated menu, and the dialog box font and point size. The font applies to all the controls on the dialog box. Beyond the first page, there are three pages of styles.

Select a control on the dialog box. Most controls have at least three property pages: one for general appearance, another for basic styles, and a third for extended styles. If a control has special properties, additional pages may appear. The combo box, for example, has a separate page for entering the initial items for its drop-down list box.

All the property sheets have a Help page. Press the Help button (next to the push pin) to view the Help page.

694. *Understanding Accelerators*

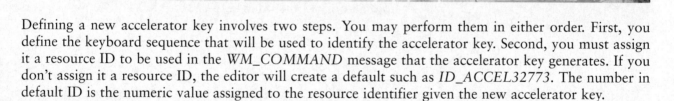

A *keyboard accelerator*, usually just referred to as an accelerator or a *shortcut key*, supercharges the keyboard in your program. It lets the user issue commands usually associated with menu or toolbar items directly from the keyboard rather than having to reach for the mouse.

Accelerators are grouped in an accelerator *table*, which can be loaded into memory from your application. The MFC AppWizard creates a default accelerator table for each application with the resource ID of *IDR_MAINFRAME*. This table is associated with the default document template and is loaded whenever a document and view are created.

Accelerators don't perform any direct action in your program. Instead, they issue *WM_COMMAND* Windows messages with their resource ID as the first argument, and how your program reacts to them depends upon how you handle the message.

An accelerator enables the user to send a command from the keyboard. Usually it's associated with a menu item or a toolbar button, but it doesn't have to be. You can set up an accelerator that works independently of any menu or toolbar.

In the next few tips, you'll add accelerators to an existing table, create a new accelerator table, and examine how your program responds to an accelerator key.

695. *Adding Accelerators to Your Program*

Defining a new accelerator key involves two steps. You may perform them in either order. First, you define the keyboard sequence that will be used to identify the accelerator key. Second, you must assign it a resource ID to be used in the *WM_COMMAND* message that the accelerator key generates. If you don't assign it a resource ID, the editor will create a default such as *ID_ACCEL32773*. The number in default ID is the numeric value assigned to the resource identifier given the new accelerator key.

In a project, open an accelerator table. Most projects have at least the *IDR_MAINFRAME* table. From the ResourceView panel, open the Accelerator tree branch and double-click on the resource ID for the accelerator table.

While the accelerator table is displayed and selected, notice that at the bottom there's a blank rectangle. This rectangle is intended to be used to create new accelerators. Right-click on this blank rectangle, and select Properties from the menu. A blank property sheet will be displayed, and you can enter the accelerator key information in it. Alternatively, you can enter a new accelerator by pressing the Insert key from any point in the accelerator table. The blank rectangle will be selected and an empty property sheet will be displayed.

On the property sheet, assign the new accelerator a resource ID, or select one from the drop-down box. The combo box control lists all resource IDs defined by the Microsoft Foundation Class resource files, as well as resource IDs from your program.

Next, select the key combination from the Modifiers group of check boxes to the right of the combo box, and then select whether the key is virtual or ASCII. A virtual key is a device-independent value that identifies the purpose of a keystroke as interpreted by the Windows keyboard device driver rather than the value of the key. An ASCII key, on the other hand, is identified by its value. Some keys inherently are virtual, such as the function and cursor keys; they have no ASCII values and can be identified only by their purpose.

Instead of selecting modifiers and key type, you can press the Next Key Typed button. When you do this, the next keystroke will be interpreted as the key that you want to use as the accelerator. Hold down the modifier keys (Ctrl, Alt, and Shift) that you want to use, and press the appropriate key. If the new accelerator key is an ASCII key, you'll still have to select the type.

Close the property sheet, or move the selection away from the blank area; the accelerator will be added to the table. A new blank area will be created at the bottom of the table.

If your new accelerator is associated with a menu item, you should modify the menu item's text to reflect the fact that there is a keyboard shortcut. Open the appropriate menu from the tree control by double-clicking on it. Select the drop-down menu from the menu bar that appears, and then right-click on the menu item and select Properties to get the Properties dialog box. In the Caption field, add a Tab character and the keyboard sequence for the shortcut key. For example, the *New* command on the File menu would be entered as "&New\tCtrl+N," meaning that the shortcut key is Ctrl+N.

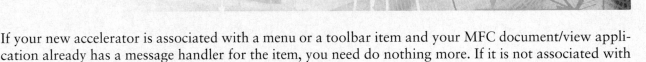

696. *Responding to Accelerator Messages*

If your new accelerator is associated with a menu or a toolbar item and your MFC document/view application already has a message handler for the item, you need do nothing more. If it is not associated with an existing item, you need to add a message handler for it.

Enter the ClassWizard and select the Message Maps page. Locate and select the resource ID in the Object ID box, and then select COMMAND in the Messages box. Press the Add Function button. When the message handler has been added, enter the appropriate code to process the message.

In an application based on the Windows API rather than MFC, the response isn't nearly so straightforward. The normal message pump in a Windows API function usually looks similar to the following code before an accelerator table has been added:

```
// Main message loop:
while (GetMessage(&msg, NULL, 0, 0))
{

    if (!PreTranslateMessage(&msg))
    {
        TranslateMessage(&msg);
        DispatchMessage(&msg);
    }
}
```

In this case, you need to load the accelerator table and modify the message loop to translate the accelerator keys before *TranslateMessage()* is called. To be effective, the accelerator keys should be processed raw; after *TranslateMessage()* is called, the keystrokes already have been turned into their ASCII equivalents and are virtually useless as accelerators.

The Windows API has only six functions to handle accelerators. To load the accelerators, use the *LoadAccelerator()* function, which returns a handle to the accelerator table. Then change the call to *PreTranslateMessage()* to *TranslateAccelerator()* as shown in the following code:

```
HACCEL hAccelTable = LoadAccelerators(hInstance,
                    MAKEINTRESOURCE(IDC_LINES));
    // Main message loop:
while (GetMessage(&msg, NULL, 0, 0))
{
```

```
    if (!TranslateAccelerator(msg.hwnd, hAccelTable, &msg))
    {
        TranslateMessage(&msg);
        DispatchMessage(&msg);
    }
}
```

Next, you need to add a *case* statement to the *WM_COMMAND* switch statement in the *WndProc()* function to handle the message.

In MFC-base programs, the *CWinThread* class contains its own *PreTranslateFunction()* that steps through the document/message-routing viewing process, giving the application class, the view class, the document class, and the frame window class an opportunity to process the message before handling it itself. If none of these classes overrides and processes the message, that message is shipped off to the *CFrameWnd::PreTranslateMessage()* function, which contains a *TranslateAccelerator()* function call.

697. Adding Accelerator Tables to Your Resources

An application may contain more than one accelerator table, but, obviously, only one can be active at any given time. In an MFC document/view application, however, it is possible to have more than one accelerator table loaded at the same time.

Create a new accelerator table by right-clicking on the Accelerator branch of the tree control and then selecting Insert Accelerator from the menu. If you need to copy an accelerator table to make modifications to it, you'll have to resort to a bit of subterfuge. With the new, empty accelerator table open, also open the table that you want to copy, and select it so that it has the keyboard focus. From the Edit menu, select the Select All item and then select Copy. Close the accelerator table and select the new table. From the Edit menu, select Paste; the contents of the first accelerator table will be pasted into you new table.

Give the accelerator table a more descriptive name than *IDR_ACCELERATOR1*, and then make any modifications that you need.

Normally, accelerator tables are loaded in the frame window class (*CMainFrame* for an SDI application or *CChildFrame* for an MDI application) because in the chain of message handling, that's where the ultimate responsibility for translating the accelerator key lies. The accelerator table gets loaded when the document template creates the view and the document. This is fine for a single-view application, but sometimes an application's window frame has more than one window, as in the case of a splitter window application, and has more than one document object in memory at the same time. You might want the accelerator table to perform differently depending upon which view is being used.

If you study the MFC source code in the *winfrm.cpp* file, you'll see that the frame window first gets the accelerator table from the active document. The default implementation of the *CDocument::GetDefaultAccelerator()* returns a NULL, so the frame window class gets the handle of any accelerator table that it has loaded and translates the key sequence from it. Thus, the document gets the first stab at translating any shortcut keys.

The *CDocument::GetDefaultAccelerator()* function is a virtual function, however, and you can override it and load accelerator tables directly into your document class. Neither the ClassWizard nor the Wizard Bar lists this function among the virtual function, but you still can override it manually.

First create the accelerator table that you want associated with your document object. Add a member variable to your document class of type *HACCEL*, and call it *m_hAccelTable*. Add the following line to the constructor for your document class, where *IDR_DOCUMENTACCEL* is the resource ID for your new accelerator table:

```
m_hAccelTable = LoadAccelerators (AfxGetInstanceHandle(),
                  MAKEINTRESOURCE(IDR_DOCUMENTACCEL));
```

Add the following function to your document class:

```
HACCEL CDummyDoc::GetDefaultAccelerator()
{
    return (m_hAccelTable);
}
```

When a view using this document object is active, its accelerator table will be referenced instead of the one in the window frame class.

698. *Understanding Menus*

A menu is a collection of items, a list of options, very much like the menu that you peruse in a restaurant. In a program, however, the items are a list of commands that will be issued to the window when one of the items is selected. In the world of Windows resources, the menu probably is the one with which users are most familiar.

When you create a Windows-based application using one of the application wizards in Visual C++, you get a default menu that is loaded when the application is run. Dialog box-based applications may omit the menu, but it is entirely possible to load a menu on a dialog box.

The menu resource defines the appearance of the menu when it is first loaded. The menu resource usually describes a menu bar that is placed on the application's window. Items on the menu bar may issue commands directly, but customarily they are associated with pop-up menus that contain one or more *subitems*. A subitem itself might be linked to another pop-up menu, or selecting it might result in a Windows message being generated.

You can create a menu resource by right-clicking the menu tree branch and selecting Insert Menu from the pop-up menu that appears. The default ID will be something like *IDR_MENU1*, so you'll probably want to give it a more descriptive resource symbol (you should use the *IDM_* prefix for menu resources). The initial menu will be blank, but you can copy another menu as the base for your new menu. Open the menu that you want to copy. Holding down the Shift or Ctrl key (the Select All menu item doesn't work here), select the first item on the menu bar, and then select the second, and so on, until you have selected all the items. Select Copy from the Visual Studio's Edit menu. Move to the new, empty menu, and select Paste from the Edit menu. All the items on the menu bar, their subitems, and all their resource IDs will be copied into the new menu, ready for you to modify as necessary.

699. *Understanding Menu Item Properties*

The appearance of menu items on the menu resource is determined by settings on the Menu Item Properties dialog box (see figure 699). Selecting an item on the menu bar reveals the drop-down menu list for that item. Bring up the property sheet by right-clicking an item, on either the menu bar or the drop-down list, and select Properties from the menu that pops up.

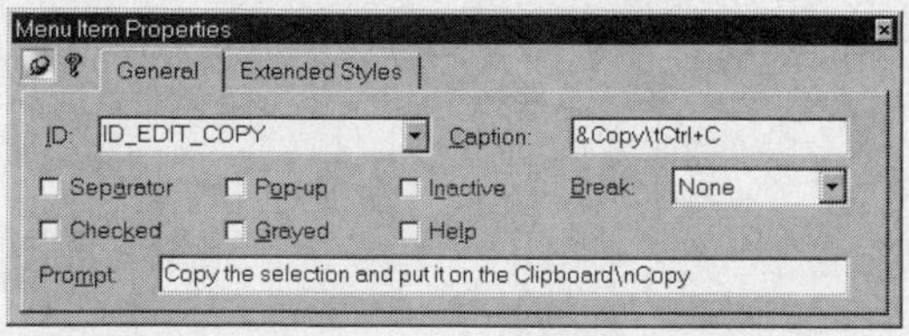

Figure 699   The menu item properties dialog box

You don't have to worry about the second page of the property sheet unless you're preparing an Arabic or Hebrew version of your menu. It contains a single check box to force the text to read from right to left.

On the first page, the ID is the resource ID associated with the menu item. It may be a resource symbol, an integer value, or a quoted string, as defined in the resource header file. In the end, however, it must translate to a number; it's the value that will be placed in the *lParam* argument when the *WM_COMMAND* message is sent to your application.

The Caption box is the text that will appear in the menu. Use an ampersand (&) to cause the following letter to have an underline, indicating that it is a shortcut to the menu item. If you need to place an ampersand in the text, use two ampersands together. "Tom & Jerry" results in text that reads "Tom _ Jerry." Instead, you would want to write "Tom && Jerry."

If you check the Separator box, the item becomes a vertical line if it's on the menu bar, or a horizontal line if it's on the drop-down menu. Checking the box disables all but the Caption field, but you still can't enter anything as a caption. Entering text here automatically unchecks the Separator box. Consider it disabled as well. Separators don't send a Windows message and so don't have an ID.

The pop-up box determines whether this item sends a Windows message or summons another menu. Its use will be discussed in Tip 700, "Adding Pop-Up Entries to a Menu."

Checking the Inactive box causes the menu item to be written in graystring when it first appears. An inactive item simply appears in the menu; it can't be selected and won't send a Windows message, although it does have a resource ID.

The Checked box determines whether the menu item will have a check mark next to it when the item first appears. The checked state can be changed programmatically using a command-enabler message handler and the *SetCheck()* function.

Selecting the Grayed box automatically sets the inactive state and disables the Inactive check box. The menu item will be written in graystring and will be inactive when the menu is created.

Help determines whether the Visual Studio creates a help ID for this menu item.

What happens when you select an optional Break style depends on whether the item is on the menu bar or a drop-down menu. If you select Column and the item is on the menu bar, the menu line is terminated, and the menu item and all those following it are set on the next line. If it's an item on a drop-down menu, it will force the end of the menu column and set the item and all the following items in a new column to the right. In both cases, the appearance in the menu editor doesn't change, however. Selecting Bar has the same effect as Column for items on the menu bar, but for drop-down items it draws a vertical line between the columns. It doesn't change the appearance in the menu editor, either.

The Prompt box contains the ToolTip text. The text up to the first newline character is drawn on the application's status bar message field, if there is one. The text after the first newline character is displayed when the mouse cursor is held over a toolbar button that has the same resource ID as the menu item. The second part of the text should be kept short. You can use this property only with applications that support the Microsoft Foundation Class library.

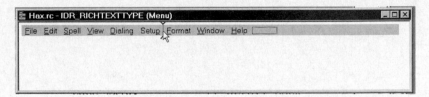

700. *Adding Pop-Up Entries to a Menu*

The top-level items on the menu bar can be rearranged in the menu editor, and new drop-down items can be added.

While a menu resource is open in the menu editor, a blank box appears on the menu bar. This is not a part of the menu, but it represents any new items that you want to add to the bar.

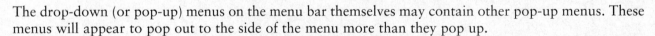

Figure 700   Attempting to drag the empty box creates an I-beam on the menu bar. When you release the mouse button, the empty box moves to the I-beam position.

To insert a new item into a particular spot, select and hold the blank box with the left mouse button. As you drag the box, an I-beam appears on the menu bar, as shown in Figure 700. When it is in the position where you want to insert a new item, release the mouse button. Begin typing the label for the new item, and the item's property sheet will appear. By default, it has the Pop-up property set.

Make any style changes to the item and add subitems as needed. Note that the only styles that have any effect on pop-up items are the Grayed and Break properties.

701. *Nesting Pop-Up Menu Items*

The drop-down (or pop-up) menus on the menu bar themselves may contain other pop-up menus. These menus will appear to pop out to the side of the menu more than they pop up.

To add a pop-up menu, click the left mouse button on the item on the menu bar where you want to insert the pop-up menu. This will cause the drop-down menu to appear. At the bottom, you'll see a blank box similar to but wider than the one on the menu bar. Grab this item with the left mouse button and drag it to the new position, as shown in Figure 702 in the next tip.

Release the mouse button, and the blank box will move to the new location. Begin typing the caption for the menu item, and the Properties box will appear. Check the pop-up box on the property sheet to create a new drop-down menu.

702. *Adding Menu Subitems*

When you drag the box on a drop-down menu, the new menu item doesn't have to be another drop-down menu. In fact, the default when you release the mouse button is to create a normal menu subitem.

When you release the mouse button and the empty box appears, start typing the caption; the Properties box will appear. Remember that if this menu item is to have a quick key, precede the letter that is to be its mnemonic with an ampersand.

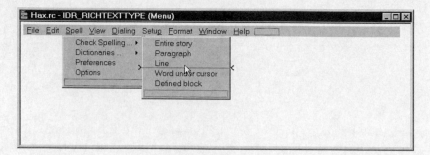

Figure 702   Dragging the empty box on a drop-down menu creates an insertion line.
The empty box will move to the location where you release the mouse button.

703. Adding Hints to Menus

Hints and ToolTips are not as important for menu items as they are for toolbar buttons. The menu item does have some text that gives away its purpose, but a toolbar button likely only has an image.

Fortunately, toolbar buttons usually share the same resource ID as menu items, and adding ToolTips and hints to menu items also adds them for the toolbars. The text is stored in the string table under the same resource ID as the menu item and toolbar button.

Add the text for the ToolTips and hints in the Prompt box at the bottom of the menu item's property sheet. The text up to the first newline character (\n) is used for the ToolTip, and the text after it is used for the flyby hint.

The text does not use escape characters, unlike the menu text, so you don't have to double up on ampersands.

704. Understanding Dialog Boxes

A *dialog box* is a window that is designed to contain *controls*. Often it is temporary with respect to the main application program, but entire applications may be built around a dialog box. A dialog box may be as simple as a message box, or it may contain several pages, each containing a large number of controls.

You use dialog boxes to communicate with users, to display program information, and to collect information needed by the program that can't normally be entered through the application's main window. The controls serve to limit the type of information. An edit control can be made to accept text or numbers only, a check box allows only yes or no information, and radio buttons allow a choice of one of many items.

You create a dialog box using a dialog box *template*, a binary description of the dialog box and the controls that you place on it. The template describes the size of the dialog box, the window style, the font it uses, and the size and placement of controls. In the Visual Studio, you create this template graphically using the dialog box editor, where you place and size the various controls, as described in Tip 707, "Creating a Dialog Box." A text version of the template is contained in the application's resource file and is compiled to binary format by the resource compiler.

In a Windows API program, a dialog box requires its own windows procedure to receive and process messages, and its window class must be registered with the operating system, the same as with the main window. In an MFC-based program, the *CDialog* class provides this procedure.

The importance of dialog boxes in a windowing environment can't be overemphasized. Windowing systems don't use the C and C++ standard input and output files, so dialog boxes are the means by which you prompt the user to perform some required action or provide some required input.

You should put a lot of thought into designing your dialog boxes. Controls dealing with related information should be grouped and arranged in a fashion that seems logical to users. For example, a dialog box that collects information for an address book should arrange the controls so that the tabbing sequence is from the entry's name to the address, then to the city and state, then the ZIP code, and finally to the telephone number. If the dialog box collects other information, related controls may be surrounded by the *group control*, which does nothing except provide a label and a line around a group of controls.

Large dialog boxes appear imposing—sometimes overwhelming—to the user. There's nothing stopping you from using the entire screen for a dialog box, but you may find that user frustration and resistance increases with the size of the dialog box. If it grows to more than a quarter of the screen, you should consider breaking it down into pages using a tab control or converting it to a property sheet (a property sheet sometimes is referred to as a "tabbed dialog box"). These methods can encapsulate a lot of controls, but they appear less threatening to a user.

705. *Understanding Modal and Modeless Dialog Boxes*

Dialog boxes come in two basic flavors, *modal* and *modeless*. Which type you choose will determine how the user interacts with your dialog box.

A modal dialog box requires the user to perform some action to dispatch the dialog box before returning to the main application. This is the most common and most easily applied type of dialog box.

In an MFC-based application, a modal dialog box usually is a transient object. You create and initialize a dialog box variable, display the dialog box, and then destroy the dialog box from within the same function. You display it by calling the *CDialog* class's *DoModal()* function.

A modeless dialog box, on the other hand, enables the user to return to the main program and perform other actions while it remains active and on the screen. An example of this type of dialog box is the Search and Replace dialog box. The user can search for a text string, return to the main program and perform some editing functions, and return to the dialog box to find the next occurrence of the string.

A modeless dialog box is revealed and hidden using the *ShowWindow()* function. It usually survives a single function call. You can elect to create a modeless dialog box in the *OnInitialUpdate()* function in a view or even the *InitInstance()* function of the application class, and then destroy it when the view or application terminates.

706. *Understanding System Modal Dialog Boxes*

A dialog box may be created as *system modal* as well, in which case it becomes "The Dialog Box that Ate Manhattan."

Functionally, a system modal dialog box performs the same as an ordinary modal dialog box. The user can't return to the application and perform other work until dispatching the dialog box. However, a system modal dialog box remains on top of everything else, even if the user switches to another application. The user can perform actions in other applications, but the dialog box will still be the topmost window and will be in the way until the user takes some action to dispatch it.

System modal dialog boxes are rare and should be used sparingly. They should be used only when a critical condition occurs that requires timely intervention by the user.

707. *Creating a Dialog Box*

To build a dialog box, open the ResourceView pane of the Workspace Window, expand the resources tree, and right-click Dialog. Then select Insert Dialog. Along with an empty dialog template (it does have OK and Cancel buttons already on it), you will get a Controls toolbar, usually to the right of the screen unless you earlier moved it elsewhere.

This toolbar is a docking toolbar and has a habit of attaching itself at odd places on the screen if you start moving it around. If it does, grab it with the mouse using the "grabber" section of the toolbar, and move it away from the frame. You should have 26 small icons on the toolbar, unless you've added some custom controls. Initially, these controls are arranged in two columns of 13 tools. The tool in the upper left is the Select arrow, and the tool at the bottom left is for custom controls. The other 24 tools represent common controls. Just let the mouse cursor hover over one for a second, and a ToolTip box will tell you which control the icon represents.

The dialog box may be resized in the dialog editor. If you click on any blank area of the new dialog box, small blue boxes will appear on the right side, the bottom, and the lower-right corner of the dialog box. Use these to increase the size of the dialog box by grabbing them with the mouse and moving the side or corner of the dialog box until it is the proper size.

After you've built the dialog box, you create a class for it using *CDialog* as the base, as described in Tip 710, "Encapsulating the Dialog Box Code in a Class."

708. *Understanding Dialog Box Properties*

Of all the resource property sheets in the Visual Studio, the dialog box probably is the most involved. A dialog box is a distinct window that is capable of containing other windows and that can be used in any of several ways, so there are lots of options and style considerations to look over. Even with all the properties listed on the four pages of the Dialog Properties dialog box, some still aren't included.

On the General page, give your dialog box a resource identifier in the ID box. Use the *IDD_* prefix for dialog boxes. To the right, the Caption box is where you enter the text that will appear in the title bar of the dialog box. You can assign a menu to this dialog by selecting it from the drop-down box in the Menu box or by entering the resource symbol of an existing menu.

The Font option selects the font that will be the default font for all controls on the dialog box. Pressing the Font button brings up a Select Font dialog box, where you can select the font name and the point size. The X Pos and Y Pos boxes specify the location in dialog units of the upper-left corner of the dialog box when it first appears on the screen. The origin for these coordinates depends on the setting of the Absolute Align check box on the More Styles page. Specify 0 and 0 to let Windows choose the position.

The Class Name box is for non-MFC applications. This is the name of a registered dialog class window and is not the C++ class name associated with the dialog box. If you have MFC features enabled, the box will be disabled. (Right-click on the root of the tree control, and select Properties from the menu. The check box on this page will tell you whether you have MFC features enabled.)

On the Styles page, select the type of window you want for the dialog box from the Style box. An overlapped window is intended as the main window for an application and should have a title bar and a border. A pop-up, the default for dialog boxes, is intended to be used for temporary windows that may appear outside an application's window boundary. Selecting Child Window will limit the dialog box to the client area of the application and generally isn't a good idea, particularly with splitter window applications.

Select a border for the dialog box. You usually don't want users to be able to resize dialog boxes, so avoid the resizing style unless you have a good reason. The Dialog Frame style is the default for dialog boxes.

The first column of check boxes deals with the title bar. If you don't check the first box, Title Bar, the rest of the column will be disabled. The second column contains options for child windows and scroll bars. If your dialog box needs scroll bars, it probably needs to be redesigned.

On the More Styles page, you'll find the check box to set System Modal mode (see Tip 706, "Understanding System Modal Dialog Boxes," the Godzilla dialog box). If the Absolute Align box is checked, the dialog box position is relative to the upper-left corner of the screen. If unchecked, the origin is the left side of the client area and the area just below the application's menu bar. The Visible check box has no visible effect on modal dialog boxes, but you should leave it unchecked for modeless dialog boxes, tab pages, and form views, and let the program control its visibility with the *ShowWindow()* function. The Disabled check box creates a dialog box that initially is disabled. Property pages should be disabled initially. Don't use this feature for ordinary dialog boxes; if you do, you'll create a dialog box that can't be closed because even the OK and Cancel buttons won't respond to user input (the Esc key will close the dialog box, however). The last check box in this column, Context Help, places a question mark box in the title bar. When the user selects this box, the cursor turns into a question mark with a pointer. When the user subsequently clicks on a control, the control receives a *WM_HELP* message, which it passes on to the parent window. To use this, your dialog box should provide a message handler for *WM_HELPINFO*. This handler is passed a context structure containing the resource ID of the control, the position of the mouse, and a context ID. Your program can call the *WinHelp()* function to provide a help message if you have prepared a help file.

The Set Foreground check box causes Windows to bring the application to the foreground when the dialog box is created by calling the *SetForegroundWindow()*. The 3-D–look box causes Windows to create the dialog box using a non-bold font and to draw 3-D borders around the controls. No-fail Create commands Windows to create the dialog box even if one or more of the controls on it fail to initialize. (A control will fail to initialize if somehow you give it illegal parameters or fail to initialize a subsystem needed by the control. A rich edit control, for example, will fail if you do not initialize the OLE subsystem in your program.) If you check the No Idle Message box, Windows won't send the dialog box any *WM_ENTERIDLE* messages when there are no messages waiting in the queue.

The Control style creates a dialog box that works as a child window to another dialog box, as in a tab control page or property page. The Center style instructs windows to place the dialog box in the center of the screen. Center Mouse attempts to center the dialog box at the mouse cursor's current position. Local Edit specifies that edit controls will use memory within the application's data segment; normally, edit controls use memory assigned to them outside the application's memory.

On the last page, you'll find check boxes to enable the dialog box extended styles. The Tool Window box creates a window with a smaller title bar and a smaller title font that is intended to be used as a floating toolbar. Client Edge creates a sunken edge around the dialog box, and Static Edge creates a border around it. Transparent lets any windows below the dialog box appear through the box. Be careful with the transparent style; depending upon the windows on your screen, it may appear that the dialog box wasn't created and displayed when it really was. (You might see a brief rectangular flash as the dialog box appears and immediately lets the windows underneath show through.)

If you check the Accept Files box, the controls on your dialog box will receive *WM_DROPFILES* messages whenever the user drags a file over the dialog box and drops it. Control Parent enables the user to tab through the child windows (controls) on the dialog box.

No Parent Notify specifies that the controls will not send *WM_PARENTNOTIFY* messages to the dialog box. Right-to-left reading order is used for languages such as Hebrew or Arabic. Right-aligned text overrides the text alignment for static controls.

709. Adding Controls to a Dialog Box

The Controls toolbar contains tool buttons that represent the Windows Common Controls that you can add to a dialog box. If you've added other controls such as ActiveX or COM controls to your project, the toolbar also will have buttons for each of them.

To place a control on your dialog box, select the button on the toolbar with the left mouse button. Move to the location on the dialog box where you want the control to appear, and then press and hold the left mouse button. As you drag the mouse cursor to the *opposite* corner of the area, a rectangle should appear. Release the mouse button. A graphic representation of the control should appear in place of the rectangle. Right-click on the control, and select Properties from the menu. Give the control a resource ID in the property sheet, and set the appropriate styles. If you have multiple dialog boxes in your application, try to develop a naming sequence for the controls. For example, if this is a dialog box dealing with communications and the control is to set the default port, name it something such as *IDC_COMM_DEFAULTPORT*. Keep the same prefix, *IDC_COMM_*, for all the controls on this dialog box. In an alphabetical listing of resource IDs, this will make all the controls for one dialog box appear together.

If you've drawn a combo box, you need to set the area for its drop-down list box. Around the combo box image are several resize boxes; some are hollow and some are solid blue. The solid boxes are the active resize boxes; if you grab one of them with the mouse, you can enlarge the combo box. Select the down arrow button on the combo box image. Notice that the only solid box is now on the bottom of the image. Select that box, and drag it downward until the drop-down box is the proper size. Then release the mouse button.

While you are in the dialog box editor, a Layout menu is available on the main menu bar. This menu contains a number of items for sizing and placing objects on the dialog box. If you select two or more controls (hold down the Shift or Ctrl keys while clicking on them), you'll notice that only one of them—the last one that you selected—has active resize buttons, the solid blue boxes along the sides. This control is the *pattern* control. When you select any of the alignment or size items from the menu, this is the control that will be used as a pattern for adjusting the sizes or positions of the other controls. If you select Align and then Left, all the other controls will be aligned with the left side of this control.

The dialog box editor will automatically arrange a group of buttons along the top-right side or centered along the bottom of the dialog box. Select the buttons that you want aligned, and then select Arrange Buttons and then Right or Bottom. The buttons will be rearranged along the side that you selected.

The Flip item is for preparing Arabic and Hebrew dialog boxes. You can create the dialog box as you would normally and then select Flip from the menu. All the controls will be rearranged in reverse order left to right, and the Mideast styles for the dialog box (Right Aligned Text, Right to Left Reading Order, and Left Scroll Bar) and all the controls will be set. Select it again, and you'll get the reverse effect.

You also need to set the tab order of the controls in your dialog box. This will determine which control gets the keyboard focus when the user presses the Tab key. Select Tab Order from the Layout menu. A number will appear next to each of the controls. This is the old tab order and, for a new dialog box, will be the order in which the controls were created. Carefully consider which control you want to be the first in the tab order. This is the control that will have the focus when the dialog box first appears. Click the left mouse button on it and the number will change to 1. Continue through the controls to set the tab order. Press the Enter key or select a blank area of the dialog box to end the tab order selection.

Every control will have a tab number, regardless of whether you've checked the Tab Stop box on the first page of the property sheet. If you unselect this box, the control still will have a position in the tab order; it just won't receive the focus when the user presses the Tab key.

Guide Settings brings up a dialog box that lets you place rulers and a grid pattern on the dialog box. These are for construction purposes only; they won't appear on the finished dialog box. The default grid is 5 dialog units, which usually is a good setting, but you can set it anywhere from 1 to 100.

Check your dialog box frequently by selecting the Test item on the Layout menu, or press Ctrl+T. Check the tab order, and test any controls that you have added since the last test. Also check the drop-down boxes for combo box controls to make sure that they appear in the right place and are the right size. To end the test, press the OK or Cancel button on the dialog box, or press the Esc key on the keyboard.

710. *Encapsulating the Dialog Box Code in a Class*

In a Windows API function, you need to create a window procedure for your new dialog box. If this is an MFC-based application, the framework will provide this procedure for you if you derive your new class from *CDialog*. You can use the ClassWizard to prepare your new class.

Right-click anywhere on the dialog box image, and select ClassWizard from the menu. For a new dialog box, you'll get the Adding a Class dialog box, where you may elect to create a new class for the dialog box or to use an existing class. Generally you will want to create a new class to encapsulate the dialog box object even if it is a simple dialog box. Press the OK button to go to the New Class dialog box.

In the New Class dialog box, the wizard preselected *CDialog* as the base class and entered the resource ID for the dialog box in the Dialog ID box. If this is a property sheet page, you should change the base class to *CPropertyPage*.

Enter a name for the new class. This should be something related to the resource ID. Later, when you have several dialog boxes in your project, you can mentally connect the class and dialog box by the similarity of names. A dialog box with an ID of *IDD_PHONERECORD* should have a class name such as *CPhoneRecordDlg*. Attaching the "Dlg" to the name identifies this class as one that encapsulates a dialog box.

As you type the dialog box class name, notice that the ClassWizard prepares a file name for you based on the class name (but missing the initial "C"). You can add the dialog box to an existing file, but the ClassWizard tends to get confused when you have more than one class in a file. Save yourself some problems now and place the dialog box class—even it it is a simple dialog box—in a file by itself.

After the class is created, add variables for all the controls for which you intend to transfer data, either to the control when the dialog box is created or from the control when the dialog box ends. Select the Member Variables page; then, select the control's resource ID and click the Add Variable button. Give the variable a name, and select a variable type. Unless you intend to access the control directly, the default variable type is acceptable. You can create two variables for a single control, using the control class for one variable and the data type for the other.

711. *Catching and Using Messages in a Dialog Box*

Most of the controls on your dialog box can send messages to the parent window. Some, such as the group box or a static text field, don't need to send messages; leave the resource ID for these as *IDC_STATIC*, and the ClassWizard will sift out the lists for member variables and messages.

Controls that need to send messages, however, should have unique resource IDs. These IDs are used in the messages that the control sends to the dialog box parent.

To catch the messages from the controls, enter the ClassWizard and select the Message Maps page. Find and select the control in the list of Object IDs. A list of the messages that the control might send to the parent will appear in the Messages box. Select the message, and press the Add Function button to add a message handler. The ClassWizard will build a default function name using the message ID and the variable name; usually, this default name is acceptable, but you can change it, if you want. For example, you might want all of your edit boxes to send their *EN_CHANGE* messages to the same function, which simply sets a member variable that the dialog controls have changed, something like *m_bModified*. When the dialog closes, you can test this variable and rewrite a record if anything has changed, or ignore it if there are no changes.

Some may have a command enabler (*UDDATE_COMMAND_UI*) listed as well. MFC dialog box classes do not support command enablers directly, but you can manually add the code to make the command enablers work. First, add the *afxpriv.h* header file to the list of include files in the dialog class source file in which you want to use command enablers. This defines the *WM_KICKIDLE* message. Next, add the following function to your dialog box class:

```
afx_msg void OnKickIdle();
```

You then need to call the *CWnd::UpdateDialogControls()* function from the *OnKickIdle()* function. *UpdateDialogControls()* needs two parameters: a pointer to the dialog window and a flag indicating whether the control should be deactivated if there is no update handler for it. Generally, for dialog boxes, you do not want to disable controls with no update handler function, so pass a *FALSE* for this parameter. In the source code file, make the body of the *OnKickIdle()* function read as shown below.

```
void CSomeDialogDlg::OnKickIdle()
{
    UpdateDialogControls (this, FALSE);
}
```

If the ClassWizard does not list *UDDATE_COMMAND_UI* as a message option, you can add enabler functions manually. Add a line to the message map for the dialog box. Of course, you add the line *outside* of the area reserved for the ClassWizard. Then, add a function to handle the update message. The following snippet would enable the OK button on a dialog box only if a member variable, *m_bModified*, is set to *true*:

```
#include  <afxpriv.h>

BEGIN_MESSAGE_MAP(CSomeDialogDlg, CDialog)
    //{{AFX_MSG_MAP(CSomeDialogDlg)
    //}}AFX_MSG_MAP
    ON_MESSAGE(WM_KICKIDLE, OnKickIdle)
    ON_UPDATE_COMMAND_UI(IDOK, OnUpdateOK)
END_MESSAGE_MAP()

void CSomeDialogDlg::OnKickIdle()
{
    UpdateDialogControls (this, FALSE);
}

void CSomeDialogDlg::OnUpdateOK(CCmdUI* pCmdUI)
{
    pCmdUI->Enable (m_bModifed == true ? TRUE : FALSE);
}
```

Windows also sends messages to the dialog box window that you may intercept and use. Select the dialog box class name in the Object IDs box to get a list of these messages. Add the message handlers the same way that you added handlers for the control messages. The list also will contain *CDialog* virtual functions that you may override. The wizard already has added the *DoDataExchange()* virtual function for you.

712. *Understanding Bitmaps*

A *bitmap* is an array of bits that describes the color of an area on the screen or output device. It may describe a single pixel or, when the bits are grouped, it may describe an entire region. Cursors and icons are really nothing more than bitmaps that have been assigned special purposes.

Figure 712 shows a hex dump of a typical bitmap, the bitmap image that is used to create the toolbar used in the *EditExplore* project. This toolbar includes the standard toolbar images included with most MFC AppWizard-generated applications, plus the four images for the list control modes. There are variants of the bitmap format, but the first 14 bytes are the same in all variants—this is referred to as the *file header*.

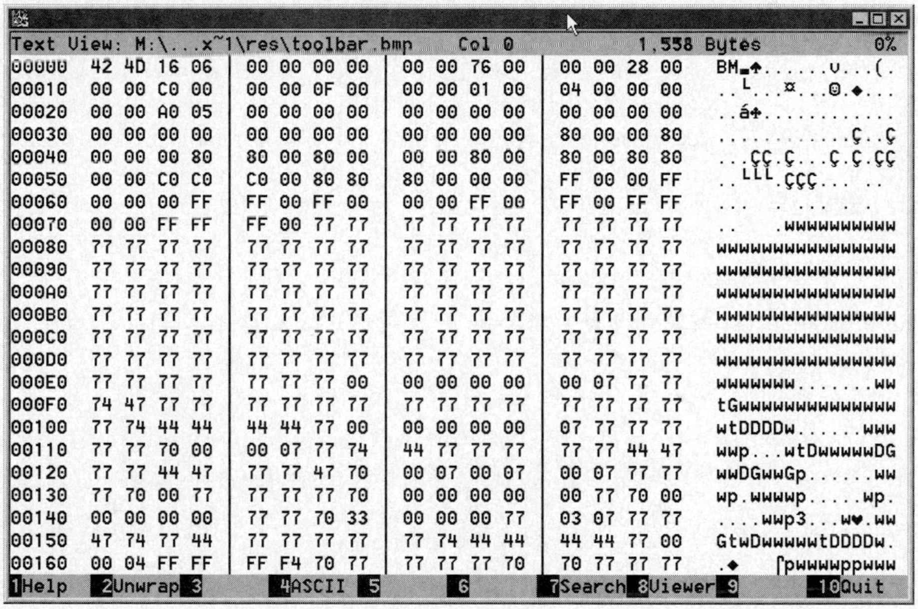

Figure 712   The first 14 bytes of a bitmap file contain the bitmap's file header

The first 2 bytes encode the letters "BM" into the file to identify it as a bitmap. The next four bytes give the size of the file, 0x616 or 1558 bytes. The next 4 bytes are reserved and usually are 0, and the 4 bytes after that give the byte offset into the file where the image data begins.

For the Windows Device Independent Bitmap format, the BITMAPINFOHEADER structure begins at offset 14. The header is described in *wingdi.h* and is listed here for reference:

```
typedef struct tagBITMAPINFOHEADER{
        DWORD       biSize;
        LONG        biWidth;
        LONG        biHeight;
```

```
            WORD        biPlanes;
            WORD        biBitCount;
            DWORD       biCompression;
            DWORD       biSizeImage;
            LONG        biXPelsPerMeter;
            LONG        biYPelsPerMeter;
            DWORD       biClrUsed;
            DWORD       biClrImportant;
} BITMAPINFOHEADER, FAR *LPBITMAPINFOHEADER,
                        *PBITMAPINFOHEADER;
```

As you can see from the hex dump, the size of the header is 0x28 or 40 bytes, which matches the sum of the sizes of the structure members. If the number of bits per pixel is 8 or less, the image must have a *color map*, which begins immediately after the header. This image has 4 bits per pixel, so a color map must follow. The size of the color map is 2, 16, or 256 entries, depending upon the bits per pixel. This one will contain 16 entries (4 bits per pixel equates to 16 possible colors). A smaller color map may be used, in which case the size is indicated in the *biClrUsed* member.

Each entry in the color map is made up of 4 bytes. The first byte is blue, the second is green, and the third is red; the fourth byte is reserved. So, the total color map size for this bitmap is 64 bytes. These are the colors that you place in the palette for the bitmap.

The color data follows the color map at the offset specified in the file header. The rows are stored with the last row first, so you'll actually be reading the bitmap from the bottom up. If you did the arithmetic, you'll see the image has 2,880 pixels, but there are only 1,440 bytes left in the file. Each pixel needs only 4 bits, so there are 2 pixels per byte. The first pixel color is obtained by shifting the first byte to the right 4 bits, and then referencing the matching color in the palette. The next pixel is obtained by *AND*'ing the first byte with 0xF and referencing the matching color in the palette. You then repeat the process on the second byte for the third and fourth pixels. This continues until you reach the end of the first row. Each row is padded with 0s to make it come out to an even 4-byte boundary. In this image, the row ends on a 4-byte boundary, but if it didn't, you would have to advance your pointer to get to the boundary. The next row would be read like the first, continuing until the first row has been read.

Create a project to read in a simple bitmap. This will be a Win32 Application on the list of project types. You can select the "Hello, world" type of project and then delete the lines that print that message. You can call the project Bitmap.

Copy the *toolbar.bmp* from the *res* directory of the EditExplore project into the directory for this project. At the top of the *Bitmap.cpp* file, add the following declarations:

```
TCHAR szBitmapFile[] = "toolbar.bmp";
void DrawBitmap (HDC hdc, HWND hWnd);
void ReadPalette (FILE *fp, int nCount,
                PALETTEENTRY *pPalette);
void ReadBitmap (FILE *fp, long lOffset, long lSize,
                BITMAPINFOHEADER &bh,
                PALETTEENTRY *pEntry,
                PALETTEENTRY *pBitmap);
```

Find the *WM_PAINT* case of the switch statement in the *WndProc()* function, and change it to read as follows:

```
hdc = BeginPaint(hWnd, &ps);
// TODO: Add any drawing code here...
DrawBitmap (hdc, hWnd);
EndPaint(hWnd, &ps);
break;
```

The program will go directly into the *DrawBitmap()* function whenever it is started. You need to add the following three functions to the code:

```c
void DrawBitmap (HDC hdc, HWND hWnd)
{
LOGPALETTE  lp;
HPALETTE    hPalette = NULL;
PALETTEENTRY *pEntry = NULL;
FILE   *fp;
TCHAR   buf[32];
    if ((fp = fopen (szBitmapFile, "rb")) == NULL)
        return;
    memset (buf, '\Ø', sizeof buf);
    fread (buf, 2, sizeof (char), fp);
    if (strcmp (buf, "BM"))
    {
        fclose (fp);
        return;
    }
    long lSize, lOffset;
    BITMAPINFOHEADER bh;
    fread (&lSize, 1, sizeof (long), fp);
// throw away reserved bytes
    fread (&lOffset, 1, sizeof (long), fp);
    fread (&lOffset, 1, sizeof (long), fp);
    fread (&bh, 1, sizeof (BITMAPINFOHEADER), fp);
//
// Can't handle compression here. Return if compression
//   field is non-zero.
    if (bh.biCompression)
    {
        fclose (fp);
        return;
    }
    int nColors;
    switch (bh.biBitCount)
    {
        case 1:
            nColors = 2;
            pEntry = new PALETTEENTRY [nColors];
            break;
        case 4:
            nColors = 16;
            pEntry = new PALETTEENTRY [nColors];
            break;
        case 8:
            nColors = 256;
            pEntry = new PALETTEENTRY [nColors];
            break;
        case 24:
            nColors = Ø;
            pEntry = NULL;
            break;
    }
    PALETTEENTRY *pBitmap = NULL;
    bh.biSizeImage = lSize - lOffset;
```

```
        if (nColors)
        {
            pBitmap = new PALETTEENTRY [bh.biSizeImage
                                    * (8 / bh.biBitCount)];
            lp.palNumEntries = nColors;
            hPalette = CreatePalette (&lp);
            int n;
            if (bh.biClrUsed)
                n = bh.biClrUsed;
            else
                n = nColors;
            PALETTEENTRY *pTemp = pEntry;

            ReadPalette (fp, n, pTemp);
        }
        else
        {
            pBitmap = new PALETTEENTRY [bh.biSizeImage];
        }
        ReadBitmap (fp, lOffset, lSize,
                    bh, pEntry, pBitmap);
        int j, n;
        for (n = bh.biHeight, j = 0; n >= 0; --n, ++j)
        {
            for (int x = 0; x < bh.biWidth; ++x)
            {
                PALETTEENTRY *p = &pBitmap [j * bh.biWidth + x];
                COLORREF cr = RGB((long) p->peRed,
                                  (long) p->peGreen,
                                  (long) p->peBlue);
                SetPixel (hdc, x, n, cr);
            }
        }

        delete pBitmap;
        delete pEntry;
        DeleteObject (hPalette);
}
//
//  Read the bitmap into memory
//
void ReadBitmap (FILE *fp,
                 long lOffset,
                 long lSize,
                 BITMAPINFOHEADER &bh,
                 PALETTEENTRY *pEntry,
                 PALETTEENTRY *pBitmap)
{
    long pos;
    long x = 0;
    long len = 0;
    fseek (fp, lOffset, SEEK_SET);
    for (pos = lOffset; pos < lSize; ++pos)
    {
    BYTE    ch;
```

```
//
//  if the end of a row, adjust for the four-byte boundary.
//
          if (len >= bh.biWidth)
          {
              len = (pos - lOffset) % 4;
              while (len--)
              {
                  fread (&ch, 1, sizeof (BYTE), fp);
              }
              len = Ø;
          }
        fread (&ch, 1, sizeof (BYTE), fp);
        switch (bh.biBitCount)
        {
            case 1:
                len += 8;
                break;
            case 4:
                pBitmap[x++] = pEntry[ch >> 4];
                pBitmap[x++] = pEntry[ch & Øx0f];
                len += 2;
                break;
            case 8:
                len += 1;
                break;
            case 24:
                pBitmap[x].peBlue = ch;
                ++pos;
                fread (&ch, 1, sizeof (BYTE), fp);
                pBitmap[x].peGreen = ch;
                ++pos;
                fread (&ch, 1, sizeof (BYTE), fp);
                pBitmap[x].peRed = ch;
                ++x;
                break;
        }
    }
}

//
//  Read the color map into the palette
//
void ReadPalette (FILE *fp, int nCount,
                PALETTEENTRY *pPalette)
{
    for (int x = Ø; x < nCount; ++x)
    {
    BYTE cr;
        fread (&cr, 1, sizeof (BYTE), fp);
        pPalette->peBlue = cr;
        fread (&cr, 1, sizeof (BYTE), fp);
        pPalette->peGreen = cr;
        fread (&cr, 1, sizeof (BYTE), fp);
        pPalette->peRed = cr;
        fread (&cr, 1, sizeof (BYTE), fp);
```

```
            pPalette->peFlags = cr;
            ++pPalette;
        }
}
```

This program won't display complicated bitmaps, nor will it decompress any compressed bitmaps. However, it at least shows you how to use the *BITMAPINFOHEADER* structure and draw the bitmap to the screen.

Also, this program reserves memory to hold the entire bitmap. For large bitmaps, that could take a large chunk, especially if your machine already is cramped for memory. You could display the bitmap on the screen as you read it in the *ReadBitmap()* function rather than keep it in memory.

713. *Understanding the Picture Control*

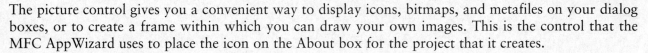

The picture control gives you a convenient way to display icons, bitmaps, and metafiles on your dialog boxes, or to create a frame within which you can draw your own images. This is the control that the MFC AppWizard uses to place the icon on the About box for the project that it creates.

The tool for the picture control is at the top of the second column of the Controls toolbar. Select the tool, and then drag the cursor across the dialog box where you want the image to appear. If you are going to insert an image into it, don't worry about sizing it. That'll be taken care of in a moment.

Right-click on the control to display the property sheet. On the first page, select the Type combo box and display the drop-down box. In addition to the icon, bitmap, and enhanced metafile, there are options for Frame and Rectangle. The Frame does nothing more than draw a line around the control area that you defined on the dialog box. You can select from a few colors for this frame border. The Rectangle option draws a filled rectangle in the same area. These options are intended to create a boundary where you can draw your own images.

Select Icon, Bitmap, or Enhanced Metafile from the control. You'll need an image that has a resource ID; the Image box won't accept the name of a file that contains an image. Select the resource ID of an image, and then click on the control. The control area should resize itself to fit the image. Move it to where you want to display it.

714. *Displaying Bitmaps*

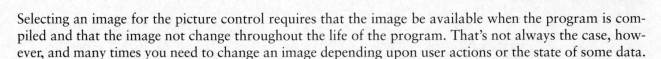

Selecting an image for the picture control requires that the image be available when the program is compiled and that the image not change throughout the life of the program. That's not always the case, however, and many times you need to change an image depending upon user actions or the state of some data.

Instead of selecting a bitmap for the picture control, select Frame to create just a rectangle around the area where you want the image to appear. In your dialog box class, add a message handler for the *WM_PAINT* message, and add the following code to it.

```
void CMyDlg::OnPaint()
{
    CPaintDC dc(this); // device context for painting
    BITMAP bm;              // Use for StretchBlt
    CBitmap bmp;
```

```
    bmp.LoadBitmap (IDB_BITMAP1);
    bmp.GetBitmap (&bm);  // Use for StretchBlt
    CRect rc;
    m_Picture.GetWindowRect (rc);
    CDC memDC;
    memDC.CreateCompatibleDC (&dc);
    ScreenToClient (rc);
    CBitmap *pOldBmp = memDC.SelectObject (&bmp);
    dc.BitBlt (rc.left, rc.top, rc.right - rc.left,
            rc.bottom - rc.top, &memDC, 0, 0, SRCCOPY);
    memDC.SelectObject (pOldBmp);
    bmp.DeleteObject ();
}
```

This code loads an image identified by *IDB_BITMAP1*, but you could assign the ID to a member variable—say, *UINT m_BmpID*—and change the value as needed to load different images.

715. *Manipulating Bitmaps*

The picture control also won't stretch or shrink an image to fit the available window size. When you assign an image to it, the control resizes itself to fit the image, whether that fits into your plans or not.

To make an image fit a specified area, you can use the *StretchBlt()* function. In the *OnPaint()* message handler, replace the call to *BitBlt()* with the following:

```
dc.StretchBlt (rc.left, rc.top, rc.right - rc.left,
            rc.bottom - rc.top, &memDC, 0, 0,
            bm.bmWidth, bm.bmHeight, SRCCOPY);
```

Ideally, the image should be one that can stand stretching or shrinking without looking skewed, such as a pattern.

To avoid distorting an image, you first find the smaller dimension and size the image to fit it, and then scale the other dimension so that the image retains its aspect ratio. The code in Tip 756, "Changing the Size of the Property Sheet Base," uses this method to draw a company logo onto the base of a property sheet without distorting the logo.

716. *Understanding Cursors*

On a character output device such as a DOS command line, the cursor is the position where the next character typed will be placed. In a Windows text window, that position is referred to as the *caret*. The word "cursor" is reserved for the name of the image that serves as the mouse pointer.

A window, even a control window, can specify the shape of the cursor when the mouse wanders into its display area. A program also may create and set its own cursor, which will appear only when the cursor is within the program's window.

You may have noticed in the EditExplore application that the cursor was a pointer when it was over the list view or the tree view, but when you moved it to the edit view, it changed to an I-beam. That's because the underlying edit control set its cursor to the I-beam, and the other two views are using the default cursor, which is the pointer, or *IDC_ARROW*.

717. *Standard Cursors*

Before you start designing your own custom cursors, the Windows API has a number of stock cursors that will meet the needs of most applications. You don't even have to add these to your resources; they are available just by loading them as described in Tip 719, "Activating a Cursor in Your Program."

The cursors and their descriptions are shown in Table 717.

Resource ID	Cursor Description
IDC_APPSTARTING	Standard arrow and small hourglass
IDC_ARROW	Standard arrow
IDC_CROSS	Crosshair
IDC_HELP	Arrow and question mark
IDC_IBEAM	I-beam
IDC_NO	Slashed circle
IDC_SIZEALL	Four-pointed arrow pointing north, south, east, and west
IDC_SIZENESW	Double-pointed arrow pointing northeast and southwest
IDC_SIZENS	Double-pointed arrow pointing north and south
IDC_SIZENWSE	Double-pointed arrow pointing northwest and southeast
IDC_SIZEWE	Double-pointed arrow pointing west and east
IDC_UPARROW	Vertical arrow
IDC_WAIT	Hourglass

Table 717   Standard Windows cursors and descriptions

If you right-click on a tree branch in the ResourceView panel and then select Insert and expand the Cursor item in the list, you'll see three additional cursors that you can add to your program. Actually, two of them aren't additional cursors, but they're copies of the standard cursors. *IDC_POINTER* is the same as the stock *IDC_ARROW*, and *IDC_NODROP* is the same as *IDC_NO*. The new addition is the *IDC_POINTER_COPY*, which is the pointer cursor with a plus sign added to it. Unlike the stock cursors, you can customize these cursor for your own needs.

718. *Using the Graphics Editor to Create Your Own Cursors*

In plenty of instances, the stock cursors just don't serve the purpose of an application. If you are designing a toolbar, for example, you might want a cursor to represent each of the tools on the toolbar. When a user selects a tool, the cursor changes to the shape of that tool.

Whatever the reason, you can design your own cursors using the cursor editor in the Visual Studio such as the fill cursor in Figure 718. From the ResourceView panel, right-click on any branch of the tree, and select Insert from the menu. In the dialog box that pops up, select Cursor from the list and press OK.

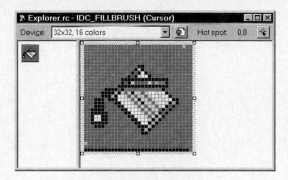

Figure 718   Designing a cursor for a fill brush toolbar

You get a 32-by-32 pixel blank layout page filled with the system mask color. You can create a custom-size cursor by selecting the New Device Image button just to the right of the combo box and filling in the information about the cursor that you want to create. Be careful with custom sizes if your program is to be used across different platforms. Windows 95, for example, requires the cursor be the same size as that returned when you call *GetSystemMetrics()* using the *SM_CXCURSOR* and *SM_CYCURSOR*. After creating the blank image, you'll be able to access it by selecting it from the combo box control.

719. *Activating a Cursor in Your Program*

You load a cursor into a program using the *LoadCursor()* or the *LoadImage()* functions. The first returns an *HCURSOR* handle, but the second must be cast to *HCURSOR*. The cursor that the window will use when it is active is specified in the *hCursor* member of the *WNDCLASS* or *WNDCLASSEX* structure when you register the window class. Any time the window is visible and the mouse moves over its territory, Windows will change the cursor to the one defined in the window class.

You can set the mouse cursor using the *SetCursor()* function, passing the handle of the new cursor to the function.

This works fine for Windows API functions, but if your application uses MFC classes, you might find it difficult to change the cursor. Try as you might, you just can't find any place in the source code where *SetCursor()* has any effect. The problem is that every time there's a mouse event, Windows resets the cursor to the one defined when the window class was registered. You can work around this in a couple of ways.

First, include a member variable in your class of type *HCURSOR*, and call it something like *m_hCursor*. Assuming that the resource ID of your cursor is *IDC_CURSOR1*, load the cursor in the class constructor using the following line:

```
m_hCursor = LoadCursor (AfxGetInstanceHandle(),
                MAKEINTRESOURCE(IDC_CURSOR1));
```

Add message handlers for the mouse events to your class, and in each of them, add the following line:

```
SetCursor (m_hCursor);
```

There's very little overhead to this function call, and this is a workable solution for temporary cursor changes. You can store the value of the current cursor in the *m_hCursor* variable, and the proper cursor is set each time there's a mouse event.

A saner method is to change the cursor in the window registration, but in an MFC-based application the framework already has registered the window, and you can't change it. Fortunately, the Windows API has a function, *SetClassLong()*, that enables you to modify many of the registered parameters. The function takes as parameters the window handle, an index into the registered values, and a handle to a cursor that already has been loaded. The cursor index is *GCL_HCURSOR*.

In the *OnInitialUpdate()* function (or the *OnInitDialog()* function, if this is a dialog box), add the following call:

```
SetClassLong (m_hWnd, GCL_HCURSOR,
        (long) LoadCursor (AfxGetInstanceHandle(),
        MAKEINTRESOURCE (IDC_CURSOR1)));
```

The function returns the old value. If this is a temporary cursor change, you might want to save it so that you can restore the old cursor later.

Neither of these methods will work if your view class uses one of the editing controls (Edit or Rich Text Edit). The control itself wants to set the cursor, and on a dialog box, the cursor will change to an I-beam when it moves over one of these controls.

720. *Setting a Cursor's Hot Spot*

Every cursor has a *hot spot*, the position on the bitmap where the action is presumed to take place. By default, this spot is the upper-left corner of the bitmap, at point (0,0), which corresponds to the tip of the arrow on the Windows pointer cursor.

However, cursors have different shapes and different places within the bitmap where you want the action to take place. In the fill cursor shown in Figure 718, for example, you would want the hot spot to be at the end of the stream of paint pouring from the bucket.

You can set the hot spot in the Visual Studio cursor editor. Open a cursor for editing, and examine the frame area to the right of the combo box. The first button is to select alternate bitmaps for the cursor. Then there's a text area that says something like "Hot spot: 0,0." After that there's another button that you use to set the hot spot.

Press the button and move the cursor over the bitmap. The cursor changes to a small circle with four pointers extruding from it. Move the cursor so that the pixel that you want to serve as the hot spot is within this circle, and press the left mouse button. The hot spot is reset to the selected pixel, and the location should be reflected in the text line at the top of the window.

721. *Using CWaitCursor*

In the Microsoft Foundation Class library, the *CWinApp()* class, which serves as the base class for most applications, loads and implements a special cursor named the *wait cursor*. The default image is an hourglass, and it is intended to be used when your application is performing a time-consuming task and you need to warn the user.

The function is implemented with the *CWinApp::DoWaitCursor()* function, which takes a positive value to start the wait cursor, a negative value to end it, and 0 to restore it (*a la* the mouse events described in Tip 719, "Activating a Cursor in Your Program").

MFC also implements a *CWaitCursor* class that makes using the wait cursor even easier. To set the wait cursor, all you need to do is declare an object of *CWaitCursor*. The class contains only three functions: the constructor, which activates the wait cursor; the destructor, which terminates the wait cursor; and *Restore()*, which restores it on a mouse event. The wait cursor appears immediately after the object is declared and will remain until the object goes out of scope and is destroyed. You can terminate the wait cursor prematurely by calling *AfxGetApp()->DoWaitCursor (-1)* without waiting for the object to go out of scope.

722. Understanding Icons

To represent programs when their windows are not visible, Windows uses small pictures named *icons*. The word "icon" comes from the Greek language and means literally "image."

Finding the proper icon is like finding a corporate logo—many companies spend a lot of money and research time on what might seem an insignificant part of a program. If it works, however, the icon and your program become synonymous. You don't have to look at the label in a list or on the desktop to know what program is represented by the icon.

Icons don't represent only programs. If your application registers a document type, you should have a distinctive icon to go with it. The icon will show on lists, trees, and other controls that list files.

723. Using Default Icons

For programs that require icons, the Visual Studio provides a few basic images. They're more of an advertisement for MFC than images for your program, however. They're placeholders, and nobody expects you to hang on to the IDE-provided icons.

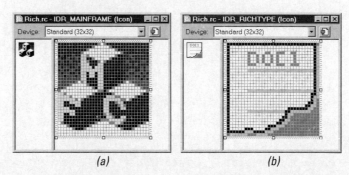

(a)   *(b)*

Figure 723   The default application icon usually has the resource ID
of IDR_MAINFRAME *and is linked with the default document template.*
The document icon is used with registered file types to provide an icon for directory lists.

You can modify the icons that Visual Studio provides as much as you want, or simply erase them and create your own.

724. *Creating Icons*

For those with an artistic bent, you can create and edit your own icons using the Visual Studio icon editor. For those without such creativity (hey, I'm an editor, not an *artiste*; I can't draw a straight line with the darned T-square nailed to the table), there are commercial icon libraries available.

To create an icon, select the ResourceView panel of the Workspace Window, and expand the tree. Right-click on any branch of the tree, and select Insert from the menu. From the dialog box that appears, select Icon and click OK.

You'll get a basic 32-by-32 pixel drawing grid filled with the system mask color. To the right are the Color and Graphics toolbars. The Color toolbar contains 16 colors, which generally is all you need for an image as small as an icon. You can change the colors in the toolbar by selecting the color on the toolbar and then selecting Adjust Colors from the Image menu.

You should prepare two icons: the 32-by-32 pixel *large* icon and a 16-by-16 pixel *small* icon. The system maintains two image lists for icons, as you saw in earlier programming examples.

725. *Assigning Icons*

If your program registers file types with the operating system, you should associate icons with it to be used when document files are displayed in a directory listing. Registering a file type allows a user to start your program and edit a file by double-clicking on the file icon.

Your application can register multiple file types at the same time. This is done after the application has created its document templates in the application class *InitIntance()* function. Associate the icon with the document type by giving the icon the same resource ID that you use to create the document template.

When all the document templates have been created for your application, call *EnableShellOpen()* to activate the double-click-to-open mechanism. After that, call *RegisterShellFileType()*, which associates each file type with your application in the registration database (the *registry*). If you want users to be able to print a document through your application without actually starting the program, pass a *TRUE* parameter to *RegisterShellFileTypes()*.

If the application has document types that it does not want to register, delay creating the document templates until after the *RegisterShellFileTypes()* call. The function call will register only document types for templates that already have been created.

If an association already exists for the file extension with another file type, the registration will not be completed. For example, Microsoft Word registers the rich-text format with an extension of *.rtf*. If you later try to register that file extension for your own application, the registration process will reject it.

726. *Understanding String Tables*

String tables provide a convenient place to collect and maintain the character strings used in an application. A string table is part of the resource file rather than the C/C++ source code, and the string entries are accessed through their resource IDs rather than string pointers.

An application can have only one string table, although you can create multiple string tables in the resource file. When the resource compiler encounters multiple string tables, it concatenates them into one table. If you examine the string table for a typical MFC AppWizard-generated application, you'll see several horizontal line separators in the string table. Each line designates a separate string table that was concatenated into the one table by the string table editor.

Each string in a string table must have a resource ID. That's the only way that your application can get to them. Some controls use string table entries as well. The ToolTip control, for example, looks for a string table entry with the same resource ID as a toolbar button or a menu item; if it finds an entry, it uses it for the tool hint and ToolTip text.

String table entries already are Unicode-enabled. You don't have to use the _TEXT_ macro on them. If Unicode is defined for your project, the strings will be compiled as Unicode.

727. *Creating String Tables*

If your project doesn't already have a string table, you can create one. If the string table already exists, you cannot create another one without specifying a different language to determine when it, rather than the original string table, is compiled as part of your application. Tip 729, "Understanding String Table Resource IDs," describes how to create alternate string tables.

From the ResourceView panel of the Workspace window, expand the tree control. If there is no branch labeled String Table, you can create one by right-clicking on any branch and selecting Insert from the menu. On the dialog that appears, select String Table and press the OK button. An empty string table will be created and added to your resources.

Alternatively, you can use the New String Table button on the Resource toolbar, or press Ctrl+8. If a string table doesn't exist, one will be created. If one already exists, it will be displayed so that you can add or edit entries.

728. *Creating String Table Entries*

You can insert new string table entries by opening the string table and pressing the Insert key, or by selecting New String from the Insert menu. Before you do, though, examine the table to see what item is selected currently.

Remember from Tip 726, "Understanding String Tables," that the horizontal separators indicate different sections of the string table in the resource file. Your new string will be added to the same section as the string that is highlighted when you press the Insert key.

When you insert a string, the Properties dialog box will appear. The default resource ID will be based on the sequence of IDs in the section in which you added the string. For example, if you select an item in the *ID_FILE_* section, your new resource ID will be the lowest available number in that sequence. The default resource symbol will be something like *IDS_STRINGnnnn*. Even if you change the resource symbol, which you probably will do, the ID number will remain the same. You would have to edit the entry in the resource symbols table to change it, and you possibly would have to delete the new string first. In short, be careful of where the current selection is before you press the Insert key.

You can edit a string table entry by double-clicking on it with the mouse, or by selecting it and pressing the Enter key. Both methods display the Properties dialog box. The string appears in the Caption box.

The string table editor will correct the string to provide the correct C++ sequences. For example, if you enter a backslash, the editor will replace it with two backslashes when it adds the entry to the table.

To produce a newline character, either enter "\n" or press Ctrl+Enter. The second method will produce a new line in the Caption box, but the string table editor will replace it with \n when the string is filed.

Don't begin and end the string with double quotes as you would with a C++ string, unless you intend for the quotes to be part of the string. The string table is compiled into binary data by the resource compiler, and the strings don't need to be quoted.

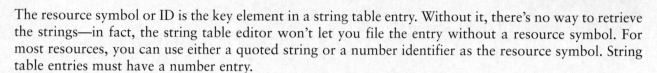

729. Understanding String Table Resource IDs

The resource symbol or ID is the key element in a string table entry. Without it, there's no way to retrieve the strings—in fact, the string table editor won't let you file the entry without a resource symbol. For most resources, you can use either a quoted string or a number identifier as the resource symbol. String table entries must have a number entry.

The resource ID is used by a number of functions in the Windows API and the Microsoft Foundation Class library. The Windows API *LoadString()* function retrieves the string using the resource ID. Assuming that you have a string identified as *IDS_TESTSTRING*, the string table entry can be retrieved by the following call:

```
TCHAR strText[_MAX_PATH];
LoadString (hInstance, IDS_TESTSTRING, strText, _
MAX_PATH);
```

The MFC *CString* class contains a similar function that is even easier to use. With *CString*, the memory allocation for the string is dynamic and expands as needed. You can retrieve the string table entry into a *CString* object with the following call:

```
CString strText;
strText.LoadString(IDS_TESTSTRING);
```

The string table is used to store ToolTips for menu items and toolbar buttons. If you enter a string with the same resource ID as the menu item, the ToolTip control will use that text to display a short help message on the status bar. If you have a toolbar button that matches the resource ID of a menu item, the same string is used for both.

730. Using Different Languages with a String Table

Most resource entries may be duplicated by using a different language for the copy or by adding a condition under which the alternate table will be compiled. String tables are slightly different; the only way to duplicate a string table is to specify an alternate language.

To create a copy of your string table, expand the tree in the ResourceView panel so that the string table entry is visible. Right-click on it and select Insert Copy from the menu. The Insert Resource Copy dialog box will appear, with the Condition field disabled. Select a new language for the string table copy, and press the OK button.

The string table editor won't translate the strings for you. You'll have to do that yourself. Nor will it update the copy when you add new strings to the original. If you are using an alternate-language string table, be sure to update all copies at the same time using the same resource identifier. It's very easy to overlook alternate tables, and later you'll have to search through them to make sure that the identifiers match.

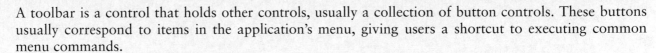

731. *Understanding Toolbars*

A toolbar is a control that holds other controls, usually a collection of button controls. These buttons usually correspond to items in the application's menu, giving users a shortcut to executing common menu commands.

Toolbars can be affixed to any side of an application's main window frame, or they can be made to "float" somewhere on the screen. They also can be made "dockable" so that the user can move them from one place to another on the window frame or leave them floating, unattached to the frame.

When you create a project using the MFC AppWizard, your application has a toolbar added to it unless you uncheck the toolbar option during the wizard steps. By default, this toolbar is dockable. You can modify the toolbar and change, add, or delete buttons as your application needs.

Toolbars are dynamic objects. They can be modified even after they are created and displayed on the main window frame. Buttons can be added or deleted even while the toolbar is actively in use.

732. *Creating a Toolbar Using the Graphics Editor*

An application isn't limited to one toolbar. You can create additional toolbars and add them to your project, displaying and hiding them as needed or by user command.

There are two ways to prepare a new toolbar in the Visual Studio. In the first method, you create or import a bitmap containing the images for the new toolbar. You can create the bitmap in the Visual Studio or in an external graphics editor, and then import it into the Visual Studio.

The normal size for a toolbar is 15 pixels deep. Each button image is 16 pixels wide. When you prepare the bitmap, the overall width should be a multiple of 16 pixels, and it should be designed so that the image boundaries fall on 16-pixel increments. Don't worry about separators; you'll add those after the bitmap has been applied to a toolbar.

You can practice the following steps using the default toolbar image, *toolbar.bmp*, which is located in the *res* directory of your project. The steps don't affect the bitmap itself. You also can use these steps to prepare a toolbar with larger or smaller buttons.

When the bitmap is finished, import it into the Visual Studio by right-clicking on any branch of the ResourceView tree control, and then select Import from the menu. In the Import Resource dialog box (which really is a File Open dialog box), locate the path and file where you saved the bitmap. Select it and press the Import button. The bitmap will be added to your resources with a resource ID of something like *IDB_BITMAP1*. Don't worry about giving it a real symbol; after the toolbar has been created, it will become a toolbar resource, and you can give it a new ID then.

With the bitmap open in the bitmap editor, select Toolbar Editor from the Image menu. You'll get a dialog box asking you to enter the width and height of the toolbar buttons. If your image was prepared for a toolbar with buttons larger or smaller than standard, enter the values here. For standard toolbars, enter "16" for the width and "15" for the height.

When you press OK, the bitmap will be transferred to a toolbar. and the Toolbar Editor will split the image into equal sections and assign the sections to the toolbar buttons. The Toolbar Editor determines from the button width and the total width of the bitmap just how many buttons to create. Notice that there is a blank button at the end that was not part of your bitmap. That button isn't part of the toolbar, but it is a template that you can use to add buttons, if needed.

You'll need to assign each button a resource ID. Select a button and press Alt+Enter, or select Properties from the View menu. The Properties dialog box will appear, and you can assign the button a resource ID. Step through each button this way. Don't assign the template button a resource ID; if you do, you'll just create a blank button on your toolbar, and a new template will appear to the right.

That's the easy way to create a new toolbar. If you have a collection of icons or small images and you want to create a toolbar using them, you can add a blank toolbar to your project and then assign the graphics to it by cutting and pasting—or, you can position the images from within your program.

Create a blank toolbar by right-clicking on any branch of the tree in the ResourceView. Select Insert from the menu and, from the Insert Resource dialog box, select Toolbar and press the New button. You'll get an empty toolbar with just a template button. Select the template button and press Alt+Enter to get the Properties dialog box. Assign the button a resource ID, and press Enter. When you do, the template button moves to the right, and a blank button is inserted into the toolbar. Continue this process until you've created all the blank buttons for your new toolbar, and then follow the steps in Tip 733, "Using the Graphics Editor to Modify Toolbars," to edit the toolbar.

733. Using the Graphics Editor to Modify Toolbars

When you've created a new toolbar, you'll need to customize it. Perhaps you need to move buttons around or add separators. Or, perhaps you want to modify an existing toolbar.

To create a separator, grab the button that you want to appear after the separator, and drag it a few pixels to the right. It will appear that you are moving one button into another's space, but when you release the mouse button, the toolbar will sort itself out and a separator will be added. You also can grab the button that you want to appear *before* the separator and drag it to the left; the Toolbar Editor doesn't care. To close up a separator, just drag one of the buttons next to it over the separator until it slightly overlaps the other button, and release the mouse button. If you overlap the other button by more than half, the Toolbar Editor will simply move the separator to the other side of the button.

To move a button from one position to another within the toolbar, grab it with the left mouse button, drag it to the new location, and release the mouse button. Unfortunately, you can't move a separator this way. Instead, to move a separator, you have to close up the old space and open a new separator.

You can copy a button from one toolbar to another, or within the same toolbar. To copy a button within the same toolbar, hold down the Ctrl key and grab the button with the left mouse button. Drag it to the new location and release the button. To copy a button from another toolbar, be sure that the source and destination toolbars are open in the Toolbar Editor. Holding down the Ctrl key, grab the button in the source toolbar and drag it to the destination toolbar. Position it in the toolbar, and release the mouse button. If you don't hold down the Ctrl key, the Toolbar Editor will move the button from one toolbar to the other rather than copy it. Give the new button a resource ID.

To add a new button to a toolbar, grab the template button at the end of the toolbar, and drag it to the location where you want the new button to appear. Use Alt+Enter to get the Properties dialog box and assign the new button a resource ID. The new button will appear, and the template button will move one button space to the right.

If you want to remove a button from the toolbar, grab it with the left mouse button, and drag it off the toolbar and drop it somewhere in space. If you accidentally remove a button from the toolbar, press the Undo button, or type Ctrl+Z.

734. *Adding a Toolbar to Your Project*

If your toolbar is ready—the buttons have been placed in the Toolbar Editor, the images are on the buttons, and the resource IDs have all been set—you can create the toolbar in the *OnCreate()* function of the main window class, or *CMainFrame* in applications generated with the MFC AppWizard.

Add a variable to the main window frame class of type *CToolbar*, and give it a descriptive name such as *m_wndFormatBar*. Locate the *OnCreate()* function in the source file, and use the toolbar class's *CreateEx()* member function to create the new toolbar, as shown here:

```
if (!m_wndFormatBar.CreateEx(this, TBSTYLE_FLAT, WS_CHILD
            | CBRS_TOP | CBRS_GRIPPER | CBRS_TOOLTIPS
            | CBRS_FLYBY | CBRS_SIZE_DYNAMIC)
        || !m_wndFormatBar.LoadToolBar(IDR_RICHTYPE))
{
    TRACE0("Failed to create Format toolbar\n");
    return -1;       // fail to create
}
```

If the toolbar is uncooked and needs to have the images placed on it or new controls added, you might want to add a function to create and load the toolbar, returning *TRUE* on success and *FALSE* if the toolbar fails to create or load. Even better, derive a new class for your toolbar using *CToolBar* as the base class, as you did in Tip 637, "Adding Menu and Toolbar Items to Support Rich Text." This will enable you to encapsulate and handle the construction and message details without making the *CMainFrame* class too messy.

735. *Adding Text, ToolTips, and Flyby Text to Toolbars*

In addition to images, toolbars support text on buttons at the same time, but achieving that is not as easy as the documentation would have you believe. You also can add ToolTips and flyby text to the toolbars, and that's quite a bit easier. In this tip, you'll do both, and you decide which you prefer. In fact, you can have button text and flyby hints simultaneously. Usually having both is redundant, though.

If the toolbar button's resource ID matches a menu item and you've already added ToolTips and flyby text for the menu item, you don't need to do anything more. The text will show up automatically in the Prompt field of the Properties dialog box. The two work together.

If you need to add the text, select the toolbar button and display the Properties dialog box by pressing Alt+Enter. In the Prompt field, enter the text that you want to appear on the status bar when the mouse cursor moves over the toolbar button. Next, enter a newline character, "\n", or press Ctrl+Enter. Now type the text that you want to appear in the hint, which will appear at the mouse cursor position when the cursor hovers over the toolbar button for a second or so. Try to keep this short, one or two words; it's a hint, not an explanation.

Adding text to the toolbar buttons is a neat effect, as you can see in Figure 735, although it does require a larger toolbar. Most of the people I know can read, and the text usually is more helpful than the image.

You could provide alternate toolbars, one with text and the other without, and let the user select via a setup dialog box or a menu item.

Create a toy project, one that you can discard when you're done. You'll need to experiment with some values to get the effect you like. The numbers in this tip are the ones that I came up with, and they look pretty good to me, but everybody's different. You may want to try different sizes to get the look and feel that you prefer. There are a couple of rules, however. First, the button width must be at least 7 logical points wider than the image width. Second, the button depth must be at least 6 logical points deeper than the image depth. This trivial information isn't in the documentation, but you'll get an assertion if you violate either.

Figure 735   Adding text to a toolbar requires the toolbar to be enlarged, but the effect is
pleasing and adds some sense of customization

First you need to increase the button width to accommodate the widest text that you will be using. Keep it reasonable to avoid a gaudy look. If you want a button to read "Statistical Analysis," try shortening it to "Stats." I set the width to 40 and haven't had any problems.

Open the toolbar in the Toolbar Editor. Select a button, and press Alt+Enter to get the Properties dialog box. Enter "40" in the Width field. The old depth of 15 is fine, unless you want to try some other sizes. This will modify the *toolbar.bmp* file by spreading out the images.

Close the toolbar, and open the *CMainFrame* class source code file, *mainfrm.cpp*. If you want to set a font for the toolbar text, add a member variable *m_ToolFont* of type *CFont*. In the source code file, add the following code *after* the toolbar has been created. The text is for the default toolbar and includes the Context Help button. If you didn't include context help, delete the last entry in the array. Of course, you'll want the text to match your own toolbar.

```
LPCTSTR btnText[] =
        {
        "New", "Open", "Save", "Cut", "Copy",
        "Paste", "Print", "About", "Help"
        };
//
//  Optional. delete the following two lines and the
//  m_ToolFont member variable to use the default font
//
    m_ToolFont.CreatePointFont (80, "Times New Roman");
    m_wndToolBar.SetFont (&m_ToolFont);
    for (int i = 0;
        i < sizeof (btnText) / sizeof (LPCTSTR);
        ++i)
    {
        m_wndToolBar.SetButtonText (i, btnText[i]);
    }
    m_wndToolBar.SetSizes (CSize(48, 40), CSize (40,15));
```

You should call *SetSizes()* after you have added text to at least one button. It really doesn't seem to make any difference whether you call it before or after adding the text, but I've read elsewhere that the size will revert to what you set it to in the Toolbar Editor if you call *SetSizes()* before adding the text. Just to be safe, I always call the function after adding the text. The first parameter to *SetSizes()* is the new button size, and the second is the new image size, which is the same as you set in the Toolbar Editor. Size the *cx* member of the button so that it is at least 7 larger than the *cx* member of the image. The *cy* members usually will be far enough apart that you don't have to worry about them, but the button *cy* must be at least 6 larger than the image *cy*. I started out with 48 and 36 for the button size because the values are easy to work with. In addition, the aspect ratio of most monitors—and, consequently, the screen resolutions—is 4:3, so *CSize(48, 36)* yields a decently square button. It looked good when the toolbar was on the top or bottom of the frame, but elsewhere it tended to chop off the bottom button. Increasing the *cy* component, as it turns out, didn't affect the shape of the button—they are still square—but it added some escapement at the bottom. At 40, the buttons didn't chop off.

736. *Understanding Dockable and Floating Toolbars*

Toolbars attach to the main window frame, but they all have a dockable property that you can enable or disable according to the needs of your application. A toolbar can be made to stay at one position on the window frame, or the user can be allowed to move it around from one location to another on the frame.

A toolbar also can be left floating, suspended somewhere on the screen and not attached to any particular object. It's still part of your application, but the user can move it out of the way as necessary, even outside the limits of the application's window. Toolbars can be forced to float and not allowed to dock anywhere on the frame, as is common with toolbars used in many graphics programs. When toolbars are forced to float all the time, they often are called "tool windows."

You set the default position for your toolbar when you create it as part of the toolbar style, the *CBRS_TOP* part of the style, but you could just as well specify *CBRS_BOTTOM*, *CBRS_LEFT*, or *CBRS_RIGHT*.

To set the allowed docking positions, you use the toolbar's *EnableDocking()* function. You pass it a value specifying the allowed docking positions, which is a combination of *CBRS_ALIGN_TOP* to allow docking at the top, *CBRS_ALIGN_BOTTOM* to allow docking at the bottom, *CRBR_ALIGN_LEFT* to allow docking on the left, and *CBRS_ALIGN_RIGHT* to allow docking on the right side of the frame. *CBRS_ALIGN_ANY* is a combination of all four of these.

Similarly, you must tell the frame window where docking is allowed by calling its *EnableDocking()* function. The flags are the same as for the toolbar's function, and you can specify a different combination.

Finally, you dock the control bar by calling the frame window's *DockControlBar()* function, passing it a pointer to the toolbar to dock.

To make a toolbar float initially, call the frame window's *FloatControlBar()* function instead of *DockControlBar()*. This function takes a pointer to the toolbar to float, a *CSize* object specifying the upper-left corner (relative to the full screen) of the floating toolbar, and an optional docking style. The following code would make the toolbar float along the right side of the main window about a third of the way down from the top of the main window frame:

```
m_wndToolBar.EnableDocking(CBRS_ALIGN_ANY);
EnableDocking(0);
CRect rcTool, rcWindow;
GetWindowRect (rcWindow);
m_wndToolBar.GetItemRect
        (m_wndToolBar.GetToolBarCtrl ().GetButtonCount() - 1,
         rcTool);
CPoint point;
point.y = rcWindow.top + (rcWindow.bottom
                        - rcWindow.top) / 3;
point.x = rcWindow.right - rcTool.right;
FloatControlBar(&m_wndToolBar, point);
```

737. *Preventing a Toolbar from Docking or Undocking*

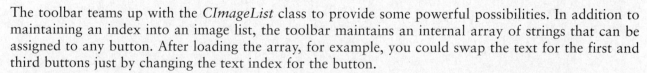

Sometimes it's necessary to keep a toolbar in one place. Perhaps it has some control that you want positioned at a particular place on the frame.

To prevent a toolbar from undocking, remove the three lines of code at the end of the *CMainFrame:: OnCreate()* function that enable docking and dock the toolbar:

```
m_wndToolBar.EnableDocking(CBRS_ALIGN_ANY);
EnableDocking(CBRS_ALIGN_ANY);
DockControlBar(&m_wndToolBar);
```

Without the first two lines, neither the frame nor the toolbar will permit docking. The toolbar will attach itself to the frame at the position specified in the style when you called the *CreateEx()* function and stay there.

Sometimes you don't want a toolbar to dock, ever. This is especially true of toolbars in graphics design programs. You want them to remain floating yet permit the user to move them around. If the toolbar is left dockable, it might attach itself to the frame in some odd locations and at unexpected times.

To keep this from happening, set the style parameter to the call to the toolbar's *EnableDocking()* and in the call to the frame window's *EnableDocking()* functions to 0 before you call *FloatControlBar()*. If you have two toolbars and want one to be dockable and the other to float forever, reset the frame window's docking flags, and then set the second toolbar's docking flags and dock the second toolbar. The following code uses two toolbars—the first cannot dock, and the second is fully dockable:

```
m_wndToolBar.EnableDocking(0);
EnableDocking(0);
FloatControlBar(&m_wndToolBar, CPoint (0, 0));
m_wndSecondBar.EnableDocking(CBRS_ALIGN_ANY);
EnableDocking(CBRS_ALIGN_ANY);
DockControlBar(&m_wndSecondBar);
```

This would place the floating toolbar in the upper-left corner of the screen. You would want to reset the values in the *CPoint* object to position your toolbar.

738. *Adding and Removing Toolbar Buttons*

The toolbar teams up with the *CImageList* class to provide some powerful possibilities. In addition to maintaining an index into an image list, the toolbar maintains an internal array of strings that can be assigned to any button. After loading the array, for example, you could swap the text for the first and third buttons just by changing the text index for the button.

In an earlier project (Tip 541, "Using the *CImageList* Class"), you saw how to insert and delete a single button that used only an icon on the button. In this project, you'll build a single toolbar using two bitmaps, an image list and the toolbar's text array. Then you'll selectively hide and show a block of buttons.

Create a new project named Buttons. The sample on the companion CD is a single-document interface using *CEditView* as the base view class. In this example, you could edit the main toolbar and add more buttons and images. This project, however, will use two bitmaps to show you how to add buttons to the toolbar after it has been created.

Open the *IDR_MAINFRAME* toolbar in the Toolbar Editor, and set the image width to 40. This will modify the *toolbar.bmp* file to give you wider images for the image list. Now delete the *IDR_MAIN-FRAME* toolbar. Insert a new toolbar, and call it *IDR_MAINFRAME*. You'll need to have at least one button, or the Toolbar Editor will delete the new toolbar when you close it. Select the pattern button and set its image width to 40, and then give it a resource ID of *ID_FILE_NEW*. Don't worry about an image for it; you'll delete this single button right after the toolbar is created.

Import the *toolbar.bmp* file as a bitmap, and give it the resource ID of *IDB_MAINFRAME*. Don't use the Toolbar Editor to convert it into a toolbar, however.

Create another bitmap 15 pixels deep and 160 pixels wide. Draw or paste four images 16 pixels wide by 15 pixels deep on this blank bitmap. You'll have 12 blank columns and then the first image, 24 blank columns, and the second image. Continue until you get to the final image. After the final image, you'll have 12 blank columns to finish out the bitmap. Fill the large white areas with the gray window frame color. This is the background color. This project uses the icons for the list control modes in a bitmap named *ViewBmp.bmp* and a resource ID of *IDB_VIEWBAR*.

Close the bitmaps and the toolbar. Open the *CMainFrame* class files *mainfrm.cpp* and *mainfrm.h*. Add a member variable of type *CImageList*, and name it *m_ToolImages*. Add two member functions, *LoadMainToolBar* and *LoadViewBarButtons()*. Both have a return type of *BOOL*. In the *OnCreate()* function, add the following code and modify the call to create the main toolbar as shown here:

```
m_ToolImages.Create (40, 15, ILC_MASK, 9, 10);
CBitmap bmp;
bmp.LoadBitmap (IDB_MAINFRAME);
m_ToolImages.Add (&bmp, GetSystemColor(COLOR_BTNFACE));
bmp.DeleteObject ();
if (!m_wndToolBar.CreateEx(this, TBSTYLE_FLAT,
                   WS_CHILD | WS_VISIBLE | CBRS_TOP
                   | CBRS_GRIPPER | CBRS_TOOLTIPS
                   | CBRS_FLYBY | CBRS_SIZE_DYNAMIC)
             || !LoadMainToolBar())
{
    TRACE0("Failed to create toolbar\n");
    return -1;      // fail to create
}
LoadViewBarButtons();
```

Instead of calling the toolbar class's *LoadToolBar()* function, you will call the local function that you just created to load the toolbar. Code the *LoadMainToolBar()* function, as shown here:

```
BOOL CMainFrame::LoadMainToolBar()
{
const UINT  uiIndex[] =
    {
    ID_FILE_NEW,
    ID_FILE_OPEN,
    ID_FILE_SAVE,
    0,
    ID_EDIT_CUT,
    ID_EDIT_COPY,
    ID_EDIT_PASTE,
    0,
    ID_FILE_PRINT,
    0,
```

```
      ID_APP_ABOUT
   };

   const char *btnText =
   {
        "New\0Open\0Save\0Cut\0Copy\0Paste\0Print\0About\0"
   };
   int x, i;
   m_wndToolBar.GetToolBarCtrl().AddStrings (
                                      (const char *) btnText);
   m_wndToolBar.GetToolBarCtrl().SetImageList
                                      (&m_ToolImages);
   m_wndToolBar.GetToolBarCtrl().DeleteButton (0);
   TBBUTTON tb;

   for (i = 0, x = 0;
        i < (sizeof (uiIndex) / sizeof (UINT));
        ++i)
   {
      tb.idCommand = uiIndex[i];
      if (!uiIndex[i])
      {
         tb.iBitmap = -1;
         tb.iString = -1;
         tb.fsStyle = TBSTYLE_SEP;
         tb.fsState = TBSTATE_INDETERMINATE;
      }
      else
      {
         tb.iBitmap = x;
         tb.iString = x++;
         tb.fsState = TBSTATE_ENABLED;
         tb.fsStyle = TBSTYLE_BUTTON;
      }
      tb.idCommand = uiIndex[i];
      m_wndToolBar.GetToolBarCtrl().InsertButton (i,&tb);
   }
   m_wndToolBar.SetSizes (CSize(48, 40), CSize (40,15));
   return (TRUE);
}
```

Make sure that the *AddViewBarButtons()* returns a dummy value, and then compile the application to make sure that the main toolbar works up to this point. If everything is kosher, add four resource symbols for the new buttons. In a real application, you would use the IDs for the menu command issued by the new buttons. The dummy IDs are for *ID_LIST_LARGEICONS*, *ID_LIST_SMALLICONS*, *ID_LIST_LIST*, and *ID_LIST_REPORT*. Also add a resource symbol for *ID_LIST_SEPARATOR*. You'll need that to hide and show the separator. Now add the new buttons in the *AddViewBarButtons()* function, as shown here:

```
//
//  The following function will insert four buttons and
//  a separator into the toolbar.
//
BOOL CMainFrame::LoadViewBarButtons()
{
TBBUTTON tb;
```

```
UINT    uiIndex[] =
    {
    ID_LIST_LARGEICONS,
    ID_LIST_SMALLICONS,
    ID_LIST_LIST,
    ID_LIST_REPORT,
    ID_LIST_SEPARATOR
    };

    const char *btnText =
    {
    "Large\ØSmall\ØList\ØReport\Ø"
    };

    int nInsertBefore =
                m_wndToolBar.CommandToIndex (ID_FILE_PRINT);
//
// Use the image count to get the index for the new
// images and strings. One string was added for each
// image, so the same value will work for both
//
    int nCount = m_ToolImages.GetImageCount();

    CBitmap bmp;
    bmp.LoadBitmap (IDB_VIEWBAR);
    m_ToolImages.Add (&bmp, GetSysColor(COLOR_BTNFACE));
    bmp.DeleteObject ();

    m_wndToolBar.GetToolBarCtrl().AddStrings (
                                    (const char *) btnText);
    int n, x;
    for (n = Ø, x = nCount;
         n < (sizeof (uiIndex) / sizeof (UINT));
        ++n)

    {
        tb.idCommand = uiIndex[n];
        if (uiIndex[n] == ID_LIST_SEPARATOR)
        {
            tb.iBitmap = -1;
            tb.iString = -1;
            tb.fsStyle = TBSTYLE_SEP;
            tb.fsState = TBSTATE_INDETERMINATE;
        }
        else
        {
            tb.iBitmap = x;
            tb.iString = x++;
            tb.fsState = TBSTATE_ENABLED;
            tb.fsStyle = TBSTYLE_BUTTON;
        }
        tb.idCommand = uiIndex[n];
        m_wndToolBar.GetToolBarCtrl().InsertButton
                                (nInsertBefore + n, &tb);
    }
    return (TRUE);
}
```

At this point, the buttons should appear on the toolbar but will be disabled. You don't have any message handlers for them at this point. To enable the new buttons, add a dummy message-handler function and add it to the message map. The sample project uses a function named *OnButtonDummy()* and adds the following four entries to the message map:

```
ON_COMMAND(ID_LIST_LARGEICONS, OnButtonDummy)
ON_COMMAND(ID_LIST_SMALLICONS, OnButtonDummy)
ON_COMMAND(ID_LIST_LIST, OnButtonDummy)
ON_COMMAND(ID_LIST_REPORT, OnButtonDummy)
```

Your own application would use real message functions to do something when a user presses one of the buttons. For this project, you just want to enable them.

That done, return to the *AddViewBarButtons()* function and change both lines that set the *tbState* members of the button structure to *TBSTATE_HIDDEN*. Now that you've enabled the buttons, you're going to hide them. Recompile the program to make sure that the new buttons *do not* appear in the toolbar.

Open the *IDR_MAINFRAME* menu in the menu editor, and add an item at the bottom of the View menu. Make the text read "Show Buttons." When you close the Properties dialog box, the editor will assign the item a resource ID of *ID_VIEW_SHOWBUTTONS*, and that's what you will use. Return to the *CMainFrame* class, and add a message handler for this item. Also add a command enabler (*UPDATE_COMMAND_UI*) for this item. The code for these functions is shown here:

```
void CMainFrame::OnViewShowbuttons()
{
UINT    uiIndex[] =
    {
    ID_LIST_LARGEICONS,
    ID_LIST_SMALLICONS,
    ID_LIST_LIST,
    ID_LIST_REPORT,
    ID_LIST_SEPARATOR
    };

    int nIndex = m_wndToolBar.CommandToIndex
                                (ID_LIST_LARGEICONS);
    int nHide;
    if (m_wndToolBar.GetToolBarCtrl().IsButtonHidden
                                (ID_LIST_LARGEICONS))
        nHide = FALSE;
    else
        nHide = TRUE;
    for (int n = 0; n < 5; ++n)
    {
        m_wndToolBar.GetToolBarCtrl().HideButton
                                (uiIndex[n], nHide);
    }
    RecalcLayout ();
    m_wndToolBar.GetToolBarCtrl().AutoSize ();
}

void CMainFrame::OnUpdateViewShowbuttons(CCmdUI* pCmdUI)
{
    if (m_wndToolBar.GetToolBarCtrl().IsButtonHidden
                                (ID_LIST_LARGEICONS))
        pCmdUI->SetText (_T("Show View Bar"));
    else
```

```
        pCmdUI->SetText (_T("Hide View Bar"));

}
```

This is the long way around, but it adds flexibility to the toolbar. By using the image list, you can change the images dynamically and hide and show the separator between the added buttons and the standard buttons. In fact, you could assign each separator a unique ID and then hide or show them as needed.

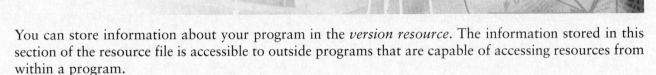

739. *Understanding the Version Resource*

You can store information about your program in the *version resource*. The information stored in this section of the resource file is accessible to outside programs that are capable of accessing resources from within a program.

From Windows Explorer, if you select an executable file and right-click on it, then select Properties from the menu, and then select the Version page of the property sheet, you'll see the information contained in this section. The version resource for the *Buttons* project from Tip 738, "Adding and Removing Toolbar Buttons," is shown in Figure 739.

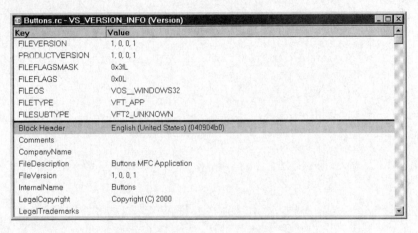

Figure 739   You store information about your program in the version resource

The Microsoft Foundation Class provides little or no support for version information. To get it and use it, you need to resort to the Windows API functions.

You can use the information here to keep your About box up to date. The default implementation of the About box does not use any of this information, but it hard-codes the display information in the dialog box resource. If you change your version number to 2.0, the dialog box still will display "Version 1.0." In the next few tips, you'll develop a *CVersion* class that will collect and encapsulate this information, and you'll use it to display current information in the About box.

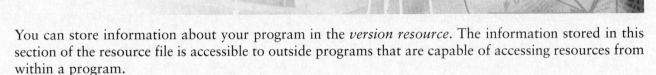

740. *Using the Version Information Editor*

A version resource has a fixed data area that is shown at the top in the version editor. All the information is numeric, and the string resource contains only one of these blocks. Below the fixed data area are one or more string information blocks. You can add additional blocks for other languages.

The FILEVERSION field has four numbers that are stored in two DWORD values. You can use these numbers as you see fit, but a common use (at least, common with me) is the major version number, the minor version number, the revision number, and the build number. If the program is a part of a larger project, you can store the product information in the PRODUCTVERSION field.

You shouldn't change anything below the PRODUCTVERSION field. None of the information that you can modify is critical to the operation of the program. You can set the operating system, for example, to any value that you want, but Visual C++ supports only 32-bit Windows applications, and that's how it will be compiled.

The blocks below the fixed data area are for strings, and you can put your name, company, copyright information, or other information here. Some of the numeric data from the fixed block—the file version and product version—is copied over to these sections as strings.

You can insert additional string blocks, but you have to give each a specific language. As with other resources, this makes building multi-language applications easier. You must provide the translation, however. Select New Version Info Block from the Insert menu, or right-click anywhere in the version resource and select New Version Info Block from the pop-up menu.

741. *Windows Functions That Access Version Information*

Before you can access any version information, you first have to get a pointer to the data block in the resource section of your program. The size for this section is variable, so it's not as simple as calling a function to get the pointer.

You first need to get the program name. Use the Windows API function *GetModuleFileName()* to get this information; it will return the full path of the program file. If you call the function with a NULL handle, it will return the path of the program that called it. We're calling it from within the program that we want information about, so you can use NULL. You also need to pass it a buffer to hold the returned name and the size of the buffer. The return value is the number of characters in the path.

When you get the path, you need to convert it to the proper character format by calling *OemToChar()*. If you're not using Unicode, the translation probably will yield the same string that you passed it. The following function lists the sequence of events. This function and the *GetProgramVersionData()* function are part of a *CVersion* class that will be introduced in the next tip:

```
bool CVersion::GetFileVersionData(LPCSTR lpstrFileName)
{
DWORD    dwSize;
char     szModuleName[_MAX_PATH];
TCHAR    ModuleName[_MAX_PATH];
HMODULE  hModule;

    if (lpstrFileName == NULL)
        hModule = NULL;
    else
        hModule = GetModulcHandle ((LPCTSTR)lpstrFileName);
    dwSize = GetModuleFileName (hModule, szModuleName,
                                sizeof (szModuleName));
    if (!dwSize)
        return (false);
    OemToChar (szModuleName, ModuleName);
    if (!GetProgramVersionData (ModuleName))
```

```
        return (false);
    return (true);
}
```

The next step is to get the size of the version data and create a buffer to hold it. You get the size by calling *GetFileVersionInfoSize()*. When you get the size and create a buffer, call *GetFileVersionInfo()* to get a copy of the data. From this point, you use the *VerQueryValue()* function to retrieve specific blocks of data.

The *VerQueryFunction()* can get pretty involved, and when you see the code in the *CVersion* class implementation, you'll appreciate the idea of encapsulating it in a class. Considering the usefulness of the version resource and the trivialness of some of the MFC classes, it's surprising that Microsoft didn't provide a class to simplify this operation.

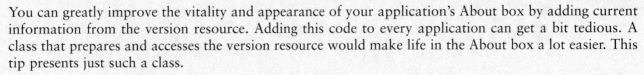

742. *Creating a CVersion Class*

You can greatly improve the vitality and appearance of your application's About box by adding current information from the version resource. Adding this code to every application can get a bit tedious. A class that prepares and accesses the version resource would make life in the About box a lot easier. This tip presents just such a class.

The *CVersion* class originally was developed to support a configuration program for a series of Windows NT service programs. The project code created by the Borland C++ 5.0 IDE served as the model for much of this class. As such, it was written to make sure that the levels of the programs match the configuration data that was being created, so it accepts either a *NULL* pointer, the default value, or a pointer to the program name for which you want to get version information. It was such a useful class that I added it to my gallery. It probably could be improved, but I'm not a professional programmer, so a lot of my code can be improved. It does work, however, which is what I care about.

You can add this class to the Buttons application from Tip 738, "Adding and Removing Toolbar Buttons." After seeing how it works, you can place it in your gallery to make it easy to add to your other applications. After building the class, you can add it to the application class to fetch version data at startup, and then use it in the About box to display current information.

Start by adding a generic class to the Buttons application. Select the ClassView panel of the Workshop Window, right-click on the project name, and select New Class from the menu. Select Generic Class from the Class Type box, and name it *CVersion*. Click the OK button to create the class using the default file names.

You'll need to add the *version.lib* library to your project. Select Settings from the Project menu, and then select All Configurations from the Settings For box at the left. There isn't a debug version of this library, so you don't need to provide separate links for the debug and release versions. Select the Link tab from the tab control to the right, and enter "version.lib" in the Object/Library Modules box. Click the OK button to close the Settings dialog box.

The class definition is in the *Version.h* file and is shown here. You'll have to spend some time adding the various functions to retrieve the separate blocks of version information.

```
class Cversion
{
public:
    CVersion();
    virtual ~CVersion();
```

```
    bool GetFileVersionData (LPCSTR lpstrFileName = NULL);
    bool GetProgramVersionData(TCHAR *ModuleName);
    bool GetProductCompanyName(Cstring
                            & strProductTrademark);
    bool GetProductCopyright (CString&
                                strProductCopyright);
    bool GetProductName(CString & strProductName);
    bool GetProductFileDescription(CString &strProductName);
    bool GetProductFileVersion(CString & strProductName);
    bool GetProductInternalName(CString & strProductName);
    bool GetProductOriginalName(CString & strProductName);
    bool GetProductVersion(CString & strProductName);
    bool GetProductVersion(DWORD & dwVersionMS,
                        DWORD & dwVersionLS);
    bool GetFileVersion(DWORD & dwVersionMS,
                        DWORD & dwVersionLS);

private:
    char *GetProductData (char *ProductData);

    char        *m_fvData;
    LPVOID      m_lpBuffer;
    VS_FIXEDFILEINFO    *m_vf;
};
```

The class initializes when you call *GetFileVersionData()*. Calling without an argument defaults to getting the version information for the current program. To get the information for another program file, specify the file's path as the only parameter in the function call.

The class implementation is listed in the following code. After that, you can add a class object to the program and use the information in the About box.

```
// Version.cpp: implementation of the CVersion class.
//
//////////////////////////////////////////////////////////
/

#include "stdafx.h"
#include "Buttons.h"
#include "Version.h"

#ifdef _DEBUG
#undef THIS_FILE
static char THIS_FILE[]=__FILE__;
#define new DEBUG_NEW
#endif

//////////////////////////////////////////////////////////
// Construction/Destruction
//////////////////////////////////////////////////////////
CVersion::CVersion()
{
    m_fvData = NULL;
}

CVersion::~CVersion()
{
```

```
    delete m_fvData;
}

bool CVersion::GetFileVersionData(LPCSTR lpstrFileName)
{
char    szModuleName[_MAX_PATH];
TCHAR   ModuleName[_MAX_PATH];

    if (lpstrFileName == NULL)
        GetModuleFileName (NULL, szModuleName,
                            sizeof (szModuleName));
    else
        strcpy (szModuleName, lpstrFileName);

    OemToChar (szModuleName, ModuleName);
    return (GetProgramVersionData (ModuleName));
}

bool CVersion::GetProgramVersionData(TCHAR *ModuleName)
{
DWORD   dwSize;
char    SubBlockName [255];
DWORD   fvHandle;
UINT    dwBytes;

    dwSize = GetFileVersionInfoSize (ModuleName, &fvHandle);
    if (!dwSize)
        return (false);
    m_fvData = new char [dwSize];
    GetFileVersionInfo (ModuleName, fvHandle, dwSize,
                        m_fvData);
    if (!dwSize)
        return (false);
    strcpy(SubBlockName, "\\VarFileInfo\\Translation");
    int result = ::VerQueryValue((LPVOID) m_fvData,
        SubBlockName,
        (void **) &m_lpBuffer,
        &dwBytes);
    *(DWORD *)m_lpBuffer =
                        MAKELONG(HIWORD(*(DWORD
*)m_lpBuffer),
                        LOWORD(*(DWORD *)m_lpBuffer));
    return (true);
}

char *CVersion::GetProductData(char * ProductData)
{
DWORD   dwSize;
char    SubBlockName[255];
char    *prodValue;

    if (!m_fvData)
        return (NULL);
    sprintf(SubBlockName, "\\StringFileInfo\\%08lx\\%s",
                *(LPWORD *)m_lpBuffer,(LPSTR) ProductData);
    if (!::VerQueryValue(m_fvData, SubBlockName,
```

```
                        (void **)&prodValue,
                        (UINT *) &dwSize))
        return (NULL);
    return (prodValue);
}

bool CVersion::GetProductFileDescription(
                              CString & strProductDesc)
{
char    *prodDesc;

    prodDesc = GetProductData ("FileDescription");
    if (prodDesc == NULL)
    {
        strProductDesc = _T("");
        return (false);
    }
    strProductDesc = prodDesc;
    return (true);
}

bool CVersion::GetProductFileVersion(
                              CString & strProductVer)
{
char    *prodVer;

    prodVer = GetProductData ("FileVersion");
    if (prodVer == NULL)
    {
        strProductVer = _T("");
        return (false);
    }
    strProductVer = prodVer;
    return (true);
}

bool CVersion::GetProductInternalName(
                              CString & strInternalName)
{
char    *prodName;

    prodName = GetProductData ("InternalName");
    if (prodName == NULL)
    {
        strInternalName = _T("");
        return (false);
    }
    strInternalName = prodName;
    return (true);
}

bool CVersion::GetProductOriginalName(
                              CString & strProductName)
{
char    *prodName;
```

```
        prodName = GetProductData ("OriginalFilename");
        if (prodName == NULL)
        {
            strProductName = _T("");
            return (false);
        }
        strProductName = prodName;
        return (true);
}


bool CVersion::GetProductVersion(DWORD & dwVersionMS,
                                      DWORD & dwVersionLS)
{
    VS_FIXEDFILEINFO    *vf;
    DWORD dwSize = 0;
    DWORD dwBytes = ::VerQueryValue(m_fvData, "\\",
                    (void **)&vf, (UINT *) &dwSize);
    if (!dwBytes)
    {
        dwVersionMS = 0;
        dwVersionLS = 0;
        return (false);
    }
    dwVersionMS = vf->dwProductVersionMS;
    dwVersionLS = vf->dwProductVersionLS;
    return (true);
}


bool CVersion::GetFileVersion(DWORD & dwVersionMS,
                                  DWORD & dwVersionLS)
{
    VS_FIXEDFILEINFO    *vf;
    DWORD dwSize = 0;
    DWORD dwBytes = ::VerQueryValue(m_fvData, "\\",
                    (void **)&vf, (UINT *) &dwSize);
    if (!dwBytes)
    {
        dwVersionMS = 0;
        dwVersionLS = 0;
        return (false);
    }
    dwVersionMS = vf->dwFileVersionMS;
    dwVersionLS = vf->dwFileVersionLS;
    return (true);
}


bool CVersion::GetProductVersion(
                                  CString & strProductVersion)
{
char    *prodVer;

    prodVer = GetProductData ("ProductVersion");
    if (prodVer == NULL)
    {
        strProductVersion = _T("");
        return (false);
```

```
    }
    strProductVersion = prodVer;
    return (true);
}


bool CVersion::GetProductCopyright(
                            CString & strProductCopyright)
{
char    *prodName;

    prodName = GetProductData ("LegalCopyright");
    if (prodName == NULL)
    {
        strProductCopyright = _T("");
        return (false);
    }
    strProductCopyright = prodName;
    return (true);
}

bool CVersion::GetProductName(CString & strProductName)
{
char    *prodName;

    prodName = GetProductData ("ProductName");
    if (prodName == NULL)
    {
        strProductName = _T("");
        return (false);
    }
    strProductName = prodName;
    return (true);
}

bool CVersion::GetProductCompanyName(
                            CString & strCompanyName)
{
    char    *prodCompanyName = NULL;
    prodCompanyName = GetProductData ("CompanyName");
    if (prodCompanyName == NULL)
    {
        strCompanyName = _T("");
        return (false);
    }
    strCompanyName = prodCompanyName;
    return (true);
}
```

The functions probably are heavy on repeated code, but I consider ease of use more important than streamlining. If a function isn't available to fetch the version information you need, copy one of the existing functions, and change the call to *GetProductData()* to get the appropriate block.

Now you can put the class to work by modifying the *CAboutDlg* class. First, add *version.h* to the *buttons.h* file, and add a *public* data member of type *CVersion*—name it *m_ver*. In the *InitInstance()* function, add the following line:

```
m_ver.GetFileVersionData ();
```

This will initialize the data in the class object.

Open the about dialog box in the dialog editor. Move the static control that says "Buttons Ver 1.0" up near the top of the dialog box. Move the other static control down a bit, and expand it so that it will hold two lines of text. Add a third static control between them. Delete all the text in the static controls, and give them unique resource IDs: *IDC_STATIC_PROGNAME*, *IDC_STATIC_BUILD*, and *IDC_STATIC_COPYRIGHT*. It should look like the image at the left in Figure 742 when you have done this (the borders were added temporarily to show the location of the controls).

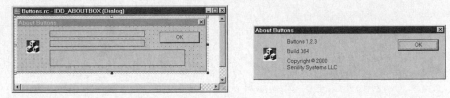

Figure 742   The left image shows the About dialog box in the dialog box editor.
At right is the finished dialog box when it appears on the screen.

Enter the ClassWizard, and select the *CAboutDlg* class (remember that this class is in the same file as the application class, so make sure that the proper class is selected). Add member variables for the static controls. The variable type is *CString*—name them *m_Copyright*, *m_ProgName*, and *m_Build*. Add the following code to the class constructor. It probably would be better to add the virtual function *OnInitDialog()* rather than place this code in the constructor, and you might consider that in real applications.

```
CAboutDlg::CAboutDlg() : CDialog(CAboutDlg::IDD)
{
    CButtonsApp *app = (CButtonsApp *) AfxGetApp();
    CString strName;
    CString strCopyright;
    app->m_ver.GetProductCopyright(strCopyright);
    app->m_ver.GetProductCompanyName (strName);
    m_Copyright.Format ("%s\n%s", (LPCSTR) strCopyright,
                                  (LPCSTR) strName);
    DWORD   dwVersionMS, dwVersionLS;
    app->m_ver.GetProductFileDescription (strName);
    app->m_ver.GetFileVersion (dwVersionMS, dwVersionLS);
    m_ProgName.Format ("%s %d.%d", (LPCSTR) strName,
                dwVersionMS >> 16, dwVersionMS & 0xffff);
    m_Build.Format ("Build %d", dwVersionLS & 0xffff);
    //{{AFX_DATA_INIT(CAboutDlg)
    //}}AFX_DATA_INIT
}
```

You could add the revision level digit by changing the *m_ProgName* initialization to the following:

```
m_ProgName.Format ("%s %d.%d.&d", (LPCSTR) strName,
                dwVersionMS >> 16,
                dwVersionMS & 0xffff,
                dwVersionLS >> 16);
```

The result should be the About box, as shown in the image to the right in Figure 742. Make some changes in the version resource to see how they are reflected in the About box. As an enhancement, you could modify the class to return the major, minor, revision, and build values in separate variables to avoid the bitwise operations when you add them to the dialog box.

743. *Keeping Your Version Information Up to Date*

If your application will be used by other people or will be released on an unsuspecting world, it's important that you keep the version information up to date. Every time you release a version with a code change, no matter how slight, it should have some identifying information on it for users.

In addition, you should save the code as it is with each release. Commercial software houses use source code control systems in which the programmer "checks out" a program, makes the necessary modifications, and returns the program. A good source code system should allow you to return to any point in the program development. There are a number of such systems on the market.

If you have several versions in the field and a user reports a problem, you could spend a lot of time trying to fix a bug that already has been fixed if you don't know the exact version number. Keep the version control resource up to date, and use the *CVersion* class with the About box. Expand the About box, and display additional information as needed.

744. *Understanding MFC Dialog and Resource Classes*

The Microsoft Foundation Class dialog and resource classes encapsulate the functions of Windows dialog boxes, user interface objects, and common dialog boxes. The base class for the dialog box classes is *CDialog*.

Through *CDialog*, MFC provides access to the Windows Common dialogs. These include the *CFileDialog* class for opening and saving files, *CFontDialog* for selecting fonts and font options, *CColorDialog* for choosing colors, *CPrintDialog* for setting print options and printing documents, and *CFindReplaceDialog* to provide a common interface for searching a document for strings and replacing them.

The user interface classes consist of classes that encapsulate Windows resource objects, such as *CMenu* for menus, *CToolBar* for toolbars, and *CBitmap* for bitmap objects.

745. *Understanding CDialog*

The *CDialog* class incorporates the dialog window class window procedure and other functions and data needed to implement a dialog box. It's the base class for all the common dialog box classes, and virtually every dialog box created in an MFC-based application will have an implementing class derived from *CDialog*.

The class has a large number of virtual functions that may be overridden, and it is rich in message functions. *CDialog* itself is derived from *CWnd*, so it has all the inherited properties and functions of an MFC window, plus those that are endemic to dialog boxes.

After you create a dialog box template using the dialog box editor, you can create a class for it by right clicking on the template and selecting ClassWizard from the menu. The wizard will prompt you through the process of creating a new dialog class.

If you create the dialog class early in the development of a dialog box template, the ClassWizard may be used throughout the process to add member variables for dialog box controls and messages needed to enable the dialog box.

746. *Understanding Data Mapping*

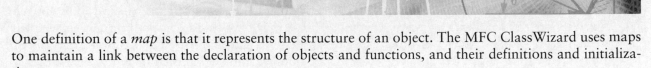

One definition of a *map* is that it represents the structure of an object. The MFC ClassWizard uses maps to maintain a link between the declaration of objects and functions, and their definitions and initializations.

Classes derived from *CDialog* contain several data mapped areas that are used by the ClassWizard to add message map functions, to override virtual functions, and to declare and intialize member variables based on the controls on a dialog box template. These areas all begin with "//{{" and end with "//}}." You should not edit areas between these marks.

The message map area is designated in the definition file (usually the header file) with *//{{AFX_MSG(class name)* and in the implementation file with *//{{AFX_MSG_MAP(class name)*. This is the area where the wizard places the declaration and message map entries for message handlers that you add.

Class member variables added by the wizard are encased in a section beginning with *//{{AFX_DATA(class name)* in the class definition and by *//{{AFX_DATA_INIT(class name)* in the implementation file. In a recordset class, this might be labeled *//AFX_FIELD* in the definition and *//{{AFX_FIELD_INIT* in the source code.

The data exchange section, the area that the wizard uses to map data in the dialog box controls to the member variables, is contained in a section beginning *//{{AFX_DATA_MAP(class name)*. In a dialog box that is used with a recordset object, this section might be labeled with *//{{AFX_FIELD_MAP*.

747. *Understanding Data Exchange*

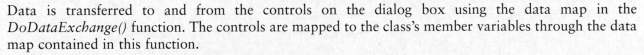

Data is transferred to and from the controls on the dialog box using the data map in the *DoDataExchange()* function. The controls are mapped to the class's member variables through the data map contained in this function.

You can call *DoDataExchange()* directly, but it's far easier to let the *CWnd* class function *UpdateData()* do the work for you. When you call *UpdateData()*, the function prepares a *CDataExchange* object that specifies whether data is being transferred to the controls or being received from the control. If you pass *UpdateData()* a *TRUE* argument, data is read from the controls and placed in the class data members. If you pass it a *FALSE* argument, the reverse transfer takes place.

Essentially, *DoDataExchange()* is the dialog box equivalent of the *Serialize()* function in a document. The class contains a member variable, *m_bSaveAndValidate*, that determines the direction of data flow.

The data exchange components also will convert control information to something usable by the program. For example, if you have a group of radio buttons, the exchange functions will convert the information to a number that serves as an index to the radio button that was selected.

You can add your own code to this function, but it should be outside the data map area used by the ClassWizard.

748. Understanding Data Validation

In addition to exchanging data with the dialog box controls, the *DoDataExchange()* validates the data if you've set limits on the information that may be entered. The validation procedures are prefixed with *DDV_*.

For example, if you've set up an edit box to be a numerical field, you can set the lower and upper boundaries on the value that a user may enter. The fields for doing this are at the bottom of the ClassWizard Member Variables page. When the user presses the OK button, or if your function calls *UpdateData()*, the field will be validated to make sure that the number falls within the range. If not, the user is told of the violation through a message box, and the dialog box won't close.

The fields on the ClassWizard page will change depending upon the data type. If the control returns a string, you can set the maximum number of characters that the user may enter. This prevents having to deal with overruns for structure or database member variables.

If your data requires additional validation beyond the capabilities of the basic validators, you can call your own functions—even use the data validation functions—but you should do so outside the data map area.

749. Embedding a Data Class into Your Dialog Class

Conventional practice holds that it's OK to declare the data members of a dialog class *public* so that they can be accessed by the function in which the dialog box was created even after the dialog box closes. This practice, however common, violates the C++ concept of having a class hoard its data members in a *private* section.

There are a couple of ways by which you can give and retrieve data from a dialog box class and still preserve the sanctity of the data members. First, you can pass pointers or references to the variables that you want set when the dialog box closes. This can be done through the constructor or the *DoModal()* member function. This works for dialog boxes with only a very few controls that need to receive and return data. It gets very clumsy, very fast.

Alternatively, you can declare a data subclass within the definition of the dialog box class. This gives you a transfer mechanism that is accessible to both the class object and the function where the dialog box was created. To be consistent, you can use the same class name across all dialog boxes that use a data subclass. If you use a common name, such as *CData*, you'll always recognize objects of that type as having the same purpose.

To embed a data class, somewhere in your dialog box class definition, just define the embedded class. Later in the definition, declare a reference to an object of this class. You then need to modify the constructor to accept a parameter that is a reference to a data class object.

Add a dialog box to the Buttons project from Tip 738, "Adding and Removing Toolbar Buttons." You don't have to make it complicated—just an edit box, maybe a check box, and some radio buttons, as shown in Figure 749. After you add the controls, select the Tab Order item from the Layout menu, and then click on the Edit box, the check box, the radio buttons (in the order they appear), the OK button, and the Cancel button. Press Return to exit the tab order. Select the first radio box, and make sure that it has the Group style checked—also make sure that the others do not have this checked. Select the OK button, and check the Group style. Setting the tab order and the group boxes, the radio controls will act as a single control, and their result can be contained in a single variable. Give all the controls unique identifiers.

Create a class for the dialog box. The sample has an ID of *IDD_RESUMEDLG* and a title of "Pet Resume," so *CResumeDlg* would be a good choice for the name. After the class has been created and you've entered the ClassWizard, add a message handler for the *WM_INITDIALOG* message. *Do not* add variables for the controls.

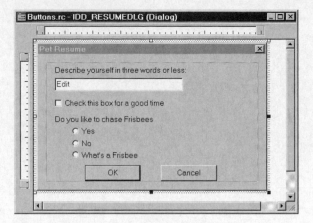

Figure 749   The dialog box added to the Buttons project in Tip 738

At the top of the dialog box class definition, add a *CData* class definition, as shown in the following code. This must be defined *before* the constructor is declared, and it should be in a *public* section. Also add a *private* data member reference of this class named *m_Data*, and change the constructor to add a reference parameter of type *CData* to it. Your class definition should look like the following:

```
// ResumeDlg.h : header file
//

/////////////////////////////////////////////////////////////
// CResumeDlg dialog

class CResumeDlg : public Cdialog
{
public:
    class Cdata
    {
    public:
        CString m_Title;
        CString m_Description;
        int     m_Frisbees;
        BOOL    m_GoodTime;
    };

// Construction
    // standard constructor
    CResumeDlg(CData & data, CWnd* pParent = NULL);

// Dialog Data
    //{{AFX_DATA(CResumeDlg)
    enum { IDD = IDD_RESUMEDLG };
    //}}AFX_DATA


// Overrides
    // ClassWizard generated virtual function overrides
    //{{AFX_VIRTUAL(CResumeDlg)
    protected:
// DDX/DDV support
    virtual void DoDataExchange(CDataExchange* pDX);
```

```
    //}}AFX_VIRTUAL

// Implementation
protected:

    // Generated message map functions
    //{{AFX_MSG(CResumeDlg)
    virtual BOOL OnInitDialog();
    //}}AFX_MSG
    CData   &m_Data;

    DECLARE_MESSAGE_MAP()
};
```

Next, you need to modify the definition for the constructor to pass the reference parameter to the *m_Data* member variable. When this is done, an instance of the class can't be declared until after an instance of the *CData* member class has been declared. The *CData* object is the key to this operation.

Why the emphasis earlier on not adding variables for the controls? Well, for one, you already added them. Referring back to Tip 747, "Understanding Data Exchange," you'll remember that you can add your own data exchange functions to the *DoDataExchange()* function, which the ClassWizard has thoughtfully provided. Instead of creating additional variables and adding overhead, you can map the controls directly into the data members of the *CData* object as shown in the following code:

```
// ResumeDlg.cpp : implementation file
//

#include "stdafx.h"
#include "Buttons.h"
#include "ResumeDlg.h"

#ifdef _DEBUG
#define new DEBUG_NEW
#undef THIS_FILE
static char THIS_FILE[] = __FILE__;
#endif

/////////////////////////////////////////////////////////////
// CResumeDlg dialog


CResumeDlg::CResumeDlg(CData& data,CWnd* pParent /*=NULL*/)
    : CDialog(CResumeDlg::IDD, pParent), m_Data (data)

{
    //{{AFX_DATA_INIT(CResumeDlg)
    //}}AFX_DATA_INIT
}

void CResumeDlg::DoDataExchange(CDataExchange* pDX)
{
    CDialog::DoDataExchange(pDX);
    //{{AFX_DATA_MAP(CResumeDlg)
    //}}AFX_DATA_MAP
    DDX_Radio(pDX, IDC_YESTOFRISBEES, m_Data.m_Frisbees);
    DDX_Text(pDX, IDC_DESCRIPTION, m_Data.m_Description);
    DDX_Check(pDX, IDC_GOODTIMECHECK, m_Data.m_GoodTime);
}
```

```
BEGIN_MESSAGE_MAP(CResumeDlg, CDialog)
    //{{AFX_MSG_MAP(CResumeDlg)
    //}}AFX_MSG_MAP
END_MESSAGE_MAP()


/////////////////////////////////////////////////////////
// CResumeDlg message handlers

BOOL CResumeDlg::OnInitDialog()
{
    CDialog::OnInitDialog();
    if (!m_Data.m_dataTitle.IsEmpty ())
        SetWindowText (m_Data.m_dataTitle);

// return TRUE unless you set the focus to a control
// EXCEPTION: OCX Property Pages should return FALSE
    return TRUE;
}
```

Now you need to provide some way for the program to get to the dialog box. Add a menu item to the *IDR_MAINFRAME* menu. It's only a test item, so the View menu is a good place. Give the menu item a resource ID of *ID_VIEW_RESUME*. Open the *ButtonsView.cpp* file, and add a message handler for the menu item ID. The code from this function is shown here:

```
/////////////////////////////////////////////////////////
// CButtonsView message handlers

void CButtonsView::OnViewResume()
{
    CResumeDlg::CData data;
    data.m_dataTitle = "Doggie Job Resume";
    data.m_dataDescription = "Darling, droopy, dachshund";
    data.m_dataFrisbees = 0;
    data.m_dataGoodTime = TRUE;
    CResumeDlg rd(data);
    if (rd.DoModal () == IDCANCEL)
        return;
    CString Message;
    Message.Format ("You are %s\n"
                    "You %swant to have a good time\n"
                    "You %s",
                    (LPCSTR) data.m_Description,
                    !data.m_GoodTime ? "don't " : "",
                    data.m_Frisbees ?
                            (data.m_Frisbees == 1
                            ? "don't like to chase Frisbees"
                            : "are hopeless")
                            : "like to chase Frisbees");
    AfxMessageBox (Message);
}
```

To create an instance of the dialog box, you must create an instance of the *CData* class. Initialize the variables, and then declare the dialog box object, passing it a reference to the data object.

Your dialog class doesn't have to initialize anything (well, we did include a variable for the window title), it doesn't have to pass any data back, and you don't have to override *OnOK()*. The View Class function, which is the only function that is concerned with the actual values of the data object members and is where you want to use the data, encapsulates the object, and the dialog class accesses it directly.

When the user clicks the OK button on the dialog box, *CDialog* updates the data object, and the dialog box closes, leaving your function with what it wants: the information that was in the dialog box. If the user pressed the Cancel button, the data object isn't updated, and you don't do anything. Otherwise, you read the data object and display a message box showing the new information.

750. *Overriding* CDialog *Functions*

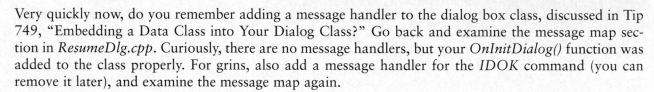

Very quickly now, do you remember adding a message handler to the dialog box class, discussed in Tip 749, "Embedding a Data Class into Your Dialog Class?" Go back and examine the message map section in *ResumeDlg.cpp*. Curiously, there are no message handlers, but your *OnInitDialog()* function was added to the class properly. For grins, also add a message handler for the *IDOK* command (you can remove it later), and examine the message map again.

So where are they?

The ClassWizard has redirected your efforts. Although you *thought* you were adding message handlers, the wizard instead merely added overrides to virtual functions. By default, *CDialog* needs to handle these two messages, but for different reasons.

CDialog handles the *WM_INITDIALOG* message in a function named *HandleInitDialog()*, where it creates the controls on the dialog box and sets the focus to the proper control. In turn, this function eventually calls *OnInitDialog()*, but because this is a virtual function that you have unwittingly overridden, it calls your function. If it didn't work this way, your code would be responsible for creating the controls and setting the focus.

The *CDialog* class also handles the *WM_SETFONT* message this way, casting the *wParam* argument to an *HFONT* value before calling your *OnSetFont()* function. The actual message-handler function is *HandleSetFont()*.

The *CDialog* class also handles the *IDOK* and *IDCANCEL* messages through virtual functions. It intercepts the messages but executes your function because its functions are virtual. The default code in *CDialog::OnOK()* calls *UpdataData(TRUE)* and then calls *EndDialog(IDOK)*, just as your function should, executing any additional commands in between.

751. *Handling Messages from Controls*

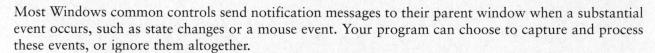

Most Windows common controls send notification messages to their parent window when a substantial event occurs, such as state changes or a mouse event. Your program can choose to capture and process these events, or ignore them altogether.

The messages differ according to the control. A button control, for example, sends only two messages to the dialog box window: *BN_CLICKED* and *BN_DOUBLECLICKED*—or, at least, those are the only two messages listed by the ClassWizard. The button control can send a number of other messages, but many of them are handled by the *CDialog* class. On the other hand, the ClassWizard lists eight messages for an edit control.

To add a message-handler function or a message generated by a control, select the ClassWizard Message Maps page, and then find the resource ID of the control in the Object IDs list. A list of available messages will appear in the Messages box. Select the appropriate message, and click the Add Function button.

In the dialog box that appears, enter the function to handle the message, or accept the default. You can have one function handle a message from more than one control. For example, suppose that your dialog box has a couple of edit boxes on it, *IDC_EDIT1* and *IDC_EDIT2*, and you want to set a flag, *m_bModified*, when the user modifies either of them. Select the *EN_CHANGE* message for the first dialog box, and press Add Function. Enter *OnEditChange()* as the function name. Select the next edit box, and also select the *EN_CHANGE* message. Enter the same function name as for the first edit box, and then add the code to the function. The message map and function would look like the following:

```
BEGIN_MESSAGE_MAP(CResumeDlg, CDialog)
    //{{AFX_MSG_MAP(CResumeDlg)
    ON_EN_CHANGE(IDC_EDIT1, OnEditChange)
    ON_EN_CHANGE(IDC_EDIT2, OnEditChange)
    //}}AFX_MSG_MAP
END_MESSAGE_MAP()

void CResumeDlg::OnEditChange()
{
    m_bModified = true;
}
```

If you have controls for which you derived your own classes to customize their operation, you might see *reflected* messages from these controls in the Messages list. These messages are preceded by an equals sign. Reflected messages are messages sent by the control to the parent window, but then sent back to the control for custom handling. Message map entries for these messages are suffixed by the word "REFLECT." The *CEditEx* class derived from *CEdit* in Tip 484, "Deriving Classes from *CEdit* and *CStatic* to Set Text Attributes," uses the reflected *WM_CTLCOLOR* message to set the background color for the control.

752. *Processing the* IDOK *and* IDCANCEL *Messages*

The *CDialog* class has a function named *EndDialog()*, which sends a message to the dialog box through the Windows API function, also named *EndDialog()*, to terminate the session and return an exit code. The default *IDOK* message handler first updates the class variables by calling *UpdateData(TRUE)* and then calls *EndDialog(IDOK)*. The default *OnCancel()* message handler simply calls *EndDialog(IDCANCEL)*.

As you saw earlier in Tip 750, "Overriding *CDialog* Functions," you can add handlers for messages using the ClassWizard or the Wizard Bar, but the IDE actually adds overrides to the virtual functions. The messages won't appear in the message map of your source code.

If you override the *OnOK()* function, you are responsible for calling *UpdateDate(TRUE)* to retrieve any new information from the dialog box controls. At the end of your handler code, you can call *EndDialog(IDOK)* or the base class *CDialog::OnOK()* function to close the dialog box.

In addition to the Cancel button, the Esc (escape) key causes the dialog box to receive an *IDCANCEL* windows command message. If you don't want the user to be able to close the dialog box using the Esc key, you can override the *OnCancel()* function and have it do nothing; then, you can assign the Cancel button a different ID such as *IDCANCEL2*. You may want to do this if you need to perform special processing before the dialog box closes.

753. *Understanding Property Sheets*

A *property sheet* is a special dialog box that implements a tab control to present tab pages similar to an index card setup. Property sheets often are used to provide setup information for an application or hardware device. The property sheet was introduced with Windows 95 and is very common in the various Windows operating systems.

The property sheet functions are encapsulated in the *CPropertySheet* class, which is similar to *CDialog* and shares many of the same functions. However, it is derived directly from *CWnd* rather than *CDialog*.

A *CPropertySheet* object contains a PROPSHEETHEADER structure used to hold the style, flags, and other control information for the property sheet that normally wouldn't be needed by a dialog box. You can access this structure to modify the property sheet, which you will do in later tips when you start building a property sheet to demonstrate the various Windows common controls.

The property sheet object is the container for one or more special dialog boxes known as *property pages*. These pages are placed on the property sheet by calling the property sheet object's *AddPage()* member function, very much like adding a page to a tab control.

Create a property sheet by adding an MFC class to your project and deriving it from *CPropertySheet*. Create a new project named PropSheet. The sample program on the companion CD uses a single-document interface and derives its view class from *CEditView*. This application won't do anything but display a property sheet (eventually), so it doesn't matter which options you select.

The first thing you do is summon the New Class dialog box. Create a new class named *CPropertyDlg*. From the Base Class box, select CPropertySheet and click the OK button.

On the IDR_MAINFRAME menu, add an item named Property Sheet, and give it a resource ID of *ID_VIEW_PROPERTYSHEET* (the default ID). Open the *CPropSheetView* class source file, and add a message handler for this function. Code it as follows:

```
//////////////////////////////////////////////////////////////
// CPropSheetView message handlers

void CPropSheetView::OnViewPropertysheet()
{
// The property sheet constructor needs a title
    CPropertyDlg pd(_T("PropSheet Application"));
    pd.DoModal ();
}
```

Compile and run the program. Select the Property Sheet item from the View menu. Nothing. Nada. Zip. Zilch. Right? You won't see anything until you add one or more pages to the sheet.

754. *Understanding Property Pages*

The *property page* also is a special dialog box, but it is designed to be placed on a property sheet. A property page contains Windows controls through which a user can enter or modify information needed by an application or hardware device. You can see an example of a multi-page property sheet by right-clicking on the Windows desktop; select Properties from the menu to see the configuration for the system monitor and display card.

You can see your own example by adding a couple of property pages to the project in Tip 753, "Understanding Property Sheets." From the ResourceView panel of the Workshop Window, right-click on any branch of the tree, and select Insert from the menu. When the Insert Resource dialog box appears, click on the "+" sign next to the Dialog entry. Select one of the *IDD_PROPPAGE* entries, and press the OK button. It really doesn't matter whether you select the Large, Medium, or Small option—you can resize it after it appears on the screen. Notice that the new object appears in the Dialog branch of the tree. Get the Properties dialog box, and give it a resource ID of *IDD_PROPPAGE_FRONTPAGE*; set the style to Child and the border to Thin. Make sure that none of the other styles is checked except for the Title Bar on the Styles page and the Disabled box on the More Styles page; the property sheet will take care of enabling and disabling the pages. Give the property page a title on the General page; that will be the text that appears in the tab.

While you're at it, add a second page. When you're finished with this exercise, we'll show you something totally useless but absolutely fascinating. Add some controls to the two pages, or change the "TODO" message so that you can tell the two pages apart when they switch.

Create classes for each of these pages. Make them *CFrontPageDlg* and *CPageTwoDlg*. Now open the *CPropertyDlg* files, both the source and the header. Add *FrontPageDlg.h* and *PageTwoDlg.h* to the list of include files at the top of *PropertyDlg.h* (well, there aren't any yet, so start an include list). Add two member variables, one of each class as shown in the following lines:

```
protected:
    CFrontPageDlg    m_FrontPage;
    CPageTwoDlg      m_PageTwo;
```

Move to the source code file, and add the following two lines to the constructor. Notice that there are two constructors. The way it was set up in Tip 753, you'll use the second constructor because you are giving it a string title rather than a resource ID for an entry in the string title. If you want to play it safe, you can add the code to both:

```
CPropertyDlg::CPropertyDlg(UINT nIDCaption,
                    CWnd* pParentWnd, UINT iSelectPage)
    :CPropertySheet(nIDCaption, pParentWnd, iSelectPage)
{
    AddPage (&m_FrontPage);
    AddPage (&m_PageTwo);
}

CPropertyDlg::CPropertyDlg(LPCTSTR pszCaption,
                    CWnd* pParentWnd, UINT iSelectPage)
    :CPropertySheet(pszCaption, pParentWnd, iSelectPage)
{
    AddPage (&m_FrontPage);
    AddPage (&m_PageTwo);
}
```

If you override the *DoModal()* virtual function, you can add these pages in that function before calling the base class *DoModal()*. Recompile the application and run it. Select the Property Sheet item from the View menu, and you should see more than you did in the last tip. In fact, you should see the property sheet appear with the two pages that you just prepared. Of course, you still have to enter all the code that you would for a dialog box. Life's not *that* easy.

And now for something completely different—or, at least, interesting. Elsewhere it was mentioned that the property sheet sometimes is referred to as a "tabbed dialog box." Actually, a property sheet is nothing more than a *CWnd*-derived pop-up window that contains a tab control. It's basically the container for the button controls and a page manager for the tab control.

There's a function, named *GetTabControl()*, that returns a pointer to the underlying tab control, and you can use it to manipulate the tab control styles and execute its member functions the same as you did in the TabView project in Tip 665, "Creating Other View Classes: *CCtrlView*."

If you design your property pages to leave some room at the bottom, and then curl up the property page window when you create it, you can move your tabs from the top to the bottom of the property sheet. Actually, you could set them on either side as well, but the property sheet class wasn't designed for you to do this (which makes it all the more fun), and it gets confused easily. Override the *OnInitDialog()* function in the *CPropertySheet* class, and add the following code to it:

```
BOOL CPropertyDlg::OnInitDialog()
{
    BOOL bResult = CPropertySheet::OnInitDialog();

    CRect rcItem;
    GetTabControl()->GetItemRect (0, rcItem);
    GetTabControl()->ModifyStyle (0, TCS_BOTTOM, TRUE);
    CRect rcPage;
    m_FrontPage.GetWindowRect (&rcPage);
    rcPage.bottom += 2 * rcItem.bottom;
    ClientToScreen (rcPage);
    m_FrontPage.MoveWindow (rcPage, TRUE);
    SetActivePage (&m_FrontPage);

    return bResult;
}
```

First you get the rectangle for the first tab on the tab control. You'll use this information to shrink the property page a bit. Then modify the tab control style to show the tabs on the bottom of the page. Next, get the rectangle of the *first* page; if you shrink this page, all the others seem to fall in line. You have to shrink the page because when you move the tabs to the bottom, they want to overlap the button controls.

Subtract twice the height of a tab from the bottom of the property page rectangle. This seems to move the tabs safely out of the way of the buttons. Convert the rectangle to screen coordinates, which is required by the *MoveWindow()* function, and move the window, causing it to shrink a bit.

For some reason, the property sheet object seems to lose track of the first page that you placed in the property sheet. Calling *SetActivePage()* with the proper first page re-establishes the natural order of things.

What good is this? For small property sheets, it seems to give a good effect, keeping the tabs and button controls near each other. For large property sheets, the user will move the mouse all over the screen anyway, and it doesn't make much difference. More importantly, it shows how you can mix your own programming style with the underlying controls in the MFC classes.

755. *Understanding the Apply Button*

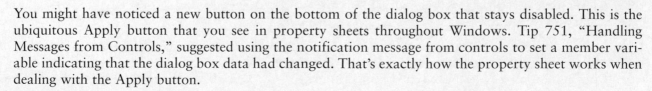

You might have noticed a new button on the bottom of the dialog box that stays disabled. This is the ubiquitous Apply button that you see in property sheets throughout Windows. Tip 751, "Handling Messages from Controls," suggested using the notification message from controls to set a member variable indicating that the dialog box data had changed. That's exactly how the property sheet works when dealing with the Apply button.

CPropertyPage contains a function, *SetModified()*, that you use to set this flag variable. When this is set, the Apply button becomes active. Add an edit control to the first property page, and call it

IDC_DESCRIPTION. Add a message handler for its *EN_CHANGE* message. In the body of this function, add a call to *SetModified()*:

```
/////////////////////////////////////////////////////////
// CFrontPageDlg message handlers

void CFrontPageDlg::OnChangeDescription()
{
    SetModified();
}
```

Compile and run the program, and add some text to the edit box. The first character that you type will light up the Apply button.

The button's ID is *PS_APPLY_NOW*, and its purpose is just what its ID implies. Your code should use this button press to save any new data or apply any changes that the user has made, and then disable the button again.

You catch these button presses by adding the virtual function *OnApply()* to each of your property pages. If a property page successfully applies the changes, it should return *TRUE* from this function, and the Apply button will be disabled again. If any of the property pages return *FALSE*, the Apply button will remain enabled. You should note, however, that if a property page has not been displayed—if the user has not selected that tab, and it is not the default page—its *OnApply()* function will not be called. In the next section on Windows common dialog boxes, you'll use this feature to set the window font and color when the Apply button is pressed.

The property sheet has uses beyond setting properties for a program or a device. You can use it as a compound dialog box to avoid having a huge dialog box on your screen. By grouping related controls and placing them on a common page, your dialog box will have less of an imposing stature when the user faces it.

In this case, you probably don't want the Apply button. The MSDN documentation suggests leaving the button alone and just never enabling it. You can see from Microsoft applications that they don't take their own advice. Personally, if it isn't needed, I prefer to remove it because at some time I'm going to get a call at home asking what *that* button is for.

With the latest release of MFC, it's fairly easy to remove the button. Before, you had to hide or destroy the button and then move the OK and Cancel buttons over to close up the hole. The PROPSHEET-HEADER structure contains a flag that determines whether the button appears. To make the button go away, in the constructor for your property sheet class, add the following line:

```
m_psh.dwFlags |= PSH_NOAPPLYNOW;
```

When you display the property sheet, the Apply button will be gone, and the OK and Cancel buttons will be placed properly.

The default message handler for the OK button will call the *OnApply()* function when the user presses the OK button, even if the Apply button has been removed. This means that you need write your update code only in one place, *OnApply()*, and you never have to add a message handler for the OK button.

756. *Changing the Size of the Property Sheet Base*

When you create a property sheet, the window will size itself to fit the property pages that you added in the constructor, plus add a margin on each side and room on the bottom to hold the button controls.

You've probably seen property sheets that have a wide margin on one side or the other, perhaps to hold a company logo or some other control, as shown in Figure 756. You can do this by adding a message handler for the *WM_CREATE* message and then expanding the window's rectangle in the *OnCreate()* function after the window has been created. (Note that this is the message handler function, *not* the *Create()* virtual function; the two are easy to get confused.)

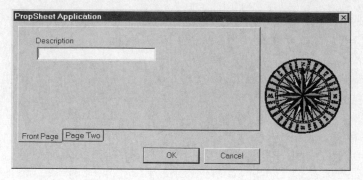

Figure 756   *The right side of the property sheet has been expanded to hold other controls—in this case, a bitmap that might serve as a company logo*

In the sample, you import a bitmap into the resources and give it a resource ID of *IDB_LOGOBMP*. Then add a member variable to the property sheet class of type *CBitmap* and name it *m_LogoBmp*. Load the bitmap in the *OnInitDialog()* function with the following line:

```
m_LogoBmp.LoadBitmap (IDB_LOGOBMP);
```

Add a message handler for the *WM_PAINT* message. You'll need to draw the image yourself. The drawing code should look like the following:

```
void CPropertyDlg::OnPaint()
{
    CPaintDC dc(this); // device context for painting

    CRect rc, rcPage;
//
// Get the client rectangle. This is the area in client
// coordinates of the property sheet.
//
    GetClientRect (rc);
//
// Get the window rectangle for a property page and convert
// it to client coordinates. This will give the offset of
// the page on the property sheet.
//
    m_FrontPage.GetWindowRect (rcPage);
    ScreenToClient (rcPage);
//
// Set the image area to the remaining area on the right.
// Add the left margin to make it match the property page,
// and subtract that much from the right margin. This
// centers the image horizontally.
//
    rc.left = rcPage.right + rcPage.left;
    rc.right -= rcPage.left;

//
// Get the bitmap structure to get the dimensions.
//
    BITMAP Bmp;
```

```
     m_LogoBmp.GetBitmap (&Bmp);
//
// Scale the height so the image isn't distorted.
//
     int nHeight = Bmp.bmHeight * (rc.right - rc.left)
                 / Bmp.bmWidth;
//
// Center the image vertically in the image area.
//
     rc.top = (rc.bottom - rc.top - nHeight) / 2;
     rc.bottom -= rc.top;
//
// Fetch the bitmap into a compatible DC
//
     CDC memDC;
     memDC.CreateCompatibleDC (&dc);
     memDC.SelectObject (&m_LogoBmp);
//
// Draw the image.
     dc.StretchBlt (rc.left, rc.top,
                    rc.right - rc.left, nHeight,
                    &memDC, 0, 0, Bmp.bmWidth, Bmp.bmHeight,
                    SRCCOPY);
// Free the DC we created
     memDC.DeleteDC();
     // TODO: Add your message handler code here

     // Do not call CPropertySheet::OnPaint() for painting messages
}
```

Recompile and run your program. Summon the property sheet. The result should be a properly sized image of your company logo on the right side of the dialog box. It doesn't add any functionality to the property sheet, but it isn't that difficult of a process, and it adds some aesthetic quality to the dialog box. Plus, it looks like you did a lot of work to customize it.

For an enhancement, you could move the image up or down a bit and add some text in this area, perhaps your company's name.

757. _Understanding Wizards_

When you understand property sheets, a wizard is surprisingly easy to implement. A wizard is a special case of the property sheet that you often see in installation programs. Instead of presenting tabs, the dialog box presents you with a series of pages that you step through in sequence using Next and Back buttons.

To create a wizard, you simply go down to your local magic shop and get a wizard gown and a magic wand. Then, whenever a user opens your property sheet, you wave the wand and it becomes a wizard instead.

Another less dramatic way is just to set the wizard flag in the PROPSHEETHEADER structure using the following line in the property sheet class's constructor or _DoModal()_ function:

```
m_psh.dwFlags |= PSH_WIZARD;
```

You also can substitute the following line:

```
SetWizardMode()
```

Now when the user summons the property sheet, "Poof, poof, piffles" (10 points to anyone who remembers that one), you've got a wizard instead of a property sheet.

Now you've got another problem facing you. Where's the OK button? How do you apply any of the data that the user just entered? You won't need the OK button because by calling property sheet functions, you'll change the Next button to a Finish button at the proper time.

758. Understanding the Next, Back, and Finish Buttons

The idea of a wizard is that the user must go through the steps of a multi-page dialog box in a given sequence. This is especially important in operations such as setting up a program. You see a wizard at work when you create new applications in the Visual Studio. You first have to select what type of application you're going to create, and that determines the steps that follow.

One of the advantages of a wizard is that only one panel shows at a time. In the absence of a tab control, the user has no idea how may pages to expect. You could have alternate pages that you step through depending upon the input from the user.

Go back to the PropSheet project and add a third page to it. Give it a resource ID of *IDD_PROP-PAGE_PAGETHREE*, and title it "Page Three." Create a class for it named *CPageThreeDlg*. Open the *CPropertyDlg* files and add a member variable to the class definition named *m_PageThree*. Add the page to the property sheet in the constructor just as you did the first two pages.

Compile and test your program. Your new wizard should have three pages to step through. Go all the way to one end and then back to the front page to verify the sequence. Now you can make it a two-page wizard with the second page, depending upon input from the user. Let's set it up so that if the user doesn't enter anything in the edit box of the front page, the wizard will skip the second page.

The problem with doing this is that you need to intercept the wizard button messages, but there are none listed in the ClassWizard for the property sheet class. So, you'll have to improvise. In case you ever need the information, the IDs for the buttons used with wizards are *ID_WIZNEXT*, *ID_WIZBACK*, *ID_WIZFINISH*, and *IDCANCEL*. You won't find them in the documentation, but you will find them in the *dlgprop.cpp* file in the MFC source directory.

(The handlers for these buttons actually are virtual function members of the *CPropertyPage* class, and Microsoft apparently expects you to handle them on a page-by-page basis. This is fine if your pages are straightforward and contain no dependencies on the data from other pages. However, venturing from the "standard" means that you'll be maintaining code in several different functions and probably in several different files, and you'll probably be calling functions in the property sheet class to handle the pages anyway. By placing these handlers in your *CPropertySheet*-derived class, you keep the paging code in one place and make it easier to maintain. It's a programmer's choice, and this code is offered as an alternative to the Microsoft method.)

Manually add message handlers for the Next and Back buttons to the *CPropertyDlg* class. The declarations in the header file should look like the following:

```
BEGIN_MESSAGE_MAP(CPropertyDlg, CPropertySheet)
    //{{AFX_MSG_MAP(CPropertyDlg)
    //}}AFX_MSG_MAP
    ON_COMMAND(ID_WIZNEXT, OnWizardNext)
```

```
    ON_COMMAND(ID_WIZBACK, OnWizardBack)
END_MESSAGE_MAP()
```

Note that you add them *outside* the ClassWizard's message map area. Add the code to these message handlers as shown here:

```
void CPropertyDlg::OnWizardNext()
{
    if (GetActivePage () == &m_FrontPage)
    {
        m_FrontPage.UpdateData ();
        if (m_FrontPage.m_Description.IsEmpty ())
            SetActivePage (&m_PageThree);
        Else
            SetActivePage (&m_PageTwo);
        return;
    }
    int nIndex = GetActiveIndex ();
    if (nIndex < (GetPageCount () - 1))
        SetActivePage (nIndex + 1);
}

void CPropertyDlg::OnWizardBack()
{
    if (GetActivePage () == &m_PageThree)
    {
        m_FrontPage.UpdateData ();
        if (m_FrontPage.m_Description.IsEmpty ())
            SetActivePage (&m_FrontPage);
        Else
            SetActivePage (&m_PageTwo);
        return;
    }
    int nIndex = GetActiveIndex ();
    if (nIndex > Ø)
        SetActivePage (nIndex - 1);
}
```

Compile and run the program. The second page is virtually invisible to the user until some text is entered in the edit box.

On the first page, you should disable the Back button, as shown in the next tip. You can enable the Finish button on any appropriate page.

Interestingly, there appears to be a bug in the MFC code that causes the Back and Next buttons to send messages even if they are disabled. This code won't respond to such stray messages.

759. *Enabling and Disabling the Next, Back, and Finish Buttons*

Typically in a wizard, you'll disable the Back button on the first page of the wizard and change the Next button to Finish on the last page. To do this, you need to call the *SetWizardButtons()* member function of the property sheet instance from the property page. The problem is that the property page doesn't store an ID for its parent.

You can get to the parent by calling *GetParent()* and downcasting the result, as in the following line:

```
CPropertySheet *pParent = STATIC_DOWNCAST (CPropertySheet,
                                           GetParent ());
```

Add the virtual function *OnSetActive()* to each of the pages on which you want to change the wizard buttons. Typically, this will be the first page, the second page, the last page, and the next-to-last page. The *OnSetActive()* function is called whenever the page comes into view, so you can do any reinitializing in this function as well. In the example, the second and next-to-last pages are the same, but both of them used the same code anyway.

In the class for the first page, make the function read as follows:

```
BOOL CFrontPageDlg::OnSetActive()
{
  CPropertySheet *pParent = STATIC_DOWNCAST (CPropertySheet,
                                             GetParent ());
  pParent->SetWizardButtons (PSWIZB_NEXT);
  return CPropertyPage::OnSetActive();
}
```

This call enables only the Next button. To enable other buttons, you would *OR* the button identifiers in the parameter list. The second and next-to-last page functions would look like the following:

```
BOOL CPageTwoDlg::OnSetActive()
{
  CPropertySheet *pParent = STATIC_DOWNCAST(CPropertySheet,
                                            GetParent ());
  pParent->SetWizardButtons (PSWIZB_NEXT | PSWIZB_BACK);
  return CPropertyPage::OnSetActive();
}
```

Finally, on the last page, you want to dump the Next button altogether and change it to a Finish button. Add the following code to the class for the *last* page of the wizard sequence:

```
BOOL CPageThreeDlg::OnSetActive()
{
  CPropertySheet *pParent = STATIC_DOWNCAST(CPropertySheet,
                                            GetParent ());
  pParent->SetWizardButtons (PSWIZB_BACK | PSWIZB_FINISH);
  return CPropertyPage::OnSetActive();
}
```

This code substitutes the Finish button for the Next button. (Don't bother trying to *OR* in the *PSWIZB_NEXT* button; the wizard accepts only two buttons in addition to the Cancel button, and you'll just get the Finish button.)

Pressing the Finish button terminates the dialog box, and you should catch the press and process the information or start whatever process you need. To do this, you need to add a message handler for the *ID_WIZFINISH* command message in the property sheet class. You won't find it in the ClassWizard or the Wizard bar, so add it the same way that you added handlers for the other buttons. After handling the message, terminate the dialog using *EndDialog(IDOK)* or some other appropriate ID other than *IDOK*.

(The *OnWizardFinish()* is a virtual function member of the *CPropertyPage* class returning type *BOOL*. You also can handle this message by overriding this function for the property page that contains the Finish button. You'll still be responsible for calling *OnUpdateData()* for each page with either method. The method presented here has the advantage of handling the button in a single function, which means that you could place the Finish button on *any* page, depending upon user actions. This method also can access all the wizard pages through member variables. Again, it's a programmer's choice, and you should try both methods to determine which you prefer.)

760. *Some Guidelines for Property Sheets and Wizards*

You've seen that property sheets and wizards are just different faces of the same class, like the push-me/pull-you of MFC. If they are the same, then, how do you decide when to use which?

Generally, if it doesn't matter what order the user processes the pages in, and if none of the pages contains critical data not initialized with defaults, you should use a property sheet. Wizards are much more difficult to code and maintain.

However, if a page contains critical information that must be entered before the other pages can be displayed, then, by all means, use a wizard. You can stop a user from going forward until some critical action is taken by disabling the Next button. To show how this is done, add a check box to the second page of the example project from Tip 757, "Understanding Wizards." Give it a resource ID of *IDC_CHECKTOCONTINUE*, and add a member variable and a message handler for its *BN_CLICKED* message. Add the following code to the function, and modify the *OnSetActive()* function as shown:

```
BOOL CPageTwoDlg::OnSetActive()
{
    CPropertySheet *pParent = STATIC_DOWNCAST
                        (CPropertySheet, GetParent ());
    UpdateData (TRUE);
    if (m_CheckToContinue == TRUE)
        pParent->SetWizardButtons (PSWIZB_NEXT
                            | PSWIZB_BACK);
    else
        pParent->SetWizardButtons (PSWIZB_BACK);
    return CPropertyPage::OnSetActive();
}

void CPageTwoDlg::OnChecktocontinue()
{
    UpdateData (TRUE);
    CPropertySheet *pParent = STATIC_DOWNCAST
                        (CPropertySheet, GetParent ());
    if (m_CheckToContinue == TRUE)
        pParent->SetWizardButtons (PSWIZB_NEXT
                            | PSWIZB_BACK);
    else
        pParent->SetWizardButtons (PSWIZB_BACK);
}
```

Once the box is checked, it will stay checked between visits to the page, but until it is checked, the Next button remains active. As soon as the user checks the box, the button becomes active. Unchecking the box makes the button revert to inactive.

Similarly, you can disable and enable the Back button in the same way.

761. *Understanding Windows Common Dialog Library*

Windows provides a collection of standard dialog boxes that are intended to serve as a common user interface to Windows operations such as selecting fonts, opening and closing files, and searching text. These *common dialog boxes* are part of the Windows API and are supported in the Microsoft Foundation Class by classes derived from *CCommonDialog*.

The dialog boxes are available on all Windows systems through a dynamic link library, *COMDLG32.DLL*. The idea behind common dialog boxes is that if applications use them, the user is presented with a consistent look for these operations. When an application displays a common dialog box, the user enters information or selects items.

Table 761 lists the common dialog boxes, their Windows API functions, their MFC classes, and their uses. None of the common dialog boxes actually performs any actions; these boxes simply deliver the user information back to the application, which is responsible for acting on it.

Windows Function	MFC Class	Purpose
ChooseColor	CColorDialog	Enables the user to select a color or to create a custom color.
ChooseFont	CFontDialog	Enables the user to select a font, a point size, text attributes, and a text color.
GetSaveFileName	CFileDialog	Creates a dialog box that lets the user enter or select a file name and a path for a file save operation.
GetOpenFileName	CFileDialog	Creates a dialog box that lets the user enter or select a file for a file open operation.
PageSetupDlg	CPageSetupDialog	Presents a dialog box that lets the user specify printer options such as margins, paper size, and orientation of the print output (landscape or portrait).
PrintDlg	CPrintDialog	Creates a dialog box that lets the user set up a printer and print a document.
FindText	CFIndReplaceDialog	Creates a modeless dialog box that enables the user to enter a search string and options for searching.
ReplaceText	CFIndReplaceDialog	Creates a modeless dialog box where the user may enter search-and-replace strings and select limited options.

Table 761   Windows common dialog boxes, their windows API functions, and their MFC classes

To allow for some customization of the common dialog boxes, Windows enables you to define a *hook procedure* to intercept and process messages and notifications sent to the common dialog box. Hook procedures are covered in Tip 804, "Understanding Hooks." You also can derive your own classes from the MFC common dialog classes to add functionality.

The common dialog boxes use companion structures to initialize them and to return information selected on the dialog box. The MFC classes incorporate the structure as a member object so that you don't have to declare it separately. The common dialog boxes do not perform any action other than collect information. It is the programmer's responsibility to use this information. The common dialog boxes are easy to use if you have a good understanding of these structures; otherwise, they may be more frustrating than useful.

762. *Understanding the Font Selection Dialog Box*

The Font Selection dialog box presents a common interface to the problem of how to display the system fonts and their attributes and then to allow the user to select among them. The dialog box contains a number of controls to accomplish this.

The Font box is a combo box that lists the available fonts according to the criteria provided when you created the font dialog box. These can be printer fonts, screen fonts, or both, or you can limit them to a subclass of fonts, such as TrueType or a particular character set. The selected or preset face name shows in the edit box of this combo control. The user can enter the name of a font here, and as the font name is typed, the dialog box will attempt to select a matching font name.

The Font Style box allows selection of only the very basic faces and weights of the font—normal, italic, bold, or bold italic. These are relative to the actual face in the font itself. For example, if a font is a light-face font, then the bold version of it might be a font with a normal weight.

The Size box lists common points sizes used for the font. The edit box portion of this combo box enables the user to enter any point size even if it is not listed in the drop-down box.

You can let the user give the font some *effects* in the group to the lower left. These include a single strikethrough line, underline, and a text color. In the rich edit control, the styles bold and italic also are considered effects.

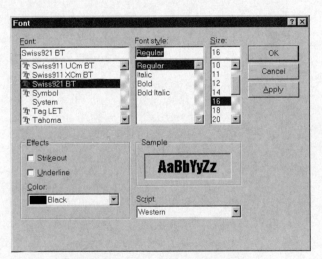

Figure 762   The font selection dialog box

The Script box is used to select from among the available language scripts for the font. The edit box of this control is not editable, and the user may select only from the available scripts. Not all fonts have alternate language scripts.

The Sample box shows how the font will appear based on the selections made in the dialog box.

The Apply button normally doesn't appear on the Font Selection dialog box. You have to add a flag to the *CHOOSEFONT* structure to enable and display this button.

763. *Understanding the* CHOOSEFONT *Structure*

The *CHOOSEFONT* structure is used to initialize the Font Selection dialog box and retrieve information entered by the user after the dialog box closes.

The *minimum* information that you must supply to the dialog box is the size of the *CHOOSEFONT* structure in the *lStructSize* member and a flag indicating what type fonts you want displayed in the *Flags* member. The font types may be screen fonts, printer fonts, or both. If you want printer fonts displayed, you also must provide a handle to a device context for the printer.

The *CHOOSEFONT* members and their uses are detailed in Table 763a.

Member Name	Use
lStructSize	The size of the *CHOOSEFONT* structure. Use the expression *sizeof(CHOOSEFONT)* to initialize this member.
hwndOwner	The handle of the window that owns the dialog box. This member may be NULL.
hDC	The handle to the printer device context. It is required if printer fonts are to be listed; it is ignored otherwise. Selecting printer fonts and setting this to the window DC effectively limits the display to screen fonts.
lpLogFont	A pointer to a *LOGFONT* structure. If you initialize a *LOGFONT* structure and use the *CF_INITTOLOGFONTSTRUCT* flag, the members of the *LOGFONT* structure will be used to set up the dialog box.
iPointSize	When the user closes the dialog box, this member is set to the point size selected by the user. If you've used *CF_INITTOLOGFONTSTRUCT*, the log font's structure's *lfHeight* member contains the size in logical screen points, and this member contains the size in tenths of a point.
Flags	A list of flags used to initialize the dialog box.
rgbColors	Sets the initial text color for the dialog box. If the user selects a different color, it is returned in this member. It is ignored if the *CF_EFFECTS* flag is not set.
lCustData	A pointer to application-defined data. This pointer is passed to the *hook* procedure, which may use it to process application data.
lpfnHook	A pointer to a *hook* procedure used to process messages intended for the dialog box.
lpTemplateName	A pointer to a string that identifies a dialog box template to be used for the standard template. The *hInstance* member must contain the handle of an object in memory that contains the template.
hInstance	If you are using a custom template, this member must contain the handle of an object in memory that contains the template.
lpszStyle	A pointer to a string *buffer* used to initialize the Font Style box in the dialog box. If the user selects a different style, it is returned in this buffer.

Table 763a The CHOOSEFONT *members and their uses with the font selection common dialog box (continued on following page)*

764. *Using* ChooseFont *Directly*

To use the Windows API, you must declare a *CHOOSEFONT* structure and initialize it at least with the size of the structure and a flag describing the font types to display. The *easiest* way to use the structure is to declare a *LOGFONT* structure and initialize its members, and then add the *CF_INITIALIZE-TOLOGFONT* flag to *CHOOSEFONT*. If you use the information returned from the dialog box, you'll need the *LOGFONT* object anyway.

Create a Win32 "Hello, World"–type application. You can name it *ChooseFont*; the name won't be used as a function and thus won't interfere with the API call. Declare two global variables, a *CHOOSEFONT* structure named *cf* and a *LOGFONT* structure named *lf*. In the application's *InitInstance()* function, initialize the structures with the following:

```
memset (&cf, '\Ø', sizeof (CHOOSEFONT));
cf.lStructSize = sizeof (CHOOSEFONT);
cf.Flags = CF_SCREENFONTS | CF_EFFECTS
        | CF_INITTOLOGFONTSTRUCT;
```

You don't need to initialize the *LOGFONT* structure because that will be done by the paint code when the program first starts. In fact, if you initialize it at this point, it will just overwrite the paint code initialization.

Add a drop-down menu to the *IDC_CHOOSEFONT* menu named Dialogs, and put a single item in it named Choose Font. Give this item a resource ID of *ID_DIALOGS_CHOOSEFONT*. Close the menu and go to the *WndProc()* function. In the switch statement for the *WM_COMMAND* message, add a case for *ID_DIALOGS_CHOOSEFONT*. The case statement should look like the following when you are finished:

```
case WM_COMMAND:
    wmId    = LOWORD(wParam);
    wmEvent = HIWORD(wParam);
    // Parse the menu selections:
    switch (wmId)
      {
          case IDM_ABOUT:
             DialogBox(hInst,(LPCTSTR)IDD_ABOUTBOX,hWnd,
                            (DLGPROC)About);
             break;
          case IDM_EXIT:
             DestroyWindow(hWnd);
             break;
          case ID_DIALOGS_CHOOSEFONT:
             cf.hwndOwner = hWnd;
             cf.lpLogFont = &lf;
             ChooseFont (&cf);
             RECT rc;
             GetClientRect (hWnd, &rc);
             InvalidateRect (hWnd, &rc, TRUE);
             break;
          default:
             return DefWindowProc(hWnd, message,
                            wParam, lParam);
      }
      break;
```

Move down to the case statement for the *WM_PAINT* message. Add the following code:

```
case WM_PAINT:
    hdc = BeginPaint(hWnd, &ps);
    if (cf.lpLogFont == NULL)
    {
        GetObject (GetStockObject (SYSTEM_FONT),
                                sizeof (LOGFONT), &lf);
    }
    HFONT font, hOldFont;
    font = CreateFontIndirect (&lf);
    RECT rt;
    hOldFont = (HFONT) SelectObject (hdc, font);
    SetTextColor (hdc, cf.rgbColors);
    GetClientRect(hWnd, &rt);
    DrawText(hdc, szHello, strlen(szHello), &rt, DT_CENTER);
    SelectObject (hdc, hOldFont);
    EndPaint(hWnd, &ps);
    DeleteObject (font);
    break;
```

The first time through the paint code, you fill in the *LOGFONT* object with the system font information, which is the font used by the GDI until you change it. You use this structure to create a font. The first time through, you'll just be duplicating the system font, but as you change the structure through successive calls to *ChooseFont()*, it will start to differ. Change the text color to that specified in the *CHOOSEFONT* structure (initially black). Paint the window, delete the font that you just created, and break from the *switch* statement.

In the handler for *ID_DIALOGS_CHOOSEFONT*, you need to add the handle only to the owner window (actually, you could let that default to NULL without any catastrophic results). Call the *ChooseFont()* function. Any changes that you make in the dialog box will be reflected in the *LOGFONT* and *CHOOSEFONT* structures. When you invalidate the client area, you force another call to the paint code, which redraws the text using the new font information.

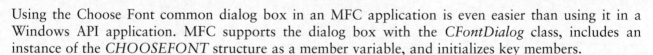

765. *Using the CFontDialog Class in MFC*

Using the Choose Font common dialog box in an MFC application is even easier than using it in a Windows API application. MFC supports the dialog box with the *CFontDialog* class, includes an instance of the *CHOOSEFONT* structure as a member variable, and initializes key members.

Using the information returned by the dialog box, however, isn't nearly as easy. With the API functions, you have a handle to the window for which you want to set the font. In an MFC application, the edit controls don't particularly like to be disturbed. You need to search through the view in the document template objects to find the window or windows that you want to modify. This is particularly true if you're working with multiple-document interface projects or you have more than one document type.

Create an MFC project named Dialogs. Make it a multiple-document interface project and select *CEditView* as the base class for the view. First, you'll want to apply the message handler and select the font from a view object to see how it works. Then you'll move the message handler to the main frame class.

Open the *IDR_DIALOGTYPE* menu in the menu editor. Add a drop-down menu named Dialogs as you did in the previous tip; then add a single item, Choose Font, and give it a resource ID of *ID_DIALOGS_ CHOOSEFONT*.

Add a property sheet class to the project. You can build upon the property sheet by adding an additional page to it later to set the window color. Name the new class *CPropertyDlg* and use *CPropertySheet* as the base class.

Add a small Property Page dialog box to the project. Use the Insert Resource dialog box, and then click on the "+" symbol next to the Dialog item. Select IDD_PROPPAGE_SMALL, and click New. Give the new property page a resource ID of *IDD_PROPPAGE_FONT*, and create a class for it named *CFontPage* derived from *CPropertyPage*. Add a button to select the font, and give it a resource ID of *IDC_FONTBUTTON* and a large static text area to display a sample of the font. Give this static control a resource ID of *IDC_STATIC_SAMPLE*.

Add an entry to the string table named *IDS_SAMPLETEXT*. Enter some text for the entry. This is the text that will be displayed in the sample window, so the content isn't important; add enough to give a good representation of the font.

Add the *CStaticEx* class to the project. If you added it to your gallery, you can select it from there. Otherwise, copy the code from Tip 484, "Deriving Classes from *CEdit* and *CStatic* to Set Text Attributes." In this project, I added a member variable of type *CFont* named *m_Font*. You'll need this to display a sample of the font in the existing window color.

Also add an *m_Font* variable of type *CFont* to the view class, *CDialogsView*. Add a message handler for the *WM_CREATE* message, and add the following code to it. You might recognize some of this from the program editor. In that project, you used a static font to set the same font for each view, but in this project, you will be setting the fonts for each view so that you can initialize it in the *OnCreate()* function. Until you set a font for the view, it will return a *NULL* when the property page attempts to get the current font.

```
int CDialogsView::OnCreate(LPCREATESTRUCT lpCreateStruct)
{
if (CEditView::OnCreate(lpCreateStruct) == -1)
        return -1;
    m_Font.CreatePointFont (120, "Courier New");
//
//  Get a reference to the window's edit control
//
    CEdit& edit = GetEditCtrl ();
//
//  If our font was created successfully, set the
//  edit control's font.
//
    if (m_Font.m_hObject != NULL)
        edit.SetFont (&m_Font);
//
//  The default of 32 dialog units sets the tab stops
//  to eight characters. We want them every four, so
//  set the tab stops at every 16 dialog units.
//
    edit.SetTabStops (16);

    return 0;
}
```

It should be noted here that Microsoft specifically warns against using the edit control to set the tab stops in a view because it also will change the tab stops for the printer output. That's a strange warning because, unless I miss my guess, you want the tab stops for both to be the same.

Also in the view class, add *PropertyDlg.h* to the list of include files in the source file. Add a message handler for the menu item *ID_DIALOGS_CHOOSEFONT*, and code it as follows:

```
/////////////////////////////////////////////////////////
// CDialogsView message handlers
```

```
void CDialogsView::OnDialogsChoosefont()
{
    CPropertyDlg pd (_T("Dialogs"));
    pd.DoModal ();
}
```

Add a member variable *m_TextColor* of type *COLORREF*, and initialize it to 0 in the constructor; then, add a member function as shown next. Override the *WM_CTLCOLOR* reflected message (the one with the equals sign in front of it), and code it as shown.

```
COLORREF CDialogsView::SetTextColor(COLORREF crText)
{
    COLORREF crOld = m_TextColor;
    m_TextColor = crText;
    return (crOld);
}

HBRUSH CDialogsView::CtlColor(CDC* pDC, UINT nCtlColor)
{
    // TODO: Change any attributes of the DC here

    pDC->SetTextColor (m_TextColor);
    return ((HBRUSH) pDC->SelectStockObject (WHITE_BRUSH));
}
```

The *CtlColor()* function first sets the text color in the device context and then returns a white brush, the color of the window's background. If you return the default *NULL*, the edit control's default handler will be called. This would reset the text color to its old value. To do it right, you should have a brush object as a member of the class and should initialize it to the window's background color. This will do for now; in Tip 771, "Using the *CColorDialog* in MFC," you'll use a member brush with this function.

You're finished with the view class, so you can close the files and move to the property sheet class, *CPropertyDlg*. Add a member variable for the Font page named *m_FontPage*. You'll also have to add *FontPage.h* to the list of include files in the class definition file (the header file). Add the page in the constructor as shown:

```
CPropertyDlg::CPropertyDlg(LPCTSTR pszCaption,
                    CWnd* pParentWnd, UINT iSelectPage)
    :CPropertySheet(pszCaption, pParentWnd, iSelectPage)
{
    AddPage (&m_FontPage);
}
```

Close the property sheet files and open the *CFontPage* files. Add a member variable for the sample text control. Name it *m_Sample* and derive it from *CStaticEx*. Add a message handler for the Font Selection button and for the *WM_INITDIALOG* message. Finally, add the virtual function *OnApply()* from the ClassWizard's list. The code for these functions is shown here:

```
/////////////////////////////////////////////////////////
// CFontPage message handlers

void CFontPage::OnFontbutton()
{
    LOGFONT lf;
    m_Sample.m_Font.GetLogFont (&lf);
    CFontDialog fd(&lf);
    fd.m_cf.Flags &= ~CF_NOFACESEL;
    if (fd.DoModal () == IDCANCEL)
```

```
        return;
    m_Sample.m_Font.DeleteObject ();
    m_Sample.m_Font.CreateFontIndirect (&lf);
    m_Sample.SetFont (&m_Sample.m_Font);
    m_Sample.SetTextColor (fd.GetColor());
    SetModified ();
}

BOOL CFontPage::OnInitDialog()
{
    CPropertyPage::OnInitDialog();

    CString strText;
    strText.LoadString (IDS_SAMPLETEXT);
    m_Sample.SetWindowText (strText);

    CMainFrame *frame = STATIC_DOWNCAST(CMainFrame,
                AfxGetApp()->GetMainWnd());
    CDialogsView *view = STATIC_DOWNCAST(CDialogsView,
                frame->GetActiveFrame()->GetActiveView());
    if (view == NULL)
        return (FALSE);
    LOGFONT lf;
    CFont *font = view->GetEditCtrl().GetFont ();
    if (font == NULL)
    {
        font = new CFont;
        font->CreatePointFont (100, "Courier New");
        font->GetLogFont (&lf);
        delete font;
    }
    else
    {
        font->GetLogFont (&lf);
    }
    if (m_Sample.m_Font.m_hObject != NULL)
        m_Sample.m_Font.DeleteObject();
    CWindowDC dc(view);
    COLORREF clr = dc.GetTextColor ();
    m_Sample.SetTextColor (clr);
    m_Sample.m_Font.CreateFontIndirect (&lf);
    m_Sample.SetFont (&m_Sample.m_Font);

    return TRUE;
}

BOOL CFontPage::OnApply()
{
    CMainFrame *frame = STATIC_DOWNCAST(CMainFrame,
                AfxGetApp()->GetMainWnd());
    CDialogsView *view = STATIC_DOWNCAST(CDialogsView,
                frame->GetActiveFrame()->GetActiveView ());
    if (view == NULL)
        return (FALSE);
    LOGFONT lf;
    CFont *font = view->GetEditCtrl().GetFont ();
```

```
      if (font == NULL)
         return (FALSE);
   m_Sample.m_Font.GetLogFont (&lf);
   font->DeleteObject ();
   font->CreateFontIndirect (&lf);
   view->SetFont (font);
   view->SetTextColor (m_Sample.GetTextColor ());
   view->Invalidate ();


   return CPropertyPage::OnApply();
}
```

Compile and run the program. Open a text file such as the *readme.txt* file, and select Choose Font from the Dialogs menu. The sample window should show the text in the current font for the active view. Press the Font Selection button to get the Font Selection dialog box. Choose a different font, and press OK. The sample window should display the new font, but it won't appear in the active view until you press Apply or OK.

766. *Setting Font Parameters in* CFontDialog

The *CFontDialog* class doesn't contain any functions to set the initial font information. To do this, you need to access the member *CHOOSEFONT* structure *m_cf*. The class initializes this structure when you declare an object, so all you have to do is modify the members that you need to change.

If you have an existing *CFont* object, the easiest way is to use the member *GetLogFont()* function to initialize a *LOGFONT* structure and then use it in the *CFileDialog* object by setting the *CF_INIT-TOLOGFONTSTRUCT* flag.

The *m_cf* structure is a public member of *CFileDialog*, so you can set its members directly as described in Tip 763, "Understanding the *CHOOSEFONT* Structure."

767. *Retrieving Font Selection Information*

Although *CFontDialog* contains no member functions for setting the initial font information, it does contain several to retrieve the selected font data after the dialog box has been closed. If you set the flag to initialize the dialog box with a *LOGFONT* structure, the information is duplicated in the *LOG-FONT* object and the member functions.

The *GetCurrentFont()* function will fill in a *LOGFONT* structure with the new font's information. After calling this function, you can use it to call *CFont::CreateFontIndirect()* using a pointer to the *LOG-FONT* object.

Table 767 summarizes the functions to retrieve specific font information.

Function	Retrieves
GetFaceName	A *CString* containing the font name
GetStyleName	A *CString* containing the style (regular, bold, italic, or bold italic)

Table 767 CFontDialog *function to retrieve information about the selected font (continued on following page)*

Function	Retrieves
GetSize	An *int* containing the size in tenths of a point
GetColor	A *COLORREF* containing the selected color
GetWeight	An *int* containing the weight of the font (thin, light, normal, bold, and so on) taken from the font record
IsStrikeOut	A *BOOL* indicating whether the strikeout effect was selected
IsUnderline	A *BOOL* indicating whether the underline effect was selected
IsBold	A *BOOL* indicating whether the selected font has the bold characteristic enabled
IsItalic	A *BOOL* indicating whether the selected font has the italic characteristic enabled

Table 767   CFontDialog function to retrieve information about the selected font (continued from previous page)

768. *Understanding the Color Selection Dialog Box*

The Color Selection common dialog box is a two-part dialog box. In its basic form, it displays a set of 48 basic colors derived from the display device and a set of custom colors that can be set by the user. Together, these form a basic 64-color set. In its expanded form, it also displays a rainbow grid on the right, enabling the user to select a color by setting the saturation and then clicking on the desired color. These colors then may be added to the Custom Color boxes on the left side. You can selectively prohibit the expanded dialog box from being displayed, or you can show the expanded dialog box when it is first displayed.

It's the programmer's responsibility to provide storage for the custom colors. These may be made persistent for the life of the program by making the array static or global. To provide persistence across instances of the program, the custom color data may be placed in the registry or in a configuration file.

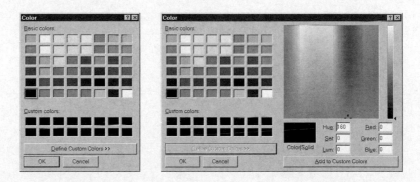

Figure 768   The basic Choose Color common dialog box is shown at left, and the expanded version resulting from pressing the Define Custom Colors button is shown at right

The Choose Color dialog box initializes itself using a *CHOOSECOLOR* structure. At the very minimum, you must initialize the *lStructSize* member to *sizeof(CHOOSECOLOR)* and provide an array of custom colors in the *lpCustColor* member.

769. *Understanding the* **CHOOSECOLOR** *Structure*

The *CHOOSECOLOR* structure supplies information to the *ChooseColor()* function to initialize the Color Selection common dialog box and to return selection information when the user closes the dialog box. This structure is not nearly as large as the *CHOOSEFONT* structure, and its members are summarized in Table 769a.

Member Name	Use
lStructSize	The size of the structure. Initialize this member with *sizeof (CHOOSECOLOR)*.
hwndOwner	Handle to the window that owns the dialog box. This may be NULL if there is no owner.
hInstance	The handle of the module that contains the dialog box template. It is ignored if a custom template is not being used.
rgbResult	On initialization, the color used for the initial color selection. On exit, the color selected by the user.
lpCustColors	Pointer to an array of 16 *COLORREF* variables. These are used to set and hold custom colors. This member must contain a valid pointer.
Flags	Initialization flags, as described in Table 769b.
lpCustData	Pointer to application-defined data. This pointer is given to the hook procedure, if one is used.
lpfnHook	Pointer to a hook procedure used to process messages for the dialog box.
lpTemplate	Pointer to a string that identifies a dialog box template in the module identified in the *hInstance* member. This is ignored if the CC_ENABLETEMPLATE flag is not set.

Table 769a   Member variables of the CHOOSECOLOR *structure and their uses*

The *Flags* member of the *CHOOSECOLOR* structure is used to set options for the dialog box. This is a *DWORD* value that is formed by OR'ing the values together. Table 769b lists the possible values for this member.

Flag	Meaning
CC_ANYCOLOR	Causes the dialog box to display all available colors.
CC_FULLOPEN	Causes the dialog box to display the custom colors section when the dialog box is first displayed.
CC_PREVENTFULLOPEN	Disables the Custom Color button and prevents the user from opening the expanded dialog box.
CC_RGBINIT	Causes the dialog box to use the color in the *rgbResult* member to select an initial color.
CC_SHOWHELP	Causes the dialog box to display a Help button. The help message is sent to the window identified in *hwndOwner*, which must supply the help text.

Table 769b   Flag values used in the Flag *member variable to initialize the color selection dialog box (continued on following page)*

Flag	Meaning
CC_SOLIDCOLOR	Causes the dialog box to display only solid colors from the set of available colors.
CC_ENABLEHOOK	Enables the hook procedure specified in *lpfnHook*.
CC_ENABLETEMPLATE	Specifies that *hInstance* and *lpTemplateName* identify a dialog box template to use instead of the default template.
CC_ENABLETEMPLATEHANDLE	Specifies that *hInstance* identifies a memory block that contains a dialog template to use in place of the default template.

Table 769b Flag values used in the Flag *member variable to initialize the color selection dialog box (continued from previous page)*

770. *Using* ChooseColor *Directly*

To use the Windows API *ChooseColor()* function, you must declare and initialize a *CHOOSECOLOR* structure and an array of 16 *COLORREF* values. The minimum requirements for the structure are its size and a pointer to the color array.

Create a new "Hello, World" Win32 application named ChooseColor, similar to the application that you created for the Font Selection dialog box. Add the Dialogs drop-down menu, and add two items to it, Background Color and Text Color. Give them resource IDs of *ID_DIALOGS_BACKCOLOR* and *ID_DIALOGS_TEXTCOLOR*.

Declare two global variables, as shown here:

```
CHOOSECOLOR     cc;
COLORREF        crCustom[16];
```

Initialize the variables in the *InitInstance()* function using the following code:

```
memset (&cc, '\0', sizeof (CHOOSECOLOR));
memset (crCustom, '\0', sizeof (crCustom));
cc.lStructSize = sizeof (CHOOSECOLOR);
cc.lpCustColors = crCustom;
```

First, add message handlers for the two menu items that you just added. These should be added to the *WM_COMMAND* switch in the *WndProc()* function. The code is shown here. You also need to add to this function three static variables, two *COLORREF* variables to hold the color results and an *HBRUSH* variable to draw the window background.

```
static crFore = RGB(0x0, 0x0, 0x0);
static crBack = RGB(0xff, 0xff, 0xff);
static HBRUSH hBrush = NULL;
// Add the following to the WM_COMMAND message handler:
        case ID_DIALOGS_BACKCOLOR:
            cc.Flags |= CC_RGBINIT | CC_ANYCOLOR;
            cc.rgbResult = crBack;
            if (ChooseColor (&cc) == IDOK)
            {
                crBack = cc.rgbResult;
```

```
                    RECT rc;
                    if (hBrush != NULL)
                    {
                        DeleteObject (hBrush);
                    }
                    hBrush = CreatSolidBrush (crBack);
                    GetClientRect (hWnd, &rc);
                    InvalidateRect (hWnd, &rc, TRUE);
                }
                break;
            case ID_DIALOGS_TEXTCOLOR:
                cc.Flags |= CC_RGBINIT | CC_ANYCOLOR;
                cc.rgbResult = crFore;
                if (ChooseColor (&cc) == IDOK)
                {
                    crFore = cc.rgbResult;
                    RECT rc;
                    GetClientRect (hWnd, &rc);
                    InvalidateRect (hWnd, &rc, TRUE);
                }
                break;
```

Setting the text color in a window is easier than setting the background color. To set the background color, you first need to fill the window area with the brush that you created in the menu item message handler. Then call *SetBkColor()* so that any text that is added subsequently will have the same background color. The code for the *WM_PAINT* message handler takes care of this:

```
case WM_PAINT:
    hdc = BeginPaint(hWnd, &ps);
    // TODO: Add any drawing code here...
    if (hBrush == NULL)

        hBrush = CreateSolidBrush(RGB(0xff,0xff,0xff));
    RECT rt;
    GetClientRect(hWnd, &rt);
    SetTextColor (hdc, crFore);
    FillRect (hdc, &rt, hBrush);
    SetBkColor (hdc, crBack);
    DrawText(hdc, szHello, strlen(szHello), &rt,
                                    DT_CENTER);
    EndPaint(hWnd, &ps);
    break;
```

Compile and run the program. You should be able to set the text color and background color separately. Experiment with the *Flags* member of the *CHOOSECOLOR* structure to see what the effects are.

771. *Using the CColorDialog in MFC*

As with *CFontDialog*, you might find that applying the results of a color dialog box to the controls underlying MFC views is a bit more difficult than using the Color Selection dialog box. In this tip, you'll completely rework the Dialogs project, offloading much of the work to the property sheet class and the views. The property pages will be responsible for handling the font and color dialog boxes and maintaining the sample window, passing the results back to the property sheet, which, when the Apply button is pressed, will pass it back to the view.

This will be more complicated than it needs to be. Both common dialog boxes easily could be handled by the same property page, but the idea of this project is to show how the dialog boxes work, as well as how to use the property sheet class to share data between the property pages.

Create a new Dialogs project similar to the one in Tip 765, "Using the *CFontDialog* Class in MFC." Make it a multi-document interface project using *CEditView* as the base class for the views. Add the Dialogs drop-down menu, and add a single item named Properties to it. The resource ID should be *ID_DIALOG_PROPERTIES*. Add your favorite sample text to the string table under the ID of *IDS_SAMPLETEXT*.

Add two small property pages to the project with resource IDs of *ID_PROPPAGE_FONT* and *ID_PROPPAGE_COLOR*. Add a property sheet class named *CPropertyDlg* to the project, and then add the *CStaticEx* class.

Make the Font property page the same as the page in Tip 765. The Color page is similar and has the same controls, but the button should have a resource ID of *ID_COLORBUTTON*.

With the construction out of the way, open the view class files *DialogsView.cpp* and *DialogsView.h*. Add message handlers for the Properties menu item, the *WM_CREATE* message, and the *WM_CTLCOLOR* reflected message. Add the *OnInitialUpdate()* virtual function. You'll also need functions to set the font, text color, and background color. When you're finished, the header file should look like the following:

```cpp
class CDialogsView : public CEditView
{
protected: // create from serialization only
    CDialogsView();
    DECLARE_DYNCREATE(CDialogsView)

// Attributes
public:
    CDialogsDoc* GetDocument();

// Operations
public:

// Overrides
    // ClassWizard generated virtual function overrides
    //{{AFX_VIRTUAL(CDialogsView)
    public:
    virtual void OnDraw(CDC* pDC);  // overridden to draw
                                    // this view
    virtual BOOL PreCreateWindow(CREATESTRUCT& cs);
    virtual void OnInitialUpdate();
    protected:
    virtual BOOL OnPreparePrinting(CPrintInfo* pInfo);
    virtual void OnBeginPrinting(CDC* pDC,
                                 CPrintInfo* pInfo);
    virtual void OnEndPrinting(CDC* pDC,CPrintInfo* pInfo);
    //}}AFX_VIRTUAL

// Implementation
public:
    BOOL SetFont  (LOGFONT &lf);
    COLORREF SetTextColor(COLORREF clrNew);
    COLORREF SetBackColor(COLORREF clrNew);
    virtual ~CDialogsView();
```

```
#ifdef _DEBUG
    virtual void AssertValid() const;
    virtual void Dump(CDumpContext& dc) const;
#endif

protected:

// Generated message map functions
protected:
    //{{AFX_MSG(CDialogsView)
    afx_msg void OnDialogsProperties();
    afx_msg HBRUSH CtlColor(CDC* pDC, UINT nCtlColor);
    afx_msg int OnCreate(LPCREATESTRUCT lpCreateStruct);
    //}}AFX_MSG
    DECLARE_MESSAGE_MAP()

    COLORREF m_clrBack;
    COLORREF m_clrText;
    CBrush m_Brush;
    CFont m_Font;
};
```

You don't need to add any code to the functions that were added by the MFC AppWizard. The code for the functions that you just added are listed here:

```
/////////////////////////////////////////////////////////////////
// CDialogsView message handlers

void CDialogsView::OnInitialUpdate()
{
    CEditView::OnInitialUpdate();
    CWindowDC dc(&GetEditCtrl());
    m_clrText = dc.GetTextColor ();
    m_clrBack = dc.GetBkColor ();
    m_Brush.CreateSolidBrush (m_clrBack);
}

void CDialogsView::OnDialogsProperties()
{
    CPropertyDlg pd ("View");
    pd.DoModal ();
}

HBRUSH CDialogsView::CtlColor(CDC* pDC, UINT nCtlColor)
{
    pDC->SetTextColor (m_clrText);
    pDC->SetBkColor (m_clrBack);
    return (m_Brush);
}

int CDialogsView::OnCreate(LPCREATESTRUCT lpCreateStruct)
{
    if (CEditView::OnCreate(lpCreateStruct) == -1)
        return -1;
//
//  Get a reference to the window's edit control
//
```

```
    CEdit& edit = GetEditCtrl ();
//
//  Create the font
//
    m_Font.CreatePointFont (120, "Courier New");
//
//  If our font was created successfully, set the
//  edit control's font.
//
    if (m_Font.m_hObject != NULL)
        edit.SetFont (&m_Font);
//
//  The default of 32 dialog units sets the tab stops
//  to eight characters. We want them every four, so
//  set the tab stops at every 16 dialog units.
//
    edit.SetTabStops (16);
    return 0;
}

COLORREF CDialogsView::SetTextColor(COLORREF clrNew)
{
    COLORREF clrOld = m_clrText;
    m_clrText = clrNew;
    return (clrOld);
}

COLORREF CDialogsView::SetBackColor(COLORREF clrNew)
{
    COLORREF clrOld = m_clrBack;
    m_clrBack = clrNew;
//
// Create a new brush. Delete the old if necessary
//
    if (m_Brush.m_hObject != NULL)
        m_Brush.DeleteObject ();
    m_Brush.CreateSolidBrush (m_clrBack);
    return (clrOld);
}

BOOL CDialogsView::SetFont(LOGFONT &lf)
{
//
// If the font already has been created, delete it
//
    if (m_Font.m_hObject != NULL)
        m_Font.DeleteObject ();
//
// Create a new font
//
    if (!m_Font.CreateFontIndirect (&lf))
        return (FALSE);
    CEditView::SetFont (&m_Font);
    return (TRUE);
}
```

Most of the work for the dialog box will be done in the property sheet class. It will store the results of the common dialog operations, and the pages will retrieve the information to set up the sample text box. This will make it possible for the Font page to display the currently selected background color and for the Color page to display the selected font and text color. You'll need to add functions to set and retrieve this information, as well as manually add message handlers for the Apply and OK buttons.

The class definition and the source code for the *CPropertyDlg* class are listed here:

```
#include    "FontPage.h"
#include    "ColorPage.h"

class CDialogsDoc;

/////////////////////////////////////////////////////////
// CpropertyDlg

class CPropertyDlg : public CPropertySheet
{
    DECLARE_DYNAMIC(CPropertyDlg)

// Construction
public:
    CPropertyDlg(UINT nIDCaption, CWnd* pParentWnd = NULL,
                                  UINT iSelectPage = 0);
    CPropertyDlg(LPCTSTR pszCaption,
            CWnd* pParentWnd = NULL, UINT iSelectPage = 0);

// Attributes
public:

// Operations
public:

// Overrides
    // ClassWizard generated virtual function overrides
    //{{AFX_VIRTUAL(CPropertyDlg)
    //}}AFX_VIRTUAL

// Implementation
public:
    BOOL SetFont (LOGFONT &lf);
    CFont * GetFont();
    void SetBackColor (COLORREF clrNew);
    void SetTextColor (COLORREF clrNew);
    COLORREF GetBackColor();
    COLORREF GetTextColor();
    virtual ~CPropertyDlg();

    // Generated message map functions
protected:
    void OnApply();
    void OnOK();
    CFont       m_Font;
    COLORREF    m_clrBack;
    COLORREF    m_clrText;

    //{{AFX_MSG(CPropertyDlg)
```

```cpp
        afx_msg int OnCreate(LPCREATESTRUCT lpCreateStruct);
        //}}AFX_MSG
        DECLARE_MESSAGE_MAP()
        CFontPage   m_FontPage;
        CColorPage  m_ColorPage;

};

/////////////////////////////////////////////////////////////
// PropertyDlg.cpp : implementation file
//

#include "stdafx.h"
#include "Dialogs.h"
#include "PropertyDlg.h"
#include "DialogsView.h"
#include "MainFrm.h"

#ifdef _DEBUG
#define new DEBUG_NEW
#undef THIS_FILE
static char THIS_FILE[] = __FILE__;
#endif

/////////////////////////////////////////////////////////////
// CpropertyDlg

IMPLEMENT_DYNAMIC(CPropertyDlg, CPropertySheet)

CPropertyDlg::CPropertyDlg(UINT nIDCaption,
                        CWnd* pParentWnd, UINT iSelectPage)
    :CPropertySheet(nIDCaption, pParentWnd, iSelectPage)
{
}

CPropertyDlg::CPropertyDlg(LPCTSTR pszCaption,
                        CWnd* pParentWnd, UINT iSelectPage)
    :CPropertySheet(pszCaption, pParentWnd, iSelectPage)
{
    AddPage (&m_FontPage);
    AddPage (&m_ColorPage);
    m_psh.dwFlags |= PSH_PROPTITLE;
}

CPropertyDlg::~CPropertyDlg()
{
}


BEGIN_MESSAGE_MAP(CPropertyDlg, CPropertySheet)
    //{{AFX_MSG_MAP(CPropertyDlg)
    ON_WM_CREATE()
    //}}AFX_MSG_MAP
    ON_COMMAND(ID_APPLY_NOW, OnApply)
    ON_COMMAND(IDOK, OnOK)
```

```
END_MESSAGE_MAP()

/////////////////////////////////////////////////////
// CPropertyDlg message handlers

int CPropertyDlg::OnCreate(LPCREATESTRUCT lpCreateStruct)
{
    if (CPropertySheet::OnCreate(lpCreateStruct) == -1)
        return -1;

    CMainFrame *frame = STATIC_DOWNCAST(CMainFrame,
                AfxGetApp()->GetMainWnd());
    CDialogsView *view = STATIC_DOWNCAST(CDialogsView,
                frame->GetActiveFrame()->GetActiveView ());
    if (view == NULL)
        return (FALSE);
    LOGFONT lf;
    CFont *font = view->GetEditCtrl().GetFont ();
    if (font == NULL)
        return (FALSE);
    font->GetLogFont (&lf);
    m_Font.CreateFontIndirect (&lf);
    CWindowDC dc(view);
    m_clrText = dc.GetTextColor ();
    m_clrBack = dc.GetBkColor ();

    return 0;
}

void CPropertyDlg::OnOK()
{

    OnApply();
    EndDialog (IDOK);
}

void CPropertyDlg::OnApply()
{

    CMainFrame *frame = STATIC_DOWNCAST(CMainFrame,
                AfxGetApp()->GetMainWnd());
    CDialogsView *view = STATIC_DOWNCAST(CDialogsView,
                frame->GetActiveFrame()->GetActiveView());
    if (view == NULL)
        return;
    LOGFONT lf;
    m_Font.GetLogFont (&lf);
    view->SetFont (lf);
    view->SetTextColor (m_clrText);
    view->SetBackColor (m_clrBack);
    m_FontPage.SetModified (FALSE);
    m_ColorPage.SetModified (FALSE);
}

COLORREF CPropertyDlg::GetTextColor()
{
    return (m_clrText);
}
```

```
COLORREF CPropertyDlg::GetBackColor()
{
    return (m_clrBack);
}

void CPropertyDlg::SetTextColor(COLORREF clrNew)
{
    m_clrText = clrNew;
}

void CPropertyDlg::SetBackColor(COLORREF clrNew)
{
    m_clrBack = clrNew;
}

CFont * CPropertyDlg::GetFont()
{
    return (&m_Font);
}

BOOL CPropertyDlg::SetFont(LOGFONT &lf)
{
    if (m_Font.m_hObject != NULL)
        m_Font.DeleteObject ();
    return (m_Font.CreateFontIndirect (&lf));
}
```

The only thing left to code are the property pages. They basically handle the common dialog boxes and their own sample window. The sample window is updated each time that the page becomes active. Thus, any changes in one page are reflected in the other page's sample window.

The property sheet object is so important in this scheme that the pages contain a member variable pointing to it. Other than that, you need to add a variable of type *CStaticEx* for the sample window, message handlers for the button, and the *WM_INITDIALOG* message, and you need to override the virtual function *OnSetActive()*. The following listing is for the Font page header and code:

```
// FontPage.h : header file
//

#include     "staticex.h"

class CPropertyDlg;

/////////////////////////////////////////////////////////
// CFontPage dialog

class CFontPage : public CpropertyPage
{
    DECLARE_DYNCREATE(CFontPage)

// Construction
public:
    CFontPage();
    ~CFontPage();

// Dialog Data
```

```
    //{{AFX_DATA(CFontPage)
    enum { IDD = IDD_PROPPAGE_FONT };
    CStaticEx   m_Sample;
    //}}AFX_DATA


// Overrides
    // ClassWizard generate virtual function overrides
    //{{AFX_VIRTUAL(CFontPage)
    public:
    virtual BOOL OnSetActive();
    protected:
    virtual void DoDataExchange(CDataExchange* pDX);
    //}}AFX_VIRTUAL

// Implementation
protected:
    // Generated message map functions
    //{{AFX_MSG(CFontPage)
    virtual BOOL OnInitDialog();
    afx_msg void OnFontbutton();
    //}}AFX_MSG
    DECLARE_MESSAGE_MAP()

    CPropertyDlg   *m_Papa;

};

//////////////////////////////////////////////////////////
// FontPage.cpp : implementation file
//

#include "stdafx.h"
#include "Dialogs.h"
#include "FontPage.h"
#include   "PropertyDlg.h"

#ifdef _DEBUG
#define new DEBUG_NEW
#undef THIS_FILE
static char THIS_FILE[] = __FILE__;
#endif

//////////////////////////////////////////////////////////
// CFontPage property page

IMPLEMENT_DYNCREATE(CFontPage, CPropertyPage)

CFontPage::CFontPage() : CPropertyPage(CFontPage::IDD)
{
    //{{AFX_DATA_INIT(CFontPage)
        // NOTE: the ClassWizard will add member
        // initialization here
    //}}AFX_DATA_INIT
}
```

```
CFontPage::~CFontPage()
{
}

void CFontPage::DoDataExchange(CDataExchange* pDX)
{
    CPropertyPage::DoDataExchange(pDX);
    //{{AFX_DATA_MAP(CFontPage)
    DDX_Control(pDX, IDC_STATIC_SAMPLE, m_Sample);
    //}}AFX_DATA_MAP
}



BEGIN_MESSAGE_MAP(CFontPage, CPropertyPage)
    //{{AFX_MSG_MAP(CFontPage)
    ON_BN_CLICKED(IDC_FONTBUTTON, OnFontbutton)
    //}}AFX_MSG_MAP
END_MESSAGE_MAP()

/////////////////////////////////////////////////////////
// CFontPage message handlers

BOOL CFontPage::OnInitDialog()
{
    CPropertyPage::OnInitDialog();

    m_Papa = STATIC_DOWNCAST(CPropertyDlg, GetParent());

    CString strText;
    strText.LoadString (IDS_SAMPLETEXT);
    m_Sample.SetWindowText (strText);

    return TRUE;  // return TRUE unless you set the
                  // focus to a control
                  // EXCEPTION: OCX Property Pages
                  // should return FALSE
}

void CFontPage::OnFontbutton()
{
    LOGFONT lf;
    m_Papa->GetFont()->GetLogFont (&lf);
    CFontDialog fd(&lf);
    fd.m_cf.Flags &= ~CF_NOFACESEL;
    fd.m_cf.Flags |= CF_EFFECTS;
    fd.m_cf.rgbColors = m_Papa->GetTextColor ();
    if (fd.DoModal () == IDCANCEL)
        return;
    m_Papa->SetFont (lf);
    m_Papa->SetTextColor (fd.GetColor());
    m_Sample.SetFont (m_Papa->GetFont());
    m_Sample.SetTextColor (fd.GetColor());
    SetModified ();
}

BOOL CFontPage::OnSetActive()
```

```
{
    m_Sample.SetBkgndColor(m_Papa->GetBackColor ());
    m_Sample.SetTextColor (m_Papa->GetTextColor ());
    m_Sample.SetFont (m_Papa->GetFont ());
    return CPropertyPage::OnSetActive();
}
```

The only difference between the code for the Font and the Color pages is in the button handler. In the Color page, the function is named *OnColorButton()* and is listed here:

```
void CColorPage::OnColorbutton()
{
    CColorDialog cd;
    cd.m_cc.rgbResult = m_Papa->GetBackColor ();
    cd.m_cc.Flags |= CC_RGBINIT | CC_ANYCOLOR;
    cd.m_cc.lpCustColors = m_clrCustom;
    if (cd.DoModal () == IDCANCEL)
        return;
    m_Papa->SetBackColor (cd.GetColor ());
    m_Sample.SetBkgndColor (cd.GetColor ());
    SetModified ();
}
```

Compile and run the program. Open a text file such as the *readme.txt* and summon the Properties dialog box. Try changing the font, text color, and background color to see how one sample window tracks the other. Then try the Apply button to impose the results of the dialog box onto the view object.

This program sets the characteristics for the active view only. You could get the application object and use the document manager to sort through the templates, find all the views of a particular type, and set the characteristics for all of them.

772. Retrieving Color Information

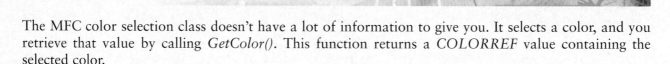

The MFC color selection class doesn't have a lot of information to give you. It selects a color, and you retrieve that value by calling *GetColor()*. This function returns a *COLORREF* value containing the selected color.

Another function, *GetSavedCustomColors()*, gives a pointer to a static array containing the object's internal collection of custom colors.

If you use a hook procedure, you can call the member function *SetColor()* at any time to force the current color selection to a particular value.

773. Saving and Reusing Custom Color Information

You must provide the Color Selection dialog box an array of type *COLORREF* large enough to hold 16 custom colors before you create the dialog box. You can provide a static array within the function that creates the dialog box to provide a consistent collection of custom colors between iterations of the dialog box. Alternatively, you can provide a global array to hold the custom colors.

If you want the colors to be persistent between instances of your program, you'll need to provide some way to write them to a file or to the system registry.

Rather than provide your own array of custom colors, you can call the *GetSavedCustomColors()* function to fill in the *lpCustColors* member of the *CHOOSECOLOR* structure as in the following line:

```
cd.m_cc.lpCustColors = cd.GetSavedCustomColors();
```

This is a static array and retains the custom colors even after the dialog box and the class object have been destroyed.

774. *Understanding the File Selection Dialog Box*

The File Selection dialog box comes in two flavors. There's a dialog box to select a file name to open and another to select a file name to save. The Open dialog box is created with the *GetOpenFileName()* function, and the Save As Dialog box is created by calling the *GetSaveFileName()* function. Both use the *OPENFILENAME* structure to initialize the dialog boxes.

In the Microsoft Foundation Class library, both of these functions and the structure are encapsulated into a single class, the *CFileDialog* class.

Using a *filter* string, these functions let you define sets of files from which the user may select. Users may be allowed to select only a single file or multiple files, depending upon flags set by the programmer.

The dialog boxes use a list control to display file names in a Windows Explorer-style format that is easily recognizable by users.

775. *Understanding the OPENFILENAME Structure*

The *OPENFILENAME* structure contains member variables that provide initialization information to the functions that create the Open and Save As dialog boxes. Both functions use the same structure, and information about the user selection is returned in this structure.

The members of the *OPENFILENAME* structure are summarized in Table 775a.

Member Name	Type	Use
lStructSize	DWORD	The size of this structure. Initialize with *sizeof(OPENFILENAME)*.
hwndOwner	HWND	A handle to the window that owns the dialog box. May be NULL.
hInstance	HINSTANCE	Handle to a module or a memory object that contains a dialog template.
lpstrFilter	LPCTSTR	Pointer to a buffer that contains null-terminated filter strings.

Table 775a OPENFILENAME *structure members, their types and uses (continued on following page)*

Member Name	Type	Use
lpstrCustomFilter	*LPTSTR*	Pointer to a static buffer that holds the filter pattern chosen by the user. The dialog box uses this to select a default pattern on successive calls to the functions.
nMaxCustFilter	*DWORD*	The size in characters of the buffer pointed to by *lpstrCustomFilter*.
nFilterIndex	*DWORD*	Used to return the 1-based index of the filter selected in the File Types box. A zero value indicates the custom filter pointed to by *lpstrCustomFilter*. You may specify an index to select a filter pattern when the dialog box is created.
lpstrFile	*LPTSTR*	On input, a pointer to a buffer to initialize the File Name box. On output, contains the full path of the selected file.
nMaxFile	*DWORD*	The size in characters of the buffer pointed to by *lpstrFile*.
lpstrFileTitle	*LPTSTR*	Pointer to a buffer to receive the file name and extension of the selected file. This returned name will not include the path. May be NULL.
nMaxFileTitle	*DWORD*	The size in characters of the buffer pointed to by *lpstrFileTitle*.
lpstrInitialDir	*LPCTSTR*	A pointer to a string that specifies the initial directory for which files are listed.
lpstrTitle	*LPCTSTR*	Pointer to a string to replace the default title for the dialog box.
Flags	*DWORD*	Values used to initialize the dialog box. See Table 775b.
nFileOffset	*WORD*	The 0-based offset in characters of the file name portion of the path pointed to by *lpstrFile*.
nFileExtension	*WORD*	The 0-based offset in characters of the extension portion of the path pointed to by *lpstrFile*.
lpstrDefExt	*LPCTSTR*	Pointer to a buffer that contains a default extension to append to a file name if the user does not enter an extension.
lCustData	*DWORD*	Application-defined data (may be a pointer). This value is passed to the function identified in the *lpfnHook* member.
lpfnHook	*LPOFNHOOKPROC*	Pointer to a hook procedure.
lpTemplateName	*LPCTSTR*	Pointer to a string containing a dialog template resource.

Table 775a OPENFILENAME *structure members, their types and uses (continued from previous page)*

The *OPENFILENAME* structure is rich in flags that may be used to initialize the dialog boxes. The *Flags* member for this structure is bidirectional. On input, the functions read the flags to initialize dialog box controls; on output, the functions set the flags to indicate user input.

The flags, summarized in Table 775b, are formed by logically *OR*'ing the values.

Flag	*Meaning*
OFN_ALLOWMULTISELECT	Enables the user to select more than one file name.
OFN_CREATEPROMPT	If the user enters the name of a file that does not exist, prompts the user for permission to create the file.
OFN_ENABLEHOOK	Enables the use of a hook function.
OFN_ENABLESIZING	If a hook procedure is provided, allows the dialog box to be resized.
OFN_ENABLETEMPLATE	Specifies that *hInstance* contains the handle of a module containing the template specified in *lpTemplateName*.
OFN_ENABLETEMPLATEHANDLE	Specifies that *hInstance* is a data block in memory of a dialog template.
OFN_EXPLORER	Specifies that any customizations to the dialog box use Explorer-style methods.
OFN_EXTENSIONDIFFERENT	On output, indicates that the user entered an extension that is different from that pointed to by *lpstrDefExt*.
OFN_FILEMUSTEXIST	Allows the user to enter only the names of existing files. Otherwise, displays a warning message.
OFN_HIDEREADONLY	Hides the Read Only check box.
OFN_READONLY	The Read Only check box is set initially. On output, it indicates the state of the check box.
OFN_NOREADONLYRETURN	On output, indicates that the Read Only check box is not set and that the file is not in a write-protected directory.
OFN_LONGNAMES	Causes old-style dialog boxes to display long file names. Explorer-style boxes always use long file names.
OFN_NOLONGNAMES	For old-style dialog boxes, only short file names are used.
OFN_NOCHANGEDIR	On output, restores the current directory to its original value if the user changed directories.
OFN_NODEREFERENCELINKS	For a shortcut file, specifies the return path is to the shortcut file, not to the file referenced by the shortcut.
OFN_NONETWORKBUTTON	Hides and disables the Network button.
OFN_NOTESTFILECREATE	The file is not created before the dialog box closes. No checking is performed for disk space, write protection, open drive door, or network restrictions.

Table 775b   The OPENFILENAME *flags and their meanings (continued on following page)*

Flag	Meaning
OFN_NOVALIDATE	The dialog box allows invalid characters in the returned file name.
OFN_OVERWRITEPROMPT	For a Save As dialog box, a warning box is displayed if the file already exists, and the user must confirm permission to overwrite the file.
OFN_PATHMUSTEXIST	Allows the user to enter only valid paths and file names. Otherwise, displays a warning prompt.
OFN_SHAREAWARE	If the file cannot be opened because of a network sharing violation, the error is ignored and the selected file name is returned.
OFN_SHOWHELP	Displays the Help button. The help message is sent to the window identified in *hwndOwner*, which is responsible for displaying the help message.

Table 775b   The OPENFILENAME *flags and their meanings (continued from previous page)*

776. *Using* GetOpenFileName() *and* GetSaveFileName() *Directly*

To use the Windows API *GetOpenFileName()* or *GetSaveFileName()* functions, you must declare and initialize an *OPENFILENAME* structure and then pass a pointer to the structure in the function call. The functions use the same dialog resource and so appear very similar when they appear on the screen.

In this tip, you'll create a Windows API program to open and display a bitmap file in a window. That's a little too simple, however, so you'll reuse this project in Tip 805, "Writing a Hook Procedure," to set up a custom template and a hook procedure to provide a preview window for the bitmap file when it's selected in the dialog box.

Create a Win32 application named *FileOpen*. In the menu, add an Open item and give it a resource ID of *IDM_OPEN*. Open the *FileOpen.cpp* source file and add the following code near the top of the file:

```
struct OPENDATA
{
    HBITMAP hBmp;
    TCHAR szFileName[_MAX_PATH];    // Buffer for file name
    TCHAR szFilePath[_MAX_PATH];    // buffer for file path
};

  BOOL   OpenBmpFile (HWND hWnd, OPENDATA &od);
```

Locate the *WndProc()* function, and find the *switch* statement that handles the *WM_COMMAND* message. You need to add code to handle the *IDM_OPEN* message, which will call a function, *OpenBmpFile()*, to display the File Selection dialog box and load the bitmap, if necessary. Also add a *static* instance of *OPENDATA*. In the *WM_PAINT* case, draw the bitmap to the screen using the *BitBlt()* function. When you're finished, the *WindProc()* code should look like the following:

```
LRESULT CALLBACK WndProc(HWND hWnd, UINT message,
                    WPARAM wParam, LPARAM lParam)
{
```

```c
static OPENDATA od = {NULL, "", ""};
int wmId, wmEvent;
PAINTSTRUCT ps;
HDC hdc;
TCHAR szHello[MAX_LOADSTRING];
LoadString(hInst, IDS_HELLO, szHello, MAX_LOADSTRING);

switch (message)
{
    case WM_COMMAND:
        wmId    = LOWORD(wParam);
        wmEvent = HIWORD(wParam);
        // Parse the menu selections:
        switch (wmId)
        {
            case IDM_ABOUT:
                DialogBox(hInst, (LPCTSTR)IDD_ABOUTBOX,
                                  hWnd, (DLGPROC)About);
                break;
            case IDM_EXIT:
                DestroyWindow(hWnd);
                break;
            case IDM_OPEN:
                if (OpenBmpFile (hWnd, od))
                {
                    if (od.hBmp != NULL)
                        DeleteObject (od.hBmp);
                    od.hBmp = (HBITMAP) LoadImage(NULL,
                            od.szFilePath, IMAGE_BITMAP,
                            0, 0, LR_LOADFROMFILE);
                    RECT rc;
                    GetClientRect (hWnd, &rc);
                    InvalidateRect (hWnd, &rc, TRUE);
                }
                break;
            default:
                return DefWindowProc(hWnd, message,
                                     wParam, lParam);
        }
        break;
    case WM_PAINT:
        hdc = BeginPaint(hWnd, &ps);
        // TODO: Add any drawing code here...
        RECT rc;
        GetClientRect(hWnd, &rc);
        if (od.hBmp != NULL)
        {
            HDC MemDC = CreateCompatibleDC (hdc);
            SelectObject (MemDC, od.hBmp);
            BitBlt (hdc, 0, 0,
                    rc.right - rc.left,
                    rc.bottom - rc.top,
                    MemDC, 0, 0, SRCCOPY);
            DeleteDC (MemDC);
        }
        EndPaint(hWnd, &ps);
```

```
                break;
        case WM_DESTROY:
            if (od.hBmp != NULL)
                DeleteObject (od.hBmp);
            PostQuitMessage(Ø);
            break;
        default:
            return DefWindowProc(hWnd, message, wParam,
                                                 lParam);
    }
    return Ø;
}
```

The *OpenBitmapFile()* does nothing more than declare an instance of the *OPENFILENAME* structure to use in a call to *GetOpenFileName()*. Afterward, it fills in the *OPENDATA* structure that was passed to it and returns to the calling function.

The code listing for *OpenBitmapFile()* is shown here:

```
//
//  FUNCTION: OpenBmpFile(HWND, OPENDATA&)
//
//  PURPOSE:  Summons the Open File common dialog.
//
//  RETURNS:  If successful, the OPENDATA structure
//            contains the selected file name and path.
//
BOOL OpenBmpFile (HWND hWnd, OPENDATA &od)
{
    TCHAR   *szFilter = "Bitmap files (*.bmp)\Ø*.bmp\Ø";
    TCHAR   szFileName[_MAX_PATH];
    TCHAR   szFilePath[_MAX_PATH];
    memset (szFileName, '\Ø', sizeof (szFileName));
    memset (szFilePath, '\Ø', sizeof (szFilePath));
    memset (od.szFileName, '\Ø', sizeof (od.szFileName));
    memset (od.szFilePath, '\Ø', sizeof (od.szFilePath));

    OPENFILENAME    ofn;
// Fill in the OPENFILENAME structure
    ofn.lStructSize       = sizeof(OPENFILENAME);
    ofn.hwndOwner         = hWnd;
    ofn.hInstance         = hInst;
    ofn.lpstrFilter       = szFilter;
    ofn.lpstrCustomFilter = NULL;
    ofn.nMaxCustFilter    = Ø;
    ofn.nFilterIndex      = Ø;
    ofn.lpstrFile         = szFilePath;
    ofn.nMaxFile          = sizeof (szFilePath);
    ofn.lpstrFileTitle    = szFileName;
    ofn.nMaxFileTitle     = sizeof (szFileName);
//
//  Set the following member to the path where you keep
//  bitmaps. The Common\graphics\bitmaps directory where
//  you installed Visual C++ is a good choice. DO NOT USE
//  forward slashes as a path delimiter. You MUST use
//  backslashes.
//
```

```
ofn.lpstrInitialDir      = NULL;
ofn.lpstrTitle           = _T("Open a Bitmap");
ofn.nFileOffset          = 0;
ofn.nFileExtension       = 0;
ofn.lpstrDefExt          = _T(".bmp");
ofn.lCustData            = 0;
ofn.lCustData            = 0;
ofn.lpfnHook             = NULL;
ofn.lpTemplateName       = 0;
ofn.Flags                = OFN_EXPLORER;

// Call the common dialog function.
if (GetOpenFileName(&ofn))
{
    strcpy (od.szFileName, szFileName);
    strcpy (od.szFilePath, szFilePath);
    return (TRUE);
}
return (FALSE);
}
```

If you've gone through the book tip by tip, you've already seen most of this, and it should be old hat by now. You've got a good base, however, for setting up a program using a custom template and a hook procedure.

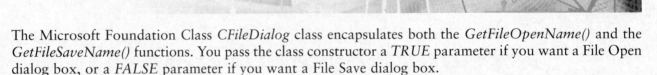

777. *Using the CFileDialog Class in MFC*

The Microsoft Foundation Class *CFileDialog* class encapsulates both the *GetFileOpenName()* and the *GetFileSaveName()* functions. You pass the class constructor a *TRUE* parameter if you want a File Open dialog box, or a *FALSE* parameter if you want a File Save dialog box.

In an MFC application, you generally don't use the File dialog box because the command is handled by the frameworks. However, if you want a single document template to handle several extensions, you need to override the frameworks message handler. The document class usually is a good place, as shown in the code that follows. This code passes *TRUE* to the constructor, meaning that it is for a File Open dialog box. The filter is a compound type that handles a number of graphics formats. This is the same function that you used in the *Graphics* project in Tip 625, "Drawing Graphics Objects in *CView*," while you were exploring the *CView* class.

Compound filters can get confusing if you try to enter everything all on one line. Each filter segment consists of two strings, and a NUL (\0) character must separate them. The first string is the text that will appear on the Files of Type box, and the second part is the filter that the dialog process uses to list files. _T("JPEG Files (*.jpg)\0*.jpg\0") would show "JPEG Files (*.jpg)" in the drop-down box of the control, and the only files that would appear in the file list would be those with a *.jpg* extension. It's like typing *DIR *.JPG*.

To make it easier to read compound filter strings, you can enter each on a separate line, as long as you don't end any lines other than the last one with any punctuation marks. *Don't* use a *CString* object for this type of filter; the last filter item must end with two NUL characters, and *CString* will allow only one at the end. You can build a filter with a *CString* object if you pass it in the constructor. The next tip will show you how.

```
///////////////////////////////////////////////////////
// CGraphicsDoc commands

void CGraphicsDoc::OnFileOpen()
{
    CFileDialog cfd (TRUE);
//
// Set the filter string to a combined string, the one
// string for each file type. This is a very long string.
// Notice that the individual filter types are separated
// by a \0.
    cfd.m_ofn.lpstrFilter =
        _T("Supported Files Types ")
        _T(" (*.bmp;*.gif;*.jpg;*.ico;*.emf;*.wmf;)\0")
        _T("*.bmp;*.gif;*.jpg;*.ico;*.emf;*.wmf;\0")
        _T("Bitmaps (*.bmp)\0*.bmp\0")
        _T("GIF Files (*.gif)\0*.gif\0")
        _T("JPEG Files (*.jpg)\0*.jpg\0")
        _T("Icons (*.ico)\0*.ico\0")
        _T("Enhanced Metafiles (*.emf)\0*.emf\0")
        _T("Windows Metafiles (*.wmf)\0*.wmf\0\0");
    cfd.m_ofn.lpstrTitle   = _T("Open Picture File");
    cfd.m_ofn.nMaxFile     = MAX_PATH;
    if (cfd.DoModal () == IDCANCEL)
        return;
    CDocument::OnNewDocument ();
    CString strPath = cfd.GetPathName();
    AfxGetApp()->OpenDocumentFile (strPath);
}
```

778. Understanding Parameters for the CFileDialog Constructor

Although the sample in the previous tip used only a single parameter, the *CFileDialog* constructor can take up to six parameters. Only the first, a *BOOL* value indicating whether the dialog box is for a file open or a file save, is required. The parameters are summarized in Table 778.

Parameter	Type	Default	Use
bOpenFileDialog	BOOL	None	Flag to indicate Open or Save dialog box
lpszDefExtension	LPCTSTR	NULL	The extension to use for a file if the user does not enter one
lpszFileName	LPCTSTR	NULL	The name that appears initially in the File Name box
dwFlags	DWORD	OFN_HIDEREAD ONLY| OFN_ OVERWRITE PROMPT	Initialization flags
lpszFilter	LPCTSTR	NULL	Filter strings
pParentWnd	CWnd*	NULL	Window that owns the dialog box

Table 778   Default parameters passed to the CFileDialog constructor

You can use a *CString* object for the filter string when you pass it in the constructor if you replace all the NUL characters with a vertical bar. You could have built the dialog box using the following syntax instead of specifying a filter in the structure:

```
CString strFilter =
        _T("Supported Types ")
        _T(" (*.bmp;*.gif;*.jpg;*.ico;*.emf;*.wmf;)|")
        _T("*.bmp;*.gif;*.jpg;*.ico;*.emf;*.wmf;|")
        _T("Bitmaps (*.bmp)|*.bmp|")
        _T("GIF Files (*.gif)|*.gif|")
        _T("JPEG Files (*.jpg)|*.jpg|")
        _T("Icons (*.ico)|*.ico|")
        _T("Enhanced Metafiles (*.emf)|*.emf|")
        _T("Windows Metafiles (*.wmf)|*.wmf||");
CFileDialog cfd (TRUE, NULL, NULL,
        OFN_HIDEREADONLY| OFN_OVERWRITEPROMPT,
        strFilter, NULL);
```

If you pass a parameter in the construction, such as the filter, and also fill in the matching member of the *OPENFILENAME* structure, the structure member will take precedence over the passed parameter.

779. Setting a Default File Name or Extension for the Dialog Box

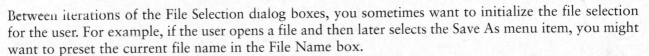

Between iterations of the File Selection dialog boxes, you sometimes want to initialize the file selection for the user. For example, if the user opens a file and then later selects the Save As menu item, you might want to preset the current file name in the File Name box.

You can do this by placing the name of the file that you want to appear in the File Name box in the buffer pointed to by the *lpstrFile* member of the *OPENFILENAME* structure. This can be the full path of the file or just the file name and extension. If you declare the buffer in global space or make it a *static* variable, the last file selected will be placed in the File Name box each time that the user opens the dialog box. In the following code, an additional string variable, *szStartPath*, has been declared, and the full path name of the file is declared static. A static variable is initialized to 0 when it is declared unless you give it another value, so this buffer will retain the name of the last file selected throughout the life of the program. The contents of the file path are used on successive calls to return to the last directory and file selected:

```
TCHAR   szFileName[_MAX_PATH];
static TCHAR   szFilePath[_MAX_PATH];
memset (szFileName, '\0', sizeof (szFileName));
TCHAR *s;
if ((s = strrchr(szFilePath, '\\')) != 0)
{
    ++s;
    strcpy (szFileName, s);
}
ofn.lpstrFile       = szFilePath;
ofn.nMaxFile        = sizeof (szFilePath);
ofn.lpstrFileTitle  = szFileName;
ofn.nMaxFileTitle   = sizeof (szFileName);
```

If your File Selection dialog box contains a compound filter, you may retain the last filter string used and reselect it by declaring a static variable of type *int* and using it for the *nFilterIndex* member of the *OPENFILENAME* structure, as in the following code:

```
    static int nFilter;
    ofn.nFilterIndex = nFilter;
```

When the user closes the dialog box, retrieve the filter index and save it in the *nFilter* variable.

```
if (GetOpenFileName(&ofn))
    {
        nFilter = ofn.nFilterIndex;
        return (TRUE);
    }
```

The filter index is 1-based. The 0 index value is used to indicate a custom filter, as described in the next tip. Tricks such as this are easily accomplished and make life a lot easier for the user.

When using the MFC *CFileDialog* class, you can specify a file name either as the third parameter to the constructor or in the *m_ofn* member structure. If you specify it in both places, the structure member will be used.

In addition, you may specify a default extension to be added to a file name if the user does not enter it when opening or saving a file. In the sample from Tip 776, "Using *GetOpenFileName()* and *GetSaveFileName()* Directly," it was set to *.bmp* using the following line:

```
ofn.lpstrDefExt       = _T(".bmp");
```

In an MFC application using *CFileDialog*, you can enter this default extension as the second parameter to the object's constructor.

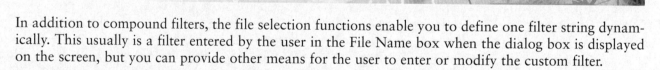

780. *Understanding Custom Filters*

In addition to compound filters, the file selection functions enable you to define one filter string dynamically. This usually is a filter entered by the user in the File Name box when the dialog box is displayed on the screen, but you can provide other means for the user to enter or modify the custom filter.

To define a custom filter, declare a *static* string (Microsoft suggests that it be at least large enough to hold 40 characters). Initialize the string with the text that you want to appear in the File of Type box, a NUL character, and the filter that you want to use as a default. The user then can type a filter in the File Name box, and the dialog procedure will replace the default filter with the one entered by the user. The following code demonstrates this:

```
    static TCHAR szCustFilter [_MAX_PATH] =
                        {"Custom Filter\0*.*"};
    ofn.lpstrCustomFilter = szCustFilter;//NULL;
    ofn.nMaxCustFilter    = sizeof (szCustFilter);
```

This code will display "Custom Filter" in the Files of Type box, and the file list will contain all the files in the directory. If the user then enters "*.cpp" in the File Name box and presses Return, the "*.*" portion of the custom filter will be changed to "*.cpp," and only files with that extension will be listed.

The custom filter is a static variable and will retain the new value the next time the user opens the File Selection dialog box.

781. *Setting a Start Directory for the Dialog Box*

You may have noticed how some programs display files from the last directory used, but your program still is opening the current directory and displaying files from it. This means that the user again must navigate to the last directory to select another file from it.

By slightly modifying the code from Tip 779, "Setting a Default File Name or Extension for the Dialog Box," you can enable this feature for your program. The *OPENFILENAME* structure contains a member, *lpstrInitialDir*, where you may specify the directory to display on startup. You already are saving the full file path in a static variable to initialize the File Name box, and that string also contains the directory information. The following modification copies the file path to a *szStartPath* buffer and then looks for the *last* backslash character. It then sets it to 0 to isolate the path and copies the remainder of the string to the *szFileName* variable:

```
TCHAR   szFileName[_MAX_PATH];
static TCHAR    szFilePath[_MAX_PATH];
TCHAR   szStartPath[_MAX_PATH];
memset (szFileName, '\Ø', sizeof (szFileName));
strcpy (szStartPath, szFilePath);
TCHAR *s;
if ((s = strrchr(szStartPath, '\\')) != Ø)
{
    *s = '\Ø';
    ++s;
    strcpy (szFileName, s);
}
ofn.lpstrFile       = szFilePath;
ofn.nMaxFile        = sizeof (szFilePath);
ofn.lpstrFileTitle  = szFileName;
ofn.nMaxFileTitle   = sizeof (szFileName);
ofn.lpstrInitialDir = szStartPath;
```

Setting the *ofn.lpstrInitialDir* pointer to this string causes the dialog box to return to the last directory selected.

782. *Retrieving File Information*

The *OPENFILENAME* structure carries information both ways. You fill the structure with initialization information, and after the user selects or saves a file and closes the dialog box, the dialog box process fills the structure with information for you.

You can read the structure directly, or, if you are using the MFC *CFileDialog* class, you can use member functions to retrieve the information. The class member functions don't return the information in the same form, however.

The *CFileDialog::GetFileTitle()* function, for example, returns the base name of the file, stripped of the path and extension. If the selected file is *C:\cfiles\visualc++\stuff.txt*, this function would return simply *stuff*. You can get the file extension separately by calling *GetFileExt()*. To get the file name, you would call *GetFileName()*; to get the full path name, you would call *GetFilePath()*.

783. *Understanding the Find and Replace Dialog Boxes*

If you created the Program Editor project beginning with Tip 81, "Creating a Project," one of the things that you probably noticed was that it didn't have text search capability. The projects generated by the MFC AppWizard are really basic, bare-bones projects. For any project involving a text editor, searching and replacing text is a basic operation, but the wizard-generated code doesn't include it for projects based on *CEditView*. If you derive your view from *CRichEditView*, these operations are included, however.

The Windows API supports text searching through the *FindText()* and *ReplaceText()* functions. These functions don't actually do any text searching or replacing. Instead, they summon common dialog boxes and send messages back to your application window, where you implement the actual search and replace operations.

Both of these functions require a pointer to a *FINDREPLACE* structure, and you must call the *RegisterWindowMessage()* function to get the identifier for the message to process the find operation.

The Microsoft Foundation Class encapsulates both the search and replace functions in the *CFindReplaceDialog* class.

784. *Understanding the FINDREPLACE Structure*

The *FINDREPLACE* structure contains the information needed by the *FindText()* and *ReplaceText()* functions. This structure is bidirectional. You initialize it with the basic information that the functions need, and the functions fill in other portions of the structure when they send messages back to your window.

At the very least, you must fill in the size of the structure, the owner window, and give it a buffer to hold the search text and enter the size of the buffer. Unlike other common dialog boxes, the owner window for this structure must not be NULL. It identifies the window to which the search-and-replace messages will be sent.

The structure members are summarized in Table 784a.

Member	Type	Use
lStructSize	DWORD	The size of the structure. Initialize this member with *sizeof(FRINDREPLACE)*.
hwndOwner	HWND	The owner of the window. This is the target for search-and-replace messages and cannot be NULL.
hInstance	HINSTANCE	Handle to a memory object containing a custom dialog template. It may be NULL if the *FR_ENABLETEMPLATE* flag is not set.
Flags	DWORD	Initialization flags. The *FindText()* and *ReplaceText()* functions also use these flags when sending messages back to your window.

Table 784a   The FINDREPLACE *structure members, their type and their uses (continued on following page)*

Member	Type	Use
lpstrFindWhat	*LPTSTR*	A pointer to a string containing the search text. Don't use a local variable here unless you declare it static.
lpstrReplaceWith	*LPTSTR*	A string pointer to a string containing the replacement text.
wFindWhatLen	*WORD*	The size in characters of *lpstrFindWhat*.
wReplaceWithLen	*WORD*	The size in characters of *lpstrReplaceWith*.
lCustData	*LPARAM*	An application-defined value. This may be a pointer cast to a *long*.
lpfnHook	*LPFRHOOKPROC*	The address of a hook procedure.
lpTemplateName	*LPCTSTR*	The name of a custom dialog template, if used by the application.

Table 784a   The FINDREPLACE *structure members, their type and their uses (continued from previous page)*

The Find and Replace dialog boxes normally are created as modeless dialog boxes, and the functions return almost immediately, leaving the dialog box displayed until dispatched by the user. It's important that you declare the structure instance and the string variables so that they don't go out of scope before the dialog box has been terminated by the user. You can declare them as *static*, declare them in global space, or dynamically allocate them using the *new* operator. A good way to handle this is to define another structure that contains a *FINDREPLACE* structure as a member along with the two string variables, and then dynamically allocate memory and place the address in the *lCustData* member. Using automatic variables is almost guaranteed to cause a program crash.

You use the *Flags* member to initialize the dialog box, and it uses the *Flags* member to communicate results of the search or replace operation and user selections to you. Your code should perform the search and replace operations using the information contained in this member; the *FindText()* and *ReplaceText()* don't do these operations for you.

The *Flags* member is summarized in Table 784b.

Flag	Meaning
FR_DIALOGTERM	The dialog box is closing, and the window handle for the dialog box no longer is valid.
FR_DOWN	The radio button for the search direction has been set to Down.
FR_ENABLEHOOK	The dialog box procedure will call the hook function in *lpfnHook* to process messages.
FR_ENABLETEMPLATE	The *lpTemplateName* contains the name of a custom dialog box template in the module identified by the *hInstance* member.
FR_ENABLETEMPLATEHANDLE	The *hInstance* member identifies the memory location of a preloaded dialog box template.
FR_FINDNEXT	The user has pressed the Find Next button.
FR_HIDEUPDOWN	This hides the Search Direction radio buttons.

Table 784b   The flags used in the text to search and replace, and their meanings (continued on following page)

Flag	Meaning
FR_NOUPDOWN	The Search Direction radio buttons are displayed but are disabled initially.
FR_HIDEMATCHCASE	This hides the Match Case check box.
FR_HIDEWHOLEWORD	This hides the Match Whole Word check box.
FR_NOWHOLEWORD	The Match Whole Word check box is displayed but is disabled initially.
FR_MATCHCASE	Hides the Match Case check box.
FR_NOMATCHCASE	The Match Case check box is displayed but is disabled initially.
FR_REPLACE	The user has clicked the Replace button.
FR_REPLACEALL	The user has clicked the Replace All button.
FR_SHOWHELP	The Help button is displayed in the dialog box and sends a *HELPMSGSTRING* message to the window identified in the *hwndOwner* member. The application is responsible for handling the help text.
FR_WHOLEWORD	The Match WholeWord Only box is checked.

Table 784b   *The flags used in the text to search and replace, and their meanings (continued from previous page)*

Many of these flags work in both directions. For example, if you set the *FR_DOWN* flag, the dialog box will display with the direction radio buttons set to Down. When you receive a message from the dialog box, this flag indicates whether the flag is still set or whether the user has changed the selection.

785. *Calling the* FindText() *Function*

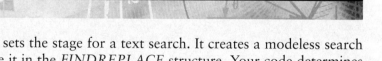

The Windows API function *FindText()* only sets the stage for a text search. It creates a modeless search dialog box based on the values that you give it in the *FINDREPLACE* structure. Your code determines how the search is performed.

To demonstrate this, create a Win32 project named Search. You can create a "Hello, World"–type application. You'll be attaching an edit control to the main window, so the message won't display anyway. You'll need to be able to open a file in the edit control, so this project will include the *GetOpenFileName()* function from the last few previous tips. In Tip 787, "Calling the *ReplaceText()* Function," you'll expand this to include the *GetSaveFileName()* function to save any changes that you make to the file.

In this project, you'll do up and down searches using case-sensitive and non–case-sensitive comparisons. To simplify matters, the Match Whole Word box will be hidden, and your code will search for string fragments that match the search string. That will give you the same search capabilities as *NotePad.exe* and a lot more than most samples we've seen. To enable the whole-word search, you need to check the character before and after the search results to make sure that it isn't an alpha character.

The sample program on the companion CD also borrows from some earlier tips to change the font (so you don't have to look at the euglee system font) and set the default tab stops in the edit control.

The program code is shown here:

```cpp
// Search.cpp : Defines the application entry point.
//

#include "stdafx.h"
#include "resource.h"
#include   <stdio.h>
#include   <commdlg.h>

#define MAX_LOADSTRING 100

struct OPENDATA
{
    TCHAR   szFileName[_MAX_PATH];  // Buffer for file name
    TCHAR   szFilePath[_MAX_PATH];  // buffer for file path
    int     nFilter;
};


// Global Variables:
HINSTANCE hInst;                            // current instance
HWND hWndEdit, hWndMain, hWndSearch;
TCHAR szTitle[MAX_LOADSTRING];          // The title bar text
TCHAR szWindowClass[MAX_LOADSTRING]; // The title bar text
// Forward declarations of functions included in
// this code module:
ATOM                MyRegisterClass(HINSTANCE hInstance);
BOOL                InitInstance(HINSTANCE, int);
LRESULT CALLBACK    WndProc(HWND, UINT, WPARAM, LPARAM);
LRESULT CALLBACK    About(HWND, UINT, WPARAM, LPARAM);
BOOL OpenTextFile (HWND hWnd, OPENDATA &od);
BOOL ReadIn (HWND hEdit, OPENDATA &od);
HWND DoFindReplaceDlg (HWND hWnd, int nStartSel = 0,
                    int nEndSel = 0,
                    bool bReplace = false);
bool DoFindText (HWND hEdit, int &nStart, int &nEnd,
                FINDREPLACE &fr);
bool DoFindNext (HWND hEdit, int &nStart, int &nEnd);
HFONT CreatePointFont (int nPoints, char *szFace, HDC hdc,
                bool bBold = false, bool bItalic = false);
HFONT CreatePointFontIndirect (LOGFONT *lf, HDC hdc);


int APIENTRY WinMain(HINSTANCE hInstance,
                    HINSTANCE hPrevInstance,
                    LPSTR     lpCmdLine,
                    int       nCmdShow)
{
    // TODO: Place code here.
    MSG msg;
    HACCEL hAccelTable;

    // Initialize global strings
    LoadString(hInstance, IDS_APP_TITLE, szTitle,
                                    MAX_LOADSTRING);
    LoadString(hInstance, IDC_SEARCH, szWindowClass,
                                    MAX_LOADSTRING);
    MyRegisterClass(hInstance);
```

```
    // Perform application initialization:
    if (!InitInstance (hInstance, nCmdShow))
    {
        return FALSE;
    }


    hAccelTable = LoadAccelerators(hInstance,
                            (LPCTSTR)IDC_SEARCH);


    // Main message loop:
    while (GetMessage(&msg, NULL, 0, 0))
    {
        if ((hWndSearch == NULL)
          || (!IsDialogMesssage (hWndSearch, &msg))
        {
            if (!TranslateAccelerator(hWndMain,
                                hAccelTable, &msg))
            {
                TranslateMessage(&msg);
                DispatchMessage(&msg);
            }
        }
    }


    return msg.wParam;
}


//
//  FUNCTION: MyRegisterClass()
//
//  PURPOSE: Registers the window class.
//
//  COMMENTS:
//
//    This function and its usage is only necessary if you
//    want this code to be compatible with Win32 systems
//    prior to the 'RegisterClassEx'

//    function that was added to Windows 95. It is important
//    to call this function so that the application will get
//    'well-formed' small icons associated with it.
//
ATOM MyRegisterClass(HINSTANCE hInstance)
{
    WNDCLASSEX wcex;

    wcex.cbSize = sizeof(WNDCLASSEX);

    wcex.style          = CS_HREDRAW | CS_VREDRAW;
    wcex.lpfnWndProc    = (WNDPROC)WndProc;
    wcex.cbClsExtra     = 0;
    wcex.cbWndExtra     = 0;
    wcex.hInstance      = hInstance;
    wcex.hIcon          = LoadIcon(hInstance,
                            (LPCTSTR)IDI_SEARCH);
    wcex.hCursor        = LoadCursor(NULL, IDC_ARROW);
```

```
    wcex.hbrBackground  = (HBRUSH)(COLOR_WINDOW+1);
    wcex.lpszMenuName   = (LPCSTR)IDC_SEARCH;
    wcex.lpszClassName  = szWindowClass;
    wcex.hIconSm        = LoadIcon(wcex.hInstance,
                                  (LPCTSTR)IDI_SMALL);


    return RegisterClassEx(&wcex);
}


//
//   FUNCTION: InitInstance(HANDLE, int)
//
//   PURPOSE: Saves instance handle and creates main window
//
//   COMMENTS:
//
//        Save the instance handle in a global variable and
//        create and display the main program window.
//        (Wow. Isn't that what PURPOSE said?)
BOOL InitInstance(HINSTANCE hInstance, int nCmdShow)
{
    HWND hWnd;

    hInst = hInstance; // Store instance handle in our
                       // global variable

    hWnd = CreateWindow(szWindowClass, szTitle,
                        WS_OVERLAPPEDWINDOW,
                        CW_USEDEFAULT, 0, CW_USEDEFAULT, 0,
                        NULL, NULL, hInstance, NULL);

    if (!hWnd)
    {
        return FALSE;
    }
    hWndMain = hWnd;
    hWndSearch = NULL

    ShowWindow(hWnd, nCmdShow);
    UpdateWindow(hWnd);

    return TRUE;
}


//
//  FUNCTION: WndProc(HWND, unsigned, WORD, LONG)
//
//  PURPOSE:  Processes messages for the main window.
//
//  WM_COMMAND  - Process the application menu
//  WM_PAINT    - Paint the main window
//  WM_DESTROY  - Post a quit message and return
//
//
LRESULT CALLBACK WndProc(HWND hWnd, UINT message,
                         WPARAM wParam, LPARAM lParam)
```

```
{
    static OPENDATA od;
    static int nStart, nEnd;
    static UINT uiFindReplaceMsg;
    static bool bSearchValid = false;
    static HINSTANCE hInstance;
    static HFONT hFont;
    int wmId, wmEvent;
    PAINTSTRUCT ps;
    HDC hdc;

    switch (message)
    {
        case WM_COMMAND:
            wmId    = LOWORD(wParam);
            wmEvent = HIWORD(wParam);
            // Parse the menu selections:
            switch (wmId)
            {
                case IDM_ABOUT:
                    DialogBox(hInst, (LPCTSTR)IDD_ABOUTBOX,
                                hWnd, (DLGPROC)About);
                    break;
                case IDM_EXIT:
                    DestroyWindow(hWnd);
                    break;
                case ID_FILE_OPEN:
                    if (OpenTextFile (hWnd, od))
                        ReadIn (hWndEdit, od);
                    break;
                case ID_SEARCH_FIND:
                    SendMessage (hWndEdit, EM_GETSEL,
                                (WPARAM) &nStart,
                                (LPARAM) &nEnd);
                    hWndSearch = DoFindReplaceDlg (hWnd,
                                    nStart, nEnd, false);
                    bSearchValid = true;
                    break;
                case ID_SEARCH_FINDNEXT:
                    if (bSearchValid)
                    {
                        DoFindNext (hWndEdit, nStart, nEnd);
                    }
                    else
                    {
                        SendMessage (hWndEdit, EM_GETSEL,
                                    (WPARAM) &nStart,
                                    (LPARAM) &nEnd);
                        hWndSearch = DoFindReplaceDlg (hWnd,
                                        nStart, nEnd, false);
                    }
                    break;
                case ID_SEARCH_REPLACE:
//
//  Reserved for search/replace code.
//
```

```
                  break;
         default:
              return DefWindowProc(hWnd, message,
                                       wParam, lParam);
    }
    break;
case WM_INITMENUPOPUP:
    switch (lParam)
    {
        case 1:     // The edit menu
             EnableMenuItem ((HMENU) wParam,
                      ID_EDIT_UNDO,
                       SendMessage (hWndEdit,
                                   EM_CANUNDO,0,0) ?
                       MF_ENABLED : MF_GRAYED);
             int nStart, nEnd;
             SendMessage (hWndEdit, EM_GETSEL,
                    (WPARAM) &nStart,(LPARAM) &nEnd);
             EnableMenuItem ((HMENU) wParam,
                       ID_EDIT_CUT,
                       nStart == nEnd ?
                       MF_GRAYED : MF_ENABLED);
             EnableMenuItem ((HMENU) wParam,
                       ID_EDIT_COPY,
                       nStart == nEnd ?
                       MF_GRAYED : MF_ENABLED);
             EnableMenuItem ((HMENU) wParam,
                     ID_EDIT_PASTE,
                     IsClipboardFormatAvailable(CF_TEXT)
                     ? MF_ENABLED : MF_GRAYED);
             EnableMenuItem ((HMENU) wParam,
                       ID_EDIT_DELETE,
                       nStart == nEnd
                       ? MF_GRAYED : MF_ENABLED);
             EnableMenuItem ((HMENU) wParam,
                       ID_EDIT_SELECTALL,
                       GetWindowTextLength (hWndEdit)
                       ? MF_ENABLED : MF_GRAYED);
             break;
        case 2:         // The Search menu
             EnableMenuItem ((HMENU) wParam,
                       ID_SEARCH_FIND,
                       GetWindowTextLength(hWndEdit) ?
                       MF_ENABLED : MF_GRAYED);
             EnableMenuItem ((HMENU) wParam,
                       ID_SEARCH_FINDNEXT,
                       bSearchValid ?
                       MF_ENABLED : MF_GRAYED);
             EnableMenuItem ((HMENU) wParam,
                       ID_SEARCH_REPLACE,
                       GetWindowTextLength(hWndEdit) ?
                       MF_ENABLED : MF_GRAYED);
             break;
        default:
             break;
    }
```

```
                    break;
          case WM_SETFOCUS:
              SetFocus (hWndEdit);
              break;
          case WM_CREATE:
              hInstance = ((CREATESTRUCT *)lParam)->hInstance;
              uiFindReplaceMsg = RegisterWindowMessage
                                          (FINDMSGSTRING);
              hWndEdit = CreateWindow (_T("edit"), NULL,
                      WS_CHILD | WS_VISIBLE | ES_NOHIDESEL |
                      WS_HSCROLL | WS_VSCROLL |
                      WS_BORDER | ES_MULTILINE |
                      ES_AUTOHSCROLL | ES_AUTOVSCROLL,
                      0, 0, 0, 0, hWnd, (HMENU) IDC_SEARCH,
                      hInst, NULL);
              hdc = GetDC (hWndEdit);
              hFont = CreatePointFont (120, "Courier New",
                                      hdc, true);
              SendMessage (hWndEdit, WM_SETFONT,
                                  (WPARAM) hFont, 0);
              {
                  int nTabs = 16;
                  SendMessage (hWndEdit, EM_SETTABSTOPS,
                              (WPARAM) 1, (LPARAM) &nTabs);
              }
              ReleaseDC (hWndEdit, hdc);
              break;
          case WM_SIZE:
              MoveWindow (hWndEdit, 0, 0, LOWORD (lParam),
                          HIWORD (lParam), TRUE);
              break;
          case WM_PAINT:
              hdc = BeginPaint(hWnd, &ps);
              // TODO: Add any drawing code here...
              RECT rt;
              GetClientRect(hWnd, &rt);
              EndPaint(hWnd, &ps);
              break;
          case WM_DESTROY:
              PostQuitMessage(0);
              DeleteObject (hFont);
              break;
          default:
              if (message == uiFindReplaceMsg)
              {
                  FINDREPLACE *pfr = (FINDREPLACE *) lParam;
                  if (pfr->Flags & FR_DIALOGTERM)
                  {
                      hWndSearch = NULL
                      return (0);
                  }
                  if (pfr->Flags & FR_FINDNEXT)
                  {
                      if (!DoFindText (hWndEdit, nStart,
                                          nEnd, *pfr))
                          break;
```

```
                            if (pfr->Flags & FR_DOWN)
                                nStart = nEnd + 1;
                        }
                        if (pfr->Flags & (FR_REPLACE
                                        | FR_REPLACEALL))
                        {
//
//  Reserved for search/replace code
//
                        }
                        if (pfr->Flags & FR_REPLACEALL)
                        {
//
//  Reserved for search/replace code
//
                        }
                        break;
                }
                return DefWindowProc(hWnd, message,
                                     wParam, lParam);
        }
    return 0;
}


// Message handler for About box.
LRESULT CALLBACK About(HWND hDlg, UINT message,
                       WPARAM wParam, LPARAM lParam)
{
    switch (message)
    {
        case WM_INITDIALOG:
                return TRUE;

        case WM_COMMAND:
            if (LOWORD(wParam) == IDOK
                || LOWORD(wParam) == IDCANCEL)
            {
                EndDialog(hDlg, LOWORD(wParam));
                return TRUE;
            }
            break;
    }
    return FALSE;
}


//
//  FUNCTION: OpenTextFile(HWND, OPENDATA&)
//
//  PURPOSE:  Summons the Open File common dialog box.
//
//  RETURNS:  If successful, the OPENDATA structure
//            contains the selected file name and path.
//
BOOL OpenTextFile (HWND hWnd, OPENDATA &od)
{
    TCHAR  *szFilter = "Text files (*.txt)\0*.txt\0"
```

```
                             "All Files (*.*)\0*.*\0";

    TCHAR   szFileName[_MAX_PATH];
    static TCHAR    szFilePath[_MAX_PATH];
    static TCHAR    szStartPath[_MAX_PATH];
    memset (szFileName, '\0', sizeof (szFileName));
    strcpy (szStartPath, szFilePath);
    TCHAR *s;
    if ((s = strrchr(szStartPath, '\\')) != 0)
    {
        *s = '\0';
        ++s;
        strcpy (szFileName, s);
    }

    memset (od.szFileName, '\0', sizeof (od.szFileName));
    memset (od.szFilePath, '\0', sizeof (od.szFilePath));

    OPENFILENAME    ofn;
    ofn.lStructSize        = sizeof(OPENFILENAME);
    ofn.hwndOwner          = hWnd;
    ofn.hInstance          = hInst;
    ofn.lpstrFilter        = szFilter;
    ofn.lpstrCustomFilter  = NULL;
    ofn.nMaxCustFilter     = 0;
    ofn.nFilterIndex       = od.nFilter;
    ofn.lpstrFile          = szFilePath;
    ofn.nMaxFile           = sizeof (szFilePath);
    ofn.lpstrFileTitle     = szFileName;
    ofn.nMaxFileTitle      = sizeof (szFileName);
//
//  Set the following member to the path where
//  you keep files
//
    ofn.lpstrInitialDir    = szStartPath;
    ofn.lpstrTitle         = _T("Open a File");
    ofn.nFileOffset        = 0;
    ofn.nFileExtension     = 0;
    ofn.lpstrDefExt        = _T(".txt");
    ofn.lCustData          = 0;
    ofn.lCustData          = 0;
    ofn.lpfnHook           = NULL;
    ofn.lpTemplateName     = 0;
    ofn.Flags              = OFN_EXPLORER;

    // Call the common dialog function.
    if (!GetOpenFileName(&ofn))
        return (NULL);
    strcpy (od.szFileName, szFileName);
    strcpy (od.szFilePath, szFilePath);
    od.nFilter = ofn.nFilterIndex;
    return (TRUE);
}


//
//  FUNCTION: ReadIn(HWND, OPENDATA&)
```

```
//
// PURPOSE:  Reads the input file and loads the text
//           into the edit control.
//
// RETURNS:  TRUE if successful, FALSE otherwise.
//
// COMMENTS: This function uses the silly Windows
//           CreateFile function to make it easier to
//           convert to Unicode later. If portability is
//           an issue, change to the C or C++ streams
//           functions (Microsoft will get over it).
//
BOOL ReadIn (HWND hEdit, OPENDATA &od)
{
    HANDLE hFile;
    hFile = CreateFile (od.szFilePath,
                        GENERIC_READ,
                        FILE_SHARE_READ,
                        NULL,
                        OPEN_EXISTING,
                        0,
                        NULL);
    if (hFile == INVALID_HANDLE_VALUE)
        return (false);
    DWORD dwLen = GetFileSize (hFile, NULL);
    TCHAR *buf = new TCHAR [dwLen + 1];
    ReadFile (hFile, buf, dwLen, &dwLen, NULL);
    buf [dwLen] = '\0';
    CloseHandle (hFile);
    SetWindowText (hEdit, buf);
    delete [] buf;
    return (TRUE);
}


//
// These variables must be declared so they won't go
// out of scope when the function exits. Declaring them
// static in global space ensures their scope and that
// they will be initialized to 0.
//
static TCHAR szSearch[48];
static TCHAR szReplace[48];
static FINDREPLACE fr;
//
// FUNCTION: DoFindReplaceDlg(HWND, int, int, bool)
//
// PURPOSE: Initialize the FINDREPLACE structure in
//          preparation for find and/or replace operation.
//
//
// RETURNS:  TRUE if successful, FALSE otherwise.
//
// COMMENTS: If text is selected when this is called,
//           the text is picked up and placed in the
//           search field.
//
```

```
HWND DoFindReplaceDlg (HWND hWnd, int nStartSel,
                       int nEndSel, bool bReplace)
{
    HWND hDlg;
    memset (&fr, '\0', sizeof (FINDREPLACE));
    fr.lStructSize = sizeof (FINDREPLACE);
    fr.hwndOwner = hWnd;
    fr.Flags |= FR_DOWN | FR_HIDEWHOLEWORD;
    if (nStartSel != nEndSel)
    {
        if ((nStartSel - nEndSel) < 48)
        {
            memset (szSearch, '\0', sizeof (szSearch));
            int nLength = GetWindowTextLength (hWndEdit);
            TCHAR *winText = new TCHAR [(nLength + 1) *
                                        sizeof (TCHAR)];
            GetWindowText (hWndEdit, winText, nLength + 1);
            _tcsncpy (szSearch, winText + nStartSel,
                      nEndSel - nStartSel);
            delete [] winText;
        }
    }
    fr.lpstrFindWhat = szSearch;
    fr.lpstrReplaceWith = szReplace;
    fr.wFindWhatLen = sizeof (szReplace);
    if (bReplace)
    {
        fr.Flags |= FR_REPLACE | FR_REPLACEALL;\
        hDlg = ReplaceText (&fr);
    }
    else
        hDlg = FindText (&fr);
    return (hDlg);
}
//
//  FUNCTION: DoFindText(HWND, int &, int &, FINDREPLACE &)
//
//  PURPOSE:  Searches the text beginning at nStart for
//            the next occurrence of a string. nStart and
//            nEnd are set to the offsets of the substring,
//            if found. Scrolls to make sure the found text
//            is at or near the top of the window.
//
//  RETURNS:  true if successful. false otherwise (the real
//            true and false; not the Microsoft version).
//
bool DoFindText (HWND hEdit, int &nStart, int &nEnd,
                                      FINDREPLACE &fr)
{
    int nLength = GetWindowTextLength (hWndEdit);
    TCHAR *winText = new TCHAR [(nLength + 1) *
                                sizeof (TCHAR)];
    GetWindowText (hWndEdit, winText, nLength + 1);
    TCHAR *szFind = new TCHAR [strlen
(fr.lpstrFindWhat)+1];
    strcpy (szFind, fr.lpstrFindWhat);
```

```
    TCHAR *szPos;
//
//  If non-case-sensitive, lowercase the string copies.
//  There is no version of tcsstr that is not
//  case-sensitive
    if (!(fr.Flags & FR_MATCHCASE))
    {
        _tcslwr (winText);
        _tcslwr (szFind);
    }
//
//  If the search is upward, terminate the string and
//  loop to the last occurrence of the find string.
//
    if (!(fr.Flags & FR_DOWN))
    {
        *(winText + nStart - 1) = _T('\0');
        szPos = NULL;
        TCHAR *t = winText;
        TCHAR *s;
        while ((s = _tcsstr (t, szFind)) != NULL)
        {
            szPos = s;
            t = s + strlen (szFind);
            nStart = szPos - winText;
            nEnd = nStart + strlen (fr.lpstrFindWhat);
        }
    }
//
//  If direction is downward, find the next occurrence
//  after the current caret position.
//
    else
    {
        szPos = _tcsstr (winText + nStart, szFind);\
        if (szPos != NULL)
        {
            nStart = szPos - winText;
            nEnd = nStart + strlen (fr.lpstrFindWhat);
        }
    }
//
//  Free the strings. All we need now are the values
//  of the pointers.
//
    delete [] winText;
    delete [] szFind;
    if (szPos == NULL)
    {
      MessageBox(fr.hwndOwner,
                _T("Search string not found"),
                _T("SearchText"), MB_OK);
      return (false);
    }
//
//  Select the text that was found.
```

```
//  Scroll to keep the selection area in the top
//  one or two lines of the visible portion of the
//  file.
//
    SendMessage (hWndEdit, EM_SETSEL, nStart, nEnd);
    SendMessage (hWndEdit, EM_SCROLLCARET, 1, 0);
    int nFirst = SendMessage (hEdit,
                           EM_GETFIRSTVISIBLELINE,0,0);
    int nCur = SendMessage (hEdit, EM_LINEFROMCHAR,
                         nStart, 0);
    if (nFirst != nCur)
    {
        SendMessage (hEdit, EM_LINESCROLL, 0,
                  nCur - nFirst - 1);
    }
    return (true);
}
//
//  FUNCTION: DoFindNext(HWND, int &, int &, FINDREPLACE &)
//
//  PURPOSE:  Implements the Find Next Command button of
//            the FindReplace common dialog box.
//
//  RETURNS:  true if successful. false otherwise.
//
bool DoFindNext (HWND hEdit, int &nStart, int &nEnd)
{
    bool bResult = DoFindText (hEdit, nStart, nEnd, fr);
    if (!bResult )
        return (false);
    nStart = nEnd + 1;
    return (true);
}


//
//  Support functions.
//
//
//  FUNCTION: CreatePointFont(int, char, HDC, bool, bool)
//
//  PURPOSE:  Create a font of a given face using the 10ths
//            of a point value and device context passed.
//            The bold and italic parameters default
//            to false.


//
//  RETURNS:  Handle to the new font, if successful.
//            NULL otherwise.
//
HFONT CreatePointFont (int nPoints, char *szFace, HDC hdc,
                            bool bBold, bool bItalic)
{
LOGFONT lf;

    memset (&lf, '\0', sizeof (LOGFONT));
    lf.lfCharSet = DEFAULT_CHARSET;
```

```
      lf.lfClipPrecision = OUT_TT_PRECIS;
      lf.lfQuality = DEFAULT_QUALITY;
      lf.lfPitchAndFamily = DEFAULT_PITCH | FF_ROMAN;
      lf.lfHeight = nPoints;
      if (bBold)
          lf.lfWeight = FW_BOLD;
      lf.lfItalic = bItalic;
      strcpy (lf.lfFaceName, szFace);
      return (CreatePointFontIndirect (&lf, hdc));
}
//
// FUNCTION: CreatePointFontIndirect(LOGFONT *, HDC)
//
// PURPOSE:  Create a font using the values in a LOGFONT
//           structure. Supports CreatePointFont().
//
// RETURNS:  Handle to the new font, if successful.
//           NULL otherwise.
//
HFONT CreatePointFontIndirect (LOGFONT *lf, HDC hdc)
{
POINT ptView;

    SetViewportOrgEx (hdc, 0, 0, &ptView);
    POINT pt;
    pt.y = ::GetDeviceCaps(hdc, LOGPIXELSY) * lf->lfHeight;
    pt.x = ::GetDeviceCaps(hdc, LOGPIXELSX) * lf->lfHeight;
    pt.y /= 720;
    pt.x /= 720;
    DPtoLP(hdc, &pt, 1);
    POINT ptOrg = { 0, 0 };
    DPtoLP(hdc, &ptOrg, 1);
    lf->lfHeight = -abs(pt.y - ptOrg.y);
    SetViewportOrgEx (hdc, ptView.x, ptView.y, NULL);
    return (CreateFontIndirect (lf));
}
```

A number of items have been added to the default menu. This project will be used through tips on the print dialog boxes, so we've prepared the menu in advance. Notice that in the *WndProc()* function, we've given you the Windows API version of command enablers for the menu items. When you open a pop-up menu, Windows sends a *WM_INITMENUPOPUP* message to the window procedure before showing the menu. Programmers usually use this opportunity to enable or disable menu items on the selected pop-up menu.

The edit control gets created in the *WM_CREATE* case statement, where you also create and attach the new font to it. Don't worry about the size of the edit control here; before the window or edit control is displayed, the program will receive a *WM_SIZE* message, and you'll use the sizes passed in the message to make the edit control size track the window size. When the window gets the focus, you use the *WM_SETFOCUS* to shift the focus to the edit control.

786. *Understanding the FINDMSGSTRING Message*

Before you can use the messages from the Search and Replace dialog boxes, you first need to get the value of the registered message that the dialog box will use to communicate with your program. You do this when the window is created, in the message case for *WM_CREATE* using *Register WindowMessage(FINDMSGSTRING)*.

The *RegisterWindowMessage()* function creates a new Windows message that is guaranteed to be unique. The string is an identifier for the new message to be registered. For the Search and Replace dialog boxes, the string is "commdlg_FindReplace."

When the user presses the Find Next, Replace, or Replace All buttons on the dialog box, or closes the dialog box by pressing the Cancel button or by using the system menu, Windows sends the button press information to your program using this registered message ID. Your program interprets the message and calls the appropriate functions to perform the necessary operations.

The message ID is a calculated value rather than a constant. It might—and likely will—change between instances of your program, so you can't set up a *case* statement for it in your *WndProc* function (in C++, the expressions used in *case* statements are evaluated at compile time). Instead, you need to catch and use the message in the *default* case using the *if (message == uiFindReplaceMsg)* syntax.

787. *Calling the ReplaceText() Function*

You've already done most of the work to create a Search and Replace dialog box. When you create the dialog box using the *ReplaceText()* function, an additional edit box is added to accept the new string that will be used to replace the search string.

Two new buttons also have been added to the dialog box, Replace and Replace All, and the Up/Down radio buttons no longer appear. The Replace function works from the caret position to the end of the file; using the common dialog box, you can't search and replace in an upward direction.

To enable the search-and-replace mechanism, you need to add code to handle the menu messages. In the program from Tip 786, "Understanding the *FINDMSGSTRING* Message," you added the menu item and reserved a case statement for it in the *WndProc()* function, and the code for the *DoFindReplaceDlg()* function was written to handle either a Search dialog box or a Search and Replace dialog box. Start by adding the following code to the *ID_SEARCH_REPLACE* case statement in *WndProc()*:

```
case ID_SEARCH_REPLACE:
    SendMessage (hWndEdit, EM_GETSEL,
              (WPARAM) &nStart, (LPARAM) &nEnd);
    hWndSearch = DoFindReplaceDlg (hWnd,
              nStart, nEnd, true);
    bSearchValid = true;
    break;
```

You also need to add code to the *default* case statement to handle the messages from the dialog box. In the earlier example, you had comment lines here to indicate that it was reserved for the replace operation. Now is the time to add that code:

```
default:
    if (message == uiFindReplaceMsg)
    {
        int nReplaced = 0;
        FINDREPLACE &fr = *((FINDREPLACE *) lParam);
        if (fr.Flags & FR_DIALOGTERM)
        {
            hWndSearch = NULL;
            return (0);
        }
        if (fr.Flags & FR_FINDNEXT)
        {
            if (!DoFindText (hWndEdit, nStart, nEnd, fr))
            {
                MessageBeep (MB_OK);
                MessageBox (hWnd,
                            _T("Search string not found"),
                            _T("Search Text"), MB_OK);
                break;
            }
            if (fr.Flags & FR_DOWN)
                nStart = nEnd + 1;
        }
        if (fr.Flags & FR_REPLACE)
        {
            if (!bLastSearchValid)
            {
                bLastSearchValid = DoFindText (hWndEdit,
                                    nStart, nEnd, fr);
            }
            else
            {
                SendMessage (hWndEdit, EM_GETSEL,
                            (WPARAM) &nStart,
                            (LPARAM) &nEnd);
                SendMessage (hWndEdit, EM_REPLACESEL,
                            (WPARAM) true,
                            (LPARAM) fr.lpstrReplaceWith);
                nEnd = nStart +
                            strlen (fr.lpstrReplaceWith);
                SendMessage (hWndEdit, EM_SETSEL,
                                    nStart, nEnd);
                SendMessage (hWndEdit, EM_SCROLLCARET,
                                    0, 0);
                ++nReplaced;
            }
            nStart = nEnd + 1;
        }
        if (fr.Flags & FR_REPLACEALL)
        {
            while (bLastSearchValid = DoFindText (hWndEdit,
                                    nStart, nEnd, fr))
```

```
        {
            SendMessage (hWndEdit, EM_GETSEL,
                         (WPARAM) &nStart,
                         (LPARAM) &nEnd);
            SendMessage (hWndEdit, EM_REPLACESEL,
                         (WPARAM) true,
                         (LPARAM) fr.lpstrReplaceWith);
            nEnd = nStart +
                         strlen (fr.lpstrReplaceWith);
            SendMessage (hWndEdit, EM_SETSEL,
                         nStart, nEnd);
            SendMessage (hWndEdit, EM_SCROLLCARET,0,0);
                  nStart = nEnd + 1;
            ++nReplaced;
        }
        TCHAR Message[64];
        _stprintf (Message, "%d string(s) replaced",
                         nReplaced);
        MessageBeep (MB_OK);
        MessageBox (hWnd, Message,
                    _T("Replace Text"), MB_OK);
    }
    break;
}
```

There are no additional functions required to support the Replace dialog box. If the message is from the Replace button, you send the edit control a message to replace the selected text (it was selected by the Find operation) with the text from the replace string in the dialog box (which you will add very shortly).

If the message is from the Replace All button, the same operation takes place, but the operation loops until the Find String operation fails. You also keep track of the number of replacements and pop up a message box telling the user how many strings were replaced.

788. *Understanding the* IsDialogMessage *Function*

You might have noticed in the message pump in the *WinMain()* function that a new conditional has been added. Before messages are processed and sent on to the application's window, they are sent through a new function, *IsDialogMessage()*.

When you have a modeless dialog box displayed, the user can set the focus either to the dialog box or to the application's main window. The problem then arises as to which window should receive a message. This is resolved by calling the *IsDialogMessage()* function.

The function is intended to be used with modeless dialog boxes, but you can use it with any window that contains controls. When it processes a message, it checks for keyboard messages and translates them into the proper commands for the dialog box. If you don't call this function, the Tab key, for example, wouldn't cause the dialog box to tab through the controls. If the message isn't for the dialog box, it returns *FALSE* and the message is sent on to the application's window for processing.

The *IsDialogMessage()* performs translation and dispatch of messages. If it handles a message, it returns *TRUE* and you must prevent it from being passed on to the application's *TranslateMessage()* and *DispatchMessage()* function.

789. *Searching and Replacing Text*

The functions presented here provide the very basic text search and replace operations. These operations are so fundamental to text processing that your application should provide at least this level of support, no matter how basic it is.

There are a number of enhancements that you could make to these functions. For example, you may have noticed that when you define a portion of text that includes a line-ending sequence (carriage return and line feed in Windows and DOS text files), the edit box displays the font's default character, usually a solid or open box. You should either strip these out of the search string or provide symbols that the user can recognize, such as "\r" or "^M" for the carriage return character. You'll have to remember to convert them back to the actual character codes for the search operations.

Extra functionality could be provided using a custom dialog box and a hook procedure, which will be covered in Tips 803, "Customizing Common Dialog Boxes," and 804, "Understanding Hooks."

790. *Understanding the* CFindReplaceDialog *Class in MFC*

Now that we've expounded on the importance of search and replace operations, you may be wondering why it wasn't included in the Program Editor project presented in Tip 81, "Creating a Project." The idea was to get a multi-document application running as quickly as possible, and adding search and replace capabilities to it was a little too advanced at the time.

Now is the time to add that capability. You're probably using the editor in the Visual Studio for most projects now and no longer need the Program Editor, but you'll need to know how to add these functions to other projects.

The *CEditView* class contains member functions for searching for text and replacing strings. It just doesn't implement the code to create the dialog box. In a single-document interface, you can add the implementing code to the view class or to the mainframe class. In a multiple-document interface, you should add it to the mainframe class to make the search strings available across documents.

What is surprising is that neither the MSDN documentation nor any of the popular books published by Microsoft Press gives you any hint about how to implement the Search and Replace mechanism in *CEditView*. They just mention that there is a common dialog box and let it go at that.

In the Program Editor project, add a Search pop-up menu to the *IDR_PROGRATYPE* menu, just as you did in the Windows API project. You can give them the same resource IDs—*ID_SEARCH_FIND*, *ID_SEARCH_FINDNEXT*, and *ID_SEARCH_REPLACE*. Add a message handler for all three of these to the *CMainFrame* class. Also add a *void* function, *DoSearchReplaceDlg(bool bSearch)*. This will be used to create the Find and Replace dialog box. The code for these three functions is listed here:

```
/////////////////////////////////////////////////////////
// CMainFrame message handlers


void CMainFrame::OnSearchFind()
{
    DoSearchReplaceDlg (true);
}
```

```
void CMainFrame::OnSearchReplace()
{
    DoSearchReplaceDlg (false);
}

void CMainFrame::OnSearchFindnext()
{
    CProgramEditorView *view = (CProgramEditorView *)
                    GetActiveFrame()->GetActiveView ();
    m_fr.lpstrFindWhat = (char *)(LPCSTR) m_strFind;
    m_fr.lpstrReplaceWith = (char *)(LPCSTR) m_strReplace;
    view->DoFindText (m_fr);
}

void CMainFrame::DoSearchReplaceDlg(bool bSearch)
{
    if (m_fd != NULL)
    {
        m_fd->SetFocus ();
        return;
    }
    m_fd = new CFindReplaceDialog;
    CView *cview = GetActiveView ();
    CProgramEditorView *view = (CProgramEditorView *)
                    GetActiveFrame()->GetActiveView ();
    CString strFind;
    strFind.Empty ();
    view->GetCurrentSelection (strFind);
    m_fd->m_fr.Flags |= FR_HIDEWHOLEWORD;
    m_fd->m_fr.hwndOwner = this->m_hWnd;
    m_fd->m_fr.lpstrFindWhat = (char *)(LPCSTR) strFind;
    m_fd->Create (bSearch, NULL, NULL, FR_DOWN, this);
    memcpy (&m_fr, &m_fd->m_fr, sizeof (FINDREPLACE));
}
```

Note that in the *DoSearchReplaceDlg()* function, the search string is being placed in the *FIND-REPLACE* structure directly, and a *NULL* is used in the call to *Create()*. If the *strFind* variable is empty, the *Create()* function would not initialize the *lpstrFindWhat* member variable. You want it initialized even if it is empty so that you can use it in a function to enable the Find Next menu item and the F3 key.

You'll need to register the Find and Replace message in the source file by adding the first line following the line toward the top of the file and the second line to the message map:

```
UINT WM_FINDREPLACE=::RegisterWindowMessage(FINDMSGSTRING);
// Add the next line to the message map
ON_REGISTERED_MESSAGE(WM_FINDREPLACE, OnFindReplace)
```

You'll have to add the *OnFindReplace()* function manually. Add the declaration to the header file. The body of the function is shown here:

```
LONG CMainFrame::OnFindReplace(UINT wParam, LONG lParam)
{
    FINDREPLACE &fr = *((FINDREPLACE *) lParam);

    memcpy (&m_fr, &fr, sizeof (FINDREPLACE));
    m_strFind = fr.lpstrFindWhat;
    m_strReplace = fr.lpstrReplaceWith;
```

```
    CProgramEditorView *view = (CProgramEditorView *)
                      GetActiveFrame()->GetActiveView();
    if (fr.Flags & FR_DIALOGTERM)
    {
        m_fd = NULL;
        return (0);
    }
    if (fr.Flags & FR_FINDNEXT)
    {
        view->DoFindText (fr);
    }
    if (fr.Flags & (FR_REPLACE | FR_REPLACEALL))
    {
        view->DoReplaceText (fr);
    }
    return (0);
}
```

Add the following member functions to the *CMainFrame* class. The Find and Replace dialog box is modeless and needs to be created on the heap. You won't have to worry about destroying it. Adding members to hold the *FINDREPLACE* structure, and the search and replace strings will let you use the F3 key to search even after you've closed and destroyed the dialog box.

```
CString m_strReplace;
CString m_strFind;
FINDREPLACE m_fr;
CFindReplaceDialog *m_fd;
```

Finally, add the view class header file to the list of include files in the mainframe source file, and then add a command enabler for the Find Next menu item. You don't need to worry about the other two menu items because the menu will be visible only when you have a document window open and in focus. The Find Next item, however, should be enabled only when there is a valid search string available.

```
// Add to the source file:
#include "Program EditorView.h"

void CMainFrame::OnUpdateSearchFindnext(CCmdUI* pCmdUI)
{
   pCmdUI->Enable(m_fr.lpstrFindWhat==NULL ? FALSE : TRUE);
}
```

You're finished with the main frame files, so close them and open the view class files. You'll need to add four functions to the class, but you'll have to add all of them manually. The first function is called by the mainframe function to get the currently selected text to initialize the Find box. The others call the *CEditView* functions to do the search and replace operations and to display a message box when the search fails.

```
void CProgramEditorView::GetCurrentSelection
                                  (CString &strFind)
{
   int nStart, nEnd;
   strFind.Empty ();
   GetEditCtrl ().GetSel (nStart, nEnd);
   if (nStart != nEnd)
       GetSelectedText (strFind);
}
```

```
void CProgramEditorView::DoFindText(FINDREPLACE &fr)
{

    OnFindNext (fr.lpstrFindWhat,
                fr.Flags & FR_DOWN ? TRUE : FALSE,
                fr.Flags & FR_MATCHCASE ? TRUE : FALSE);

    int nStart, nEnd;
    GetEditCtrl ().GetSel (nStart, nEnd);
    int nFirst = GetEditCtrl().GetFirstVisibleLine ();
    int nCur = GetEditCtrl().LineFromChar (nStart);
    if (nFirst != nCur)
    {
        GetEditCtrl().LineScroll (nCur - nFirst - 1, 0);
    }
}

void CProgramEditorView::DoReplaceText(FINDREPLACE &fr)
{
    if (fr.Flags & FR_REPLACEALL)
        OnReplaceAll (fr.lpstrFindWhat,
                      fr.lpstrReplaceWith,
                      fr.Flags & FR_MATCHCASE
                             ? TRUE : FALSE);
    else
    {
        OnReplaceSel (fr.lpstrFindWhat,
                      fr.Flags & FR_DOWN ? TRUE : FALSE,
                      fr.Flags & FR_MATCHCASE ? TRUE : FALSE,
                      fr.lpstrReplaceWith);
        int nStart, nEnd;
        GetEditCtrl ().GetSel (nStart, nEnd);
        int nFirst = GetEditCtrl().GetFirstVisibleLine ();
        int nCur = GetEditCtrl().LineFromChar (nStart);
        if (nFirst != nCur)
        {
            GetEditCtrl().LineScroll(nCur - nFirst - 1, 0);
        }
    }
}

void CProgramEditorView::OnTextNotFound(LPCTSTR lpszFind)
{
    MessageBeep (MB_OK);
    AfxMessageBox ("Search string not found");
}
```

Compile and run the program. Test both the forward and the backward searches, and test the replace function (replace operations only go forward in the text). Try the F3 key by creating the dialog box, entering your search string, performing one search, and then pressing the Cancel button. The member variables that you added to the mainframe class will be initialized, and you can use the F3 key to continue your searches even though the dialog box has been destroyed.

791. *Using the* ON_REGISTERED_MESSAGE *Message Map Macro*

As you saw earlier, the *RegisterWindowsMessage()* function creates a custom message that your program can use. The message ID is guaranteed to be unique throughout the system.

Because the message IDs are tailored for your program, the Microsoft Foundation Class library has no way of knowing how to handle it through normal message map entries, so you use the macro *ON_REGISTERED_MESSAGE* to map to your application's function to handle the message. The message handler must have a return value of *LONG* and must accept two parameters, a *WPARAM* and an *LPARAM*.

For the *CFindReplaceDialog* class, the *LPARAM* argument contains a pointer to the class object's *FIND-REPLACE* member.

792. *Using the* CFindReplaceDialog *Functions*

The *CFindReplaceDialog* class contains several member functions to retrieve information from the class object's member structure. Whether you use these or test the *Flags* member directly is a matter of programmer preference.

The class also has a static function to locate any instance of a class object using the *lParam* value passed to the *OnFindReplace()* message handler. If you don't need a pointer to the object outside this function, you don't need to declare a member pointer to a class object as you did in the previous example. However, we used the pointer variable in another function to shift the focus to the dialog box if the user selected the Find or Replace menu items when the dialog was displayed (it's a modeless dialog box, so this is possible). We couldn't have done that without the pointer.

The class functions and their uses are summarized in Table 792.

Member Function	Return Type	Use
FindNext	BOOL	Indicates whether the user pressed the Find Next button.
GetFindString	CString	Retrieves the *lpstrFindWhat* string.
GetReplaceString	CString	Retrieves the *lpstrReplaceWith* string.
IsTerminating	BOOL	Indicates whether the user is closing the dialog box.
MatchCase	BOOL	Retrieves the state of the Match Case check box.
MatchWholeWord	BOOL	Retrieves the state of the Match Whole Word check box.
ReplaceAll	BOOL	Indicates whether the user pressed the Replace All button on the dialog box.
ReplaceCurrent	BOOL	Indicates whether the user pressed the Replace button on the dialog box.

Table 792 CFindReplaceDialog's *list of functions (continued on following page)*

Member Function	Return Type	Use
SearchDown	BOOL	Retrieves the state of the Up and Down radio buttons. 0 indicates an upward search and a non-0 indicates a downward search.
GetNotifier	pointer	A static function used to find the current instance of the dialog box. The *lParam* argument of the message handler is used to locate the instance.

Table 792 CFindReplaceDialog's *list of functions (continued from previous page)*

Truly, these functions simply add another level of abstraction and make the program code more difficult to follow.

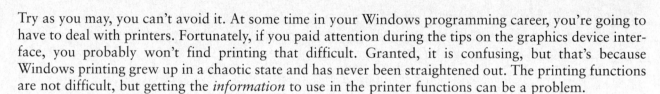

793. *Understanding the Print Dialog Boxes*

Try as you may, you can't avoid it. At some time in your Windows programming career, you're going to have to deal with printers. Fortunately, if you paid attention during the tips on the graphics device interface, you probably won't find printing that difficult. Granted, it is confusing, but that's because Windows printing grew up in a chaotic state and has never been straightened out. The printing functions are not difficult, but getting the *information* to use in the printer functions can be a problem.

Despite all this, and despite common beliefs, printing from Windows isn't that daunting. It's almost as easy as drawing or placing text on the screen. You just have to remember that a printer is a page-oriented device, and you have to take a few extra steps. In Windows, there are two important concepts that you should understand:

1. To allow processes to share devices, Windows uses print *spooling* to store printer jobs while they are waiting for the printer to become free. A spooler is a queue where jobs are stored temporarily. To access a printer, you must start a queue operation to reserve a location in the spooler and then end the operation when your job is complete. This is done using the *StartDoc()* and *EndDoc()* functions.

2. Unlike a screen, where you can just slap on some scroll bars and let the user move the data about the screen, the printer page isn't rewritable. You also must split your document into pages. This is done with the *StartPage()* and *EndPage()* functions.

Once you understand these functions, printing is no more difficult than drawing or writing to the screen. The same GDI functions that you use to display text or graphics on the screen are used to send text and graphics to the printer.

The printer dialog boxes in the common dialog boxes set go a long way toward making life easier when you are using a printer. Working with these dialog boxes involves working with global memory handles, a leftover from the Pre-Windows 95 days.

794. *Understanding the Page Setup Dialog Box*

The Page Setup dialog box provides controls for the user to specify the attributes of the printed page. These include the orientation—landscape or portrait—the size and source of the paper, and the page margins.

You create the Page Setup dialog box by calling the *PageSetupDlg()* function and passing it a pointer to a *PAGESETUPDLG* structure. To use the function with the system default printer, you can call it with an empty structure (containing only the structure size in the *lStructSize* member). Assuming that the user didn't press the Cancel button, the structure will be filled in when the function returns.

795. *Understanding the* **PAGESETUPDLG** *Structure*

The *PAGESETUPDLG* structure contains information to initialize the Page Setup common dialog box through the *PageSetupDlg()* function. When the function returns, it places default or user selection information in the structure.

The structure contains global memory handles for the *DEVNAMES* and *DEVMODE* structures, which are needed by several other printer functions and may be used to get this information for the system default printer without displaying the dialog box. Zero the structure, set the size in the *lStructSize* member, and set the *PSD_RETURNDEFAULT* bit in the *Flags* member, as shown in the following snippet:

```
PAGESETUPDLG    ps;
memset (&ps, '\0', sizeof (PAGESETUPDLG));
ps.lStructSize = sizeof (PAGESETUPDLG);
ps.Flags = PSD_RETURNDEFAULT;
PageSetupDlg (&ps);
```

By adding a few more lines, you can get the name of the default system printer:

```
TCHAR szPrinterName[_MAX_PATH];
DEVMODE *pDM = (DEVMODE *) GlobalLock (ps.hDevMode);
strcpy (szPrinterName, (char *) pDM->dmDeviceName);
GlobalUnlock (ps.hDevMode);
```

When the function returns, other members of this structure contain the printer margins and the paper size. The *DEVMODE* structure also contains information about the printer.

Figure 795 shows the Page Setup dialog boxes.

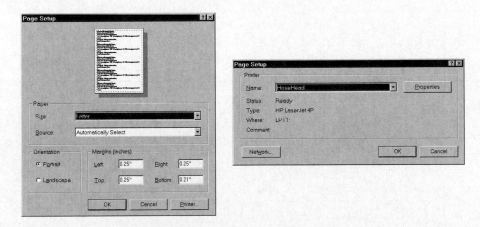

Figure 795   *The new Page Setup dialog box is on the left. This requires the user to call a second dialog box, shown at the right, using the Printer button to change to another printer, encapsulating different functions in different dialog boxes.*

Copy the Search and Replace project from Tip 787, "Calling the *ReplaceText()* Function," and add a couple of items to the File menu. Name them Print and Page Setup, and give them resource IDs of *ID_FILE_PRINT* and *ID_FILE_PAGESETUP*. Add a global variable of type *TCHAR* named *szPrinterName[_MAX_PATH]*, and add the following code at the bottom of the *InitInstance()* function (this is another way to get the default printer name):

```
TCHAR buffer[256];
memset (buffer, '\0', sizeof (buffer));

GetProfileString("windows", "device", ",,,",
                  buffer, sizeof(buffer));
char *s = strchr (buffer, ',');
if (s != NULL)
{
    *s = '\0';
    strcpy (szPrinterName, buffer);
}
else
{
    MessageBox (hWnd,_T("Cannot find default printer"),
                  _T("InitInstance"), MB_OK);
}
```

Add a case statement to the *WM_COMMAND* switch in the *WndProc()* function:

```
case ID_FILE_PAGESETUP:
    DoPageSetup (hWnd);
    break;
```

Add the *DoPageSetup()* function to summon the Page Setup dialog box. The first time through, it will display the system default printer information, and the user will have the opportunity here to change the printer. The change is not permanent, and it affects only this instance of the program. Additional invocations of the function will display information about the currently selected printer. You'll also have to add *<winspool.h>* to the list of include files.

There is a second method of setting up a printer, which is used by applications created by the MFC AppWizard although Microsoft says that new applications should not use it. According to the MSDN documentation, new programs should use the *PageSetupDlg()* function. The MFC method calls the *PrintDlg()* function with the PD_PRINTSETUP bit set in the *Flags* member of *PRINTDLG*. This next function contains alternate code to use the old method. Just #define *ALTERNATE_PRINT_SETUP* in the program file, and the alternate code will be compiled.

```
//
//   FUNCTION: DoPageSetup (HWND)
//
//   PURPOSE:  Handles user setup and selection of the
//             printer.
//
//   RETURNS:  void function.
//
void DoPageSetup (HWND hWnd)
{
TCHAR   buffer[256];
HANDLE hPrinter;


//
// Get the default printer
```

```
//
    strcpy (buffer, szPrinterName);
    PAGESETUPDLG    ps;

    memset (&ps, '\Ø', sizeof (PAGESETUPDLG));
    ps.lStructSize = sizeof (PAGESETUPDLG);
//
// Get a pointer to the DEVMODE structure for the
// current printer.
//
    OpenPrinter (buffer, &hPrinter, NULL);
    DWORD dwBytesReturned, dwBytesNeeded;
    GetPrinter(hPrinter, 2, NULL, Ø, &dwBytesNeeded);
    PRINTER_INFO_2* pInfo2 =
                    (PRINTER_INFO_2*)GlobalAlloc(GPTR,
                                        dwBytesNeeded);
    if (GetPrinter(hPrinter, 2, (LPBYTE)pInfo2,
                                dwBytesNeeded,
                                &dwBytesReturned) == Ø)
    {
        GlobalFree(pInfo2);
        ClosePrinter(hPrinter);
        return;
    }
//
// Use the DEVMODE to initialize the dialog box using
// the currently selected printer.
//
    HGLOBAL phDevMode = GlobalAlloc(GPTR, sizeof(DEVMODE));
    DEVMODE *pTempDM = (DEVMODE *) GlobalLock (phDevMode);
    memcpy (pTempDM, pInfo2->pDevMode, sizeof (DEVMODE));

#ifdef _ALTERNATE_PRINT_SETUP
    PRINTDLG pd;
    memset (&pd, '\Ø', sizeof (PRINTDLG));
    pd.lStructSize = sizeof (PRINTDLG);
    pd.Flags = PD_PRINTSETUP;
    pd.hDevMode = phDevMode;

    if (!PrintDlg (&pd))
    {
        GlobalFree (phDevMode);
        return;
    }
    DEVMODE *pDM = (DEVMODE *) GlobalLock(pd.hDevMode);

#else
    ps.hDevMode = phDevMode;

    if (!PageSetupDlg (&ps))
    {
        GlobalFree (phDevMode);
        return;
    }
    DEVMODE *pDM = (DEVMODE *) GlobalLock(pd.hDevMode);
```

```
//
//  Get a copy of the new DEVMODE structure. This
//  contains any changes that the user made in the
//  dialog box.
//
#endif

    DEVMODE dm;
    memcpy (&dm, pDM, sizeof (DEVMODE));
//
//  If the selected printer changed, close the
//  current printer and reopen the new one.
//
    if (strcmp ((char *)dm.dmDeviceName, buffer))
    {
        ClosePrinter (hPrinter);
        strcpy (buffer, (char *) dm.dmDeviceName);
        OpenPrinter (buffer, &hPrinter, NULL);
        if (hPrinter == NULL)
        {
            TCHAR Message[256] = {"Cannot open "};
            strcat (Message, buffer);
            MessageBox (hWnd, Message, _T("Page Setup"),
                                                MB_OK);
            return;
        }
        strcpy (szPrinterName, buffer);
    }
//
//  Free the old PRINTER_INFO_2 structure and get
//  a new one.
//
    GlobalFree (pInfo2);
    GetPrinter(hPrinter, 2, NULL, 0, &dwBytesNeeded);
    pInfo2 = (PRINTER_INFO_2*)GlobalAlloc(GPTR,
        dwBytesNeeded);
    if (GetPrinter(hPrinter, 2, (BYTE *)pInfo2,
                              dwBytesNeeded,
                              &dwBytesReturned) == 0)
    {
        GlobalFree(pInfo2);
        ClosePrinter(hPrinter);
        return;
    }
    pInfo2->pDevMode = &dm;
    DWORD dwResult = SetPrinter (hPrinter, 2,
                              (BYTE *) pInfo2, 0);
    if (!dwResult)
    {
        TCHAR Message[256];
        dwResult = GetLastError ();
        if (dwResult == 5)
            strcpy (Message,_T("Access to printer denied"));
        else
            sprintf (Message, "Error %d setting printer",
                              dwResult);
```

```
        MessageBox (hWnd, Message, "Printer Setup", MB_OK);
    }
    ClosePrinter (hPrinter);
    GlobalUnlock(ps.hDevMode);
    GlobalUnlock(ps.hDevNames);
    GlobalFree(pInfo2);
}
```

The function first opens the printer by name and uses the handle to get a *DEVINFO* structure for the printer. It uses that structure to initialize the dialog box. If a *NULL* were used, the dialog box would list settings for the default printer. If the user has changed the selected printer, this ensures that the correct printer settings will be displayed.

This dialog box also can be used to change the printer selection. After it returns, you need to check the name in the *hDevMode* member of the *PAGESETUPDLG* structure. If the names don't match, close the printer and open the one indicated in the structure. Then apply the new settings to the new printer.

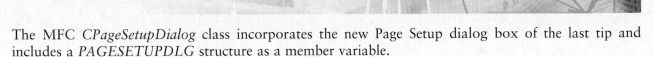

796. *Using the CPageSetupDialog Class*

The MFC *CPageSetupDialog* class incorporates the new Page Setup dialog box of the last tip and includes a *PAGESETUPDLG* structure as a member variable.

Projects created by the MFC AppWizard don't use this dialog box. Instead, they use the old Page Setup dialog box, which Microsoft recommends that you don't use. You'll look at this dialog box in Tip 802, "Understanding the Print Setup Dialog Box," but meanwhile, you can easily see the difference between the new and the old in the same program.

If you open the Program Editor project and examine the *ProgramEditor.cpp* file, you'll see an entry in the message map like the following:

```
ON_COMMAND(ID_FILE_PRINT_SETUP, CWinApp::OnFilePrintSetup)
```

Run the program and select Print Setup from the File menu to see what the old Print Setup dialog box looks like. Then comment out this line and add a message handler to the *ProgramEditorApp* class for *ID_FILE_PRINT_SETUP* using the ClassWizard. The code for this new function should look like the following:

```
void CProgramEditorApp::OnFilePrintSetup()
{
    CPageSetupDialog psd;
    if (psd.DoModal () == IDCANCEL)
        return;
    CString strDev = psd.GetDeviceName ();
    HANDLE hPrinter;
    DWORD dwBytesNeeded, dwBytesReturned;
    TCHAR szDev[128];
    strcpy (szDev, (LPCSTR) strDev);
    OpenPrinter (szDev, &hPrinter, NULL);
    GetPrinter(hPrinter, 2, NULL, 0, &dwBytesNeeded);
    PRINTER_INFO_2 *pInfo2 =
                    PRINTER_INFO_2*)GlobalAlloc(GPTR,
                    dwBytesNeeded);
    if (GetPrinter(hPrinter, 2, (BYTE *)pInfo2,
```

```
                              dwBytesNeeded,
                              &dwBytesReturned) == 0)
    {
        ClosePrinter(hPrinter);
        GlobalFree(pInfo2);
        return;
    }
    pInfo2->pDevMode = psd.GetDevMode ();
    DWORD dwResult = SetPrinter (hPrinter, 2,
                              (BYTE *) pInfo2, 0);
    if (!dwResult)
    {
        TCHAR Message[256];
        dwResult = GetLastError ();
        if (dwResult == 5)
            strcpy (Message,_T("Access to printer denied"));
        else
            sprintf (Message, "Error %d setting printer",
                              dwResult);
        AfxMessageBox (Message, MB_OK);
    }
    ClosePrinter (hPrinter);
    GlobalFree(pInfo2);
}
```

Recompile and run the program, and you'll see the new breed of Page Setup dialog box. In fact, a lot of the code for this function was lifted out of the Windows API application in the previous tip. If you decide to stick with the new dialog box, you might want to include the code that allows you to change printers. This would mean that your application class would have to maintain some additional printer information.

797. *Understanding the Print Dialog Box*

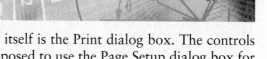

The last stop before the document is committed to the printer itself is the Print dialog box. The controls on this dialog box offer limited printer options (the user is supposed to use the Page Setup dialog box for page and printer options), but by pressing the Properties button, some printer functions may be modified.

The user has one last chance on this dialog box to change printers. Other than that, the only controls are to set the print range and the number of copies.

The Print dialog box is controlled by the *PRINTDLG* structure and is summoned by calling the Windows API *PrintDlg()* function. The structure and calls to the Windows API function are encapsulated in the MFC *CPrintDialog* class.

As with most common dialog box functions and control structures, the *PRINTDLG* structure is a bidirectional affair. You can set members to initialize controls on the dialog box when it first shows on the screen. When the *PrintDlg()* function exits, it sets the members to indicate user input.

798. *Understanding the* **PRINTDLG** *Structure*

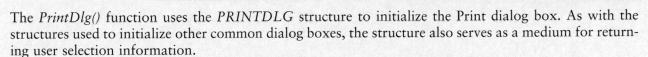

The *PrintDlg()* function uses the *PRINTDLG* structure to initialize the Print dialog box. As with the structures used to initialize other common dialog boxes, the structure also serves as a medium for returning user selection information.

If passed an empty structure, *PrintDlg()* will display and collect print information for the system default printer. To make it select another printer, you need to fill in the *hDevMode* member with information about the selected printer. You can get a handle to a *DEVMODE* structure the same way that you got it for the Page Setup dialog box. In the next tip, you'll add printing code to a Windows API project that gets a global *DEVMODE* structure.

The *PRINTDLG* structure contains pagination information and the number of copies. You can use this information to adjust your printer output loop.

799. *Calling* **PrintDlg()** *Directly*

You call the *PrintDlg()* function with a pointer to a *PRINTDLG* structure. The function presents the user with a Print Dialog box, which, when dispatched, returns with some details about the print job.

At this point, the user expects to see some printer action. Windows 95 and beyond use printer spooling and place the jobs in a queue. You get a slot in the queue by calling the *StartDoc()* function. The job stays in the queue until you close it with the *EndDoc()* function, at which time the Windows print spooler sends it to the printer. If there are multiple jobs in the spooler, which you might find on a shared printer in a moderately busy office, the job will be held until those ahead of it have printed. Windows will print no line before its time.

Open the project from Tip 795, "Understanding the *PAGESETUPDLG* Structure," in which you added the printer setup code. It's time to make it actually print something. The code in the tip is basic printing code, and you should understand how the page and document functions work. The loop that outputs the text uses the *DrawText()* function, the same one that you used in earlier examples using the graphics device interface. You could use any of the GDI output functions—*Rectangle()*, *Ellipse()*, *LineTo()*—to draw graphics on the printer, or the other text functions—*TextOut()* and *TabbedTextOut()*, for example—to output the text.

The menu for the project should already have a Print item on the File menu. If not, add it now and give it a resource ID of *ID_FILE_PRINT*. In the *WndProc()* function, add a case statement for this ID right after the one for the printer setup item. It should call a function named *DoPrint()*:

```
case ID_FILE_PRINT:
    DoPrint (hWndEdit);
    break;
```

The *DoPrint()* function is where all the work is being done. Don't forget to prototype the function near the top of the file—and, while you're at it, also prototype a function named *PrintPage()*:

```
void DoPrint (HWND hWnd);
bool PrintPage (HWND hWnd, PRINTDLG &pd);
```

After setting up the printer structures and calling the Print dialog box, *DoPrint()* will call *StartDoc()* to open the spooler location and then loop until all the text in the file has been printed. The code for the two functions is listed here:

```
//
//  FUNCTION: DoPrint (HWND)
//
//  PURPOSE:  Displays the Print Dialog box for the
//            currently selected printer. After the
//            dialog box is closed, it continues and
//            prints the document.
//
//  RETURNS:  void function.
//
//  COMMENTS: The HWND parameter is a handle to an edit
//            control from which the text to be printed
//            will be take.
//
void DoPrint (HWND hWnd)
{
PRINTDLG pd;
char    buffer[256];

    memset (buffer, '\0', sizeof (buffer));
    memset (&pd, '\0', sizeof (PRINTDLG));
    pd.lStructSize = sizeof (PRINTDLG);

    HANDLE hPrinter;
    OpenPrinter (szPrinterName, &hPrinter, NULL);
//
//  Get a pointer to the DEVMODE structure for the
//  current printer.
//
    DWORD dwBytesReturned, dwBytesNeeded;
    GetPrinter(hPrinter, 2, NULL, 0, &dwBytesNeeded);
    PRINTER_INFO_2* pInfo2 =
        (PRINTER_INFO_2*)GlobalAlloc(GPTR,dwBytesNeeded);
    if (GetPrinter(hPrinter, 2, (LPBYTE)pInfo2,
                              dwBytesNeeded,
                              &dwBytesReturned) == 0)
    {
        GlobalFree(pInfo2);
        ClosePrinter(hPrinter);
        return;
    }
//
//  Use the DEVMODE to initialize the dialog box.
//
    HANDLE phDevMode = GlobalAlloc(GPTR, sizeof (DEVMODE));
    DEVMODE *pTempDM = (DEVMODE *) GlobalLock (phDevMode);
    memcpy (pTempDM, pInfo2->pDevMode, sizeof (DEVMODE));
    pd.hDevMode = phDevMode;
    if (!PrintDlg (&pd))
    {
        GlobalFree (phDevMode);
        return;
```

```
    }
    DEVMODE* pDevMode = (DEVMODE*)GlobalLock(pd.hDevMode);
    strcpy (buffer, (char *) pDevMode->dmDeviceName);
    GlobalUnlock(pd.hDevMode);

    pd.hDC = CreateDC (NULL, buffer, NULL, NULL);

    DOCINFO di = {sizeof (DOCINFO), "Test", NULL, NULL, 0};

    HFONT hFont = CreatePointFont (100, "Courier New",
                                   pd.hDC, true, false);
    SelectObject (pd.hDC, hFont);

    pd.nFromPage = 1;
    pd.nMaxPage = -1;

    StartDoc (pd.hDC, &di);

    while (PrintPage (hWnd, pd) == false)
        ++pd.nFromPage;

    EndDoc (pd.hDC);
    GlobalFree (pd.hDevMode);
    GlobalFree (pd.hDevNames);
    DeleteDC (pd.hDC);
}

bool PrintPage (HWND hWnd, PRINTDLG &pd)
{
char    buffer[256];

    memset (buffer, '\0', sizeof (buffer));
    static int nLine;
    static int nLines;
    if (pd.nFromPage == 1)
    {
        nLines = SendMessage (hWnd, EM_GETLINECOUNT, 0, 0);
        nLine = 0;
    }
    DEVMODE* pDevMode = (DEVMODE*)GlobalLock(pd.hDevMode);

    TEXTMETRIC tm;
    GetTextMetrics (pd.hDC, &tm);
    int cyChar = tm.tmHeight + tm.tmExternalLeading;
    int nMarginX = GetDeviceCaps (pd.hDC, PHYSICALOFFSETX);
    int nMarginY = GetDeviceCaps (pd.hDC, PHYSICALOFFSETY);
    int nPageX = GetDeviceCaps (pd.hDC, PHYSICALWIDTH);
    int nPageY = GetDeviceCaps (pd.hDC, PHYSICALHEIGHT);
    int nPageMax = nPageY - 2 * nMarginY;
    SaveDC (pd.hDC);
    StartPage (pd.hDC);
    int nPos = cyChar + nMarginY;
    UINT uFormat =  DT_EXPANDTABS | DT_TABSTOP | 0x400;
    RECT rc;
    rc.left = nMarginX;
    rc.top = nMarginY;
```

```
        rc.right = nPageX - nMarginX;
        rc.bottom = rc.top + cyChar;
        for ( ; nLine < nLines; ++nLine)
        {
            memset (buffer, '\0', sizeof (buffer));
            WORD *pBuf = (WORD *) buffer;
            *pBuf = (WORD) sizeof (buffer);
            SendMessage (hWnd, EM_GETLINE, (WPARAM) nLine,
                                          (LPARAM) buffer);
            char *s;
            if ((s = strchr (buffer, 0x0d)) != NULL)
                StripChar (s);
            if ((s = strchr (buffer, 0x0a)) != NULL)
                StripChar (s);
            DrawText (pd.hDC, buffer, strlen (buffer),
                         &rc, uFormat);
            rc.top += cyChar;
            rc.bottom += cyChar;
            if (rc.bottom > nPageMax)
                break;
        }
    ++nLine;
    EndPage (pd.hDC);
    RestoreDC (pd.hDC, -1);
    if (nLine <= nLines)
        return (false);
    return (true);
}
```

Each time that the bottom of the bounding rectangle for the text exceeds the page depth minus the printer's page offset, *PrintPage()* exits the *for* loop and issues an *EndPage()* command, forcing the printer to eject the page. If it hasn't reached the end of the text in the edit control, it returns *false*, forcing *DoPrint()* to call it again.

Before calling *PrintPage()*, *DoPrint()* issued a *StartDoc()* command. When *PrintPage()* returns *true*, indicating that it has finished all the text, *DoPrint()* will issue an *EndDoc()* command, closing the spooler job.

800. *Using the CPrintDialog Class*

The MFC *CPrintDialog* class encapsulates the *PRINTDLG* structure and the *PrintDlg()*. Normally in an MFC application, the frameworks takes care of the printing dialog boxes, and you never get close to the implementation code.

However, you can override the frameworks printing functions to provide your own printing functions. To use *CPrintDialog*, you declare an instance of it. Once it is constructed, you need to initialize the members of the *PRINTDLG* structure, *m_pd*. Do this the same way you did in the Windows API function. If you handle the printing yourself, you are responsible for calling *GlobalFree()* to release the global memory used by the dialog box.

Unlike the Windows API function, which returns 0 or non-0 results to indicate failure or success, the *CPrintDialog::DoModal()* returns *IDOK* or *IDCANCEL*.

The MSDN documentation tells you that you can retrieve information about the currently selected printer by calling *CPrintDialog::GetDefaults()*. In fact, this function simply calls *PrintDlg()* using the *PD_RETURNDEFAULT* flag, which means that it retrieves information for the current system default printer, not the program's currently selected printer. The two printers aren't necessarily the same; in the next tip, we'll give you a couple of functions to get global handles to the *DEVMODE* and *DEVNAMES* structures for any printer.

801. *Retrieving Printer Information Without Displaying the Print Dialog Box*

The problem with using the *RETURNDEFAULT* flags of the printer dialog functions is that they can retrieve information only about the current system default printer. Your program, however, may be using other printers such as a plotter or labeler, while the system default may remain the trusty old laser printer.

These two functions will enable you to get global handles to *DEVMODE* and *DEVNAMES* structures initialized for a particular printer without having to go through the printer setup or printer dialog box process. Most of the code for these functions was gleaned from the Microsoft Web site (despite my rantings about Microsoft, the programmers there are professional, while I'm just *idiot savant*, so I do plunder its Web site from time to time) while I was working on a service program to print order tickets for advertisements. One type of order had to be printed on pink paper, another type had to be printed on blue paper, and dedicated printers were set aside for each color. So, the program had to switch printers without human intervention, depending upon the information sent to it.

The first function returns a global handle to a *DEVMODE* structure. It's the one that you'll probably need most. Remember, it's a global handle, so to convert it to a pointer, you have to use the return value from *GlobalLock()*. Afterward, you'll have to call *GlobalUnlock()* for each time you call *GlobalLock()* on a handle. Also, your code is responsible for freeing the global memory when you are finished with it; call *GlobalFree(handle)*.

```
//
// FUNCTION: GetDevModes (LPTSTR)
//
// PURPOSE:  Allocates global memory for a DEVMODE
//           structure. The caller is responsible for
//           calling GlobalFree.
//
// RETURNS:  If successful, an HGLOBAL handle to a
//           printer DEVMODE structure. NULL if
//           not successful.
//
HGLOBAL GetDevMode (LPTSTR pszPrinterName)
{
//
// Open printer to get a handle to it.
//
    HANDLE hPrinter;
    if (OpenPrinter(pszPrinterName, &hPrinter, NULL)
                                        == FALSE)
        return FALSE;
```

```
//
// Get a PRINTER_INFO_2 structure
//
   DWORD dwBytesReturned, dwBytesNeeded;
   GetPrinter(hPrinter, 2, NULL, 0, &dwBytesNeeded);
   PRINTER_INFO_2* pInfo2 =
                   (PRINTER_INFO_2*)GlobalAlloc(GPTR,
                        dwBytesNeeded);
   if (GetPrinter(hPrinter, 2,
                (BYTE *)pInfo2,
                dwBytesNeeded,
                &dwBytesReturned) == 0)
   {
      GlobalFree(pInfo2);
      ClosePrinter(hPrinter);
      return FALSE;
   }
//
// Don't need the printer handle now, so dump it.
//
   ClosePrinter(hPrinter);
//
// Allocate a global handle for DEVMODE
//
   HGLOBAL  hDevMode = GlobalAlloc(GHND,
                        sizeof(*pInfo2->pDevMode) +
                        pInfo2->pDevMode->dmDriverExtra);
   if (hDevMode == NULL)
   {
      GlobalFree (pInfo2);
      return (NULL);
   }
//
// Get a pointer to the DEVMODE structure.
//
   DEVMODE* pDevMode = (DEVMODE*)GlobalLock(hDevMode);
   if (pDevMode == NULL)
   {
      GlobalFree (pInfo2);
      GlobalFree (hDevMode);
      return (NULL);
   }
//
// Copy the DEVMODE structure from the PRINTER_INFO_2
// structure's pDevMode member.
//
   memcpy(pDevMode, pInfo2->pDevMode,
                sizeof(*pInfo2->pDevMode) +
                pInfo2->pDevMode->dmDriverExtra);
//
// Unlock the global memory and free the pInfo2 structure.
//
   GlobalUnlock(hDevMode);
   GlobalFree (pInfo2);
//
// Return the global handle
```

```
//
    return (hDevMode);
}
```

The second function returns a global handle to a *DEVNAMES* structure. The *DEVNAMES* structure is a collection of offsets, and the information that you want actually follows immediately after the structure memory. Each member of the structure is an offset from the beginning of the structure. To get the printer name, for example, you would add the address of the structure to the *wDeviceOffset* member to get a pointer to the string containing the printer name. This name is identical to the *dmDeviceName* member of the *DEVMODE* structure.

```
//
//  FUNCTION: GetDevNames (LPTSTR)
//
//  PURPOSE:  Allocates global memory for a DEVNAME
//            structure. The caller is responsible for
//            calling GlobalFree.
//
//  RETURNS:  If successful, an HGLOBAL handle to a
//            printer DEVNAMES structure. NULL if
//            not successful.
//
HGLOBAL GetDevNames (LPTSTR pszPrinterName)
{
//
//  Open printer to get a handle to it.
//
    HANDLE hPrinter;
    if (OpenPrinter(pszPrinterName, &hPrinter, NULL)
                                        == FALSE)

        return (NULL);


//
//  Get a PRINTER_INFO_2 structure
//
    DWORD dwBytesReturned, dwBytesNeeded;
    GetPrinter(hPrinter, 2, NULL, 0, &dwBytesNeeded);
    PRINTER_INFO_2* pInfo2 =
                    (PRINTER_INFO_2*)GlobalAlloc(GPTR,
                    dwBytesNeeded);
    if (GetPrinter(hPrinter, 2,
                (BYTE *)pInfo2,
                dwBytesNeeded,
                &dwBytesReturned) == 0)
    {
        GlobalFree(pInfo2);
        ClosePrinter(hPrinter);
        return (NULL);
    }
//
//  Don't need the printer handle now, so dump it.
//
    ClosePrinter(hPrinter);


//
//  The DEVNAMES structure size varies (it's actually a
```

```
//  a group of offsets to strings that are placed just
//  after the structure). Get the size of the members from
//  the PRINTER_INFO_2 structure and add them to get
//  the structure size.
//
//  First the driver name
    DWORD drvNameLen = lstrlen(pInfo2->pDriverName)+1;
//  The printer name
    DWORD ptrNameLen = lstrlen(pInfo2->pPrinterName)+1;
//  and the port name
    DWORD porNameLen = lstrlen(pInfo2->pPortName)+1;
//
//  Allocate enough global memory to hold DEVNAMES.
//
    HGLOBAL hDevNames = GlobalAlloc(GHND,
                         sizeof(DEVNAMES) +
                         (drvNameLen + ptrNameLen +
                         porNameLen)*sizeof(TCHAR));
    if (hDevNames == NULL)
    {
        GlobalFree(pInfo2);
        return (NULL);
    }
    DEVNAMES* pDevNames = (DEVNAMES*)GlobalLock(hDevNames);
    if (pDevNames == NULL)
    {
        GlobalFree (pInfo2);
        GlobalFree (hDevNames);
        return (NULL);
    }
// Copy the DEVNAMES information from PRINTER_INFO_2
// tcOffset = TCHAR Offset into structure
    int tcOffset = sizeof(DEVNAMES)/sizeof(TCHAR);

    pDevNames->wDriverOffset = tcOffset;
    memcpy((LPTSTR)pDevNames + tcOffset,
                    pInfo2->pDriverName,
                    drvNameLen*sizeof(TCHAR));
    tcOffset += drvNameLen;

    pDevNames->wDeviceOffset = tcOffset;
    memcpy((LPTSTR)pDevNames + tcOffset,
                    pInfo2->pPrinterName,
                    ptrNameLen*sizeof(TCHAR));
    tcOffset += ptrNameLen;

    pDevNames->wOutputOffset = tcOffset;
    memcpy((LPTSTR)pDevNames + tcOffset,
                    pInfo2->pPortName,
                    porNameLen*sizeof(TCHAR));
    pDevNames->wDefault = 0;
//
//  Unlock the global memory and free the pInfo2 structure.
//
    GlobalUnlock(hDevNames);
    GlobalFree(pInfo2);
```

```
//
//  return the global handle to the DEVNAMES structure
//
    return (hDevNames);
}
```

802. Understanding the Print Setup Dialog Box

The Print Setup dialog box is an anachronism. The MSDN documentation states, "The Print Setup dialog box should not be used in new applications. It has been superseded by the Page Setup common dialog box created by the *PageSetupDlg()* function." Curiously, however, projects created by the MFC AppWizard continue to use the old Print Setup dialog box.

The Print Setup dialog box shown in Figure 802 doesn't offer the options and controls available on the Page Setup dialog box. For one, Print Setup provides no method for the user to set margins.

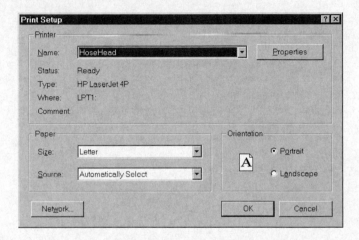

Figure 802   The old Printer Setup dialog allowed selection of another printer without summoning another dialog box

The Page Setup dialog box is more compact than Print Setup. The printer selection portion of the dialog box has been moved to a second dialog box that you get to by pressing the Printer button, where you also get access to the Properties dialog box.

Page Setup also offers a small preview page that you can draw yourself by providing a paint hook procedure.

803. Customizing Common Dialog Boxes

The common dialog boxes provide the basic necessities for displaying and collecting information for their assigned tasks. For most projects, that's all you will need. There are times, however, when some additional controls would provide functions you need on these dialog boxes.

The structures associated with the common dialog boxes all contain entries for custom dialog templates. This doesn't mean that you have to redraw the dialog box completely. The common dialog code contains a mechanism that lets you *embed* the common dialog box in your own template so that you don't have to reinvent the wheel every time you need to add a control or two to a common dialog box.

Prior to Windows 95, the common dialog box templates were part of the Windows software development kit (SDK), and you built your custom dialog box around the template. You can still do this, but the templates no longer are provided, and all your code has to be rolled by hand. You can get the common dialog templates by selecting Open from the File menu in the Visual Studio. At the bottom of the Open dialog box, select Resources in the Open As box, and select Executable Files in the Files of Type box. Track to your Windows system directory and select the *commdlg.dll* file. Under the Dialogs listing, you'll find the templates for all the common dialog boxes. When you open one of the templates, use the Select All item on the Edit menu to put the controls in the Clipboard. Close the file and return to your project, and then paste the controls onto your own dialog box.

An easier way is to embed the existing common dialog box into your own dialog box. In your project, create a dialog box to hold the controls that you want to add to the common dialog box. On the Styles page of the Properties dialog box, you should check the Clip Siblings box. On the More Styles page, check the Control, 3-D-Look, and Visible boxes. Select Child as the window style.

Add the controls that you want, and close the dialog box editor. In your program code where you set up the structure to initialize the common dialog box, add the ID for your custom dialog box to the *lpTemplateName* member using the *MAKEINTRESOURCE* macro. For example, you have a custom template for the File Open common dialog box with a resource ID of *IDD_FILEOPEN*. In the structure, use the following line:

```
ofn.lpTemplateName    = MAKEINTRESOURCE(IDD_FILEOPEN);
```

You also must specify the instance handle of your program. For a Windows API application, this value is passed to the *WinMain()* function. For an MFC project, you can get the handle by calling *AfxGet InstanceHandle()*.

Compile and run your program. When you select the common dialog box, your controls will be added *below* the common dialog box's controls. If you want your controls to appear this way, that's all you need to do. However, suppose that you want your controls above or to one side of the common dialog box's image. You can do this by drawing a static control on your custom template and giving it the special resource ID of *stc32*. If the common dialog box code finds a control with this ID on a custom template, it positions your controls *relative* to the location of this static control.

The actual size of the *stc32* control doesn't matter. The keyword here is *relative*. The common dialog box code will expand the static control to hold the common dialog box, and then add your controls around it in the same relative positions as the dialog template shows. You might have to experiment with placement a bit to get the exact position you want.

Before you add the static control, however, add the *dlgs.h* file to your resource script. In the ResourceView pane of the Workshop Window, right-click on the root tree item and select Resource Includes from the menu. In the dialog box, add "#include <dlgs.h>" to the Read-Only Symbol Directives box. Compile your program. Now when you add the static control, you can select *stc32* from the drop-down list of the ID control. Don't type in the ID directly. If you do, the resource editor will add a new value to your *resource.h* file, and you'll get a redefinition error when you compile the program.

In the FileOpen project from Tip 776, "Using *GetOpenFileName()* and *GetSaveFileName()* Directly," you can add a control to display a preview of the selected bitmap file so that you know what it looks like before you open it. For a text-based project, you could display the first line or two of the file in this box. The custom dialog template is shown in Figure 803. We've drawn a border around the *stc32* control and put some text in it to make it visible on the image, but your template should remove these.

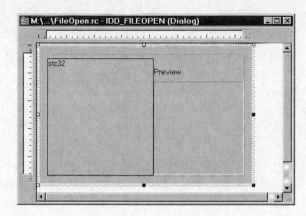

Figure 803   The custom dialog template shows the relative placement of the common dialog box controls and the preview window

The static control isn't drawn to size. We're interested only in the *relative* placement of the controls on the right side of the common dialog box, so we've made it just big enough to position the preview window and a label just above it. The control that will hold the preview has a sunken property. When you use the File Open dialog box with this custom template, you should see a sunken gray area to the right of the common dialog box controls.

To make this work, you need to provide a *hook* procedure to draw the bitmap image in the preview area. Hook procedures are discussed in the next tip; in Tip 805, "Writing a Hook Procedure," you'll add the code to display the image.

804. *Understanding Hooks*

Custom templates for the common dialog boxes don't make a lot of sense without hook procedures. You can add controls, but the code in the common dialog box DLL doesn't know anything about them. It can't update them because even if it were aware of the additional controls, it wouldn't have any idea what to draw in them.

The hook procedure is where you maintain and draw your controls. Essentially, a hook procedure is a message monitor. It's a hook into the message flow so that your program can act on messages intended for controls that you've added to the custom dialog box.

Your hook procedure doesn't necessarily receive all messages for the dialog box. With the *OPENFILE-NAME* structure, you can use the newer style dialog boxes by setting the *OFN_EXPLORER* bit in the *Flags* member. In this case, your hook procedure receives messages intended for the controls on your custom dialog box template, plus notification messages and a few other messages. Generally, the hook procedure receives messages before the dialog box procedure, with the exception of *WM_INITDIALOG*, which it receives after it has been processed by the dialog box procedure.

To use a hook procedure with a common dialog box, you must set the *ENABLEHOOK* flag in the controlling structure before opening the dialog box. The exact flag varies according to the dialog box. For the *OPENFILENAME* structure, it is *OFN_ENABLEHOOK*; for the *CHOOSEFONT* structure it is *CF_ENABLEHOOK*, and so on. Usually the hook flag is set along with the *ENABLETEMPLATE* flag, indicating that you are providing a custom dialog template.

805. *Writing a Hook Procedure*

Hook procedures and custom templates can turn the common dialog boxes into something not so common and can add a great deal of functionality in the process. In this tip, you'll add a preview window to the File Open common dialog box and use the hook procedure to keep it updated, redrawing a new bitmap in the preview window as the user selects different files as shown in Figure 805.

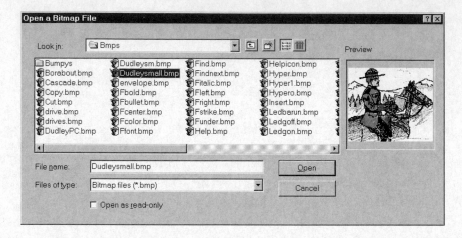

Figure 805   Adding a preview window to a File Open common dialog box gives the user a chance
to see the contents of a file before committing to opening it in the application. You can do this easily
using a hook procedure and a custom dialog box template.

If you didn't already add the custom dialog template in Tip 803, "Customizing Common Dialog Boxes," add it now or use the code on the companion CD-ROM. In the *OpenBmpFile()* function, modify the last three lines of the *OPENFILENAME* structure to read as follows:

```
ofn.lpfnHook          = OpenFileHookProc;
ofn.lpTemplateName    = MAKEINTRESOURCE(IDD_FILEOPEN);
ofn.Flags             = OFN_EXPLORER | OFN_ENABLEHOOK
                        | OFN_ENABLETEMPLATE;
```

You'll also need to add three new functions, so prototype them in the *FileOpen.h* file, which is listed here:

```
#if _MSC_VER > 1000
#pragma once
#endif // _MSC_VER > 1000

#include <commdlg.h>    // includes common dialog box
                        // functionality
#include <dlgs.h>       // includes common dialog box
                        // template defines
#include <cderr.h>      // includes the common dialog box
                        // error codes

struct OPENDATA
{
    HBITMAP  hBmp;
    char szFileName[_MAX_PATH];   // Buffer for file name
    char szFilePath[_MAX_PATH];   // buffer for file path
```

```
};

BOOL OpenBmpFile (HWND hWnd, OPENDATA &od);
UINT CALLBACK OpenFileHookProc(HWND, UINT, WPARAM, LPARAM);
BOOL NEAR PASCAL DoNotify(HWND hDlg, LPOFNOTIFY pofn);
void DrawPreview (HWND hOwner, HBITMAP hBmp);
```

The hook procedure is *OpenFileHookProc()*. It handles the basic messages sent by the dialog box procedure, including *WM_INITDIALOG*. Particularly important for your controls is the *WM_PAINT* message. The added controls get paint messages, and text controls such as static and edit boxes will redraw themselves. However, any special drawing, such as placing the bitmap image in the preview window, will have to be done in your code.

The source code in the *FileOpen.cpp* file is listed here:

```
// FileOpen.cpp : Defines the entry point for the
// application.
//

#include "stdafx.h"
#include "resource.h"
#include "FileOpen.h"

#define MAX_LOADSTRING 100

HINSTANCE hInst;                        // current instance
TCHAR szTitle[MAX_LOADSTRING];          // The title bar text
TCHAR szWindowClass[MAX_LOADSTRING]; // The title bar text

// Forward declarations of functions in this code module:
ATOM                MyRegisterClass(HINSTANCE hInstance);
BOOL                InitInstance(HINSTANCE, int);
LRESULT CALLBACK    WndProc(HWND, UINT, WPARAM, LPARAM);
LRESULT CALLBACK    About(HWND, UINT, WPARAM, LPARAM);

int APIENTRY WinMain(HINSTANCE hInstance,
                     HINSTANCE hPrevInstance,
                     LPSTR     lpCmdLine,
                     int       nCmdShow)
{
    // TODO: Place code here.
    MSG msg;
    HACCEL hAccelTable;

    // Initialize global strings
    LoadString(hInstance, IDS_APP_TITLE, szTitle,
            MAX_LOADSTRING);
    LoadString(hInstance, IDC_FILEOPEN, szWindowClass,
            MAX_LOADSTRING);
    MyRegisterClass(hInstance);

    // Perform application initialization:
    if (!InitInstance (hInstance, nCmdShow))
    {
        return FALSE;
    }
```

```
    hAccelTable = LoadAccelerators(hInstance,
                               (LPCTSTR)IDC_FILEOPEN);


    // Main message loop:
    while (GetMessage(&msg, NULL, 0, 0))
    {
        if (!TranslateAccelerator(msg.hwnd,
                               hAccelTable, &msg))

        {
            TranslateMessage(&msg);
            DispatchMessage(&msg);
        }
    }

    return msg.wParam;
}



//
//  FUNCTION: MyRegisterClass()
//
//  PURPOSE: Registers the window class.
//
//  COMMENTS:
//
//    This function and its usage is necessary only if you
//    want this code to be compatible with Win32 systems
//    prior to the 'RegisterClassEx' function that was
//    added to Windows 95 It is important to call this
//    function so that the application will get
//    'well-formed' small icons associated with it.
//
ATOM MyRegisterClass(HINSTANCE hInstance)
{
    WNDCLASSEX wcex;

    wcex.cbSize = sizeof(WNDCLASSEX);

    wcex.style          = CS_HREDRAW | CS_VREDRAW;
    wcex.lpfnWndProc    = (WNDPROC)WndProc;
    wcex.cbClsExtra     = 0;
    wcex.cbWndExtra     = 0;
    wcex.hInstance      = hInstance;
    wcex.hIcon          = LoadIcon(hInstance,
                            (LPCTSTR)IDI_FILEOPEN);
    wcex.hCursor        = LoadCursor(NULL, IDC_ARROW);
    wcex.hbrBackground  = (HBRUSH)(COLOR_WINDOW+1);
    wcex.lpszMenuName   = (LPCSTR)IDC_FILEOPEN;
    wcex.lpszClassName  = szWindowClass;
    wcex.hIconSm        = LoadIcon(wcex.hInstance,
                            (LPCTSTR)IDI_SMALL);

    return RegisterClassEx(&wcex);
}
```

```
//
//   FUNCTION: InitInstance(HANDLE, int)
//
//   PURPOSE: Saves instance handle and creates main window
//
//   COMMENTS:
//
//        In this function, we save the instance handle in
//        a global variable and create and display the main
//        program window.
//
BOOL InitInstance(HINSTANCE hInstance, int nCmdShow)
{
   HWND hWnd;

  // Store instance handle in our global variable
   hInst = hInstance;
   hWnd = CreateWindow(szWindowClass, szTitle,
                     WS_OVERLAPPEDWINDOW,
                     CW_USEDEFAULT, 0, CW_USEDEFAULT,
                     0, NULL, NULL, hInstance, NULL);

   if (!hWnd)
   {
      return FALSE;
   }

   ShowWindow(hWnd, nCmdShow);
   UpdateWindow(hWnd);

   return TRUE;
}


//
//  FUNCTION: WndProc(HWND, unsigned, WORD, LONG)
//
//  PURPOSE:  Processes messages for the main window.
//
//  WM_COMMAND  - process the application menu
//  WM_PAINT    - Paint the main window
//  WM_DESTROY  - post a quit message and return
//
//
LRESULT CALLBACK WndProc(HWND hWnd, UINT message,
                         WPARAM wParam, LPARAM lParam)
{
   static OPENDATA od = {NULL, "", ""};
   int wmId, wmEvent;
   PAINTSTRUCT ps;
   HDC hdc;

   switch (message)
   {
      case WM_COMMAND:
         wmId    = LOWORD(wParam);
         wmEvent = HIWORD(wParam);
```

```
            // Parse the menu selections:
            switch (wmId)
            {
                case IDM_ABOUT:
                    DialogBox(hInst, (LPCTSTR)IDD_ABOUTBOX,
                              hWnd, (DLGPROC)About);
                    break;
                case IDM_EXIT:
                    DestroyWindow(hWnd);
                    break;
                case IDM_OPEN:
                {
                    OpenBmpFile (hWnd, od);
                    RECT rc;
                    GetClientRect (hWnd, &rc);
                    InvalidateRect (hWnd, &rc, TRUE);
                    break;
                }
                default:
                    return DefWindowProc(hWnd, message,
                                         wParam, lParam);
            }
            break;
        case WM_PAINT:
            hdc = BeginPaint(hWnd, &ps);
            // TODO: Add any drawing code here...
            if (od.hBmp != NULL)
            {
                RECT rt;
                GetClientRect(hWnd, &rt);
                HDC MemDC = CreateCompatibleDC (hdc);
                SelectObject (MemDC, od.hBmp);
                BitBlt (hdc, 0, 0, rt.right - rt.left,
                        rt.bottom - rt.top, MemDC, 0, 0,
                        SRCCOPY);
                DeleteDC (MemDC);
            }
            EndPaint(hWnd, &ps);
            break;
        case WM_DESTROY:
            if (od.hBmp != NULL)
            {
                DeleteObject (od.hBmp);
                od.hBmp = NULL;
            }
            PostQuitMessage(0);
            break;
        default:
            return DefWindowProc(hWnd, message,
                                 wParam, lParam);
    }
    return 0;
}

// Message handler for About box.
LRESULT CALLBACK About(HWND hDlg, UINT message,
```

```
                    WPARAM wParam, LPARAM lParam)
{
    switch (message)
    {
        case WM_INITDIALOG:
                return TRUE;


        case WM_COMMAND:
            if (LOWORD(wParam) == IDOK || LOWORD(wParam)
                                      == IDCANCEL)
            {
                EndDialog(hDlg, LOWORD(wParam));
                return TRUE;
            }
            break;
    }
    return FALSE;
}

BOOL OpenBmpFile (HWND hWnd, OPENDATA &OpenData)
{
    TCHAR       szFile[MAX_PATH]    = "\0";
    TCHAR  *szFilter = "Bitmap files (*.bmp)\0*.bmp\0";
                    ;
    memset (szFile, '\0', sizeof (szFile));

    OPENDATA od = {NULL, "", ""};

    OPENFILENAME   ofn;
// Fill in the OPENFILENAME structure to support
// a template and a hook.
    ofn.lStructSize       = sizeof(OPENFILENAME);
    ofn.hwndOwner         = hWnd;
    ofn.hInstance         = hInst;
    ofn.lpstrFilter       = szFilter;
    ofn.lpstrCustomFilter = NULL;
    ofn.nMaxCustFilter    = 0;
    ofn.nFilterIndex      = 0;
    ofn.lpstrFile         = szFile;
    ofn.nMaxFile          = sizeof(szFile);
    ofn.lpstrFileTitle    = NULL;
    ofn.nMaxFileTitle     = 0;
    ofn.lpstrInitialDir   = NULL;
    ofn.lpstrTitle        = "Open a Bitmap File";
    ofn.nFileOffset       = 0;
    ofn.nFileExtension    = 0;
    ofn.lpstrDefExt       = NULL;
    ofn.lCustData         = (LPARAM) &od;
    ofn.lpfnHook          = OpenFileHookProc;
    ofn.lpTemplateName    = MAKEINTRESOURCE(IDD_FILEOPEN);
    ofn.Flags             = OFN_EXPLORER | OFN_ENABLEHOOK
                          | OFN_ENABLETEMPLATE;

    DrawPreview (hWnd, od.hBmp);

    // Call the common dialog function.
```

```
        if (GetOpenFileName(&ofn))
        {
//
// Use this conditional block to preprocess any file
// information. Return TRUE. If the bitmap isn't NULL,
// copy the data into the OPENDATA structure that was
// passed as a parameter.
//
            if (od.hBmp != NULL)
            {
                memcpy (&OpenData, &od, sizeof (OPENDATA));
            }
            return (TRUE);
        }
        return (FALSE);
}

UINT CALLBACK OpenFileHookProc(HWND hDlg, UINT uMsg,
                               WPARAM wParam, LPARAM lParam)
{
    switch (uMsg)
    {
//
// The dialog procedure already has processed the
// WM_INITDIALOG message, so we can safely assume that the
// hDlg parameter is valid. Save the address of the
// of the OPENFILENAME structure in the window long.
//
        case WM_INITDIALOG:
            SetWindowLong(hDlg, DWL_USER, lParam);
            break;
        case WM_NCPAINT:
        case WM_PAINT:
        {
            OPENDATA &od = *(OPENDATA *)((OPENFILENAME *)
              (GetWindowLong (hDlg,DWL_USER)))->lCustData;
            DrawPreview (hDlg, od.hBmp);
            return (FALSE);
        }
        case WM_NOTIFY:
            DoNotify(hDlg, (LPOFNOTIFY)lParam);
            return (FALSE);
        default:
            break;
    }
    return (FALSE);
}

BOOL PASCAL DoNotify(HWND hDlg, LPOFNOTIFY pofn)
{

    OPENDATA &od = *(OPENDATA *)((OPENFILENAME *)
          (GetWindowLong (hDlg, DWL_USER)))->lCustData;

    switch (pofn->hdr.code)
    {
```

```
//
// The user has selected a new file. If it's a bitmap
// file, dump the old bitmap and display the new one.
// If it's a directory, just dump the bitmap.
//
      case CDN_SELCHANGE:
      {
//
// Get the path of the selected file. To get just the
// file name without the complete path, call
//        CommDlg_OpenSave_GetSpec(GetParent(hDlg),
//            szFile, sizeof(szFile));

          CommDlg_OpenSave_GetFilePath(GetParent(hDlg),
              od.szFilePath, sizeof(od.szFilePath));
          WIN32_FIND_DATA fd;
          HANDLE hFind;
          hFind = FindFirstFile(od.szFilePath, &fd);
          if (hFind == NULL)
              break;
          FindClose (hFind);
          if (od.hBmp != NULL)
          {
              DeleteObject (od.hBmp);
              od.hBmp = NULL;
          }
          if (!(fd.dwFileAttributes &
                FILE_ATTRIBUTE_DIRECTORY))
          {
              od.hBmp = (HBITMAP) LoadImage (NULL,
                        od.szFilePath, IMAGE_BITMAP,
                        0, 0, LR_LOADFROMFILE);
          }
          DrawPreview (hDlg, od.hBmp);
      }
      break;
//
// The folder has changed, which means there no longer
// is a file selected. Delete the bitmap and erase it
// from the preview window.
//
      case CDN_FOLDERCHANGE:
      {
          if (od.hBmp != NULL)
          {
              DeleteObject (od.hBmp);
              od.hBmp = NULL;
          }
          memset (od.szFileName, '\0',
                  sizeof (od.szFileName));
          memset (od.szFilePath, '\0',
                  sizeof (od.szFilePath));
          DrawPreview (hDlg, od.hBmp);
      }
      break;
//
```

```
//  CDN_FILEOK is sent when the user presses the OK
//  button, which is labeled Open or Save, depending
//  upon whether this is a File Open or File Save
//  dialog box.
//
        case CDN_FILEOK:
            SetWindowLong(hDlg, DWL_MSGRESULT, 1L);
            break;
//
//  CDN_SHAREVIOLATION is sent when the user presses
//  the OK button and a network-sharing violation
//  occurs on the selected file.
//
        case CDN_SHAREVIOLATION:
            MessageBox(hDlg, "Network sharing violation",
                            "Open Bitmap File", MB_OK);
            break;
    }

    return(TRUE);
}

void DrawPreview (HWND hOwner, HBITMAP hBmp)
{

    HWND hPreview = GetDlgItem (hOwner,IDC_STATIC_PREVIEW);
    if (hPreview == NULL)
        return;
    RECT rc;
//
//  Get the control rectangle and fill it with the
//  light gray background brush.
//
    GetClientRect (hPreview, &rc);
    rc.right -= rc.left;
    rc.bottom -= rc.top;
    rc.top = rc.left = 0;
    HDC PrevDC = GetDC(hPreview);
    FillRect (PrevDC, &rc,
            (HBRUSH) GetStockObject (LTGRAY_BRUSH));
//
//  If there's no bitmap, just leave the control with
//  the gray background.
//
    if (hBmp == NULL)
        return;
//
//  Adjust the right and bottom of the rectangle so that
//  we can add a margin later.
//
    rc.right -= 4;
    rc.bottom -= 4;
//
//  Create the memory DC to hold the bitmap image for
//  the StretchBlt operation. Select the image and get
//  the BITMAP structure for it. You'll need the structure
```

```
//   to get the size for the StretchBlt function.
//
     HDC MemDC = CreateCompatibleDC (PrevDC);
     SelectObject (MemDC, hBmp);
     BITMAP bmp;
     GetObject (hBmp, sizeof (BITMAP), &bmp);
//
//   Scale the image so that it will fit in the preview
//   window. Take the larger side and make it fit, and
//   then scale the smaller side accordingly. If the
//   bitmap is square, the StretchBlt function will
//   make it fit.
//
     int nHeight, nWidth;
     if (bmp.bmWidth > bmp.bmHeight)
     {
         nWidth = rc.right;
         nHeight = bmp.bmHeight * rc.right / bmp.bmWidth;
         rc.top = (rc.bottom - nHeight) / 2;
         rc.bottom = rc.top + nHeight;
     }
     else if (bmp.bmHeight > bmp.bmWidth)
     {
         nHeight = rc.bottom;
         nWidth = bmp.bmWidth * rc.bottom / bmp.bmHeight;
         rc.left = (rc.right - nWidth) / 2;
         rc.right = rc.left + nWidth;
     }
//
//   Add a wee bit of offset to the sides so the control
//   edges show through. Note that we already had subtracted
//   4 from the bottom and right sides to account for this.
//
     rc.top += 2, rc.left += 2;
     rc.right += 2, rc.bottom += 2;
//
//   Draw the image and free the DCs. DO NOT delete the
//   preview window's DC; just release it. Delete the
//   memory DC, though.
//
     StretchBlt (PrevDC, rc.left, rc.top,
                        rc.right - rc.left,
                        rc.bottom - rc.top,
                        MemDC, 0, 0, bmp.bmWidth,
                        bmp.bmHeight, SRCCOPY);
     ReleaseDC (hPreview, PrevDC);
     DeleteDC (MemDC);
}
```

Separating the code that actually draws the bitmap makes it easier to extend the program to include other file types. You could write other drawing functions and select them according to the file type.

If you provide a template with multiple file types, Windows will send you a *CDN_TYPECHANGE* message when the user changes the selection in the Files of Type box. You can use this to adjust parameters for drawing other information in the preview control.

806. *Providing Help for a Common Dialog Box*

The common dialog boxes enable you to display a Help button, but they don't provide the help file that you need to process the resulting information. When the Help button is pressed, the dialog box procedure sends a *CDN_HELP* message to your hook procedure. Use this message to call the *WinHelp()* function to display your application's help file.

Help files are prepared using a rich text editor. The editor should be capable of displaying footnotes. WordPerfect and Microsoft Word are good editors for help files—and in this case, I would have to give the edge to Word. Add a section to your help file describing the common dialog box operations. You should include topics for the basic controls in addition to any that you've added through a custom template.

Once you've prepared the help file, you compile it using the Help Workshop, *hcw.exe*. The Help Workshop program doesn't appear on the Tools menu of the Visual Studio, but a copy of it should have been installed when you installed Visual Studio. It's in the *COMMON\TOOLS* subdirectory in the Visual Studio directory.

Building a good help file is a project in itself, and we won't have room in this book to cover the steps in preparing a help file. Unfortunately, there's not a lot of literature on writing help files, either. It's the forgotten topic of computer books, but Nancy Hickman does a good job of covering the process in her book, *Building Windows 95 Help*.

807. *Understanding Controls in the Windows Environment*

In Windows, a *control* is a child window that an application uses to perform input and output operations. Controls usually are associated with a dialog box, but they may be used in conjunction with any window. In fact, in a typical application, the user is confronted with a number of controls, although they may not be as obvious as dialog box controls. The menu is a control; the toolbar is a collection of button controls and is a control itself. Often, the main window is associated with an underlying control such as an edit control for a *CEditView* application or a rich-text control for a *CRichEditView* application.

Controls are always child windows. When the runtime code creates controls for a dialog box, they are child windows of the dialog box. Each control on the main window frame is a child of the frame window. This parent-child relationship is a key element in the operation of a Windows application. Controls send messages to their parents when events occur. These messages are known as *notification* messages and usually occur as the result of some action by the user, such as a button press or a typed character. The application uses these messages to react to user actions. In the other direction, the application can send messages to the control windows.

Each control has its own windows procedure, just as your Windows API programs have had their *WndProc()* functions. This procedure determines what messages a control will receive and respond to, and determines what action will be taken. Most controls respond to the Windows management messages such as *WM_SHOWWINDOW*, *WM_ENABLE*, and *WM_SETFOCUS*.

808. *Understanding the Common Controls*

Windows provides a number of controls that programmers may use directly in their applications and dialog boxes. These controls are known as *common controls* and are contained in the common control library, *comctl32.dll*. This library contains all the controls that were used in the old 16-bit windows but are converted for use in a 32-bit environment such as Windows 95 and Windows NT. In addition, since the introduction of Windows 95, a number of additional controls have been added to the library, and there are some controls contained in the ActiveX library *comctl32.ocx*. In all, the default control toolbar in the Visual Studio contains buttons and icons for 24 different common controls (plus a 25th button for custom controls).

Many of the common controls, particularly the newer ones, have *Owner Draw* style settings so that you can customize the appearance and operation of the control. The Owner Draw mechanism will vary by control. For buttons, the application (the *owner*) is responsible for drawing the control. For other controls such as list boxes, combo boxes, and list controls, the control itself draws the frame, and the application is responsible for drawing the contents.

The controls provide a common user interface between programs. Unless you modify it with one of the customization options such as Owner Draw, a control from the library looks and acts the same in every program that uses it. This shortens the time that it takes users to learn how to use a program. Thus, you should customize a control only when necessary and then maintain as much of the common base control as possible.

The advantage of using a common control is that much of the work is done for you. The more work a control does, the less programming you have to do. The trade-off, of course, is that your program looks and feels more like other programs when you use the basic, uncooked controls. The edit control is a good example. It provides keyboard processing, character translation, cursor movement, and, when used as a multi-line control, word wrapping. All of this is done without you having to write a single line of code.

Unless your application is a very unusual one, you'll use several of the basic controls somewhere in your program. Even the basic common dialog boxes use edit and static controls.

809. *Understanding Common Control Window Classes*

Because they are windows, each control has a window class. Don't confuse this with a C++ class; the window class is the definition that you give it using the *WNDCLASS* and *WNDCLASSEX* structures when you call the *RegisterClass()* function. You don't use this in your application because the window classes for the controls already are registered. You don't have to do it unless you are creating a custom control.

Each window class has a Windows procedure defined for it. This procedure is responsible for handling incoming messages and sending messages out to the parent window (the control is always a child window, remember, so it has a parent).

Not all common controls have distinct window classes. Many share the same window class. For example, the pushbutton, radio buttons, check boxes, and group boxes all have the same registered class name, BUTTON. This is why, in the ClassWizard, you'll see *BN_CLICKED* and *BN_DOUBLE CLICKED* messages available for all these controls even though the group box doesn't respond to button clicks and will never send these messages.

The common control window classes are summarized in Table 809.

Window Class	Controls
Button	Pushbutton, radio button, check box, group box
ListBox	List box, check list box, drag list box
Edit	Edit box
Static	Static text (label), picture
Scrollbar	Scroll bar
msctls_updown32	Spin control
msctls_progress32	Progress control
msctls_trackbar32	Slider control
msctls_hotkey32	Hotkey control
SysListView32	List control (not the same as a list box control)
SysTreeView32	Tree control
SysTabControl32	Tab control
SysAnimate32	Animation control
RICHEDIT	Rich edit control
SysDateTimePick32	Date and time picker control
SysMonthCal32	Calendar (monthly) control
SysIPAddress32	IP address control
ComboBoxEx32	Extended combo box control

Table 809 The window classes used by the Windows common control library

Copy these into a file someplace where you can get to it readily. You'll need these window class names if you ever have to create a control using the *CreateEx()* function. I've never found a comprehensive list of them in the MSDN library (it might be there, but it's well hidden). I compiled this list by creating each control on a dialog box, and then checked the template to see what Window class name the resource editor gave each control.

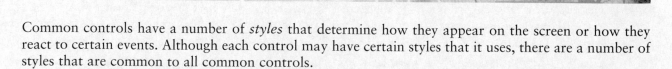

810. *Understanding Common Control Styles*

Common controls have a number of *styles* that determine how they appear on the screen or how they react to certain events. Although each control may have certain styles that it uses, there are a number of styles that are common to all common controls.

In the dialog box editor, the styles that are listed on the General page of a control's property sheet usually are styles that are common to most controls, but some of them are spread out on other pages. The first page usually contains four styles that are common to all controls: visible, disabled, group, and tab stop. A fifth check box on the General page, Help ID, is not a style but a flag to the resource editor to create an ID for the control in the help file. These styles are indicated by individual bits that are either set or reset in a control value—a 32-bit unsigned integer. In most Windows code, you'll see this value indicated by the variable name *dwStyle*.

These styles are summarized in Table 810. Some of them you won't see in the dialog editor, but you can use them when you create the control using the *Create()* or *CreateEx()* functions. For example, the *WS_CAPTION* doesn't appear in the Edit box styles in the dialog editor, but it is possible to create an edit control box that has its own title bar using the create functions.

Style	Value	Meaning
WS_VISIBLE	0x10000000	Indicates whether the control is visible when it is first created.
WS_DISABLED	0x08000000	Indicates whether the control is disabled (grayed) when it is first created.
WS_GROUP	0x00020000	Indicates the first control in a group of controls through which the user can move using the cursor keys. Only the first control of the group has this style set, and the next control containing this style terminates the current group. An example of a group is a set of radio buttons.
WS_TABSTOP	0x00010000	When set, the user may use the Tab key to access the control. The Tab key sequentially selects controls with this bit set.
WS_CHILD	0x40000000	Creates a child window. Controls are all child windows.
WS_CLIPCHILDREN	0x02000000	Prevents drawing in the client area of the main window from drawing over child windows. Used with parent windows.
WS_CLIPSIBLINGS	0x04000000	Clips the region of child windows when they overlap.
WS_CAPTION	0x00C00000	Creates a window that has a title bar. This is a combination of *WS_BORDER* and *WS_DLGFRAME*.
WS_BORDER	0x00800000	Specifies that the control has a border around it.
WS_VSCROLL	0x00200000	Creates a control with a vertical scroll bar.
WS_HSCROLL	0x00100000	Creates a control with a horizontal scroll bar
WS_DLGFRAME	0x00400000	Creates a window with a double border. This style cannot be used with the *WS_CAPTION* style.

Table 810   *Window styles used with common controls*

Notice that none of these styles uses bits in the low-order word (the 16 least significant bits). These bits are reserved for styles that are particular to individual control types. These styles—and other window styles—are defined in the *winuser.h* header file.

In addition to these styles, you'll see *extended* styles used by controls. Not all the styles used by controls in 32-bit windows can be contained in the upper 16 bits of the style value. To accommodate these additional styles, Windows uses an extended style value, which you'll usually see in Windows programming using the variable name *dwStyleEx* or *dwExStyle*.

811. *Windows Notification Messages Used by Common Controls*

All controls are child windows and communicate with their parent windows through notification messages. These messages are usually generated as the result of some action by the user. For example, when the user checks or unchecks a selection box, the control sends a *BN_CLICKED* message to the parent window. It is the parent window's responsibility to act on the message.

Simple notification messages such as *BN_CLICKED* are sent as *WM_COMMAND* messages with the notification code (*BN_CLICKED*) and the control's ID in the *wParam* argument and the control's handle in the *lParam* argument. In an MFC program that uses message map macros, you'll see it in the message map as *ON_BN_CLICKED(IDC_BUTTONID, OnButtonID)*.

Frequently, however, controls need to give their parents more information than just simple events. There are a number of special-purpose notification messages such as *WM_CTLCOLOR*, *WM_VSCROLL*, and *WM_DRAWITEM* that cover many of these cases.

With Windows 95, controls have become considerably more complex, and the amount of information that has to be sent back to the parent has increased. To cover all these cases, the Microsoft designers came up with the *WM_NOTIFY* message, which allows a control to pass any amount of information in a standard fashion. These messages contain the ID of the control in the *wParam* argument and a pointer to a structure in the *lParam*. This structure is always cast to an *NMHDR* structure (Notification Message HeaDeR), but in fact it may be a pointer to any type of structure required by the control and message. For a list control asking for display information, for example, the parameter is actually a pointer to a structure of type *LV_DISPINFO*, and you need to cast it to the proper type before you can use it.

812. *Macros Used by Common Controls*

When you build your program using the Microsoft Foundation Class library, notification messages have an added dimension. The notification messages may be handled either by the parent window class or by the control class through a process known as message *reflection*.

Message reflection is a new feature of MFC beginning with version 4.0. It is *not* a feature of the Windows API, and you can use it only if you base your application on MFC and the parent window for the controls is a descendant of *CWnd*.

Normally in a Windows program, when a control sends a notification message to its parent window, the parent is responsible for handling the message. This means that the code for handling these messages to customize controls must be in all classes that need to handle that message. You could derive a custom base class for all these parent windows to contain the message handlers, but then you have the problem of identifying a particular control that you want to customize.

Reflection provides a better method of customizing the controls by allowing the control itself to handle the notification messages. To use it, you derive your own class from the control class and add handlers for the reflected messages. When the parent window receives a message from the control, it reflects it back to the control, which has the first chance to handle the message. If the child window—the control—doesn't handle the message, it comes back to the parent window for processing. You don't see this happening in your program; the code to handle message reflection is contained in the *CWnd* class.

Let's assume that you have a control that sends a notification message to the parent window. This message is intercepted by the code in *CWnd* before it can get to your parent window class's message map. *CWnd* routes the message through the control's window procedure. If the procedure returns *TRUE*, the control has handled the message. If it returns *FALSE*, the control did not handle the message, and it is passed on to the parent window's message map. So, to handle reflected messages in a control, you must derive your own class from the control's base class and add these messages to your message map.

An extended form of message reflection, which you'll see in the following tables, allows both the control and the parent window to handle the notification message. In this case, if the control's window procedure returns *TRUE*, the message will be passed on to the parent window as well. If it returns *FALSE*, the message stops at the control level. Note that the sense of the return type is just the reverse of normal reflection.

The generalized form of the reflected message macro is *ON_NOTIFY_REFLECT* to handle messages sent as *WM_NOTIFY*, and *ON_CONTROL_REFLECT* to handle messages sent as *WM_COMMAND*. Each of these macros requires two arguments—the first is the notification code, and the second is the address of the handler function.

Some messages have specific macros usually because the information to the handling function differs enough from the general macro to require special handling. In these cases, there are no arguments to the macro, and you don't specify a message-handler function. Instead, you must use a predefined function name. The macro name is formed by adding "ON_" to the beginning of the message name and then appending "_REFLECT." The macro to handle the *WM_CTLCOLOR* message then becomes *ON_WM_CTLCOLOR_REFLECT*.

The message map macros for reflected messages showing the parameters to the macro and the proper function prototype are summarized in Table 812. Note particularly the first four items, which include the extended reflection macros. The functions here return type *BOOL* rather than the *void* type returned by the non-extended functions. This allows the *CWnd* code to decide whether to pass the message on to the parent window.

Macro	Prototype
ON_CONTROL_REFLECT(wNotifyCode,Func)	afx_msg void Func();
ON_CONTROL_REFLECT_EX(wNotifyCode,Func)	afx_msg BOOL Func();
ON_NOTIFY_REFLECT(wNotifyCode,Func)	afx_msg void Func(NMHDR *, LRESULT *) ;
ON_NOTIFY_REFLECT_EX(wNotifyCode,Func)	afx_msg BOOL Func(NMHDR *, LRESULT *);
ON_WM_CTLCOLOR_REFLECT()	afx_msg HBRUSH CtlColor(CDC *, UINT);
ON_WM_DRAWITEM_REFLECT()	afx_msg void DrawItem (DRAWITEMSTRUCT *);
ON_WM_MEASUREITEM_REFLECT()	afx_msg void MeasureItem (MEASUREITEMSTRUCT *);
ON_WM_DELETEITEM_REFLECT()	afx_msg void DeleteItem (DELETEITEMSTRUCT *);
ON_WM_COMPAREITEM_REFLECT()	afx_msg int CompareItem (COMPAREITEMSTRUCT *);
ON_WM_CHARTOITEM()	afx_msg int CharToItem(UINT nKey, UINT nIndex);

Table 812   Reflected message macros and prototypes for functions to handle them (continued on following page)

Macro	Prototype
ON_WM_VKEYTOITEM()	afx_msg int VKToItem(UINT nKey, UINT nIndex);
ON_WM_HSCROLL_REFLECT()	afx_msg void HScroll(UINT nSBCode, UINT nPos);
ON_WM_VSCROLL_REFLECT()	afx_msg void VScroll(UINT nSBCode, UINT nPos);
ON_WM_PARENTNOTIFY_REFLECT()	afx_msg void ParentNotify (UINT message, LPARAM lParam);

Table 812   Reflected message macros and prototypes for functions to handle them (continued from previous page)

The key to using the reflected messages is deriving your own classes from the MFC controls. These can be specific or generalized handlers. The MSDN documentation shows an example of how to set the background color of a control to a specific color. *CStaticEx* and *CEditEx*, discussed in Tip 484, "Deriving Classes from *CEdit* and *CStatic* to Set Text Attributes," carry this a step further and allow you to change the background color programmatically. You'll revisit derived classes in Tip 817, "Deriving Custom Classes from the MFC Control Classes."

813. Structures Used by the Common Controls Library

The older common controls are simple enough to use. You create the control and display your data in it, whether it's a text box containing a string or a list box containing a number of strings.

Since the advent of Windows 95, however, many of the newer controls have greater flexibility in how you enter and display your data. This flexibility comes at the cost of complexity. To encapsulate and manage the information contained in the controls, many of them use *item* structures.

For example, adding a line to an older *list box control* is as simple as sending it an *LB_ADDSTRING* message with a pointer to the string to be added. In the case of the MFC *CListBox* class, you call the *AddString()* member function.

The newer *list control*, however, has far greater flexibility in displaying the information. An entry easily can be broken down into columns, and the control might have an image list associated with it to select an icon to display. To make the addition of items to the list control easier, it uses an *LVITEM* structure where you define the item's text, its column, its state, and perhaps an image to associate with it. You must fill out this structure to add any item to the list control.

You'll find the item structures common in the newer controls. The combo box control gets its name from the fact that it is a combination of the edit box and list box controls. The extended combo box, on the other hand, only *appears* similar to the old combo box control, and you use them in very different ways. Both the list and edit portions of the control have added functionality, and you use a *COMBOBOX-EXITEM* structure to contain and manipulate the data.

The item structure mechanism makes sense in an environment that changes as quickly as Windows. It allows the control to grow in flexibility as Windows evolves. We're already seeing this. The tree control started out using a *TVITEM* structure as its control mechanism, but already Microsoft has introduced a *TVITEMEX* structure with an enhancement that enables you to give individual tree items extra height when needed.

Not all the newer controls use an item structure. The animation control, for example, is a simple control that displays a sequence of bitmaps. It would gain little from an item structure and as yet does not require one.

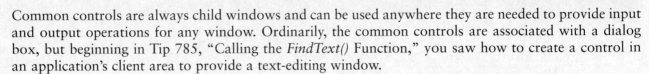

814. Using Common Controls

Common controls are always child windows and can be used anywhere they are needed to provide input and output operations for any window. Ordinarily, the common controls are associated with a dialog box, but beginning in Tip 785, "Calling the *FindText()* Function," you saw how to create a control in an application's client area to provide a text-editing window.

All the common controls are represented in the Microsoft Foundation Class library. In some cases, MFC uses the common control's base class to create other controls. For example, *CCheckListBox* and *CDragListBox* are derivations of the *CListBox* control class.

To use a common control in a dialog box, use the Dialog Editor to draw the control in the location and size on the dialog box where you want it to appear. Use the Properties dialog box to set the properties and appearance of the control.

The control sends notification messages to its parent window, so in a Windows API program, you add *case* statements to the dialog box's window procedure to intercept and use the messages. The *DialogBox()* function takes care of creating the controls based upon the dialog template created by the Dialog Editor when you drew the controls on the dialog box image. After the dialog box and the controls are created, Windows sends your application a *WM_INITDIALOG* message, and you can use this message to initialize the controls with your own data. When the dialog box is closed, the *EndDialog()* function destroys the controls.

In a dialog box used with an MFC class derived from *CDialog*, the controls are created when you declare an instance of the dialog box class and call its *DoModal()* member function, or create the dialog box by calling the *Create()* or *CreateEx()* member functions. In both cases, another member function, *OnInitDialog()*, gets called. It is in this function that the controls actually get created. This is an important step to remember because you can't manipulate the controls—set the window text, draw button images, resize the controls, and so on—until they have been created in this function. If you try to manipulate a control before this, such as in the dialog box class constructor, you'll get a program error because the controls don't yet exist.

Outside a dialog box, you'll have to create a control by calling its *Create()* or *CreateEx()* member function. Most of the control classes in MFC don't list *CreateEx()* as a member function, but it is inherited from *CWnd*, which is the base class for all the common controls. In the next section, you'll use *CreateEx()* to repeatedly create and destroy a control to change its appearance on the sample dialog box.

815. Determining the Revision Level of the Common Controls DLL

Getting the revision level of the common controls DLL from the desktop is a pretty simple matter. You open your Windows system directory, right-click on *comctl32.dll*, and select Properties from the context menu.

Sometimes, however, you need to determine this information from within a program so that your application can decide on alternate sections of code based on the version of the common controls DLL. Your program can't reach out of the screen and click your mouse buttons. Even if it could, it might tend to scare off a few users.

Most of the later Windows shell DLLs contain a function named *DLLGetVersion()*, which you may call after getting the function's address using the Windows API function *GetProcAddress()*. In the case of *ComCtl32.dll*, the function was available in versions after 4.0. So, if you query the DLL for the address of the function and the query fails, you know that the revision level is 4.0 or earlier. If the call succeeds, then you can use the function address to get the specific revision level. The following function implements that capability. You'll need to include *shlwapi.h* in the list of include files in the source file where you implement this function.

```
//
//  Get the revision level of the common controls DLL
//
bool GetCommonControlsVersion(DWORD &dwMajor,DWORD &dwMinor)
{
HINSTANCE    hInstCtrl;
DLLGETVERSIONPROC pfDllGetVersion;
bool         bResult;

    if ((hInstCtrl = LoadLibrary ("ComCtl32.dll")) == NULL)
        return (false);
    pfDllGetVersion =
            (DLLGETVERSIONPROC)GetProcAddress(hInstCtrl,
            _T("DllGetVersion"));

    if(pfDllGetVersion)
    {
        DLLVERSIONINFO    dvi;
        memset (&dvi, '\0', sizeof(dvi));
        dvi.cbSize = sizeof(dvi);
        if(SUCCEEDED((*pfDllGetVersion)(&dvi)))
        {
            dwMajor = dvi.dwMajorVersion;
            dwMinor = dvi.dwMinorVersion;
            bResult = true;
        }
        else
        {
            bResult = false;
        }
    }
    else
    {
//
//  If the call to GetProcAddress failed, then the DLL is
//  is 4.0 or earlier.
//
        dwMajor = 4;
        dwMinor = 0;
        bResult = true;
    }

    FreeLibrary(hInstCtrl);
```

Control	MFC Class	Description
ReBar	CReBar	A control bar that provides layout, persistence, and state information for its controls.
Rich edit	CRichEditCtrl	Edit control that allows multiple character, paragraph and color formatting. Often used as the underlying control for a document window.
Scroll bar	CScrollBar	Scroll bar used inside a dialog box.
Slider	CSliderCtrl	Similar to a sliding control used as volume control on audio equipment.
Spin button	CSpinButtonCtrl	A pair of arrow buttons to increment or decrement a value.
Static text	CStatic	An edit control for labeling other controls.
Status bar	CStatusBarCtrl	A bar to display information such as the state of the Insert or NumLock keys, or to write status or help messages.
Tab	CTabCtrl	Is used in property sheets. Similar to notebook tabs.
Toolbar	CToolBarCtrl	Contains buttons to generate command messages.
ToolTip	CToolTipCtrl	A small pop-up window that describes the use of a button or tool.
Tree	CTreeCtrl	Displays a hierarchical list.

Table 816   The Windows common controls showing their associated MFC classes (continued from previous page)

The MFC library also provides a *CDragListBox* control derived from *CListBox* that enables users to move the strings around in a list box; a *CCheckListBox* control, also derived from *CListBox*, which includes a check box control to the left of each string; and a *CBitmapButton* control, derived from *CButton*, which uses a series of four bitmaps to draw the state of a button.

Beginning in the next section, you'll build a property sheet containing all these controls that will include programming samples and determine how and when to use the various classes.

Begin by creating a new project named Controls. Unfortunately, the MFC AppWizard doesn't have an option to create a project based on a property sheet, but you can start off by building a dialog-based class and then delete the dialog box and class created by the AppWizard.

The application on the companion CD doesn't use the About box, so you can unselect the box on the second page of the wizard. If you include the About box, you'll have to provide some way to display it. Accept the rest of the options as they are, and create the project.

In the ResourceView pane of the Workshop Window, delete the default dialog box created by the AppWizard. Just select it and hit the Delete key. On the FileView pane, select and delete the *ControlsDlg.h* and *ControlsDlg.cpp* files. This won't actually delete the files, but it will remove them from the project. If you want to delete the files themselves (you won't need them), do it from Explorer or a directory list.

Open the *Controls.cpp* file and delete the line that includes *ControlsDlg.h*. Using the New Class dialog, create a new class named *CControlsProp* and select *CPropertySheet* as the base class. Add *ControlsProp.h* to the list of include files in *Controls.cpp*. You need to modify the *InitInstance()* function to reflect these changes to call the property sheet *DoModal()* function rather than the default dialog box function. You'll also need to initialize the rich edit control here. When you are finished, the *InitInstance()* function should look as follows:

```
    return (true);
}
```

You could modify this function to pass the name of the DLL for which you want to get the revision level. In addition, *DLLGetVersion()* in the DLLs returns an OLE-specific error, so if you need to know the exact reason that no version number could be found, you could modify the function to return this code rather than a simple *true* or *false*.

816. *Charting the Windows Common Controls*

The Microsoft Foundation Class contains classes for all the Windows common controls, encapsulating most of their functions and messages into a single object. Using the MFC classes greatly simplifies the use and manipulation of the controls.

The common controls and their MFC classes are summarized in Table 816. In addition, there are additional control classes that are derived from these base classes to provide even more controls.

Control	MFC Class	Description
Animation	CAnimate	Displays successive frames of an AVI video clip.
Button	CButton	Buttons such as OK or Cancel.
Calendar	CMonthCalCtrl	Displays a simple calendar from which a date may be selected.
Combo box	CComboBox	Edit box and list box combination.
Data/time picker	CDateTimeCtrl	Interface to display and enter date and time information.
Extended combo box	CComboBoxEx	Extended version of the combo box that may use an image list to include icons in the list box.
Edit box	CEdit	Boxes for entering text. Often used as the underlying control in a document window.
Header	CHeaderCtrl	Buttons above a column of text, such as in a list control in report mode.
Hotkey	CHotKeyCtrl	Enables user to create a "hotkey" to perform an action quickly.
Image list	CImageList	Is used to manage large sets of icons or bitmaps. (This is not a true control, but it supports lists used by other controls.)
IP address	CIPAddressCtrl	Enables the user to enter and display a number in Internet Protocol format.
List	CListCtrl	Displays a list of text with icons.
List box	CListBox	Contains a list of strings.
Progress	CProgressCtrl	A bar that indicates the progress of an operation.

Table 816   *The Windows common controls showing their associated MFC classes (continued on following page)*

```
BOOL CControlsApp::InitInstance()
{

//
//  Initialize the rich edit control.
//
    if (!AfxInitRichEdit ())
    {
        AfxMessageBox(_T("Rich edit control "
                        "initialization failed"));
        return FALSE;
    }

#ifdef _AFXDLL
    Enable3dControls();         // Call this when using MFC
                                // in a shared DLL
#else
    Enable3dControlsStatic();   // Call this when linking
                                // to MFC statically
#endif

    CControlsProp cp (_T("Common Controls Examples"));
    cp.DoModal ();
    return (false);
}
```

Open the *ControlProp.cpp* file, and add the following two lines to the constructors. You won't have any need for the Apply or Help buttons.

```
m_psh.dwFlags |= PSH_NOAPPLYNOW;
m_psh.dwFlags &= ~PSH_HASHELP;
```

Using the ClassWizard, add the *OnInitDialog()* virtual function and add the following code to it. You won't need the OK button either, so you can hide it, and you can rename the Cancel button to something like Close or Exit.

```
BOOL CControlsProp::OnInitDialog()
{
    BOOL bResult = CPropertySheet::OnInitDialog();
    CWnd *button = GetDlgItem (IDOK);
    button->ShowWindow (SW_HIDE);
    button = GetDlgItem (IDCANCEL);
    button->SetWindowText (_T("Close"));
    return bResult;
}
```

If you've done everything right, you've created the perfect application. It does nothing. It shows nothing on the screen. In fact, it exits right after it starts. Users can't have any problems using it because they don't have a chance to make a mistake.

Not to worry. In Tip 820, "Using the *CStatic* Class," you'll add the first property page to the project, and it will (should) display something.

817. Deriving Custom Classes from the MFC Control Classes

The nature of a class library is that its classes should be reusable—that is, you should be able to derive your own classes from the library to create your functionality and appearance. No matter how good it is, no class library is ever going to meet the needs of all programmers.

It almost seems sometimes that the Microsoft Foundation Class tries to hide some of the functionality and possibilities from you, and the MSDN documentation really doesn't do a great job of describing all the functions that can be overridden and how to use them. You should make it a practice to study the MFC code when deriving a custom class rather than rely on the MSDN documentation. You'd be surprised at what you'll find that isn't even hinted about in MSDN.

If you're planning to use reflected messages, such as to draw the control background in a custom color or to implement an owner-drawn control, you'll need to derive your own class. Even if a base class function can't be overridden, it's possible that you can capture the message and process it before the base class has a chance at it.

In the following tips, you'll derive classes from many of the MFC base classes.

818. Understanding the Static Text Control

Controls on a dialog box by themselves aren't always self-explanatory. Sometimes they need a bit of text or a label to explain their purposes. The static text control serves that purpose. Other than the button class of controls, which generally contain their own labels, almost every control on a dialog box can benefit from the help of a static text control.

Unchanging labels are created using the resource ID of *ID_STATIC*, or –1. You can't use the *GetDlg Item()* function to get a static text control's window, so you can't move it or change the text in it. It truly is static.

You can, however, give an individual static text control a unique resource ID and use that to get the underlying window. Once you have the window (an HWND variable, in the case of a Windows API program or the pointer to the *CWnd* object in MFC) you can move and resize the control using the *MoveWindow()* function or change its text using the *SetWindowText()* function. This makes the control useful for more than just displaying text. It can be the recipient of a bitmap, for example, or another object.

819. Deriving a Custom Class from CStatic *to Gain Functionality*

The *CStatic* class encompasses the Windows static control. It's usually nothing more than a blank area on the dialog box, but by setting various styles, you can make it appear with a border, as a sunken area or as a raised area.

To effectively show all the possibilities of the *CStatic* class, you'll need to derive a custom class from it, which you did earlier. If you added the *CStaticEx* class from Tip 484, "Deriving Classes from *CEdit* and *CStatic* to Set Text Attributes," to your gallery, add it to the *Controls* project. Otherwise, create a new class named *CStaticEx* and copy the code from Tip 484 (the ClassWizard really doesn't like it if you just copy files over and add them to the project—when you try to add member variables based on the derived class, it may not recognize it). Recompile the program so that the ClassWizard will recognize the new class.

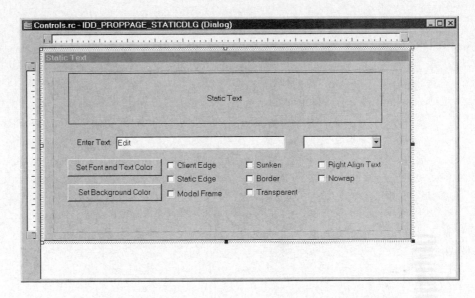

Figure 819   The controls and labels for the Static Text property page

Add a large property sheet to the project. Select Insert from the ResourceView's context menu, and then expand the Dialog item on the Insert Resource dialog box. You should see an item labeled *IDD_PROP-PAGE_LARGE*. Select it and click New. The resulting dialog template probably isn't big enough to hold everything that you will place on it, so resize it to 325 by 155. If you select a resize button on the template, the size of the dialog box will appear in the far right of the Visual Studio's status bar. Set the title to Static Text, and give it a resource ID of *IDD_PROPPAGE_STATICDLG*.

Add controls to the dialog box, as shown in Figure 819. The large static text area is shown with a border to give you an idea of how large it should be. The only style box that should be checked is the Visible and Center Vertically check box.

Add a class named *CStaticPage* to the project for this property page. Make sure that it is derived from *CPropertyPage* rather than *CDialog*. Label the controls, give them resource IDs, and create member variables for them, as shown in Table 819.

Resource ID	Label	Variable	Variable Type
IDC_STATICSAMPLE	Static Text	m_StaticSample	CStaticEx
IDC_STATICTEXT	None	m_StaticText	CString
IDC_STATICALIGNTEXT		m_TextAlign	CString
IDC_SETSTATICFONT	Set Font and Text Color	None	None
IDC_SETSTATICCOLOR	Set Background Color	None	None
IDC_STATICCLIENT	Client Edge	m_ClientEdge	BOOL
IDC_STATICSTATIC	Static Edge	m_StaticEdge	BOOL

Table 819   Resource IDs and control variables for the static text property page (continued on following page)

Resource ID	Label	Variable	Variable Type
IDC_STATICMODAL	Modal Edge	m_ModalEdge	BOOL
IDC_STATICSUNKEN	Sunken	m_Sunken	BOOL
IDC_STATICBORDER	Border	m_Border	BOOL
IDC_STATICTRANSPARENT	Transparent	m_Transparent	BOOL
IDC_STATICRIGHTTEXT	Right-Align Text	m_RightText	BOOL
IDC_STATICNOWRAP	Nowrap	m_NoWrap	BOOL

Table 819   Resource IDs and control variables for the static text property page (continued from previous page)

Some of the styles used by the static control can't be changed after you've created the control, so you need to add a function, *RecreateWindow()*, to destroy the control and then re-create it using the new styles.

The following sample of a class derived from *CStatic* draws a custom progress bar. Later versions of the common controls for use with 32-bit Windows include a *CProgressCtrl* class that implements a progress bar. That wasn't always the case, and in older versions, programmers wanting a progress bar had to draw it themselves.

The *CProgressBar* class shown here won't work in 16-bit Windows because it uses a thread to update the static control and draw the progress bar. It does, however, provide mechanisms to set the color of the control's background and the progress indicator, and to use custom colors for the indicator text. It also provides a solid progress bar rather than the questionable broken bar of the *CProgressCtrl*.

```
// ProgressBar.h : header file
//

/////////////////////////////////////////////////////////
// CProgressBar window

class CProgressBar : public Cstatic
{
// Construction
public:
    CProgressBar();

// Attributes
public:

// Operations
public:

// Overrides
    // ClassWizard generated virtual function overrides
    //{{AFX_VIRTUAL(CProgressBar)
    //}}AFX_VIRTUAL

// Implementation
public:
    COLORREF SetBackTextColor (COLORREF clrBar);
    COLORREF SetBackColor (COLORREF clrBar);
    COLORREF SetBarTextColor (COLORREF clrBarText);
    COLORREF SetBarColor (COLORREF clrBar);
    void UsePercent (bool bUsePct = true);
```

```cpp
   void SetBarText (CString strText);
   void SetBarText (char *szText);
   void Update();
   UINT SetPosition (UINT nPos);
   void SetMinMax (UINT nMin, UINT nMAX);
   virtual ~CProgressBar();

   // Generated message map functions
protected:
   void DrawVerticalBar (CWindowDC &dc);
   void DrawBar (CWindowDC &dc);
   void DoRedraw();
   static UINT CProgressBar::UpdateThread(void *pParam);
 //{{AFX_MSG(CProgressBar)
   afx_msg void OnPaint();
   //}}AFX_MSG

   DWORD      m_dwThread;
   UINT       m_nMin;
   UINT       m_nMax;
   UINT       m_nPos;
   CString    m_strBarText;

   COLORREF   m_clrBar;
   COLORREF   m_clrBarText;
   COLORRFF   m_clrBackText;
   COLORREF   m_clrBackGnd;

   CFont      m_Font;
   bool       m_bUsePercent;

   DECLARE_MESSAGE_MAP()
private:
   HANDLE m_hDrawEvent;
};

///////////////////////////////////////////////////////
// ProgressBar.cpp : implementation file
//

#include "stdafx.h"
#include "Controls.h"
#include "ProgressBar.h"

#ifdef _DEBUG
#define new DEBUG_NEW
#undef THIS_FILE
static char THIS_FILE[] = __FILE__;
#endif

///////////////////////////////////////////////////////
// CprogressBar

CProgressBar::CProgressBar()
{
    m_nMin = 0;
```

```
    m_nMax = 100;
    m_nPos = 0;
    m_bUsePercent = true;
    m_strBarText = _T("");
    m_hDrawEvent =  CreateEvent (NULL, FALSE, FALSE, NULL);
    m_clrBar = RGB (0x00, 0x00, 0xff);
    m_clrBackGnd = GetSysColor (COLOR_ACTIVEBORDER);
    m_clrBarText = RGB (0xff, 0xff, 0xff);
    m_clrBackText = RGB (0x00, 0x00, 0x00);
    AfxBeginThread (UpdateThread, (LPVOID) this)
}

CProgressBar::~CProgressBar()
{
}


//
//  The draw code for the progress bar happens in the
//  background. This makes it possible to update the
//  bar while other processing is going on.
//
UINT CProgressBar::UpdateThread(void *pParam)
{

    CProgressBar &Bar = (*(CProgressBar *) pParam);
    HANDLE hDraw = Bar.m_hDrawEvent;
    while (1)
    {
        DWORD dwResult = WaitForSingleObject (hDraw, 1000);
        switch (dwResult)
        {
            case WAIT_OBJECT_0:
                Bar.DoRedraw ();
                break;
            case WAIT_TIMEOUT:
                continue;
        }
    }

    return (0);
}

//
//  Update() sets the event, triggering a redraw of
//  the progress bar.
//
void CProgressBar::Update()
{
    SetEvent (m_hDrawEvent);
}

BEGIN_MESSAGE_MAP(CProgressBar, CStatic)
    //{{AFX_MSG_MAP(CProgressBar)
    ON_WM_PAINT()
    //}}AFX_MSG_MAP
END_MESSAGE_MAP()
```

```
//////////////////////////////////////////////////////////
// CProgressBar message handlers
//
//  You need to handle the WM_PAINT messages. If the
//  control is ever hidden by another window and later
//  later comes into view, Windows sends the WM_PAINT
//  message to redrawthe control.
void CProgressBar::OnPaint()
{
    CPaintDC dc(this); // device context for painting
    DoRedraw ();
}


void CProgressBar::DoRedraw()
{
    CWindowDC dc(this);
    DrawBar (dc);
}


void CProgressBar::DrawBar(CWindowDC &dc)
{
    CRect rc;
    GetWindowRect (rc);
//
//  If the window is taller than it is wide, assume that
//  it is a vertical progress bar.
//
    if ((rc.right - rc.left) < (rc.bottom - rc.top))
    {
        DrawVerticalBar (dc);
        return;
    }
    CPen pen;
    CBrush brushBack;
    CString strText = _T("");
    brushBack.CreateSolidBrush (m_clrBackGnd);
//
//  Get the window rectangle and draw a 3D rectangle.
//  Then shrink the rectangle by one point so that it will
//  fit inside the 3D rectangle.
//
    GetWindowRect (rc);
    ScreenToClient (rc);
    dc.Draw3dRect (rc, GetSysColor (COLOR_3DDKSHADOW),
                   GetSysColor (COLOR_3DHIGHLIGHT));

    rc.left += 1;
    rc.right -= 1;
    rc.top += 1;
    rc.bottom -= 1;
//
//  Fill the inner rectangle with the background
//  brush to erase any previous drawing.
//
    dc.FillRect (rc, &brushBack);
```

```
        int nPos = m_nPos * 100 / m_nMax;

    CRect rcBar = rc;

    rcBar.right = (rcBar.right - rcBar.left) * nPos / 100;
    CRect rcRest = rc;
    rcRest.left = rcBar.right;
    if (nPos)
    {
        CBrush  brushBar;
        CPen    penBar;
        brushBar.CreateSolidBrush (m_clrBar);
        dc.SelectObject (&brushBar);
        penBar.CreatePen (PS_SOLID, 1, m_clrBar);
        dc.SelectObject (&penBar);
        dc.Rectangle (rcBar);
    }
    else
        rcBar.right = rcBar.left;

    if (m_Font.m_hObject == NULL)
    {
        CFont *font = GetFont ();
        LOGFONT lf;
        font->GetLogFont (&lf);
        lf.lfHeight = (rc.bottom - rc.top) * 80 / 100;
        lf.lfWeight = FW_BOLD;
        strcpy (lf.lfFaceName, "Arial");
        m_Font.CreateFontIndirect (&lf);
    }
    dc.SelectObject (&m_Font);
    dc.SetBkMode (TRANSPARENT);
//
// Output the text, clipping the right side of
// the control so that the text within the bar can
// be a different color than the text outside.
//
    if (m_bUsePercent)
        strText.Format ("%d%%", nPos);
    else
        strText = m_strBarText;
    CSize sz = dc.GetTextExtent ((LPCSTR) strText,
                                 strText.GetLength());
    rc.top = (rc.bottom - rc.top - sz.cy) / 2;
    if (nPos)
    {
        dc.SaveDC ();
        dc.ExcludeClipRect(rcRest);
        dc.SetTextColor (m_clrBarText);
        dc.DrawText (strText, rc, DT_CENTER | DT_NOPREFIX);
        dc.RestoreDC (-1);
    }
    dc.SaveDC ();
//
// Clip the other part of the control, and redraw
// the text in the background text color.
```

```
//
    dc.ExcludeClipRect(rcBar);
    dc.SetTextColor (m_clrBackText);
    dc.DrawText (strText, rc, DT_CENTER | DT_NOPREFIX);
    dc.RestoreDC (-1);
}

void CProgressBar::DrawVerticalBar(CWindowDC &dc)
{
    CPen pen;
    CRect rc;
    CBrush brushBack;
    CString strText = _T("");
    brushBack.CreateSolidBrush (m_clrBackGnd);
//
//  Get the window rectangle and draw a 3D rectangle.
//  Then shrink the rectangle by one point so that it will
//  fit inside the 3D rectangle.
//
    GetWindowRect (rc);
    ScreenToClient (rc);
    dc.FillRect (rc, &brushBack);
    dc.Draw3dRect (rc, GetSysColor (COLOR_3DDKSHADOW),
                   GetSysColor (COLOR_3DHIGHLIGHT));

    rc.left += 1;
    rc.right -= 1;
    rc.top += 1;
    rc.bottom -= 1;
//
//  Fill the inner rectangle with the background
//  brush to erase any previous drawing.
//
    int nPos = m_nPos * 100 / m_nMax;

    CRect rcBar = rc;

    rcBar.top = rcBar.bottom - (rcBar.bottom - rcBar.top)
                               * nPos / 100;
    CRect rcRest = rc;
    rcRest.bottom = rcBar.top;
    if (nPos)
    {
        CBrush  brushBar;
        CPen    penBar;
        brushBar.CreateSolidBrush (m_clrBar);
        dc.SelectObject (&brushBar);
        penBar.CreatePen (PS_SOLID, 1, m_clrBar);
        dc.SelectObject (&penBar);
        dc.Rectangle (rcBar);
    }
    else
        rcBar.bottom = rcBar.top;

    if (m_Font.m_hObject == NULL)
    {
```

```
            CFont *font = GetFont ();
            LOGFONT lf;
            font->GetLogFont (&lf);
            lf.lfHeight = (rc.right - rc.left) * 80 / 100;
            strcpy (lf.lfFaceName, "Arial");
            lf.lfHeight *= -1;
            lf.lfEscapement = lf.lfOrientation = 901;
            lf.lfWeight = FW_BOLD;
            m_Font.CreateFontIndirect (&lf);
        }
        dc.SelectObject (&m_Font);
        dc.SetBkMode (TRANSPARENT);
//
//  Output the text, clipping the right side of
//  the control so that the text within the bar can
//  be a different color than the text outside.
//
        if (m_bUsePercent)
            strText.Format ("%d%%", nPos);
        else
            strText = m_strBarText;
        CSize sz = dc.GetTextExtent ((LPCSTR) strText,
                                strText.GetLength());
        int cxText = (rc.right - sz.cy) / 2;
        if (nPos)
        {
            dc.SaveDC ();
            dc.ExcludeClipRect(rcRest);
            dc.SetTextColor (m_clrBarText);
            dc.TextOut (cxText, rc.bottom / 2 + sz.cx / 2,
                        (LPCSTR) strText, strText.GetLength());
            dc.RestoreDC (-1);
        }
        dc.SaveDC ();
//
//  Clip the other part of the control, and redraw
//  the text in the background text color.
//
        dc.ExcludeClipRect(rcBar);
        dc.SetTextColor (m_clrBackText);
        dc.SetTextAlign (TA_LEFT);
        dc.TextOut (cxText, rc.bottom / 2 + sz.cx / 2,
                    (LPCSTR) strText, strText.GetLength());
        dc.RestoreDC (-1);
}


/////////////////////////////////////////////////
/ Functions to set progress bar parameters.
//
void CProgressBar::SetMinMax(UINT nMin, UINT nMax)
{
    if (nMax <= nMin)
        return;
    m_nMin = nMin;
    if (nMax > 0)
        m_nMax = nMax;
```

```
        else
            m_nMax = 1;
        if (m_nPos < m_nMin)
            m_nPos = m_nMin;
        if (m_nPos > m_nMax)
            m_nPos = m_nMax;
}

UINT CProgressBar::SetPosition(UINT nPos)
{
    UINT oldPos = m_nPos;
    if (nPos > m_nMax)
        m_nPos = m_nMax;
    else if (nPos < m_nMin)
        m_nPos = m_nMin;
    else
        m_nPos = nPos;
    return (oldPos);
}

void CProgressBar::SetBarText(char *szText)
{
    m_strBarText = szText;
}

void CProgressBar::SetBarText(CString strText)
{
    m_strBarText = strText;
}

//
//  If m_bUsePercent is true, the ratio or the bar
//  to the full width times 100 will be displayed in
//  the progress bar along with a % sign. If false,
//  the text in m_strBarText is used.
//
void CProgressBar::UsePercent(bool bUsePct)
{
    m_bUsePercent = bUsePct;
}

//
//  Set custom color information for the progress bar.
//
COLORREF CProgressBar::SetBarColor(COLORREF clrBar)
{
    COLORREF clrOld = m_clrBar;
    m_clrBar = clrBar;
    return (clrOld);
}

COLORREF CProgressBar::SetBarTextColor(COLORREF clrBarText)
{
    COLORREF clrOld = m_clrBarText;
    m_clrBarText = clrBarText;
    return (clrOld);
```

```
}

COLORREF CProgressBar::SetBackColor(COLORREF clrBack)
{
    COLORREF clrOld = m_clrBackGnd;
    m_clrBackGnd = clrBack;
    return (clrOld);
}

COLORREF CProgressBar::SetBackTextColor(COLORREF
                                        clrBackText)
{
    COLORREF clrOld = m_clrBackText;
    m_clrBackText = clrBackText;
    return (clrOld);
}
```

To set the text as a percentage in the center of the progress bar, call *UsePercent(true)*. To set your own text in place of the percentage, call *UsePercent(false)* and then set your own text using *SetBarText()*, passing it the string that you want displayed. To display nothing as the progress bar moves across the control, set *UsePercent()* to false and call *SetBarText()* with an empty string.

Notice the text is written twice, once using the rectangle for the color bar as the bounding box. The text is in the color *m_clrBarText*, which defaults to white. The rectangle clips the text at the end of the bar. The second text output uses the rest of the control as the clipping rectangle. The text color here is *m_clrBackText*, which defaults to black. As a result, the bar seems to slide through the text, changing its color on the way. You can change all four colors—the bar color, the background color, the bar text color, and the background text color—using member functions.

The control measures its own rectangle. If the control is taller than it is wide, it draws a vertical progress bar. Otherwise, it draws a horizontal progress bar. You don't have to set any flags.

You'll use this progress bar later in the discussion on scroll bars to represent the window that receives scroll bar messages. You might want to consider expanding this class to suit your own needs and add it to your gallery. The common controls library does have a progress bar control, but it really has limited functionality.

820. *Using the CStatic Class*

The static control doesn't do much except be there and look pretty, if you can call a block of text in that ugly system font pretty. The *CStatic* class doesn't have a lot of member functions, either, and these are mostly related to images that can be displayed in a static area. You'll use those later to draw bitmaps and such in static areas. About the only message that you can get from it is when the user mouse-clicks in the control area.

CStatic, however, is derived from *CWnd* and thus inherits all the functions of that class. You can use these functions the same as you would any other control, to move the window, change the text, and change styles, to some extent.

Now for the bad news about the *CStaticDlg* class. You have to add message handlers for all of those checkboxes, the combo box, the edit box, and the font and color buttons. To make things easier, the code is listed here:

```cpp
#include    "StaticEx.h"

/////////////////////////////////////////////////////////
// CStaticPage dialog

class CStaticPage : public CpropertyPage
{
    DECLARE_DYNCREATE(CStaticPage)

// Construction
public:
    CStaticPage();
    ~CStaticPage();

// Dialog Data
    //{{AFX_DATA(CStaticPage)
    enum { IDD = IDD_PROPPAGE_STATICDLG };
    CStaticEx    m_StaticSample;
    CString m_TextAlign;
    BOOL    m_bRightText;
    CComboBox    m_TextAlignBox;
    CEdit    m_StaticText;
    CButton m_SetFont;
    CButton m_SetColor;
    BOOL     m_bBorder;
    BOOL     m_bClientEdge;
    BOOL     m_bModalFrame;
    BOOL     m_bNoWrap;
    BOOL     m_bStatic;
    BOOL     m_bSunken;
    BOOL     m_bTransparent;
    //}}AFX_DATA

// Overrides
    // ClassWizard generate virtual function overrides
    //{{AFX_VIRTUAL(CStaticPage)
    protected:
        // DDX/DDV support
        virtual void DoDataExchange(CDataExchange* pDX);
//}}AFX_VIRTUAL

// Implementation
protected:
    // Generated message map functions
    //{{AFX_MSG(CStaticPage)
    afx_msg void OnChangeStatictext();
    virtual BOOL OnInitDialog();
    afx_msg void OnSelchangeStaticaligntext();
    afx_msg void OnStaticrighttext();
    afx_msg void OnSetstaticfont();
    afx_msg void OnSetstaticcolor();
    afx_msg void OnStaticsunken();
    afx_msg void OnStaticstatic();
    afx_msg void OnStatictransparent();
    afx_msg void OnStaticnowrap();
    afx_msg void OnStaticmodal();
```

```
        afx_msg void OnStaticclient();
        afx_msg void OnStaticborder();
    //}}AFX_MSG
    DECLARE_MESSAGE_MAP()

    CFont m_Font;
    DWORD m_dwStyle;
    DWORD m_dwStyleEx;
    void RecreateWindow();
};
// StaticPage.cpp : implementation file
//

#include "stdafx.h"
#include "Controls.h"
#include "StaticPage.h"

#ifdef _DEBUG
#define new DEBUG_NEW
#undef THIS_FILE
static char THIS_FILE[] = __FILE__;
#endif

/////////////////////////////////////////////////////////
// CStaticPage property page

IMPLEMENT_DYNCREATE(CStaticPage, CPropertyPage)

CStaticPage::CStaticPage()
                    : CPropertyPage(CStaticPage::IDD)
{
    //{{AFX_DATA_INIT(CStaticPage)
    m_TextAlign = _T("");
    m_bBorder = FALSE;
    m_bClientEdge = FALSE;
    m_bRightText = FALSE;
    m_bModalFrame = FALSE;
    m_bNoWrap = FALSE;
    m_bStatic = FALSE;
    m_bSunken = FALSE;
    m_bTransparent = FALSE;
    //}}AFX_DATA_INIT
    m_psp.dwFlags &= ~PSP_HASHELP;
}

CStaticPage::~CStaticPage()
{
}

void CStaticPage::DoDataExchange(CDataExchange* pDX)
{
    CPropertyPage::DoDataExchange(pDX);
    //{{AFX_DATA_MAP(CStaticPage)
    DDX_Control(pDX, IDC_STATICSAMPLE, m_StaticSample);
    DDX_CBString(pDX, IDC_STATICALIGNTEXT, m_TextAlign);
    DDX_Check(pDX, IDC_STATICRIGHTTEXT, m_bRightText);
```

```
        DDX_Control(pDX, IDC_STATICALIGNTEXT, m_TextAlignBox);
        DDX_Control(pDX, IDC_STATICTEXT, m_StaticText);
        DDX_Control(pDX, IDC_SETSTATICFONT, m_SetFont);
        DDX_Control(pDX, IDC_SETSTATICCOLOR, m_SetColor);
        DDX_Check(pDX, IDC_STATICBORDER, m_bBorder);
        DDX_Check(pDX, IDC_STATICCLIENT, m_bClientEdge);
        DDX_Check(pDX, IDC_STATICMODAL, m_bModalFrame);
        DDX_Check(pDX, IDC_STATICNOWRAP, m_bNoWrap);
        DDX_Check(pDX, IDC_STATICSTATIC, m_bStatic);
        DDX_Check(pDX, IDC_STATICSUNKEN, m_bSunken);
        DDX_Check(pDX, IDC_STATICTRANSPARENT, m_bTransparent);
    //}}AFX_DATA_MAP
}


BEGIN_MESSAGE_MAP(CStaticPage, CPropertyPage)
    //{{AFX_MSG_MAP(CStaticPage)
    ON_EN_CHANGE(IDC_STATICTEXT, OnChangeStatictext)
    ON_CBN_SELCHANGE(IDC_STATICALIGNTEXT,
                     OnSelchangeStaticaligntext)
    ON_BN_CLICKED(IDC_STATICRIGHTTEXT, OnStaticrighttext)
    ON_BN_CLICKED(IDC_SETSTATICFONT, OnSetstaticfont)
    ON_BN_CLICKED(IDC_SETSTATICCOLOR, OnSetstaticcolor)
    ON_BN_CLICKED(IDC_STATICSUNKEN, OnStaticsunken)
    ON_BN_CLICKED(IDC_STATICSTATIC, OnStaticstatic)
    ON_BN_CLICKED(IDC_STATICTRANSPARENT,
                     OnStatictransparent)
    ON_BN_CLICKED(IDC_STATICNOWRAP, OnStaticnowrap)
    ON_BN_CLICKED(IDC_STATICMODAL, OnStaticmodal)
    ON_BN_CLICKED(IDC_STATICCLIENT, OnStaticclient)
    ON_BN_CLICKED(IDC_STATICBORDER, OnStaticborder)
    //}}AFX_MSG_MAP
END_MESSAGE_MAP()

/////////////////////////////////////////////////////////
// CStaticPage message handlers

BOOL CStaticPage::OnInitDialog()
{
    CPropertyPage::OnInitDialog();

    CString text;
    LOGFONT lf;
    COLORREF clr=(COLORREF)GetSysColor(COLOR_ACTIVEBORDER);
    m_StaticSample.SetBkgndColor (clr);
    m_StaticSample.GetWindowText (text);
    m_StaticText.SetWindowText (text);
    m_TextAlignBox.SelectString (-1, "Center");
    CFont *font = GetFont();
    font->GetLogFont (&lf);
    m_Font.CreateFontIndirect (&lf);
    m_StaticSample.SetFont (&m_Font);
    m_dwStyleEx = 0;
    m_dwStyle = m_StaticSample.GetStyle ();


    return TRUE;  // return TRUE unless you set the focus
```

```
                    // to a control
                    // EXCEPTION: OCX Property Pages should
                    // return FALSE
}

void CStaticPage::OnChangeStatictext()
{
    CString text;
    m_StaticText.GetWindowText (text);
    m_StaticSample.SetWindowText (text);
}

void CStaticPage::OnSelchangeStaticaligntext()
{
    int sel = m_TextAlignBox.GetCurSel ();
    switch (sel)
    {
        case 0:                 //  Left align
            m_dwStyle &= ~(SS_CENTER | SS_RIGHT);
            m_dwStyle |= SS_LEFT;
            m_StaticSample.ModifyStyle(SS_CENTER | SS_RIGHT,
                                       SS_LEFT);
            break;
        case 1:                 //  Right align
            m_dwStyle &= ~(SS_LEFT | SS_CENTER);
            m_dwStyle |= SS_RIGHT;
            m_StaticSample.ModifyStyle (SS_CENTER | SS_LEFT,
                                        SS_RIGHT);
            break;
        case 2:                 //  Center align
            m_dwStyle &= ~(SS_LEFT | SS_RIGHT);
            m_dwStyle |= SS_CENTER;
            m_StaticSample.ModifyStyle (SS_LEFT | SS_RIGHT,
                                        SS_CENTER);
            break;
        default:
            break;
    }
    m_StaticSample.Invalidate ();
}

void CStaticPage::OnStaticrighttext()
{
    UpdateData (TRUE);
    if (m_bRightText)
    {
        m_dwStyleEx |= WS_EX_RIGHT;
        RecreateWindow();
    }
    else
    {
        m_dwStyleEx &= ~WS_EX_RIGHT;
        RecreateWindow();
    }
```

```
}

void CStaticPage::OnSetstaticfont()
{
    LOGFONT     lf;
    m_Font.GetLogFont (&lf);
    CFontDialog cf (&lf);
    cf.m_cf.rgbColors = m_StaticSample.GetTextColor();
    if (cf.DoModal() == IDCANCEL)
        return;
    cf.GetCurrentFont (&lf);
    m_StaticSample.SetTextColor (cf.GetColor());
    if (m_Font.m_hObject != NULL)
    {
        m_Font.DeleteObject ();
    }
    m_Font.CreateFontIndirect (&lf);
    m_StaticSample.SetFont (&m_Font);
}

void CStaticPage::OnSetstaticcolor()
{

    CColorDialog cc (m_StaticSample.GetBkgndColor ());
    if (cc.DoModal () != IDCANCEL)
    {
        bkcr = cc.GetColor ();
        m_StaticSample.SetBkgndColor (cc.GetColor ());
    }
}

void CStaticPage::OnStaticsunken()
{
    UpdateData (TRUE);
    if (m_bSunken == TRUE)
    {
        m_dwStyle |= SS_SUNKEN;
    }
    else
    {
        m_dwStyle &= ~SS_SUNKEN;
    }
    RecreateWindow();
}

void CStaticPage::OnStatictransparent()
{
}

void CStaticPage::OnStaticnowrap()
{
    // TODO: Add your control notification
    // handler code here

}
```

```
void CStaticPage::OnStaticstatic()
{
    UpdateData (TRUE);
    if (m_bStatic == TRUE)
    {
        m_dwStyleEx |= WS_EX_STATICEDGE;
    }
    else
    {
        m_dwStyleEx &= ~WS_EX_STATICEDGE;
    }
    RecreateWindow ();
}

void CStaticPage::OnStaticmodal()
{
    UpdateData (TRUE);
    if (m_bModalFrame == TRUE)
    {
        m_dwStyleEx |= WS_EX_DLGMODALFRAME;
    }
    else
    {
        m_dwStyleEx &= ~WS_EX_DLGMODALFRAME;
    }
    RecreateWindow ();
}

void CStaticPage::OnStaticclient()
{
    UpdateData (TRUE);
    if (m_bClientEdge == TRUE)
    {
        m_dwStyleEx |= WS_EX_CLIENTEDGE;
    }
    else
    {
        m_dwStyleEx &= ~WS_EX_CLIENTEDGE;
    }
    RecreateWindow ();
}

void CStaticPage::OnStaticborder()
{
    UpdateData (TRUE);
    if (m_bBorder == TRUE)
    {
        m_dwStyle |= WS_BORDER;
    }
    else
    {
        m_dwStyle &= ~WS_BORDER;
    }
    RecreateWindow ();
}
```

```
void CStaticPage::RecreateWindow()
{
    CString str;
    m_StaticSample.GetWindowText (str);
    DWORD dwStyle = m_StaticSample.GetStyle ();
    DWORD dwStyleEx = m_StaticSample.GetExStyle ();
    m_StaticSample.ShowWindow (SW_HIDE);
    CRect rc;
    m_StaticSample.GetWindowRect (&rc);
    ScreenToClient (rc);

    m_StaticSample.DestroyWindow();
    m_StaticSample.CreateEx (m_dwStyleEx,
                        "Static",
                        "Static",
                        m_dwStyle,
                        rc,
                        this,
                        IDC_STATICSAMPLE);
    m_StaticSample.ShowWindow (SW_SHOWNORMAL);
    m_StaticSample.SetWindowText (str);
    m_StaticSample.SetFont (&m_Font);
}
```

On several occasions, such as when you change the window frame, the code destroys and re-creates the sample window. This is fairly trivial for the text controls because they are children of the dialog box. The creation is done using the *CWnd::CreateEx* class rather than the *CStatic* member *Create()*. Another method is to call the *SetWindowPos()* API function, which forces the control to reread its style values. You'll see both methods in the code as you build property pages for the various controls. Feel free to experiment.

Compile and run the program. You should have broken perfection, and the program now will display a property sheet with a single page on it. Try changing the various frame styles and mixing font, text color, and background color. Use this page as a preview to see what a customized static box will look like in your own application before you commit a combination to code.

821. *Understanding the Edit Control*

The edit control, sometimes known as a *text box*, provides a place for the user to interact with the program by entering text. You also may set the control's text to provide a default entry. Unlike the static control, the edit control can send several different messages and can have scroll bars embedded in it.

The control often is associated with client windows to provide a general editing window where text files may be dumped, modified, and saved. It's the underlying control for the MFC *CEditView* class as well.

You can create an edit control on a dialog box by drawing the object in the dialog editor and then letting the *OnDialogInit()* function handle the creations details. You also can create it by calling the class's *Create()* member function or the *CWnd::CreateEx()* function. The latter gives you more control over the creation parameters.

When used on the dialog box, the control is destroyed automatically when the dialog box terminates. If you create a control using one of the create functions, you'll have to call *DestroyWindow()* to get rid of it.

822. *Using the CEdit Class*

The edit control is a primary tool for Windows projects. In the tips involving searching and replacing, you saw how it was created and attached to the project's client window area and then dynamically resized to maintain the same size as the client window. The files were read in the edit control and were operated on, and the user never saw the underlying window.

It's also a primary control for dialog boxes. Its collection of message events allows the program to monitor the text content constantly and to react instantly to user input. The control responds to a number of messages to manipulate the control and its text content.

With the MFC *CEdit* class, you have a number of functions to use with the control and manipulate text. Eventually these member functions boil down to sending messages to the control, but the end result for you is that they are much easier to use, and the code is much easier to follow. *CEdit* inherits a lot of its functionality from the *CWnd* base class.

823. *Deriving a Custom Class from CEdit*

As with the *CStatic* example, to handle the reflected messages sent by the edit control, the Edit Page of the Controls property sheet uses a class derived from *CEdit*, the *CEditEx* class from Tip 484, "Deriving Classes from *CEdit* and *CStatic* to Set Text Attributes."

Some parts of the Edit Page will be similar to the Static Page. The edit and static controls share some styles, but the edit control has a number of styles that the static control does not. The edit box does not have the sunken style available to the static control, however. The additional check boxes enable and disable these styles. In addition, a group of scroll-bar check boxes will be added to the page (you can add scroll bars to a static control as well, but they generally aren't very useful). At the bottom of the page, a text area will display the last message sent from the sample edit box. The layout of the property page is shown in Figure 823.

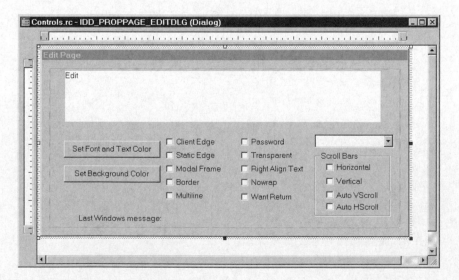

Figure 823   The arrangement of controls on the Edit Page shows additional controls used by the edit control

Add another page to the *Controls* project. Again use the Large Property Page selection, and make the size 325 by 155. Give the property page a resource ID of *IDD_PROPPAGE_EDITDLG*. For this page, the control IDs are all prefixed by *EDIT* instead of *STATIC*, so *ID_STATICBORDER* becomes *ID_EDITBORDER*. The additional controls and their variable types are listed in Table 823.

Resource ID	Label	Variable	Variable Type
IDC_EDITSAMPLE	Static Text	m_StaticSample	CStaticEx
IDC_EDITMULTILINE	Multi-line	m_bMultiline	BOOL
IDC_EDITPASSWORD	Password	m_bPassword	BOOL
IDC_EDITWANTRETURN	Want Return	m_bWantReturn	BOOL
IDC_EDITHORZSCROLL	Horizontal	m_bHorzScroll	BOOL
IDC_EDITVERTSCROLL	Vertical	m_bVertScroll	BOOL
IDC_EDITAUTOVSCROLL	Auto VScroll	m_bAutoVScroll	BOOL
IDC_EDITAUTOHSCROLL	Auto HScroll	m_bAutoHScroll	BOOL
IDC_EDITMESSAGE	None	m_EditMessage	CStatic

Table 823   Additional resource IDs and control variables needed for the Edit Page property page

The header and source files for the property page are shown here. In the next tip, you'll add message handlers to capture the messages sent back by the edit control and display them at the bottom of the property page.

```
#include   "EditEx.h"

/////////////////////////////////////////////////////////////
// CEditPage dialog

class CEditPage : public CpropertyPage
{
    DECLARE_DYNCREATE(CEditPage)

// Construction
public:
    CEditPage();
    ~CEditPage();

// Dialog Data
    //{{AFX_DATA(CEditPage)
    enum { IDD = IDD_PROPPAGE_EDITDLG };
    CEditEx m_EditSample;
    CStatic m_EditMessage;
    CString m_TextAlign;
    BOOL    m_bRightText;
    CComboBox    m_TextAlignBox;
    CButton m_SetFont;
    CButton m_SetColor;
    BOOL    m_bBorder;
    BOOL    m_bClientEdge;
    BOOL    m_bModalFrame;
    BOOL    m_bNoWrap;
    BOOL    m_bStatic;
```

```
    BOOL    m_bPassword;
    BOOL    m_bTransparent;
    BOOL    m_bHorzScroll;
    BOOL    m_bMultiline;
    BOOL    m_bVertScroll;
    BOOL    m_bWantReturn;
    BOOL    m_bAutoVScroll;
    BOOL    m_bAutoHScroll;
 //}}AFX_DATA


// Overrides
    // ClassWizard generate virtual function overrides
    //{{AFX_VIRTUAL(CEditPage)
    protected:
    virtual void DoDataExchange(CDataExchange* pDX);
    // DDX/DDV support
    //}}AFX_VIRTUAL

// Implementation
protected:
    // Generated message map functions
    //{{AFX_MSG(CEditPage)
    virtual BOOL OnInitDialog();
    afx_msg void OnSelchangeEditaligntext();
    afx_msg void OnEditrighttext();
    afx_msg void OnSetEditfont();
    afx_msg void OnSetEditcolor();
    afx_msg void OnEditpassword();
    afx_msg void OnEditstatic();
    afx_msg void OnEdittransparent();
    afx_msg void OnEditnowrap();
    afx_msg void OnEditmodal();
    afx_msg void OnEditclient();
    afx_msg void OnEditborder();
    afx_msg void OnEdithorzscroll();
    afx_msg void OnEditmultiline();
    afx_msg void OnEditvertscroll();
    afx_msg void OnEditautovscroll();
    afx_msg void OnEditwantreturn();
    afx_msg void OnEditautohscroll();
    //}}AFX_MSG
    DECLARE_MESSAGE_MAP()

    void RecreateWindow();

    CFont   m_Font;
    DWORD   m_dwStyle;
    DWORD   m_dwStyleEx;

};


// EditPage.cpp : implementation file
//

#include "stdafx.h"
```

```
#include "Controls.h"
#include "EditPage.h"

#ifdef _DEBUG
#define new DEBUG_NEW
#undef THIS_FILE
static char THIS_FILE[] = __FILE__;
#endif

/////////////////////////////////////////////////////////
// CEditPage property page

IMPLEMENT_DYNCREATE(CEditPage, CPropertyPage)

CEditPage::CEditPage() : CPropertyPage(CEditPage::IDD)
{
    //{{AFX_DATA_INIT(CEditPage)
    m_TextAlign = _T("");
    m_bRightText = FALSE;
    m_bBorder = FALSE;
    m_bClientEdge = FALSE;
    m_bModalFrame = FALSE;
    m_bNoWrap = FALSE;
    m_bStatic = FALSE;
    m_bPassword = FALSE;
    m_bTransparent = FALSE;
    m_bHorzScroll = FALSE;
    m_bMultiline = FALSE;
    m_bVertScroll = FALSE;
    m_bWantReturn = FALSE;
    m_bAutoVScroll = FALSE;
    m_bAutoHScroll = FALSE;
    //}}AFX_DATA_INIT
    m_psp.dwFlags &= ~PSP_HASHELP;
}

CEditPage::~CEditPage()
{
}

void CEditPage::DoDataExchange(CDataExchange* pDX)
{
    CPropertyPage::DoDataExchange(pDX);
    //{{AFX_DATA_MAP(CEditPage)
    DDX_Control(pDX, IDC_EDITSAMPLE, m_EditSample);
    DDX_Control(pDX, IDC_EDITMESSAGE, m_EditMessage);
    DDX_CBString(pDX, IDC_EDITALIGNTEXT, m_TextAlign);
    DDX_Check(pDX, IDC_EDITRIGHTTEXT, m_bRightText);
    DDX_Control(pDX, IDC_EDITALIGNTEXT, m_TextAlignBox);
    DDX_Control(pDX, IDC_SETEDITFONT, m_SetFont);
    DDX_Control(pDX, IDC_SETEDITCOLOR, m_SetColor);
    DDX_Check(pDX, IDC_EDITBORDER, m_bBorder);
    DDX_Check(pDX, IDC_EDITCLIENT, m_bClientEdge);
    DDX_Check(pDX, IDC_EDITMODAL, m_bModalFrame);
    DDX_Check(pDX, IDC_EDITNOWRAP, m_bNoWrap);
    DDX_Check(pDX, IDC_EDITSTATIC, m_bStatic);
```

```
        DDX_Check(pDX, IDC_EDITPASSWORD, m_bPassword);
        DDX_Check(pDX, IDC_EDITTRANSPARENT, m_bTransparent);
        DDX_Check(pDX, IDC_EDITHORZSCROLL, m_bHorzScroll);
        DDX_Check(pDX, IDC_EDITMULTILINE, m_bMultiline);
        DDX_Check(pDX, IDC_EDITVERTSCROLL, m_bVertScroll);
        DDX_Check(pDX, IDC_EDITWANTRETURN, m_bWantReturn);
        DDX_Check(pDX, IDC_EDITAUTOVSCROLL, m_bAutoVScroll);
        DDX_Check(pDX, IDC_EDITAUTOHSCROLL, m_bAutoHScroll);
        //}}AFX_DATA_MAP
}


BEGIN_MESSAGE_MAP(CEditPage, CPropertyPage)
    //{{AFX_MSG_MAP(CEditPage)
    ON_CBN_SELCHANGE(IDC_EDITALIGNTEXT,
                        OnSelchangeEditaligntext)
    ON_BN_CLICKED(IDC_EDITRIGHTTEXT, OnEditrighttext)
    ON_BN_CLICKED(IDC_SETEDITFONT, OnSetEditfont)
    ON_BN_CLICKED(IDC_SETEDITCOLOR, OnSetEditcolor)
    ON_BN_CLICKED(IDC_EDITPASSWORD, OnEditpassword)
    ON_BN_CLICKED(IDC_EDITSTATIC, OnEditstatic)
    ON_BN_CLICKED(IDC_EDITTRANSPARENT, OnEdittransparent)
    ON_BN_CLICKED(IDC_EDITNOWRAP, OnEditnowrap)
    ON_BN_CLICKED(IDC_EDITMODAL, OnEditmodal)
    ON_BN_CLICKED(IDC_EDITCLIENT, OnEditclient)
    ON_BN_CLICKED(IDC_EDITBORDER, OnEditborder)
    ON_BN_CLICKED(IDC_EDITHORZSCROLL, OnEdithorzscroll)
    ON_BN_CLICKED(IDC_EDITMULTILINE, OnEditmultiline)
    ON_BN_CLICKED(IDC_EDITVERTSCROLL, OnEditvertscroll)
    ON_BN_CLICKED(IDC_EDITAUTOVSCROLL, OnEditautovscroll)
    ON_BN_CLICKED(IDC_EDITWANTRETURN, OnEditwantreturn)
    ON_BN_CLICKED(IDC_EDITAUTOHSCROLL, OnEditautohscroll)
    //}}AFX_MSG_MAP
END_MESSAGE_MAP()

/////////////////////////////////////////////////////////////////////////////
// CEditPage message handlers

BOOL CEditPage::OnInitDialog()
{
    CPropertyPage::OnInitDialog();
    LOGFONT lf;
    m_TextAlignBox.SelectString (-1, "Left");
    CFont *font = GetFont();
    font->GetLogFont (&lf);
    m_Font.CreateFontIndirect (&lf);
    m_EditSample.SetFont (&m_Font);
    m_dwStyleEx = 0;
    m_dwStyle = m_EditSample.GetStyle ();
    return TRUE;  // return TRUE unless you set the focus
                  // to a control
                  // EXCEPTION: OCX Property Pages should
                  // return FALSE
}

void CEditPage::OnSelchangeEditaligntext()
```

```
{
    int sel = m_TextAlignBox.GetCurSel ();
    switch (sel)
    {
        case 0:                    //  Left align
            m_dwStyle &= ~(ES_CENTER | ES_RIGHT);
            m_dwStyle |= ES_LEFT;
            m_EditSample.ModifyStyle (ES_CENTER | ES_RIGHT,
                                      ES_LEFT);
            break;
        case 1:                    //  Right align
            m_dwStyle &= ~(ES_LEFT | ES_CENTER);
            m_dwStyle |= ES_RIGHT;
            m_EditSample.ModifyStyle (ES_CENTER | ES_LEFT,
                                      ES_RIGHT);
            break;
        case 2:                    //  Center align
            m_dwStyle &= ~(ES_LEFT | ES_RIGHT);
            m_dwStyle |= ES_CENTER;
            m_EditSample.ModifyStyle (ES_LEFT | ES_RIGHT,
                                      ES_CENTER);
            break;
        default:
            break;
    }
//  m_EditSample.Invalidate ();
    RecreateWindow ();
}

void CEditPage::OnEditrighttext()
{
    UpdateData (TRUE);
    if (m_bRightText)
    {
        m_dwStyleEx |= WS_EX_RIGHT;
        RecreateWindow();
    }
    else
    {
        m_dwStyleEx &= ~WS_EX_RIGHT;
        RecreateWindow();
    }

}

void CEditPage::OnSetEditfont()
{
    LOGFONT    lf;
    m_Font.GetLogFont (&lf);
    CFontDialog cf (&lf);
    cf.m_cf.rgbColors = m_EditSample.GetTextColor();
    if (cf.DoModal() == IDCANCEL)
        return;
    cf.GetCurrentFont (&lf);
    m_EditSample.SetTextColor (cf.GetColor());
    if (m_Font.m_hObject != NULL)
```

```cpp
    {
        m_Font.DeleteObject ();
    }
    m_Font.CreateFontIndirect (&lf);
    m_EditSample.SetFont (&m_Font);
}

void CEditPage::OnSetEditcolor()
{
    COLORREF clrBack = m_EditSample.GetBkgndColor ();
    CColorDialog cc (clrBack);
    if (cc.DoModal () != IDCANCEL)
        m_EditSample.SetBkgndColor (cc.GetColor ());
}

void CEditPage::OnEditpassword()
{
    UpdateData (TRUE);
    if (m_bPassword == TRUE)
    {
        m_dwStyle |= ES_PASSWORD;
    }
    else
    {
        m_dwStyle &= ~ES_PASSWORD;
    }
    RecreateWindow();
}

void CEditPage::OnEdittransparent()
{
}

void CEditPage::OnEditnowrap()
{
    // TODO: Add your control notification handler code here

}

void CEditPage::OnEditstatic()
{
    UpdateData (TRUE);
    if (m_bStatic == TRUE)
    {
        m_dwStyleEx |= WS_EX_STATICEDGE;
    }
    else
    {
        m_dwStyleEx &= ~WS_EX_STATICEDGE;
    }
    RecreateWindow ();
}

void CEditPage::OnEditmodal()
{
    UpdateData (TRUE);
```

```
        if (m_bModalFrame == TRUE)
        {
            m_dwStyleEx |= WS_EX_DLGMODALFRAME;
        }
        else
        {
            m_dwStyleEx &= ~WS_EX_DLGMODALFRAME;
        }
        RecreateWindow ();
}

void CEditPage::OnEditclient()
{
        UpdateData (TRUE);
        if (m_bClientEdge == TRUE)
        {
            m_dwStyleEx |= WS_EX_CLIENTEDGE;
        }
        else
        {
            m_dwStyleEx &= ~WS_EX_CLIENTEDGE;
        }
        RecreateWindow ();
}

void CEditPage::OnEditborder()
{
        UpdateData (TRUE);
        if (m_bBorder == TRUE)
        {
            m_dwStyle |= WS_BORDER;
        }
        else
        {
            m_dwStyle &= ~WS_BORDER;
        }
        RecreateWindow ();
}

void CEditPage::RecreateWindow()
{
        CString str;
        m_EditSample.GetWindowText (str);
        DWORD dwStyle = m_EditSample.GetStyle ();
        DWORD dwStyleEx = m_EditSample.GetExStyle ();
        m_EditSample.ShowWindow (SW_HIDE);
        CRect rc;
        m_EditSample.GetWindowRect (&rc);
        ScreenToClient (rc);

        int nStart, nEnd;
        m_EditSample.GetSel (nStart, nEnd);

        m_EditSample.DestroyWindow();
        m_EditSample.CreateEx (m_dwStyleEx,
                                "Edit",
```

```
                            "Edit",
                            m_dwStyle,
                            rc,
                            this,
                            IDC_EDITSAMPLE);
    m_EditSample.ShowWindow (SW_SHOWNORMAL);
    m_EditSample.SetWindowText (str);
    m_EditSample.SetFont (&m_Font);
    m_EditSample.SetSel (nStart, nEnd);
}

void CEditPage::OnEdithorzscroll()
{
    UpdateData (TRUE);
    if (m_bHorzScroll == TRUE)
    {
        m_dwStyle |= WS_HSCROLL;
    }
    else
    {
        m_dwStyle &= ~WS_HSCROLL;
    }
    RecreateWindow ();
}

void CEditPage::OnEditvertscroll()
{
    UpdateData (TRUE);
    if (m_bVertScroll == TRUE)
    {
        m_dwStyle |= WS_VSCROLL;
    }
    else
    {
        m_dwStyle &= ~WS_VSCROLL;
    }
    RecreateWindow ();
}

void CEditPage::OnEditmultiline()
{
    UpdateData (TRUE);
    if (m_bMultiline == TRUE)
    {
        m_dwStyle |= ES_MULTILINE;
    }
    else
    {
        m_dwStyle &= ~ES_MULTILINE;
    }
    RecreateWindow ();
}

void CEditPage::OnEditautohscroll()
{
    UpdateData (TRUE);
```

```
        if (m_bAutoHScroll == TRUE)
        {
            m_dwStyle |= ES_AUTOHSCROLL;
        }
        else
        {
            m_dwStyle &= ~ES_AUTOHSCROLL;
        }
        RecreateWindow ();
}

void CEditPage::OnEditautovscroll()
{
    UpdateData (TRUE);
    if (m_bAutoVScroll == TRUE)
    {
        m_dwStyle |= ES_AUTOVSCROLL;
    }
    else
    {
        m_dwStyle &= ~ES_AUTOVSCROLL;
    }
    RecreateWindow ();
}

void CEditPage::OnEditwantreturn()
{
    UpdateData (TRUE);
    if (m_bAutoVScroll == TRUE)
    {
        m_dwStyle |= ES_WANTRETURN;
    }
    else
    {
        m_dwStyle &= ~ES_WANTRETURN;
    }
    RecreateWindow ();
}
```

Include any additional functionality that you need in the *CEditEx* class, and add controls to the property page to reflect those changes. Keep the property page up to date, and you'll find that it comes in very handy in the selection of designs—you'll have some sample code that you can lift out and place in your own application.

824. Adding Message Handlers for an Edit Control

An edit control has eight notification messages that it sends to the parent window when events or errors occur that affect the control. These messages are sent as *WM_COMMAND* messages and are summarized in Table 824.

Message	Meaning
EN_CHANGE	The text in the control has been altered. Sent after the control has been updated.
EN_ERRSPACE	The control cannot allocate enough memory to perform a request.
EN_HSCROLL	The user has clicked on the control's horizontal scroll bar. Sent before the screen is updated.
EN_KILLFOCUS	The control has lost the keyboard focus.
EN_MAXTEXT	The current insertion would exceed the control's maximum text length. Also sent when the insertion would exceed the control's width and the *ES_AUTOHSCROLL* style is not set, or when the insertion would exceed the height of the control and the *ES_AUTOVSCROLL* style is not set.
EN_SETFOCUS	The control has received the keyboard focus.
EN_UPDATE	The control is about to display altered text. Sent after the text is formatted but before the text is displayed. Use this message to resize the control, if necessary.
EN_VSCROLL	The user has clicked on the control's vertical scroll bar. Sent before the screen is updated.

Table 824   Notification messages used by the edit control to inform the parent window of changes and events affecting the control

The Edit Page property page in the *Controls* project contains a static control at the bottom to display the messages. Add handlers for these messages using the ClassWizard to enable this display. The code is shown here:

```
//
//   Function prototypes in the editpage .h file
//
    afx_msg void OnChangeEditsample();
    afx_msg void OnErrspaceEditsample();
    afx_msg void OnHscrollEditsample();
    afx_msg void OnKillfocusEditsample();
    afx_msg void OnMaxtextEditsample();
    afx_msg void OnSetfocusEditsample();
    afx_msg void OnUpdateEditsample();
    afx_msg void OnVscrollEditsample();
//
//   Message map entries in the editpage.cpp file
//
    ON_EN_CHANGE(IDC_EDITSAMPLE, OnChangeEditsample)
    ON_EN_ERRSPACE(IDC_EDITSAMPLE, OnErrspaceEditsample)
    ON_EN_HSCROLL(IDC_EDITSAMPLE, OnHscrollEditsample)
    ON_EN_KILLFOCUS(IDC_EDITSAMPLE, OnKillfocusEditsample)
    ON_EN_MAXTEXT(IDC_EDITSAMPLE, OnMaxtextEditsample)
    ON_EN_SETFOCUS(IDC_EDITSAMPLE, OnSetfocusEditsample)
    ON_EN_UPDATE(IDC_EDITSAMPLE, OnUpdateEditsample)
    ON_EN_VSCROLL(IDC_EDITSAMPLE, OnVscrollEditsample)
//
//   Handlers for messages sent from the edit control
//   in the editpage.cpp file.
//
```

```cpp
void CEditPage::OnChangeEditsample()
{
    CString Message;
    Message.Format ("EN_CHANGE (%d)", EN_CHANGE);
    m_EditMessage.SetWindowText (Message);
}

void CEditPage::OnErrspaceEditsample()
{
    CString Message;
    Message.Format ("EN_ERRSPACE (%d)", EN_ERRSPACE);
    m_EditMessage.SetWindowText (Message);
}

void CEditPage::OnHscrollEditsample()
{
    CString Message;
    Message.Format ("EN_HSCROLL (%d)", EN_HSCROLL);
    m_EditMessage.SetWindowText (Message);
}

void CEditPage::OnKillfocusEditsample()
{
    CString Message;
    Message.Format ("EN_KILLFOCUS (%d)", EN_KILLFOCUS);
    m_EditMessage.SetWindowText (Message);
}

void CEditPage::OnMaxtextEditsample()
{
    CString Message;
    Message.Format ("EN_MAXTEXT (%d)", EN_MAXTEXT);
    m_EditMessage.SetWindowText (Message);
}

void CEditPage::OnSetfocusEditsample()
{
    CString Message;
    Message.Format ("EN_SETFOCUS (%d)", EN_SETFOCUS);
    m_EditMessage.SetWindowText (Message);
}

void CEditPage::OnUpdateEditsample()
{
    CString Message;
    Message.Format ("EN_CHANGE (%d)", EN_CHANGE);
    m_EditMessage.SetWindowText (Message);
}

void CEditPage::OnVscrollEditsample()
{
    CString Message;
    Message.Format ("EN_VSCROLL (%d)", EN_VSCROLL);
    m_EditMessage.SetWindowText (Message);
}
```

825. *Understanding the Button Control*

The button control is used to signal a single input event when it is pressed by the user. The control draws a rectangular area that may be raised or flat. It's a flexible control; it can be used as a plain-face object, or it may contain a bitmap, an icon, or text. More often than not, it's used with text on the face.

The window class for this control, Button, is the same window class used by the check box and the radio button controls. Just by changing the styles for these last two controls, they can be made to look like buttons but still perform as check boxes or radio buttons.

In the case of the check box, the button will remain in a depressed state (the "check" is set) when the user presses it and returns to the up position (the "check" is not set) when pressed again.

For radio buttons, pressing one button causes the check to disappear from any other button in the same group and to appear in the pressed button's image.

826. *Using the* CButton *Class*

The *CButton* class encapsulates the button window class as an MFC object and includes functions to set the text of the button, to set the bitmap or icon if the button contains an image, and to get and set the check and state of the button.

Add a property page to the *Controls* project by inserting a large property sheet. The size should be the same as the others, but it isn't critical. When the property sheet appears, Windows will make all the property pages the same. For this page, you'll have to hire some outside bitmaps to represent LEDs, and one to place on the button when it has the *BS_BITMAP* style set (see Figure 826). You can collect your own or use the ones on the companion CD-ROMs.

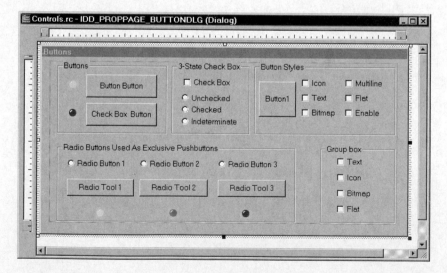

Figure 826   *The Buttons page demonstrates how the button control can be configured using the different styles*

Create a class for this property page named *CButtonPage*. Add a member variable to the *CControlsProp* class, and add the page to the property sheet in the *CConstrolsProp* constructors.

The Button object is a standard pushbutton that releases after the user releases the mouse button. It controls the LED to the left, shifting from green to yellow to red. Just below it is a check box that has the Push Like style set so that it appears every bit like a button. At the bottom left of the page are two sets of radio buttons, one with the Push Like style set. These buttons will be programmed to mirror the state of the other. Pushbutton check boxes and pushbutton radio buttons will be discussed in Tips 830, "Using a Pushbutton Check Box," and 833, "Using Pushbuttons for Radio Boxes."

In the upper middle is a check box with the 3-State style set. Its check is controlled by the three radio buttons just below it. This check box can have one of three states: 0, or unchecked; 1, or checked; or 2, indicating an indeterminate state.

At the upper right is a plain button that will change styles according to the check marks just to the right of it. You can see the different effect of the styles on the appearance of the button.

At the lower right is a group box sample. The label for a group box may be assigned text, an icon, or a bitmap. The group box border may be normal or may have the Flat style, and actually the normal style looks more flat than the Flat style. The check boxes here let you see how each of the styles affects the look.

Except for the bitmaps, all these controls use the button window class and can be considered a button of one form or another. Even the two group boxes derive from the button window class. In the next tip, you'll add the code for the various messages that these buttons generate.

827. *Adding Message Handlers for a Button Control*

Almost everything that happens with a button generates a message or is the result of a message. The button can send a number of messages back to its parent window, but most of them are hangers-on from the old 16-bit Windows. Only four messages are pertinent to 32-bit windows and, in fact, are not available in Windows versions prior to Windows 95. *BN_CLICKED* is sent when the user presses the button, and *BN_DOUBLECLICKED* is sent when the user double-clicks the button. *BN_SETFOCUS* is sent when the button receives the keyboard focus, and *BN_KILLFOCUS* is sent when it loses the keyboard focus. The last two messages are sent only if you select the Notify box on the Styles page of the property sheet when you design the dialog box.

This property page includes a lot of message handlers, mostly *BN_CLICKED*. The header and source code for the *CButtonPage* class is shown here:

```
// ButtonPage.h : header file
//

/////////////////////////////////////////////////////////
// CButtonPage dialog

class CButtonPage : public CpropertyPage
{
    DECLARE_DYNCREATE(CButtonPage)

// Construction
public:
    CButtonPage();
    ~CButtonPage();

// Dialog Data
```

```cpp
    //{{AFX_DATA(CButtonPage)
    enum { IDD = IDD_PROPPAGE_BUTTONDLG };
    CButton m_GroupSample;
    CButton m_StyleButton;
    CStatic m_ButtonButtonLed;
    CStatic m_CheckBoxLed;
    CStatic m_RadioLedRed;
    CStatic m_RadioLedYellow;
    CStatic m_RadioLedGreen;
    int     m_nRadioButton;
    int     m_nRadioTool;
    BOOL    m_bFlat;
    BOOL    m_bIcon;
    BOOL    m_bMultiline;
    BOOL    m_bBitmap;
    BOOL    m_bCheckBoxButton;
    BOOL    m_bText;
    BOOL    m_bEnable;
    BOOL    m_bGroupBitmap;
    BOOL    m_bGroupFlat;
    BOOL    m_bGroupIcon;
    BOOL    m_bGroupText;
    int     m_CheckState;
    //}}AFX_DATA


// Overrides
    // ClassWizard generate virtual function overrides
    //{{AFX_VIRTUAL(CButtonPage)
    protected:
    virtual void DoDataExchange(CDataExchange* pDX);
    // DDX/DDV support
    //}}AFX_VIRTUAL


// Implementation
protected:
    // Generated message map functions
    //{{AFX_MSG(CButtonPage)
    virtual BOOL OnInitDialog();
    afx_msg void OnRadiotool();
    afx_msg void OnRadioButton();
    afx_msg void OnButtonbutton();
    afx_msg void OnCheckboxbutton();
    afx_msg void OnButtonflat();
    afx_msg void OnButtonicon();
    afx_msg void OnButtonmultiline();
    afx_msg void OnButtonbitmap();
    afx_msg void OnButtontext();
    afx_msg void OnButtonenable();
    afx_msg void OnGroupicon();
    afx_msg void OnGroupbitmap();
    afx_msg void OnGroupflat();
    afx_msg void OnGrouptext();
    afx_msg void OnUncheckedradio();
    afx_msg void OnCheckradio();
    afx_msg void OnIndetermradio();
```

```
      afx_msg void OnChecksample();
   //}}AFX_MSG
   DECLARE_MESSAGE_MAP()

   CBitmap m_bmpRedOn;
   CBitmap m_bmpRedOff;
   CBitmap m_bmpGreenOn;
   CBitmap m_bmpGreenOff;
   CBitmap m_bmpYellowOn;
   CBitmap m_bmpYellowOff;
   CBitmap m_bmpDudleyPC;
   HICON   m_icoMainframeLarge;
   HICON   m_icoMainframeSmall;
};

/////////////////////////////////////////////////////////
// ButtonPage.cpp : implementation file
//

#include "stdafx.h"
#include "Controls.h"
#include "ButtonPage.h"

#ifdef _DEBUG
#define new DEBUG_NEW
#undef THIS_FILE
static char THIS_FILE[] = __FILE__;
#endif

/////////////////////////////////////////////////////////
// CButtonPage property page

IMPLEMENT_DYNCREATE(CButtonPage, CPropertyPage)

CButtonPage::CButtonPage() : CPropertyPage(CButtonPage::IDD)
{
   //{{AFX_DATA_INIT(CButtonPage)
   m_nRadioButton = 0;
   m_nRadioTool = 0;
   m_bFlat = FALSE;
   m_bIcon = FALSE;
   m_bMultiline = FALSE;
   m_bBitmap = FALSE;
   m_bCheckBoxButton = FALSE;
   m_bText = TRUE;
   m_bEnable = TRUE;
   m_bGroupBitmap = FALSE;
   m_bGroupFlat = FALSE;
   m_bGroupIcon = FALSE;
   m_bGroupText = TRUE;
   m_CheckState = 0;
   //}}AFX_DATA_INIT
   m_psp.dwFlags &= ~PSP_HASHELP
}

CButtonPage::~CButtonPage()
```

```
{
    m_psp.dwFlags &= ~PSP_HASHELP;
}

void CButtonPage::DoDataExchange(CDataExchange* pDX)
{
    CPropertyPage::DoDataExchange(pDX);
    //{{AFX_DATA_MAP(CButtonPage)
    DDX_Control(pDX, IDC_CHECKSAMPLE, m_CheckSample);
    DDX_Control(pDX, IDC_GROUPSAMPLE, m_GroupSample);
    DDX_Control(pDX, IDC_STYLEBUTTON, m_StyleButton);
    DDX_Control(pDX, IDC_BUTTONBUTTONLED,
                     m_ButtonButtonLed);
    DDX_Control(pDX, IDC_CHECKBUTTONLED, m_CheckBoxLed);
    DDX_Control(pDX, IDC_RADIOTOOLLED3, m_RadioLedRed);
    DDX_Control(pDX, IDC_RADIOTOOLLED2, m_RadioLedYellow);
    DDX_Control(pDX, IDC_RADIOTOOLLED1, m_RadioLedGreen);
    DDX_Radio(pDX, IDC_RADIOBUTTON1, m_nRadioButton);
    DDX_Radio(pDX, IDC_RADIOTOOL1, m_nRadioTool);
    DDX_Check(pDX, IDC_BUTTONFLAT, m_bFlat);
    DDX_Check(pDX, IDC_BUTTONICON, m_bIcon);
    DDX_Check(pDX, IDC_BUTTONMULTILINE, m_bMultiline);
    DDX_Check(pDX, IDC_BUTTONBITMAP, m_bBitmap);
    DDX_Check(pDX, IDC_CHECKBOXBUTTON, m_bCheckBoxButton);
    DDX_Check(pDX, IDC_BUTTONTEXT, m_bText);
    DDX_Check(pDX, IDC_BUTTONENABLE, m_bEnable);
    DDX_Check(pDX, IDC_GROUPBITMAP, m_bGroupBitmap);
    DDX_Check(pDX, IDC_GROUPFLAT, m_bGroupFlat);
    DDX_Check(pDX, IDC_GROUPICON, m_bGroupIcon);
    DDX_Check(pDX, IDC_GROUPTEXT, m_bGroupText);
    DDX_Radio(pDX, IDC_UNCHECKEDRADIO, m_CheckState);
    //}}AFX_DATA_MAP
}


BEGIN_MESSAGE_MAP(CButtonPage, CPropertyPage)
    //{{AFX_MSG_MAP(CButtonPage)
    ON_BN_CLICKED(IDC_RADIOTOOL1, OnRadiotool)
    ON_BN_CLICKED(IDC_RADIOBUTTON1, OnRadioButton)
    ON_BN_CLICKED(IDC_BUTTONBUTTON, OnButtonbutton)
    ON_BN_CLICKED(IDC_CHECKBOXBUTTON, OnCheckboxbutton)
    ON_BN_CLICKED(IDC_BUTTONFLAT, OnButtonflat)
    ON_BN_CLICKED(IDC_BUTTONICON, OnButtonicon)
    ON_BN_CLICKED(IDC_BUTTONMULTILINE, OnButtonmultiline)
    ON_BN_CLICKED(IDC_BUTTONBITMAP, OnButtonbitmap)
    ON_BN_CLICKED(IDC_BUTTONTEXT, OnButtontext)
    ON_BN_CLICKED(IDC_BUTTONENABLE, OnButtonenable)
    ON_BN_CLICKED(IDC_GROUPICON, OnGroupicon)
    ON_BN_CLICKED(IDC_GROUPBITMAP, OnGroupbitmap)
    ON_BN_CLICKED(IDC_GROUPFLAT, OnGroupflat)
    ON_BN_CLICKED(IDC_GROUPTEXT, OnGrouptext)
    ON_BN_CLICKED(IDC_RADIOTOOL2, OnRadiotool)
    ON_BN_CLICKED(IDC_RADIOTOOL3, OnRadiotool)
    ON_BN_CLICKED(IDC_RADIOBUTTON2, OnRadioButton)
    ON_BN_CLICKED(IDC_RADIOBUTTON3, OnRadioButton)
    ON_BN_CLICKED(IDC_UNCHECKEDRADIO, OnUncheckedradio)
```

```
        ON_BN_CLICKED(IDC_CHECKRADIO, OnCheckradio)
        ON_BN_CLICKED(IDC_INDETERMRADIO, OnIndetermradio)
        ON_BN_CLICKED(IDC_CHECKSAMPLE, OnChecksample)
        //}}AFX MSG_MAP
END_MESSAGE_MAP()

/////////////////////////////////////////////////////////////////////
// CButtonPage message handlers

BOOL CButtonPage::OnInitDialog()
{
    CPropertyPage::OnInitDialog();

    m_bmpRedOn.LoadBitmap (IDB_LEDREDON);
    m_bmpRedOff.LoadBitmap (IDB_LEDREDOFF);
    m_bmpGreenOn.LoadBitmap (IDB_LEDGREENON);
    m_bmpGreenOff.LoadBitmap (IDB_LEDGREENOFF);
    m_bmpYellowOn.LoadBitmap (IDB_LEDYELLOWON);
    m_bmpYellowOff.LoadBitmap (IDB_LEDYELLOWOFF);

    m_bmpDudleyPC.LoadBitmap (IDB_DUDLEYPC);

    m_ButtonButtonLed.SetBitmap (m_bmpGreenOn);
    m_CheckBoxLed.SetBitmap (m_bmpRedOff);

    m_icoMainframeSmall = (HICON) LoadImage
                        (AfxGetInstanceHandle(),
                         MAKEINTRESOURCE (IDR_MAINFRAME),
                         IMAGE_ICON,
                         16, 16, 0);
    m_icoMainframeLarge = (HICON) LoadImage
                        (AfxGetInstanceHandle(),
                         MAKEINTRESOURCE (IDR_MAINFRAME),
                         IMAGE_ICON,
                         32, 32, 0);
    return TRUE;  // return TRUE unless you set the focus
                  // to a control
                  // EXCEPTION: OCX Property Pages should
                  // return FALSE
}

void CButtonPage::OnRadiotool()
{
    UpdateData (TRUE);
    switch (m_nRadioTool)
    {
        case 0:
            m_RadioLedRed.SetBitmap (m_bmpRedOff);
            m_RadioLedGreen.SetBitmap (m_bmpGreenOn);
            m_RadioLedYellow.SetBitmap (m_bmpYellowOff);
            break;
        case 1:
            m_RadioLedRed.SetBitmap (m_bmpRedOff);
            m_RadioLedYellow.SetBitmap (m_bmpYellowOn);
            m_RadioLedGreen.SetBitmap (m_bmpGreenOff);
            break;
```

```
            case 2:
                m_RadioLedRed.SetBitmap (m_bmpRedOn);
                m_RadioLedYellow.SetBitmap (m_bmpYellowOff);
                m_RadioLedGreen.SetBitmap (m_bmpGreenOff);
                break;
            default:
                return;
        }
    m_nRadioButton = m_nRadioTool;
    UpdateData (FALSE);
}

void CButtonPage::OnRadioButton()
{
    UpdateData (TRUE);
    m_nRadioTool = m_nRadioButton;
    UpdateData (FALSE);
    OnRadiotool ();
}

void CButtonPage::OnButtonbutton()
{
    static int nPress = 0;
    ++nPress;
    if (nPress > 2)
        nPress = 0;
    switch (nPress)
    {
        case 0:
            m_ButtonButtonLed.SetBitmap (m_bmpGreenOn);
            break;
        case 1:
            m_ButtonButtonLed.SetBitmap (m_bmpYellowOn);
            break;
        case 2:
            m_ButtonButtonLed.SetBitmap (m_bmpRedOn);
            break;
        default:
            break;
    }
}

void CButtonPage::OnCheckboxbutton()
{
    UpdateData (TRUE);
    if (m_bCheckBoxButton)
        m_CheckBoxLed.SetBitmap (m_bmpRedOn);
    else
        m_CheckBoxLed.SetBitmap (m_bmpRedOff);
}

void CButtonPage::OnButtonflat()
{
    UpdateData (TRUE);
    if (m_bFlat)
        m_StyleButton.ModifyStyle (0, BS_FLAT, TRUE);
```

```
    else
        m_StyleButton.ModifyStyle (BS_FLAT, 0, TRUE);
    m_StyleButton.Invalidate ();
}

void CButtonPage::OnButtonicon()
{
    UpdateData (TRUE);
    if (m_bIcon)
    {
        m_bBitmap = FALSE;
        m_bText = FALSE;
        m_StyleButton.ModifyStyle (BS_BITMAP,
                                BS_ICON, TRUE);
        m_StyleButton.SetIcon (m_icoMainframeLarge);
        m_StyleButton.SetWindowText (_T("Button"));
    }
    else
    {
        m_bIcon = FALSE;
        m_bBitmap = FALSE;
        m_bText = TRUE;
        m_StyleButton.ModifyStyle (BS_ICON, 0, TRUE);
        if (m_bMultiline)
          m_StyleButton.SetWindowText(_T("Button Button"));
        else
          m_StyleButton.SetWindowText (_T("Button"));
        m_StyleButton.SetIcon (NULL);
    }
    UpdateData (FALSE);
}

void CButtonPage::OnButtonbitmap()
{
    UpdateData (TRUE);
    if (m_bBitmap)
    {
        m_bIcon = FALSE;
        m_bText = FALSE;
        m_StyleButton.ModifyStyle (BS_ICON,
                                BS_BITMAP, TRUE);
        m_StyleButton.SetWindowText (_T("Button"));
        m_StyleButton.SetBitmap (m_bmpDudleyPC);
    }
    else
    {
        m_bIcon = FALSE;
        m_bBitmap = FALSE;
        m_bText = TRUE;
        m_StyleButton.ModifyStyle (BS_BITMAP, 0, TRUE);
        if (m_bMultiline)
          m_StyleButton.SetWindowText(_T("Button Button"));
        else
          m_StyleButton.SetWindowText (_T("Button"));
        m_StyleButton.SetBitmap (NULL);
    }
```

```
    UpdateData (FALSE);
}

void CButtonPage::OnButtontext()
{
    UpdateData (TRUE);
    if (m_bText)
    {
        m_bIcon = FALSE;
        m_bBitmap = FALSE;
        m_StyleButton.ModifyStyle (BS_ICON | BS_BITMAP,
                                    Ø, TRUE);
        if (m_bMultiline)
          m_StyleButton.SetWindowText(_T("Button Button"));
        else
          m_StyleButton.SetWindowText (_T("Button"));
    }
    else
    {
        if (m_bIcon | m_bBitmap)
        {
            m_bText = FALSE;
        }
        else
        {
            m_bText = TRUE;
            if (m_bMultiline)
                m_StyleButton.SetWindowText
                                (_T("Button Button"));
            else
                m_StyleButton.SetWindowText (_T("Button"));
        }
    }
    UpdateData (FALSE);
}

void CButtonPage::OnButtonmultiline()
{
    UpdateData (TRUE);
    if (m_bMultiline)
    {
        m_StyleButton.ModifyStyle (Ø, BS_MULTILINE, TRUE);
        m_StyleButton.SetWindowText (_T("Button Button"));
    }
    else
    {
        m_StyleButton.ModifyStyle (BS_MULTILINE, Ø, TRUE);
        m_StyleButton.SetWindowText (_T("Button"));
    }

}

void CButtonPage::OnButtonenable()
{
    UpdateData (TRUE);
    if (m_bEnable)
```

```
        m_StyleButton.EnableWindow (FALSE);
    else
        m_StyleButton.EnableWindow (TRUE);
}

void CButtonPage::OnGroupicon()
{
    UpdateData (TRUE);
    if (m_bGroupIcon)
    {
        m_bGroupBitmap = FALSE;
        m_bGroupText = FALSE;
        m_GroupSample.ModifyStyle (BS_BITMAP,
                                   BS_ICON, TRUE);
        m_GroupSample.SetIcon (m_icoMainframeSmall);
    }
    else
    {
        m_GroupSample.ModifyStyle (BS_BITMAP, 0, TRUE);
    }
    UpdateData (FALSE);
}

void CButtonPage::OnGroupbitmap()
{
    UpdateData (TRUE);
    if (m_bGroupBitmap)
    {
        m_bGroupIcon = FALSE;
        m_bGroupText = FALSE;
        m_GroupSample.ModifyStyle (BS_ICON,
                                   BS_BITMAP, TRUE);
        m_GroupSample.SetBitmap (m_bmpGreenOn);
    }
    else
    {
        m_GroupSample.ModifyStyle (BS_ICON, 0, TRUE);
    }
    UpdateData (FALSE);
}

void CButtonPage::OnGrouptext()
{
    UpdateData (TRUE);
    if (m_bGroupText)
    {
        m_bGroupIcon = FALSE;
        m_bGroupBitmap = FALSE;
        m_GroupSample.ModifyStyle (BS_ICON | BS_BITMAP,
                                   0, TRUE);
        m_GroupSample.SetWindowText (_T("Group Box"));
    }
    else
    {
        m_GroupSample.ModifyStyle (BS_ICON, 0, TRUE);
    }
```

```
        UpdateData (FALSE);
}

void CButtonPage::OnGroupflat()
{
        UpdateData (TRUE);
        if (m_bGroupFlat)
            m_GroupSample.ModifyStyle (0, BS_FLAT, TRUE);
        else
            m_GroupSample.ModifyStyle (BS_FLAT, 0, TRUE);
        m_GroupSample.Invalidate ();
}
void CButtonPage::OnUncheckedradio()
{
        m_CheckSample.SetCheck (0);
}

void CButtonPage::OnCheckradio()
{
        m_CheckSample.SetCheck (1);
}

void CButtonPage::OnIndetermradio()
{
        m_CheckSample.SetCheck (2);
}

void CButtonPage::OnChecksample()
{
        UpdateData (TRUE);
        m_CheckState = m_CheckSample.GetCheck ();
        UpdateData (FALSE);
}
```

All the button controls derive from *CWnd* and thus inherit all the major window functions. You can hide and show them using the *ShowWindow()* function, or move and resize them using the *MoveWindow()* function.

828. Using Command Update to Enable or Disable a Button

When used with dialog box controls, command enablers don't work very well. In fact, they're downright fatal to the application. Other class libraries such as the Object Windows Library seem to implement them in dialog boxes without any great problems, but Microsoft hasn't shown any indication that it is less than happy with the situation as it is. In fact, the *ON_UPDATE_COMMAND_UI* message doesn't even appear in the list of available messages for a control on a dialog box.

In dialog boxes, then, you'll have to use timers or catch the *WM_IDLE* message and use the *CWnd:: EnableWindow()* function to enable or disable button controls. The *CButton* class also has a *SetCheck()* function that you can use to make the button appear pressed or unpressed.

When used on the main window frame or in a toolbar, the command enablers function normally, and you can use the *ON_UPDATE_COMMAND_UI* message to set the state and check of a button.

829. *Understanding Check Boxes*

The Check Box common control usually is used to indicate a true or false condition—it is either checked or unchecked. It combines a square box to hold the check mark and a label. A 3-State style allows a third condition for the check box, an indeterminate state in which the box is both checked and grayed.

Several cases of the check box are shown on the Button property page. Most of these are used as control selections for the associated buttons, but two cases demonstrate the properties of check boxes.

At the upper center of the page is a group box labeled 3-State Check Box that shows the various states of the check box. Successively clicking the box or label will move the box from unchecked to checked to grayed. You also can select one of the radio buttons below it to set the state. This code demonstrates how to interpret the state from user input and how to set it programmatically.

In the Microsoft Foundation Class, the check box is represented by the *CButton* class, the same as the pushbutton control. The class produces a check box button when you give it the *BS_CHECKBOX* style.

830. *Using a Pushbutton Check Box*

The other case of the check box control shows a control that looks and operates like a button control, with one major difference. When it is pressed, it doesn't return to the up state when the user releases the mouse button. Instead, it toggles the current state. If the button is up—the check is not set—when pressed, it will go into the down state—the check is set—and stay there. If it's down, it will go to the up state and stay there.

The lower button in the group box at the upper left, labeled Buttons, demonstrates this style of check box. In this sample, it's used to turn the LED to the left on and off.

The check box uses the same window class as the standard button control and thus is drawn by the same window procedure that draws the button.

831. *Understanding Radio Buttons*

The Radio Button control is designed to be used in a group to enable the user to select an exclusive item from several. In a group of radio buttons, only one may be selected at any given time, and selecting another unselects the previous selection. The control gets its name from this operation, similar to the buttons on a car radio.

By default, the control draws an open circle as an indicator. When a button is selected, a smaller, solid circle appears inside the selected button. A label usually is used to the right or left of the indicator.

The radio button is created from the Button window class. Like the check box control, the radio button control is represented in the Microsoft Foundation Class by the *CButton* class. The styles *BS_RADIOBUTTON* and *BS_AUTORADIOBUTTON* convert it to the radio button appearance. Buttons formed with the *BS_RADIOBUTTON* style must have their check states changed by the program, but the system is responsible for maintaining the state of those formed with the *BS_AUTORA-DIOBUTTON* style.

832. Grouping Radio Buttons

The radio button control can be used as a single selection object, the same as an ordinary button or a check box. Its best use, though, is the way it was intended to be used: in a group of similar buttons like those on a radio.

When grouped, only one radio button in the group may be selected at any time. When the buttons are created using the *BS_AUTORADIOBUTTON* style, the system unchecks any buttons other than the current selection.

To group radio buttons, create them in sequence, setting Group style on the first button only. For buttons after the first, make sure that the Group style is unchecked. When you come to the end of the group, the *next* control created should have the Group style checked. This will terminate the previous group, the radio button collection.

If you've already created the controls and are not sure of the sequence, or if you later need to add another radio button to the group, select the Tab Order item from the Layout menu, or press Ctrl+D with the dialog box template. Set the new tab order so that the radio buttons appear in order in the tab sequence. This will change the creation order as well and place the radio buttons in a group. Finally, check the next control in the tab order to make sure that it has the Group style checked.

When you create a member variable in the dialog box class using the ClassWizard, the wizard will list only one resource ID for the button group, the button containing the Group style. The value of the button press is an integer, beginning with 0 for the first button in the group and incrementing for each button in the group, with the next button in the tab order getting the next value. If you have a group of four radio buttons, for example, and you create a variable named *m_RadioValue*, if the user selects the first button in the group, *m_RadioValue* will contain 0. When the second button is selected, *m_RadioValue* will be 1, continuing with a value of 2 for the third button, and 3 for the fourth and final button in the tab order.

833. Using Pushbuttons for Radio Boxes

Because they use the same window class as the standard button control, radio buttons can be made to appear as ordinary buttons but still behave as radio buttons. Essentially, this was how you set up the toolbar buttons for the *Explorer* project in Tip 671, "Saving the Status Bar Message," to select one of the four views for the list view. Toolbars, of course, don't have the advantage of the Group style used with dialog boxes, so the exclusive property was done in code, the same as if the buttons had the *BS_RADIOBUTTON* style rather than the *BS_AUTORADIOBUTTON* style set.

To create a pushbutton-style radio button, select the Push Like style in the dialog editor when you design the dialog box. Not all the radio buttons in a group need to have this style. You could have one button with the Push Like style and the others without.

When a button with the Push Like style set is pressed, it changes to a down state and remains there until another button is pressed. All the other buttons in the group, including any previous selection, are set to the up position.

If you examine the button in the group box at the lower left of the Buttons page, you'll notice that the row of three pushbuttons actually are radio buttons with the Push Like style set. Because they are grouped, only one of them can be pressed at once, and pressing another releases any other pressed button.

834. Using Bitmaps and Icons on Check Boxes and Radio Buttons

Buttons, check boxes, and radio buttons have a lot in common. They use the same window class and the same *CButton* class in the Microsoft Foundation Class. Although the dialog editor has separate buttons for them on its toolbar, they are not listed as separate controls in the list of Windows common controls.

In effect, they are different faces of the same control. You've seen how one can be made to mimic the other. What you haven't seen yet is a check box or radio button with an image on it. Placing images on a button control is a common practice, and it's almost expected if you are preparing a toolbar.

You can place an icon, bitmap, or cursor image on a button control or a Push Like check box or radio button. When you are designing the dialog box, select the Icon or Bitmap button on the Styles page of the property sheet. In the *OnInitDialog()* function—or after the control has been created, if it is on the main window frame—use the *CButton::SetIcon()*, *CButton::SetBitmap()*, or *CButton::SetCursor()* function, as appropriate to connect the control with the image.

Figure 834   Some additional buttons will let you experiment with check and radio styles

Let's go back to the dialog template for the Buttons page and add some check boxes to the group labeled Button Styles. Add check boxes for Push Like, Radio, and Check. When you select the Radio check box, the sample button won't have any way to become unchecked, so we'll add a hidden radio button labeled Uncheck, which will become visible only when the Radio style is selected. Set the Group style on the sample button.

Add member variables for these controls. The check boxes are all type *BOOL* variables, and the hidden radio button is a *CButton* control. The hidden button won't show in the ClassWizard, so you'll have to check the Group box for it temporarily, create the variable, and then uncheck the Group box. Be sure that the Visible box for the hidden button on the General page is *unchecked*.

Add handler function for the *BN_CLICKED* message for the three new check boxes. You won't need a message handler for the hidden button. The variable and new function declarations in the header file should look like the following:

```
//
// New variables
    CButton  m_UncheckButton;
    BOOL     m_bButtonCheckStyle;
    BOOL     m_bButtonRadioStyle;
    BOOL     m_bButtonPushStyle;
//
// New message handlers
    afx_msg void OnButtonradiostyle();
    afx_msg void OnButtoncheckstyle();
    afx_msg void OnButtonpushstyle();
```

Implement these new buttons and message handlers with the following code in the source file:

```cpp
//
//  New message handlers for the sample style button
//  implementing radio and check box styles.
//
void CButtonPage::OnButtonradiostyle()
{
    UpdateData (TRUE);
    if (m_bButtonRadioStyle)
    {
        m_StyleButton.ModifyStyle(BS_AUTOCHECKBOX,
                                  BS_AUTORADIOBUTTON, TRUE);
        m_bButtonCheckStyle = FALSE;
        m_UncheckButton.ShowWindow (SW_SHOWNORMAL);
    }
    else
    {
        m_StyleButton.ModifyStyle (BS_AUTORADIOBUTTON,
                                   0, TRUE);
        m_UncheckButton.ShowWindow (SW_HIDE);
    }
    UpdateData (FALSE);
    m_StyleButton.Invalidate ();
}

void CButtonPage::OnButtoncheckstyle()
{
    UpdateData (TRUE);
    if (m_bButtonCheckStyle)
    {
        m_StyleButton.ModifyStyle (BS_AUTORADIOBUTTON,
                                   BS_AUTOCHECKBOX, TRUE);
        m_bButtonRadioStyle = FALSE;
        m_UncheckButton.ShowWindow (SW_HIDE);
    }
    else
        m_StyleButton.ModifyStyle (BS_AUTOCHECKBOX,
                                   0, TRUE);
    UpdateData (FALSE);
    m_StyleButton.Invalidate ();
}

void CButtonPage::OnButtonpushstyle()
{
    UpdateData (TRUE);
    if (m_bButtonPushStyle)
        m_StyleButton.ModifyStyle (0, BS_PUSHLIKE, TRUE);
    else
        m_StyleButton.ModifyStyle (BS_PUSHLIKE, 0, TRUE);
    m_StyleButton.Invalidate ();
}
```

At this point, your sample page now can display virtually any permutation of the button control. If you find any that we've missed, add them. The page is getting a bit crowded, but you can add another tab or place additional samples on an embedded tab control, as you'll do shortly with the list box control.

835. Understanding the Group Control

The final stop on the tour of the button control is the *group* control, that sunken line with a label that you use to isolate a collection of related controls. It may sound strange, but the group control is nothing more than a case of the button control. It uses the Button window class, and if you declare a variable of it in MFC using the ClassWizard, the variable will be of type *CButton*.

You can see this in the header and source files for the Buttons property page. To change the label from text to bitmap to icon, we declared a control variable named *m_GroupSample*, and it is indeed of type *CButton*.

Because it is a button control, you can use many of the same styles on a group control. Setting the bitmap or icon buttons changes the label from a string to a picture. Setting the Flat style, well, that kind of makes it look less flat.

We have one word of caution when using a bitmap or icon with the group box control. Don't make the image larger than a single line of text. If you do and subsequently change the style, the dialog box procedure won't erase the entire image. It'll only redraw the area where a line of text would appear. If you want a large image, you'll have to take care of erasing the remnants yourself.

836. Understanding the List Box Control

For all its simplicity, the list box control sure is a versatile critter. Until the new list control came along with Windows 95, the list box was the only control available for listing a collection of objects (the drop-down box of a combo control is really a list box). Over the years, a selection of useful functions was developed to make use of it.

Although the list control with its different views is the primary method of listing the contents of directories, that wasn't so before Windows 95. Most applications in earlier versions of Windows used the list box for directory information, and a Windows message, *LB_DIR*, is dedicated to adding a selected group of file names to a list box control. You'll look at this message and the MFC *CListBox::Dir()* function in Tip 840, "Using the List Box *Dir()* Function."

Unless you override the drawing code for a list box by setting the Owner Draw style, a list box can contain and display only strings. Each string entry can have an associated 32-bit value that can be just an ordinary number or a pointer to a structure containing information about the list box entry.

When a list box is displayed, Windows will try to size the depth of the box so that a partial string is not visible at the bottom of the box, and it may not appear exactly as you drew it in the dialog editor. If you need the box to appear an exact size, you can avoid this by setting the *LBS_NOINTEGRALHEIGHT* style. Just check the No Integral Height box on the Style page of the properties dialog box.

837. Using the CListBox Class

The Microsoft Foundation Class implements the list box in three different classes. The first, *CListBox*, encapsulates an ordinary list box control and provides functions to manipulate the list box and the strings that it contains.

The other two classes are derived from *CListBox* and impart special properties on the list box control. The *CCheckListBox* class creates an Owner Draw list box (the Owner Draw part is taken care of by the class code) that includes check boxes to the left of each string. A user may select items by placing checks in the boxes rather than highlighting the strings in a multiple selection box. To create this style of box, you must select Fixed from the Owner Draw box on the Styles page of the Properties sheet when you place the list box on your dialog box. The Selection should be Single, and the Has Strings box must be checked.

The *CDragListBox* class creates a list box that incorporates OLE drag-and-drop operations so that the user can rearrange the strings by dragging them with the mouse and dropping them in a different location. When you create this type of list box, you should use the Single option in the Selection box and uncheck the Sort box on the Styles page.

The ClassWizard doesn't list *CCheckListBox* or *CDragListBox* among the base class possibilities. To create a dialog class member variable using these, you can select *CListBox* as the base class and then edit the header file to change the base class name. Alternatively, you can enter the variables manually, but remember to include them in the *DoDataExchange()* function.

The List Box page of the *Controls* property sheet project will demonstrate all three list box classes and show how to use two list box controls as a selection control. We can't contain all these samples on a single property page, however, so we'll resort to adding a tab control to the property page and place them on a couple of tab pages.

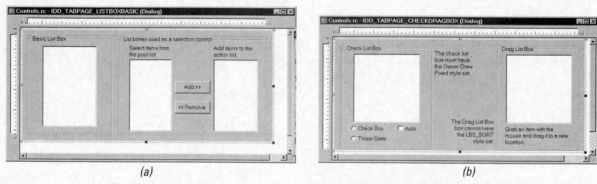

(a)   (b)

*Figures 837a and 837b   Two tab sheets will be used on the List Box page of the
property sheet to demonstrate variations of the list box control*

First create the dialog boxes to contain the list box samples. These should be 312 units wide by 137 deep; you'll need every pixel to draw the samples. Unselect all styles for these dialog boxes, and make sure this is a child window with a border of None. Unlike the property pages, these dialog boxes should not have a title bar and should be left enabled. Add the controls as shown in Figures 837a and 837b. The dialog box in Figure 837a should be given a resource ID of *IDD_TABPAGE_LISTBOXBASIC*, and the dialog box in Figure 837b should be given a resource ID of *IDD_TABPAGE_CHECKDRAGBOX*. Create classes for these dialog boxes. The classes should be derived from *CDialog* rather than *CPropertyPage* because you will be adding them to a tab control. Name the classes *CListBoxBasicDlg* and *CCheckDragDlg*. The code will be shown later, but right now you need them for the tab control page.

Add a large property sheet to the *Controls* project. Make it the same size as the other pages, 325 by 155. In this case, the size of the property page is important. Remove the blue constraining line from the property page using the rules at the top and left sides of the dialog editor window. Select Tab Control from the toolbar, and draw a control that fills the entire dialog box, corner to corner. Make sure that none of the style boxes is checked, but you may select the Hot Track style. Give the tab control a resource ID of *IDC_LISTBOXTABS* and the property sheet a resource ID of *IDD_PROPPAGE_LISTBOXDLG*.

Create a class for this property sheet named *CListBoxDlg*. From the ClassWizard, add a member variable for the tab control named *m_ListBoxTabs*. Select the Messages page and select the *IDC_LIST-BOXTABS* entry. Add handlers for the *TCH_SELCHANGE* and *TCN_SELCHANGING* messages.

The header and implementation code for this class is shown here. Don't worry about the mechanisms of the tab control in this section; later, you'll create a property sheet for the tab control itself and have a sample that will demonstrate the options for you.

```
// ListBoxDlg.h : header file
//

#include "ListBoxBasicDlg.h"
#include "CheckDragDlg.h"


/////////////////////////////////////////////////////////////
// CListBoxDlg dialog

class CListBoxDlg : public CpropertyPage
{
    DECLARE_DYNCREATE(CListBoxDlg)

// Construction
public:
    CListBoxDlg();
    ~CListBoxDlg();

// Dialog Data
    //{{AFX_DATA(CListBoxDlg)
    enum { IDD = IDD_PROPPAGE_LISTBOXDLG };
    CTabCtrl    m_ListBoxTabs;
    //}}AFX_DATA


// Overrides
    // ClassWizard generate virtual function overrides
    //{{AFX_VIRTUAL(CListBoxDlg)
    protected:
    virtual void DoDataExchange(CDataExchange* pDX);
    // DDX/DDV support
    //}}AFX_VIRTUAL

// Implementation
protected:
    // Generated message map functions
    //{{AFX_MSG(CListBoxDlg)
    virtual BOOL OnInitDialog();
    afx_msg void OnSelchangeListboxtabs(NMHDR* pNMHDR,
                                        LRESULT* pResult);
    afx_msg void OnSelchangingListboxtabs(NMHDR* pNMHDR,
                                          LRESULT* pResult);
    //}}AFX_MSG
    DECLARE_MESSAGE_MAP()

    CListBoxBasicDlg    m_BasicPage;
    CCheckDragDlg       m_CheckDragPage;

};


/////////////////////////////////////////////////////////////
// ListBoxDlg.cpp : implementation file
//
```

```cpp
#include "stdafx.h"
#include "Controls.h"
#include "ListBoxDlg.h"

#ifdef _DEBUG
#define new DEBUG_NEW
#undef THIS_FILE
static char THIS_FILE[] = __FILE__;
#endif

/////////////////////////////////////////////////////////////
// CListBoxDlg property page

IMPLEMENT_DYNCREATE(CListBoxDlg, CPropertyPage)

CListBoxDlg::CListBoxDlg() : CPropertyPage(CListBoxDlg::IDD)
{
    //{{AFX_DATA_INIT(CListBoxDlg)
        // NOTE: the ClassWizard will add member
        // initialization here
    //}}AFX_DATA_INIT
    m_psp.dwFlags &= ~PSP_HASHELP;
}

CListBoxDlg::~CListBoxDlg()
{
}

void CListBoxDlg::DoDataExchange(CDataExchange* pDX)
{
    CPropertyPage::DoDataExchange(pDX);
    //{{AFX_DATA_MAP(CListBoxDlg)
    DDX_Control(pDX, IDC_LISTBOXTABS, m_ListBoxTabs);
    //}}AFX_DATA_MAP
}


BEGIN_MESSAGE_MAP(CListBoxDlg, CPropertyPage)
    //{{AFX_MSG_MAP(CListBoxDlg)
    ON_NOTIFY(TCN_SELCHANGE, IDC_LISTBOXTABS,
            OnSelchangeListboxtabs)
    ON_NOTIFY(TCN_SELCHANGING, IDC_LISTBOXTABS,
            OnSelchangingListboxtabs)
    //}}AFX_MSG_MAP
END_MESSAGE_MAP()

/////////////////////////////////////////////////////////////
// CListBoxDlg message handlers

 BOOL CListBoxDlg::OnInitDialog()
{
    CPropertyPage::OnInitDialog();

    m_BasicPage.Create(IDD_TABPAGE_LISTBOXBASIC,
                    GetDlgItem (IDC_LISTBOXTABS));
    m_CheckDragPage.Create(IDD_TABPAGE_CHECKDRAGBOX,
```

```
                        GetDlgItem (IDC_LISTBOXTABS));

    TC_ITEM TabItem;
    TabItem.mask = TCIF_TEXT | TCIF_PARAM;
    TabItem.iImage = 0;

    TabItem.lParam = (long) &m_BasicPage;
    TabItem.pszText = _T("Basic List Box");
    m_ListBoxTabs.InsertItem (0, &TabItem);

    TabItem.lParam = (long) &m_CheckDragPage;
    TabItem.pszText = "Check and Drag Boxes";
    m_ListBoxTabs.InsertItem (1, &TabItem);

//
// Size the dialog boxes to fit the tab control, giving
// just a bit of breathing room around the edges.
//
    CRect r, rc;
    m_ListBoxTabs.GetItemRect (0, &r);
    rc.top = r.bottom + 2;
    rc.left = r.left + 2;
    m_ListBoxTabs.GetClientRect (&r);
    rc.bottom = r.bottom - 2;
    rc.right = r.right - rc.left - 2;

    m_BasicPage.MoveWindow (rc);
    m_CheckDragPage.MoveWindow (rc);

    m_BasicPage.ShowWindow (SW_NORMAL);

    return TRUE;  // return TRUE unless you set the focus
                  // to a control
                  // EXCEPTION: OCX Property Pages should
                  // return FALSE
}

void CListBoxDlg::OnSelchangeListboxtabs(NMHDR* pNMHDR,
                                         LRESULT* pResult)
{
TC_ITEM     ti;
CWnd*       cDlg;
int         result;

    int sel = m_ListBoxTabs.GetCurSel();
    ti.mask = TCIF_PARAM | TCIF_IMAGE;
    result = m_ListBoxTabs.GetItem (sel, &ti);
    cDlg = (CWnd *) ti.lParam;
    if (cDlg)
        cDlg->ShowWindow (true);
    ti.mask = TCIF_IMAGE;
    ti.iImage += 1;
    m_ListBoxTabs.SetItem (sel, &ti);

    *pResult = 0;
}
```

```
void CListBoxDlg::OnSelchangingListboxtabs(NMHDR* pNMHDR,
                                           LRESULT* pResult)
{
TC_ITEM    ti;
CWnd*      cDlg;
int        result;

    int sel = m_ListBoxTabs.GetCurSel();
    ti.mask = TCIF_PARAM | TCIF_IMAGE;
    result = m_ListBoxTabs.GetItem (sel, &ti);
    cDlg = (CWnd *) ti.lParam;
    if (cDlg)
        cDlg->ShowWindow (false);
    ti.mask = TCIF_IMAGE;
    ti.iImage -= 1;
    m_ListBoxTabs.SetItem (sel, &ti);

    *pResult = 0;
}
```

Add a member variable for this class to the *CControlsProp* class named *m_ListBoxPage*, and add it to the property sheet in the constructors.

Compile the program and run it to make sure that everything is working up to this point. You should have a total of four property pages, including this new one. When you select the List Box tab, the tab control should become visible, allowing you to select between the two dialog boxes that you just created.

Now you need to code the dialog box classes. Start with the *CListBoxBasicDlg* class. Add member variables for all three list boxes. The list box on the left is *m_BasicList*, and the two on the right are *m_PoolList* and *m_ActionList*. The two buttons are *m_AddButton* and *m_RemoveButton*.

The header and source files for the *CListBoxBasicDlg* are shown here:

```
// ListBoxBasicDlg.h : header file
//

/////////////////////////////////////////////////////////////
// CListBoxBasicDlg

class CListBoxBasicDlg : public CDialog
{
    DECLARE_DYNAMIC(CListBoxBasicDlg)

// Construction
public:
    CListBoxBasicDlg(CWnd* pParent = NULL);
    virtual ~CListBoxBasicDlg();

// Attributes
public:

// Operations
public:

// Overrides
    // ClassWizard generated virtual function overrides
    //{{AFX_VIRTUAL(CListBoxBasicDlg)
    protected:
```

```cpp
    virtual void DoDataExchange(CDataExchange* pDX);
    // DDX/DDV support
    //}}AFX_VIRTUAL

// Implementation
public:

// Dialog Data
    //{{AFX_DATA(CListBoxBasicDlg)
    enum { IDD = IDD_TABPAGE_LISTBOXBASIC };
    CButton m_RemoveButton;
    CButton m_AddButton;
    CListBox    m_BasicList;
    CListBox    m_ActionList;
    CListBox    m_PoolList;
    //}}AFX_DATA

    // Generated message map functions
protected:
    //{{AFX_MSG(CListBoxBasicDlg)
    virtual BOOL OnInitDialog();
    afx_msg void OnSelchangeActionlist();
    afx_msg void OnSelchangePoollist();
    afx_msg void OnDblclkPoollist();
    afx_msg void OnDblclkActionlist();
    afx_msg void OnSelcancelActionlist();
    afx_msg void OnSelcancelBasiclist();
    afx_msg void OnSelcancelPoollist();
    afx_msg void OnSelchangeBasiclist();
    afx_msg void OnDblclkBasiclist();
    afx_msg void OnAddbutton();
    afx_msg void OnRemovebutton();
    //}}AFX_MSG
    DECLARE_MESSAGE_MAP()
    afx_msg void OnCancel();
};

/////////////////////////////////////////////////////////////
// ListBoxBasicDlg.cpp : implementation file
//

#include "stdafx.h"
#include "Controls.h"
#include "ListBoxBasicDlg.h"

#ifdef _DEBUG
#define new DEBUG_NEW
#undef THIS_FILE
static char THIS_FILE[] = __FILE__ ;
#endif

/////////////////////////////////////////////////////////////
// CListBoxBasicDlg

IMPLEMENT_DYNAMIC(CListBoxBasicDlg, CDialog)
```

```cpp
CListBoxBasicDlg::CListBoxBasicDlg(CWnd* pParent)
    :CDialog (IDD, pParent)
{
    //{{AFX_DATA_INIT(CListBoxBasicDlg)
    //}}AFX_DATA_INIT
}


CListBoxBasicDlg::~CListBoxBasicDlg()
{
}



void CListBoxBasicDlg::DoDataExchange(CDataExchange* pDX)
{
    CDialog::DoDataExchange(pDX);
    //{{AFX_DATA_MAP(CListBoxBasicDlg)
    DDX_Control(pDX, IDC_REMOVEBUTTON, m_RemoveButton);
    DDX_Control(pDX, IDC_ADDBUTTON, m_AddButton);
    DDX_Control(pDX, IDC_BASICLIST, m_BasicList);
    DDX_Control(pDX, IDC_ACTIONLIST, m_ActionList);
    DDX_Control(pDX, IDC_POOLLIST, m_PoolList);
    //}}AFX_DATA_MAP
}

BEGIN_MESSAGE_MAP(CListBoxBasicDlg, CDialog)
    //{{AFX_MSG_MAP(CListBoxBasicDlg)
    ON_LBN_SELCHANGE(IDC_ACTIONLIST, OnSelchangeActionlist)
    ON_LBN_SELCHANGE(IDC_POOLLIST, OnSelchangePoollist)
    ON_LBN_DBLCLK(IDC_POOLLIST, OnDblclkPoollist)
    ON_LBN_DBLCLK(IDC_ACTIONLIST, OnDblclkActionlist)
    ON_LBN_SELCANCEL(IDC_ACTIONLIST, OnSelcancelActionlist)
    ON_LBN_SELCANCEL(IDC_BASICLIST, OnSelcancelBasiclist)
    ON_LBN_SELCANCEL(IDC_POOLLIST, OnSelcancelPoollist)
    ON_LBN_SELCHANGE(IDC_BASICLIST, OnSelchangeBasiclist)
    ON_LBN_DBLCLK(IDC_BASICLIST, OnDblclkBasiclist)
    ON_BN_CLICKED(IDC_ADDBUTTON, OnAddbutton)
    ON_BN_CLICKED(IDC_REMOVEBUTTON, OnRemovebutton)
    //}}AFX_MSG_MAP
    ON_COMMAND(IDCANCEL, OnCancel)
END_MESSAGE_MAP()

/////////////////////////////////////////////////////////////////////
////
// CListBoxBasicDlg message handlers

void CListBoxBasicDlg::OnCancel()
{
}


BOOL CListBoxBasicDlg::OnInitDialog()
{
    CDialog::OnInitDialog();

//
//  Load the lists with file names.
//
```

```
    WIN32_FIND_DATA fd;
    HANDLE hFind;
    if ((hFind = FindFirstFile (_T("*.*"), &fd)) != NULL)
    {
        do
        {
            if (fd.cFileName[0] == '.')
                continue;
            m_BasicList.AddString (fd.cFileName);
            m_PoolList.AddString (fd.cFileName);
        } while (FindNextFile (hFind, &fd) == TRUE);
    }

    m_BasicList.SetCurSel (0);
    m_PoolList.SetCurSel (0);

    m_AddButton.EnableWindow (FALSE);
    m_RemoveButton.EnableWindow (FALSE);

    return TRUE;  // return TRUE unless you set the focus
                  // to a control
                  // EXCEPTION: OCX Property Pages should
                  // return FALSE
}

/////////////////////////////////////////////////////////////
// Functions for m_BasicList

void CListBoxBasicDlg::OnSelcancelBasiclist()
{
    // TODO: Add your control notification handler code here

}

void CListBoxBasicDlg::OnSelchangeBasiclist()
{
    // TODO: Add your control notification handler code here

}

void CListBoxBasicDlg::OnDblclkBasiclist()
{
    // TODO: Add your control notification handler code here

}

/////////////////////////////////////////////////////////////
// Functions for m_PoolList

void CListBoxBasicDlg::OnSelchangePoollist()
{
    if (m_PoolList.GetSelCount ())
        m_AddButton.EnableWindow (TRUE);
    else
        m_AddButton.EnableWindow (FALSE);
}
```

```
void CListBoxBasicDlg::OnDblclkPoollist()
{
    OnAddbutton ();
}

void CListBoxBasicDlg::OnSelcancelPoollist()
{
    OnSelchangePoollist();
}

////////////////////////////////////////////////////////////
// Functions for m_ActionList

void CListBoxBasicDlg::OnSelchangeActionlist()
{
    if (m_ActionList.GetSelCount ())
       m_RemoveButton.EnableWindow (TRUE);
    else
       m_RemoveButton.EnableWindow (FALSE);
}

void CListBoxBasicDlg::OnDblclkActionlist()
{
    OnRemovebutton();
}

void CListBoxBasicDlg::OnSelcancelActionlist()
{
    OnSelchangeActionlist();
}

////////////////////////////////////////////////////////////
// Button functions

void CListBoxBasicDlg::OnAddbutton()
{

    int Count = m_PoolList.GetSelCount ();
    if (!Count)
        return;
    int *SelItems = new int [Count];
    m_PoolList.GetSelItems (Count, SelItems);
    for (int i = 0; i < Count; ++i)
    {
    CString strText;
    int iIndex;

        m_PoolList.GetText (SelItems[i], strText);
//
// The item data is a user specified number. It usually is
// a pointer to a structure containing detailed information
//
        DWORD dwData = m_PoolList.GetItemData (SelItems[i]);
        iIndex = m_ActionList.AddString ((LPCSTR) strText);
        m_ActionList.SetItemData (iIndex, dwData);
```

```
        }
//
//   Delete the selected items from the highest
//   index to the lowest. Deleting the lowest
//   index first changes the relative index of the
//   higher index selected items.
//
        for (i = Count - 1; i >= 0; --i)
        {
            m_PoolList.DeleteString (SelItems[i]);
        }
        delete [] SelItems;
        m_PoolList.SetSel (-1, false);
        if (m_PoolList.GetSelCount ())
            m_AddButton.EnableWindow (true);
        else
            m_AddButton.EnableWindow (false);
        if (m_ActionList.GetSelCount ())
        {
            m_RemoveButton.EnableWindow (true);
        }
        else
        {
            m_RemoveButton.EnableWindow (false);
        }
}

void CListBoxBasicDlg::OnRemovebutton()
{

    int Count = m_ActionList.GetSelCount ();
    if (!Count)
        return;
    int *SelItems = new int [Count];
    m_ActionList.GetSelItems (Count, SelItems);
    for (int i = 0; i < Count; ++i)
    {
    CString strText;
    int iIndex;

        m_ActionList.GetText (SelItems[i], strText);
        DWORD dwData=m_ActionList.GetItemData (SelItems[i]);
        iIndex = m_PoolList.AddString ((LPCSTR) strText);
        m_PoolList.SetItemData (iIndex, dwData);
    }
//
//   Delete the selected items from the highest
//   index to the lowest. Deleting the lowest
//   index first changes the relative index of the
//   higher index selected items.
//
        for (i = Count - 1; i >= 0; --i)
            m_ActionList.DeleteString (SelItems[i]);

        delete [] SelItems;
        m_ActionList.SetSel (-1, false);
```

```
        if (m_PoolList.GetSelCount ())
            m_AddButton.EnableWindow (true);
        else
            m_AddButton.EnableWindow (false);
        if (m_ActionList.GetSelCount ())
        {
            m_RemoveButton.EnableWindow (true);
        }
        else
        {
            m_RemoveButton.EnableWindow (false);
        }
}
```

The second tab page gives examples of the *CCheckListBox* and the *CDragListBox* classes. These are MFC-derived variants on the list box, so they can be used only in MFC-based projects.

Check the tab order to make sure that the two radio buttons are together. The check list box should be the first in the tab order; this will give it the focus when the dialog box appears. Next should be the two radio buttons, then the check box, and finally the drag list box. The first radio button (the one labeled Check Box) and the Auto check box should have the Group style set.

Notice that in the following two classes, we add a message handler for the *IDCANCEL* message. You don't have a Cancel button on the pages that you created for the tab control, but these classes are derived from *CDialog*, and the default handler will respond to the *IDCANCEL* message when the user presses the Esc key, will close the dialog box, and will leave you with a blank tab page. By providing a handler that does nothing, the *IDCANCEL* message gets sent back to the property sheet class, where the handler there closes the application.

You don't have a Cancel button, so the resource ID won't show up in the ClassWizard or the Wizard Bar. You'll have to add the message handler by hand.

Following is the code for *CCheckDragDlg*:

```
// CheckDragDlg.h : header file
//


/////////////////////////////////////////////////////////////////
// CCheckDragDlg dialog

class CCheckDragDlg : public CDialog
{
// Construction
public:
// standard constructor
    CCheckDragDlg(CWnd* pParent = NULL);

// Dialog Data
    //{{AFX_DATA(CCheckDragDlg)
    enum { IDD = IDD_TABPAGE_CHECKDRAGBOX };
    CDragListBox    m_DragList;
    CCheckListBox   m_CheckList;
    BOOL    m_bAuto;
    int     m_nCheckBoxType;
    //}}AFX_DATA



// Overrides
```

```cpp
    // ClassWizard generated virtual function overrides
    //{{AFX_VIRTUAL(CCheckDragDlg)
    protected:
    virtual void DoDataExchange(CDataExchange* pDX);
    // DDX/DDV support
    //}}AFX_VIRTUAL

// Implementation
protected:
    DWORD m_dwCheckListStyle;
    void RecreateCheckList();
    void LoadLists(CListBox &lb);

    // Generated message map functions
    //{{AFX_MSG(CCheckDragDlg)
    virtual BOOL OnInitDialog();
    afx_msg void OnCheck3statebox();
    afx_msg void OnCheckCheckbox();
    afx_msg void OnCheckAutobox();
    afx_msg void OnDblclkChecklist();
    //}}AFX_MSG
    afx_msg void OnCancel();
    DECLARE_MESSAGE_MAP()
};

/////////////////////////////////////////////////////////
// CheckDragDlg.cpp : implementation file
//

#include "stdafx.h"
#include "Controls.h"
#include "CheckDragDlg.h"

#ifdef _DEBUG
#define new DEBUG_NEW
#undef THIS_FILE
static char THIS_FILE[] = __FILE__;
#endif

struct CHECKBOXDATA
    {
    bool    bCheck;
    DWORD   dwData;
    CString strData;
    };

/////////////////////////////////////////////////////////
// CCheckDragDlg dialog

CCheckDragDlg::CCheckDragDlg(CWnd* pParent /*=NULL*/)
    : CDialog(CCheckDragDlg::IDD, pParent)
{
    //{{AFX_DATA_INIT(CCheckDragDlg)
    m_bAuto = TRUE;
    m_nCheckBoxType = 0;
    //}}AFX_DATA_INIT
```

```
        m_dwCheckListStyle = BS_AUTOCHECKBOX;
}


void CCheckDragDlg::DoDataExchange(CDataExchange* pDX)
{
    CDialog::DoDataExchange(pDX);
    //{{AFX_DATA_MAP(CCheckDragDlg)
    DDX_Control(pDX, IDC_DRAGLIST, m_DragList);
    DDX_Control(pDX, IDC_CHECKLIST, m_CheckList);
    DDX_Check(pDX, IDC_CHECK_AUTOBOX, m_bAuto);
    DDX_Radio(pDX, IDC_CHECK_CHECKBOX, m_nCheckBoxType);
    //}}AFX_DATA_MAP
}


BEGIN_MESSAGE_MAP(CCheckDragDlg, CDialog)
    //{{AFX_MSG_MAP(CCheckDragDlg)
    ON_BN_CLICKED(IDC_CHECK_3STATEBOX, OnCheck3statebox)
    ON_BN_CLICKED(IDC_CHECK_CHECKBOX, OnCheckCheckbox)
    ON_BN_CLICKED(IDC_CHECK_AUTOBOX, OnCheckAutobox)
    ON_LBN_DBLCLK(IDC_CHECKLIST, OnDblclkChecklist)
    //}}AFX_MSG_MAP
    ON_COMMAND(IDCANCEL, OnCancel)
END_MESSAGE_MAP()

//////////////////////////////////////////////////////////
// CCheckDragDlg message handlers
void CCheckDragDlg::OnCancel()
{
}

BOOL CCheckDragDlg::OnInitDialog()
{
    CDialog::OnInitDialog();

// CCheckBoxes must be
// LBS_OWNERDRAWFIXED | LBS_OWNERDRAWVARIABLE
//
// CDragList cannot have LBS_SORT or LBS_MULTISELECT
//
//  AUTOCHECKBOX provides a box that is either checked
//  or unchecked.
//  AUTO3STATE provides a three-state checkbox. The first
//  click checks it, the second puts it into an indeterminate
//  state, and the third unchecks it.
//
//  Fill the lists with file names for sample data.
//
    CFont *font = GetFont();
    m_DragList.SetFont (font);
    m_CheckList.SetFont (font);
    LoadLists (m_DragList);
    LoadLists (m_CheckList);

    return TRUE;  // return TRUE unless you set the focus
```

```
                // to a control
                // EXCEPTION: OCX Property Pages should
                // return FALSE
}

void CCheckDragDlg::LoadLists(CListBox &lb)
{
    WIN32_FIND_DATA fd;
    HANDLE hFind;
    if ((hFind = FindFirstFile (_T("*.*"), &fd)) == NULL)
        return;
    do
    {
        if (fd.cFileName[0] == '.')
            continue;
        lb.AddString (fd.cFileName);
    } while (FindNextFile (hFind, &fd) == TRUE);
    FindClose (hFind);
}

void CCheckDragDlg::OnCheck3statebox()
{
    if (m_bAuto)
        m_dwCheckListStyle = BS_AUTO3STATE;
    else
        m_dwCheckListStyle = BS_3STATE;
    m_nCheckBoxType = 1;
    RecreateCheckList ();
    UpdateData (FALSE);
}

void CCheckDragDlg::OnCheckCheckbox()
{
    if (m_bAuto)
        m_dwCheckListStyle = BS_AUTOCHECKBOX;
    else
        m_dwCheckListStyle = BS_CHECKBOX;
    m_nCheckBoxType = 0;
    RecreateCheckList ();
    UpdateData (FALSE);
}

void CCheckDragDlg::OnCheckAutobox()
{
    UpdateData (TRUE);
    if (m_bAuto)
    {
        switch (m_dwCheckListStyle)
        {
            case BS_CHECKBOX:
                m_dwCheckListStyle = BS_AUTOCHECKBOX;
                break;
            case BS_3STATE:
                m_dwCheckListStyle = BS_AUTO3STATE;
                break;
        }
```

```
        }
        else
        {
            switch (m_dwCheckListStyle)
            {
                case BS_AUTOCHECKBOX:
                    m_dwCheckListStyle = BS_CHECKBOX;
                    break;
                case BS_AUTO3STATE:
                    m_dwCheckListStyle = BS_3STATE;
                    break;
            }
        }
    RecreateCheckList ();
}

void CCheckDragDlg::RecreateCheckList()
{
CHECKBOXDATA *cbd;

    CRect rc;
    DWORD dwStyle = m_CheckList.GetStyle ();
    DWORD dwStyleEx = m_CheckList.GetExStyle ();
    m_CheckList.GetWindowRect (&rc);
    ScreenToClient (rc);
    CFont *font = GetFont ();
    int nCount = m_CheckList.GetCount ();
    int nSel = m_CheckList.GetCurSel ();
    if (nCount)
    {
        cbd = new CHECKBOXDATA [nCount];
        for (int n = Ø; n < nCount; ++n)
        {
            cbd[n].bCheck = m_CheckList.GetCheck(n)
                                         ? true : false;
            cbd[n].dwData = m_CheckList.GetItemData (n);
            m_CheckList.GetText (n, cbd[n].strData);
        }
    }
    m_CheckList.ResetContent ();
    m_CheckList.DestroyWindow ();
    m_CheckList.CreateEx (dwStyleEx, "listbox", NULL,
                            dwStyle, rc, this,
                            IDC_CHECKLIST, NULL);
    m_CheckList.SetCheckStyle (m_dwCheckListStyle);
    m_CheckList.SetFont (font);
    m_CheckList.ShowWindow (SW_SHOWNORMAL);
    if (nCount)
    {
        for (int n = Ø; n < nCount; ++n)
        {
            int nIndex = m_CheckList.AddString
                                ((LPCSTR) cbd[n].strData);
            m_CheckList.SetCheck (nIndex, cbd[n].bCheck);
            m_CheckList.SetItemData (nIndex,
cbd[n].dwData);
```

```
        }
        delete [] cbd;
    }
    m_CheckList.SetCurSel (nSel);
}


//
//  If auto is selected, return or we'll just be
//  unsetting a just set check.
//  By unselecting auto, we can let the user select
//  or unselect and item by double-clicking anywhere
//  on the line.
//
void CCheckDragDlg::OnDblclkChecklist()
{
    if (m_bAuto)
        return;
    int nIndex = m_CheckList.GetCurSel ();
    int nCheck = m_CheckList.GetCheck (nIndex);
    if (m_dwCheckListStyle == BS_CHECKBOX)
    {
        m_CheckList.SetCheck (nIndex, nCheck
                                    ? FALSE : TRUE);
    }
    else
    {
        ++nCheck;
        if (nCheck > 2)
            nCheck = 0;
        m_CheckList.SetCheck (nIndex, nCheck);
    }
}
```

The message handler *OnDblclkChecklist()* for the double-click event on the check list box gives you a chance to provide the user with another option. Notice that when the Auto Checkbox style is set, the user must click directly on the check box to change the state. With the Auto style turned off, you let the user check the box by double-clicking anywhere on the line. Even if the selection changes during the double-click, the first click changes the selection, and the second sets the check box to the next state.

838. *Understanding List Box Messages*

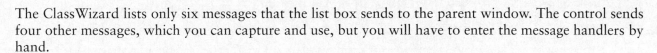

The ClassWizard lists only six messages that the list box sends to the parent window. The control sends four other messages, which you can capture and use, but you will have to enter the message handlers by hand.

The messages and their meanings are summarized in Table 838. The first six messages in the table are listed in the ClassWizard Message page.

List Box Message	Meaning
LBN_SELCHANGE	The selection in the list box control is about to change.
LBN_DBLCLK	The user has double-clicked an entry in the list box.
LBN_ERRSPACE	The list box procedure failed to allocate memory for an operation.
LBN_KILLFOCUS	The list box is about to lose the input focus.
LBN_SELCANCEL	The list box selection has been canceled.
LBN_SETFOCUS	The list box is about to receive the input focus.
WM_CHARTOITEM	This is sent by a list box in response to a *WM_CHAR* message. The *LBS_WANTKEYBOARDINPUT* style must be set for this message to be sent.
WM_CTLCOLORLISTBOX	This is sent by a list box before the control is redrawn. You can use this message to set the text and background colors of the list box.
WM_DELETEITEM	This is sent when items are removed from the list box. This can be when the control is destroyed or in response to delete string or reset contents operations.
WM_VKEYTOITEM	This is sent by a list box in response to a *WM_KEYDOWN* message. The *LBS_WANTKEYBOARDINPUT* style must be set for this message to be sent.

Table 838   Control messages sent to the parent window by a list box control

There are a number of messages that you can send to a list box control as well. These are mostly useful when you are using the Windows API; with MFC, the messages are wrapped into member functions of the *CListBox* class. You can get a list of the messages in the MSDN documentation under List Box Messages, but you can't get to it directly. In the Index box, enter *LB_ADDFILE* and press Return to get the page. Scroll to the bottom and select the link labeled List Box Messages.

839. Using List Box String Functions

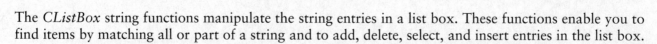

The *CListBox* string functions manipulate the string entries in a list box. These functions enable you to find items by matching all or part of a string and to add, delete, select, and insert entries in the list box.

The functions are summarized in Table 839. The string functions eventually send messages to the list box, the same as you would in a Windows API function.

Function	Message	Use
AddString()	LB_ADDSTRING	Adds a string entry to the list box. Returns the index of the added string.
DeleteString()	LB_DELETESTRING	Deletes the string at an index. Returns a count of the strings remaining.
InsertString()	LB_INSERTSTRING	Inserts a string at a given index. Returns the index where the string was inserted.

Table 839   String functions in the CListBox *Class and their associated messages (continued on following page)*

Function	Message	Use
ResetContent()	*LB_RESETCONTENT*	Clears all the strings in a list box. No return value.
Dir()	*LB_DIR*	Inserts a list of files from a given directory into the list box. Returns the index of the last file name. See Tip 840, "Using the List Box *Dir()* Function."
FindString()	*LB_FINDSTRING*	Searches for the first string that matches a string fragment. Returns the index of the match, or *LB_ERR* if no match was made. Does not select the matched string. Not case sensitive.
FindStringExact()	*LB_FINDSTRINGEXACT*	Attempts to find an entry that is an exact match of a string. Not case sensitive. Returns the index of the match or *LB_ERR*.
SelectString()	*LB_SELECTSTRING*	Similar to *FindString()*, except that the match list box item is selected automatically.

Table 839   String functions in the CListBox *Class and their associated messages (continued from previous page)*

The list box contains only strings unless you set the Owner Draw style and draw the control with other objects such as icons or bitmaps. Even in an Owner Draw box, the string functions still will work if you set the *LBS_HASSTRINGS* style.

840. *Using the List Box* Dir() *Function*

Because the list box was a primary means of listing a directory for many applications under 16-bit versions of Windows, an API function was provided to make this operation easier. The function, *DlgDirList()*, is encased in the *CListBox::Dir()* function. Other functions work in reverse and convert the selection back to a file name, a directory name, or a drive letter.

The function—either *DlgDirList()* or *CListBox::Dir()*—takes a list of file specifications encoded into an unsigned *int* and extracts the file types from the directory. Passing the function a 0 lists only "normal" files, those that are available for reading and writing.

The specification is formed by *OR*'ing together items from Table 840. There are no macros #*define*'ed for these values, but many of them are enumerated in the *CFile* class. Table 840 lists the enumerated symbol in *CFile* along with the value.

Value	CFile *enum*	Meaning
0x0000	*normal*	Only files that are available for reading and writing. This excludes directories and drives.
0x0001	*readOnly*	Include read-only files.
0x0002	*hidden*	Include files with the hidden attribute.
0x0004	*system*	Include files with the system attribute.
0x0010	*directory*	Show subdirectories.

Table 840   Attribute bits used by the list box directory operations (continued on following page)

Value	CFile *enum*	*Meaning*
0x0020	*archive*	Include files with the archive attribute.
0x4000	(none)	Show drives.
0x8000	(none)	Don't include "normal" files. Show only the files for which attributes are given.

Table 840   Attribute bits used by the list box directory operations (continued from previous page)

If you are going to list more than just files, you'll want to turn off sorting for the list box (uncheck the Sort option). Drives and directories are listed inside square brackets ("[" and "}"). Drive letters also are surrounded by hyphens.

To list everything—the files in the current directory, the subdirectories, and the drives on the system—you would set the flags to 0x4037. The problem with this is that the drives are listed at the bottom of the list box, and the subdirectories are mixed in with the file names. Usually in a directory list, you want the drives first, then the directories, and then the file names. You can do this by successively calling the function, first for the drives, again for the subdirectories, and finally for the files:

```
m_BasicList.Dir (0x4000 | 0x8000, "");
m_BasicList.Dir (0x0010 | 0x8000, "*.*");
m_BasicList.Dir (0x0007, "*.*");
```

Or, use the following enumerated *Attribute* values from *CFile*:

```
m_BasicList.Dir (0x4000 | 0x8000, "");
m_BasicList.Dir (CFile::Attribute::directory |
                 0x8000, "*.*");
m_BasicList.Dir (CFile::Attribute::readOnly |
                 CFile::Attribute::hidden |
                 CFile::Attribute::system, "*.*");
```

Using just "*.*" will list the current directory, but you may include a directory path as well. The following lists all the files in the *WinNT* directory regardless of the current directory:

```
m_BasicList.Dir (0x0007, "C:\\WinNT\\*.*");
```

The Windows API also has a function for working the other way, getting a selection from the list box and turning it back into its path form. Unfortunately, this function, *DlgDirSelectEx()*, never found its way into the *CListBox* class. However, by providing a couple of extra bits of information, you can call it for a *CListBox* object.

You can use the *CListBox::GetText()* function to get the text of the selected string. However, if it's, say, the drive C: entered by the *Dir()* function, *GetText()* will return "[-c:-]," not exactly something that you could plug directly into a path string.

If you use the following line to retrieve the entry, it will strip the brackets and hyphens from the entry and return "c:," ready to insert into a path:

```
DlgDirSelectEx (this->m_hWnd, str,
               _MAX_PATH, IDC_BASICLIST);
```

The first argument is the handle of the window that owns the list box. The second is the address of a buffer to contain the returned string. The third is the size of the buffer, and the fourth is the resource ID of the list box containing the string.

The function assumes that the entry was placed there with the *CListBox::Dir()* or *DlgDirList()* function. If the entry is a directory, it will string the brackets. In any case, the returned string will be ready for use in a path.

DlgDirSelectEx() is a Windows API function, so you don't need to base your program on MFC to use it.

841. *Understanding the Combo Box Control*

The combo box control takes its name from the fact that it uses an edit box in combination with a list box to provide a mechanism for user selection. The edit box can be set up so that the user can enter a list item directly, or it can be used just to display the current selection.

Internet Explorer did two good things for us. First, it got Microsoft in trouble with the law and revealed the company's tactics to the world. Second, it gave us some new controls to work with. One of these is an enhanced combo box control that enables programmers to list items with images without resorting to owner draw methods. It's not the best of the new controls, but it does have some uses. Let's take a look at the old combo box first; then, we'll look into the new extended combo box beginning with Tip 859, "Understanding the Extended Combo Box Control."

The combo box appears in three incarnations. In the simple form, it's an edit control on top of a list box that is always visible. Its second visage, the drop-down box, is the same as the simple combo box, except that the list is not displayed until the user presses a down button on the edit box. The third form, the drop-down list, substitutes a static text control for the edit box, which is used to display the current selection; the user may not use the text area to enter data.

Because it is built with a list box, the combo box has many of the list box functions available to it, including the *Dir()* function and the string manipulation functions.

842. *Using the CComboBox Class*

The standard combo box control is encapsulated in the MFC *CComboBox* class and the extended combo box in the *CComboBoxEx* class. In this tip, you'll build a property page that will demonstrate many of the properties of the combo box and use *CComboBox* member functions to manipulate the control. The page will include a sample of the extended combo box, but we won't deal with it here. That will have to wait for Tip 859, "Understanding the Extended Combo Box Control." Also, you'll do an Owner Draw combo box in Tip 856, "Adding an Image List to a Control."

Create a new large property page in the Controls project, and add the controls as shown in Figure 842. Give the page a resource ID of *IDD_PROPPAGE_COMBOBOXDLG*. Using the ClassWizard, create a class for the property page named *CComboBoxDlg*, making sure that it is derived from *CPropertyPage*.

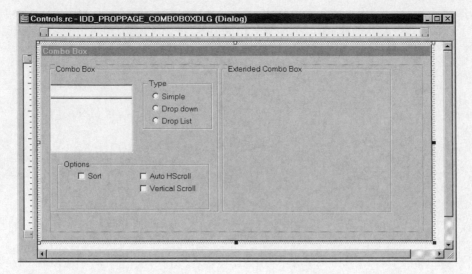

Figure 842   The combo box sample page contains an example of the standard combo box control. Save room for the extended combo box control, which you will include in Tip 860, "Using the CComboBoxEx Class."

Set the combo boxes up using the Simple style to begin. You'll be able to change the style from the property page. Make sure that the set of radio buttons is grouped properly, and add variables for the controls. The standard combo box is *m_ComboSample*. The header file is shown here:

```
// ComboBoxDlg.h : header file
//

#include <afxtempl.h>

struct COMBODATA
    {
    CString strData;
    DWORD   dwData;
    };

//////////////////////////////////////////////////////////
// CComboBoxDlg dialog

class CComboBoxDlg : public CpropertyPage
{
    DECLARE_DYNCREATE(CComboBoxDlg)

// Construction
public:
    CComboBoxDlg();
    ~CComboBoxDlg();

// Dialog Data
    //{{AFX_DATA(CComboBoxDlg)
    enum { IDD = IDD_PROPPAGE_COMBOBOXDLG };
    CComboBox   m_ComboSample;
    CComboBox   m_stylebox;
    int      m_nComboType;
    CString m_strComboSample;
    BOOL    m_bComboVScroll;
    BOOL    m_bComboAutoHScroll;
```

```
    //}}AFX_DATA


// Overrides
    // ClassWizard generate virtual function overrides
    //{{AFX_VIRTUAL(CComboBoxDlg)
    protected:
    virtual void DoDataExchange(CDataExchange* pDX);
    // DDX/DDV support
    //}}AFX_VIRTUAL

// Implementation
protected:
    DWORD m_dwComboStyle;
    CRect m_rcCombo;
    CRect m_rcDrop;
    CFont m_Font;
    void RecreateComboBox();
    // Generated message map functions
    //{{AFX_MSG(CComboBoxDlg)
    afx_msg void OnComboSimple();
    afx_msg void OnComboDroplist();
    afx_msg void OnComboDropdown();
    virtual BOOL OnInitDialog();
    afx_msg void OnEditchangeComboSample();
    afx_msg void OnComboVscrollbox();
    afx_msg void OnDestroy();
    afx_msg void OnComboAutohscrollbox();
    //}}AFX_MSG
    DECLARE_MESSAGE_MAP()
};
```

The structure at the top of the file, *COMBOBOXDATA*, will be used to store the contents of the combo box when it is destroyed and re-created using different styles.

```
// ComboBoxDlg.cpp : implementation file
//

#include "stdafx.h"
#include "Controls.h"
#include "ComboBoxDlg.h"

#ifdef _DEBUG
#define new DEBUG_NEW
#undef THIS_FILE
static char THIS_FILE[] = __FILE__;
#endif

/////////////////////////////////////////////////////////////
// CComboBoxDlg property page

IMPLEMENT_DYNCREATE(CComboBoxDlg, CPropertyPage)

CComboBoxDlg::CComboBoxDlg() : CPropertyPage(CComboBoxDlg::IDD)
{
    //{{AFX_DATA_INIT(CComboBoxDlg)
```

```
        m_nComboType = 0;
        m_strComboSample = _T("");
        m_bComboVScroll = FALSE;
        m_bComboAutoHScroll = FALSE;
        //}}AFX_DATA_INIT
        m_psp.dwFlags &= ~PSP_HASHELP;
}

CComboBoxDlg::~CComboBoxDlg()
{
}

void CComboBoxDlg::DoDataExchange(CDataExchange* pDX)
{
        CPropertyPage::DoDataExchange(pDX);
        //{{AFX_DATA_MAP(CComboBoxDlg)
        DDX_Control(pDX, IDC_COMBO_SAMPLE, m_ComboSample);
        DDX_Radio(pDX, IDC_COMBO_SIMPLE, m_nComboType);
        DDX_CBString(pDX, IDC_COMBO_SAMPLE, m_strComboSample);
        DDX_Check(pDX, IDC_VSCROLLBOX, m_bComboVScroll);
        DDX_Check(pDX, IDC_AUTOHSCROLLBOX, m_bComboAutoHScroll);
        //}}AFX_DATA_MAP
}


BEGIN_MESSAGE_MAP(CComboBoxDlg, CPropertyPage)
        //{{AFX_MSG_MAP(CComboBoxDlg)
        ON_BN_CLICKED(IDC_COMBO_SIMPLE, OnComboSimple)
        ON_BN_CLICKED(IDC_COMBO_DROPLIST, OnComboDroplist)
        ON_BN_CLICKED(IDC_COMBO_DROPDOWN, OnComboDropdown)
        ON_CBN_EDITCHANGE(IDC_COMBO_SAMPLE,
                            OnEditchangeComboSample)
        ON_BN_CLICKED(IDC_VSCROLLBOX, OnComboVscrollbox)
        ON_WM_DESTROY()
        ON_BN_CLICKED(IDC_AUTOHSCROLLBOX, OnComboAutohscrollbox)
        //}}AFX_MSG_MAP
END_MESSAGE_MAP()

/////////////////////////////////////////////////////////////
// CComboBoxDlg message handlers

BOOL CComboBoxDlg::OnInitDialog()
{
        CPropertyPage::OnInitDialog();

        CFont *font = GetFont ();
        LOGFONT lf;
        font->GetLogFont (&lf);
        m_Font.CreateFontIndirect (&lf);
        m_ComboSample.SetFont (&m_Font);

        m_ComboSample.Dir (0, "*.*");

        m_ComboSample.GetDroppedControlRect (m_rcDrop);
        m_ComboSample.GetWindowRect (m_rcCombo);
        ScreenToClient (m_rcCombo);
```

```
    m_dwComboStyle = m_ComboSample.GetStyle ();
    m_ComboSample.SetCurSel (0);

    return TRUE;  // return TRUE unless you set the focus
                  // to a control
                  // EXCEPTION: OCX Property Pages should
                  // return FALSE
}

void CComboBoxDlg::OnDestroy()
{
    CPropertyPage::OnDestroy();
}

//////////////////////////////////////////////////////////////
// Combo Box Functions

void CComboBoxDlg::OnComboSimple()
{
    UpdateData (TRUE);
    m_dwComboStyle &= ~(CBS_DROPDOWN | CBS_DROPDOWNLIST);
    m_dwComboStyle |= CBS_SIMPLE;
    RecreateComboBox();
    m_ComboSample.SetFocus ();
}

void CComboBoxDlg::OnComboDroplist()
{
    UpdateData (TRUE);
    m_dwComboStyle &= ~(CBS_DROPDOWN | CBS_SIMPLE);
    m_dwComboStyle |= CBS_DROPDOWNLIST;
    RecreateComboBox();
    m_ComboSample.SetFocus ();
    if (m_ComboSample.GetDroppedState ())
        m_ComboSample.ShowDropDown (FALSE);
}

void CComboBoxDlg::OnComboDropdown()
{
    UpdateData (TRUE);
    m_dwComboStyle &= ~(CBS_DROPDOWNLIST | CBS_SIMPLE);
    m_dwComboStyle |= CBS_DROPDOWN;
    RecreateComboBox();
    m_ComboSample.SetFocus ();
    if (m_ComboSample.GetDroppedState ())
        m_ComboSample.ShowDropDown (FALSE);
}

void CComboBoxDlg::RecreateComboBox()
{
    int nSel = m_ComboSample.GetCurSel ();
    int nCount = m_ComboSample.GetCount ();
    COMBODATA *pData = new COMBODATA [nCount];
    for (int n = 0; n < nCount; ++n)
    {
```

```
            m_ComboSample.GetLBText(n, pData[n].strData);
            pData[n].dwData = m_ComboSample.GetItemData (n);
        }
        m_ComboSample.ResetContent();
        m_ComboSample.DestroyWindow ();
        m_ComboSample.Create (m_dwComboStyle, m_rcCombo,
                              this, IDC_COMBO_SAMPLE);
        for (n = 0; n < nCount; ++n)
        {
          int nIndex=m_ComboSample.AddString (pData[n].strData);
          m_ComboSample.SetItemData (nIndex, pData[n].dwData);
        }
        delete [] pData;
        m_ComboSample.SetFont (&m_Font);
        m_ComboSample.SetCurSel (nSel);
}

void CComboBoxDlg::OnEditchangeComboSample()
{
        CString strText;
        m_ComboSample.GetWindowText (strText);
        DWORD dwSel = m_ComboSample.GetEditSel();
        int nStart = LOWORD (dwSel);
        int nEnd = HIWORD (dwSel);
        if (!m_ComboSample.GetDroppedState())
            m_ComboSample.ShowDropDown (TRUE);
        int nSel = m_ComboSample.GetCurSel ();
        int nLoc = m_ComboSample.FindString (nSel,
                                 (LPCSTR) strText);
        if (nLoc >= 0)
            m_ComboSample.SetCurSel (nLoc);
        m_ComboSample.SetEditSel (nStart, -1);
        m_ComboSample.Invalidate();
}

void CComboBoxDlg::OnComboVscrollbox()
{
        UpdateData (TRUE);
        if (m_bComboVScroll)
            m_dwComboStyle |= WS_VSCROLL;
        else
            m_dwComboStyle &= ~WS_VSCROLL;
        RecreateComboBox ();
}

void CComboBoxDlg::OnComboAutohscrollbox()
{
        UpdateData (TRUE);
        if (m_bComboAutoHScroll)
        {
            m_dwComboStyle |= CBS_AUTOHSCROLL;
        }
        else
        {
            m_dwComboStyle &= ~CBS_AUTOHSCROLL;
        }
```

```
        RecreateComboBox ();
}
```

The combo box control doesn't take kindly to changing its basic styles once the control has been created, so don't plan on using the *ModifyStyle()* function to switch styles. If you create the control as a simple combo box, it will be a simple combo box until it is destroyed.

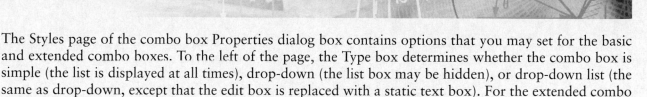

843. *Understanding the Combo Box Styles*

The Styles page of the combo box Properties dialog box contains options that you may set for the basic and extended combo boxes. To the left of the page, the Type box determines whether the combo box is simple (the list is displayed at all times), drop-down (the list box may be hidden), or drop-down list (the same as drop-down, except that the edit box is replaced with a static text box). For the extended combo box, this is the only style selection you have; the rest of the page is blank.

You can select other options for the standard combo box using the Owner Draw selection box. If you select Fixed, your code is responsible for drawing the list box item. You would use this style to draw items that might include icons and text with the same height. The Variable option is used where the list box items might have different heights, such as mixing large and small icons, or bitmaps of different sizes.

If you select one of the Owner Draw options other than No, the Has Strings check box will be enabled. This is an important option for owner draw boxes. If the list box will contain strings, you can set this option, and the system will maintain pointers to the strings contained in the control. You then can get the text of the item by calling *CComboBox::GetLBText* or by using the *LB_GETTEXT* message. If you don't select this option and your control contains strings, you'll have to maintain the pointers yourself.

The Sort option causes the control to sort the entries in the list box portion alphabetically. The sort is not case sensitive, so you can mix uppercase and lowercase strings and still have them sorted properly.

Vertical Scroll causes the control to include a vertical scroll bar on the right side of the list box. The scroll bar appears when the number of items exceeds the height of the list box, and it is hidden otherwise unless you set the Disable No Scroll option.

No Integral Height specifies that you want the control drawn in exactly the size that you drew it on the dialog box template. By default, Windows will resize the control so that a partial string won't appear at the bottom of the list box when it is first displayed, so the control may not appear the same as you drew it. Select this option to override this behavior.

Select OEM Convert to have Windows convert the text in the control to the OEM character set before displaying it. When the text is retrieved, it is converted back to the Windows character set. This is useful in controls that display file names.

When the user enters text in the combo box edit control, it will accept text up to the width of the edit box and then will start issuing beeps when additional text is typed. If you set the Auto Hscroll option, the edit box will automatically scroll when the user types beyond the end of the line.

Disable No Scroll is used in combination with the Vertical Scroll style. When this option is set, the vertical scroll bar will appear even if the number of items in the list box doesn't exceed the height of the box. In this case, it will appear disabled and will switch to enabled when enough items have been added that scrolling becomes necessary.

Finally, the Uppercase and Lowercase options convert all the entries in the list box and the edit box to the same case.

844. *Understanding Combo Box Messages*

Because the combo box control contains a list box, it sends the same notification messages to the parent window as the list box does, except that the message definitions are prefixed with a *CBN_* instead of an *LBN_*. Thus, an *LBN_DBLCLK* for the list box becomes *CBN_DBLCLK* for the combo box.

The combo box is a more complicated control, so it needs more notification messages. In addition to the list box notifications, the combo box needs to notify the parent of events that happen in the edit box. Table 844 summarizes the notification messages sent by a combo box.

List Box Message	Meaning
CBN_CLOSEUP	Is sent when the list box has been closed.
CBN_DROPDOWN	Is sent when the drop-down box is displayed.
CBN_EDITCHANGE	Indicates that the user has modified the contents of the edit control.
CBN_EDITUPDATE	Altered text is about to be displayed. The text has been formatted but not yet drawn to the control.
CBN_SELENDCANCEL	Ignores the user's selection. The user selected an item but then selected another control or closed the dialog box.
CBN_SELENDOK	The user selected an item and then closed the list. The selection should be processed.
CBN_SELCHANGE	The selection in the list box control is about to change.
CBN_DBLCLK	The user has double-clicked an entry in the list box.
CBN_ERRSPACE	The list box procedure failed to allocate memory for an operation.
CBN_KILLFOCUS	The list box is about to lose the input focus.
CBN_SETFOCUS	The list box is about to receive the input focus.

Table 844   Notification messages sent by a combo box control to its parent window

Messages sent to a combo box are encapsulated in the *CComboBox* member functions.

It is notable, however, that the combo box has its own form of the directory function, *DirDlgListComboBox()*, and a companion function to retrieve and format a selection from the combo box, *DlgDirSelectComboBox()*. The function works the same as the list box functions.

845. *Understanding the Scroll Bar Control*

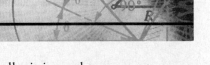

The scroll bar is a very basic part of the Windows user interface. Generally, it is used to convert mouse or keyboard input into messages that a window procedure can use to shift the contents of the window to one side or vertically.

The scroll bar is an elongated window that consists of a directional arrow at either end and a scroll box—usually known as the *thumb*—that moves between the arrows. The window area between the directional arrows usually is a lighter gray than the rest of the control window.

You should include a scroll bar in any window in which the contents extend beyond the visible window. The Windows interface allows two types of scroll bars, a horizontal and a vertical scroll bar, which are distinguished by the messages they send. The horizontal scroll bar sends a *WM_HSCROLL* message to the parent window when the user modifies the scroll bar, and the vertical scroll bar sends a *WM_VSCROLL* message.

846. *Adding Scroll Bars to a View*

Scroll bars don't automatically appear when the contents of your window extend beyond the window boundaries. In some cases, such as with the Microsoft Foundation Class *CScrollView* class, it's almost automatic; you set the size of your window content, and the view calculates the scroll information and displays the scroll bars, if necessary.

If your application will need scroll bars, you should create the views using the *WS_HSCROLL* and *WS_VSCROLL* styles. This will create a window with both scroll bars. If you don't want the scroll bars to show until you need them, you can hide them with the *ShowScrollBar()* function.

Many of the MFC view classes handle the details of sizing the scroll bar thumbs and setting them to the correct position. All you need do is to make the scroll bar visible. Others, such as the basic *CView* class, have no concept of scroll bars in their code. In this case, it's your responsibility to handle the scroll data and make the scroll bars appear properly. You do this by setting the members of a *SCROLLINFO* structure and calling *SetScrollInfo()*. Tip 848, "Understanding the *SCROLLINFO* Structure," discusses the *SCROLLINFO* structure and how to use it.

847. *Adding Scroll Bars to Controls*

In a dialog box, you can't always provide a control large enough to display all the information that you need to place in it. Many controls, such as the edit box and list box, often can benefit from a scroll bar.

In these controls, the user can scroll through the windows without a scroll bar by using the cursor keys. If the text in a multi-line edit control extends beyond the bottom of the window, the cursor keys will cause the window to scroll even without a scroll bar. However, adding scroll bars makes life easier for the user. Scroll bars provide easy navigation through a long list of information and generally provide an analog feedback to the user by indicating the current position relative to the entire window.

You can add scroll bars to just about any of the Windows common controls by specifying the *WS_HSCROLL* window style to display a horizontal scroll bar, or *WS_VSCROLL* style to display a vertical scroll bar. If you have the warped and twisted mind typical of programmers, you probably asked whether you can add scroll bars to scroll bars. Yes, you can, but the dialog editor doesn't contain check boxes to do that. You can edit your resource file and add the *WS_VSCROLL* or *WS_HSCROLL* styles to a scroll bar control. Handling the appearance and the messages might be a bit tricky. Like a number of the common controls, the scroll bar was never intended to have scroll bars and doesn't handle the scroll messages.

For controls that were designed to use scroll bars, however, the sizing and positioning of the scroll bar and its thumb usually are handled by the control itself. These controls also respond to scroll bar messages.

The edit control uses special style flags to provide automatic display of scroll bars. With this control, you may specify *ES_AUTOVSCROLL* or *ES_AUTOHSCROLL* styles. When the contents of the control exceed the window size, the control will display the proper scroll bar automatically.

848. Understanding the SCROLLINFO Structure

Information is passed between the application and a scroll bar using the *SCROLLINFO* structure and the *GetScrollInfo()* and *SetScrollInfo()* functions. The structure contains the information that the scroll bar needs to set its current position and to size the scroll bar thumb.

```
typedef struct tagSCROLLINFO { // si
UINT cbSize;
    UINT fMask;
    int nMin;
    int nMax;
    UINT nPage;
    int nPos;
    int nTrackPos;
} SCROLLINFO; typedef SCROLLINFO FAR *LPSCROLLINFO;
```

Use the *fMask* member to indicate which members of the structure are valid, as shown in Table 848. When you are getting scroll information using the *GetScrollInfo()*, the flag bits in this member will indicate which of the returned values are valid.

Flag	Meaning
SIF_ALL	All the structure members are valid.
SIF_DISABLENOSCROLL	This is used to set the scroll bar's parameters. If the limits make the scroll bar unnecessary, it will be disabled.
SIF_PAGE	The *nPage* member is valid and contains the page size.
SIF_POS	The *nPos* member is valid and contains the current position of the thumb. This value is not updated while the user is dragging the thumb. See *SIF_TRACKPOS*.
SIF_RANGE	The *nMin* and *nMax* members are valid and indicate the upper and lower limits of the scroll range.
SIF_TRACKPOS	The *nTrackPos* member contains the position of the thumb while the user is dragging it.

Table 848 SCROLLINFO flag bits and their use

The scroll bar doesn't scroll your window. You have to do that in your code, and most of the MFC view classes have supporting scroll functions, but in those cases you probably won't have to deal with the *SCROLLINFO* structure anyway. After scrolling the window, you set the new values in the *SCROLLINFO* structure and call *SetScrollInfo()* to update the scroll bar. You must set the appropriate flags in the *fMask* member; only the parameters with the flags set are updated.

849. *Understanding the CScrollBar Class*

The scroll bar control is encapsulated in the Microsoft Foundation Class *CScrollBar* class. The scroll bar sends only one message: *WM_VSCROLL* if it's a vertical scroll bar, and *WM_HSCROLL* if it's a horizontal scroll bar. The MFC class doesn't have a lot to do, then, so it's full of member functions to set the scroll bar parameters without resorting to a *SCROLLINFO* structure.

The function and their uses are described in Table 849.

CScrollBar *Function*	*Use*
GetScrollPos()	Retrieves the current position of the thumb.
SetScrollPos()	Sets the position of the thumb.
GetScrollRange()	Gets the upper- and lower-position limits for a scroll bar.
SetScrollRange()	Sets the upper- and lower-position limits for a scroll bar.
ShowScrollBar()	Hides and displays a scroll bar.
EnableScrollBar()	Enables or disables one or both arrows on a scroll bar.
GetScrollInfo()	Retrieves scroll bar information in a *SCROLLINFO* structure.
SetScrollInfo()	Sets scroll bar information using a *SCROLLINFO* structure.
GetScrollLimit()	Retrieves the upper limit of a scroll bar. This *is not* the same as the *nMax* structure member.

Table 849   CScrollBar *member functions*

There's not much to display on a scroll bar sample property page, but you can use it in Tip 852, "Using the Scroll Bar as an Input Control," when you use the scroll bar to cause some event other than scrolling a window. Add a large property page to the Controls project, and draw a horizontal and vertical scroll bar in it. You could do this just as easily by checking the Horizontal Scroll and Vertical Scroll style boxes, but the page is going to be empty enough as it is.

Along each scroll bar, draw a static text control. Make them the same size, as if a mirror image of each scroll bar. Don't set any styles for them, and erase the Static text. They'll appear invisible on the dialog template, but remember that they are there.

Give the horizontal scroll bar a resource ID of *IDC_HORZSCROLLBAR* and the vertical scroll bar an ID of *IDC_VERTSCROLLBAR*. The static box next to the horizontal scroll bar should have an ID of *IDC_HORZPROGRESSBAR*, and the one next to the vertical scroll bar should be an ID of *IDC_VERTPROGRESSBAR*.

Give the dialog box a resource ID of *IDD_PROPPAGE_SCROLLBARDLG* and create a class, *CScrollBarDlg*, for it. In the constructor, add the following line:

```
m_psp.dwFlags &= ~PSP_HASHELP;
```

Create member variables for the scroll bars. The horizontal scroll bar is *m_HorzScroll*, and the vertical scroll bar is *m_VertScroll*. Don't worry about the static fields yet. Also add two *protected* or *private* member variables of type *SCROLLINFO*, and name them *m_siHorz* and *m_siVert*.

Add message handlers for the *WM_VSCROLL* and *WM_HSCROLL* messages. The ClassWizard won't list any messages if you select the scroll bar variables, so you'll have to select the dialog class and use its message events. Scroll bars drawn on the page or attached to it will send the same messages.

Finally, add an instance of the class to *CControlsProp*. Add *ScrollBarDlg.h* to the list of include files for *ControlsProp.h*, and add a member variable, *m_ScrollBarPage*. Add the following line to the constructors in *ControlsProp.cpp* (as long as you've got at least one page in the constructors, you can add the line just to the *OnInitDialog()* function):

```
AddPage (&m_ScrollBarPage);
```

Compile and run the program. Amazingly, the scroll bars do nothing. As you move the thumb, it just snaps right back to the home position. Actually, the scroll bars are busy sending a lot of *WM_HSCROLL* and *WM_VSCROLL* messages. You just don't have any code in the message handlers yet.

850. *Hiding and Showing Scroll Bars*

Scroll bars don't have to be dead weight for your application's window. You can show or hide them as needed using the *ShowScrossBar()* function. This function has three incarnations. There's one in the Windows API, one in the MFC *CWnd* class, and a third in the *CScrollBar* class. Each needs a different number of parameters.

The Windows API function's parameters are a handle to the window that owns the scroll bars, a code indicating which scroll bar you want to show or hide, and a Boolean value indicating whether you want to show or hide the scroll bar. The scroll bar code can be *SB_HORZ* for the horizontal scroll bar, *SB_VERT* for the vertical scroll bar, or *SB_BOTH* for both scroll bars. The final parameter may be *TRUE* to show the scroll bar or *FALSE* to hide it.

The *CWnd* version doesn't need the handle to the window. The class member function takes it from the member variable *m_hWnd*, so you need to supply only the last two parameters. The Boolean value defaults to *TRUE*. You use this function when you've added scroll bars to your window by setting the style bits.

The *CScrollBar::ShowScrollBar()* function needs only the Boolean value, and it defaults to *TRUE*. Use this function when you've created a scroll bar as a tool on a dialog box or such in an MFC-based application.

Return to the scroll bar property page and select the Horizontal Scroll and Vertical Scroll style boxes. Then add two check boxes to the property page. There's plenty of room, so you shouldn't have any trouble finding an empty spool. Give the first check box a resource ID of *IDC_SHOWVERTICAL*, and change the label to read Show Vertical Scroll Bar. The second check box should have a resource ID of *IDC_SHOWHORIZONTAL*. Label it Show Horizontal Scroll Bar. Add member variables (use the BOOL value option) and message handlers for both check boxes. The message handlers are simple affairs; you can use the values returned from the check boxes as the Boolean parameter:

```
void CScrollBarDlg::OnShowvertical()
{
    UpdateData (TRUE);
    ShowScrollBar (SB_VERT, m_bShowVertical);
//  ::ShowScrollBar (this->m_hWnd, SB_VERT,
//               m_bShowVertical);
}

void CScrollBarDlg::OnShowhorizontal()
{
    UpdateData (TRUE);
```

```
    ShowScrollBar (SB_HORZ, m_bShowHorizontal);
// ::ShowScrollBar (this->m_hWnd, SB_HORZ,
//           m_bShowHorizontal);
}
```

The alternate code in the message handlers calls the Windows API version of the same function, so it passes the window handle as the first parameter. Try using the alternate code, and you should get the same results.

851. Interpreting Scroll Bar Messages

Scroll bar messages contain a code indicating what part of the scroll bar generated the message. If your program processes scroll bar messages, it should use the code to perform specific actions, as listed in Table 851.

Horizontal Code	Vertical Code	Action
SB_LEFT	SB_TOP	Scroll to far left or top.
SB_ENDSCROLL	Same	End scroll.
SB_LINELEFT	SB_LINEUP	Scroll left one character or up one line.
SB_LINERIGHT	SB_LINEDOWN	Scroll right one character or down one line.
SB_PAGELEFT	SB_PAGEUP	Scroll one page left or up.
SB_PAGERIGHT	SB_PAGEDOWN	Scroll one page right or down.
SB_RIGHT	SB_BOTTOM	Scroll to far right or bottom.
SB_THUMBPOSITION	Same	Scroll to absolute position. The current position is specified by the *nPos* parameter.
SB_THUMBTRACK	Same	Drag scroll box to specified position. The current position is specified by the *nPos* parameter

Table 851   Scroll bar codes included in the scroll bar messages

A single action on the part of the user may cause a message to repeat. For example, if the user clicks and holds a direction arrow at one end of the scroll bar, a series of line scroll messages will be sent. When the user releases the mouse button, an *SB_ENDSCROLL* message will be sent.

Usually, you'll handle the different codes in a *switch* statement in your scroll bar message handler, with a separate case for each code.

In Table 851, entries on the same line have the same numeric value. For example, *SB_LINEUP* and *SB_LINELEFT* have the same value and may be used interchangeably. For readability, the proper symbol should be used in a horizontal or vertical scroll message, however.

In addition to the scroll code, the message contains a value that indicates the current position of the thumb if the scroll code is *SB_THUMBPOSITION* or *SB_THUMBTRACK*. This value is compatible with older versions of Windows and is only a 16-bit value, which effectively limits the scroll position to a maximum value of 65,535.

You'll use all of these scroll bar codes in the message handlers in the next tip.

When you apply this information to a real scroll bar, you'll notice an anomaly that you as a programmer have to deal with. If you set the range of a scroll bar to, say, 0 to 100, the end buttons will be capable of scrolling the entire range. But if the user drags the thumb across the scroll bar, the position parameter to the message handler tracks the back side of the thumb. Thus, by dragging the thumb, the position parameter can never attain the value specified in the *nMax* member of the *SCROLLINFO* structure. For a range of 0 to 100, the maximum position value is going to be something like 91 when the thumb is butted up against the far stop and can't move any farther.

You can get the maximum value that the thumb can attain by calling the *GetScrollLimit()* function. You can use this value to adjust the scroll limit for your application, or you can ignore it and let the user apply the arrow button to scroll the rest of the way through a document. Different applications handle it differently, but you should be aware that it exists when your application starts showing strange scroll behavior. In the next tip, you'll see how it affects the maximum value that may be obtained by the progress bar.

852. *Using the Scroll Bar as an Input Control*

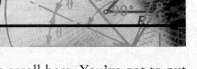

OK, you can't have a property page that does nothing but show and hide scroll bars. You've got to put something on the page to get some action out of it. Before the slider control, which you'll see shortly, the scroll bar commonly was used to get quasi-analog position information on a dialog box. You could use this position information to set a volume level, a color saturation, or anything that required a large range of values from the user. In this tip, you'll use it to set the position of a home-grown progress bar.

Add the *CProgressBar* class from Tip 819, "Deriving a Custom Class from *CStatic* to Gain Functionality," to the project. If you added it to your gallery, put it in the application using the Components and Controls option after selecting the Add to Project item on the Project menu. Otherwise, copy the files into the project directory and use the File option from the same menu.

Add member variables for the static text fields on the property page that you created in Tip 849, "Understanding the *CScrollBar* Class." The variable for the static field next to the horizontal scroll bar should be *m_HorzProgress*, and the one next to the vertical scroll bar should be *m_VertProgress*.

The header file for the *CScrollBarDlg* property page is listed here:

```
// ScrollBarDlg.h : header file
//

#include    "ProgressBar.h"

/////////////////////////////////////////////////////////
// CScrollBarDlg dialog

class CScrollBarDlg : public CpropertyPage
{
    DECLARE_DYNCREATE(CScrollBarDlg)

// Construction
public:
    CScrollBarDlg();
    ~CScrollBarDlg();

// Dialog Data
    //{{AFX_DATA(CScrollBarDlg)
```

```
    enum { IDD = IDD_PROPPAGE_SCROLLBARDLG };
    CScrollBar  m_VertScroll;
    CScrollBar  m_HorzScroll;
    CProgressBar    m_VertProgress;
    CProgressBar    m_HorzProgress;
    BOOL    m_bShowHorizontal;
    BOOL    m_bShowVertical;
    //}}AFX_DATA


// Overrides
    // ClassWizard generate virtual function overrides
    //{{AFX_VIRTUAL(CScrollBarDlg)
    protected:
    virtual void DoDataExchange(CDataExchange* pDX);
    // DDX/DDV support
    //}}AFX_VIRTUAL


// Implementation
protected:
    SCROLLINFO m_siVert;
    SCROLLINFO m_siHorz;
    // Generated message map functions
    //{{AFX_MSG(CScrollBarDlg)
    afx_msg void OnHScroll(UINT nSBCode, UINT nPos,
                        CScrollBar* pScrollBar);
    afx_msg void OnVScroll(UINT nSBCode, UINT nPos,
                        CScrollBar* pScrollBar);
    virtual BOOL OnInitDialog();
    afx_msg void OnShowvertical();
    afx_msg void OnShowhorizontal();
    //}}AFX_MSG
    DECLARE_MESSAGE_MAP()

};
```

In the source code, you'll see two sets of function calls that set the maximum values for the progress bars. The first set places the maximum values the same as the *nMax* member of the *SCROLLINFO* structures. When you run the code, you'll see that the maximum value that can be attained by dragging the thumb is 91 percent, but then you can use the arrow button to go the extra distance.

The second set of function calls sets the maximum values for the progress bars to the value returned by *GetScrollLimit()*. This allows the thumb movements to sct the progress bars to 100 percent. The arrow buttons still will issue scroll messages, but the progress bar code restricts any further input.

```
// ScrollBarDlg.cpp : implementation file
//

#include "stdafx.h"
#include "Controls.h"
#include "ScrollBarDlg.h"

#ifdef _DEBUG
#define new DEBUG_NEW
#undef THIS_FILE
static char THIS_FILE[] = __FILE__;
```

```
#endif

/////////////////////////////////////////////////////////
// CScrollBarDlg property page

IMPLEMENT_DYNCREATE(CScrollBarDlg, CPropertyPage)

CScrollBarDlg::CScrollBarDlg() : CPropertyPage(CScrollBarDlg::IDD)
{
    //{{AFX_DATA_INIT(CScrollBarDlg)
    m_bShowHorizontal = FALSE;
    m_bShowVertical = FALSE;
    //}}AFX_DATA_INIT
    m_psp.dwFlags &= ~PSP_HASHELP;
    m_HorzProgress.SetMinMax (0, 100);
    m_VertProgress.SetMinMax (0, 100);
}

CScrollBarDlg::~CScrollBarDlg()
{
}

void CScrollBarDlg::DoDataExchange(CDataExchange* pDX)
{
    CPropertyPage::DoDataExchange(pDX);
    //{{AFX_DATA_MAP(CScrollBarDlg)
    DDX_Control(pDX, IDC_VERTSCROLLBAR, m_VertScroll);
    DDX_Control(pDX, IDC_HORZSCROLLBAR, m_HorzScroll);
    DDX_Control(pDX, IDC_VERTPROGRESSBAR, m_VertProgress);
    DDX_Control(pDX, IDC_HORZPROGRESSBAR, m_HorzProgress);
    DDX_Check(pDX, IDC_SHOWHORIZONTAL, m_bShowHorizontal);
    DDX_Check(pDX, IDC_SHOWVERTICAL, m_bShowVertical);
    //}}AFX_DATA_MAP
}

BEGIN_MESSAGE_MAP(CScrollBarDlg, CPropertyPage)
    //{{AFX_MSG_MAP(CScrollBarDlg)
    ON_WM_HSCROLL()
    ON_WM_VSCROLL()
    ON_BN_CLICKED(IDC_SHOWVERTICAL, OnShowvertical)
    ON_BN_CLICKED(IDC_SHOWHORIZONTAL, OnShowhorizontal)
    //}}AFX_MSG_MAP
END_MESSAGE_MAP()

/////////////////////////////////////////////////////////
// CScrollBarDlg message handlers

BOOL CScrollBarDlg::OnInitDialog()
{
    CPropertyPage::OnInitDialog();

    memset (&m_siHorz, '\0', sizeof (SCROLLINFO));
    m_siHorz.cbSize = sizeof (SCROLLINFO);
    m_siHorz.nMin = 0;
    m_siHorz.nMax = 100;
    m_siHorz.nPage = 10;
```

```
    m_siHorz.nPos = 0;
    m_siHorz.fMask = SIF_ALL;
    m_HorzScroll.SetScrollInfo (&m_siHorz);
    SetScrollInfo (SB_HORZ, &m_siHorz);

    memset (&m_siVert, '\0', sizeof (SCROLLINFO));
    m_siVert.cbSize = sizeof (SCROLLINFO);
    m_siVert.nMin = 0;
    m_siVert.nMax = 100;
    m_siVert.nPage = 10;
    m_siVert.nPos = 100;
    m_siVert.fMask = SIF_ALL;
    m_VertScroll.SetScrollInfo (&m_siVert);
    SetScrollInfo (SB_VERT, &m_siVert);

//
//  Alternate code for setting the progress bar levels
//
    m_HorzProgress.SetMinMax (m_siHorz.nMin, m_siHorz.nMax);
    m_VertProgress.SetMinMax (m_siVert.nMin, m_siVert.nMax);

    ShowScrollBar (SB_HORZ, m_bShowHorizontal);
    ShowScrollBar (SB_VERT, m_bShowVertical);

    return TRUE;  // return TRUE unless you set the focus
                  // to a control
                  // EXCEPTION: OCX Property Pages should
                  // return FALSE
}

void CScrollBarDlg::OnHScroll(UINT nSBCode, UINT nPos,
                            CScrollBar* pScrollBar)
{
//
//  The scroll bar isn't the only control that sends
//  scroll messages. On a dialog box, always test for
//  the identity of a scroll bar.
//
    if (pScrollBar != &m_HorzScroll)
    {
        CDialog::OnHScroll(nSBCode, nPos, pScrollBar);
        return;
    }
    switch (nSBCode)
    {
        case SB_LEFT:           //  Scroll to far left.
            m_siHorz.nPos = m_siHorz.nMin;
            break;
        case SB_ENDSCROLL:      //  End scroll.
            return;
        case SB_LINELEFT:       //  Scroll left.
            m_siHorz.nPos -= 1;
            if (m_siHorz.nPos < m_siHorz.nMin)
                m_siHorz.nPos = m_siHorz.nMin;
            break;
        case SB_LINERIGHT:      //  Scroll right.
```

```
                m_siHorz.nPos += 1;
                if (m_siHorz.nPos > m_siHorz.nMax)
                    m_siHorz.nPos = m_siHorz.nMax;
                break;
            case SB_PAGELEFT:       // Scroll one page left.
                m_siHorz.nPos -= m_siHorz.nPage;
                if (m_siHorz.nPos < m_siHorz.nMin)
                    m_siHorz.nPos = m_siHorz.nMin;
                break;
            case SB_PAGERIGHT:      // Scroll one page right.
                m_siHorz.nPos += m_siHorz.nPage;
                if (m_siHorz.nPos > m_siHorz.nMax)
                    m_siHorz.nPos = m_siHorz.nMax;
                break;
            case SB_RIGHT:          // Scroll to far right.
                m_siHorz.nPos = m_siHorz.nMax;
                break;
            case SB_THUMBPOSITION:  // Scroll to absolute
                                    // position. The current
                                    // position is specified
                                    // by the nPos parameter.
                m_siHorz.nPos = nPos;
                break;
            case SB_THUMBTRACK:     // Drag scroll box to
                                    // specified position. The
                                    // current position is
                                    // specified by the nPos
                                    // parameter
                m_siHorz.nPos = nPos;
                break;
    }
    m_siHorz.fMask = SIF_ALL;
    m_HorzScroll.SetScrollInfo (&m_siHorz, TRUE);
//  SetScrollInfo (SB_HORZ, &m_siHorz);
    m_HorzProgress.SetPosition (m_siHorz.nPos);
    m_HorzProgress.Update ();
    ShowScrollBar (SB_HORZ, m_bShowHorizontal);
}

void CScrollBarDlg::OnVScroll(UINT nSBCode, UINT nPos,
                             CScrollBar* pScrollBar)
{
    if (pScrollBar != &m_VertScroll)
    {
        CDialog::OnHScroll(nSBCode, nPos, pScrollBar);
        return;
    }
    switch (nSBCode)
    {
    case SB_TOP:            // Scroll to top.
        m_siVert.nPos = m_siVert.nMin;
        break;
    case SB_ENDSCROLL:      // End scroll.
        return;
    case SB_LINEUP:     // Scroll up.
        m_siVert.nPos -= 1;
```

```
                    if (m_siVert.nPos < m_siVert.nMin)
                        m_siVert.nPos = m_siVert.nMin;
                    break;
              case SB_LINEDOWN:      //  Scroll down.
                    m_siVert.nPos += 1;
                    if (m_siVert.nPos > m_siVert.nMax)
                        m_siVert.nPos = m_siVert.nMax;
                    break;
              case SB_PAGEUP:     //  Scroll one page up.
                    m_siVert.nPos -= m_siVert.nPage;
                    if (m_siVert.nPos < m_siVert.nMin)
                        m_siVert.nPos = m_siVert.nMin;
                    break;
              case SB_PAGEDOWN:       //  Scroll one page down
                    m_siVert.nPos += m_siVert.nPage;
                    if (m_siVert.nPos > m_siVert.nMax)
                        m_siVert.nPos = m_siVert.nMax;
                    break;
              case SB_BOTTOM:         //  Scroll to far right
                    m_siVert.nPos = m_siVert.nMax;
                    break;
              case SB_THUMBPOSITION:  //  Scroll to absolute
                                      //  position. The current
                                      //  position is specified
                                      //  by the nPos parameter.
                    m siVert.nPos = nPos;
                    break;
              case SB_THUMBTRACK:     //  Drag scroll box to
                                      //  specified position. The
                                      //  current position is
                                      //  specified by the nPos
                                      //  parameter
                    m_siVert.nPos = nPos;
                    break;
        }
    m_siVert.fMask = SIF_ALL;
    m_VertScroll.SetScrollInfo (&m_siVert, TRUE);
//  SetScrollInfo (SB_VERT, &m_siVert);
    m_VertProgress.SetPosition
            (m_VertScroll.GetScrollLimit() -
            m_siVert.nPos + m_siVert.nMin);
    m_VertProgress.Update ();
    ShowScrollBar (SB_VERT, m_bShowVertical);
}

void CScrollBarDlg::OnShowvertical()
{
    UpdateData (TRUE);
    ShowScrollBar (SB_VERT, m_bShowVertical);
//  Alternate code for showing the property page scroll bar
//  ::ShowScrollBar (this->m_hWnd, SB_VERT,
//                   m_bShowVertical);
}

void CScrollBarDlg::OnShowhorizontal()
{
```

```
    UpdateData (TRUE);
    ShowScrollBar (SB_HORZ, m_bShowHorizontal);
//  Alternate code for showing the property page scroll bar
//  ::ShowScrollBar (this->m_hWnd, SB_HORZ,
//                   m_bShowHorizontal);
}
```

At the beginning of each scroll message handler, the code tests the scroll bar pointer passed as a parameter against the address of your class member scroll bar. On a dialog box—or property sheet—the scroll bar might not be the only object sending scroll messages. The slider and spinner controls also send scroll bar messages, and this is where you will distinguish between them. If you have another control that sends scroll messages, you will want to call a handler function for it at this point.

There's only one *WM_HSCROLL* and one *WM_VSCROLL* message, regardless of the control that sends it. To effectively demonstrate this, comment out the tests in each message handler, and then remove the comment from the *SetScrollInfo()* function call at the bottom of each handler. Run the program and show the dialog box scroll bars. You'll see that the handler responds to messages from the window scroll bars *and* those that you added as controls to the property page.

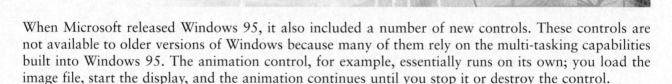

853. *Understanding the 32-Bit Controls*

When Microsoft released Windows 95, it also included a number of new controls. These controls are not available to older versions of Windows because many of them rely on the multi-tasking capabilities built into Windows 95. The animation control, for example, essentially runs on its own; you load the image file, start the display, and the animation continues until you stop it or destroy the control.

Some of these new controls—the rich edit control, the list control, and the tree control, for example— serve as the basis for new view classes that can be used only with 32-bit versions of Windows.

Even since the introduction of Windows 95, a number of new controls have been introduced, some of them primarily to support Microsoft's Web browser, Internet Explorer. Table 853 lists the controls available since Windows 95.

Control	MFC Class	Purpose
Image list	*CImageList*	Stores and manipulates collections of images for other controls.
Extended combo box	*CComboBoxEx*	Acts as an extension to the combo box control to support image lists.
Spinner	*CSpinCtrl*	Increments or decrements the value in an associated control.
Progress bar	*CProgressCtrl*	Implements a simple progress bar.
Slider	*CSliderCtrl*	Is used like a scroll bar to adjust a value or a display.
Hotkey	*CHotKeyCtrl*	Allows a user to enter a hotkey quickly. Hotkeys are similar to keyboard accelerators.
List	*CListCtrl*	Displays a list of items using columns or icons.
Tree	*CTreeCtrl*	Displays items in an hierarchical list.

Table 853   The common controls available in 32-bit windows since Windows 95 was introduced (continued on following page)

Control	MFC Class	Purpose
Tab	*CTabCtrl*	Displays a set of tabs that can be used to select alternate controls or dialog boxes.
Animation	*CAnimateCtrl*	Displays successive frames from an AVI file.
Rich edit	*CRichEditCtrl*	Provides character and paragraph formatting within a control.
Date and time picker	*CDateTimeCtrl*	Presents a control already formatted for date and time display.
Monthly calendar	*CMonthCalCtrl*	Displays a calendar for one month.
IP address	*CIPAddressCtrl*	Presents a control already formatted for display and input of an address in Internet Protocol format.

Table 853   *The common controls available in 32-bit windows since Windows 95 was introduced (continued from previous page)*

With a couple of notable exceptions, you can recognize the MFC classes for these new controls by looking for the "Ctrl" prefix on the class names. The image list and the extended combo box don't follow this rule. The image list isn't a true control, but it is used to support other controls; the extended combo box is a derivative of the basic combo box and is used to support Internet Explorer.

854. *Understanding the Image List Control*

An *image list* is a collection of bitmapped images stored like a C++ array. The images are all the same size and may be referenced by their zero-based index. The image list isn't a true control, but it is an object that is used to support other classes that need an image control object.

Images in an image list are stored in a single bitmap in screen format. Windows API functions enable you to add to or delete from the list, replace individual images, draw individual images, and merge them.

An image list is referenced by its *handle* using the symbol *HIMAGELIST*. Image lists may be non-masked or masked. In the non-masked image list, the images are contained in a single color bitmap. The masked version contains two bitmaps, one to contain the images and the second to contain a sequence of monochrome bitmaps that serve as masks for the image list. There is one mask image for every image in the list.

A *mask* is used to screen out bits selectively and thus let the image blend in with the background. When a non-masked image is drawn, it is copied bit for bit to the output device, the screen. The image pixels destroy any existing pixels on the screen. When a masked image is drawn, however, the bits in the image are combined with the mask bits, producing a transparent area where the original screen pixels may be seen. This is how an icon normally is drawn on the screen.

Image lists weren't necessarily new with the introduction of Windows 95. Programmers have created and used them in one form or another under older versions of Windows. The addition to the control list simply formalizes them and provides a consistent set of operations to create and manipulate the images.

Several of the 32-bit controls use and benefit from the image list, notably the list, tree, tab, and extended combo box controls. The image list isn't limited to those controls—they just have built-in functions to use the image list—and you can use an image list even with the older controls.

The MFC *CImageList* class encapsulates the image list control and the functions used to access and manipulate the images. The function also contains code to draw an image.

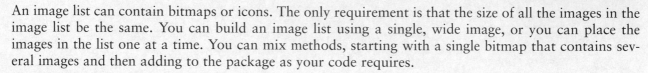

855. *Building an Image List*

An image list can contain bitmaps or icons. The only requirement is that the size of all the images in the image list be the same. You can build an image list using a single, wide image, or you can place the images in the list one at a time. You can mix methods, starting with a single bitmap that contains several images and then adding to the package as your code requires.

When you've established a size for the images, you can add an icon of any size, and the image list control will size it to fit, stretching or shrinking as necessary. In the next tip, for example, you build an image list based on a bitmap containing seven images, each 20 pixels wide. After the list is created, you add some small icons, which are only 16 pixels wide, to it. The icons are stretched to fit and show perfectly in the list box.

Bitmaps are a different story. A bitmap can be used to insert multiple images with one operation, and the *Add()* function implies the number of images from the size of the bitmap. This means that bitmaps must be multiples of the image size when you add them. You can use the *LoadImage()* function to load and resize a bitmap to fit, however.

After you've built the image list, you can retrieve information about the images by calling *CImageList:: GetImageInfo()*, passing the index of the image and a pointer to an *IMAGEINFO* structure. This structure contains a handle to the bitmap image and the rectangle of the image within the bitmap. If it's a single-image bitmap, the rectangle will be the size of the bitmap, reduced or enlarged to fit into the image list.

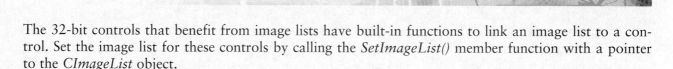

856. *Adding an Image List to a Control*

The 32-bit controls that benefit from image lists have built-in functions to link an image list to a control. Set the image list for these controls by calling the *SetImageList()* member function with a pointer to the *CImageList* object.

The list control may contain as many as three image lists—one for the small icons, another for large icons, and yet a third to contain images to represent the items in a user-defined state. The *SetImageList()* member function for the list control includes a flag indicating which image list is to be set. *SetImageList (CImageList *pImages, LVSIL_NORMAL)* sets the large image list for the list control. Substituting *LVSIL_SMALL* sets the small image list, and *LVSIL_STATE* sets the state image list.

The tree control can contain two image lists, one for the normal icons and another for user-defined state icons. *SetImageList (CImageList *pImages, TVSIL_NORMAL)* sets the normal image list, and *SetImage List (CImageList *pImages, TVSIL_STATE)* sets the state image list.

Some of the basic controls inherited from 16-bit Windows also can benefit from image lists, but you have to provide the code to link the image list to the control. The best way to do this is to derive new classes from the MFC class, set the owner draw style, and provide the code to link the image list and provide the drawing code. In this tip, you'll add a property page for image lists that will include an Owner Draw list box and an Owner Draw combo box.

Several of the pages in the *Controls* application, including the one you are about to add, will access the system image list for examples. Unfortunately, an application may attach to the system image list only once, so you need to add code to the application class to create a centralized location for the image list.

Add the following member variables to the *ControlsApp* class header file, *Controls.h*:

```
HIMAGELIST    m_hSmallImages;
HIMAGELIST    m_hLargeImages;
CImageList    m_SmallImages;
CImageList    m_LargeImages;
```

In the source code file, *Controls.cpp*, at the beginning of the *InitInstance()* function, add the following two lines of code to initialize the image list handles to *NULL*. You can add these at any point before the call to *DoModal()*:

```
m_hSmallImages = NULL;
m_hLargeImages = NULL;
```

Also add a member function, *GetSystemImageList()*, as shown here, and override the *ExitInstance()* virtual function. Especially when using Windows 95 and 98, you must remember to detach the system image lists before the *CImageList* objects that use them go out of scope. If you don't, you'll have to reboot your machine to recover the desktop (and directory) icons. The *CImageList* destructor automatically frees the images when the object is destroyed unless you first detach the object.

```
int CControlsApp::ExitInstance()
{
    if (m_hSmallImages != NULL)
        m_SmallImages.Detach ();
    if (m_hLargeImages != NULL)
        m_LargeImages.Detach ();
    return CWinApp::ExitInstance();
}

CImageList *CControlsApp::GetSystemImageList(bool bSmall)
{
    if (bSmall)
    {
        if (m_hSmallImages != NULL)
            return (&m_SmallImages);
        SHFILEINFO sfiInfo;
        memset(&sfiInfo, Ø, sizeof(SHFILEINFO));
        m_hSmallImages = (HIMAGELIST) (
                SHGetFileInfo (
                "C:\\",
                Ø,
                &sfiInfo,
                sizeof(sfiInfo),
                SHGFI_SYSICONINDEX | SHGFI_SMALLICON)
        );
        m_SmallImages.Attach(m_hSmallImages);
        return (&m_SmallImages);
    }
    if (m_hLargeImages != NULL)
            return (&m_LargeImages);
    SHFILEINFO sfiInfo;
    memset(&sfiInfo, Ø, sizeof(SHFILEINFO));
    m_hLargeImages = (HIMAGELIST) (
```

```
        SHGetFileInfo (
        "C:\\",
        0,
        &sfiInfo,
        sizeof(sfiInfo),
        SHGFI_SYSICONINDEX | SHGFI_LARGEICON)
    );
    m_LargeImages.Attach (m_hLargeImages);
    return (&m_LargeImages);
}
```

This code calls the Windows shell function to get a handle to the system image lists—both large and small—and attaches them to the *CImageList* objects. Successive calls simply return a pointer to the *CImageList* objects.

The combo box on this property page uses the system image list. The list box will contain two image lists that you will build, one large and one small. They both will start with basic images built from a bitmap containing seven images to start, and then you'll add images of different sizes.

Add a new property page to the *Controls* application. Give this new sheet a title of Image List and a resource ID of *IDD_PROPPAGE_IMAGELISTDLG*. Add a list box control and a combo box control, as shown in Figure 856. Select the Owner Draw Variable style for the list box, but do not check the Has Strings box. For the combo box, select the Owner Draw Variable style, but select the Has Strings option. Figure 856 shows the combo box with the Simple style set, but you may use the Drop Down or Drop list styles as well. Below the list box, add a couple of radio buttons and label them Small Image List and Large Image List. Set the group style for the first button but not for the second. Give the list box a resource ID of *IDC_LISTBOX_IMAGES* and the combo box a resource ID of *IDC_COMBO_IMAGES*.

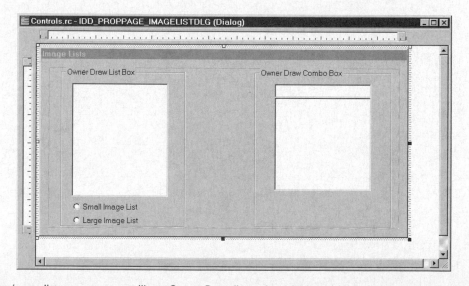

Figure 856   The image list property page will use Owner Draw list and combo boxes to display images along with the list items

Create a class for this property page using the ClassWizard. Name it *CImageListDlg*, and set the base class to *CPropertyPage*. Add message handlers for the two radio buttons. Also create a member variable, *m_nImageList*, for the radio buttons using the *int* data type.

Add two new classes to the project. The first is *CImageListBox*, and its base class should be *CListBox* (be sure *not* to select *CListCtrl*). The second is *CImageComboBox*, using a base class of *CComboBox*. Add the header files for these two classes to the *ImageListDlg.h* file. Now add member variables for the list box and the combo box. The list box variable is *m_ImageListBox*, and the combo box is *m_ImageComboBox*. For both of these, select Control as the category and the new class you created for them as the Variable Type.

Before you can compile and display this page, you must override the *MeasureItem()* and *DrawItem()* functions. For Owner Draw controls, the framework will call the *MeasureItem()* function when the control is created. The *DrawItem()* function gets called when any item in the control needs to be repainted. The application will assert if you don't override these functions for Owner Draw controls.

In the header for each of these classes, add *afxtempl.h* to the include files. For each of these classes, you'll also need to define structures for the data; you'll use *CList* objects to contain the data. In the sample code on the companion CD, these structures are defined in the header files for the classes, as shown in the code here.

For each, you'll need to add *SetImageList()* and *AddItem()* member functions, and a pointer to a *CImageList* member variable. The header files for *CImageListBox* and *CImageComboBox* are shown here:

```
// ImageListBox.h : header file
//

/////////////////////////////////////////////////////////////
// CImageListBox window

#include    "afxtempl.h"

struct LISTIMAGEDATA
    {
    int    nItem;
    int    nImage;
    CString Text;
    };

class CImageListBox : public ClistBox
{
// Construction
public:
    CImageListBox();

// Attributes
public:

// Operations
public:

// Overrides
    // ClassWizard generated virtual function overrides
    //{{AFX_VIRTUAL(CImageListBox)
    public:
    virtual void DrawItem(LPDRAWITEMSTRUCT
                        lpDrawItemStruct);
    virtual void MeasureItem(LPMEASUREITEMSTRUCT
                            lpMeasureItemStruct);
    //}}AFX_VIRTUAL

// Implementation
public:
    int AddItem (LISTIMAGEDATA &ld);
```

```
        void SetImageList (CImageList *pImages);
        virtual ~CImageListBox();

        // Generated message map functions
protected:
        CImageList *m_pImages;
        //{{AFX_MSG(CImageListBox)
            // NOTE - the ClassWizard will add and remove member functions here.
        //}}AFX_MSG

        DECLARE_MESSAGE_MAP()

        CList<LISTIMAGEDATA, LISTIMAGEDATA&> m_ListData;
};

// ImageComboBox.h : header file
//

/////////////////////////////////////////////////////////////
// CImageComboBox window

#include <afxtempl.h>

struct COMBOIMAGEDATA
    {
    int     nItem;
    int     nParentItem;
    int     nImage;
    CString Text;
    bool    Expanded;
    int     nIndent;
    int     nMode;
    };

class CImageComboBox : public CcomboBox
{
// Construction
public:
    CImageComboBox();
    enum Modes
    {
        mShort = 0,
        mDetail,
        mExpanded
    };

// Attributes
public:

// Operations
public:

// Overrides
    // ClassWizard generated virtual function overrides
    //{{AFX_VIRTUAL(CImageComboBox)
    public:
```

```
        virtual void DrawItem(LPDRAWITEMSTRUCT
                                lpDrawItemStruct);
        virtual void MeasureItem(LPMEASUREITEMSTRUCT
                                    lpMeasureItemStruct);
    //}}AFX_VIRTUAL

// Implementation
public:
    void SetImageList (CImageList *pImages);
    void AddItem (COMBOIMAGEDATA &cd);
    virtual ~CImageComboBox();

    // Generated message map functions
protected:
    CImageList *m_pImages;
    //{{AFX_MSG(CImageComboBox)
        // NOTE - the ClassWizard will add and remove member
        // functions here.
    //}}AFX_MSG

    DECLARE_MESSAGE_MAP()

    CList<COMBOIMAGEDATA, COMBOIMAGEDATA&> m_ComboData;
};
```

You'll add the drawing code for these classes in the next tip, but for now you need to finish the property page to display these controls.

Open the *ImageListDlg.cpp* source file and *ImageListDlg.h* header file. Override the *OnInitDialog()* virtual function. Next, add three *CImageList* objects to *CImageListDlg* class, *m_LargeImages*, *m_Small Images*, and *m_ComboImages*. You'll also need to add some support functions. Some of these, such as *GetSystemImageList()* and *GetIconIndex()*, are familiar from previous tips. Others will be used to support the Owner Draw list box and combo box. The header file for *CImageListDlg* is listed here:

```
// ImageListDlg.h : header file
//

/////////////////////////////////////////////////////
// CImageListDlg dialog

#include    "ImageListBox.h"
#include    "ImageComboBox.h"

class CImageListDlg : public CpropertyPage
{
    DECLARE_DYNCREATE(CImageListDlg)

// Construction
public:
    CImageListDlg();
    ~CImageListDlg();

// Dialog Data
    //{{AFX_DATA(CImageListDlg)
    enum { IDD = IDD_PROPPAGE_IMAGELISTDLG };
    CImageListBox    m_ImageListBox;
```

```
    CImageComboBox  m_ImageComboBox;
    //}}AFX_DATA


// Overrides
    // ClassWizard generate virtual function overrides
    //{{AFX_VIRTUAL(CImageListDlg)
    protected:
    virtual void DoDataExchange(CDataExchange* pDX);
    // DDX/DDV support
    //}}AFX_VIRTUAL


// Implementation
protected:
    void AddNode (TCHAR *szName, int nNode,
                  int nType, int nMode);
    void LoadComboBox();
    void RecreateListBox();
    int GetIconIndex (CString strFileName,
                      DWORD dwAttributes);
    // Generated message map functions
    //{{AFX_MSG(CImageListDlg)
    afx_msg void OnRadioLargeimagelist();
    afx_msg void OnRadioSmallimagelist();
    virtual BOOL OnInitDialog();
    //}}AFX_MSG
    DECLARE_MESSAGE_MAP()

};
```

The companion CD contains two bitmaps, one with small images representing drives and another with large images. You should copy these files, *drives.bmp* and *largedn.bmp*, and import them into the project as *IDB_SMALLDRIVES* and *IDB_LARGEDRIVES*.

Create the image lists in the *OnInitDialog()* function. Also set up some strings for the list box. The code for *ImageListDlg.cpp* is shown here:

```
// ImageListDlg.cpp : implementation file
//

#include "stdafx.h"
#include "Controls.h"
#include "ImageListDlg.h"

#ifdef _DEBUG
#define new DEBUG_NEW
#undef THIS_FILE
static char THIS_FILE[] = __FILE__;
#endif


/////////////////////////////////////////////////////////
// CImageListDlg property page

IMPLEMENT_DYNCREATE(CImageListDlg, CPropertyPage)

CImageListDlg::CImageListDlg()
                    : CPropertyPage(CImageListDlg::IDD)
```

```
{
    //{{AFX_DATA_INIT(CImageListDlg)
    m_nImageList = 0;
    //}}AFX_DATA_INIT
    m_psp.dwFlags &= ~PSP_HASHELP;
}

CImageListDlg::~CImageListDlg()
{
}

void CImageListDlg::DoDataExchange(CDataExchange* pDX)
{
    CPropertyPage::DoDataExchange(pDX);
    //{{AFX_DATA_MAP(CImageListDlg)
    DDX_Control(pDX, IDC_LISTBOX_IMAGES, m_ImageListBox);
    DDX_Control(pDX, IDC_COMBO_IMAGES, m_ImageComboBox);
    DDX_Radio(pDX, IDC_RADIO_SMALLIMAGELIST, m_nImageList);
    //}}AFX_DATA_MAP
}


BEGIN_MESSAGE_MAP(CImageListDlg, CPropertyPage)
    //{{AFX_MSG_MAP(CImageListDlg)
    ON_BN_CLICKED(IDC_RADIO_LARGEIMAGELIST,
                  OnRadioLargeimagelist)
    ON_BN_CLICKED(IDC_RADIO_SMALLIMAGELIST,
                  OnRadioSmallimagelist)
    //}}AFX_MSG_MAP
END_MESSAGE_MAP()

/////////////////////////////////////////////////////////
// CImageListDlg message handlers

void CImageListDlg::OnRadioLargeimagelist()
{
    m_ImageListBox.SetImageList (&m_LargeImages);
    RecreateListBox ();
}

void CImageListDlg::OnRadioSmallimagelist()
{
    m_ImageListBox.SetImageList (&m_SmallImages);
    RecreateListBox ();
}

BOOL CImageListDlg::OnInitDialog()
{
    CPropertyPage::OnInitDialog();

    const TCHAR *szItems[] =
        {
        "Folder",
        "Open Folder",
        "Floppy Drive",
        "Hard Drive",
```

```
            "Network Drive",
            "CD-ROM",
            "Audio CD"
            };

    m_SmallImages.Create (IDB_SMALLDRIVES, 20, 10,
                          RGB (0x00, 0x80, 0x80));
    m_LargeImages.Create (IDB_LARGEDRIVES, 32, 10,
                          RGB (0x00, 0x80, 0x80));

    CFont *font = GetFont ();
    m_ImageListBox.SetFont (font);

    int nCount = sizeof (szItems) / sizeof (char *);

    m_ImageListBox.SetImageList (&m_SmallImages);
    for (int n = 0; n < nCount; ++n)
    {
        LISTIMAGEDATA ld;
        ld.nItem = n;
        ld.nImage = n;
        ld.Text = szItems[n];
        m_ImageListBox.AddItem (ld);
    }
    m_ImageListBox.SetCurSel (0);

    CControlsApp *app = (CControlsApp *) AfxGetApp();
    m_ImageComboBox.SetImageList(app->GetSystemImageList());

    LoadComboBox();

    return TRUE;
}

//////////////////////////////////////////////////////////
// CImageListBox support functions

//
//  The owner draw box's MeasureItem() function is
//  called only when the list box is created, so to
//  change image sizes, we need to re-create the box.
//
void CImageListDlg::RecreateListBox()
{
    DWORD dwStyle = m_ImageListBox.GetStyle ();
    dwStyle |= WS_BORDER | LBS_NOINTEGRALHEIGHT
            | LBS_NOTIFY | WS_VSCROLL;
    int nCount = m_ImageListBox.GetCount ();
    int nSel = m_ImageListBox.GetCurSel ();
    CRect rc;
    m_ImageListBox.GetWindowRect (rc);
    ScreenToClient (rc);
    m_ImageListBox.DestroyWindow ();
    m_ImageListBox.Create (dwStyle, rc, this,
                           IDC_LISTBOX_IMAGES);
    CFont *font = GetFont ();
```

```
    m_ImageListBox.SetFont (font);
    for (int n = 0; n < nCount; ++n)
    {
        m_ImageListBox.AddString ("");
    }
    m_ImageListBox.SetCurSel (nSel);
}


/////////////////////////////////////////////////////////
// CImageComboBox support functions

int CImageListDlg::GetIconIndex(CString strFileName,
                                DWORD dwAttributes)
{
    SHFILEINFO sfi;
    memset(&sfi, 0, sizeof(sfi));
    if (dwAttributes & FILE_ATTRIBUTE_DIRECTORY)
    {
        SHGetFileInfo (
            strFileName,
            FILE_ATTRIBUTE_DIRECTORY,
            &sfi,
            sizeof(sfi),
            SHGFI_SMALLICON |
                SHGFI_SYSICONINDEX |
                SHGFI_USEFILEATTRIBUTES |
                (dwAttributes & SHGFI_OPENICON)
            );
        return (sfi.iIcon);
    }
    else
    {
        SHGetFileInfo (
            strFileName,
            FILE_ATTRIBUTE_NORMAL,
            &sfi,
            sizeof(sfi),
            SHGFI_SMALLICON | SHGFI_SYSICONINDEX
                | (dwAttributes & SHGFI_OPENICON)
            );
        return sfi.iIcon;
    }
    return (-1);
}

void CImageListDlg::LoadComboBox()
{
char        drives [_MAX_PATH];
char *aDrive, *s;   // = drives;

//  Get the drive string. This is a double NUL terminated
//  list, with each item terminated with a NUL.
//
    if (::GetLogicalDriveStrings(_MAX_PATH, drives))
    {
    char    CurDrive[64];       // We need the copy
```

```
                                    //   because we are going to
                                    //   remove any trailing
                                    //   backslash, which would
                                    //   screw up our double NUL
                                    //   terminated list.
        aDrive = drives;
//  Parse the drives
        do
        {
        UINT    type;
//  Get a drive
            strcpy (CurDrive, aDrive);
            type = ::GetDriveType(CurDrive);

            if ((s = strchr (CurDrive, '\\')) != NULL)
                *s = '\0';
//  Make sure that the drive letter is caps, and add
//  the node for the drive.
            strupr (CurDrive);
            AddNode(CurDrive, -1, type,
                    CImageComboBox::mShort);
            aDrive += strlen (aDrive) + 1;
        } while(strlen (aDrive));
    }
}


void CImageListDlg::AddNode(TCHAR *szName, int nNode,
                            int nType, int nMode)
{
    if (nType >= DRIVE_REMOVABLE)
    {
    char    VolName[24];
    char    RootName[10];
    DWORD   dwCompLen, dwFlags;
    DWORD   dwAttributes;
    COMBOIMAGEDATA  cd;

        dwAttributes = FILE_ATTRIBUTE_SYSTEM;
        sprintf (RootName, "%s\\", szName);
        memset (VolName, '\0', sizeof (VolName));
        GetVolumeInformation (RootName, VolName, 24, NULL,
                        &dwCompLen, &dwFlags, NULL, 0);
        CString fn;
        fn = RootName;
        if (strlen (VolName))
        {
            cd.Text.Format ("%s (%s)", szName, VolName);
        }
        else
            cd.Text.Format ("%s", szName);
        cd.nImage = GetIconIndex (fn, dwAttributes);
        cd.nParentItem = -1;
        cd.Expanded = false;
        cd.nMode = CImageComboBox::mShort;
        m_ImageComboBox.AddItem (cd);
    }
}
```

In case some of this looks familiar, yes, it was lifted from an earlier tree view example and modified slightly to fit the combo box requirements. The code and the data structure associated with the combo box are setting you up to build a tree-like structure in the combo box.

You can compile and display the page at this point, but you need to add the code to draw the list and combo box items. Remember, it *is* "owner draw."

857. *Drawing Images from an Image List*

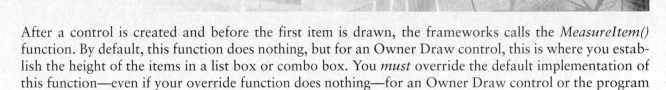

After a control is created and before the first item is drawn, the frameworks calls the *MeasureItem()* function. By default, this function does nothing, but for an Owner Draw control, this is where you establish the height of the items in a list box or combo box. You *must* override the default implementation of this function—even if your override function does nothing—for an Owner Draw control or the program will assert.

When the frameworks finishes with the *MeasureItem()* function, it begins to call *DrawItem()* for Owner Draw controls. This function, too, must be overridden, but if you do nothing in this function, you'll see nothing on the screen. This is where the items for the list box and the combo box on this property page get displayed.

To draw the image for the item, you can use the *CImageList::Draw()* member function. It doesn't matter whether you draw the text or the image first. Usually, however, the image is on the left of an item, and it's easier to draw it first and then calculate the rectangle for any text.

For the *CImageListBox* and *CImageComboBox* classes, most of the work is done in the *DrawItem()* function. The implementation code for the *CImageListBox* class is listed here.

```cpp
// ImageListBox.cpp : implementation file
//

#include "stdafx.h"
#include "Controls.h"
#include "ImageListBox.h"

#ifdef _DEBUG
#define new DEBUG_NEW
#undef THIS_FILE
static char THIS_FILE[] = __FILE__;
#endif


/////////////////////////////////////////////////////////
// CimageListBox

CImageListBox::CImageListBox()
{
    m_pImages = NULL;
}

CImageListBox::~CImageListBox()
{
}
```

```cpp
BEGIN_MESSAGE_MAP(CImageListBox, CListBox)
    //{{AFX_MSG_MAP(CImageListBox)
        // NOTE - the ClassWizard will add and remove
        // mapping macros here.
    //}}AFX_MSG_MAP
END_MESSAGE_MAP()

/////////////////////////////////////////////////////////
// CImageListBox message handlers

#ifdef _FULLFOCUSRECT
void CImageListBox::DrawItem(LPDRAWITEMSTRUCT
                               lpDrawItemStruct)
{
    UINT nItem = lpDrawItemStruct->itemID;
    if (nItem == (UINT) -1)
        return;
    CDC dc;
    dc.Attach (lpDrawItemStruct->hDC);
    CBrush brush;

    CRect rc = lpDrawItemStruct->rcItem;

    brush.CreateSolidBrush (GetSysColor (
                lpDrawItemStruct->itemState & ODS_SELECTED
                 ? COLOR_HIGHLIGHT : COLOR_WINDOW));
    dc.SetTextColor (GetSysColor (
                lpDrawItemStruct->itemState & ODS_SELECTED
                 ? COLOR_HIGHLIGHTTEXT : COLOR_WINDOWTEXT));
    dc.FillRect (rc, &brush);
    dc.SetBkMode (TRANSPARENT);
    POSITION pos = m_ListData.FindIndex (nItem);
    LISTIMAGEDATA ld = m_ListData.GetAt (pos);
    if (lpDrawItemStruct->itemState & ODS_FOCUS)
        dc.DrawFocusRect (&rc);

    if (m_pImages != NULL)
    {
        IMAGEINFO ii;
        m_pImages->Draw (&dc, ld.nImage, CPoint(rc.left,
                        rc.top), ILD_NORMAL);
        m_pImages->GetImageInfo(ld.nImage, &ii);
        rc.left += ii.rcImage.right - ii.rcImage.left;
    }
//
// Add 4 pixels to the left margin to keep from
// butting up against the wall or image.
//
    rc.left += 4;

    CSize sz = dc.GetTextExtent (ld.Text);
    rc.top += (rc.bottom - rc.top - sz.cy) / 2;

    dc.DrawText (ld.Text, &rc, DT_VCENTER);
    dc.Detach ();
}
```

```
#else

void CImageListBox::DrawItem
                       (LPDRAWITEMSTRUCT lpDrawItemStruct)
{
    UINT nItem = lpDrawItemStruct->itemID;
    if (nItem == (UINT) -1)
        return;
    CDC dc;
    dc.Attach (lpDrawItemStruct->hDC);
    CBrush brushWhite;
    CBrush brushSel;
    CRect rc = lpDrawItemStruct->rcItem;

    brushWhite.CreateSolidBrush(GetSysColor(COLOR_WINDOW));
    brushSel.CreateSolidBrush (GetSysColor
                (lpDrawItemStruct->itemState & ODS_SELECTED
                ? COLOR_HIGHLIGHT : COLOR_WINDOW));

    dc.SetTextColor (GetSysColor (
                lpDrawItemStruct->itemState & ODS_SELECTED
? COLOR_HIGHLIGHTTEXT : COLOR_WINDOWTEXT));
    dc.FillRect (rc, &brushWhite);
    dc.SetBkMode (TRANSPARENT);

    POSITION pos = m_ListData.FindIndex (nItem);
    LISTIMAGEDATA ld = m_ListData.GetAt (pos);

    if (m_pImages != NULL)
    {
        IMAGEINFO ii;
        m_pImages->Draw (&dc, ld.nImage, CPoint(rc.left,
                rc.top), lpDrawItemStruct->itemState
                & ODS_SELECTED ? ILD_BLEND : ILD_TRANSPARENT);
        m_pImages->GetImageInfo(ld.nImage, &ii);
        rc.left += ii.rcImage.right - ii.rcImage.left;
    }
//
//  Add 4 pixels to the left margin to keep from
//  butting up against the wall or image.
//
    rc.left += 4;
    dc.FillRect (rc, &brushSel);
    if (lpDrawItemStruct->itemState & ODS_FOCUS)
        dc.DrawFocusRect (&rc);

    if (lpDrawItemStruct->itemState & ODS_FOCUS)
        dc.DrawFocusRect (&rc);

    CSize sz = dc.GetTextExtent (ld.Text);
    rc.top += (rc.bottom - rc.top - sz.cy) / 2;

    dc.DrawText (ld.Text, &rc, DT_VCENTER);
    dc.Detach ();
}
```

```
#endif  //  _FULLFOCUSRECT

void CImageListBox::MeasureItem
              (LPMEASUREITEMSTRUCT lpMeasureItemStruct)
{
    if (m_pImages != NULL)
    {
        IMAGEINFO ii;
        m_pImages->GetImageInfo(
                    lpMeasureItemStruct->itemID, &ii);
        lpMeasureItemStruct->itemHeight = ii.rcImage.bottom
                                - ii.rcImage.top + 4;
    }
}

void CImageListBox::SetImageList(CImageList *pImages)
{
    m_pImages = pImages;
}

int CImageListBox::AddItem(LISTIMAGEDATA &ld)
{
    AddString ("");
    return (m_ListData.AddTail (ld) == NULL ? -1 : 0);
}
```

There are two *DrawItem()* functions in this code. One of them draws a full-focus rectangle when the selected item has the focus. When you do this, you want to draw the image using the *ILD_NORMAL* style to make it stand out from the focus rectangle (the images were created with a blend background).

Alternatively, you can draw the focus rectangle so that it doesn't envelop the image. In this case, if the item has the focus, you want to draw it with the *ILD_BLEND* style to give it some focus color. If it doesn't have the focus, draw it with the *ILD_TRANSPARENT* style to make the background color disappear.

Neither way is right or wrong. It's a programmer preference, and you'll see both methods used in various applications. By default, the list box is drawn without the full-focus rectangle. Choose the one you like better. To try the other method, add the following line somewhere near the top of the file:

```
#define   _FULLFOCUSRECT
```

The drawing code for the combo box is almost identical. The *MeasureItem()* function does nothing because we're using only small icons and the default size is satisfactory. The code is shown here:

```
// ImageComboBox.cpp : implementation file
//

#include "stdafx.h"
#include "Controls.h"
#include "ImageComboBox.h"

#ifdef _DEBUG
#define new DEBUG_NEW
#undef THIS_FILE
static char THIS_FILE[] = __FILE__;
#endif
```

```
///////////////////////////////////////////////////////
// CimageComboBox

CImageComboBox::CImageComboBox()
{
    m_pImages = NULL;
}

CImageComboBox::~CImageComboBox()
{
}


BEGIN_MESSAGE_MAP(CImageComboBox, CComboBox)
    //{{AFX_MSG_MAP(CImageComboBox)
        // NOTE - the ClassWizard will add and remove
        // mapping macros here.
    //}}AFX_MSG_MAP
END_MESSAGE_MAP()

///////////////////////////////////////////////////////
// CImageComboBox message handlers

void CImageComboBox::DrawItem(LPDRAWITEMSTRUCT
                              lpDrawItemStruct)
{
    UINT nItem = lpDrawItemStruct->itemID;
    if (nItem == (UINT) -1)
        return;
    CDC dc;
    dc.Attach (lpDrawItemStruct->hDC);
    CBrush brushWhite;
    CBrush brushSel;
    CRect rc = lpDrawItemStruct->rcItem;

    brushWhite.CreateSolidBrush(GetSysColor(COLOR_WINDOW));
    brushSel.CreateSolidBrush (GetSysColor
                (lpDrawItemStruct->itemState & ODS_SELECTED
                ? COLOR_HIGHLIGHT : COLOR_WINDOW));

    dc.SetTextColor (GetSysColor
                (lpDrawItemStruct->itemState & ODS_SELECTED
                ? COLOR_HIGHLIGHTTEXT : COLOR_WINDOWTEXT));
    dc.FillRect (rc, &brushWhite);
    dc.SetBkMode (TRANSPARENT);
    POSITION pos = m_ComboData.FindIndex (nItem);
    COMBOIMAGEDATA ld = m_ComboData.GetAt (pos);

    if (m_pImages != NULL)
    {
        IMAGEINFO ii;
        m_pImages->Draw (&dc, ld.nImage,
                CPoint(rc.left, rc.top),
                lpDrawItemStruct->itemState & ODS_SELECTED
                ? ILD_BLEND : ILD_TRANSPARENT);
        m_pImages->GetImageInfo(ld.nImage, &ii);
```

```
                    rc.left += ii.rcImage.right - ii.rcImage.left;
        }
//
//  Add 4 pixels to the left margin to keep from
//  butting up against the wall or image.
//
        rc.left += 4;
        dc.FillRect (rc, &brushSel);

        if (lpDrawItemStruct->itemState & ODS_FOCUS)
            dc.DrawFocusRect (&rc);

        CSize sz = dc.GetTextExtent (ld.Text);
        rc.top += (rc.bottom - rc.top - sz.cy) / 2;

        dc.DrawText (ld.Text, &rc, DT_VCENTER);
        dc.Detach ();
}

void CImageComboBox::MeasureItem(LPMEASUREITEMSTRUCT
                                 lpMeasureItemStruct)
{
}

void CImageComboBox::AddItem(COMBOIMAGEDATA &cd)
{
    if (cd.nParentItem == -1)
    {
        m_ComboData.AddTail (cd);
        AddString (cd.Text);
        return;
    }
}

void CImageComboBox::SetImageList(CImageList *pImages)
{
    m_pImages = pImages;
}
```

858. *Managing and Manipulating Image Lists*

When you've created and assigned the image list to a control, it isn't necessarily a fixed object, set in stone and incapable of being changed. In many cases, the image list is more flexible than the control that uses it. After you assign a size to the images, you can assign larger or smaller icons to it, and the image list will take care of sizing them to fit.

Say that you want to add some icons to the image list. The bitmap for the small list was drawn 20 pixels wide, and small icons are 16 pixels wide. You also can replace an individual image, even one on the original bitmap. The code that follows adds three icons and a large bitmap, and then replaces the 3.5-inch drive image with a better one.

This is all done in the *OnInitDialog()* function, as shown here. Actually, you can change the image list at any time, but be sure that your controls are updated at the same time to reflect the change.

```cpp
BOOL CImageListDlg::OnInitDialog()
{
    CPropertyPage::OnInitDialog();

    const TCHAR *szItems[] =
        {
        "Folder",
        "Open Folder",
        "3.5-Inch Floppy",
        "Hard Drive",
        "Network Drive",
        "CD-ROM",
        "Audio CD",
        "Desktop",
        "My Computer",
        "Puters in the Hood",
        "Dudley"
        };

    m_SmallImages.Create (IDB_SMALLDRIVES, 20, 10,
                          RGB (0x00, 0x80, 0x80));
    m_LargeImages.Create (IDB_LARGEDRIVES, 32, 10,
                          RGB (0x00, 0x80, 0x80));

//*******************************************
//  New images are added here.
//*******************************************
//  First the small image list.
//
    HICON hIcon = (HICON) LoadImage(AfxGetInstanceHandle(),
                        MAKEINTRESOURCE(IDI_DESKTOP),
                        IMAGE_ICON, 16, 16, LR_DEFAULTSIZE);
    m_SmallImages.Add (hIcon);
    DeleteObject (hIcon);
    hIcon = (HICON) LoadImage (AfxGetInstanceHandle (),
                        MAKEINTRESOURCE(IDI_MYPUTER),
                        IMAGE_ICON, 16, 16, LR_DEFAULTSIZE);
    m_SmallImages.Add (hIcon);
    DeleteObject (hIcon);
    hIcon = (HICON) LoadImage (AfxGetInstanceHandle (),
                        MAKEINTRESOURCE(IDI_THEHOOD),
                        IMAGE_ICON, 16, 16, LR_DEFAULTSIZE);
    m_SmallImages.Add (hIcon);
    DeleteObject (hIcon);

//
//   Load a bitmap, resizing it to the image size.
//
    HBITMAP hBmp=(HBITMAP)LoadImage(AfxGetInstanceHandle(),
            MAKEINTRESOURCE(IDB_DUDLEYPC), IMAGE_BITMAP,
            20, 16, LR_DEFAULTCOLOR);
    CBitmap bmp;
    bmp.Attach (hBmp);
```

```
      m_SmallImages.Add (&bmp, (COLORREF) 0);
      bmp.Detach ();
      DeleteObject (hBmp);
//
//  Replace the floppy icon with a better one
//  Notice that we use the large icon even for the small
//  image list.
      hIcon = (HICON) LoadImage (AfxGetInstanceHandle (),
                        MAKEINTRESOURCE(IDI_35INCHDRIVE),
                        IMAGE_ICON, 32, 32, LR_DEFAULTSIZE);
      m_SmallImages.Replace (2, hIcon);
//
//  Now do the same for the large image list. The
//  large floppy icon already is loaded, so replace
//  it first.
//
      m_LargeImages.Replace (2, hIcon);
      DeleteObject (hIcon);

      hIcon = (HICON) LoadImage (AfxGetInstanceHandle (),
                        MAKEINTRESOURCE(IDI_DESKTOP),
                        IMAGE_ICON, 32, 32, LR_DEFAULTSIZE);
      m_LargeImages.Add (hIcon);
      DeleteObject (hIcon);
      hIcon = (HICON) LoadImage (AfxGetInstanceHandle (),
                        MAKEINTRESOURCE(IDI_MYPUTER),
                        IMAGE_ICON, 32, 32, LR_DEFAULTSIZE);
      m_LargeImages.Add (hIcon);
      DeleteObject (hIcon);
      hIcon = (HICON) LoadImage (AfxGetInstanceHandle (),
                        MAKEINTRESOURCE(IDI_THEHOOD),
                        IMAGE_ICON, 32, 32, LR_DEFAULTSIZE);
      m_LargeImages.Add (hIcon);
      DeleteObject (hIcon);
//
//  Now add that Dudley bitmap.
//
      hBmp = (HBITMAP) LoadImage (AfxGetInstanceHandle (),
                    MAKEINTRESOURCE(IDB_DUDLEYPC),
                    IMAGE_BITMAP, 32, 32, LR_DEFAULTCOLOR);
      bmp.Attach (hBmp);
      m_LargeImages.Add (&bmp, (COLORREF) 0);
      bmp.Detach ();
      DeleteObject (hBmp);

//*****************************************
// End of new code
//*****************************************
      CFont *font = GetFont ();
      m_ImageListBox.SetFont (font);

      int nCount = sizeof (szItems) / sizeof (char *);

      m_ImageListBox.SetImageList (&m_SmallImages);
      for (int n = 0; n < nCount; ++n)
      {
```

```
        LISTIMAGEDATA ld;
        ld.nItem = n;
        ld.nImage = n;
        ld.Text = szItems[n];
        m_ImageListBox.AddItem (ld);
    }
    m_ImageListBox.SetCurSel (0);

    CControlsApp *app = (CControlsApp *) AfxGetApp();
    m_ImageComboBox.SetImageList(app->GetSystemImageList());

    LoadComboBox();
    TCHAR szPath[_MAX_PATH];
    GetCurrentDirectory (_MAX_PATH, szPath);
    TCHAR szDrive[_MAX_PATH], szDir[_MAX_PATH],
        szName[_MAX_PATH], szExt[_MAX_PATH];
    _splitpath (szPath, szDrive, szDir, szName, szExt);
    if (m_ImageComboBox.SelectString (-1, szDrive)
                                == CB_ERR)
        m_ImageComboBox.SetCurSel (0);

    return (TRUE);
}
```

Adding a bitmap of odd size to the image list involves a bit more work than an icon, but in practical applications, most of the images that you run across are going to be bitmaps. You are going to need to add a bitmap at least as often as you need to add an icon. The *LoadImage()* function can resize a bitmap when it loads the image; just don't include the *LR_DEFAULTSIZE* flag in the function call.

859. Understanding the Extended Combo Box Control

The extended combo box is an "enhancement" to the standard combo box. The biggest claim about it is that it lets you include an image with the list box entry, but the cost of this is very high. This version of the combo box implements only as much functionality as Internet Explorer needs, and don't labor under the mistaken impression that Microsoft created it to make life easier for programmers. You lose most of the flexibility afforded by the string functions, and the extended combo box won't do any sorting for you. It works best in the drop-down or drop list incarnations. Fortunately, that's probably the only way you would use it. Otherwise, your coding requirements are such that you might as well design your own Owner Draw combo box from the standard control.

Either the documentation on this control is very poor or the control is not well constructed. I've never been able to access the edit box portion of the control when using it in the Simple style. The only samples that you see of this control in the Microsoft literature concentrate on its Explorer qualities.

You can't add a string directly to an extended combo box. Instead, you have go through an item structure, which is why you lose the string functionality of the combo box. This control doesn't really benefit from an item structure, and it has all the appearance that the item structure was added to the control out of some sort of Dilbertish corporate directive.

OK, let's put the soap box away. On the positive side, the control did serve us well in the *FontView* project from Tip 485, "A GDI Example: Drawing a Character Map," where it was used in the drop list style. One thing you might have noticed—actually, it was difficult to miss—is that the extended combo box did not sort the font list. Instead, the function to enumerate the fonts built a sorted list, and only after the list was complete did you add the fonts to the extended combo box. Using a *CList* object makes the task a bit easier, but you'll have to go through the sorting process every time you want a sorted list in an extended combo box. In Tip 865, "Understanding the *CRichEditCtrl* Class," you'll use the same process of enumerating the fonts, but this time you'll sort the list and use *LPSTR_TEXTCALLBACK* to display the items.

860. *Using the CComboBoxEx Class*

The MFC *CComboBoxEx* encapsulates the extended combo box control and provides the functions used to manipulate the control and list items. Almost everywhere that the MSDN documentation touches on the *CComboBoxEx*, it touts the control's capacity to incorporate an image list. The control also supports text callback, in which the control itself doesn't store the display information but instead calls your application to get the display string when it needs to redraw an item. It doesn't support image callback.

In Tip 857, "Drawing Images from an Image List," you saw how easy it was to link an image list to a standard combo box. The drawing code in that sample also provided the functionality of text and image callback by storing the pertinent information in a structure and then retrieving it to draw the item.

Return to the combo box page in the *Controls* application. Add a new class to the project named *CPathBox*, and use *CComboBoxEx* as the base class. In this class, you'll build an extended combo box with images that display the drives and then expand your current directory under the proper drive.

The items in the extended combo box will be stored in a *CList* object, so you'll use text callback to draw the items to save memory. The listing for the *CPathBox* is shown here:

```
// PathBox.h : header file
//

/////////////////////////////////////////////////////////
// CPathBox window

#include    <afxtempl.h>

class CPathBox : public CcomboBoxEx
{
// Construction
public:
    CPathBox();

// Attributes
public:
    class CpathData
    {
    public:
        CPathData ();
        CString    strName;
        int        nItem;
        POSITION   ParentItem;
        int        nImage;
        int        nSelImage;
        DWORD      dwData;
```

```
        bool        Expanded;
        int         nIndent;
        int         nMode;\
        int         nLevel;
        bool        bVisible;
    };

// Operations
public:

// Overrides
    // ClassWizard generated virtual function overrides
    //{{AFX_VIRTUAL(CPathBox)
    //}}AFX_VIRTUAL

// Implementation
public:
    POSITION GetSelPosition();
    virtual ~CPathBox();
    BOOL SetPath (LPCTSTR pszPath);
    void UpdateDisplay(POSITION &posSel);

    // Generated message map functions
protected:
    void ExpandItem (CString &strPath);
    void InitialUpdate(CString &strPath);
    int GetIconIndex(CString &strFile,
                DWORD dwAttributes = FILE_ATTRIBUTE_NORMAL);

    //{{AFX_MSG(CPathBox)
    afx_msg void OnGetdispinfo(NMHDR* pNMHDR,
                                LRESULT* pResult);
    //}}AFX_MSG

    DECLARE_MESSAGE_MAP()

    CList<CPathData, CPathData&>    m_PathData;
};
```

The source file and the sample on the companion CD include alternate code to build just the current path or to expand the combo box to show all the directories in the current path, sort of like a single-branch tree. This is done in the *ExpandItem()* function. Try them both out; you'll probably find that the full branch is a bit busy for a combo box, but there may be some applications for which you'll need it. To use the alternate code, just include a *#define _FULLDIRTREE* statement near the top of the file. The listing that follows shows the implementation code for the *CPathBox* class:

```
// PathBox.cpp : implementation file
//

#include "stdafx.h"
#include "controls.h"
#include "PathBox.h"

#ifdef _DEBUG
#define new DEBUG_NEW
#undef THIS_FILE
```

```cpp
static char THIS_FILE[] = __FILE__;
#endif

/////////////////////////////////////////////////////////
// CpathBox

CPathBox::CPathBox()
{
}

CPathBox::~CPathBox()
{
}


BEGIN_MESSAGE_MAP(CPathBox, CComboBoxEx)
    //{{AFX_MSG_MAP(CPathBox)
    ON_NOTIFY_REFLECT(CBEN_GETDISPINFO, OnGetdispinfo)
    //}}AFX_MSG_MAP
END_MESSAGE_MAP()

/////////////////////////////////////////////////////////
// CPathBox message handlers
BOOL CPathBox::SetPath(LPCTSTR pszPath)
{
    CString strPath = pszPath;
    InitialUpdate (strPath);
    ExpandItem (strPath);
    return (TRUE);
}

void CPathBox::InitialUpdate(CString &strPath)
{
    if (GetImageList() != NULL)
       return;
    TCHAR   szCurDrive[3];
    strncpy (szCurDrive, (LPCSTR) strPath, 2);
    szCurDrive [2] = _T('\0');
//
//  Get the system image list and attach to it.
//
    CControlsApp *app = (CControlsApp *) AfxGetApp();
    CImageList *Images = app->GetSystemImageList();
    SetImageList (Images);

    int nPos = 0;
    int nCount = 0;
    CString strDrives = _T ("?:\\");

    DWORD dwDrives = ::GetLogicalDrives ();

    POSITION pos = NULL;
    while (dwDrives)
    {
        if (dwDrives & 1)
        {
```

```
                strDrives.SetAt (Ø, _T ('A') + nPos);
                CString strDrive = strDrives.Left (2);
                UINT nType = ::GetDriveType (strDrives);
                CString strRoot;
                strRoot = strDrive + '\\';
                CPathData PathData;
                PathData.strName = strDrive;
                PathData.bVisible = true;
                PathData.nLevel = Ø;
                PathData.nIndent = Ø;
                PathData.nImage = GetIconIndex (strRoot,
                                 FILE_ATTRIBUTE_SYSTEM);
                pos = m_PathData.AddTail (PathData);
            }
        dwDrives >>= 1;
        nPos++;
    }
    UpdateDisplay (pos);
}

void CPathBox::UpdateDisplay(POSITION &posSel)
{
    ResetContent ();
    int nCount = Ø;
    POSITION pos = m_PathData.GetHeadPosition ();
    while (pos != NULL)
    {
        COMBOBOXEXITEM cbei;
        cbei.lParam = (LPARAM) pos;
        CPathData pb = m_PathData.GetNext (pos);
        if (pb.bVisible == false)
            continue;
        cbei.mask = CBEIF_TEXT | CBEIF_IMAGE
                  | CBEIF_SELECTEDIMAGE | CBEIF_LPARAM
                  | CBEIF_INDENT;
        cbei.iItem = nCount++;
        cbei.iIndent = pb.nIndent;
        cbei.pszText = LPSTR_TEXTCALLBACK;
        cbei.iImage = pb.nImage;
        cbei.iSelectedImage = cbei.iImage;
        int nItem = InsertItem (&cbei);
        if ((POSITION) cbei.lParam == posSel)
            SetCurSel (nItem);
    }
}

void CPathBox::ExpandItem(CString &strPath)
{
    TCHAR   szCurDrive[3];
    strncpy (szCurDrive, (LPCSTR) strPath, 2);
    szCurDrive [2] = _T('\Ø');
    int nSel = FindStringExact (-1, szCurDrive);
    if (nSel < Ø)
        return;
    SetCurSel (nSel);
    POSITION pos = (POSITION) GetItemData (nSel);
```

```
        POSITION next = pos;
        CPathData pf = m_PathData.GetNext (next);
        POSITION parent = pf.ParentItem;
        CString strFile = strPath;
        int nCount = 0;
        int nIndex = 0;
        while ((nIndex = strPath.Find ('\\', nIndex)) >= 0)
        {
            ++nIndex;
            ++nCount;
        }
        ++nCount;
        CString *strElems = new CString [nCount];
        int nStart = 0;
        for (nIndex = 0; nIndex < nCount; ++nIndex)
        {
            int nEnd = strPath.Find ('\\', nStart);
            if (nEnd < 0)
            {
                strElems[nIndex] =
                  strPath.Right (strPath.GetLength() - nStart);
                break;
            }
            strElems [nIndex] = strPath.Mid (nStart,
                                            nEnd - nStart);

            nStart = nEnd + 1;
        }

#ifndef _FULLDIRTREE

        CString strItemPath = szCurDrive;
        for (nIndex = 1; nIndex < nCount; ++nIndex)
        {
            strItemPath += '\\';
            strItemPath += strElems[nIndex];
            CPathData pfNew;
            pfNew.strName = strElems[nIndex];
            pfNew.ParentItem = next;
            pfNew.bVisible = true;
            pfNew.nImage = GetIconIndex (strItemPath,
                              FILE_ATTRIBUTE_DIRECTORY);
            pfNew.nSelImage = pfNew.nImage;
            pfNew.nIndent = 2 * nIndex;
            pos = m_PathData.InsertAfter (pos, pfNew);
        }
        UpdateDisplay (pos);
        delete [] strElems;

#else
//
//   Alternate display code.
//
        POSITION nextpos = pos;
        POSITION selpos = pos;
        CString strLevel = _T("");
        for (nIndex = 0; nIndex < nCount; ++nIndex)
```

```
    {
        strLevel += strElems[nIndex] + '\\';
        CString strTest =
                    strPath.Left (strLevel.GetLength());
        if (nIndex < (nCount - 1))
        {
            strTest += strElems[nIndex + 1];
        }
        else
            strTest.Empty ();
        CString strLevelPath = strLevel + "*.*";

        WIN32_FIND_DATA fd;
        int nItem = GetCount ();
        HANDLE hFind = FindFirstFile ((LPCSTR)
                                        strLevelPath, &fd);

        if (hFind == NULL)
            break;
        do
        {
            if (!(fd.dwFileAttributes
                    & FILE_ATTRIBUTE_DIRECTORY))
                continue;
            if (*(fd.cFileName) == '.')
                continue;
            CPathData PathData;
            PathData.strName = fd.cFileName;
            PathData.bVisible = true;
            PathData.nLevel = 1;
            PathData.ParentItem = parent;
            CString strData;
            strData.Format ("%s%s", (LPCSTR) strLevel,
                            fd.cFileName);
            PathData.nImage = GetIconIndex (strData,
                                FILE_ATTRIBUTE_DIRECTORY);
            PathData.nIndent = pf.nIndent + 2;
            pos = m_PathData.InsertAfter (next, PathData);
            if (!strTest.Compare ((LPCSTR) strData))
            {
                nextpos = pos;
                selpos = pos;
            }
            next = pos;
        } while (FindNextFile (hFind, &fd));
        next = nextpos;
        pf = m_PathData.GetNext(nextpos);
        FindClose (hFind);
    }
    UpdateDisplay (selpos);
#endif     // _FULLDIRTREE
}

POSITION CPathBox::GetSelPosition()
{
    int nSel = GetCurSel ();
    if (nSel < 0)
```

```
        return (NULL);
    POSITION pos = (POSITION) GetItemData (nSel);
    return (pos);
}


int CPathBox::GetIconIndex(CString &strFile,
                           DWORD dwAttributes)
{
    SHFILEINFO sfi;
    memset(&sfi, 0, sizeof(sfi));
    SHGetFileInfo (strFile, dwAttributes,
           &sfi, sizeof(sfi),
           SHGFI_SMALLICON | SHGFI_SYSICONINDEX |
           SHGFI_USEFILEATTRIBUTES);
    return (sfi.iIcon);
}


void CPathBox::OnGetdispinfo(NMHDR* pNMHDR,
                             LRESULT* pResult)
{
    NMCOMBOBOXEX *pData = (NMCOMBOBOXEX *) pNMHDR;
    COMBOBOXEXITEM *pItem = &pData->ceItem;
    if (pItem->mask & CBEIF_TEXT)
    {
        CPathData pd = m_PathData.GetAt ((POSITION)
                                          pItem->lParam);
        ::lstrcpy (pItem->pszText, (LPCSTR) pd.strName);
    }
    *pResult = 0;
}


//
// Constructor for the data class
//
CPathBox::CPathData::CPathData ()
{
    strName = _T("");
    nItem = 0;
    ParentItem = NULL;
    nImage = -1;
    nSelImage = -1;
    dwData = 0;
    Expanded = false;
    nIndent = 0;
    nMode = 0;
    nLevel = 0;
    bVisible = false;
}
```

This will provide a basic class that you can build upon, but in real-world applications you might find the extended combo box a frustrating control. If you want to build another Internet Explorer, it's a good control, but Internet Explorer is a lot like NotePad—one per world is plenty.

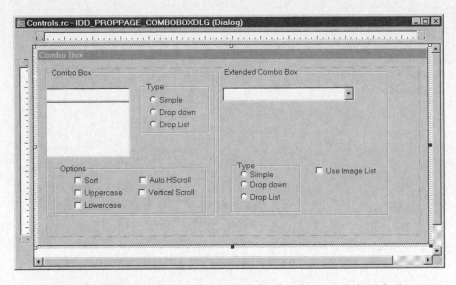

Figure 860   The Combo Box property page showing the extended combo box

Add the controls to the extended combo box group, as shown in Figure 860. The Simple check box doesn't have the Visible style, but the button and the handler code are included in case you want to experiment with them. Draw the extended combo box wider than you normally would. When you start expanding the subdirectories with indents, the image could get fairly wide.

Add the *PathBox.h* file to the list of include files in *ComboBoxDlg.h*. Add a member variable for the extended combo box, making sure that it is of type *CPathBox*. If the class wizard doesn't list *CPathBox* in the control type, make it *CComboBoxEx* and edit the header file to change it. Also add member variables for the radio buttons and the Use Image List check box. Add message handlers for the radio buttons and check box.

Replace the *CComboBoxDlg* constructor and add the virtual function *OnInitDialog()* as shown here:

```
CComboBoxDlg::CComboBoxDlg() :
                  CPropertyPage(CComboBoxDlg::IDD)
{
    //{{AFX_DATA_INIT(CComboBoxDlg)
    m_nComboType = 0;
    m_nComboExType = 1;
    m_strComboSample = _T("");
    m_bComboVScroll = FALSE;
    m_bUseImageList = TRUE;
    //}}AFX_DATA_INIT
    m_psp.dwFlags &= ~PSP_HASHELP;
}
BOOL CComboBoxDlg::OnInitDialog()
{
    CPropertyPage::OnInitDialog();

    m_ComboSample.Dir (0, "*.*");

    char szDir[ MAX_PATH];
    memset (szDir, '\0', sizeof (szDir));
    GetCurrentDirectory (_MAX_PATH, szDir);
    CString strDir;
```

```
    m_ComboExSample.SetPath (szDir);
    CFont *font = GetFont ();
    LOGFONT lf;
    font->GetLogFont (&lf);
    m_Font.CreateFontIndirect (&lf);
    m_ComboSample.SetFont (&m_Font);

    m_ComboSample.GetDroppedControlRect (m_rcDrop);
    m_ComboSample.GetWindowRect (m_rcCombo);
    ScreenToClient (m_rcCombo);
//
//  Set up a rectangle for the extended combo box.
//
    m_ComboExSample.GetWindowRect (m_rcComboEx);
    ScreenToClient (m_rcComboEx);
    m_rcComboEx.bottom += 4 * (m_rcComboEx.bottom
                             - m_rcComboEx.top);
//
//  Save the combo box styles for later use.
//
    m_dwComboStyle = m_ComboSample.GetStyle ();
    m_dwComboExStyle = m_ComboExSample.GetStyle ();
    m_dwComboExStyleEx = m_ComboExSample.GetExStyle ();
//
//  Select the first item in the combo box. The CpathBox
//  class will set its own selection.
//
    m_ComboSample.SetCurSel (0);

    return TRUE;
}
```

The rest of the code to support the extended combo box will consist of message handlers. Most of the implementation code is in the *CPathBox* class. You will need to add a function, *RecreateComboBoxEx*, to destroy and re-create the extended combo box when one of the radio buttons is selected. The added code is shown in the listing that follows.

```
/////////////////////////////////////////////////////////
// Extended Combo Box Functions

void CComboBoxDlg::RecreateComboExBox()
{
    POSITION pos = m_ComboExSample.GetSelPosition();
    m_ComboExSample.ResetContent();
    m_ComboExSample.DestroyWindow ();
    m_ComboExSample.Create (m_dwComboExStyle, m_rcComboEx,
                            this, IDC_COMBOEX_SAMPLE);
    m_ComboExSample.SetExtendedStyle (m_dwComboExStyleEx,
                                      m_dwComboExStyleEx);
    m_ComboExSample.SetFont (&m_Font);
    m_ComboExSample.UpdateDisplay (pos);
    CControlsApp *app = (CControlsApp *) AfxGetApp();
    m_ComboExSample.SetImageList(app->GetSystemImageList());
}

void CComboBoxDlg::OnComboexSimple()
```

```
{
    UpdateData (TRUE);
    m_dwComboExStyle &= ~(CBS_DROPDOWN | CBS_DROPDOWNLIST);
    m_dwComboExStyle |= CBS_SIMPLE;
    RecreateComboExBox();
    m_ComboExSample.Invalidate ();
}

void CComboBoxDlg::OnComboexDroplist()
{
    UpdateData (TRUE);
    m_dwComboExStyle &= ~(CBS_DROPDOWN | CBS_SIMPLE);
    m_dwComboExStyle |= CBS_DROPDOWNLIST;
    RecreateComboExBox();
}

void CComboBoxDlg::OnComboexDropdown()
{
    Invalidate ();
    UpdateData (TRUE);
    m_dwComboExStyle &= ~(CBS_DROPDOWNLIST | CBS_SIMPLE);
    m_dwComboExStyle |= CBS_DROPDOWN;
    RecreateComboExBox();
    if (m_ComboExSample.GetDroppedState ())
        m_ComboExSample.ShowDropDown (FALSE);
}

void CComboBoxDlg::OnComboexUseimagelist()
{
    UpdateData (TRUE);
    if (m_bUseImageList)
        m_dwComboExStyleEx &= ~(CBES_EX_NOEDITIMAGE
                                | CBES_EX_NOEDITIMAGEINDENT);
    else
        m_dwComboExStyleEx |= CBES_EX_NOEDITIMAGE
                                | CBES_EX_NOEDITIMAGEINDENT;
    RecreateComboExBox();
}
```

861. *Adding Items to an Extended Combo Box*

The extended combo box does derive some benefit from the use of an item structure, but whether it is worth the loss of the string functions is a matter of opinion. You must use the item structure, *COMBOBOXEXITEM*, when you add an item to an extended combo box. You can't just add a string directly.

The item structure lets you set the index of the item's image and the amount to tab the text from the image, or the left side of the drop-down box, if no image is used.

The indent is in units of 10 pixels. A standard small icon is 16 pixels and, allowing for a 4-pixel buffer between the icon and the text, an indent of 2 will move the item to the right so that it appears directly below the text for the previous item.

To add an item to the extended combo box, set the member variables to the proper values. You must set the *mask* variable to indicate which items you want to set. Any variable that doesn't have the flag set in *mask* will be ignored.

After you've set the structure members, call the *CComboBoxEx* class's *InsertItem()* member function, passing the address of the item structure as a parameter. The function will return the 0-based index at which the item was inserted, or −1 if the operation didn't succeed. Also, the parent window will be sent a *CBEN_INSERTITEM* message through the notification message process.

862. *Using* CImageList *with* CComboBoxEx

Like many of the newer controls, the extended combo box includes support for an image list. In fact, if you don't use an image list with it, there's little advantage to using the extended combo box over the standard control.

You can use images of any size. The extended combo box control will size the height of items according to the size of the images in the image list, much as the Owner Draw control did in the tips on image lists.

Assign an image list to the control by calling the *SetImageList()* member function, passing a pointer to a *CImageList* object. By default, the image list is *NULL* until you set it. You can retrieve a pointer to the image list by calling the *GetImageList()* member function. The pointer returned by this function is a moveable pointer, and you should use it immediately after retrieving it; don't store it for later use because it probably won't be valid after the next idle time processing.

863. *Understanding* CComboBoxEx *Operations*

The *CComboBoxEx* class contains member functions for adding, deleting, and manipulating items in the control. The extended control is built on top of a standard combo box control, and you can use some of the standard control's functions by getting a pointer to the *CListBox* class object that encapsulates it.

The pointer to the *CListBox* object is obtained by calling *GetComboBoxCtrl()*. You can't, however, use this pointer to perform string functions that the extended control doesn't include. To add, retrieve, or modify entries, you must go through the process of getting or filling out an item structure, and then call the *CComboBoxEx* function to perform the operation. You can delete an entry the same as you would with the standard control, using the index of the item.

Add items by calling the *InsertItem()* function, and retrieve them by calling *GetItem()*. Both of these functions take a pointer to a *COMBOBOXEXITEM* structure as the only parameter. After you retrieve an item with *GetItem()*, you can modify the structure and set the changes by calling *SetItem()*, using a pointer to the modified item structure as a pointer.

You can get a pointer to the extended combo box's edit control by calling *GetEditCtrl()*. This works only when using the drop-down style. The drop list style doesn't use an edit control, and the call always returns a *NULL* pointer when using the simple style. Typical of Microsoft documentation, the MSDN literature doesn't tell you that you can't use the Simple style, but then it doesn't tell anything useful about using the extended combo box control when you create it using the Simple style.

864. *Understanding the Rich Edit Control*

Although it is available on Windows versions only since Windows 95 and Windows NT 3.51, the rich edit control has its roots in 16-bit Windows. It originally was created to support a DOS version of Microsoft Word, but it wasn't added to the common controls until Windows 95 was released.

The control provides an interface for entering and editing text, much like the edit control. Unlike the edit control, however, it also supports text formatting in different colors, attributes, fonts, and point sizes within the same control, and it may contain embedded OLE objects. It also supports paragraph formatting, including styles such as bullets and number lists.

The rich edit control provides only the interface for these styles and formats. You, the programmer, have to provide the code that lets a user access these functions. You may limit the selection or colors and fonts as required by your application, and you may set restrictions on paragraph formatting.

The rich edit control functions are contained in their own library, *riched32.dll*, and before you can use it, you must load the library module. In an MFC application using the *CRichEditCtrl* class, you do this by calling *AfxInitRichEdit()* once before creating the control, either on a dialog box or in memory. Typically, you would include this call in the application class *InitInstance()* function. After calling the function successfully, you can create multiple rich edit controls without calling it again.

The rich edit control is the underlying control for the *CRichEditView* class. When using this class in a document/view project, the call to *AfxInitRichEdit()* is embedded in the *PreCreateWindow()* member function.

The rich edit control is a "bottomless" text control. Under Windows 95 and 98, the standard edit control has a limit of 65,537 bytes, but the rich edit control may be set to virtually any size. The effective limit is 4,294,967,295, the maximum value that may be contained in an unsigned integer under 32-bit Windows. (Under Windows NT, the standard edit control also has a limit of 4,294,967,295 bytes).

The rich edit control isn't a perfect control. You'll notice some quirks about it that belie its origin. For example, if you cut and paste text that contains "smart" quotes—the trans-ASCII characters for open and closed single- and double-quote marks—the paste operation will change them back to standard ASCII characters, losing the directional information. This happens even with cut-and-paste operations within the same control. You have to write code to change them back, usually making a "best guess" as to which they should be.

In programming, you want the standard ASCII quote marks. In text processing, however, the direction of the quote is extremely important, and this sort of behavior by the rich edit control can only be called idiotic. When I asked Microsoft reps about it some years ago, they told me simply that if it's a problem, don't use it. That's a pretty good cop-out. The next time my wife tells me that the washing machine is broken, I'll just tell her, "If it's a problem, don't use it."

865. *Understanding the CRichEditCtrl Class*

The MFC *CRichEditCtrl* class encapsulates the rich edit control and contains functions to access the control and to perform character and paragraph formatting. The *CRichEditView* class uses this class as its underlying edit control.

You've already used the rich edit control in a document/view application, so in this tip you'll add a property page for the control and implement the functions to use it in a dialog box. The rich edit control isn't often found on a dialog box; the basic edit control usually serves the purpose of most user input applications. There's no reason you can't use it, however.

Add a property page to the *Controls* application. Make it the same size as the other property pages. Give it a resource ID of *IDD_PROPERTYPAGE_RICHEDITDLG*, and title it Rich Edit. Add the same buttons that you used for the edit control page to access the font and color common dialog boxes, but don't add the various check boxes to change the appearance of the control. The appearance will be the same as for the edit and static controls, so there's no need to repeat them on this property page. Instead, you'll add a group of buttons with icons on them to access the character and paragraph formatting and indenting operations.

The character-formatting buttons are check box controls with the Push Like style set. The paragraph-formatting buttons are radio buttons, also with the Push Like style set. The first two indenting are a radio button group, and the third is a check box. Draw the group boxes around these sets of large buttons, and place the buttons at the bottom of the group box, leaving plenty of room at the top. You'll be adding legends to the buttons directly on the dialog box. The finished property page is shown in Figure 865.

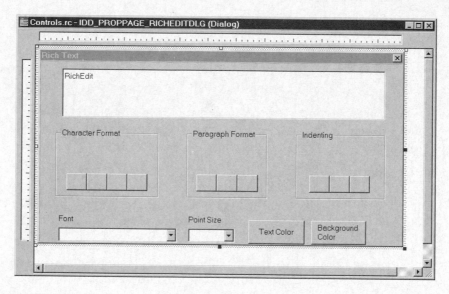

Figure 865   Lay out the rich edit sample page carefully, allowing lots of room above the formatting buttons for labels

This version of the rich edit control isn't going to be a full-fledged text editor. Instead, it's going to be more like a way of entering blocks of formatted text. For one thing, you can't handle the buttons the same you did using *CRichEditView* because the command enablers don't work in a dialog box (Microsoft still hasn't figured that out). Just do the best you can using the cursor movement keys, and maybe you can sneak some code in here and there to keep the buttons updated.

The rich edit control is much more complicated than the standard edit control, so it's going to take more handling. Individual characters may have their own attributes, while in the standard edit control, all characters have the same attributes. You have to consider that when responding to a button press. If more than one character is selected, you need to operate on the entire selection.

An important point to remember—and, if you get nothing else from this tip, remember this point—is that after you perform a formatting operation, return the focus *immediately* to the rich edit control, particularly if there is no selected text in the control. You can't rely on the user to click the mouse at the proper point, and even a single pixel error in the mouse click can cause you to lose your new formatting. If you return the focus in your code, the caret will be in the proper position. If the user then moves it, well, you can't do much about that.

Create a class, *CRichEditDlg*, for this page, using *CPropertyPage* as the base class. The header file is shown here:

```
// RichEditDlg.h : header file
//

#include    <afxtempl.h>

/////////////////////////////////////////////////////////
// CRichEditDlg dialog

class CRichEditDlg : public CpropertyPage
{
    DECLARE_DYNCREATE(CRichEditDlg)

// Construction
public:
    CRichEditDlg();
    ~CRichEditDlg();

    class CfontData
    {
    public:
        CFontData () {
                    m_strName = _T("");
                    m_nIcon = 0;
                 }
        ~CFontData () { }
        CString m_strName;
        int     m_nIcon;
    };

// Dialog Data
    //{{AFX_DATA(CRichEditDlg)
    enum { IDD = IDD_PROPPAGE_RICHEDITDLG };
    CButton m_ctlParaIndentBullets;
    CComboBox   m_ctlPointBox;
    CComboBoxEx m_ctlFontBox;
    CButton m_ctlParaRight;
    CButton m_ctlParaCenter;
    CButton m_ctlParaLeft;
    CButton m_ctlParaIndentMore;
    CButton m_ctlParaIndentLess;
    CButton m_ctlFormatUnderline;
    CButton m_ctlFormatStrikeout;
    CButton m_ctlFormatItalic;
    CButton m_ctlFormatBold;
    CRichEditCtrl   m_RichSample;
    int     m_nFormatItalic;
    int     m_nFormatBold;
    int     m_nFormatStrikout;
    int     m_nFormatUnderline;
    int     m_nParaAlign;
    BOOL    m_nParaIndentBullets;
    //}}AFX_DATA

    COLORREF    m_clrBack;
    COLORREF    m_clrCustom[16];
```

```
// Overrides
    // ClassWizard generate virtual function overrides
    //{{AFX_VIRTUAL(CRichEditDlg)
    protected:
    virtual void DoDataExchange(CDataExchange* pDX);
    // DDX/DDV support
    //}}AFX_VIRTUAL

    CHARFORMAT  m_CharFormat;

// Implementation
protected:
    CImageList m_imageFonts;
    static int CALLBACK AddFontName(ENUMLOGFONT *lpelfe,
                    NEWTEXTMETRIC *lpntme, int FontType,
                    LPARAM lParam);
    // Generated message map functions
    //{{AFX_MSG(CRichEditDlg)
    virtual BOOL OnInitDialog();
    afx_msg void OnRichsetcolor();
    afx_msg void OnPaint();
    afx_msg void OnSelchangeFontbox();
    afx_msg void OnSelchangePointbox();
    afx_msg void OnRichsettextcolor();
    afx_msg void OnFormatBold();
    afx_msg void OnFormatItalic();
    afx_msg void OnFormatStrikeout();
    afx_msg void OnFormatUnderline();
    afx_msg void OnParagraphleft();
    afx_msg void OnParagraphcenter();
    afx_msg void OnParagraphright();
    afx_msg void OnIndentless();
    afx_msg void OnIndentmore();
    afx_msg void OnIndentbullets();
    afx_msg void OnMsgfilterRichSample(NMHDR* pNMHDR,
                                         LRESULT* pResult);
    afx_msg void OnGetdispinfoFontbox(NMHDR* pNMHDR,
                                         LRESULT* pResult);
    //}}AFX_MSG
    DECLARE_MESSAGE_MAP()

    CList <CFontData, CFontData&> m_FontData;

};
```

Notice that *afxtempl.h* has been included in this file, along with the definition of an embedded class, *CFontData*. At the bottom of the header file is a *CList* object declaration for this class. This is how you will sort the font names, using the sorting process from Tip 498, "Array, List, and Map Classes."

The source file for *CRichEditDlg* is shown here:

```
// RichEditDlg.cpp : implementation file
//

#include "stdafx.h"
#include "Controls.h"
#include "RichEditDlg.h"
```

```
#ifdef _DEBUG
#define new DEBUG_NEW
#undef THIS_FILE
static char THIS_FILE[] = __FILE__;
#endif

struct FONTDATA
    {
    CString         strFont;
    CComboBoxEx     *FontBox;
    CRichEditDlg    *Papa;
    };

#define    EDIT_STYLES    ES_MULTILINE | \
                          ES_AUTOVSCROLL | \
                          ES_WANTRETURN
#define    EDIT_EX_STYLES WS_EX_DLGMODALFRAME | \
                          WS_EX_CLIENTEDGE | \
                          WS_EX_STATICEDGE


/////////////////////////////////////////////////////////
// CRichEditDlg property page

IMPLEMENT_DYNCREATE(CRichEditDlg, CPropertyPage)

CRichEditDlg::CRichEditDlg()
              : CPropertyPage(CRichEditDlg::IDD)
{

    //{{AFX_DATA_INIT(CRichEditDlg)
    m_nFormatItalic = FALSE;
    m_nFormatBold = FALSE;
    m_nFormatStrikout = FALSE;
    m_nFormatUnderline = FALSE;
    m_nParaAlign = 0;
    m_nParaIndentBullets = FALSE;
    //}}AFX_DATA_INIT
    m_clrBack = GetSysColor (COLOR_WINDOW);
    for (int i = 0; i < 16; ++i)
        m_clrCustom[i] = RGB (0xff, 0xff, 0xff);
    m_psp.dwFlags &= ~PSP_HASHELP;
}

CRichEditDlg::~CRichEditDlg()
{
}

void CRichEditDlg::DoDataExchange(CDataExchange* pDX)
{
    CPropertyPage::DoDataExchange(pDX);
    //{{AFX_DATA_MAP(CRichEditDlg)
    DDX_Control(pDX, IDC_INDENTBULLETS,
                     m_ctlParaIndentBullets);
    DDX_Control(pDX, IDC_POINTBOX, m_ctlPointBox);
    DDX_Control(pDX, IDC_FONTBOX, m_ctlFontBox);
```

```
        DDX_Control(pDX, IDC_PARAGRAPHRIGHT, m_ctlParaRight);
        DDX_Control(pDX, IDC_PARAGRAPHCENTER, m_ctlParaCenter);
        DDX_Control(pDX, IDC_PARAGRAPHLEFT, m_ctlParaLeft);
        DDX_Control(pDX, IDC_INDENTMORE, m_ctlParaIndentMore);
        DDX_Control(pDX, IDC_INDENTLESS, m_ctlParaIndentLess);
        DDX_Control(pDX, IDC_FORMATUNDERLINE,
                         m_ctlFormatUnderline);
        DDX_Control(pDX, IDC_FORMATSTRIKEOUT,
                         m_ctlFormatStrikeout);
        DDX_Control(pDX, IDC_FORMATITALIC, m_ctlFormatItalic);
        DDX_Control(pDX, IDC_FORMATBOLD, m_ctlFormatBold);
        DDX_Control(pDX, IDC_RICH_SAMPLE, m_RichSample);
        DDX_Check(pDX, IDC_FORMATITALIC, m_nFormatItalic);
        DDX_Check(pDX, IDC_FORMATBOLD, m_nFormatBold);
        DDX_Check(pDX, IDC_FORMATSTRIKEOUT, m_nFormatStrikout);
        DDX_Check(pDX,IDC_FORMATUNDERLINE, m_nFormatUnderline);
        DDX_Radio(pDX, IDC_PARAGRAPHLEFT, m_nParaAlign);
        DDX_Check(pDX,IDC_INDENTBULLETS, m_nParaIndentBullets);
        //}}AFX_DATA_MAP
}


BEGIN_MESSAGE_MAP(CRichEditDlg, CPropertyPage)
    //{{AFX_MSG_MAP(CRichEditDlg)
    ON_BN_CLICKED(IDC_RICHSETCOLOR, OnRichsetcolor)
    ON_WM_PAINT()
    ON_CBN_SELCHANGE(IDC_FONTBOX, OnSelchangeFontbox)
    ON_CBN_SELCHANGE(IDC_POINTBOX, OnSelchangePointbox)
    ON_BN_CLICKED(IDC_RICHSETTEXTCOLOR, OnRichsettextcolor)
    ON_BN_CLICKED(IDC_FORMATBOLD, OnFormatBold)
    ON_BN_CLICKED(IDC_FORMATITALIC, OnFormatItalic)
    ON_BN_CLICKED(IDC_FORMATSTRIKEOUT, OnFormatStrikeout)
    ON_BN_CLICKED(IDC_FORMATUNDERLINE, OnFormatUnderline)
    ON_BN_CLICKED(IDC_PARAGRAPHLEFT, OnParagraphleft)
    ON_BN_CLICKED(IDC_PARAGRAPHCENTER, OnParagraphcenter)
    ON_BN_CLICKED(IDC_PARAGRAPHRIGHT, OnParagraphright)
    ON_BN_CLICKED(IDC_INDENTLESS, OnIndentless)
    ON_BN_CLICKED(IDC_INDENTMORE, OnIndentmore)
    ON_BN_CLICKED(IDC_INDENTBULLETS, OnIndentbullets)
    ON_NOTIFY(EN_MSGFILTER, IDC_RICH_SAMPLE,
                         OnMsgfilterRichSample)
    ON_NOTIFY(CBEN_GETDISPINFO, IDC_FONTBOX,
                           OnGetdispinfoFontbox)
    //}}AFX_MSG_MAP
END_MESSAGE_MAP()


/////////////////////////////////////////////////////////
// CRichEditDlg message handlers

BOOL CRichEditDlg::OnInitDialog()
{

    CPropertyPage::OnInitDialog();

    long mask = m_RichSample.GetEventMask();
    m_RichSample.SetEventMask (mask | ENM_UPDATE |
                    ENM_KEYEVENTS | ENM_MOUSEEVENTS);
```

```
m_CharFormat.dwEffects &= ~(CFM_ITALIC | CFM_BOLD |
                            CFM_UNDERLINE |
                            CFM_STRIKEOUT | CFM_COLOR |
                            CFM_SIZE | CFM_FACE);


HICON hIcon = (HICON)LoadImage (AfxGetInstanceHandle(),
                   MAKEINTRESOURCE (IDI_FORMATBOLD),
                   IMAGE_ICON,
                   16, 16, 0);
m_ctlFormatBold.SetIcon (hIcon);
DeleteObject (hIcon);
hIcon = (HICON) LoadImage (AfxGetInstanceHandle (),
                   MAKEINTRESOURCE (IDI_FORMATITALIC),
                   IMAGE_ICON,
                   16, 16, 0);
m_ctlFormatItalic.SetIcon (hIcon);
DeleteObject (hIcon);
hIcon = (HICON) LoadImage (AfxGetInstanceHandle (),
                   MAKEINTRESOURCE(IDI_FORMATUNDERLINE),
                   IMAGE_ICON,
                   16, 16, 0);
m_ctlFormatUnderline.SetIcon (hIcon);
DeleteObject (hIcon);
hIcon = (HICON) LoadImage (AfxGetInstanceHandle (),
                   MAKEINTRESOURCE(IDI_FORMATSTRIKEOUT),
                   IMAGE_ICON,
                   16, 16, 0);
m_ctlFormatStrikeout.SetIcon (hIcon);
DeleteObject (hIcon);


hIcon = (HICON) LoadImage (AfxGetInstanceHandle (),
                   MAKEINTRESOURCE (IDI_PARAGRAPHLEFT),
                   IMAGE_ICON,
                   16, 16, 0);
m_ctlParaLeft.SetIcon (hIcon);
DeleteObject (hIcon);
hIcon = (HICON) LoadImage (AfxGetInstanceHandle (),
                   MAKEINTRESOURCE(IDI_PARAGRAPHCENTER),
                   IMAGE_ICON,
                   16, 16, 0);
m_ctlParaCenter.SetIcon (hIcon);
DeleteObject (hIcon);
hIcon = (HICON) LoadImage (AfxGetInstanceHandle (),
                   MAKEINTRESOURCE (IDI_PARAGRAPHRIGHT),
                   IMAGE_ICON,
                   16, 16, 0);
m_ctlParaRight.SetIcon (hIcon);
DeleteObject (hIcon);


hIcon = (HICON) LoadImage (AfxGetInstanceHandle (),
                   MAKEINTRESOURCE (IDI_INDENTMORE),
                   IMAGE_ICON,
                   16, 16, 0);
m_ctlParaIndentMore.SetIcon (hIcon);
DeleteObject (hIcon);
```

```
        hIcon = (HICON) LoadImage (AfxGetInstanceHandle (),
                        MAKEINTRESOURCE (IDI_INDENTLESS),
                        IMAGE_ICON,
                        16, 16, 0);
        m_ctlParaIndentLess.SetIcon (hIcon);
        DeleteObject (hIcon);
        hIcon = (HICON) LoadImage (AfxGetInstanceHandle (),
                        MAKEINTRESOURCE (IDI_INDENTBULLETS),
                        IMAGE_ICON,
                        16, 16, 0);
        m_ctlParaIndentBullets.SetIcon (hIcon);
        DeleteObject (hIcon);

        m_imageFonts.Create (16, 16, ILC_MASK, 2, 2);
        hIcon = (HICON) LoadImage (AfxGetInstanceHandle (),
                        MAKEINTRESOURCE (IDI_TRUETYPEFONTS),
                        IMAGE_ICON, 16, 16, 0);
        m_imageFonts.Add (hIcon);
        DeleteObject (hIcon);
        hIcon = (HICON) LoadImage (AfxGetInstanceHandle (),
                        MAKEINTRESOURCE (IDI_PRINTERFONTS),
                        IMAGE_ICON, 16, 16, 0);
        m_imageFonts.Add (hIcon);
        DeleteObject (hIcon);

        m_ctlFontBox.SetImageList (&m_imageFonts);

//
// Get an enumerated list of fonts and place them
// in a sorted list.
//
        CWindowDC dc(this);
        FONTDATA fd;
        CString strFont = _T("Times New Roman");
        fd.FontBox = &m_ctlFontBox;
        fd.strFont = strFont;
        fd.Papa = this;
        ::EnumFontFamilies ((HDC) dc, NULL,
                        (FONTENUMPROC) AddFontName,
                        (LPARAM) &fd);
//
// Use the sorted list to load the font combo box.
//
        int nCount = m_FontData.GetCount ();
        POSITION pos = m_FontData.GetHeadPosition ();
        CFontData font = m_FontData.GetHead ();
        for (int n = 0; pos != NULL; ++n)
        {
            font = m_FontData.GetNext (pos);
            COMBOBOXEXITEM cbi;
            memset (&cbi, '\0', sizeof (COMBOBOXEXITEM));
            cbi.iItem = n;
            cbi.mask = CBEIF_IMAGE | CBEIF_TEXT |
                        CBEIF_SELECTEDIMAGE | CBS_SORT;
            cbi.iImage = font.m_nIcon;
            cbi.iSelectedImage = font.m_nIcon;
```

```
        cbi.pszText = LPSTR_TEXTCALLBACK;
        m_ctlFontBox.InsertItem (&cbi);
        if (!font.m_strName.CompareNoCase (strFont))
            m_ctlFontBox.SetCurSel (n);
    }

    CHARFORMAT cf;
    memset (&cf,'\0', sizeof (CHARFORMAT));
    strcpy (cf.szFaceName, _T("Times New Roman"));
    cf.yHeight = 20 * 10;
    cf.dwMask = CFM_FACE | CFM_SIZE;
    m_RichSample.SetDefaultCharFormat (cf);
    m_RichSample.SetSel (-1, -1);
    m_ctlPointBox.SelectString (-1, _T("10"));
    m_RichSample.ReplaceSel (_T(""));

    m_RichSample.SetFocus ();
    return FALSE;
}

void CRichEditDlg::OnRichsetcolor()
{
    CColorDialog    cc (m_clrBack);
    cc.m_cc.lpCustColors = m_clrCustom;
    if (cc.DoModal () == IDCANCEL)
        return;
    m_clrBack = cc.GetColor();
    m_RichSample.SetBackgroundColor (false, m_clrBack);
    m_RichSample.SetFocus ();
}

void CRichEditDlg::OnRichsettextcolor()
{
    CHARFORMAT cf;
    memset (&cf, '\0', sizeof (CHARFORMAT));
    cf.dwMask = CFM_COLOR;
    m_RichSample.GetSelectionCharFormat (cf);
    CColorDialog cc (cf.crTextColor);
    cc.m_cc.lpCustColors = m_clrCustom;
    if (cc.DoModal () == IDCANCEL)
        return;
    cf.dwMask = CFM_COLOR;
    cf.dwEffects &= ~CFE_AUTOCOLOR;
    cf.crTextColor  = cc.GetColor ();
    m_RichSample.SetSelectionCharFormat (cf);
    m_RichSample.SetFocus ();
}

void CRichEditDlg::OnPaint()
{
    CPaintDC dc(this); // device context for painting
//
// Create a font slanted at a 60-degree angle. This will
// be used to set legends for the various buttons.
//
    CFont *font = GetFont ();
```

```
    LOGFONT lf;
    font->GetLogFont (&lf);
    lf.lfEscapement = 600;
    lf.lfOrientation = 600;
    lf.lfQuality = PROOF_QUALITY;
    lf.lfUnderline = TRUE;
    strcpy (lf.lfFaceName, "Arial Bold");
    CFont SlantFont;
    SlantFont.CreateFontIndirect (&lf);
    CFont *fontOld = dc.SelectObject (&SlantFont);

//
//  Draw the legends, approximately centering the origin
//  of the text at the middle top of each button.
//  To do this, we need to get the rectangle of each
//  button and convert it to client coordinates.
//
    CRect rc;
    m_ctlFormatBold.GetWindowRect (&rc);
    ScreenToClient (&rc);
    CString text = "Bold";
    dc.SetTextAlign (TA_BASELINE);
    dc.TextOut (rc.left + (rc.right - rc.left) / 2,
                rc.top - 2, text);

    m_ctlFormatItalic.GetWindowRect (&rc);
    ScreenToClient (&rc);
    text = "Italic";
    dc.TextOut (rc.left + (rc.right - rc.left) / 2,
                rc.top - 2, text);

    m_ctlFormatUnderline.GetWindowRect (&rc);
    ScreenToClient (&rc);
    text = "Underline";
    CSize sz = dc.GetTextExtent(text);
    dc.TextOut (rc.left + (rc.right - rc.left) / 2,
                rc.top - 2, text);

    m_ctlFormatStrikeout.GetWindowRect (&rc);
    ScreenToClient (&rc);
    text = "Strikeout";
    dc.TextOut (rc.left + (rc.right - rc.left) / 2,
                rc.top - 2, text);

    m_ctlParaLeft.GetWindowRect (&rc);
    ScreenToClient (&rc);
    text = "Left";
    dc.TextOut (rc.left + (rc.right - rc.left) / 2,
                rc.top - 2, text);

    m_ctlParaRight.GetWindowRect (&rc);
    ScreenToClient (&rc);
    text = "Right";
    dc.TextOut (rc.left + (rc.right - rc.left) / 2,
                rc.top - 2, text);
```

```
    m_ctlParaCenter.GetWindowRect (&rc);
    ScreenToClient (&rc);
    text = "Center";
    dc.TextOut (rc.left + (rc.right - rc.left) / 2,
                rc.top - 2, text);

    m_ctlParaIndentLess.GetWindowRect (&rc);
    ScreenToClient (&rc);
    text = "Less";
    dc.TextOut (rc.left + (rc.right - rc.left) / 2,
                rc.top - 2, text);

    m_ctlParaIndentMore.GetWindowRect (&rc);
    ScreenToClient (&rc);
    text = "More";
    dc.TextOut (rc.left + (rc.right - rc.left) / 2,
                rc.top - 2, text);

    m_ctlParaIndentBullets.GetWindowRect (&rc);
    ScreenToClient (&rc);
    text = "Bullets";
    dc.TextOut (rc.left + (rc.right - rc.left) / 2,
                rc.top - 2, text);
    dc.SelectObject (fontOld);
}

int CALLBACK CRichEditDlg::AddFontName(ENUMLOGFONT *lpelfe,
                            NEWTEXTMETRIC *lpntme,
                            int FontType, LPARAM lParam)
{
    static int nItem = 0;

    FONTDATA *fd = (FONTDATA *) lParam;
    CFontData font;
    CRichEditDlg *edit = fd->Papa;
    font.m_strName = lpelfe->elfLogFont.lfFaceName;
    switch (FontType)
    {
        case RASTER_FONTTYPE:
        case DEVICE_FONTTYPE:
            font.m_nIcon = 1;
            break;
        case TRUETYPE_FONTTYPE:
            font.m_nIcon = 0;
            break;
    }
    POSITION pos;
    if (edit->m_FontData.GetCount () == 0)
    {
        edit->m_FontData.AddHead (font);
        return (TRUE);
    }
    pos = edit->m_FontData.GetHeadPosition ();
    CFontData data;
    int nCount = edit->m_FontData.GetCount ();
    data = edit->m_FontData.GetHead ();
```

```
        for (int n = 0; n < nCount; ++n)
        {
            int nResult =
                data.m_strName.CompareNoCase(font.m_strName);
            if (nResult > 0)
                break;
            data = edit->m_FontData.GetNext (pos);
        }
        if (pos == NULL)
        {
            if (font.m_strName.CompareNoCase(data.m_strName) < 0)
                {
                    pos = edit->m_FontData.GetTailPosition ();
                    edit->m_FontData.InsertBefore (pos, font);
                }
                else
                    edit->m_FontData.AddTail (font);
                return (TRUE);
        }
        edit->m_FontData.GetPrev (pos);
        edit->m_FontData.InsertBefore (pos, font);
        return (TRUE);
}

void CRichEditDlg::OnSelchangeFontbox()
{
    CHARFORMAT cf;
    DWORD dwMask = m_RichSample.GetSelectionCharFormat(cf);
    int nSel = m_ctlFontBox.GetCurSel ();
    long nStart, nEnd;
    m_RichSample.GetSel (nStart, nEnd);
    COMBOBOXEXITEM cbi;
    memset (&cbi, '\0', sizeof (COMBOBOXEXITEM));
    cbi.iItem = nSel;
    cbi.mask = CBEIF_TEXT;
    TCHAR   szFont[_MAX_PATH];
    cbi.pszText = szFont;
    cbi.cchTextMax = _MAX_PATH;
    m_ctlFontBox.GetItem (&cbi);
    cf.dwMask = CFM_FACE;
    strcpy (cf.szFaceName, szFont);
    m_RichSample.SetSelectionCharFormat (cf);
    m_RichSample.SetFocus ();
}

void CRichEditDlg::OnSelchangePointbox()
{
    CHARFORMAT cf;
    DWORD dwMask = m_RichSample.GetSelectionCharFormat(cf);
    int nSel = m_ctlPointBox.GetCurSel ();
    if (nSel < 0)
        return;
    CString strSel;
    m_ctlPointBox.GetLBText (nSel, strSel);
    int nSize = atoi ((LPCSTR) strSel);
    if (nSize < 6)
```

```
        return;
    cf.yHeight = 20 * nSize;
    cf.dwMask = CFM_SIZE;
    m_RichSample.SetSelectionCharFormat (cf);
    m_RichSample.SetFocus ();
}

void CRichEditDlg::OnFormatBold()
{
    CHARFORMAT cf;
    m_RichSample.GetSelectionCharFormat (cf);
    cf.dwMask |= CFM_BOLD;
    cf.dwEffects ^= CFE_BOLD;
    m_RichSample.SetSelectionCharFormat (cf);
    m_ctlFormatBold.SetCheck (
                    cf.dwEffects & CFE_BOLD ?
                    1 : 0);
    if (cf.dwEffects & CFE_BOLD)
        m_ctlFormatBold.SetCheck (1);
    else
        m_ctlFormatBold.SetCheck (0);
    m_RichSample.SetFocus ();
}

void CRichEditDlg::OnFormatItalic()
{
    CHARFORMAT cf;
    m_RichSample.GetSelectionCharFormat (cf);
    cf.dwMask |= CFM_ITALIC;
    cf.dwEffects ^= CFE_ITALIC;
    m_RichSample.SetSelectionCharFormat (cf);
    m_ctlFormatItalic.SetCheck (
                    cf.dwEffects & CFE_ITALIC ?
                    1 : 0);
    m_RichSample.SetFocus ();
}

void CRichEditDlg::OnFormatStrikeout()
{
    CHARFORMAT cf;
    m_RichSample.GetSelectionCharFormat (cf);
    cf.dwMask |= CFM_STRIKEOUT;
    cf.dwEffects ^= CFE_STRIKEOUT;
    m_RichSample.SetSelectionCharFormat (cf);
    m_ctlFormatStrikeout.SetCheck (
                    cf.dwEffects & CFE_STRIKEOUT ?
                    1 : 0);
    m_RichSample.SetFocus ();
}

void CRichEditDlg::OnFormatUnderline()
{
    CHARFORMAT cf;
    m_RichSample.GetSelectionCharFormat (cf);
    cf.dwMask |= CFM_UNDERLINE;
    cf.dwEffects ^= CFE_UNDERLINE;
```

```cpp
    m_RichSample.SetSelectionCharFormat (cf);
    m_ctlFormatUnderline.SetCheck (
                    cf.dwEffects & CFE_UNDERLINE ?
                    1 : 0);
    m_RichSample.SetFocus ();
}

void CRichEditDlg::OnParagraphleft()
{
    PARAFORMAT pf;
    m_RichSample.GetParaFormat(pf);
    pf.dwMask = PFM_ALIGNMENT;
    pf.wAlignment = PFA_LEFT;
    m_RichSample.SetParaFormat(pf);
    m_RichSample.SetFocus ();
}

void CRichEditDlg::OnParagraphcenter()
{
    PARAFORMAT pf;
    m_RichSample.GetParaFormat(pf);
    pf.dwMask = PFM_ALIGNMENT;
    pf.wAlignment = PFA_CENTER;
    m_RichSample.SetParaFormat(pf);
    m_RichSample.SetFocus ();
}

void CRichEditDlg::OnParagraphright()
{
    PARAFORMAT pf;
    m_RichSample.GetParaFormat(pf);
    pf.dwMask = PFM_ALIGNMENT;
    pf.wAlignment = PFA_RIGHT;
    m_RichSample.SetParaFormat(pf);
    m_RichSample.SetFocus ();
}

void CRichEditDlg::OnIndentless()
{
PARAFORMAT  pf;
CHARFORMAT  cf;

    memset (&pf, '\0', sizeof (PARAFORMAT));
    pf.cbSize = sizeof (PARAFORMAT);
    m_RichSample.GetParaFormat (pf);
    m_RichSample.GetSelectionCharFormat (cf);
    pf.dwMask = PFM_STARTINDENT | PFM_RIGHTINDENT;
    if (pf.dxRightIndent)
        pf.dxRightIndent -= cf.yHeight;
    if (pf.dxStartIndent)
        pf.dxStartIndent -= cf.yHeight;
    m_RichSample.SetParaFormat (pf);
    m_RichSample.SetFocus ();
}

void CRichEditDlg::OnIndentmore()
```

```
{
PARAFORMAT  pf;
CHARFORMAT  cf;

    memset (&pf, '\0', sizeof (PARAFORMAT));
    pf.cbSize = sizeof (PARAFORMAT);
    m_RichSample.GetParaFormat (pf);
    m_RichSample.GetSelectionCharFormat (cf);
    pf.dwMask = PFM_STARTINDENT | PFM_RIGHTINDENT;
    pf.dxStartIndent += cf.yHeight;
    pf.dxRightIndent += cf.yHeight;
    m_RichSample.SetParaFormat (pf);
    m_RichSample.SetFocus ();
}

void CRichEditDlg::OnIndentbullets()
{
PARAFORMAT  pf;
CHARFORMAT  cf;

    memset (&pf, '\0', sizeof (PARAFORMAT));
    pf.cbSize = sizeof (PARAFORMAT);
    m_RichSample.GetParaFormat (pf);
    m_RichSample.GetSelectionCharFormat (cf);
    pf.dwMask = PFM_NUMBERING | PFM_OFFSET;
    pf.wNumbering ^= PFN_BULLET;
    if (pf.wNumbering & PFN_BULLET)
    {
        pf.dxOffset = cf.yHeight;
    }
    else
    {
        pf.dwMask |= PFM_STARTINDENT | PFM_RIGHTINDENT;
        pf.dxOffset = 0;
        pf.dxStartIndent = 0;
        pf.dxRightIndent = 0;
    }
    m_RichSample.SetParaFormat (pf);
    m_RichSample.SetFocus ();
}

void CRichEditDlg::OnMsgfilterRichSample(NMHDR* pNMHDR,
                                         LRESULT* pResult)
{
    MSGFILTER *pMsgFilter =
                reinterpret_cast<MSGFILTER *>(pNMHDR);
    // TODO: The control will not send this notification
    // unless you override the
    // CPropertyPage::OnInitDialog()function to send the
    // EM_SETEVENTMASK message to the control with either
    // the ENM_KEYEVENTS or ENM_MOUSEEVENTS flag ORed into
    // the lParam mask.

    PARAFORMAT  pf;
    CHARFORMAT  cf;
```

```
        *pResult = 0;

        memset (&pf, '\0', sizeof (PARAFORMAT));
        pf.cbSize = sizeof (PARAFORMAT);
        m_RichSample.GetParaFormat (pf);
        m_RichSample.GetSelectionCharFormat (cf);
//
//  Select the proper items in the combo boxes
//
        if (cf.dwMask & CFM_FACE)
        {
            int nCount = 0;
            POSITION pos = m_FontData.GetHeadPosition ();
            while (pos != NULL)
            {
                CFontData data = m_FontData.GetNext (pos);
                if (!strcmp ((LPCSTR) data.m_strName,
                             cf.szFaceName))
                    break;
                ++nCount;
            }
            if (pos != NULL)
                m_ctlFontBox.SetCurSel (nCount);
        }
        else
            m_ctlFontBox.SetCurSel (-1);

        if (cf.dwMask & CFM_SIZE)
        {
            CString strText;
            strText.Format ("%d", cf.yHeight / 20);
            int nPos = m_ctlPointBox.FindStringExact (-1,
                                       (LPCSTR) strText);
            if (nPos >= 0)
                m_ctlPointBox.SetCurSel (nPos);
        }
        else
            m_ctlPointBox.SetCurSel (-1);
//
//  The format buttons are tri-state. Set their
//  proper states.
//
        if (cf.dwMask & CFM_BOLD)
            m_ctlFormatBold.SetCheck (cf.dwEffects &
                                CFE_BOLD ? 1 : 0);
        Else
            m_ctlFormatBold.SetCheck (2);
        if (cf.dwMask & CFM_ITALIC)
            m_ctlFormatItalic.SetCheck (cf.dwEffects &
                                CFE_ITALIC ? 1 : 0);
        Else
            m_ctlFormatItalic.SetCheck (2);

        if (cf.dwMask & CFM_UNDERLINE)
            m_ctlFormatUnderline.SetCheck (cf.dwEffects &
                                CFE_UNDERLINE ? 1 : 0);
```

```
        Else
            m_ctlFormatUnderline.SetCheck (2);

        if (cf.dwMask & CFM_STRIKEOUT)
            m_ctlFormatStrikeout.SetCheck (cf.dwEffects &
                                    CFE_STRIKEOUT ? 1 : 0);
        Else
            m_ctlFormatStrikeout.SetCheck (2);

        if (pf.dwMask = PFM_ALIGNMENT)
        {
            switch (pf.wAlignment)
            {
                case PFA_LEFT:
                    m_ctlParaLeft.SetCheck (1);
                    m_ctlParaRight.SetCheck (0);
                    m_ctlParaCenter.SetCheck (0);
                    break;
                case PFA_RIGHT:
                    m_ctlParaLeft.SetCheck (0);
                    m_ctlParaRight.SetCheck (1);
                    m_ctlParaCenter.SetCheck (0);
                    break;
                case PFA_CENTER:
                    m_ctlParaLeft.SetCheck (0);
                    m_ctlParaRight.SetCheck (0);
                    m_ctlParaCenter.SetCheck (1);
                    break;
            }
        }
        else
        {
            m_ctlParaLeft.SetCheck (2);
            m_ctlParaRight.SetCheck (2);
            m_ctlParaCenter.SetCheck (2);
        }
}

void CRichEditDlg::OnGetdispinfoFontbox(NMHDR* pNMHDR,
                                        LRESULT* pResult)
{
    // TODO: Add your control notification
    // handler code here
    NMCOMBOBOXEX *pData = (NMCOMBOBOXEX *) pNMHDR;
    COMBOBOXEXITEM *pItem = &pData->ceItem;
    if (pItem->mask & CBEIF_TEXT)
    {
        POSITION pos = m_FontData.FindIndex (pItem->iItem);
        CFontData cfd = m_FontData.GetAt (pos);
        ::lstrcpy (pItem->pszText, (LPCSTR) cfd.m_strName);
    }
    *pResult = 0;
}
```

The formatting, event mask, and notification messages will be covered in the next few tips, but there are a couple of things about this property page not related to the rich edit control that need explanation.

When you enumerate the fonts, the function doesn't add the font to the extended combo box directly. Remember that the extended combo box doesn't do any sorting, and you want this font list to be sorted. Instead, the fonts are sorted by name as they are delivered by the enumeration function and are stored in a *CList* object, *m_FontData*. After all the font names have been stored, they are read back and entered in the extended combo box. Because the class instance is storing the names, there's no reason to waste the memory to have the control hold the names as well, so you'll use *LPSTR_TEXTCALLBACK* in the text member of the *COMBOBOXEXITEM* structure. When the control needs to draw an item, it calls you back and you give it the text to draw, one item at a time, in the *OnGetdispinfoFontbox()* function.

This class also draws directly on the dialog box outside the control areas to write the legends for the buttons at a 60-degree angle. You don't need a control to draw on a dialog box; it's a fairly good drawing surface even if the documentation tells you that you need a control. Just add a message handler for the *ON_PAINT* message, and draw your own lines, boxes, text, or whatever—even add graphics, if you want. In this case, you want to have legends for the buttons, and they just aren't wide enough to accept the text. The static text control produces a rectangle, so even if you used it, the width of the boxes would overlap, and you would have to derive a class and add the draw code anyway. So, you create a font that is tilted clockwise 60 degrees, locate the center of each box, and draw its legend directly on the dialog box surface. It's clean, it's easy, and it works.

866. *Character Formatting in a Rich Edit Control*

Character formatting consists of setting the text attributes—bold, italic, underline, and strikeout—and its font, size, and color. The *CRichEditCtrl* class contains member functions to perform all of these operations as well as to retrieve the current character formatting.

Paragraph formatting consists of setting the attributes for an entire paragraph (a paragraph is the block of text between newline characters). These include the alignment—left, right, or center—and the tabs, indents, and numbering. The *CRichEditCtrl* class also contains members to set the paragraph format and to retrieve the current paragraph format.

Character formatting is achieved using the *CHARFORMAT* structure, setting the individual member variables, and then setting the flags to indicate which format items you want to modify. Then you call *SetSelectionCharFormat()* to set the new formats. If you don't set the proper flag, the rich edit control won't change the format.

You can retrieve the current character formatting by calling *GetSelectionCharFormat()*, passing a *reference* to a *CHARFORMAT* structure as the only parameter. You don't have to set the flag bits to retrieve the current character formatting. When the function returns, the rich edit control will have set the flag bits to indicate which structure members are valid. If there is no selected text in the control, all the members should be valid. If there is text selected and the selection spans a format change, the mask bit for that format won't be set. For example, if you select some text in the control and that selection includes some bold and some non-bold text, the *CFM_BOLD* bit won't be set when the *GetSelection CharFormat()* function returns. You can use this fact to set or unset the bold button, or to set it to an indeterminate state.

For each of the four formatting buttons, you're interested in only one value, so the code sets that bit in the *dwFlags* member. The effects bit is *XOR*'d with the current value. Remember that the *XOR* operator sometimes is known as the "toggle" operator because if you *XOR* a bit with a 1, it always toggles the bit value. The button either is being pressed down or is being released, in each case from an opposite state, so the toggle works just fine on it. Then you set the selection to the new value by calling *SetSelectionCharFormat()*, and you set the check on the button (up or down), depending upon the result of the *XOR* operation. Finally, the focus is returned to the rich edit control.

The *CRichEditCtrl* class also has functions for getting and setting the default character format. If you are not planning to use the default font (you know, that euglee one) or other default values such as point size, you should call *SetDefaultCharFormat()* immediately after the control is created to set your own defaults. If you don't and the user presses Ctrl+End, the caret will go to the very end of the text in the control and revert to the default format. Setting your own defaults ensures that this won't happen.

Paragraph formatting is achieved in much the same way as character formatting, but using the *PARAFORMAT* structure instead. You can use *CRichEditCtrl* member functions to format paragraphs and to retrieve formatting information. Paragraph-formatting attributes include alignment, tabs, and indents. You can get the current paragraph formatting by calling *GetParaFormat()* and passing a *reference* to a *PARAFORMAT* structure.

As with the character formatting, you must set the proper bit in the *dwMask* member, or the control won't apply the new format. The new value is entered in the proper member variable. For the three alignment buttons, this is the *wAlignment* member, which can have one and only one of three values: *PFA_LEFT*, *PFA_CENTER*, and *PFA_RIGHT*. To set this value, you must set the *PFM_ALIGNMENT* bit in the *dwMask* member.

To set an indented paragraph, you set the *PFM_STARTINDENT* or *PFM_RIGHTINDENT* flags, or both. The amount of the left indent is placed in the *dxStartIndent* member, and the right indent value is placed in the *dxRightIndent* member. In this sample, the indent amount is the height of a line of text, and it is applied to both the left and the right sides of the paragraph. You can apply separate values to the indents. You apply paragraph formatting by using the *SetParaFormat()* member function.

When the user presses the Increase Indent button, the indent is added to any previous indent. The Decrease Indent button subtracts from the indent. The control won't indent with a value of less than 0, so you don't need to test for and avoid a negative indent.

867. *Setting Colors in a Rich Edit Control*

The rich edit control permits you to set the color of the text and the control's background color. You don't have to handle the *WM_CTLCOLOR* message to set the background color. Without providing your own drawing code, you can't set the background color for individual characters; you can set only the background color for the entire control.

Set the background color by calling the *SetBackgroundColor()* member function. This function takes two parameters. The first is a Microsoft *BOOL* value indicating whether the background should be set to the system color. The second parameter is a *COLORREF* value indicating the new background color. If the first parameter is *TRUE*, the *COLORREF* value is ignored and the background is set to *COLOR_WINDOW*, which usually is white. If the first parameter is *FALSE*, the background is set to the value of the *COLORREF* parameter.

Setting the color of the text itself involves the character-formatting structure, *CHARFORMAT*. As with the formatting buttons, you must set a flag, *CFM_COLOR*, in the *dwFlags* member to set the color. You then set the *crTextColor* member to the *COLORREF* value for the text color and then call *SetSelectionCharFormat()* to activate the new color. You can change the color at the same time that you set other formats by OR'ing the mask values into the *dwMask* member.

If you change the text color, you also should turn off the *CFE_AUTOCOLOR* bit in the *dwEffects* member variable. If this bit is set, the text color always will be the result of *GetSys Color(COLOR_WINDOWTEXT)*, which is usually black, and setting your own color won't have any effect. Turn off the autocolor bit using *cf.dwEffects &= ~CFE_AUTOCOLOR*, where *cf* is the *CHAR-*

FORMAT instance. Setting the auto color effects bit is controlled using the *CFM_COLOR* bit in the *dwMask* member variable.

868. Understanding the Rich Edit Event Mask

The rich edit control is a polite control. Although it is capable of sending a rich selection of messages back to its parent window, it won't fetter your program with a lot of messages that you don't want to see. You have to tell it specifically what messages you want to receive. You do this by sending the control an *EM_SETEVENTMASK* message with a set of flags in the *lParam* argument. When you are using the *CRichEditCtrl* class, you can call the *SetEventMask()* member function.

If you intend to process any messages from the control, you must set the proper bit in the event mask. The MSDN documentation doesn't contain a concise list of the flags and their meanings, but you'll find them defined in *richedit.h*. They are listed in Table 868.

Event Mask	Value	Meaning
ENM_NONE	0x00000000	No event flags are set.
ENM_CHANGE	0x00000001	The user has taken some action that might have altered the text in the control. This is sent after updated text has been displayed. See *ENM_UPDATE*.
ENM_UPDATE	0x00000002	Notifies the parent when altered text is about to be displayed. The text has been formatted for display but has not yet been displayed.
ENM_SCROLL	0x00000004	Notifies the parent when the text scrolls.
ENM_KEYEVENTS	0x00010000	Notifies the parent of keyboard events.
ENM_MOUSEEVENTS	0x00020000	Notifies the parent of mouse events.
ENM_REQUESTRESIZE	0x00040000	Notifies the parent when the control's contents are either larger or smaller than the control's window.
ENM_SELCHANGE	0x00080000	Notifies the parent when the character selection in the control changes.
ENM_DROPFILES	0x00100000	The user is attempting to drop a file into the control's window using drag and drop.
ENM_PROTECTED	0x00200000	The user is attempting to change a block of text that is protected.
ENM_CORRECTTEXT	0x00400000	Is used to signal a selection event when a pen is used.
ENM_SCROLLEVENTS	0x00000008	Notifies the parent of a scrollbar event.
ENM_DRAGDROPDONE	0x00000010	The parent window is notified when a drag-and-drop operation has been completed.

Table 868   Mask bits used to set the rich edit control's event mask. Only notification messages with the event mask bit set will be sent to the parent window.

Combine these flags by *OR*'ing them together in a *DWORD* variable or directly in the call to *SetEventMask()*. You can get the current event mask by calling *GetEventMask()*. In the sample control, you want to be notified when the text has been changed (in case you want to set a flag indicating that the text has been modified) and when a mouse or keyboard event occurs, so the event mask is set using the following two lines:

```
long mask = m_RichSample.GetEventMask();
m_RichSample.SetEventMask (mask | ENM_UPDATE
                | ENM_KEYEVENTS | ENM_MOUSEEVENTS);
```

Actually, the default mask is *ENM_NONE*, indicating that no event notification is requested, so the first line could be eliminated.

869. Understanding Rich Edit Control Notification Messages

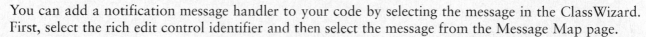

You can add a notification message handler to your code by selecting the message in the ClassWizard. First, select the rich edit control identifier and then select the message from the Message Map page.

Most of the notification messages are listed, and their names match those in the event mask list shown in Tip 868, "Understanding the Rich Edit Event Mask," but you'll notice a particularly odd one in the list: *EN_MSGFILTER*. Rather than send a cacophony of keyboard messages such as *WM_KEY-DOWN*, *WM_KEYUP*, and *WM_CHAR*, and mouse messages such as *WM_MOUSEMOVE* and a slough of click and double-click events, the control groups them all together in a single message, *EN_MSGFILTER*. This enables you to have a single message handler to process all the keyboard and mouse messages.

This is particularly handy when using a rich edit control because you want to know when the user changes the text or caret position so that you can update your button controls and perhaps member variables for the dialog box.

The *EN_MSGFILTER* message is sent *before* the messages have been processed by the rich edit control, so you have an opportunity to handle them first, intercede with some operations of your own, or simply pass them on to the control for handling. In the sample code, the *OnMsgfilterRichSample()* function uses these messages to get the character and paragraph formatting and to update the other controls on the dialog box.

The message information in contained in a pointer to a *MSGFILTER* structure, which is cast to a *NMHDR* (Notification Message HeaDeR) pointer in the parameter list. Just cast it back to a *MSGFIL-TER* pointer. The message ID is in the *msg* member, and the *lParam* and *wParam* members are the same as for any message event.

If you handle a message and do not want the control to process it, set the **pResult* variable to a non-zero value. If you want the control to process the message as well, set the value to 0. For example, suppose that you want the control to handle all the character and mouse events, but you want to intercept the Enter key and add a paragraph mark, a newline character, and a tab. In this case, you wouldn't want the control to process the message as well, so you would add the following code:

```
MSGFILTER *pMsgFilter =
            reinterpret_cast<MSGFILTER *>(pNMHDR);
if (pMsgFilter->msg == WM_CHAR)
{
    if (pMsgFilter->wParam == 0x0d)
```

```
        {
            TCHAR text[] = {_T((char) 0xB6),
                            _T((char) 0x0a), _T(0x09), 0};
            m_RichSample.ReplaceSel (text, TRUE);
            *pResult = 1;
        }
    }
```

This snippet tests only for the Enter key. In a real application, you might want to check the flag in the *lParam* member of the *MSGFILTER* structure to test for combinations of the Ctrl, Alt, and Shift keys.

870. *Understanding the Progress Control*

When time-consuming operations are being performed, it's a good idea to show the user some action on the dialog box or window frame so that he doesn't think that the program has "locked up," tempting him to reach for the Big Red Switch (you'd be surprised at how many Windows users don't know how to kill a process).

You can do this with the progress bar control, which simply draws a rectangle with a color bar to indicate the progress of an operation. The bar usually is set to indicate the portion of the operation that has been completed.

In its default state, the control draws "chunks" in the rectangle. It does have a solid bar setting, but in its default form it looks like a half-hearted attempt to simulate the bar LEDs used for indicators on stereo equipment. In real life, those bar LEDs are simulating an analog meter, and if it were economically feasible, engineers would make the LED display continuous rather than broken. So, you have a Windows control emulating a device that is emulating another device. It's like using a copy machine to reproduce a photograph and then making a copy of that reproduction. Somewhere along the line, something gets lost.

What's lost in the progress bar is precision, as you'll see in the next few tips. You might think of this as the "peanut butter control" because it comes in two styles, chunky and creamy. For all that it does, it might as well be peanut butter.

The progress bar may be oriented horizontally or vertically, but it isn't smart enough to figure out from its own size what orientation it should take. It defaults to horizontal, and if you want a vertical control, you must specifically set that style.

871. *Using the* CProgressCtl *Class*

For a class library that purports to be a leader in the field, some of the Microsoft Foundation Class implementations are pretty dismal. The *CProgressCtrl* is one of these. There are better implementations of the progress bar control in free libraries that are available on the Web.

CProgressCtrl gives you only basic functionality. You can draw a color bar in the control, period. There are no tick marks, no text, and no other information that you can display with this control. In Tip 819, "Deriving a Custom Class from *CStatic* to Gain Functionality," you saw how easy it was to implement this basic functionality using only the static text control.

But, sigh, you want to use the progress bar control anyway. OK, create a new property page for the Controls project. Name it *IDD_PROPPAGE_PROGRESSBARDLG*, and title it Progress Bar. Add the controls as shown in Figure 871. The three scroll-like controls off to the right are spinner controls. Don't worry about sizing them or where you place them; you'll "buddy" them with the edit controls, and the dialog box procedure will take care of that for you. (You'll learn about buddy controls in the tips on spinner controls beginning with Tip 882, "Understanding the Spin Control.")

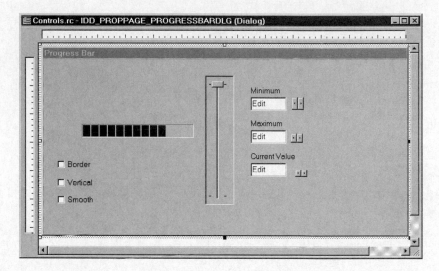

Figure 871   The Progress Bar page is fairly simple because the control has limited functionality

Set the tab order so that the edit control next to each spinner falls just before the spinner control. Get the Properties dialog box for the spinner control, and check the Auto Buddy and Set Buddy Integer styles. Also set the Orientation to Horizontal and the Alignment to Right. This will join the spinners and edit controls so that the spinners appear in the right side of the edit controls.

Create a new class for this property page named *CProgressBarDlg*. Make sure that it is derived from *CPropertyPage* (hate to keep reminding you, but it is pretty easy to overlook this step, or to select the wrong base class). The header file is shown here:

```
// ProgressBarDlg.h : header file
//

/////////////////////////////////////////////////////////////////
// CProgressBarDlg dialog

class CProgressBarDlg : public CPropertyPage
{
    DECLARE_DYNCREATE(CProgressBarDlg)

// Construction
public:
    CProgressBarDlg();
    ~CProgressBarDlg();

// Dialog Data
    //{{AFX_DATA(CProgressBarDlg)
    enum { IDD = IDD_PROPPAGE_PROGRESSBARDLG };
    CProgressCtrl   m_ctlProgBarSample;
    CSliderCtrl m_ctlProgBarSlider;
    CSpinButtonCtrl m_ctlSpinMin;
```

```
    CSpinButtonCtrl m_ctlSpinMax;
    CSpinButtonCtrl m_ctlSpinCur;
    BOOL    m_bProgBarVertical;
    BOOL    m_bProgBarSmooth;
    BOOL    m_bProgBarBorder;
    int     m_nProgBarSlider;
    int     m_nRangeMax;
    int     m_nRangeCur;
    int     m_nRangeMin;
    //}}AFX_DATA

// Overrides
    // ClassWizard generate virtual function overrides
    //{{AFX_VIRTUAL(CProgressBarDlg)
    protected:
    virtual void DoDataExchange(CDataExchange* pDX);
    // DDX/DDV support
    //}}AFX_VIRTUAL

// Implementation
protected:
    void AdjustSliderRect(CSliderCtrl &ctlSlider);
 DWORD m_dwProgBarStyle;
    int m_nStep;
    void RecreateProgBar(bool bOrientation = false);
    // Generated message map functions
    //{{AFX_MSG(CProgressBarDlg)
    afx_msg void OnProgbarVertical();
    afx_msg void OnProgbarSmooth();
    afx_msg void OnProgbarBorder();
    virtual BOOL OnInitDialog();
    afx_msg void OnHScroll(UINT nSBCode, UINT nPos,
                       CScrollBar* pScrollBar);
    afx_msg void OnVScroll(UINT nSBCode, UINT nPos,
                       CScrollBar* pScrollBar);
    afx_msg void OnChangeProgbarRangemax();
    afx_msg void OnChangeProgbarRangemin();
    afx_msg void OnChangeProgbarRangecur();
    //}}AFX_MSG
    DECLARE_MESSAGE_MAP()

};
```

There are a lot of message handlers in this code but none for the progress bar itself. That's because the control doesn't send any, other than a notification that it is out of memory, and that's not likely to happen. The code for the implementation is shown here:

```
// ProgressBarDlg.cpp : implementation file
//

#include "stdafx.h"
#include "controls.h"
#include "ProgressBarDlg.h"

#ifdef _DEBUG
#define new DEBUG_NEW
```

```cpp
#undef THIS_FILE
static char THIS_FILE[] = __FILE__;
#endif


/////////////////////////////////////////////////////////////
// CProgressBarDlg property page
// ProgressBarDlg.cpp : implementation file
//

#include "stdafx.h"
#include "controls.h"
#include "ProgressBarDlg.h"

#ifdef _DEBUG
#define new DEBUG_NEW
#undef THIS_FILE
static char THIS_FILE[] = __FILE__;
#endif

/////////////////////////////////////////////////////////////
// CProgressBarDlg property page

IMPLEMENT_DYNCREATE(CProgressBarDlg, CPropertyPage)

CProgressBarDlg::CProgressBarDlg()
                : CPropertyPage(CProgressBarDlg::IDD)
{
    //{{AFX_DATA_INIT(CProgressBarDlg)
    m_bProgBarVertical = FALSE;
    m_bProgBarSmooth = FALSE;
    m_bProgBarBorder = FALSE;
    m_nRangeMax = 100;
    m_nRangeCur = 0;
    m_nRangeMin = 0;
    m_nStep = 1;
    m_nProgBarSlider = 0;
    //}}AFX_DATA_INIT
    m_psp.dwFlags &= ~PSP_HASHELP;
}


CProgressBarDlg::~CProgressBarDlg()
{
}


void CProgressBarDlg::DoDataExchange(CDataExchange* pDX)
{
    CPropertyPage::DoDataExchange(pDX);
    //{{AFX_DATA_MAP(CProgressBarDlg)
    DDX_Control(pDX, IDC_SPIN_MIN, m_ctlSpinMin);
    DDX_Control(pDX, IDC_SPIN_MAX, m_ctlSpinMax);
    DDX_Control(pDX, IDC_SPIN_CURVAL, m_ctlSpinCur);
    DDX_Control(pDX, IDC_PROGBAR_SAMPLE,
                     m_ctlProgBarSample);
    DDX_Control(pDX, IDC_PROGBAR_SLIDER,
                     m_ctlProgBarSlider);
    DDX_Check(pDX, IDC_PROGBAR_VERTICAL,
```

```
                        m_bProgBarVertical);
    DDX_Check(pDX, IDC_PROGBAR_SMOOTH, m_bProgBarSmooth);
    DDX_Check(pDX, IDC_PROGBAR_BORDER, m_bProgBarBorder);
    DDX_Slider(pDX, IDC_PROGBAR_SLIDER, m_nProgBarSlider);
    DDX_Text(pDX, IDC_PROGBAR_RANGEMAX, m_nRangeMax);
    DDX_Text(pDX, IDC_PROGBAR_RANGECUR, m_nRangeCur);
    DDX_Text(pDX, IDC_PROGBAR_RANGEMIN, m_nRangeMin);
    //}}AFX_DATA_MAP
}


BEGIN_MESSAGE_MAP(CProgressBarDlg, CPropertyPage)
    //{{AFX_MSG_MAP(CProgressBarDlg)
    ON_BN_CLICKED(IDC_PROGBAR_VERTICAL, OnProgbarVertical)
    ON_BN_CLICKED(IDC_PROGBAR_SMOOTH, OnProgbarSmooth)
    ON_BN_CLICKED(IDC_PROGBAR_BORDER, OnProgbarBorder)
    ON_WM_HSCROLL()
    ON_WM_VSCROLL()
    ON_EN_CHANGE(IDC_PROGBAR_RANGEMAX,
                    OnChangeProgbarRangemax)
    ON_EN_CHANGE(IDC_PROGBAR_RANGEMIN,
                    OnChangeProgbarRangemin)
    ON_EN_CHANGE(IDC_PROGBAR_RANGECUR,
                    OnChangeProgbarRangecur)
    //}}AFX_MSG_MAP
END_MESSAGE_MAP()

/////////////////////////////////////////////////////////
// CProgressBarDlg message handlers

BOOL CProgressBarDlg::OnInitDialog()
{
    CPropertyPage::OnInitDialog();

    m_ctlProgBarSample.SetRange (m_nRangeMin, m_nRangeMax);
    m_ctlProgBarSlider.SetRange (m_nRangeMin, m_nRangeMax);
    m_ctlSpinMin.SetRange32 (m_nRangeMin, m_nRangeMax);
    m_ctlSpinMax.SetRange32 (m_nRangeMin, m_nRangeMax);
    m_ctlSpinCur.SetRange32 (m_nRangeMin, m_nRangeMax);
    m_ctlProgBarSample.SetPos (m_nRangeCur);
    m_ctlProgBarSlider.SetPos (m_nRangeMax);
    m_dwProgBarStyle = m_ctlProgBarSample.GetStyle ();
    AdjustSliderRect (m_ctlProgBarSlider);
    return TRUE;
}


void CProgressBarDlg::OnProgbarVertical()
{
    UpdateData (TRUE);
    if (m_bProgBarVertical)
    {
        m_dwProgBarStyle |= PBS_VERTICAL;
    }
    else
    {
        m_dwProgBarStyle &= ~PBS_VERTICAL;
```

```
    }
    RecreateProgBar (true);
}

void CProgressBarDlg::OnProgbarSmooth()
{
    UpdateData (TRUE);
    if (m_bProgBarSmooth)
    {
        m_dwProgBarStyle |= PBS_SMOOTH;
    }
    else
    {
        m_dwProgBarStyle &= ~PBS_SMOOTH;
    }
    RecreateProgBar ();
}

void CProgressBarDlg::OnProgbarBorder()
{
    UpdateData (TRUE);
    if (m_bProgBarBorder)
    {
        m_dwProgBarStyle |= WS_BORDER;
    }
    else
    {
        m_dwProgBarStyle &= ~WS_BORDER;
    }
    RecreateProgBar ();
}

void CProgressBarDlg::RecreateProgBar(bool bOrientation)
{
    CRect rc;
    m_ctlProgBarSample.GetWindowRect (&rc);
    ScreenToClient (&rc);
    int nUpper, nLower;
    m_ctlProgBarSample.GetRange (nLower, nUpper);
    int nPos = m_ctlProgBarSample.GetPos ();
    m_ctlProgBarSample.DestroyWindow ();
    CRect rcNew = rc;
    if (bOrientation)
    {
        CPoint ptMid;
        ptMid.x = rc.left + (rc.right - rc.left) / 2;
        ptMid.y = rc.top + (rc.bottom - rc.top) / 2;
        if (m_dwProgBarStyle & PBS_VERTICAL)
        {
            int nHeight = rc.right - rc.left;
            int nWidth = rc.bottom - rc.top;
            rcNew.top = ptMid.y - nHeight / 2;
            rcNew.bottom = ptMid.y + nHeight / 2;
            rcNew.left = ptMid.x - nWidth / 2;
            rcNew.right = ptMid.x + nWidth / 2;
        }
```

```cpp
        else
        {
            int nHeight = rc.right - rc.left;
            int nWidth = rc.bottom - rc.top;
            rcNew.top = ptMid.y - nHeight / 2;
            rcNew.bottom = ptMid.y + nHeight / 2;
            rcNew.left = ptMid.x - nWidth / 2;
            rcNew.right = ptMid.x + nWidth / 2;
        }
    }
    m_ctlProgBarSample.Create (m_dwProgBarStyle,
                        rcNew, this, IDC_PROGBAR_SAMPLE);
    m_ctlProgBarSample.SetRange32 (nLower, nUpper);
    m_ctlProgBarSlider.SetRange (nLower, nUpper);
    m_ctlProgBarSample.SetPos (nPos);
}

void CProgressBarDlg::OnHScroll(UINT nSBCode, UINT nPos,
                                CScrollBar* pScrollBar)
{

    CPropertyPage::OnHScroll(nSBCode, nPos, pScrollBar);
}

void CProgressBarDlg::OnVScroll(UINT nSBCode,
                                UINT nPos,
                                CScrollBar* pScrollBar)
{
    UpdateData (TRUE);
    if (pScrollBar == (CScrollBar *) &m_ctlProgBarSlider)
    {
        int nPos = m_nProgBarSlider;
        int nLower, nUpper;
        m_ctlProgBarSample.GetRange (nLower, nUpper);
        int nActual = nLower + nUpper - nPos;
        m_ctlProgBarSample.SetPos (nActual);
        m_nRangeCur = nActual;
        UpdateData (FALSE);
        return;
    }
    CPropertyPage::OnVScroll(nSBCode, nPos, pScrollBar);
}

//
// The following three functions get called even
// before the dialog box is created. Test whether
// the progress bar window is NULL, and return
// if so.
//
void CProgressBarDlg::OnChangeProgbarRangemax()
{
    if (m_ctlProgBarSample.m_hWnd == NULL)
        return;
    int nRangeOld = m_nRangeMax;
    UpdateData (TRUE);
    int nLower, nUpper;
```

```
        m_ctlProgBarSample.GetRange (nLower, nUpper);
        if (m_nRangeMax <= nLower)
        {
            m_nRangeMax = nRangeOld;
            UpdateData (FALSE);
            return;
        }
        m_ctlProgBarSample.SetRange32 (nLower, m_nRangeMax);
        m_ctlProgBarSlider.SetRange (nLower, m_nRangeMax);
        m_nProgBarSlider = nLower + nUpper - m_nRangeCur;
        if (m_nRangeMax < m_nRangeCur)
        {
            m_nRangeCur = m_nRangeMax;
            m_ctlProgBarSample.SetPos (m_nRangeMax);
        }
        UpdateData (FALSE);
}

void CProgressBarDlg::OnChangeProgbarRangemin()
{
        if (m_ctlProgBarSample.m_hWnd == NULL)
            return;
        int nRangeOld = m_nRangeMin;
        UpdateData (TRUE);
        int nLower, nUpper;
        m_ctlProgBarSample.GetRange (nLower, nUpper);
        if (m_nRangeMin >= nUpper)
        {
            m_nRangeMin = nRangeOld;
            UpdateData (FALSE);
            return;
        }
        m_ctlProgBarSample.SetRange32 (m_nRangeMin, nUpper);
        m_ctlProgBarSlider.SetRange (m_nRangeMin, nUpper);
        m_nProgBarSlider = nLower + nUpper - m_nRangeCur;
        if (m_nRangeMin > m_nRangeCur)
        {
            m_nRangeCur = m_nRangeMin;
            m_ctlProgBarSample.SetPos (m_nRangeMin);
        }
        UpdateData (FALSE);
}

void CProgressBarDlg::OnChangeProgbarRangecur()
{
        if (m_ctlProgBarSample.m_hWnd == NULL)
            return;
        int nRangeOld = m_nRangeCur;
        UpdateData (TRUE);
        int nLower, nUpper;
        m_ctlProgBarSample.GetRange (nLower, nUpper);
        if (m_nRangeCur < nLower)
        {
            m_nRangeCur = nRangeOld;
            UpdateData (FALSE);
            return;
```

```
        }
        if (m_nRangeCur > nUpper)
        {
            m_nRangeCur = nRangeOld;
            UpdateData (FALSE);
            return;
        }
        m_ctlProgBarSample.SetPos (m_nRangeCur);
        m_nProgBarSlider = nLower + nUpper - m_nRangeCur;
        UpdateData (FALSE);
    }


    void CProgressBarDlg::AdjustSliderRect(
                                    CSliderCtrl &ctlSlider)
    {
        int nExtra = 0;
        DWORD dwSliderStyle = ctlSlider.GetStyle ();
        DWORD dwSliderStyleEx = ctlSlider.GetExStyle ();
    //
    //  If the control has a border or edge, give it a bit
    //  extra on the right or bottom to account for the edge.
    //
        if ((dwSliderStyle & WS_BORDER) ||
            (dwSliderStyleEx & (WS_EX_CLIENTEDGE
                            | WS_EX_STATICEDGE
                            | WS_EX_DLGMODALFRAME)))
            nExtra = 4;

        CRect rcThumb, rcSlider;
        ctlSlider.GetThumbRect (&rcThumb);
        ctlSlider.GetWindowRect (&rcSlider);
        ScreenToClient (&rcSlider);
        if (dwSliderStyle & TBS_VERT)
        {
            rcSlider.right = rcSlider.left + rcThumb.left
                        + rcThumb.right + nExtra;
        }
        else
            rcSlider.bottom = rcSlider.top + rcThumb.top
                        + rcThumb.bottom + nExtra;
        ctlSlider.MoveWindow (&rcSlider, TRUE);
    }
```

In the *OnVScroll()* message handler, make sure that you test the identity of the control before executing the scroll code. On this page, the three spinner controls as well as the slider control send scroll messages. You want to respond only to the slider control. The spin controls are buddies with the edit controls, and you get their new values by responding to the edit control *EN_CHANGE* messages.

The last function in the source file, *AdjustSliderRect()*, handles a problem with the slider control itself. You'll see why you need this function in Tip 877, "Using Slider Controls."

872. *Understanding Progress Bar Styles*

The progress control is a little short on style, and it's short on styles that you can set as well. Other than the usual *WS_BORDER* and the extended frame styles, you have only two options. You can set it to be a vertical progress bar, and you can change it from chunky to smooth.

You can't, however, change these styles once the control has been created. If you want it smooth or vertical, or both, you must select those styles before the progress bar is put together.

In the sample code for the progress bar in Tip 871, "Using the *CProgressCtl* Class," you used the trick of saving the pertinent information and then destroying the control. It gets re-created with the new style, and the upper and lower bounds and the current position are restored. In *RecreateProgBar()*, if the modification is to change the orientation, you find the center of the control and then rotate its rectangle 90 degrees clockwise or counterclockwise before re-creating the control.

873. *Setting the Progress Bar Range and Position*

The default range for a progress bar is 0 through 100, but you can set these to any value that your application needs. Get the current range by calling *GetRange()* and the current position by calling *GetPos()*. To set the range, call *SetRange()* or *SetRange32()*; to set the current position, call *SetPos()*.

In the sample code, there are four different controls that act on the range and position values, so the code is a little more complicated than you would have in a typical application. The two spinners set the maximum and minimum positions, while the slider and the third spinner set the current position.

The range minimum must be less than the range maximum, but it doesn't have to start at 0. There are two functions to set the range. The first, *SetRange()*, takes two short integers (16-bit values) as arguments. The second, *SetRange32()*, takes two integers as arguments.

874. *Understanding Progress Bar Operations*

If you want accuracy in a progress bar, you should avoid the progress control's chunky mode. As a result of its double agent act of trying to emulate a digital device emulating an analog device, the control loses significant accuracy in the chunky mode.

The purpose of a progress bar is to keep users apprised of the state of a lengthy operation so that they don't get tempted to hit the reset button, erroneously thinking that the machine is hung up. In the chunky mode, the Windows progress bar shows a full bar long before you have set its position to the maximum value.

Select the Progress Bar page of the *Controls* application, and make sure that the progress bar is in chunky mode (the Smooth style is unchecked); then, move the slider so that the progress bar shows about 80 or 85 percent of maximum. You can read this value in the Current Value edit box.

Using the spinner control that's buddied with the Current Value edit box, slowly raise the value for the progress bar. The slider control should move up as you do. When you reach about 93, the progress bar shows 100 percent. If this indeed is a lengthy operation, taking perhaps several minutes, then the user has a lot of time between the time that the progress bar reaches maximum and the time that the operation is completed to ponder the effects of a system crash. You need to take this into account in chunky style and not set the value to greater than 93 percent until the operation truly is complete.

The situation doesn't improve by increasing the range. With a range of 0 to 1,000, the progress bar shows full throttle when its value is only 921. The indicator also jumps in chunks and doesn't draw a partial rectangle as its value increases. Because of this, the chunky style should be considered as a flashy style rather than a substantial style.

You'll notice that in most of Microsoft's applications, such as installations and updates, the smooth style rather than the chunky style is used.

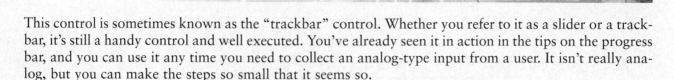

875. *Understanding the Slider Control*

This control is sometimes known as the "trackbar" control. Whether you refer to it as a slider or a trackbar, it's still a handy control and well executed. You've already seen it in action in the tips on the progress bar, and you can use it any time you need to collect an analog-type input from a user. It isn't really analog, but you can make the steps so small that it seems so.

The control gets its name—the "slider" name, that is—from the fact that it looks like the slide potentiometers used as volume controls on audio equipment. It can be oriented horizontally or vertically. But, like the progress bar control, it can't tell from its own size which orientation it should have. You have to set the style option when you create the control. For this control, however, that's understandable because the selection will determine what type of message is sent back to the parent window.

The slider replaces the scroll bar that you used in Tip 852, "Using the Scroll Bar as an Input Control," to get input from the user. In fact, the slider control sends scroll messages to the parent window. In horizontal mode, it sends a *WM_HSCROLL* message when the user adjusts the control, and in its vertical style it sends a *WM_VSCROLL* message.

Like the scroll bar, it has a "thumb" that the user can grab to pull the control up or down (or right to left). However, it doesn't have the end arrows of the scroll bar, but a user can click the mouse along the track bar and move the thumb a page at a time. The control captures the keyboard input when it has the focus, and all the cursor movement keys—Home, Page Up, the arrow keys, and so on—can be used to move the thumb in lieu of grabbing the thumb with the mouse.

The slider can be constructed with tick marks along either or both sides, and it can contain a highlighted selection range that can be programmed to follow the thumb movements—essentially its own progress bar. Tick marks can be added automatically with a specified frequency, or you can program them manually.

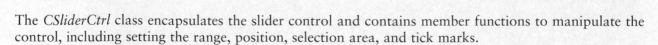

876. *Understanding the CSliderCtrl Class*

The *CSliderCtrl* class encapsulates the slider control and contains member functions to manipulate the control, including setting the range, position, selection area, and tick marks.

The slider is a versatile control and can be configured in many different ways. The control's styles can be changed on the fly in your application code without having to destroy and re-create the control or call the *SetWindowPos()* function.

```
    int     m_nVertSelMin;
    int     m_nVertSelMax;
};
```

The last two variables above—*m_nVertSelMin* and *m_nVertSelMax*—will contain the upper and lower limits of the fixed selection area for the vertical slider. For the horizontal slider, the selection will follow the thumb, which is why there's a message handler for *WM_HSCROLL* but none for *WM_VSCROLL*.

The source file is shown here:

```
// SliderDlg.cpp : implementation file
//

#include "stdafx.h"
#include "controls.h"
#include "SliderDlg.h"

#ifdef _DEBUG
#define new DEBUG_NEW
#undef THIS_FILE
static char THIS_FILE[] = __FILE__;
#endif


/////////////////////////////////////////////////////////////
// CSliderDlg property page

IMPLEMENT_DYNCREATE(CSliderDlg, CPropertyPage)

CSliderDlg::CSliderDlg() : CPropertyPage(CSliderDlg::IDD)
{
    //{{AFX_DATA_INIT(CSliderDlg)
    m_bVertTickMarks = FALSE;
    m_bVertAutoTick = FALSE;
    m_nVertPoints = 0;
    m_bVertEnableSel = FALSE;
    m_nVertLowerLimit = 0;
    m_nVertUpperLimit = 100;
    m_nVertSlider = 0;
    m_nVertTickFreq = 2;
    m_bHorzAutoTick = FALSE;
    m_bHorzEnableSel = FALSE;
    m_nHorzLowerLimit = 0;
    m_nHorzPoints = 0;
    m_nHorzSlider = 0;
    m_bHorzTickMarks = FALSE;
    m_nHorzUpperLimit = 100;
    m_nHorzTickFreq = 1;
    //}}AFX_DATA_INIT
    m_psp.dwFlags &= ~PSP_HASHELP;
    m_nVertSelMin = -1;
    m_nVertSelMax = -1;
}

CSliderDlg::~CSliderDlg()
{
}
```

```cpp
void CSliderDlg::DoDataExchange(CDataExchange* pDX)
{
    CPropertyPage::DoDataExchange(pDX);
    //{{AFX_DATA_MAP(CSliderDlg)
    DDX_Control(pDX, IDC_HORZ_TICKFREQEDIT,
                m_ctlHorzTickFreq);
    DDX_Control(pDX, IDC_HORZ_TICKFREQSPIN,
                m_ctlHorzTickFreqSpinner);
    DDX_Control(pDX, IDC_HORZ_SLIDER, m_ctlHorzSlider);
    DDX_Control(pDX, IDC_VERT_SLIDER, m_ctlVertSlider);
    DDX_Control(pDX, IDC_VERT_TICKFREQEDIT,
                m_ctlVertTickFreq);
    DDX_Control(pDX, IDC_VERT_TICKFREQSPIN,
                m_ctlVertTickFreqSpinner);
    DDX_Check(pDX, IDC_VERT_TICKMARKS, m_bVertTickMarks);
    DDX_Check(pDX, IDC_VERT_AUTOTICK, m_bVertAutoTick);
    DDX_Radio(pDX, IDC_VERT_POINTSBOTH, m_nVertPoints);
    DDX_Check(pDX, IDC_VERT_ENABLESEL, m_bVertEnableSel);
    DDX_Text(pDX, IDC_VERT_LOWEREDIT, m_nVertLowerLimit);
    DDX_Text(pDX, IDC_VERT_UPPEREDIT, m_nVertUpperLimit);
    DDX_Slider(pDX, IDC_VERT_SLIDER, m_nVertSlider);
    DDX_Text(pDX, IDC_VERT_TICKFREQEDIT, m_nVertTickFreq);
    DDX_Check(pDX, IDC_HORZ_AUTOTICK, m_bHorzAutoTick);
    DDX_Check(pDX, IDC_HORZ_ENABLESEL, m_bHorzEnableSel);
    DDX_Text(pDX, IDC_HORZ_LOWEREDIT, m_nHorzLowerLimit);
    DDX_Radio(pDX, IDC_HORZ_POINTSBOTH, m_nHorzPoints);
    DDX_Slider(pDX, IDC_HORZ_SLIDER, m_nHorzSlider);
    DDX_Check(pDX, IDC_HORZ_TICKMARKS, m_bHorzTickMarks);
    DDX_Text(pDX, IDC_HORZ_UPPEREDIT, m_nHorzUpperLimit);
    DDX_Text(pDX, IDC_HORZ_TICKFREQEDIT, m_nHorzTickFreq);
    //}}AFX_DATA_MAP
}


BEGIN_MESSAGE_MAP(CSliderDlg, CPropertyPage)
    //{{AFX_MSG_MAP(CSliderDlg)
    ON_BN_CLICKED(IDC_HORZ_ENABLESEL, OnHorzEnablesel)
    ON_EN_CHANGE(IDC_HORZ_LOWEREDIT, OnChangeHorzLoweredit)
    ON_BN_CLICKED(IDC_HORZ_POINTSBOTH, OnHorzPoints)
    ON_BN_CLICKED(IDC_HORZ_TICKMARKS, OnHorzTickmarks)
    ON_EN_CHANGE(IDC_HORZ_UPPEREDIT, OnChangeHorzUpperedit)
    ON_BN_CLICKED(IDC_HORZ_AUTOTICK, OnHorzAutotick)
    ON_EN_CHANGE(IDC_HORZ_TICKFREQEDIT,
                OnChangeHorzTickfreqedit)
    ON_BN_CLICKED(IDC_VERT_ENABLESEL, OnVertEnablesel)
    ON_EN_CHANGE(IDC_VERT_LOWEREDIT, OnChangeVertLoweredit)
    ON_BN_CLICKED(IDC_VERT_POINTSBOTH, OnVertPoints)
    ON_BN_CLICKED(IDC_VERT_TICKMARKS, OnVertTickmarks)
    ON_EN_CHANGE(IDC_VERT_UPPEREDIT, OnChangeVertUpperedit)
    ON_BN_CLICKED(IDC_VERT_AUTOTICK, OnVertAutotick)
    ON_EN_CHANGE(IDC_VERT_TICKFREQEDIT,
                OnChangeVertTickfreqedit)
    ON_WM_HSCROLL()
    ON_BN_CLICKED(IDC_CLEARVERTSEL, OnClearvertsel)
    ON_BN_CLICKED(IDC_SETVERTSEL, OnSetvertsel)
```

```
    ON_BN_CLICKED(IDC_HORZ_POINTSBOTTOM, OnHorzPoints)
    ON_BN_CLICKED(IDC_HORZ_POINTSTOP, OnHorzPoints)
    ON_BN_CLICKED(IDC_VERT_POINTSRIGHT, OnVertPoints)
    ON_BN_CLICKED(IDC_VERT_POINTSLEFT, OnVertPoints)
    //}}AFX_MSG_MAP
END_MESSAGE_MAP()


/////////////////////////////////////////////////////////
// CSliderDlg message handlers
/////////////////////////////////////////////////////////
// Functions common to horizontal and vertical sliders
/////////////////////////////////////////////////////////

BOOL CSliderDlg::OnInitDialog()
{
    CPropertyPage::OnInitDialog();
    AdjustSliderRect (m_ctlVertSlider);
    AdjustSliderRect (m_ctlHorzSlider);
    m_ctlVertSlider.SetSelection (m_nVertLowerLimit,
                                  m_nVertUpperLimit);
    m_ctlHorzSlider.SetRange (m_nHorzLowerLimit,
                              m_nHorzUpperLimit, TRUE);
    m_ctlVertSlider.SetRange (m_nVertLowerLimit,
                              m_nVertUpperLimit, TRUE);
    m_ctlVertSlider.SetPos (m_nVertUpperLimit);
    m_ctlVertSlider.SetTicFreq (m_nVertTickFreq);
    ::EnableWindow (GetDlgItem (IDC_CLEARVERTSEL)->m_hWnd,
                               FALSE);
    ::EnableWindow (GetDlgItem (IDC_SETVERTSEL)->m_hWnd,
                               FALSE);
    return TRUE;
}


void CSliderDlg::AdjustSliderRect(CSliderCtrl &ctlSlider)
{
    int nExtra = 0;
    DWORD dwSliderStyle = ctlSlider.GetStyle ();
    DWORD dwSliderStyleEx = ctlSlider.GetExStyle ();
//
//  If the control has a border or edge, give it a bit
//  extra on the right or bottom to account for the edge.
//
    if ((dwSliderStyle & WS_BORDER) ||
        (dwSliderStyleEx & (WS_EX_CLIENTEDGE
                          | WS_EX_STATICEDGE
                          | WS_EX_DLGMODALFRAME)))
        nExtra = 4;

    CRect rcThumb, rcSlider;
    ctlSlider.GetThumbRect (&rcThumb);
    ctlSlider.GetWindowRect (&rcSlider);
    ScreenToClient (&rcSlider);
    if (dwSliderStyle & TBS_VERT)
    {
//
//  If the point is on the right only and there are
```

```
//  ticks, add enough room to draw the tick marks.
//
        if (!(dwSliderStyle & TBS_NOTICKS))
        {
            if (!(dwSliderStyle & (TBS_LEFT | TBS_BOTH)))
                nExtra += 4;
        }
        rcSlider.right = rcSlider.left + rcThumb.left
                       + rcThumb.right + nExtra;
    }
    else
        rcSlider.bottom = rcSlider.top + rcThumb.top
                        + rcThumb.bottom + nExtra;
    ctlSlider.MoveWindow (&rcSlider, TRUE);
}


/////////////////////////////////////////////////////////
// CSliderDlg message handlers
/////////////////////////////////////////////////////////
// Horizontal Slider Functions
/////////////////////////////////////////////////////////

void CSliderDlg::OnChangeHorzLoweredit()
{
    if (m_ctlHorzSlider.m_hWnd == NULL)
        return;
    int nMin, nMax;
    UpdateData (TRUE);
    if (m_nHorzLowerLimit >= m_nHorzUpperLimit)
    {
        nMin = m_ctlHorzSlider.GetRangeMin ();
        m_nHorzLowerLimit = nMin;
        UpdateData (FALSE);
        return;
    }
    m_ctlHorzSlider.GetRange (nMin, nMax);
    m_ctlHorzSlider.SetRange (m_nHorzLowerLimit,
                              nMax, TRUE);
    if (m_ctlHorzSlider.GetStyle () & TBS_ENABLESELRANGE)
        m_ctlHorzSlider.SetSelection (m_nHorzLowerLimit,
                                m_ctlHorzSlider.GetPos ());
    m_ctlHorzSlider.Invalidate ();
}

void CSliderDlg::OnChangeHorzUpperedit()
{
    if (m_ctlHorzSlider.m_hWnd == NULL)
        return;
    int nMin, nMax;
    UpdateData (TRUE);
    if (m_nHorzUpperLimit <= m_nHorzLowerLimit)
    {
        nMax = m_ctlHorzSlider.GetRangeMax ();
        m_nHorzUpperLimit = nMax;
        UpdateData (FALSE);
        return;
```

```
    }
    m_ctlHorzSlider.GetRange (nMin, nMax);
    m_ctlHorzSlider.SetRange (nMin, m_nHorzUpperLimit,
                              TRUE);
}

void CSliderDlg::OnHorzPoints()
{
    UpdateData (TRUE);
    switch (m_nHorzPoints)
    {
        case 0:
            m_ctlHorzSlider.ModifyStyle (TBS_BOTTOM
                                | TBS_TOP, TBS_BOTH, TRUE);
            break;
        case 1:
            m_ctlHorzSlider.ModifyStyle (TBS_BOTTOM
                                | TBS_BOTH, TBS_TOP, TRUE);
            break;
        case 2:
            m_ctlHorzSlider.ModifyStyle (TBS_BOTH
                                | TBS_TOP, TBS_BOTTOM, TRUE);
            break;
    }
}

void CSliderDlg::OnHorzTickmarks()
{
    UpdateData (TRUE);
    int nMin, nMax;
    m_ctlHorzSlider.GetRange (nMin, nMax);
    if (m_bHorzTickMarks)
    {
        if (m_bHorzAutoTick)
        {
            m_ctlHorzSlider.ModifyStyle (TBS_NOTICKS,
                                         0, TRUE);
            m_ctlHorzSlider.SetTicFreq (-1);
        }
        else
        {
            m_ctlHorzSlider.ModifyStyle (0,
                                    TBS_AUTOTICKS, TRUE);
            m_ctlHorzSlider.SetTicFreq (-1);
            m_ctlHorzSlider.ModifyStyle (TBS_NOTICKS
                            | TBS_AUTOTICKS, 0, TRUE);
            m_ctlHorzSlider.SetTicFreq (m_nHorzTickFreq);
        }
    }
    else
    {
        m_ctlHorzSlider.ModifyStyle (0, TBS_NOTICKS, TRUE);
    }
    AdjustSliderRect (m_ctlHorzSlider);
    m_ctlHorzSlider.SetRange (nMin, nMax, TRUE);
}
```

```
void CSliderDlg::OnHorzAutotick()
{
    UpdateData (TRUE);
    int nMin, nMax;
    m_ctlHorzSlider.GetRange (nMin, nMax);
    if (m_bHorzAutoTick)
    {
        m_ctlHorzSlider.SetTicFreq (-1);
        m_ctlHorzSlider.ModifyStyle (0,
                                     TBS_AUTOTICKS, TRUE);
        m_ctlHorzTickFreq.EnableWindow (FALSE);
        m_ctlHorzTickFreqSpinner.EnableWindow (FALSE);
    }
    else
    {
        m_ctlHorzSlider.ModifyStyle (TBS_AUTOTICKS,
                                     0, TRUE);
        m_ctlHorzSlider.SetTicFreq (m_nHorzTickFreq);
        m_ctlHorzTickFreq.EnableWindow (TRUE);
        m_ctlHorzTickFreqSpinner.EnableWindow (TRUE);
    }
    m_ctlHorzSlider.SetRange (nMin, nMax, TRUE);
}

void CSliderDlg::OnHorzEnablesel()
{
    UpdateData (TRUE);
    if (m_bHorzEnableSel)
    {
        m_ctlHorzSlider.ModifyStyle (0,
                                  TBS_ENABLESELRANGE, TRUE);
        m_ctlHorzSlider.SetSelection (

                          m_ctlHorzSlider.GetRangeMin(),
                          m_ctlHorzSlider.GetPos());
    }
    else
    {
        m_ctlHorzSlider.ClearSel ();
        m_ctlHorzSlider.ModifyStyle (TBS_ENABLESELRANGE,
                                     0, TRUE);
    }
    m_ctlHorzSlider.Invalidate ();
}

void CSliderDlg::OnChangeHorzTickfreqedit()
{
    if (m_ctlHorzSlider.m_hWnd == NULL)
        return;
    UpdateData (TRUE);
    m_ctlHorzSlider.SetTicFreq (m_nHorzTickFreq);
    m_ctlHorzSlider.Invalidate ();
}

void CSliderDlg::OnHScroll(UINT nSBCode, UINT nPos,
```

```
                            CScrollBar* pScrollBar)
{
    if (pScrollBar != (CScrollBar *) &m_ctlHorzSlider)
    {
        CPropertyPage::OnHScroll(nSBCode,nPos,pScrollBar);
        return;
    }
    if (m_ctlHorzSlider.GetStyle () & TBS_ENABLESELRANGE)
    {
        m_ctlHorzSlider.SetSelection (
                            m_ctlHorzSlider.GetRangeMin(),
                            m_ctlHorzSlider.GetPos());
        m_ctlHorzSlider.Invalidate ();
    }
}


///////////////////////////////////////////////////////
// CSliderDlg message handlers
///////////////////////////////////////////////////////
// Vertical Slider Functions
///////////////////////////////////////////////////////

void CSliderDlg::OnChangeVertLoweredit()
{
    if (m_ctlVertSlider.m_hWnd == NULL)
        return;
    int nMin, nMax;
    UpdateData (TRUE);
    if (m_nVertLowerLimit >= m_nVertUpperLimit)
    {
        nMin = m_ctlVertSlider.GetRangeMin ();
        m_nVertLowerLimit = nMin;
        UpdateData (FALSE);
        return;
    }
    m_ctlVertSlider.GetRange (nMin, nMax);
    m_ctlVertSlider.SetRange (m_nVertLowerLimit,
                            nMax, TRUE);
}

void CSliderDlg::OnChangeVertUpperedit()
{
    if (m_ctlVertSlider.m_hWnd == NULL)
        return;
    int nMin, nMax;
    UpdateData (TRUE);
    if (m_nVertUpperLimit <= m_nVertLowerLimit)
    {
        nMax = m_ctlVertSlider.GetRangeMax ();
        m_nVertUpperLimit = nMax;
        UpdateData (FALSE);
        return;
    }
    m_ctlVertSlider.GetRange (nMin, nMax);
    m_ctlVertSlider.SetRange (nMin,
                            m_nVertUpperLimit, TRUE);
```

```
}

void CSliderDlg::OnVertPoints()
{
    UpdateData (TRUE);
    switch (m_nVertPoints)
    {
        case 0:
            m_ctlVertSlider.ModifyStyle (TBS_BOTTOM
                            | TBS_TOP, TBS_BOTH, TRUE);
            break;
        case 1:
            m_ctlVertSlider.ModifyStyle (TBS_BOTTOM
                            | TBS_BOTH, TBS_TOP, TRUE);
            break;
        case 2:
            m_ctlVertSlider.ModifyStyle (TBS_BOTH
                            | TBS_TOP, TBS_BOTTOM, TRUE);
            break;
    }
}

void CSliderDlg::OnVertTickmarks()
{
    UpdateData (TRUE);
    int nMin, nMax;
    m_ctlVertSlider.GetRange (nMin, nMax);
    if (m_bVertTickMarks)
    {
        if (m_bVertAutoTick)
        {
            m_ctlVertSlider.ModifyStyle (TBS_NOTICKS,
                                0, TRUE);
            m_ctlVertSlider.SetTicFreq (-1);
        }
        else
        {
            m_ctlVertSlider.ModifyStyle (0,
                                TBS_AUTOTICKS, TRUE);
            m_ctlVertSlider.SetTicFreq (-1);
            m_ctlVertSlider.ModifyStyle (TBS_NOTICKS
                                | TBS_AUTOTICKS, 0, TRUE);
            m_ctlVertSlider.SetTicFreq (m_nVertTickFreq);
        }
    }
    else
    {
        m_ctlVertSlider.ModifyStyle (0, TBS_NOTICKS, TRUE);
    }
    AdjustSliderRect (m_ctlVertSlider);
    m_ctlVertSlider.SetRange (nMin, nMax, TRUE);
}

void CSliderDlg::OnVertAutotick()
{
    UpdateData (TRUE);
```

```
    int nMin, nMax;
    m_ctlVertSlider.GetRange (nMin, nMax);
    if (m_bVertAutoTick)
    {
        m_ctlVertSlider.SetTicFreq (-1);
        m_ctlVertSlider.ModifyStyle (0,
                                TBS_AUTOTICKS, TRUE);
        m_ctlVertTickFreq.EnableWindow (FALSE);
        m_ctlVertTickFreqSpinner.EnableWindow (FALSE);
    }
    else
    {
        m_ctlVertSlider.ModifyStyle (TBS_AUTOTICKS,
                                0, TRUE);
        m_ctlVertSlider.SetTicFreq (m_nVertTickFreq);
        m_ctlVertTickFreq.EnableWindow (TRUE);
        m_ctlVertTickFreqSpinner.EnableWindow (TRUE);
    }
    m_ctlVertSlider.SetRange (nMin, nMax, TRUE);
}

void CSliderDlg::OnVertEnablesel()
{
    UpdateData (TRUE);
    if (m_bVertEnableSel)
    {
        m_ctlVertSlider.ModifyStyle (0, TBS_ENABLESELRANGE,
                                TRUE);
        ::EnableWindow (GetDlgItem(IDC_SETVERTSEL)->m_hWnd,
                                TRUE);
        ::EnableWindow (GetDlgItem
                    (IDC_CLEARVERTSEL)->m_hWnd, FALSE);
    }
    else
    {
        m_ctlVertSlider.ClearSel (TRUE);
        m_nVertSelMax = m_nVertSelMin = -1;
        m_ctlVertSlider.ModifyStyle (TBS_ENABLESELRANGE,
                                0, TRUE);
        ::EnableWindow (GetDlgItem(IDC_SETVERTSEL)->m_hWnd,
                                FALSE);
        ::EnableWindow (GetDlgItem
                    (IDC_CLEARVERTSEL)->m_hWnd, FALSE);
    }
    AdjustSliderRect (m_ctlVertSlider);
}

void CSliderDlg::OnChangeVertTickfreqedit()
{
    if (m_ctlVertSlider.m_hWnd == NULL)
        return;
    UpdateData (TRUE);
    m_ctlVertSlider.SetTicFreq (m_nVertTickFreq);
    m_ctlVertSlider.Invalidate ();
}
```

```
void CSliderDlg::OnClearvertsel()
{
    m_nVertSelMax = m_nVertSelMin = -1;
    m_ctlVertSlider.ClearSel (TRUE);
    ::EnableWindow (
                GetDlgItem (IDC_CLEARVERTSEL)->m_hWnd,
                FALSE);
    ::EnableWindow (GetDlgItem (IDC_SETVERTSEL)->m_hWnd,
                TRUE);
}

void CSliderDlg::OnSetvertsel()
{
    if ((m_nVertSelMax < 0) && (m_nVertSelMin < 0))
    {
        m_nVertSelMax = m_ctlVertSlider.GetPos ();
        return;
    }
    m_nVertSelMin = m_ctlVertSlider.GetPos ();
    if (m_nVertSelMin < m_nVertSelMax)
    {
        int temp = m_nVertSelMin;
        m_nVertSelMin = m_nVertSelMax;
        m_nVertSelMax = temp;
    }
    m_ctlVertSlider.SetSelection (m_nVertSelMax,
                            m_nVertSelMin);
    m_ctlVertSlider.Invalidate ();
    ::EnableWindow (GetDlgItem (IDC_SETVERTSEL)->m_hWnd,
                FALSE);
    ::EnableWindow (GetDlgItem (IDC_CLEARVERTSEL)->m_hWnd,
                TRUE);
}
```

When you change the selection in a slider control, the control doesn't update itself automatically. You have to invalidate the control each time. The same is true if you change the tick frequency. The tick marks won't change until you call the *Invalidate()* function to force the control to redraw itself.

Test the controls to make sure that everything works. You should be able to change slider styles and still maintain a proper focus rectangle. Enable the selection on both controls. The horizontal selection should follow the thumb, but on the vertical you'll have to set it by pressing the Set button for the first point; then, move the thumb and press the button again to get the second point. On the vertical control, notice that when you set a selection area, the control adds a couple of wider tick marks at the ends of the selection.

Go back to the dialog template and place a border around one of the slider controls, and go through the same process. Add and remove the tick marks to make sure that the control resizes itself properly.

877. *Using Slider Controls*

The slider control does have a couple of quirks that you have to program around. First, it's a scroll bar, and in the vertical style, the minimum value is at the top and the maximum value at the bottom. This is the default Windows coordinate system. This is just the opposite of how slider pots appear in the real world, unless the engineer had some good reason for reversing the wiring. The same quirk appears in the spinner and progress bar controls.

Second, the control won't center itself properly in its rectangle. If it's a vertical slider, it positions itself to the left of the rectangle; a horizontal slider positions itself to the top of the rectangle. The right or bottom margins also will change, depending upon the resolution of the monitor on which it is being displayed. You can carefully draw the control on the dialog template to account for this, but if it's subsequently displayed on a monitor with a different resolution, or if you programmatically change styles, the whole thing is thrown off. As a result, you usually have to draw the control rectangle larger than the control.

You can see this anomaly in Microsoft products. From the desktop, select the Start menu and then Programs, Accessories, Multimedia, and finally Volume Control. Select the Play Control volume slider, and look at the focus rectangle around it. Now select the volume slider for the next device, probably CD Audio, and compare the focus rectangle. The rectangles are of different size, but in neither case is the control in the middle of the focus rectangle. It's always to the left.

In addition, the control won't adjust its position for any border that you place around it. It will always position itself to the left or the top, and you have to draw any control with a border very, very carefully. This is why you rarely see this control in any configuration other than flat.

You can adjust for this quirk using the *AdjustSliderRect()* function shown in the sample code. Each time you change styles that affect the width (or depth for a horizontal slider) of the control, call this function to adjust the rectangle. The function first gets the rectangle of the thumb. This rectangle is relative to the control's rectangle and will be used as the basis for adjusting the control rectangle. Then it gets the rectangle for the control itself and adjusts it for the dialog box coordinates (the client coordinates).

Using the left side of the control's rectangle as a base, add the amount of space to the thumb, which is the *left* value of the thumb rectangle. Also add to it the *right* value of the thumb rectangle and set the control rectangle's *right* member to this sum. You've now adjusted the right side of the control's rectangle to give it the same space as on the left. For a horizontal control, substitute *top* for *left* and *bottom* for *right*.

Finally, if there's a border around the control such as with the *WS_BORDER* style or one of the extended border styles, you need to add a few points to the right (or bottom) edge to compensate. Empirically, 4 points is about right.

When you draw the control, don't be concerned with the actual size of the rectangle. Make the control as long or as tall as you need it, but make sure that the thumb is visible in the rectangle. Before you display the control, and each time that you modify the style, call *AdjustSliderRect()* to recalculate the rectangle. The control should remain in the center of the rectangle, whether it's the focus rectangle or a border rectangle.

878. *Interpreting Slider Control Messages*

The slider control doesn't send a wide variety of messages to the parent window. The most commonly used message is the trusty old scroll message, either *WM_HSCROLL* or *WM_VSCROLL*. Other than that, the slider sends only three other messages. One of them, *NM_OUTOFMEMORY*, is a notification that the control can't allocate memory, and you probably will never see that message under the new Windows operating systems.

Another is *NM_RELEASECAPTURE*, which notifies the parent window when the control has released the mouse capture. You can use this to delay updating any other controls until the user has released the mouse button.

The most interesting and useful of the three messages is *NM_CUSTOMDRAW*. This message enables you to custom draw a portion or all of the control without having to set an Owner Draw style. In fact, the slider control doesn't even have an Owner Draw style. This message requires some explanation. It works only with version 4.70 and above of the common controls library.

There are three parts to the slider control that you may opt to draw yourself: the thumb, the channel in which the thumb slides, and the tick marks along the edges. When the control is ready to redraw itself, it will send an *NM_CUSTOMDRAW* message to the parent window. This message basically asks whether you want to draw any part of the control yourself. If you do, then you reply "Yes" by setting the return value to *CDRF_NOTIFYITEMDRAW*. As the control draws each of the three available items, it again sends the *NM_CUSTOMDRAW* message to the parent window. This time it identifies the item and asks whether you want to draw it. If so, go ahead and draw the item with your own code, and then tell the control that you took care of it by setting the return value to *CDRF_SKIPDEFAULT*.

This is much easier to do than it sounds. Suppose that when the slider selection is displayed, you want to draw a green section to indicate a safety zone, and anything out of that zone will be yellow. Your control shouldn't let a danger zone be selected, but you could expand this example to include one. You want to do this only when the selection is displayed and a selection range has been set.

Add the *NM_CUSTOMDRAW* message handler for the slider that you want to use. In this sample, it's the vertical slider on the property page. The code for this handler is shown here:

```cpp
void CSliderDlg::OnCustomdrawVertSlider(NMHDR* pNMHDR,
                                        LRESULT* pResult)
{
    NMCUSTOMDRAW *pNMCustomDraw = (LPNMCUSTOMDRAW) pNMHDR;

    if (pNMCustomDraw->dwDrawStage == CDDS_PREPAINT)
    {
        *pResult = CDRF_NOTIFYITEMDRAW;
        return;
    }
    if ((pNMCustomDraw->dwDrawStage == CDDS_ITEMPREPAINT)
        && (pNMCustomDraw->dwItemSpec == TBCD_CHANNEL)
        && (m_ctlVertSlider.GetStyle ()
                    & TBS_ENABLESELRANGE))
    {
        if ((m_nVertSelMin < 0) || (m_nVertSelMax < 0))
        {
            *pResult = 0;
            return;
        }
        CBrush brYellow;
        CBrush brGreen;
        CDC dc;
        dc.Attach (pNMCustomDraw->hdc);
        brYellow.CreateSolidBrush (RGB (0xff, 0xff, 0x00));
        brGreen.CreateSolidBrush (RGB (0x00, 0xff, 0x00));
        dc.FillRect (&pNMCustomDraw->rc, &brYellow);
        CRect rc = pNMCustomDraw->rc;
        int nMin, nMax;
        m_ctlVertSlider.GetRange (nMin, nMax);
        int nTop = rc.top;
```

```
        CRect rcThumb;
        m_ctlVertSlider.GetThumbRect (&rcThumb);
        rc.top = m_nVertSelMin * (rc.bottom - nTop)
                        / (nMax-nMin) +
                        + rcThumb.bottom - rcThumb.top;
        rc.bottom = m_nVertSelMax * (rc.bottom - nTop)
                        / (nMax - nMin)
                        + rcThumb.bottom - rcThumb.top;
        dc.FillRect (&rc, &brGreen);
        dc.Draw3dRect (&pNMCustomDraw->rc,
                    GetSysColor (COLOR_3DDKSHADOW),
                    GetSysColor (COLOR_3DHIGHLIGHT));
        dc.Detach ();
        *pResult = CDRF_SKIPDEFAULT;
        return;
    }
    *pResult = 0;
}
```

Cast the *pNMHDR* parameter to a *NMCUSTOMDRAW* structure pointer. Check the *dwDrawStage* member to see if it is *CDDS_PREPAINT*. This means that the control hasn't been drawn yet. Set the **pResult* to *CDRF_NOTIFYITEMDRAW* and return without doing anything else.

The control then sends this message three more times, first to draw the tick marks, then to draw the channel, and finally to draw the thumb. When the *dwItemSpec* member is *TBCD_CHANNEL*, do your custom drawing and return *CDRF_SKIPDEFAULT* to let the control know that you drew the item.

In the draw code, first check that the selection area is displayed. If not, just return 0 and let the control draw the channel. Otherwise, first draw the rectangle with a solid yellow color. The structure contains a handle to the control's device context, so just attach that to the drawing.

Using the range minimums and maximums, the thumb rectangle and the channel rectangle passed in the notification structure, calculate the top and bottom of the green rectangle and draw it. Finally, draw the 3-D rectangle to make the selection area stand out.

Add the code to your project and test it (we've already added it to the code on the companion CD—just remove the comment markers). Check the Enable Selection box. Move the slider thumb to your upper "safe" range limit and press the Set button once. Then move the thumb to the lower end of the "safe" range and press Set again. The control should respond immediately by filling in the channel with yellow and the area between the selection points with green. The code disables the Set button and enables the Clear button.

879. *Understanding Slider Styles*

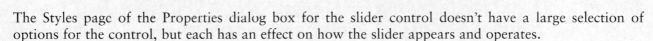

The Styles page of the Properties dialog box for the slider control doesn't have a large selection of options for the control, but each has an effect on how the slider appears and operates.

Referring to Figure 879, the Orientation box enables you to set the control vertically or horizontally. This is the only style option that can't be changed once the control has been created. The Points box refers to the thumb and whether you want the side of it to come to a point. Selecting Both strangely removes the points altogether. Selecting Right makes a pointed tip on the right side of the thumb; selecting Left places the tip on the left side of the thumb.

Figure 879   Style options for the slider control

Tick Marks places short lines on one or both sides of the control, depending upon the Point selection. To draw the ticks automatically when the range is set or changed, select Auto Ticks. You must select Tick Marks as well if you select Auto Ticks. Enable Selection displays the progress bar-like rectangle in the slider channel.

Border is the familiar *WS_BORDER* style, but in this case, the control will draw itself slightly depressed from the dialog box surface.

880. *Setting Tick Marks*

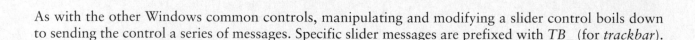

If the range of the slider control is coarse, the thumb will move in jumps from one integer value to the next. You can test the smoothness of the control by setting the tick marks at intervals of 1 and setting the Tick Marks style. If the tick marks are close together, the thumb operation should be smooth; the tick marks indicate the actual position where the thumb will land.

However, if you have a large range for the slider, an interval of 1 produces nearly a black line along the side of the control. You can open this up by changing the frequency of the tick marks. The actual frequency will depend upon the size of the control. The longer the channel, the more often you can display tick marks and still make them distinct.

You can't set the frequency for the Auto Tick style, however, and for a control with a wide range, you'll probably find that this style is good only for drawing dark black lines along the side of the control. In this case, you're better off without Auto Tick and setting the frequency to something that appears decent.

The tick marks will appear on the side with the point, or both sides if you've got the *TBS_BOTH* style set.

Alternatively, you have the option of drawing your own tick marks using the *NM_CUSTOMDRAW* message handler. The *dwItemSpec* value is set to *TBCD_TICS* (note no "K") when the control is ready to draw the tick marks.

881. *Using* **CSliderCtrl** *Member Functions*

As with the other Windows common controls, manipulating and modifying a slider control boils down to sending the control a series of messages. Specific slider messages are prefixed with *TB_* (for *trackbar*).

When using the *CSliderCtrl* class, you circumvent the message process. The member functions handle the details of sending the message to the control. All you do is call the function and pass it the required parameters.

The control class has some scroll bar-like functions. For example, you can set the line size, which determines how far the thumb will move in one increment. The page size also can be modified. This is the amount that the thumb will jump when the user clicks the channel rather than the thumb. You can think of the channel as the open space between the end arrows on a scroll bar.

882. *Understanding the Spin Control*

Imagine a scroll bar with no thumb and no bar, only the arrow buttons at the ends. Then flip the arrows so that they point away from each other. A control of this type is variously known as a spin control, a spinner, or an up-down control. It's designed to send the increment/decrement messages associated with a scroll bar (the line up and line down conditions), but without complicating the operation with thumb-track and page scroll messages. In essence, it's an empty scrollbar.

Spinners typically are used to provide a mechanism by which the user can increment or decrement a value by clicking on one of the buttons. It's commonly used in the buddy system, where it's attached to another control and transfers the results of the clicks to the buddy control. You've seen them used as support controls for the progress bar and slider controls in the last few tips.

If the user clicks and holds the arrow button, the internal value of the spinner control continues to increment and decrement until it reaches a preset limit. After an arrow button has been held down for a few seconds, the rate at which the value changes increases. The rate of change (sound like as elementary calculus class?) can be modified by the programmer.

883. *Understanding the CSpinButtonCtrl Class*

The *CSpinButtonCtrl* class encapsulates the spin button common control and provides functions for accessing and manipulating the control.

The spinner control operates within a range that is adjustable by the programmer. The default range is 100 to 0. Before you ask, yes, the default range actually is backward, going from a lower limit of 100 to an upper limit of 0. Unlike the slider and progress bar controls, it is OK to reverse the range limits to a value higher than the upper end. Doing so switches the operation of the buttons.

In this sense, the spinner works in the reverse direction of a slider. If you get the default range of a slider control, you'll see that the lower limit is 0 and the upper limit is 100. This might be a bit confusing to you if you are just getting started with these controls. If you ponder it a while, though, you'll realize that the programmer who put the spinner control together actually was thinking about the user and those of us who must program these controls (that person must be a rare bird at Microsoft). By making it so that the upper button increases the value and the lower button decreases it, you get a more intuitive user action. Then, by setting the default range so that the upper limit is lower than the lower limit, the default operation of the control *appears* to be the same as the slider and progress bar. Unfortunately, it means that the default behavior of the control in a horizontal orientation appears to be the reverse of the slider and progress controls, but this really isn't very significant; the control mostly is used in a vertical orientation.

In the tips on the slider control, you might have noticed that to decrease the value using the spinner controls, you pressed the *upper* button; to increase it, you pressed the *lower* button. That's because the controls used the default range. In Tip 885, "Using *CSpinButtonCtrl* Member Functions," you'll return to that code, add member variables for the spinners, and reverse the button operation.

You've already seen the spinner control in action and as a buddy to an edit control, so in this sample code, you'll learn how to program other aspects of the spinner. Create a new property sheet for the Controls project with a resource ID of *IDD_PROPPAGE_SPINNERDLG*, as shown in Figure 883. Title it Spinners.

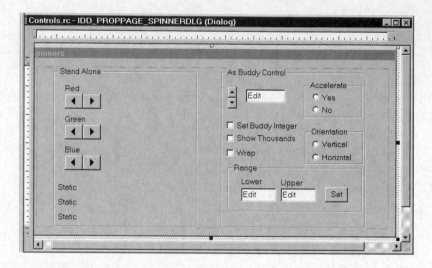

Figure 883   The spinner control property page has stand-alone and buddy spinners

The three static fields at the bottom of the Stand Alone group are the progress bars that you derived from the *CStatic* class in Tip 819, "Deriving a Custom Class from *CStatic* to Gain Functionality." You can't use the common progress bar control here because you'll need to change the color to match the spinner button titles. There's also a large square to the right of the color buttons that will show a mixture of the three colors; it's derived from *CStaticEx*. Make sure that the two sets of radio buttons are properly grouped.

Create a class for this property page named *CSpinnerDlg*. The header file is shown here:

```
// SpinnerDlg.h : header file
//


#include    "StaticEx.h"
#include    "ProgressBar.h"


/////////////////////////////////////////////////////////
// CSpinnerDlg dialog

class CSpinnerDlg : public CpropertyPage
{
    DECLARE_DYNCREATE(CSpinnerDlg)

// Construction
public:
    CSpinnerDlg();
    ~CSpinnerDlg();

// Dialog Data
```

```
    //{{AFX_DATA(CSpinnerDlg)
    enum { IDD = IDD_PROPPAGE_SPINNERDLG };
    CProgressBar    m_SoloBlueBar;
    CProgressBar    m_SoloGreenBar;
    CProgressBar    m_SoloRedBar;
    CSpinButtonCtrl m_SoloRedSpinner;
    CSpinButtonCtrl m_SoloGreenSpinner;
    CSpinButtonCtrl m_SoloBlueSpinner;
    CStaticEx   m_ctlShowColors;
    CButton m_btnSetRange;
    CEdit   m_BuddyEdit;
    CSpinButtonCtrl m_ctlBuddySpinner;
    BOOL    m_bBuddyWrap;
    BOOL    m_bBuddyInteger;
    BOOL    m_bBuddyThousands;
    int     m_nBuddyUpper;
    int     m_nBuddyLower;
    int     m_nBuddyOrientation;
    int     m_nBuddyAccelerate;
    //}}AFX_DATA


// Overrides
    // ClassWizard generate virtual function overrides
    //{{AFX_VIRTUAL(CSpinnerDlg)
    protected:
    virtual void DoDataExchange(CDataExchange* pDX);
    // DDX/DDV support
    //}}AFX_VIRTUAL


// Implementation
protected:
    void RecreateBuddy();
    DWORD m_dwBuddyStyle;
    // Generated message map functions
    //{{AFX_MSG(CSpinnerDlg)
    afx_msg void OnHScroll(UINT nSBCode, UINT nPos,
                        CScrollBar* pScrollBar);
    virtual BOOL OnInitDialog();
    afx_msg void OnBuddySetinteger();
    afx_msg void OnBuddyThousands();
    afx_msg void OnBuddyWrap();
    afx_msg void OnBuddySetrange();
    afx_msg void OnChangeBuddyRange();
    afx_msg void OnBuddyOrientation();
    afx_msg void OnBuddyAccelerate();
    //}}AFX_MSG
    DECLARE_MESSAGE_MAP()

};
```

The code will use the *WM_HSCROLL* message to update the progress bars and static text window. There are several controls that send this message in addition to the spinner control, so your message handler will have to sort them out. If you later change the orientation of the spinner, you'll have to move the code from *OnHScroll()* to *OnVScroll()*. In Tip 886, "Interpreting Spin Control Messages," you'll amend this code a bit to allow you to use a message directly from the spinner control to update the bars and avoid the scroll message handlers altogether. That's the reason for the *#define _USEDELTAPOS* statement near the top of the file.

The source file is shown here:

```
// SpinnerDlg.cpp : implementation file
//

#include "stdafx.h"
#include "Controls.h"
#include "SpinnerDlg.h"

#ifdef _DEBUG
#define new DEBUG_NEW
#undef THIS_FILE
static char THIS_FILE[] = __FILE__;
#endif

// #define _USEDELTAPOS

/////////////////////////////////////////////////////////
// CSpinnerDlg property page

IMPLEMENT_DYNCREATE(CSpinnerDlg, CPropertyPage)

CSpinnerDlg::CSpinnerDlg()
                    : CPropertyPage(CSpinnerDlg::IDD)
{
    //{{AFX_DATA_INIT(CSpinnerDlg)
    m_bBuddyWrap = FALSE;
    m_bBuddyInteger = TRUE;
    m_bBuddyThousands = FALSE;
    m_nBuddyUpper = 10000;
    m_nBuddyLower = 0;
    m_nBuddyOrientation = 0;
    m_nBuddyAccelerate = 0;
    //}}AFX_DATA_INIT
    m_psp.dwFlags &= ~PSP_HASHELP;
}

CSpinnerDlg::~CSpinnerDlg()
{
}

void CSpinnerDlg::DoDataExchange(CDataExchange* pDX)
{
    CPropertyPage::DoDataExchange(pDX);
    //{{AFX_DATA_MAP(CSpinnerDlg)
    DDX_Control(pDX, IDC_SOLO_BLUEBAR, m_SoloBlueBar);
    DDX_Control(pDX, IDC_SOLO_GREENBAR, m_SoloGreenBar);
    DDX_Control(pDX, IDC_SOLO_REDBAR, m_SoloRedBar);
    DDX_Control(pDX,IDC_SOLO_REDSPINNER,m_SoloRedSpinner);
    DDX_Control(pDX, IDC_SOLO_GREENSPINNER,
                                    m_SoloGreenSpinner);
    DDX_Control(pDX, IDC_SOLO_BLUESPINNER,
                                    m_SoloBlueSpinner);
```

```
        DDX_Control(pDX, IDC_STATIC_SHOWCOLORS,
                                        m_ctlShowColors);
        DDX_Control(pDX, IDC_BUDDY_SETRANGE, m_btnSetRange);
        DDX_Control(pDX, IDC_BUDDY_EDIT, m_BuddyEdit);
        DDX_Control(pDX, IDC_BUDDY_SPINNER, m_ctlBuddySpinner);
        DDX_Check(pDX, IDC_BUDDY_WRAP, m_bBuddyWrap);
        DDX_Check(pDX, IDC_BUDDY_SETINTEGER, m_bBuddyInteger);
        DDX_Check(pDX, IDC_BUDDY_THOUSANDS, m_bBuddyThousands);
        DDX_Text(pDX, IDC_BUDDY_UPPER, m_nBuddyUpper);
        DDX_Text(pDX, IDC_BUDDY_LOWER, m_nBuddyLower);
        DDX_Radio(pDX, IDC_BUDDY_VERTICAL,
                                        m_nBuddyOrientation);
        DDX_Radio(pDX, IDC_BUDDY_ACCELERATE,
                                        m_nBuddyAccelerate);
    //}}AFX_DATA_MAP
}


BEGIN_MESSAGE_MAP(CSpinnerDlg, CPropertyPage)
    //{{AFX_MSG_MAP(CSpinnerDlg)
    ON_WM_HSCROLL()
    ON_BN_CLICKED(IDC_BUDDY_SETINTEGER, OnBuddySetinteger)
    ON_BN_CLICKED(IDC_BUDDY_THOUSANDS, OnBuddyThousands)
    ON_BN_CLICKED(IDC_BUDDY_WRAP, OnBuddyWrap)
    ON_BN_CLICKED(IDC_BUDDY_SETRANGE, OnBuddySetrange)
    ON_EN_CHANGE(IDC_BUDDY_LOWER, OnChangeBuddyRange)
    ON_BN_CLICKED(IDC_BUDDY_VERTICAL, OnBuddyOrientation)
    ON_BN_CLICKED(IDC_BUDDY_ACCELERATE, OnBuddyAccelerate)
    ON_EN_CHANGE(IDC_BUDDY_UPPER, OnChangeBuddyRange)
    ON_BN_CLICKED(IDC_BUDDY_HORIZONTAL, OnBuddyOrientation)
    ON_BN_CLICKED(IDC_BUDDY_NOACCELERATE,OnBuddyAccelerate)
    ON_NOTIFY(UDN_DELTAPOS, IDC_SOLO_REDSPINNER,
                            OnDeltaposSoloRedspinner)
    ON_NOTIFY(UDN_DELTAPOS, IDC_SOLO_GREENSPINNER,
                            OnDeltaposSoloGreenspinner)
    ON_NOTIFY(UDN_DELTAPOS, IDC_SOLO_BLUESPINNER,
                            OnDeltaposSoloBluespinner)
    //}}AFX_MSG_MAP
END_MESSAGE_MAP()

/////////////////////////////////////////////////////////
// CSpinnerDlg message handlers

BOOL CSpinnerDlg::OnInitDialog()
{
    CPropertyPage::OnInitDialog();
    m_ctlBuddySpinner.SetRange (m_nBuddyLower,
                                m_nBuddyUpper);
    m_dwBuddyStyle = m_ctlBuddySpinner.GetStyle ();
    m_dwBuddyStyle &= ~UDS_AUTOBUDDY;
    m_btnSetRange.EnableWindow (FALSE);

    m_SoloRedSpinner.SetRange (0, 255);
    m_SoloRedSpinner.SetPos (255);
    m_SoloGreenSpinner.SetRange (0, 255);
    m_SoloGreenSpinner.SetPos (255);
```

```
        m_SoloBlueSpinner.SetRange (0, 255);
        m_SoloBlueSpinner.SetPos (255);

        UDACCEL Accel[] =
            {
            0, 1,
            5, 10,
            10, 100
            };
        BOOL bResult = m_ctlBuddySpinner.SetAccel(3, Accel);

        m_SoloRedBar.SetBarColor (RGB (0xff, 0x0, 0x0));
        m_SoloRedBar.SetMinMax (0, 255);
        m_SoloRedBar.UsePercent (false);
        m_SoloRedBar.SetBarText (_T("Red = 255"));
        m_SoloRedBar.SetPosition (255);

        m_SoloGreenBar.SetBarColor (RGB (0x0, 0xff, 0x0));
        m_SoloGreenBar.SetBarTextColor (RGB (0x0, 0x0, 0x0));
        m_SoloGreenBar.SetMinMax (0, 255);
        m_SoloGreenBar.UsePercent (false);
        m_SoloGreenBar.SetBarText (_T("Green = 255"));
        m_SoloGreenBar.SetPosition (255);

        m_SoloBlueBar.SetBarColor (RGB (0x0, 0x0, 0xff));
        m_SoloBlueBar.SetMinMax (0, 255);
        m_SoloBlueBar.UsePercent (false);
        m_SoloBlueBar.SetBarText (_T("Blue = 255"));
        m_SoloBlueBar.SetPosition (255);

        return TRUE;
}

void CSpinnerDlg::OnHScroll(UINT nSBCode, UINT nPos,
                            CScrollBar* pScrollBar)
{
    static int nRed = 255;
    static int nGreen = 255;
    static int nBlue = 255;
//
//  Don't need to deal with the end scroll.
//
    if (nSBCode == SB_ENDSCROLL)
        return;
#ifndef _USEDELTAPOS
    if (pScrollBar == (CScrollBar *) &m_SoloRedSpinner)
    {
        CString strText;
        nRed = nPos;
        strText.Format ("Red = %d", nPos);
        m_SoloRedBar.SetBarText (strText);
        m_SoloRedBar.SetPosition (nPos);
        m_SoloRedBar.Update ();
        m_ctlShowColors.SetBkgndColor (RGB(nRed, nGreen,
                                      nBlue));
        return;
```

```
    }
    if (pScrollBar == (CScrollBar *) &m_SoloBlueSpinner)
    {
        CString strText;
        nBlue = nPos;
        strText.Format ("Blue = %d", nPos);
        m_SoloBlueBar.SetBarText (strText);
        m_SoloBlueBar.SetPosition (nPos);
        m_SoloBlueBar.Update ();
        m_ctlShowColors.SetBkgndColor (RGB(nRed, nGreen,
                                    nBlue));

        return;
    }
    if (pScrollBar == (CScrollBar *) &m_SoloGreenSpinner)
    {
        CString strText;
        nGreen = nPos;
        strText.Format ("Green = %d", nPos);
        m_SoloGreenBar.SetBarText (strText);
        m_SoloGreenBar.SetPosition (nPos);
        m_SoloGreenBar.Update ();
        m_ctlShowColors.SetBkgndColor (RGB(nRed, nGreen,
                                    nBlue));

        return;
    }
#endif
}

void CSpinnerDlg::OnBuddySetinteger()
{
    UpdateData (TRUE);
    if (m_bBuddyInteger)
    {
        m_dwBuddyStyle |= UDS_SETBUDDYINT;
    }
    else
    {
        m_dwBuddyStyle &= ~UDS_SETBUDDYINT;
    }
    RecreateBuddy ();
}

void CSpinnerDlg::OnBuddyThousands()
{
    UpdateData (TRUE);
    if (m_bBuddyThousands)
    {
        m_dwBuddyStyle &= ~UDS_NOTHOUSANDS;
    }
    else
    {
        m_dwBuddyStyle |= UDS_NOTHOUSANDS;
    }
    RecreateBuddy ();
}
```

```
void CSpinnerDlg::OnBuddyWrap()
{
    UpdateData (TRUE);
    if (m_bBuddyWrap)
    {
        m_dwBuddyStyle |= UDS_WRAP;
    }
    else
    {
        m_dwBuddyStyle &= ~UDS_WRAP;
    }
    RecreateBuddy ();
}

void CSpinnerDlg::RecreateBuddy()
{
    CRect rc, rcEdit;
    m_ctlBuddySpinner.GetWindowRect (&rc);
    m_BuddyEdit.GetWindowRect (&rcEdit);
    rcEdit.left = rc.left;
    ScreenToClient (&rc);
    ScreenToClient (&rcEdit);
    int nLower, nUpper, nPos;
    m_ctlBuddySpinner.GetRange32 (nLower, nUpper);
    nPos = m_ctlBuddySpinner.GetPos ();
    m_ctlBuddySpinner.DestroyWindow ();
    m_ctlBuddySpinner.Create (m_dwBuddyStyle, rc, this,
                              IDC_BUDDY_SPINNER);
    m_BuddyEdit.MoveWindow (&rcEdit, TRUE);
    m_ctlBuddySpinner.SetBuddy (&m_BuddyEdit);
    m_ctlBuddySpinner.SetRange32 (nLower, nUpper);
    m_ctlBuddySpinner.SetPos (nPos);
    m_BuddyEdit.SetFocus ();
}

void CSpinnerDlg::OnBuddySetrange()
{
    UpdateData (TRUE);
    m_ctlBuddySpinner.SetRange32 (m_nBuddyLower,
                                  m_nBuddyUpper);
    m_btnSetRange.EnableWindow (FALSE);
}

void CSpinnerDlg::OnChangeBuddyRange()
{
    m_btnSetRange.EnableWindow (TRUE);
}

void CSpinnerDlg::OnBuddyOrientation()
{
    UpdateData (TRUE);
    if (m_nBuddyOrientation == 0)
    {
        m_dwBuddyStyle &= ~UDS_HORZ;
    }
    else
```

```
    {
        m_dwBuddyStyle |= UDS_HORZ;
    }
    RecreateBuddy ();
}


void CSpinnerDlg::OnBuddyAccelerate()
{
    UpdateData (TRUE);
    if (m_nBuddyAccelerate == 0)
    {
    UDACCEL Accel[] =
        {
        0, 1,
        2, 10,\
        5, 25,
        8, 100,
        10, 250
        };
        m_ctlBuddySpinner.SetAccel(5, Accel);
    }
    else
    {
    UDACCEL Accel[] =
        {
        0, 1,
        };
        m_ctlBuddySpinner.SetAccel(1, Accel);
    }
}
```

The code overrides the default acceleration and increments for the spinner in the Buddy Control group, and you set your own accelerator table. The control has a wide range, from 0 to 10,000, so you'll want to speed it up a bit to get from one end to the other. You'll see how to use the acceleration and increment functions in Tip 885, "Using *CSpinButtonCtrl* Member Functions."

884. *Understanding Spin Button Styles*

The spin control properties are fixed when you create the control. You can't change them programmatically, so you have to decide beforehand how you want the control to appear and perform. The sample code in the previous tip destroys the control and then re-creates with the new styles according to the selection on the property page.

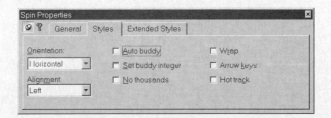

Figure 884   The Styles page of the spinner control's property page.
The Hot Track item is new and is not covered in the MSDN documentation.

The Orientation property determines whether the control will appear with the arrows pointing up and down (Vertical) or left and right (Horizontal). It also determines whether the control will send the *WM_VSCROLL* or *WM_HSCROLL* message when the user presses one of the buttons.

Alignment is used with the buddy system and determines whether the control will attach itself to the left or right side of the buddy control, or whether it will be unattached. The spinner control will buddy with virtually any control, but it won't perform like a buddy unless the other control is designed to accept a buddy control.

The Auto Buddy property determines whether the control will attach itself to another control when it is created. When the spinner control attaches to buddy control, the width of the buddy is decreased by the width of the spinner. You can change the buddy control programmatically, but the buddy control being shunned won't resize itself. You can take care of that by getting the width of both controls with *GetWindowRect()* and adjusting the left or right side of the buddy rectangle; then, call *MoveWindow()* after the buddy control has changed.

Set Buddy Integer allows the spinner control to format a string with its current position and set the text in the buddy control. Any control that can set text—the edit control, the static control, buttons, and so on—can be used with this property, although with some of them it doesn't make much sense.

By default, when the spinner control formats a string for display using the Buddy Integer property, it inserts commas to delimit thousands. Setting the No Thousands style prevents this, and the string is inserted as a plain number.

When the user presses one of the spinner buttons and the control reaches either end of its range, it won't advance any farther. If you set the Wrap property, the position automatically starts over at the opposite end of the range. In the sample code in Tip 883, "Understanding the *CSpinButtonCtrl* Class," the range is from 0 to 10,000. If the position is 0 and the user presses the Down button, the control will wrap to 10,000 and continue downward. Similarly, if the current position is 10,000 and the user presses the Up key, it will wrap to 0 and continue counting upward. This is how the control got its nickname "spinner." The value spins around constantly while one of the buttons is held down. Without the Wrap property, it is really an Up Down control, which is its official name.

The arrow keys allow the user to use the cursor movement keys to increment or decrement the position when the spinner is linked to a buddy control.

Hot Track is a new property not explained in the help file or the MSDN documentation. It appears to do nothing, so we assume that it will be implemented in a later service pack. With other controls that contain this property, the accompanying text is displayed in the system highlight color when the mouse moves over it, and it reverts to the default color when the mouse leaves.

885. *Using* CSpinButtonCtrl *Member Functions*

The *CSpinButtonCtrl* class contains member functions for manipulating control and retrieving its current values.

There are two versions to set the range of the control. The first, *SetRange()*, takes two integers as parameters for the upper and lower limits. Using this function, the upper limit is 32,767 and the lower limit is 32,768. A further condition is that the difference between the upper and lower limits cannot be more then 32,767. These are curious conditions because the control is capable of handling greater extremes, but the MFC code does not allow testing to enforce these limits. If you exceed them, however, the results are unpredictable. You can retrieve the range using *GetRange()*.

The *SetRange32()* function allows you to exceed the limits imposed by *SetRange()*. We've set spinner ranges to well over a million without problems except that, with a buddy control, it won't format the entire number properly. For example, 1,000,000 shows in the buddy window as 1000,000. You can get the 32-bit range by calling *GetRange32()*.

There is an overloaded *GetRange()* function that takes no parameters and returns the range as two 16-bit values packed into a *DWORD* return value. The low-order word is the upper-range limit, and the high-order word is the lower-range limit. Don't ask—that's not very intuitive, and we don't know why.

The *GetBuddy()* function enables you to retrieve a pointer to the control's buddy control as a *CWnd* object. If there is no buddy, the function returns *NULL*. You can change the buddy control—even if it was attached using the Auto Buddy property—by calling *SetBuddy()* and passing a pointer to the new buddy window as a *CWnd* object. You have to be careful with this, however. When the spinner releases from a buddy, it doesn't restore the buddy's original size. That's not very buddy-like, but you can fix it by first getting the size of the buddy window and the spinner control, and then adjusting the buddy window's size. You can see an example of this in the *RecreateBuddy()* function in the sample code.

By default, when a spinner sets the text in a buddy window, it uses decimal notation. You can use hexadecimal notation by setting the base to 16. The *SetBase()* function will accept 10 or 16 as the number base. You can retrieve the current base setting using *GetBase()*.

Finally, the accelerator functions let you change the speed and default increments the spinner uses. For a large range, continually bumping up the rate of change makes it possible to get through the entire range quickly, yet still get to the intermediate values by releasing and pressing the button again. This resets the acceleration to its starting point.

The default acceleration and increments for a buddy control are set to three steps. When you first press a button, the control increments by 1 for the first 2 seconds. Then it shifts into second gear and increments by 5 for the next 3 seconds, when it shifts into high gear and increments by 20. For most applications, that's a pretty good setting, but you might want to change it for very large ranges. In the sample code, the range maximum is 10,000, so the acceleration was bumped up to 5 steps so that after 10 seconds, it is incrementing by steps of 250.

You can get the current accelerator list by calling the *GetAccel()* function. If you don't know the size of the list, you can call the function first with a 0 for the size and a *NULL* as the pointer to your array. The function then will return the number of entries in the list, and you can allocate memory to hold them before calling the function a second time with the proper parameters. The following code demonstrates this:

```
    UDACCEL *pAccel;
    int nCount = m_ctlBuddySpinner.GetAccel(0, NULL);
    pAccel = new UDACCEL [nCount];
    m_ctlBuddySpinner.GetAccel(nCount, pAccel);
//
//  Do something with the accelerator table
//
    delete [] pAccel;
```

A *UDACCEL* structure contains two members. The first, *nSec*, is the time to wait before the new acceleration takes effect. The second, *nInc*, is the amount to increment the current position with each step. The *nSec* value is cumulative. You set it from the beginning of time, not from the value of the last list entry. The following code from the sample sets up an array of five entries and then sets the acceleration to that table:

```
UDACCEL Accel[] =
{
    0, 1,
    2, 10,
```

```
    5, 25,
    8, 100,
    10, 250
};
m_ctlBuddySpinner.SetAccel(5, Accel);
```

The table starts at the beginning of time with an increment of 1. After 2 seconds, it shifts to an increment of 10. Three seconds later, or 5 seconds after the beginning of time, it shifts to an increment of 25, then to 100 after another 3 seconds, and finally to an increment of 250 at 10 seconds after the button was first pressed. On a fast machine, the last increment won't be reached, but even on slower machines, the entire range is covered in about 15 seconds.

When you let up on the button, the sequence repeats. So, the first run-through gets you near the right value, and then you release the button and restart to get to the precise value that you want.

886. *Interpreting Spin Control Messages*

When the user presses a button on a spinner control, Windows sends a scroll message, either *WM_VSCROLL* or *WM_HSCROLL*, depending upon the orientation of the control, to the control's parent window. It's possible to have more than one spinner on a dialog box all sending the same message, plus the slider and scroll bars sending the same messages. This means that your handler for these messages could become bloated and busy. The scroll message is sent after the control has updated its position.

The spinner control has two notification messages that it can send to the parent window. The first is the familiar *NM_OUTOFMEMORY*. The second, *UDN_DELTAPOS*, is more interesting and useful.

This message is sent to the control's parent when the control is about to modify its position, but it is sent *before* the update is performed. This means that you can examine user input and modify or use it before it becomes final. You can even have the control reject the operation. In addition, the message is sent for each control, so you can have separate handlers for each spinner control.

The property page code on the companion CD has message handlers for the spinners that control the red, green, and blue color bars in the Stand Alone group. The code for these functions in shown here. To enable them and disable the code in the *OnHScroll()* function, just uncomment the *#define* *_USEDELTAPOS* macro at the top of the file.

```cpp
void CSpinnerDlg::OnDeltaposSoloRedspinner(NMHDR* pNMHDR,
                                LRESULT* pResult)
{
    NMUPDOWN* pNMUpDown = (NMUPDOWN*)pNMHDR;
    // TODO: Add your control notification handler
    // code here

#ifdef _USEDELTAPOS

    CString strText;
    int nRed = pNMUpDown->iPos + pNMUpDown->iDelta;
    int nGreen = m_SoloGreenBar.GetPosition ();
    int nBlue = m_SoloBlueBar.GetPosition ();
    if (nRed < 0)
        nRed = 0;
    if (nRed > 255)
```

```
        nRed = 255;
    strText.Format ("Red = %d", nRed);
    m_SoloRedBar.SetBarText (strText);
    m_SoloRedBar.SetPosition (nRed);
    m_SoloRedBar.Update ();
    m_ctlShowColors.SetBkgndColor (RGB(nRed,
                                    nGreen, nBlue));
#endif

    *pResult = 0;
}

void CSpinnerDlg::OnDeltaposSoloGreenspinner(NMHDR* pNMHDR,
                                    LRESULT* pResult)
{
    NMUPDOWN* pNMUpDown = (NMUPDOWN*)pNMHDR;
    // TODO: Add your control notification handler
    // code here

#ifdef _USEDELTAPOS

    CString strText;
    int nGreen = pNMUpDown->iPos + pNMUpDown->iDelta;
    int nRed = m_SoloRedBar.GetPosition ();
    int nBlue = m_SoloBlueBar.GetPosition ();
    if (nGreen < 0)
        nGreen = 0;
    if (nGreen > 255)
        nGreen = 255;
    strText.Format ("Green = %d", nGreen);
    m_SoloGreenBar.SetBarText (strText);
    m_SoloGreenBar.SetPosition (nGreen);
    m_SoloGreenBar.Update ();
    m_ctlShowColors.SetBkgndColor (RGB(nRed,
                                    nGreen, nBlue));

#endif

    *pResult = 0;
}

void CSpinnerDlg::OnDeltaposSoloBluespinner(NMHDR* pNMHDR,
                                    LRESULT* pResult)
{
    NMUPDOWN* pNMUpDown = (NMUPDOWN*)pNMHDR;
    // TODO: Add your control notification handler
    // code here

#ifdef _USEDELTAPOS

    CString strText;
    int nBlue = pNMUpDown->iPos + pNMUpDown->iDelta;
    int nRed = m_SoloRedBar.GetPosition ();
    int nGreen = m_SoloGreenBar.GetPosition ();
    if (nBlue < 0)
        nBlue = 0;
```

```
        if (nBlue > 255)
            nBlue = 255;
        strText.Format ("Blue = %d", nBlue);
        m_SoloBlueBar.SetBarText (strText);
        m_SoloBlueBar.SetPosition (nBlue);
        m_SoloBlueBar.Update ();
        m_ctlShowColors.SetBkgndColor (RGB(nRed,
                                      nGreen, nBlue));

#endif

    *pResult = 0;
}
```

You can see that the slight disadvantage is that without resorting to global or class members, you can't have shared variables for the three colors. With these controls it's no problem because we've added a function to the custom progress bar to retrieve the current value.

The *NMUPDOWN* structure contains three members. The first is a *NMHDR* structure that is used with most notification messages. The second is *iPos*, which gives the control's current position *before* the operation takes place. The third is *iDelta*, which contains the amount by which the position will change. The last parameter may be positive or negative, depending upon the button pressed.

By setting **pResult* to 0, the control will go ahead and process the operation and update its position. You can handle all the details of the operation in the message handler yourself and return a non-zero value, in which case the control won't process the message.

887. *Understanding the Header Control*

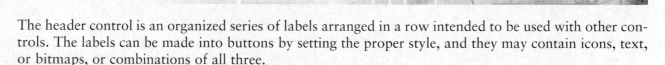

The header control is an organized series of labels arranged in a row intended to be used with other controls. The labels can be made into buttons by setting the proper style, and they may contain icons, text, or bitmaps, or combinations of all three.

Typically, the header control is used to delimit columns for a list or table. When used with the list control, another 32-bit control, it can be used to dynamically reorder columns and send messages that enable you to re-sort columns in the table.

Documentation on the header control is scarce, and much of it, including the MSDN documentation with the Visual Studio, is ambiguous and at times incorrect. If you follow the MSDN steps to create a header control outside a list control, it just won't work as advertised. For example, the MSDN documentation tells you to "use ClassWizard to create an *OnChildNotify* handler function" to process the notification messages from the control. Well, there is no *WM_CHILDNOTIFY* Windows message to handle. There is an *OnChildNotify()* virtual function in the *CWnd* class, and most of the view and many of the control classes, but if you override it, few of the header controls' notification messages show up. The control *does* send notification messages; you can catch them in a Windows API program, but somehow they get lost in MFC.

For this reason, most books—including those from Microsoft Press—simply skip this control, merely noting its existence. The MSDN samples sidestep this issue by limiting their examples to programs that use the header control with a list control. That's too bad because this overlooked control has a lot of potential. Even when used with the list control, the MSDN documentation really doesn't give you much information on how to use and manipulate the header control.

The notification messages are there, but you have to add a handler for the *WM_NOTIFY* message to catch them. When the *wParam* argument for this message equals the resource ID for your header control, cast the *lParam* argument to an *NMHDR* structure, and you'll find the notification message in the *code* member of this structure. To add this function to your code, the Class Wizard lists it among the virtual functions rather than the messages, so you need to select *OnNotify* from the Messages list of the Message Map page.

888. *Using the* CHeaderCtrl *Class*

If you're looking for the header control on the Controls toolbar in Visual Studio, look no further. It isn't there. The header control wasn't designed for mere mortals to tinker with, and presumably that includes you and me. That won't stop us, though.

Actually, the header control isn't a control that you can just draw on a dialog box. It wouldn't make much sense. You could use it as a collection of pushbuttons, but it would be much easier to program the buttons than the header control. To be really useful, the header control needs to be teamed with another control, and the faithful old list box is a good example.

In this tip, you'll build a property page with two samples on it. The first links a header control with an ordinary list box to show you how you can use it to label columns and set their widths for a tabulated list box. This control will show dynamic column ordering. The second is a list control operating in report mode, which shows off some of the advanced features such as dynamic column sizing. The drag-and-drop feature to reorder the columns doesn't work with the list control, but you'll see it in operation in the list box that you put together.

Your new property page should have a resource ID of *IDD_PROPPAGE_HEADERDLG*, and you can title it Headers. Figure 888a shows how it should look. The Basic group is empty except for the single check box. Don't draw anything else inside this area. You'll create a *CWnd* object in here the same size as the list control in the With List Control group and then use it to hold the header and list box controls.

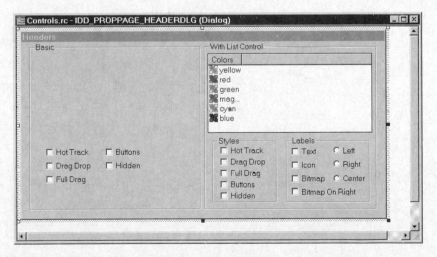

Figure 888a   The header control sample page contains a large open area where you'll build a custom list box to join with a header control. To the right is a list control where you can experiment with its header styles.

You'll need to add a class for the parent control to contain the list box, and a class for the list box to provide Owner Draw capability. Without Owner Draw, the header control capability is lost on the list box. When you're done, you'll find it difficult to distinguish between the list control in report mode and your Owner Draw list box. The list control, however, has a lot more capabilities than you're going to put into the simple list box, as you'll see shortly in the tips on the list control beginning with Tip 892, "Understanding the List Control." Eventually, you could add automatic horizontal scrolling and images to the list box, but right now our focus is on the header control, not the list box.

Add two new classes to your project. The first one is *CHeaderWnd*. Derive it from the Generic CWnd class in the New Class dialog box. This will be the container for the list box and the header control. The second new class is *CheaderListBox*, and its base class should be *CListBox*. This will be your Owner Draw list box where you'll draw columns of text. Let's start with the *CHeaderWnd* class. The header and source file for it are shown here:

```cpp
// HeaderWnd.h : header file
//

#include    "HeaderListBox.h"

/////////////////////////////////////////////////////////
// CHeaderWnd window

class CHeaderWnd : public CWnd
{
// Construction
public:
    CHeaderWnd();

// Attributes
public:

// Operations
public:

// Overrides
    // ClassWizard generated virtual function overrides
    //{{AFX_VIRTUAL(CHeaderWnd)
    protected:
    virtual BOOL OnNotify(WPARAM wParam, LPARAM lParam,
                        LRESULT* pResult);
    //}}AFX_VIRTUAL

// Implementation
public:
    int SetSelection(int nSel);
    void AddListItem(WIN32_FIND_DATA &fd);
    void HideHeader (bool bHide = false);
    CHeaderCtrl * GetHeaderCtrl();
    bool Initialize();
    virtual ~CHeaderWnd();

    // Generated message map functions
protected:
    CImageList m_imageOneTwoThree;
    //{{AFX_MSG(CHeaderWnd)
    //}}AFX_MSG
    DECLARE_MESSAGE_MAP()

    CHeaderCtrl m_Header;
```

```
        CHeaderListBox  m_List;
};


/////////////////////////////////////////////////////
//
// HeaderWnd.cpp : implementation file
//

#include "stdafx.h"
#include "Controls.h"
#include "HeaderWnd.h"

#ifdef _DEBUG
#define new DEBUG_NEW
#undef THIS_FILE
static char THIS_FILE[] = __FILE__;
#endif

/////////////////////////////////////////////////////
// CheaderWnd

CHeaderWnd::CHeaderWnd()
{
}

CHeaderWnd::~CHeaderWnd()
{
}


BEGIN_MESSAGE_MAP(CHeaderWnd, CWnd)
    //{{AFX_MSG_MAP(CHeaderWnd)
    //}}AFX_MSG_MAP
END_MESSAGE_MAP()


/////////////////////////////////////////////////////
// CHeaderWnd message handlers

bool CHeaderWnd::Initialize()
{
    CRect rc;
    ::GetWindowRect (this->m_hWnd, &rc);
    CFont *font = GetParent()->GetFont();
    LOGFONT lf;
    font->GetLogFont (&lf);
    CRect rcHeader;
    rcHeader.top = 0;
    rcHeader.left = 2;
    rcHeader.bottom = 3 * lf.lfHeight / 2;
    if (rcHeader.bottom < 0)
        rcHeader.bottom *= -1;
    rcHeader.right = rc.right - rc.left - 2;
    m_Header.CreateEx (0, WC_HEADER, NULL,
            WS_VISIBLE | WS_CHILD | HDS_HORZ,
            rcHeader, this,
```

```
                IDC_HEADER_LISTHEADER);
    m_Header.ShowWindow (SW_SHOWNORMAL);
    m_Header.SetFont (font);

    CRect rcList (rcHeader);
    rcList.top = rcList.bottom;
    rcList.bottom = rc.bottom - rc.top;
    m_List.Create (LBS_OWNERDRAWFIXED | WS_VSCROLL
                | WS_VISIBLE | LBS_NOINTEGRALHEIGHT
                | WS_CHILD, rcList, this,
                 IDC_HEADER_LISTBOX);
    m_List.ShowWindow (SW_SHOWNORMAL);
    m_List.SetFont (font);

    m_imageOneTwoThree.Create (IDB_ONETWOTHREE, 16, 2,
                            RGB(0x00, 0x80, 0x80));
    m_Header.SetImageList (&m_imageOneTwoThree);

    HDITEM hi;
    memset (&hi, '\0', sizeof (HDITEM));
    hi.mask = HDI_WIDTH | HDI_TEXT
            | HDI_ORDER | HDI_LPARAM
            | HDI_IMAGE | HDI_FORMAT;
    hi.iOrder = 0;
    hi.lParam = 0;
    hi.iImage = 0;
    hi.fmt = HDF_IMAGE | HDF_STRING;
    hi.cxy = rcHeader.right / 3;
    hi.pszText = "File";
    m_Header.InsertItem (0, &hi);
    hi.pszText = "Size";
    hi.iOrder = 1;
    hi.lParam = 1;
    hi.iImage = 1;
    m_Header.InsertItem (1, &hi);
    hi.cxy -= 2;
    hi.pszText = "Created";
    hi.iOrder = 2;
    hi.lParam = 2;
    hi.iImage = 2;
    m_Header.InsertItem (2, &hi);

    return (true);
}

BOOL CHeaderWnd::OnNotify(WPARAM wParam, LPARAM lParam,
                        LRESULT* pResult)
{
    if (wParam == IDC_HEADER_LISTHEADER)
    {
        NMHDR *pNMHDR = (NMHDR *) lParam;
        switch (pNMHDR->code)
        {
            case HDN_ENDDRAG:
            case HDN_ENDTRACK:
                m_List.Invalidate ();
                *pResult = 0;
```

```
                return (TRUE);
            default:
                break;
        }
    }
    return CWnd::OnNotify(wParam, lParam, pResult);
}


CHeaderCtrl * CHeaderWnd::GetHeaderCtrl()
{
    return (&m_Header);
}


//
//  HDS_HIDDEN appears to be a style engineered
//  for the list control. You can set the style and
//  the control will disappear, but removing the
//  style won't make the control reappear.
//
void CHeaderWnd::HideHeader(bool bHide)
{
    CRect rcHeader, rcList;
    m_List.GetWindowRect (&rcList);
    m_Header.GetWindowRect (&rcHeader);
    if (bHide)
    {
        m_Header.ShowWindow (SW_HIDE);
        rcList.right = rcList.right - rcList.left;
        rcList.bottom = rcList.bottom - rcList.top
                        + rcHeader.bottom - rcHeader.top;
        rcList.left = rcList.top = 0;
        m_List.MoveWindow (rcList);
    }
    else
    {
        rcList.right = rcList.right - rcList.left;
        rcList.bottom = rcList.bottom - rcList.top;
        rcList.left = 0;
        rcList.top = rcHeader.bottom - rcHeader.top;
        m_list.MoveWindow (rcList);
        m_Header.ShowWindow (SW_SHOWNORMAL);
    }

}


void CHeaderWnd::AddListItem(WIN32_FIND_DATA &fd)
{
    m_List.AddListItem (fd);
    return;
}


int CHeaderWnd::SetSelection(int nSel)
{
    int nCur = m_List.GetCurSel ();
    m_List.SetCurSel (nSel);
    return (nCur);
}
```

Now you need an Owner Draw list box. This won't be anything fancy, but combined with a header control, you easily can tabulate the columns and let the user change the width by sliding the buttons on the header control. The code will access the header control to find out how wide each column should be. The code is shown here:

```cpp
// HeaderListBox.h : header file
//

#include    <afxtempl.h>

/////////////////////////////////////////////////////////
// CHeaderListBox window

class CHeaderListBox : public CListBox
{
// Construction
public:
    CHeaderListBox();

// Attributes
public:

// Operations
public:

// Overrides
    // ClassWizard generated virtual function overrides
    //{{AFX_VIRTUAL(CHeaderListBox)
    public:
    virtual void DrawItem(LPDRAWITEMSTRUCT
                                    lpDrawItemStruct);
    virtual void MeasureItem(LPMEASUREITEMSTRUCT
                                    lpMeasureItemStruct);
    //}}AFX_VIRTUAL

// Implementation
public:
    void AddListItem(WIN32_FIND_DATA &fd);
    virtual ~CHeaderListBox();

    // Generated message map functions
protected:
    void InsertChar (TCHAR *sz, TCHAR ch);
    void FormatNumber (CString& strText, ULONG ulSize);
    //{{AFX_MSG(CHeaderListBox)
        // NOTE - the ClassWizard will add and remove
        // member functions here.
    //}}AFX_MSG

    DECLARE_MESSAGE_MAP()

    CList<WIN32_FIND_DATA, WIN32_FIND_DATA&> m_ListData;

};

/////////////////////////////////////////////////////////
```

```cpp
// HeaderListBox.cpp : implementation file
//

#include "stdafx.h"
#include "Controls.h"
#include "HeaderListBox.h"
#include "HeaderWnd.h"

#ifdef _DEBUG
#define new DEBUG_NEW
#undef THIS_FILE
static char THIS_FILE[] = __FILE__;
#endif

/////////////////////////////////////////////////////////
// CHeaderListBox

CHeaderListBox::CHeaderListBox()
{
}

CHeaderListBox::~CHeaderListBox()
{
}


BEGIN_MESSAGE_MAP(CHeaderListBox, CListBox)
    //{{AFX_MSG_MAP(CHeaderListBox)
        // NOTE - the ClassWizard will add and
        // remove mapping macros here.
    //}}AFX_MSG_MAP
END_MESSAGE_MAP()

/////////////////////////////////////////////////////////
// CHeaderListBox message handlers

void CHeaderListBox::DrawItem(
                    LPDRAWITEMSTRUCT lpDrawItemStruct)
{
    if (lpDrawItemStruct->itemID == (UINT) -1)
        return;
    int nItem = lpDrawItemStruct->itemID;
    CDC* pDC = CDC::FromHandle(lpDrawItemStruct->hDC);

//
// If this item is selected, paint it in white text
// with a blue background (the system colors).
//
    CBrush brush;
    if (lpDrawItemStruct->itemState & ODS_SELECTED)
    {
        brush.CreateSolidBrush (GetSysColor
                              (COLOR_HIGHLIGHT));
        pDC->SetTextColor (GetSysColor
                              (COLOR_HIGHLIGHTTEXT));
    }
```

```
//
//  Otherwise paint it, paint it, paint it black with
//  a white background.
//
    else
    {
        brush.CreateSolidBrush (GetSysColor(COLOR_WINDOW));
        pDC->SetTextColor (GetSysColor(COLOR_WINDOWTEXT));
    }
    pDC->FillRect (&lpDrawItemStruct->rcItem, &brush);
    pDC->SetBkMode (TRANSPARENT);
    CRect rcItem(lpDrawItemStruct->rcItem);
    rcItem.InflateRect(-2, -2);

    CRect rc (rcItem);
    HDITEM hi;

    CHeaderCtrl *Header = ((CHeaderWnd *)
                          GetParent())->GetHeaderCtrl ();
    memset (&hi, '\0', sizeof (HDITEM));
    hi.mask = HDI_WIDTH | HDI_ORDER;

    Header->GetItemRect (0, rcItem);
    rc.left = rcItem.left + 2;
    rc.right = rc.left + rcItem.right - rcItem.left - 2;
    POSITION pos = m_ListData.FindIndex (nItem);
    if (pos == NULL)
        return;
    WIN32_FIND_DATA fd = m_ListData.GetAt (pos);
    CString strText = fd.cFileName;
    pDC->DrawText (strText, &rc, DT_END_ELLIPSIS);

    Header->GetItemRect (1, rcItem);
    rc.left = rcItem.left + 2;
    rc.right = rc.left + rcItem.right - rcItem.left - 2;
    FormatNumber (strText, fd.nFileSizeLow);
    pDC->DrawText (strText, &rc, DT_END_ELLIPSIS);

    Header->GetItemRect (2, rcItem);
    rc.left = rcItem.left + 2;
    rc.right = rc.left + rcItem.right - rcItem.left - 2;

    CTime Now = fd.ftCreationTime;
    strText.Format ("%02d/%02d/%02d %02d:%02d",
        Now.GetMonth(), Now.GetDay(),
        Now.GetYear() % 100,
        Now.GetHour(), Now.GetMinute());
    pDC->DrawText (strText, &rc, DT_END_ELLIPSIS);

    // Focus rect
    if (lpDrawItemStruct->itemAction & ODA_FOCUS)
        pDC->DrawFocusRect(&lpDrawItemStruct->rcItem);
}

void CHeaderListBox::MeasureItem(LPMEASUREITEMSTRUCT
                                 lpMeasureItemStruct)
```

```
{
    if (lpMeasureItemStruct->itemID != IDC_HEADER_LISTBOX)
        return;
    CWindowDC (this);
    LOGFONT lf;
    CFont *font = GetFont();
    font->GetLogFont (&lf);
    lpMeasureItemStruct->itemHeight = lf.lfHeight;
    if (lpMeasureItemStruct->itemHeight < 0)
        lpMeasureItemStruct->itemHeight *= -1;
    CHeaderCtrl *Header = ((CHeaderWnd *)
                    GetParent())->GetHeaderCtrl ();
    CRect rcItem;
    Header->GetItemRect (2, rcItem);
    lpMeasureItemStruct->itemWidth = rcItem.right;
}

void CHeaderListBox::AddListItem(WIN32_FIND_DATA &fd)
{

    POSITION pos = m_ListData.AddTail (fd);
    AddString ((LPCSTR) pos);
}

void CHeaderListBox::FormatNumber(CString &strText,
                                  ULONG ulSize)
{

    TCHAR szBuf[32];

    strText.Empty();
    memset (szBuf, '\0', sizeof (szBuf));
    sprintf (szBuf + 1, "%ld", ulSize);
    TCHAR *psz = szBuf + strlen (szBuf + 1);
    for (int i = 1; *(psz - 1); ++i, -psz)
    {
        if (!(i%3))
            InsertChar (psz, ',');
    }
    strText = (szBuf + 1);
}

void CHeaderListBox::InsertChar(TCHAR *sz, TCHAR ch)
{
    char *s = sz + strlen (sz);
    while (s > sz)
    {
        *s = *(s-1);
        -s;
    }
    *s = ch;
}
```

When you put these together with the following code to create a new property page, the newly created window along with its header control should appear as in Figure 888b.

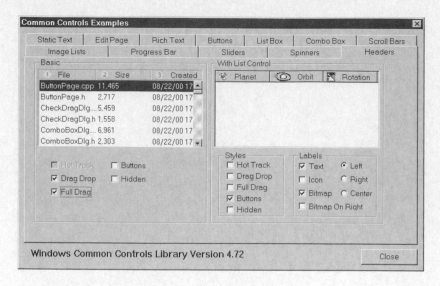

Figure 888b   The control on the left is the one that you just created using a CWnd *object.*
It's an ordinary list box with column listings similar to the list control on the right.
The difference is that in your control, the user may change the order of the column by dragging the header columns.

That done, you can go ahead and implement the property page class. Make sure that it's derived from *CpropertyPage*, and name it *CHeaderDlg*. Add it to the property sheet. This code will create and initialize the *CHeaderWnd* object, which in turn will create and initialize the *CHeaderListBox* object, along with a header control to go with it.

Not all the styles will be implemented on both controls. For example, the left, right, and center formats will be used only on the list control, but there's nothing stopping you from using the same technique to add the styles to the header control in the Basic group. In fact, more styles are available for the Basic list box because the list control doesn't permit dragging and dropping the header columns. We've opted to add the icons with the numbers to the Basic header control so that you can see the original order of the columns. You could remove these easily and use bitmaps, or just plain text.

The class also will be a repository for the image list and bitmaps that will be used with the list control's header. The *HeaderDlg.h* file is listed here:

```
// HeaderDlg.h : header file
//

#include   "HeaderWnd.h"


/////////////////////////////////////////////////////
// CHeaderDlg dialog

class CHeaderDlg : public CpropertyPage
{
    DECLARE_DYNCREATE(CHeaderDlg)

// Construction
public:
    CImageList m_imageOneTwoThree;
    CHeaderDlg();
    ~CHeaderDlg();

// Dialog Data
    //{{AFX_DATA(CHeaderDlg)
```

```
    enum { IDD = IDD_PROPPAGE_HEADERDLG };
    CListCtrl   m_HeaderListCtrl;
    BOOL    m_bListHotTrack;
    BOOL    m_bListButtons;
    BOOL    m_bListFullDrag;
    BOOL    m_bListDragDrop;
    BOOL    m_bBasicHotTrack;
    BOOL    m_bBasicHidden;
    BOOL    m_bBasicFullDrag;
    BOOL    m_bBasicDragDrop;
    BOOL    m_bBasicButtons;
    BOOL    m_bListHidden;
    BOOL    m_bListIcon;
    BOOL    m_bListText;
    BOOL    m_bListBitmap;
    int     m_nListFormat;
    BOOL    m_bListBmpOnRight;
    //}}AFX_DATA


// Overrides
    // ClassWizard generate virtual function overrides
    //{{AFX_VIRTUAL(CHeaderDlg)
    protected:
    virtual void DoDataExchange(CDataExchange* pDX);
    //}}AFX_VIRTUAL


// Implementation
protected:
    // Generated message map functions
    //{{AFX_MSG(CHeaderDlg)
    virtual BOOL OnInitDialog();
    afx_msg void OnHeaderListbuttons();
    afx_msg void OnHeaderListhottrack();
    afx_msg void OnHeaderListfulldrag();
    afx_msg void OnHeaderListdragdrop();
    afx_msg void OnHeaderBasicdragdrop();
    afx_msg void OnHeaderBasicbuttons();
    afx_msg void OnHeaderBasicfulldrag();
    afx_msg void OnHeaderBasichidden();
    afx_msg void OnHeaderBasichottrack();
    afx_msg void OnHeaderListtext();
    afx_msg void OnHeaderListicon();
    afx_msg void OnHeaderListbitmap();
    afx_msg void OnFormatLabel();
    afx_msg void OnHeaderListBmponRight();
    afx_msg void OnHeaderListhidden();
    //}}AFX_MSG
    DECLARE_MESSAGE_MAP()

    CHeaderWnd  m_ListParent;

    HBITMAP     m_hBmpPlanet;
    HBITMAP     m_hBmpOrbit;
    HBITMAP     m_hBmpRotate;
};
```

You'll load the bitmaps using the *LoadImage()* function. You could use *Cbitmap* objects, but with small images, *Cbitmap* seems to reserve a little extra memory—and when you use the *m_hObject* member, you get some black space to the right. *LoadImage()* is a bit more complicated, but it doesn't cause this. The object created is a resource object, an *HBITMAP*, so remember that they must be deleted when the class is destroyed (OK, old habit, I know—later versions of Windows do clean up after you, but deleting unused resources is a good habit to form).

The source code for the *CHeaderDlg* file is shown here:

```cpp
// HeaderDlg.cpp : implementation file
//

#include "stdafx.h"
#include "Controls.h"
#include "HeaderDlg.h"

#ifdef _DEBUG
#define new DEBUG_NEW
#undef THIS_FILE
static char THIS_FILE[] = __FILE__;
#endif


/////////////////////////////////////////////////////////
// CHeaderDlg property page

IMPLEMENT_DYNCREATE(CHeaderDlg, CPropertyPage)

CHeaderDlg::CHeaderDlg() : CPropertyPage(CHeaderDlg::IDD)
{
    //{{AFX_DATA_INIT(CHeaderDlg)
    m_bListHotTrack = FALSE;
    m_bListButtons = TRUE;
    m_bListFullDrag = FALSE;
    m_bListDragDrop = FALSE;
    m_bBasicHotTrack = FALSE;
    m_bBasicHidden = FALSE;
    m_bBasicFullDrag = FALSE;\
    m_bBasicDragDrop = FALSE;
    m_bBasicButtons = FALSE;
    m_bListHidden = FALSE;
    m_bListIcon = FALSE;
    m_bListText = TRUE;
    m_bListBitmap = FALSE;
    m_nListFormat = 0;
    m_bListBmpOnRight = FALSE;
    //}}AFX_DATA_INIT
    m_psp.dwFlags &= ~PSP_HASHELP;
    m_hBmpPlanet = NULL;
    m_hBmpOrbit = NULL;
    m_hBmpRotate = NULL;
}

CHeaderDlg::~CHeaderDlg()
{
    if (m_hBmpPlanet != NULL)
        DeleteObject (m_hBmpPlanet);
```

```
    if (m_hBmpOrbit != NULL)
        DeleteObject (m_hBmpOrbit);
    if (m_hBmpRotate != NULL)
        DeleteObject (m_hBmpRotate);
}


void CHeaderDlg::DoDataExchange(CDataExchange* pDX)
{
    CPropertyPage::DoDataExchange(pDX);
    //{{AFX_DATA_MAP(CHeaderDlg)
    DDX_Control(pDX, IDC_HEADER_LISTCONTROL,
                m_HeaderListCtrl);
    DDX_Check(pDX, IDC_HEADER_LISTHOTTRACK,
              m_bListHotTrack);
    DDX_Check(pDX, IDC_HEADER_LISTBUTTONS, m_bListButtons);
    DDX_Check(pDX, IDC_HEADER_LISTFULLDRAG,
                m_bListFullDrag);
    DDX_Check(pDX, IDC_HEADER_LISTDRAGDROP,
                m_bListDragDrop);
    DDX_Check(pDX, IDC_HEADER_BASICHOTTRACK,
                m_bBasicHotTrack);
    DDX_Check(pDX, IDC_HEADER_BASICHIDDEN, m_bBasicHidden);
    DDX_Check(pDX, IDC_HEADER_BASICFULLDRAG,
                m_bBasicFullDrag);
    DDX_Check(pDX, IDC_HEADER_BASICDRAGDROP,
                m_bBasicDragDrop);
    DDX_Check(pDX, IDC_HEADER_BASICBUTTONS,
                m_bBasicButtons);
    DDX_Check(pDX, IDC_HEADER_LISTHIDDEN, m_bListHidden);
    DDX_Check(pDX, IDC_HEADER_LISTICON, m_bListIcon);
    DDX_Check(pDX, IDC_HEADER_LISTTEXT, m_bListText);
    DDX_Check(pDX, IDC_HEADER_LISTBITMAP, m_bListBitmap);
    DDX_Radio(pDX, IDC_HEADER_LISTLEFT, m_nListFormat);
    DDX_Check(pDX, IDC_HEADER_LISTBMPONRIGHT,
                m_bListBmpOnRight);
    //}}AFX_DATA_MAP
}


BEGIN_MESSAGE_MAP(CHeaderDlg, CPropertyPage)
    //{{AFX_MSG_MAP(CHeaderDlg)
    ON_BN_CLICKED(IDC_HEADER_LISTBUTTONS,
                OnHeaderListbuttons)\
    ON_BN_CLICKED(IDC_HEADER_LISTHOTTRACK,
                OnHeaderListhottrack)
    ON_BN_CLICKED(IDC_HEADER_LISTFULLDRAG,
                OnHeaderListfulldrag)
    ON_BN_CLICKED(IDC_HEADER_LISTDRAGDROP,
                OnHeaderListdragdrop)
    ON_BN_CLICKED(IDC_HEADER_BASICDRAGDROP,
                OnHeaderBasicdragdrop)
    ON_BN_CLICKED(IDC_HEADER_BASICBUTTONS,
                OnHeaderBasicbuttons)
    ON_BN_CLICKED(IDC_HEADER_BASICFULLDRAG,
                OnHeaderBasicfulldrag)
    ON_BN_CLICKED(IDC_HEADER_BASICHIDDEN,
                OnHeaderBasichidden)
```

```
        ON_BN_CLICKED(IDC_HEADER_BASICHOTTRACK,
                        OnHeaderBasichottrack)
        ON_BN_CLICKED(IDC_HEADER_LISTTEXT, OnHeaderListtext)
        ON_BN_CLICKED(IDC_HEADER_LISTICON, OnHeaderListicon)
        ON_BN_CLICKED(IDC_HEADER_LISTBITMAP,
                                    OnHeaderListbitmap)
        ON_BN_CLICKED(IDC_HEADER_LISTLEFT, OnFormatLabel)
        ON_BN_CLICKED(IDC_HEADER_LISTBMPONRIGHT,
                        OnHeaderListBmponRight)
        ON_BN_CLICKED(IDC_HEADER_LISTRIGHT, OnFormatLabel)
        ON_BN_CLICKED(IDC_HEADER_LISTCENTER, OnFormatLabel)
        ON_BN_CLICKED(IDC_HEADER_LISTHIDDEN,
                                    OnHeaderListhidden)
    //}}AFX_MSG_MAP
END_MESSAGE_MAP()


///////////////////////////////////////////////////////////
// CHeaderDlg message handlers

BOOL CHeaderDlg::OnInitDialog()
{
char *szTitles [] =
    {
    "Planet",
    "Orbit",
    "Rotation"
    };
#define TITLES (sizeof(szTitles)/sizeof(char *))

    CPropertyPage::OnInitDialog();

    CRect rc;
    m_HeaderListCtrl.GetWindowRect (&rc);
    CHeaderCtrl *header = m_HeaderListCtrl.GetHeaderCtrl();
    LV_COLUMN   lc;
    HDITEM      hi;

    memset (&lc, '\0', sizeof (LV_COLUMN));
    memset (&hi, '\0', sizeof (HDITEM));
    lc.mask = LVCF_TEXT | LVCF_WIDTH | LVCF_SUBITEM;
    for (int sub = 0; sub < TITLES; ++sub)
    {
        lc.iImage = sub;
        lc.pszText = szTitles[sub];
        lc.cx = (rc.right - rc.left) / 3 - 2;
        lc.iSubItem = sub;
        m_HeaderListCtrl.InsertColumn (sub, &lc);
    }
//
// Calculate the parent window for the list box
// so it is the same size as the list control.
//
    CRect rcAdv;
    ::GetWindowRect (
        GetDlgItem(IDC_HEADER_ADVANCED)->m_hWnd, rcAdv);
    ScreenToClient (&rcAdv);
```

```
    CRect rcBasic;
    ::GetWindowRect (
         GetDlgItem(IDC_HEADER_BASIC)->m_hWnd, rcBasic);
    ScreenToClient (&rcBasic);
    CRect rcCtrl;
    m_HeaderListCtrl.GetWindowRect (&rcCtrl);
    ScreenToClient (&rcCtrl);
    CRect rcListBox (rcBasic);
    rcListBox.left += rcCtrl.left - rcAdv.left;
    rcListBox.right -= rcAdv.right - rcCtrl.right;
    rcListBox.top = rcCtrl.top;
    rcListBox.bottom = rcCtrl.bottom;
//
//  Create the list box parent window. Use the
//  static window type.
//
    m_ListParent.CreateEx (0, "static", NULL, WS_CHILD
                        | WS_VISIBLE | SS_SUNKEN,
                          rcListBox, this,
                          IDC_HEADER_LISTBOX);
    m_ListParent.ShowWindow (SW_SHOWNORMAL);
//
//  Initialize the window variables. This will
//  create the list box and its header control.
//
    m_ListParent.Initialize ();
//
//  Load the owner draw list box with file structures.
//
    WIN32_FIND_DATA fd;
    HANDLE hFind;
    int nItem = 0;
    if ((hFind = FindFirstFile (_T("*.*"), &fd)) != NULL)
    {
        do
        {
            if (fd.cFileName[0] == '.')
                continue;
            m_ListParent.AddListItem (fd);
        } while (FindNextFile (hFind, &fd) == TRUE);
    }
    m_ListParent.SetSelection (0);
//
//  Disable the Hot Track button in the basic group
//  and the Bitmap on Right button in the list box
//  group. Hot Track requires button style, and
//  Bitmap on Right requires bitmap format.
//
    ::EnableWindow (GetDlgItem (
               IDC_HEADER_BASICHOTTRACK)->m_hWnd, FALSE);
    ::EnableWindow (
               GetDlgItem(
               IDC_HEADER_LISTBMPONRIGHT)->m_hWnd, FALSE);
//
//  Load the bitmaps for the list control header.
//
```

```
        HINSTANCE hInst = AfxGetInstanceHandle ();
        m_hBmpPlanet=(HBITMAP)LoadImage(hInst,
                    MAKEINTRESOURCE(IDB_HEADER_SMALLEARTH),
                    IMAGE_BITMAP, 16, 16, LR_DEFAULTCOLOR);
        m_hBmpOrbit = (HBITMAP) LoadImage (hInst,
                    MAKEINTRESOURCE(IDB_HEADER_ORBIT),
                    IMAGE_BITMAP, 32, 16, LR_DEFAULTCOLOR);
        m_hBmpRotate = (HBITMAP) LoadImage (hInst,
                    MAKEINTRESOURCE(IDB_HEADER_DAYNIGHT),
                    IMAGE_BITMAP, 16, 16, LR_DEFAULTCOLOR);
//
//  Set the image list for the list control header.
//  Note that this image list is completely separate
//  from the other two that may be used with the
//  list control.
//
        m_imageOneTwoThree.Create (IDB_ONETWOTHREE, 16, 2,
                                RGB(0x00, 0x80, 0x80));
        header->SetImageList (&m_imageOneTwoThree);
        return (TRUE);
}


/////////////////////////////////////////////////////////
// Basic group handler functions

void CHeaderDlg::OnHeaderBasicdragdrop()
{
    UpdateData (TRUE);
    if (m_bBasicDragDrop)
    {
        m_ListParent.GetHeaderCtrl()->ModifyStyle (0,
                                HDS_DRAGDROP, TRUE);
    }
    else
    {
        m_ListParent.GetHeaderCtrl()->ModifyStyle(
                                HDS_DRAGDROP, 0, TRUE);
    }
}

void CHeaderDlg::OnHeaderBasicbuttons()
{
    UpdateData (TRUE);
    if (m_bBasicButtons)
    {
        ::EnableWindow (GetDlgItem
                (IDC_HEADER_BASICHOTTRACK)->m_hWnd, TRUE);
        m_ListParent.GetHeaderCtrl()->ModifyStyle (0,
                                HDS_BUTTONS, TRUE);
    }
    else
    {
        m_bBasicHotTrack = FALSE;
        ::EnableWindow (
                GetDlgItem(IDC_HEADER_BASICHOTTRACK)->m_hWnd,
                FALSE);
```

```
                m_ListParent.GetHeaderCtrl()->ModifyStyle (
                                HDS_BUTTONS, Ø, TRUE);
    }
    UpdateData (FALSE);
}

void CHeaderDlg::OnHeaderBasicfulldrag()
{
    UpdateData (TRUE);
    if (m_bBasicFullDrag)
    {
        m_ListParent.GetHeaderCtrl()->ModifyStyle (Ø,
                                HDS_FULLDRAG, TRUE);
    }
    else
    {
        m_ListParent.GetHeaderCtrl()->ModifyStyle (
                                HDS_FULLDRAG, Ø, TRUE);
    }
}

void CHeaderDlg::OnHeaderBasichidden()
{
    UpdateData (TRUE);
    if (m_bBasicHidden)
    {
        m_ListParent.HideHeader(true);
    }
    else
    {
        m_ListParent.HideHeader(false);
    }
}

void CHeaderDlg::OnHeaderBasichottrack()
{
    UpdateData (TRUE);
    if (m_bBasicHotTrack)
    {
        m_ListParent.GetHeaderCtrl()->ModifyStyle (Ø,
                                HDS_HOTTRACK, TRUE);
    }
    else
    {
        m_ListParent.GetHeaderCtrl()->ModifyStyle (
                                HDS_HOTTRACK, Ø, TRUE);
    }
}

//////////////////////////////////////////////////////
// List control group handler functions

void CHeaderDlg::OnHeaderListbuttons()
{
    UpdateData (TRUE);
    if (m_bListButtons)
```

```
    {
        ::EnableWindow (
             GetDlgItem (IDC_HEADER_LISTHOTTRACK)->m_hWnd,
             TRUE);
        m_HeaderListCtrl.GetHeaderCtrl()->ModifyStyle (0,
                                         HDS_BUTTONS, TRUE);
    }
    else
    {
        ::EnableWindow (
             GetDlgItem (IDC_HEADER_LISTHOTTRACK)->m_hWnd,
             FALSE);
        m_HeaderListCtrl.GetHeaderCtrl()->ModifyStyle (
                                         HDS_BUTTONS, 0, TRUE);
    }
}

void CHeaderDlg::OnHeaderListhottrack()
{
    UpdateData (TRUE);
    if (m_bListHotTrack)
    {
        m_HeaderListCtrl.GetHeaderCtrl()->ModifyStyle (0,
                                         HDS_HOTTRACK, TRUE);
    }
    else
    {
        m_HeaderListCtrl.GetHeaderCtrl()->ModifyStyle (
                                         HDS_HOTTRACK, 0, TRUE);
    }
}

void CHeaderDlg::OnHeaderListfulldrag()
{
    UpdateData (TRUE);
    if (m_bListFullDrag)
    {
        m_HeaderListCtrl.GetHeaderCtrl()->ModifyStyle (0,
                                         HDS_FULLDRAG, TRUE);
    }
    else
    {
        m_HeaderListCtrl.GetHeaderCtrl()->ModifyStyle (
                                         HDS_FULLDRAG, 0, TRUE);
    }
}

void CHeaderDlg::OnHeaderListdragdrop()
{
    UpdateData (TRUE);
    if (m_bListDragDrop)
    {
        m_HeaderListCtrl.GetHeaderCtrl()->ModifyStyle (0,
                                         HDS_DRAGDROP, TRUE);
    }
    else
```

```
        {
            m_HeaderListCtrl.GetHeaderCtrl()->ModifyStyle (
                                HDS_DRAGDROP, Ø, TRUE);
        }
}

void CHeaderDlg::OnHeaderListtext()
{
    UpdateData (TRUE);
    HDITEM hi;
    memset (&hi, '\Ø', sizeof (HDITEM));
    CHeaderCtrl *header = m_HeaderListCtrl.GetHeaderCtrl();
    hi.mask = HDI_FORMAT;

    header->GetItem (Ø, &hi);
    if (m_bListText)
    {
        hi.mask = HDI_FORMAT;
        hi.fmt |= HDF_STRING;
        hi.iImage = Ø;
        header->SetItem (Ø, &hi);
        hi.iImage = 1;
        header->SetItem (1, &hi);
        hi.iImage = 2;
        header->SetItem (2, &hi);
    }
    else
    {
        hi.mask = HDI_FORMAT;
        hi.fmt &= ~HDF_STRING;
        header->SetItem (Ø, &hi);
        header->SetItem (1, &hi);
        header->SetItem (2, &hi);
    }
}

void CHeaderDlg::OnHeaderListicon()
{
    UpdateData (TRUE);
    HDITEM hi;
    memset (&hi, '\Ø', sizeof (HDITEM));
    CHeaderCtrl *header = m_HeaderListCtrl.GetHeaderCtrl();
    hi.mask = HDI_FORMAT;

    header->GetItem (Ø, &hi);
    if (m_bListIcon)
    {
        hi.mask = HDI_IMAGE | HDI_FORMAT;
        hi.fmt |= HDF_IMAGE;
        hi.iImage = Ø;
        header->SetItem (Ø, &hi);
        hi.iImage - 1;
        header->SetItem (1, &hi);
        hi.iImage = 2;
        header->SetItem (2, &hi);
    }
```

```
        else
        {
            hi.mask = HDI_FORMAT;
            hi.fmt &= ~HDF_IMAGE;
            header->SetItem (0, &hi);
            header->SetItem (1, &hi);
            header->SetItem (2, &hi);
        }
}

void CHeaderDlg::OnHeaderListbitmap()
{
    UpdateData (TRUE);
    HDITEM hi;
    memset (&hi, '\0', sizeof (HDITEM));
    CHeaderCtrl *header = m_HeaderListCtrl.GetHeaderCtrl();
    hi.mask = HDI_FORMAT;

    header->GetItem (0, &hi);
    if (m_bListBitmap)
    {
        hi.mask = HDI_BITMAP | HDI_FORMAT;
        hi.fmt |= HDF_BITMAP;
        hi.hbm = m_hBmpPlanet;
        header->SetItem (0, &hi);
        hi.hbm = m_hBmpOrbit;
        header->SetItem (1, &hi);
        hi.hbm = m_hBmpRotate;
        header->SetItem (2, &hi);
        ::EnableWindow (
                GetDlgItem(
                    IDC_HEADER_LISTBMPONRIGHT)->m_hWnd, TRUE);
    }
    else
    {
        hi.mask = HDI_FORMAT;
        hi.fmt &= ~HDF_BITMAP;
        header->SetItem (0, &hi);
        header->SetItem (1, &hi);
        header->SetItem (2, &hi);
        ::EnableWindow (
            GetDlgItem(IDC_HEADER_LISTBMPONRIGHT)->m_hWnd,
            FALSE);
    }
}

void CHeaderDlg::OnFormatLabel()
{
    UpdateData (TRUE);
    HDITEM hi;
    memset (&hi, '\0', sizeof (HDITEM));
    CHeaderCtrl *header = m_HeaderListCtrl.GetHeaderCtrl();
    hi.mask = HDI_FORMAT;
    header->GetItem (0, &hi);
    hi.fmt &= ~(HDF_LEFT | HDF_RIGHT | HDF_CENTER);
    switch (m_nListFormat)
```

```
    {
        case 0:     // Left
            hi.fmt |= HDF_LEFT;
            break;
        case 1:     // Right
            hi.fmt |= HDF_RIGHT;
            break;
        case 2:     // Center
            hi.fmt |= HDF_CENTER;
            break;
        default:
            return;
    }
    header->SetItem (0, &hi);
    header->SetItem (1, &hi);
    header->SetItem (2, &hi);
}

void CHeaderDlg::OnHeaderListBmponRight()
{
    UpdateData (TRUE);
    HDITEM hi;
    memset (&hi, '\0', sizeof (HDITEM));
    CHeaderCtrl *header = m_HeaderListCtrl.GetHeaderCtrl();
    hi.mask = HDI_FORMAT;
    header->GetItem (0, &hi);
    if (m_bListBmpOnRight)
    {
        hi.fmt |= HDF_BITMAP_ON_RIGHT;
    }
    else
    {
        hi.fmt &= ~HDF_BITMAP_ON_RIGHT;
    }
    header->SetItem (0, &hi);
    header->SetItem (1, &hi);
    header->SetItem (2, &hi);
}

void CHeaderDlg::OnHeaderListhidden()
{
    UpdateData (TRUE);
    if (m_bListHidden)
    {
        m_HeaderListCtrl.ModifyStyle (0,
                                      LVS_NOCOLUMNHEADER,
                                      TRUE);
    }
    else
    {
        m_HeaderListCtrl.ModifyStyle (LVS_NOCOLUMNHEADER,
                                      0,
                                      TRUE);
    }
}
```

One thing that you will want to check is the *HDS_FULLDRAG* style. Using this style, you should be able to grab the separator between two columns in the header and change the relative size of a column. As you move, the header control should redraw itself, showing the new size of the column being dragged and the new positions of the columns to the right. Without this style, the header control will not redraw itself until you release the mouse button. In both cases, the list below the header should redraw itself to reflect the new column sizes and positions.

889. *Using Dynamic Reordering of Header Fields*

One of the better features of the header control is its capability to create a drag image for you and to let the user move the fields around. When this feature is enabled, the user left-clicks the mouse on the field to be moved. Then, holding the mouse button, the user drags it to the new location and releases. The header column assumes the new position.

Of course, the header control only moves the header column around. It doesn't do anything to the control associated with it. That is your responsibility. With the multi-column list box, the *ON_NOTIFY* message informs the parent of the header field movement, and the parent then invalidates the list box, causing it to redraw itself, as in the following code. You should note that in this sense multi-column is not the same as selecting the style on the list box property page in the dialog editor. In this code, you are creating the columns, not the list box.

```
BOOL CHeaderWnd::OnNotify(WPARAM wParam, LPARAM lParam,
                          LRESULT* pResult)
{
    if (wParam == IDC_HEADER_LISTHEADER)
    {
        NMHDR *pNMHDR = (NMHDR *) lParam;
        switch (pNMHDR->code)
        {
            case HDN_ENDDRAG:
            case HDN_ENDTRACK:
                m_List.Invalidate ();
                *pResult = 0;
                return (TRUE);
            default:
                break;
        }
    }
    return CWnd::OnNotify(wParam, lParam, pResult);
}
```

The code sets **pResult* to zero and returns *TRUE*. Returning *TRUE* effectively keeps the ancestor class code from continuing to process this message, and setting **pResult* to 0 lets the header control continue to process it. When you receive this message, the operation hasn't been completed yet; if you set **pResult* to anything other than zero, the header control will cancel the operation. A non-zero result tells the header control that you processed the message.

When you've received notification that a drag-and-drop operation involving the header control has been completed, you can use that information to perform any operation that your code needs to do. In this sample, the Owner Draw list box uses the location information in the header control to draw the text in the proper place.

Unfortunately, the list control doesn't implement this feature of the header control. We know from the code for our Basic section that simply modifying the style turns on the code, but it doesn't work with the list control. Given the features of the list control, however, it would take more coding than our example provided to implement drag-and-drop reordering.

One final note about this header control style: You can turn it off and on, along with the column resizing, by setting the control to *WS_DISABLED*. Unlike most of the controls, the header control doesn't gray out the surface. It looks normal, but the drag and drop, column resizing, and pushbutton operations don't work.

890. *Enabling Hot Tracking in the Header Control*

The header control can be set to watch for mouse-over events and highlight the text in the button where the mouse is lingering—or rushing pell mell to get away from *le matou*, for that matter.

This is known as *hot tracking* and is enabled by setting the header control style *HDS_HOTTRACK*. Hot tracking works both in the list control header and in any header that you create. To enable it, you also must set the *HDS_BUTTONS* style; it won't work with flat column headers.

In a program using MFC, you can call the *CWnd* function *ModifyStyle()* to turn the style on or off. In the following two lines, the first will activate the style and the second will deactivate it:

```
ModifyStyle (0, HDS_HOTTRACK, TRUE);
ModifyStyle (HDS_HOTTRACK, 0, TRUE);
```

Use this form if you've derived a class from *CHeaderCtrl* and you need to change it from within the class implementation code. If you want to change the hot track style in a list control, you need to call the *CListCtrl::GetHeaderCtrl()* function to get a pointer to the list control's header.

The highlighted text is blue, and with small fonts, it doesn't show up very well.

Alternatively, you can modify the control's style using the *GetWindowLong()* function to retrieve the current style, set the proper bits, and then call *SetWindowLong()*, as in the following code:

```
DWORD dwStyle = GetWindowLong (hWnd, GWL_STYLE);
dwStyle |= HDS_HOTTRACK;
SetWindowLong (hWnd, GWL_STYLE, dwStyle);
```

This sets the style for the control identified by the handle *hWnd*. This method works with either MFC-based programs or Windows API applications.

891. *Using Image Lists with the Header Control*

The header control is very versatile when it comes to the button or column display. It can contain text, an icon, a bitmap, or any combination of the three. The bitmap may be displayed on the left or right side of the text, depending upon the format mode.

Text is displayed in the control's current font. You can call *SetFont()* to change it. Icons should be the standard small 16-by-16-pixel variety and must be contained in an image list object.

Bitmaps, on the other hand, can be any size. They shouldn't exceed the button width or depth, of course, and you need to make them small enough to leave room for any text that you want to display. The bitmaps for individual buttons don't have to be the same size, and the sample code in the Controls project purposely includes a bitmap that is twice as wide as the others to demonstrate that. The Orbit bitmap is 16 pixels deep by 32 pixels wide, while the others are only 16 pixels wide.

By default, the control displays nothing but a blank button or column header. You need to set some information in the control's memory using an *HDITEM* structure. The text, icon, and bitmap identifiers are contained in separate members of the variable. To use text, set the *pszText* member to the string that you want to display, and then set the *mask* bit for *HDI_TEXT* to indicate that the text is valid. Similarly, for an icon, set the *iImage* member to the index of the image in the image list, and then set the *HDI_IMAGE* flag in the *mask*. For bitmaps, set the *hbm* member to the *handle* of the bitmap that you want to display, and set the *HDI_BITMAP* flag. Finally, call the *CHeaderControl::SetItem()* function.

If you are loading the item initially, you don't need to set the format flags. However, if later you want to change things programmatically, you need to set the *HDI_FORMAT* flag in the *mask* member and then set the *fmt* variable with the proper flags: *HDF_STRING* to display text, *HDF_IMAGE* to display the icon, and *HDF_BITMAP* to display the bitmap. As with the *mask* member, you can *OR* these values together.

Other format flags let you set the text and images in the center of the button, or set the bitmap to the right of the text. The normal order for drawing items on the header button is image, text, and then bitmap when the alignment is set to *HDF_LEFT* or *HDF_CENTER*. With *HDF_RIGHT*, the order is bitmap, image, and then text.

892. *Understanding the List Control*

Probably the most versatile and useful—and certainly one of the most commonly used—of the new 32-bit controls is the *list control*. This isn't to be confused with the *list box* control, which is one of the carryovers from 16-bit Windows. They are different animals, and each serves a different purpose.

This is the control you see when you open a directory view in Windows. Double-click on the My Computer icon on the desktop, and you'll get a list view showing the drives available on your computer.

The list control modes permit different views of the same collections of items. You can view the collection as large or small icons, or as a list arranged in rows across the control. Each of these views contains a single piece of text to label the item. The fourth view—the report mode—lists the collection in a column down the control and may contain additional columns to display additional information about the objects in the collection.

Each mode may be used with an image list. In fact, the large and small icon modes are almost useless without an image list. The control can contain two images lists, one for the large icons that is used only in the large icon mode and another for the small icons used in the other three modes. In addition, in the report mode the control incorporates a header control, which itself can contain a third image list.

893. *Using the CListCtrl Class*

The Microsoft Foundation Class library's *CListCtrl* class encapsulates the list control and contains member functions to access and maintain the contents of the control and to manipulate the list and its associated header control.

The control has some quirks you should know about, but overall it's a very good control. It won't replace the trusty old list box control—even in owner-draw mode, the list control can't match the possibilities of an owner-draw list box. But for those occasions when you need to list information in columns or in icon form, it's an easy control to master and use.

The example will use text and image callback. Text callback is the most efficient method of using the list control. Your program stores the data and feeds it to the control when requested. Storing the data in the program solves a lot of problems by making the uncooked data immediately available. The list control requires strings to display, but a lot of the information that you will place in a list control may be numerical, or a combination of numbers or characters. That's why we chose the planets as the subject for this list control example. The entries contain a mixed sample of numbers and characters.

You'll also have the option of *not* using text and image callback to see the difference. Simply remove or comment out the *#define _USETEXTCALLBACK* near the top of the source file, and recompile the code. Notice how much more complicated the code has become, and just to make it easier, the column formatting has been changed so that the number can be compared more easily.

Also, to sort the items, you need to get the text out of the control. The control is a member of the class, and the sort function is a callback function, which means that it must be *static* and therefore doesn't have access to non-*static* class members (don't try making the list control variable *static*—that will really confound things). To fix this, you have to declare a global pointer to the list control just to be able to sort.

To implement the full row selection, you'll need to add a new control class, *CListCtrlEx*, and derive it from *CListCtrl*. The code is exactly the same as the *CListViewEx* class from Tip 655, "Using the Owner Draw Property to Create a Full Line Selection." Just change the references to *CListViewEx* to *CListCtrlEx* and the reference to *CListView* to *CListCtrl*. Also remove any references to the underlying list control. For example, instead of *GetListCtrl().GetImageList()*, you need only *GetImageList()*. I've already done this for you and the source code for *CListCtrlEx* is on the companion CD-ROM but because it is so similar to the earlier project code, it won't be listed again. The files on the CD-ROM that you will need are *ListCtrlEx.cpp* and *ListCtrlEx.h*.

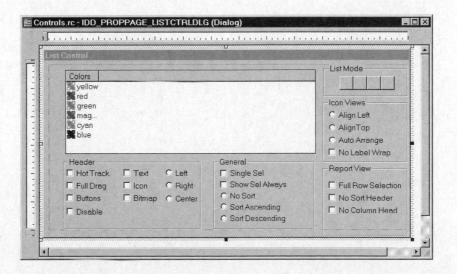

Figure 893   The List Control property page contains a number of controls for experimenting with the control's styles

Go ahead and create a new property page for the Controls project. Title it List Control, and give it a resource ID of *IDD_PROPPAGE_LISTCTRLDLG*. Figure 893 shows the controls on this page. Create a class named *ClistCtrlDlg*, and derive it from *CPropertyPage*. The header file is shown here:

```cpp
// ListCtrlDlg.h : header file
//

#include    "ListCtrlEx.h"

struct ROTATION
{
    int Days;
    int Hours;
    int Minutes;
};

struct PLANET
    {
    char    Planet[12];
    char    Desc[32];
    int     Orbit;
    ROTATION    Rotation;
    int     Diameter;
    int     nIcon;
    };

/////////////////////////////////////////////////////////
// CListCtrlDlg dialog

class CListCtrlDlg : public CPropertyPage
{
    DECLARE_DYNCREATE(CListCtrlDlg)

// Construction
public:
    int SetSelectedItem(int nSel);
    int GetSelectedItem();
    CListCtrlDlg();
    ~CListCtrlDlg();

// Dialog Data
    //{{AFX_DATA(CListCtrlDlg)
    enum { IDD = IDD_PROPPAGE_LISTCTRLDLG };
    CListCtrlEx m_ctlList;
    int     m_nListMode;
    int     m_nIconAlign;
    int     m_nListSort;
    int     m_nHeaderAlign;
    BOOL    m_bBitmap;
    BOOL    m_bButtons;
    BOOL    m_bFullDrag;
    BOOL    m_bFullRowSel;
    BOOL    m_bHotTrack;
    BOOL    m_bIcon;
    BOOL    m_bNoColHeader;
    BOOL    m_bNoLabelWrap;
    BOOL    m_bNoSortHeader;
    BOOL    m_bShowSelAlways;
    BOOL    m_bSingleSel;
    BOOL    m_bText;
```

```
    BOOL    m_bDisableHeader;
    //}}AFX_DATA


// Overrides
    // ClassWizard generate virtual function overrides
    //{{AFX_VIRTUAL(CListCtrlDlg)
    protected:
    virtual void DoDataExchange(CDataExchange* pDX);
    // DDX/DDV support
    //}}AFX_VIRTUAL


// Implementation
protected:
    static int CALLBACK CompareFunction(LPARAM lParam1,
                        LPARAM lParam2, LPARAM lParamSort);
    void FreeItemMemory();
    void AddItem (int nIndex, PLANET *planet);
    void LoadListControl();
    BOOL OnToolTipNotify(UINT nID, NMHDR *pTTTStruct,
                        LRESULT *pResult);
    // Generated message map functions
    //{{AFX_MSG(CListCtrlDlg)
    virtual BOOL OnInitDialog();
    afx_msg void OnListMode();
    afx_msg void OnIconAlign();
    afx_msg void OnListSort();
    afx_msg void OnHeaderAlign();
    afx_msg void OnListctrlNolabelwrap();
    afx_msg void OnListctrlFullrowsel();
    afx_msg void OnListctrlNosortheader();
    afx_msg void OnListctrlNocolumnheader();
    afx_msg void OnListctrlSinglesel();
    afx_msg void OnListctrlShowselalways();
    afx_msg void OnListctrlHottrack();
    afx_msg void OnListctrlFulldrag();
    afx_msg void OnListctrlButtons();
    afx_msg void OnListctrlText();
    afx_msg void OnListctrlIcon();
    afx_msg void OnListctrlBitmap();
    afx_msg void OnListctrlDisableheader();
    afx_msg void OnGetdispinfoListctrlListctrl(
                        NMHDR* pNMHDR, LRESULT* pResult);
    afx_msg void OnColumnclickListctrlListctrl(
                        NMHDR* pNMHDR, LRESULT* pResult);
    afx_msg void OnDestroy();
    //}}AFX_MSG
    DECLARE_MESSAGE_MAP()

CImageList      m_HeaderIcons;
    CImageList      m_SmallPlanets;
    CImageList      m_LargePlanets;
    HBITMAP         m_hBmpPlanet;
    HBITMAP         m_hBmpOrbit;
    HBITMAP         m_hBmpRotate;
    HBITMAP         m_hBmpDiameter;
};
```

The sample also will include some of the functions from the header control sample because, well, the header is a part of the list control, and the purpose of this exercise is to give you some real-world samples of how the control works. This time, however, you can have text or an icon, or both, or a bitmap. If you have the bitmap, the text and icon boxes will be disabled. The custom bitmaps for these columns will include the icon and text, but in a stylized format. The font used is nothing but the Comic MS font colored red, but you can see the visual impact that it makes.

The source file for the *CListCtrlDlg* class is shown here:

```cpp
// ListCtrlDlg.cpp : implementation file
//

#include "stdafx.h"
#include "Controls.h"
#include "ListCtrlDlg.h"

#ifdef _DEBUG
#define new DEBUG_NEW
#undef THIS_FILE
static char THIS_FILE[] = __FILE__;
#endif

#define MAX_STRING      256

PLANET  Planets[] =
    {
    "Mercury", "- The Messenger", 579, 58, 0, 0,
                38 * 12756 / 100, 0,
    "Venus", "- The Messenger", 1082, 243, 0, 0,
                95 * 12756 / 100, 1,
    "Earth", "- Our Home Planet", 1302, 0, 23, 56,
                100 * 12756 / 100, 2,
    "Mars", "- The Red Planet", 2279, 1, 0, 37,
                53 * 12756 / 100, 3,
    "Jupiter", "- The Giant Planet", 7790, 0, 9, 55,
                1121 * 12756 / 100, 4,
    "Saturn", "- The Ringed Planet", 14320, 0, 10, 40,
                914 * 12756 / 100, 5,
    "Uranus", "- The Green Giant", 28000, 0, 17, 14,
                400 * 12756 / 100, 6,
    "Neptune", "- The Blue Planet", 45000, 0, 16, 7,
                390 * 12756 / 100, 7,
    "Pluto", "- The Farthest Planet", 59000, 6, 9, 17,
                18 * 12756 / 100, 8
    };
#define    PLANETS    (sizeof(Planets)/sizeof(PLANET))

#undef STATEMASK
#define    STATEMASK   0

#define _USETEXTCALLBACK

//
//  The following is needed only if you are NOT using
//  LPSTR_TEXTCALLBACK and you need to sort.
//
```

```
static CListCtrlEx  *g_pctlList;

//////////////////////////////////////////////////////
// CListCtrlDlg property page

IMPLEMENT_DYNCREATE(CListCtrlDlg, CPropertyPage)

CListCtrlDlg::CListCtrlDlg()
                    : CPropertyPage(CListCtrlDlg::IDD)
{
    //{{AFX_DATA_INIT(CListCtrlDlg)
    m_nListMode = 0;
    m_nIconAlign = 0;
    m_nListSort = 0;
    m_nHeaderAlign = 0;
    m_bBitmap = FALSE;
    m_bButtons = TRUE;
    m_bFullDrag = FALSE;
    m_bFullRowSel = FALSE;
    m_bHotTrack = FALSE;
    m_bIcon = FALSE;
    m_bNoColHeader = FALSE;
    m_bNoLabelWrap = FALSE;
    m_bNoSortHeader = FALSE;
    m_bShowSelAlways = FALSE;
    m_bSingleSel = FALSE;
    m_bText = TRUE;
    m_bDisableHeader = FALSE;
    //}}AFX_DATA_INIT
    m_psp.dwFlags &= ~PSP_HASHELP;
    m_hBmpPlanet = NULL;
    m_hBmpOrbit = NULL;
    m_hBmpRotate = NULL;
    m_hBmpDiameter = NULL;
}

CListCtrlDlg::~CListCtrlDlg()
{
    if (m_hBmpPlanet != NULL)
        DeleteObject (m_hBmpPlanet);
    if (m_hBmpOrbit != NULL)
        DeleteObject (m_hBmpOrbit);
    if (m_hBmpRotate != NULL)
        DeleteObject (m_hBmpRotate);
    if (m_hBmpDiameter)
        DeleteObject (m_hBmpDiameter);
}

void CListCtrlDlg::DoDataExchange(CDataExchange* pDX)
{
    CPropertyPage::DoDataExchange(pDX);
    //{{AFX_DATA_MAP(CListCtrlDlg)
    DDX_Control(pDX, IDC_LISTCTRL_LISTCTRL, m_ctlList);
    DDX_Radio(pDX, IDC_LIST_LARGEICON, m_nListMode);
    DDX_Radio(pDX, IDC_LISTCTRL_ALIGNLEFT, m_nIconAlign);
    DDX_Radio(pDX, IDC_LISTCTRL_NOSORT, m_nListSort);
```

```
        DDX_Radio(pDX, IDC_LISTCTRL_LEFT, m_nHeaderAlign);
        DDX_Check(pDX, IDC_LISTCTRL_BITMAP, m_bBitmap);
        DDX_Check(pDX, IDC_LISTCTRL_BUTTONS, m_bButtons);
        DDX_Check(pDX, IDC_LISTCTRL_FULLDRAG, m_bFullDrag);
        DDX_Check(pDX, IDC_LISTCTRL_FULLROWSEL, m_bFullRowSel);
        DDX_Check(pDX, IDC_LISTCTRL_HOTTRACK, m_bHotTrack);
        DDX_Check(pDX, IDC_LISTCTRL_ICON, m_bIcon);
        DDX_Check(pDX, IDC_LISTCTRL_NOCOLUMNHEADER,
                                        m_bNoColHeader);
        DDX_Check(pDX, IDC_LISTCTRL_NOLABELWRAP,
                                        m_bNoLabelWrap);
        DDX_Check(pDX, IDC_LISTCTRL_NOSORTHEADER,
                                        m_bNoSortHeader);
        DDX_Check(pDX, IDC_LISTCTRL_SHOWSELALWAYS,
                                      m_bShowSelAlways);
        DDX_Check(pDX, IDC_LISTCTRL_SINGLESEL, m_bSingleSel);
        DDX_Check(pDX, IDC_LISTCTRL_TEXT, m_bText);
        DDX_Check(pDX, IDC_LISTCTRL_DISABLEHEADER,
                                      m_bDisableHeader);

    //}}AFX_DATA_MAP
}

BEGIN_MESSAGE_MAP(CListCtrlDlg, CPropertyPage)
    //{{AFX_MSG_MAP(CListCtrlDlg)
    ON_BN_CLICKED(IDC_LIST_LARGEICON, OnListMode)
    ON_BN_CLICKED(IDC_LISTCTRL_ALIGNLEFT, OnIconAlign)
    ON_BN_CLICKED(IDC_LISTCTRL_SORTASCENDING, OnListSort)
    ON_BN_CLICKED(IDC_LISTCTRL_LEFT, OnHeaderAlign)
    ON_BN_CLICKED(IDC_LISTCTRL_NOLABELWRAP,
                            OnListctrlNolabelwrap)
    ON_BN_CLICKED(IDC_LISTCTRL_FULLROWSEL,
                            OnListctrlFullrowsel)
    ON_BN_CLICKED(IDC_LISTCTRL_NOSORTHEADER,
                            OnListctrlNosortheader)
    ON_BN_CLICKED(IDC_LISTCTRL_NOCOLUMNHEADER,
                            OnListctrlNocolumnheader)
    ON_BN_CLICKED(IDC_LISTCTRL_SINGLESEL,
                            OnListctrlSinglesel)
    ON_BN_CLICKED(IDC_LISTCTRL_SHOWSELALWAYS,
                            OnListctrlShowselalways)
    ON_BN_CLICKED(IDC_LISTCTRL_HOTTRACK,OnListctrlHottrack)
    ON_BN_CLICKED(IDC_LISTCTRL_FULLDRAG,OnListctrlFulldrag)
    ON_BN_CLICKED(IDC_LISTCTRL_BUTTONS, OnListctrlButtons)
    ON_BN_CLICKED(IDC_LISTCTRL_TEXT, OnListctrlText)
    ON_BN_CLICKED(IDC_LISTCTRL_ICON, OnListctrlIcon)
    ON_BN_CLICKED(IDC_LISTCTRL_BITMAP, OnListctrlBitmap)
    ON_BN_CLICKED(IDC_LISTCTRL_DISABLEHEADER,
                            OnListctrlDisableheader)
    ON_NOTIFY(LVN_GETDISPINFO, IDC_LISTCTRL_LISTCTRL,
                            OnGetdispinfoListctrlListctrl)
    ON_NOTIFY(LVN_COLUMNCLICK, IDC_LISTCTRL_LISTCTRL,
                            OnColumnclickListctrlListctrl)
    ON_BN_CLICKED(IDC_LIST_LIST, OnListMode)
    ON_BN_CLICKED(IDC_LIST_REPORT, OnListMode)
    ON_BN_CLICKED(IDC_LIST_SMALLICON, OnListMode)
    ON_BN_CLICKED(IDC_LISTCTRL_ALIGNTOP, OnIconAlign)
```

```
    ON_BN_CLICKED(IDC_LISTCTRL_AUTOARRANGE, OnIconAlign)
    ON_BN_CLICKED(IDC_LISTCTRL_SORTDESCENDING, OnListSort)
    ON_BN_CLICKED(IDC_LISTCTRL_CENTER, OnHeaderAlign)
    ON_BN_CLICKED(IDC_LISTCTRL_RIGHT, OnHeaderAlign)
    ON_BN_CLICKED(IDC_LISTCTRL_NOSORT, OnListSort)
    ON_WM_DESTROY()
    //}}AFX_MSG_MAP
    ON_NOTIFY_EX(TTN_NEEDTEXT, 0, OnToolTipNotify)
END_MESSAGE_MAP()

/////////////////////////////////////////////////////////
// CListCtrlDlg message handlers

BOOL CListCtrlDlg::OnInitDialog()
{
    CPropertyPage::OnInitDialog();
    CImageList Images;
    Images.Create (IDB_LISTMODES, 16, 4,
                    GetSysColor (COLOR_BTNFACE));
    ((CButton *)GetDlgItem(IDC_LIST_LARGEICON))->SetIcon(
                                    Images.ExtractIcon (0));
    ((CButton *)GetDlgItem(IDC_LIST_SMALLICON))->SetIcon(
                                    Images.ExtractIcon (1));
    ((CButton *)GetDlgItem(IDC_LIST_LIST))->SetIcon (
                                    Images.ExtractIcon (2));
    ((CButton *)GetDlgItem(IDC_LIST_REPORT))->SetIcon (
                                    Images.ExtractIcon (3));


//
//  Load the bitmaps for the list control header.
//
    HINSTANCE hInst = AfxGetInstanceHandle ();
    m_hBmpPlanet = (HBITMAP) LoadImage (hInst,
                    MAKEINTRESOURCE(IDB_LISTCTRL_PLANET),
                    IMAGE_BITMAP, 80, 16, LR_DEFAULTCOLOR);
    m_hBmpOrbit = (HBITMAP) LoadImage (hInst,
                    MAKEINTRESOURCE(IDB_LISTCTRL_ORBIT),
                    IMAGE_BITMAP, 80, 16, LR_DEFAULTCOLOR);
    m_hBmpRotate = (HBITMAP) LoadImage (hInst,
                    MAKEINTRESOURCE(IDB_LISTCTRL_DAYNIGHT),
                    IMAGE_BITMAP, 80, 16, LR_DEFAULTCOLOR);
    m_hBmpDiameter = (HBITMAP) LoadImage (hInst,
                    MAKEINTRESOURCE(IDB_LISTCTRL_DIAMETER),
                    IMAGE_BITMAP, 80, 16, LR_DEFAULTCOLOR);
//
//  If you are planning to modify the header at any time,
//  ALWAYS create the control in report view, then change
//  the style to what you want in this function. This will
//  ensure the header gets created with the control.
//  Otherwise, you might get a rude shock (called an
//  "access violation") when you try to modify the header.
//
    m_ctlList.ModifyStyle (LVS_SMALLICON | LVS_LIST
                        | LVS_REPORT, LVS_ICON, TRUE);
    LoadListControl();
//
```

```
//  Set the global variable to point to the list control.
//
    g_pctlList = &m_ctlList;
    return TRUE;
}


BOOL CListCtrlDlg::OnToolTipNotify(UINT nID,
                    NMHDR *pTTTStruct, LRESULT *pResult)
{
    TOOLTIPTEXT *pTTT = (TOOLTIPTEXT *)pTTTStruct;
    UINT nCtrlID =pTTTStruct->idFrom;
    if (pTTT->uFlags & TTF_IDISHWND)
    {
//
// For ToolTips, the nID parameter is always 0.
// The ID in the ToolTip structure actually is
// the HWND of the tool.
//
        nCtrlID = ::GetDlgCtrlID((HWND)nCtrlID);
        if(nCtrlID)
        {
            TCHAR szTip[MAX_STRING];
            if (!LoadString (AfxGetInstanceHandle (),
                        nCtrlID, szTip, MAX_STRING))
                return (FALSE);
            char *pszShort = strchr (szTip, '\n');
            if (pszShort != NULL)
                pTTT->lpszText = pszShort + 1;
            else
                pTTT->lpszText = MAKEINTRESOURCE(nCtrlID);
            pTTT->hinst = AfxGetResourceHandle();
            return(TRUE);
        }
    }
    return(FALSE);
}


void CListCtrlDlg::OnListMode()
{
    UpdateData (TRUE);
    switch (m_nListMode)
    {
        case 0:    // ID_LIST_LARGEICON
            m_ctlList.ModifyStyle (LVS_SMALLICON
                            | LVS_LIST | LVS_REPORT
                            | LVS_OWNERDRAWFIXED,
                            LVS_ICON, TRUE);
            break;
        case 1:    // ID_LIST_SMALLICON
            m_ctlList.ModifyStyle (LVS_ICON | LVS_LIST
                            | LVS_REPORT
                            | LVS_OWNERDRAWFIXED,
                            LVS_SMALLICON, TRUE);
            break;
        case 2:    // ID_LIST_LIST
            m_ctlList.ModifyStyle (LVS_ICON | LVS_SMALLICON
```

```
                              | LVS_REPORT
                              | LVS_OWNERDRAWFIXED,
                              LVS_LIST, TRUE);
            break;
        case 3:     // ID_LIST_REPORT
            m_ctlList.ModifyStyle (LVS_ICON | LVS_LIST
                              | LVS_SMALLICON,
                              LVS_REPORT, TRUE);
            if (m_bFullRowSel)
                m_ctlList.ModifyStyle (Ø,
                              LVS_OWNERDRAWFIXED, TRUE);
            break;
    }
}

void CListCtrlDlg::OnIconAlign()
{
    UpdateData (TRUE);
    switch (m_nIconAlign)
    {
        case Ø:     // Align Left
            m_ctlList.ModifyStyle (LVS_ALIGNTOP
                              | LVS_AUTOARRANGE,
                              LVS_ALIGNLEFT, TRUE);
            break;
        case 1:     // Align Top
            m_ctlList.ModifyStyle (LVS_ALIGNLEFT
                              | LVS_AUTOARRANGE,
                              LVS_ALIGNTOP, TRUE);
            break;
        case 2:     // Auto Arrange
            m_ctlList.ModifyStyle (LVS_ALIGNTOP
                              | LVS_ALIGNLEFT,
                              LVS_AUTOARRANGE, TRUE);
            break;
    }
}

void CListCtrlDlg::OnListSort()
{
    UpdateData (TRUE);
    switch (m_nListSort)
    {
        case Ø:     // No Sort
            m_ctlList.ModifyStyle (LVS_SORTDESCENDING
                              | LVS_SORTASCENDING,
                              Ø, TRUE);
            break;
        case 1:     // Sort Ascending
            m_ctlList.ModifyStyle (LVS_SORTDESCENDING,
                              LVS_SORTASCENDING, TRUE);
            break;
        case 2:     // Align Top
            m_ctlList.ModifyStyle (LVS_SORTASCENDING,
                              LVS_SORTDESCENDING, TRUE);
            break;
```

```cpp
    }
}

void CListCtrlDlg::OnHeaderAlign()
{
    UpdateData (TRUE);
    HDITEM hi;
    memset (&hi, '\0', sizeof (HDITEM));
    CHeaderCtrl *header = m_ctlList.GetHeaderCtrl ();
    hi.mask = HDI_FORMAT;
    header->GetItem (0, &hi);
    hi.fmt &= ~(HDF_LEFT | HDF_RIGHT | HDF_CENTER);
    switch (m_nHeaderAlign)
    {
        case 0:     // Left
            hi.fmt |= HDF_LEFT;
            break;
        case 1:     // Right
            hi.fmt |= HDF_RIGHT;
            break;
        case 2:     // Center
            hi.fmt |= HDF_CENTER;
            break;
        default:
            return;
    }
    header->SetItem (0, &hi);
    header->SetItem (1, &hi);
    header->SetItem (2, &hi);
}

void CListCtrlDlg::OnListctrlNolabelwrap()
{
    UpdateData (TRUE);
    if (m_bNoLabelWrap)
        m_ctlList.ModifyStyle (0, LVS_NOLABELWRAP, TRUE);
    else
        m_ctlList.ModifyStyle (LVS_NOLABELWRAP, 0, TRUE);
}

void CListCtrlDlg::OnListctrlFullrowsel()
{
    UpdateData (TRUE);
    int nType = m_ctlList.GetStyle () & LVS_TYPEMASK;
    if (nType != LVS_REPORT)
        return;
    int nSel = GetSelectedItem();
    if (m_bFullRowSel)
        m_ctlList.ModifyStyle (0, LVS_OWNERDRAWFIXED, TRUE);
    else
        m_ctlList.ModifyStyle (LVS_OWNERDRAWFIXED, 0, TRUE);
    m_ctlList.SetFocus ();
    SetSelectedItem (nSel);
}

void CListCtrlDlg::OnListctrlNosortheader()
```

```
{
    UpdateData (TRUE);
    if (m_bNoSortHeader)
        m_ctlList.ModifyStyle (0, LVS_NOSORTHEADER, TRUE);
    else
        m_ctlList.ModifyStyle (LVS_NOSORTHEADER, 0, TRUE);
}

void CListCtrlDlg::OnListctrlNocolumnheader()
{
    UpdateData (TRUE);
    if (m_bNoColHeader)
        m_ctlList.ModifyStyle (0, LVS_NOCOLUMNHEADER, TRUE);
    else
        m_ctlList.ModifyStyle (LVS_NOCOLUMNHEADER, 0, TRUE);
}

void CListCtrlDlg::OnListctrlSinglesel()
{
    UpdateData (TRUE);
    if (m_bSingleSel)
        m_ctlList.ModifyStyle (0, LVS_SINGLESEL, TRUE);
    else
        m_ctlList.ModifyStyle (LVS_SINGLESEL, 0, TRUE);
}

void CListCtrlDlg::OnListctrlShowselalways()
{
    UpdateData (TRUE);
    if (m_bShowSelAlways)
        m_ctlList.ModifyStyle (0, LVS_SHOWSELALWAYS, TRUE);
    else
        m_ctlList.ModifyStyle (LVS_SHOWSELALWAYS, 0, TRUE);
//
// Give the list control the focus, and then yank it
// back. This will make the style take effect.
//
    CWnd *wnd = m_ctlList.SetFocus();
    wnd->SetFocus();
}

void CListCtrlDlg::OnListctrlHottrack()
{
    UpdateData (TRUE);
    if (m_bHotTrack)
    {
        m_ctlList.GetHeaderCtrl()->ModifyStyle (0,
                                    HDS_HOTTRACK, TRUE);
    }
    else
    {
        m_ctlList.GetHeaderCtrl()->ModifyStyle (
                                    HDS_HOTTRACK, 0, TRUE);
    }
}
```

```
void CListCtrlDlg::OnListctrlFulldrag()
{
    UpdateData (TRUE);
    if (m_bFullDrag)
    {
        m_ctlList.GetHeaderCtrl()->ModifyStyle (Ø,
                                   HDS_FULLDRAG, TRUE);
    }
    else
    {
        m_ctlList.GetHeaderCtrl()->ModifyStyle (
                                   HDS_FULLDRAG, Ø, TRUE);
    }
}

void CListCtrlDlg::OnListctrlButtons()
{
    UpdateData (TRUE);
    if (m_bButtons)
    {
        ::EnableWindow (
                GetDlgItem (IDC_LISTCTRL_HOTTRACK)->m_hWnd,
                TRUE);
        m_ctlList.GetHeaderCtrl()->ModifyStyle (Ø,
                HDS_BUTTONS, TRUE);
    }
    else
    {
        ::EnableWindow (
                GetDlgItem (IDC_LISTCTRL_HOTTRACK)->m_hWnd,
                FALSE);
        m_ctlList.GetHeaderCtrl()->ModifyStyle (HDS_BUTTONS,
                                        Ø, TRUE);
    }
}

void CListCtrlDlg::OnListctrlText()
{
    UpdateData (TRUE);
    HDITEM hi;
    memset (&hi, '\Ø', sizeof (HDITEM));
    CHeaderCtrl *header = m_ctlList.GetHeaderCtrl ();
    hi.mask = HDI_FORMAT;

    header->GetItem (Ø, &hi);
    if (m_bText)
    {
        hi.mask = HDI_FORMAT;
        hi.fmt |= HDF_STRING;
        hi.iImage = Ø;
        header->SetItem (Ø, &hi);
        hi.iImage = 1;
        header->SetItem (1, &hi);
        hi.iImage = 2;
        header->SetItem (2, &hi);
        hi.iImage = 2;
```

```
            header->SetItem (3, &hi);
        }
        else
        {
            hi.mask = HDI_FORMAT;
            hi.fmt &= ~HDF_STRING;
            header->SetItem (0, &hi);
            header->SetItem (1, &hi);
            header->SetItem (2, &hi);
            header->SetItem (3, &hi);
        }
}

void CListCtrlDlg::OnListctrlIcon()
{
    UpdateData (TRUE);
    HDITEM hi;
    memset (&hi, '\0', sizeof (HDITEM));
    CHeaderCtrl *header = m_ctlList.GetHeaderCtrl ();
    hi.mask = HDI_FORMAT;

    header->GetItem (0, &hi);
    if (m_bIcon)
    {
        hi.mask = HDI_IMAGE | HDI_FORMAT;
        hi.fmt |= HDF_IMAGE;
        hi.iImage = 0;
        header->SetItem (0, &hi);
        hi.iImage = 1;
        header->SetItem (1, &hi);
        hi.iImage = 2;
        header->SetItem (2, &hi);
        hi.iImage = 3;
        header->SetItem (3, &hi);
    }
    else
    {
        hi.mask = HDI_FORMAT;
        hi.fmt &= ~HDF_IMAGE;
        header->SetItem (0, &hi);
        header->SetItem (1, &hi);
        header->SetItem (2, &hi);
        header->SetItem (3, &hi);
    }
}

void CListCtrlDlg::OnListctrlBitmap()
{
    UpdateData (TRUE);
    HDITEM hi;
    memset (&hi, '\0', sizeof (HDITEM));
    CHeaderCtrl *header = m_ctlList.GetHeaderCtrl ();
    hi.mask = HDI_FORMAT;

    header->GetItem (0, &hi);
    if (m_bBitmap)
```

```
                {
                    hi.mask = HDI_BITMAP | HDI_FORMAT;
                    hi.fmt |= HDF_BITMAP;
                    hi.fmt &= ~(HDF_STRING | HDF_IMAGE);
                    hi.hbm = m_hBmpPlanet;
                    header->SetItem (0, &hi);
                    hi.hbm = m_hBmpOrbit;
                    header->SetItem (1, &hi);
                    hi.hbm = m_hBmpRotate;
                    header->SetItem (2, &hi);
                    hi.hbm = m_hBmpDiameter;
                    header->SetItem (3, &hi);
                    ::EnableWindow (
                            GetDlgItem (IDC_LISTCTRL_TEXT)->m_hWnd,
                            FALSE);
                    ::EnableWindow (
                            GetDlgItem (IDC_LISTCTRL_ICON)->m_hWnd,
                            FALSE);
                }
                else
                {
                    ::EnableWindow (
                            GetDlgItem (IDC_LISTCTRL_TEXT)->m_hWnd,
                            TRUE);
                    ::EnableWindow (
                            GetDlgItem (IDC_LISTCTRL_ICON)->m_hWnd,
                            TRUE);
                    hi.mask = HDI_FORMAT;
                    hi.fmt &= ~HDF_BITMAP;
                    header->SetItem (0, &hi);
                    header->SetItem (1, &hi);
                    header->SetItem (2, &hi);
                    header->SetItem (3, &hi);
                    if (m_bText)
                        OnListctrlText();
                    if (m_bIcon)
                        OnListctrlIcon();
                }
        UpdateData (FALSE);
}

void CListCtrlDlg::OnListctrlDisableheader()
{
    UpdateData (TRUE);
    if (m_bDisableHeader)
        m_ctlList.GetHeaderCtrl()->EnableWindow (FALSE);
    else
        m_ctlList.GetHeaderCtrl()->EnableWindow (TRUE);
}

void CListCtrlDlg::LoadListControl()
{
char *szTitles [] =
    {
    "Planet",
    "Orbit",
```

```
    "Rotation",
    "Diameter"
    };
int nWidths [] = {100, 100, 100, 100};

#define TITLES (sizeof(szTitles)/sizeof(char *))

    LV_COLUMN    lc;

//
//  Create and load the header icons into its image list.
//  DO NOT attach the image list to the header control yet.
//
    m_HeaderIcons.Create (IDB_LISTCTRL_ICONS, 16, 2,
                          RGB(0x00, 0x80, 0x80));
    memset (&lc, '\0', sizeof (LV_COLUMN));
    lc.mask = LVCF_TEXT | LVCF_WIDTH | LVCF_SUBITEM;
    for (int sub = 0; sub < TITLES; ++sub)
    {
        lc.iImage = sub;
        lc.pszText = szTitles[sub];
        lc.cx = nWidths[sub];
        lc.iSubItem = sub;
        m_ctlList.InsertColumn (sub, &lc);
    }
//
//  Create and load the large and small images lists that
//  will be used by header control.
//
    m_SmallPlanets.Create (IDB_LISTCTRL_SMALLPLANETS,
                           16, 2, RGB(0x00, 0x80, 0x80));
    m_LargePlanets.Create (IDB_LISTCTRL_LARGEPLANETS,
                           32, 2, RGB(0x00, 0x80, 0x80));
    m_ctlList.SetImageList (&m_LargePlanets, LVSIL_NORMAL);
    m_ctlList.SetImageList (&m_SmallPlanets, LVSIL_SMALL);
//
//  Set the header control image list last. If you set it
//  too early, the list control will assign its small image
//  list to the header control.
//
    m_ctlList.GetHeaderCtrl()->SetImageList(&m_HeaderIcons);
//
//  Load the data into the list control.
//
    for (int i = 0; i < PLANETS; ++i)
        AddItem (i, &Planets[i]);
}


//
//  NOTA BENE: The following block of code will be compiled
//  ONLY if the _USETEXTCALLBACK macro is not defined. The
//  definition is at the top of this file.
//
#ifndef _USETEXTCALLBACK

void CListCtrlDlg::AddItem(int nIndex, PLANET *pPlanet)
```

```
{
    CString string;
    LV_ITEM lvitem;
    memset ((char *) &lvitem, '\0', sizeof (LV_ITEM));

//
//  Insert the planet's name in the first column. This also
//  will be the text used by the other three modes.
//
    string = pPlanet->Planet;
    string += pPlanet->Desc;
    lvitem.mask = LVIF_TEXT | LVIF_IMAGE | LVIF_PARAM
                | LVIF_STATE;
    lvitem.iItem = nIndex;
    lvitem.iSubItem = 0;
    lvitem.stateMask = STATEMASK;
    lvitem.iImage = pPlanet->nIcon;
    lvitem.pszText = (char *)(LPCSTR) string;
    lvitem.lParam = nIndex;
    m_ctlList.InsertItem (&lvitem);
//
//  Insert the orbit into the second column.
//
    m_ctlList.FormatNumber (string, pPlanet->Orbit);
    string += ",000 km";
    lvitem.mask = LVIF_TEXT;
    lvitem.iItem = nIndex;
    lvitem.iSubItem = 1;
    lvitem.pszText = (char *)(LPCSTR) string;
    m_ctlList.SetItemText (nIndex, 1, (LPCSTR) string);
//
//  The rotation period goes in the third column.
//
    if (pPlanet->Rotation.Days)
    {
        string.Format ("%dd %02dh %02dm",
            pPlanet->Rotation.Days,
            pPlanet->Rotation.Hours,
            pPlanet->Rotation.Minutes);
    }
    else
    {
        string.Format ("%02dh %02dm",
            pPlanet->Rotation.Hours,
            pPlanet->Rotation.Minutes);
    }
    lvitem.mask = LVIF_TEXT;
    lvitem.iItem = nIndex;
    lvitem.iSubItem = 2;
    lvitem.pszText = (char *)(LPCSTR) string;
    m_ctlList.SetItemText (nIndex, 2, (LPCSTR) string);
//
//  Finally, the diameter goes in the fourth column.
//
    m_ctlList.FormatNumber (string, pPlanet->Diameter);
    string += " km";
```

```
    lvitem.mask = LVIF_TEXT;
    lvitem.iItem = nIndex;
    lvitem.iSubItem = 3;
    lvitem.pszText = (char *)(LPCSTR) string;
    m_ctlList.SetItemText (nIndex, 3, (LPCSTR) string);
}

int CALLBACK CListCtrlDlg::CompareFunction(LPARAM lParam1,
                       LPARAM lParam2, LPARAM lParamSort)
{
    CString strItem1;
    CString strItem2;
    int nResult;
    int nSortOrder = 1;
    if (lParamSort < 0)
    {
        lParamSort *= -1;
        nSortOrder = -1;
    }
    switch (lParamSort)
    {
        case 0:     // Sort by planet name
            strItem1 = g_pctlList->GetItemText (lParam1, 0);
            strItem2 = g_pctlList->GetItemText (lParam2, 0);
            nResult = strItem1.Compare ((LPCSTR) strItem2);
            break;
        case 1:     // Sort by orbit
        {
            strItem1 = g_pctlList->GetItemText (lParam1, 1);
            DWORD dwOne = g_pctlList->UnformatNumber (
        strItem1);
            strItem2 = g_pctlList->GetItemText (lParam2, 1);
            DWORD dwTwo = g_pctlList->UnformatNumber (
        strItem2);
            nResult = (int) (dwOne - dwTwo);
        }
            break;
        case 2:     // Sort by rotation
        {
            strItem1 = g_pctlList->GetItemText (lParam1, 2);
            DWORD dwOne = g_pctlList->UnformatNumber (
        strItem1);
            strItem2 = g_pctlList->GetItemText (lParam2, 2);
            DWORD dwTwo = g_pctlList->UnformatNumber (
        strItem2);
            nResult = (int) (dwOne - dwTwo);
        }
            break;
        case 3:     // Sort by diameter
        {
            strItem1 = g_pctlList->GetItemText (lParam1, 3);
            DWORD dwOne = g_pctlList->UnformatNumber (
        strItem1);
            strItem2 = g_pctlList->GetItemText (lParam2, 3);
            DWORD dwTwo = g_pctlList->UnformatNumber (
        strItem2);
```

```
                nResult = (int) (dwOne - dwTwo);
            }
            break;
        default:
            nResult = 0;
            break;
    }
    return (nResult * nSortOrder);
}

void CListCtrlDlg::OnDestroy()
{
    CPropertyPage::OnDestroy();
}

void CListCtrlDlg::OnColumnclickListctrlListctrl(NMHDR* pNMHDR, LRESULT* pResult)
{
    if (!(m_ctlList.GetStyle() & (LVS_SORTDESCENDING
                              | LVS_SORTASCENDING)))
    {
        return;
    }
    NM_LISTVIEW* pNMListView = (NM_LISTVIEW*)pNMHDR;
    int nSortBy = pNMListView->iSubItem;
    if (m_ctlList.GetStyle () & LVS_SORTDESCENDING)
        nSortBy *= -1;
    m_ctlList.SortItems (CompareFunction, nSortBy);

    int nCount = m_ctlList.GetItemCount ();
    for (int i = 0; i < nCount; ++i)
        m_ctlList.SetItemData (i, (LPARAM) i);

    *pResult = 0;
}

#else
//
//  NOTA BENE: The following block of code implements
//  text callback. To implement it, make sure that the
//  _USETEXTCALLBACK macro is defined. The definition
//  is at the top of this file.
//
void CListCtrlDlg::AddItem(int nIndex, PLANET *planet)
{
PLANET  *pPlanet;
LV_ITEM lvitem;

    memset ((char *) &lvitem, '\0', sizeof (LV_ITEM));
    try
    {
        pPlanet = new PLANET;
    }
    catch (CMemoryException *e)
    {
        e->Delete ();
        return;
```

```
    }
    memcpy (pPlanet, planet, sizeof (PLANET));

    lvitem.mask = LVIF_TEXT | LVIF_IMAGE | LVIF_PARAM
                | LVIF_STATE;
    lvitem.iItem = nIndex;
    lvitem.iSubItem = 0;
    lvitem.stateMask = STATEMASK;
    lvitem.iImage = I_IMAGECALLBACK;
    lvitem.pszText = LPSTR_TEXTCALLBACK;
    lvitem.lParam = (LPARAM) pPlanet;
    m_ctlList.InsertItem (&lvitem);
}

int CALLBACK CListCtrlDlg::CompareFunction(LPARAM lParam1,
                        LPARAM lParam2, LPARAM lParamSort)
{
    int nResult;
    int nSortOrder = 1;
    if (lParamSort < 0)
    {
        lParamSort *= -1;
        nSortOrder = -1;
    }
    PLANET *pPlanet1 = (PLANET *) lParam1;
    PLANET *pPlanet2 = (PLANET *) lParam2;
    switch (lParamSort)
    {
        case 0:     // Sort by planet name
            nResult = strcmp (pPlanet1->Planet,
                            pPlanet2->Planet);
            break;
        case 1:     // Sort by orbit
            nResult = (int) (pPlanet1->Orbit
                        - pPlanet2->Orbit);
            break;
        case 2:     // Sort by rotation
            if (pPlanet1->Rotation.Days ==
                pPlanet2->Rotation.Days)
            {
                if (pPlanet1->Rotation.Hours ==
                    pPlanet2->Rotation.Hours)
                    nResult = pPlanet1->Rotation.Minutes
                            - pPlanet2->Rotation.Minutes;
                else
                    nResult = pPlanet1->Rotation.Hours
                            - pPlanet2->Rotation.Hours;
            }
            else
                nResult = pPlanet1->Rotation.Days
                        - pPlanet2->Rotation.Days;
            break;
        case 3:     // Sort by diameter
            nResult = pPlanet1->Diameter
                    - pPlanet2->Diameter;
            break;
```

```
            default:
                nResult = 0;
                break;
        }
        return (nResult * nSortOrder);
}


void CListCtrlDlg::OnDestroy()
{
    FreeItemMemory ();
    CPropertyPage::OnDestroy();
}


void CListCtrlDlg::OnColumnclickListctrlListctrl(NMHDR* pNMHDR, LRESULT* pResult)
{
    if (!(m_ctlList.GetStyle() & (LVS_SORTDESCENDING
                                | LVS_SORTASCENDING)))
        return;
    NM_LISTVIEW* pNMListView = (NM_LISTVIEW*)pNMHDR;
    int nSortBy = pNMListView->iSubItem;
    if (m_ctlList.GetStyle () & LVS_SORTDESCENDING)
        nSortBy *= -1;
    m_ctlList.SortItems (CompareFunction, nSortBy);

    *pResult = 0;
}


#endif       // _USETEXTCALLBACK
//
// This is the end of the alternate code block. The
// balance of the code will be compiled for both versions.
//

void CListCtrlDlg::FreeItemMemory()
{
    int nCount = m_ctlList.GetItemCount ();
    for (int i = 0; i < nCount; ++i)
        delete (PLANET *) m_ctlList.GetItemData (i);
    m_ctlList.DeleteAllItems ();
}


//
// The following is the text callback function. It is
// not called unless the text members of any item or
// subitem is set to LPSTR_TEXTCALLBACK.
//
void CListCtrlDlg::OnGetdispinfoListctrlListctrl(
                    NMHDR* pNMHDR, LRESULT* pResult)
{
CString     string;
PLANET      *pPlanet;

    LV_DISPINFO* pDispInfo = (LV_DISPINFO*)pNMHDR;
    pPlanet = (PLANET *) pDispInfo->item.lParam;

    if (pDispInfo->item.mask & LVIF_TEXT)
```

```
    {
        switch (pDispInfo->item.iSubItem)
        {
            case 0:           // Need Planet name
                string = pPlanet->Planet;
                {
//
//  Include the description only in the icon views.
//
                    DWORD dwStyle = m_ctlList.GetStyle ()
                                    & LVS_TYPEMASK;
                    if (!(dwStyle & 1))
                        string += pPlanet->Desc;
                }
                ::lstrcpy (pDispInfo->item.pszText,
                        (LPCSTR) string);
                break;
            case 1:           // Needs Orbit
                m_ctlList.FormatNumber (string,
                                    pPlanet->Orbit);
                string += ",000 km";
                ::lstrcpy (pDispInfo->item.pszText,
                        (LPCSTR) string);
                break;
            case 2:           // Needs Rotation
                if (pPlanet->Rotation.Days)
                {
                    string.Format ("%dd %dh %dm",
                        pPlanet->Rotation.Days,
                        pPlanet->Rotation.Hours,
                        pPlanet->Rotation.Minutes);
                }
                else
                {
                    string.Format ("%dh %dm",
                        pPlanet->Rotation.Hours,
                        pPlanet->Rotation.Minutes);
                }
                ::lstrcpy (pDispInfo->item.pszText,
                        (LPCSTR) string);
                break;
            case 3:           // Needs Diameter
                m_ctlList.FormatNumber (string,
                        pPlanet->Diameter);
                string += " km.";
                ::lstrcpy (pDispInfo->item.pszText,
                        (LPCSTR) string);
                break;
        }
    }

    if (pDispInfo->item.mask & LVIF_IMAGE)
    {
        pDispInfo->item.iImage = pPlanet->nIcon;
    }
    *pResult = 0;
```

```
}

//
//  Get the index of the first selected item. If you have
//  multiple selection set, you can use the pos variable
//  to loop through and get all the selected items.
//
int CListCtrlDlg::GetSelectedItem()
{
    if (!m_ctlList.GetItemCount ())
        return (-1);
    POSITION pos = m_ctlList.GetFirstSelectedItemPosition();
    if (pos == NULL)
        return (-1);
    return (m_ctlList.GetNextSelectedItem(pos));
}

//
//  Set the selection to focused and selected.
//
int CListCtrlDlg::SetSelectedItem(int nSel)
{
    int nOldSel = GetSelectedItem();
    m_ctlList.SetItemState (nSel, LVIS_SELECTED
                                | LVIS_FOCUSED,
                                  LVIS_SELECTED | LVIS_FOCUSED);
    return (nOldSel);
}
```

There are a couple of important notes about this code. First, notice the complexity of the code when you don't use text callback. Sorting can become a nightmare. When you insert formatted numbers into an item, you have to unformat them to compare them. Also, you must set the text for each subitem. With text callback, you need only set the first column; *LPSTR_TEXTCALLBACK* is the default for the subitems. Text and image callback will be discussed in more detail in Tip 898, "Understanding LPSTR_TEXTCALLBACK and I_IMAGECALLBACK Modes."

894. *Understanding List Control Styles*

The list control contains a variety of styles for manipulating the control and its associated header control. These include styles for setting the list mode to one of the four view options, arranging the icons, and selecting sort options.

All but one, the *LVS_NOSORTHEADER*, may be modified after the control is created. The No Sort header option causes the header to appear flat instead of as buttons and not to generate column click messages, so it's easy to program around it. The list control styles are shown in Table 894.

You can set the header styles individually using the *CListCtrl::GetHeaderCtrl()* function to get a pointer to the function, and then call *ModifyStyle()* to change the style.

Style	Purpose
LVS_ICON	The items are displayed using large icons. Only the text from the first column is displayed.
LVS_SMALLICON	The items are displayed using small icons. Only the text from the first column is displayed.
LVS_LIST	The items are displayed using small icons in list form horizontally. Only the text from the first column is displayed.
LVS_REPORT	The items are displayed in a vertical list along with the text in the subcolumns. The items may be displayed with or without icons.
LVS_ALIGNTOP	Items are aligned with the top of the control in large and small icon views.
LVS_ALIGNLEFT	Items are aligned with the left side of the control in large and small icon views.
LVS_AUTOARRANGE	Items are arranged automatically in large and small icon views.
LVS_EDITLABELS	This provides an edit control in place for editing the item labels. In report mode, this applies only to the first column. The application must process the *LVN_ENDLABEL* notification message.
LVS_NOCOLUMNHEADER	This hides the control's associated header control.
LVS_NOLABELWRAP	In large icon view, the text for individual items is displayed on a single line rather than wrapped.
LVS_NOSCROLL	This disables scrolling.
LVS_NOSORTHEADER	This displays the header control's columns in flat rather than button style.
LVS_OWNERDRAWFIXED	This causes the control to send *WM_DRAWITEM* messages when an item needs to be painted. This applies only to report mode.
LVS_SHAREIMAGELISTS	The control doesn't destroy its image lists when it is destroyed. This allows images lists to be shared between list controls. Note, however, that other controls that use image lists may not have this style.
LVS_SHOWSELALWAYS	Always shows the current selection, if any. When the control doesn't have the focus, the selection will appear with a grayed background.
LVS_SINGLESEL	This limits the user to selecting only one item.
LVS_SORTASCENDING	This sorts items in ascending order based on text.
LVS_SORTDESCENDING	This sorts items in descending order based on text.

Table 894   The styles used to manipulate the list control and its header

Some of these styles affect the header display, and you may adjust the header styles afterward by accessing the header control separately. See Tips 887, "Understanding the Header Control," to 891, "Using Image Lists with the Header Control," for a discussion on using the header control.

895. *Enabling Full Row Select in Report View Style*

One of the quirks of the list control is that in report view, it displays only the selection on the first column and responds only to mouse clicks on the first column. The limited visibility of the selected item means that narrow items can be lost visually. The mouse response means that the user must move the mouse to the far left of the control to select an item or to change the selection.

You can correct the mouse situation by providing the handler for the *NM_CLICK* message, which is sent any time that the user clicks the left mouse button on the control. The code for this handler is shown here:

```
void CListCtrlDlg::OnClickListctrlListctrl(NMHDR* pNMHDR,
                                LRESULT* pResult)
{
    if (m_ctlList.GetStyle () & LVS_REPORT)
    {
        LPNMLISTVIEW lpnmlv = (LPNMLISTVIEW) pNMHDR;
        int nIndex;
        CPoint point (lpnmlv->ptAction);
        point.x = 2;
        if ((nIndex = m_ctlList.HitTest (point, NULL))
                                 != -1)
        {
            m_ctlList.SetItemState (nIndex, LVIS_SELECTED
                                        | LVIS_FOCUSED,
                        LVIS_SELECTED | LVIS_FOCUSED);
        }
    }
    *pResult = 0;
}
```

This function performs a hit test to see if the point is inside a list item line. First, set the x member to a value to ensure that it is inside the first column, and then perform the hit test. If the point is valid, the control will return the index of the item clicked, and you can set the focus and selection to that item.

The selection problem is a little more complicated. To extend the selection to include the full width of the item, you will have to draw it. This means providing code for the *WM_DRAWITEM* message and setting the list control to *LVS_OWNERDRAWFIXED*. The easiest way to do this is to provide an owner draw class for the list control. In the sample code, this is *ListCtrlEx*.

The owner draw code—your implementation of *OnDraw()*—is summoned only when the control is in the *LVS_REPORT* view mode, so you don't need to provide custom drawing code for all four modes. In Tip 655, "Using the Owner Draw Property to Create a Full Line Selection," you created a custom class derived from *CListView* that provided a full line selection. That code contained the nucleus of the list control's *OnDraw()* function, and you can use the same code for an owner-draw list control. The code can be modified easily to become the mechanism for an owner-draw list control. Just follow a few simple steps:

- Copy the *ListViewEx.cpp* and *ListViewEx.h* files, and name them *ListCtrlEx.cpp* and *ListCtrlEx.h*.

- In both files, search for *CListView* and *CListViewEx* and replace them with *CListCtrl* and *ClistCtrlEx*, respectively.

- Any time there is a reference to the underlying control, remove it. Most of these references are in the *OnDraw()* function. This class *is* the list control, so you can call the member functions directly.

In the code for the sample property page, we've included a couple of extra functions to unformat a number when you are not using text callback.

896. Adding Items to a List Control

As with most of the 32-bit controls, adding an item to the list control involves an item structure, in this case *LVITEM*. The structure is used to add the item and the text for the first column only. The text for other columns is set by calling member function *SetItemText()*.

To add an item to a list control, or to retrieve an item, you initialize the appropriate members of the *LVITEM* structure and set the mask to indicate which members are valid. The *LVITEM* structure is shown here:

```
typedef struct _LVITEM {
    UINT    mask;
    int     iItem;
    int     iSubItem;
    UINT    state;
    UINT    stateMask;
    LPTSTR  pszText;
    int     cchTextMax;
    int     iImage;
    LPARAM  lParam;
#if (_WIN32_IE >= 0x0300)
    int iIndent;
#endif
} LVITEM, FAR *LPLVITEM;
```

The *mask* member indicates which items are valid. You must set this before calling *InsertItem()* to add the item to the list or *SetItem()* to modify an entry. If you don't, the results are unpredictable. When retrieving an item with the *GetItem()* function, the control will set this member to indicate which of the other members are valid. The *mask* member may contain any of the flags shown in Table 896.

Flag	Purpose
LVIF_TEXT	The *pszText* member is valid, and you must provide a pointer to a string to be displayed.
LVIF_IMAGE	The *iImage* member is valid, and you must provide an index into the image list for the icon to be used.
LVIF_INDENT	The *iIndent* member is valid, and you must provide a value in icon units.
LVIF_PARAM	The *lParam* member is valid. The control will store whatever value is in the member.
LFIF_STATE	The *state* member is valid and must be set. The state determines whether the item is selected or focused and also specifies which overlay image to use.

Table 896   The format masks used with the LVITEM structure to determine valid entries (continued on following page)

Flag	Purpose
LVIF_NORECOMPUTE	This informs the control not to call the function to get the display information when the *GetItem()* function is called. The *pszText* member will contain *LPSTR_TEXTCALLBACK* when the *GetItem()* function returns. This item does not map to a structure variable.
LVID_DI_SETITEM	This is used in the function to get display information. This tells the control to store the current string and not to ask for it again. This item does not map to a structure variable.

Table 896   The format masks used with the LVITEM structure to determine valid entries (continued from previous page)

The *iIndent* member and its corresponding flag, *LVIF_INDENT*, were added with the controls library released with Internet Explorer 3.0. If you set this flag in the *mask* member, you must include a value in the *iIndent* member. The value is in icon units, so a value of 1 will indent the text by the width of an icon, 2 will indent twice the width of an icon, and so forth. The indent applies only to the first column in *LVS_REPORT* display mode.

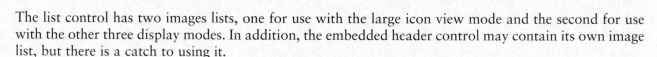

897. *Using an Image List with the List Control*

The list control has two images lists, one for use with the large icon view mode and the second for use with the other three display modes. In addition, the embedded header control may contain its own image list, but there is a catch to using it.

In anything but *LVS_REPORT* display mode, image lists are almost required. You can add an item without an image and display it in one of the icon modes, but only the text will be displayed and it looks, um, rather strange. There's a blank area where the image should be, and the display looks unfinished.

The *SetImageList()* function for the list control takes two parameters (with most other controls you need only pass a pointer to an image list). You must provide it with a pointer to an image list and a flag specifying whether it is the large or small image list. The following two lines set both the large and the small image lists:

```
m_ctlList.SetImageList (&m_LargePlanets, LVSIL_NORMAL);
m_ctlList.SetImageList (&m_SmallPlanets, LVSIL_SMALL);
```

Usually you use 32-by-32-pixel images for the large icons and 16-by-16-pixel images for the small icons, but there's no rule saying that you can't have larger or smaller images. The control will adjust its layout for larger or smaller icons.

The header control, however, requires a small icon size image, 16 by 16 pixels. The header won't argue with a larger image size, and it will display the proper image. If it's larger than 16 by 16, the image will be clipped to fit the header size.

When you set the small image list for the list control, it also assigns the same image list to the header. This can be a problem if you've already set the header image list. The trick here is to set the image lists for the list control first and then set the image list for the header control. Any time you call the list control's *SetImageList()* function to modify the assigned image list, call the header control's *SetImageList()* function as well to assign the proper image list to it.

898. *Understanding* LPSTR_TEXTCALLBACK *and* I_IMAGECALLBACK *Modes*

When you use text callback, the control doesn't store the strings that it displays in the list. Instead, when it needs data for painting, it calls your application using the *LVN_GETDISPINFO* message through *WM_NOTIFY*. Your application responds by filling in the string member of the *item.pszText* member of the *LV_DISPINFO* passed in the message.

Usually, your application needs to store the display information anyway, so the idea of giving it to the control as needed can amount to a large memory savings, especially on long lists.

You use text callback by assigning the *pszText* member of the *LVITEM* structure the value *LPSTR_TEXTCALLBACK*, which is nothing more than a –1 cast to a string pointer. You need to do this only for the first column. Subcolumns in report mode default to *LPSTR_TEXTCALLBACK*; unless you explicitly assign a string to them with the *SetItemText()* function, the control will call back for display information. The item *mask* member will have the *LVIF_TEXT* bit set.

Actually, we could have just assigned an index into the Planets array and saved allocating space on the heap. In the real world, however, you probably won't know just how many structures to create for your application, so the idea of storing them in the heap and then putting the address into the *lParam* member of the item structure saves having to do a count first. When you do this, remember to add a message handler for the *WM_DESTROY* message and to free the allocated memory *before* the base class *OnDestroy()* function is called. If you wait, the list control will be destroyed, and you won't be able to get the pointers to the memory items.

There is one catch to using text callback. If you have one of the list control's sort styles set, either ascending or descending, text callback will fail when you add the items. You can add the sorting styles after the items are added, but because sorting is done when the items are added, that means sorting will be your responsibility. The next tip will discuss sorting in a list control.

If you use text callback, you'll greatly simplify your programming life.

Image callback works much the same way, except that you don't realize a memory savings like you do with text callback. To use image callback, assign *I_IMAGECALLBACK* instead of an image number to the *iImage* member of the *LVITEM* structure. This value also is –1, but it's an integer. When the control needs the image number, it will use the same message as text callback, except that the *mask* member of the structure will have the *LVIF_IMAGE* bit set. To respond to it, set the item's *iImage* member to the index of the image in the image list.

One advantage to using text and image callback is that you can tailor the display for the current mode. In the sample property page, the icon views have a short description tacked onto them, but in list and report modes this isn't the case. We did this to give some more text to show how the *LVS_NOLABEL-WRAP* style works, but it's applicable to real programs as well.

899. *Sorting a List Control Based on a Header Field Selection*

Sorting with a list control can provide some powerful capabilities by letting the user sort the list by clicking any of the column headers. That's the traditional way of handling sorting because the list control sends an *LVN_COLUMNCLICK* notification message when one of the column headers is clicked. You can provide alternate methods of getting to the sort mechanism.

The list control sorts the list when you call the *SortItems()* member function. Actually, the control doesn't do any sorting. You pass it the address of a sort function in the call to *SortItems()*, along with a *DWORD* value that your sort function can use to determine how the data should be sorted.

The sort function is a callback function and thus must be declared *static* in your class or declared in global space. This means that it doesn't have access to the *this* pointer. You can use the *DWORD* value to pass the address of a structure containing all the sort information, or simply pass the identifier for the column.

Sorting can be as simple or as complex as you want. In the list control sample property page, the function simply returned the result of a numerical comparison or a mathematical subtraction. Earlier, however, in the *EditExplore* project, the code tested whether the entry was a directory and then sorted it so that the directory entries would remain at the top of the list, regardless of alphabetical or numerical order.

The list control will sort the data according to the first column when the items are added to the control. Its sorting responsibility is done at that point. If you're using text callback, you can't use the sort styles when you add items. In this case, add your data in any order, and then call the *SortItem()* function to sort the list accordingly.

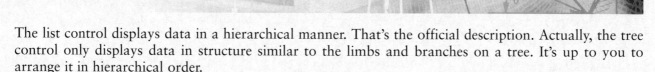

900. *Understanding the Tree Control*

The list control displays data in a hierarchical manner. That's the official description. Actually, the tree control only displays data in structure similar to the limbs and branches on a tree. It's up to you to arrange it in hierarchical order.

The tree control starts out with a root node, the top item in a descending list. Usually, you arrange the branches so that the most general piece of information is at the root node and then work down to the most specific. You may have more than one node at the root level. In a collection of books, for example, the root nodes may be Fiction and Non-fiction. Opening one of the nodes might reveal the titles of books, which, when opened, might reveal a list of chapters in the book.

This control has been undergoing some changes recently. As with the list control, there are differences between the appearance of certain styles on a machine with Visual Studio Service Pack 4 applied and a machine without the service pack. For example, when the full row selection style is used on the SP4 machine with a control having lines, the selection begins at the left margin, breaks at the lines, and then continues from the icon to the right margin. On the machine without SP4, the selection simply begins at the icon and continues to the right margin. Microsoft's documentation does say that full row selection should not be used with the Has Lines style.

So, we're not sure which styles will work on your machine or how they will appear. We'll program and test on both machines, but you definitely should experiment with the code for this control. That's the reason I wrote the *Contols* application originally—to test changes in the controls when Microsoft updates the common controls library.

901. *Understanding the CTreeCtrl Class*

The tree control is represented in the Microsoft Foundation Class by the *CTreeCtrl* class, which encapsulates the control and contains functions to manipulating the styles and data in the tree.

In this tip, you'll build a property page to demonstrate the various tree control styles. It will include a button that will summon a dialog box to choose a directory path from a tree control. You'll notice a number of quirks with the control, particularly recent incarnations. The new *TVS_CHECKBOXES* style enables you to include check boxes with the branch items, but once you add them, you can't remove them. You can remove the style, and the check boxes won't respond to user clicks, but they still will be visible in the control. To get rid of them, you'll have to click the Recreate Tree button. We've included this button rather than automatically rebuild the tree so that you can get an idea of the interaction between the various styles.

You should create the tree with the buttons, lines, and lines at root styles selected, and then remove them in the *OnInitDialog()* function if you don't want them. On some machines, we've noticed that the tree will set up its own boundary rectangle within the control's rectangle when it is created. When you later add the lines and buttons, and then expand the tree, the draw operation will clip the text that extends beyond the original boundary. This happens on the machine with Service Pack 4, and we're not sure exactly what causes it. To be safe, include the styles, load the tree, and then remove the styles that you don't want, or maybe you just want to wait for Service Pack 5 (there's some lore on the Web about never installing even-numbered service packs from Microsoft).

Create the property page with a resource ID of *IDD_PROPPAGE_TREECTRLDLG*, and label it Tree Control. Figure 901 shows the controls on this page.

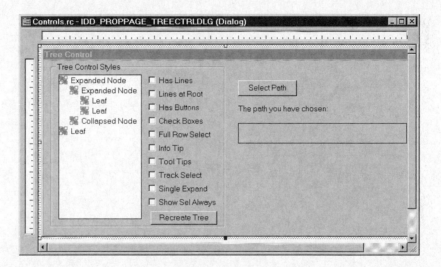

Figure 901   The Tree Control property page with the controls for demonstrating styles and selecting a directory

To the right of the property page is a button to select a directory. This is a dialog box that you can use in your applications, and you'll create it separately so that you can place it in your gallery. Let's get into the property page code first and then go over the dialog box. The header file for *CTreeCtrlDlg* is shown here:

```
// TreeCtrlDlg.h : header file
//


/////////////////////////////////////////////////////
// CTreeCtrlDlg dialog

class CTreeCtrlDlg : public CpropertyPage
{
    DECLARE_DYNCREATE(CTreeCtrlDlg)

// Construction
```

```
public:
    CTreeCtrlDlg();
    ~CTreeCtrlDlg();

// Dialog Data
    //{{AFX_DATA(CTreeCtrlDlg)
    enum { IDD = IDD_PROPPAGE_TREECTRLDLG };
    CTreeCtrl   m_ctlTree;
    BOOL    m_bCheckBoxes;
    BOOL    m_bFullRowSel;
    BOOL    m_bHasButtons;
    BOOL    m_bHasLines;
    BOOL    m_bInfoTip;
    BOOL    m_bLinesAtRoot;
    BOOL    m_bShowSelAlways;
    BOOL    m_bSingleExpand;
    BOOL    m_bToolTips;
    BOOL    m_bTrackSelect;
    //}}AFX_DATA


// Overrides
    // ClassWizard generate virtual function overrides
    //{{AFX_VIRTUAL(CTreeCtrlDlg)
    protected:
    virtual void DoDataExchange(CDataExchange* pDX);
    // DDX/DDV support
    virtual BOOL OnNotify(WPARAM wParam, LPARAM lParam,
                          LRESULT* pResult);
    //}}AFX_VIRTUAL


// Implementation
protected:
    BOOL m_bCheckBoxesAreVisible;
    CImageList m_Images;
    void LoadTree();
    // Generated message map functions
    //{{AFX_MSG(CTreeCtrlDlg)
    virtual BOOL OnInitDialog();
    afx_msg void OnTreeRecreatetree();
    afx_msg void OnTreeSelectpath();
    //}}AFX_MSG
    DECLARE_MESSAGE_MAP()
    afx_msg void OnTreeCheckboxes(UINT nID);

};
```

In this tip, you'll get an introduction to the *ON_COMMAND_RANGE* macro, which will be used to handle the messages from all the check boxes. If you use this macro, you'll probably have to edit the *resource.h* file to make sure that all of the control identifiers fall within a contiguous range. Microsoft says that you shouldn't edit this file, but it's really a practical necessity because it's unlikely that the ClassWizard will assign contiguous identifiers to the controls. If you *never* edit your dialog boxes and *never* make any changes to the control identifiers, and if you create all the controls for the *ON_COM-MAND_RANGE* one after the other with nothing in between and *never* change them, then you probably won't have to edit the file.

That *never* happens for me, though.

An interesting addition to the tree control's styles list is the *TVS_INFOTIP* style. If you create your tree with the *TVS_TOOLTIPS* style, then whenever the mouse cursor moves over an item that goes outside the control's boundary, the ToolTip will pop up with the full name of the item. That's really handy because it saves the user from having to scroll over to see the full name.

Even handier are the info tips. If you set this style (you have to set the ToolTips style as well), you can replace the text in the ToolTip with your own. In addition, the ToolTip will show even though the item isn't partially obscured by the edge of the control. You can catch the message that sets the text here by overriding the *OnNotify()* function, and then set your own text. In the following code, you'll notice that we've replaced the members of the *PLANET* structure with strings; then, when we added the items to the tree, we made the item's parameter point to these strings. Thus, when Info Tips is checked and the mouse cursor moves over an item, the contents of the string are displayed. The documentation for this style is less ambiguous than the *WM_NOTIFY* information for the header control because, well, it tells you even less. The source code is shown here:

```cpp
// TreeCtrlDlg.cpp : implementation file
//


#include "stdafx.h"
#include "Controls.h"
#include "TreeCtrlDlg.h"
#include   "ChooseDirectory.h"
#ifdef _DEBUG
#define new DEBUG_NEW
#undef THIS_FILE
static char THIS_FILE[] = __FILE__;
#endif


/////////////////////////////////////////////////////////////
// CTreeCtrlDlg property page

 struct TREEPLANET
    {
//  HTREEITEM   hItem;
    char    Planet[12];
    char    Desc[32];
    char    Orbit[24];
    char    Rotation[24];
    char    Diameter[24];
    int     nIcon;
    };

static TREEPLANET   Planets[] =
    {
    "Mercury", "The Messenger", "58 million km",
            "58d 0h 0m", "4847 km", 0,
    "Venus", "The Nearest Planet", "108 million km",
            "243d 0h 0m", "12,118 km", 1,
    "Earth", "Our Home Planet", "130 million km",
            "23h 56m", "12,756 km", 2,
    "Mars", "The Red Planet", "228 million km",
            "1d 0h 37m", "6,761 km", 3,
    "Jupiter", "The Giant Planet", "779 million km",
            "9h 55m", "142,994 km", 4,
    "Saturn", "The Ringed Planet", "1,432 million km",
```

```
               "10h 40m", "116,589 km", 5,
    "Uranus",  "The Green Giant", "2,800 million km",
               "17h 14m", "51,024 km", 6,
    "Neptune", "The Blue Planet", "4,500 million km",
               "16h 7m", "49,748 km", 7,
    "Pluto",   "The Farthest Planet", "5,900 million km",
               "6d 9h 17m", "2,296 km", 8
    };
#define    PLANETS    (sizeof(Planets)/sizeof(TREEPLANET))

#define MAX_STRING     256

IMPLEMENT_DYNCREATE(CTreeCtrlDlg, CPropertyPage)

CTreeCtrlDlg::CTreeCtrlDlg()
                    : CPropertyPage(CTreeCtrlDlg::IDD)
{
    //{{AFX_DATA_INIT(CTreeCtrlDlg)
    m_bCheckBoxes = FALSE;
    m_bFullRowSel = FALSE;
    m_bHasButtons = TRUE;
    m_bHasLines = TRUE;
    m_bInfoTip = FALSE;
    m_bLinesAtRoot = TRUE;
    m_bShowSelAlways = FALSE;
    m_bSingleExpand = FALSE;
    m_bToolTips = TRUE;
    m_bTrackSelect = FALSE;
    m_bCheckBoxesAreVisible = FALSE;
    //}}AFX_DATA_INIT
    m_psp.dwFlags &= ~PSP_HASHELP;
}


CTreeCtrlDlg::~CTreeCtrlDlg()
{
}


void CTreeCtrlDlg::DoDataExchange(CDataExchange* pDX)
{
    CPropertyPage::DoDataExchange(pDX);
    //{{AFX_DATA_MAP(CTreeCtrlDlg)
    DDX_Control(pDX, IDC_TREE_TREECTRL, m_ctlTree);
    DDX_Check(pDX, IDC_TREE_CHECKBOXES, m_bCheckBoxes);
    DDX_Check(pDX, IDC_TREE_FULLROWSEL, m_bFullRowSel);
    DDX_Check(pDX, IDC_TREE_HASBUTTONS, m_bHasButtons);
    DDX_Check(pDX, IDC_TREE_HASLINES, m_bHasLines);
    DDX_Check(pDX, IDC_TREE_INFOTIP, m_bInfoTip);
    DDX_Check(pDX, IDC_TREE_LINESATROOT, m_bLinesAtRoot);
    DDX_Check(pDX, IDC_TREE_SHOWSELALWAYS,
                           m_bShowSelAlways);
    DDX_Check(pDX, IDC_TREE_SINGLEEXPAND, m_bSingleExpand);
    DDX_Check(pDX, IDC_TREE_TOOLTIPS, m_bToolTips);
    DDX_Check(pDX, IDC_TREE_TRACKSELECT, m_bTrackSelect);
    //}}AFX_DATA_MAP
}
```

```
BEGIN_MESSAGE_MAP(CTreeCtrlDlg, CPropertyPage)
    //{{AFX_MSG_MAP(CTreeCtrlDlg)
    ON_BN_CLICKED(IDC_TREE_RECREATETREE,OnTreeRecreatetree)
    ON_BN_CLICKED(IDC_TREE_SELECTPATH, OnTreeSelectpath)
    //}}AFX_MSG_MAP
    ON_COMMAND_RANGE(IDC_TREE_HASBUTTONS,
                     IDC_TREE_HASLINES, OnTreeCheckboxes)
END_MESSAGE_MAP()

//////////////////////////////////////////////////////
// CTreeCtrlDlg message handlers

BOOL CTreeCtrlDlg::OnInitDialog()
{
    CPropertyPage::OnInitDialog();
    m_Images.Create (IDB_TREECTRL_PLANETS, 16, 2,
                     RGB (0x00, 0x80, 0x80));
    m_ctlTree.SetImageList (&m_Images, TVSIL_NORMAL);
    LoadTree();
    return (TRUE);
}

void CTreeCtrlDlg::OnTreeCheckboxes(UINT nID)
{
    UpdateData (TRUE);
    UINT indent = m_ctlTree.GetIndent();
    DWORD dwStyle = GetWindowLong (m_ctlTree, GWL_STYLE);
    switch (nID)
    {
        case IDC_TREE_HASBUTTONS:
            if (m_bHasButtons)
            {
                dwStyle |= TVS_HASBUTTONS | TVS_LINESATROOT;
                m_bLinesAtRoot = TRUE;
            }
            else
                dwStyle &= ~TVS_HASBUTTONS;
            break;
        case IDC_TREE_TOOLTIPS:
            if (m_bToolTips)
                dwStyle &= TVS_NOTOOLTIPS;
            else
            {
                dwStyle |= TVS_NOTOOLTIPS;
                dwStyle &= ~TVS_INFOTIP;
                m_bInfoTip = FALSE;
            }
            break;
        case IDC_TREE_TRACKSELECT:
            if (m_bTrackSelect)
                dwStyle |= TVS_TRACKSELECT;
            else
                dwStyle &= ~TVS_TRACKSELECT;
            break;
        case IDC_TREE_SINGLEEXPAND:
            if (m_bSingleExpand)
```

```
                dwStyle |= TVS_SINGLEEXPAND;
        else
                dwStyle &= ~TVS_SINGLEEXPAND;
        break;
    case IDC_TREE_SHOWSELALWAYS:
        if (m_bShowSelAlways)
                dwStyle |= TVS_SHOWSELALWAYS;
        else
                dwStyle &= ~TVS_SHOWSELALWAYS;
        break;
    case IDC_TREE_INFOTIP:
        if (m_bInfoTip)
                dwStyle |= TVS_INFOTIP;
        else
                dwStyle &= ~TVS_INFOTIP;
        break;
    case IDC_TREE_LINESATROOT:
        if (m_bLinesAtRoot)
        {
                dwStyle |= TVS_LINESATROOT | TVS_HASLINES;
                m_bHasLines = TRUE;
        }
        else
        {
                dwStyle &= ~TVS_LINESATROOT
                            | TVS_HASBUTTONS;
                m_bHasButtons = FALSE;
        }
        break;
    case IDC_TREE_FULLROWSEL:
        if (m_bFullRowSel)
                dwStyle |= TVS_FULLROWSELECT;
        else
                dwStyle &= ~TVS_FULLROWSELECT;
        break;
    case IDC_TREE_CHECKBOXES:
        if (m_bCheckBoxes)
        {
                dwStyle |= TVS_CHECKBOXES;
                m_bCheckBoxesAreVisible = TRUE;
        }
        else
        {
                HIMAGELIST hImages =
                        (HIMAGELIST) m_ctlTree.GetImageList
                                    (TVSIL_STATE);
                if (hImages != NULL)
                    DeleteObject (hImages);
                dwStyle &= ~TVS_CHECKBOXES;
                SetWindowLong (m_ctlTree, GWL_STYLE,
                            dwStyle);
                return;
        }
        break;
    case IDC_TREE_HASLINES:
        if (m_bHasLines)
```

```
                    dwStyle |= TVS_HASLINES;
            else
            {
                dwStyle &= ~(TVS_HASLINES | TVS_LINESATROOT
                         | TVS_HASBUTTONS);
                m_bLinesAtRoot = FALSE;
                m_bHasButtons = FALSE;
            }
        default:
            break;
    }
    UpdateData (FALSE);
    SetWindowLong (m_ctlTree, GWL_STYLE, dwStyle);
    indent = m_ctlTree.GetIndent();
    m_ctlTree.Invalidate (TRUE);
}

void CTreeCtrlDlg::LoadTree()
{
    HTREEITEM hItem;
    TVITEM tvi;
    memset (&tvi, '\0', sizeof (TVITEM));
    HTREEITEM hRoot = m_ctlTree.InsertItem ("Astronomy",
                        18, 18);
    m_ctlTree.SetItemData (hRoot, NULL);
    HTREEITEM hPlanets = m_ctlTree.InsertItem
                        ("The Planets", 0, 0, hRoot);
    m_ctlTree.SetItemData (hPlanets, NULL);
    for (int i = 0; i < PLANETS; ++i)
    {
        HTREEITEM hPlanet = m_ctlTree.InsertItem
                        (Planets[i].Planet,
                         Planets[i].nIcon + 1,
                         Planets[i].nIcon + 1, hPlanets);
        m_ctlTree.SetItemData (hPlanet,
                         (LPARAM) Planets[i].Desc);
        hItem = m_ctlTree.InsertItem ("Orbit", 10, 10,
                         hPlanet);
        m_ctlTree.SetItemData (hItem,
                         (LPARAM) Planets[i].Orbit);
        hItem = m_ctlTree.InsertItem ("Rotation", 11, 11,
                         hPlanet);
        m_ctlTree.SetItemData (hItem,
                         (LPARAM) Planets[i].Rotation);
        hItem = m_ctlTree.InsertItem ("Diameter", 12, 12,
                         hPlanet);
        m_ctlTree.SetItemData (hItem,
                         (LPARAM) Planets[i].Diameter);
    }

    HTREEITEM hStars = m_ctlTree.InsertItem ("The Stars",
                                        13, 13, hRoot);
    m_ctlTree.SetItemData (hStars, NULL);
    hItem = m_ctlTree.InsertItem ("Vega", 15, 15, hStars);
    m_ctlTree.SetItemData (hItem, NULL);
    hItem = m_ctlTree.InsertItem ("Betelgeuse", 16, 16,
```

```
                                            hStars);
    m_ctlTree.SetItemData (hItem, NULL);
    hItem = m_ctlTree.InsertItem ("Cor Coroli", 17, 17,
                                        hStars);
    m_ctlTree.SetItemData (hItem, NULL);
    hItem = m_ctlTree.InsertItem ("Albireo", 14, 14,
                                        hStars);
    m_ctlTree.SetItemData (hItem, NULL);
}

BOOL CTreeCtrlDlg::OnNotify(WPARAM wParam, LPARAM lParam,
                            LRESULT* pResult)
{
    NMHDR *pNMHDR = (NMHDR *) lParam;
    if (wParam == IDC_TREE_TREECTRL)
    {
        switch (pNMHDR->code)
        {
            case TVN_GETINFOTIP:
            {
                NMTVGETINFOTIP *TTInfo =
                            (NMTVGETINFOTIP *) lParam;
                char *pszText = (char *) TTInfo->lParam;
                TTInfo->pszText = pszText;
                *pResult = 0;
                return (TRUE);
            }
            default:
                break;
        }
    }
    return CPropertyPage::OnNotify(wParam,lParam,pResult);
}

void CTreeCtrlDlg::OnTreeRecreatetree()
{
    CRect rc;
    DWORD dwStyle = m_ctlTree.GetStyle();
    dwStyle |= TVS_HASLINES | TVS_LINESATROOT
            | TVS_HASBUTTONS | WS_BORDER;
    dwStyle &= ~(TVS_CHECKBOXES | TVS_INFOTIP
            | TVS_NOTOOLTIPS);
    m_ctlTree.GetWindowRect (rc);
    ScreenToClient (rc);
    if (m_bCheckBoxesAreVisible)
    {
        HIMAGELIST hImages =
                m_ctlTree.GetImageList(
                            TVSIL_STATE)->m_hImageList;
        if (hImages != NULL)
            DeleteObject (hImages);
    }
    m_ctlTree.DestroyWindow ();
    m_ctlTree.Create(dwStyle, rc, this, IDC_TREE_TREECTRL);
    m_ctlTree.SetImageList (&m_Images, TVSIL_NORMAL);
    m_ctlTree.ShowWindow (SW_NORMAL);
```

```
    LoadTree();
    m_bHasLines = TRUE;
    m_bLinesAtRoot = TRUE;
    m_bHasButtons = TRUE;
    m_bToolTips = TRUE;
    m_bCheckBoxes = FALSE;
    m_bInfoTip = FALSE;
    UpdateData (FALSE);
}

void CTreeCtrlDlg::OnTreeSelectpath()
{
CChooseDirectory::CData data;

    TCHAR *szDir;
    DWORD dwLen = GetCurrentDirectory (0, NULL);
    if (!dwLen)
        return;
    try
    {
        szDir = new TCHAR [dwLen + 1];
    }
    catch (CMemoryException *e)
    {
        e->Delete ();
        return;
    }
    GetCurrentDirectory (dwLen + 1, szDir);
    data.m_OldPath = szDir;
    CChooseDirectory ccd(data);
    if (ccd.DoModal () == IDCANCEL)
        return;
    ::SetWindowText (GetDlgItem (
                    IDC_TREE_CHOSENPATH)->m_hWnd,
                    (LPCSTR) data.m_DirPath);
    ::ShowWindow (GetDlgItem (
                    IDC_TREE_SHOWPATH)->m_hWnd,
                    SW_SHOWNORMAL);
}
```

Compile and run the *Controls* application, and select the Tree Control page. Select Check Boxes, and you'll see the effect of adding the check boxes to the control. Unselect it, and the check boxes remain, but you no longer can check them. You can re-enable them, but you can't get rid of them without destroying the control and creating it again. Microsoft recommends that if you do this, you get the handle to the state image list and delete it as well. The state image list will be covered in Tip 904, "Using an Image List with the Tree Control."

The tree control, like the list control and the animation control that follows, is a fun control to work with. Albert Einstein once said that imagination is more important than knowledge. If you let your imagination run with this control, you can create some interesting effects. No one ever said that dialog boxes have to be dull. You can't "break" any of these controls; the worst you can do is lock up your machine and have to reboot from time to time, which is a good idea when using Windows anyway.

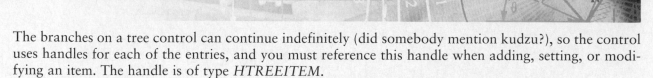

902. *Adding a Branch to a Tree Control*

The branches on a tree control can continue indefinitely (did somebody mention kudzu?), so the control uses handles for each of the entries, and you must reference this handle when adding, setting, or modifying an item. The handle is of type *HTREEITEM*.

When you use the *InsertItem()* function, you specify the parent's *HTREEITEM* handle. If you don't, the handle will default to the root item, and you'll add another major limb to the tree.

The *InsertItem()* function is overloaded and comes in four different forms. With the first, you use a *TVINSERTSTRUCT* structure to specify the details of the insertion. This structure includes an item structure, a union containing *TVITEM* and *TVITEMEX* structures. The *TVITEMEX* structure is available only if you've installed Internet Explorer 4.0 or later.

Using the insert structure, the loop to insert the planet names and details in the tree control looks as follows:

```
TVINSERTSTRUCT tvis;
memset (&tvis, '\0', sizeof (TVINSERTSTRUCT));
for (int i = 0; i < PLANETS; ++i)
{
    tvis.item.mask = TVIF_TEXT | TVIF_IMAGE
                   | TVIF_SELECTEDIMAGE | TVIF_PARAM;
    tvis.hParent = hPlanets;
    tvis.item.pszText = Planets[i].Planet;
    tvis.item.iImage = Planets[i].nIcon + 1;
    tvis.item.iSelectedImage = Planets[i].nIcon + 1;
    tvis.item.lParam = (LPARAM) Planets[i].Desc;
    hItem = m_ctlTree.InsertItem (&tvis);

    tvis.item.pszText = "Orbit";
    tvis.item.iImage =  10;
    tvis.item.iSelectedImage = 10;
    tvis.hParent = hItem;
    tvis.item.lParam = (LPARAM) Planets[i].Orbit;
    m_ctlTree.InsertItem (&tvis);

    tvis.item.pszText = "Rotation";
    tvis.item.iImage =  11;
    tvis.item.iSelectedImage = 11;
    tvis.hParent = hItem;
    tvis.item.lParam = (LPARAM) Planets[i].Rotation;
    m_ctlTree.InsertItem (&tvis);

    tvis.item.pszText = "Diameter";
    tvis.item.iImage =  11;
    tvis.item.iSelectedImage = 11;
    tvis.hParent = hItem;
    tvis.item.lParam = (LPARAM) Planets[i].Diameter;
    m_ctlTree.InsertItem (&tvis);
}
```

For a simple tree such as the one we've created, the insert structure is overkill. But for more complicated trees, you might consider using it rather than the other overloads.

The second form of *InsertItem()* is a little strange. You have to set a mask parameter similar to the *mask* member of the item structure and then pass all of the items that you normally would put into the item structure. None of the parameters has defaults, so if you don't need a parameter, you must pass a bogus value (it can be 0).

The third form is the simplest. The only required parameter is the text that you want to appear in the control. The other parameters are the parent node, which defaults to *TVI_ROOT*, and the item after which you want to insert the new item. The last parameter defaults to *TVI_LAST*, which means that you want it as the last item in the node specified in the parent parameter. It also may be *TVI_FIRST* to place it at the beginning, or *TVI_SORT*, which instructs the control to sort the node's child items alphabetically.

The fourth form is the one shown in the sample code. You specify the text, the image index, the index of the selected image, the parent node, which defaults to *TVI_ROOT*, and the node to insert after, which defaults to *TVI_LAST*.

903. *Understanding Tree Control Styles*

The tree control is undergoing some changes, and as a result, not all of the styles used by the control are documented in the MSDN literature. In this tip, you'll go over the tried-and-true styles plus some of the new ones, but for updated documentation, you can go to Microsoft's Web site, *msdn.microsoft.com*, and do a search on the style. Table 903 summarizes the tree control's styles.

Style	Effect
TVS_HASLINES	This produces lines linking child items and their parents.
TVS_LINESATROOT	The root items have lines linking them to their children.
TVS_HASBUTTONS	A box containing a "+" symbol is added to the left of each parent item. Clicking on the symbol expands the items, and the symbol changes to "–". Clicking it again collapses the branch.
TVS_EDITLABELS	This provides an edit control so that the user can edit the item labels.
TVS_SHOWSELALWAYS	The selection is always highlighted even if the control doesn't have the focus.
TVS_DISABLEDRAGDROP	This keeps the control from sending the *TVN_BEGINDRAG* message.
TCS_NOTOOLTIPS	The control doesn't use ToolTips. If ToolTips were enabled initially and they are later disabled in code by setting this style, they cannot be re-enabled.
TVS_SINGLEEXPAND	Changing the selection causes the new selection to expand and the item losing the selection to collapse. This applies to single-clicking on the item text. The user still may expand and collapse other items by selecting the appropriate button.

Table 903   The styles used with the tree control. This is not a comprehensive list, and the meanings of the styles are subject to change (continued on following page).

Style	Effect
TVS_CHECKBOXES	This causes a check box to appear next to each item in the tree. Once this style is enabled, it cannot be removed. However, removing the style disables the check boxes. (This style may not be supported by the compiler provided with this book).
TVS_FULLROWSELECT	This causes the selection indicator to extend from the left to right margins of the control. When used with the TVW_LINE-SATROOT style, this style is unpredictable. (This style may not be supported by the compiler provided with this book).
TVS_INFOTIP	Instead of ToolTips, the control sends a *WM_NOTIFY* message containing the ID of the tree control and information about the item whenever the mouse cursor hovers over an item. You may insert your own ToolTip text for this item. (This style may not be supported by the compiler provided with this book).
TVS_TRACKSELECT	This is the tree control's version of hot tracking. When the mouse passes over an item, the item text is displayed in highlighted text and underlined. (This style may not be supported by the compiler provided with this book).

Table 903   The styles used with the tree control. This is not a comprehensive list, and the meanings of the styles are subject to change (continued from previous page).

Many of these styles interact with one another, and enabling one might have an effect on the appearance of another style. Use the tree control sample to experiment with the various styles.

904. Using an Image List with the Tree Control

The tree control uses only one size image, a 16-by-16-pixel, icon-sized image, to display items. However, you can set two different image lists, one for the normal images and another for the *state* images. The latter image list is used when an item is placed in a programmer-defined state.

In addition, two image indexes may be assigned to an item, the regular image and the image to use when the item is selected. You may assign the same image to both. This is how a folder icon, for example, can show as closed when it isn't selected, but change to an open folder when it gets selected. Both icons must be in the same image list.

The state image list and an item's state help to keep track of the current condition of an item. You can use the state information to set an item's text in bold, and by retrieving the state, you can tell whether a parent item has ever been expanded. The last case can be useful in building a directory tree, which is a common use for the tree control. A full directory tree can take a long time to build, and users can become restless while this is happening. Instead of loading the entire tree, you build only as much as you need for the initial display. Then, when an item is opened, you check the state to see whether it has ever been expanded and, if not, build that part of the tree.

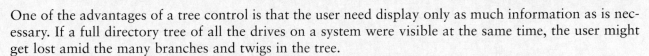

905. *Expanding and Collapsing a Branch*

One of the advantages of a tree control is that the user need display only as much information as is necessary. If a full directory tree of all the drives on a system were visible at the same time, the user might get lost amid the many branches and twigs in the tree.

Similarly, when the items contained in a branch no longer are needed, the user can close up the items and move on to the next branch. This gives the tree a much more orderly appearance than its name would imply.

Setting the *TVW_SINGLEEXPAND* style does this for you and makes it possible to open a branch with a single click. If a branch is on the same level as the one being selected by the user, it is collapsed automatically and the selected branch is expanded.

To expand or collapse a branch in code, you use the *Expand()* member function of *CTreeCtrl*. This function takes as parameters an *HTREEITEM* handle to the node that you want to change and a code indicating how you want to change it.

Passing *TVE_COLLAPSE* always will collapse an expanded node. If the node already is collapsed, the function call will have no effect. If you pass, *TVE_COLLAPSERESET* will collapse the node and remove any child nodes. If the node isn't already expanded, it will remove the child nodes.

Passing *TVE_EXPAND* will expand the node with the same results as *TVE_COLLAPSE*.

A final modifier, *TVE_TOGGLE*, will collapse the node if it is expanded, and expand the node if it is collapsed. You don't need to query the control for the current state of the node; the result is the opposite of its current state. If the node has no children, the modifier has no effect.

906. *Understanding the Animation Control*

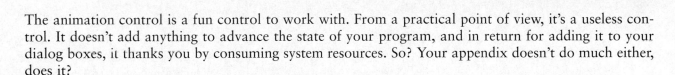

The animation control is a fun control to work with. From a practical point of view, it's a useless control. It doesn't add anything to advance the state of your program, and in return for adding it to your dialog boxes, it thanks you by consuming system resources. So? Your appendix doesn't do much either, does it?

The animation control has very few styles and sends and responds to very few messages. It's really an easy control to master, but based on that, it isn't as common as you might expect. What isn't easy to master is the technique of creating the animation files used by the control. Unless you're an artist or are adept at working with bitmaps (well, that leaves me out), creating the *.avi* files can be a bit of a chore.

It's a good user feedback device. The control works in the background, using a separate thread to produce the moving effect, and thus it really doesn't interfere with the operation of your program. The thread starts when you issue the *Play()* command.

The control displays consecutive bitmaps at a preset rate. It can play *.avi* files with two tracks, one video and the other audio, but the audio track is ignored. The Visual Studio comes with a set of *.avi* files that you'll find in the *COMMON\GRAPHICS\VIDEO* subdirectory where you installed the Visual Studio.

907. *Using the* **CAnimateCtrl** *Class*

The animation control is wrapped in the Microsoft Foundation Class library in the *CAnimateCtrl* class, which includes the few functions and styles that the control needs.

There's not a lot to demonstrate with the animation control. The command has very few functions and sends only two notification messages back to the parent window: *ACN_START* when the play begins and *ACN_STOP* when the play ends. Capturing and using these messages will be covered at the end of this tip.

Create the animation property page with a resource ID of *IDD_PROPPAGE_ANIMATEDLG*, and title it Animation, as shown in Figure 907. Set the Auto Play property on the animation controls but not the Border property. This will make the controls appear flat on the screen and begin running when you first open the page.

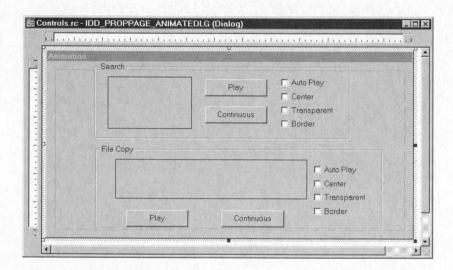

Figure 907   The Animation property page shows the few styles that are available for the control

The sample will use a couple of the stock animation files from the Visual Studio collection: *filecopy.avi* and *search.avi*. You've seen both of these at some time in Windows. The file copy has a sheet of paper flying between two open folders. The search animation features a flashlight trying to find something in the dark.

The code is really fairly simple, and the header and implementation files are listed here:

```
// AnimationDlg.h : header file
//

/////////////////////////////////////////////////////////
// CAnimationDlg dialog

class CAnimationDlg : public CPropertyPage
{
    DECLARE_DYNCREATE(CAnimationDlg)

// Construction
public:
    CAnimationDlg();
```

```
    ~CAnimationDlg();

// Dialog Data
    //{{AFX_DATA(CAnimationDlg)
    enum { IDD = IDD_PROPPAGE_ANIMATEDLG };
    CAnimateCtrl    m_ctlCopy;
    CAnimateCtrl    m_ctlSearch;
    BOOL    m_bCopyAutoPlay;
    BOOL    m_bCopyBorder;
    BOOL    m_bCopyCenter;
    BOOL    m_bCopyTransparent;
    BOOL    m_bSearchAutoPlay;
    BOOL    m_bSearchBorder;
    BOOL    m_bSearchCenter;
    BOOL    m_bSearchTransparent;
    //}}AFX_DATA


// Overrides
    // ClassWizard generate virtual function overrides
    //{{AFX_VIRTUAL(CAnimationDlg)
    public:
    protected:
    // DDX/DDV support
    virtual void DoDataExchange(CDataExchange* pDX);
//}}AFX_VIRTUAL

// Implementation
protected:
    DWORD m_dwCopyStyle;
    DWORD m_dwSearchStyle;
    void OnCopyStop();
void OnSearchStop();
    void OnCopyStart();
    void OnSearchStart();
    bool m_bSearchRunning;
    bool m_bCopyRunning;
    void RecreateControl (UINT nID);
    // Generated message map functions
    //{{AFX_MSG(CAnimationDlg)
    virtual BOOL OnInitDialog();
    //}}AFX_MSG
    DECLARE_MESSAGE_MAP()
    afx_msg void OnCopyCommands(UINT nID);
    afx_msg void OnSearchCommands(UINT nID);

};

/////////////////////////////////////////////////////
// AnimationDlg.cpp : implementation file
//

#include "stdafx.h"
#include "Controls.h"
#include "AnimationDlg.h"
```

```
#ifdef _DEBUG
#define new DEBUG_NEW
#undef THIS_FILE
static char THIS_FILE[] = __FILE__;
#endif


/////////////////////////////////////////////////////////
// CAnimationDlg property page

IMPLEMENT_DYNCREATE(CAnimationDlg, CPropertyPage)

CAnimationDlg::CAnimationDlg()
                      : CPropertyPage(CAnimationDlg::IDD)
{
    //{{AFX_DATA_INIT(CAnimationDlg)
    m_bCopyAutoPlay = TRUE;
    m_bCopyBorder = FALSE;
    m_bCopyCenter = FALSE;
    m_bCopyTransparent = FALSE;
    m_bSearchAutoPlay = TRUE;
    m_bSearchBorder = FALSE;
    m_bSearchCenter = FALSE;
    m_bSearchTransparent = FALSE;
    //}}AFX_DATA_INIT
    m_psp.dwFlags &= ~PSP_HASHELP;
}


CAnimationDlg::~CAnimationDlg()
{
}

void CAnimationDlg::DoDataExchange(CDataExchange* pDX)
{
    CPropertyPage::DoDataExchange(pDX);
    //{{AFX_DATA_MAP(CAnimationDlg)
    DDX_Control(pDX, IDC_ANI_COPY, m_ctlCopy);
    DDX_Control(pDX, IDC_ANI_SEARCH, m_ctlSearch);
    DDX_Check(pDX, IDC_ANICOPY_AUTOPLAY, m_bCopyAutoPlay);
    DDX_Check(pDX, IDC_ANICOPY_BORDER, m_bCopyBorder);
    DDX_Check(pDX, IDC_ANICOPY_CENTER, m_bCopyCenter);
    DDX_Check(pDX, IDC_ANICOPY_TRANSPARENT,
                             m_bCopyTransparent);
    DDX_Check(pDX, IDC_ANISEARCH_AUTOPLAY,
                             m_bSearchAutoPlay);
    DDX_Check(pDX, IDC_ANISEARCH_BORDER, m_bSearchBorder);
    DDX_Check(pDX, IDC_ANISEARCH_CENTER, m_bSearchCenter);
    DDX_Check(pDX, IDC_ANISEARCH_TRANSPARENT,
                             m_bSearchTransparent);
    //}}AFX_DATA_MAP
}


BEGIN_MESSAGE_MAP(CAnimationDlg, CPropertyPage)
    //{{AFX_MSG_MAP(CAnimationDlg)
    //}}AFX_MSG_MAP
    ON_COMMAND_RANGE(IDC_ANICOPY_CENTER,
```

```
                        IDC_ANICOPY_PLAY, OnCopyCommands)
    ON_COMMAND_RANGE(IDC_ANISEARCH_CENTER,
                        IDC_ANISEARCH_PLAY, OnSearchCommands)
    ON_CONTROL(ACN_STOP, IDC_ANI_COPY, OnCopyStop)
    ON_CONTROL(ACN_STOP, IDC_ANI_SEARCH, OnSearchStop)
    ON_CONTROL(ACN_START, IDC_ANI_COPY, OnCopyStart)
    ON_CONTROL(ACN_START, IDC_ANI_SEARCH, OnSearchStart)
END_MESSAGE_MAP()

/////////////////////////////////////////////////////
// CAnimationDlg message handlers

BOOL CAnimationDlg::OnInitDialog()
{
    CPropertyPage::OnInitDialog();
    m_ctlCopy.Open (MAKEINTRESOURCE (IDR_AVI_FILECOPY));

    m_ctlSearch.Open (MAKEINTRESOURCE (IDR_AVI_SEARCH));

    return TRUE;
}

void CAnimationDlg::OnCopyCommands(UINT nID)
{
    UpdateData (TRUE);
    switch (nID)
    {
        case IDC_ANICOPY_CENTER:
            if (m_bCopyCenter)
                m_ctlCopy.ModifyStyle (0,ACS_CENTER,TRUE);
            else
                m_ctlCopy.ModifyStyle (ACS_CENTER,0,TRUE);
            break;
        case IDC_ANICOPY_TRANSPARENT:
            if (m_bCopyTransparent)
                m_ctlCopy.ModifyStyle (0, ACS_TRANSPARENT,
                                        TRUE);
            Else
                m_ctlCopy.ModifyStyle (ACS_TRANSPARENT, 0,
                                        TRUE);
            break;
        case IDC_ANICOPY_BORDER:
            m_ctlCopy.Stop ();
            if (m_bCopyBorder)
                m_ctlCopy.ModifyStyle (0, WS_BORDER, TRUE);
            else
                m_ctlCopy.ModifyStyle (WS_BORDER, 0, TRUE);
            break;
        case IDC_ANICOPY_AUTOPLAY:
            if (m_bCopyAutoPlay)
                m_ctlCopy.ModifyStyle (0, ACS_AUTOPLAY,
                                        TRUE);
            else
                m_ctlCopy.ModifyStyle (ACS_AUTOPLAY, 0,
                                        TRUE);
            break;
```

```
            case IDC_ANICOPY_CONTINUOUS:
                m_ctlCopy.Play (0, -1, -1);
                return;
            case IDC_ANICOPY_PLAY:
                if (m_bCopyRunning)
                {
                    m_ctlCopy.Stop ();
                }
                else
                {
                    m_ctlCopy.Play (0, 0xffff, 1);
                }
                return;
    }
    RecreateControl (IDC_ANI_COPY);
    UpdateData (FALSE);
}

void CAnimationDlg::OnSearchCommands(UINT nID)
{
    UpdateData (TRUE);
    switch (nID)
    {
        case IDC_ANISEARCH_CENTER:
            if (m_bSearchCenter)
                m_ctlSearch.ModifyStyle (0, ACS_CENTER,
                                            TRUE);
            else
                m_ctlSearch.ModifyStyle (ACS_CENTER, 0,
                                            TRUE);
            break;
        case IDC_ANISEARCH_TRANSPARENT:
            if (m_bSearchTransparent)
                m_ctlSearch.ModifyStyle (0,ACS_TRANSPARENT,
                                            TRUE);
            Else
                m_ctlSearch.ModifyStyle (ACS_TRANSPARENT,0,
                                            TRUE);
            break;
        case IDC_ANISEARCH_BORDER:
            m_ctlSearch.Stop ();
            if (m_bSearchBorder)
                m_ctlSearch.ModifyStyle (0, WS_BORDER,
                                            TRUE);
            else
                m_ctlSearch.ModifyStyle (WS_BORDER, 0,
                                            TRUE);
            break;
        case IDC_ANISEARCH_AUTOPLAY:
            if (m_bSearchAutoPlay)
                m_ctlSearch.ModifyStyle (0, ACS_AUTOPLAY,
                                            TRUE);
            else
                m_ctlSearch.ModifyStyle (ACS_AUTOPLAY, 0,
                                            TRUE);
            break;
```

```
            case IDC_ANISEARCH_CONTINUOUS:
                m_ctlSearch.Play (0, -1, -1);
                return;
            case IDC_ANISEARCH_PLAY:
                if (m_bSearchRunning)
                {
                    m_ctlSearch.Stop ();
                }
                else
                {
                    m_ctlSearch.Play (0, 0xffff, 1);
                }
                return;
    }
    RecreateControl (IDC_ANI_SEARCH);
    UpdateData (FALSE);
}

void CAnimationDlg::RecreateControl(UINT nID)
{
    CAnimateCtrl *ctlAnimate;
    switch (nID)
    {
        case IDC_ANI_COPY:
            ctlAnimate = &m_ctlCopy;
            break;
        case IDC_ANI_SEARCH:
            ctlAnimate = &m_ctlSearch;
            break;
        default:
            return;
    }
//
//  Get the rectangle.
//
    CRect rc;
    ctlAnimate->GetWindowRect (rc);
    ctlAnimate->Stop();
    ctlAnimate->Close();

//
// Calling SetWindowPos forces the window to
// re-read its style
//
    ctlAnimate->SetWindowPos(NULL, 0, 0, rc.Width(),
                        rc.Height(),
                        SWP_NOZORDER | SWP_NOMOVE
                      | SWP_NOACTIVATE | SWP_SHOWWINDOW);
    if (nID == IDC_ANI_COPY)
        ctlAnimate->Open(MAKEINTRESOURCE(IDR_AVI_FILECOPY));
    else
        ctlAnimate->Open(MAKEINTRESOURCE (IDR_AVI_SEARCH));
}
//
//  The notification message handlers are called when
//  the play stops or starts. Use them to change the button
```

```
//  text and keep track of the running flags.
//
void CAnimationDlg::OnCopyStop()
{
    ::SetWindowText (GetDlgItem (
                     IDC_ANICOPY_PLAY)->m_hWnd, "Play");
    m_bCopyRunning = false;
}

void CAnimationDlg::OnCopyStart()
{
    ::SetWindowText (GetDlgItem (IDC_ANICOPY_PLAY)->m_hWnd,
                               "Stop");
    m_bCopyRunning = true;
}
void CAnimationDlg::OnSearchStop()
{
    ::SetWindowText (GetDlgItem (
                     IDC_ANISEARCH_PLAY)->m_hWnd, "Play");
    m_bSearchRunning = false;
}

void CAnimationDlg::OnSearchStart()
{
    ::SetWindowText (GetDlgItem (
                     IDC_ANISEARCH_PLAY)->m_hWnd, "Stop");
    m_bSearchRunning = true;
}
```

The animation control doesn't like to be destroyed and re-created, so this sample uses a trick that I picked up from some Microsoft sample code. Calling *SetWindowPos()* makes the window reread its style. The animation control won't redisplay the new styles while it has an animation object open, so you have to stop and close the object first. There should be one close for each open, according to Microsoft, to avoid resource leaks.

What makes the buttons work are the notification messages from the control, and each control uses "all both" of them. If you're into masochism, try deciphering the MSDN documentation on how to use these messages. Here's the complete text of the documentation on the *ACN_STOP* message:

"Notifies an animation control's parent window that the associated AVI clip has stopped playing. This notification message is sent in the form of a *WM_COMMAND* message.

"The return value is ignored."

Typically, Microsoft doesn't *misinform* you, but then it really doesn't tell you anything. As it works out, you use the *ON_CONTROL* macro to handle these notification messages. The macro needs three parameters, the message ID, the ID of the control sending the message, and the address of the handler function.

908. *Understanding* CAnimateCtrl *Member Functions*

The *CAnimateCtrl* derives from *CWnd* and thus inherits a large body of member functions. The class itself, however, has only five member functions other than the basic *Create()* function. The uses for these function are summarized in Table 908.

Member Function	Use
Open	Opens an AVI resource or file.
Close	Closes the AVI resource or file. If the open object is a resource, this frees it. There should be one *Close()* for each *Open()*.
Play	Starts the animation playing. The parameters are the first frame to play, the last frame to play (–1 indicates the last frame), and the number of times to repeat the play (–1 to play continuously).
Stop	Stops the animation.
Seek	Seeks a particular frame in the animation file or resource. 0 is the first frame, and –1 is taken to be the last frame.

Table 908   The animation control member functions

The frame values are 16-bit values, but you can pass them integers as long as they do not exceed 65,536. C++ automatically casts them to unsigned integers. All the functions return type *BOOL*, with *TRUE* indicating success and *FALSE* indicating failure.

909. *Creating an Animation File*

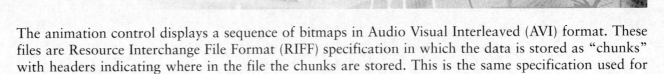

The animation control displays a sequence of bitmaps in Audio Visual Interleaved (AVI) format. These files are Resource Interchange File Format (RIFF) specification in which the data is stored as "chunks" with headers indicating where in the file the chunks are stored. This is the same specification used for WAVE and MIDI files.

You can create your own animation files using an AVI editor. There's a simple editor among the MSDN sample programs on the CD that you got with Visual Studio. Look for it in the *\SAMPLES\VC98\SDK\ DKTOOLS\AVIEDIT* subdirectory on the CD. The program runs by itself if you want to sample *.avi* files, but if you want to edit or create frames or a new file, you'll also need *IMAGEDIT.EXE*, which you'll find in the *SDKTOOLS* subdirectory.

910. *Adding an AVI Image File to Your Project*

The Visual Studio doesn't have a built-in resource type for AVI files, so adding an animation object to the resources isn't as simple as importing an icon or a bitmap file. Instead, you have to create a custom resource.

The first time that you import an AVI file, the Visual Studio will prompt you for a custom resource type with a dialog box as shown in Figure 910.

Summon the resource menu by right-clicking in the ResourceView panel of the Workspace Window, and select Import. When the dialog box appears, enter "AVI" as the new resource type, and press the OK button. A new branch of the tree named "AVI" (containing the quote marks) will appear in the ResourceView panel, and the imported file will open in a binary text editor.

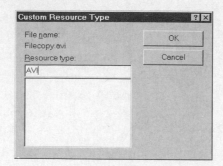

Figure 910   You can create new resource types using the Custom Resource Type dialog box

The Visual Studio doesn't contain an editor for AVI files, so if you want to edit the new resource in the studio, you'll have to edit the binary values of the file. Otherwise, you need to use an AVI editor such as the one provided as part of the MSDN sample code.

After you've added the new resource type, you can import additional AVI files using it. Each time, the Visual Studio will prompt you with the same dialog box shown in Figure 910, but after the first import, the AVI type will be listed in the large box. Just select it and press the OK button.

911. *Playing, Pausing, and Stopping an Animation*

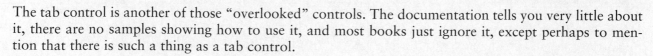

With such a limited number of functions, there's not a lot you can do with the *CAnimateCtrl* class except start the show and sit back and watch. The animation runs in its own thread, so once you start it, your program can get back to whatever it was doing. When the reason for the animation object has completed, you can stop and destroy the control.

The animation control values for all the functions are all unsigned integers and must be less than 65,536. Anything larger will return an error, a *FALSE*. The sole exception is –1, which is used to indicate the last frame of the object and continuous mode in the *Play()* function.

Call the *Play()* function with the start frame, the end frame, and the number of times to repeat the play. If the repeat count is 0, the animation won't play.

All the *CAnimateCtrl* functions return type *BOOL*, including the *Stop()* function, so there's no effective way of restarting animation from the same frame where you stopped it. You can pass a value of –1 as the start frame, and the animation will pick up at the last frame it played, but you run the risk of not being able to restart it when it reaches the last frame.

912. *Understanding the Tab Control*

The tab control is another of those "overlooked" controls. The documentation tells you very little about it, there are no samples showing how to use it, and most books just ignore it, except perhaps to mention that there is such a thing as a tab control.

This control is the basis of the Windows property sheet dialog box. It presents a group of tabs (or tab—there can be just one) that the user can select. The tabs can be arranged in a single row with a scroll button at the side if the total width of the tabs exceeds the control's width, or the tabs can be tiered as in the property sheet. The tabs may be placed at the top or bottom of the control, or on either side.

The tab control isn't an easy control to use or master, but once you understand just what the control does—and, more importantly, what it doesn't do—it loses a lot of its mystique.

The tab control only manages the tabs. Just because the user selects a tab doesn't mean that another dialog box or set of controls is going to be displayed. The actual page management is the responsibility of the program using the tab control. Its operation often is compared with the dividing tabs on a notebook or the labels on a file cabinet.

It can be the basis of a dialog box, as in the property sheet, or a tab control may be placed on a dialog box just as any other control. Used effectively, it can help to sort out densely populated dialog boxes by grouping related data elements.

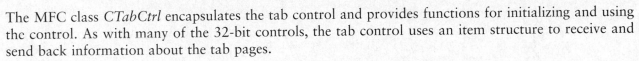

913. *Understanding the CTabCtrl Class*

The MFC class *CTabCtrl* encapsulates the tab control and provides functions for initializing and using the control. As with many of the 32-bit controls, the tab control uses an item structure to receive and send back information about the tab pages.

When you create a tab control, you may place controls directly on a page, or create a group of controls in a dialog box and place the dialog box on a tab page. In this sample, both approaches will be taken so that you can judge the relative merits of each.

The tab control uses a single image list, and if you plan to use different images for a page when it is selected and when it is not, you'll need to keep them both in the same image list object.

By now, your Controls property sheet should be getting a little full. There should be 15 pages at this point, and you can have up to 24 in a single property sheet. That means there's enough room for a tab control sheet.

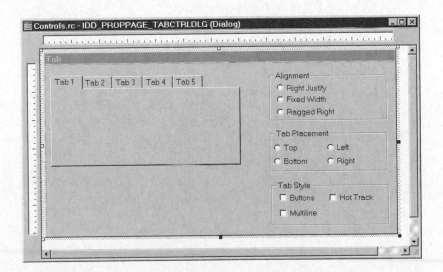

Figure 913a   The tab control property page shows a small tab control, which will present a maintenance challenge

Add a property page to the Controls project, as shown in Figure 913a. Give this property page a resource ID of *IDD_PROPPAGE_TABCTRLDLG*, and title it Tab Control. The tab control on this page is none too big, and it should present some interesting problems in managing the pages. Each page will have to be relatively small, and any misplacement will show up right away.

Create a class for the property page named *CTabCtrlDlg*. For this page, you'll also need to add a couple of minor classes for the two dialog boxes that will go on pages 2 and 5. These will be *CTabSampleDlg1* and *CTabSampleDlg2*. They won't do a lot, and you can create them in the same file, *TabSamplesDlg.cpp*. The dialog boxes are shown in Figures 913b and 913c, and the code for them follows. Derive these dialog boxes from *CPropertyPage*, but make sure that the Disabled box is unchecked on the More Styles page.

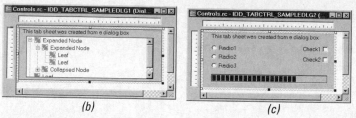

(b)   *(c)*

Figures 913b and 913c   The (very) small dialog boxes that will be placed on the tab control property sheet

```cpp
// TabSamplesDlg.h : header file
//


/////////////////////////////////////////////////////////////
// CTabSampleDlg1 dialog

class CTabSampleDlg1 : public CpropertyPage
{
// Construction
public:
    CTabSampleDlg1(CWnd* pParent = NULL);
    // standard constructor

// Dialog Data
    //{{AFX_DATA(CTabSampleDlg1)
    enum { IDD = IDD_TABCTRL_SAMPLEDLG1 };
    CTreeCtrl   m_TabTree;
    //}}AFX_DATA



// Overrides
    // ClassWizard generated virtual function overrides
    //{{AFX_VIRTUAL(CTabSampleDlg1)
    protected:
    virtual void DoDataExchange(CDataExchange* pDX);
    // DDX/DDV support
    //}}AFX_VIRTUAL


// Implementation
protected:

    // Generated message map functions
    //{{AFX_MSG(CTabSampleDlg1)
    virtual BOOL OnInitDialog();
    //}}AFX_MSG
    DECLARE_MESSAGE_MAP()
```

```cpp
};

//////////////////////////////////////////////////////
// CTabSampleDlg2 dialog

class CTabSampleDlg2 : public CDialog
{
// Construction
public:
    CTabSampleDlg2(CWnd* pParent = NULL);
    // standard constructor

// Dialog Data
    //{{AFX_DATA(CTabSampleDlg2)
    enum { IDD = IDD_TABCTRL_SAMPLEDLG2 };
    CProgressCtrl    m_progress;
    //}}AFX_DATA


// Overrides
    // ClassWizard generated virtual function overrides
    //{{AFX_VIRTUAL(CTabSampleDlg2)
    protected:
    virtual void DoDataExchange(CDataExchange* pDX);
    // DDX/DDV support
    //}}AFX_VIRTUAL

// Implementation
protected:

    // Generated message map functions
    //{{AFX_MSG(CTabSampleDlg2)
    afx_msg void OnTimer(UINT nIDEvent);
    virtual BOOL OnInitDialog();
    //}}AFX_MSG
    DECLARE_MESSAGE_MAP()
};
// TabSamplesDlg.cpp : implementation file
//

#include "stdafx.h"
#include "Controls.h"
#include "TabSamplesDlg.h"

#ifdef _DEBUG
#define new DEBUG_NEW
#undef THIS_FILE
static char THIS_FILE[] = __FILE__;
#endif


//////////////////////////////////////////////////////
// CTabSampleDlg1 dialog

//////////////////////////////////////////////////////
// CTabSampleDlg1 dialog
```

```
CTabSampleDlg1::CTabSampleDlg1(CWnd* pParent /*=NULL*/)
    : CPropertyPage(CTabSampleDlg1::IDD)
{
    //{{AFX_DATA_INIT(CTabSampleDlg1)
    //}}AFX_DATA_INIT
}


void CTabSampleDlg1::DoDataExchange(CDataExchange* pDX)
{
    CDialog::DoDataExchange(pDX);
    //{{AFX_DATA_MAP(CTabSampleDlg1)
    DDX_Control(pDX, IDC_TABCTRL_SHEET1TREE, m_TabTree);
    //}}AFX_DATA_MAP
}

BEGIN_MESSAGE_MAP(CTabSampleDlg1, CDialog)
    //{{AFX_MSG_MAP(CTabSampleDlg1)
    //}}AFX_MSG_MAP
END_MESSAGE_MAP()

/////////////////////////////////////////////////////////
// CTabSampleDlg1 message handlers

BOOL CTabSampleDlg1::OnInitDialog()
{
TV_INSERTSTRUCT TreeItem;

    CDialog::OnInitDialog();

    TreeItem.hParent = TVI_ROOT;
    TreeItem.hInsertAfter = TVI_LAST;\
    TreeItem.item.mask = TVIF_TEXT | TVIF_PARAM;
    TreeItem.item.pszText = "Animals";
    TreeItem.item.lParam = 0;
    HTREEITEM hAnimal1 = m_TabTree.InsertItem(&TreeItem);

    TreeItem.item.pszText = "Plants";
    TreeItem.item.lParam = 1;
    HTREEITEM hPlants1 = m_TabTree.InsertItem(&TreeItem);

    TreeItem.item.mask = TVIF_TEXT | TVIF_PARAM;
    TreeItem.item.iImage = -1;
    TreeItem.item.iSelectedImage = -1;
    TreeItem.hParent = hAnimal1;
    TreeItem.item.pszText = "Domesticated";
    TreeItem.item.lParam = 100;
    HTREEITEM hAnimal2 = m_TabTree.InsertItem(&TreeItem);

    TreeItem.item.pszText = "Wild and Free";
    TreeItem.item.lParam = 100;
    HTREEITEM hAnimal3 = m_TabTree.InsertItem(&TreeItem);

    TreeItem.hParent = hAnimal2;
    TreeItem.item.pszText = "Dogs";
```

```
        TreeItem.item.lParam = 101;
        m_TabTree.InsertItem(&TreeItem);

        TreeItem.item.pszText = "Cats";
        TreeItem.item.lParam = 102;
        m_TabTree.InsertItem(&TreeItem);

        TreeItem.item.pszText = "Hamsters";
        TreeItem.item.lParam = 103;
        m_TabTree.InsertItem(&TreeItem);

        TreeItem.hParent = hAnimal3;
        TreeItem.item.pszText = "Tigers";
        TreeItem.item.lParam = 111;
        m_TabTree.InsertItem(&TreeItem);

        TreeItem.item.pszText = "Lions";
        TreeItem.item.lParam = 112;
        m_TabTree.InsertItem(&TreeItem);

        TreeItem.item.pszText = "Gerbils";
        TreeItem.item.lParam = 113;
        m_TabTree.InsertItem(&TreeItem);

        return TRUE;
}

/////////////////////////////////////////////////////////
// CTabSampleDlg2 dialog

CTabSampleDlg2::CTabSampleDlg2(CWnd* pParent /*=NULL*/)
    : CDialog(CTabSampleDlg2::IDD, pParent)
{
    //{{AFX_DATA_INIT(CTabSampleDlg2)
        // NOTE: the ClassWizard will add
        // member initialization here
    //}}AFX_DATA_INIT
}


void CTabSampleDlg2::DoDataExchange(CDataExchange* pDX)
{
    CDialog::DoDataExchange(pDX);
    //{{AFX_DATA_MAP(CTabSampleDlg2)
    DDX_Control(pDX, IDC_TABCTRL_SHEET2PROGRESS1,
                m_progress);
    //}}AFX_DATA_MAP
}


BEGIN_MESSAGE_MAP(CTabSampleDlg2, CDialog)
    //{{AFX_MSG_MAP(CTabSampleDlg2)
    ON_WM_TIMER()
    //}}AFX_MSG_MAP
END_MESSAGE_MAP()
```

```
//////////////////////////////////////////////////////
// CTabSampleDlg2 message handlers

BOOL CTabSampleDlg2::OnInitDialog()
{
    CDialog::OnInitDialog();

    // TODO: Add extra initialization here

    m_progress.SetRange (0, 100);
    m_progress.SetStep (1);
    m_progress.SetPos (0);

    SetTimer (1, 100, NULL);
    return TRUE;
}

void CTabSampleDlg2::OnTimer(UINT nIDEvent)
{
    m_progress.StepIt();
}
```

The code for the tab control page will let you explore the different styles for the control—buttons or tabs and hot tracking—and place the tabs on any of the four sides. For simplicity, the image list will use only three different colors of LEDs, which you can load from icons. It's a lot easier to draw the LEDs than real icons, and any time I can get out of work is fine with me. The header file for the *CTabCtrlDlg* class is shown here:

```
// TabCtrlDlg.h : header file
//

#include     "TabSamplesDlg.h"

//////////////////////////////////////////////////////
// CTabCtrlDlg dialog

class CTabCtrlDlg : public CpropertyPage
{
    DECLARE_DYNCREATE(CTabCtrlDlg)

// Construction
public:
    virtual void InitializeTree (CTreeCtrl *tree);
    CTabCtrlDlg();
    ~CTabCtrlDlg();

// Dialog Data
    //{{AFX_DATA(CTabCtrlDlg)
    enum { IDD = IDD_PROPPAGE_TABCTRLDLG };
    CButton m_StyleMultilineCtrl;
    CTabCtrl    m_tab;
    int     m_Align;
    int     m_TabsLocation;
    BOOL    m_StyleButtons;
    BOOL    m_StyleHotTrack;
    BOOL    m_StyleMultiline;
```

```
        TabItem.pszText = "Seventh";
        TabItem.iImage = 0;
        m_tab.InsertItem (6, &TabItem);
}


void CTabCtrlDlg::DeleteTabItems()
{
    m_tab.DeleteAllItems ();
}


void CTabCtrlDlg::OnSelchangeSampletab(NMHDR* pNMHDR,
                                       LRESULT* pResult)
{
TC_ITEM     ti;
CWnd*       cDlg;
int         result;

    // TODO: Add your control notification handler
    // code here

    int sel = m_tab.GetCurSel();
    ti.mask = TCIF_PARAM | TCIF_IMAGE;
    result = m_tab.GetItem (sel, &ti);
    cDlg = (CWnd *) ti.lParam;
    if (cDlg)
        cDlg->ShowWindow (true);
    ti.mask = TCIF_IMAGE;
    ti.iImage += 1;
    m_tab.SetItem (sel, &ti);

    *pResult = 0;
}


void CTabCtrlDlg::OnSelchangingSampletab(NMHDR* pNMHDR,
                                         LRESULT* pResult)
{
TC_ITEM     ti;
CWnd*       cDlg;
int         result;

    // TODO: Add your control notification handler
    // code here

    int sel = m_tab.GetCurSel();
    ti.mask = TCIF_PARAM | TCIF_IMAGE;
    result = m_tab.GetItem (sel, &ti);
    cDlg = (CWnd *) ti.lParam;
    if (cDlg)
        cDlg->ShowWindow (false);
    ti.mask = TCIF_IMAGE;
    ti.iImage -= 1;
    m_tab.SetItem (sel, &ti);
    *pResult = 0;
}
```

```
                  r.bottom - r.top,
              this->m_hWnd, NULL, NULL);// IDC_TABEDIT);
   m_edit.SetWindowText ("This is a multiline edit "
                         "control without scrolling.");

   InitializeTree (&m_tree);
//
//  Insert the tab pages. Seven in all.
//
   AddTabItems ();
   AlignTabsAtTop();
//
//  Show the first control or dialog
//
   m_tab.ShowWindow (true);
   m_tree.ShowWindow (SW_NORMAL);

   return TRUE;
}

void CTabCtrlDlg::AddTabItems()
{
   TC_ITEM TabItem;
   TabItem.mask = TCIF_TEXT | TCIF_IMAGE | TCIF_PARAM;
   TabItem.iImage = 1;
   TabItem.lParam = (long) &m_tree;
   TabItem.pszText = "First";
   m_tab.InsertItem (0, &TabItem);

   TabItem.iImage = 2;
   TabItem.lParam = (long) &m_tabboxes;
   TabItem.pszText = "Second";
   m_tab.InsertItem (1, &TabItem);

   TabItem.iImage = 4;
   TabItem.pszText = "Third";
   TabItem.lParam = (long) &m_list;
   m_tab.InsertItem (2, &TabItem);

   TabItem.pszText = "Fourth";
   TabItem.lParam = (long) &m_edit;
   TabItem.iImage = 0;
   m_tab.InsertItem (3, &TabItem);

   TabItem.pszText = "Fifth";
   TabItem.lParam = (long) &m_tabtree;
   TabItem.iImage = 2;
   m_tab.InsertItem (4, &TabItem);

//
//  The next two pages are blank.
//
   TabItem.pszText = "Sixth";
   TabItem.lParam = 0L;
   TabItem.iImage = 4;
   m_tab.InsertItem (5, &TabItem);
```

```
      m_Images.Add(hIcon);
      DeleteObject (hIcon);
      hIcon = AfxGetApp()->LoadIcon (IDI_GREENONLED);
      m_Images.Add(hIcon);
      DeleteObject (hIcon);

      hIcon = AfxGetApp()->LoadIcon (IDI_YELLOWOFFLED);
      m_Images.Add(hIcon);
      DeleteObject (hIcon);
      hIcon = AfxGetApp()->LoadIcon (IDI_YELLOWONLED);
      m_Images.Add(hIcon);
      DeleteObject (hIcon);
      m_tab.SetImageList (&m_Images);

//
//  Create the dialog box items. These will be placed
//  on the tab page. Other pages will be created with
//  the controls in place.
//
      m_tabtree.Create(
                  MAKEINTRESOURCE(IDD_TABCTRL_SAMPLEDLG1),
                  GetDlgItem (IDD_PROPPAGE_TABCTRLDLG));
      m_tabtree.ModifyStyle (WS_CAPTION, 0, FALSE);
      m_tabboxes.Create(
                  MAKEINTRESOURCE(IDD_TABCTRL_SAMPLEDLG2),
                  GetDlgItem (IDD_PROPPAGE_TABCTRLDLG));
      m_tabboxes.ModifyStyle (WS_CAPTION, 0, FALSE);

      CRect r;
      m_tab.GetClientRect (&r);
      m_tab.GetWindowRect (m_rcBase);
      ScreenToClient (m_rcBase);
      m_tab.GetItemRect (0, &m_rcTab);
//
//  Create the individual controls. Notice they are
//  sized to the client rectangle, which is the client
//  area of a tab page.
      CRect rcControl;
      r = m_rcBase;
      r.top += m_rcTab.bottom - m_rcTab.top;
      m_list.CreateEx (0, "SysListView32",
            NULL, WS_CHILD, r.left, r.top,
            r.right - r.left, r.bottom - r.top,
            this->m_hWnd, NULL, NULL);//IDC_TABLIST);
      m_list.ModifyStyle (WS_CAPTION, 0, TRUE);

      DWORD dwStyle = TREE_STYLES;
      m_tree.CreateEx (0, "SysTreeView32",
            NULL, TREE_STYLES, r.left, r.top,
            r.right - r.left, r.bottom - r.top,
            this->m_hWnd, NULL, NULL);// IDC_TABTREECTRL);
      m_tree.ModifyStyle (WS_CAPTION, 0, TRUE);

      m_edit.CreateEx (0, "Edit",
            "", EDIT_STYLES | WS_CHILD,
            r.left, r.right, r.right - r.left,
```

```
    //}}AFX_DATA_MAP
}

BEGIN_MESSAGE_MAP(CTabCtrlDlg, CPropertyPage)
    //{{AFX_MSG_MAP(CTabCtrlDlg)
    ON_NOTIFY(TCN_SELCHANGE, IDC_TABCTRL_SAMPLETAB,
                            OnSelchangeSampletab)
    ON_NOTIFY(TCN_SELCHANGING, IDC_TABCTRL_SAMPLETAB,
                            OnSelchangingSampletab)
    ON_WM_DESTROY()
    ON_BN_CLICKED(IDC_TABCTRL_STYLE_MULTILINE,
                            OnStyleMultiline)
    ON_BN_CLICKED(IDC_TABCTRL_TABS_TOP, OnPlaceTabs)
    ON_BN_CLICKED(IDC_TABCTRL_ALIGN_FIXEDWIDTH,
                            OnAlignFixedwidth)
    ON_BN_CLICKED(IDC_TABCTRL_ALIGN_RIGHTJUSTIFY,
                            OnAlignRightjustify)
    ON_BN_CLICKED(IDC_TABCTRL_ALIGN_RAGGEDRIGHT,
                            OnAlignRaggedright)
    ON_BN_CLICKED(IDC_TABCTRL_STYLE_BUTTONS,OnStyleButtons)
    ON_BN_CLICKED(IDC_TABCTRL_STYLE_HOTTRACK,
                            OnStyleHottrack)
    ON_BN_CLICKED(IDC_TABCTRL_TABS_BOTTOM, OnPlaceTabs)
    ON_BN_CLICKED(IDC_TABCTRL_TABS_LEFT, OnPlaceTabs)
    ON_BN_CLICKED(IDC_TABCTRL_TABS_RIGHT, OnPlaceTabs)
    //}}AFX_MSG_MAP
END_MESSAGE_MAP()

/////////////////////////////////////////////////////////
// CTabCtrlDlg message handlers

BOOL CTabCtrlDlg::OnInitDialog()
{

    CPropertyPage::OnInitDialog();

    GetClientRect (m_rcBase);
    m_rcBase.right = 60 * m_rcBase.right / 100;
    m_rcBase.bottom = m_rcBase.bottom / 2 + 20;
    m_rcBase.left += 5;
    m_rcBase.top += 10;
    m_tab.Create (WS_VISIBLE | TCS_FOCUSNEVER
                | TCS_SINGLELINE, m_rcBase, this,
                IDC_TABCTRL_SAMPLETAB);
    CFont* font = GetFont ();
    m_tab.SetFont (font);

    m_Images.Create (16, 16, ILC_MASK, 6, 4);
    HICON hIcon = AfxGetApp()->LoadIcon (IDI_REDOFFLED);
    m_Images.Add(hIcon);
    DeleteObject (hIcon);
    hIcon = AfxGetApp()->LoadIcon (IDI_REDONLED);
    m_Images.Add(hIcon);
    DeleteObject (hIcon);

    hIcon = AfxGetApp()->LoadIcon (IDI_GREENOFFLED);
```

```cpp
// TabCtrlDlg.cpp : implementation file
//

#include "stdafx.h"
#include "Controls.h"
#include "TabCtrlDlg.h"

#ifdef _DEBUG
#define new DEBUG_NEW
#undef THIS_FILE
static char THIS_FILE[] = __FILE__;
#endif

#define     TREE_STYLES     (TVS_HASBUTTONS | TVS_HASLINES\
                            | TVS_LINESATROOT\
                            | TVS_SHOWSELALWAYS | WS_CHILD)
#define     EDIT_STYLES      (ES_MULTILINE | ES_WANTRETURN\
                            | WS_CHILD)

#define     TCS_MULTISEL    0x04

/////////////////////////////////////////////////////////////
// CTabCtrlDlg property page

IMPLEMENT_DYNCREATE(CTabCtrlDlg, CPropertyPage)

CTabCtrlDlg::CTabCtrlDlg()
                    : CPropertyPage(CTabCtrlDlg::IDD)
{
    //{{AFX_DATA_INIT(CTabCtrlDlg)
    m_Align = 0;
    m_TabsLocation = 0;
    m_StyleButtons = FALSE;
    m_StyleHotTrack = FALSE;
    m_StyleMultiline = FALSE;
    //}}AFX_DATA_INIT
    m_psp.dwFlags &= ~PSP_HASHELP;
}

CTabCtrlDlg::~CTabCtrlDlg()
{
}

void CTabCtrlDlg::DoDataExchange(CDataExchange* pDX)
{
    CPropertyPage::DoDataExchange(pDX);
    //{{AFX_DATA_MAP(CTabCtrlDlg)
    DDX_Control(pDX, IDC_TABCTRL_STYLE_MULTILINE,
                    m_StyleMultilineCtrl);
    DDX_Radio(pDX, IDC_TABCTRL_ALIGN_RIGHTJUSTIFY,m_Align);
    DDX_Radio(pDX, IDC_TABCTRL_TABS_TOP, m_TabsLocation);
    DDX_Check(pDX, IDC_TABCTRL_STYLE_BUTTONS,
                    m_StyleButtons);
    DDX_Check(pDX, IDC_TABCTRL_STYLE_HOTTRACK,
                    m_StyleHotTrack);
    DDX_Check(pDX, IDC_TABCTRL_STYLE_MULTILINE,
                    m_StyleMultiline);
```

```
    //}}AFX_DATA
    CImageList  m_Images;
    CTabSampleDlg1  m_tabtree;
    CTabSampleDlg2  m_tabboxes;
    CListCtrl    m_list;
    CEdit        m_edit;
    CTreeCtrl    m_tree;

// Overrides
    // ClassWizard generate virtual function overrides
    //{{AFX_VIRTUAL(CTabCtrlDlg)
    protected:
    virtual void DoDataExchange(CDataExchange* pDX);
    // DDX/DDV support
    //}}AFX_VIRTUAL

// Implementation
protected:
    void GetTabRects (CRect &r, CRect &rc);
    bool m_bMultiline;
    void RecreateWindow (DWORD dwStyle, DWORD dwStyleEx);
    void DeleteTabItems();
    void AddTabItems();
    void AlignTabsAtRight();
    void AlignTabsAtLeft();
    CRect m_rcTab;
    void AlignTabsAtBottom();
    CRect m_rcBase;
    void AlignTabsAtTop();
    // Generated message map functions
    //{{AFX_MSG(CTabCtrlDlg)
    virtual BOOL OnInitDialog();
    afx_msg void OnSelchangeSampletab(NMHDR* pNMHDR,
                                      LRESULT* pResult);
    afx_msg void OnSelchangingSampletab(NMHDR* pNMHDR,
                                        LRESULT* pResult);
    afx_msg void OnDestroy();
    afx_msg void OnStyleMultiline();
    afx_msg void OnPlaceTabs();
    afx_msg void OnAlignFixedwidth();
    afx_msg void OnAlignRightjustify();
    afx_msg void OnAlignRaggedright();
    afx_msg void OnStyleButtons();
    afx_msg void OnStyleHottrack();
    //}}AFX_MSG
    DECLARE_MESSAGE_MAP()
};
```

Finally, the source listing for the *CTabCtrlDlg* class. The messages sent by the tab control are more straightforward than you're accustomed to. In the header and animation classes, you had to hunt for the proper macro or virtual function to use to catch the notification messages. With the tab control, the messages come as simple old *WM_NOTIFY* messages, and you can catch them with the *ON_NOTIFY* macro in the message map. On top of that, they're even listed in the ClassWizard's message list.

```
//
//  All controls that were not created on a dialog box must
//  be destroyed here.
//
void CTabCtrlDlg::OnDestroy()
{
    m_list.DestroyWindow ();
    m_edit.DestroyWindow ();
    m_tree.DestroyWindow ();
    m_tab.DestroyWindow ();
    CPropertyPage::OnDestroy();
}

void CTabCtrlDlg::InitializeTree(CTreeCtrl * tree)
{
TV_INSERTSTRUCT TreeItem;

    // TODO: Add extra initialization here
    TreeItem.hParent = TVI_ROOT;
    TreeItem.hInsertAfter = TVI_LAST;
    TreeItem.item.mask = TVIF_TEXT | TVIF_PARAM;
    TreeItem.item.pszText = "Animals";
    TreeItem.item.lParam = 0;
    HTREEITEM hAnimal1 = tree->InsertItem(&TreeItem);

    TreeItem.item.pszText = "Plants";
    TreeItem.item.lParam = 1;
    HTREEITEM hPlants1 = tree->InsertItem(&TreeItem);

    TreeItem.item.mask = TVIF_TEXT | TVIF_PARAM;
    TreeItem.item.iImage = -1;
    TreeItem.item.iSelectedImage = -1;
    TreeItem.hParent = hAnimal1;
    TreeItem.item.pszText = "Domesticated";
    TreeItem.item.lParam = 100;
    HTREEITEM hAnimal2 = tree->InsertItem(&TreeItem);

    TreeItem.item.pszText = "Wild and Free";
    TreeItem.item.lParam = 100;
    HTREEITEM hAnimal3 = tree->InsertItem(&TreeItem);

    TreeItem.hParent = hAnimal2;
    TreeItem.item.pszText = "Dogs";
    TreeItem.item.lParam = 101;
    tree->InsertItem(&TreeItem);

    TreeItem.item.pszText = "Cats";
    TreeItem.item.lParam = 102;
    tree->InsertItem(&TreeItem);

    TreeItem.item.pszText = "Hamsters";
    TreeItem.item.lParam = 103;
    tree->InsertItem(&TreeItem);

    TreeItem.hParent = hAnimal3;
    TreeItem.item.pszText = "Tigers";
```

```
        TreeItem.item.lParam = 111;
        tree->InsertItem(&TreeItem);

        TreeItem.item.pszText = "Lions";
        TreeItem.item.lParam = 112;
        tree->InsertItem(&TreeItem);

        TreeItem.item.pszText = "Gerbils";
        TreeItem.item.lParam = 113;
        tree->InsertItem(&TreeItem);
}

void CTabCtrlDlg::OnStyleMultiline()
{
    UpdateData (TRUE);
    if (m_StyleMultiline == TRUE)
    {
        m_tab.ModifyStyle (TCS_SINGLELINE | TCS_MULTISEL,
                            TCS_MULTILINE, TRUE);
        m_tab.Invalidate ();
    }
    else
    {
        m_tab.ModifyStyle (TCS_MULTILINE | TCS_MULTISEL,
                            TCS_SINGLELINE, TRUE);
        m_tab.Invalidate ();
    }
    switch (m_TabsLocation)
    {
        case 0:     // At the top
            AlignTabsAtTop();
            break;
        case 1:     // At the bottom
            AlignTabsAtBottom ();
            break;
        case 2:     // At the left
            AlignTabsAtLeft();
            break;
        case 3:     // At the right
            AlignTabsAtRight();
            break;
    }
    TC_ITEM     ti;
    int nSel = m_tab.GetCurSel ();
    ti.mask = TCIF_PARAM | TCIF_IMAGE;
    m_tab.GetItem (nSel, &ti);
    CWnd *cDlg = (CWnd *) ti.lParam;
    if (cDlg != NULL)
        cDlg->Invalidate ();
}

void CTabCtrlDlg::OnPlaceTabs()
{
DWORD dwStyle, dwStyleEx;

    UpdateData (TRUE);
```

```
    switch (m_TabsLocation)
    {
        case 0:       // At the top
            m_tab.ModifyStyle (TCS_BOTTOM | TCS_VERTICAL,
                               0, TRUE);
            dwStyle = m_tab.GetStyle();
            dwStyleEx = m_tab.GetExStyle();
            RecreateWindow (dwStyle, dwStyleEx);
            m_StyleMultilineCtrl.EnableWindow(TRUE);
            AlignTabsAtTop();
            break;
        case 1:       // At the bottom
            m_tab.ModifyStyle (TCS_VERTICAL, TCS_BOTTOM,
                               TRUE);
            dwStyle = m_tab.GetStyle();
            dwStyleEx = m_tab.GetExStyle();
            RecreateWindow (dwStyle, dwStyleEx);
            AlignTabsAtBottom ();
            m_StyleMultilineCtrl.EnableWindow(TRUE);
            break;
        case 2:       // At the left
            m_tab.ModifyStyle (TCS_BOTTOM, TCS_VERTICAL,
                               TRUE);
            dwStyle = m_tab.GetStyle();
            dwStyleEx = m_tab.GetExStyle();
            RecreateWindow (dwStyle, dwStyleEx);
            AlignTabsAtLeft();
            m_StyleMultiline = TRUE;
            UpdateData (FALSE);
            OnStyleMultiline ();
            m_StyleMultilineCtrl.EnableWindow(FALSE);
            break;
        case 3:       // At the right
            m_tab.ModifyStyle (0, TCS_BOTTOM
                                  | TCS_VERTICAL,
                                  TRUE);
            dwStyle = m_tab.GetStyle();
            dwStyleEx = m_tab.GetExStyle();
            RecreateWindow (dwStyle, dwStyleEx);
            m_StyleMultiline = TRUE;
            UpdateData (FALSE);
            OnStyleMultiline ();
            m_StyleMultilineCtrl.EnableWindow(FALSE);
            AlignTabsAtRight();
            break;
    }
}

void CTabCtrlDlg::AlignTabsAtTop()
{
CRect   r, rc;

    int nRows = m_tab.GetRowCount ();
//
// Get the image area and resize all the controls.
//
```

```
    GetTabRects (r, rc);
    if (nRows == 1)
        rc.bottom = m_rcBase.bottom;
    else
        rc.bottom += (r.bottom - r.top) * (nRows - 1);

    m_tab.MoveWindow (rc, TRUE);

    CRect rcClient;
    CRect rcTab;

    rc = m_rcBase;
    rc.top += (r.bottom - r.top) * nRows + 6;
    rc.bottom += (r.bottom - r.top) * nRows - 30;
    rc.left += 6;
    rc.right -= 6;
    m_list.MoveWindow (rc, TRUE);
    m_edit.MoveWindow (rc, TRUE);
    m_tree.MoveWindow (rc, TRUE);

    m_tab.GetWindowRect (rcClient);
    ScreenToClient (rcClient);
    rc.top += rcClient.top + 42;
    rc.left += 10;
    rc.right += 10;
    rc.bottom += 56;
    m_tabtree.MoveWindow (rc, TRUE);
    m_tabboxes.MoveWindow (rc, TRUE);
}

void CTabCtrlDlg::AlignTabsAtBottom()
{
CRect   r, rc;

    int nRows = m_tab.GetRowCount ();
//
//  Get the image area and resize all the controls.
//
    GetTabRects (r, rc);
    if (nRows == 1)
        rc.bottom = m_rcBase.bottom;
    else
        rc.bottom = m_rcBase.bottom + (r.bottom - r.top)
                    * (nRows - 1);
    m_tab.MoveWindow (rc, TRUE);

    rc.top += 6;
    rc.bottom -= (r.bottom - r.top) * nRows + 10;
    rc.left += 6;
    rc.right -= 6;
    m_list.MoveWindow (rc, TRUE);
    m_edit.MoveWindow (rc, TRUE);
    m_tree.MoveWindow (rc, TRUE);

    CRect rcClient;
    m_tab.GetWindowRect (rcClient);
```

```
    ScreenToClient (rcClient);
    rc.top += rcClient.top + 42;
    rc.left += 10;
    rc.right += 10;
    rc.bottom += 56;
    m_tabtree.MoveWindow (rc, TRUE);
    m_tabboxes.MoveWindow (rc, TRUE);
}

void CTabCtrlDlg::AlignTabsAtLeft()
{
CRect   r, rc;

    int nRows = m_tab.GetRowCount ();
//
//  Get the image area and resize all the controls.
//
    GetTabRects (r, rc);
    m_tab.MoveWindow (rc, TRUE);

    rc.left += (r.right - r.left) * nRows + 6;
    rc.top += 6;
    rc.bottom -= 6;
    rc.right -= 6;
    m_list.MoveWindow (rc, TRUE);
    m_edit.MoveWindow (rc, TRUE);
    m_tree.MoveWindow (rc, TRUE);

    CRect rcClient;
    m_tab.GetWindowRect (rcClient);
    ScreenToClient (rcClient);
    rc.top += rcClient.top + 42;
    rc.left += 10;
    rc.right += 10;
    rc.bottom += 56;
    m_tabtree.MoveWindow (rc, TRUE);
    m_tabboxes.MoveWindow (rc, TRUE);
}

void CTabCtrlDlg::AlignTabsAtRight()
{
CRect   r, rc;

    int nRows = m_tab.GetRowCount ();
//
//  Get the image area and resize all the controls.
//
    GetTabRects (r, rc);
    rc = m_rcBase;
    m_tab.MoveWindow (rc, TRUE);

    rc.right -= (r.right - r.left) * nRows + 6;
    rc.top += 6;
    rc.bottom -= 6;
    rc.left += 6;
    m_list.MoveWindow (rc, TRUE);
```

```
        m_edit.MoveWindow (rc, TRUE);
        m_tree.MoveWindow (rc, TRUE);

        CRect rcClient;
        m_tab.GetWindowRect (rcClient);
        ScreenToClient (rcClient);
        rc.top += rcClient.top + 42;
        rc.left += 10;
        rc.right += 10;
        rc.bottom += 56;
        m_tabtree.MoveWindow (rc, TRUE);
        m_tabboxes.MoveWindow (rc, TRUE);
}

void CTabCtrlDlg::OnAlignFixedwidth()
{
        m_tab.ModifyStyle (TCS_RAGGEDRIGHT, TCS_FIXEDWIDTH,
                            TRUE);
        RecreateWindow (m_tab.GetStyle(), m_tab.GetExStyle ());
        switch (m_TabsLocation)
        {
            case 0:     // At the top
                AlignTabsAtTop();
                break;
            case 1:     // At the bottom
                AlignTabsAtBottom ();
                break;
            case 2:     // At the left
                AlignTabsAtLeft();
                break;
            case 3:     // At the right
                AlignTabsAtRight();
                break;
        }
}

void CTabCtrlDlg::OnAlignRightjustify()
{
        m_tab.ModifyStyle (TCS_RAGGEDRIGHT | TCS_FIXEDWIDTH,
                            0, TRUE);
        RecreateWindow (m_tab.GetStyle(), m_tab.GetExStyle ());
        switch (m_TabsLocation)
        {
            case 0:     // At the top
                AlignTabsAtTop();
                break;
            case 1:     // At the bottom
                AlignTabsAtBottom ();
                break;
            case 2:     // At the left
                AlignTabsAtLeft();
                break;
            case 3:     // At the right
                AlignTabsAtRight();
                break;
        }
```

```
}

void CTabCtrlDlg::OnAlignRaggedright()
{
    m_tab.ModifyStyle (TCS_FIXEDWIDTH, TCS_RAGGEDRIGHT,
                        TRUE);
    RecreateWindow (m_tab.GetStyle(), m_tab.GetExStyle ());
    switch (m_TabsLocation)
    {
        case 0:     // At the top
            AlignTabsAtTop();
            break;
        case 1:     // At the bottom
            AlignTabsAtBottom ();
            break;
        case 2:     // At the left
            AlignTabsAtLeft();
            break;
        case 3:     // At the right
            AlignTabsAtRight();
            break;
    }
}

void CTabCtrlDlg::RecreateWindow(DWORD dwStyle,
                                 DWORD dwStyleEx)
{
    TC_ITEM     ti;

    UpdateData (TRUE);
    CWnd *parent;
    int nSel = m_tab.GetCurSel ();
    ti.mask = TCIF_PARAM | TCIF_IMAGE;
    m_tab.GetItem (nSel, &ti);
    CWnd *cDlg = (CWnd *) ti.lParam;
    if (cDlg != NULL)
        cDlg->ShowWindow (SW_HIDE);
    CRect rc;
    m_tab.GetWindowRect (rc);
    DeleteTabItems ();
    parent = m_tab.GetParent();
    m_tab.DestroyWindow ();
    m_tab.Create (dwStyle, rc, parent,
                IDC_TABCTRL_SAMPLETAB);
    m_tab.ShowWindow (SW_SHOWDEFAULT);
    if (m_StyleMultiline == TRUE)
    {
        m_tab.ModifyStyle (TCS_SINGLELINE, TCS_MULTILINE,
                            TRUE);
    }
    else
    {
        m_tab.ModifyStyle (TCS_MULTILINE, TCS_SINGLELINE,
                            TRUE);
    }
    CFont* font = GetFont ();
```

```
        m_tab.SetFont (font);
        m_tab.SetImageList (&m_Images);
        AddTabItems ();
        m_tab.SetCurSel (nSel);
        if (cDlg != NULL)
            cDlg->ShowWindow (SW_SHOWNORMAL);
}

void CTabCtrlDlg::OnStyleButtons()
{
    UpdateData (TRUE);
    if (m_StyleButtons == TRUE)
    {
        m_tab.ModifyStyle (Ø, TCS_BUTTONS, TRUE);
        m_tab.Invalidate ();
    }
    else
    {
        m_tab.ModifyStyle (TCS_BUTTONS, Ø, TRUE);
        m_tab.Invalidate ();
    }
    TC_ITEM    ti;
    int nSel = m_tab.GetCurSel ();
    ti.mask = TCIF_PARAM | TCIF_IMAGE;
    m_tab.GetItem (nSel, &ti);
    CWnd *cDlg = (CWnd *) ti.lParam;
    if (cDlg != NULL)
        cDlg->Invalidate ();
}

void CTabCtrlDlg::OnStyleHottrack()
{
    DWORD dwStyle, dwStyleEx;

    UpdateData (TRUE);
    if (m_StyleHotTrack == TRUE)
    {
        m_tab.ModifyStyle (Ø, TCS_HOTTRACK, TRUE);
        dwStyle = m_tab.GetStyle ();
        dwStyleEx = m_tab.GetExStyle ();
        RecreateWindow (dwStyle, dwStyleEx);
    }
    else
    {
        m_tab.ModifyStyle (TCS_HOTTRACK, Ø, TRUE);
        dwStyle = m_tab.GetStyle ();
        dwStyleEx = m_tab.GetExStyle ();
        RecreateWindow (dwStyle, dwStyleEx);
    }
    switch (m_TabsLocation)
    {
        case Ø:     // At the top
            AlignTabsAtTop();
            break;
        case 1:     // At the bottom
            AlignTabsAtBottom ();
```

```
              break;
      case 2:        // At the left
          AlignTabsAtLeft();
          break;
      case 3:        // At the right
          AlignTabsAtRight();
          break;
   }
}

void CTabCtrlDlg::GetTabRects(CRect &r, CRect &rc)
{
    int nSel = m_tab.GetCurSel ();
    m_tab.SetCurSel (0);
    m_tab.GetItemRect (0, &r);
    m_tab.GetClientRect (rc);
    rc.left += m_rcBase.left;
    rc.top += m_rcBase.top;
    rc.right += m_rcBase.left;
    rc.bottom += m_rcBase.top;
    m_tab.SetCurSel (nSel);
}
```

When you first select the page and set the tabs at the bottom, you'll recognize the placement as the same used by the Workspace window.

The second and fifth pages are created using the small dialog boxes that you created earlier. Notice that they don't size as well as the pages with individual controls. To place and size the controls, you measure from the upper left of the tab control itself. However, the dialog boxes are descendents of the property page, and to place them you must measure from the upper left of the property page. When you change their sizes, the edge of the dialog box clips the controls, and you need to add scroll bars to the dialog boxes themselves. To avoid this, you could add code to the two dialog box classes to shrink or expand the controls as needed to fit into the rectangle.

914. *Adding Pages to a Tab Control*

To insert and maintain tabs, the tab control uses an item structure, which should be familiar to you by now. To add a tab page to the control, you need to fill out the members of a *TABITEM* structure. This sample is an old property page prepared using Visual Studio 5.0, so it still shows the item structure as *TC_ITEM*. Microsoft has been updating the item structures for the various controls and making the names and member variables conform to a single style, so a more modern version would use the *TABITEM* structure.

To set the data for an item, you must set the flags in the item structure's *mask* member variable to indicate which the control should use and which it should ignore. The following code, for example, sets up the first tab declaring the *pszText*, *iImage*, and *lParam* members to be valid:

```
TC_ITEM TabItem;
memset (&TabItem, '\0', sizeof (TC_ITEM));
TabItem.mask = TCIF_TEXT | TCIF_IMAGE | TCIF_PARAM;
TabItem.iImage = 1;
TabItem.lParam = (long) &m_tree;
```

```
TabItem.pszText = "First";
m_tab.InsertItem (0, &TabItem);
```

The *lParam* member may be any number that you want, including a pointer to another structure that might contain other information about the tab. In the sample code, the member was used to point to the control or dialog box that occupied the tab. The *lParam* value is included in the *WM_NOTIFY* messages, and the sample code used it to hide or display the tab page, depending upon whether it was currently selected or just becoming selected.

915. *Using an Image List with a Tab Control*

You can use a single image list with the tab control to place icons on the tabs. The tabs will accommodate text at the same time as icons. The control doesn't distinguish between normal and selected icons, so it won't display an alternative icon when the user presses a tab button. You can take care of that in your code, however, by getting the current selection in the handler code for the *TCN_SELCHANGE* message.

Build the image list as you would for any other control, but add the alternative selected icons if you intend to use them. The sample code uses on and off LED icons to indicate the selected and unselected tabs, and they are arranged one after the other. The off LED is placed first, and the on LED is next. This allows selection of the proper icon simply by incrementing or decrementing the *iImage* member of the *TABITEM* structure and then calling *SetItem()* to inform the tab control that the icon has changed.

The tab control does have the capability to delete an icon from the image list using the *RemoveImage()* function. When you remove an image, the tab control adjusts each tab's image index to the proper icon remains associated with the tab. There is no similar *AddImage()* function that performs the same purpose; presumably, you would just add the new image at the end of the image list, or replace an existing image.

916. *Adding Controls on the Fly to a Blank Tab Control Page*

The sample property page has left you two blank pages on the tab control for your experimentation. Actually, we wanted to show you what the control would look like if you tried to stuff a lot of tabs into it, but you still can use these blank pages to create your own controls or dialog boxes.

You can insert additional pages as you need, but as small as the control in the sample code is, you might consider expanding the size.

The tab control doesn't handle the tab pages themselves, so it really doesn't care what's on a page, a control or a dialog box. For example, suppose that you wanted to replace the tree control on the first page with a tab control at some time during your application's run. You can add a button to the bottom of the property page to switch controls. The following function handles that nicely:

```
void CTabCtrlDlg::OnTabctrlSwitchcontrols()
{
    TC_ITEM ti;
    ti.mask = TCIF_PARAM;
    m_tab.GetItem (0, &ti);
    CTreeCtrl *tree = (CTreeCtrl *) ti.lParam;
    tree->SetParent (&m_tab);
```

```
        CRect rc;
        tree->GetWindowRect (rc);
        m_tab.ScreenToClient (rc);
        if (tree->IsKindOf (RUNTIME_CLASS(CTreeCtrl)))
        {
            tree->DestroyWindow ();
            m_AltList.Create (LVS_REPORT | WS_BORDER,
                                rc, &m_tab, 0);
            ti.lParam = (LPARAM) &m_AltList;
            m_FirstPageControl = &m_AltList;
            ::SetWindowText (
                GetDlgItem(IDC_TABCTRL_SWITCHCONTROLS)->m_hWnd,
                "Use Tree Control");
        }
        else
        {
            tree->DestroyWindow ();
            m_tree.Create (TREE_STYLES, rc, &m_tab, 0);
            ti.lParam = (LPARAM) &m_tree;
            m_tab.SetItem (0, &ti);
            int nCur = m_tab.GetCurSel ();
            if (nCur == 0)
                m_tree.ShowWindow (SW_SHOWNORMAL);
            InitializeTree (&m_tree);
            m_FirstPageControl = &m_tree;
            ::SetWindowText (
                GetDlgItem(IDC_TABCTRL_SWITCHCONTROLS)->m_hWnd,
                "Use List Control");
        }
        m_tab.SetItem (0, &ti);
        int nCur = m_tab.GetCurSel ();
        if (nCur == 0)
            m_FirstPageControl->ShowWindow (SW_SHOWNORMAL);
        m_FirstPageControl->SetParent (this);
}

void CTabCtrlDlg::InitializeList(CListCtrl *list)
{
char *szTitles [] =
    {
    "Life Form",
    "Type",
    "Status"
    };

#define TITLES (sizeof(szTitles)/sizeof(char *))

    LV_COLUMN    lc;
    CRect rc;
    list->GetWindowRect (rc);
    int nWidth = (rc.right - rc.left) / 3;
    memset (&lc, '\0', sizeof (LV_COLUMN));
    lc.mask = LVCF_TEXT | LVCF_WIDTH | LVCF_SUBITEM;
    for (int sub = 0; sub < TITLES; ++sub)
    {
        lc.pszText = szTitles[sub];
```

```
        lc.cx = nWidth;
        lc.iSubItem = sub;
        list->InsertColumn (sub, &lc);
    }
}
```

The sample on the companion CD includes this button and function. Of course, we've added the *InitializeList()* function along with a class variable *m_FirstPageControl*, which is a *CWnd* pointer, and initialized it to the tree control in *OnInitDialog()*. Then in several functions, we've changed the reference to *m_tree* to *m_FirstPageControl*. The old lines of code are still there; they're commented out so that you can see where the changes were made.

In the function to switch controls, we change the parent to the tab control to get the proper rectangle. Then, after the new control has been created using the tab control as the parent, we switch back to the property page as the parent. The only reason for this is because we are destroying the tab control whenever you select a different style. That means that the control's children also will be destroyed, and we wouldn't want that. Unfortunately, the *SetWindowPos()* method won't work here because the tab control won't change its font orientation when you switch to tabs on the left or right side. Ordinarily, you won't be destroying your tab control, so you won't have to worry about the parent.

Alternatively, you could create the list control in the *OnInitDialog()* function and then simply switch pointers when you want to swap controls.

917. *Interpreting Tab Control Messages*

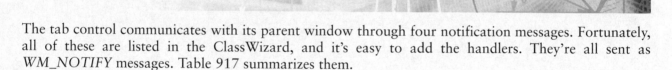

The tab control communicates with its parent window through four notification messages. Fortunately, all of these are listed in the ClassWizard, and it's easy to add the handlers. They're all sent as *WM_NOTIFY* messages. Table 917 summarizes them.

Tab Control Message	Purpose
TCN_GETOBJECT	Sent when the object of a drag-and-drop operation is dragged over a tab. This message is sent only if the *TCS_EX_REGISTERDROP* extended style is set.
TCN_KEYDOWN	Sent when the tab control has the focus and the user presses a key.
TCN_SELCHANGING	Sent when the selected tab on the control is about to change. The current selection hasn't changed yet.
TCN_SELCHANGE	Sent when the selected tab has changed. The current selection has changed when this message is sent.

Table 917   The tab control notification messages sent to its parent window

You can use the *TCN_SELCHANGING* message to perform any actions that you need before the selection change finishes, such as hiding the controls on the current page, or you can even prevent the selection change if your code detects something that requires attention. If your message handler returns *TRUE*, the selection change will continue. However, if you return *FALSE* from the handler, the selection change is aborted.

The *TCN_SELCHANGE* message may be used to set up the newly selected page, initialize any controls or dialog boxes, and display them.

918. *Understanding the Status Bar Control*

The status bar is one of the four controls that make up the control bar group. The other three control bars are the toolbar, the dialog bar, and the rebar controls. You've met the control bar group indirectly in the form of the *CStatusBar* class, which is used to attach a status bar to the main window frame of a document/view application.

A status bar is a horizontal window—it doesn't have a vertical style—that you usually place at the bottom of a larger window to display status information and program messages. There's no requirement that it be at the bottom of its parent window, and, in fact, the status bar has a style to make it attach to the top of the parent window.

You can subdivide the status bar into smaller windows to display different pieces of information simultaneously. You can even build controls onto it. A couple of common controls for this window are a combo box or a progress bar. It's a convenient place to put them if they are needed repeatedly by an application.

You can place a status bar on a dialog box, including a property page. In fact, you can even place a status bar on a property sheet. You'll do that in the next few tips.

919. *Using the* CStatusBarCtrl *Class*

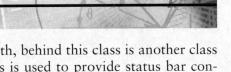

Although the *CStatusBar* class is the one most programmers deal with, behind this class is another class that encapsulates the status bar control—*CStatusBarCtrl*. This class is used to provide status bar control functionality in the Microsoft Foundation Class. It contains member functions to manipulate and modify the basic status bar and to access the individual panes you may place on the control.

If you're going to place a status bar on a dialog box or other non-mainframe object, the *CStatusBarCtrl* class is the one you will use.

Create a property page with the resource ID of *IDD_PROPPAGE_STATUSBARDLG* and label it "Status Bar." Make this property page a little wider than the others—say 345 by 155. The property sheet will resize it, and you'll want to make sure the status bar spans the width of the property page. The status bar will size itself according to the size of the parent unless you include the *CCS_NOPARENTAL-IGN* style. You'll use that style in Tip 921, "Adding Controls to a Status Bar," when you place a status bar on the property sheet. But for the one on the property page, you'll want it to size itself according to the page size. The property sheet is a simple one, as shown in Figure 919.

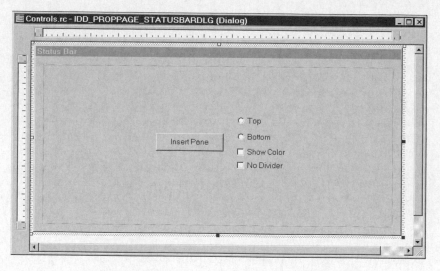

Figure 919   The status bar control's property page is mostly open space.
The status bar will be created in the property page setup code.

You'll need a couple of radio buttons to switch the status bar from the bottom to the top of the property page, a check box to modify the highlight style, and another check box to color the status bar. Then you'll need a button to insert a new panel and delete it. The header file also is fairly simple and is shown below:

```cpp
// StatusBarDlg.h : header file
//


/////////////////////////////////////////////////////////////
// CStatusBarDlg dialog

class CStatusBarDlg : public CPropertyPage
{
    DECLARE_DYNCREATE(CStatusBarDlg)

// Construction
public:
    CStatusBarDlg();
    ~CStatusBarDlg();

// Dialog Data
    //{{AFX_DATA(CStatusBarDlg)
    enum { IDD = IDD_PROPPAGE_STATUSBARDLG };
    int     m_nStatusBarPos;
    BOOL    m_bColor;
    BOOL    m_bNoDivider;
    //}}AFX_DATA


// Overrides
    // ClassWizard generate virtual function overrides
    //{{AFX_VIRTUAL(CStatusBarDlg)
    protected:
    virtual void DoDataExchange(CDataExchange* pDX);
    // DDX/DDV support
    //}}AFX_VIRTUAL
```

```
// Implementation
protected:
    void SetBarParts(UINT *pInd, int nCount);
    CStatusBarCtrl m_SampleBar;
    // Generated message map functions
    //{{AFX_MSG(CStatusBarDlg)
    virtual BOOL OnInitDialog();
    afx_msg void OnStatusbarPosition();
    afx_msg void OnTimer(UINT nIDEvent);
    afx_msg void OnStatusbarColor();
    afx_msg void OnStatusbarNodivider();
    //}}AFX_MSG
    DECLARE_MESSAGE_MAP()
};
```

The code will create a status bar, which will align itself at the bottom of the property page by default. Then you'll add some panes to it with text, and another to show the current date and time, which will be updated every five seconds using a timer.

You'll also be able to set the background color of the status bar to cyan, which will show the effect (or lack of effect) of the *CCS_NODIVIDER* style.

```
// StatusBarDlg.cpp : implementation file
//

#include "stdafx.h"
#include "Controls.h"
#include "StatusBarDlg.h"

#ifdef _DEBUG
#define new DEBUG_NEW
#undef THIS_FILE
static char THIS_FILE[] = __FILE__;
#endif

/////////////////////////////////////////////////////////
// CStatusBarDlg property page

#define    PANEOFFSET    6

IMPLEMENT_DYNCREATE(CStatusBarDlg, CPropertyPage)

static UINT indicators[] =
{
    ID_SEPARATOR,            // status line indicator
    ID_INDICATOR_CAPS,
    ID_INDICATOR_NUM,
    ID_INDICATOR_SCRL,
    ID_INDICATOR_TIME
};

CStatusBarDlg::CStatusBarDlg() : CPropertyPage(CStatusBarDlg::IDD)
{
    //{{AFX_DATA_INIT(CStatusBarDlg)
    m_nStatusBarPos = 1;
```

```
        m_bColor = FALSE;
        m_bNoDivider = TRUE;
        //}}AFX_DATA_INIT
        m_psp.dwFlags &= ~PSP_HASHELP;
//    m_psp.pszTitle = "Status Bar";
}

CStatusBarDlg::~CStatusBarDlg()
{
}

void CStatusBarDlg::DoDataExchange(CDataExchange* pDX)
{
    CPropertyPage::DoDataExchange(pDX);
    //{{AFX_DATA_MAP(CStatusBarDlg)
    DDX_Radio(pDX, IDC_STATUSBAR_TOP, m_nStatusBarPos);
    DDX_Check(pDX, IDC_STATUSBAR_COLOR, m_bColor);
    DDX_Check(pDX, IDC_STATUSBAR_NODIVIDER, m_bNoDivider);
    //}}AFX_DATA_MAP
}


BEGIN_MESSAGE_MAP(CStatusBarDlg, CPropertyPage)
    //{{AFX_MSG_MAP(CStatusBarDlg)
    ON_BN_CLICKED(IDC_STATUSBAR_TOP, OnStatusbarPosition)
    ON_WM_TIMER()
    ON_BN_CLICKED(IDC_STATUSBAR_COLOR, OnStatusbarColor)
    ON_BN_CLICKED(IDC_STATUSBAR_NODIVIDER,
                                    OnStatusbarNodivider)
    ON_BN_CLICKED(IDC_STATUSBAR_BOTTOM, OnStatusbarPosition)
    ON_BN_CLICKED(IDC_STATUSBAR_INSERTPANE,
                                    OnStatusbarInsertpane)

    //}}AFX_MSG_MAP
END_MESSAGE_MAP()

/////////////////////////////////////////////////////////////
// CStatusBarDlg message handlers

BOOL CStatusBarDlg::OnInitDialog()
{
    CPropertyPage::OnInitDialog();

    CRect rc;
    GetWindowRect (rc);
    ScreenToClient (rc);
// Note: the CCS_NOHILITE style is no longer supported
// so it is commented out in the line below.
    m_SampleBar.Create (CCS_NODIVIDER |// CCS_NOHILITE |
                        WS_CHILD |
                        WS_VISIBLE |
                        CCS_BOTTOM |
                        CCS_ADJUSTABLE,
                        CRect (0, 0, 0, 0), this, 0);

    CFont *font = GetFont ();
    m_SampleBar.SetFont (font);
```

```
        SetBarParts (indicators,
                     sizeof(indicators)/sizeof(UINT));

    m_SampleBar.GetRect (1, rc);
    rc.bottom += 4 * (rc.bottom - rc.top);

    SetTimer (42, 5000, NULL);
    return TRUE;
}

void CStatusBarDlg::OnStatusbarPosition()
{
    UpdateData (TRUE);
    switch (m_nStatusBarPos)
    {
        case 0:     // Status bar on Top
            m_SampleBar.ModifyStyle (CCS_BOTTOM,
                                     CCS_TOP, TRUE);
            break;
        case 1:     // Status bar on Bottom
            m_SampleBar.ModifyStyle (CCS_TOP,
                                     CCS_BOTTOM, TRUE);
            break;
        default:
            return;
    }
    m_SampleBar.SetWindowPos (NULL, 0, 0, 0, 0,
                             SWP_NOZORDER | SWP_NOMOVE |
                             SWP_NOACTIVATE | SWP_SHOWWINDOW);
}

void CStatusBarDlg::SetBarParts(UINT *pInd, int nCount)
{

    CRect rc;
//  m_SampleBar.GetWindowRect (rc);
    GetWindowRect (rc);
    ScreenToClient (rc);
    int nWidth = rc.right - rc.left;
    int *Indicators = new int [nCount];
    CWindowDC dc(&m_SampleBar);
    CSize sz;
    memset (Indicators, '\0', sizeof (int) * nCount);
    CTime Now = CTime::GetCurrentTime ();
    CString strTime = Now.Format ("%A, %B %d, %Y %H:%M");
    for (int pos = nCount - 1; pos >= 0; --pos)
    {
        switch (pInd[pos])
        {
            case ID_SEPARATOR:      // status line indicator
                Indicators[pos] = nWidth;
                break;
            case ID_INDICATOR_CAPS:
                Indicators[pos] = nWidth;
                sz = dc.GetTextExtent ("CAPS", 4);
                nWidth -= sz.cx + PANEOFFSET;
```

```
                break;
            case ID_INDICATOR_NUM:
                Indicators[pos] = nWidth;
                sz = dc.GetTextExtent ("NUM", 3);
                nWidth -= sz.cx + PANEOFFSET;
                break;
            case ID_INDICATOR_SCRL:
                Indicators[pos] = nWidth;
                sz = dc.GetTextExtent ("SCRL", 4);
                nWidth -= sz.cx + PANEOFFSET;
                break;
            case ID_INDICATOR_TIME:
                Indicators[pos] = nWidth;
                sz = dc.GetTextExtent (strTime);
                nWidth -= sz.cx + PANEOFFSET;
                break;
            default:
                break;
        }
    }
    m_SampleBar.SetParts (nCount, Indicators);
    m_SampleBar.GetParts (nCount, Indicators);
    m_SampleBar.SetParts (nCount, Indicators);
    for (pos = nCount - 1; pos > 0; --pos)
    {
        switch (pInd[pos])
        {
            case ID_SEPARATOR:      // status line indicator
                m_SampleBar.SetText (_T("Stuff"), pos, 0);
                break;
            case ID_INDICATOR_CAPS:
                m_SampleBar.SetText (_T("CAPS"), pos, 0);
                break;
            case ID_INDICATOR_NUM:
                m_SampleBar.SetText (_T("NUM"), pos, 0);
                break;
            case ID_INDICATOR_SCRL:
                m_SampleBar.SetText (_T("SCRL"), pos, 0);
                break;
            case ID_INDICATOR_TIME:
                m_SampleBar.SetText((LPCSTR)strTime,pos,0);
                break;
            default:
                break;
        }
    }
    delete [] Indicators;
}

void CStatusBarDlg::OnTimer(UINT nIDEvent)
{
    switch (nIDEvent)
    {
        case 42:
        {
            int nCount = m_SampleBar.GetParts (0, NULL);
```

```
            CWindowDC dc(this);
            CTime Now = CTime::GetCurrentTime();
            CString strTime;
            strTime = m_SampleBar.GetText (nCount - 1);
            CSize szOld = dc.GetTextExtent (strTime);
            strTime = Now.Format ("%A, %B %d, %Y %H:%M");
            CSize sz = dc.GetTextExtent (strTime);
            if (sz.cx != szOld.cx)
            {
                int *Indicators = new int [nCount];
                CString *strText = new CString [nCount];
                for (int i = 0; i < nCount; ++i)
                {
                    TCHAR szText[40];
                    m_SampleBar.GetText (szText, i);
                    strText[i] = szText;
                }
                strText[nCount-1] = (LPCSTR) strTime;
                m_SampleBar.GetParts (nCount, Indicators);
                for (i = (nCount - 1); i > 0; --i)
                {
                    sz = dc.GetTextExtent (strText[i]);
                    Indicators[i-1] = Indicators[i]
                                        - sz.cx + PANEOFFSET;
                }
                m_SampleBar.SetParts (nCount, Indicators);
                for (i = 0; i < nCount; ++i)
                    m_SampleBar.SetText (strText[i], i, 0);
                delete [] Indicators;
                delete [] strText;

            }
            else
                m_SampleBar.SetText (strTime,
                                    nCount - 1, 0);

            return;
        }
        default:
            break;
    }
    CPropertyPage::OnTimer(nIDEvent);
}

void CStatusBarDlg::OnStatusbarColor()
{
    UpdateData (TRUE);
    if (m_bColor)
        m_SampleBar.SetBkColor (RGB(0x00, 0xff, 0xff));
    else
        m_SampleBar.SetBkColor(GetSysColor (COLOR_BTNFACE));
}

void CStatusBarDlg::OnStatusbarNodivider()
{
    UpdateData (TRUE);
    DWORD dwStyle;
    dwStyle = GetWindowLong (m_SampleBar.m_hWnd, GWL_STYLE);
```

```
        if (m_bNoDivider)
            dwStyle |= CCS_NODIVIDER;
        else
            dwStyle &= ~CCS_NODIVIDER;
        SetWindowLong (m_SampleBar.m_hWnd, GWL_STYLE, dwStyle);
        CRect rc;
        m_SampleBar.GetWindowRect (rc);
        m_SampleBar.SetWindowPos(NULL, 0, 0,
                            rc.Width(), rc.Height(),
                            SWP_NOZORDER | SWP_NOMOVE |
                            SWP_NOACTIVATE | SWP_SHOWWINDOW);
}

void CStatusBarDlg::OnStatusbarInsertpane()
{
    int nInsertAt = 4;
    int nCount = m_SampleBar.GetParts (0, NULL);
    if (nCount == 6)
    {
        DeletePane (nInsertAt);
        return;
    }

    int *Indicators = new int [nCount + 1];
    CString *strText = new CString [nCount + 1];
    m_SampleBar.GetParts (nCount, Indicators);
    for (int i = 0; i < nCount; ++i)
    {
        TCHAR szText[40];
        m_SampleBar.GetText (szText, i);
        strText[i] = szText;
    }
    for (i = nCount; i > nInsertAt; --i)
    {
        Indicators [i] = Indicators[i - 1];
        strText[i] = (LPCSTR)strText [i - 1];
    }
    strText [i] = _T("INS");
    CWindowDC dc(&m_SampleBar);
    CSize sz = dc.GetTextExtent (strText[i]);
    for (i = nInsertAt + 1; i > 0; --i)
    {
        sz = dc.GetTextExtent (strText[i]);
        Indicators [i-1] = Indicators[i]
                        - sz.cx - PANEOFFSET;
    }
    --i;
    m_SampleBar.SetParts (nCount + 1, Indicators);
    for (i = 0; i < (nCount + 1); ++i)
        m_SampleBar.SetText ((LPCSTR)strText[i], i, 0);
    delete [] Indicators;
    delete [] strText;
    CWnd *button = GetDlgItem (IDC_STATUSBAR_INSERTPANE);
    button->SetWindowText (_T("Delete Pane"));
}
```

```
void CStatusBarDlg::DeletePane(int nPane)
{
    int nCount = m_SampleBar.GetParts (Ø, NULL);
    int *Indicators = new int [nCount + 1];
    CString *strText = new CString [nCount + 1];
    m_SampleBar.GetParts (nCount, Indicators);
    for (int i = Ø; i < nCount; ++i)
    {
        TCHAR szText[4Ø];
        m_SampleBar.GetText (szText, i);
        strText[i] = szText;
    }
//
//  Remove the text from item 3;
//
    for (i = nPane; i < (nCount - 1); ++i)
    {
        strText[i] = strText[i + 1];
    }
//
//  Put the time indicator width in the next
//  lower array member
    Indicators[nCount-2] = Indicators[nCount-1];
    CWindowDC dc(&m_SampleBar);
    CSize sz;
    for (i = (nCount-2); i > Ø; --i)
    {
        sz = dc.GetTextExtent (strText[i]);
        Indicators[i-1] = Indicators [i] - sz.cx
                                    - PANEOFFSET;
    }
    m_SampleBar.SetParts (nCount - 1, Indicators);
    for (i = Ø; i < (nCount - 1); ++i)
        m_SampleBar.SetText ((LPCSTR)strText[i], i, Ø);
    CWnd *button = GetDlgItem (IDC_STATUSBAR_INSERTPANE);
    button->SetWindowText (_T("Insert Pane"));
}
```

Notice that when the panel widths are set based on the width of the text, an offset is added to the size. The status bar control draws a three-pixel border around each pane, and that's included in the size you get to use. To make the text fit, you have to add six to offset the border on the left and right.

You're going to find some discrepancies in the documentation for the control bar classes, and for *CStatusBarCtrl*, particularly. They all list a nonexistent style, *CCS_NOHILITE*. The bar used to draw a one-pixel separator line above itself to distinguish it from other controls it touches. This style removed that line, but it apparently has been dropped in favor of *CCS_NODIVIDER*, which, according to the MSDN documentation, prevents a control bar from drawing a *two-pixel* divider. For the status bar class, this style apparently has no effect.

Pane management, when using the *CStatusBarCtrl* class is, at best, a pain. You'll look at that in the next tip. You will then truly appreciate some of the tasks that are performed by *CStatusBar* to handle the individual panes.

920. *Setting Indicators on the Status Bar Control*

Another curiosity about the *CStatusBarCtrl* class is the method of setting the indicators themselves. First, let's look at what the MSDN documentation says:

"Each element in the array specifies the position, in client coordinates, of the right edge of the corresponding part. If an element is –1, the position of the right edge for that part extends to the right edge of the control."

According to this, to set the parts—or panes—in the status bar, you need to declare an array of type *int* to hold the position of the right side of each pane. The implication here is that you can set the indicators in any order, you just need to specify the right side of the pane.

In addition, the only place where the –1 width may be used is in the far right pane, where it really isn't of much use. You have to get the width of the control (using *GetWindowRect()*), so you automatically have a value for the right edge of this pane. If you use it in any other position, it will simply wipe out the pane to its immediate right. By default, the status bar control contains one pane when it is created, and its width is set to –1;

To see this, try setting a random pane in the sample code's array to –1 and see the result. Then, try swapping a couple of array elements using code similar to that below:

```
int temp = Indicators [3];
Indicators [3] = Indicators [4];
Indicators [4] = temp;
```

You'll see that the order is important, and the first element of the array must be the far-right pane. Then you can work your way back to the far-right pane in the last element.

In addition, you can't just add a pane to the exiting set. You have to get the current pane positions using the *GetParts()* member function, open up a member of the array where you want to place the new pane, and recompute all of the pane positions. You can see this in the *OnStatusbarInsertpane()* function from the sample code in the previous tip (this function is the message handler for the Insert Pane button).

Once you manage the panes on a status bar control yourself, the *CStatusBar* class gets a bit friendlier. *CStatusBar* maintains the panes in structures containing the text, position, and any associated styles. In our code, you've used only the default style, which is for each pane to be sunken.

921. *Adding Controls to a Status Bar*

A status bar also may be a container for controls. You need to add a panel large enough to hold the control, then create it with the control's *Create()* function using the status bar as the parent window. The MFC status bar control class can't handle the control's notification messages, however, so you'll want to derive a new class from *CStatusBarCtrl*. You can use this derived class to pass the messages back to the status bar's parent.

Before adding a status bar to the property sheet, you need to prepare it for the combo box control that will go in the status bar. You'll need to add the title to the *m_psp* member of the property pages. It's getting a little cumbersome adding the pages to both constructors, so let's create a new function in *CControlsProp* to handle adding the pages and setting this text. Both constructors will just call this function.

Now you'll need to add a new class, *CPropStatusBar* derived from *CStatusBarCtrl*. Add a variable of this class to the property sheet class and call it *m_wndStatusBar*. You'll also need to add a *CComboBox* variable called *m_wndCombo*. The status bar will contain a pane showing the common control library version, and a combo box that will arrange the property pages alphabetically. Rather than hunt through the tabs, you'll be able to select a page from the combo box and go directly to it. To do this, the derived class for the status bar will pass the combo box message back using *WM_NOTIFY* and you'll need to add *OnNotify* to the property sheet class.

Lastly, you'll need to add a resource ID for the combo box. Name it *IDC_PROPSHEET_COMBO* and accept whatever value the resource editor gives it.

The header and source files for the *CPropStatusBar* class are shown below. It's a simple class. The only reason you need it is to catch the combo box selection change message and pass it back to the property sheet. In a real application where you are adding controls, you probably would want to add other message handlers to it.

```cpp
// PropStatusBar.h : header file
//


/////////////////////////////////////////////////////////////////
// CPropStatusBar window

class CPropStatusBar : public CStatusBarCtrl
{
// Construction
public:
    CPropStatusBar();

// Attributes
public:

// Operations
public:

// Overrides
    // ClassWizard generated virtual function overrides
    //{{AFX_VIRTUAL(CPropStatusBar)
    //}}AFX_VIRTUAL

// Implementation
public:
    virtual ~CPropStatusBar();

    // Generated message map functions
protected:
    void OnSelChange();
    //{{AFX_MSG(CPropStatusBar)
    //}}AFX_MSG

    DECLARE_MESSAGE_MAP()
};


/////////////////////////////////////////////////////////////////
// PropStatusBar.cpp : implementation file
/////////////////////////////////////////////////////////////////
```

```cpp
#include "stdafx.h"
#include "Controls.h"
#include "PropStatusBar.h"

#ifdef _DEBUG
#define new DEBUG_NEW
#undef THIS_FILE
static char THIS_FILE[] = __FILE__;
#endif

/////////////////////////////////////////////////////////
// CPropStatusBar

CPropStatusBar::CPropStatusBar()
{
}

CPropStatusBar::~CPropStatusBar()
{
}


BEGIN_MESSAGE_MAP(CPropStatusBar, CStatusBarCtrl)
    //{{AFX_MSG_MAP(CPropStatusBar)
    //}}AFX_MSG_MAP
    ON_CBN_SELCHANGE(IDC_PROPSHEET_COMBO, OnSelChange)
END_MESSAGE_MAP()

/////////////////////////////////////////////////////////
// CPropStatusBar message handlers

void CPropStatusBar::OnSelChange()
{
    static NMHDR nmHdr;
    static long lResult;
    nmHdr.hwndFrom = m_hWnd;
    nmHdr.idFrom = IDC_PROPSHEET_COMBO;
    nmHdr.code = CBN_SELCHANGE;
    GetParent()->SendMessage (WM_NOTIFY,
                              IDC_PROPSHEET_COMBO,
                              (LPARAM) &nmHdr);
}
```

You'll need to add code to the *OnInitDialog()* function in the *CControlsProp* class to create the status bar and the combo box. The new source file for *ControlsProp.cpp* is shown below:

```cpp
// ControlsProp.cpp : implementation file
//

#include "stdafx.h"
#include "Controls.h"
#include "ControlsProp.h"

#ifdef _DEBUG
#define new DEBUG_NEW
#undef THIS_FILE
```

```cpp
static char THIS_FILE[] = __FILE__;
#endif

bool GetCommonControlsVersion(DWORD &dwMajor,
                              DWORD &dwMinor);


/////////////////////////////////////////////////////////////
// CControlsProp

IMPLEMENT_DYNAMIC(CControlsProp, CPropertySheet)

CControlsProp::CControlsProp(UINT nIDCaption,
        CWnd* pParentWnd, UINT iSelectPage)
      : CPropertySheet(nIDCaption, pParentWnd, iSelectPage)
{
    AddPages ();
}

CControlsProp::CControlsProp(LPCTSTR pszCaption,
        CWnd* pParentWnd, UINT iSelectPage)
      : CPropertySheet(pszCaption, pParentWnd, iSelectPage)
{
    AddPages ();
}

void CControlsProp::AddPages()
{
    AddPage (&m_StaticPage);
    m_StaticPage.m_psp.pszTitle = _T("Static Text");
    AddPage (&m_EditPage);
    m_EditPage.m_psp.pszTitle = _T("Edit");
    AddPage (&m_RichEditPage);
    m_RichEditPage.m_psp.pszTitle = _T("Rich Edit");
    AddPage (&m_ButtonPage);
    m_ButtonPage.m_psp.pszTitle = _T("Buttons");
    AddPage (&m_ListBoxPage);
    m_ListBoxPage.m_psp.pszTitle =  T("List Box");
    AddPage (&m_ComboBoxPage);
    m_ComboBoxPage.m_psp.pszTitle = _T("Combo Box");
    AddPage (&m_ScrollBarPage);
    m_ScrollBarPage.m_psp.pszTitle = _T("Scroll Bar");
    AddPage (&m_ImageListPage);
    m_ImageListPage.m_psp.pszTitle = _T("Image List");
    AddPage (&m_ProgressBarPage);
    m_ProgressBarPage.m_psp.pszTitle = _T("Progress Bar");
    AddPage (&m_SliderPage);
    m_SliderPage.m_psp.pszTitle = _T("Slider");
    AddPage (&m_SpinnerPage);
    m_SpinnerPage.m_psp.pszTitle = _T("Spinner");
    AddPage (&m_HeaderPage);
    m_HeaderPage.m_psp.pszTitle = _T("Header");
    AddPage (&m_ListCtrlPage);
    m_ListCtrlPage.m_psp.pszTitle = _T("List Control");
    AddPage (&m_TreeCtrlPage);
    m_TreeCtrlPage.m_psp.pszTitle = _T("Tree Control");
    AddPage (&m_AnimationPage);
```

```
        m_AnimationPage.m_psp.pszTitle = _T("Animation");
        AddPage (&m_TabCtrlPage);
        m_TabCtrlPage.m_psp.pszTitle = _T("Tab Control");
        AddPage (&m_StatusBarPage);
        m_StatusBarPage.m_psp.pszTitle = _T("Status Bar");

        m_psh.dwFlags |= PSH_NOAPPLYNOW;
        m_psh.dwFlags &= ~PSH_HASHELP;
}

CControlsProp::~CControlsProp()
{
}

BEGIN_MESSAGE_MAP(CControlsProp, CPropertySheet)
    //{{AFX_MSG_MAP(CControlsProp)
    //}}AFX_MSG_MAP
END_MESSAGE_MAP()

/////////////////////////////////////////////////////////////
// CControlsProp message handlers

BOOL CControlsProp::OnInitDialog()
{
    BOOL bResult = CPropertySheet::OnInitDialog();
//
//  Get a pointer to the OK button and change its text
//  to Close.
//
    CWnd *button = GetDlgItem (IDOK);
    button->ShowWindow (SW_HIDE);
    button = GetDlgItem (IDHELP);
    button->ShowWindow (SW_HIDE);
    button = GetDlgItem (IDCANCEL);
    button->SetWindowText (_T("Close"));
//
//  Get the button's rectangle. The status bar will be
//  aligned with the button.
//
    CRect rc;
    button->GetWindowRect (rc);
    ScreenToClient (rc);
    rc.right = rc.left - 15;
    rc.left = 5;
//
//  Use the CCS_NOPARENTALIGN style so the status bar
//  can be placed using the rectangle.
//
    m_wndStatusBar.Create (WS_CHILD
                         | WS_VISIBLE
                         | CCS_NOPARENTALIGN
                         | CCS_BOTTOM,
                           rc, this, 0);
//
//  The control bar will have two parts. The first will be
//  the combo box at the right side. The second will hold
```

```
//   the string containing the common controls version.
//
     int nParts [] = {rc.right - 120, -1};
     m_wndStatusBar.SetParts (2, nParts);
//
// Get the rectangle of the right part and create a
// combo box in it. Use CBS_SORT so the property sheets
// will be in alphabetical order.
//
     m_wndStatusBar.GetRect (1, rc);
     rc.bottom += 4 * (rc.bottom - rc.top);
     m_wndCombo.Create (CBS_DROPDOWNLIST
                        | WS_VISIBLE
                        | WS_CHILD | WS_BORDER
                        | CBS_SORT
                        | WS_VSCROLL,
                        rc, &m_wndStatusBar,
                        IDC_PROPSHEET_COMBO);
//
// The status bar sets its own font, but we need to set
// it for the new combo box.
//
     CFont *font = GetFont ();
     m_wndCombo.SetFont (font);
//
// Load the combo box with the titles of the property
// pages. Put a pointer to the property page in the
// item data pointer variable.
//
     int nPageCount = GetPageCount ();
     for (int i = 0; i < nPageCount; ++i)
     {
         CPropertyPage *page = GetPage (i);
         int nIndex = m_wndCombo.AddString
                                   (page->m_psp.pszTitle);
         m_wndCombo.SetItemDataPtr (nIndex, page);
     }
//
// Select the first page, which will be visible when the
// property sheet first appears.
//
     m_wndCombo.SelectString (-1,
                          GetPage(0)->m_psp.pszTitle);
//
// Get the version of the common controls library and
// make a string out of it. Put the string in the left
// side of the status bar.
//
     DWORD dwMajor, dwMinor;

     GetCommonControlsVersion(dwMajor, dwMinor);
     CString strText;
     strText.Format
         ("Windows Common Controls Library Version %d.%02d",
          dwMajor, dwMinor);
     m_wndStatusBar.SetText ((LPCSTR) strText, 0, 0);
```

```
//
//  Just for the sake of appearance, make the Close button
//  the same height as the status bar.
//
    CRect rcButton;
    m_wndStatusBar.GetWindowRect (rc);
    button->GetWindowRect (rcButton);
    rcButton.top = rc.top;
    ScreenToClient (rcButton);
    button->MoveWindow (rcButton, TRUE);
    return bResult;
}
//  When the selection changes because the mouse was clicked
//  on a tab, change the combo box selection to match.
//  Also, when the status bar tells us the combo box
//  selection has changed, get the pointer to the new page
//  and set it as the active page.
//
BOOL CControlsProp::OnNotify(WPARAM wParam,
                             LPARAM lParam, LRESULT* pResult)
{
NMHDR *pNMHDR = (NMHDR *) lParam;
    switch (pNMHDR->code)
    {
        case TCN_SELCHANGE:
        {
            int nIndex = GetActiveIndex ();
            CPropertyPage *active = GetPage (nIndex);
            int nCount = GetPageCount ();
            for (int i = 0; i < nCount; ++i)
            {
                if (m_wndCombo.GetItemDataPtr (i) == active)
                {
                    m_wndCombo.SetCurSel (i);
                    break;
                }
            }
        }
        break;
        case CBN_SELCHANGE:
        {
            int nSel = m_wndCombo.GetCurSel ();
            CPropertyPage *page =
                        (CPropertyPage *)
                        m_wndCombo.GetItemDataPtr (nSel);
            SetActivePage (page);
            return (TRUE);
        }
    }
    return (CPropertySheet::OnNotify(wParam,
                                    lParam, pResult));
}
```

The *TCN_SELCHANGE* case in the *OnNotify()* function gets the *index* of the active page from the property sheet control, then, using the index, the code gets a pointer to the page. If you call *GetActivePage()* here, you'll get a pointer to the page that is losing focus, which is a curious condition. Getting the newly activated page and setting the combo box to that page assures the selected item tracks whether you pick it from a tab or select it from the combo box.

Keeping the combo box a child of the status bar makes positioning it easy, but it complicates the message handling. Given a choice, it's safer to keep the status bar the parent window. If you ever have to resize the property sheet, the status bar and combo box will reposition themselves accordingly.

922. *Understanding the Toolbar Control*

The toolbar control is the second in the set of control bar controls. Toolbars have been around for a long time and the most common use for them is to provide a convenient place to collect related button controls. You can, however, include other controls on a toolbar.

Usually, the button controls in a toolbar are associated with the application's menus and provide an alternate means for user input. This is only a convention, however, and you can create toolbars that contain objects that don't correspond to menu items.

The control is the underlying control for the MFC *CToolBar* class, which is used to place toolbars on the main frame of an application window. Unlike the status bar control, toolbars may be vertical or horizontal.

923. *Using the* **CToolBar** *Class*

Most often the toolbar is associated with a window frame in the document/view architecture, and in earlier tips, you saw how to manipulate and modify the toolbar in those applications. Those programs used the *CToolBar* class, which includes a toolbar control.

The MFC *CToolBarCtrl* class is the class that actually encapsulates the toolbar control and provides the functions, variables, and data structures to implement the control. It doesn't have to be used on a window frame, and you can create one on a dialog box or, in the case of our *Controls* application, on a property sheet.

In its latest incarnation, the toolbar control supports three image lists. One is for the normal image. The second is for the *hot* image, which is displayed when the mouse moves over a toolbar control (on a dialog box, the hot image list seems to be used only when a button is in the checked state). The third image list is for the disabled images, which are displayed when a toolbar control is set to disabled.

The page for this sample will have the resource ID of *IDD_PROPPAGE_TOOLBARCTRL* and has controls as shown in Figure 923. Create a class for it called *CToolBarDlg* and add it to the property sheet.

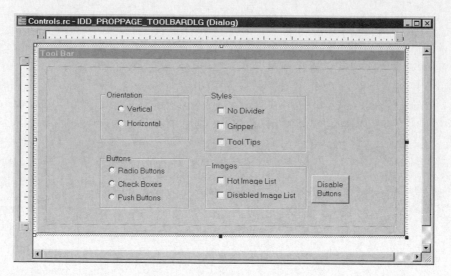

Figure 923   The toolbar control property page shows how to use a toolbar on a dialog box

This won't be a comprehensive demonstration of the toolbar control's capabilities. Much of that was covered in the document/view section, located in Tips 610 to 672. Instead, this code will demonstrate some of the differences when you use a toolbar control on a dialog box.

```cpp
// ToolBarDlg.h : header file
//


/////////////////////////////////////////////////////////////
// CToolBarDlg dialog

class CToolBarDlg : public CPropertyPage
{
    DECLARE_DYNCREATE(CToolBarDlg)

// Construction
public:
    CToolBarDlg();
    ~CToolBarDlg();

// Dialog Data
    //{{AFX_DATA(CToolBarDlg)
    enum { IDD = IDD_PROPPAGE_TOOLBARDLG };
    BOOL    m_bNoDivider;
    int     m_nOrientation;
    BOOL    m_bGripper;
    BOOL    m_bToolTips;
    int     m_nButtonStyle;
    BOOL    m_bDisabledList;
    BOOL    m_bHotList;
    //}}AFX_DATA


// Overrides
    // ClassWizard generate virtual function overrides
    //{{AFX_VIRTUAL(CToolBarDlg)
    protected:
```

```
    virtual void DoDataExchange(CDataExchange* pDX);
    // DDX/DDV support
    //}}AFX_VIRTUAL

// Implementation
protected:
    void CreateToolBar(DWORD dwStyle);
    BOOL OnToolTipText (UINT id, NMHDR * pTTTStruct,
                        LRESULT * pResult);
    CImageList m_imageNormal;
    CImageList m_imageDisabled;
    CImageList m_imageHot;
    CToolBarCtrl m_ToolBar;
    // Generated message map functions
    //{{AFX_MSG(CToolBarDlg)
    virtual BOOL OnInitDialog();
    afx_msg void OnToolbarNodivider();
    afx_msg void OnToolbarOrientation();
    afx_msg void OnToolbarGripper();
    afx_msg void OnToolbarTooltips();
    afx_msg void OnButtonStyle();
    afx_msg void OnToolbarHotlist();
    afx_msg void OnToolbarDisabledlist();
    afx_msg void OnToolbarDisablebutton();
    //}}AFX_MSG
    DECLARE_MESSAGE_MAP()
};
```

The toolbar control itself doesn't automatically display ToolTips. In document/view applications, that is handled by the *CToolBar* class, which includes a toolbar control. The ToolTips are actually handled by the *CWnd* ancestor class for the property page. Unfortunately, you can't just declare a toolbar object and start handing out your own ToolTips in your own style. It's a little more complicated than that, and you'll learn how to deal with the ToolTip control beginning in Tip 925, "Understanding the ToolTip Control." So, in our code, you have to add the handler for the *TTN_NEEDTEXT* message from the ToolTip control. The source code file is shown below:

```
// ToolBarDlg.cpp : implementation file
//

#include "stdafx.h"
#include "Controls.h"
#include "ToolBarDlg.h"

#ifdef _DEBUG
#define new DEBUG_NEW
#undef THIS_FILE
static char THIS_FILE[] = __FILE__;
#endif


/////////////////////////////////////////////////////////////
// CToolBarDlg property page

IMPLEMENT_DYNCREATE(CToolBarDlg, CPropertyPage)

CToolBarDlg::CToolBarDlg() : CPropertyPage(CToolBarDlg::IDD)
{
```

```
    //{{AFX_DATA_INIT(CToolBarDlg)
    m_bNoDivider = FALSE;
    m_nOrientation = 1;
    m_bGripper = FALSE;
    m_bToolTips = FALSE;
    m_nButtonStyle = 0;
    m_bDisabledList = FALSE;
    m_bHotList = FALSE;
    //}}AFX_DATA_INIT
}

CToolBarDlg::~CToolBarDlg()
{
}

void CToolBarDlg::DoDataExchange(CDataExchange* pDX)
{
    CPropertyPage::DoDataExchange(pDX);
    //{{AFX_DATA_MAP(CToolBarDlg)
    DDX_Check(pDX, IDC_TOOLBAR_NODIVIDER, m_bNoDivider);
    DDX_Radio(pDX, IDC_TOOLBAR_VERTICAL, m_nOrientation);
    DDX_Check(pDX, IDC_TOOLBAR_GRIPPER, m_bGripper);
    DDX_Check(pDX, IDC_TOOLBAR_TOOLTIPS, m_bToolTips);
    DDX_Radio(pDX, IDC_TOOLBAR_RADIOBUTTONS,
                                        m_nButtonStyle);
    DDX_Check(pDX, IDC_TOOLBAR_DISABLEDLIST,
                                        m_bDisabledList);
    DDX_Check(pDX, IDC_TOOLBAR_HOTLIST, m_bHotList);
    //}}AFX_DATA_MAP
}


BEGIN_MESSAGE_MAP(CToolBarDlg, CPropertyPage)
    //{{AFX_MSG_MAP(CToolBarDlg)
    ON_BN_CLICKED(IDC_TOOLBAR_NODIVIDER, OnToolbarNodivider)
    ON_BN_CLICKED(IDC_TOOLBAR_HORIZONTAL,
                                        OnToolbarOrientation)
    ON_BN_CLICKED(IDC_TOOLBAR_GRIPPER, OnToolbarGripper)
    ON_BN_CLICKED(IDC_TOOLBAR_TOOLTIPS, OnToolbarTooltips)
    ON_BN_CLICKED(IDC_TOOLBAR_RADIOBUTTONS, OnButtonStyle)
    ON_BN_CLICKED(IDC_TOOLBAR_VERTICAL,
                                        OnToolbarOrientation)
    ON_BN_CLICKED(IDC_TOOLBAR_PUSHBUTTONS, OnButtonStyle)
    ON_BN_CLICKED(IDC_TOOLBAR_CHECKBUTTONS, OnButtonStyle)
    ON_BN_CLICKED(IDC_TOOLBAR_HOTLIST, OnToolbarHotlist)
    ON_BN_CLICKED(IDC_TOOLBAR_DISABLEDLIST,
                                        OnToolbarDisabledlist)
    ON_BN_CLICKED(IDC_TOOLBAR_DISABLEBUTTON,
                                        OnToolbarDisablebutton)
    //}}AFX_MSG_MAP
    ON_NOTIFY_EX(TTN_NEEDTEXT, 0, OnToolTipText)
END_MESSAGE_MAP()

/////////////////////////////////////////////////////////
// CToolBarDlg message handlers
```

```cpp
BOOL CToolBarDlg::OnInitDialog()
{
    CPropertyPage::OnInitDialog();
    m_imageNormal.Create (IDB_TOOLBAR_ENABLED,
                          16, 4, ILC_MASK);
    m_imageDisabled.Create (IDB_TOOLBAR_DISABLED,
                          16, 4, ILC_MASK);
    m_imageHot.Create (IDB_TOOLBAR_HOT, 16, 4, ILC_MASK);
    CreateToolBar (WS_CHILD | WS_VISIBLE | CCS_NOPARENTALIGN
                    | TBSTYLE_WRAPABLE | TBSTYLE_TOOLTIPS);
    return TRUE;
}

void CToolBarDlg::CreateToolBar(DWORD dwStyle)
{
TBBUTTON ButtonData[4] =
    {
    0, ID_LIST_LARGEICON, TBSTATE_ENABLED | TBSTATE_CHECKED,
            TBSTYLE_BUTTON | TBSTYLE_CHECKGROUP, 0, 0, 0, -1,
    1, ID_LIST_SMALLICON, TBSTATE_ENABLED,
            TBSTYLE_BUTTON | TBSTYLE_CHECKGROUP, 0, 0, 0, -1,
    2, ID_LIST_LIST, TBSTATE_ENABLED,
            TBSTYLE_BUTTON | TBSTYLE_CHECKGROUP, 0, 0, 0, -1,
    3, ID_LIST_REPORT, TBSTATE_ENABLED,
            TBSTYLE_BUTTON | TBSTYLE_CHECKGROUP, 0, 0, 0, -1
    };

    CRect rc = CRect (0, 0, 0, 0);
    rc.bottom = 18;
    rc.right = 4 * 24 + 6;
    m_ToolBar.Create (dwStyle,
                      rc,
                      this, 0);
    m_ToolBar.SetImageList (&m_imageNormal);
    m_ToolBar.AddButtons (4, ButtonData);
    m_ToolBar.GetToolTips ()->Activate (FALSE);
}

void CToolBarDlg::OnToolbarNodivider()
{
    UpdateData (TRUE);
    CRect rcBar;
    m_ToolBar.GetWindowRect (rcBar);
    ScreenToClient (rcBar);
    if (m_bNoDivider)
    {
        m_ToolBar.ModifyStyle (0, CCS_NODIVIDER, TRUE);
        rcBar.bottom -= 2;
    }
    else
    {
        m_ToolBar.ModifyStyle (CCS_NODIVIDER, 0, TRUE);
        rcBar.bottom += 2;
    }
    m_ToolBar.SetWindowPos (NULL, rcBar.left, rcBar.top,
                rcBar.Width (), rcBar.Height(),
```

```
                     SWP_NOZORDER | SWP_NOACTIVATE |
                     SWP_SHOWWINDOW);
}


BOOL CToolBarDlg::OnToolTipText(UINT id, NMHDR *pNMHDR,
                               LRESULT *pResult)
{
    TOOLTIPTEXT *pTTT = (TOOLTIPTEXT *)pNMHDR;
    UINT nID =pNMHDR->idFrom;
// is idFrom actually the HWND of the tool?
    if (pTTT->uFlags & TTF_IDISHWND)
        nID = ::GetDlgCtrlID((HWND)nID);
    if(nID)
    {
        pTTT->lpszText = MAKEINTRESOURCE(nID);
        pTTT->hinst = AfxGetResourceHandle();
        return(TRUE);
    }
    return(FALSE);
}


void CToolBarDlg::OnToolbarOrientation()
{
    int nOld = m_nOrientation;
    UpdateData (TRUE);
    if (nOld == m_nOrientation)
        return;
    CRect rcBar;
    m_ToolBar.GetWindowRect (rcBar);
    ScreenToClient (rcBar);
    DWORD dwSize = m_ToolBar.GetButtonSize ();
    int nCount = m_ToolBar.GetButtonCount ();
    int nWidth = LOWORD (dwSize);
    int nHeight = HIWORD (dwSize);
//
// Leave the left and top as is. Make the toolbar
// as wide as it is deep and as deep as it is wide
//
    if (!m_bNoDivider)
        rcBar.top -= 6;
    if (m_nOrientation)     // Horizontal
    {
        rcBar.right = rcBar.left + nCount * nWidth + 2;
        rcBar.bottom = rcBar.top + nHeight;
        if (m_bGripper)
            rcBar.right += 6;
    }
    else                    // Vertical
    {
        if (m_bGripper)
            nWidth += 6;
        rcBar.right = rcBar.left + nWidth;
        rcBar.bottom = rcBar.top + nCount * nHeight + 2;
    }
    m_ToolBar.SetWindowPos (NULL, rcBar.left, rcBar.top,
```

```
                   rcBar.Width (), rcBar.Height(),
               SWP_NOZORDER | SWP_NOACTIVATE |
               SWP_SHOWWINDOW);
}

void CToolBarDlg::OnToolbarGripper()
{
    UpdateData (TRUE);
    CRect rcBar;
    m_ToolBar.GetWindowRect (rcBar);
    ScreenToClient (rcBar);
    if (!m_bNoDivider)
        rcBar.top -= 4;
    if (m_bGripper)
    {
        m_ToolBar.ModifyStyle (0, CBRS_GRIPPER, TRUE);
        rcBar.right += 6;
    }
    else
    {
        m_ToolBar.ModifyStyle (CBRS_GRIPPER, 0, TRUE);
        rcBar.right -= 6;
    }
    m_ToolBar.SetWindowPos (NULL, rcBar.left, rcBar.top,
               rcBar.Width (), rcBar.Height(),
               SWP_NOZORDER | SWP_NOACTIVATE |
               SWP_SHOWWINDOW);
    InvalidateRect (rcBar);
}

void CToolBarDlg::OnToolbarTooltips()
{
    UpdateData (TRUE);
    if (m_bToolTips)
        m_ToolBar.GetToolTips ()->Activate (TRUE);
    else
        m_ToolBar.GetToolTips ()->Activate (FALSE);
}

void CToolBarDlg::OnButtonStyle()
{
    UpdateData (TRUE);
    int nCount = m_ToolBar.GetButtonCount ();
    BYTE NewStyle;
    switch (m_nButtonStyle)
    {
        case 0:     // Radio Buttons
            NewStyle = TBSTYLE_CHECKGROUP;
            break;
        case 1:     // Check Buttons
            NewStyle = TBSTYLE_CHECK;
            break;
        case 2:     // Push Buttons
            NewStyle = TBSTYLE_BUTTON;
```

```
                break;
        }
        for (int i = 0; i < nCount; ++i)
        {
            TBBUTTON tb;
            TBBUTTONINFO tbi;
            m_ToolBar.GetButton (i, &tb);
            tbi.cbSize = sizeof (TBBUTTONINFO);
            m_ToolBar.GetButtonInfo (tb.idCommand, &tbi);
            tbi.fsStyle = NewStyle;
            if (NewStyle == TBSTYLE_BUTTON)
                tbi.fsState &= ~TBSTATE_CHECKED;
            if (NewStyle == TBSTYLE_CHECKGROUP)
            {
                if (i)
                    tbi.fsState &= ~TBSTATE_CHECKED;
                else
                    tbi.fsState |= TBSTATE_CHECKED;
            }
            tbi.dwMask = TBIF_STYLE | TBIF_STATE;
            m_ToolBar.SetButtonInfo (tb.idCommand, &tbi);
        }
}


void CToolBarDlg::OnToolbarHotlist()
{
    UpdateData (TRUE);
    if (m_bHotList)
        m_ToolBar.SetHotImageList (&m_imageHot);
    else
        m_ToolBar.SetHotImageList (NULL);
    m_ToolBar.Invalidate ();
}


void CToolBarDlg::OnToolbarDisabledlist()
{
    UpdateData (TRUE);
    if (m_bDisabledList)
        m_ToolBar.SetDisabledImageList (&m_imageDisabled);
    else
        m_ToolBar.SetDisabledImageList (NULL);
    m_ToolBar.Invalidate ();
}


void CToolBarDlg::OnToolbarDisablebutton()
{
    UpdateData (TRUE);
    int nCount = m_ToolBar.GetButtonCount ();
    TBBUTTONINFO tbi;
    for (int i = 0; i < nCount; ++i)
    {
        TBBUTTON tb;
        m_ToolBar.GetButton (i, &tb);
        tbi.cbSize = sizeof (TBBUTTONINFO);
        m_ToolBar.GetButtonInfo (tb.idCommand, &tbi);
        tbi.fsState ^= TBSTATE_ENABLED;
```

```
        tbi.dwMask = TBIF_STATE;
        m_ToolBar.SetButtonInfo (tb.idCommand, &tbi);
    }
    CWnd *button = GetDlgItem (IDC_TOOLBAR_DISABLEBUTTON);
    if (tbi.fsState & TBSTATE_ENABLED)
        button->SetWindowText ("Disable\nButtons");
    else
        button->SetWindowText ("Enable\nButtons");
}
```

By default, a toolbar control wants to place itself at the upper-left corner of its parent's window and it will size itself to be as wide as the parent window. You can force it to the bottom of the window using the *CCS_BOTTOM* style in the call to *Create()*. Using either of these styles, the rectangle parameter is ignored, and you don't need to calculate the control's size. In fact, you can pass *CRect(0,0,0,0)* as the value for this parameter.

Attaching to the upper or lower corner of the window is fine for a frame window application, but on a dialog box, you probably will want to use the *CCS_NOPARENTALIGN* style. In this case, the *Create()* function will use the *rect* parameter and position itself according to the rectangle's values. You have to specify a width for the toolbar, but a height is optional; the control will size itself to fit the button images.

With the *CCS_NOPARENTALIGN*, the toolbar control will adjust itself to fit the rectangle. If you make the rectangle one button wide and deep enough to accommodate all the buttons, the toolbar will assume vertical orientation.

924. *Using Image Lists with the Toolbar Control*

The toolbar control uses up to three image lists, although none of them is required; you can use text labels on toolbar buttons as though they were ordinary button controls. The first list is the normal image list and is loaded using the *CToolBarCtrl*'s member function *SetImageList()*. This is the image list used for all the button's states if none of the other image lists are loaded. When the button is disabled, the image will be grayed out.

The second image list is the *hot* image list. On a mainframe application, the toolbar control will use this image list when the mouse cursor moves over a button, or when the button is in a checked (pushed down) state. On a dialog application, however, the toolbar control uses this image list only when the button is checked. In the sample code provided, a hot image list with the colors of the items slightly changed is shown.

Although the *CToolBar* class has no function for setting the hot image list, the *CToolBarCtrl* does, and you can set it using the *GetToolBarCtrl()* function in *CToolBar*, then use the control object to set the hot image list, as shown in the following line.

```
m_wndToolBar.GetToolTips()->SetHotImageList (&m_imageList);
```

Typically, you would make this call in the *CMainFrame* class where the toolbar is created.

The disabled image list is used whenever a button is set to the disabled state, except on a dialog box. The image for a checked button won't change, although the button may, in fact, be disabled. You can provide an alternate image for the disabled button rather than resort to the graying out technique. The sample duplicates the normal images, but a red "X" is drawn in the upper-right corner.

925. *Understanding the ToolTip Control*

A *ToolTip* is a small pop-up window that is usually associated with a control or menu item that contains a brief description of the item's purpose. Usually, the window will appear about a half second after the mouse cursor has lingered—or hovered, to be more programmatic—over the item, and will disappear about four or five seconds later, or when the user clicks on the control or moves the mouse cursor away from it.

These ToolTips are provided by the ToolTip control, which provides a set of notification messages to your application to get the text for the pop-up window. It also notifies your program when a ToolTip window is about to be displayed or hidden. Your application can intercept these messages and modify the behavior of the control.

In an MFC document/view application, the framework provides for the ToolTip control and handles the messages. All you need do is provide the text for any controls you add to the frame. In the document/view architecture, you add this to the properties box when you create the control, as shown in Figure 925. The resource editor creates a string table entry for the control. In the MFC scheme, the framework displays only the text up to the newline (\n) on the frame's status bar. The text after the newline is the ToolTip text.

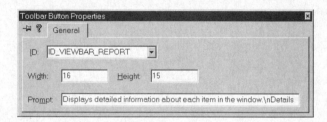

Figure 925   Enter the prompt and ToolTip text in the Prompt box of the Toolbar Button Properties dialog box.
The portion up to the newline character will be display on the status bar when the mouse cursor moves over the button.
The portion after the newline character is the text for the ToolTip.

Outside the document/view system, however, you need to add these string table entries yourself because the structure passed by the *TTN_NEEDTEXT* message requires a resource ID for the text rather than a string. It then gets the string from the string table.

Alternatively, you can use the *TTN_GETDISPINFO* message to copy a string directly into the ToolTip control. Although it isn't really pointed out anywhere, ToolTip messages do have a size limit. The buffer is 80 characters, which means you may have up to 79 characters in a ToolTip message, plus the terminating *NUL* character. This applies whether you're using the string table or the *TTN_GETDISPINFO* message.

The ToolTip notification messages will be covered in Tip 927, "Understanding the Hot Key Control."

926. *Using the CToolTipCtrl Class*

The *CToolTipCtrl* class encapsulates the ToolTip control and provides member functions to manipulate the control, including setting hover and display times for the ToolTip windows. You also can set the size and color of the ToolTip window along with the text color.

A single ToolTip control—and thus a single *CToolTipCtrl* object—can manage the ToolTips for a number of controls. When you create a ToolTip control object, the control always uses the *WS_POPUP* and *WS_EX_TOOLWINDOW* styles regardless of whether you specify them in the call to *Create()*. You can use other standard window styles, but the ToolTip control has only two styles that are specific.

The *TTS_ALWAYSTIP* style specifies that the tip window will appear even when a control is disabled or inactive. If you don't set this style, the tip will be displayed only when the control is active. The *TTS_NOPREFIX* disables stripping the ampersand character from a tip string. Normally, the control will strip ampersands so the same string may be used for menu text. If you don't use this style, it makes adding an ampersand character to the string a bit strange. One ampersand will be stripped. Two will cause the following character to be underscored. Three will produce a genuine ampersand character. It's best to use "and" in a ToolTip string.

Objects derived from *CWnd*—that includes dialog boxes and property sheets—have ToolTip capability. You actually could use a statement such as *EnableToolTip(TRUE)*. In your *OnInitDialog()* function, enter the text for the ToolTips in your string table and provide a message handler for the *TTN_NEEDTEXT* message. You have instant ToolTips.

You have no control over that specific ToolTip control, however, other than to set the text it will display. You can't set the text or background colors, and you can't change the width or the hover or display times. To do that, you have to create your own ToolTip control.

The easiest way to get your own ToolTip control working in an MFC dialog box is to derive your own class for the control and *subclass* it. Subclassing is the process of deriving from a parent control class and wrapping your new class around the control. It's usually done when you create a new ActiveX control using one of the MFC control classes.

The problem is the way Windows handles messages. The ToolTip contains a function for relaying mouse messages to it, and you could include handlers for the mouse messages and relay them to your tool tip control. But Windows sends messages to the window under the cursor, and you would have to derive classes for all the controls on your dialog box and provide the same capability.

Fortunately, this problem was recognized when the control was developed, so *CToolTipCtrl* has the mechanism for subclassing itself built into the control. All you have to do is derive a class from it and provide a single function for adding controls to the ToolTip. Such a class is shown below.

```
// ToolTips.h : header file
//


/////////////////////////////////////////////////////////////
// CToolTips window

class CToolTips : public CToolTipCtrl
{
// Construction
public:
    CToolTips();

// Attributes
public:

// Operations
public:

// Overrides
    // ClassWizard generated virtual function overrides
    //{{AFX_VIRTUAL(CToolTips)
    //}}AFX_VIRTUAL
```

```cpp
// Implementation
public:
    BOOL AddRect (CWnd *pParent, UINT nID, CRect &rc,
                    LPCSTR pszText= LPSTR_TEXTCALLBACK);
    BOOL AddControl(CWnd *pCtrl, UINT nID);
    BOOL AddControl(CWnd *pCtrl,
                    LPCSTR pszText= LPSTR_TEXTCALLBACK);
    virtual ~CToolTips();

    // Generated message map functions
protected:
    //{{AFX_MSG(CToolTips)
        // NOTE - the ClassWizard will add and remove member functions here.
    //}}AFX_MSG

    DECLARE_MESSAGE_MAP()
};

/////////////////////////////////////////////////////////////
// ToolTips.cpp : implementation file
/////////////////////////////////////////////////////////////
#include "stdafx.h"
#include "Controls.h"
#include "ToolTips.h"

#ifdef _DEBUG
#define new DEBUG_NEW
#undef THIS_FILE
static char THIS_FILE[] = __FILE__;
#endif

/////////////////////////////////////////////////////////////
// CToolTips

CToolTips::CToolTips()
{
}

CToolTips::~CToolTips()
{
}


BEGIN_MESSAGE_MAP(CToolTips, CToolTipCtrl)
    //{{AFX_MSG_MAP(CToolTips)
        // NOTE - the ClassWizard will add and remove mapping macros here.
    //}}AFX_MSG_MAP
END_MESSAGE_MAP()

/////////////////////////////////////////////////////////////
// CToolTips message handlers

BOOL CToolTips::AddControl(CWnd *pCtrl, LPCSTR pszText)
{
    TOOLINFO ti;
```

```
    ti.cbSize = sizeof (TOOLINFO);
    ti.uFlags = TTF_IDISHWND | TTF_SUBCLASS;
    ti.hwnd = pCtrl->GetParent()->GetSafeHwnd();
    ti.uId = (UINT) pCtrl->GetSafeHwnd ();
    ti.hinst = AfxGetInstanceHandle ();
    ti.lpszText = (LPTSTR) pszText;

    BOOL bResult = SendMessage (TTM_ADDTOOL,0,(LPARAM) &ti);
    return (bResult);
}

BOOL CToolTips::AddControl(CWnd *pCtrl, UINT nID)
{
    return (AddControl(pCtrl, MAKEINTRESOURCE(nID)));
}

BOOL CToolTips::AddRect(CWnd *pParent, UINT nID,
                        CRect &rc, LPCSTR pszText)
{
    TOOLINFO ti;
    ti.cbSize = sizeof (TOOLINFO);
    ti.uFlags = 0;//TTF_TRACK;
    ti.hwnd = pParent->m_hWnd;
    ti.uId = nID;
    ti.hinst = AfxGetInstanceHandle ();
    ti.lpszText = (LPTSTR) pszText;
    ti.rect = rc;
    BOOL bResult = SendMessage (TTM_ADDTOOL, 0,
                                (LPARAM) &ti);
    return (bResult);
}
```

This derived ToolTip control provides two methods of adding a control: by passing the string to be displayed or by passing the resource ID of the control. If you let the string default to *LPSTR_TEXTCALLBACK*, the control will send a notification message to its parent window whenever it needs text, and you can change it on-the fly. Notice the controls are all type *CWnd*. Under the C++ rules, you can cast a class to its parent safely.

Most important, examine the line in *AddControl()* where the *uFlags* member of the *TOOLINFO* structure is set. Each control will have the *TTF_SUBCLASS* flag set. The documentation on this flag is subtle, and it isn't indexed. You have to select the Search tab on the MSDN library and perform a search on it. You'll find it in three articles. Between the three, you'll find information on how to do this.

In addition, the *AddRect()* lets you define any rectangular area that you want to generate a ToolTip. Many books will show you how to do a rectangular ToolTip area, but usually this information isn't very useful. How many times will you want a blank area generating a ToolTip? Usually, what you will want to do is define a static control area such as one that holds a label or image to pop up a ToolTip.

There's a problem with this, however. Static controls don't generate the messages for ToolTips. You can't just get the rectangle of a static control and add it using *AddRect()*. The problem is that when the mouse is over a control, the control is getting the mouse messages. In the case of a static control, these are not passed on to your dialog box, so you don't get a ToolTip.

You can, however, intercept the *WM_MOUSEMOVE* message and pass it on to the ToolTip control using the *RelayEvent()* function. Suddenly, you've got ToolTips where you couldn't get them before. You'll see this at work in the sample code that follows. The ToolTip property page uses the *CStaticEx* class to draw the color boxes you will use to set the ToolTip text and background colors.

That's all you need to make your ToolTip control work. When you add a ToolTip control to your dialog box class, make sure it is declared as a variable of your ToolTip class, not *CToolTipCtrl*.

Now you can create the property page for ToolTips. The control layout is shown in Figure 926. Give it a resource ID of *IDD_PROPPAGE_TOOLTIPDLG* and label it "Tool Tips."

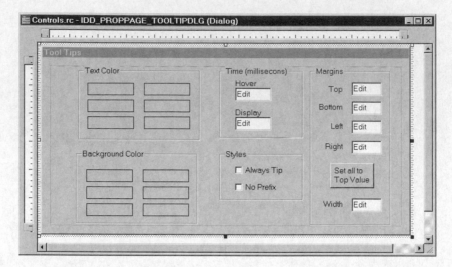

Figure 926   The ToolTips property page. The rectangles in the color areas are static controls with the Border style set. You will use these areas to set the text and background colors of the ToolTips.

Create a class for the property page dialog box named *CToolTipDlg*. Make the color selection controls of type *CStaticEx* and the ToolTip control of your derived class, *CToolTips*, in the sample. The header file is listed below.

```
#include    "StaticEx.h"
#include    "ToolTips.h"


/////////////////////////////////////////////////////////
// CToolTipDlg dialog

class CToolTipDlg : public CPropertyPage
{
    DECLARE_DYNCREATE(CToolTipDlg)

// Construction
public:
    CToolTips & GetToolTipControl();
    CToolTipDlg();
    ~CToolTipDlg();

// Dialog Data
    //{{AFX_DATA(CToolTipDlg)
    enum { IDD = IDD_PROPPAGE_TOOLTIPDLG };
    CStaticEx   m_ctlBackYellow;
    CStaticEx   m_ctlBackWhite;
    CStaticEx   m_ctlBackMagenta;
    CStaticEx   m_ctlBackGreen;
    CStaticEx   m_ctlBackCyan;
    CStaticEx   m_ctlBackBlack;
    CStaticEx   m_ctlTextBlack;
    CStaticEx   m_ctlTextBlue;
```

```
    CStaticEx   m_ctlTextGray;
    CStaticEx   m_ctlTextGreen;
    CStaticEx   m_ctlTextRed;
    CStaticEx   m_ctlTextWhite;
    int      m_nHoverTime;
    int      m_nDisplayTime;
    int      m_nBottomMargin;
    int      m_nLeftMargin;
    int      m_nRightMargin;
    int      m_nTopMargin;
    int      m_nWidth;
    BOOL     m_bAlwaysTip;
    BOOL     m_bNoPrefix;
    //}}AFX_DATA


// Overrides
    // ClassWizard generate virtual function overrides
    //{{AFX_VIRTUAL(CToolTipDlg)
    protected:
    // DDX/DDV support
    virtual void DoDataExchange(CDataExchange* pDX);
    //}}AFX_VIRTUAL

// Implementation
protected:
    BOOL OnToolTipText(UINT id, NMHDR *pNMHDR,
                       LRESULT *pResult);
    void AddControls();
    // Generated message map functions
    //{{AFX_MSG(CToolTipDlg)
    afx_msg void OnTooltipAlwaystip();
    afx_msg void OnTooltipNoprefix();
    afx_msg void OnChangeTooltipTopmargin();
    afx_msg void OnChangeTooltipBottommargin();
    afx_msg void OnChangeTooltipLeftmargin();
    afx_msg void OnChangeTooltipRightmargin();
    afx_msg void OnTooltipHoverstatic();
    afx_msg void OnChangeTooltipDisplaytime();
    afx_msg void OnTooltipSetall();
    virtual BOOL OnInitDialog();
    afx_msg void OnLButtonDblClk(UINT nFlags,CPoint point);
    afx_msg void OnChangeTooltipWidth();
    afx_msg void OnMouseMove(UINT nFlags, CPoint point);
    //}}AFX_MSG

    afx_msg void OnTooltipTextblack();
    afx_msg void OnTooltipTextblue();
    afx_msg void OnTooltipTextgray();
    afx_msg void OnTooltipTextgreen();
    afx_msg void OnTooltipTextred();
    afx_msg void OnTooltipTextwhite();

    afx_msg void OnTooltipBackblack();
    afx_msg void OnTooltipBackcyan();
    afx_msg void OnTooltipBackgreen();
```

```
    afx_msg void OnTooltipBackmagenta();
    afx_msg void OnTooltipBackwhite();
    afx_msg void OnTooltipBackyellow();

    DECLARE_MESSAGE_MAP()

    CToolTips   m_ToolTips;
};
```

Notice the *OnMouseMove()* message handler. As you learned earlier, static areas don't relay ToolTip information, but this function will intercept the mouse movement and pass it on to the ToolTip control before it gets to the static controls. This will allow our color areas to generate ToolTips. Feel free to experiment with the colors.

Add the ToolTip property page to the property sheet, making sure you include the line to set the title text. The title is now used by the combo box on the property sheet status bar. The source code listing is shown below.

```
// ToolTipDlg.cpp : implementation file
//

#include "stdafx.h"
#include "Controls.h"
#include "ToolTipDlg.h"

#ifdef _DEBUG
#define new DEBUG_NEW
#undef THIS_FILE
static char THIS_FILE[] = __FILE__;
#endif

/////////////////////////////////////////////////////////
// CToolTipDlg property page

IMPLEMENT_DYNCREATE(CToolTipDlg, CPropertyPage)

CToolTipDlg::CToolTipDlg()
                    : CPropertyPage(CToolTipDlg::IDD)
{
    //{{AFX_DATA_INIT(CToolTipDlg)
    m_nHoverTime = 0;
    m_nDisplayTime = 0;
    m_nBottomMargin = 0;
    m_nLeftMargin = 0;
    m_nRightMargin = 0;
    m_nTopMargin = 0;
    m_nWidth = 0;
    m_bAlwaysTip = FALSE;
    m_bNoPrefix = FALSE;
    //}}AFX_DATA_INIT
    m_psp.dwFlags &= ~PSP_HASHELP;
}

CToolTipDlg::~CToolTipDlg()
{
}
```

```
void CToolTipDlg::DoDataExchange(CDataExchange* pDX)
{
    CPropertyPage::DoDataExchange(pDX);
    //{{AFX_DATA_MAP(CToolTipDlg)
    DDX_Control(pDX, IDC_TOOLTIP_BACKYELLOW,
                                    m_ctlBackYellow);
    DDX_Control(pDX, IDC_TOOLTIP_BACKWHITE,m_ctlBackWhite);
    DDX_Control(pDX, IDC_TOOLTIP_BACKMAGENTA,
                                    m_ctlBackMagenta);
    DDX_Control(pDX, IDC_TOOLTIP_BACKGREEN,m_ctlBackGreen);
    DDX_Control(pDX, IDC_TOOLTIP_BACKCYAN, m_ctlBackCyan);
    DDX_Control(pDX, IDC_TOOLTIP_BACKBLACK,m_ctlBackBlack);
    DDX_Control(pDX, IDC_TOOLTIP_TEXTBLACK,m_ctlTextBlack);
    DDX_Control(pDX, IDC_TOOLTIP_TEXTBLUE, m_ctlTextBlue);
    DDX_Control(pDX, IDC_TOOLTIP_TEXTGRAY, m_ctlTextGray);
    DDX_Control(pDX, IDC_TOOLTIP_TEXTGREEN, m_ctlTextGreen);
    DDX_Control(pDX, IDC_TOOLTIP_TEXTRED, m_ctlTextRed);
    DDX_Control(pDX, IDC_TOOLTIP_TEXTWHITE, m_ctlTextWhite);
    DDX_Text(pDX, IDC_TOOLTIP_HOVERTIME, m_nHoverTime);
    DDX_Text(pDX, IDC_TOOLTIP_DISPLAYTIME, m_nDisplayTime);
    DDX_Text(pDX, IDC_TOOLTIP_BOTTOMMARGIN,
                                    m_nBottomMargin);
    DDX_Text(pDX, IDC_TOOLTIP_LEFTMARGIN, m_nLeftMargin);
    DDX_Text(pDX, IDC_TOOLTIP_RIGHTMARGIN, m_nRightMargin);
    DDX_Text(pDX, IDC_TOOLTIP_TOPMARGIN, m_nTopMargin);
    DDX_Text(pDX, IDC_TOOLTIP_WIDTH, m_nWidth);
    DDX_Check(pDX, IDC_TOOLTIP_ALWAYSTIP, m_bAlwaysTip);
    DDX_Check(pDX, IDC_TOOLTIP_NOPREFIX, m_bNoPrefix);
    //}}AFX_DATA_MAP
}

BEGIN_MESSAGE_MAP(CToolTipDlg, CPropertyPage)
    //{{AFX_MSG_MAP(CToolTipDlg)
    ON_BN_CLICKED(IDC_TOOLTIP_ALWAYSTIP,OnTooltipAlwaystip)
    ON_BN_CLICKED(IDC_TOOLTIP_NOPREFIX, OnTooltipNoprefix)
    ON_EN_CHANGE(IDC_TOOLTIP_TOPMARGIN,
                                    OnChangeTooltipTopmargin)
    ON_EN_CHANGE(IDC_TOOLTIP_BOTTOMMARGIN,
                                    OnChangeTooltipBottommargin)
    ON_EN_CHANGE(IDC_TOOLTIP_LEFTMARGIN,
                                    OnChangeTooltipLeftmargin)
    ON_EN_CHANGE(IDC_TOOLTIP_RIGHTMARGIN,
                                    OnChangeTooltipRightmargin)
    ON_BN_CLICKED(IDC_TOOLTIP_HOVERSTATIC,
                                    OnTooltipHoverstatic)
    ON_EN_CHANGE(IDC_TOOLTIP_DISPLAYTIME,
                                    OnChangeTooltipDisplaytime)
    ON_BN_CLICKED(IDC_TOOLTIP_SETALL, OnTooltipSetall)
    ON_WM_LBUTTONDBLCLK()
    ON_EN_CHANGE(IDC_TOOLTIP_WIDTH, OnChangeTooltipWidth)
    ON_WM_MOUSEMOVE()
    ON_WM_PAINT()
    //}}AFX_MSG_MAP
    ON_NOTIFY_EX(TTN_GETDISPINFO, 0, OnToolTipText)
END_MESSAGE_MAP()
```

```
/////////////////////////////////////////////////////
// CToolTipDlg message handlers

BOOL CToolTipDlg::OnInitDialog()
{
    CPropertyPage::OnInitDialog();

    CRect rc;
    m_ctlTextWhite.SetBkgndColor (RGB(0xff, 0xff, 0xff));
    m_ctlTextRed.SetBkgndColor (RGB(0xff, 0x00, 0x00));
    m_ctlTextGreen.SetBkgndColor (RGB(0x00, 0xff, 0x00));
    m_ctlTextGray.SetBkgndColor (RGB(0xc0, 0xc0, 0xc0));
    m_ctlTextBlue.SetBkgndColor (RGB(0x00, 0x00, 0xff));
    m_ctlTextBlack.SetBkgndColor (RGB(0x00, 0x00, 0x00));

    m_ctlBackBlack.SetBkgndColor (RGB(0x00, 0x00, 0x00));
    m_ctlBackYellow.SetBkgndColor (RGB(0xff, 0xff, 0xa0));
    m_ctlBackMagenta.SetBkgndColor (RGB(0xff, 0xa0, 0xff));
    m_ctlBackGreen.SetBkgndColor (RGB(0x90, 0xff, 0x90));
    m_ctlBackCyan.SetBkgndColor (RGB(0xa0, 0xff, 0xff));
    m_ctlBackWhite.SetBkgndColor (RGB(0xff, 0xff, 0xff));

    m_ToolTips.Create (this);
    AddControls ();
    m_ToolTips.Activate (TRUE);
    m_ToolTips.GetMargin (rc);
    m_nTopMargin = rc.top;
    m_nBottomMargin = rc.bottom;
    m_nLeftMargin = rc.left;
    m_nRightMargin = rc.right;

    m_ToolTips.EnableToolTips ();

    int nDelay = m_ToolTips.GetDelayTime (TTDT_INITIAL);
    m_nHoverTime = nDelay;
    nDelay = m_ToolTips.GetDelayTime (TTDT_AUTOPOP);
    m_nDisplayTime = nDelay;
    m_nWidth = m_ToolTips.GetMaxTipWidth ();

    UpdateData (FALSE);

    return TRUE;
}


BOOL CToolTipDlg::OnToolTipText(UINT id, NMHDR *pNMHDR,
                                LRESULT *pResult)
{
    TOOLTIPTEXT *pTTT = (TOOLTIPTEXT *)pNMHDR;
    UINT nID =pNMHDR->idFrom;
// is idFrom is actually the HWND of the tool?
    if (pTTT->uFlags & TTF_IDISHWND)
    {
        nID = ::GetDlgCtrlID((HWND)nID);
    }
    if(nID)
```

```
    {
        pTTT->lpszText = MAKEINTRESOURCE(nID);
        pTTT->hinst = AfxGetResourceHandle();
        return(TRUE);
    }
    return(FALSE);
}

void CToolTipDlg::AddControls()
{
const UINT nCtrlIDs [] =
    {
// The time group
    IDC_TOOLTIP_HOVERTIME, IDC_TOOLTIP_DISPLAYTIME,
// The margins group
    IDC_TOOLTIP_TOPMARGIN, IDC_TOOLTIP_BOTTOMMARGIN,
    IDC_TOOLTIP_LEFTMARGIN, IDC_TOOLTIP_RIGHTMARGIN,
    IDC_TOOLTIP_WIDTH, IDC_TOOLTIP_SETALL,
// The style group
    IDC_TOOLTIP_ALWAYSTIP, IDC_TOOLTIP_NOPREFIX
    };

    CRect rc;
    UINT n;
    for (n = 0; n < 10; ++n)
    {
        m_ToolTips.AddControl (GetDlgItem(nCtrlIDs[n]));
    }

    const UINT nRectIDs [] =
    {
    IDC_TOOLTIP_TEXTWHITE, IDC_TOOLTIP_TEXTBLACK,
    IDC_TOOLTIP_TEXTGREEN, IDC_TOOLTIP_TEXTGRAY,
    IDC_TOOLTIP_TEXTBLUE, IDC_TOOLTIP_TEXTRED,
    IDC_TOOLTIP_BACKWHITE, IDC_TOOLTIP_BACKBLACK,
    IDC_TOOLTIP_BACKCYAN, IDC_TOOLTIP_BACKMAGENTA,
    IDC_TOOLTIP_BACKYELLOW, IDC_TOOLTIP_BACKGREEN
    };

    for (n = 0; n < (sizeof(nRectIDs)/sizeof (int)); ++n)
    {
        ::GetWindowRect (GetDlgItem
                        (nRectIDs[n])->m_hWnd, rc);
        ScreenToClient (rc);
        m_ToolTips.AddRect (this, nRectIDs[n], rc);
    }
    CRect rcBlank;
    ::GetWindowRect (GetDlgItem
                    (IDC_TOOLTIP_STYLEGROUP)->m_hWnd, rc);
    ScreenToClient (rc);
    rcBlank.top = rc.bottom + 10;

    ::GetWindowRect (GetDlgItem
                (IDC_TOOLTIP_BACKCOLORGROUP)->m_hWnd, rc);
    ScreenToClient (rc);
    rcBlank.left = rc.right + 10;
```

```
            rcBlank.bottom = rc.bottom;


        ::GetWindowRect (GetDlgItem
                         (IDC_TOOLTIP_MARGINSGROUP)->m_hWnd, rc);
        ScreenToClient (rc);
        rcBlank.right = rc.left - 10;
        m_ToolTips.AddRect (this, IDS_BLANKSPOT, rcBlank);
}

void CToolTipDlg::OnTooltipAlwaystip()
{
    UpdateData (TRUE);
    if (m_bAlwaysTip)
        m_ToolTips.ModifyStyle (0, TTS_ALWAYSTIP, TRUE);
    else
        m_ToolTips.ModifyStyle (TTS_ALWAYSTIP, 0, TRUE);
}

void CToolTipDlg::OnChangeTooltipWidth()
{
    UpdateData (TRUE);
    m_ToolTips.SetMaxTipWidth (m_nWidth);
}

void CToolTipDlg::OnChangeTooltipTopmargin()
{
    UpdateData (TRUE);
    CRect rc;
    m_ToolTips.GetMargin (rc);
    rc.top = m_nTopMargin;
    m_ToolTips.SetMargin (rc);
}

void CToolTipDlg::OnChangeTooltipBottommargin()
{
    UpdateData (TRUE);
    CRect rc;
    m_ToolTips.GetMargin (rc);
    rc.bottom = m_nBottomMargin;
    m_ToolTips.SetMargin (rc);
}

void CToolTipDlg::OnChangeTooltipLeftmargin()
{
    UpdateData (TRUE);
    CRect rc;
    m_ToolTips.GetMargin (rc);
    rc.left = m_nLeftMargin;
    m_ToolTips.SetMargin (rc);
}

void CToolTipDlg::OnChangeTooltipRightmargin()
{
    UpdateData (TRUE);
    CRect rc;
```

```
    m_ToolTips.GetMargin (rc);
    rc.right = m_nRightMargin;
    m_ToolTips.SetMargin (rc);
}

void CToolTipDlg::OnTooltipHoverstatic()
{
    UpdateData (TRUE);
    m_ToolTips.SetDelayTime (m_nHoverTime, TTDT_INITIAL);
}

void CToolTipDlg::OnChangeTooltipDisplaytime()
{
    UpdateData (TRUE);
    m_ToolTips.SetDelayTime (m_nDisplayTime, TTDT_AUTOPOP);
}

void CToolTipDlg::OnTooltipSetall()
{
    UpdateData (TRUE);
    CRect rc;
    m_nBottomMargin = m_nTopMargin;
    m_nLeftMargin = m_nTopMargin;
    m_nRightMargin = m_nTopMargin;
    rc.top = m_nTopMargin;
    rc.bottom = m_nBottomMargin;
    rc.left = m_nLeftMargin;
    rc.right = m_nRightMargin;
    m_ToolTips.SetMargin (rc);
    UpdateData (FALSE);
}

void CToolTipDlg::OnLButtonDblClk(UINT nFlags, CPoint point)
{
    CRect rc;
    ::GetWindowRect (GetDlgItem(
                IDC_TOOLTIP_TEXTCOLORGROUP)->m_hWnd, rc);
    ScreenToClient (rc);
    if (rc.PtInRect (point))
    {
        ::GetWindowRect (GetDlgItem
                    (IDC_TOOLTIP_TEXTBLACK)->m_hWnd, rc);
        ScreenToClient (rc);
        if (rc.PtInRect (point))
        {
            OnTooltipTextblack();
            return;
        }
        ::GetWindowRect (GetDlgItem
                    (IDC_TOOLTIP_TEXTGREEN)->m_hWnd, rc);
        ScreenToClient (rc);
        if (rc.PtInRect (point))
        {
            OnTooltipTextgreen();
            return;
        }
```

```
        ::GetWindowRect (GetDlgItem
                    (IDC_TOOLTIP_TEXTBLUE)->m_hWnd, rc);
    ScreenToClient (rc);
    if (rc.PtInRect (point))
    {
        OnTooltipTextblue();
        return;
    }
    ::GetWindowRect (GetDlgItem
                    (IDC_TOOLTIP_TEXTGRAY)->m_hWnd, rc);
    ScreenToClient (rc);
    if (rc.PtInRect (point))
    {
        OnTooltipTextgray();
        return;
    }
    ::GetWindowRect (GetDlgItem
                    (IDC_TOOLTIP_TEXTRED)->m_hWnd, rc);
    ScreenToClient (rc);
    if (rc.PtInRect (point))
    {
        OnTooltipTextred();
        return;
    }
    ::GetWindowRect (GetDlgItem
                    (IDC_TOOLTIP_TEXTWHITE)->m_hWnd, rc);
    ScreenToClient (rc);
    if (rc.PtInRect (point))
    {
        OnTooltipTextwhite();
        return;
    }
}
::GetWindowRect (GetDlgItem
            (IDC_TOOLTIP_BACKCOLORGROUP)->m_hWnd, rc);
ScreenToClient (rc);
if (rc.PtInRect (point))
{
    ::GetWindowRect (GetDlgItem
                (IDC_TOOLTIP_BACKWHITE)->m_hWnd, rc);
    ScreenToClient (rc);
    if (rc.PtInRect (point))
    {
        OnTooltipBackwhite();
        return;
    }
    ::GetWindowRect (GetDlgItem
                (IDC_TOOLTIP_BACKMAGENTA)->m_hWnd, rc);
    ScreenToClient (rc);
    if (rc.PtInRect (point))
    {
        OnTooltipBackmagenta();
        return;
    }
    ::GetWindowRect (GetDlgItem
                (IDC_TOOLTIP_BACKYELLOW)->m_hWnd, rc);
```

```
        ScreenToClient (rc);
        if (rc.PtInRect (point))
        {
            OnTooltipBackyellow();
            return;
        }
        ::GetWindowRect (GetDlgItem
                    (IDC_TOOLTIP_BACKGREEN)->m_hWnd, rc);
        ScreenToClient (rc);
        if (rc.PtInRect (point))
        {
            OnTooltipBackgreen();
            return;
        }
        ::GetWindowRect (GetDlgItem
                    (IDC_TOOLTIP_BACKCYAN)->m_hWnd, rc);
        ScreenToClient (rc);
        if (rc.PtInRect (point))
        {
            OnTooltipBackcyan();
            return;
        }
        ::GetWindowRect (GetDlgItem
                    (IDC_TOOLTIP_BACKBLACK)->m_hWnd, rc);
        ScreenToClient (rc);
        if (rc.PtInRect (point))
        {
            OnTooltipBackblack();
            return;
        }
    }
    CPropertyPage::OnLButtonDblClk(nFlags, point);
}

void CToolTipDlg::OnTooltipNoprefix()
{
    UpdateData (TRUE);
    if (m_bAlwaysTip)
        m_ToolTips.ModifyStyle (0, TTS_NOPREFIX, TRUE);
    else
        m_ToolTips.ModifyStyle (TTS_NOPREFIX, 0, TRUE);
}

void CToolTipDlg::OnTooltipBackblack()
{
    CStaticEx *color =
        (CStaticEx *) GetDlgItem(IDC_TOOLTIP_BACKBLACK);
    m_ToolTips.SetTipBkColor (color->GetBkgndColor());
    m_ToolTips.Update ();
}

void CToolTipDlg::OnTooltipBackcyan()
{
    CStaticEx *color = (CStaticEx *) GetDlgItem
                            (IDC_TOOLTIP_BACKCYAN);
    m_ToolTips.SetTipBkColor (color->GetBkgndColor());
```

```
        m_ToolTips.Update ();
}

void CToolTipDlg::OnTooltipBackgreen()
{
    CStaticEx *color = (CStaticEx *) GetDlgItem
                             (IDC_TOOLTIP_BACKGREEN);
    m_ToolTips.SetTipBkColor (color->GetBkgndColor());
    m_ToolTips.Update ();
}

void CToolTipDlg::OnTooltipBackmagenta()
{
    CStaticEx *color = (CStaticEx *) GetDlgItem
                             (IDC_TOOLTIP_BACKMAGENTA);
    m_ToolTips.SetTipBkColor (color->GetBkgndColor());
    m_ToolTips.Update ();
}

void CToolTipDlg::OnTooltipBackwhite()
{
    CStaticEx *color = (CStaticEx *) GetDlgItem
                             (IDC_TOOLTIP_BACKWHITE);
    m_ToolTips.SetTipBkColor (color->GetBkgndColor());
    m_ToolTips.Update ();
}

void CToolTipDlg::OnTooltipBackyellow()
{
    CStaticEx *color = (CStaticEx *) GetDlgItem
                             (IDC_TOOLTIP_BACKYELLOW);
    m_ToolTips.SetTipBkColor (color->GetBkgndColor());
    m_ToolTips.Update ();
}

void CToolTipDlg::OnTooltipTextblack()
{
    CStaticEx *color = (CStaticEx *) GetDlgItem
                             (IDC_TOOLTIP_TEXTBLACK);
    m_ToolTips.SetTipTextColor (color->GetBkgndColor());
    m_ToolTips.Update ();
}

void CToolTipDlg::OnTooltipTextblue()
{
    CStaticEx *color = (CStaticEx *) GetDlgItem
                             (IDC_TOOLTIP_TEXTBLUE);
    m_ToolTips.SetTipTextColor (color->GetBkgndColor());
    m_ToolTips.Update ();
}

void CToolTipDlg::OnTooltipTextgray()
{
    CStaticEx *color = (CStaticEx *) GetDlgItem
                             (IDC_TOOLTIP_TEXTGRAY);
    m_ToolTips.SetTipTextColor (color->GetBkgndColor());
    m_ToolTips.Update ();
```

```
}

void CToolTipDlg::OnTooltipTextgreen()
{
    CStaticEx *color = (CStaticEx *) GetDlgItem
                                (IDC_TOOLTIP_TEXTGREEN);
    m_ToolTips.SetTipTextColor (color->GetBkgndColor());
    m_ToolTips.Update ();
}

void CToolTipDlg::OnTooltipTextred()
{
    CStaticEx *color = (CStaticEx *) GetDlgItem
                                (IDC_TOOLTIP_TEXTRED);
    m_ToolTips.SetTipTextColor (color->GetBkgndColor());
    m_ToolTips.Update ();
}

void CToolTipDlg::OnTooltipTextwhite()
{
    CStaticEx *color = (CStaticEx *) GetDlgItem
                                (IDC_TOOLTIP_TEXTWHITE);
    m_ToolTips.SetTipTextColor (color->GetBkgndColor());
    m_ToolTips.Update ();
}

CToolTips & CToolTipDlg::GetToolTipControl()
{
    return (m_ToolTips);
}

void CToolTipDlg::OnMouseMove(UINT nFlags, CPoint point)
{
    int xPos, yPos;
    xPos = point.x;
    yPos = point.y;
    MSG msg;
    msg.hwnd = this->m_hWnd;
    msg.message = WM_MOUSEMOVE;
    msg.wParam = (WPARAM) nFlags;
    msg.lParam = MAKELONG (xPos, yPos);
    m_ToolTips.RelayEvent (&msg);
    CPropertyPage::OnMouseMove(nFlags, point);
}
```

Now you have to add entries to the string table for each of these ToolTips as shown below:

Resource ID	Add This Text
IDC_TOOLTIP_RIGHTSTATIC	"Label for right margin field"
IDC_TOOLTIP_LEFTSTATIC	"Label for left margin field"
IDC_TOOLTIP_TOPSTATIC	"Label for top margin field"
IDC_TOOLTIP_BOTTOMSTATIC	"Label for bottom margin field"

Table 926   Add the strings in the table to the Controls project string table using the indicated resource ID (continued on following page)

Resource ID	Add This Text
IDC_TOOLTIP_TEXTBLACK	"Set the text color to Black"
IDC_TOOLTIP_TEXTBLUE	"Set the text color to Blue"
IDC_TOOLTIP_TEXTRED	"Set the text color to Red"
IDC_TOOLTIP_TEXTGREEN	"Set the text color to Green"
IDC_TOOLTIP_TEXTGRAY	"Set the text color to Gray"
IDC_TOOLTIP_TEXTWHITE	"Set the text color to White"
IDC_TOOLTIP_BACKWHITE	"Set the background color to White"
IDC_TOOLTIP_BACKBLACK	"Set the background color to Black"
IDC_TOOLTIP_BACKYELLOW	"Set the background color to Yellow"
IDC_TOOLTIP_BACKCYAN	"Set the background color to Cyan"
IDC_TOOLTIP_BACKMAGENTA	"Set the background color to Magenta"
IDC_TOOLTIP_BACKGREEN	"Set the background color to Green"
IDC_TOOLTIP_WIDTH	"Set the maximum width in pixels for the tip window. Text will be wrapped"
IDS_BLANKSPOT	"This is a blank area to test tool tips"

Table 926   Add the strings in the table to the Controls project string table using the indicated resource ID (continued from previous page)

After compiling the program, double-click on one of the color areas to change the ToolTip color. You can change either the background or the text color. The text or background color should change immediately. If a ToolTip is not being displayed when you double-click on one of the colors, it will display in the color you selected. Try different margins and widths. Sometimes a deeper, but narrower tip box is more attention getting to the user.

The ToolTip control has a limited number of notification messages it sends back to the parent window. Two of them, *TTN_GETDISPINFO* and *TTN_NEEDTEXT*, actually are the same message. New programs should use the *TTN_GETDISPINFO* message. It's part of Microsoft's effort to standardize control structures and messages.

You can use the *ON_NOTIFY* or *ON_NOTIFY_EX* macros to handle the *TTN_NEEDTEXT* (or *TTN_GETDISPINFO*) messages. You gave the ToolTip control the text for all the control when you added them, so actually you don't need to handle this message. You've included it, and the message macro, in case you do want to use *LPSTR_TEXTCALLBACK*, in which case, the ToolTip control will ask for the tip window text.

There are two other notification messages from the ToolTip control. *TTN_SHOW* is sent when a tip window is about to be shown, and *TTN_POP* is sent when the window is about to be hidden. You can intercept these messages and use them to prevent the action by taking place.

927. *Understanding the Hotkey Control*

A *hotkey* is a keyboard combination the user can press to perform an action quickly. It's virtually the same as an accelerator key, but it doesn't have to be attached to a particular view or perform a menu operation.

Hotkey support is provided by the hotkey control, which produces a window and waits for a keystroke combination. The combined keystroke then is available to the application. You register the combination with the operating system, which then will send your application a *WM_HOTKEY* message when the key combination is pressed.

The message includes an identifier and the key combination that was pressed. It's up to your application to interpret the message and perform the appropriate action.

928. *Using the* **CHotKeyCtrl** *Class*

The hotkey is really an easy key to master and use when used within the same thread. It is possible to send a hotkey to another application using *global hotkeys*, but that is beyond the scope of this book.

You can set rules on what key combinations may be used. As with most of the windows controls, the hot key control has its own particular set of quirks, as you'll see shortly.

For this one, you won't even have to include the *OnInitDialog()* function. Add another property page to the *Controls* project as shown in Figure 928. Give it a resource ID of *DDD_PROPPAGE_HOTKEY-DLG* and label it "Hot Key."

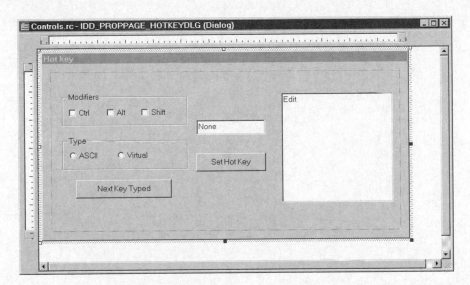

Figure 928   *The hotkey property page gives you the controls you need to define a hotkey, which will be used to toggle the edit window on the right on and off*

The edit window on the right side of the property sheet is the target for the hotkeys. When you select a hotkey, it will alternately display and hide the window. The sample code has the Visible flag turned off, but it doesn't make any difference. When you register the hotkey, you can toggle the window on and off even if you have another property sheet selected. You can also give the focus to another application, assuming, of course, that that application hasn't registered the same hotkey. You could use this to bring your own application to the top of the Z order.

Create a class for the property page called *CHotKeyDlg*. The header code is listed below.

```
// HotKeyDlg.h : header file
//

/////////////////////////////////////////////////////////////////
```

```
// CHotKeyDlg dialog

class CHotKeyDlg : public CPropertyPage
{
    DECLARE_DYNCREATE(CHotKeyDlg)

// Construction
public:
    CHotKeyDlg();
    ~CHotKeyDlg();

// Dialog Data
    //{{AFX_DATA(CHotKeyDlg)
    enum { IDD = IDD_PROPPAGE_HOTKEYDLG };
    CEdit   m_ctlEdit;
    CHotKeyCtrl m_HotKey;
    BOOL    m_bAlt;
    BOOL    m_bCtrl;
    BOOL    m_bShift;
    int     m_nType;
    //}}AFX_DATA


// Overrides
    // ClassWizard generate virtual function overrides
    //{{AFX_VIRTUAL(CHotKeyDlg)
    protected:
    virtual void DoDataExchange(CDataExchange* pDX);
    // DDX/DDV support
    //}}AFX_VIRTUAL


// Implementation
protected:
    WORD m_wModifiers;
    WORD m_wVirtual;
    afx_msg void OnHotKey (WPARAM wParam, LPARAM lParam);
    void GetKeyCombs (WORD &wBanned, WORD &wDefault);
    // Generated message map functions
    //{{AFX_MSG(CHotKeyDlg)
    afx_msg void OnHotkeyGethotkey();
    afx_msg void OnHotkeyAlt();
    afx_msg void OnHotkeyCtrl();
    afx_msg void OnHotkeyShift();
    afx_msg void OnHotkeyType();
    afx_msg void OnHotkeyNexttyped();
    //}}AFX_MSG
    DECLARE_MESSAGE_MAP()

};
```

Without setting any rules on the hotkey combination, the control can return any combination of any key combined with the control, alternate, and shift keys. But, not setting any rules avoids much of the functionality of the control.

One of the problems newcomers to this control run into is the fact that the allowed keys in the *SetRules()* function use a different set of flags than the disallowed keys. Then, when you get ready to register a hotkey, you find the *RegisterHotKey()* function takes a third set of flags. Throughout your code, you have to keep translating these flags, as you can see in the code below. Well, something *had* to be done to make it less than easy-to-use.

```cpp
// HotKeyDlg.cpp : implementation file
//

#include "stdafx.h"
#include "Controls.h"
#include "HotKeyDlg.h"

#ifdef _DEBUG
#define new DEBUG_NEW
#undef THIS_FILE
static char THIS_FILE[] = __FILE__;
#endif

/////////////////////////////////////////////////////////
// CHotKeyDlg property page


//
//  A couple of macros will reduce our typing. And
//  help us not forget the flags are different.
//
#define ALL_KEYS      HKCOMB_A | HKCOMB_C | HKCOMB_CA | \
                      HKCOMB_NONE | IIKCOMB_S | HKCOMB_SA | \
                      HKCOMB_SC | HKCOMB_SCA

#define ALL_MODIFIERS   HOTKEYF_SHIFT | HOTKEYF_EXT | \
                        HOTKEYF_CONTROL | HOTKEYF_ALT

IMPLEMENT_DYNCREATE(CHotKeyDlg, CPropertyPage)

CHotKeyDlg::CHotKeyDlg() : CPropertyPage(CHotKeyDlg::IDD)
{
    //{{AFX_DATA_INIT(CHotKeyDlg)
    m_bAlt = FALSE;
    m_bCtrl = FALSE;
    m_bShift = FALSE;
    m_nType = 0;
    //}}AFX_DATA_INIT
    m_psp.dwFlags &= ~PSP_HASHELP;
    m_wVirtual = 0;
    m_wModifiers = 0;
}

CHotKeyDlg::~CHotKeyDlg()
{
}

void CHotKeyDlg::DoDataExchange(CDataExchange* pDX)
{
    CPropertyPage::DoDataExchange(pDX);
    //{{AFX_DATA_MAP(CHotKeyDlg)
    DDX_Control(pDX, IDC_HOTKEY_EDIT, m_ctlEdit);
    DDX_Control(pDX, IDC_HOTKEY_HOTKEY, m_HotKey);
```

```
        DDX_Check(pDX, IDC_HOTKEY_ALT, m_bAlt);
        DDX_Check(pDX, IDC_HOTKEY_CTRL, m_bCtrl);
        DDX_Check(pDX, IDC_HOTKEY_SHIFT, m_bShift);
        DDX_Radio(pDX, IDC_HOTKEY_ASCII, m_nType);
    //}}AFX_DATA_MAP
}


BEGIN_MESSAGE_MAP(CHotKeyDlg, CPropertyPage)
    //{{AFX_MSG_MAP(CHotKeyDlg)
    ON_BN_CLICKED(IDC_HOTKEY_GETHOTKEY, OnHotkeyGethotkey)
    ON_BN_CLICKED(IDC_HOTKEY_ALT, OnHotkeyAlt)
    ON_BN_CLICKED(IDC_HOTKEY_CTRL, OnHotkeyCtrl)
    ON_BN_CLICKED(IDC_HOTKEY_SHIFT, OnHotkeyShift)
    ON_BN_CLICKED(IDC_HOTKEY_ASCII, OnHotkeyType)
    ON_BN_CLICKED(IDC_HOTKEY_VIRTUAL, OnHotkeyType)
    ON_BN_CLICKED(IDC_HOTKEY_NEXTTYPED, OnHotkeyNexttyped)
    //}}AFX_MSG_MAP
    ON_MESSAGE(WM_HOTKEY, OnHotKey)
END_MESSAGE_MAP()

/////////////////////////////////////////////////////////////
// CHotKeyDlg message handlers

//
//    Flags specific to the RegisterHotKey() function.
//
//    MOD_ALT Either alt key must be held down.
//    MOD_CONTROL Either ctrl key must be held down.
//    MOD_SHIFT Either shift key must be held down.
//    MOD_WIN Either WINDOWS key was held down. These keys
//    are labeled with the Microsoft Windows logo.
//
void CHotKeyDlg::OnHotkeyGethotkey()
{
    WORD wVirtual, wModifiers;
    m_HotKey.GetHotKey (wVirtual, wModifiers);
    if (!(wVirtual | wModifiers))
        return;
    CWnd *button = GetDlgItem (IDC_HOTKEY_GETHOTKEY);
    if (!(m_wVirtual | m_wModifiers))
    {
        UINT nModifers = 0;
        if (wModifiers & HOTKEYF_ALT)
            nModifers |= MOD_ALT;
        if (wModifiers & HOTKEYF_CONTROL)
            nModifers |= MOD_CONTROL;
        if (wModifiers & HOTKEYF_SHIFT)
            nModifers |= MOD_SHIFT;
        BOOL bResult = RegisterHotKey (this->m_hWnd,
                                    1, nModifers, wVirtual);
        button->SetWindowText (_T("Remove Hot Key"));
        m_wVirtual = wVirtual;
        m_wModifiers = wModifiers;
    }
    else
```

```
    {
        UnregisterHotKey (this->m_hWnd, 1);
        m_HotKey.SetHotKey (0, 0);
        button->SetWindowText (_T("Set Hot Key"));
        m_wVirtual = 0;
        m_wModifiers = 0;
    }
}


//
//  This is the message handler that does the work
//  when the system sends us the WM_HOTKEY message.
//
//  wParam contains the id.
//  lParam contains the key in the upper word,
//      the modifiers in the lower word.
//
void CHotKeyDlg::OnHotKey(WPARAM wParam, LPARAM lParam)
{
    if (m_ctlEdit.IsWindowVisible ())
        m_ctlEdit.ShowWindow (SW_HIDE);
    else
    {
        m_ctlEdit.ShowWindow (SW_SHOWNORMAL);
        m_ctlEdit.SetFocus ();
    }
}


void CHotKeyDlg::OnHotkeyAlt()
{
    UpdateData (TRUE);
    WORD wBanned, wDefault;
    GetKeyCombs (wBanned, wDefault);
    m_HotKey.SetRules (wBanned, wDefault);
    m_HotKey.SetFocus ();
}


void CHotKeyDlg::OnHotkeyCtrl()
{
    UpdateData (TRUE);
    WORD wBanned, wDefault;
    GetKeyCombs (wBanned, wDefault);
    m_HotKey.SetRules (wBanned, wDefault);
    m_HotKey.SetFocus ();
}


void CHotKeyDlg::OnHotkeyShift()
{
    UpdateData (TRUE);
    WORD wBanned, wDefault;
    GetKeyCombs (wBanned, wDefault);
    m_HotKey.SetRules (wBanned, wDefault);
    m_HotKey.SetFocus ();
}


//
```

```cpp
// ASCII keys allow any combination. Virtual keys
// may be used only with or without the Alt key.
//
void CHotKeyDlg::OnHotkeyType()
{
    static BOOL bOldCtrl = FALSE;
    static BOOL bOldShift = FALSE;
    UpdateData (TRUE);
    WORD wBanned, wDefault;
    switch (m_nType)
    {
        case 0:      // ASCII
            m_bCtrl = bOldCtrl;
            m_bShift = bOldShift;
            ::EnableWindow (
                        GetDlgItem (IDC_HOTKEY_CTRL)->m_hWnd,
                        TRUE);
            ::EnableWindow (
                        GetDlgItem (IDC_HOTKEY_SHIFT)->m_hWnd,
                        TRUE);
            UpdateData (FALSE);
            GetKeyCombs (wBanned, wDefault);
            break;
        case 1:      // Virtual
            bOldCtrl = m_bCtrl;
            bOldShift = m_bShift;
            m_bCtrl = FALSE;
            m_bShift = FALSE;
            ::EnableWindow (
                        GetDlgItem (IDC_HOTKEY_CTRL)->m_hWnd,
                        FALSE);
            ::EnableWindow (
                        GetDlgItem (IDC_HOTKEY_SHIFT)->m_hWnd,
                        FALSE);
            UpdateData (FALSE);
            GetKeyCombs (wBanned, wDefault);
            break;
        default:
            return;
    }
    m_HotKey.SetRules (wBanned, wDefault);
    m_HotKey.SetFocus ();
}

void CHotKeyDlg::OnHotkeyNexttyped()
{
//
// No holds barred. Any combination is possible.
// Ignore, but don't change, the check and radio
// box settings.
//
    m_HotKey.SetRules (0, 0);
    m_HotKey.SetHotKey (0, 0);
    m_HotKey.SetFocus ();
}
```

```
void CHotKeyDlg::GetKeyCombs (WORD &wBanned, WORD &wDefault)
{
//
//  At first, all key combinations are banned and
//  no combinations are allowed.
//
    WORD wNoNo = ALL_KEYS;
    WORD wOkay = 0;
    if (m_bShift)
        wOkay |= HOTKEYF_SHIFT;
    if (m_bCtrl)
        wOkay |= HOTKEYF_CONTROL;
    if (m_bAlt)
        wOkay |= HOTKEYF_ALT;
    switch (wOkay)
    {
        case 0:                // Any key allowed
            break;
        case HOTKEYF_SHIFT: //  Shifted keys only
            wNoNo &= ~(HKCOMB_S);
            wNoNo |= (HKCOMB_SCA);
            wNoNo |= (HKCOMB_A);
            wNoNo |= (HKCOMB_C);
            wNoNo |= (HKCOMB_SC);
            wNoNo |= (HKCOMB_SA);
            wNoNo |= (HKCOMB_CA);
            break;
        case HOTKEYF_CONTROL:   // Control keys only
            wNoNo &= ~(HKCOMB_C);
            wNoNo |= (HKCOMB_S);
            wNoNo |= (HKCOMB_A);
            wNoNo |= (HKCOMB_SCA);
            wNoNo |= (HKCOMB_SC);
            wNoNo |= (HKCOMB_SA);
            wNoNo |= (HKCOMB_CA);
            break;
        case HOTKEYF_ALT:       // Alt keys only
            wNoNo &= ~(HKCOMB_A);
            wNoNo |= (HKCOMB_S);
            wNoNo |= (HKCOMB_SCA);
            wNoNo |= (HKCOMB_C);
            wNoNo |= (HKCOMB_SC);
            wNoNo |= (HKCOMB_SA);
            wNoNo |= (HKCOMB_CA);
            break;
                            // Shift + Ctrl combinations
        case HOTKEYF_SHIFT | HOTKEYF_CONTROL:
            wNoNo &= ~(HKCOMB_SC);
            wNoNo |= (HKCOMB_S);
            wNoNo |= (HKCOMB_A);
            wNoNo |= (HKCOMB_C);
            wNoNo |= (HKCOMB_SCA);
            wNoNo |= (HKCOMB_SA);
            wNoNo |= (HKCOMB_CA);
            break;
                            // Shift + Alt combinations
```

```
        case HOTKEYF_SHIFT | HOTKEYF_ALT:
            wNoNo &= ~(HKCOMB_SA);
            wNoNo |= (HKCOMB_S);
            wNoNo |= (HKCOMB_A);
            wNoNo |= (HKCOMB_C);
            wNoNo |= (HKCOMB_SC);
            wNoNo |= (HKCOMB_SCA);
            wNoNo |= (HKCOMB_CA);
            break;
                        // Alt + Ctrl combinations
        case HOTKEYF_CONTROL | HOTKEYF_ALT:
            wNoNo &= ~(HKCOMB_CA);
            wNoNo |= (HKCOMB_S);
            wNoNo |= (HKCOMB_S);
            wNoNo |= (HKCOMB_C);
            wNoNo |= (HKCOMB_SC);
            wNoNo |= (HKCOMB_SA);
            wNoNo |= (HKCOMB_SCA);
            break;
                        // Alt + Ctrl + Shift
        case HOTKEYF_SHIFT | HOTKEYF_CONTROL | HOTKEYF_ALT:
            wNoNo &= ~(HKCOMB_SCA);
            wNoNo |= (HKCOMB_S);
            wNoNo |= (HKCOMB_A);
            wNoNo |= (HKCOMB_C);
            wNoNo |= (HKCOMB_SC);
            wNoNo |= (HKCOMB_SA);
            wNoNo |= (HKCOMB_CA);
            break;
    }
    wBanned = wNoNo;
    wDefault = wOkay;
}
```

In this dialog box, it isn't necessary to keep returning the focus to the hot key control, but there's really no other place for it to be other than the edit control. However, the edit control isn't always there. To enter a hotkey, the control has to have the focus anyway, so that's a good place to leave it.

There's probably an easier way than the long *switch* statement in *GetKeyCombs()* to set the various flags, but this method is simple, easy to troubleshoot, and it works.

When you compile the program, assign a hotkey, then move to another property page and type the hotkey combination. Return to the hotkey page. The edit window should have the opposite visibility. Try switching to another application and try the hotkey. It still works even though the *Controls* application doesn't have the focus.

929. Setting and Using a Hotkey

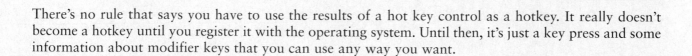

There's no rule that says you have to use the results of a hot key control as a hotkey. It really doesn't become a hotkey until you register it with the operating system. Until then, it's just a key press and some information about modifier keys that you can use any way you want.

The Visual Studio resource editor uses this control when you add or edit keyboard accelerators to an application. In case you didn't recognize it, the property sheet sample was patterned after the Visual Studio dialog box.

Assuming you do want to use the information for a hotkey, you'll have to register it with the operating system using the *RegisterHotKey()* function. You can set as many hotkeys as you want (there is a finite number of combinations, however), but each one must have its own identifier number. The hotkey is valid until your application exits, or until you unregister it. You can save the key combination in the registry or an *.INI* file and re-register it the next time your application starts, however.

As parameters, the *RegisterHotKey()* function requires the handle of the window registering the hotkey. You can't have a hotkey without a window. The handle is the public *m_hWnd* member of the *CWnd* object and is available to every class object that is derived from *CWnd*. Also, it needs the unique identifier number. That's just an integer in the range of 0 to 0xBFFF. A *DLL* uses identifiers larger than that. It also needs a flag set indicating which modifier keys are required with the keystroke. This is the third flag set you will use with the hot key control, and their names and meanings are listed in the sample code just after the message map. Lastly, it needs the virtual key code for the primary key in the hotkey combination. This is the same value returned from the call to *GetHotKey()* and doesn't require any further translation.

930. *Understanding the Date and Time Picker Control*

Providing a safe means of accepting date and time information from a user always has been a challenge to programmers. You have to parse the incoming information continuously to prevent user errors such as a date of June 31, or an hour of 25 (or even 13 if you're using a 12-hour format).

The date and time picker control provides a formatted interface to allow the user to select or enter a specific date or time. The control may be initialized to accept or display a date or a time, or both if you use a custom format.

When initialized as a date picker, the control features a drop-down calendar control (much like the drop-down list box of a combo control) from which the user may select a date. When a date is selected from the calendar control, it collapses, leaving only your date and time picker control. You can prevent the calendar display by providing the control with a spinner control rather than the drop-down button.

By default, the date and time picker displays and accepts dates and times according to the system-defined format, but you may use your own format strings with it. The components—month, day, and year for a date or hour, minute and second for a time—are displayed in discrete fields in the control. The user can't overstrike the formatting characters such as the "/" or ":".

931. *Using the CDateTimeCtrl Class*

The Microsoft Foundation Class library encapsulates the date and time picker control in the *CDateTimeCtrl* class, which provides functions to initialize and manipulate the control and its contents.

The class object allows you to initialize the control using a *CTime* class object, s *SYSTEMTIME* structure, or a *COleDateTime* object. You also may specify a range for the date or time.

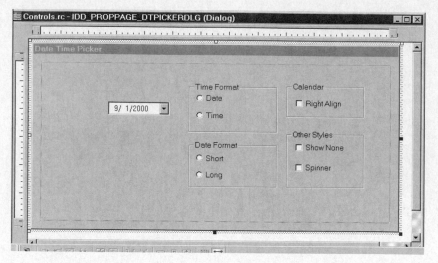

Figure 931   You only need a few controls to experiment with the date and time picker control

Create a property page with a resource ID of *IDD_PROPPAGE_DTPICKERDLG* as shown in Figure 931. Label it "Date Time Picker," then create a class for the dialog called *CDateTimePickerDlg*. Add the class to the property sheet. The controls on this property page will allow you to experiment with the various styles for the date and time picker. The header file containing the class definition is listed below:

```
// DateTimePickerDlg.h : header file
//

/////////////////////////////////////////////////////////
// CDateTimePickerDlg dialog

class CDateTimePickerDlg : public CPropertyPage
{
    DECLARE_DYNCREATE(CDateTimePickerDlg)

// Construction
public:
    CDateTimePickerDlg();
    ~CDateTimePickerDlg();

// Dialog Data
    //{{AFX_DATA(CDateTimePickerDlg)
    enum { IDD = IDD_PROPPAGE_DTPICKERDLG };
    CDateTimeCtrl    m_ctlDTPicker;
    BOOL     m_bRightAlign;
    BOOL     m_bShowNone;
    BOOL     m_bSpinner;
    CTime    m_timeDTPicker;
    int      m_nDateFormat;
    int      m_nDateOrTime;
    //}}AFX_DATA


// Overrides
    // ClassWizard generate virtual function overrides
    //{{AFX_VIRTUAL(CDateTimePickerDlg)
    protected:
```

```
    virtual void DoDataExchange(CDataExchange* pDX);
    // DDX/DDV support
    //}}AFX_VIRTUAL

// Implementation
protected:
    CRect m_rcWide;
    CRect m_rcNarrow;
    DWORD m_dwStyle;
    void RecreateControl(int nSize = 0);
    // Generated message map functions
    //{{AFX_MSG(CDateTimePickerDlg)
    afx_msg void OnDatetimeRightalign();
    afx_msg void OnDatetimeShownone();
    afx_msg void OnDateFormat();
    afx_msg void OnDateOrTime();
    afx_msg void OnDatetimeSpinner();
    virtual BOOL OnInitDialog();
    //}}AFX_MSG
    DECLARE_MESSAGE_MAP()

};
```

The control doesn't have a lot of styles from which to choose, so the class definition is relatively simple. Many of the styles can't be changed once the control has been created, so you'll have to result to destroying and re-creating the control when some of the styles change.

Two rectangles are stored for the control. The time format and the short date format are relatively short strings when compared with the long date format. You'll expand the width when the long date format is used. You probably won't want to switch between these formats in an application.

```
// DateTimePickerDlg.cpp : implementation file
//

#include "stdafx.h"
#include "Controls.h"
#include "DateTimePickerDlg.h"

#ifdef _DEBUG
#define new DEBUG_NEW
#undef THIS_FILE
static char THIS_FILE[] = __FILE__;
#endif


/////////////////////////////////////////////////////////////
// CDateTimePickerDlg property page

#define TIMEFORMAT    _T("hh':'mm':'ss''ddd MMM dd','yyy")

IMPLEMENT_DYNCREATE(CDateTimePickerDlg, CPropertyPage)

CDateTimePickerDlg::CDateTimePickerDlg()
                : CPropertyPage(CDateTimePickerDlg::IDD)
{
    //{{AFX_DATA_INIT(CDateTimePickerDlg)
    m_bRightAlign = FALSE;
    m_bShowNone = FALSE;
```

```
        m_bSpinner = FALSE;
        m_timeDTPicker = 0;
        m_nDateFormat = 0;
        m_nDateOrTime = 0;
        //}}AFX_DATA_INIT
        m_psp.dwFlags &= ~PSP_HASHELP;
}


CDateTimePickerDlg::~CDateTimePickerDlg()
{
}


void CDateTimePickerDlg::DoDataExchange(CDataExchange* pDX)
{
    CPropertyPage::DoDataExchange(pDX);
    //{{AFX_DATA_MAP(CDateTimePickerDlg)
    DDX_Control(pDX, IDC_DATETIME_DTPICKER, m_ctlDTPicker);
    DDX_Check(pDX, IDC_DATETIME_RIGHTALIGN, m_bRightAlign);
    DDX_Check(pDX, IDC_DATETIME_SHOWNONE, m_bShowNone);
    DDX_Check(pDX, IDC_DATETIME_SPINNER, m_bSpinner);
    DDX_DateTimeCtrl(pDX, IDC_DATETIME_DTPICKER,
                                        m_timeDTPicker);
    DDX_Radio(pDX, IDC_DATETIME_SHORTDATE, m_nDateFormat);
    DDX_Radio(pDX, IDC_DATETIME_SHOWDATE, m_nDateOrTime);
    //}}AFX_DATA_MAP
}


BEGIN_MESSAGE_MAP(CDateTimePickerDlg, CPropertyPage)
    //{{AFX_MSG_MAP(CDateTimePickerDlg)
    ON_BN_CLICKED(IDC_DATETIME_RIGHTALIGN,
                                    OnDatetimeRightalign)
    ON_BN_CLICKED(IDC_DATETIME_SHOWNONE, OnDatetimeShownone)
    ON_BN_CLICKED(IDC_DATETIME_SHORTDATE, OnDateFormat)
    ON_BN_CLICKED(IDC_DATETIME_SHOWDATE, OnDateOrTime)
    ON_BN_CLICKED(IDC_DATETIME_SPINNER, OnDatetimeSpinner)
    ON_BN_CLICKED(IDC_DATETIME_LONGDATE, OnDateFormat)
    ON_BN_CLICKED(IDC_DATETIME_SHOWTIME, OnDateOrTime)
    //}}AFX_MSG_MAP
END_MESSAGE_MAP()

//////////////////////////////////////////////////////////
// CDateTimePickerDlg message handlers

BOOL CDateTimePickerDlg::OnInitDialog()
{
    CPropertyPage::OnInitDialog();

    m_dwStyle = m_ctlDTPicker.GetStyle ();
    m_timeDTPicker = CTime::GetCurrentTime ();
    m_ctlDTPicker.GetWindowRect (m_rcWide);
    ScreenToClient (m_rcWide);
    m_rcNarrow = m_rcWide;
    m_rcWide.left -= m_rcWide.Width();
    UpdateData (FALSE);
```

```
        return TRUE;
}

void CDateTimePickerDlg::OnDatetimeRightalign()
{
    UpdateData (TRUE);
    if (m_bRightAlign)
    {
        m_ctlDTPicker.ModifyStyle (0, DTS_RIGHTALIGN, TRUE);
        m_dwStyle |= DTS_RIGHTALIGN;
    }
    else
    {
        m_ctlDTPicker.ModifyStyle (DTS_RIGHTALIGN, 0, TRUE);
        m_dwStyle &= ~DTS_RIGHTALIGN;
    }
}

void CDateTimePickerDlg::OnDatetimeShownone()
{
    UpdateData (TRUE);
    if (m_bShowNone)
    {
        m_dwStyle |= DTS_SHOWNONE;
        m_ctlDTPicker.ModifyStyle (0, DTS_SHOWNONE, TRUE);
    }
    else
    {
        m_dwStyle &= ~DTS_SHOWNONE;
        m_ctlDTPicker.ModifyStyle (DTS_SHOWNONE, 0, TRUE);
    }
    RecreateControl ();

}

void CDateTimePickerDlg::OnDateFormat()
{
    UpdateData (TRUE);
    switch (m_nDateFormat)
    {
        case 0:     // Short time
            m_dwStyle &= ~DTS_LONGDATEFORMAT;
            m_dwStyle |= DTS_SHORTDATEFORMAT;
            RecreateControl (2);
            break;
        case 1:
            m_dwStyle |= DTS_LONGDATEFORMAT;
            m_dwStyle &= ~DTS_SHORTDATEFORMAT;
            RecreateControl (1);
            break;
        default:
            return;
    }
    m_timeDTPicker = CTime::GetCurrentTime ();
    UpdateData (FALSE);
}
```

```cpp
void CDateTimePickerDlg::OnDateOrTime()
{
    UpdateData (TRUE);
    CWnd *shortDate = GetDlgItem (IDC_DATETIME_SHORTDATE);
    CWnd *longDate = GetDlgItem (IDC_DATETIME_LONGDATE);
    switch (m_nDateOrTime)
    {
        case 0:      // Short time
            m_dwStyle &= ~DTS_TIMEFORMAT;
            m_ctlDTPicker.ModifyStyle (DTS_TIMEFORMAT,
                                                     0, TRUE);
            RecreateControl (m_nDateFormat ? 1 : 2);
            shortDate->EnableWindow (TRUE);
            longDate->EnableWindow (TRUE);
            m_bSpinner = FALSE;
            break;
        case 1:
            m_dwStyle |= DTS_TIMEFORMAT;
            m_ctlDTPicker.ModifyStyle (0, DTS_TIMEFORMAT,
                                                     TRUE);
            RecreateControl (2);
            shortDate->EnableWindow (FALSE);
            longDate->EnableWindow (FALSE);
            m_bSpinner = TRUE;
            break;
        default:
            return;
    }
    m_timeDTPicker = CTime::GetCurrentTime ();
    UpdateData (FALSE);
}

void CDateTimePickerDlg::OnDatetimeSpinner()
{
    UpdateData (TRUE);
    if (m_bSpinner)
        m_dwStyle |= DTS_UPDOWN;
    else
        m_dwStyle &= ~DTS_UPDOWN;
    RecreateControl ();
}

void CDateTimePickerDlg::RecreateControl(int nSize)
{
    CRect rc;
    switch (nSize)
    {
        case 0:      // S'alright. Do nothing
            m_ctlDTPicker.GetWindowRect (rc);
            ScreenToClient (rc);
            break;
        case 1:      // Size for long date
            rc = m_rcWide;
            break;
        case 2:      // Size for short date
```

```
          rc = m_rcNarrow;
          break;
      }
      CFont *font = GetFont ();
      m_ctlDTPicker.DestroyWindow ();
      m_ctlDTPicker.Create (m_dwStyle, rc, this,
                                    IDC_DATETIME_DTPICKER);
      m_ctlDTPicker.SetFont (font);
}
```

The *CDateTimeCtrl* only contains a dozen member functions, including the constructor and the *Create()* function. About half of those member functions deal with the embedded calendar control. The functions allow you to set and get the date and time from the control, set and get a range of dates and set the display format string.

932. *Understanding Date and Time Control Styles*

The date and time picker control styles are as limited at the *CDateTimeCtrl* functions. Of the seven styles available, three of them deal with the date and time display format, which will be covered in Tip 933, "Understanding Date and Time Formats."

Of the others, *DTN_RIGHTALIGN* aligns the drop-down calendar with the right side of the edit box. Without it, the left side of the calendar will be aligned with the left side of the edit box.

The *DTN_SHOWNONE* style produces a check box on the left side of the edit fields. While this box is unchecked, the control won't provide any date or time information to your program. To enter a date or time, the user must check the box. Selecting the down arrow button to display the calendar automatically selects the date on the calendar and checks the box.

You can change the down arrow button to a spinner control by specifying the *DTN_UPDOWN* style. With a spinner, the drop-down calendar is not available, and the user can change the current display by selecting a field, then pressing one of the buttons on the spinner.

Curiously, the control provides a spinner automatically when you specify the time format when the control is created. You can get rid of the spinner and add the down arrow button (to display the calendar) by destroying the control and re-creating it without the *DTN_UPDOWN* flag in the *dwStyle* parameter to *Create()*. Simply modifying the style or calling *SetWindowPos()* to force the control to reread its style won't do the trick. Creating the spinner for a time format is logical, because the drop-down calendar provides only date information.

Using the *DTS_APPCANPARSE* style for the control is like releasing the safety on a rifle. The control won't assure that the characters entered in the control by the user are valid for the date or time format. Essentially, the control becomes an edit box. It's up to your application to parse the string and make sure it conforms to a valid date or time format. When you draw the control, the properties dialog box doesn't provide a check box to include this style, but you can add it using the *ModifyStyle()* function in your dialog box's *OnInitDialog()* function. Actually, the control provides excellent parsing. With the ability to set a custom format string, there's little reason to use this style.

To process the *DTS_APPCANPARSE* style, you'll have to add the *OnNotify()* virtual function to your dialog box class as shown in the following code:

```
BOOL CDateTimePickerDlg::OnNotify(WPARAM wParam,
                      LPARAM lParam, LRESULT* pResult)
{
```

```
    NMHDR *pNMHDR = (NMHDR *) lParam;
    if (pNMHDR->idFrom == IDC_DATETIME_DTPICKER)
    {
        NMDATETIMESTRING *nmDT =
                        (NMDATETIMESTRING *) pNMHDR;
        if (nmDT->nmhdr.code == DTN_USERSTRING)
        {
// Handle the string parsing here
            return (TRUE);
        }
    }
    return CPropertyPage::OnNotify(wParam, lParam, pResult);
}
```

Look for the ID of the control in the *idFrom* member of the *NMHDR* structure, then recast the structure to a pointer to *NMDATETIMESTRING*. Check the code to make sure it is a *DTN_USERSTRING* message. If all this is true, parse the string and beep the evil user for entering an invalid character. (Actually, you'll get this message even if the string conforms to the date or time format.)

933. *Understanding Date and Time Formats*

The date and time picker control has three preset formats that you can specify in the style member when you create the control. When drawing the control on a dialog box in the dialog editor, these formats are provided in a combo box on the Styles page of the control's property sheet. All three preset styles use the system settings.

The *DTS_TIMEFORMAT* style produces a control that presents the time according to the *LOCALE_STIMEFORMAT* system parameter. Usually this produces a format such as hour:minute:second, but that may vary according to the regional settings for your computer.

The *DTS_SHORTDATEFORMAT* causes the control to display the date as MM/DD/YY, or however your *LOCALE_SSHORTDATE* is configured. The *DTS_LONGDATEFORMAT* uses the *LOCALE_SLONGDATEFORMAT* setting to format a string that includes the day of the week. Usually this will be something like "Tuesday, February 07, 2012."

You can specify a custom date or time string for the date and time picker control using the *SetFormat()* member of *CDateTimeCtrl*. The format characters are similar to the time formatting string on other systems, but the list does have some modifications for Windows. Table 933 lists the formatting strings the control will recognize.

String	Meaning
d	A one- or two-digit day
dd	A two-digit day left padded with a 0
dddd	The full weekday name
h	A one- or two-digit hour in 12-hour format
hh	A two-digit hour in 12-hour format left padded with a 0
H	A one- or two-digit hour in 24-hour format
HH	A two-digit hour in 24-hour format left padded with a 0

Table 933 The formatting sequences used for the date and time picker control (continued on following page)

String	Meaning
m	The minute one- or two-digit number
mm	The minute as a two-digit number left padded with a 0
M	The month as a one- or two-digit number
MM	The month as a two-digit number left padded with a 0
MMM	The months as a three-character abbreviation
MMMM	The full month name
s	A one-digit second
ss	A two-digit second left padded with a 0
t	A one-letter abbreviation for AM or PM
tt	A two-letter abbreviation for AM or PM
X	A callback field. When the control encounters an X in the format string, it queries the application to fill in the X. You must handle the *DTN_WMKEY-DOWN, DTN_FORMAT,* and *DTN_FORMATQUERY* notification message. Multiple X's designate separate fields. For example, "X" and "XX" are both single unique fields.
y	A one-digit year using the last digit of the year.
yy	A two-digit year using the last two digits of the year.
yyy	The year using all four digits (but note there are only three y's).

Table 933   The formatting sequences used for the date and time picker control (continued from previous page)

The seconds entries in the table are not documented, and the MSDN documentation is not entirely truthful. It isn't inaccurate, but in keeping with Microsoft policy, it just doesn't tell you everything you need to know. The fields in the control apparently have some preset minimum widths, and yield some peculiar results. When specified as single-digit fields, the hours, minutes, and seconds will display in two character positions, when the first character displays a space if the number contains a 0 there. Thus, an indication specified as "s" would read " 4" when the second is 4, but "12" when the second is 12.

The month field also seems to be padded to allow for the longest month name, September, and the weekday field is wide enough for the longest day, Wednesday (as a matter of fact for you nitpickers, D-Day didn't fall on a Wednesday). If you enter a format such as "ddddMMMMd" and set the date to a Friday in May, you're going to get something like "Friday   May   2". But advance the date to a Wednesday in September and you'll get "WednesdaySeptember24" Would you buy a car or a piece of furniture in this condition? Does Microsoft—the company that wants to dominate the software business—really think this is acceptable?

You'll have to take this into account when you prepare your custom format strings. Obviously, three-letter abbreviations for the months and days of the week, and full two-digit representations of hours, minutes, and seconds, and even the day of the month, is the safer way to go. Unfortunately, the default setting for the *LOCALE_LONGDATEFORMAT* is to use the full name, and that's what the control will use if you just select *DTS_LONGDATEFORMAT* as the style. When you use this style, it's best to have your own format string.

Try using the TIMEFORMAT macro defined at the top of the *DateTimePickerDlg.cpp* file. Modify it using the formatting strings in Table 933 to see what effect the changes have on the display.

In the format string, any characters included between single quote marks are interpreted as literals. They are displayed as entered in the string. To include a single quote in the string, you need to double it, as in

Assembly language. To produce an output such as "Today's date: February 7, 2012" you would enter a string such as shown below

```
"'Today''s date: ' MMMM d',' yyy"
```

Any delimiting characters, such as the semicolon in a time string, also must be enclosed in single quotes. To display "The time is 17:42:42" you would enter a string such as the following:

```
"'The time is' HH':'mm':'ss"
```

The text between the single quote marks is protected from user tampering unless you include the *DTS_APPCANPARSE* style. When the user moves across the control, literals are skipped.

934. *Understanding the Calendar Control*

The monthly calendar control has been available in the common controls library only since version 4.70. It provides a child window that displays a complete month at a time in calendar format.

Over the last few years, there have been a number of calendar controls available as commercial products or free on the Web. It was only a matter of time before Microsoft included one in the common controls library. It isn't the best of the lot, and in terms of functionality, it probably falls in the lower half of the list. But it is a calendar control, comes at no extra charge, and it is adequate for most tasks.

The MSDN documentation tells you the calendar control is highly customizable "by applying a variety of styles to the object when you create it." That *variety* is a grand total of five style options, far less than those available to controls that aren't so-called customizable. It's customizable in the sense that you can set the colors for the various elements on the control. Other than that, it's no more customizable than any other control. You can use inherited *CWnd* functions such as *SetFont()* to set certain attributes, but the MFC class itself doesn't provide any more customization functions.

Apparently, much of the documentation for the calendar control was written before the control was completed or released. Some of it even reminds you of "vaporware." For example, if you look up the calendar control in the glossary (it's under "month calendar control"), it states that the "calendar can display one or more months at a time." The documentation doesn't explain how, but if you change the size of the control's rectangle, it will display more than one month. For example, to make it display two months, use the following code:

```
m_ctlCalendar.GetWindowRect (rc);
ScreenToClient (rc);
int iWidth = rc.right - rc.left;
iWidth *= 2;
rc.right = rc.left + iWidth + 6;
m_ctlCalendar.MoveWindow (rc);
```

Notice that when adjusting the size of the rectangle, you had to add about six pixels for the space between the month displays. If you want to display three months, change the multiplier for *iWidth* to 3 and add about 12 pixels for the space between the month displays.

In addition, it has a serious bug in it that makes it touchy when you try to retrieve a selected date from the control. You'll see how to program around this bug in the next tip.

The spinner control on the year allows you to display months back to 1753 and as far in advance as 2999. The British empire—and the American colonies—adopted the Gregorian calendar in 1752, so presumably this is the reason for the lower limit. Month calculations before 1753 can be tricky because the year ended on March 25 (which is why George Washington was born in 1731 *and* 1732). I don't know the reason for the upper limit of 2999 because my college courses on the history of the British empire didn't go that far.

(Lest you think the Gregorian calendar was developed for better timekeeping purposes, it was an attempt to better track the proper dates for Easter. If it weren't for the fact that it was becoming difficult under the Julian calendar, we still would be celebrating New Year's on March 25.)

Using the delta control on the calendar allows you to go back to 1601. That's as far back as the Microsoft time scheme can count. The results are unreliable, though, and based on the Gregorian rather than the Julian calendar. Although the spinner control on the year stops at 2999, you can display years as high as 9999 with questionable reliability.

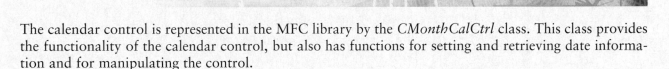

935. *Using the CMonthCalCtrl Class*

The calendar control is represented in the MFC library by the *CMonthCalCtrl* class. This class provides the functionality of the calendar control, but also has functions for setting and retrieving date information and for manipulating the control.

Figure 935 shows the layout for a property page for the calendar control. The control has only one size, and you can see that it was only partially drawn on the dialog box. The *CMonthCalCtrl* class has functions for resizing the control after it has been created.

Drawing a larger control on the dialog box doesn't produce a bigger calendar. It just makes a bigger control with a lot of white space. Instead, just draw it approximately on the dialog box and use the *SizeMinReq()* function to draw the entire control in the minimum space.

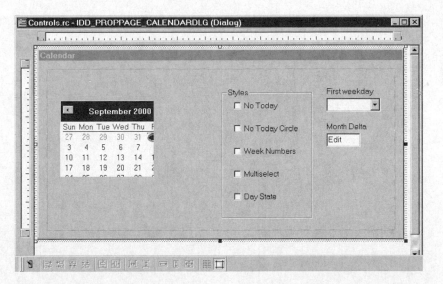

Figure 935   Position the upper-left corner of the calendar control, but don't worry about getting it sized just right

Create the property page with a resource ID of *IDD_PROPPAGE_CALENDARDLG* and label it "Calendar." The controls in the property page will let you experiment with all the calendar control-specific styles. Unseen at the bottom of the page are two static controls that will show the selection obtained by handling the *MCN_SELCHANGE* notification. The header and source files are listed as follows:

```cpp
// CalendarDlg.h : header file
//


/////////////////////////////////////////////////////////
// CCalendarDlg dialog

class CCalendarDlg : public CPropertyPage
{
    DECLARE_DYNCREATE(CCalendarDlg)

// Construction
public:
    CCalendarDlg();
    ~CCalendarDlg();

// Dialog Data
    //{{AFX_DATA(CCalendarDlg)
    enum { IDD = IDD_PROPPAGE_CALENDARDLG };
    CMonthCalCtrl   m_ctlCalendar;
    BOOL    m_bDayState;
    BOOL    m_bMultiselect;
    BOOL    m_bNoToday;
    BOOL    m_bNoTodayCircle;
    BOOL    m_bWeekNumbers;
    int     m_nFirstWeekDay;
    int     m_nMonthDelta;
    //}}AFX_DATA


// Overrides
    // ClassWizard generate virtual function overrides
    //{{AFX_VIRTUAL(CCalendarDlg)
    protected:
    virtual void DoDataExchange(CDataExchange* pDX);
    // DDX/DDV support
    virtual BOOL OnNotify(WPARAM wParam, LPARAM lParam,
                          LRESULT* pResult);
    //}}AFX_VIRTUAL


// Implementation
protected:
    void ShowDates (CTime &timeStart, CTime &timeEnd);
    void SetDayStateBits (MONTHDAYSTATE &month,
                          int nCount, ...);
    void RecreateControl();
    DWORD m_dwStyle;
    // Generated message map functions
    //{{AFX_MSG(CCalendarDlg)
    afx_msg void OnNoToday();
    afx_msg void OnNoTodayCircle();
    afx_msg void OnDayState();
    afx_msg void OnMultiselect();
    afx_msg void OnWeekNumbers();
    virtual BOOL OnInitDialog();
    afx_msg void OnSelchangeFirstWeekDay();
    afx_msg void OnChangeCalendarDelta();
```

```
    //}}AFX_MSG
    DECLARE_MESSAGE_MAP()

};
```

The *CMonthCalCtrl* functions are a little choosy about how you get the current selection. If you are in single-selection mode, you must use the *GetCurSel()* function. When you are in multi-selection mode, you must use *GetSelRange()*. Using the wrong function will cause your program to assert. Also, *GetCurSel()* has a bug in it that isn't shared by *GetSelRange()*. This will be covered after the source code listing.

```cpp
// CalendarDlg.cpp : implementation file
//

#include "stdafx.h"
#include "Controls.h"
#include "CalendarDlg.h"
#include   <stdarg.h>

#ifdef _DEBUG
#define new DEBUG_NEW
#undef THIS_FILE
static char THIS_FILE[] = __FILE__;
#endif

/////////////////////////////////////////////////////////////
// CCalendarDlg property page

static TCHAR *szMonths[] =
    {
    "January", "February", "March", "April", "May",
    "June", "July", "August", "September",
    "October", "November","December"
    };
static TCHAR *szDays[] =
    {
    "Sunday", "Monday", "Tuesday", "Wednesday",
    "Thursday", "Friday", "Saturday"
    };

IMPLEMENT_DYNCREATE(CCalendarDlg, CPropertyPage)

CCalendarDlg::CCalendarDlg()
                        : CPropertyPage(CCalendarDlg::IDD)
{
    //{{AFX_DATA_INIT(CCalendarDlg)
    m_bDayState = FALSE;
    m_bMultiselect = FALSE;
    m_bNoToday = FALSE;
    m_bNoTodayCircle = FALSE;
    m_bWeekNumbers = FALSE;
    m_nFirstWeekDay = Ø;
    m_nMonthDelta = Ø;
    //}}AFX_DATA_INIT
    m_psp.dwFlags &= ~PSP_HASHELP;
}
```

```
CCalendarDlg::~CCalendarDlg()
{
}

void CCalendarDlg::DoDataExchange(CDataExchange* pDX)
{
    CPropertyPage::DoDataExchange(pDX);
    //{{AFX_DATA_MAP(CCalendarDlg)
    DDX_Control(pDX, IDC_CALENDAR_CALENDAR, m_ctlCalendar);
    DDX_Check(pDX, IDC_CALENDAR_DAYSTATE, m_bDayState);
    DDX_Check(pDX, IDC_CALENDAR_MULTISELECT,
                                        m_bMultiselect);
    DDX_Check(pDX, IDC_CALENDAR_NOTODAY, m_bNoToday);
    DDX_Check(pDX, IDC_CALENDAR_NOTODAYCIRCLE,
                                        m_bNoTodayCircle);
    DDX_Check(pDX, IDC_CALENDAR_WEEKNUMBERS,
                                        m_bWeekNumbers);
    DDX_CBIndex(pDX, IDC_CALENDAR_FIRSTWEEKDAY,
                                        m_nFirstWeekDay);
    DDX_Text(pDX, IDC_CALENDAR_DELTA, m_nMonthDelta);
    DDV_MinMaxInt(pDX, m_nMonthDelta, 0, 1200);
    //}}AFX_DATA_MAP
}


BEGIN_MESSAGE_MAP(CCalendarDlg, CPropertyPage)
    //{{AFX_MSG_MAP(CCalendarDlg)
    ON_BN_CLICKED(IDC_CALENDAR_NOTODAY, OnNoToday)
    ON_BN_CLICKED(IDC_CALENDAR_NOTODAYCIRCLE,
                                        OnNoTodayCircle)
    ON_BN_CLICKED(IDC_CALENDAR_DAYSTATE, OnDayState)
    ON_BN_CLICKED(IDC_CALENDAR_MULTISELECT, OnMultiselect)
    ON_BN_CLICKED(IDC_CALENDAR_WEEKNUMBERS, OnWeekNumbers)
    ON_CBN_SELCHANGE(IDC_CALENDAR_FIRSTWEEKDAY,
                                    OnSelchangeFirstWeekDay)
    ON_EN_CHANGE(IDC_CALENDAR_DELTA, OnChangeCalendarDelta)
    //}}AFX_MSG_MAP
END_MESSAGE_MAP()

/////////////////////////////////////////////////////////
// CCalendarDlg message handlers

BOOL CCalendarDlg::OnInitDialog()
{
    CPropertyPage::OnInitDialog();
    CRect rc;
    m_ctlCalendar.SizeMinReq(TRUE);
    m_ctlCalendar.SetCurSel (CTime::GetCurrentTime ());
    m_dwStyle = m_ctlCalendar.GetStyle ();
    UpdateData (FALSE);
    return TRUE;
}

void CCalendarDlg::OnNoToday()
{
```

```
    UpdateData (TRUE);
    if (m_bNoToday)
    {
        m_dwStyle |= MCS_NOTODAY;
        m_ctlCalendar.ModifyStyle (0, MCS_NOTODAY, TRUE);
    }
    else
    {
        m_dwStyle &= ~MCS_NOTODAY;
        m_ctlCalendar.ModifyStyle (MCS_NOTODAY, 0, TRUE);
    }
    m_ctlCalendar.SizeMinReq(TRUE);
}

void CCalendarDlg::OnNoTodayCircle()
{
    UpdateData (TRUE);
    if (m_bNoTodayCircle)
    {
        m_dwStyle |= MCS_NOTODAYCIRCLE;
        m_ctlCalendar.ModifyStyle (0, MCS_NOTODAYCIRCLE,
                                   TRUE);
    }
    else
    {
        m_dwStyle &= ~MCS_NOTODAYCIRCLE;
        m_ctlCalendar.ModifyStyle (MCS_NOTODAYCIRCLE, 0,
                                   TRUE);
    }
}

void CCalendarDlg::OnDayState()
{
    UpdateData (TRUE);
    if (m_bDayState)
    {
        m_dwStyle |= MCS_DAYSTATE;
        m_ctlCalendar.ModifyStyle (0, MCS_DAYSTATE, TRUE);
    }
    else
    {
        m_dwStyle &= ~MCS_DAYSTATE;
        m_ctlCalendar.ModifyStyle (MCS_DAYSTATE, 0, TRUE);
    }
    RecreateControl ();
}

void CCalendarDlg::OnMultiselect()
{
    UpdateData (TRUE);
    if (m_bMultiselect)
        m_dwStyle |= MCS_MULTISELECT;
    else
        m_dwStyle &= ~MCS_MULTISELECT;
    RecreateControl ();
}
```

```
void CCalendarDlg::OnWeekNumbers()
{
    UpdateData (TRUE);
    if (m_bWeekNumbers)
    {
        m_dwStyle |= MCS_WEEKNUMBERS;
        m_ctlCalendar.ModifyStyle (0, MCS_WEEKNUMBERS,
                                    TRUE);
    }
    else
    {
        m_dwStyle &= ~MCS_WEEKNUMBERS;
        m_ctlCalendar.ModifyStyle (MCS_WEEKNUMBERS, 0,
                                    TRUE);
    }
    m_ctlCalendar.SizeMinReq(TRUE);
}

void CCalendarDlg::RecreateControl()
{
    UpdateData (TRUE);
    CRect rc;
    m_ctlCalendar.GetWindowRect (rc);
    ScreenToClient (rc);
    CTime dateStart, dateEnd;
    DWORD dwStyle = m_ctlCalendar.GetStyle ();
    bool bMultisel = false;
    if (dwStyle & MCS_MULTISELECT)
    {
        bMultisel = true;
        m_ctlCalendar.GetSelRange (dateStart, dateEnd);
    }
    else
    {
        SYSTEMTIME st;
        m_ctlCalendar.GetCurSel (&st);
        st.wHour = 8;
        st.wMinute = st.wSecond = st.wMilliseconds = 0;
        CTime sel(st);
        dateStart = sel;
        dateEnd = sel;
    }
    m_ctlCalendar.DestroyWindow ();
    m_ctlCalendar.Create (m_dwStyle, rc,
                        this, IDC_CALENDAR_CALENDAR);
    if (m_dwStyle & MCS_MULTISELECT)
        m_ctlCalendar.SetSelRange (dateStart, dateStart);
    else
        m_ctlCalendar.SetCurSel (dateStart);
    ShowDates (dateStart, dateEnd);
    m_ctlCalendar.SetFirstDayOfWeek (m_nFirstWeekDay == 0
                            ? 6 : (m_nFirstWeekDay - 1));
    m_ctlCalendar.SizeMinReq(TRUE);

    MONTHDAYSTATE month;
```

```
    SetDayStateBits (month, 3, 2, 12, 18);
    m_ctlCalendar.SetDayState (1, &month);
}

void CCalendarDlg::OnSelchangeFirstWeekDay()
{
    UpdateData (TRUE);
    int nWeekDay = m_nFirstWeekDay;
    if (nWeekDay == 0)
        nWeekDay = 0;
    --nWeekDay;
    if (nWeekDay < 0)
        return;
    m_ctlCalendar.SetFirstDayOfWeek (nWeekDay);
    m_ctlCalendar.SetFocus();
}

void CCalendarDlg::OnChangeCalendarDelta()
{
    UpdateData (TRUE);
    m_ctlCalendar.SetMonthDelta (m_nMonthDelta);
}

void CCalendarDlg::SetDayStateBits(MONTHDAYSTATE &month,
                                   int nCount, ...)
{
va_list va;

    int i;
    month = 0;
    int count;
    va_start (va, nCount);
    for (count = 0; count < nCount; ++count)
    {
        i = va_arg(va, int);
        if (i < 32)
            month |= 1 << (i - 1);
    }
    va_end (va);
}

BOOL CCalendarDlg::OnNotify(WPARAM wParam, LPARAM lParam,
                            LRESULT* pResult)
{
    NMHDR *pNMHDR = (NMHDR *) lParam;
    if (pNMHDR->idFrom == IDC_CALENDAR_CALENDAR)
    {
        NMSELCHANGE *nmDT = (NMSELCHANGE *) pNMHDR;
        if (nmDT->nmhdr.code == MCN_SELCHANGE)
        {
            CTime selStart (nmDT->stSelStart);
            CTime selEnd (nmDT->stSelEnd);
            ShowDates (selStart, selEnd);
        }
    }
    return CPropertyPage::OnNotify(wParam, lParam, pResult);
```

```
}

void CCalendarDlg::ShowDates(CTime &timeStart,
                             CTime &timeEnd)
{
    CString strStart, strEnd;
    bool bMultisel = (m_ctlCalendar.GetStyle()
                            & MCS_MULTISELECT)
                ? true : false;
    strStart.Format ("%sSelection: %s %s %d, %04d",
            bMultisel ? "Begin " : "",
            szDays[timeStart.GetDayOfWeek() - 1],
            szMonths[timeStart.GetMonth() - 1],
            timeStart.GetDay(), timeStart.GetYear());
    if (bMultisel)
    {
        strEnd.Format ("End Selection: %s %s %d, %04d",
            szDays[timeEnd.GetDayOfWeek() - 1],
            szMonths[timeEnd.GetMonth() - 1],
            timeEnd.GetDay(), timeEnd.GetYear());
    }
    else
        strEnd = _T("");
    ::SetWindowText (
            GetDlgItem(IDC_CALENDAR_SELBEGIN)->m_hWnd,
            (LPCSTR) strStart);
    ::SetWindowText (
            GetDlgItem(IDC_CALENDAR_SELEND)->m_hWnd,
            (LPCSTR) strEnd);
}
```

When you call *GetCurSel()* using a *CTime* object, it has a tendency to put junk in the members that it doesn't use—the hour, minute, and seconds. The *CTime* object's value really is nothing more than a *time_t* value, so the conversion tends to skew things a bit. Theoretically, you should be able to call *GetCurSel(CTime object)*, then turn around in the next statement and call *SetCurSel(CTime object)*, and nothing should change. Give it a try. Execute the code repeatedly and your selected date is going to jump around like a bunny rabbit that just ate hot peppers.

The trick here is to catch it before the conversion is done, mop up the mess and get along with what you were doing. You can use the overloaded *GetCurSel()* that takes a *SYSTEMTIME* structure pointer as its parameter. You've still got some garbage in there, and you need to clean it up before you convert it to a *CTime* value. Set the minutes and seconds to zero (you don't have to worry about milliseconds; *CTime* doesn't use that) and the hour to eight, then pass the *SYSTEMTIME* to the constructor for a *CTime* object.

When you make date conversions without regard to the time of day, always pick a "safe" hour, one way from midnight—when the civil and military day changes—and noon—when the Julian (no relation to the Julian calendar) day changes. The only computer time that has proven to be reliable *and* consistent over the years is the UNIX-based system, which counts the number of seconds since Jan. 1, 1970. This is the time held by the MFC *Ctime* class. The UNIX system uses a signed value and will expire in 2037. There's also the system used by the UNIX *rdate* program, which uses an epoch of 1900 and stores the value in an unsigned long.

A sample of the conversion is shown in the *RecreateControl()* function, where the current selection is saved and restored after the control is destroyed and re-created.

Compile and run the application. Select the Calendar page and test the calendar. To move from month to month, click one of the arrow buttons at the upper left and upper right. To change from one month to another, click on the month name at the top and you'll get a menu of the months; select one to move directly to it. To change from one year to another, click on the year in the title bar and you'll get a spinner control next to the year.

Try changing the month delta. This determines how far the month will change when you click the arrow buttons. You can set it to move, say, six months at a time. On each month's display, a few days from the month before and the month after are shown. You can click on one of those dates to move to that month, bypassing the delta setting.

936. *Customizing Calendar Controls*

This tip is included only because the Microsoft hoopla about this control leads you to believe it is highly customizable and you're going to want to know how to customize it. The only customization provided by the control is to set the colors for the various elements in the control.

You can retrieve a current color by naming *GetColor()* and specifying the region, such as the title, the text, etc. Select the region from Table 936. The return value is a *COLORREF* of the color for that region.

To set a color, use the *SetColor()* function, passing the region identifier from Table 936 and a *COLORREF* value for the requested color

Calendar Color	Applies to
MCSC_TEXT	The date numbers for the current month
MCSC_BACKGROUND	The background color between months (this apparently was set before the control was completed; it appears to have no effect and doesn't appear in the ActiveX properties)
MCSC_MONTHBK	The background color for the entire control (the name is slightly misleading. Instead of just the month, the control's rectangle appears to be painted in this color before the elements are drawn on it)
MCSC_TITLEBK	The background for the title bar and the selected day, and the text color for the days of the week
MCSC_TITLETEXT	The text color for the month name and year in the title bar
MCSC_TRAILINGTEXT	The text color for the days in the preceding and following months

Table 936   The color macros for the calendar control and the portions they affect when used in the SetColor() *function*

You can set the font using the *CWnd::SetFont()* function. You don't need to qualify it because it is inherited by the *CMonthCalCtrl* class. There are some problems with setting the font. Changing the font changes it for all the text on the control; you can't access certain parts of the control to set individual fonts.

Anytime you change the control's font, be sure to call *SizeMinReq()* after setting the font to make the control resize itself for the new font. If you don't, you'll likely end up with a display that is either too small or too large for the control's rectangle.

937. *Understanding Calendar Control Properties*

If you look at the control in the Visual Studio ActiveX container, you'll also see the control's properties that you can modify along with those you can't.

To do this, select ActiveX Control Test Container from the Tools menu in Visual Studio. When the test container starts, select Insert New Control from its Edit menu. From the list, find and select Microsoft MonthView Control. Now return to the Edit menu and select Properties at the bottom of the menu. You'll be able to view and modify any properties from the property sheet. This is a good way to examine and test any new ActiveX control, by the way.

The properties you can modify are enabled; those you can't are disabled or grayed out. For example, select the Color page then select a region to modify and select a new color. Press the Apply button to make the change appear on the control sample.

Move back to the General page and examine the *MaxSelCount* property at the lower right. It's grayed out, indicating you can't change that property. That's curious because *CMonthCalCtrl* provides a member function for modifying this property. If, however, you call this function with a new value, it doesn't change. *MaxSelCount* will always be seven, and that's the maximum selection range for the control.

938. *Using Calendar Messages*

The calendar control sends three notification messages to the parent window. The first is the *MCN_SELCHANGE*, which is sent whenever the month changes. The *MCN_SELECT* message is sent whenever the user selects a date in the month being displayed. The third message is *MCN_GETDAYSTATE*, which is sent when the control needs to know what days of the month to set in boldface.

You can handle these messages in two different ways. You can process them in the *OnNotify()* function, or you can add message handlers for them using the ClassWizard. The sample code on the companion CD contains both methods for you to try.

When the control sends the *MCN_GETDAYSTATE* message, it is asking for the days of the month to emphasize by setting them in bold type. The control always asks for the day state information for three months. You must pass it back the address of a three-element array of type *MONTHDAYSTATE* (type *DWORD* also is acceptable). The first member of this array is for the month preceding the currently selected month. The second is the currently selected month, and the third is the following month. Some dates from the preceding and following months are always shown on the control, and it uses this information to set them in a bolder type.

You could use this information to set, say, the holidays or your days off in the month when it is selected. You could inspect a schedule and boldface those dates on which you have meetings. There's just one small problem with this, however, and I haven't found an adequate workaround for it. When the selection changes, this message is sent at the wrong time.

If the user selects a new month for the calendar, Windows sends this message *before* the selection change takes place. If you get the current selection, you're going to get the month that is being left behind, and you have no way of knowing what month is about to be displayed. You can't assume the following month. Suppose the user presses the button to select the preceding month, or changes the selection from the year spinner or month menu.

The *CMonthCalCtrl* class has a member function, *SetDayState()* that, according to the documentation, sets the day states for you. It appears to do nothing, however, and the control still calls your code for day state information. If you don't give it the information in the message handler, the day states on the displayed month won't be what you want. Unless you're very lucky, of course.

939. *Other Control Classes in the MFC Library*

Your *Controls* property sheet should be getting pretty full by now. You can have up to 24 pages, and the calendar control makes it 22. You'll add just one more, a page for other controls, leaving you an open spot for experimenting with any new controls that may be released, or for your own custom controls.

There are two controls of interest left. One is the bitmap button control, which is a button that contains a set of four bitmaps for its different states. The second is the IP address control, which provides a safe method for obtaining IP address information from a user.

Two other controls of interest are the *CDragListBox* and the *CCheckListBox* controls, which are MFC class derivations of the list box control. They were covered in Tip 836, "Understanding the List Box Control" and examples of them appear on the List Box page of the *Controls* project.

Create another property page, *IDD_PROPPAGE_OTHERDLG*, and label it "Other Controls." Create a class for it called *COtherDlg* and add it to the property sheet. In the next two tips you'll add controls to this page.

940. *Understanding the Bitmap Button Control*

The bitmap button is more of a ho-hum control than a useful object. You'd do much better creating your own Owner Draw button class and use it with an image list to draw the bitmaps on the button. Having gone through the control samples in this book, you should be able to do that easily.

For one, the bitmap button can handle only four images (only one is required). If you want it to appear as a button, you have to draw the highlight rectangles as part of the images. Then, if you later want to change it to a flat button, you have to go back and redraw all the images. The images must be separate bitmaps with their own identifiers.

Still, you may find some use for it, and the sample code shows two ways to create a bitmap button. In the first, you create it from a button drawn on the dialog box. When you draw the button, the size isn't important; just make sure the upper-left corner is properly placed. Give the button a label; you need this to match it up to the bitmaps. Also give it a numerical resource ID; you'll need this for the *AutoLoad()* function. Set the Owner Draw style and add a *CBitmapButton* object in your dialog class. Don't use the ClassWizard to add the variable. If you do, it will be added to the *DoDataExchange()* function and created when the *CDialog::OnInitDialog()* function is executed. This will cause your program to assert when you try to load the bitmaps.

Create one to four bitmaps. The bitmap for the up state is required, but the other three are optional. Draw the images (they should all be the same size; 32 by 32 is a good button size). Give the bitmaps *string* resource IDs that are the same as the label for your button, but append a "U" to the up image, a D to the down image, an "F" for the focused image and an "X" for the disabled image. If you labeled your button "HeeHaw," you'll have four bitmaps with string identifiers of "HeeHawU," "HeeHawD," "HeeHawF" and "HeeHawX."

The following step assumes you gave the button a numerical resource ID of *IDC_HEEHAWBUTTON* and the variable is *m_btnHeeHaw*. In the *OnInitDialog()* function of your dialog class, add the following line:

```
m_btnHeeHaw.AutoLoad (IDC_HEEHAWBUTTON, this);
```

The *AutoLoad()* function will read the label for the button and match it up with the similarly named bitmaps and resize the button to match the size of the bitmaps. You can use the button as an ordinary button, processing the notification messages as though it were a *CButton* object.

In the second method, you create a button in memory without drawing it on the dialog box. Instead, you'll calculate its position based on other controls. In the sample code, the button is surrounded by a group box, so you can use that as the reference.

For this method, your bitmaps may have numerical or string identifiers. For simplicity, you'll use the same images as for the other buttons. Add a *CBitmapButton* variable to the dialog class. Again, do this manually; there's no object for the ClassWizard to work with anyway. If you intend to use messages from this button, add a resource ID for it manually.

Assuming the group box ID is *IDC_GROUPBOX*, the button's resource ID is *IDC_HAWHEEBUTTON*, and the variable's identifier is *m_btnHawHee*, add the following code to the *OnInitDialog()* function:

```
m_btnHawHee.Create ("", WS_VISIBLE | BS_OWNERDRAW,
                CRect(0,0,0,0), this,
                IDC_HAWHEEBUTTON);
m_btnHawHee.LoadBitmaps ("BitButtonU", "BitButtonD",
                "BitButtonF", "BitButtonX");
m_btnHawHee.SizeToContent ();
CRect rcGroup, rcButton;
m_btnHawHee.GetWindowRect (rcButton);
::GetWindowRect (GetDlgItem(IDC_OTHER_GROUP)->m_hWnd,
                rcGroup);
ScreenToClient (rcGroup);
ScreenToClient (rcButton);
int nHeight = rcButton.bottom - rcButton.top;
int nMid = rcGroup.left +
        (rcGroup.right - rcGroup.left) / 2;
int nHalf = (rcButton.right - rcButton.left) / 2;
rcButton.left = nMid - nHalf;
rcButton.right = nMid + nHalf;
nMid = rcGroup.top + (rcGroup.bottom - rcGroup.top) / 2;
rcButton.top = nMid - nHalf + 4;
rcButton.bottom = nMid + nHalf + 4;
m_btnHawHee.SetWindowPos (NULL, rcButton.left,
                rcButton.top, rcButton.Width (),
                rcButton.Height (),
                SWP_NOZORDER | SWP_NOACTIVATE
                | SWP_SHOWWINDOW);
```

Because there's no button object on the dialog box for the ClassWizard to work with, you'll have to add message handlers and message map entries for this button manually.

941. _Understanding the IP Address Control_

The usefulness of the IP address control makes up for the silliness of the bitmap button control. This control offers a safe method to get an IP address from a user. It's formatted with four fields separated by periods in the style of an IP address. It won't let the user enter anything but a number, and it won't accept a number larger than 255. If you try to enter anything larger, it will default to the upper limit for the field, which you can set for each field individually.

It's an easy control to master. There are no styles other than the standard Windows control styles, and there are only four notification messages, three of which are familiar edit control messages.

The notification messages are _EN_SETFOCUS_ and _EN_KILLFOCUS_. These are sent whenever the control gets or loses the focus. Whenever a user changes contents of the control, the _EN_CHANGE_ message is sent. The one notification message endemic to the IP address control is _IPN_FIELDCHANGED_. This is sent whenever the user changes the contents of a field, or moves the caret from one field to another.

There's not a lot to handle on the IP address control. The code shows you how to set the ranges and to set and get an IP address. The header and source code for _COtherDlg_ is shown below:

```
// OtherDlg.h : header file
//


/////////////////////////////////////////////////////////
// COtherDlg dialog

class COtherDlg : public CPropertyPage
{
    DECLARE_DYNCREATE(COtherDlg)

// Construction
public:
    COtherDlg();
    ~COtherDlg();

// Dialog Data
    //{{AFX_DATA(COtherDlg)
    enum { IDD = IDD_PROPPAGE_OTHERDLG };
    CIPAddressCtrl  m_ctlIPUpper;
    CIPAddressCtrl  m_ctlIPLower;
    CIPAddressCtrl  m_ctlIPAddress;
    CBitmapButton   m_BitButton1;
    CBitmapButton   m_BitButton2;
    //}}AFX_DATA


// Overrides
    // ClassWizard generate virtual function overrides
    //{{AFX_VIRTUAL(COtherDlg)
    protected:
    virtual void DoDataExchange(CDataExchange* pDX);
    // DDX/DDV support
    //}}AFX_VIRTUAL
```

```cpp
// Implementation
protected:
    // Generated message map functions
    //{{AFX_MSG(COtherDlg)
    afx_msg void OnPaint();
    virtual BOOL OnInitDialog();
    afx_msg void OnOtherDisable();
    afx_msg void OnSetIPRange();
    afx_msg void OnIPSetRange();
    //}}AFX_MSG
    DECLARE_MESSAGE_MAP()

};


/////////////////////////////////////////////////////////////
// OtherDlg.cpp : implementation file
/////////////////////////////////////////////////////////////

#include "stdafx.h"
#include "Controls.h"
#include "OtherDlg.h"

#ifdef _DEBUG
#define new DEBUG_NEW
#undef THIS_FILE
static char THIS_FILE[] = __FILE__;
#endif


/////////////////////////////////////////////////////////////
// COtherDlg property page

IMPLEMENT_DYNCREATE(COtherDlg, CPropertyPage)

COtherDlg::COtherDlg() : CPropertyPage(COtherDlg::IDD)
{
    //{{AFX_DATA_INIT(COtherDlg)
        // NOTE: the ClassWizard will add member initialization here
    //}}AFX_DATA_INIT
    m_psp.dwFlags &= ~PSP_HASHELP;
}

COtherDlg::~COtherDlg()
{
}

void COtherDlg::DoDataExchange(CDataExchange* pDX)
{
    CPropertyPage::DoDataExchange(pDX);
    //{{AFX_DATA_MAP(COtherDlg)
    DDX_Control(pDX, IDC_OTHER_IPUPPER, m_ctlIPUpper);
    DDX_Control(pDX, IDC_OTHER_IPLOWER, m_ctlIPLower);
    DDX_Control(pDX, IDC_OTHER_IPADDRESS, m_ctlIPAddress);
    //}}AFX_DATA_MAP
}
```

```
BEGIN_MESSAGE_MAP(COtherDlg, CPropertyPage)
    //{{AFX_MSG_MAP(COtherDlg)
    ON_WM_PAINT()
    ON_BN_CLICKED(IDC_OTHER_DISABLE, OnOtherDisable)
    ON_BN_CLICKED(IDC_OTHER_IPSETRANGE, OnIPSetRange)
    //}}AFX_MSG_MAP
END_MESSAGE_MAP()


/////////////////////////////////////////////////////////////
// COtherDlg message handlers

BOOL COtherDlg::OnInitDialog()
{
    CPropertyPage::OnInitDialog();


//
//  Initialize the button portion of the page
//
    m_BitButton1.AutoLoad (IDC_OTHER_BITBUTTON, this);

    m_BitButton2.Create ("", WS_VISIBLE | BS_OWNERDRAW
                         | BS_AUTOCHECKBOX, CRect(0,0,0,0),
                         this, IDC_OTHER_BITBUTTON);
    m_BitButton2.LoadBitmaps ("BitButtonU", "BitButtonD",
                              "BitButtonF", "BitButtonX");
    m_BitButton2.SizeToContent ();
    CRect rcGroup, rcButton;
    m_BitButton2.GetWindowRect (rcButton);
    ::GetWindowRect (GetDlgItem(IDC_OTHER_GROUP)->m_hWnd,
                                rcGroup);
    ScreenToClient (rcGroup);
    ScreenToClient (rcButton);
    int nHeight = rcButton.bottom - rcButton.top;
    int nMid = rcGroup.left
                        + (rcGroup.right - rcGroup.left) / 2;
    int nHalf = (rcButton.right - rcButton.left) / 2;
    rcButton.left = nMid - nHalf;
    rcButton.right = nMid + nHalf;
    nMid = rcGroup.top + (rcGroup.bottom - rcGroup.top) / 2;
    rcButton.top = nMid - nHalf + 4;
    rcButton.bottom = nMid + nHalf + 4;
    m_BitButton2.SetWindowPos (NULL, rcButton.left,
                                rcButton.top,
                                rcButton.Width (),
                                rcButton.Height (),
                                SWP_NOZORDER | SWP_NOACTIVATE
                                | SWP_SHOWWINDOW);
//
//  Initialize the IP portion of the page. You can use
//  either a single four-by value, or individual values
//  for the address elements.
//
    m_ctlIPUpper.SetAddress (0xFFFFFFFF);
    m_ctlIPLower.SetAddress (0, 0, 0, 0);
    m_ctlIPAddress.SetAddress (0);
    return TRUE;
```

```
}

void COtherDlg::OnPaint()
{
    CPaintDC dc(this); // device context for painting

    CRect rc;
    GetWindowRect (rc);
    ScreenToClient (rc);
    CRect rcPage (rc);
    int nMid = (rc.right - rc.left) / 2;
    rc.left = rc.left + nMid - 2;
    rc.right = rc.left + 4;
    CBrush brush(RGB(0x00, 0x00, 0x00));
    dc.FillRect (rc, &brush);
    rc = rcPage;
    rc.right = nMid - 2;
    rc.top += 10;
    CFont *font = GetFont ();
    LOGFONT lf;
    font->GetLogFont (&lf);
    lf.lfHeight *= 2;
    strcpy (lf.lfFaceName, "Times New Roman");
    CFont newFont;
    newFont.CreateFontIndirect (&lf);
    dc.SelectObject (&newFont);
    dc.DrawText (CString (_T("Bitmap Button")), rc,
                           DT_CENTER);
    rc.left = rc.right + 4;
    rc.right = rcPage.right;
    dc.DrawText (CString (_T("IP Address")), rc, DT_CENTER);
}

//////////////////////////////////////////////////////////
// Bitmap Button message handlers
//////////////////////////////////////////////////////////

void COtherDlg::OnOtherDisable()
{
    if (m_BitButton1.IsWindowEnabled ())
    {
        m_BitButton1.EnableWindow (FALSE);
        ::SetWindowText (GetDlgItem (
                    IDC_OTHER_DISABLE)->m_hWnd, "Enable");
    }
    else
    {
        m_BitButton1.EnableWindow (TRUE);
        ::SetWindowText (GetDlgItem (
                    IDC_OTHER_DISABLE)->m_hWnd, "Disable");
    }
}

//////////////////////////////////////////////////////////
// IP control message handlers
//////////////////////////////////////////////////////////
```

```
void COtherDlg::OnIPSetRange()
{
    BYTE cUpperAddr1, cUpperAddr2, cUpperAddr3, cUpperAddr4;
    BYTE cLowerAddr1, cLowerAddr2, cLowerAddr3, cLowerAddr4;
    BYTE cAddr1, cAddr2, cAddr3, cAddr4;
    m_ctlIPUpper.GetAddress (cUpperAddr1, cUpperAddr2,
                             cUpperAddr3, cUpperAddr4);
    m_ctlIPLower.GetAddress (cLowerAddr1, cLowerAddr2,
                             cLowerAddr3, cLowerAddr4);
    if ((cUpperAddr1 < cLowerAddr1) ||
        (cUpperAddr2 < cLowerAddr2) ||
        (cUpperAddr3 < cLowerAddr3) ||
        (cUpperAddr4 < cLowerAddr4))
    {
        AfxMessageBox ("Lower limits cannot be greater"
                       " than upper limits");
        return;
    }
//
//  Set the ranges for the fields.
//
    m_ctlIPAddress.SetFieldRange (0, cLowerAddr1,
                                     cUpperAddr1);
    m_ctlIPAddress.SetFieldRange (1, cLowerAddr2,
                                     cUpperAddr2);
    m_ctlIPAddress.SetFieldRange (2, cLowerAddr3,
                                     cUpperAddr3);
    m_ctlIPAddress.SetFieldRange (3, cLowerAddr4,
                                     cUpperAddr4);
//
//  Make sure the current values aren't outside the range.
//  If they are, adjust them to the nearest value within
//  range. After that, the control will take care of the
//  adjustments.
//
    m_ctlIPAddress.GetAddress (cAddr1, cAddr2,
                               cAddr3, cAddr4);
    if (cAddr1 > cUpperAddr1)
        cAddr1 = cUpperAddr1;
    else if (cAddr1 < cLowerAddr1)
        cAddr1 = cLowerAddr1;

    if (cAddr2 > cUpperAddr2)
        cAddr2 = cUpperAddr2;
    else if (cAddr2 < cLowerAddr2)
        cAddr2 = cLowerAddr2;

    if (cAddr3 > cUpperAddr3)
        cAddr3 = cUpperAddr3;
    else if (cAddr3 < cLowerAddr3)
        cAddr3 = cLowerAddr3;

    if (cAddr4 > cUpperAddr4)
        cAddr4 = cUpperAddr4;
    else if (cAddr4 < cLowerAddr4)
```

```
        cAddr4 = cLowerAddr4;

    m_ctlIPAddress.SetAddress (cAddr1, cAddr2,
                               cAddr3, cAddr4);
}
```

If you've stayed with us through the entire controls section, you deserve a pat on the back—or a kick in the *derriere*. If you've learned anything, it should be that you should experiment with the controls. Derive your own classes from the MFC classes, or create your own from scratch. You can't break any of the controls, so you have nothing to lose and plenty to gain.

Never blindly assume the MSDN documentation is correct. It usually is, but at times we've found it to be misleading and conspicuously missing some important information that is needed to make a control work.

942. Understanding Programs and Processes

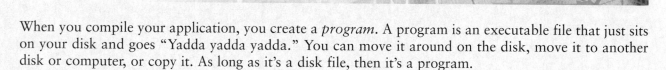

When you compile your application, you create a *program*. A program is an executable file that just sits on your disk and goes "Yadda yadda yadda." You can move it around on the disk, move it to another disk or computer, or copy it. As long as it's a disk file, then it's a program.

When you load the program into memory and run it, it takes on some magical qualities. It can read, create, and store data. It can interact with a user by displaying data in different forms. It uses system resources and has its own address space. It can crash. It's now called a *process*.

A program becomes a process when you load it into memory and give it a *point of execution*. The Visual Studio compiler reads your source code and converts it to a sequence of numbers. The sequence of numbers is instructions to your computer's central processing unit (CPU). The point of execution is the number in the address contained in the CPU's *instruction pointer* register.

This execution point also is called a *thread*. A thread is the basic execution unit to which the Windows operating system will assign CPU time. The thread has access to the process's virtual address space, including code, data, and stack segments of its memory space. The virtual address space doesn't have to be in memory alone. Part or all of it can be on disk or another storage medium.

DOS and 16-bit Windows are *single-threaded* and *single-tasking* operating systems. When a program is running under DOS (actually, 16-bit Windows is nothing more than an application running under DOS), no other process can execute. DOS contains only one execution point. The 16-bit versions of Windows provided what appeared to be multi-tasking by sharing its CPU time with Windows applications; the operating system had no part in this time-sharing.

Under a multi-tasking operating system, more than one program can be loaded into memory and executed at the same time. The operating system assigns a process CPU time during which it executes instructions. The operating system then yanks the CPU away from the process and gives the next process a chance to execute. The operating system takes care of swapping the CPU registers for the various processes. It does so quickly enough that the processes appear to run simultaneously.

In a multi-threaded operating system, a single process may contain more than one execution point, but in effect it is another process operating in the same address space as the first, or primary, thread. You'll learn more about threads in Tip 945, "Understanding Threads."

943. *Understanding* exec *and* spawn

A process can create another process by loading it into memory and starting its execution through two mechanisms that are built into the C and C++ standard runtime code. It can *exec* another process, in which case it replaces itself with the new process. It can also *spawn* a new process, in which case both it and the new process are active in memory and both are running.

The *exec* and *spawn* mechanisms come in several different flavors indicated by appending one to three letters to the function name as shown in Table 943a. These different functions allow you to pass different sets of parameters to the new process, including defining some environment variables that will be available only to the new process.

Suffix	Parameter List
l	A fixed number of command-line arguments is passed to the new process.
e	An array of pointers to environment strings is passed to the new process.
p	This specifies the operating system using the PATH environment variable to find the program file.
v	An array of pointers-to-command-line-arguments is passed to the new process along with a count of the arguments (the familiar *argc* and *argv* you see so often in C and C++ programming).

Table 943a   *Suffixes used with* exec *and* spawn *displaying the parameters used*

In Visual C++, the names of the functions are all prefixed with an underscore, which means they are not portable without some modification. A function name may include more than one letter from the list. For example, *_execvpe* and *_spawnvpe* include all the options from e, p, and v. The l and v suffixes are mutually exclusive. A function name won't include both l and v.

The *spawn* functions also require a mode indicating how the operating system is to deal with the parent process. Mode flag definitions are listed in Table 943b. Note the leading underscore, which is used only with Visual C++. Other development environments and compilers on other platforms usually use these definitions without the leading underscore. So if you need to port your code, removing the underscore is another useless step created by Microsoft.

spawn *Mode*	Meaning
_P_WAIT	The parent process is suspended until the child process completes execution.
_P_NOWAIT	Continues to run the parent process while the child process runs. The function returns the child process ID, so the parent can wait for completion using *cwait* or *wait*.
_P_NOWAITO	Identical to *P_NOWAIT* except that the child process ID isn't saved by the operating system, so the parent process can't wait for it using *cwait* or *wait*.
_P_DETACH	Identical to *P_NOWAITO*, except that the child process is executed in the background with no access to the keyboard or the display. No process ID is returned.
_P_OVERLAY	Overlays child process in memory location formerly occupied by parent. Same as an *exec* call.

Table 943b   *Mode flags used in calls to* spawn *functions*

If you're writing portable code, you should use these functions. The Windows API, however, provides another means of starting a new process that is neither portable nor as functional as the C/C++ library functions. The *CreateProcess()* function returns Windows-specific information to the creating process. In a UNIX environment, for example, a process may create a number of child processes, each performing specific tasks. Terminating the parent process also terminates the child processes without any further action from the parent process. The *CreateProcess()*, on the other hand, only creates detached processes. Your program must maintain information about any child processes and your program must specifically terminate them before it exits or they will remain active.

The UNIX method of creating and controlling processes and process-ownership is simple, elegant, easy-to-use, and works very well. It has been duplicated on other operating systems with equal success. The Windows-specific functions are inconsistent and behave differently on various versions of the operating system. You should stick with the standard function calls where possible; there's no sense building non-portability into your programs unless you have to.

To demonstrate the differences between *exec()*, *spawn()*, and *CreateProcess()*, create a dialog-based application in the Visual Studio called *NewProc*. The dialog box will have three buttons, one for each method of starting a new process as shown in Figure 943.

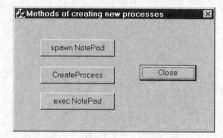

Figure 943   The NewProc *dialog box has buttons to launch NotePad.exe*

The first two buttons will start a copy of NotePad.exe after first checking whether it already has started a copy and whether that process is still running. The third button will simply ask whether you want to continue; answering "Yes" will terminate the application and start NotePad.exe.

The application is fairly simple, and the header and source codes for the dialog box class *CNewProcDlg* are listed below.

```
/////////////////////////////////////////////////////////////
// CNewProcDlg dialog
class CNewProcDlg : public Cdialog
{
// Construction
public:
    PROCESS_INFORMATION m_pi;
    CNewProcDlg(CWnd* pParent = NULL);
  // standard constructor
// Dialog Data
    //{{AFX_DATA(CNewProcDlg)
    enum { IDD = IDD_NEWPROC_DIALOG };
        // NOTE: the ClassWizard will add data members here
    //}}AFX_DATA

    // ClassWizard generated virtual function overrides
    //{{AFX_VIRTUAL(CNewProcDlg)
    protected:
    virtual void DoDataExchange(CDataExchange* pDX);
    // DDX/DDV support
```

```
    //}}AFX_VIRTUAL

// Implementation
protected:
    HICON m_hIcon;

    // Generated message map functions
    //{{AFX_MSG(CNewProcDlg)
    virtual BOOL OnInitDialog();
    afx_msg void OnPaint();
    afx_msg HCURSOR OnQueryDragIcon();
    afx_msg void OnCreateprocess();
    afx_msg void OnExecnotepad();
    afx_msg void OnSpawnnotepad();
    //}}AFX_MSG
    DECLARE_MESSAGE_MAP()
};

// NewProcDlg.cpp : implementation file
//

#include "stdafx.h"
#include "NewProc.h"
#include "NewProcDlg.h"
#include    <process.h>

#ifdef _DEBUG
#define new DEBUG_NEW
#undef THIS_FILE
static char THIS_FILE[] = __FILE__;
#endif

/////////////////////////////////////////////////////////////
// CNewProcDlg dialog

CNewProcDlg::CNewProcDlg(CWnd* pParent /*=NULL*/)
    : CDialog(CNewProcDlg::IDD, pParent)
{
    //{{AFX_DATA_INIT(CNewProcDlg)
        // NOTE: the ClassWizard will add member
        // initialization here
    //}}AFX_DATA_INIT
    // Note that LoadIcon does not require a subsequent
    // DestroyIcon in Win32
    m_hIcon = AfxGetApp()->LoadIcon(IDR_MAINFRAME);
    memset (&m_pi, '\0', sizeof (PROCESS_INFORMATION));
}

void CNewProcDlg::DoDataExchange(CDataExchange* pDX)
{
    CDialog::DoDataExchange(pDX);
    //{{AFX_DATA_MAP(CNewProcDlg)
    // NOTE: the ClassWizard will add DDX and DDV calls here
    //}}AFX_DATA_MAP
}
```

```
BEGIN_MESSAGE_MAP(CNewProcDlg, CDialog)
    //{{AFX_MSG_MAP(CNewProcDlg)
    ON_WM_SYSCOMMAND()
    ON_WM_PAINT()
    ON_WM_QUERYDRAGICON()
    ON_BN_CLICKED(IDC_CREATEPROCESS, OnCreateprocess)
    ON_BN_CLICKED(IDC_EXECNOTEPAD, OnExecnotepad)
    ON_BN_CLICKED(IDC_SPAWNNOTEPAD, OnSpawnnotepad)
    //}}AFX_MSG_MAP
END_MESSAGE_MAP()

/////////////////////////////////////////////////////////
// CNewProcDlg message handlers

BOOL CNewProcDlg::OnInitDialog()
{
    CDialog::OnInitDialog();

    // Set the icon for this dialog.
    //  The framework does this automatically
    //  when the application's main window is not a dialog
    SetIcon(m_hIcon, TRUE);          // Set big icon
    SetIcon(m_hIcon, FALSE);         // Set small icon

    // TODO: Add extra initialization here

    return TRUE;
}

void CNewProcDlg::OnPaint()
{
    if (IsIconic())
    {
        CPaintDC dc(this); // device context for painting

        SendMessage(WM_ICONERASEBKGND,
                    (WPARAM) dc.GetSafeHdc(), 0);

        // Center icon in client rectangle
        int cxIcon = GetSystemMetrics(SM_CXICON);
        int cyIcon = GetSystemMetrics(SM_CYICON);
        CRect rect;
        GetClientRect(&rect);
        int x = (rect.Width() - cxIcon + 1) / 2;
        int y = (rect.Height() - cyIcon + 1) / 2;

        // Draw the icon
        dc.DrawIcon(x, y, m_hIcon);
    }
    else
    {
        CDialog::OnPaint();
    }
}

// The system calls this to obtain the cursor to display
```

```
// while the user drags the minimized window.
HCURSOR CNewProcDlg::OnQueryDragIcon()
{
    return (HCURSOR) m_hIcon;
}


void CNewProcDlg::OnCreateprocess()
{
STARTUPINFO          si;

    if (m_pi.dwProcessId)
    {
        DWORD dwCode;
        GetExitCodeProcess ((HANDLE) pi.hProcess, &dwCode);
        if (dwCode == STILL_ACTIVE)
        {
            AfxMessageBox ("Another copy of NotePad.exe "
                          " was started by CreateProcess\n"
                          "It will be stopped first.");
            TerminateProcess (m_pi.hProcess, 0);
        }
    }
    memset ((char *) &si, '\0', sizeof (STARTUPINFO));
    si.cb = sizeof (STARTUPINFO);
    TCHAR szDir[_MAX_PATH];
    GetWindowsDirectory (szDir, _MAX_PATH);
    CString strProgPath, strProgParms;
    strProgPath.Format ("%s\\NotePad.exe", szDir);
    GetCurrentDirectory (_MAX_PATH, szDir);
    strProgParms.Format ("notepad %s\\readme.txt", szDir);
    if (!CreateProcess((LPCTSTR) strProgPath,
                (char *)(LPCSTR) strProgParms,
                (LPSECURITY_ATTRIBUTES) NULL,
                (LPSECURITY_ATTRIBUTES) NULL,
                false,
                DETACHED_PROCESS,
                (LPVOID) NULL,
                szDir,
                (LPSTARTUPINFO) &si,
                (LPPROCESS_INFORMATION) &m_pi))
    {
        AfxMessageBox ("CreateProcess failed", MB_ICONSTOP);
    }
}


void CNewProcDlg::OnExecnotepad()
{
    if (AfxMessageBox("This will terminate your "
                     "Application. Do you want to "
                     "continue?", MB_YESNO) == IDNO)
        return;
    if (_execlp ("NotePad", "NotePad.Exe",
                "readme.txt", NULL) < 0)
    {
        CString Message;
        Message.Format ("Error %d exec'ing process", errno);
```

```
        AfxMessageBox (Message);
    }
}

void CNewProcDlg::OnSpawnnotepad()
{
    static int nPID = 0;
    CString Message;
    if (nPID)
    {
        DWORD dwCode;
        GetExitCodeProcess ((HANDLE) nPID, &dwCode);
        if (dwCode == STILL_ACTIVE)
        {
            switch (AfxMessageBox ("Another copy of NotePad"
                                   "has been started by "
                                   "spawn and will be "
                                   "terminated. Do you want "
                                   "to continue?",
                                   MB_YESNO))
            {
                case IDNO:
                    return;
                case IDYES:
                    TerminateProcess ((HANDLE) nPID, 0);
                    break;
                default:
                    return;
            }
        }
    }
    nPID = _spawnlp (_P_NOWAIT, "NotePad",
                     "NotePad.Exe", "readme.txt", NULL);
    if (nPID < 0)
    {
        CString Message;
        Message.Format ("Error %d exec'ing process", errno);
        AfxMessageBox (Message);
        nPID = 0;
    }
}
```

The *spawn* functions appear to return the process ID of the newly created process, but not really. The return value is an *int* to make it compatible with the library specifications. A value of -1 indicates the call failed. If the return value is valid, however, the return value is not the process ID, but a handle to the process. You can use this handle to inquire about the status of the process or to stop it, but you first must cast the integer to a *HANDLE*. Don't do it when you're catching the return value because a handle is an unsigned quantity. The test for -1 will never be true. If you use a handle for the *spawn* return value, test for *INVALID_HANDLE_VALUE*, which is the equivalent of -1 as an unsigned quantity. Examples of both are shown in the code.

If you've programmed under the UNIX operating system, you've probably encountered the *fork* function as well. With *fork*, the process copies itself and both copies begin executing at the same point. This is the next instruction after the *fork* call. It is not implemented in Visual C++ because the operating system is multi-threaded and virtually the same result may be obtained by starting a new thread.

944. *Handling an Unsuccessful exec*

There is no return from a successful *exec()* call. The memory space for parent process is overlaid with that of the child process; the parent ceases to exist. A successful *exec()* call, however, doesn't mean a successful execution of the new process. The newly started process may encounter a program error and then crash and burn. The operation was a success but the patient died. The *exec()* call was successful and your parent application has gone away.

There's not a lot you can do about that situation. It is possible for a call to *exec()* to fail, however, and your program should be prepared to handle it. The program file for the new process might have been moved, or there might have been a file read error, or not enough memory to load it.

The *exec()* function returns a -1 if it fails. Your program should check for that and give the user a chance to recover, perhaps popping up a file open common dialog box to let the user find the proper file.

945. *Understanding Threads*

As you've seen, a thread is an execution point in a process. A single process might have more than one thread running at any given time. For all intents and purposes, additional threads are like additional processes, but they all share the same address space, the same data and code, and the same system resources. The difference is that the additional threads have their own execution points and receive their share of the CPU time to execute.

You were introduced to multiple threads in Tip 819, "Deriving a Custom Class from *CStatic* to Gain Functionality." You created a simple progress bar from a static text control then gave the progress bar its own thread. This allows the progress bar to redraw the position of the progress indicator even when your process was executing other code.

Each thread in a process has its own stack space that is separate from and inaccessible by other threads. This makes C and C++ ideal languages for multi-threaded applications. The parameters and variables local to a function are stored on the stack. This means that more than one thread may execute the same function code at the same time without interfering with each other. Indeed, more than one thread may execute the same *statement* at the same time.

Global and static data are shared between threads in the same process, however. Unless you absolutely need data with these storage classes, you should avoid using them in favor of automatic variables, even for a single-threaded application. This will keep the application open to adding additional threads in the future without considerable reworking of the code.

In Tip 819, the *CProgressBar* class used the *AfxBeginThread()* function in the constructor. This is the primary method of starting *worker* threads when using the Microsoft Foundation Class. There is an overloaded version for *user interface* threads, which you will see shortly.

The primary method of creating a thread in the Windows API is the *CreateThread()* function. This function takes six required parameters. The first parameter is a pointer to a *SECURITY_ATTRIBUTES* structure. Usually this can be *NULL*, and on Windows 95, it is ignored altogether. (Windows 95, 98, and ME don't use security attributes.) The second parameter is the stack size, which, when set to 0, will be the same size as the calling thread's stack.

The third parameter is the starting address of the new thread. This must be the address of a function that will be executed by the new thread and cannot be *NULL*. It's a callback function, so it must be defined as a global function, or declared *static* if it is a member of a class. You should remember that *static* functions in a class do not have access to *non-static* variables and functions. When the thread returns from this function, it terminates.

The fourth parameter is an application-defined parameter. You may pass any value in this parameter, including a pointer or *NULL*.

The next parameter is the creation flag. Only two values are supported in this parameter. If this parameter is 0, the thread starts executing immediately. If it is *CREATE_SUSPENDED*, the thread will not start running until the creating thread calls the *ResumeThread()* function.

The sixth and last parameter is a pointer to a 32-bit variable that will receive the new thread's ID. On Windows NT, this parameter may be *NULL*, but on Windows 95 and Windows 98, it must be a valid pointer.

If the function is successful, it will return the handle to the thread. It's a good idea to save this handle in a *static* or class member variable. You use it to suspend and resume threads, or to terminate a thread if necessary.

In addition, the C runtime library provides a *_beginthread()* function that is portable across multi-threaded operating systems. This function takes as parameters the address of a startup function, the stack size, and a pointer to an application-defined value. The constraints are the same as *CreateThread()*, and the application-defined value usually is a pointer to a string containing startup arguments. Threads started with this function must be terminated with the *_endthread()* function, but they will terminate automatically when the application exits.

If you haven't worked with multi-threaded applications, you should take the time to experiment with some test code. Multi-threading is one of the major benefits of 32-bit Windows, and you're passing up a good tool if you don't learn it. Obviously, not every application can benefit from multiple threads, but you'll find them surprisingly easy to work with. Often, additional threads will perk up an application's responsiveness.

Threads don't have to live for the lifetime of the application. If you have a particular operation that is time-consuming, try passing it off to a thread.

946. *Using MFC Thread Classes*

The primary thread in an application, based on the Microsoft Foundation Class, is contained in the *CWinApp* class object. Every document/view application and every dialog-based application created using the Visual Studio MFC AppWizard contains a class derived from *CwinApp*. An application can have only one instance of a *CWinApp*-derived class active at any time.

In addition, MFC provides the *CWinThread* class used to create class objects that will run their own threads. MFC defines two types of threads—user interface and worker—which you'll meet shortly. Threads that use a *CWinThread*-derived class object are user interface threads.

Any thread that uses MFC code must be created by MFC code so that MFC can safely manage the thread data and information. If you create a thread using the *_beginthread()* function, you can't execute MFC functions or access MFC class objects.

You don't, however, need to derive a *CWinThread* class for every thread you start. MFC provides another mechanism, the *AfxBeginThread()* function, that creates a *CWinThread* object for you, then called *CreateThread()*. There are two versions of this function, one for worker and another for user-interface threads. They are global functions that return a pointer to the *CWinApp* object, so you don't have to create a class object to use them.

947. *Understanding How Windows Schedules Threads*

Part of the Windows operating system—or any multi-tasking operating system for that matter—is a process scheduler, which determines which of the competing threads will get the next available slice of the central processor unit's time.

The Windows scheduler is *preemptive*, meaning it gets control of the processor every time a clock interrupt occurs. That happens just under two million times a second. Modern CPUs operate with clocks that run at hundreds of millions of cycles per second, so there are plenty of CPU clock cycles available between each clock interrupt.

When the scheduler gets control, it decrements the count of the time slice allotted for the currently executing thread. When that count gets to zero, it uses a set of priorities to determine which thread gets the next time slice. Threads have priorities, which you'll look at in the next tip, and the scheduler maintains a queue of threads in each priority level. When a thread finishes its time slice, it goes to the back of the queue.

When the scheduler decides what thread is to get the next time slice, it saves the context of the currently executing thread and loads the context of the next thread to execute, and the thread gets its time to run. Threads that are sleeping or blocked—such as waiting for keyboard input or an event to occur—are not considered for scheduling.

The scheduler's decision is based on three criteria: the process's priority class, the thread priority, and a dynamic priority boost the system may apply to the thread. The third criterion is based on system activity. If the window was waiting for input such as a key press or mouse move that suddenly occurs, the scheduler boosts the thread priority. After boosting priority, the scheduler bumps it down one notch for each time slice the thread receives until the priority is back to its original level. In addition, the scheduler gives the boosts to the priority of the window that has the foreground so that it is higher than the background processes.

Process priorities fall into four categories as summarized in Table 947. You can assign your process to one of the priority classes by calling *SetPriorityClass()*.

Priority Class	Meaning
IDLE_PRIORITY_CLASS	The process threads are given time only when the system is idle. They are preempted when a thread of a higher class requests time.
NORMAL_PRIORITY_CLASS	No special scheduling is needed.
HIGH_PRIORITY_CLASS	A process that performs time-critical operations.
REALTIME_PRIORITY_CLASS	The highest priority. A process in this class can preempt any other thread, including system threads.

Table 947 Process priority classes used by the Windows scheduler

Obviously, the *HIGH_PRIORITY_CLASS* should be used rarely, and then for very short intervals. A CPU-intensive process in this class easily can consume all available cycles. The *REALTIME_PRIORITY_CLASS* level should be used less often. Processes at this level can prevent flushing of disk caches or even stop mouse movements. When it is used, it should be only for the briefest of time.

948. *Understanding Thread Priorities*

Threads are not created equal. They don't all get even slices of the processor's time. That's not unreasonable because some tasks are more time-consuming than others and some events are more important than others.

You saw how the Windows scheduler ranks processes by their priority class. The scheduler's second criterion for allocating a time slice is based on the thread priority within that class. A process can set this priority by calling the *SetThreadPriority()* function.

A thread can have a priority ranging from a base of 1 for an idle thread to 15 for a time-critical thread. A thread in the *REALTIME_PRIORITY_CLASS* can have a priority from 16 for an idle thread to 31 for a time-critical thread.

In between is the *THREAD_PRIORITY_NORMAL* priority. The other priority definitions are relative to this normal priority. The thread priorities are summarized in Table 948.

Priority	Meaning
THREAD_PRIORITY_IDLE	Base priority of 1 except for the real-time priority class where it is a base of 16.
THREAD_PRIORITY_LOWEST	2 points below normal priority.
THREAD_PRIORITY_BELOW_NORMAL	1 point below normal priority
THREAD_PRIORITY_NORMAL	Normal priority for the class.
THREAD_PRIORITY_ABOVE_NORMAL	1 point above normal priority.
THREAD_PRIORITY_HIGHEST	2 points above normal priority.
THREAD_PRIORITY_TIME_CRITICAL	Priority of 15 except for the real-time priority class, where it is 31.

Table 948 Individual thread priority levels within a process class

The scheduler determines the overall priority by combining class priority with the thread's priority. The scheme means that processes that need more CPU time will get it, and those that are idle or working at a low priority level will get less time.

Compare this system to the old 16-bit system of timeshare. All processes, whether idle or trying to dodge bullets, got the same amount of time in a rotating cycle.

949. *Using Worker Threads*

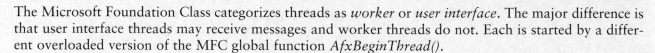

The Microsoft Foundation Class categorizes threads as *worker* or *user interface*. The major difference is that user interface threads may receive messages and worker threads do not. Each is started by a different overloaded version of the MFC global function *AfxBeginThread()*.

Worker threads require at least two parameters: the address of the controlling function as the first parameter and a pointer to an application-defined parameter as the second. Additional optional parameters, in order, are the thread priority (from Table 948), the stack size, creation flags (only 0 and

CREATE_SUSPENDED are permitted), and finally, a pointer to a security attributes structure, which is only used with Windows NT.

The controlling function for a worker thread must be prototyped as returning an *unsigned int* and taking a single parameter, a *void* pointer, as in the following line:

```
UINT ThreadFunction(void *pParam);
```

In addition, if it is a member function of a class, it must be declared *static*. If the function will need access to non-*static* class objects, pass a pointer to the class object as *pParam* (it's the *this* pointer), or pass the address of a structure that contains the class object's address as a member.

Typically, you would use a worker thread as a background thread that doesn't require user intervention. This might include a spreadsheet recalculation, printing operations, or spell checker.

950. *Using User Interface Threads*

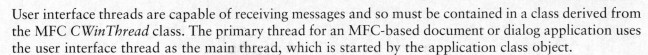

User interface threads are capable of receiving messages and so must be contained in a class derived from the MFC *CWinThread* class. The primary thread for an MFC-based document or dialog application uses the user interface thread as the main thread, which is started by the application class object.

Classes of this type must use the *DECLARE_DYNACREATE* macro in the class definition and the *IMPLEMENT_DYNACREATE* macro in the source code file. You also must provide a default constructor that takes no parameters.

The *AfxBeginThread()* overloaded function to start a user interface thread only requires a single parameter, and the runtime class of your *CWinThread* derived class. Four optional parameters are the same as the last four parameters for the worker thread version of *AfxBeginThread()*.

To start the thread, declare a pointer to an object of your thread class, then call the *AfxBeginThread()* function. Assuming your thread class is *CTestThread*, the following will start the thread:

```
CTestThread *pThread;
pThread = (CTestThread *)AfxBeginThread
                        (RUNTIME_CLASS(CTestThread));
```

You should save the pointer if you need to communicate with the thread or to stop it before your application ends. The thread will die normally when you exit the application, but you can terminate it sooner by sending it a *WM_QUIT* message. That's covered shortly.

Normally, in a *CWinThread*-derived class, you will override the *InitInstance()* member function to provide startup code for your thread. You also will want to override *ExitInstance()* to provide cleanup code. *Don't* call the base class *ExitInstance()* until you have executed your cleanup code; that function deletes the class object.

CWinThread-derived classes usually are message-driven objects, so to begin the thread you can call the base class *Run()* function. That starts the message pump. The *Run()* function is *virtual* and you can override it, but if you do you'll have to provide your own message pump (see the code in the *thrdcore.cpp* file in the MFC source directory) or eventually call the base class function.

You can process Standard Window messages as you would for any other object that receives messages. User messages, on the other hand, require special handling in a *CWndThread* object. Using the standard *ON_MESSAGE* handler won't work.

To use a *WM_USER* message, you'll have to implement the *ON_THREAD_MESSAGE* macro, using the message ID and a pointer to the handling function. For example, to receive the *WM_USER+20* message, you would add the following macro to the message map and the function to the thread class:

```
ON_THREAD_MESSAGE(WM_USER+20, OnUserMessage20)

void CTestThread::OnUserMessage20(WPARAM wParam,
                                  LPARAM lParam)
{
    // Handle the message in the body of the function
}
```

When you want to send this message to the thread, you would use the following syntax from someplace else in your code, replacing the *wParam* and *lParam* values with your own:

```
pThread->PostThreadMessage(WM_USER+20, wParam, lParam);
```

The ClassWizard won't be any help to you in creating the message handlers. You'll have to do it the old-fashioned way by tying it in yourself.

951. *Terminating and Suspending a Thread*

Some threads will last the lifetime of the process and will die naturally when the program terminates. Some threads, particularly worker threads, might be temporary and need to terminate at some point in the process's run.

A worker thread can terminate itself simply by returning from the controlling function, as you specified in the call to *AfxBeginThread()*. It can use either a *return()* statement with a return value, or it can call *AftEndThread()*, passing the exit code as a parameter. *AfxEndThread()* can be executed at any time by the thread that is terminating.

A user interface thread can exit by calling the Windows API function *::PostQuitMessage()* using the exit code as a parameter. This will place a *WM_QUIT* message in the thread's message queue.

You should follow one of these methods to allow a thread to terminate itself. This will stop thread execution, detach any DLLs that were attached to the thread, deallocate the stack, and remove the thread object from memory.

If you are using a thread created by one of the MFC methods, terminating the thread will determine how you started the thread. If you used the *CreateThread()* Windows API function, you should call the *EndThread()* API function to stop the thread, specifying the exit code as a parameter. You then can use *GetExitCodeThread()* to retrieve the exit code if necessary. *ExitThread()* must be called by the thread that is terminating.

You should remember that *ExitThread()* does not close the thread handle, and your program should call *CloseHandle()* after the thread exits to close the handle. If this function returns *STILL_ACTIVE* (a value of 259, or 0x103), the thread is still running.

If you started the thread with the runtime library function *_beginthread()*, the thread should call the *_endthread()*. You *can* terminate the thread by calling *ExitThread()*, but you'll find some small memory leaks as the result of improper cleanup. This function will close the thread handle and you should not subsequently call *CloseHandle()* if the thread exited through this function.

952. *Terminating a Thread from Another Thread*

Threads have internal methods for doing themselves in, but suppose the occasion arises where you need to stop a thread prematurely from code outside the thread? There is no "AfxKillThread()" function that you can call from outside the thread to stop it.

Posting a quit message to a user interface thread's message queue will signal it to stop, but that's only one of several possible thread types you may have. For other threads, you have to set up some sort of communication between them.

You can signal a user interface thread to terminate by calling the *PostThreadMessage()* function and passing it a *WM_QUIT* message. Use either the library *PostThreadMessage()* function or the one in the *CWinThread* class with the following syntax:

```
    ::PostThreadMessage(pThread->m_nThreadID, WM_QUIT,
                    nExitCode, 0);
or
    pThread->PostThreadMessage(WM_QUIT, nExitCode, 0);
```

The *nExitCode* parameter is the value you will retrieve when you call the *GetExitCodeThread()* function.

Worker threads, and those started by the standard functions, require different handling. They don't have message queues so you can't simply send them a *WM_QUIT* message.

One way is to set up a Boolean variable and have the thread check it between jobs. If it's *false*, the thread continues to run. If it's *true*, have the thread call the *AfxEndThread()*, *_endthread()*, or *ExitThread()* function, depending upon how you started the thread.

A more elegant method is to create an event or a semaphore, then have the thread check it from time to time. Those objects will be covered shortly.

953. *Getting a Thread's Return Code*

A thread is an execution point in a process, so it has an exit code like the main thread. The difference between the main thread and any other thread is that you retrieve the main thread's exit code from *outside* the process. It's the value returned by the *WinMain()* or *man()* function. You get the exit codes for other threads from within your program.

For a user interface thread, the return value is the one delivered through the *PostQuitMessage()* or the *PostThreadMessage()* functions, regardless of whether you sent the message from within the thread.

For worker threads, the return value is passed as the only parameter to the *AfxEndThread()* function. Threads created using the Windows API function *CreateThread()* deliver their return codes through the *ExitThread()* function. Threads created by the *_beginthread()* library function and terminated with the *_endthread()* function don't have return codes.

You retrieve this code by calling the *GetExitCodeThread()*, which is very similar in operation to the *GetExitCodeProcess()* function that you used in the *spawn* example in Tip 943, "Understanding *exec* and *spawn*." The function takes as parameters a handle to the thread and a pointer to a *DWORD* variable to hold the exit code. You should call this function before you call *CloseHandle()* for the thread object.

With user interface threads, the *CWinThread* class takes care of cleaning up after the thread, and this usually includes calling *CloseHandle()* and destroying the thread object. This can be a problem if you want to retrieve the exit code for the thread.

The *CWinThread* class contains a public variable, *m_bAutoDelete*, which controls whether the object is deleted automatically. By default, this variable is set to *TRUE*, indicating that the object will delete itself. If you need to retrieve the exit code for a *CWinThread* object, set this variable to *FALSE*.

This means that you will be responsible for destroying the thread object. That's not a real problem if you saved the pointer to the thread object. Simply enter the statement *delete pThread;*. You don't have to close the handle; that's taken care of by the *CWinThread* destructor.

954. *Suspending and Resuming a Thread*

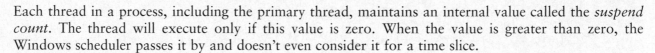

Each thread in a process, including the primary thread, maintains an internal value called the *suspend count*. The thread will execute only if this value is zero. When the value is greater than zero, the Windows scheduler passes it by and doesn't even consider it for a time slice.

You don't have direct access to this counter, but you may affect its value with two Windows API functions, *SuspendThread()*, and *ResumeThread()*. Each time you call *SuspendThread()*, the thread increments its suspend count by 1. Each time you call *ResumeThread()*, the thread decrements its suspend count by 1 until it reaches 0; it won't decrement any further if the count already is 0.

Be careful with the *SuspendThread()* function. Because the scheduler never gives the thread any CPU time, a thread that suspends itself has no way of resuming itself. You must call *ResumeThread* from outside the thread.

Some confusion occurs because there are two *SuspendThread()* functions when using MFC. There's the Windows API version, which takes a handle to the thread as its only parameter, and there's a *SuspendThread()* member in *CWnd*, which takes no parameters. The *CWnd* function suspends the current thread, so if you call it from a view, dialog, or even the application class, your caret is going to stop blinking, you won't be able to access the menus, and you can't exit the application gracefully. As a result, you should call the *CWnd* function *only* from the thread you want to suspend.

The *CWnd* function simply calls the API function, so it's safer to always make it practice to use the API function, avoiding the *CWnd* variation. It's no more of a problem; you only need to remember to pass the handle of the thread. (You did save the handle in a safe place, didn't you?) For a user interface thread, it's the *m_hThread* member of *CWinThread*. For other threads, it's the return value when you start the thread.

955. *Sharing Objects Between Threads*

All the threads in a given process run in the same process space. Except for the stack, the threads share the same data and code. Automatic variables local to a function are protected from tampering because other threads can't access the current thread's stack. Static and global variables have a different fate, however.

All the threads in a process can access global memory, and because there's only one copy of a *static* variable created, even in a function definition, all the threads must share it. This can produce some interesting problems, particularly with an optimizing compiler, such as that in Visual Studio. Optimization is turned off when you compile your debug code, so your release code may experience some problems you never encountered during the development stage.

An optimizing compiler may take the value of a variable several instruction cycles before it actually uses it. If it's a static variable, another thread may modify the variable between the time the variable's value is loaded into a CPU register and the time it's actually used.

It's best to avoid this situation by not allowing more than one thread to use a global or static variable. If you must give more than one thread access to such a variable and there is a possibility that more than one thread may access it at the same time, declare it *volatile*. This will keep the compiler from loading the variable's value ahead of its use, and it won't take the value until it actually is used.

956. Synchronizing Threads

It's not always possible to declare a variable *volatile*. Suppose you have an application where one thread reads a packet of data from a serial line or network connection. The connection is asynchronous, and the thread doesn't have time to process the data before the next packet arrives. So, you stuff it into a memory queue and create a second thread to pull it off the queue and process it.

Obviously, you can't have both threads adjusting the memory pointers in the queue at the same time. You need some way to *synchronize* the threads.

The first thing you can do is to create an *event* and have the second thread, the one that is reading from the queue, wait for the first thread to signal the event. The second thread won't use any processing time until the first thread signals the event, at which time the second thread will check the queue and remove everything on the queue and process it.

That action will synchronize the operation of the threads, but it won't solve the problem of both threads adjusting the queue at the same time. For that, you have to look into the synchronization objects available in Windows. These are the mutex, semaphores, and critical sections.

957. Understanding Mutexes and Semaphores

A *mutex* is a locking device that can be locked by only one object. Once it's locked and another object tries to unlock it, it will make the second object sleep until the first object unlocks it. It's like using a bathroom stall. One person comes in, enters the stall and locks it. Another person comes in, finds the stall locked and waits for it to become unlocked. When the first person unlocks the stall and exits, the second person enters and locks the stall. No one else can get in until the second person unlocks the stall.

OK, lousy metaphor, but you get the idea. Let's see how it works in C++. Create a dialog-based project called *Mutex*. You don't need an about box, but other than that, accept the defaults through the MFC AppWizard steps.

After you create the project, you'll need a random number function, so create a *utility.cpp* file and add the following two functions to it:

```
//
// utility.cpp. Some useful routines to make life easier
//
```

```
#include "stdafx.h"

void Randomize ()
{
time_t      t;
unsigned int    n;

/*

   Get the current time. That will be used to seed the
   random number function.
*/
   time (&t);

/*

  srand() requires an unsigned int, but time returns an
  unsigned long.

  Mask off any unused bits at the top in case there are
  any errors in typecasting (we want the lower part of
  the time because it should always be different, and
  sizeof (time_t) and sizeof (int) may not be the same on
  all systems).
*/
   n = (unsigned int) (t & ((long) ((unsigned int) -1)));

/*

   Now, use that value as the random number seed.
*/
   srand (n);
}

/*

   Return a random number in the range 0 to num-1. If 0 is
   passed, return it. If a negative number is passed,
   return the random number.
*/

int Random (int num)
{
   if (!num)
      return (0);
   if (num < 0)
      return (rand ());
   return (rand () % num);
}
```

Keep these functions around. I wrote them a long time ago in C and have used them on several platforms. They do a pretty good job of giving random numbers. The *Randomize()* function isn't dependent upon the size of an integer or the byte order in which it is stored.

In the *CMutexDlg* class you'll need to add *afxmt.h* to the list of included files in the class's header file. This header file defines the synchronization objects. The *MutexDlg.h* file is listed below.

```
////////////////////////////////////////////////////////////
// CMutexDlg dialog

#include    <afxmt.h>
```

```
struct QUEUEITEM
    {
    char    szText[80];
    QUEUEITEM  *pPrev;
    QUEUEITEM  *pNext;
    };

class CMutexDlg : public Cdialog
{
// Construction
public:
    static UINT StartProcessor (void *pParam);
    static UINT StartReceiver (void *pParam);
    void DeleteItemFromQueue (QUEUEITEM *pItem);
    void AddItemToQueue (QUEUEITEM *pItem);
    CMutexDlg(CWnd* pParent = NULL); // standard constructor

// Dialog Data
    //{{AFX_DATA(CMutexDlg)
    enum { IDD = IDD_MUTEX_DIALOG };
    CStatic m_strProcessor;
    CStatic m_strReceiver;
    //}}AFX_DATA
//  CStatic m_strReceiver;
//  CStatic m_strProcessor;

    // ClassWizard generated virtual function overrides
    //{{AFX_VIRTUAL(CMutexDlg)
    protected:
    virtual void DoDataExchange(CDataExchange* pDX);
    // DDX/DDV support
    //}}AFX_VIRTUAL

// Implementation
protected:
    HICON m_hIcon;

    CMutex  m_Mutex;

    // Generated message map functions
    //{{AFX_MSG(CMutexDlg)
    virtual BOOL OnInitDialog();
    afx_msg void OnPaint();
    afx_msg HCURSOR OnQueryDragIcon();
    //}}AFX_MSG
    DECLARE_MESSAGE_MAP()
};
```

For this text, we'll use a couple of worker threads. The mutex is what is of interest, and the code will work with whatever type of thread you use.

Assume the receiver thread gets a record from the serial line or network connect at random intervals of up to two seconds. It tucks these items into a linked list (for simplicity, the linked list won't be created, but you already know how to do that) then goes back to wait for another. The processor thread takes the item from the list and processes it. This processing takes up to 500 milliseconds. The random number function will use exact time, and the disparity should make the threads lose sync rapidly.

Each thread will write to a field on the dialog box informing you what it's doing. If it has the queue locked, you'll see it on the dialog box. To make it even more apparent, when a thread locks the queue, it'll draw a key next to the message line and erase it when it unlocks the queue. You should never see the key next to both message lines at the same time, although there may be brief periods when neither displays the key.

```cpp
// MutexDlg.cpp : implementation file
//

#include "stdafx.h"
#include "Mutex.h"
#include "MutexDlg.h"

#ifdef _DEBUG
#define new DEBUG_NEW
#undef THIS_FILE
static char THIS_FILE[] = __FILE__;
#endif

void Randomize ();
int Random (int num);

/////////////////////////////////////////////////////////////
// CMutexDlg dialog

CMutexDlg::CMutexDlg(CWnd* pParent /*=NULL*/)
    : CDialog(CMutexDlg::IDD, pParent)
{
    //{{AFX_DATA_INIT(CMutexDlg)
        // NOTE: the ClassWizard will add member
        // initialization here
    //}}AFX_DATA_INIT
    // Note that LoadIcon does not require a subsequent
    // DestroyIcon in Win32
    m_hIcon = AfxGetApp()->LoadIcon(IDR_MAINFRAME);
}

void CMutexDlg::DoDataExchange(CDataExchange* pDX)
{
    CDialog::DoDataExchange(pDX);
    //{{AFX_DATA_MAP(CMutexDlg)
    DDX_Control(pDX, IDC_MESSAGE_PROCESSOR, m_strProcessor);
    DDX_Control(pDX, IDC_MESSAGE_RECEIVER, m_strReceiver);
    //}}AFX_DATA_MAP
}

BEGIN_MESSAGE_MAP(CMutexDlg, CDialog)
    //{{AFX_MSG_MAP(CMutexDlg)
    ON_WM_PAINT()
    ON_WM_QUERYDRAGICON()
    //}}AFX_MSG_MAP
END_MESSAGE_MAP()


/////////////////////////////////////////////////////////////
// CMutexDlg message handlers
```

```
BOOL CMutexDlg::OnInitDialog()
{
    CDialog::OnInitDialog();

    // Set the icon for this dialog.  The framework does
    // this automatically when the application's main
    // window is not a dialog
SetIcon(m_hIcon, TRUE);          // Set big icon
    SetIcon(m_hIcon, FALSE);         // Set small icon

    Randomize ();
    m_bmpKey.LoadBitmap (IDB_MUTEXKEY);
    m_Images.Create (IDB_MUTEXKEY, 32, 2, ILC_MASK);

    m_strReceiver.GetWindowRect (m_rcReceiver);
    m_strProcessor.GetWindowRect (m_rcProcessor);
    ScreenToClient (m_rcReceiver);
    ScreenToClient (m_rcProcessor);
    m_rcReceiver.right = m_rcReceiver.left - 10;
    m_rcReceiver.left = m_rcReceiver.right - 32;
    m_rcProcessor.left = m_rcReceiver.left;
    m_rcProcessor.right = m_rcReceiver.right;
//
// For a dialog box, ScreenToClient includes the title
// bar, so adjust for it.
//
    m_rcProcessor.top += 16;
    m_rcProcessor.bottom += 16;
    m_rcReceiver.top += 16;
    m_rcReceiver.bottom += 16;

    AfxBeginThread (StartReceiver, this);
    AfxBeginThread (StartProcessor, this);

    return TRUE;
}

// If you add a minimize button to your dialog, you will
// need the code below to draw the icon.  For MFC
// applications using the document/view model, this is
// automatically done for you by the framework.

void CMutexDlg::OnPaint()
{
    if (IsIconic())
    {
        CPaintDC dc(this); // device context for painting

        SendMessage(WM_ICONERASEBKGND,
                    (WPARAM) dc.GetSafeHdc(), 0);

        // Center icon in client rectangle
        int cxIcon = GetSystemMetrics(SM_CXICON);
        int cyIcon = GetSystemMetrics(SM_CYICON);
        CRect rect;
        GetClientRect(&rect);
```

```cpp
            int x = (rect.Width() - cxIcon + 1) / 2;
            int y = (rect.Height() - cyIcon + 1) / 2;

            // Draw the icon
            dc.DrawIcon(x, y, m_hIcon);
        }
        else
        {
            CDialog::OnPaint();
        }
}


// The system calls this to obtain the cursor to display
// while the user drags the minimized window.
HCURSOR CMutexDlg::OnQueryDragIcon()
{
    return (HCURSOR) m_hIcon;
}


void CMutexDlg::AddItemToQueue(QUEUEITEM *pItem)
{
    m_strReceiver.SetWindowText ("Waiting for queue");
    m_Mutex.Lock ();
    DrawKey (m_rcReceiver, true);
    m_strReceiver.SetWindowText ("Queue is locked");
    Sleep (Random(1500));
    m_Mutex.Unlock ();
    DrawKey (m_rcReceiver, false);
    m_strReceiver.SetWindowText ("Queue is unlocked");
}


void CMutexDlg::DeleteItemFromQueue(QUEUEITEM *pItem)
{
    m_strProcessor.SetWindowText ("Waiting for queue");
    m_Mutex.Lock ();
    DrawKey (m_rcProcessor, true);
    m_strProcessor.SetWindowText ("Queue is locked");
    Sleep (Random(1500));
    m_Mutex.Unlock ();
    DrawKey (m_rcProcessor, false);
    m_strProcessor.SetWindowText ("Queue is unlocked");
}

UINT CMutexDlg::StartReceiver(void *pParam)
{
    CMutexDlg *pOwner = (CMutexDlg *) pParam;
    QUEUEITEM qi;
    while (1)
    {
        pOwner->m_strReceiver.SetWindowText
                                    ("Receiving item");
        Sleep (Random (1000));
        pOwner->AddItemToQueue (&qi);
    }
    return (0);
}
```

```
UINT CMutexDlg::StartProcessor(void *pParam)
{
    CMutexDlg *pOwner = (CMutexDlg *) pParam;
    QUEUEITEM qi;
    while (1)
    {
        pOwner->m_strProcessor.SetWindowText
                                    ("Processing item");
        Sleep (Random (500));
        pOwner->DeleteItemFromQueue (&qi);
    }
    return (0);
}

void CMutexDlg::DrawKey(CRect &rc, bool bDraw)
{

    CWindowDC dc(this);
    if (bDraw == false)
        m_Images.Draw (&dc, 1, CPoint (rc.left, rc.top),
                    ILC_MASK);
    else
        m_Images.Draw (&dc, 0, CPoint (rc.left, rc.top),
                    ILC_MASK);
}
```

If you have more than one exit point in the function that locks the mutex, you can create a lock object from *CSingleLock* that will lock the mutex. When it goes out of scope and is destroyed, it will unlock the mutex for you.

To show how this works, change the *AddItemToQueue()* and *DeleteItemFromQueue()* functions so they look like the following:

```
void CMutexDlg::AddItemToQueue(QUEUEITEM *pItem, int nID)
{
    m_strReceiver.SetWindowText ("Waiting for queue");
    CSingleLock AddQueue (&m_Mutex);
    AddQueue.Lock ();
    DrawKey (m_rcReceiver, true);
    m_strReceiver.SetWindowText ("Queue is locked");
    Sleep (Random(1500));
    DrawKey (m_rcReceiver, false);
    m_strReceiver.SetWindowText ("Queue is unlocked");
}

void CMutexDlg::DeleteItemFromQueue(QUEUEITEM *pItem,
                                    int nID)
{
    m_strProcessor.SetWindowText ("Waiting for queue");
    CSingleLock DeleteQueue (&m_Mutex);
    DeleteQueue.Lock ();
    DrawKey (m_rcProcessor, true);
    m_strProcessor.SetWindowText ("Queue is locked");
    Sleep (Random(1500));
    DrawKey (m_rcProcessor, false);
    m_strProcessor.SetWindowText ("Queue is unlocked");
}
```

When you use this method, you're virtually assured the mutex will be unlocked. If you should leave the mutex locked, the next call to it will block indefinitely (forever?).

You don't need to declare the mutex as the member of a class. You can create a named mutex any time you need it and lock it. There can be only one mutex with a given name, and if another function tries to create it, it will attach to the existing mutex and effectively lock out the second thread.

The code below is an example of a named mutex that is created as needed:

```
void CMutexDlg::AddItemToQueue(QUEUEITEM *pItem)
{
    m_strReceiver.SetWindowText ("Waiting for queue");
    CMutex mutex (FALSE, "QueueLock");
    mutex.Lock ();
    DrawKey (m_rcReceiver, true);
    m_strReceiver.SetWindowText ("Queue is locked");
    Sleep (Random(1500));
    DrawKey (m_rcReceiver, false);
    m_strReceiver.SetWindowText ("Queue is unlocked");
    mutex.Unlock ();
}

void CMutexDlg::DeleteItemFromQueue(QUEUEITEM *pItem)
{
    m_strProcessor.SetWindowText ("Waiting for queue");
    CMutex mutex (FALSE, "QueueLock");
    mutex.Lock ();
    DrawKey (m_rcProcessor, true);
    m_strProcessor.SetWindowText ("Queue is locked");
    Sleep (Random(1500));
    DrawKey (m_rcProcessor, false);
    m_strProcessor.SetWindowText ("Queue is unlocked");
    mutex.Unlock ();
}
```

The code on the companion CD has all three methods.

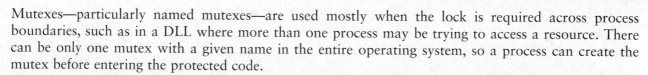

958. *Understanding Critical Sections*

Mutexes—particularly named mutexes—are used mostly when the lock is required across process boundaries, such as in a DLL where more than one process may be trying to access a resource. There can be only one mutex with a given name in the entire operating system, so a process can create the mutex before entering the protected code.

For resources that will be accessed solely by threads within a process, a better choice is the *CCriticalSection*. A critical section object is faster than a mutex, but not as flexible. You should create a separate global or class member variable for each resource you want to protect with a critical section, then use its *Lock()* and *Unlock()* member functions.

You can use the same sample that you used for the mutex to experiment with critical sections. First, add a *CCriticalSection* object to the class definition called *m_cs*. Modify the *AddItemToQueue()* and *DeleteItemFromQueue()* functions to look like the code below:

```
void CMutexDlg::AddItemToQueue(QUEUEITEM *pItem)
{
```

```
    m_strReceiver.SetWindowText ("Waiting for queue");
    m_cs.Lock ();
//  CSingleLock DeleteQueue (&m_cs);
//  DeleteQueue.Lock ();

    DrawKey (m_rcReceiver, true);
    m_strReceiver.SetWindowText ("Queue is locked");
    Sleep (Random(1500));
    DrawKey (m_rcReceiver, false);
    m_strReceiver.SetWindowText ("Queue is unlocked");
    m_cs.Unlock ();
}

void CMutexDlg::DeleteItemFromQueue(QUEUEITEM *pItem)
{
    m_strProcessor.SetWindowText ("Waiting for queue");
    m_cs.Lock ();

    DrawKey (m_rcProcessor, true);
    m_strProcessor.SetWindowText ("Queue is locked");
    Sleep (Random(1500));
    DrawKey (m_rcProcessor, false);
    m_strProcessor.SetWindowText ("Queue is unlocked");
    m_cs.Unlock ();
}
```

This is very similar to using a mutex, but inherently faster. If you need to protect a resource and speed is a factor, and you don't need to access the lock object across process boundaries (you can't create a named critical section object), then *CCriticalSection* is the choice.

You also can use a *CCriticalSection* object with a *CSingleLock* to provide automatic unlocking when you exit a function. The code above has the lines to do this commented out. Comment out the *m_cs.Lock()* and *m_cs.Unlock()* lines and remove the comment markers from the *CSingleLock* lines to test it.

The code on the sample CD implements both mutex and critical section objects.

959. *Understanding Events*

Have the thread that does the processing repeatedly check the queue to see if there's anything that is wasting CPU time. In a real situation, unless you're processing a lot of records continuously, the thread is going to find the queue empty most of the time. Wouldn't it be handy if we had some way to pause the processor thread until the receiver thread put something into the queue?

You could suspend the processing thread, then let the receiver thread resume it when a record arrives. The question then becomes one of when to suspend the processor thread and when to resume it. Examining this situation, it would be possible to have the processing thread suspended while a record is waiting in the queue.

The solution to this is to have the receiving thread set an *event* every time it receives a record. Even if the processing thread is busy when the new record arrives, when it returns to check, the event it will find it set. If no new record is available, the processing thread will simply wait for the receiving thread to set the event. In the meantime, it won't be consuming any processing time.

Both the Windows API and MFC provide event mechanisms. The MFC implementation is a wrapper for the API event functions, and neither is easier to use. We'll use the MFC *CEvent* class for this sample, then in Tip 994, "Creating a Named Event," when you look at using events across process boundaries, you'll use the API method. To use an event across process boundaries, you need to create a named event. You can't create a named event as a member of a class using *CEvent* because the constructor assumes default values, and uses *NULL* as the event name.

960. *Waiting for a Single Event*

Create a new project called *Events*. The code will be essentially the same as for the *Mutex* project, except instead of having the processor thread sleep for lengthy periods, it will wait for an event. Things will start off a bit slow at first to give you a chance to see how it works, but it will gradually speed up until the wait time (while the queue is locked in) is only 100 milliseconds. Depending upon the random sleep interval for the receiver thread, you may see the queue bump up to a dozen items or so, then, it will gradually work its way down.

The assumption is that it takes the processing thread much longer to process the record than it does for the receiving thread to receive it. The processing thread may have to collect information from other sources—an account database, a customer service database, etc.—then index the record into another database. These circumstances occur in real life, especially when you are transferring records from one system to another.

To simulate bursts of records, the receiver thread will sleep for a random number of seconds, then receive a random number of records and place them in the queue, setting the event for each record. The receiving thread will add records to the tail of the queue, and the processing thread will take them off the head of the queue in a first-in, first-out scheme.

The header file for the *CEventDlg* class is shown below:

```
/////////////////////////////////////////////////////////////
// CEventsDlg dialog

#include    <afxmt.h>

struct QUEUEITEM
    {
    char    szText[80];
    QUEUEITEM   *pPrev;
    QUEUEITEM   *pNext;
    };

class CEventsDlg : public Cdialog
{
// Construction
public:
    static UINT StartProcessor (void *pParam);
    static UINT StartReceiver (void *pParam);
    int DeleteItemFromQueue (QUEUEITEM *pItem);
    void AddItemToQueue (QUEUEITEM *pItem);
    CEventsDlg(CWnd* pParent = NULL);// standard constructor

// Dialog Data
```

```
    //{{AFX_DATA(CEventsDlg)
    enum { IDD = IDD_EVENTS_DIALOG };
        // NOTE: the ClassWizard will add data members here
    //}}AFX_DATA
    CStatic m_strProcessor;
    CStatic m_strReceiver;

    // ClassWizard generated virtual function overrides
    //{{AFX_VIRTUAL(CEventsDlg)
    protected:
    virtual void DoDataExchange(CDataExchange* pDX);
    // DDX/DDV support
    //}}AFX_VIRTUAL

// Implementation
protected:
    int m_nQueueCount;
    HICON m_hIcon;

    CRect m_rcProcessor;
    CRect m_rcReceiver;
    void DrawKey (CRect &rc, bool bDraw = false);

    CEvent  m_QueueEvent;

    CCriticalSection m_cs;
    CBitmap m_bmpKey;
    CImageList  m_Images;
    // Generated message map functions
    //{{AFX_MSG(CEventsDlg)
    virtual BOOL OnInitDialog();
    afx_msg void OnPaint();
    afx_msg HCURSOR OnQueryDragIcon();
    //}}AFX_MSG
    DECLARE_MESSAGE_MAP()
};
```

An event is a two-state object. It is either set or reset. When the receiver thread sets the event, the processor thread goes to work, looping through until the *DeleteItemFromQueue()* returns 0. If the receiver thread adds records to the queue interval between the time the processor thread empties the queue and gets back to wait for an event, it will find the event set and get right back to work. Otherwise, it'll wait for the event. The source code is shown below:

```
// EventsDlg.cpp : implementation file
//

#include "stdafx.h"
#include "Events.h"
#include "EventsDlg.h"

#ifdef _DEBUG
#define new DEBUG_NEW
#undef THIS_FILE
static char THIS_FILE[] = __FILE__;
#endif
```

```cpp
///////////////////////////////////////////////////////////
// CEventsDlg dialog

void Randomize ();
int Random (int num);

static int  g_nWaitTime = 1500;

CEventsDlg::CEventsDlg(CWnd* pParent /*=NULL*/)
    : CDialog(CEventsDlg::IDD, pParent)
{
    //{{AFX_DATA_INIT(CEventsDlg)
        // NOTE: the ClassWizard will add member
        // initialization here
    //}}AFX_DATA_INIT
    // Note that LoadIcon does not require a subsequent
    // DestroyIcon in Win32
    m_hIcon = AfxGetApp()->LoadIcon(IDR_MAINFRAME);
}

void CEventsDlg::DoDataExchange(CDataExchange* pDX)
{
    CDialog::DoDataExchange(pDX);
    //{{AFX_DATA_MAP(CEventsDlg)
    //}}AFX_DATA_MAP
    DDX_Control(pDX, IDC_MESSAGE_PROCESSOR, m_strProcessor);
    DDX_Control(pDX, IDC_MESSAGE_RECEIVER, m_strReceiver);
}

BEGIN_MESSAGE_MAP(CEventsDlg, CDialog)
    //{{AFX_MSG_MAP(CEventsDlg)
    ON_WM_PAINT()
    ON_WM_QUERYDRAGICON()
    //}}AFX_MSG_MAP
END_MESSAGE_MAP()

///////////////////////////////////////////////////////////
// CEventsDlg message handlers

BOOL CEventsDlg::OnInitDialog()
{
    CDialog::OnInitDialog();

    // Set the icon for this dialog.  The framework does
    // this automatically when the application's main
    // window is not a dialog

    SetIcon(m_hIcon, TRUE);         // Set big icon
    SetIcon(m_hIcon, FALSE);        // Set small icon

    Randomize ();
    m_bmpKey.LoadBitmap (IDB_MUTEXKEY);
    m_Images.Create (IDB_MUTEXKEY, 32, 2, ILC_MASK);

    m_strReceiver.GetWindowRect (m_rcReceiver);
    m_strProcessor.GetWindowRect (m_rcProcessor);
```

```
      ScreenToClient (m_rcReceiver);
      ScreenToClient (m_rcProcessor);
    m_rcReceiver.right = m_rcReceiver.left - 10;
    m_rcReceiver.left = m_rcReceiver.right - 32;
    m_rcProcessor.left = m_rcReceiver.left;
    m_rcProcessor.right = m_rcReceiver.right;
//
//  For a dialog box, ScreenToClient includes the title
//  bar, so adjust for it.
//
    m_rcProcessor.top += 16;
    m_rcProcessor.bottom += 16;
    m_rcReceiver.top += 16;
    m_rcReceiver.bottom += 16;

    m_nQueueCount = 0;
    ::SetWindowText (
            GetDlgItem(IDC_STATIC_QUEUECOUNT)->m_hWnd, "0");
    AfxBeginThread (StartReceiver, this);
    AfxBeginThread (StartProcessor, this);

    return TRUE;
}


// If you add a minimize button to your dialog, you will
// need the code below to draw the icon.  For MFC
// applications using the document/view model,
//  this is automatically done for you by the framework.

void CEventsDlg::OnPaint()
{
    if (IsIconic())
    {
        CPaintDC dc(this); // device context for painting

        SendMessage(WM_ICONERASEBKGND,
                (WPARAM) dc.GetSafeHdc(), 0);

        // Center icon in client rectangle
        int cxIcon = GetSystemMetrics(SM_CXICON);
        int cyIcon = GetSystemMetrics(SM_CYICON);
        CRect rect;
        GetClientRect(&rect);
        int x = (rect.Width() - cxIcon + 1) / 2;
        int y = (rect.Height() - cyIcon + 1) / 2;

        // Draw the icon
        dc.DrawIcon(x, y, m_hIcon);
    }
    else
    {
        CDialog::OnPaint();
    }
}

// The system calls this to obtain the cursor to display
```

```cpp
// while the user drags the minimized window.
HCURSOR CEventsDlg::OnQueryDragIcon()
{
    return (HCURSOR) m_hIcon;
}


void CEventsDlg::AddItemToQueue(QUEUEITEM *pItem)
{
    m_strReceiver.SetWindowText ("Waiting for queue");
    CSingleLock QueueLock(&m_cs);
    QueueLock.Lock ();
    DrawKey (m_rcReceiver, true);
    m_strReceiver.SetWindowText ("Queue is locked");
    Sleep (Random(g_nWaitTime));
    DrawKey (m_rcReceiver, false);
    m_strReceiver.SetWindowText ("Queue is unlocked");
    ++m_nQueueCount;
    CString strText;
    strText.Format ("%d", m_nQueueCount);
    ::SetWindowText (
                GetDlgItem(IDC_STATIC_QUEUECOUNT)->m_hWnd,
                (LPCSTR) strText);
}


int CEventsDlg::DeleteItemFromQueue(QUEUEITEM *pItem)
{
    if (!m_nQueueCount)
        return (0);
    m_strProcessor.SetWindowText ("Waiting for queue");
    CSingleLock QueueLock(&m_cs);
    QueueLock.Lock ();
    DrawKey (m_rcProcessor, true);
    m_strProcessor.SetWindowText ("Queue is locked");
    Sleep (Random(g_nWaitTime));
    DrawKey (m_rcProcessor, false);
    m_strProcessor.SetWindowText ("Queue is unlocked");
    --m_nQueueCount;
    CString strText;
    strText.Format ("%d", m_nQueueCount);
    ::SetWindowText (
                GetDlgItem(IDC_STATIC_QUEUECOUNT)->m_hWnd,
                (LPCSTR) strText);
    int nCount = m_nQueueCount;
    return (nCount);
}

UINT CEventsDlg::StartReceiver(void *pParam)
{
    CEventsDlg *pOwner = (CEventsDlg *) pParam;
    QUEUEITEM qi;
    while (1)
    {
        if (g_nWaitTime > 100)
            g_nWaitTime -= 100;
        pOwner->m_strReceiver.SetWindowText
                                    ("Receiving item");
```

```
        int nWaitTime, nCount;
        nWaitTime = Random (7000)+ 3000;
           ;
        Sleep (nWaitTime);
        nCount = Random (7) + 1;
        while (nCount--)
        {
            pOwner->AddItemToQueue (&qi);
            pOwner->m_QueueEvent.SetEvent ();
        }
    }
    return (0);
}

UINT CEventsDlg::StartProcessor(void *pParam)
{
    CEventsDlg *pOwner = (CEventsDlg *) pParam;
    QUEUEITEM qi;
    while (1)
    {
        DWORD dwEvent = WaitForSingleObject
                        (pOwner->m_QueueEvent, INFINITE);
        switch (dwEvent)
        {
            case WAIT_OBJECT_0:
                pOwner->m_strProcessor.SetWindowText
                            ("Processing item");
                while (pOwner->DeleteItemFromQueue (&qi))
                    Sleep (1000);
                continue;
            case WAIT_TIMEOUT:
                continue;
            default:
                return (-1);
        }
    }
    return (0);
}

void CEventsDlg::DrawKey(CRect &rc, bool bDraw)
{

    CWindowDC dc(this);
    if (bDraw == false)
        m_Images.Draw (&dc, 1, CPoint (rc.left, rc.top),
                    ILC_MASK);
    else
        m_Images.Draw (&dc, 0, CPoint (rc.left, rc.top),
                    ILC_MASK);
}
```

Notice that the queue counter is within the critical sections of code. One thread can't increment it while the other is in the process of decrementing it.

The *WaitForSingleObject()* function takes, as arguments, a handle to the event to wait for and an integer value specifying the number of milliseconds to wait. The value *INFINITE* means no timeout, and the thread will wait until the event is set or the event is destroyed when the class object goes out of scope (in this case, when the program ends).

When a successful wait returns, the value for *WaitForSingleObject()* should be *WAIT_OBJECT_0*. If you specified a wait time and the event timed out, the return value will be *WAIT_TIMEOUT*. If you want your thread to wake up and smell the roses periodically, you can put a value *in milliseconds* in this argument. Any other value is an error, and the thread exits with a return code of -1.

961. *Waiting for Multiple Events*

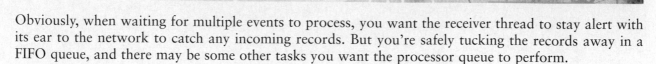

Obviously, when waiting for multiple events to process, you want the receiver thread to stay alert with its ear to the network to catch any incoming records. But you're safely tucking the records away in a FIFO queue, and there may be some other tasks you want the processor queue to perform.

You can wait for multiple events by calling the *WaitForMultipleObjects()* function rather than the *WaitForSingleObject()* function. The parameters for this function are a bit different. The first is a pointer to an array of event handles; the second is the number of events in that array. The third parameter is a Boolean flag that we'll explain in the next paragraph. Finally, the fourth parameter is the timeout value.

The flag specifies how you want to wait for the event. If you enter *TRUE*, the *wait* won't return until all of the events in the array have been set. This might be useful if you're waiting for more than one thread to complete tasks asynchronously. The return value is the last event to be set. If you set it to *TRUE*, the *wait* will return when only one event is set, and the return value is the event that caused the return.

Events are counted upward from *WAIT_EVENT_0* (the second event is *WAIT_EVENT_0 + 1*, the third is *WAIT_EVENT_0 + 2*, and so forth). *WAIT_TIMEOUT* is returned when the interval you specified has been reached. The interval is reset each time you call the function.

Let's give the processor thread something extra to do. Add a second event to the *CEventsDlg* class called *m_DrawEvent*, then add a *SetTimer()* call in *OnInitDialog()* to go off every ten seconds. The handler function will do no more than set the *m_DrawEvent*. Change the call in its control function to *WaitForMultipleObjects()* as shown in the code below:

```
// EventsDlg.cpp : implementation file
//

#include "stdafx.h"
#include "Events.h"
#include "EventsDlg.h"

#ifdef _DEBUG
#define new DEBUG_NEW
#undef THIS_FILE
static char THIS_FILE[] = __FILE__;
#endif


/////////////////////////////////////////////////////////////
// CEventsDlg dialog

void Randomize ();
int Random (int num);
```

```
static int  g_nWaitTime = 1500;

CEventsDlg::CEventsDlg(CWnd* pParent /*=NULL*/)
    : CDialog(CEventsDlg::IDD, pParent)
{
    //{{AFX_DATA_INIT(CEventsDlg)
        // NOTE: the ClassWizard will add member
        // initialization here
    //}}AFX_DATA_INIT
    // Note that LoadIcon does not require a subsequent
    // DestroyIcon in Win32
    m_hIcon = AfxGetApp()->LoadIcon(IDR_MAINFRAME);
}

void CEventsDlg::DoDataExchange(CDataExchange* pDX)
{
    CDialog::DoDataExchange(pDX);
    //{{AFX_DATA_MAP(CEventsDlg)
    //}}AFX_DATA_MAP
    DDX_Control(pDX, IDC_MESSAGE_PROCESSOR, m_strProcessor);
    DDX_Control(pDX, IDC_MESSAGE_RECEIVER, m_strReceiver);
}

BEGIN_MESSAGE_MAP(CEventsDlg, CDialog)
    //{{AFX_MSG_MAP(CEventsDlg)
    ON_WM_PAINT()
    ON_WM_QUERYDRAGICON()
    ON_WM_TIMER()
    //}}AFX_MSG_MAP
END_MESSAGE_MAP()

/////////////////////////////////////////////////////////
// CEventsDlg message handlers

BOOL CEventsDlg::OnInitDialog()
{
    CDialog::OnInitDialog();

    // Set the icon for this dialog.  The framework does
    // this automatically when the application's main
    // window is not a dialog

    SetIcon(m_hIcon, TRUE);         // Set big icon
    SetIcon(m_hIcon, FALSE);        // Set small icon

    Randomize ();
    m_bmpKey.LoadBitmap (IDB_MUTEXKEY);
    m_Images.Create (IDB_MUTEXKEY, 32, 2, ILC_MASK);

    m_strReceiver.GetWindowRect (m_rcReceiver);
    m_strProcessor.GetWindowRect (m_rcProcessor);
    ScreenToClient (m_rcReceiver);
    ScreenToClient (m_rcProcessor);
    m_rcReceiver.right = m_rcReceiver.left - 10;
    m_rcReceiver.left = m_rcReceiver.right - 32;
    m_rcProcessor.left = m_rcReceiver.left;
```

```
        m_rcProcessor.right = m_rcReceiver.right;
//
//  For a dialog box, ScreenToClient includes the title
//  bar, so adjust for it.
//
    m_rcProcessor.top += 16;
    m_rcProcessor.bottom += 16;
    m_rcReceiver.top += 16;
    m_rcReceiver.bottom += 16;

    m_nQueueCount = 0;
    ::SetWindowText (
            GetDlgItem(IDC_STATIC_QUEUECOUNT)->m_hWnd, "0");
    AfxBeginThread (StartReceiver, this);
    AfxBeginThread (StartProcessor, this);

    SetTimer (42, 10000, NULL);

    return TRUE;
}


// If you add a minimize button to your dialog, you will
// need the code below to draw the icon.  For MFC
// applications using the document/view model,
//  this is automatically done for you by the framework.

void CEventsDlg::OnPaint()
{
    if (IsIconic())
    {
        CPaintDC dc(this); // device context for painting

        SendMessage(WM_ICONERASEBKGND, (WPARAM)
                    dc.GetSafeHdc(), 0);

        // Center icon in client rectangle
        int cxIcon = GetSystemMetrics(SM_CXICON);
        int cyIcon = GetSystemMetrics(SM_CYICON);
        CRect rect;
        GetClientRect(&rect);
        int x = (rect.Width() - cxIcon + 1) / 2;
        int y = (rect.Height() - cyIcon + 1) / 2;

        // Draw the icon
        dc.DrawIcon(x, y, m_hIcon);
    }
    else
    {
        CDialog::OnPaint();
    }
}

// The system calls this to obtain the cursor to display
// while the user drags the minimized window.
HCURSOR CEventsDlg::OnQueryDragIcon()
{
```

```
    return (HCURSOR) m_hIcon;
}

void CEventsDlg::AddItemToQueue(QUEUEITEM *pItem)
{
    m_strReceiver.SetWindowText ("Waiting for queue");
    CSingleLock QueueLock(&m_cs);
    QueueLock.Lock ();
    DrawKey (m_rcReceiver, true);
    m_strReceiver.SetWindowText ("Queue is locked");
    Sleep (Random(g_nWaitTime));
    DrawKey (m_rcReceiver, false);
    m_strReceiver.SetWindowText ("Queue is unlocked");
    ++m_nQueueCount;
    CString strText;
    strText.Format ("%d", m_nQueueCount);
    ::SetWindowText (
                GetDlgItem(IDC_STATIC_QUEUECOUNT)->m_hWnd,
                (LPCSTR) strText);
}

int CEventsDlg::DeleteItemFromQueue(QUEUEITEM *pItem)
{
    if (!m_nQueueCount)
        return (0);
    m_strProcessor.SetWindowText ("Waiting for queue");
    CSingleLock QueueLock(&m_cs);
    QueueLock.Lock ();
    DrawKey (m_rcProcessor, true);
    m_strProcessor.SetWindowText ("Queue is locked");
    Sleep (Random(g_nWaitTime));
    DrawKey (m_rcProcessor, false);
    m_strProcessor.SetWindowText ("Queue is unlocked");
    --m_nQueueCount;
    CString strText;
    strText.Format ("%d", m_nQueueCount);
    ::SetWindowText (
                GetDlgItem(IDC_STATIC_QUEUECOUNT)->m_hWnd,
                (LPCSTR) strText);
    int nCount = m_nQueueCount;
    return (nCount);
}

UINT CEventsDlg::StartReceiver(void *pParam)
{
    CEventsDlg *pOwner = (CEventsDlg *) pParam;
    QUEUEITEM qi;
    while (1)
    {
        if (g_nWaitTime > 100)
            g_nWaitTime -= 100;
        pOwner->m_strReceiver.SetWindowText
                                    ("Receiving item");
        int nWaitTime, nCount;
        nWaitTime = Random (7000)+ 3000;
            ;
```

```
            Sleep (nWaitTime);
            nCount = Random (7) + 1;
            while (nCount--)
            {
                pOwner->AddItemToQueue (&qi);
                pOwner->m_QueueEvent.SetEvent ();
            }
        }
        return (0);
}

UINT CEventsDlg::StartProcessor(void *pParam)
{
        CEventsDlg *pOwner = (CEventsDlg *) pParam;
        QUEUEITEM qi;
        HANDLE  hEvents[2];
        hEvents[0] = pOwner->m_QueueEvent;
        hEvents[1] = pOwner->m_DrawEvent;
        while (1)
        {
            pOwner->m_strProcessor.SetWindowText ("Waiting");
            DWORD dwEvent = WaitForMultipleObjects (2, hEvents,
                                            FALSE, INFINITE);
            switch (dwEvent)
            {
                case WAIT_OBJECT_0:
                    pOwner->m_strProcessor.SetWindowText
                                            ("Processing item");
                    while (pOwner->DeleteItemFromQueue (&qi))
                    {
                        pOwner->m_strProcessor.SetWindowText
                                        ("Processing");
                        Sleep (1000);
                    }
                    continue;
                case WAIT_OBJECT_0 + 1:
                    pOwner->DrawThis (pOwner);
                    continue;
                case WAIT_TIMEOUT:
                    continue;
                default:
                    return (-1);
            }
        }
        return (0);
}

void CEventsDlg::DrawKey(CRect &rc, bool bDraw)
{

        CWindowDC dc(this);
        if (bDraw == false)
            m_Images.Draw (&dc, 1, CPoint (rc.left, rc.top),
                        ILC_MASK);
        else
            m_Images.Draw (&dc, 0, CPoint (rc.left, rc.top),
```

```
                    ILC_MASK);
}

void CEventsDlg::DrawThis(CEventsDlg *pPaPa)
{
    CRect rc, rcRx, rcPr;
    pPaPa->m_strReceiver.GetWindowRect (rcRx);
    pPaPa->m_strProcessor.GetWindowRect (rcPr);
    pPaPa->ScreenToClient (rcRx);
    pPaPa->ScreenToClient (rcPr);
    CBrush *brushOld;
    CBrush brushNew (GetSysColor (COLOR_ACTIVEBORDER));
    CWindowDC dc(pPaPa);
    pPaPa->GetWindowRect (rc);
    ScreenToClient (rc);
    rc.top += 50;
    rc.left = rcRx.right;
    CRect rcClear (rc);
    rcClear.top = rcRx.top;
    rcClear.left = rcRx.right + 8;
    rcClear.right -= 4;
    rcClear.bottom = rcPr.bottom + 32;
    dc.FillRect (rcClear, &brushNew);
    rc.left = rcRx.right + (rc.right - rcRx.right) / 2;
    rc.top = rcRx.bottom + (rcPr.top - rcRx.bottom) / 2
                        + 22;
    rc.bottom = rc.top;
    rc.right = rc.left;
    for (int i = 0; i < 50; ++i)
    {
        rc.InflateRect (2,2,2,2);
        dc.Ellipse (rc.left, rc.top, rc.right, rc.bottom);
        brushOld = (CBrush *) dc.SelectObject (brushNew);
        rc.InflateRect (-1,-1,-1,-1);
        dc.Ellipse (rc.left, rc.top, rc.right, rc.bottom);
        Sleep (50);
    }
}

void CEventsDlg::OnTimer(UINT nIDEvent)
{
    if (nIDEvent == 42)
        m_DrawEvent.SetEvent ();
    CDialog::OnTimer(nIDEvent);
}
```

When the processor thread sees the *m_DrawEvent*, it'll head off to do another task. We'll make it time-consuming and have it draw an expanding circle on the right side of the dialog box. This should take it just under three seconds. During this time, the receiver thread may add items to the queue, but the processor thread won't see them. When it returns from its night on the circle, it will find the *m_QueueEvent* set, and start processing the queue.

Similarly, while it's processing the queue items and the timer sets its event, the processor thread won't see the *m_DrawEvent* timer until it finishes with the queue. When it returns, it will head off to draw the circle. If more than one timer interrupts occur, the thread will see only one of them.

Note also—and with a word of caution—that the processor thread calls the *DrawThis()* function with a pointer to the dialog box class, and the rectangles and device context are all referenced to this pointer. The thread doesn't have access to the *this* pointer, even when it is in a member function of *this* because the control function is *static*. It's generally unsafe to call functions and access objects created by other threads. In this case, we're safe because the threads were started by the dialog class, but don't try to call other objects created by other threads. In a debug version, your program may assert, and in a release version it may simply crash.

962. *Using Multi-Threaded C Runtime Libraries*

Several C runtime library functions use static variables to store intermediate data. This can cause problems if more than one thread uses these functions. The *strtok()* function, for example, stores an intermediate pointer in a static variable that it uses on successive calls to return the next token.

Several of the time functions use static variables to store a *tm* structure or a string containing the time. The *localtime()*, *gmtime()*, and *mktime()* all use the same static *tm* structure, and *asctime()* uses a static string. Each of these is overwritten each time the function is called.

This can be a problem if more than one thread calls the same function. One or more calls are likely to produce the wrong information.

Visual C++ includes both single- and multi-threaded versions of the C runtime library and for the Microsoft Foundation Library. Usually the IDE will select the proper settings, but if you are switching over from a single-threaded application, you might want to check the settings to make sure the multi-threaded versions of the libraries are being used.

Select the Settings item from the Project menu in Visual Studio. First, check the General page to see if you are using MFC as a static library or a shared DLL, then select the C/C++ tab. In the Category box, select Code Generation. At the upper right there will be a combo box labeled "Use runtime library."

If you open the drop-down list box for this control, you'll find six settings, three for release builds and three for debug builds. The single-threaded item has an asterisk after it indicating it is the default setting. For your release builds (check the Settings For combo box at the upper left) you'll want to use the Multi-threaded setting for static library linking and the Multi-threaded DLL setting if you are using MFC as a shared DLL.

Similarly, for the debug builds you'll want to use Debug Multi-threaded for static linking and Debug Multi-threaded DLL for dynamic linking.

Static linking for the MFC library, by the way, is available only on the Professional and Enterprise editions of Visual Studio. If you have the Standard edition, you may see only four options in this combo box.

963. *Understanding the ASSERT Macro*

Before getting into exceptions, you should understand the difference between an exception and an assertion. We've talked about programs asserting, and briefly touched on its meaning earlier, but we've never discussed it as a tool.

The *ASSERT* macro is one of a pair of MFC macros that can help you debug your programs. The other is the *VERIFY* macro. Their difference is very subtle, but you should understand it.

ASSERT in a debug version of an MFC application will test a Boolean expression. If the result is *false*, it will *assert*, meaning it will stop the program and display a message. You can press the Retry button and the debugger will take you to the statement that caused the assertion. In the release version of the same program, the *ASSERT* macro does nothing. It will not evaluate the expression and it won't halt the program. For debugging, you can include *ASSERT* statements and not have to remove them for the release build.

The *VERIFY* macro performs much the same purpose, except in the release build, it will evaluate the expression but it won't halt the program. In the debug version, it behaves like the *ASSERT* macro.

Consider the following snippet:

```
int x = 1;
int y = 0;
ASSERT (y = x);
CString Message;
Message.Format ("Result is y = %d", y);
AfxMessageBox (Message);
```

In the debug version of the code, the message box will inform you that *y* is equal to 1. The expression was evaluated, the result was non-zero, so the program did not assert.

Now compile the same code for release and run it. The message box will inform you that the value of *y* is zero. Of course, the program didn't assert because the *ASSERT* macro doesn't do that in release code.

Now change the *ASSERT* macro in the above code to a *VERIFY* macro statement, then compile and run it for both debug and release versions. In both cases, the expression *was* evaluated and the value of *y* is 1.

You can use both of these macros in your debugging efforts. If the test is simply a check-point and you don't need the result of the expression, use *ASSERT*. If the expression must be evaluated as part of the program and you want to test for its value in debugging, use the *VERIFY* macro.

964. *Understanding Exceptions*

An *exception* is an interruption of the normal program flow resulting from an unexpected or abnormal event. Exceptions are a part of the C++ language specification and give the programmer an opportunity to handle these conditions rather than simply halting the program because of the error condition. If the programmer doesn't handle the exception, generally it will cause the program to terminate.

An *exception handler* allows you to provide an alternate block of code to handle the condition and allow your program to recover from it gracefully.

Exceptions may be generated—they are said to be *raised* or *thrown*—under three conditions:

- They may be thrown as the result of a hardware problem, such as an attempt to divide by zero or to access an invalid memory address.

- They may be generated when the software encounters a problem that keeps it from completing a task, such as a request to allocate an invalid block of memory or an invalid handle or pointer.

- Finally, the programmer may elect to throw an exception to signal an error condition as a means of aborting a block of code. For example, if a file that is needed for a block of code doesn't exist, the programmer may throw in an exception that will execute a block of code to create the file first.

You don't *have* to handle an exception. If you don't, you'll usually get an error message from the runtime code and your program will terminate. However, C++ provides a simple method for you to catch these conditions and adjust your program stream.

Exceptions are *caught* by executing a *guarded section* of code within a *try* block, then providing a *catch* block to handle them. As you will see, you can have multiple catch blocks to handle different types of exceptions that may be raised.

In addition, the Microsoft Foundation Class provides a set of exception macros and a collection of classes intended to make it even easier to handle exceptions.

965. *Throwing Exceptions*

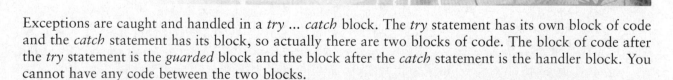

The C++ language provides a mechanism for raising an exception at any time by using the *throw* keyword. Several runtime library routines will execute *throw* statements when error conditions arise, but your program may use it to execute alternate blocks of code.

Let's say your program needs to retrieve some basic operating conditions from an initialization file that must be in a particular format. If this is the first time the program has been run, the file may not exist, or it might have been deleted by a user, or it simply may be corrupt and the operating system can't open it.

In Visual C++, an exception raised by the program code in a debug build won't necessarily cause the process to terminate. It will pause the process and display a warning about the exception, giving you the chance to examine the code to determine why it occurred. Thus, you can use the exception handling mechanism as a debugging tool.

In a release build, however, it will display a message about "Abnormal program termination" and end the program. Unless you catch the exception, the program won't continue beyond the point where the exception was thrown.

A *throw* statement doesn't have to return an argument, but as you will see in the next tip, each *catch* block must contain an argument. If you *throw* an exception without an argument, what happens will be determined by where you executed the *throw* statement.

966. *Understanding the* try ... catch *block*

Exceptions are caught and handled in a *try ... catch* block. The *try* statement has its own block of code and the *catch* statement has its block, so actually there are two blocks of code. The block of code after the *try* statement is the *guarded* block and the block after the *catch* statement is the handler block. You cannot have any code between the two blocks.

Each block must be a compound statement enclosed between curly braces ("{" and "}") even if there is only a single statement in the block.

The *try* and *catch* statements operate in pairs; you can't use one without the other. In other words, you can't have a *try* block and not have it followed immediately by a *catch* block. It wouldn't make much sense not to do it that way, and the C++ language doesn't allow it.

You may, however, have multiple *catch* blocks after a single *try* block. For example, you can have a *catch* block to handle a type *int* exception, another for a character pointer, and still another for a *long*.

Remember that variables follow the scope rules of C++ even within *try* and *catch* blocks. If you declare a variable within one block, it won't be available in other blocks, or in the normal program code outside the block. If you need to use a variable or object outside the blocks, or within other blocks of the *try ... catch* syntax, declare them with function scope and assign them values in the blocks.

967. *Understanding the* throw *Statement*

The syntax of a *throw* statement is the same as a return statement. Generally, it will cause the currently executing function to return abnormally. You're not limited, however, to using the function's return type as the object of a *throw* statement. You can return an object or value of any type, but your code must be ready to *catch* that type or the exception will be considered unhandled.

The simplest form of the *throw* statement is just that: *throw*. When executed within a *catch* block, it will rethrow the same type of exception. But when issued outside any *catch* block, the exception type is undefined and can't be caught. It *will* cause your program to terminate. It should be used only in the direst of circumstances where you absolutely need to force the program to end. Before using it, you should provide whatever shutdown code your program needs because no statements will be executed after the program encounters the statement.

Usually, however, you'll provide an argument with the *throw* statement, and the argument *type* will be used to catch the exception. The syntax of several possible *throw* examples is shown below. The parentheses are optional.

```
throw (-1);          //  may be caught by a catch statement
                     // using an integer argument
throw (-1L);         //  may be caught by a catch statement
                     // using a long argument
throw ("Error condition"); // May be caught by a catch
              // statement using a character pointer
              // argument
```

As pointed out, the *catch* statement must use the same variable type or the exception or it won't be caught. As you'll see in the next tip, it is possible to provide multiple *catch* blocks to handle different types of exceptions.

968. *Catching Exceptions*

A thrown exception is handled in a block of code using the *catch* keyword. The syntax of a *catch* statement is the same as a function statement except the argument list may not be empty. You must provide one, and only one, argument, and its type must be the same as that used by the *throw* statement.

Each section of guarded code within a *try* block must be followed immediately by at least one *catch* block. When a guarded block of code is executed and an exception is raised, program control transfers to the *catch* block, whose argument type matches that used by the *throw* statement.

The following snippet shows how to *throw* and *catch* an integer exception:

```
BOOL MyDlg::OnInitDialog()
{
    try
```

```
    {
        TestIntFunc ();
    }
    catch (int x)
    {
        AfxMessageBox ("Caught int exception");
        return (FALSE);
    }
    return (TRUE);
}
int CEventsDlg::TestIntFunc()
{
    throw (-1);
    return (0);
}
```

The call to *TestIntFunc()* is contained in a block of code guarded by the *try* statement. When the exception is thrown using an integer argument, control will pass to the *catch* statement. Immediately following, a message box will be displayed and the function will return *FALSE*. You don't have to return from a function in the *catch* block. You could handle or adjust for the error condition, then let the program flow naturally to the next statement.

You may provide multiple catch blocks to handle different error conditions. To do this, simply write the *catch* blocks one after another *with no intervening code* as though each were the only *catch* block. Tip 969, "Using Multiple *catch* Statements," shows an example of how to do this.

There are times when you may find yourself having to catch exceptions, but you may not know the data type at the time you write your code. A special case of the *catch* statement allows you to catch every exception regardless of the data type. This form is written using the ellipsis as the argument to the *catch* statement and is coded with the following syntax:

```
try
{
    // code for the guarded block.
}
catch (...)
{
    // General exception handling for unknown
    // data types.
}
```

You can use this generalized *catch* block in a sequence of catch blocks, but it should be the last block in the sequence. Only one exception handler will be used, and they are tried in the order in which they are written. If this block isn't the last, the *catch* blocks that follow will never be used.

Exception objects don't have to be one of the basic C++ data types. You may use your own derived data types, including pointers to classes and structures. In Tip 977, "Creating Your Own Exception Classes," you'll create a class to open a file that will be used in an exception handler to make sure a file is open before the code may proceed.

969. *Using Multiple catch Statements*

Suppose you execute three function calls within a guarded block. You could have code similar to the code that follows. This sample will use some global variables that will be initialized in the functions to show you the problem with using calls to more than one function that might throw an exception. The following program is a command-line program. Compile it with the command line shown at the top of the listing.

```cpp
#include    <windows.h>
#include    <stdio.h>
#include    <iostream.h>
//
// excep1.cpp. Test program for exception handling.
// compile this program with the following command line
//
//          cl -GX excep1.cpp user32.lib
//
// The -GX enables exception handling. The user32.lib
// provides the MessageBox function.
//
void TestFileFunc ();
void TestCharFunc ();
void TestIntFunc ();

int g_Var1 = 0;
int g_Var2 = 0;
int g_Var3 = 0;

main ()
{
    try
    {
        TestIntFunc ();
        TestCharFunc ();
        TestFileFunc ();
    }
    catch (char *ErrorMsg)
    {
        MessageBox (NULL, ErrorMsg, "Howdy", MB_OK);
    }
    catch (int x)
    {
        MessageBox (NULL, "Caught int exception",
                    "Howdy", MB_OK);
    }
    catch (long lx)
    {
        MessageBox (NULL, "Caught long exception",
                    "Howdy", MB_OK);
    }
    cout << "g_Var1 = " << g_Var1 << endl;
    cout << "g_Var2 = " << g_Var2 << endl;
    cout << "g_Var3 = " << g_Var3 << endl;
}

void TestIntFunc()
{
    throw (-1);
    g_Var1 = 10;
}
```

```
void TestCharFunc()
{
    throw ("Error condition");
    g_Var2 = 20;
}

void TestFileFunc()
{
    throw (-1L);
    g_Var3 = 30;
}
```

When you run this program, you should get the output shown below. Notice that all the global variables are still 0:

```
g_Var1 = 0
g_Var2 = 0
g_Var3 = 0
```

When the exception was thrown, control passed immediately to the handler block. The *g_Var1* initialization came after the *throw*, so it never was performed, and the second two functions in the *try* block never were called.

You can see there's some risk when you put too much code in a *try* block. Anything after the exception is passed over, and even if you catch and process the exception you still didn't complete the initialization. This code would better be written with multiple *try ... catch* blocks as shown below:

```
#include    <windows.h>
#include    <stdio.h>
#include    <iostream.h>
//
//  excep2.cpp. Test program for exception handling.
//  compile this program with the following command line
//
//          cl -GX excep2.cpp user32.lib
//
//  The -GX enables exception handling. The user32.lib
//  provides the MessageBox function.
//
void TestFileFunc ();
void TestCharFunc ();
void TestIntFunc ();

int g_Var1 = 0;
int g_Var2 = 0;
int g_Var3 = 0;

main ()
{
    try
    {
        TestCharFunc ();
    }
    catch (char *ErrorMsg)
    {
        MessageBox (NULL, ErrorMsg, "Howdy", MB_OK);
```

```
   }
   try
   {
       TestIntFunc ();
   }
   catch (int x)
   {
       MessageBox (NULL, "Caught int exception",
                   "Howdy", MB_OK);
   }
   try
   {
       TestFileFunc ();
   }
   catch (long lx)
   {
       MessageBox (NULL, "Caught long exception",
                   "Howdy", MB_OK);
   }
   cout << "g_Var1 = " << g_Var1 << endl;
   cout << "g_Var2 = " << g_Var2 << endl;
   cout << "g_Var3 = " << g_Var3 << endl;
}

void TestIntFunc()
{
   g_Var1 = 10;
   throw (-1);
}

void TestCharFunc()
{
   g_Var2 = 20;
   throw ("Error condition message");
}

void TestFileFunc()
{
   g_Var3 = 30;
   throw (-1L);
}
```

970. *Handling Errors*

Exception handling is a clean and elegant method of handling potential problem spots in your program. Control passes quickly and automatically to a known block of code, which usually is designed specifically to handle errors.

When you write the code in the *catch* block, you have three possibilities to consider:

1. If the error isn't serious, you can make adjustments for it and continue the program. If it's a simple matter of not being able to open a file, you can provide some means for the user to enter a different path or file name. A memory allocation error, on the other hand, might be more serious and you might want to consider more drastic action.

2. You can do some cleanup tasks, close open files, deallocate memory the program allocated, and exit the program if the error is so severe that the program can't continue. After cleanup, you can terminate the program by calling *exit*.

3. Finally, you may decide to let another exception handler make the decision. You might have a handler in a function where the guarded section calls another function that contains an exception handler. That handler will get the first crack at the exception. If it can't handle it adequately, you can execute the *throw* statement to rethrow the exception. The handler block will terminate and control will then pass to the next higher exception handler. If none is found, an abnormal program termination will result.

If your error is three or four function calls deep, you don't need to provide error checking at every level. Even if your program does nothing but exit gracefully, it's still better than the "abnormal program termination" that occurs when an exception is unhandled.

971. *Using Exceptions to Signal Failed Objects*

Error checking is particularly good for signaling when the constructor for a C++ class fails to initialize everything properly. A constructor can't have a return type, so it can't inform you of any errors. To assure proper construction, you would have to check the data members of the class to make sure they have valid values.

By throwing an exception in a constructor when an object creation attempt fails, control returns to the function that created the object. You can take corrective measures at that point.

The Microsoft Foundation Class uses this technique in several places. The *CFile* class, for example, has an overloaded constructor that takes as arguments the name of a file and a set of open flags. On construction, it attempts to open the file. If it fails, it throws a *CFileException* and control returns to your program code. You can elect to handle the exception, as in Tip 968, "Catching Exceptions," or let the program bomb.

MFC provides a number of exception classes and some macros to help make the exception process less painless. We'll look at the macros first, then the exception classes.

972. *Understanding the TRY, CATCH, and END_CATCH Macros*

Except for the fact that you have to end the try and catch macros with another macro, using the MFC exception macros is not much different from using the exception statements built into the C++ language. The MFC macros do have the advantage of automatically deleting the exception object when one of the MFC exception classes is used.

To use the MFC macros, start the *try* block with an uppercase *TRY*. Write the *try* block code as you normally would, but using calls to MFC objects. For example, to open a file, you would use the MFC *CFile* class rather than call a function that uses the C *fopen()* function.

show you the problem with using calls to more than one function that might throw an exception. The following program is a command-line program. Compile it with the command line shown at the top of the listing.

```cpp
#include    <windows.h>
#include    <stdio.h>
#include    <iostream.h>
//
//  excep1.cpp. Test program for exception handling.
//  compile this program with the following command line
//
//          cl -GX excep1.cpp user32.lib
//
//  The -GX enables exception handling. The user32.lib
//  provides the MessageBox function.
//
void TestFileFunc ();
void TestCharFunc ();
void TestIntFunc ();

int g_Var1 = 0;
int g_Var2 = 0;
int g_Var3 = 0;

main ()
{
    try
    {
        TestIntFunc ();
        TestCharFunc ();
        TestFileFunc ();
    }
    catch (char *ErrorMsg)
    {
        MessageBox (NULL, ErrorMsg, "Howdy", MB_OK);
    }
    catch (int x)
    {
        MessageBox (NULL, "Caught int exception",
                    "Howdy", MB_OK);
    }
    catch (long lx)
    {
        MessageBox (NULL, "Caught long exception",
                    "Howdy", MB_OK);
    }
    cout << "g_Var1 = " << g_Var1 << endl;
    cout << "g_Var2 = " << g_Var2 << endl;
    cout << "g_Var3 = " << g_Var3 << endl;
}

void TestIntFunc()
{
    throw (-1);
    g_Var1 = 10;
}
```

```
void TestCharFunc()
{
    throw ("Error condition");
    g_Var2 = 20;
}

void TestFileFunc()
{
    throw (-1L);
    g_Var3 = 30;
}
```

When you run this program, you should get the output shown below. Notice that all the global variables are still 0:

```
g_Var1 = 0
g_Var2 = 0
g_Var3 = 0
```

When the exception was thrown, control passed immediately to the handler block. The *g_Var1* initialization came after the *throw*, so it never was performed, and the second two functions in the *try* block never were called.

You can see there's some risk when you put too much code in a *try* block. Anything after the exception is passed over, and even if you catch and process the exception you still didn't complete the initialization. This code would better be written with multiple *try ... catch* blocks as shown below:

```
#include    <windows.h>
#include    <stdio.h>
#include    <iostream.h>
//
//  excep2.cpp. Test program for exception handling.
//  compile this program with the following command line
//
//          cl -GX excep2.cpp user32.lib
//
//  The -GX enables exception handling. The user32.lib
//  provides the MessageBox function.
//
void TestFileFunc ();
void TestCharFunc ();
void TestIntFunc ();

int g_Var1 = 0;
int g_Var2 = 0;
int g_Var3 = 0;

main ()
{
    try
    {
        TestCharFunc ();
    }
    catch (char *ErrorMsg)
    {
        MessageBox (NULL, ErrorMsg, "Howdy", MB_OK);
```

For the *catch* block, use an uppercase *CATCH*. Two arguments are required, however. The first is the MFC exception class being used, and the second is a pointer to an exception class object. You can define your own exception classes, but if you are going to use them in a *CATCH* macro, they must be derived from the MFC *CException* class.

Finally, end the *TRY ... CATCH* with an *END_CATCH* macro. This will end the exception block and that assures the exception object is deleted automatically.

If you need to rethrow an exception within an MFC block, use the *THROW_LAST* macro rather than the *throw* statement.

Suppose you were using MFC and wanted to open a file using the *CFile* class. *CFile* throws a *CFileException* if it can't open the file, so you want to declare the object at least in function scope and call the *Open* member function in a guarded section of code. Here's what it would look like:

```
CFile   file;

TRY
{
    file.Open ("MyProg.ini", CFile::modeRead
                        | CFile::typeBinary);
}
CATCH (CFileException, e)
{
    // write code here to process a failed open
}
END_CATCH
```

Just as with the C++ exception handlers, you can use multiple *CATCH* statements, but the second and following catch macros must be *AND_CATCH* rather than simply *CATCH*. Use only one *END_CATCH* macro, which must be after the last *AND_CATCH* block. All the blocks must be contiguous; there can be no program statements between them.

973. *Understanding the* **CATCH_ALL** *and* **END_CATCH_ALL** *Macros*

One advantage of the MFC exception macros is that they provide some nifty macros for catching *any* exception using one of the MFC exception classes. You can also sort it out in the handler code by testing for the runtime class of the exception handler.

To use the *CATCH_ALL* macro, use it in place of the *CATCH* macro, but use only the pointer to the exception object as a parameter. You don't need the exception class name. Within the code block you can test the exception object to find out what type of exception was thrown. End the *TRY ... CATCH* block with the *END_CATCH_ALL* macro.

Suppose the *TRY* block from the previous example might generate more than one MFC exception. You could rewrite the code as follows:

```
CFile   file;

TRY
{
    file.Open ("MyProg.ini", CFile::modeRead
```

```
                    | CFile::typeBinary);
}
CATCH_ALL (e)
{
    if (e->IsKindOf((RUNTIME_CLASS(CFileException)))
    {
        //  Write code here to handle the specific
        //  CFileException instance
    }
    else
    {
        //  write code here to process all other possible
        //  exception classes
    }
}
END_CATCH
```

The *CATCH_ALL* macro is particularly good when dealing with databases. There is a *CDBException* class, but a recordset object may generate more than just that one exception. You can test the *IsKindOf()* function specifically for a *CDBException*, then a *CMemoryException,* and then process all other types.

MFC also provides another macro, *AND_CATCH_ALL*, which may be used as the last in a sequence of catch blocks. If you use it, then it *must* be the last catch block. Suppose in the above example, you first want to catch a file exception, then a memory exception, and finally a database exception. If none of those occurred, you would want to process any other exception. The sequence would look like this:

```
CFile   file;

TRY
{
    file.Open ("MyProg.ini", CFile::modeRead
                        | CFile::typeBinary);
}
CATCH (CFileException, e)
{
    //  Write code here to handle the specific
    //  CFileException instance
}
AND_CATCH (CMemoryException, e)
{
    //  Write code here to process a memory failure.
}
AND_CATCH (CDBException, e)
{
    //  Write code here to process a database exception.
}
AND_CATCH_ALL (e)
{
    //  write code here to process all other possible
    //  exception classes
}
END_CATCH_ALL
```

(Be sure to include the *afxdb.h* header file to get the definition of the *CDBException* class.)

Now that you know how to *use* them, let's take a look at the various MFC exception classes and what they are.

974. *Understanding the MFC Exception Classes*

As of this writing, MFC provides 11 specific exception handling classes and one general class from which the others are derived.

The *CException* class is the base class for all of the specific exception classes. *CException* is the type of object used with the *CATCH_ALL* macros. It contains basic functions for retrieving an error message and reporting the error message in a message box, along with a function to delete the exception object.

The other exception classes are summarized in Table 974.

Exception Class	When Used
CArchiveException	When a *CArchive* exception occurs
CDaoException	Used with the data access object classes
CDBException	Used by the database and recordset classes
CMemoryException	When a memory error such as an allocation attempt occurs
CNotSupportedException	Thrown when an unsupported operation occurs
CFileException	Used by *CFile* and its derivatives (*CMemoryFile*, *CFtpFile*, etc)
CResourceException	When a Windows resource can't be found or created
COleException	An exception thrown by an OLE operation
COleDispatchException	Exceptions specific to the OLE *IDispatch* interface, a key element in automation
CInternetException	Exceptions related to the Internet classes
CUserException	A generic exception class

Table 974   *The exception classes defined by the Microsoft Foundation Class library*

The *CException* class holds the error that caused the exception in a string. The other classes hold error code numbers and/or the context of the error that caused the exception.

975. *Retrieving and Interpreting Exception Class Error Information*

You can retrieve the error string from the *CException* class by calling its member function *GetError Message()*. This function takes a string array and the size of the array as parameters. The string can be used directly in a message box, or mixed with your own diagnostic message.

The following code snippet used within an MFC *CATCH* block will retrieve the error text and display it in a message box:

```
char errmsg [256];
e->GetErrorMessage (errmsg, 256);
AfxMessageBox (errmsg);
```

You must use this code within the *CATCH* block because the exception pointer has scope only within that block. Once the block exits, the MFC class automatically deletes the object, so assigning it to a variable in function scope will not be a valid operation.

Strings are not easy to parse when your code is trying to figure out an error and take appropriate action. The *CException* class itself doesn't contain a numerical error code, but the derived classes contain error code where appropriate. That "appropriate" qualifier is important because not all classes contain error codes. The *CMemoryException* class, for example, has no need for an error code because the error was caused by an out-of-memory condition, period.

The *CArchiveException*, on the other hand, contains an integer member variable, called *m_cause*, which contains a specific error code that may be used in a *switch* statement. The *CFileException* class contains two error codes. The first, *m_cause*, contains an error code that is portable across operating systems (such as UNIX) and the other, *m_IOsError*, contains a Windows error code.

976. Deleting Exception Objects

If you use a pointer to a user-defined data type in the *throw* function call, you must take care to assure that the life of the object survives the scope of the function when the exception was called. Using a pointer to an object declared locally within the function is likely to lead to some drastic results, or at least unpredictable results.

For this reason, objects used in a *throw* call usually are created on the heap using the *new* operator or by calling *malloc()*. The pointer then is delivered to your *catch* block.

A problem arises because once the *throw* has been executed, the pointer variable goes out of scope and is destroyed. (The actual object remains on the heap, however.) The pointer that is given to your *catch* block has scope only within that block. If you don't delete it in the *catch* block, you'll lose the address of the object permanently, and you will have a memory leak when your program exits.

MFC exception objects are destroyed when the macro sequence ends. You can use the MFC exception classes without the macros, but you will be responsible for deleting the object before its pointer goes out of scope.

977. Creating Your Own Exception Classes

You may throw an exception using a pointer to an object such as a class or a structure. These are user-defined data types in C++, and that's how the MFC exception classes work. When, say, a *CFile* error occurs, the MFC code creates an object of type *CFileException* and then calls *throw*, using the *CFileException* object as the data type.

The object may include the means for the user to recover from the error, or to gracefully exit the program. In the following code, you create a file open common dialog box to allow the user to hunt down a file, then create an object of that dialog class and use it in the *throw* statement. This is all contained in a class, *COpenFile*. The *TestFileFunc()* function attempts to open a file. If it can't, it creates an object of *COpenFile* and throws an exception using the object. The *catch* statement uses an object of this type as well.

As long as *TestFileFunc()* throws an exception, the *break* statement that would cause the program to exit the loop is never executed. The only other way to get out of the loop is by pressing the Cancel button on the dialog box, which exits the program.

```cpp
#include    <windows.h>
#include    <stdio.h>
#include    <iostream.h>
//
//  excep3.cpp. Test program for exception handling.
//  compile this program with the following command line
//
//          cl -GX excep3.cpp user32.lib comdlg32.lib
//
//  The -GX enables exception handling. The user32.lib
//  provides the MessageBox function. comdlg32 is used
//  for the open/save file common dialog box.
//
FILE *TestFileFunc (char *szFile);

class CopenFileError
{
    public:
        COpenFile();
        ~COpenFile();

        OPENFILENAME m_ofn;

        int m_errno;
        int GetFileName (char *szName, int nSize);
};


main ()
{
    char fn[_MAX_PATH] = {"DooWop.Diddly"};
    FILE *fp;
    while (1)
    {
        try
        {
            fp = TestFileFunc (fn);
            break;
        }
        catch (COpenFile *of)
        {
            int nResult = of->GetFileName (fn, _MAX_PATH);
            delete of;
            if (nResult == IDCANCEL)
                return (-1);
        }
    }
    fclose (fp);
    cout << "Open file " << fn << endl;
}


FILE *TestFileFunc(char *szFile)
```

```
{
    FILE *fp = fopen (szFile, "rb");
    if (fp == NULL)
    {
        int err = errno;
        COpenFile *of = new COpenFile;
        of->m_errno = err;
        throw (of);
    }
    return (fp);
}


COpenFile::COpenFile()
{
    memset (&m_ofn, '\Ø', sizeof (OPENFILENAME));
    m_ofn.lStructSize = sizeof (OPENFILENAME);
}


COpenFile::~COpenFile()
{

}


int COpenFile::GetFileName (char *szName, int nSize)
{
    m_ofn.lpstrFile = szName;
    m_ofn.nMaxFile = nSize;
    m_ofn.lpstrTitle = "Open a File";
    m_ofn.lpstrFilter = "All files (*.*)\Ø*.*\Ø";
    BOOL bResult = GetOpenFileName (&m_ofn);
    return (bResult ? IDOK : IDCANCEL);
}
```

The program enters a forever loop that the program can exit in only two ways. Either a file is opened successfully, in which case the *break* statement is executed, or the user presses the Cancel button on the dialog box. As long as the user enters an invalid file name and presses the OK button, the loop will continue.

In the above program, note the statement where the exception object was deleted when it was no longer needed. As you learned in Tip 976, "Deleting Exception Objects," when you return a pointer to an object that was created on the heap, your exception handler is responsible for deleting it.

The *COpenFile* class also stores the system-wide *errno* value, which your code may examine for the specific error. When you get this value, do it immediately after the error occurs, even if it means intermediate storage. There's only one *errno*, and another statement may change its value.

978. *Nesting* try ... catch *Blocks*

Whether you are using the C++ exception statements or the MFC exception macros, you can nest exception handlers by placing additional *try ... catch* blocks within a guarded *try* block or within a *catch* block.

The following code shows how this would be done and is a legal construction in C++:

```
try
{
    //  code for the guarded block.
    try     // Inner try block
    {
        // code for inner try guarded block
    }
    catch(char *e)
    {
        // code for inner catch block
    }
}
catch (...) //  Any catch block
{
    try      // Inner try block in catch block
    {
        // code for inner try in catch block
    }
    catch(char *e)
    {
        // code for inner catch block
    }
}
```

The technique could be used to handle the situation in Tip 969, "Using Multiple *catch* Statements," where three function calls were executed within the guarded block. This would assure that all the global variables are initialized by calling each function within its own guarded block of code. At any point, if your code decides the problem is too severe to continue, it could rethrow the exception within an inner block and have the exception handled by the outer block.

Exception handlers may also be nested by placing them in functions that are called from within a guarded block. In the following snippet, *FuncA* is called from a guarded block in *FuncB*:

```
void FuncA ()
{
try     // Inner try block
    {
        // code for inner try guarded block
    }
    catch(char *e)
    {
        // code for inner catch block
    }
}

void FuncB ()
{
    try
    {
        FuncA ();
    }
    catch (...)
    {
        // Code for outer catch block
    }
}
```

If an exception occurs in *FuncA* that the *catch* block can't handle, the block can rethrow the exception and control would transfer to the outer *catch* block in *FuncB*, the same as if you had written them in the same function using a nested *try ... catch*.

979. *Understanding Interprocess Communications*

The C and C++ languages have always had close ties with the UNIX operating system. Probably because of this association, many of the concepts of UNIX have worked their way into the language specifications.

One of these concepts is *interprocess communications*. From its inception, UNIX has been a multi-tasking operating system, and at any given time, a number of processes, including system processes, might be running. Many of these processes are related or perform related functions and need some method of conveying information from one to another.

To handle this, several mechanisms to allow processes to communicate with others were developed. Some, such as the *signal* mechanism, were simple. Signals allow one process to interrupt the normal program flow in another process by sending it an integer value. A signal handler could be set up in the receiving process based on this number.

Other systems are more complex. *Pipes* and *shared memory* allow the transfer of any type of program data. *Semaphores* provide a mechanism to synchronize process execution and limit access to system resources so they aren't competing for the same resource at the same time.

Not all of these mechanisms have been implemented in their entirety on Windows. Signals, for example, incorporate only a subset of the many possible values on UNIX. Signals basically are a mechanism to allow a process to interrupt itself. One reason is that Windows was born from a single-tasking operating system (DOS) and many of these operations didn't have any meaning. Others were implemented in a different fashion. The message queue on a Windows system, for example, is very different from the message queue on a UNIX system.

980. *Understanding Handles*

If you are going to do any serious programming in the Windows operating system, you are going to run across *handles*. You need to have a working idea of what handles are and how they work.

From the header files supplied with Visual C++, we can see that the type *HANDLE* is *typedef*'ed simply as a pointer to type *void*, which is a pointer to an uncertain data type:

```
typedef void *HANDLE;
```

That doesn't tell the whole story, however, because a handle is more than just a pointer to any data type. It's a pointer to a pointer that points to a data object. The use of handles dates from early Windows when it ran on machines with limited memory (if you think memory is expensive today, it wasn't long ago that 64 *kilo*bytes of memory for the IBM PC sold for well over $200). To keep enough memory free to run other programs, Windows often had to move objects around in memory. But if a process already had a pointer to the object, moving the object would invalidate the pointer.

To get around this, Microsoft used a system of pointers to keep track of objects. Instead of using a pointer directly, a program would use a handle which would reference containing the address of the real object. This way, Windows could safely move objects around as necessary, then update the pointer in the reference and allow the processes a safe means of accessing the object.

When a process needs to access an object using a handle, it calls *GlobalLock()* to freeze the object in memory. In return, Windows would pass the actual address of the object and the process could safely read or write to the object. As long as an object is locked by a process, Windows won't move it. The handle contains more than just the object's address; for example, it contains a lock count indicating how many processes have requested the address of the object. As long as the lock count is greater than zero, Windows will not move the object.

The idea got expanded so that eventually most objects, including files, were identified by their handles.

A *handle*, then, is a pointer to an object that contains a pointer to another object. It's slightly archaic on modern machines. When Windows made the transition from a simple time-shared program to a multitasking operating system, there was so much legacy code that needed to run under the new operating system that the handle survived the transition.

981. *Understanding Process Control Routines*

Among the interprocess communications mechanisms are a number of functions that are intended to start, stop, and control processes from within a program. These are the *process control routines*. You met some of them in the earlier discussion on *exec* and *spawn*.

On Windows, there are other process control routines; most are intended to provide control of the currently executing process. They are summarized in Table 981.

Function	Purpose
abort	Causes an abrupt program termination. Prints "Abnormal program termination," then raises the *SIGABRT* signal. You can provide some cleanup code for an abnormal termination by handling the SIGABRT signal.
atexit	Schedules a function to execute when the program exits. The function must be prototyped as *void _cdecl Func();*.
exit	Terminates the process after cleanup. (The *_exit* version terminates immediately without cleanup.)
_cexit	Causes the program to execute cleanup functions as though it were exiting, but actually returns to caller.
getpid	Returns the process ID for the currently executing process.
signal	Sets a handler function for a signal. The function must be prototyped as *void _cdecl Func (int sig);* where *sig* is the signal identifier that caused the call to the function.
raise	Raises a signal. By default, causes the process to terminate with a status code of 3.
system	Executes a system command and returns to the caller.

Table 981   Process control routines

The obvious question raised by Table 981 is, "Can I provide some cleanup code for an unhandled exception by setting a handler for *SIGABRT*." The answer is yes, as you'll see in the next tip, "Understanding Signals." You can't stop the abnormal termination, but you can do some end-game processing.

982. Understanding Signals

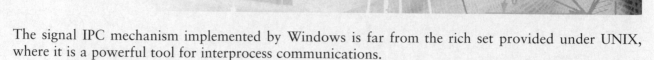

The signal IPC mechanism implemented by Windows is far from the rich set provided under UNIX, where it is a powerful tool for interprocess communications.

Under Windows, signals are mostly useful for *intra*process communication, and may be used to invoke a program abort (the default) or unscheduled processing. Windows defines only six of the wide range of signals implemented by UNIX, as shown in Table 982:

Signal	Meaning
SIGABRT	Abnormal termination
SIGFPE	Floating point error
SIGILL	Illegal instruction
SIGINT	Ctrl+C signal
SIGSEGV	Access violation
SIGTERM	Termination request

Table 982   The six signals defined for Windows and their meanings

You can set a handler for any of these signals by calling the *signal()* function and specifying its address. Your program may generate one of these signals by calling the *raise()* function, which forces a call to the function you set in the call to *signal()*. If no function address has been set, the program will exit with a result code of 3 when you call *raise()*.

The following short program shows how you can handle the abnormal termination signal to provide some emergency shutdown operations. Signals occur asynchronously—they can happen at any time—and your handler code should avoid any system calls (such as *time()*), any calls that use the heap, and any low-level function calls such as *printf()*.

```
#include    <windows.h>
#include    <stdio.h>
#include    <signal.h>
//
//  sigtest.cpp. Test program for signal handling.
//  compile this program with the following command line
//
//          cl -GX sigtest.cpp user32.lib
//
//  The -GX enables exception handling. The user32.lib
//  provides the MessageBox function.
//


//
//  Prototype for signal handler
//
```

```
void _cdecl HandleAbort (int sig);


//
//  Save the old signal function if any
//
void (*func)(int sig);

main ()
{
    func = signal (SIGABRT, HandleAbort);
    throw;
    MessageBox (NULL, "Abort handled", "Abort", MB_OK);
}

void _cdecl HandleAbort (int sig)
{
    MessageBox (NULL, "Handling abort", "Abort", MB_OK);
    if (func != NULL)
        func(sig);
}
```

The call to *signal()* sets the signal handler for the specified signal, and returns the address of any previous handler, so you save that address in the *void (*func)(int sig)* variable. If the system already has set a handler, you can call it after your function executes.

The *throw* statement will cause the program to terminate because there is no exception handler. An unhandled exception prints "abnormal program termination" and raises the *SIGABRT* signal. When that happens, your *HandleAbort()* function will be called.

The statement after the *throw* statement that displays a second message box will not be executed. The program will terminate when your *HandleAbort()* function returns.

983. *Using Windows Messages Between Processes*

Windows processes communicate with one another through the Windows message system. You can send a message to any window as long as you know its window handle, the HWND value. You can also post a message to another thread, including a thread in another process, if you know the thread ID.

When you start a process using the *CreateProcess()* function, which is the preferred method, Windows will fill in a *PROCESS_INFORMATION* structure that contains the process ID and handle, along with the thread ID and handle.

You can use this thread ID to post messages to the process's main thread using the *PostThreadMessage()* function. This function posts the message to the thread, but it doesn't wait for the thread to process it, so it won't hang up your processes.

In the sample code from Tip 943, "Understanding *exec* and *spawn*," where you used the *CreateProcess()* function to start a copy of *NotePad.exe*, the code stopped any previous process using the *Terminate Process()* function. That's really a rude method of stopping a process, and it doesn't give the process a chance to close any other processes or DLLs it might have open.

A better method of stopping the old process would have been to post the *WM_QUIT* message to the process's main thread using the following syntax:

```
PostThreadMessage (pi.dwThreadId, WM_QUIT, 0, 0);
```

The Windows API defines a block of message IDs that are reserved for use by programs. You can use this block to pass messages between processes that respond to them in their message maps. The block begins at *WM_USER*, which is defined at 0x400, and continues through 0x7FFF.

984. *Understanding Queued and Non-Queued Messages*

Because Windows can display several windows on the desktop at the same time, it needs some way of sorting out the messages to the various windows. It does this through message *queues*. Windows maintains a single system message queue and one message queue for each thread in the system.

Device drivers, such as the program that controls the keyboard, receive information from a device to place it in the system message queue. Windows takes the messages off the system queue one at a time, determines which window should receive it, and then places it in the thread message queue for the thread that created the destination window.

Windows always posts the messages at the end of the thread message queue, so the thread receives them in a first in, first out sequence. The exception is the *WM_PAINT* message. Windows keeps the *WM_PAINT* message in the queue until the thread's message queue is empty. Multiple *WM_PAINT* messages are then combined into one and the message is placed in the thread message queue. Processing a *WM_PAINT* message can be costly in terms of CPU time, and this method minimizes the number of times a window must redraw its client area.

These are *queued* messages. Some messages, however, are too important to wait. Typically, these are event notification messages that affect a window. For these, Windows bypasses the system queue and sends the messages directly to the head of the thread's message queue. These are *non-queued* messages.

Suppose a user is typing and one series of keystrokes is intended to bring another window into focus. If this message had to wait its turn in the queue, further keystrokes would be directed to the window that currently has the focus, not the intended window. When a situation such as this occurs, Windows bypasses the system message queue and sends the *WM_ACTIVATE, WM_SETFOCUS,* and *WM_SET CURSOR* messages directly to the thread, assuring the proper window is brought to the top.

985. *Understanding Pipes*

A *pipe* is an interprocess communications mechanism that allows processes to transfer information to one another as though they were reading and writing to a file.

You've probably met a pipe on the Windows console command line. The pipe is represented by the vertical bar symbol ("|"). On the command line, this symbol instructs the command interpreter to use the output of the program on the left side of the symbol and send it to the input of the program on the right side. The output is passed through a *pipe* from one process to another. An example of this might be the following command line:

```
C:>type stuff.cpp | grep -i printf
```

This command would list every line in the *stuff.cpp* program file where you used the *printf()* function. The *type* command reads the *stuff.cpp* file one line at a time and sends it to the *grep* process.

Pipes don't have to be used only from the command line. You can create an *unnamed* or *anonymous* pipe that can be used between related processes, such as a parent process and one that it spawned, or a *named* pipe that can be used between unrelated processes, even a process on a remote computer.

986. *Using Unnamed Pipes for Interprocess Communications*

Pipes are inherently two-way objects, although a process normally either writes to the pipe or reads from it. It needs two file descriptors, one for the write half of the pipe and another for the read half. When you write something to the write pipe, it appears at the other end in the read half.

In case you're wondering, the read and write ends are the same on both ends of the pipe.

A pipe has only two ends, one for the sender and another for the receiver. In UNIX, a construction called a "tee" allows the pipe to have more than two endpoints. This has not been implemented in Windows.

Create a pipe using the *_pipe()* function or the *CreatePipe()* function. You'll look at the standard C *_pipe()* function first and create a project using it. Windows, of course, wants to do things a little differently, so your code won't be portable. In Tip 988, "Using Named Pipes for Interprocess Communications," you'll re-create the project using the *CreatePipe()* function, which will allow it to be inherited through *CreateProcess()*.

As parameters for the *_pipe()* call, you'll need the address of an array of two integers to hold the file descriptors, the number of bytes of memory to reserve for the pipe, and the mode, which is taken from the low-level C *open()* flags. This can be *O_TEXT*, *O_BINARY*, and so on. Normally, you'll open a pipe with the *O_BINARY* flags. The following snippet shows a typical open:

```
int    hPipe[2];
if (_pipe(hPipe, 512, O_BINARY) == -1)
    return (FALSE);
```

The same process can both read and write the pipe, so it can be used for intraprocess communications as well. The pipe has no identifiers other than the open descriptors, so it can only be used between related processes, such as a parent and child or two-child processes. To do this, the pipe must be opened before the other process is created so it can inherit the open descriptors.

The open file descriptors are inherited through the *exec* or *spawn* processes. Of course, because the *exec* process leaves no parent, the second child to use the pipe must already have been created.

Create a single-document application called *Anon* using the *CEditView* base class. At startup, the program will open a pipe with the standard C function, and spawn a copy of itself passing the descriptor to the read half of the pipe as a parameter. After adding message handlers for the keyboard messages, the parent process will pass the messages through the pipe to the child process. In the child process, the view class will spawn a thread to read the pipe. As each keystroke is sent through the pipe, the message will be re-sent to the child process's view. When you type a character in the parent process, it should appear in the child window as well.

When you run the application, you should see two copies of it appear side by side at the top of your screen as shown in Figure 986.

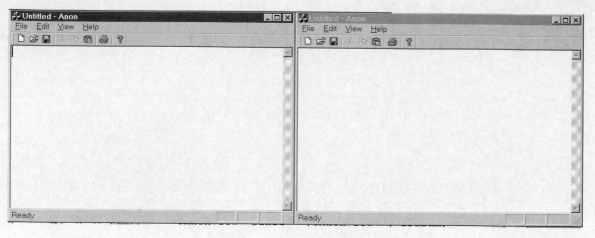

Figure 986   *The anonymous pipe sender on the left will send keyboard messages through a pipe to
the receiver on the right. You should see the characters appear simultaneously.*

Once the project has been created, add the virtual function *OnExitInstance()* to the application class.
You'll need to add a couple of global variables as well, as shown in the following listing:

```cpp
// Anon.cpp : Defines the class behaviors for the application.
//

#include "stdafx.h"
#include "Anon.h"

#include "MainFrm.h"
#include "AnonDoc.h"
#include "AnonView.h"

#ifdef _DEBUG
#define new DEBUG_NEW
#undef THIS_FILE
static char THIS_FILE[] = __FILE__;
#endif

/////////////////////////////////////////////////////////////
// CAnonApp

int g_hPipe[2];
int g_pid;
bool    g_bReceive;

BEGIN_MESSAGE_MAP(CAnonApp, CWinApp)
    //{{AFX_MSG_MAP(CAnonApp)
    ON_COMMAND(ID_APP_ABOUT, OnAppAbout)
        // NOTE - the ClassWizard will add and remove mapping macros here.
        //    DO NOT EDIT what you see in these blocks of generated code!
    //}}AFX_MSG_MAP
    // Standard file based document commands
    ON_COMMAND(ID_FILE_NEW, CWinApp::OnFileNew)
    ON_COMMAND(ID_FILE_OPEN, CWinApp::OnFileOpen)
    // Standard print setup command
    ON_COMMAND(ID_FILE_PRINT_SETUP, CWinApp::OnFilePrintSetup)
END_MESSAGE_MAP()
```

```
/////////////////////////////////////////////////////////
// CAnonApp construction

CAnonApp::CAnonApp()
{
    // TODO: add construction code here,
    // Place all significant initialization in InitInstance
}

/////////////////////////////////////////////////////////
// The one and only CAnonApp object

CAnonApp theApp;

/////////////////////////////////////////////////////////
// CAnonApp initialization

BOOL CAnonApp::InitInstance()
{

    HWND hTop = GetDesktopWindow();
    HDC hdc = GetDC (hTop);
    int nWidth = GetDeviceCaps (hdc, HORZRES) / 2;
    int nHeight = GetDeviceCaps (hdc, VERTRES) / 2;
    ReleaseDC (hTop, hdc);
//
//  Open the pipe to the child process
//
    g_hPipe[0] = g_hPipe[1] = 0;
    char *szCmdLine = GetCommandLine ();
    char *s = strrchr (szCmdLine, '.');
    if (s == NULL)
        return (FALSE);
    szCmdLine = s;
    s = strchr (szCmdLine, ' ');
    if (s == NULL)
    {
        if (_pipe(g_hPipe, 512, O_BINARY) == -1)
            return (FALSE);
        CString strArgs;
        strArgs.Format ("%d", g_hPipe[0]);
        char szDir[_MAX_PATH];
        GetModuleFileName(NULL, szDir, _MAX_PATH);
        if ((g_pid = spawnl (P_NOWAIT, szDir, szDir,
                             (LPCSTR) strArgs, NULL)) < 0)
            return (FALSE);
        g_bReceive = false;
    }
    else
    {
        sscanf (s, " %d %d", &g_hPipe[0], g_hPipe[1]);
        g_bReceive = true;
    }

    AfxEnableControlContainer();
```

```
#ifdef _AFXDLL
    Enable3dControls();          // Call this when using MFC
                                 // in a shared DLL
#else
    Enable3dControlsStatic();    // Call this when linking to
                                 // MFC statically
#endif

    // Change the registry key under which our settings
    // are stored.
    // TODO: You should modify this string to be something
    // appropriate such as the name of your company or
    // organization.
    SetRegistryKey(_T(
             "Local AppWizard-Generated Applications"));

    LoadStdProfileSettings();  // Load standard INI file
                               // options (including MRU)

    // Register the application's document templates.
    // Document templates serve as the connection between
    // documents, frame windows and views.

    CSingleDocTemplate* pDocTemplate;
    pDocTemplate = new CSingleDocTemplate(
        IDR_MAINFRAME,
        RUNTIME_CLASS(CAnonDoc),
        RUNTIME_CLASS(CMainFrame),  // main SDI frame window
        RUNTIME_CLASS(CAnonView));
    AddDocTemplate(pDocTemplate);

    // Parse command line for standard shell commands, DDE,
    // file open
    CCommandLineInfo cmdInfo;
//
// Set the shell command for FileNew and comment out the
// line to parse the shell command.
//
    cmdInfo.m_nShellCommand = CCommandLineInfo::FileNew;
//  ParseCommandLine(cmdInfo);

    // Dispatch commands specified on the command line
    if (!ProcessShellCommand(cmdInfo))
        return FALSE;
//
// Create the applications so their windows are side by side
//
    if (g_hPipe[1])
    {
        m_pMainWnd->SetWindowPos (NULL, 0, 0,
                                  nWidth, nHeight, 0);
    }
    else
    {
        m_pMainWnd->SetWindowPos (NULL, nWidth, 0,
```

```
                              nWidth, nHeight, 0);
    }

    // The one and only window has been initialized,
    // so show and update it.
    m_pMainWnd->ShowWindow(SW_SHOW);
    m_pMainWnd->UpdateWindow();

    return TRUE;
}

//////////////////////////////////////////////////////////////
// CAnonApp message handlers

int CAnonApp::ExitInstance()
{
    if (g_pid)
    {
        TerminateProcess ((HANDLE) g_pid, 0);
        close(g_hPipe[0]);
        close(g_hPipe[1]);
    }
    return CWinApp::ExitInstance();
}

//////////////////////////////////////////////////////////////
// CAboutDlg dialog used for App About

class CAboutDlg : public CDialog
{
public:
    CAboutDlg();

// Dialog Data
    //{{AFX_DATA(CAboutDlg)
    enum { IDD = IDD_ABOUTBOX };
    //}}AFX_DATA

    // ClassWizard generated virtual function overrides
    //{{AFX_VIRTUAL(CAboutDlg)
    protected:
    virtual void DoDataExchange(CDataExchange* pDX);    // DDX/DDV support
    //}}AFX_VIRTUAL

// Implementation
protected:
    //{{AFX_MSG(CAboutDlg)
        // No message handlers
    //}}AFX_MSG
    DECLARE_MESSAGE_MAP()
};

CAboutDlg::CAboutDlg() : CDialog(CAboutDlg::IDD)
{
    //{{AFX_DATA_INIT(CAboutDlg)
    //}}AFX_DATA_INIT
```

```
}

void CAboutDlg::DoDataExchange(CDataExchange* pDX)
{
    CDialog::DoDataExchange(pDX);
    //{{AFX_DATA_MAP(CAboutDlg)
    //}}AFX_DATA_MAP
}

BEGIN_MESSAGE_MAP(CAboutDlg, CDialog)
    //{{AFX_MSG_MAP(CAboutDlg)
        // No message handlers
    //}}AFX_MSG_MAP
END_MESSAGE_MAP()

// App command to run the dialog
void CAnonApp::OnAppAbout()
{
    CAboutDlg aboutDlg;
    aboutDlg.DoModal();
}
```

If the process is on the receiving end of the pipe, the *CAnonView* class will start a thread to read the pipe, sending any messages that are received to the view where they will duplicate keystrokes in the parent process's window. The code for the *CAnonView* class is shown below:

```
// AnonView.cpp : implementation of the CAnonView class
//

#include "stdafx.h"
#include "Anon.h"

#include "AnonDoc.h"
#include "AnonView.h"

#ifdef _DEBUG
#define new DEBUG_NEW
#undef THIS_FILE
static char THIS_FILE[] = __FILE__;
#endif

/////////////////////////////////////////////////////////
// CAnonView

extern int g_hPipe[2];
extern bool g_bReceive;

IMPLEMENT_DYNCREATE(CAnonView, CEditView)

BEGIN_MESSAGE_MAP(CAnonView, CEditView)
    //{{AFX_MSG_MAP(CAnonView)
    ON_WM_KEYDOWN()
    ON_WM_KEYUP()
    ON_WM_CHAR()
    //}}AFX_MSG_MAP
    // Standard printing commands
```

```
    ON_COMMAND(ID_FILE_PRINT, CEditView::OnFilePrint)
    ON_COMMAND(ID_FILE_PRINT_DIRECT, CEditView::OnFilePrint)
    ON_COMMAND(ID_FILE_PRINT_PREVIEW,
                CEditView::OnFilePrintPreview)
END_MESSAGE_MAP()

/////////////////////////////////////////////////////////////
// CAnonView construction/destruction

CAnonView::CAnonView()
{
    // TODO: add construction code here
    if (g_bReceive)
        AfxBeginThread (ReadFromPipe, this);
}

CAnonView::~CAnonView()
{
}

BOOL CAnonView::PreCreateWindow(CREATESTRUCT& cs)
{
    BOOL bPreCreated = CEditView::PreCreateWindow(cs);
    cs.style &= ~(ES_AUTOHSCROLL|WS_HSCROLL);
    // Enable word-wrapping

    return bPreCreated;
}

/////////////////////////////////////////////////////////////
// CAnonView drawing

void CAnonView::OnDraw(CDC* pDC)
{
    CAnonDoc* pDoc = GetDocument();
    ASSERT_VALID(pDoc);
    // TODO: add draw code for native data here
}

/////////////////////////////////////////////////////////////
// CAnonView printing

BOOL CAnonView::OnPreparePrinting(CPrintInfo* pInfo)
{
    // default CEditView preparation
    return CEditView::OnPreparePrinting(pInfo);
}

void CAnonView::OnBeginPrinting(CDC* pDC, CPrintInfo* pInfo)
{
    // Default CEditView begin printing.
    CEditView::OnBeginPrinting(pDC, pInfo);
}

void CAnonView::OnEndPrinting(CDC* pDC, CPrintInfo* pInfo)
{
```

```cpp
    // Default CEditView end printing
    CEditView::OnEndPrinting(pDC, pInfo);
}


/////////////////////////////////////////////////////////
// CAnonView diagnostics

#ifdef _DEBUG
void CAnonView::AssertValid() const
{
    CEditView::AssertValid();
}


void CAnonView::Dump(CDumpContext& dc) const
{
    CEditView::Dump(dc);
}


CAnonDoc* CAnonView::GetDocument() // non-debug version is inline
{
    ASSERT(m_pDocument->IsKindOf(RUNTIME_CLASS(CAnonDoc)));
    return (CAnonDoc*)m_pDocument;
}
#endif //_DEBUG


/////////////////////////////////////////////////////////
// CAnonView message handlers

void CAnonView::OnKeyDown(UINT nChar, UINT nRepCnt,
                          UINT nFlags)
{
    WriteToPipe (WM_KEYDOWN, nChar, nRepCnt, nFlags);
    CEditView::OnKeyDown(nChar, nRepCnt, nFlags);
}


void CAnonView::OnKeyUp(UINT nChar, UINT nRepCnt,
                        UINT nFlags)
{
    WriteToPipe (WM_KEYUP, nChar, nRepCnt, nFlags);
    CEditView::OnKeyUp(nChar, nRepCnt, nFlags);
}


void CAnonView::OnChar(UINT nChar, UINT nRepCnt,
                       UINT nFlags)
{
    WriteToPipe (WM_CHAR, nChar, nRepCnt, nFlags);
    CEditView::OnChar(nChar, nRepCnt, nFlags);
}


void CAnonView::OnSysKeyDown(UINT nChar, UINT nRepCnt,
                             UINT nFlags)
{
    WriteToPipe (WM_SYSKEYDOWN, nChar, nRepCnt, nFlags);
    CEditView::OnSysKeyDown(nChar, nRepCnt, nFlags);
}
```

```
void CAnonView::OnSysKeyUp(UINT nChar, UINT nRepCnt,
                           UINT nFlags)
{
    WriteToPipe (WM_SYSKEYUP, nChar, nRepCnt, nFlags);
    CEditView::OnSysKeyUp(nChar, nRepCnt, nFlags);
}

void CAnonView::OnSysChar(UINT nChar, UINT nRepCnt,
                          UINT nFlags)
{
    WriteToPipe (WM_SYSCHAR, nChar, nRepCnt, nFlags);
    CEditView::OnSysChar(nChar, nRepCnt, nFlags);
}

void CAnonView::WriteToPipe(UINT message, UINT nChar,
                            UINT nRepCnt, UINT nFlags)
{
    if (g_bReceive)
        return;
    MSG msg;
    msg.message = message;
    msg.lParam = MAKELONG (nRepCnt, nFlags);
    msg.wParam = nChar;
    msg.time = time (0);
    msg.hwnd = NULL;
    write (g_hPipe[1], (char *) &msg, sizeof (MSG));

UINT CAnonView::ReadFromPipe(void *lParam)
{
    CAnonView *pThis = (CAnonView *) lParam;
    while (1)
    {
        MSG msg;
        if (read (g_hPipe[0], &msg, sizeof (MSG)) < 1)
            break;
        pThis->SendMessage (msg.message, msg.wParam,
                            msg.lParam);
    }
    return (0);
}
```

Try typing in the left window client area and you should see the keystrokes duplicated nearly simultaneously in the right window's client area. It doesn't work the other way around, however.

987. *Using* **CreatePipe()**

The above method works well for creating and using a pipe. However, in Windows, the preferred method of creating a child process is to use the *CreateProcess()* function. The problem with *Create Process()* and *_pipe()* is that the pipe function opens the pipe using low-level file descriptors. These are inherited when you create a new process using one of the standard C functions such as *spawn()*. They are not inherited, however, when you use *CreateProcess()*.

To use the *CreatePipe()* function, you get to meet another of Microsoft's inane creations, the *SECURITY_ATTRIBUTES* structure. The only reason you need it is for the *bInheritHandle* flag, which permits the pipe handles to be inherited by the child process. Except for that, the structure is ignored on Windows 98 and 95.

(I've always chuckled at the Windows NT security system, which in the end, doesn't work as well as the UNIX system. The designers compromise half of the security by forcing you to have a user named "Administrator." Any time you sit down to hack a Windows NT machine, you *know* there's a user named Administrator, so you're halfway in. At least in UNIX, you can change the super-user name. Have you ever tried changing the name of the Administrator user on NT? Have your install CD ready.)

Enough digression. The source for the *CreatePipe()* version of the *Anon* project's application class is shown below:

```cpp
// Anon.cpp : Defines the class behaviors for the application.
//

#include "stdafx.h"
#include "Anon.h"

#include "MainFrm.h"
#include "AnonDoc.h"
#include "AnonView.h"

#ifdef _DEBUG
#define new DEBUG_NEW
#undef THIS_FILE
static char THIS_FILE[] = __FILE__;
#endif

/////////////////////////////////////////////////////////////
// CAnonApp

HANDLE  g_hRead, g_hWrite;
bool    g_bReceive;

BEGIN_MESSAGE_MAP(CAnonApp, CWinApp)
    //{{AFX_MSG_MAP(CAnonApp)
    ON_COMMAND(ID_APP_ABOUT, OnAppAbout)
        // NOTE - the ClassWizard will add and remove mapping macros here.
        //    DO NOT EDIT what you see in these blocks of generated code!
    //}}AFX_MSG_MAP
    // Standard file based document commands
    ON_COMMAND(ID_FILE_NEW, CWinApp::OnFileNew)
    ON_COMMAND(ID_FILE_OPEN, CWinApp::OnFileOpen)
    // Standard print setup command
    ON_COMMAND(ID_FILE_PRINT_SETUP, CWinApp::OnFilePrintSetup)
END_MESSAGE_MAP()

/////////////////////////////////////////////////////////////
// CAnonApp construction

CAnonApp::CAnonApp()
{
    // TODO: add construction code here,
    // Place all significant initialization in InitInstance
}
```

```
///////////////////////////////////////////////////////
// The one and only CAnonApp object

CAnonApp theApp;

///////////////////////////////////////////////////////
// CAnonApp initialization

BOOL CAnonApp::InitInstance()
{

    HWND hTop = GetDesktopWindow();
    HDC hdc = GetDC (hTop);
    int nWidth = GetDeviceCaps (hdc, HORZRES) / 2;
    int nHeight = GetDeviceCaps (hdc, VERTRES) / 2;
    ReleaseDC (hTop, hdc);
    memset (&m_pi, '\0', sizeof (PROCESS_INFORMATION));
    char *szCmdLine = GetCommandLine ();
    char *s = strrchr (szCmdLine, '.');
    if (s == NULL)
        return (FALSE);
    szCmdLine = s;
    s = strchr (szCmdLine, ' ');
    if (s == NULL)
    {
        SECURITY_ATTRIBUTES sa;
        memset (&sa, '\0', sizeof (SECURITY_ATTRIBUTES));
        sa.nLength = sizeof (SECURITY_ATTRIBUTES);
        sa.bInheritHandle = TRUE;
        sa.lpSecurityDescriptor = NULL;
//
//  Open the pipe to the child process
//
        if (!CreatePipe (&g_hRead, &g_hWrite, &sa, 512))
            return (FALSE);
        STARTUPINFO si;
        memset (&si, '\0', sizeof (STARTUPINFO));
        si.cb = sizeof (STARTUPINFO);

        si.dwXSize = nWidth;
        si.dwYSize = nHeight;
        si.dwX = nWidth;
        si.dwY = 0;
        si.dwFlags = STARTF_USESIZE | STARTF_USEPOSITION;
        g_bReceive = false;

        CString strArgs, strPath;
        char szDir[_MAX_PATH];
        GetModuleFileName(NULL, szDir, _MAX_PATH);
        strPath = szDir;
        GetCurrentDirectory (_MAX_PATH, szDir);
        strArgs.Format ("%s %ld %ld", (LPCSTR) strPath,
                        g_hRead, g_hWrite);
        BOOL bResult = CreateProcess((LPCTSTR) strPath,
                (char *)(LPCSTR) strArgs,
```

```
                    (LPSECURITY_ATTRIBUTES) NULL,
                    (LPSECURITY_ATTRIBUTES) NULL,
                    TRUE,
                    DETACHED_PROCESS,
                    (LPVOID) NULL,
                    szDir,
                    (LPSTARTUPINFO) &si,
                    (LPPROCESS_INFORMATION) &m_pi);
        if (!bResult)
        {
            AfxMessageBox ("CreateProcess failed",
                        MB_ICONSTOP);
            return (FALSE);
        }

    }
    else
    {
        sscanf (s, " %ld %ld", &g_hRead, &g_hWrite);
        g_bReceive = true;
    }

    AfxEnableControlContainer();

    // Standard initialization

#ifdef _AFXDLL
    Enable3dControls();        // Call this when using MFC
                               // in a shared DLL
#else
    Enable3dControlsStatic();  // Call this when linking to
                               // MFC statically
#endif

    // Change the registry key under which our settings are
    // stored.
    // TODO: You should modify this string to be something
    // appropriate such as the name of your company or
    // organization.
    SetRegistryKey(_T(
            "Local AppWizard-Generated Applications"));

    LoadStdProfileSettings();  // Load standard INI file
                               // options (including MRU)

    // Register the application's document templates.
    // Document templates serve as the connection between
    // documents, frame windows and views.

    CSingleDocTemplate* pDocTemplate;
    pDocTemplate = new CSingleDocTemplate(
        IDR_MAINFRAME,
        RUNTIME_CLASS(CAnonDoc),
        RUNTIME_CLASS(CMainFrame),  // main SDI frame window
        RUNTIME_CLASS(CAnonView));
    AddDocTemplate(pDocTemplate);
```

```cpp
    // Parse command line for standard shell commands, DDE,
    // file open
    CCommandLineInfo cmdInfo;
//
// Set the shell command for FileNew and comment out the
// line to parse the shell command.
//
    cmdInfo.m_nShellCommand = CCommandLineInfo::FileNew;
//  ParseCommandLine(cmdInfo);

    // Dispatch commands specified on the command line
    if (!ProcessShellCommand(cmdInfo))
        return FALSE;

    if (!g_bReceive)
    {
        m_pMainWnd->SetWindowPos (NULL, 0, 0, nWidth,
                                    nHeight, 0);
        m_pMainWnd->SetFocus ();
    }

    // The one and only window has been initialized,
    // so show and update it.
    m_pMainWnd->ShowWindow(SW_SHOW);
    m_pMainWnd->UpdateWindow();

    return TRUE;
}


/////////////////////////////////////////////////////////////
// CAboutDlg dialog used for App About

class CAboutDlg : public CDialog
{
public:
    CAboutDlg();

// Dialog Data
    //{{AFX_DATA(CAboutDlg)
    enum { IDD = IDD_ABOUTBOX };
    //}}AFX_DATA


    // ClassWizard generated virtual function overrides
    //{{AFX_VIRTUAL(CAboutDlg)
    protected:
    virtual void DoDataExchange(CDataExchange* pDX);
    // DDX/DDV support
    //}}AFX_VIRTUAL

// Implementation
protected:
    //{{AFX_MSG(CAboutDlg)
        // No message handlers
    //}}AFX_MSG
```

```
    DECLARE_MESSAGE_MAP()
};

CAboutDlg::CAboutDlg() : CDialog(CAboutDlg::IDD)
{
    //{{AFX_DATA_INIT(CAboutDlg)
    //}}AFX_DATA_INIT
}

void CAboutDlg::DoDataExchange(CDataExchange* pDX)
{
    CDialog::DoDataExchange(pDX);
    //{{AFX_DATA_MAP(CAboutDlg)
    //}}AFX_DATA_MAP
}

BEGIN_MESSAGE_MAP(CAboutDlg, CDialog)
    //{{AFX_MSG_MAP(CAboutDlg)
        // No message handlers
    //}}AFX_MSG_MAP
END_MESSAGE_MAP()

// App command to run the dialog
void CAnonApp::OnAppAbout()
{
    CAboutDlg aboutDlg;
    aboutDlg.DoModal();
}


/////////////////////////////////////////////////////////////////
// CAnonApp message handlers


int CAnonApp::ExitInstance()
{
    if (m_pi.hProcess)
    {
        ::PostThreadMessage (m_pi.dwThreadId,WM_QUIT, 0, 0);
        CloseHandle (g_hWrite);
        CloseHandle (m_pi.hProcess);
    }
    return CWinApp::ExitInstance();
}
```

Hot dog! You've gone through twice the work and achieved the same result. Actually, considering the inherent instability of the Windows platform, this method probably would be safer than using the low-level C functions.

988. Using Named Pipes for Interprocess Communications

Named pipes can be used by unrelated processes. All a process needs to know is the name of the pipe to open it. In addition, named pipes may be used by clients on remote computers across your network.

A named pipe is created using the *CreateNamedPipe()* function, specifying the Uniform Naming Convention (UNC) name of the pipe, including the network node, and a passel of attributes. If the pipe is to be used by processes on the same computer, you can use a period as the network node name, as shown in the following example. The first line shows *adamselene* as the network node, and the second uses an unspecified node name:

```
"\\\\adamselene\\pipe\\pipename"
"\\\\.\\pipe\\pipename"
```

The node name follows, then another backslash, the word "pipe," another backslash, and finally the name of the pipe.

The client process opens the pipe with the *CreateFile()* function as though it were an ordinary file. It specified *OPEN_EXISTING* in the open flags, so a file is not actually created.

For consistency and so you can compare the various pipe methods, you'll do the same thing as we did for the anonymous pipe examples. This time, however, the processes don't have to be related. Create a workspace called *Pipes* and then create two projects in it, one named *Write* and the second named—you've got it—*Read*. When a keystroke appears in the *Write* project, it will be sent to the *Read* project, and should appear simultaneously.

The code for *Write.cpp* is listed below. This process is responsible for creating the named pipe.

```cpp
// Write.cpp : Defines the class behaviors
// for the application.
//

#include "stdafx.h"
#include "Write.h"

#include "MainFrm.h"
#include "WriteDoc.h"
#include "WriteView.h"

#ifdef _DEBUG
#define new DEBUG_NEW
#undef THIS_FILE
static char THIS_FILE[] = __FILE__;
#endif

/////////////////////////////////////////////////////////////
// CWriteApp

HANDLE  g_hPipe;

BEGIN_MESSAGE_MAP(CWriteApp, CWinApp)
    //{{AFX_MSG_MAP(CWriteApp)
    ON_COMMAND(ID_APP_ABOUT, OnAppAbout)
        // NOTE - the ClassWizard will add and remove
        //mapping macros here.
        //    DO NOT EDIT what you see in these blocks
        // of generated code!
    //}}AFX_MSG_MAP
    // Standard file based document commands
    ON_COMMAND(ID_FILE_NEW, CWinApp::OnFileNew)
    ON_COMMAND(ID_FILE_OPEN, CWinApp::OnFileOpen)
    // Standard print setup command
```

```
        ON_COMMAND(ID_FILE_PRINT_SETUP,
                  CWinApp::OnFilePrintSetup)
END_MESSAGE_MAP()

/////////////////////////////////////////////////////////////
// CWriteApp construction

CWriteApp::CWriteApp()
{
    // TODO: add construction code here,
    // Place all significant initialization in InitInstance
}

/////////////////////////////////////////////////////////////
// The one and only CWriteApp object

CWriteApp theApp;

/////////////////////////////////////////////////////////////
// CWriteApp initialization

BOOL CWriteApp::InitInstance()
{

    HWND hTop = GetDesktopWindow();
    HDC hdc = GetDC (hTop);
    int nWidth = GetDeviceCaps (hdc, HORZRES) / 2;
    int nHeight = GetDeviceCaps (hdc, VERTRES) / 2;
    ReleaseDC (hTop, hdc);
//
//  Open the pipe to the client process
//

    g_hPipe = CreateNamedPipe ("\\\\.\\pipe\\pipename",
                  PIPE_ACCESS_DUPLEX | FILE_FLAG_OVERLAPPED,
                  PIPE_TYPE_BYTE | PIPE_READMODE_BYTE,
                  PIPE_NOWAIT,
                  PIPE_UNLIMITED_INSTANCES,
                  512, NMPWAIT_USE_DEFAULT_WAIT,
                  NULL);

    if (g_hPipe == INVALID_HANDLE_VALUE)
    {
        CString Message;
        Message.Format ("CreateNamedPipe failed. Error %ld",
                      GetLastError ());
        AfxMessageBox (Message);
        return (FALSE);
    }

    AfxEnableControlContainer();

    // Standard initialization

#ifdef _AFXDLL
    Enable3dControls();
#else
```

```
        Enable3dControlsStatic();
#endif

    // Change the registry key under which our settings
    // are stored.
    // TODO: You should modify this string to be something
    // appropriate such as the name of your company or
    // organization.
    SetRegistryKey(_T(
            "Local AppWizard-Generated Applications"));

    LoadStdProfileSettings();  // Load standard INI file
                               // options (including MRU)

    // Register the application's document templates.
    // Document templates serve as the connection between
    // documents, frame windows and views.

    CSingleDocTemplate* pDocTemplate;
    pDocTemplate = new CSingleDocTemplate(
        IDR_MAINFRAME,
        RUNTIME_CLASS(CWriteDoc),
        RUNTIME_CLASS(CMainFrame),  // main SDI frame window
        RUNTIME_CLASS(CWriteView));
    AddDocTemplate(pDocTemplate);

    // Parse command line for standard shell commands, DDE,
    // file open
    CCommandLineInfo cmdInfo;
    cmdInfo.m_nShellCommand = CCommandLineInfo::FileNew;
    ParseCommandLine(cmdInfo);

    // Dispatch commands specified on the command line
    if (!ProcessShellCommand(cmdInfo))
        return FALSE;

    // The one and only window has been initialized, so show
    // and update it.

    m_pMainWnd->ShowWindow(SW_SHOW);
    m_pMainWnd->UpdateWindow();
//
//  Make the window appear in the upper left quadrant
//
    m_pMainWnd->SetWindowPos (NULL,0,0,nWidth,nHeight,0);

    return (TRUE);
}


/////////////////////////////////////////////////////////////
// CAboutDlg dialog used for App About

class CAboutDlg : public CDialog
{
public:
    CAboutDlg();
```

```
// Dialog Data
    //{{AFX_DATA(CAboutDlg)
    enum { IDD = IDD_ABOUTBOX };
    //}}AFX_DATA

    // ClassWizard generated virtual function overrides
    //{{AFX_VIRTUAL(CAboutDlg)
    protected:
    // DDX/DDV support
    virtual void DoDataExchange(CDataExchange* pDX);
    //}}AFX_VIRTUAL

// Implementation
protected:
    //{{AFX_MSG(CAboutDlg)
        // No message handlers
    //}}AFX_MSG
    DECLARE_MESSAGE_MAP()
};

CAboutDlg::CAboutDlg() : CDialog(CAboutDlg::IDD)
{
    //{{AFX_DATA_INIT(CAboutDlg)
    //}}AFX_DATA_INIT
}

void CAboutDlg::DoDataExchange(CDataExchange* pDX)
{
    CDialog::DoDataExchange(pDX);
    //{{AFX_DATA_MAP(CAboutDlg)
    //}}AFX_DATA_MAP
}

BEGIN_MESSAGE_MAP(CAboutDlg, CDialog)
    //{{AFX_MSG_MAP(CAboutDlg)
        // No message handlers
    //}}AFX_MSG_MAP
END_MESSAGE_MAP()

// App command to run the dialog
void CWriteApp::OnAppAbout()
{
    CAboutDlg aboutDlg;
    aboutDlg.DoModal();
}

/////////////////////////////////////////////////////////////
// CWriteApp message handlers

int CWriteApp::ExitInstance()
{
    if (g_hPipe != INVALID_HANDLE_VALUE)
        CloseHandle (g_hPipe);
    return CWinApp::ExitInstance();
}
```

Although you've been using message structures, you can send virtually any type of data through a pipe, assuming the receiving process has some idea of its form and how to handle it.

Except for the portion where the pipe is created, this class looks very similar to the previous projects. The view class for the *Write* program, however, needs some special attention. The pipe server and pipe client are unrelated processes, so the *Write* program isn't starting the client reader. Further, you don't know when, if ever, a client is going to attach to the pipe.

The pipe has been created, but you don't want to write to it until a client has attached. You need to wait for a connection, but then again, you don't want to tie up your view class while waiting. So, you need to set a global Boolean value to *false*. As long as it's false, the *WriteToThread()* function simply returns.

More interesting, however, is the global *OVERLAPPED* structure. You created the pipe with the *FILE_FLAG_OVERLAPPED* flag set, which means you can use overlapped I/O on it. The overlapped procedure puts the wait in the background, and sets a member event when the I/O is completed. The view class is free to go about its business. We create a worker thread that waits for that event, sets the Boolean flag to true, and returns. The event becomes set when a client attaches. The *WriteToThread()* function will now deliver the messages to the client. The code for the *CWriteView* class is shown below:

```cpp
// WriteView.cpp : implementation of the CWriteView class
//

#include "stdafx.h"
#include "Write.h"

#include "WriteDoc.h"
#include "WriteView.h"

#ifdef _DEBUG
#define new DEBUG_NEW
#undef THIS_FILE
static char THIS_FILE[] = __FILE__;
#endif

/////////////////////////////////////////////////////////////
// CWriteView

extern HANDLE g_hPipe;
bool    g_bConnected;

IMPLEMENT_DYNCREATE(CWriteView, CEditView)

BEGIN_MESSAGE_MAP(CWriteView, CEditView)
    //{{AFX_MSG_MAP(CWriteView)
    ON_WM_KEYDOWN()
    ON_WM_KEYUP()
    ON_WM_CHAR()
    //}}AFX_MSG_MAP
    // Standard printing commands
    ON_COMMAND(ID_FILE_PRINT, CEditView::OnFilePrint)
    ON_COMMAND(ID_FILE_PRINT_DIRECT, CEditView::OnFilePrint)
    ON_COMMAND(ID_FILE_PRINT_PREVIEW,
               CEditView::OnFilePrintPreview)
END_MESSAGE_MAP()


/////////////////////////////////////////////////////////////
// CWriteView construction/destruction
```

```
CWriteView::CWriteView()
{
    g_bConnected = false;
    AfxBeginThread (WaitForConnect, this);
}


CWriteView::~CWriteView()
{
}


BOOL CWriteView::PreCreateWindow(CREATESTRUCT& cs)
{
    // TODO: Modify the Window class or styles here by modifying
    //  the CREATESTRUCT cs

    BOOL bPreCreated = CEditView::PreCreateWindow(cs);
// Enable word-wrapping
    cs.style &= ~(ES_AUTOHSCROLL|WS_HSCROLL);

    return bPreCreated;
}


/////////////////////////////////////////////////////////////
// CWriteView drawing

void CWriteView::OnDraw(CDC* pDC)
{
    CWriteDoc* pDoc = GetDocument();
    ASSERT_VALID(pDoc);
    // TODO: add draw code for native data here
}


/////////////////////////////////////////////////////////////
// CWriteView printing

BOOL CWriteView::OnPreparePrinting(CPrintInfo* pInfo)
{
    // default CEditView preparation
    return CEditView::OnPreparePrinting(pInfo);
}

void CWriteView::OnBeginPrinting(CDC* pDC, CPrintInfo* pInfo)
{
    // Default CEditView begin printing.
    CEditView::OnBeginPrinting(pDC, pInfo);
}

void CWriteView::OnEndPrinting(CDC* pDC, CPrintInfo* pInfo)
{
    // Default CEditView end printing
    CEditView::OnEndPrinting(pDC, pInfo);
}


/////////////////////////////////////////////////////////////
// CWriteView diagnostics
```

```cpp
#ifdef _DEBUG
void CWriteView::AssertValid() const
{
    CEditView::AssertValid();
}


void CWriteView::Dump(CDumpContext& dc) const
{
    CEditView::Dump(dc);
}


CWriteDoc* CWriteView::GetDocument()
{
    ASSERT(m_pDocument->IsKindOf(RUNTIME_CLASS(CWriteDoc)));
    return (CWriteDoc*)m_pDocument;
}
#endif //_DEBUG

/////////////////////////////////////////////////////////////////
// CWriteView message handlers

void CWriteView::OnKeyDown(UINT nChar, UINT nRepCnt,
                           UINT nFlags)
{
    WriteToPipe (WM_KEYDOWN, nChar, nRepCnt, nFlags);
    CEditView::OnKeyDown(nChar, nRepCnt, nFlags);
}

void CWriteView::OnKeyUp(UINT nChar, UINT nRepCnt,
                         UINT nFlags)
{
    WriteToPipe (WM_KEYUP, nChar, nRepCnt, nFlags);
    CEditView::OnKeyUp(nChar, nRepCnt, nFlags);
}

void CWriteView::OnChar(UINT nChar, UINT nRepCnt,
                        UINT nFlags)
{
    WriteToPipe (WM_CHAR, nChar, nRepCnt, nFlags);
    CEditView::OnChar(nChar, nRepCnt, nFlags);
}

void CWriteView::OnSysKeyDown(UINT nChar, UINT nRepCnt,
                              UINT nFlags)
{
    WriteToPipe (WM_SYSKEYDOWN, nChar, nRepCnt, nFlags);
    CEditView::OnSysKeyDown(nChar, nRepCnt, nFlags);
}

void CWriteView::OnSysKeyUp(UINT nChar, UINT nRepCnt,
                            UINT nFlags)
{
    WriteToPipe (WM_SYSKEYUP, nChar, nRepCnt, nFlags);
    CEditView::OnSysKeyUp(nChar, nRepCnt, nFlags);
}
```

```
void CWriteView::OnSysChar(UINT nChar, UINT nRepCnt,
                             UINT nFlags)
{
    WriteToPipe (WM_SYSCHAR, nChar, nRepCnt, nFlags);
    CEditView::OnSysChar(nChar, nRepCnt, nFlags);
}

void CWriteView::WriteToPipe(UINT message, UINT nChar,
                             UINT nRepCnt, UINT nFlags)
{
    if (!g_bConnected)
        return;
    DWORD dwWritten;
    MSG msg;
    msg.message = message;
    msg.lParam = MAKELONG (nRepCnt, nFlags);
    msg.wParam = nChar;
    msg.time = time (0);
    msg.hwnd = NULL;
    if (!WriteFile (g_hPipe, (char *) &msg,
                    sizeof (MSG), &dwWritten, NULL))
    {
        DWORD dwError = GetLastError ();
        if (dwError == PIPE_CLOSED)
        {
            g_bConnected = false;
            DisconnectNamedPipe (g_hPipe);
            AfxBeginThread (WaitForConnect, this);
        }
    }
}

UINT CWriteView::WaitForConnect(void *lParam)
{
    OVERLAPPED o;
    memset (&o, '\0', sizeof (OVERLAPPED));
    o.hEvent = CreateEvent (NULL, TRUE, FALSE, NULL);
    ConnectNamedPipe (g_hPipe, &o);
    WaitForSingleObject (o.hEvent, INFINITE);
    g_bConnected = true;
    CloseHandle (o.hEvent);
    return (0);
}
```

If the *WriteToPipe()* function detects that the pipe has closed because the client either disconnected or terminated, it sets the connected flag to false and restarts a wait thread. When another client connects, the messages will be forwarded again.

The read client is more straightforward. The only thing you do in the *InitInstance()* function is resize the window so it fits next to the server window at the top of the screen. That's just for appearance for this demonstration, of course, and the code essentially is the same as the resizing code in the anonymous pipe tips. Let's just review the *Read* process's view code here:

```
// ReadView.cpp : implementation of the CReadView class
//
```

```
#include "stdafx.h"
#include "Read.h"

#include "ReadDoc.h"
#include "ReadView.h"

#ifdef _DEBUG
#define new DEBUG_NEW
#undef THIS_FILE
static char THIS_FILE[] = __FILE__;
#endif


/////////////////////////////////////////////////////////
// CReadView


#define    PIPE_CLOSED    232
#define    PIPE_ENDED     109


HANDLE g_hPipe;


IMPLEMENT_DYNCREATE(CReadView, CEditView)


BEGIN_MESSAGE_MAP(CReadView, CEditView)
    //{{AFX_MSG_MAP(CReadView)
        // NOTE - the ClassWizard will add and remove mapping macros here.
        //    DO NOT EDIT what you see in these blocks of generated code!
    //}}AFX_MSG_MAP
    // Standard printing commands
    ON_COMMAND(ID_FILE_PRINT, CEditView::OnFilePrint)
    ON_COMMAND(ID_FILE_PRINT_DIRECT, CEditView::OnFilePrint)
    ON_COMMAND(ID_FILE_PRINT_PREVIEW,
               CEditView::OnFilePrintPreview)
END_MESSAGE_MAP()


/////////////////////////////////////////////////////////
// CReadView construction/destruction


CReadView::CReadView()
{
    g_hPipe = INVALID_HANDLE_VALUE;
    AfxBeginThread (ReadFromPipe, this);
}


CReadView::~CReadView()
{
}


BOOL CReadView::PreCreateWindow(CREATESTRUCT& cs)
{
    // TODO: Modify the Window class or styles here by modifying
    //  the CREATESTRUCT cs

    BOOL bPreCreated = CEditView::PreCreateWindow(cs);
    cs.style &= ~(ES_AUTOHSCROLL|WS_HSCROLL);  // Enable word-wrapping

    return bPreCreated;
```

```
}

//////////////////////////////////////////////////////////
// CReadView drawing

void CReadView::OnDraw(CDC* pDC)
{

    CReadDoc* pDoc = GetDocument();
    ASSERT_VALID(pDoc);
    // TODO: add draw code for native data here
}


//////////////////////////////////////////////////////////////
// CReadView printing

BOOL CReadView::OnPreparePrinting(CPrintInfo* pInfo)
{
    // default CEditView preparation
    return CEditView::OnPreparePrinting(pInfo);
}

void CReadView::OnBeginPrinting(CDC* pDC, CPrintInfo* pInfo)
{
    // Default CEditView begin printing.
    CEditView::OnBeginPrinting(pDC, pInfo);
}

void CReadView::OnEndPrinting(CDC* pDC, CPrintInfo* pInfo)
{
    // Default CEditView end printing
    CEditView::OnEndPrinting(pDC, pInfo);
}


//////////////////////////////////////////////////////////////
// CReadView diagnostics

#ifdef _DEBUG
void CReadView::AssertValid() const
{
    CEditView::AssertValid();
}

void CReadView::Dump(CDumpContext& dc) const
{
    CEditView::Dump(dc);
}

CReadDoc* CReadView::GetDocument() // non-debug version is inline
{
    ASSERT(m_pDocument->IsKindOf(RUNTIME_CLASS(CReadDoc)));
    return (CReadDoc*)m_pDocument;
}
#endif //_DEBUG


//////////////////////////////////////////////////////////////
// CReadView message handlers
```

```
UINT CReadView::ReadFromPipe(void *lParam)
{
    CReadView *pThis = (CReadView *) lParam;
    while (1)
    {
        while (g_hPipe == INVALID_HANDLE_VALUE)
        {
            g_hPipe = CreateFile("\\\\.\\pipe\\pipename",
                GENERIC_READ | GENERIC_WRITE,
                FILE_SHARE_READ | FILE_SHARE_WRITE,
                NULL,
                OPEN_EXISTING,
                FILE_ATTRIBUTE_NORMAL | FILE_FLAG_OVERLAPPED,
                NULL);
            if (g_hPipe == INVALID_HANDLE_VALUE)
            {
                if (GetLastError () == 50)
                {
                    AfxMessageBox ("The network does not "
                                    "support this operation");
                    return (0);
                }
                Sleep (1000);
            }
        }
        while (1)
        {
            DWORD dwRead, dwAvailable, dwLeft;
            MSG msg;
            BOOL bResult;
            bResult = PeekNamedPipe (g_hPipe, &msg,
                                    sizeof (MSG), &dwRead,
                                    &dwAvailable, &dwLeft);
            if (!bResult)
            {
                DWORD dwError = GetLastError ();
                CloseHandle (g_hPipe);
                if (dwError == PIPE_ENDED)
                {
                    AfxMessageBox (
                            "The pipe has been closed");
                    g_hPipe = INVALID_HANDLE_VALUE;
                }
                break;
            }
            bResult = ReadFile (g_hPipe, &msg,
                                sizeof (MSG), &dwRead, NULL);
            if (dwRead < sizeof (MSG))
                continue;
            pThis->SendMessage (msg.message, msg.wParam,
                                msg.lParam);
        }
        if (g_hPipe != INVALID_HANDLE_VALUE)
            break;
    }
    return (0);
}
```

The constructor sets the pipe handle to *INVALID_HANDLE_VALUE*. That's the same as the unsigned int –1. It serves as our signal that we haven't connected to the pipe yet. Seeing this, the *ReadFromPipe()* function in the worker thread connects to the pipe. If it fails because the network doesn't support named pipes, it returns after displaying a message. Otherwise, it sleeps for a second and then retries the connection, assuming the server hasn't started up.

This code uses the *PeekNamedPipe()* function so the program will not block on the call to *ReadFile()*. If the thread detects the pipe has been closed, it pops up a message box, closes its end of the pipe, and returns to the outer forever loop to try to reconnect. (You actually could do without the *Peek NamedPipe()* function here because a closed pipe will cause the *ReadFile()* function to return with an error.)

989. Understanding Pipe Operations

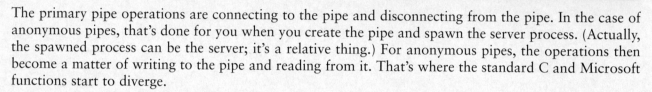

The primary pipe operations are connecting to the pipe and disconnecting from the pipe. In the case of anonymous pipes, that's done for you when you create the pipe and spawn the server process. (Actually, the spawned process can be the server; it's a relative thing.) For anonymous pipes, the operations then become a matter of writing to the pipe and reading from it. That's where the standard C and Microsoft functions start to diverge.

The C functions treat an anonymous pipe created with *_pipe()* as files, and use low-level file operations on them. When you create the pipe with *CreatePipe()*, the Microsoft functions also treat the pipe as a file, but the reading and writing are at a high level, accessing the pipe through handles rather than file descriptors.

Beginning with named pipes, the operations get a lot more complex. You get a lot for that complexity, however. You get a very powerful programming tool. This is one place where Microsoft did a better than average job. The named pipe mechanism is a powerful and flexible IPC mechanism.

Unfortunately, MSDN did it again. The documentation on named pipes is scattered and not indexed. If you know where to look, it's not hard to find, however. Enter "Pipe Reference" in the keyword field and press Enter. What you get isn't a complete pipe reference, but a list of *some* of the functions that are used with pipes. The named pipe functions are there, though, and, in fact, all but one of them, *CreatePipe()*, deal with named pipes.

990. Connecting and Disconnecting a Pipe

You connect to an anonymous pipe when the pipe is created, and you disconnect from it either by exiting the program or by closing the file descriptors, in the case of the C library pipe, or the pipe handle, in the case of the Microsoft version.

Named pipes present more of a challenge. You could have gotten away without the *Connect NamedPipe()* operation in the sample code because you are only writing to the pipe. Microsoft warns that blocking reads from the pipe should not be performed until a client has connected or a race condition may result.

To make it safe for you to experiment with a two-way pipe, code is included on the CD-ROM.

The pipe is already connected when you create the pipe. Using the *ConnectNamedPipe()* simply assures that you won't do any operations on the pipe until there is a process at the other end.

If the pipe server fails or exits for any reason, you must close the pipe in all the processes that have it open. If you don't, the resource won't be released and the server won't be able to re-create the pipe. If this happens, the *ReadFile()* and *PeekNamedPipe()* function will return with an error, and when you call *GetLastError()* the error code will be 109.

991. *Closing a Pipe*

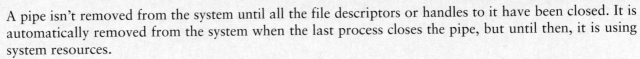

A pipe isn't removed from the system until all the file descriptors or handles to it have been closed. It is automatically removed from the system when the last process closes the pipe, but until then, it is using system resources.

Windows can support a limited number of pipes. If a pipe is no longer needed, your processes should close it as soon as possible, freeing the resources for other processes. This is especially important on servers where you may be running a SQL Server, an Internet Server, or any number of server programs that might use pipes.

To close a pipe created with the low-level C function, close the file descriptors using the low-level *close()* function. Remember to close both ends of the pipe; there are two file descriptors in the array.

To close an anonymous pipe created with the Windows API function, *CreatePipe()*, you need to close both handles that were passed back to you. In the example in Tip 987, "Using *CreatePipe()*," these are the *g_hRead* and *g_hWrite* variables that were passed in the call to *CreatePipe()*. Close these handles by calling the *CloseHandle()* function.

Closing a named pipe is easiest of all. This pipe is truly bidirectional, and reads and writes are performed on it using only a single handle. Close this handle by calling the *CloseHandle()* function.

992. *Using the _popen Function*

The last pipe mechanism you should know about isn't a mechanism by itself, but a curious and sometimes useful function called *_popen()*. This function creates a pipe and then spawns a copy of the system command processor, *command.exe* in Windows. The command processor can be used to run a system command or start another program. Using the pipe, you can write to the program's (or command's) standard input or read its standard output in your program.

It's a handy function for sucking system information into your program so you can thrash it about and extract the parts you want. You also can output data from your program to another. For example, the *grep* program can take its standard input from a pipe, so you could open the pipe to write to its standard input, and perform a *grep* on data internal to your program.

The following program, *Popen.exe*, uses the command interpreter's *dir* command to pipe directory information into the program. It then parses it and stores the entries in a linked list. Then it outputs the directory in a fashion similar to the UNIX *ls* program. The project is a command-line program, but it was created to support MFC so you can use it as a starting point for another project.

```
// Popen.cpp : Defines the entry point for the
// console application.
```

```
//

#include "stdafx.h"
#include "Popen.h"
#include <stdio.h>
#include <stdlib.h>

#ifdef _DEBUG
#define new DEBUG_NEW
#undef THIS_FILE
static char THIS_FILE[] = __FILE__;
#endif

/////////////////////////////////////////////////////////////
// The one and only application object

struct ENTRY
{
    char    szFile[_MAX_PATH];
    char    mod [20];
    int     size;
    ENTRY   *prev;
    ENTRY   *next;
};

ENTRY   *pHead, *pTail;

void StripChar (char *s);
void StripWhite (char *str);
void ListOne ();
void ListColumns();
void LongList ();
void FormatNumber (char *szBuf, long size);
void InsertChar (TCHAR *sz, TCHAR ch);

CWinApp theApp;

using namespace std;

int _tmain(int argc, TCHAR* argv[], TCHAR* envp[])
{
    int nRetCode = 0;
    pHead = pTail = NULL;
// initialize MFC and print an error on failure
    if (!AfxWinInit(::GetModuleHandle(NULL), NULL,
                ::GetCommandLine(), 0))
    {
        // TODO: change error code to suit your needs
        cerr << _T("Fatal Error: MFC initialization failed")
            << endl;
        return (1);
    }

    char    szBuffer[128];
    FILE    *dir;
//
```

```
//  Use the dir command and read its output through
//  a pipe. Open the pipe with a read text attribute.
//  The /on flag lists the files in alphabetical order.
//
    if( (dir = _popen( "dir *.* /on", "rt" )) == NULL )
        return (1);
//
//  Read the pipe as a file. When the command finishes,
//  it will return eof.
//
    while( !feof(dir))
    {
//
//  Junk lines all start with a space or carriage return,
//  so skip them.
//
        if( fgets( szBuffer, 128, dir) == NULL )
            continue;
        if (*szBuffer <= ' ')
            continue;
        char *s = szBuffer + 38;
        *(s++) = '\Ø';
//
//  Don't list the current and parent directories
//
        if (*s == '.')
            continue;
//
//  Strip to bare file name.
//
        StripWhite (s);
//
//  Get a place for this entry on the heap.
//
        ENTRY *pEntry = new ENTRY;
        memset (pEntry, '\Ø', sizeof (ENTRY));
        strcpy (pEntry->szFile, s);
//
//  Add it to the end of the linked list.
//
        if (pHead == NULL)
            pHead = pTail = pEntry;
        else
        {
            pTail->next = pEntry;
            pEntry->prev = pTail;
            pTail = pEntry;
        }
//
//  Get the size as a number
//
        s = szBuffer + 25;
        while (*s)
        {
            if (!isdigit(*s))
                StripChar (s);
```

```
            else
                ++s;
        }
        s = szBuffer + 25;
        pEntry->size = atol (s);
        szBuffer[16] = '\0';
        StripWhite (szBuffer);
        strcpy (pEntry->mod, szBuffer);
    }
//
//  Check the flags to see how to output the
//  directory list.
//
    char cFlag;
    if (argc < 2)
        cFlag = 'c';
    else if (*argv[1] != '-')
        cFlag = '\0';
    else
        cFlag = tolower (*(argv[1] + 1));
    switch (cFlag)
    {
        case 'c':       // List in columns
            ListColumns();
            break;
        case '1':       // List one file per line
            ListOne ();
            break;
        case 'l':       // Long list
            LongList ();
            break;
        default:
            fprintf (stderr, "Invalid flag %s\n\n",
                             argv[1]);
            break;
    }
//
//  Free the linked list.
//
    ENTRY *pCur = pHead;
    while (pCur)
    {
        ENTRY *pTemp = pCur->next;
        delete pCur;
        pCur = pTemp;
    }

    return (nRetCode);
}


//
//  Strip all leading and trailing white space
//  from a string.
//
void StripWhite (char *str)
{
```

```c
char    *s, *t;

//
//  First strip off any leading white space
//
    s = str;
    while (*s <= ' ')
    {
        if (!*s)
            break;
        StripChar ((char *) s);
    }
//
//  Now go to the end of the string and backtrack until we
//  find a non-white character
//
    s = str;
    t = str + strlen (str) - 1;
    while (t >= s)
    {
        if (*t > ' ')
            break;
        *t = '\0';
        --t;
    }
}


//
//  Remove the character at *s from the string it
//  is in.
//
void StripChar (char *s)
{
    while (*s)
    {
        *s = *(s+1);
        ++s;
    }
}


//
//  List the directory in columns
//
void ListColumns()
{
    ENTRY *pCur = pHead;
    int nLongest = 0;
    while (pCur)
    {
        int len = strlen (pCur->szFile);
        if (len > nLongest)
            nLongest = len;
        pCur = pCur->next;
    }
    nLongest += 2;
    int nCols = 79 / nLongest;
```

```
        TCHAR szBuf [128];
        pCur = pHead;
        while (pCur != NULL)
        {
            memset (szBuf, '\0', sizeof (szBuf));
            for (int i = 0; i < nCols; ++i)
            {
                TCHAR *szName = new char [nLongest + 1];
                memset (szName, '\0', nLongest + 1);
                strcpy (szName, pCur->szFile);
                for (int x = strlen (szName); x < nLongest; ++x)
                    szName[x] = ' ';
                strcat (szBuf, szName);
                delete [] szName;
                pCur = pCur->next;
                if (pCur == NULL)
                    break;
            }
            if (strlen (szBuf))
                printf ("%s\n", szBuf);
        }
}

void ListOne ()
{
    ENTRY *pCur = pHead;
    while (pCur)
    {
        printf ("%s\n", pCur->szFile);
        pCur = pCur->next;
    }
}

void LongList ()
{
    TCHAR szLine[512];
    memset (szLine, '\0', sizeof (szLine));
    ENTRY *pCur = pHead;
    while (pCur != NULL)
    {
        TCHAR szSize [16];
        memset (szSize, '\0', sizeof (szSize));
        FormatNumber (szSize, pCur->size);
        printf ("%s  % 13s %s\n", pCur->mod,
                    szSize, pCur->szFile);
        pCur = pCur->next;
    }
}

void FormatNumber (char *szBuf, long size)
{
    TCHAR szTemp [32];
    memset (szTemp, '\0', sizeof (szTemp));
    sprintf (szTemp + 1, "%ld", size);
    TCHAR *psz = szTemp + strlen (szTemp + 1);
    for (int i = 1; *(psz - 1); ++i, --psz)
```

```
    {
        if (!(i%3))
            InsertChar (psz, ',');
    }
    strcpy (szBuf, psz);
}

void InsertChar (TCHAR *sz, TCHAR ch)
{
    char *s = sz + strlen (sz);
    while (s > sz)
    {
        *s = *(s-1);
        --s;
    }
    *s = ch;
}
```

By default, the program outputs the directory using the file names only in columns across the screen after first determining how many columns will fit. This is the same as using the –c flag. This is similar to the default action of the UNIX *ls* command. A flag of –1 causes it to list the file names only in a single column down the screen. This always was a handy option with the *ls* command because the output then could be used as the input for another program or script.

Finally, the –l option outputs the directory in long format, similar to but not quite the same as the command interpreter's default action.

993. *Understanding Events as an IPC Device*

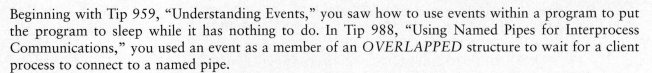

Beginning with Tip 959, "Understanding Events," you saw how to use events within a program to put the program to sleep while it has nothing to do. In Tip 988, "Using Named Pipes for Interprocess Communications," you used an event as a member of an *OVERLAPPED* structure to wait for a client process to connect to a named pipe.

An event is an all-or-nothing mechanism. An event state is either *TRUE* when it is set or *FALSE* when it is reset. You can set it 10 times, but its state still will be set and it will return to the *FALSE* state with a single reset.

You use an event to signal a thread that a device or data is ready for it to use. This keeps the thread from munching on an incomplete object while another thread is trying to prepare it. It also keeps the thread from consuming CPU time while it isn't doing anything; while a thread is waiting for an event, the scheduler doesn't give it any CPU time. Multiple threads may wait for an event, but all of them will be released at the same time when you set the event. Thus, it's difficult to use events to control access to an object for multiple threads.

Events may be anonymous or they may be named, just like pipes. To use an anonymous event, the process or thread must know the handle for the event. It's generally used only between threads within a single process.

Events may be used across process boundaries by creating a *named event*. Any process that knows the name of an event may use it, regardless of whether the process is related to the one that originally created the event.

994. *Creating a Named Event*

Suppose, for example, you have a process watching a directory where you put raw information destined for a printer—a daemon process. This process takes the raw information and prepares a form, then places the bits of data at the correct position on the form.

You could have the process sleep for a few seconds, wake up, and check the directory. It would go to work if it finds anything in the directory, or go back to sleep for another cycle if the directory is empty.

Odds are that the process is going to find the directory empty most of the time, and much of its processing time is going to be consumed with unproductive activity. Plus, disk access is one of the most time-consuming activities for a program.

Alternatively, you could create a named event that any process that wants to place data in the directory could use to signal the daemon that a file is ready for printing. The daemon gets the signal when the event it set, wakes up, and prints any forms that are waiting, then goes back to sleep until the next process signals it.

If you enter "events" in the keyword field of the MSDN documentation, you'll get a long list of event items dealing with ActiveX, Internet Server, etc., but nothing about events. The best way to find information on event processes is to enter "CreateEvent" in the keyword field and follow the links at the bottom of the item.

Create a named event using the *CreateEvent()* function, the same function you used to create anonymous events. However, as the fourth and final parameter, use the name you want to give the event. The name may be a string constant, or it may be a variable containing a string. Here's the statement we'll use in a shared memory file in Tip 1001, "Understanding Shared Memory," to create an event that will signal another process that we wrote something to the file:

```
const char *szFileEvent = {"JAMSA"};
m_hevMemFile = CreateEvent (NULL, FALSE, TRUE, szFileEvent);
```

The first parameter is a pointer to a *SECURITY_ATTRIBUTES* structure. You'll need this to set the *bInheritHandle* member to *TRUE* if you intend for the handle to be inherited by child processes. Other than that, the *SECURITY_ATTRIBUTES* structure isn't used on Windows 95 and 98. If you set this member to *NULL*, the handle can't be inherited by child processes.

The next parameter determines how the event will be reset. If you set it to *TRUE*, the event will be reset automatically when the process waiting for it gets the event signal. If you set it to *FALSE*, it won't be reset, and you'll have to call *ResetEvent()* to reset it.

The third parameter is the initial state of the event. Normally you'll want to set this to *FALSE* so it isn't set when it is created. In this case, however, you'll want the other process to be alerted immediately so it can read and clean out the memory file when it first starts. So, the initial state has been set to *TRUE*.

The last parameter is the name. Without a name (the parameter is *NULL*), the event is an anonymous event and can be used only within the process or by related processes that inherit the handle (if, of course, you set the *bInheritHandle* flag to *TRUE*).

To attach to a named event and wait for it, an unrelated process can call the *OpenEvent()* function, which returns a handle to the event. The following line shows how the *ReDraw* process in the shared memory file sample opens the event we just created:

```
const char *szFileEvent = {"JAMSA"};
m_hevMemFile = OpenEvent (EVENT_ALL_ACCESS, TRUE,
                          szFileEvent);
```

The first parameter is the access you want to the event. On Windows 95 and 98, you have two choices. *EVENT_ALL_ACCESS* gives you full access to the event. You can set and reset it and you can use it in a wait function. *EVENT_MODIFY_STATE* only enables you to set or reset the event. On Windows NT, a third option, *SYNCHRONIZE*, enables you to use the event only in a wait function, but you can't set or reset it.

The second parameter is the inheritance flag. If you intend to spawn other processes using the *Create Process()* function and you want the child processes to be able to use this handle, you must set this flag to *TRUE*.

The last parameter is the event name. This parameter must match exactly the name you used when you created the event in the other process. It is case sensitive, so if you used a mixture of upper- and lower-case letters in the name, you'll have to repeat it exactly in this parameter.

995. *Understanding Semaphores as an IPC Device*

While most lock objects such as mutexes and critical sections and the event mechanism, are two-state devices—they are set or not set—the *semaphore* is a locking device that can maintain a count. You can use it to limit the number of threads that can access an object or a block of code or data at the same time.

The semaphore often is used as a synchronization object across process boundaries, but you just as easily can use it to synchronize threads within the same process. How you create it determines how it will be used.

The semaphore maintains two values. The first is its maximum value. This is the number of locks it will permit before it blocks any additional threads. The second is the current count. When no threads are accessing a guarded object, this value will be the same as the maximum count. Each time a thread locks the semaphore, the current count is decremented by 1. When it reaches 0, no more threads will be allowed to lock the semaphore and will be forced to wait until the count is non-zero. When a thread releases, or unlocks, the semaphore, the count is incremented by one. The current count can never be less than zero nor more than the maximum value.

996. *Creating and Removing Semaphores*

The Windows API has functions for creating and manipulating semaphores, and the Microsoft Foundation class encapsulates these functions in its *CSemaphore* class. You can mix the two methods, and in the case of a semaphore used across process boundaries, you can use the MFC class object even if another process, even the one that created the semaphore, is using the Windows API method. The next tip will look at using the semaphore as an MFC object.

Create a semaphore using the Windows API *CreateSemaphore()* function. The first parameter is a pointer to a *SECURITY_ATTRIBUTES* structure, which you'll need to let child processes inherit the semaphore handle.

The second parameter is the initial count for the semaphore. You can create the semaphore with a count less than the initial count. For example, if you want to block processes from accessing a resource while your application is initializing, you can create it with an initial count of 0. This effectively will keep the wolves away from the door until you raise the count as described in Tip 998, "Locking and Unlocking Semaphores." The value can't be less than 0 or more than the maximum count.

The third parameter is the maximum count. This is the maximum number of locks a semaphore will permit before it causes threads to wait, and is the maximum value you can specify for the initial count.

The last parameter is the semaphore's name. This is required only if it will be used across process boundaries by unrelated processes. To create an anonymous semaphore, use *NULL* for this parameter.

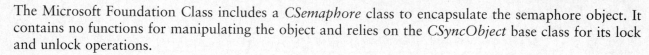

997. *Using MFC Semaphore Classes*

The Microsoft Foundation Class includes a *CSemaphore* class to encapsulate the semaphore object. It contains no functions for manipulating the object and relies on the *CSyncObject* base class for its lock and unlock operations.

The order of arguments to the *CSemaphore* constructor differs from the Windows API function, but it is in a logical order for using default values for the lesser-needed parameters. The first parameter is the initial count, the second is the maximum count, the third is the semaphore name, and the last is a pointer to a *SECURITY_ATTRIBUTES* structure.

All of the arguments to the constructor have default values. The initial and maximum count values default to 1 and the name and security descriptor pointer default to *NULL*.

The *Draw* and *Redraw* applications in Tip 1000, "Understanding Memory Mapped Files," contain examples of semaphores using both the Windows API and the MFC *CSemaphore* class.

998. *Locking and Unlocking Semaphores*

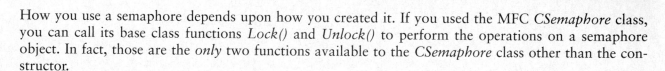

How you use a semaphore depends upon how you created it. If you used the MFC *CSemaphore* class, you can call its base class functions *Lock()* and *Unlock()* to perform the operations on a semaphore object. In fact, those are the *only* two functions available to the *CSemaphore* class other than the constructor.

Using the MFC version, you also can use the *CSingleLock* and *CMultiLock* objects to lock the semaphore and provide automatic unlocking when the object goes out of scope. To do this, first declare the object using a pointer to the semaphore class object, then call the *Lock()* function as shown in the snippet below:

```
CScmaphore sem(2, 2, NULL, NULL);
void OneFunction()
{
    CSingleLock QueueLock (&sem);
    QueueLock.Lock();
// some lines of code here.
}
```

In this snippet, you don't have to call *QueueLock.Unlock()* to release the semaphore. It will be taken care of when QueueLock goes out of scope. However, if you do call *QueueLock.Unlock()*, it won't cause a double unlock on the semaphore object.

You also can use the *CSemaphore* object in any of the Windows API functions by using its *m_hObject* member variable. This is the handle to the semaphore object contained in the class object.

For a semaphore object created using the Windows API, get a fresh 16-penny nail and a 28-ounce framer's hammer and firmly affix it to the wall. It's locked. If you're out of 16-penny nails you can use the semaphore handle in a call to *WaitForSingleObject()* or as a member of an array of handles in a call to *WaitForMultipleObjects()*. If the semaphore's count is not zero, the wait will return immediately and the semaphore's count will be decremented.

To unlock a semaphore object, call the *ReleaseSemaphore()* function. The first parameter is a handle to the semaphore object, the second parameter is the amount by which to increment the semaphore's count, and the last is a pointer to a *long* variable to hold the previous count.

Locking a semaphore decrements its count by one. When you are finished with the semaphore, the *ReleaseSemaphore()* function allows you to increment it by more than one. However, if the value you specify would increase the current count to more than the maximum count, the function call won't have any effect. It's best to increment it only by the amount you decremented it, usually 1. In addition, you can't use 0 for this argument.

The last parameter points to a variable of type *long* to hold the semaphore's count before you changed it. If you don't need this count, you can pass a *NULL* for this parameter. You can't get the count without adjusting the semaphore's current count. Passing a 0 for the increment value simply results in an error and the *long* variable is unchanged.

Before leaving semaphores, the MSDN documentation mentions a *SignalObjectAndWait()* function as the method of locking a semaphore. You should know that this function is available only for programs running on Windows NT 4.0 and above. You should avoid this function unless you are absolutely certain your program will never be run on Windows 95 or 98, or on a version of Windows NT below 4.0. This might apply to a Windows service program, but applications are less certain.

999. *Understanding Mapped Files*

Before looking at the memory-mapped file as an interprocess communications device, you should understand the concept of file mapping. Mainframe and minicomputers have used file mapping for a long time to extend the addressing capabilities of the machines beyond physical memory. A machine might have had as little as 32- or 64-kilobytes of memory, but addressed memory in the megabyte range when files were mapped into a program's address space.

File mapping allows a program to treat the contents of a file as though the file were part of the process's physical address space. When a file is mapped, the program can use pointers to objects in the file and modify them directly rather than having to read the objects into memory, modify them, and then rewrite them back to the file.

Don't get a mapped file confused with a memory file. A lot of references treat them as the same animal, but there are some distinct differences. In Windows, a memory file is the Windows implementation of the *shared memory* IPC mechanism. You create mapped files and memory files with the same functions.

A mapped file is a disk file that is first opened as an ordinary file using the Windows API function *CreateFile()*. A file-mapping object is then applied to it using the handle returned by *CreateFile()*, and then the contents of the file are mapped into the process's address space. In a true mapped file scheme, the file normally isn't read into memory. Blocks of it usually are read into memory when the contents are changed, and then swapped back to the disk file because of the physical constraints of disk operations. Rarely is a truly mapped file read into memory in its entirety.

A memory file, on the other hand, is *never* opened. In fact, the file handle you pass to the mapping object to create the memory-mapped file is *INVALID_HANDLE_VALUE*. The Windows API's mapping functions recognize that as a request to create a mapped memory file, thus creating a shared memory file.

The *INVALID_HANDLE_VALUE* macro, by the way, applies only to files and not to other objects that use handles. Its value is 0xFFFFFFFF, the unsigned equivalent of a −1. This value dates back to the 1970s when CP/M—Control Program/Monitor—was the dominant operating system for microcomputers. It returned a 0xFF, the byte equivalent of a −1, when it failed to open a file. When Tim Patterson of Seattle Computers cloned CP/M for the Intel 8086 processor, he used the same scheme. Then Patterson's operating system became MS-DOS (no, Bill Gates didn't write it), and −1 was the standard for failure to open a file. Today, there's so much programming based on that value that it hangs around in the form of *INVALID_HANDLE_VALUE* for files while other objects that use handles return *NULL* on failure.

From a programmer's point of view, there's little difference between a mapped file and a memory file. You access the data in both using pointers as though it were a part of the process's physical address space.

Both objects are sharable as IPC devices. Child processes may inherit the mapping object's handle, or the mapping object may be created with a name, allowing unrelated processes to access it as long as they know the object's name.

1000. *Understanding Memory Mapped Files*

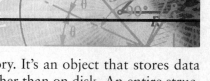

A memory file is the Windows method of implementing shared memory. It's an object that stores data in much the same way as a disk file, but the data is kept in memory rather than on disk. An entire structured data file can be read into memory and placed in a memory file, giving rapid access to the file during the lifetime of a program. When the program exits, any modified records can be rewritten to disk by retrieving them from the memory file. This doesn't imply that a memory file must be used with a disk file; it can be used without ever creating a disk file.

Windows uses the global allocation system to create memory files. The memory file is a moveable object, so you access it using handles. Calling the *GlobalLock()* function freezes the memory address of the file and returns a character pointer to the memory.

More than one process may use a memory file, in which case it is called *shared memory*. Functionally, there's no difference between a memory file and a shared memory file. The former is sharable, but only if you permit it by giving the object a name. In fact, the MFC *CSharedFile* class is derived directly from the *CMemFile* class.

To create a memory file, call the *CreateFileMapping()* function specifying the macro *INVALID_HANDLE_VALUE* for the handle to the file to map. The Windows API recognizes this as a request to map a memory block as a file. This function will return a handle to the file-mapping object that you then pass on to *MapViewOfFile()*. The return is a void pointer to the beginning of the mapped address space, and you may cast it to a pointer of any data type.

In the next tip, you'll use a memory file as a shared object to allow one process to pass mouse strokes it uses to draw lines on to another process, where the lines will be duplicated in its client window.

1001. *Understanding Shared Memory*

Shared memory is a block of memory that more than one process can access. This allows processes to pass large blocks of data from one to another without resorting to breaking it down into smaller packets for transfer by another IPC device.

For example, a pipe has limited storage that you set at the time you create the pipe. Once that limit has been reached, you can't write any more data to the pipe until a client process begins taking it out of the other end.

With shared memory, you can dynamically reallocate the size of the block to hold whatever data you need to transfer to another process. Shared memory is an important component of the UNIX IPC system, where it is treated the same as any other memory block to which the process has access.

On Windows, shared memory is implemented as a memory-mapped file, an object that is mapped similar to a disk file. A process creates it as a memory file then accesses it as though it were ordinary memory. You can copy the object to it using the standard *memcpy()* function and store variables and other data in it as necessary.

Create a *workspace* called *MemFile*. In this workspace, create two projects, one called *Draw* and the other called *Redraw*. Create the single-document application projects using the MFC AppWizard, but unselect the box on the first page of the wizard labeled "Document/view architecture support." Accept the other defaults throughout the wizard. At the end, you won't have any choice on the base class for the view, so just click Finish and create the projects.

In this sample, when you draw lines on the *Draw* window using the right mouse button, the movements will be tracked and written to a memory file, which will be shared with the *Redraw* process. When you write data to the file, you'll set an event that will make the *Redraw* process read the file and draw the same lines in its window. To keep both processes from accessing the file at the same time, we'll use a semaphore. The application class for both *Draw* and *Redraw* is the stock code prepared by the AppWizard. All the work is done in the view classes. The header and source code for the *CChildView* class for *Draw* is shown below:

```
///////////////////////////////////////////////////////////////
// CChildView window for the Draw program
// ChildViewTx.h
//
class CChildView : public CWnd
{
// Construction
public:
    CChildView();

// Attributes
public:

// Operations
public:

// Overrides
    // ClassWizard generated virtual function overrides
    //{{AFX_VIRTUAL(CChildView)
    protected:
    virtual BOOL PreCreateWindow(CREATESTRUCT& cs);
    //}}AFX_VIRTUAL
```

```cpp
// Implementation
public:
    virtual ~CChildView();

    // Generated message map functions
protected:
    PROCESS_INFORMATION m_pi;
    BOOL StartReceiver();
    void DoMouseLine (CWindowDC& dc, POINT & ptLineStart,
                      POINT & ptLineEnd);
    void DoMouseEvent (UINT message, UINT nFlags,
                       POINT & point);
    bool m_bTracking;
    //{{AFX_MSG(CChildView)
    afx_msg void OnPaint();
    afx_msg void OnLButtonDown(UINT nFlags, CPoint point);
    afx_msg void OnLButtonUp(UINT nFlags, CPoint point);
    afx_msg void OnMouseMove(UINT nFlags, CPoint point);
    afx_msg void OnRButtonDown(UINT nFlags, CPoint point);
    afx_msg void OnRButtonUp(UINT nFlags, CPoint point);
    //}}AFX_MSG
    DECLARE_MESSAGE_MAP()

    BYTE      *m_sfBuf;
    HANDLE    m_hMap;
    HANDLE    m_hevMemFile;

    POINT  m_ptLineStart;
    POINT  m_ptLineEnd;
    POINT  m_ptLast;

};

// ChildViewTx.cpp : implementation of the CChildView class
//

#include "stdafx.h"
#include "Draw.h"
#include "ChildViewTx.h"
#include    <accctrl.h>
#include    <aclapi.h>

#ifdef _DEBUG
#define new DEBUG_NFW
#undef THIS_FILE
static char THIS_FILE[] = __FILE__;
#endif

CSemaphore  g_sem (1, 1, "JAMSAMEDIA");

const char *szFileEvent = {"JAMSA"};
const char *szMemFile = {"JAMSAFILE"};

/////////////////////////////////////////////////////////////
// CChildView
```

```
CChildView::CChildView()
{
    m_hMap = CreateFileMapping (INVALID_HANDLE_VALUE, NULL,
                        PAGE_READWRITE, 0, 4096, szMemFile);
    if (m_hMap != NULL)
        m_sfBuf = (BYTE *) MapViewOfFile (m_hMap,
                                FILE_MAP_WRITE, 0, 0, 0);
    else
        m_sfBuf = NULL;
    CSingleLock semLock (&g_sem);
    semLock.Lock ();
    m_bTracking = false;
    m_hevMemFile = CreateEvent (NULL, FALSE, TRUE,
                                szFileEvent);
    if (m_hevMemFile == NULL)
    {
        AfxMessageBox ("MemFile event is NULL");
    }
    m_ptLineStart.x = -1;
    m_ptLineStart.y = -1;
    if (!StartReceiver ())
    {
      AfxMessageBox(_T("Could not start receiver process"));
    }
    semLock.Unlock ();
}

CChildView::~CChildView()
{
    if (m_hevMemFile != NULL)
        CloseHandle (m_hevMemFile);
    if (m_pi.hProcess)
        ::PostThreadMessage (m_pi.dwThreadId, WM_QUIT,
                        0, 0);
}

BEGIN_MESSAGE_MAP(CChildView,CWnd )
    //{{AFX_MSG_MAP(CChildView)
    ON_WM_PAINT()
    ON_WM_LBUTTONDOWN()
    ON_WM_LBUTTONUP()
    ON_WM_MOUSEMOVE()
    ON_WM_RBUTTONDOWN()
    ON_WM_RBUTTONUP()
    //}}AFX_MSG_MAP
END_MESSAGE_MAP()

/////////////////////////////////////////////////////////
// CChildView message handlers

BOOL CChildView::PreCreateWindow(CREATESTRUCT& cs)
{
    if (!CWnd::PreCreateWindow(cs))
        return FALSE;
```

```cpp
        cs.dwExStyle |= WS_EX_CLIENTEDGE;
        cs.style &= ~WS_BORDER;
        cs.lpszClass =
                      AfxRegisterWndClass(
CS_HREDRAW|CS_VREDRAW|CS_DBLCLKS,
                            ::LoadCursor(NULL, IDC_ARROW),
                            HBRUSH(COLOR_WINDOW+1), NULL);

    return TRUE;
}


void CChildView::OnPaint()
{
    CPaintDC dc(this); // device context for painting

    // TODO: Add your message handler code here

    // Do not call CWnd::OnPaint() for painting messages
}


void CChildView::OnLButtonDown(UINT nFlags, CPoint point)
{
    DoMouseEvent (WM_LBUTTONDOWN, nFlags, point);
}

void CChildView::OnLButtonUp(UINT nFlags, CPoint point)
{
    DoMouseEvent (WM_LBUTTONUP, nFlags, point);
}

void CChildView::OnRButtonDown(UINT nFlags, CPoint point)
{
    DoMouseEvent (WM_RBUTTONDOWN, nFlags, point);
}

void CChildView::OnRButtonUp(UINT nFlags, CPoint point)
{
    DoMouseEvent (WM_RBUTTONUP, nFlags, point);
}

void CChildView::OnMouseMove(UINT nFlags, CPoint point)
{
    DoMouseEvent (WM_MOUSEMOVE, nFlags, point);
}


void CChildView::DoMouseEvent(UINT message, UINT nFlags,
                              POINT &point)
{
CWindowDC          dc (this);
static             int nPoints = 0;
static             unsigned char *buf = m_sfBuf;
CString Message;
CSingleLock semLock (&g_sem);

    switch (message)
```

```
{
    case WM_LBUTTONDOWN:
        m_ptLineStart = point;
        break;
    case WM_LBUTTONUP:
        m_bTracking = false;
        m_ptLineStart.x = -1;
        m_ptLineStart.y = -1;
        break;
    case WM_RBUTTONUP:
        semLock.Lock();
        m_ptLast.x = -1;
        m_ptLast.y = -1;
        buf = m_sfBuf;
        memcpy (buf, &nPoints, sizeof (int));
        semLock.Unlock ();
        SetEvent (m_hevMemFile);
        nPoints = 0;
        break;
    case WM_RBUTTONDOWN:
        dc.SetPixel (point, 0);
        semLock.Lock();
        if (m_ptLast.x >= 0)
        {
            DoMouseLine (dc, m_ptLast, point);
            memcpy (buf, &point, sizeof (POINT));
            buf += sizeof (POINT);
            ++nPoints;
        }
        else
        {
            memcpy (buf, &nPoints, sizeof (int));
            buf += sizeof (int);
        }
        semLock.Unlock();
        m_ptLast = point;
        break;
    case WM_MOUSEMOVE:
        if (nFlags & MK_RBUTTON)
        {
            DoMouseEvent (WM_RBUTTONDOWN, nFlags,
                        point);
            break;
        }
        if (!(nFlags & MK_LBUTTON))
            return;
        if (m_bTracking)
        {
            POINT pt;
            pt = point;
            if (m_ptLineStart.x >= 0)
            {
                DoMouseLine (dc, m_ptLineStart,
                        m_ptLineEnd);
                DoMouseLine (dc, m_ptLineStart, pt);
            }
```

```
            }
            m_ptLineEnd = point;
            m_bTracking = true;
            break;
    }
}


void CChildView::DoMouseLine(CWindowDC &dc,
                                POINT &ptLineStart,
                                POINT &ptLineEnd)
{
CPen    *penOld, Pen;

    Pen.CreatePen (PS_SOLID, 2, (COLORREF) 0x00ffffff);
    int nOldMode = dc.SetROP2 (R2_XORPEN);// R2_NOT);
    dc.MoveTo (ptLineStart);
    penOld = dc.SelectObject (&Pen);
    dc.LineTo (ptLineEnd);
    dc.SetROP2 (nOldMode);
    dc.SelectObject (penOld);
    Pen.DeleteObject ();
    Pen.CreatePen (PS_SOLID, 1, (COLORREF) 0x0);
}


BOOL CChildView::StartReceiver()
{
STARTUPINFO          si;

    memset ((char *) &si, '\0', sizeof (STARTUPINFO));
    memset ((char *) &m_pi, '\0',
                        sizeof (PROCESS_INFORMATION));
    si.cb = sizeof (STARTUPINFO);

    CWindowDC dc(GetDesktopWindow());
    int nWidth = GetDeviceCaps (dc.m_hDC, HORZRES) / 2;
    int nDepth = GetDeviceCaps (dc.m_hDC, VERTRES) / 2;
    si.dwXSize = nWidth;
    si.dwYSize = nDepth;
    si.dwX = nWidth;
    si.dwY = 0;
    si.dwFlags = STARTF_USESIZE | STARTF_USEPOSITION;

    int nBytes = GetCurrentDirectory (0, NULL);
    if (!nBytes)
        return (FALSE);
    ++nBytes;
    char *dir = new char [nBytes];
    GetCurrentDirectory (nBytes, dir);
    if (dir == NULL)
        return (FALSE);
    char *s = strrchr (dir, '\\');
    if (s == NULL)
    {
        delete [] dir;
        return (FALSE);
    }
```

```
    *s = '\0';
    CString strDir = dir;
    delete [] dir;

    CString ProgPath=strDir + "\\Redraw\\Debug\\Redraw.exe";
    CString ProgParam = ProgPath;
    CString StartPath = strDir + "\\Redraw";
    BOOL bResult = CreateProcess((LPCTSTR) ProgPath,
                (char *) (LPCSTR) ProgParam,
                (LPSECURITY_ATTRIBUTES) NULL,
                (LPSECURITY_ATTRIBUTES) NULL,
                false,
                DETACHED_PROCESS,
                (LPVOID) NULL,
                (LPCTSTR) StartPath,
                (LPSTARTUPINFO) &si,
                (LPPROCESS_INFORMATION) &m_pi);
    return (bResult);
}
```

This program uses several IPC mechanisms, and they are all set up in the *CChildView* constructor. The shared memory is created using the *CreateFileMapping()* and passing it *INVALID_HANDLE_VALUE*. The second parameter is a pointer to a *SECURITY_ATTRIBUTES* structure, which you will need if this object is to be inherited by child processes. Our child process will be opening it as a shared object so we don't need the security attributes and pass a *NULL* here.

The third parameter is the protection for the file view. There are three options, *PAGE_READONLY*, *PAGE_READWRITE*, and *PAGE_WRITECOPY*. The last option allows you to modify the file object, but the modifications are swapped out in memory and don't go to the original file. For a mapped file, the options must be consistent with the access used to open the file with *CreateFile()*.

The next two parameters are the high-order 32 bits for the maximum file size, and the low-order 32 bits for the maximum file size. You won't have any use for the high-order bits because right now pointers greater than that allowed in the low-order 32 bits can't be used. That doesn't mean that future machines and operating systems won't be able to use it, however.

The last parameter is the name of the file-mapping object. If you specify *NULL*, the object can't be used by unrelated processes, but the handle may be inherited by child processes, depending upon how you set the *bInheritHandle* flag in the security descriptor. By giving it a name, you make it sharable by any process that knows its name (like Cheers, where everybody knows your name).

Next we map the view of the file using the handle returned by *CreateFileMapping()*. The parameters after the handle are the access mode, which must be consistent with the mode in the call to *CreateFileMapping()*. The next two parameters form a 64-bit memory address where you want to place the file. Specify 0 to let the system decide. Finally, you tell the system how many pages of the file to map. Entering 0 maps the entire file.

In the *Redraw* program, except for the protection flags we use the same mapping arguments, but we don't have to. We could have specified 65536 as the maximum file size, but that wouldn't change the mapping for the *Draw* process.

The header file and the source code for *Redraw* view class are shown below:

```
////////////////////////////////////////////////////////////
// CChildView window
// Declarations for the Redraw view class


class CChildView : public CWnd
```

```cpp
{
// Construction
public:
    CChildView();

// Attributes
public:

// Operations
public:

// Overrides
    // ClassWizard generated virtual function overrides
    //{{AFX_VIRTUAL(CChildView)
    protected:
    virtual BOOL PreCreateWindow(CREATESTRUCT& cs);
    //}}AFX_VIRTUAL

// Implementation
public:
    virtual ~CChildView();

    // Generated message map functions
protected:
    void DoMouseLine(CWindowDC &dc, POINT &ptLineStart,
                     POINT &ptLineEnd);
    afx_msg void OnUser (WPARAM wparam, LPARAM lparam);
    static DWORD WINAPI StartUpdateThread(void *pParam);
    //{{AFX_MSG(CChildView)
    afx_msg void OnPaint();
    afx_msg void OnDestroy();
    //}}AFX_MSG
    DECLARE_MESSAGE_MAP()

    BYTE        *m_sfBuf;
    HANDLE      m_hMap;
    HANDLE      m_hevMemFile;
    HANDLE      m_hevDieMoFo;
    DWORD       m_dwThread;
};
// ChildViewRx.cpp : implementation of the CChildView class
//

#include "stdafx.h"
#include "Redraw.h"
#include "ChildViewRx.h"

#ifdef _DEBUG
#define new DEBUG_NEW
#undef THIS_FILE
static char THIS_FILE[] = __FILE__;
#endif

#define     ONESECOND       1000
#define     ONEMINUTE       (60 * ONESECOND)
```

```
CSemaphore  g_sem (1, 1, "JAMSA MEDIA");

const char *szFileEvent = {"JAMSA"};
const char *szMemFile = {"JAMSAFILE"};


struct THREADPARMS
    {
    HANDLE  hevMemFile;
    HANDLE  hevDieMoFo;
    CChildView  *Papa;
    };
THREADPARMS parms;


/////////////////////////////////////////////////////////////
// CChildView

CChildView::CChildView()
{
    m_dwThread = 0;
    m_hevDieMoFo = CreateEvent (NULL, TRUE, FALSE, NULL);
    m_hevMemFile = OpenEvent (EVENT_ALL_ACCESS, TRUE,
                              szFileEvent);
    if (m_hevDieMoFo == NULL)
        AfxMessageBox ("Terminate event is NULL");
    if (m_hevMemFile == NULL)
        AfxMessageBox ("MemFile event is NULL");
    parms.hevDieMoFo = m_hevDieMoFo;
    parms.hevMemFile = m_hevMemFile;
    parms.Papa = this;
    ::CreateThread (NULL, 0, StartUpdateThread,
                    (LPVOID) &parms, 0, &m_dwThread);
}

CChildView::~CChildView()
{
}

BEGIN_MESSAGE_MAP(CChildView,CWnd )
    //{{AFX_MSG_MAP(CChildView)
    ON_WM_PAINT()
    ON_WM_DESTROY()
    ON_MESSAGE(WM_USER+40, OnUser)
    //}}AFX_MSG_MAP
END_MESSAGE_MAP()


/////////////////////////////////////////////////////////////
// CChildView message handlers

BOOL CChildView::PreCreateWindow(CREATESTRUCT& cs)
{
    if (!CWnd::PreCreateWindow(cs))
        return FALSE;

    cs.dwExStyle |= WS_EX_CLIENTEDGE;
```

```
        cs.style &= ~WS_BORDER;
        cs.lpszClass =
                    AfxRegisterWndClass(
CS_HREDRAW|CS_VREDRAW|CS_DBLCLKS,
                        ::LoadCursor(NULL, IDC_ARROW),
                        HBRUSH(COLOR_WINDOW+1), NULL);

    return TRUE;
}


void CChildView::OnPaint()
{
    CPaintDC dc(this); // device context for painting

    // TODO: Add your message handler code here

    // Do not call CWnd::OnPaint() for painting messages
}


void CChildView::OnDestroy()
{
    CWnd ::OnDestroy();
    SetEvent (m_hevDieMoFo);
}


DWORD WINAPI CChildView::StartUpdateThread(void *pParam)
{
HANDLE  hWaitFor [2];
DWORD   dwSignal;
THREADPARMS parms;

    memcpy (&parms, (THREADPARMS *) pParam,
            sizeof (THREADPARMS));
    hWaitFor [0] = parms.hevMemFile;
    hWaitFor [1] = parms.hevDieMoFo;
    if (hWaitFor[0] == NULL)
    {
        AfxMessageBox ("hevMemFile is null");
        return (-1);
    }
    if (hWaitFor[1] == NULL)
    {
        AfxMessageBox ("hevDieMoFo is null");
        return (-1);
    }
    for (;;)
    {
        dwSignal = WaitForMultipleObjects (2, hWaitFor,
                                        FALSE, INFINITE);
        switch (dwSignal)
        {
            case WAIT_OBJECT_0:            // Memory file event
                ::SendMessage  (parms.Papa->m_hWnd,
                            WM_USER+40,
                            (WPARAM) (WM_USER+40),
                            (LPARAM) 0);
```

```
                    break;
            case WAIT_OBJECT_0 + 1:    // Terminate
                return (0);
            case WAIT_TIMEOUT:
                continue;
        }
    }
    return (0);
}

void CChildView::OnUser(WPARAM wparam, LPARAM lparam)
{
BYTE    *b;

    CSingleLock semLock (&g_sem);
    semLock.Lock();
    m_hMap = CreateFileMapping (INVALID_HANDLE_VALUE, NULL,
                        PAGE_READWRITE, 0, 4096, szMemFile);
    if (m_hMap != NULL)
        m_sfBuf = (BYTE *) MapViewOfFile (m_hMap,
                                    FILE_MAP_READ, 0, 0, 0);
    else
        m_sfBuf = NULL;
    if (m_sfBuf == NULL)
    {
        AfxMessageBox ("File mapping failed");
        return;
    }
    b = m_sfBuf;
    CWindowDC dc(this);
    int nPoints = (int) *b;

    b += sizeof (int);
    POINT ptStart = (POINT) (*((POINT*)b));
    for (int i = 1; i < nPoints; ++i)
    {
    POINT pt;

        pt = (POINT) (*((POINT*)b));
        dc.SetPixel (pt, (COLORREF) 0);
        b += sizeof (POINT);
        DoMouseLine (dc, ptStart, pt);
        ptStart = pt;
    }
    semLock.Unlock ();
}

void CChildView::DoMouseLine(CWindowDC &dc,
                    POINT &ptLineStart, POINT &ptLineEnd)
{
CPen    *penOld, Pen;

    Pen.CreatePen (PS_SOLID, 2, (COLORREF) 0x00ffffff);
    int nOldMode = dc.SetROP2 (R2_XORPEN);// R2_NOT);
    dc.MoveTo (ptLineStart);
    penOld = dc.SelectObject (&Pen);
```

```
    dc.LineTo (ptLineEnd);
    dc.SetROP2 (nOldMode);
    dc.SelectObject (penOld);
    Pen.DeleteObject ();
    Pen.CreatePen (PS_SOLID, 1, (COLORREF) 0x0);
}
```

When you run these programs, the path to the *Redraw.exe* program on the right is relative and assumes you are running *Draw.exe* (the one on the left) from the Visual Studio. If you run *Draw.exe* from the command line, it will not start the *Redraw.exe* process.

Index

About the CD-ROMs that accompany this book: